PSYCHOLOGY
in PERSPECTIVE

1817

HARPER & ROW, PUBLISHERS, New York
Cambridge, Philadelphia, St. Louis, San Francisco,
London, Singapore, Sydney, Tokyo

SECOND EDITION

PSYCHOLOGY *in* PERSPECTIVE

JAMES HASSETT
KATHLEEN M. WHITE
Boston University

To our editors, past and present:
Without their help, guidance, support, and friendship,
this book easily could have been mediocre.
And to our loved ones, Pat, Eileen, Richard, Sarah, and Barbara:
Without them, our lives could have been mediocre, too.

A list of text, table, and illustration credits appears as a "Credits" section at the back of this book and is hereby made part of this copyright page.

Editor in Chief: Judith Rothman
Sponsoring Editor: Laura Pearson
Development Editor: Louise Hockett
Project Editor: Donna DeBenedictis
Cover Design: Karen Salsgiver
Text Line Art: Vantage Art, Inc.
Text Anatomical Art: Mei-Ku Huang, M.D./Evelyne Johnson Associates
Photo Research: Roberta Guerette/Omni-Photo Communications
Production Manager: Willie Lane
Compositor: Arcata Graphics/Kingsport
Printer and Binder: Arcata Graphics/Kingsport
Cover Printer: New England Book Components, Inc.
Cover Separator: Jen Mar Graphics, Inc.

Psychology in Perspective, Second Edition

Library of Congress Cataloging-in-Publication Data
Hassett, James.
    Psychology in perspective / James Hassett, Kathleen M. White.—
2nd ed.
      p. cm.
    Includes index.
    ISBN 0-06-042696-9
    1. Psychology.   I. White, Kathleen M., 1940–   II. Title.
BF121.H26 1989
150—dc19   88–24590
                                        CIP

88 89 90 91 9 8 7 6 5 4 3 2 1

CONTENTS IN BRIEF

v

CONTENTS IN DETAIL

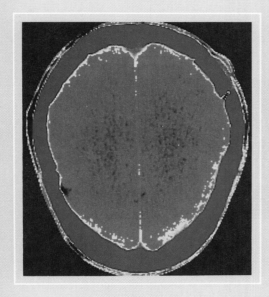

Cognitive Processes

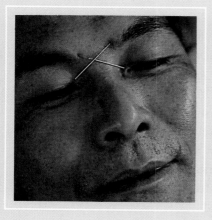

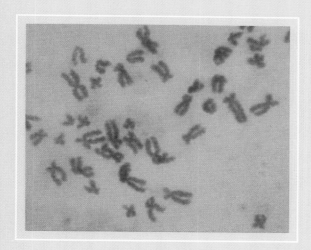

Developmental Processes

Emotion and Personality

CHAPTER 11
MOTIVATION AND EMOTION   **419**

Abnormal Behavior

Social and Applied Psychology

CRITICAL THINKING EXERCISES

TO THE INSTRUCTOR

*T*he second edition of *Psychology in Perspective* marks the beginning of a new collaboration. Users of the first edition were enthusiastic about my approach to making the scientific method accessible to all students. Now, for the second edition, I am pleased to be joined by a long-time colleague on the faculty at Boston University, Dr. Kathleen M. White. To complement my background in experimental psychology, Kathie adds her areas of expertise, personality and human development across the life span. The balance provided by this merging of minds has strengthened the book and led to an increased emphasis on critical thinking.

Much of the acceptance of the first edition was based on its success in teaching students to think more critically about behavior. A good text should be more than a list of facts to be memorized; it should explain psychology as an ongoing process of gaining insights into the awe-inspiring complexity of human thought and action. The second edition of *Psychology in Perspective* continues in the tradition of teaching students to think critically by distinguishing between claims based on scientifically sound evidence, weak evidence, or no evidence at all.

Critical Thinking Exercises

A major goal of this revision was to broaden the most popular feature of the first edition: the critical thinking exercises. The most obvious method to achieve this goal was the addition of a new series of exercises entitled **Applying Scientific Concepts**. These exercises challenge students to go beyond the information provided in the text and consider, from a critical perspective, the roles of psychological theories and data in understanding new situations and problems. One exercise, for example, is built around a case from neurologist Oliver Sacks's 1986 book, *The Man Who Mistook His Wife for a Hat and Other Clinical Tales*. The text provides a clinical portrait of Mrs. S. and asks students to draw on the material in Chapter 3, "The Nervous System," to answer several questions and infer which part of her brain was damaged.

The **Becoming a Critical Consumer** exercises, an extremely popular feature in the first edition, present passages from the popular media that relate to topics covered in the text. These accounts—ranging from an excerpt from *Walden Two* to articles from the *New York Times*—ask students to compare the claims made therein with the relevant discussions in the text. We retained the most popular excerpts and added new ones where appropriate.

Understanding the Scientific Method, which was called **How Do They Know?** in the first edition, is designed to show students how scientists use the scientific method to solve psychological problems. Case study techniques, for example, are discussed in the story of Phineas Gage as well as what this unfortunate victim of brain damage can teach us about the relationship between biology and behavior (Chapter 3). Similarly, replication is presented not in an isolated list of scientific methods but as a way of understanding possible sex differences in fear of success (Chapter 12).

In each chapter, the specific critical thinking skills best suited to the exercises are described in a brief discussion section at the end of the chapter, following the summary. For example, in the exercise based on *The Man Who Mistook His Wife for a Hat,* the discussion focuses on the process of making inferences and how that process can lead to the conclusion that Mrs. S. suffered damage to the right side of her brain.

The Process of Scientific Study

Many introductory psychology texts discuss history, but most students—and some professors—find this material boring or irrelevant or both. If covering history means defining structuralism and functionalism in the first chapter and never mentioning them again, they may be right. However, in order for students to understand where psychology is today, they need to know where it came from. Thus, we highlighted history throughout the text, not by attempting to list all the important names and dates, but by emphasizing scientific study as an active, ongoing process; by describing how that process has led to the development of major psychological concepts and theories; and by demonstrating the connection between original research and follow-up research. Chapter 7, for example, begins with an explanation of Ebbinghaus's first attempts to make a scientific study of memory, and then goes on to show how his efforts influenced the work and beliefs of several generations of researchers.

We also tried to enliven history by emphasizing the human side of science—describing, for example, how Skinner accidentally discovered extinction when a food dispenser broke (Chapter 6); how Piaget's study of his own children helped him form theories about childhood development (Chapter 9); and how Freud's analysis of his own dreams contributed to his views on the workings of the subconscious (Chapter 12). Our marginal biographies of theorists and famous subjects mentioned in the text add some personal insights to our understanding of these people. Rorschach, for example, had the childhood nickname *Klex,* meaning "painter" or "inkblot."

Focusing on the *process* of scientific study should inspire students to learn about psychology. While the questions that psychologists study have been fascinating enough to motivate thousands of people to devote their lives to the field, introductory texts often lack any sense of human drama. In *Psychology in Perspective,* we involve students in the excitement of the scientific approach, from the breakthrough of each new discovery to the inevitable frustration of discovering that behavior is always more complex than it first seems.

In-Depth Coverage of Selected Topics

Virtually all psychology instructors agree that an introductory course should familiarize students with certain basic facts and phenomena, such as classical and operant conditioning, attribution theory, and psychoanalysis. However, too many textbooks overwhelm students with an abundance of theories, names, and details that interfere with their understanding of the origins of those "facts" and what they really mean.

In *Psychology in Perspective,* we take the approach that it is far more important for introductory students to gain a firm grasp of the nature of the psychoanalytic approach, for example, than to memorize the differences between the individual psychoanalytic theories of Freud, Jung, Adler, and Horney. Our emphasis on this type of in-depth coverage is evident throughout the text. For example, Chapter 12, "Personality," provides a detailed overview of one theorist for each of the major theoretical approaches. Similarly, Chapter 14, "Diagnosing Abnormal Behavior," provides a detailed discussion of four major categories of disorders—personality, anxiety, affective, and schizophrenic—rather than devoting the available space to a laundry list of DSM-III-R's 17 major categories and hundreds of subdivisions.

New to This Edition

In addition to thoroughly updating the research and selectively rewriting to improve clarity, we substantially reorganized the chapters and added or expanded a number of topics, pedagogical aids, and design elements.

Content

Three new chapters were added to the second edition:

- **Chapter 2, "The Scientific Method."** Because first-edition users requested additional basic coverage of the scientific method at the beginning of the book, we expanded this topic into a separate chapter.

- **Chapter 4, "Consciousness."** The first edition included a "psychobiology" chapter that covered sleep, drugs, genetics, and stress. The new consciousness chapter reflects a more traditional organization, with expanded material on sleep and drugs, along with new material on meditation and hypnosis. Genetics is relocated to Chapter 9, "Infancy and Childhood," and stress is now discussed in Chapter 17 under the section on health psychology.

- **Chapter 17, "Applied Psychology."** Due to the growing importance of applied psychology in recent years—and to student and instructor interest—we added a separate chapter on this topic. Chapter 17 includes an entirely new section on industrial/organizational psychology, as well as expanded coverage of environmental and health psychology.

We reorganized and expanded many sections within chapters in an effort to facilitate student comprehension and to remain current in a constantly changing field. For example,

- **Chapter 1, "Introduction: Psychology in Perspective,"** now includes a presentation of the SQ3R method in a section on how to study.
- **Chapter 2, "Psychology as a Human Science,"** contains new research on the validity of common sense, although there are also frequent references to its shortcomings; in particular, the effects of biases and expectations on everyday observation are extensively discussed.
- **Chapter 7, "Remembering and Forgetting,"** discusses Alzheimer's disease in detail.
- **Chapter 8, "Thought and Language,"** has an expanded section on language development, including a new section on the mastery of reading.
- **Chapter 10, "Adolescence and Adulthood,"** has expanded sections on intimacy, AIDS and current trends in sexual behavior, and marriage and divorce.
- **Chapter 11, "Motivation and Emotion,"** has an expanded section on eating disorders, with new material on anorexia nervosa and bulimia.
- **Chapter 13, "Measuring Intelligence,"** has an extensive discussion of the misunderstandings that surround face validity and psychological tests.
- **Chapter 14, "Diagnosing Abnormal Behavior,"** now includes a detailed explanation of DSM-III-R.

Pedagogy

In addition to the new critical thinking exercise, **Applying Scientific Concepts,** several other new pedagogical aids were designed to help students comprehend and review the material more efficiently.

- **Chapter outlines,** listing the main headings and critical thinking exercise titles, provide students with a convenient overview of the chapter contents.
- **Chapter summaries** were rewritten in a new format that closely follows the chapter organization, thus making it easier for students to review the material.

- A **running glossary** was added that corresponds to the boldfaced terms in the text.

- In addition to the end-of-book **statistical appendix**, **glossary**, and **bibliography**, the second edition includes an **author index** as well as a **subject index**.

New Design and Art

The second edition was completely redesigned for a brighter, more open look. The larger dimensions of the book accommodate new pedagogical aids, such as the running glossary, and a greater number of photographs and illustrations without producing a cluttered appearance. The overall effect is one that makes the book both more functional and more aesthetically appealing.

The full four-color design has been used innovatively throughout the text. In particular, color is used to its greatest advantage by Mei-Ku Huang, M.D., who rendered new, highly creative anatomical art for Chapter 3, "The Nervous System," and Chapter 5, "Sensation and Perception." Dr. Huang, a practicing diagnostic radiologist, studied medicine at Georgetown University and studio art at Duke University and Parsons School of Design in New York City. His careful attention to accuracy and detail was invaluable to us.

Supplements

Psychology in Perspective is accompanied by a completely redesigned learning and teaching package. Wherever possible, the supplements have been integrated in a common critical thinking approach, and each is keyed to the text.

STUDY GUIDE

The *Study Guide* provides a solid review of the text. Prepared by Dr. Therese Herman-Sissons of Montclair State College, the guide is organized according to a five-step, SQ3R-oriented format. Built into each step are the critical thinking skills students can use to criticize, analyze, interpret, and evaluate whatever they are learning both in *Psychology in Perspective* and in other textbooks as well.

INSTRUCTOR'S MANUAL

This manual will ease the burdens of new instructors and harried veterans alike. Kathie White has provided lecture suggestions, topics and issues for discussion, and activities and exercises that are oriented to critical thinking.

TEST BANK AND HARPER TEST

Therese Herman-Sissons has generated a *Test Bank* consisting of approximately 4,000 multiple-choice and essay questions. The questions vary in difficulty level and are designed to test application of concepts as well as knowledge of facts.

The *Test Bank* is available as a printed manual and on Harper Test. Harper Test is a computerized test-generation system with full word-processing capabilities. It produces customized tests and allows instructors to scramble and/or add new test items. Harper Test is available for the Apple II and IBM PC and PS2 families of computers.

TRANSPARENCIES AND IBM SIMULATION

Available to the instructor are a set of approximately 100 transparencies, many in full color, for use in the introductory psychology course. An accompanying handbook will help instructors select and coordinate transparencies with their lectures. An IBM simulation for introductory psychology also has been developed.

Acknowledgments

A number of people have provided valuable input to the second edition. Drs. Esther Greif and Sheree Dukes Kohak drafted several sections regarding new research developments and made other extremely significant contributions to the book.

Additionally, the following professors provided many constructive comments and suggestions that significantly helped to focus and polish the first and second editions of this text:

Clifford Abrams
Penn Valley Community College

James Ackil
Western Illinois University

Robert Arkin
University of Missouri

Joel Aronoff
Michigan State University

Pietro Badia
Bowling Green University

Susan Belmore
University of Kentucky

Michael Bergmire
Jefferson College

Sheila Bienenfeld
San Jose State University

Elizabeth Blanchard
San Joaquin Delta Community College

Burton I. Blau
University of Central Florida

David Bolocofsky
University of Northern Colorado

Kenneth S. Bordens
Indiana University–Purdue
Indiana University at Fort Wayne

Donald Border
Wenatchee Valley College

Scott Borrelli
Boston University

Donald Bowers
Philadelphia Community College

Michael Brailoff
College of Marin

Sharon S. Brehm
University of Kansas

Gwen J. Broude
Vassar College

Larry Brown
Oklahoma State University

Francis B. Colavita
University of Pittsburgh

Eric Cooley
Western Oregon State University

Stanley Coren
University of British Columbia

James Coyne
University of California

Linda K. Davis
Mount Hook Community College

Gerald C. Davison
University of Southern California

Nancy Denney
University of Kansas

Jerry P. Dodson
Boise State University

Leonard A. Eiserer
Elizabethtown College

Del Ellsworth
Elizabethtown College

Pamela S. Engram
Ithaca College

Warren Fass
University of Pittsburgh at Bradford

Charles R. Fletcher
University of Minnesota

William Ford
Bucks County Community College

Phyllis R. Freeman
SUNY at New Paltz

Bruce Fretz
University of Maryland

Louis Fusilli
Monroe Community College

Norman L. Garrett
Los Angeles City College

Meg Gerrard
Iowa State University

Alan Glaros
University of Missouri–Kansas City

Leonard Goodstein
University Associates

Bernard Gorman
Nassau Community College

Kenneth F. Green
California State University, Long Beach

Larry Gregory
New Mexico State University

Richard A. Griggs
University of Florida

Charles G. Halcomb
Texas Tech University

Gordon Hammerle
Adrian College

Michael Haney
University of San Diego

Therese Herman-Sissons
Montclair State College

Leslie Hicks
Howard University

Annette Hiedemann
West Virginia Wesleyan College

Gladys Hiner
Rose State College

Michael P. Hoff
Dalton College

James Howell
Portland Community College

Phyllis Rash Hughes
Parkland College

Michael Hughmanick
West Valley College

Bruce Hunsberger
Wilfrid Laurier University

Fabio Idrobo
Boston University

Margaret Jean Intons-Peterson
Indiana University

Mary Ivory
Henry Ford Community College

James J. Johnson
Illinois State University

Edwin Kahn
Queensborough Community College–CUNY

Chadwick Karr
Portland State University

Richard Kasschau
University of Houston

Harold O. Kiess
Framingham State College

Wright Killian
Pembroke State University

John M. Knight
Central State University

Edward Krupat
Massachusetts College of Pharmacy
and Allied Health Sciences

Tim Lehmann
Valencia Community College

Manuel Leon
Boise State University

Robert Levy
Indiana State University

Kenneth Livingston
Vassar College

William Mackavey
Boston University

Brendan A. Maher
Harvard University

Henry Marcucella
Boston University

Michele Martel
Northeast Missouri State
University

Donald McBurney
University of Pittsburgh

Duane G. McClearn
University of Colorado, Boulder

Donald McCoy
University of Kentucky

Kathleen McNamara
Colorado State University

Frances McSweeney
Washington State University

Danica Mijovic
Boston University

Donald E. Mitchell
Dalhousie University

Christopher Monte
Manhattanville College

Douglas G. Mook
University of Virginia

Bert Moore
University of Texas at Dallas

David Mostofsky
Boston University

Chris Munson
Monroe Community College

Robert A. Neimeyer
Memphis State University

Nora Newcombe
Temple University

Edward O'Day
San Diego State University

Wendy Palmquist
Plymouth State College

David Pomerantz
SUNY at Stony Brook

William Ray
Pennsylvania State University

Freda Rebelsky Camp
Boston University

Marylou Robbins
San Jacinto College–South

Nicholas Rohrman
Colby College

Billy B. Rose
San Antonio College

Andrew Sagar
Elizabethtown College

Richard Schuberth
Rice University

Jonathan Segal
Trinity College

Paul Sheldon
Villanova University

Charles Sheridan
University of Missouri, Kansas City

Joan Sieber
California State University–
Hayward

Charlotte Simon
Montgomery College

Roy H. Smith
Mary Washington College

Steven M. Smith
Texas A&M University

David R. Soderquist
University of North Carolina at
Greensboro

Mary Helen Spear
Prince George's Community
College

James R. Speer
Stephen F. Austin State University

Fred E. Stickle
Western Kentucky University

D. Theron Stimmel
Southwest Texas State University

Maria Taranto
Nassau Community College

Ronald D. Taylor
University of Kentucky, Fort Knox

Paul E. Thetford
Texas Woman's University

Ronald N. Tietbohl
Wesley College

Rodney Triplet
Northern State College

Jeffrey Turner
Mitchell College

Norris Vestre
Arizona State University

Ann Weber
University of North Carolina
at Asheville

Michael Wessells
Randolph–Macon College

Robert L. Williams
Washington University

Warner Wilson
Wright State University

Peter Worms
Montclair State College

Paul F. Zelhart
East Texas State University

We also want to thank those who assisted in preparing the manuscript: Dorothy Farrell, Audrey Staub, and Joanne DiPlacido for helping with the research; Barbara B. Malley, Nancy Lerner, and Connie Cassarino for typing and proofreading; and Marcia Johnston and Mary Perry for carrying out the many secretarial tasks.

Harper & Row must be commended for its continued support throughout the first and second editions of this text. Special thanks go to Judith Rothman for never wavering in her commitment to making the second edition a success; Louise Hockett for her help in developing each chapter with a professional's eye; and Donna DeBenedictis for her expert management of the book through the production stages.

Finally, we are deeply indebted to our families, friends, and colleagues for their patience and understanding throughout this project. Their unstinting support has been a source of constant inspiration and, thus, constitutes a vital contribution to the success of this text. For that, we are eternally grateful.

James Hassett

Kathleen M. White

TO THE STUDENT

*E*ach year, more than one million college students take courses in introductory psychology, and a large number of people go on to take advanced degrees in this field. Did you know that about 10 percent of all the science and engineering Ph.D.s awarded in the United States are in psychology?

There is good reason for this academic popularity. What could be more fascinating than the basic subject of psychology—you and me? Why do we think and act as we do? How can we better understand ourselves, our families, our friends, the people we love, even the person who delivers our mail?

"Sure," you might say, "I'm as interested as anyone in finding out what makes people tick. But I don't want to read a bunch of facts. How can a textbook teach me what I need to know and make it interesting as well?"

First of all, you won't find a lot of dry facts in *Psychology in Perspective*. For every research statistic we cite, we also discuss applications to everyday life. Nor will you find simple answers to the questions raised in our book, because human behavior is very complex and there is still much uncharted territory. But we do tell you about what psychologists have learned already and how they go about studying human behavior. And you'll read about a wide range of topics, such as what happens chemically in the brain to produce "runner's high," what kinds of intimate relationships young adults tend to develop, and how different types of psychologists explain and treat personality disorders.

How these topics are discussed is as important as the topics themselves. Therefore, throughout the text you'll find interesting case studies—such as one about a man whose behavior changed dramatically after he suffered brain damage—and descriptions about some fascinating research programs, such as the short- and long-term effects of divorce on children. We have also included exercises in each chapter that allow you to try your hand at applying psychological concepts to real life situations and that test your ability to be a "critical consumer" of the kind of "pop psych" articles found in popular newspapers and magazines.

We wrote this book because we wanted to encourage you to ask questions about human thought and action and to evaluate explanations proposed by others, not because we expected to teach you pat answers. And we wanted to share our enthusiasm about how far psychology has come in a little over 100 years, and our excitement over how much more it is likely to progress in the next few decades.

James Hassett

Kathleen M. White

PSYCHOLOGY
in PERSPECTIVE

INTRODUCTION: PSYCHOLOGY IN PERSPECTIVE

Chapter 1

*S*tudents take their first psychology course for all kinds of reasons, ranging from the mundane to the sublime. One of the authors of this book tells his classes the following anecdote to explain how he embarked on his profession.

My older brother was the first to tell me the truth about psychology. We were waiting for the Q36 bus on Hillside Avenue in Queens, New York. The subject came up because one of his college friends had just decided to major in psychology. I knew nothing about this mysterious subject.

"What do psychologists do?" I asked.

"Well," my brother replied, "they try to predict how people will act."

"What does that mean?"

"A psychologist might try to predict what a person will do when he walks into a room."

"They can't do that, can they?" I asked uneasily. Like many eighth-graders, I had a number of habits that I preferred to keep to myself.

"Of course not," he replied, with the total intellectual assurance that only college sophomores can master. "It's supposed to be a science, but they really don't know anything yet."

Thus, my first reaction to psychology consisted of equal parts of awe and skepticism—awe that scientists might someday know what I would do even before I did and skepticism that they would ever be able to pull it off.

Many years, countless psychology credits, and several degrees later, I still react to psychology with awe and skepticism. And, like most teachers, I secretly want you to feel the same way I do. So throughout, this book is intended to amaze you with all the things that psychologists know—without ever losing sight of all the things that still remain to be learned.

I must admit that it was neither awe nor skepticism that led me to major in psychology. I was trying to impress a girl who was breathlessly thrilled at the prospect of understanding what makes people tick. I went along because psychology didn't seem too difficult and majoring in it required only one year of French—at a time when many majors required two years of a foreign language.

When I lined up to register as a psychology major in my freshman year, I found myself standing next to a shelf of books with forbidding titles such as *Journal of Experimental Psychology,* Volume 67, 1964, and *Journal of Abnormal and Social Psychology,* Volume 28, 1933. I took one of these hefty volumes off the shelf and opened it at random to an article entitled "The Robustness of the Chi-Square Statistic." I looked again at the cover of the book to make sure it said psychology. It did. I turned to another article. And another. Though some of the articles seemed to have some vague relation to people, none of them made a lot of sense to me. If I had not already been waiting in line for one-and-a-half hours, I might have headed for the history department.

I have since learned that psychology is an incredibly diverse field that raises hundreds of questions I had never thought about—from the way nerve cells in the eye distinguish between red and orange to the mental processes involved in understanding a joke. I can't say that I came to psychology to learn about all these things, but I can say that most of them proved to be pretty interesting.

For example, because I now know a bit about human memory, I know that the anecdotes I've been reporting are probably only partly true. The bus my brother and I were waiting for might have been the Q1 or the Q43, or maybe we were discussing sociology while waiting for the subway in Brooklyn. I have learned that human memory is constructive: We tend to fill in the details of a story. In time, we may remember these manufactured details as vividly as we remember the original events.

At least one more psychological phenomenon relates to these anecdotes. Most people tend to assume that their experiences are typical and that other people are generally like them. Thus we assume that you may be like us, that you come to your first psychology course with only a vague idea of what this subject is all about. And so the obvious place to begin this text is with a brief description of what psychology is and what it is not.

What Is Psychology?

Psychology can be defined as the scientific study of behavior and mental processes. The intellectual roots of this subject can be traced back at least as far as Aristotle, the Greek philosopher who analyzed the nature of thought and memory more than three centuries before the birth of Christ.

For more than 2,000 years, scholars have tried to understand human nature. From Homer's *Odyssey* to Chaucer's *Canterbury Tales,* from the *Analects* of Confucius to Machiavelli's *The Prince,* philosophers and theologians, playwrights and politicians, have explored the workings of the human mind. But

psychology The scientific study of behavior and mental processes.

**WILHELM WUNDT
(1832–1920)**

Wundt founded the first laboratory of experimental psychology in 1879 at the University of Leipzig in Germany. Many of his studies were based on introspection—the careful, rigorous, and disciplined analysis of one's own thoughts by highly trained observers. At first, university administrators were unenthusiastic about Wundt's laboratory because they feared that "prolonged use of [his] introspection techniques by psychology students was likely to drive them insane" (Fancher, 1979, p. 134). It did not, but neither did it have the impact on the development of psychology Wundt had hoped for. The behaviorists later rejected the introspectionists' study of internal mental processes.

it was only a little over a century ago that psychology emerged as a distinct discipline.

According to most historians, psychology was born in 1879, when Wilhelm Wundt founded the first psychological laboratory at the University of Liepzig in Germany. But in a larger sense, psychology was one of several social sciences that emerged from nineteenth-century philosophy partly as a result of that discipline's growing involvement with the scientific method. Other social sciences that were born at about the same time include sociology—the study of society, groups, and social institutions—and anthropology—the study of the origins and characteristics of different cultures.

Thus, psychologists do not hold a monopoly on the study of human behavior. The boundaries between psychology and other sciences are often blurred. Sociologists, anthropologists, biologists, physicians, and others sometimes pursue the same problems from similar perspectives. In this section, we shall not attempt to define the precise compartments into which every scientist and nonscientist can be fitted. Rather, we shall try to convey a sense of the vast scope of psychology—the wide range of topics that psychologists study, the variety of their theoretical orientations, and the different professional activities they engage in. Only after reviewing this diversity shall we summarize the goals that all psychologists share.

A Variety of Questions

One way to get a feeling for the wide range of topics that psychologists have studied is simply to preview some of the research that will be described in this text.

For example: *Are children's thought processes qualitatively different from those of adults?* In the chapter on infancy and childhood, we review Jean Piaget's studies suggesting that a rational child is not merely a miniature version of a rational adult; children may actually think and perceive the world in a different way.

Why do women get drunk more easily than men? It is not simply because they weigh less. A 140-pound woman who has three drinks in one hour will ordinarily feel the effects more than a 140-pound man who drinks the same amount in the same time. The discussion of alcohol in the chapter on consciousness explains how physical differences between the sexes affect the psychological response to alcohol.

Can lie detectors really determine when people are telling the truth? In the chapter on motivation and emotion, we examine how lie detectors work and review the evidence concerning their accuracy.

Why do tape recordings of your own voice so often sound odd or unfamiliar? The answer lies partly in the physical structure of the ear, as explained in the chapter on sensation and perception.

Will pets learn faster if they are rewarded for good behavior or punished for being bad? The chapter on learning provides relevant data and describes many other general principles that apply to both animals and humans.

When is depression normal and when does it cross the line into mental illness? What can be done to cure depression? Some tentative answers appear in the two chapters on abnormal psychology.

As you read this text, you will learn about these topics and many more. Any student who is still reluctant to abandon the stereotype that psychologists deal only with personal problems should simply turn to the table of contents. The chapters cover everything from learning to language, attitudes to adolescence, and personality to perception. In short, psychologists study a wide range of topics that can be applied to every aspect of human behavior and experience.

A Variety of Theoretical Perspectives

In dealing with such a wide range of problems, psychologists have developed several theoretical perspectives. This can sometimes be confusing for introductory students. When people hear that psychology is a science, they often expect it to consist of a series of well-established facts of the sort one might learn in physics or astronomy. However, psychology is one of the younger sciences, and there are still disputes over some fundamental questions.

In his influential book *The Structure of Scientific Revolutions,* Thomas Kuhn (1970)[*] used the word **paradigm** to refer to a common set of beliefs and assumptions shared by a particular group of scientists. In a young, dynamic, and changing science like psychology, several contradictory paradigms may coexist. In this section, we introduce five major psychological paradigms: psychoanalytic, behavioral, humanistic, cognitive, and biological. Each provides a different way of looking at the complexity of behavior and experience. The influence of these paradigms on the development of psychology will be examined throughout the text.

THE PSYCHOANALYTIC APPROACH

The first complete and systematic theory of human behavior was proposed around the turn of the century by a Viennese neurologist named Sigmund Freud. Based on his experience in treating people with emotional problems, Freud developed the **psychoanalytic approach,** which stresses the importance of unconscious conflicts and biological instincts in the determination of complex human behavior.

Freud believed that inborn sexual and aggressive instincts could be transformed in the course of development to determine everything from a man's relationships with his parents to his choice of a career and a spouse. Freud argued further that people are not ordinarily aware of the actual causes of their behavior; the critical transformations of instinctual energy ordinarily remain hidden in the unconscious mind. He was also one of the first to stress the importance of early childhood experiences in shaping adult personality.

Freud and his followers—including Carl Jung, Alfred Adler, and Erik Erikson—developed rich, complex, and ambitious theories that attempted to explain every aspect of human behavior, from trivial events, such as slips of the tongue, to the highest artistic and cultural achievements of the human race. All these psychoanalytic theories were deterministic, because they implied

paradigm A common set of beliefs and assumptions shared by a particular group of scientists.

psychoanalytic approach A paradigm that stresses the importance of unconscious conflicts and biological instincts in determining behavior.

[*]In psychology, references are usually cited by listing the name of the author and the year of publication. See the bibliography for complete references.

that every act and feeling is the inevitable result of natural forces and previous events.

The influence of psychoanalytic thought on modern research can be seen in the use of *projective tests* to assess unconscious motivations. In projective testing, individuals are presented with an ambiguous stimulus, such as an inkblot or a picture, designed to evoke inner feelings and conflicts. Such tests are particularly relevant to the psychoanalytic approach because of their assumed ability to tap unconscious concerns—just the sort of thing that made our "author as a young man" very nervous.

Examples of projective tests are the Rorschach inkblot test (described in Chapter 13) and the Thematic Apperception Test. In the latter, subjects are asked to tell stories in response to a series of somewhat ambiguous pictures. It is assumed that the stories reflect motives and needs of which the subjects are not even aware. Analyses of these stories have focused on the need for achievement, power, and affiliation. In individuals undergoing transitions (e.g., change of residence or job, marriage, divorce), stories have been analyzed for the recurrence of conflicts going back to the early psychosexual stages described by Freud (see Chapter 12). Stories have also been analyzed for a motive known as "fear of success" (see "Understanding the Scientific Method," Chapter 11).

THE BEHAVIORAL APPROACH

Like the psychoanalytic approach, behaviorism assumes that every act is caused by natural forces. But this determinism is virtually the only point of agreement. The **behavioral approach** focuses on the systematic study of observable behavior. While Freud was willing to speculate about the internal workings of the unconscious mind, the first behaviorists limited themselves to that which can be observed and measured directly: physical stimuli and behavioral responses. Thus behaviorism was sometimes referred to as S-R psychology.

John B. Watson, the most influential of the pioneer behaviorists, argued that psychology's early studies (by Wundt and others) of the nature of mental life had produced only confusion and inconsistency. In his presidential address to the American Psychological Association in 1915, Watson also argued that virtually all behavior was learned. Therefore, psychologists should seek to discover the basic laws of learning that apply to both animals and humans and provide the foundation for a natural science of behavior.

The behavioral approach dominated American psychology at least until the 1950s and, in modified form, is still influential. Perhaps most important, the behaviorists established a strong tradition of laboratory research with humans and lower animals. The most famous of Watson's intellectual descendants is B. F. Skinner, who is known both for his pioneering laboratory research on animal learning and for his more speculative writings, such as the novel *Walden Two,* in which he described a utopian community designed on scientific behavioral principles (see Chapter 6).

Researchers in the behavioral tradition are best known for their laboratory investigations of learning in humans and lower animals. However, a number of contemporary behaviorists are interested in applying behavioral principles to improve the quality of life. Such behaviorists take the position that if individu-

behavioral approach   A paradigm that focuses on the systematic study of observable behavior.

als understand the laws of learning, they can use these laws for their own benefit—for example, to lose weight, stop smoking, overcome shyness, and reduce anxiety over stressful events, such as taking an exam. Books like the still-popular *Don't Say Yes When You Want to Say No* (Fensterheim & Baer, 1975), designed to help people become more assertive, derive from this tradition. We provide some advice on starting a self-modification program in the Chapter 6 "Applying Scientific Concepts" exercise.

THE HUMANISTIC APPROACH

While Freud saw human choices as an inevitable result of hidden instinctual forces and the early behaviorists portrayed humans as mechanically responding to stimuli and rewards, humanistic psychology provided a more optimistic view. Instead of accepting determinism, this theory argued that free will allows people to make conscious choices to grow and become better human beings. Thus the **humanistic approach** is concerned with human values, subjective experience, and the uniqueness of each individual. Abraham Maslow, for example, studied the characteristics of people who used all their talents to achieve their full potential as human beings; he called these people *self-actualized*.

Many humanistic psychologists believe that science will never be able to comprehend fully the infinite complexity of human behavior and experience. Nevertheless, they have been active in the *applied* domain of psychology. Carl Rogers is probably the best known of the humanistic therapists (see Chapter 15 for a brief description of his approach), but many of the current "self-help" books in psychology have a humanistic orientation. Indeed, in such books as *A Couple's Guide to Communication* (Gottman, Notarius, Gonso, & Markman, 1976)—a classic guide for both clients and therapists—one can find a blending of humanistic and behavioral approaches.

THE COGNITIVE APPROACH

The **cognitive approach** emphasizes the active internal nature of higher mental processes involved in such areas as attention, perception, memory, language, imagery, and reasoning. When behaviorists first focused on the stimuli that produced certain responses, they were unwilling to speculate about what went on inside the organism to form an intermediate link. For example, a strict behaviorist would study the way a child learned to speak only by considering the words and symbols the child was exposed to (stimuli) and the child's actual utterances (responses). A cognitive psychologist would use the same observations to try to deduce the internal linguistic rules the child had learned. Hearing a 2-year-old say, "You breaked it," a cognitive psychologist would infer that this error tells us something about a rule the child had deduced to form the past tense. Twenty-five years ago, few researchers favored such a cognitive approach; today, it may be the most influential paradigm in psychology.

Many cognitive psychologists are interested in *information processing*—the way our brains filter, select, process, store, and retrieve information coming in from the environment. Some of these cognitive psychologists develop computer models of the brain. Their efforts are directed at identifying the ways

humanistic approach A paradigm that is concerned with human values, subjective experience, and the uniqueness of each individual.

cognitive approach A paradigm that emphasizes the active internal nature of higher mental processes.

in which the operation of the human brain is like the operation of a computer. In a way, a cognitive psychologist is like an engineer who tries to understand an automobile engine by studying the performance of the car. Inferences about internal structures are indirect, based on what can be seen. In contrast, the biological approach to psychology is roughly analogous to opening the hood and trying to take the engine apart.

THE BIOLOGICAL APPROACH

The **biological approach** to psychology analyzes the physiological events associated with behavior and experience. For example, Chapter 7 on memory begins with an account of an unfortunate patient who had a brain operation on a structure called the hippocampus and, as a result, lost most of his ability to learn anything new. When he read a newspaper, for example, he forgot what it said within 15 minutes, and thus could read the same paper over and over without realizing he had seen it before. Although such dramatic cases are rare, they give biological psychologists fascinating clues to how the human brain functions under normal conditions.

At times, it is difficult to draw a line between the biological approach to psychology and the subject of biology itself. For example, some of the material in Chapter 3 on the structure of the nervous system could be covered in a biology course in much the same way. But researchers in this field seldom worry about keeping biology separate from psychology. Instead they use any techniques that will help them understand how psychological and biological influences work together to affect behavior and experience.

Biological psychologists have done much of the research on neuro-transmitters (see Chapter 3). By tracking these chemical messengers of the nervous system, they have discovered how a number of psychoactive drugs work. As you will see in Chapter 4, drugs such as morphine and heroin seem to affect people so strongly because they mimic some of the body's natural painkilling chemicals. Biological psychologists have made important discoveries in a broad range of other areas, including sensation and perception, health and illness, and abnormal behavior.

THE VALUE OF MULTIPLE PERSPECTIVES

To understand the implications of these five approaches, it is helpful to consider how each might try to understand the problems of a college student who is anxious about grades. From a psychoanalytic perspective, this anxiety might reflect an unconscious conflict caused by an aggressive impulse that has been channeled into competition with other people over grades. From a behavioral perspective, the origins of this anxiety are likely to seem more straightforward: Perhaps the student was severely punished for poor performance in the first grade and has learned to fear the results of tests. From a humanistic perspective, the problem may revolve around self-concept, the gap between what a person would like to be and how she perceives herself. From a biological perspective, this problem may be caused partly by a genetic predisposition to become anxious. Finally, the cognitive approach might explore the way this person interprets the meaning of a grade.

These different explanations might be useful for understanding different

biological approach A paradigm that analyzes the physiological events associated with behavior and experience.

TABLE 1.1

A Preview of Research Based on Five Theoretical Paradigms

The Paradigm	The Research
Psychoanalytic approach: stresses how unconscious conflicts and biological instincts determine complex human behavior	Freud and Breuer analyzed the case of Anna O., a disturbed young woman whose symptoms included visual problems that were not caused by physical illness. They discovered that one evening, when Anna was caring for her dying father, he asked what time it was, but the tears in her eyes prevented her from seeing her watch. Anna didn't want to upset her father by crying, so she tried to strangle her powerful emotions. This conflict was buried in her unconscious mind, and later led to visual problems (see Chapter 12).
Behavioral approach: systematically studies observable behavior	Ayllon and Azrin created a token economy to change the behavior of seriously disturbed mental patients. Desirable behaviors (such as getting dressed alone or making a bed) were systematically rewarded with tokens that could be redeemed for cigarettes, candy, etc. (see Chapter 6).
Humanistic approach: studies human values, subjective experience, and the uniqueness of each individual	Maslow studied extremely well-adjusted individuals, such as Eleanor Roosevelt and Albert Einstein, to try to discover the general characteristics of self-actualized people who used their talents to live up to their full potential (see Chapter 12).
Cognitive approach: emphasizes active internal nature of higher mental processes	Bartlett studied the way people remembered stories they had heard hours, days, or months before. He found that people often remembered a limited number of details and invented new material to fill in for what they had forgotten. He called this phenomenon *constructive memory* (see Chapter 7).
Biological approach: analyzes physiological events associated with behavior and experience	Broca studied the brains of patients who developed severe language problems. He consistently found damage in the same area on the left side of the brain (see Chapter 3).

people—not everyone worries about grades for the same reason. Different types of psychotherapy are associated with these paradigms, and the type that actually works may depend on both the problem and the person. For this reason, most psychotherapists call themselves eclectic, implying that they do not always use the same approach (see Chapter 15).

Thus, each of the five paradigms provides a different way of looking at a person or situation, and each has proved its value in research and clinical practice (see Table 1.1). As psychology continues to develop, we can expect new paradigms to offer further insights.

A Variety of Professional Activities

Another way to demonstrate the diversity of psychology is to consider the different activities in which psychologists engage and the impact of their work on our society.

Sooner or later psychology touches your life. For example, almost everyone who goes to school in the United States takes aptitude and achievement tests designed by psychologists. The popularity of these tests can be traced to World War I, when psychologists were called on to develop simple exams to screen out draftees who were not intelligent enough to function in the armed forces. The Army Alpha Test (for those who could read) and the Army Beta Test (for those who could not) were so successful that mass mental testing became an accepted feature of American society.

The first mass testing in history took place during World War I when the U.S. Army used intelligence tests to screen out recruits who were intellectually unable to perform as soldiers. This photograph shows recruits taking the Army intelligence test at Camp Lee in 1917.

One group of experts who had worked on the army intelligence tests went on to develop a short objective test to evaluate college applicants. This test was introduced in June 1926 and became known as the Scholastic Aptitude Test (SAT). Every year, millions of students take the SAT and its many offspring, including the Graduate Record Examination, the Law School Admissions Test, and the Medical College Admissions Test.

Psychologists have also worked behind the scenes to help shape twentieth-century technology. In one famous example (Lachman, Lachman, & Butterfield, 1979), psychologists helped discover why a particular airplane designed in the 1940s had a long history of crash landings. When engineers could find nothing wrong with the mechanical function of the plane, psychologists analyzed the cockpit design to try to determine the errors a human operator might make under stress. The psychologists discovered that the brake lever was located near a similar lever that raised the landing gear. When pilots were unable to take their eyes off the runway during stressful landings, they sometimes identified the wrong control by touch, retracted the landing gear when they wanted to put on the brakes, and crash-landed the plane on its belly.

Once this flaw in design had been located, the solution was obvious: Cockpit controls were redesigned so that completely different arm motions were required to put on the brakes and to retract the landing gear. Since then, in order to avoid such flaws, psychologists have worked closely with engineers on the design of many new machines.

Even the humanities have been touched by psychology. F. Scott Fitzgerald studied Freudian psychoanalysis before writing *Tender Is the Night* (Hoffman,

1945), and Thomas Mann, when writing *The Magic Mountain,* was heavily influenced by Freud's theories (Brennan, 1942).

Our legal system, too, has been affected by psychology. In *Brown v. The Board of Education of Topeka,* the 1954 landmark decision that called for the desegregation of public schools, the Supreme Court cited studies of the effects of segregation on personality (Rosen, 1972). In a more recent Supreme Court case on the ideal size for juries, the majority opinion drew so heavily on research about small groups that at times it sounded more like an article in a social psychology journal than a legal document (Tanke & Tanke, 1979).

Thus psychology has influenced our laws, our literature, and even the way we live. In some cases this influence has been immediate and intentional; in other cases the impact has been less direct.

Basic and Applied Psychology

In every science, including psychology, there is a distinction between basic and applied research. In psychology, **basic research** uses the scientific method to try to understand fundamental laws of the mind and behavior; **applied research** tries to solve specific problems by applying scientific principles and knowledge.

Thus, for example, basic researchers might look for fundamental laws of learning, while applied researchers would try to find the best way to teach an IBM employee to use a new computer. Or basic researchers might look for differences in the brain chemistry of schizophrenics versus other clinical patients, while applied researchers would more likely focus on evaluating a particular drug used to treat schizophrenia. Similarly, basic researchers might investigate the nature of intelligence, while applied researchers would try to improve a particular IQ test.

Note that in each of these examples, the applied researchers focus on a more immediate problem, while the basic researchers provide the foundation for applied work. Thus understanding of the nature of intelligence may be required to produce the best intelligence tests, and knowledge of the brain chemistry of schizophrenia may lead to the discovery of new drugs to treat or even cure it.

BASIC RESEARCH SPECIALTIES

Basic research is designed to answer fundamental questions about behavior, such as: How is stress related to disease? Or: What brain areas are related to thirst? The answers may at times lead to practical applications. For example, we shall see in Chapter 12 that the study of personality characteristics associated with heart disease has led to therapeutic programs that are designed to promote healthier lifestyles. But basic research is not designed to solve practical problems; rather, basic researchers seek knowledge for its own sake.

Basic researchers who call themselves **experimental psychologists** typically conduct laboratory studies in such areas as learning, human memory, and sensation and perception. Many experimental psychologists work with animals to unravel mysteries concerning the effects of different patterns of reward and punishment, the development of addictions, and the ability to

basic research The use of the scientific method to try to understand fundamental laws of the mind and behavior.

applied research The application of scientific principles and knowledge to solve specific problems.

experimental psychologists Basic researchers who typically conduct laboratory studies in such areas as learning, human memory, and sensation and perception.

discriminate among various stimuli (does a monkey see a triangle as different from a square?). They also study infants to learn more about the basic competencies (visual, auditory, conceptual) with which babies are born and the ways these basic competencies are modified by experience.

Physiological psychologists study the biological bases of behavior: how the structure of the brain is related to experience, for example, or how genetics influence behavior. Physiological psychologists have helped us learn more about how the human senses work—discovering, for example, that pilots flying at night can see better out of the sides of their eyes than straight ahead. They have also collected a great deal of important data on sleep, jet lag, and human vigilance. And their work on neurotransmitters has already led to more effective ways of dealing with neurological problems such as Parkinson's disease.

Developmental psychologists focus on the physical, emotional, and intellectual changes associated with aging. Most developmental psychologists today work within a *life span developmental framework;* they recognize that development is a lifelong process that continues from cradle to grave. While some developmental psychologists focus on the characteristics and behaviors of infants and toddlers, others are more interested in older children and adolescents. Still others attempt to identify and study the major patterns of development that occur during mid-life and old age.

Contemporary **personality psychologists** are more empirical in their approach and focus on more limited problems than the whole person. Nevertheless, many of these psychologists work within the tradition of Sigmund Freud and Erik Erikson. For example, they may try to investigate unconscious motives that underlie and give direction to behavior. They believe that there's more to personality than meets the eye, and that we need to know *why* people behave as they do, not just *what* they do.

Social psychologists are concerned with the way people respond to other human beings and how they interact with one another. They study such issues as impression formation, attitude change, and obedience to authority. Their emphasis is on how social forces, not internal psychological processes, influence what people do. In doing basic research, social psychologists, like other basic researchers, try to add to our knowledge about human behavior. Other psychologists are more interested in how this basic knowledge can be applied to solve human problems.

APPLIED PSYCHOLOGY SPECIALTIES

As you can see in Figure 1.1, more than three out of every four psychologists work in applied areas. **Clinical psychology** involves the diagnosis and treatment of abnormal behavior. It is closely related to **counseling psychology**, which specializes in helping people solve everyday problems such as marital difficulties. As we shall see in the chapters on abnormal behavior, it is not always easy to draw a firm line between the normal and the abnormal, so these specialties are not always easy to differentiate. More than half of all psychologists identify themselves as specialists in the clinical or counseling fields. (These groups often work closely with **psychiatrists**, licensed physicians who are trained in medicine before they specialize in the treatment of mental and emotional problems.)

physiological psychologists
Psychologists who study the biological bases of behavior.

developmental psychologists
Psychologists who study the physical, intellectual, and emotional changes associated with aging.

personality psychologists
Psychologists who focus on the problem of individual differences and how they develop.

social psychologists Psychologists who study the way people respond to and interact with others.

clinical psychology The diagnosis and treatment of abnormal behavior.

counseling psychology A specialty that emphasizes normal adjustment rather than abnormal function.

psychiatrists Licensed physicians who specialize in the treatment of mental and emotional problems.

APPLIED PSYCHOLOGY   **BASIC PSYCHOLOGY**

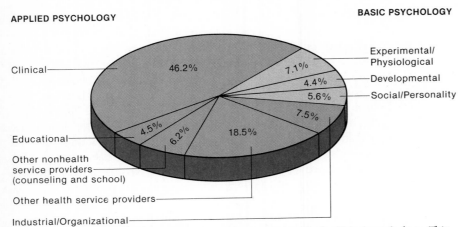

Clinical — 46.2%

7.1% — Experimental/Physiological

4.4% — Developmental

5.6% — Social/Personality

7.5%

4.5%   6.2%   18.5%

Educational —

Other nonhealth service providers (counseling and school) —

Other health service providers —

Industrial/Organizational —

Figure 1.1 Most psychologists work in applied areas, particularly clinical psychology. This graph summarizes the distribution of full-time psychologists who are members of the American Psychological Association and hold doctoral degrees.

School psychologists provide counseling to students among other services.

There are several other applied specialties in which large numbers of psychologists work. **School psychologists** provide advice and guidance in school systems. For example, they conduct testing programs to identify and help people with special needs, such as students with learning disabilities or those with unusually high intelligence. **Educational psychologists** work in the same general area but tend to be more concerned with ways of increasing teacher effectiveness. **Industrial/organizational psychologists** apply research findings to the work world. They might help to select personnel, for example, or to restructure jobs to increase worker satisfaction. **Health psychologists** typically work in medical settings, where they bring a psychological perspective to the understanding of "physical" problems. Such problems include illnesses

school psychologists Psychologists who provide advice and guidance in school systems.

educational psychologists Psychologists who work within school systems to find ways of increasing teacher effectiveness.

industrial/organizational psychologists Psychologists who apply research findings to the work world.

health psychologists Psychologists who apply a psychological perspective to stress-related diseases or other physical disorders.

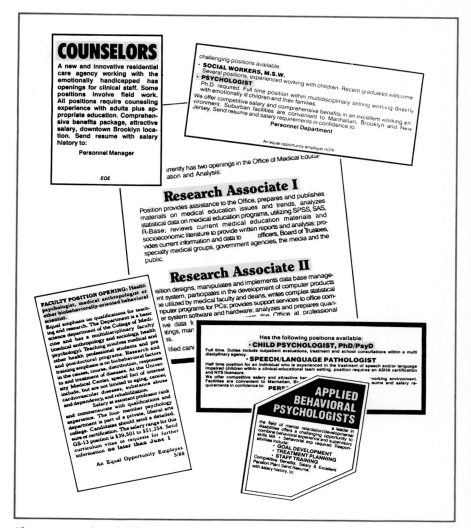

There are a number of different career paths open to those who pursue a career in psychology.

traditionally considered to have a psychological basis (e.g., asthma) as well as other illnesses now recognized to have a stress-related component (e.g., high blood pressure and diabetes mellitus). Health psychologists have also developed useful strategies for dealing with conditions such as epilepsy.

Most psychologists who work in these areas have completed advanced postgraduate training and have received a Ph.D., Ed.D., M.A., or similar degree. Undergraduate training in psychology almost always focuses on the basic scientific foundations of these specialties. The American Psychological Association has a booklet called *Careers in Psychology* that provides more information about the kinds of career paths open to psychologists.[*]

[*]To obtain this booklet, you can write to: The American Psychological Association, Publications Office, 1400 North Uhle Street, Arlington, VA 22201.

Some Common Goals

Thus far, this introduction to the nature of psychology has stressed diversity in research questions, theoretical approaches, and professional activities. Given all these differences, what do psychologists have in common?

The most obvious basis for unity is the nearly universal belief that the scientific method is a useful way to *understand, predict,* and *control* behavior. In one way or another, all scientists share these three major goals. A physicist, for example, may try to understand the principles involved in rocket propulsion, to predict how a certain rocket will take off, and to control the forces that can propel a rocket to the moon. Similarly, a psychologist might try to understand the laws of social interaction in order to predict how a certain group will make a decision. And ultimately the psychologist too might try to apply this understanding to control behavior—suggesting, for example, what types of groups would be most efficient at making certain types of decisions.

Most people agree that it is useful for scientists to understand and predict natural phenomena. But as soon as scientists use this knowledge to change the physical or social environment, value judgments and ethical issues become involved. Behavior control can raise especially difficult problems. Indeed, the very expression *behavior control* has a rather ominous tone. Few people object to psychologists' attempts to change abnormal or troublesome behavior, as when a therapist helps a business executive overcome a fear of flying. But, as we shall see later, when psychologists recommend how prisons should be organized or how parents should raise their children, the ethical issues become more complex.

Before such issues can be addressed, however, we must understand what the scientific method really involves. Chapter 2 explains how valuable a scientific approach to behavior can be and why common sense and casual observations are often misleading. It also describes the scientific method in some detail.

Here we want merely to note that there is no single set of procedures called *the scientific method*. Rather, science is in many ways an attitude—a rational and skeptical approach to knowledge. Because scientists are skeptical, psychologists are not willing to accept any generalization on faith or because an expert seems trustworthy. They insist that every claim be tested against observable evidence.

This questioning attitude is an essential element in the scientist's repertoire of critical thinking skills. Indeed, the ability to think critically is another shared characteristic of all scientists. To do their work, scientists must be able to draw inferences from a set of data, recognize unstated assumptions, weigh evidence and determine whether particular generalizations are warranted, and distinguish between weak and strong arguments in support of a particular inference—all of which constitute critical thinking skills. They also need considerable expertise in their area of specialization, which includes not just a set of facts that have been gathered but also a set of methodological tools for gathering new data.

If psychologists hear people say, "Did you know that happy infants always develop into optimistic adults?" or "It seems that most American women are afraid to succeed at their careers," their response is always the same: How do they know? It is this critical questioning of every claim, even if it is made by another scientist, that lies at the very heart of science in general and psychology as a discipline.

Psychologists use their critical thinking skills to evaluate both the claims that are made and the means that are used to support the claims. And ultimately, they demand that every claim be tested against observable evidence. Indeed, scientists love to ask: "What are the data?"

To help you develop critical thinking skills, this text includes a number of exercises designed to engage you in the type of analysis that is crucial to the scientific method. These critical thinking exercises are divided into three types, each one aimed at a different aspect of critical thinking.

The first group of exercises—"Understanding the Scientific Method"— explains how specific techniques have led to greater understanding of various topics—for example, how the brain works, the effects of punishment, and the nature of madness. These exercises reflect the general emphasis of this text, which is on evaluating the claims of the experts by examining the evidence and reaching your own conclusions. Inevitably, this means learning about research methodology. Students are sometimes impatient with scientific controversies; they are more interested in the conclusions themselves than in understanding how they were reached. Or, as George Miller put it, methodological issues that are "bread and butter to the working scientist can be spinach to everyone else" (Lachman, Lachman, & Butterfield, 1979, p. 13).

To understand psychology fully and appreciate its significance, you must learn to tell the difference between a conclusion based on a strong study and one based on a weak study or on no study at all. Whenever you hear a wondrous new claim about an advance in understanding human behavior, your reaction should always be the same: How do they know? Only when you understand the evidence that lies behind the claim will you be able to make an intelligent assessment of its value and validity (correctness). The critical thinking exercises called "Understanding the Scientific Method" are designed to share with you the tools scientists use to gather their evidence— tools that may lead to quite different conclusions from the ones reached by a neighbor reading a popular magazine or making observations from the porch. (See "Understanding the Scientific Method," which explains critical thinking skills in more detail.)

Another group of critical thinking exercises focuses on popular renditions of psychological concepts. As psychologists have grown in number and influence, almost every American has become a "consumer" of psychological knowledge and services. Many people learn about psychology primarily through newspaper and magazine articles that tell them how to develop more satisfying friendships, fulfill their potential, and determine if their pet goldfish is neurotic. Some of these articles are accurate and some are not. In this text, the "Becoming a Critical Consumer" exercises contain excerpts from popular literature that you are encouraged to read carefully in order to determine their strengths and weaknesses. Our goal is to have every student learn to become a critical consumer of psychological knowledge. The very nature of psychology as an ongoing process of discovery demands that students learn not just *what* the experts have said, but also *why* they have said it.

Finally, the critical thinking exercises called "Applying Scientific Concepts" are designed to give you practice in using psychological concepts to complete scientific problems or determine how theories and research findings

What Are Critical Thinking Skills?

Scientists, like other people, come in different shapes and sizes. They subscribe to different theories and study a wide range of different problems. But, as we have noted, they also share similarities. In their drive to understand, predict, and learn to control behavior, they honor the scientific method—relying on systematic observation of behavior and subjecting their hypotheses to empirical tests through the systematic collection of data. We discuss the nature of the scientific method in some depth in Chapter 2.

Scientists also share the ability to think critically. A number of years ago, two psychologists, Goodwin Watson and Edward Maynard Glaser (1952), developed a test called the Critical Thinking Appraisal. The critical thinking abilities assessed by this test continue to be an important part of a scientific approach. These skills include the following:

1. Inference—the ability to make judgments about the probability of inferences drawn from a set of facts.
2. Recognition of assumptions—the ability to recognize unstated assumptions underlying particular assertions.
3. Interpretation—the ability to weigh evidence and to distinguish between unwarranted generalizations and inferences supported by the data.
4. Evaluation of arguments—the ability to distinguish between arguments that are strong and important to the question and those that are weak or irrelevant.

While acknowledging the importance of critical thinking skills, psychologists have also come to emphasize the advantage of in-depth knowledge in particular areas. Indeed, John Bransford and his colleagues (Bransford, Sherwood, Vye, & Rieser, 1986) argue that specific knowledge about an area (e.g., psychological research methods) and the ability to think critically about that area develop hand-in-hand. This text is intended to provide you with important knowledge about psychology. The critical thinking exercises have been created to help you develop critical thinking skills in relation to psychology as you master specific psychological content.

relate to your everyday experience. For example, this chapter has an exercise on using your critical thinking skills (see "Applying Scientific Concepts"). Subsequent chapters provide opportunities for applying new concepts to diagnose a case of brain damage, develop a program to modify your own behavior, and make judgments about the capacity for intimacy in some of your favorite television characters. The more you struggle to use new concepts and the more you use them in a meaningful way, the more likely you will be to develop critical thinking abilities.

In addition to helping you become critical thinkers, we also want to instill an appreciation for the many mysteries with which psychologists are still grappling. However, you should also understand that even though psychologists are scientists who still are looking for answers, this does not mean

Using Your Critical Thinking Skills

In your daily life you are exposed to numerous assertions, many of which are not backed up by scientific data; they simply represent people's beliefs. Critical thinking skills allow you to evaluate assertions, make your own inferences from a set of data, and consider the logical implications of particular sets of information. This exercise provides the opportunity to practice using critical thinking to reason about assertions and types of information that interest psychologists. (A discussion of this exercise appears after the "Summary" at the end of this chapter.)

1. You read an article about dozens of experiments in which researchers give rats food pellets, first for approaching, then for touching, and finally for pushing a bar, always in the presence of a red light. The rats gradually begin to press the bar whenever the red light goes on. What *inference* can you draw from this information?

2. You read in your psychology textbook about the results of several studies showing that people are attracted to others who are similar to themselves, thus supporting the adage that "birds of a feather flock together." Your Uncle Albert, on the other hand, insists that "opposites attract." After all, he notes, he married Aunt Edna, who is always after him to go dancing when he'd rather bowl. Which position is the stronger—your psychology textbook's or Uncle Albert's? Why?

3. Several of your friends urge you not to vote for candidate X. The reason they give is that he underwent electroshock therapy several years ago. Evaluate the strength of their argument.

4. Your sister reads an article in the newspaper saying that day care is bad for children. Consequently, she decides to reject her husband's suggestion that she resume her career while their children are still preschoolers. Is her conclusion valid? Why or why not?

that psychology has nothing to offer at present. Life does not wait for research psychologists to complete their investigations; applied psychologists must deal with today's problems as best they can, given what they have learned thus far.

For example, if a man consults a therapist because he has an anxiety attack whenever he has to get on an airplane, the mental health professional does not have the luxury of saying, "I'm sorry, but psychology is not yet sure how it should deal with your problem. Why don't you come back and see me in a few years?" Instead, she must consider the relevant available evidence and recommend the best course of therapy she can. In this regard, psychology is like medicine, where information necessary to diagnosis and cure is often incomplete.

Many students agree that their study habits could be far more efficient.

Applying Psychology

Throughout this text—particularly in Chapter 17, "Applied Psychology"—we shall provide many examples of the ways in which psychology can be applied to solve a wide range of problems, from the evaluation of eyewitness testimony to the design of industrial training programs. We provide our first example of the application of psychological principles to everyday life by considering a problem relevant to all students: learning material and studying for exams.

How to Study

According to the educational psychologist Francis P. Robinson (1970, p. 13), many of the techniques students use to master their lessons are "not very efficient." For example, given an assignment to read Chapter 1 of this text, the typical student might begin by finding the first and last pages and holding the chapter between two fingers to measure its thickness. This tactile assessment of the weightiness of the material might be followed by a frown of concentration and a detailed reading of each page. The entire process might be punctuated by mumbles of "mmhm" and "aha" and occasional comparisons of the thickness of the material read with that which remains.

If our mythical student were asked at the beginning of this process what the assignment was about, he or she might well reply, "About 35 pages." This example suggests a common concentration on the mere length of an assignment, rather than on the identification and mastery of key concepts contained in it.

The SQ3R method has been shown to be an effective technique for making study more efficient.

SQ3R method A method for efficient study consisting of five steps: survey, question, read, recite, and review.

More conscientious students might review the chapter four or five times. But while additional readings do improve knowledge of the material, the improvement may be painfully slow. For example, in one study of reading comprehension, the average person scored 69% on a test after one reading of the material, 74% after two readings, and 75% after three (English, Welborn, and Killian, 1934).

Of course, the actual rate of improvement for a particular student will depend on a number of variables, including the level of difficulty of the material and the test and the time lapse between readings. But the general point is that while simple repetition helps, it is often not the most efficient way to master material.

Many students would probably agree that they do not study in the most efficient possible manner. There are a number of guides written by psychologists to help students develop better study skills and habits. (See, for example, Carman & Adams, 1972; or Pauk, 1974.) One of the most influential is Robinson's *Effective Study*. Its first edition was published in 1941; the most recent revision, the fourth edition, appeared in 1970. In it he outlines a set of procedures designed to help students select the most important ideas from material they read, and comprehend and remember them as rapidly as possible.

For efficient study, Robinson proposed the **SQ3R method**, which consists of the following five steps: survey, question, read, recite, and review. (Note that the acronym SQ3R can help you remember these five steps by focusing your attention on the first letter in each word. Chapter 7 of our text includes a discussion of this memory aid and several others.) The following explanation of these five steps illustrates how they can be applied in the study of our book.

According to Robinson, study should begin with a short *survey* to identify the most critical concepts in a chapter or article. In reading this textbook, you can accomplish this step by looking at the table of contents at the beginning of each chapter. These headings and subheadings identify the most important material and can help you organize your thoughts before actually reading the chapter. Robinson (1970, p. 28) suggests that this initial survey "should not take more than a minute."

The real work of studying begins at the next step, when you must turn each heading into a *question* to arouse your curiosity and focus your attention. For example, in Chapter 1, when you see the heading "A Variety of Theoretical Perspectives," you should make a conscious effort to focus on the most important point by asking yourself: What are the key theories in psychology?

Then *read* the material to answer the question. In this example, you will find the answers in the second paragraph under the heading: The five major approaches are the psychoanalytic, behavioral, humanistic, cognitive, and biological.

Once you have read a particular section, turn away from the book and try to *recite* the answer to your own question. Reciting will be most effective if you use your own words and try to give an example of each key concept. This step will be particularly helpful if you "recite" by writing down a very brief outline of the key ideas.

These three critical steps—questioning, reading, and reciting—should be repeated for each of the headings in the chapter. For example, your next subheading question in Chapter 1 could be: What is the psychoanalytic approach? You would read for the answer and then turn away from the book to "recite" by jotting down your answer.

Finally, after the entire chapter has been completed in this manner, you should proceed to the fifth and final step: *review*. If you have been taking good notes throughout the process, you can simply look them over to get "the big picture" of how the ideas in the chapter are related. Further, you can check your memory by covering up portions of the notes to see whether you have mastered the main points and each of the subtopics.

Robinson (1970) has cited many studies which show that the SQ3R method increases comprehension speed and improves test performance. It accomplishes this by requiring each student to become an active learner who seeks out knowledge and tries to organize it, rather than a passive "couch potato" who waits inertly for facts to fill his or her brain.

Using Robinson's findings, and those of other educational psychologists, this book has been designed to make it easier for you to learn about psychology. In addition to using the SQ3R method as discussed above, the wise student will take advantage of its features by reading the chapter summary section first as a preview and later as a reminder of the most critical material in each chapter. Students can also benefit by focusing on the headings and subheadings, which organize the material, and on the definitions of key terms, which are written in **boldface**.

How to Take Tests

Students' success in studying is usually measured by their performance on classroom tests. Although some may wish to argue about the wisdom of judging achievement in college by grades, it is a fact of life that this is often done. Since test performance may be affected by variables above and beyond a student's knowledge of the material, it is in each student's interest to understand these other factors.

According to a study by Murray (1980), many college students are overly optimistic in predicting their performance on tests and, in fact, are often underprepared. One way to combat this natural optimism is to **overlearn** material by continuing to study beyond the point where material is first remembered. (See Chapter 7 for a further discussion of this point.)

In terms of more specific test-taking strategies, one of the more interesting lines of research concerns changing responses on objective exams. According to traditional folk wisdom, a person's first response to an objective test item is more likely to be correct than her second; therefore, it is assumed that students should stick with their first choices.

Several surveys have found that about three out of four students agree with this theory, along with a majority of teachers. Indeed, in a survey at Texas A & M University, about 20% of the faculty members directly advised their students not to change responses because doing so would probably result in lower grades (Benjamin, Cavell, & Shallenberger, 1984).

However, when the researchers who conducted this survey went on to review earlier studies regarding this question, they found that this advice was probably wrong. These studies showed that most people do change some answers and are likely to achieve higher tests scores as a result. That is,

overlearn To practice beyond the point of mastery.

Test performance is affected by a number of factors above and beyond a student's knowledge of the material.

people are more likely to *correct* an error when they change an answer than they are to introduce a new mistake. Further, these researchers "noted a remarkable consistency of results across 33 separate investigations . . . [a] kind of consistency [that] is rare in psychology. . . ." (Benjamin et al., 1984, p. 140).

The researchers also noted, perhaps inevitably, that further investigation will be required to resolve this question fully. Some of the more recent research has focused on such issues as item difficulty and reasons for changing answers. Ramsey, Ramsey, and Barnes (1987), like Skinner (1983), found that students are more likely to improve their scores when they change answers on easy items rather than on difficult ones. Moreover, scores are more likely to improve when students are highly confident about their changes than when they are less confident—although even when they are only 75% confident, some improvement in performance is likely.

Ramsey, Ramsey, and Barnes (1987) also found that the reason for making a change is significantly related to better scores. For example, changing answers to questions that students realize they have misread or misinterpreted increases scores significantly more than changing answers for other reasons, such as to correct a clerical error. These investigators came up with quite a different conclusion than the advice professors often give their students: "The evidence clearly indicates that students who change answers are likely to benefit" (p. 209). We suggest that the debate will go on, and that further investigation will be needed to clarify the circumstances under which answer changing is likely to improve test scores. Nevertheless, students who blindly follow the advice "Never change an answer" are likely to be doing themselves a disservice.

Our excursion into applied psychology brings us to an important conclusion that will be echoed in the chapters to come: Psychology is a science that can help us solve the mysteries of human behavior and improve the way we live our lives. Throughout this text, there will be a strong emphasis on research methods. Hopefully, this exposure to scientific methods will teach you to think more clearly and objectively about people. And along the way, it will also help you to understand the most fascinating organisms on the face of the earth—yourself and others.

Summary

What Is Psychology?

- **Psychology** can be defined as the scientific study of behavior and mental processes. Psychologists conduct research on a wide variety of topics, including the brain, learning and memory, thought, sensation and perception, normal and abnormal personality, and social psychology.

A Variety of Theoretical Approaches

- A **paradigm** is a common set of beliefs and assumptions shared by a particular group of scientists. In a young, dynamic, and changing science like psychology, several contradictory paradigms may coexist.

- **Psychoanalysts** emphasize the role of unconscious processes and biological instincts in motivating behavior. **Behaviorists** emphasize systematic studies of observable behavior. **Humanistic psychologists** are particularly concerned with human values, subjective experience, and the uniqueness of the individual. **Cognitive psychologists** study the active internal nature of higher mental processes involved in attention, perception, memory, language, imagery, and reasoning. **Biological psychologists** analyze the physiological events associated with behavior and experience.

A Variety of Professional Activities

- **Basic research** psychologists use the scientific method to try to understand fundamental laws of the mind and behavior. **Applied research** psychologists try to solve specific problems by applying scientific principles and knowledge. In practice, many psychologists are involved in both types of activities.

- In the basic research group, **experimental psychologists** typically conduct laboratory studies in such areas as learning, human memory, and sensation and perception. **Physiological psychologists** study the biological bases of behavior. **Developmental psychologists** focus on the physical, intellectual, and emotional changes associated with aging. **Personality psychologists** focus on individual differences and how they develop. **Social psychologists** are concerned with the way people respond to other human beings and how they interact with one another.

- In the applied group are **clinical psychologists**, who diagnose and treat abnormal behavior. **Counseling psychologists** specialize in helping people solve everyday problems, such as marital difficulties. Both groups work closely with **psychiatrists**, licensed physicians who are trained in medicine before they specialize in the treatment of mental and emotional problems. There are also **school psychologists**, who provide advice and guidance in school systems; **educational psychologists**, who tend to be more concerned with ways of increasing teacher effectiveness; **industrial/organizational psychologists**, who apply research findings to the work world; and **health psychologists**, who apply a psychological perspective to stress-related diseases or other physical disorders.

Applying Psychology

- Francis P. Robinson's book, *Effective Study,* proposed the **SQ3R method** for efficient study, which consists of five steps: survey, question, read, recite, and review.

- One way to counteract students' tendency for being overly optimistic in predicting their test performance is to **overlearn** material, that is, to continue to study beyond the point where material is first remembered.

Critical Thinking Exercise Discussion

Using Your Critical Thinking Skills

1. The major allowable inference based on the experiments is that rats can learn to press bars in the presence of a red light when they are reinforced for doing so. It would be unjustified, for example, to infer that rats are smart or dumb. The available data simply do not support such conclusions. (Chapter 6 discusses such learning in rats.)

2. Your textbook has the stronger argument, as it reports the results of systematic research designed to test the hypothesis that "birds of a feather flock together." (See Chapter 16 for a discussion of research on attraction.)

3. Your friends' argument rests on some unstated and probably unexamined assumptions—for example, that people who have undergone electroshock therapy are crazy, unfit to govern, and so forth. Unless they can provide evidence supportive of their unstated assumption, their argument is a weak one. (Electroshock therapy is discussed in Chapter 15.)

4. Your sister would do well to read the original research on which the newspaper article was based as well as other research relevant to the topic. (In this text, especially in the "Becoming a Critical Consumer" boxes, the popular media are shown often to fail to follow the canons of good scientific reporting and critical thinking when writing for the public.)

PSYCHOLOGY AS A HUMAN SCIENCE

Chapter 2

Around 1900, the Berlin press discovered Clever Hans. Hans was a trotting horse who could add, subtract, multiply, divide, and more. Or could he?

Every day around noon, a retired mathematics teacher named Herr von Osten gave a free demonstration of his favorite horse's astounding abilities. "How much is $\frac{2}{5}$ and $\frac{1}{2}$?" Hans's trainer might ask. Hans would pause thoughtfully, tap his front right foot 9 times, pause again, and tap 10 times for the answer, $\frac{9}{10}$. "If the eighth day of the month comes on a Tuesday, what is the date of the following Friday?" While some members of the audience were still trying to figure that one out, Hans would tap 11 times and stop. "Which of these cards says *horse,* Hans?" Hans would carefully examine the printed cards placed before him and point to the correct card with his nose. (Naturally the card said *Pferd,* since Hans spoke only German.) "Which hand is that gentleman raising, Hans?" Hans would correctly move his head to the right. And so on.

Hans could count the number of men or women in the audience or the number of people wearing eyeglasses. He could answer questions by shaking his head *yes* or *no,* solve simple algebra problems, and tell time. He could even spell out words using an elaborate code of foot taps developed by Herr von Osten. German educators concluded that Hans had the intelligence of a 13- or 14-year-old human.

Clever Hans became the rage of Germany and then of the world. His story was told in newspapers, magazines, and books. There were Clever Hans postcards and Clever Hans toys. In the meantime, the experts debated whether

Hans was a miraculous freak, a fraud, or a living example of what horses everywhere could achieve with proper education.

Some experts believed that Hans really was a thinking horse. Others argued that he wasn't really intelligent, he just had a fantastic memory. A few said that Hans was stupid but telepathic—he got the answers from "thought waves which radiate from the brain of his master" (Pfungst, 1911, p. 28).

But human nature being what it is, many people suspected Herr von Osten of trickery. An informal commission was appointed to investigate the charge. In September 1904, 13 experts (including a circus manager, a veterinarian, a teacher, and several zoologists and psychologists) reported that Herr von Osten was not guilty of using intentional signals or "unintentional signals of the kind which are presently familiar" (Pfungst, 1911, p. 254).

But Oskar Pfungst, an associate of one of the psychologists of the committee, was not convinced. He proceeded to plan a series of experiments under more carefully controlled conditions. Clever Hans was high-strung and moody and had a tendency to bite his new trainers whenever he got excited. But the horse gradually learned to answer questions posed by the psychologist, and the research went on for two hours each day, four days a week.

Pfungst planned to vary systematically the conditions under which Hans was tested. First, he would ask Hans questions when Herr von Osten was not around. Later, Hans would wear large blinders so he could not receive visual cues. Cotton would be stuffed in Hans's ears to avoid unintentional auditory cues. Pfungst even considered obscuring the horse's sense of smell. The ultimate test of Hans's reasoning ability would be somehow to give him

Clever Hans prepares to answer a question during a test performed in Berlin in 1904.

a problem to which no one present knew the answer. Throughout all this, conditions were to be kept as natural as possible, and each test would be repeated many times.

This type of careful, systematic observation gradually revealed Hans's secret. When the horse had to read a number from a card, he was right 98% of the time if the experimenter had looked at the card first, but only 8% of the time if he had not. Tests with written words yielded the same result. When the experimenter knew the answer, Hans had no trouble; when all around him were ignorant, so was Clever Hans. Later tests revealed the importance of visual cues. Hans became very upset when he had to wear blinders and spent much of his time trying to get a peek at his inquisitors. When he could not see the questioner, he could not get the right answer.

Armed with this information, Pfungst began watching Hans's performances more closely. He noticed that whenever anyone asked Hans a question, there was a natural tendency for the questioner to lean forward very slightly to watch the horse's foot. When Hans reached the right number of taps, the questioner would involuntarily jerk his head slightly upward. After Pfungst discovered this, he could make Hans tap as many times as he wanted by consciously leaning forward and then subtly jerking his head back. Other unintentional cues could explain Hans's other tricks.

Oskar Pfungst succeeded where so many had failed not because he was smarter than others who had studied Clever Hans or even because he was a more astute observer of animal behavior. Pfungst's advantage was his careful application of the scientific method.

He began by identifying variables that might affect Hans's performance, such as the presence of visual or auditory cues. He then went on to perform a series of experiments to test the importance of each variable. For example, in one experiment Pfungst put cotton in Hans's ears to eliminate auditory cues. He then compared the percentage of problems that Hans solved under these conditions with his normal performance. This experiment suggested that auditory cues were not a critical factor.

However, when Pfungst eliminated visual cues by placing blinders on the horse, suddenly Hans was not so clever. The dramatic drop in the percentage of correct answers was also seen on several other occasions. This led Pfungst to conclude that Hans's real cleverness lay not in his ability to solve equations, but rather in his ability to read the faces and body language of his inquisitors, and to stop tapping when he reached the number that they knew was correct.

Thus, Herr von Osten was innocent of trickery but guilty of not being careful enough. When it became clear that the psychologists were going to issue an unfavorable report, von Osten flew into a rage and forbade further experiments. He continued to believe in Hans and to exhibit him, apparently to his dying day. Pfungst went back to his laboratory and experimented with an elaborate device that measured very small movements of people's heads. And Clever Hans, we might guess, was left to wonder whatever happened to all those pompous men who used to ask him questions and why he was no longer on the front pages of *Frankfurter Zeitung*.

How can we characterize Oscar Pfungst's approach to the case of the mysterious counting horse? Essentially, he was objective and systematic in his observations. He formulated hypotheses and then tested them in light of empirical evidence. In short, he behaved like a scientist.

The Need for a Scientific Approach to Behavior

Why, you might ask, is it important to learn new methods in order to take a scientific approach to behavior? After all, you already try to understand, predict, and control behavior just like a psychologist. It does seem likely that at one time or another, each of us has tried to understand why a friend seemed upset, to predict what Dad would say when he "found out," or to change the bad habits of a loved one. However, to solve these ordinary problems in living, the ordinary person uses common sense—some combination of lessons learned from the past and intuitions about the future. Unfortunately, common sense and personal experience can be misleading. This creates unique problems for both teachers and students of psychology.

If a physics teacher tells a class that force equals mass times acceleration, few students are likely to object that this goes against common sense, that in their experience force equals mass times acceleration squared. Similarly, students of basic chemistry usually accept the periodic chart of elements without debate. But by the time you read your first psychology book, you will have dealt with people for many years, and, in all probability, you will have developed strong opinions about human nature.

For example, consider the following study. Researchers who studied 30 Boston area couples found that when husbands described themselves as warm, empathic, understanding, and nurturant, their wives were very comfortable with the marriage (White et al., 1986). However, when wives described themselves in those same terms, the husbands were quite dissatisfied with the relationship. How would you explain such findings? If you are a woman who thinks that any man who describes himself as warm and empathic must be a wimp and you wouldn't want anything to do with him, you probably will doubt the study, even though it involved the systematic collection of data and careful statistical analyses. When scientific findings conflict with common sense or personal experience, people often reject the scientific conclusion rather than question whether their experiences are typical and their observations accurate.

A Test of Common Beliefs

To see whether students do indeed come to psychology classes with many misconceptions, psychologist Eva Vaughan developed the Test of Common Beliefs, which includes 80 statements about behavior. Eight of these items are listed here. Before reading on, decide whether you think each is true or false.

1. A schizophrenic is someone with a split personality.
2. Boys and girls exhibit no behavioral differences until environmental influences begin to produce such differences.
3. Genius is closely akin to insanity.
4. To change people's behavior toward members of ethnic minority groups, we must first change their attitudes.

5. The basis of a baby's love for its mother is the fact that the mother meets the baby's physiological needs for food, water, and so on.
6. Children's IQ scores have very little to do with how well they perform in school.
7. The best way to ensure that a behavior will persist after training is to reward the behavior every time it occurs throughout training rather than reward it only once in a while.
8. Under hypnosis people can perform feats of physical strength that they could never do otherwise (adapted from Vaughan, 1977).

In Vaughan's original study, each of these eight statements was accepted by at least half a group of 119 college students. If you are like most people, you probably believe that at least some of these statements are true. In fact, however, scientific research has shown that every one of them is false.

To make matters worse, incorrect opinions like these are often hard to change. In one study, Lamal (1979) compared students' scores on a modified version of the Test of Common Beliefs before and after they took an introductory psychology course. Although there was some improvement at the end of the course, the average student still accepted 38% of the false statements. Education can gradually correct mistaken beliefs, but the process is often slower than we might hope.

Evaluating Common Sense

Why are such misconceptions so difficult to correct? Part of the answer involves the way the human mind works, or, as a psychologist might say, the way people process information. Many people rely heavily on common sense, but there are a number of ways in which common sense is systematically wrong.

EXPECTATIONS AND BIAS

The ability of the human mind to distort the facts is awe-inspiring. For example, a few weeks after Arthur Bremer shot presidential candidate George Wallace, *Life* magazine interviewed Bremer's mother to see what evil influences could have led to this assassination attempt. His mother explained, "I still think it was something he ate that didn't agree with him. Why else would he do such a thing? He didn't care about politics, at least not that I know of. . . . It *had* to be something he ate" (quoted in Wittner, 1972, p. 32).

Perhaps the mothers of Hitler, Mussolini, and Jack the Ripper had similar explanations for their sons' lapses. While few psychologists would have the nerve to attack motherly love, it is quite clear that in this case, Mrs. Bremer was not being entirely objective.

Many psychologists have studied how expectations and bias influence what we perceive and remember. In one classic study of subjectivity, psychologists asked undergraduates from Dartmouth and Princeton to review films of a controversial football game between the two schools (Hastorf & Cantril, 1954). Sports fans will not be surprised to learn that Princeton students thought the Dartmouth team deserved more penalties for breaking the rules, whereas

Dartmouth students noticed more infractions by the Princeton team. Two other classic demonstrations of the effect of expectations are illustrated in Figures 2.1 and 2.2.

Biases and expectations shape people's beliefs in a number of different ways. For one thing, people tend to seek out information that agrees with what they already believe and to ignore or avoid information that disagrees with their perceptions. In one ingenious experiment (Block & Balloun, 1967), people were asked to listen to two tape-recorded speeches about cigarette smoking. One speech summarized the evidence that smoking causes cancer; the other argued that this was a myth. Each subject was told that unfortunately the speeches had been recorded under poor conditions and were sometimes hard to hear unless the listener pressed a button to reduce static. Interestingly, nonsmokers tended to press the button to hear the antismoking message clearly, and smokers were more likely to press the button to listen to the prosmoking speech.

Not only do our biases and expectations affect what we pay attention to in the first place, but they can even change what we remember. In one study (Snyder & Uranowitz, 1978), 212 students read the fictitious life story

FIGURE 2.1 How many aces of spades do you see? For most people, a quick glance yields three. If you agree, go back and count again. Expectations can influence perception. Because you expect an ace of spades to be black, you can easily miss the two red ones. The correct total is five.

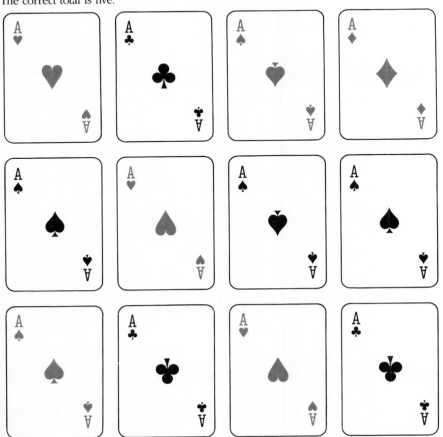

FIGURE 2.2 This picture of an argument was used in a classic study of the psychology of rumors. One person saw this picture and described it to a second person; the second described it to a third; and so on. As the story was repeated, the details were altered to fit the cultural stereotypes of the 1940s, when the study was performed. More than half the time, the sixth person in the rumor chain said that the black man, not the white man, held the razor.

of Betty K. After they had spent a few minutes thinking about what Betty was like, some were told she was a lesbian; others heard that she was heterosexual. A week later people from the second group described Betty as an attractive woman who had had a steady boyfriend in high school and a tranquil childhood. Although they had read the same life history, the people who had been told that Betty was a lesbian said she was rather unattractive, had never had a steady boyfriend, and had an abusive father. Stereotypes about sexual prefer-ences had actually changed the way people remembered this fictional young woman.

Further complicating casual observations of behavior are **self-fulfilling prophecies**—expectations that come true partly because people believe them. If everyone believes that inflation is here to stay, they will spend more and increase inflation. If you think your new roommate is inconsiderate, you may treat her in such an unpleasant way that she will retaliate by behaving inconsiderately. Numerous studies have shown that one person's expectations can influence another's behavior (Snyder, 1982).

Self-fulfilling prophecies can be important not just in dealing with others but even in dealing with ourselves. Psychologists have shown that people who expect to fail often do; those with higher opinions of themselves are more likely to succeed (Jones, 1977). Thus, biases and expectations can influ-ence not just what people attend to and remember but even what happens to them.

self-fulfilling prophecies
Expectations that come true partly because people believe they will.

THE IMPACT OF VIVID EXAMPLES

Still another problem with common sense is the fact that people are often overly impressed by vivid examples. Imagine how you might react in the following situation:

> Let us suppose that you wish to buy a new car and have decided that on grounds of economy and longevity you want to purchase one of those solid, stalwart, middle-class Swedish cars—either a Volvo or a Saab. As a prudent and sensible buyer, you go to *Consumer Reports,* which informs you that the consensus of their experts is that the Volvo is mechanically superior, and the consensus of the readership is that the Volvo has the better repair record. Armed with this information, you decide to go and strike a bargain with the Volvo dealer before the week is out. In the interim, however, you go to a cocktail party where you announce this intention to an acquaintance. He reacts with disbelief and alarm: "A Volvo! You've got to be kidding. My brother-in-law had a Volvo. First, the fancy fuel injection computer thing went out. 250 bucks. Next he started having trouble with the rear end. Had to replace it. Then the transmission and the clutch. Finally sold it in three years for junk." (Nisbett, Borgida, Crandall, & Reed, 1976, p. 129)

If you are totally rational and logical, this alarming report should not have a major impact on your plans. After all, if the *Consumer Reports* survey summarized the experiences of 900 Volvo owners, you now have information on 901. The averages still look very good. But you may not be totally rational and logical. Abstract averages lack the dramatic impact of one concrete, vivid case and often seem less convincing (Nisbett & Ross, 1980).

How often have you heard a cigarette smoker argue that no matter what the Surgeon General says, "I know a man who smoked three packs a day and lived to be 86"? Common sense may tell us that all the scientists' fancy charts and technical reports are less convincing than a case you can see with your own eyes. But in this respect common sense is extremely misleading. The fact that one heavy smoker lives to be 86 does *not* disprove the general rule: On the average, smokers still die younger than nonsmokers. This vivid example merely reminds us that statistical predictions about large groups do not apply to every individual, that there are often exceptions to the rule.

In a systematic demonstration of the impact of vivid examples, Borgida and Nisbett (1977) directly contrasted the influence of abstract and concrete information on students' course choices. One group of psychology majors was given course evaluations based on the average ratings of large groups of students who had taken the courses. When the psychology majors later indicated what courses they themselves planned to take, they apparently ignored these abstract recommendations. In contrast, another group heard individual students describe what they had liked or disliked about specific courses. Although this concrete information only reflected the opinion of two or three individuals, students were more likely to follow this advice.

Even highly sophisticated observers may be fooled by common sense. In a discussion of the history of medicine, Crichton (1970) notes that nineteenth-century surgeons resisted change in operating-room procedures long after researchers had provided statistical evidence that the sterilization of instruments reduced the risk of infection. One reason was that every surgeon could cite many examples of patients he had successfully operated on without washing his hands or sterilizing his instruments. These vivid examples seemed more convincing than abstract surveys showing that on the average more patients recovered when sterile procedures were observed. Many patients died because these surgeons based their practice on common sense.

Psychology students should try to avoid this error in reasoning. A particular claim about human behavior should always be carefully evaluated in terms of the evidence on which it is based. The fact that you know someone who is an exception does not disprove the rule.

20/20 HINDSIGHT

Sometimes, students have the opposite problem. Instead of arguing that a specific research conclusion goes against common sense and therefore must be wrong, they complain that a certain study simply confirms common sense and therefore seems trivial—they knew it all along. This criticism says as much about the way the human mind works as it does about psychology. No one should be surprised if some psychological research agrees with common sense. Sometimes common sense is right and sometimes it is wrong, and one goal of psychology is to find out which times are which. But when we say we could easily have predicted how an experiment would turn out, it may just be the wisdom of hindsight.

Most people tend to overrate their own success in predicting the future. If your best friend announces that he is getting married, you are likely to say to yourself, "I knew this would be the one." But if he announces instead that the relationship has ended, you would probably say to yourself, "I knew it wouldn't last." No matter what happens, we tend to think we knew it all along. Everybody is an expert in hindsight. Every sports fan can tell you what the coach should have done—after the game is over.

Many studies have shown that after people hear the results of a scientific experiment, a historical conflict, or a medical diagnosis (Arkes, Wortman, Saville, & Harkness, 1981), they think they could easily have predicted the results on the basis of common sense. But when other people were asked to *predict* the same results beforehand, they were not particularly successful. The answer was obvious only after the fact.

WHEN COMMON SENSE SUCCEEDS

The findings discussed above, and others like them, stirred up a controversy about the limits and implications of human reasoning power. Many critics asked whether the picture could really be as gloomy as these defects of common sense seemed to suggest. If human beings are really so far out of touch with reality, how did they create the pyramids, Hoover Dam, and the ice cream sandwich?

As a result of this skepticism, other studies were done that examined human reasoning in many different contexts in order to learn more not only about its weaknesses, but also about its strengths. For example, Nisbett and Kunda (1985) examined people's perceptions about their own social groups. In this study, a group of introductory psychology students at the University of Michigan were asked to predict their classmates' responses to a questionnaire.

Some questions concerned typical behavior, such as: How often do you have trouble getting to sleep? And: How often do you go to bars or nightclubs? Others concerned attitudes, such as: How do you feel about women being allowed to have an abortion on demand? And: How do you feel about increasing defense spending? The final group of questions regarded how much the students liked or disliked people and things, such as *Star Wars,* Jane Fonda, Pepperidge Farm cookies, and Saudi Arabians.

When these researchers compared the actual responses of one group of students to the predictions of their classmates, they did find systematic and predictable errors. For example, people tended to assume that others were like them and therefore weighted the distributions in their own direction. However, the overall success of their estimates was far more impressive than the failures. Indeed, the researchers later wrote: "We were quite surprised by the accuracy subjects displayed" (Nisbett & Kunda, 1985, p. 310).

CONCLUSION

These results and others emphasize the fact that common sense and everyday observation have strengths as well as weaknesses. The problem is learning when to trust common sense and when to beware of it.

After analyzing several different meanings of the term *common sense,* Fletcher (1984, p. 212) described how common sense can be "a valuable resource that can be utilized in various ways by psychologists." However, he noted that this resource is also "difficult and dangerous," because it can exert "a powerful hidden influence over psychologists' thinking that is often both unanalyzed and unevaluated."

There are many situations in which this hidden influence may lead in the wrong direction. We tend to filter the world through our biases, paying attention to and remembering facts that are consistent with our prior beliefs. Self-fulfilling prophecies can cause our false beliefs to become true. We are overly impressed by concrete evidence. And we tend to think we knew something all along even when we did not.

The limitations of human processes of thinking and judgment do not mean that all observations must be discarded, but they do mean that we must learn to be cautious in our generalizations. As Jepson, Krantz, and Nisbett (1983, p. 495) put it: "Induction [an inference based on several observations] is a skill in which learning plays an important role." Less formally, we might say that experience is the best teacher only after we have learned to become good students.

It will be useful to keep these conclusions about common sense in mind as you read this textbook and others. For example, as you read the findings of a specific study, you will sometimes be tempted to say to yourself, "That's so true, I've felt that way myself," or, "Baloney! I know that's not right." Your personal experiences may be convincing, but remember that, by themselves, they have little scientific validity. Whatever happened to you is just one person's experience, and there is a good chance that you are not able to be objective about it anyway. Intuitive opinions must be verified by a more systematic and objective approach to behavior and experience. And that is precisely what the scientific method provides.

An Introduction to Scientific Methods

The next section reviews the principal methods psychologists use when they collect data as part of their research: behavioral observations, interviews, questionnaires, and case studies. The section that follows it describes correlational and experimental research designs. Table 2.1 gives actual examples of correlational and experimental studies for each of the major types of data collection methods.

TABLE 2.1

Examples of Principal Data Collection Methods

Method	Description	Correlation Study Example	Experimental Study Example[a]
Behavioral observation	Systematic observation, recording, and analysis of behavior of humans or lower animals. May involve manual coding (categorizing), audiotaping, or videotaping of behavior.	Jean Piaget's theory of cognitive development, especially during infancy, was stimulated by his naturalistic observations of his own three children. (Piaget, 1954, Chapter 9.)	Children in experimental groups watched models attack a "Bobo" doll. Children in control groups were not exposed to this aggressive behavior. The subsequent behavior of all children was observed and recorded. (Bandura, 1977, Chapter 6.)
Interview	Questions on such issues as the individual's thoughts, feelings, and experiences; typically administered in a one-on-one format, in person or over the phone.	In the famous Kinsey study, thousands of volunteers participated in long interviews concerning their sexual behavior. ("Understanding the Scientific Method," Chapter 9.)	Subjects were interviewed after their participation in an experiment on obedience to determine the effectiveness of the experimental manipulation (i.e., did they think they were administering real shocks to the other subject? (Milgram, 1974, Chapter 16.)
Questionnaire	Questions on such issues as the individual's attitudes, beliefs, opinions, and experiences; typically self-administered. Can be completed in large groups or as part of mail or telephone *surveys*.	Adult householders filled in responses to questions on a postcard concerning the candidate for whom they would vote in the 1936 presidential election. ("Understanding the Scientific Method," Chapter 10.)	Subjects read questionnaires presumably filled out by a "stranger" but actually structured by the investigator so that the stranger would seem similar to the subject in specified ways. Subjects then completed questionnaires indicating how much they thought they would like this stranger. (Byrne, 1971, Chapter 16.)
Case study	Detailed description of life experiences and/or behavior patterns of a single individual.	Phineas Gage survived a serious head injury from a crowbar accident. His subsequent behavior and personality were assessed with a variety of instruments and described in the case study report. ("Understanding the Scientific Method," Chapter 3.)	John, an autistic child who had to be restrained from hurting himself, underwent therapy with behavior modification techniques. The details of John's behavior before, during, and after therapy, as well as the details of the therapeutic intervention, were fully described. ("Understanding the Scientific Method," Chapter 6.)

[a] Cross references to chapters in this text are in parenthesis.

Methods of Collecting Data

One common method that psychologists use to collect data is **systematic observation**—the careful observation, recording, and analysis of behavior. Observation of behavior often takes place in a psychological *laboratory,* where the investigator has control over many aspects of the experimental situation. Behavior can also be observed in *naturalistic* settings, where the researcher has less control over variables but the behavior is closer to "real life." Helping behavior is a good example of behavior that has been observed both in the laboratory and in naturalistic settings. The question frequently asked in these studies is: Are people more likely to help somebody in need if they have just had the opportunity to watch somebody else (a *model*) providing assistance?

Interviews and questionnaires are common forms of *self-report* measures. You have undoubtedly already completed a number of interviews and questionnaires in your life, as part of registering for school or to vote, applying for a job, getting medical assistance—perhaps even as a courteous response to a "telecommunications" voice beseeching your attention over the phone. In formal terms, **interviews** are direct interpersonal communications between an interviewer and a respondent—either face-to-face or over the phone. **Questionnaires** are self-administered measures that can be completed without any personal interaction with the information seeker. While interviews are more personal and allow the interviewer to give or seek clarifications, they are not as practical as questionnaires for obtaining a lot of information from large groups of people at the same time.

Many studies make use of more than one type of data collection. Data from interviews, questionnaires, and other sources may be summarized in a **case history**, a detailed description of the life experiences and behavior patterns of a single individual. Clinical psychologists often find the case-history method helpful in understanding the problems of their clients. In Chapter 3, we describe one of the most famous case histories in psychology, that of Phineas Gage, an accident victim whose personality changed dramatically after specific areas in his brain were damaged.

While case histories focus on a single individual, **surveys** measure the behavior of large groups of people, usually by summarizing information from many interviews or questionnaires. In Chapter 10, we contrast several famous surveys of sexual behavior to illustrate the importance of beginning with a **representative sample**, a group in which subjects are systematically chosen to represent some larger population. Selecting a representative sample is absolutely crucial if survey researchers are to make correct predictions about the behavior of a whole population. For example, until pollsters learned how to identify samples that were truly representative of the voting public, they were unable to predict election results accurately.

Experimental Research Designs

The experiment is generally considered the most powerful research technique available in psychology. When it is possible to bring a phenomenon into the laboratory for a closer look through an experimental study, many researchers prefer this technique over other alternatives. Scientists conduct experiments, or other types of investigations, to study the relationships among *variables*—

Although psychology is often associated with the image of a laboratory rat learning to run through a maze, this is just one technique among many.

systematic observation The careful observation, recording, and analysis of behavior.

interviews Systematic discussions of a person's experiences and feelings.

questionnaires Written lists of questions to which people are asked to respond.

case history A detailed description of the life experiences and behavior patterns of a single individual.

surveys Summaries of information drawn from many interviews or questionnaires in order to measure the behavior of large groups of people.

representative sample A group in which subjects are systematically chosen to represent some larger population.

that is, factors that can vary or change. Almost any interesting characteristic of people, animals, or situations can be a variable in a scientific study.

An **experiment** is a scientific study in which a researcher tries to establish a causal link (i.e., a cause-effect relationship) between two variables by manipulating one variable and observing changes in the other. The factor that the experimenter manipulates is called the **independent variable**. The **dependent variable** is the factor that may be affected; it is called dependent because the experiment is set up so that any changes that occur in this factor depend on changes in the independent variable. (Table 2.2 gives examples of independent and dependent variables. In "Applying Scientific Concepts," you are asked to identify independent and dependent variables on your own.)

Suppose, for example, that you are interested in learning how alcohol consumption affects the quickness with which drivers react on the road. In this case, alcohol consumption will be the independent variable, and speed of response will be the dependent variable. Both the independent and the dependent variables will have to be precisely defined for purposes of the experiment. Will the term *alcohol consumption* refer to beer, wine, or spirits? How much alcohol will you be considering, and over what period of time will it be consumed? Even the brand of liquor and its proof might be considered in the definition of the independent variable. Such a definition is called an *operational definition,* since it summarizes the operations used, or the steps taken, to define the variable. Similarly, speed of response must be defined. Will it apply to a simple task with limited possible responses, such as a driver applying the brakes upon seeing a red light? Or will you be looking at response time in a complex situation with a number of possible reactions, such as a driver seeing a shape move suddenly on the side of the road and having to decide whether to ignore it, change direction, or hit the brakes?

Let us assume that in this case, the independent variable of alcohol consumption will be defined as drinking 2 ounces of vodka within 30 minutes; the dependent variable of response speed will be defined by a reaction time

experiment A scientific attempt to establish a causal link between two variables by manipulating one and observing changes in the other.

independent variable The factor in an experiment that the experimenter manipulates.

dependent variable The factor that is affected by an experimenter's manipulations.

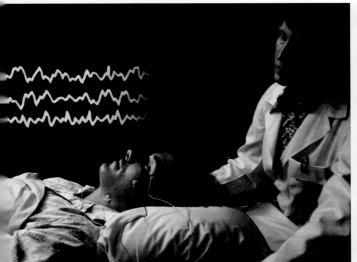

In sleep research, the dependent variables can be the frequency and amplitude of brain waves.

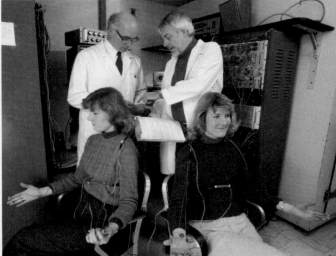

Studies of twins can provide important insights into the relative influence of heredity and environment.

TABLE 2.2

Independent and Dependent Variables in an Experimental Design

Type of Variable	Description	Example
Independent	These are variables that are manipulated by the researcher using an experimental design. To manipulate the independent variable, the investigator actively produces or creates *levels* of the variable to determine its effects on a dependent variable.	An investigator is interested in how children's aggressive behavior is affected by viewing somebody else (known in psychological parlance as a "model") behave aggressively. One group of children (the experimental group) views an aggressive model beating up an innocent "Bobo" doll. Another group of children (the control group) is spared the R-rated violence. Here there are two levels to the independent variable: (1) aggressive model present (the experimental group), and (2) aggressive model absent (the control group).
Dependent	These are the outcome variables, or effects, that are presumed to be *dependent* on the operation of the independent variable that the investigator is manipulating. When an investigator is interested in determining the causes of aggressiveness, cancer, or loving-kindness, it is aggressiveness, cancer, and loving-kindness that are the dependent variables.	In the experiment described above, it is the child's own aggressiveness that is the dependent variable of interest. After exposing the experimental group to the aggressive model, the investigator would observe all children (experimental and control) to determine the extent to which the experimental group was more aggressive. Specific aggressive behaviors, such as hitting, kicking, biting, and swearing, would be selected as the precise dependent variables to be analyzed.

device in which a person must press a switch as quickly as possible as soon as a light goes on.

Note that these choices brought the original question into focus by forcing specificity. It would be impossible to design a single experiment that would answer the general question: How does alcohol consumption affect the speed of response? To answer such a broad question, we would need to perform a series of experiments with different definitions of alcohol consumption and different measures of response speed. Although it is possible to imagine many measures of response speed that resemble driving more closely than this task, laboratory researchers often prefer to start by trying to understand very simple and "pure" behaviors.

Every experiment requires a comparison between at least one **experimental condition** (in which the independent variable is manipulated) and at least one **control condition** (with no special treatments or manipulations). Thus, to perform our hypothetical study of alcohol, you would need to compare the speed of response under two conditions: drinking vodka (the experimental condition) and not drinking vodka (the control condition).

One way to make this comparison is by studying different groups of people. Here, the *experimental group* would have their reaction times tested 30 minutes after they drank the vodka. The *control group* would get the same tests, but no vodka. Of course, if different people are recruited for the two groups, it is important that they be similar in ways that might affect the tests.

Suppose that by chance or accident the control group contained a large proportion of young athletes with quick reflexes, while the experimental group happened to have more middle-aged people with slower reflexes. It

experimental condition The manipulation of the independent variable to test its effect.

control condition The part of an experiment lacking special treatments or manipulations, allowing a basis for comparison with the experimental condition.

APPLYING SCIENTIFIC CONCEPTS

Identifying Independent and Dependent Variables

This chapter introduces you to the idea of independent and dependent variables. While the material probably makes sense to you while you are reading it, reading about new concepts and using them are two very different skills. In this exercise, you are asked to try to master these new concepts by applying them to unfamiliar research problems. As you complete the exercise, try to recall the particular critical thinking skills involved in each of the following applications of the new concepts. (A discussion of this exercise appears after the "Summary" at the end of this chapter.)

1. Dr. Sy conducted an experiment with kindergarten children to test the hypothesis that frustration causes aggression. In each of several kindergarten classrooms, he randomly assigned all the children to one of two play groups. Play group A, the "frustrated play group," was put in a playroom with attractive toys but was not allowed to play with them. Children in play group B were put in a playroom where they could play as much as they wanted with the same attractive toys. During each group's time in the playroom, Dr. Sy observed the children's behavior and made note of all aggressive acts, such as hitting, kicking, biting, shoving, swearing, name-calling, and grabbing.

What was the independent variable in this experiment?

How many levels did it have?

What was the dependent variable in this experiment?

2. Dr. Kol used a sample of college men and women to test the hypothesis that students form impressions of strangers partly on the basis of ethnic characteristics. Each participant in the study was asked to read a description of a mythical student (student X) and then to check off adjectives (e.g., affectionate, bossy, cautious, devious, exciting, fanciful) that seemed to apply to student X. Half the subjects received descriptions in which student X was said to be of the same race as the subject, and the other half were given descriptions where student X was said to be of a different race. The descriptions were the same in every other way. Dr. Kol compared average number of positive characteristics checked when student X was the same race as the subjects, and when student X was a different race.

What was the independent variable in this experiment?

How many levels did the independent variable have?

What was the dependent variable?

3. Dr. O'Gee is interested in the effects of bug size on the eating behavior of young birds. He presents the young birds with artificial (but very realistic and tasty) bugs in one of four sizes: slightly smaller than the bugs they normally eat, identical in size to the bugs they normally eat, slightly largely than their normal fare, and much larger than their normal fare but still easily ingestable. Dr. O'Gee then records whether or not each young bird eats the "bug."

What was the independent variable in this experiment?

How many levels did the independent variable have?

What was the dependent variable?

is likely that if neither group drank, the average reaction time for the younger control group would be shorter. But if the study measured the experimental group's reaction times only when they were drinking, this underlying difference in age and reflex speed would confuse the issue by introducing what are known as *confounding variables*.

Several techniques are used to avoid complications of this sort. The simplest is to assign people to the experimental and control groups at random. A second possibility is to pretest the reaction speed of each person and then form them into subject pairs with roughly equal reaction times. One person from each of these pairs would then be randomly assigned to the experimental condition and the other to the control condition. This has many advantages over using two different groups, but it also requires that each subject be tested twice, and it is thus more expensive and time-consuming.

A third possibility is to have the subjects act as their own controls. Here each person would be tested once when they were drinking and once when they were not. This is a very sophisticated technique. But it too is expensive, and it introduces new statistical complexities. Since people may do better the second time around, it is important that equal numbers of similar people take the drinking test first and others, the nondrinking test first.

In some cases, the "ideal" technique for a particular experiment might be difficult, impossible, or unethical. For example, it would be inhumane and impossible to do an experiment in which some human beings were required to smoke three packs of cigarettes a day to see if they died sooner of lung cancer.

Many of the complications and fine points of experimental methods will be discussed in detail in later chapters. Here the most important point is that experimental methods allow a researcher more control over the environment than other research methods, and thus can permit inferences about causality that would not be possible otherwise.

Correlational Research Designs

In cases where true experiments are unethical or difficult and costly to perform, researchers turn to correlational designs. Indeed, for some research problems, a correlational design is intrinsically more appropriate than an experimental design. Suppose you are interested in exploring differences between groups that already differ in some characteristic (e.g., sex, age, birth order). Here, a correlational design would be the method of choice. For example, assume you are interested in learning whether there are differences in emotional expressiveness between men and women. In this case, you obviously could not randomly assign subjects to either group and then look at their emotional expressiveness. Similarly, if you wanted to test the hypothesis that teenagers are more self-conscious than grade-school children, you could not randomly assign children to the younger or older age group. You *could* select children who are either adolescent or in grade school and compare their degree of self-consciousness, but you would not be using an experimental design. Age (like sex in the preceding example) is not a variable you can manipulate; you can only select subjects who already differ in this variable and then compare their scores on some other variable (e.g., emotional expressiveness, self-consciousness).

Correlational designs also are used to determine whether two characteristics are *associated* with each other. When research on the effects of smoking is conducted with laboratory animals, experimental techniques can be used. That is, animals can be randomly assigned to "treatment groups" receiving specified amounts of smoke at specified intervals. Research on smoking and cancer in humans, on the other hand, has relied on correlational techniques. Although one cannot infer cause-effect relationships from a correlation between variables, data on correlations provide useful information in situations where the use of experimental techniques would be unethical. For example, researchers correlating amount of smoking with incidence of lung cancer have demonstrated a positive association between these variables: The more people smoke, the more likely they are to contract lung cancer.

When the purpose of a correlational study is to determine whether two or more variables are *correlated* (associated with each other), researchers typically compute a **correlation coefficient**. This statistic, described more fully in Chapter 13 and the Appendix, provides a precise statistical expression of the relationship between two variables. The correlation may be *positive,* as when increases in one variable (e.g., skiing) are associated with increases in another variable (e.g., bruises), or it may be *negative,* as when increases in one variable (e.g., cursing) are associated with decreases in another variable (e.g., smiles from Mom). Correlation coefficients are not the only statistic used in correlational studies. Sometimes, the purpose of a correlational study is to determine whether particular differences between groups are **statistically significant** (see "Understanding the Scientific Method" in this chapter). In these cases, the correlational researcher might use any of the statistical tests also used by experimentalists.

Whichever approach—experimental or correlational—researchers use, it is their goal to achieve replicable results. **Replications** are repetitions of a study to see whether similar results are obtained each time. If a psychologist published a study showing that redheaded children are prone to temper tantrums, but nobody else could replicate those findings, the research would not be accepted as providing valid evidence about redheaded children.

The Human Side of Science

In reading a textbook, it is easy to forget that the principal actors in the drama of science are themselves living, breathing human beings. Like lawyers, accountants, and bus drivers, psychologists come in a variety of sizes, shapes, and temperaments. Some are driven by a desire for fame, some by financial pressures, some by an idealistic determination to improve the world, some by all these factors and more. And the way a researcher pursues a given problem may depend on his or her personality as well as training.

Trying to understand science simply by memorizing its rules is a bit like trying to understand how Congress works by studying the U.S. Constitution and Robert's Rules of Order. To understand Congress, one must also know about lobbyists, political deals, and the nature of power. To understand a scientific result, one must also know about the historical events and the human

---

correlation coefficient A precise statistical expression of the relationship between two variables.

statistically significant Unlikely to have occurred by chance according to some predetermined criterion, usually a probability of less than .05.

replications Repetitions of a study to see whether similar results are found.

background—the egotistical desire for fame, the spark of genius, and the fortunate accident. One of the goals of this textbook is to take you behind the scenes to glimpse the people and cultural forces that have shaped psychology.

The Scientific Method in Action

An introductory text must teach you the meaning of key terms, such as *correlation* and *case history,* but abstract definitions can make science seem rather dry and boring. Nothing could be further from the truth. A scientist is like a detective in a murder novel, trying to solve the mysteries of nature by carefully analyzing its cryptic clues. We end this chapter with an example of the scientific method in action in order to provide a more realistic picture of how psychology works.

The Case of the Biased Teachers

Although the case of Clever Hans provides an excellent introduction to the application of scientific methods, psychologists usually study more general questions than whether a particular horse can solve math problems. Our next case explores one of the most famous experiments in the recent history of psychology to show how the results of one study can be challenged by another.

As noted earlier, psychologists have long been interested in the effects of self-fulfilling prophecies—predictions that come true partly because people believe them. In 1968, Robert Rosenthal and Lenore Jacobson published a book called *Pygmalion in the Classroom,* which seemed to prove that teachers' high expectations can raise students' IQs. The cautious phrase *seemed to prove* is quite intentional; as we shall see, other researchers found that teacher expectations have an effect, but not on IQ.

Rosenthal and Jacobson's research had begun several years earlier, in the spring of 1964, when they administered the Harvard Test of Inflected Acquisition to every student at a public elementary school. Teachers were told that this test would identify children who could be expected to show a sudden improvement in their academic work. They were informed that although the current classroom performance of these late-bloomers might seem quite ordinary or even below average, they would soon improve dramatically.

On the first day of the next semester, each teacher in the first through sixth grades was given a list of the pupils who had been identified by the test. But this list was purposely misleading. In fact, the Harvard Test of Inflected Acquisition was simply an IQ test. And the late-bloomers had not been identified by their test scores. Their names had been picked randomly out of a hat.

The independent variable in this study involved teachers' expectations. Out of every five students, one was randomly identified as a late-bloomer. These made up the experimental group—subjects who had received a critical treatment to determine its effects. In contrast, the remaining children formed the control group—subjects who had not received any special experimental treatment.

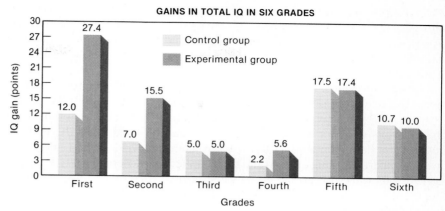

FIGURE 2.3 IQ gains of children identified as late-bloomers compared with normal controls (Rosenthal & Jacobson, 1968). Although this study showed dramatic gains in the first two grades, later replications led to more moderate conclusions.

The dependent variable in this study was performance on a similar test 12 months later. The control group provided a baseline estimate of how children from this elementary school changed in a year under normal conditions. Results for the experimental group should have been different only if teachers' expectations really had an effect on IQ.

As Figure 2.3 shows, the effects on first- and second-graders were quite dramatic. In both grades the gains in IQ for the late-bloomers were more than double those for the rest of the class. Because the only difference between the groups was what their teachers expected of them, these expectations seemed to be a very important factor. But what about the fourth grade, where the difference between the groups was only a few points, or the fifth and sixth grades, where there was even a slight tendency for the control group to do better? Do these small differences really mean something, or are they too small to have any importance? To answer such questions, psychologists turn to the study of statistics to determine whether a particular result is statistically significant, that is, if it is unlikely to have occurred by chance according to some predetermined criterion, usually a probability of less than 5%. The details of this criterion and of Rosenthal and Jacobson's results are described in "Understanding the Scientific Method." Statistical analysis revealed that there was a significant difference between the experimental and control groups in the first and second grades but not in the third, fourth, fifth, or sixth grades.

The general conclusion was widely reported in the press (for one example, see "Becoming a Critical Consumer" [page 46]), and many experts speculated that low teacher expectations were often responsible for students' problems in school. The scientific community, however, was far more cautious.

Like many dramatic reports, the Rosenthal and Jacobson study created a tremendous amount of controversy. Other researchers examined the details closely and discovered many flaws that led to serious doubts. One critic (Thorndike, 1968, p. 708) charged that the study was "so defective technically that one can only regret that it ever got beyond the eyes of the original investigators!"

In 1971, Janet Elashoff and Richard Snow, eds., published *Pygmalion*

Reconsidered, a critical analysis of technical and statistical details that was almost as long as the original report. They raised doubts about whether the IQ test Rosenthal and Jacobson used provided valid results for young children— a particularly damaging criticism because only the youngest group had shown gains in IQ.

One of the most important checks on the accuracy of research is replication—the repetition of a study to see whether the results are similar. In one chapter of *Pygmalion Reconsidered,* Baker and Christ (1971) summarized the attempts of other investigators to replicate the original study. If many researchers had been able to show that teacher expectations had raised IQs in many different settings, that would have implied that Rosenthal and Jacobson's conclusions were not the result of some idiosyncracy of the original study. But the nine studies that measured IQs all found that positive teacher expectations failed to raise IQ.

Other researchers, however, showed that high teacher expectations can have more subtle effects. In one typical follow-up study (Rubovits & Maehr, 1971), 26 college students taught sample lessons to groups of four grade-school children. Each group consisted of two children who were identified as gifted and two who were described as nongifted (though all children were actually similar in ability). A neutral observer carefully recorded the teachers' behavior according to a precise rating system and discovered that the student teachers asked the supposedly gifted students more questions and praised their answers more often.

Most of the studies of teacher behavior reviewed by Baker and Christ (14 of 17) revealed that expectations did make a difference. And some studies of student performance (6 of 12) found that high teacher expectations could indeed improve performance on non-IQ tests such as classroom examinations. Baker and Christ (1971) concluded, "The question for future research is not whether there are expectancy effects, but how they operate in school situations" (p. 64).

But the controversy did not end. In 1978, Robert Rosenthal and Donald

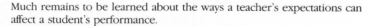

Much remains to be learned about the ways a teacher's expectations can affect a student's performance.

Statistical Significance: When Do Teachers' Expectations Make a Difference?

Whenever psychologists quantify psychological variables, they are faced with the problem of interpreting the observed numbers. In most cases this begins with a *test of statistical significance* to determine whether a particular mathematical result is likely to have occurred by chance.

Although many students are intimidated by the very word *statistics,* each of us intuitively applies certain laws of probability in everyday life. This is particularly true for people who spend a lot of time in casinos in Las Vegas or Atlantic City. Gamblers are continually faced with the problem of figuring the odds to choose a good bet.

Suppose that, during a semester break visit to a gambling resort, you meet a young man who offers to bet you $10 on the flip of a coin: If heads comes up, he pays you $10; if it's tails, you pay him $10. You accept. He flips the coin and it comes up tails. You mumble something about bad luck and ask if he would like to go for double or nothing. He does and it's tails again, and a third time, and a fourth time. By now you are down $80 and beginning to wonder if he takes credit cards. In your desperation you decide to keep doubling the bet until you win.

But suppose the two of you bet 20 more times and the coin comes up tails every time. One tails is bad luck, 4 in a row is *very* bad luck, but 24 in a row seems suspiciously like cheating. (A statistician could tell you that 24 tails in a row would occur by chance—that is, by accident—less than 1 out of every 10 million times.) You form a new theory: The man offered to bet in the first place because he is actually a coin shark, a person who cheats unwitting opponents out of their money with trick coin flips. Note that it is possible that you are wrong—he may just be lucky. But you

believe that this is far less likely than some other explanation, and you will probably be willing to act on this estimate of probability—possibly by asking several large friends over to discuss the coin flipper's success in detail.

The psychologist who is trying to decide what to conclude on the basis of certain numerical results is faced with a similar problem in probabilities. In the Rosenthal and Jacobson experiment, IQs were measured before some children were identified as late-bloomers and then again one year later. It is not surprising that changes in the two groups were not identical. The question is, how big a difference would you expect to see by chance, even if the two groups were basically the same.

To answer this question psychologists use statistical procedures to determine the precise odds that a particular result did not occur by chance. For a variety of reasons, psychologists have agreed to accept findings that could be expected to occur by chance no more than 5 times out of every 100 (Cowles & Davis, 1982). This is often symbolized by the expression $p < .05$, which means that the probability that something will occur by chance is less than 5%. Psychologists who wish to be more conservative and take a smaller chance of accepting incorrect research results often use a cutoff point of 1 out of every 100 times ($p < .01$). Thus, a particular finding is said to be *statistically significant* if the odds against its occurrence by chance exceed some predetermined criterion, usually $p < .05$.

Thus, the first step Rosenthal and Jacobson took after collecting the data shown in Figure 2.3 was to perform a series of standard calculations (called an *analysis of variance*) to see whether the overall

(box continues on next page)

results were statistically significant. They were. The probability was less than .02 that the observed differences in IQ between experimental and control groups would have occurred by chance. They then did a separate analysis (using a different statistical procedure called a *t-test*) for each grade. For the first grade, the difference between the experimental and control groups was highly significant ($p < .002$). The results were also significant for second-graders ($p < .02$). But the smaller differences observed in the third, fourth, fifth, and sixth grades might have resulted from random variation; none of these probabilities met the criterion of $p < .05$.

Thus statistical analyses of the Rosenthal and Jacobson data revealed that teacher expectations affected performance only in the first and second grades.

Tests of statistical significance like this are a critical element in most psychological studies. A survey of journals published by the American Psychological Association found that more than nine out of every ten articles included significance tests (Eddington, 1974). The vast majority of the research findings described in this book were subjected to tests of statistical significance to be certain that they should not be attributed to chance.

BECOMING A CRITICAL CONSUMER

Teacher Expectations and IQ

On September 20, 1968, *Time* magazine (p. 62) published an article describing Rosenthal's and Jacobson's research. As you read the excerpt, compare it to our description of the same research. Does the article accurately describe the major findings? Do you agree with the final conclusion? (A short discussion of these issues appears after the "Summary" at the end of this chapter.)

TEACHERS
Blooming by Deception

Critics of the public schools, particularly in urban ghettos, have long argued that many children fail to learn simply because their teachers do not expect them to. That proposition is effectively documented in a new book called *Pygmalion in the Classroom*. . . . [The authors] told the teachers that a new test could predict which slow-learning students were likely to "show an unusual forward spurt of academic and intellectual functioning." The exam, actually a routine but unfamiliar intelligence test, was given to all pupils. Teachers were then told which students had displayed a high potential for improvement. The names were actually drawn out of a hat.

When tested later, the designated late-bloomers showed an average IQ gain of 12.22 points, while the rest of the student body gained 8.42 points. The gains were most dramatic in the lowest grades. First-graders whose teachers expected them to advance intellectually jumped 27.4 points, second-graders 16.5 points. There were similar gains in reading ability. One young Mexican American, who had been classified as mentally retarded with an IQ of 61, scored 106 after his selection as a late-bloomer.

Rosenthal and Jacobson politely refrain from moralizing, suggesting only that "teachers' expectations of their pupils' performance may serve as self-fulfilling prophecies." But the findings raise some fundamental questions about teacher training. They also cast doubt on the wisdom of assigning children to classes according to presumed ability, which may only mire the lowest groups into self-confining ruts. If children tend to become the kind of students their teachers expect them to be, the obvious need is to raise the teachers' sights. Or, as Eliza Doolittle says in Shaw's *Pygmalion,* "The difference between a lady and a flower girl is not how she behaves, but how she's treated."

Rubin published a summary of the literature on self-fulfilling prophecies, "Interpersonal Expectancy Effects: The First 345 Studies." These studies went far beyond teacher expectations; they documented the effects of expectations on the behavior of such groups as employers, therapists, and scientific researchers. After reviewing the wide range of methods used in these studies and the consistency of the effects, Rosenthal and Rubin concluded that expectations do indeed affect behavior.

But even this impressive summary did not settle the issue. Twenty-nine criticisms and commentaries by other experts were published along with this article, challenging many of the details and conclusions.

Some students are distressed by continuing controversies of this sort; they would like to know the truth and not be bothered with the details. But human behavior is extremely complex, and science often progresses by controversy. Psychology does not have a final set of answers to every question; it is a continuing process of searching for the truth.

As this process goes on, it often raises new issues and provides insights into new areas. For example, Eden and Shani (1982) went beyond the elementary school classroom in a study they called "Pygmalion Goes to Boot Camp." They studied the effects of expectations on the performance of 105 Israeli soldiers in a combat command course that lasted 16 hours a day for 15 weeks. Trainees who had been identified to their instructors as having "high command potential" before the course began later reported more satisfaction with the results. They also scored higher than their classmates on objective tests in the subjects they were taught, including combat tactics, topography, and navigation. The authors concluded that the implications of the Pygmalion effect may go far beyond the traditional classroom, and predicted, for example, that "the performance of civilian production workers would improve if their immediate supervisors expected more of them" (Eden & Shani, 1982, p. 197).

If there is one lesson to be learned from this review of the Rosenthal and Jacobson research and the many studies that followed it, it is that no single study ever settles an issue. Journalists often make this mistake, reporting the latest finding by a psychologist (or a sociologist or a cancer researcher) as if that one study provided the answer the human race had been searching for since the dawn of time. Life is not that simple. A well-designed study tells us more than a poorly designed one, and any study at all provides more information than an unconfirmed or biased opinion. But there is always more to be learned and more data to be collected.

Summary

The Need for a Scientific Approach to Behavior

● **Self-fulfilling prophecies** are expectations that come true partly because people believe in them. People are often overly impressed by vivid information, even when abstract information is more trustworthy. Further, people often feel that they knew something all along, even when they did not. As a result, psychologists mistrust common sense and casual observations and rely instead on scientific methods to provide a more rational and skeptical approach to knowledge.

An Introduction to Scientific Methods

- Data collection methods in psychology include **systematic observation**—the careful observation, recording, and analysis of behavior. In **interviews**, psychologists directly ask people questions about their experiences and feelings. **Questionnaires** are self-administered measures that can be completed without any personal interaction. Data from these and other sources may be summarized in a **case history**, a detailed description of the life experiences and behavior patterns of a single individual.

- **Surveys** measure the behavior of large groups of people, usually by summarizing information from many interviews or questionnaires.

- A **representative sample** is a group in which subjects are systematically chosen to represent some larger population.

- An **experiment** is a scientific study in which a researcher tries to establish a causal link between two variables by manipulating one variable and observing changes in the other. The factor that the experimenter manipulates is called the **independent variable**; the **dependent variable** is the factor that may be affected. It is called dependent because the experiment is set up so that any changes that occur in this factor depend on changes in the other variable.

- In the **experimental condition**, the independent variable is manipulated to test its effect. This is compared to a **control condition**, in which there are no special treatments or manipulations and which thus serves as a basis for comparison.

- A **correlation coefficient** is computed by researchers to obtain a precise statistical expression of the relationship between two variables.

- Two groups may be compared to see if the differences between them are **statistically significant**—that is, unlikely to have occurred by chance.

- **Replications** are repetitions of a study to see if similar results can be obtained.

Critical Thinking Exercises Discussions

Identifying Independent and Dependent Variables

First, consider the answers to each of the problems posed in the exercise. Then consider the critical thinking skills needed to arrive at the correct solutions.

ANSWERS FOR EXAMPLE 1:
The independent variable was type of play group.

There were two levels to the independent variable: frustrated and nonfrustrated.

The dependent variable was aggression—operationalized as specific aggressive acts.

ANSWERS FOR EXAMPLE 2:
The independent variable was the racial characterization of student X.

The independent variable had two levels: The race was either the same as or different from the subject's.

The dependent variable was the number of positive characteristics attributed to student X.

ANSWERS FOR EXAMPLE 3:
The independent variable was the size of the artificial bug.

The independent variable had four levels: the four different sizes of artificial bugs.

The dependent variable was the eating behavior of the young birds, that is, whether they ate the artificial bug or not.

This exercise called on a number of critical thinking skills—in particular, discriminating among concepts and generalizing your learning. You had to discriminate the nuances among three interrelated concepts: independent variable, levels of an independent variable, and dependent variable. To make this discrimination, you may have had to look at the definition of each term and examples of each several times. You also had to generalize the meaning of these concepts to new situations. Such generalization involves holding onto the basic meaning of each concept while deciding how it applies to an example you have not seen before.

Teacher Expectations and IQ

While the *Time* article presents a clear picture of the research, it is less careful in its presentation of the implications of research. For example, it states correctly that the gains were most dramatic in the lowest grades, but it does not note that the same research found that teachers' expectations did not have significant effects in the third, fourth, fifth, and sixth grades.

The last paragraph contains some sweeping conclusions for educational reform. Note that the researchers themselves do not fall prey to the desire to overextend the data their study has yielded. Thinking critically means resisting the tendency to draw conclusions that are not firmly grounded in evidence. That doesn't mean that you can't have fun speculating as to the broader implications of a given set of data. It does mean that untested ideas, no matter how promising or exciting, should be set forth as part of a tentative hypothesis that can be tested.

Interestingly, most newspapers and magazines that enthusiastically reported this study did not report on later challenges. As noted in the text, subsequent studies revealed that expectations can influence teacher behavior but that they do not affect IQ.

THE NERVOUS SYSTEM

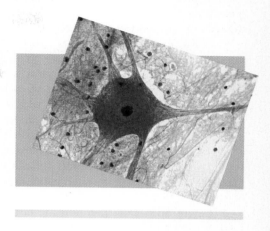

Chapter 3

$\mathcal{T}$he human brain is profoundly mysterious. How could this soggy mess of tissue create the Golden Gate Bridge and the Mona Lisa, the Roman Empire and the Russian Revolution, nuclear weapons and the Big Mac? How does this tangled network of cells regulate our heartbeat, our breathing, and the temperature of our bodies? And, as it oversees the thankless task of keeping us alive, where does the brain find time to marvel at the beauty of a sunset or wonder at the mystery of itself?

As psychologists have tried to develop a science of behavior and experience, they have often found themselves asking basic biological questions about how the nervous system works. In later chapters, when we discuss the nature of memory or sensation or motivation or abnormal behavior, we too shall often return to a discussion of the brain. Thus, it seems sensible to begin the study of psychology here, by showing how the biological paradigm tries to understand human thought and action on the physiological level.

Most of the time, people fumble along through life without paying much attention to their biological nature. But if a friend is paralyzed after his spinal cord is damaged in an auto accident or a relative has difficulty speaking after she has a stroke, we are all too grimly reminded of how truly fragile and intricate are the relationships between brain, behavior, and experience.

One way that scientists learn how the brain relates to behavior is by studying cases in which something goes wrong. For example, a **stroke** (technically known as a cerebrovascular accident) occurs when a blood vessel in the brain is blocked or broken. When brain tissue is deprived of the oxygen and nutrients carried in the blood, it dies. Depending on the location and

stroke A cerebrovascular accident that occurs when a blood vessel is blocked or broken and brain tissue is damaged.

the amount of dead tissue, the effects of a stroke can range from a mild passing dizziness or disorientation to death. Students of brain function are most interested in those intermediate cases in which permanent damage to the brain produces behavioral changes.

The term **aphasia** refers to a disturbance in the ability to speak or understand language caused by damage to the brain. There are many different types of aphasia, and a casual visitor to an aphasia clinic would probably be bewildered by the many different ways in which language can go wrong. For example, when a stroke victim with one type of aphasia was asked what he did on a typical day in the hospital, he replied: "Me go, er, uh, P.T. nine o'cot, speech . . . two times . . . read . . . wr . . . ripe, er, rike, er, write . . . practice . . . get-ting better" (Gardner, 1974, p. 61). In contrast to this slow and labored speech, some aphasia patients speak fluently but do not make any sense. When one such patient was asked why he was in the hospital, he replied: "Boy I'm sweating, I'm awful nervous, you know, once in a while I get caught up, I can't mention the tarripoi, a month ago, quite a little I've done a lot well, I'm pose a lot, while, on the other hand, you know what I mean" (Gardner, 1974, p. 68).

To a person who knows nothing about the structure and organization of the brain, the contrast between these patients is baffling. Why did the strokes affect their language abilities in such dramatically different ways?

Before the nineteenth century, scientists knew very little about strokes and aphasia. The French physician Paul Broca opened the door to a solution with an insight that now seems simple: He studied the brains of aphasia victims after they died. Beginning in 1861, Broca published a series of papers that described the results of his autopsies on the brains of aphasia patients. In every case, Broca found that damage was located near the front of the brain on the left side. This part of the brain is now called Broca's area (Figure 3.1) and is located next to brain areas that control the movements of muscles involved in speaking, such as the lips, jaw, tongue, and vocal cords. Broca's area seems to be responsible for coordinating these muscles during speech. When brain tissue in this area is damaged, the result is likely to be **expressive aphasia** (also known as Broca's aphasia), in which a person understands what others say but has difficulty speaking. Obviously, this was the problem of the first patient described above, who had so much trouble explaining that he went to P.T. (physical therapy) every day.

In 1874, a few years after Broca's discovery, Carl Wernicke published a paper describing how autopsies of another group of patients revealed that damage to a different area on the left side of the brain led to a different type of linguistic problem. Wernicke's area, as this part of the brain became known, is closer to the back of the brain and is located near areas involved with hearing. Damage here produces **receptive aphasia** (or Wernicke's aphasia), a syndrome involving difficulties in understanding speech. A patient with receptive aphasia can speak fluently but has problems using the right words and phrases. In extreme cases, speech becomes totally nonsensical, as it did for the second patient described above.

Today, more than a century after the pioneering efforts of Broca and Wernicke, advances in medical technology have substantially improved diagnosis. One hundred years ago, the site of brain damage could be precisely

aphasia A disturbance in the ability to speak or understand language caused by damage to the brain.

expressive aphasia Difficulty in speaking resulting from tissue damage in Broca's area.

receptive aphasia Difficulty in understanding language resulting from tissue damage in Wernike's area.

determined only after a patient had died and the brain could be dissected in a laboratory. Aside from its macabre overtones, this procedure implied that diagnosis in living patients was based largely on guesswork.

As we shall see in this chapter, CAT scans and other techniques are now available to pinpoint damage in the living brain. These technological advances have helped scientists to learn a great deal about the structure and function of both damaged and undamaged brains. For example, later researchers have verified Broca's observation that when brain damage produces permanent language disabilities, the problem is almost always on the left side of the brain. But in a few cases (roughly about 3%), damage to the right side of the brain produces similar problems, particularly among people who are left-handed. This observation has led brain scientists to study differences between right-handed and left-handed individuals, as described toward the end of this chapter.

But despite the many advances in technique and knowledge, much remains to be learned. Brain scientists know little about how nerve cells in Broca's and Wernicke's areas perform their functions or even precisely what these functions are. On a more practical level, there is no known cure for aphasia. Some patients may improve dramatically as a result of speech therapy,

FIGURE 3.1 For most people, the left side of the brain controls language. Damage to specific areas produces different types of aphasia. Broca's area is adjacent to the motor strip that controls movement of muscles involved in speaking; damage here produces Broca's aphasia, which involves difficulty coordinating these muscles in speech. Wernicke's area is adjacent to the area in which information from the ear is first analyzed by the cortex; damage here produces Wernicke's aphasia, characterized by difficulties in understanding speech.

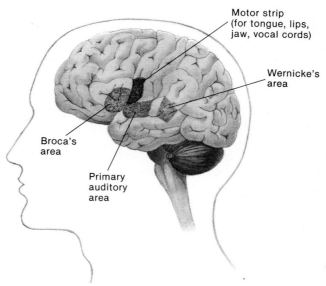

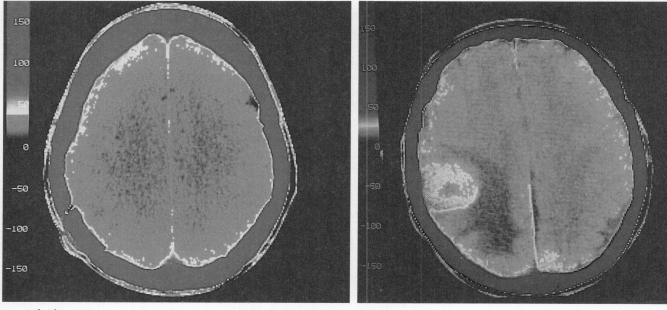

Left: This CAT scan is a three dimensional image generated from a computer analysis of some X-rays of a normal brain. *Right*: This CAT scan is of a patient with a brain tumor.

but others respond less well to this treatment. This disparity between the progress that has been made in the last century and the mysteries that remain is a theme that recurs throughout this chapter and, indeed, throughout this book.

In any case, the study of aphasia leaves no doubt that if we want to understand human behavior and experience fully, we must learn about their biological bases. In this chapter, we focus on the structure and function of the nervous system and its relation to behavior. In later chapters, which consider such topics as the effects of drugs (Chapter 5) and behavioral genetics (Chapter 9), additional examples are cited of the intricate and complex relationships between biology and behavior.

How Scientists Study the Brain

The clinical studies of aphasia patients described here provide a good introduction to the brain, because the effects of damage are vivid and undeniable. But, from a scientific point of view, such clinical cases are limited in a number of ways. For example, a stroke may affect several brain structures at once, making it hard to determine which brain areas are responsible for specific behaviors. Further, there are a number of reasons why it is dangerous to generalize from a case study of a single individual. (See "Understanding the Scientific Method" on page 85.) Thus, it seems reasonable to begin our introduction to the nervous system with an overview of other techniques now available to study the brain, what they can tell us, and how they have evolved over the centuries. A summary of each of the processes and examples of their use can be found in Table 3.1.

TABLE 3.1

Methods of Studying the Brain

Procedure	*Process*	*Examples of use of techniques*
Ablation	Brain tissue is surgically removed or destroyed; an invasive technique.	In the 1820s, Flourens removed slices of the cerebellum in animals and identified its role in muscular coordination.
Electrical stimulation	Brain tissue is stimulated by an electric current, typically through electrodes; an invasive technique.	In 1870, Fritsch and Hitzig began mapping brain functions by applying weak currents through electrodes to specific points in animal brains. Gol (1967) used electrical stimulation to the brain to reduce pain.
Electrical recording	Normal electrical activity of the brain is monitored—e.g., through an electroencephalogram (EEG) recording of electrical activity at the surface of the skull; less invasive than ablation or electrical stimulation.	EEGs are used diagnostically to identify potential problems in brain functioning.
CAT scan	Computed Axial Tomography: Involves injecting dyes into the circulatory system of the brain, taking X-rays from many different angles, and obtaining a computer-generated three-dimensional picture of the brain and any particular slice of tissue within the brain; a noninvasive technique.	CAT scans are used to help neurologists diagnose such problems as brain tumors, cerebral blood clots, and multiple sclerosis.
PET scan	Position Emission Tomography: Involves measurement of radioactive glucose injected into individuals; allows computer to generate a motion picture of consumption of glucose in brain; a noninvasive technique.	PET scans are used to identify abnormal brain areas in patients with aphasia and epilepsy.

Neuroanatomical Studies

Neuroanatomical studies focus on the physical structure of the brain, spinal cord, and rest of the nervous system. The earliest brain scientists began on this level, by describing what the brain looked like and how it was put together. Removed from the skull, the brain looks a little like a 3-pound walnut composed of very soft cream-colored clay. It is covered with wrinkles and, like a walnut, can be neatly split down the middle into two symmetrical halves.

When anatomists began to cut into the brain, they soon realized that it is not a uniform structure but is composed of a number of separate parts. Names we use today for these structures are often derived from the Latin or Greek terms that described their appearance. One structure deep inside the brain was called the *amygdala,* because it looked like an almond; another became known as the *hippocampus,* because its shape reminded some ancient anatomist of a seahorse. These and other basic structures of the human brain have been known since the time of Galen, a famous physician who lived about one-and-a-half centuries after Christ.

The next major advances in understanding the anatomy of the brain came after the invention of the microscope made it possible to magnify tissue many hundreds of times. Under the microscope, a plain, untreated slice of tissue taken from the brain reveals little; everything is packed so tightly together

neuroanatomical studies Studies that focus on the physical structure of the brain, spinal cord, and nervous system.

that one hardly sees more than a smear. But in 1875, Camillo Golgi discovered that when nerve tissue is treated with silver nitrate, a very small proportion of the cells became clearly visible under the microscope. Golgi thus discovered that neurons, or nerve cells, are the fundamental building blocks of the nervous system. The Golgi stain revealed that many neurons had a rather oddly shaped cell body with a number of long branches.

Although no one has discovered how or why the Golgi stain works, this technical advance enabled the Spanish anatomist Santiago Ramón y Cajal to chart the connections between cells in every part of the nervous system. (Golgi and Cajal shared a Nobel Prize for this work in 1906.) In the late 1800s, biologists had believed that the nervous system was composed of tubes through which electricity flowed, just as blood flowed through the arteries and veins. But Cajal believed that the nervous system was discontinuous, that there were very small gaps between neighboring cells. It was not until the early 1950s that Cajal was finally proved correct. The gap between neurons is only about 100 angstroms wide (an angstrom is 1 ten-billionth of a meter) and could be seen only by means of the incredible magnification of the electron microscope.

These are exciting times for neuroanatomists, as advances in technology, such as the CAT scan, allow them to probe ever more deeply into the structure of the brain. This knowledge provides the foundation on which psychologists build when they study the function of various brain structures.

Ablation Studies

One way to try to understand how the brain actually works is to observe the effects of damage to certain structures. We have already seen how this applies to aphasia patients: Specific linguistic problems have been linked to different types of brain damage, suggesting that these structures play an important role in normal language use.

A similar rationale applies in **ablation studies**, which involve surgically removing or destroying brain tissue and observing the effects on behavior. For obvious reasons, this type of research should never be practiced on humans. But scientists have learned a great deal about the nervous system by performing ablation studies on animals. The resulting knowledge has contributed to human welfare and the saving of human lives.

Pierre Flourens pioneered this technique in the 1820s, when he removed thin slices of tissue from the cerebellum (located near the back of the brain) of birds, rabbits, and dogs. After he nursed the animals back to health, Flourens found that most lacked muscular coordination and had a poor sense of balance. Since this appeared to be the only effect of the operation, Flourens concluded that under normal conditions the cerebellum played an important role in muscular coordination and balance. Later studies using a variety of other techniques verified this finding.

The basic logic of ablation studies is still the same today, but surgical techniques have advanced considerably. Very small and precisely localized areas of the brain can be removed with miniaturized vacuum pumps, cauterized with heated probes, destroyed by electrical stimulation, or damaged by drugs

ablation studies Studies in which surgical removal or destruction of brain tissue is followed by observation of the effects on behavior.

that affect only one type of neuron. Regardless of the technique used, ablation studies allow researchers to study specific brain **lesions** (wounds or injuries) in a way that would not be possible if they were able to study only diseased or accidentally damaged brains.

Of course, human brain surgery is sometimes performed to treat medical problems, such as brain tumors and certain types of epilepsy. Brain surgery patients are often followed carefully by research teams who are interested in side effects on behavior. For example, later in this chapter we discuss a group of epileptics who volunteered for an experimental operation in which the two sides of the brain were surgically separated so that, in a way, they had two minds in a single skull. We also examine the use of frontal lobotomy (in which portions of the frontal cortex are destroyed) to treat mental illness. Although such operations were motivated by a desire to help particular patients, research on the behavioral results can be seen as a kind of ablation study of the human brain.

Electrical Stimulation

Another way to study brain function is to activate specific structures in the brain. In **electrical stimulation studies**, brain tissue is stimulated by an electric current while the effects on behavior are observed. The rationale for such studies can be traced to 1786, when Luigi Galvani discovered that a mild electric shock could contract the muscle in a dead frog's leg and cause the leg to twitch. Galvani believed that he had discovered the vital life force, and some observers predicted that scientists would soon be able to bring the dead back to life. They were wrong.

But in 1870, two German physiologists, Gustav Fritsch and Eduard Hitzig, were able to produce specific movements in living animals by applying a weak electric current to electrodes inserted in specific sites in the brain. (An **electrode** is simply a conductor of electrical activity that is placed in contact with biological tissue.) Although the electrical stimulation they used was not identical to the normal electrical and chemical signals of the brain, it was close enough to elicit specific muscular responses. For example, they found that stimulation of one spot on a dog's brain led to a leg twitch, another spot to a facial movement, a third spot to the contraction of a muscle in the neck, and so on. In this way, they were able to draw an early map of brain functions, relating specific anatomic areas to particular muscle movements.

Some of the earliest findings on areas of specialization in the human cortex come from the electrical stimulation studies of Wilder Penfield. A neurosurgeon at the Montreal Neurological Institute, Penfield often performed surgery on epileptic patients (people with a convulsive brain disorder associated with abnormal electrical activity in the brain). In order to minimize the disruption of normal functions following removal of damaged tissues, Penfield (1947) used the electrical stimulation technique to "map" the cortex, indicating what portions of the cortex performed what functions.

As electrical stimulation techniques have become more sophisticated, they have provided a great deal of information about the workings of the brain. In a few cases, electrical stimulation devices have been experimentally

lesions Wounds or injuries.

electrical stimulation studies Studies in which brain tissue is stimulated by an electric current while the effects on behavior are observed.

electrode An electrical conductor that is placed in contact with biological tissue.

implanted in human patients to treat otherwise incurable conditions. For example, Gol (1967) reported the case of a man who was dying from cancer and suffered from such acute pain that he groaned continuously. After all other treatments failed, electrical stimulation of the brain relieved this man's continual pain. The value of this extreme and unorthodox treatment is still being tested in further research.

Electrical Recording

Electrical recording studies involve measuring the normal electrical activity of the brain. Both ablation and electrical stimulation are invasive techniques: They interfere with brain processes in the hope of understanding normal function. In contrast, electrical recording studies try to monitor the ordinary electrical activity of the brain with as little interference as possible.

An **electroencephalogram**, or **EEG**, is a recording of the electrical activity at the surface of the brain or on the skull. In 1929, an Austrian psychiatrist named Hans Berger announced that he had recorded the electrical activity of the human brain through electrodes attached to the skull. At first, many believed it would be possible to study the physical correlates of human thought. This led to tremendous excitement: Scientists hurried to build EEG machines of their own, and science-fiction writers plotted stories about learning to read people's minds by studying their brain waves.

EEG recordings proved to be very useful in the diagnosis of certain medical conditions, particularly epilepsy. Epileptic seizures involve disordered bursts of electrical activity throughout the brain, and the electrical signs of even very minor seizures were quite dramatic (see Figure 3.2). As we shall see in Chapter 4, EEG recordings also help to identify several stages of sleep and provide insights into the hidden world of dreams.

But early EEG researchers soon discovered they would not be reading minds for quite some time. Recordings from the surface of the skull reflected the simultaneous activity of millions of neurons and were quite difficult to interpret. Some researchers, therefore, looked for more sophisticated recording techniques. One involved **microelectrodes**, wires small enough to record

FIGURE 3.2 Typical EEG recordings. The first two were recorded at the same time from two different spots on the skull of a relaxed adult. The third was recorded during a petit mal epileptic seizure and shows dramatic spiking.

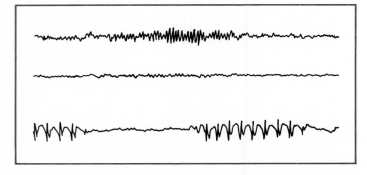

the electrical activity of a single nerve cell at a time. The diameter of the tip of a microelectrode is measured in microns (millionths of a meter), and it can detect an electrical charge of one-millionth of a volt. Single-cell recordings of this sort have provided many insights, particularly into the workings of the visual system. But since microelectrodes must be inserted into the brain and can destroy brain tissue, these studies have ordinarily been limited to nonhumans.

Chemical Studies

Chemical studies, also an invasive procedure, involve introducing a chemical into the brain to determine its behavioral and physiological effects. Typically, a miniature hypodermic needle is implanted into an animal's brain, and then a very small quantity of a particular chemical is pumped through the needle to specific brain tissues.

A number of such chemical techniques have been developed for studying the structure and function of the brain. For example, Louis Sokoloff and his colleagues at the National Institute of Mental Health developed a way of tracing anatomic pathways in the brain. Active neurons consume glucose (a form of sugar) more rapidly than inactive neurons. In Sokoloff's procedure, 2-deoxyglucose, a type of sugar, is produced in a radioactive form. An animal is required to perform a certain task, such as visually distinguishing between a circle and a square, soon after an injection of radioactive 2-deoxyglucose. Brain cells involved in making this visual distinction consume more sugar, and radioactivity builds up in them. The animal is then destroyed, the brain is frozen, and very thin slices of brain tissue are pressed against a piece of photographic film (which is sensitive to radioactivity). The developed photograph thus provides a picture of the brain cells that are especially active during performance of the task.

Advances in Noninvasive Techniques

Except for EEG studies, all the procedures described thus far require neurosurgery and alterations to brain tissue. This feature obviously limits their use with humans. However, major advances are now being made with a family of **noninvasive techniques**—techniques that do not require brain surgery and that can be used to study function in the normal human brain. The most familiar of these are *CAT scans* (computed axial tomography).

For many years, neurologists have studied brain damage by taking X-rays of the head (typically, dyes are injected into the circulatory system of the brain to make blood vessels more visible). However, since a person's head is about 6 inches wide from ear to ear and at least as long from front to back, the flat, two-dimensional picture yielded by a traditional X-ray can be extremely confusing. In the **CAT scan**, X-rays are taken from many different angles, and a computer analyzes these X-rays to generate a three-dimensional picture of the brain. The researcher or clinician can then ask the computer for a picture of any slice of tissue within the brain.

CAT scans were introduced around 1973, and the first major studies

electrical recording studies
Studies that measure the normal electrical activity of the brain.

electroencephalogram (EEG) A recording of the electrical activity at the surface of the brain or on the skull.

microelectrodes Wires small enough to record the electrical activity of a single nerve cell.

chemical studies Procedures involving introducing a chemical into the brain to determine its behavioral and physiological effects.

noninvasive techniques
Nonsurgical techniques for studying function in the normal brain.

CAT scan A technique in which X-rays taken from many different angles are analyzed by computer to generate a three-dimensional picture of the brain.

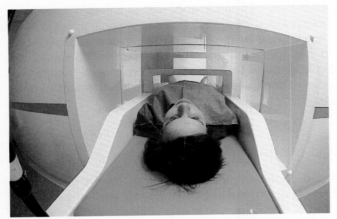

Computed axial tomography, or a CAT scan, is an example of the kind of new technology that is revolutionizing our knowledge of brain function.

that applied this technique to aphasia were published in 1977. This research has shown a "remarkable consistency" in verifying the theories of Broca and Wernicke described at the beginning of this chapter (Damasio and Geschwind, 1982, p. 131). CAT scans are now routinely used by neurologists to assess brain damage caused by strokes, tumors, and other disorders.

A more detailed three-dimensional image of brain structures can be produced as a result of another new technological advance called *NMR* (nuclear magnetic resonance). Here, a person is enclosed in a magnetic field, and radio waves are reflected from internal brain structures to reveal their characteristics.

The CAT scan and NMR provide the equivalent of a still photograph of a cross-section of the brain. Several other new techniques provide a "moving picture" of the brain as it responds to external stimuli. One class of techniques measures cerebral blood flow, the rate at which blood flows to different brain areas. In one procedure, a person inhales a slightly radioactive gas. When the radioactivity passes from the lungs into the blood, the blood flow through the circulatory system becomes radioactive for the next 15 minutes or so. During this time, the circulation of blood to different brain areas provides a general index of the activation of neurons. The sophisticated devices to measure radioactivity have made it possible literally to watch blood flow to the front of a person's brain while he or she considers an abstract problem, and then flow to speech centers in the left hemisphere as the person begins to talk about it (Ingvar & Lassen, 1975).

PET scans (positron emission tomography) also rely on the measurement of radioactive substances, in this case radioactive glucose, which is injected into the subject. More active brain sites consume more of the sugar, and a computer can generate a "moving picture" of this use of energy (Fox, 1984).

For our purposes, the details of these procedures are less important than the fact that new techniques are constantly being developed to examine the brain in new ways.

localization   The theory that different areas of the brain are responsible for different psychological functions.

holism   The theory that each psychological function is controlled by a wide variety of cells throughout the entire brain.

phrenology   The outdated theory that the brain consists of several different organs, each responsible for a particular human trait.

Left: In NMR, or nuclear magnetic resonance, a person is enclosed in a magnetic field and radio waves are reflected to reveal internal brain structures. *Right*: This is an NMR scan of a normal brain.

FIGURE 3.3 A phrenologist's model illustrating one nineteenth-century theory about localization of personality traits in the brain. Although phrenology helped set the stage for early brain research, it was quite wrong.

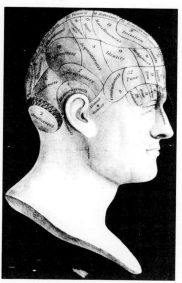

Converging Lines of Evidence and Localization of Function

Each method described in this section looks at the brain from a slightly different perspective. Scientists look for several lines of evidence that all lead to, or converge on, a single conclusion.

A good example of the way different scientific methods gradually lead to the same conclusion can be seen in the historical controversy over localization of functions. According to the theory of **localization**, different areas of the brain are responsible for different psychological functions. The alternative theory, **holism**, claims that each psychological function is controlled by a wide variety of cells throughout the entire brain rather than being concentrated in a few discrete areas. Theorists who accept the idea of localization might believe, for example, that aggression is controlled by a single group of neurons in one location of the brain. On the other hand, theorists adopting the holist position would argue that many different areas of the brain are involved in aggressive responses.

Medical historians usually trace the idea of localization to a controversial German physician named Franz Joseph Gall. Around 1800, Gall proposed the theory of **phrenology**, which held that the brain consists of a number of separate organs, each responsible for a specific human trait. Unusual growth of any of these organs creates a bump on the skull; the pattern of bumps reveals a person's character. According to one phrenological chart (see Figure 3.3), a woman with a bump on one spot near the top of her head would have an overdeveloped organ of imitation; she could therefore be expected to study religiously the latest fashions in *Vogue* magazine so that she would always know what clothes she was supposed to wear. If the bump were a little farther back, it would indicate an overactive organ of hope, and she might be a Chicago Cubs fan, believing every spring that this was the year that unfortunate team would finally win the pennant.

We now know that this theory is quite wrong. Skull shape does not conform to brain shape, and Gall's entire classification scheme has been discredited. But, as Edmund G. Boring (1950, p. 57) stated in *A History of Experimental Psychology,* phrenology was "an instance of a theory which, while essentially wrong, was just enough right to further scientific thought." Many of the landmark discoveries that we described earlier in this section can be traced back to Gall.

When Pierre Flourens refined the technique of ablation in the 1820s, he was trying to refute Gall's claim that the cerebellum was the "organ of amativeness." Since removal of this area of the brain affected animals' coordination and balance rather than their sexual activities, Flourens felt that he had disproved at least this one claim of phrenology.

When Flourens went on to remove larger portions of the brain, he found little evidence of specific deficits. Thus he came to favor the view now known as holism. But later researchers, using other methods, disagreed. Broca's findings of specific deficits in the brains of aphasia patients supported the theory of localization. So did Fritsch and Hitzig's report that electrical stimulation of specific brain areas caused a dog to move particular muscles. The controversy over which theory was correct, localization or holism, went on for more than a century.

Gradually, however, various lines of evidence converged on the same conclusion. Basic sensory and motor functions are localized in fairly specific areas of the brain. But a rule of thumb might be that the more complex the psychological function, the less likely it is to be located in only one area of the brain. Thus, a sensory impression of a spot of light is highly localized; the larger perception of a pattern of light and dark areas that leads you to recognize a photograph of Tom Cruise is less clearly localized; and a reaction of sexual excitement to this picture involves still more complex interactions between different brain areas.

In the case of vision, simple sensations are localized in an area near the back of the brain called the occipital lobe (described on page 76). This conclusion is based on several converging lines of evidence. When a particular area of the occipital lobe is destroyed, through surgery or accident, a person or animal becomes partially blind. EEGs and other electrical recordings from the occipital area change systematically when a person looks at a stimulus. Simple electrical stimulation of the occipital cortex produces a sensation of a light flashing in a particular spot. Since these and other studies all led to the same conclusion, scientists accepted the idea that simple visual sensations were located in a particular area of the brain.

But the scientific community has been slower to agree on whether complex psychological functions—such as hunger, aggression, and sexuality—are localized. In part, that is because various lines of evidence have not yet converged on a single conclusion; there is still a great deal of controversy over studies of these more complicated behavior patterns.

FRANZ JOSEPH GALL (1758–1828)

A brilliant anatomist, Gall was the first to trace fibers through the central nervous system to show how information crossed from one side of the body to the opposite side of the brain. But Gall is best remembered for phrenology—his attempts to relate character to the shape of the skull. In his autobiography, Gall traced this curious idea to an observation he had made as a schoolboy. Students who got better grades than he often did not seem brighter, but they did have protruding eyes, which he later attributed to overdeveloped verbal memories in the front of the skull. Unfortunately, the evidence behind phrenology rarely rose above this level. According to one nineteenth-century scientist's joke, after Gall's death, measurements of his own skull revealed that it was twice as thick as average.

For example, in one of the most famous experiments on electrical stimulation of the brain, Dr. José Delgado implanted electrodes deep in the brain of a bull that had been bred for bullfighting and charging human beings. A special radio receiver attached to the bull's horns provided electrical stimulation through the electrodes to the bull's brain whenever Delgado pressed a button on a small transmitter. The scientist went into the bullring armed only with a cape and his transmitter. As the bull charged, Delgado pressed his button. Happily, the electrical stimulation caused the animal to stop its charge and turn aside. This demonstration was cited widely as proof that Delgado had located an aggressive center in the bull's brain (for an example, see "Becoming a Critical Consumer"). Advocates of this point of view believed that electrical stimulation reduced or interfered with the activity of a localized area of the brain that controlled aggression.

Other brain scientists, however, disagreed. Eliot Valenstein (1973) examined a film of this demonstration and noted that whenever the bull stopped its charge, it turned in one direction. He concluded that the electrical stimulation actually activated a brain area that controlled muscular movement. The bull turned aside not because its aggressiveness was curbed but because the electrical stimulation produced a turning movement.

Given the ambiguity of most complex behavior patterns and the fact that they can be influenced by such a wide variety of external stimuli, controversies over the localization of complex psychological functions are likely to continue. But, over time, scientific consensus should result as evidence from many sources and types of studies gradually converge on a single conclusion.

Electrical stimulation can be used to study the behavioral functions associated with different areas of the brain.

Electrical Stimulation of the Brain

Compare this description of advances in brain research from an article in the *New York Times* (Rensberger, 1971), to our account of the same research. How is this selection inaccurate or misleading? (A short discussion appears after the "Summary" at the end of this chapter.)

> Over the last few years, [scientists] have been learning to tinker with the brains of animals and men and to manipulate their thoughts and behavior.
>
> Though their methods are still crude and not always predictable, there can remain little doubt that the next few years will bring a frightening array of refined techniques for making human beings act according to the will of the psychotechnologist. . . .

Perhaps the most famous demonstration of the potential of psychotechnology was an experiment carried out several years ago by Yale University's José M. R. Delgado.

Dr. Delgado implanted a radio-controlled electrode deep within the brain of a "brave bull," a variety bred to respond with a raging charge when it sees any human being. But when Dr. Delgado pressed a button on a transmitter, sending a signal to a battery-powered receiver attached to the bull's horns, an impulse went into the bull's brain and the animal would cease his charge.

After several stimulations, the bull's naturally aggressive behavior disappeared. It was as placid as Ferdinand.

In the meantime, it is important to remember that there is still considerable controversy over the localization of complex functions.

As we review brain structures later in this chapter, it may be hard to resist asking which psychological function is regulated by the hippocampus, or the cerebellum, or the frontal cortex. Because introductory textbooks are required to simplify complex material, they sometimes may make the brain seem more localized and simple than it really is. As you read the section, try to remember that the brain is an extremely sophisticated system that we are just beginning to comprehend.

The Structure and Function of the Nervous System

When a songwriter suggests that love and marriage go together like a horse and carriage, and you can't have one without the other, he is linking a function (love) with a social structure (marriage). Much of the research on the brain has focused on the link between *brain functions* (activities) and *physical structures* (parts). Whether considering the brain as a whole or in terms of its smallest component elements, neuroscientists have attempted to identify particular functions associated with particular structures.

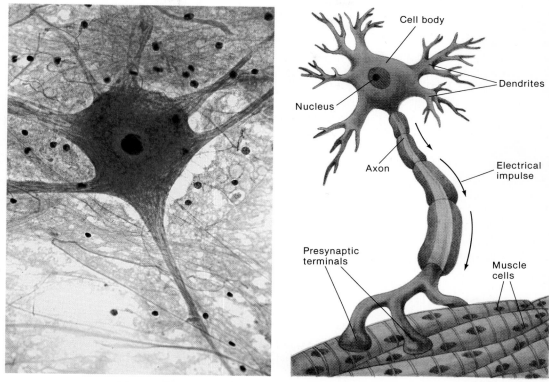

FIGURE 3.4 *Left*: Motor neuron in the spinal cord, stained to increase visibility and enlarged through a microscope. *Right*: The major structures of a neuron. The arrows show the pathway in which electrochemical impulses travel.

The Neuron

The basic building blocks of the nervous system are called nerve cells, or neurons. A **neuron** can be defined as a cell that processes information and transmits information by means of electrochemical impulses. Each neuron has three major functions: receiving messages, responding to them, and sending messages. These functions are handled through three different structures: the dendrites, the cell body, and the axon. The neuron receives electrical and chemical messages from other cells through its dendrites, responds to that information in some way in the cell body, and sends messages on to other neurons through the axon.

More specifically, the **dendrite** is the part of a neuron that usually receives electrical and chemical messages from other nerve cells. The word *dendrite* comes from the Greek word for trees; as you can see in Figure 3.4, the cell body is connected to many dendrites, which extend from it like the branches of a tree. The **cell body** is the central part of the neuron that responds to incoming information and manufactures chemicals required for the cell's nutrition and normal function. Finally, a single **axon** usually transmits electrical impulses away from the cell body to other neurons. As Figure 3.4 shows, axons tend to be much longer and thinner than dendrites.

neuron An individual nerve cell, the fundamental building block of the nervous system.

dendrite The part of a neuron that usually receives electrical and chemical messages from other neurons.

cell body The central part of the neuron.

axon The part of a neuron that transmits electrical impulses to other neurons.

Electrical messages ordinarily travel in only one direction: Information comes into a cell through a dendrite, is processed in the cell body, and passes through the axon. When we say that "information is processed" in the cell body, we mean that the cell body analyzes the information being communicated by the dendrite activity, and, based on this analysis, either sends a particular kind of electrochemical message or does not respond.

Ordinarily, information is transmitted from the axon of one cell to the dendrite of another. However, in some cases, an axon transmits information directly to the cell body of another neuron. Either way, the signal is transmitted at the **synapse**, the space across which the axon of one neuron can stimulate the dendrite or cell body of another (see Figure 3.5). Neurons communicate with one another at the synapse in a complex electrochemical code that scientists are just beginning to understand.

In one sense, the neuron can be considered a miniature battery that communicates with other neurons by *firing,* or sending a small electrical charge along the length of its axon. This process is called *electrochemical* to distinguish the movement of this charge from the movement of an electrical current, such as the one that flows through the power cord of your VCR. The electrical charge in the neuron travels down the axon by means of a chemical process that is different from, and much slower than, a household electrical current.

The firing of a neuron is said to obey the "all-or-none principle"; that is, at any given moment, a neuron either transmits its maximum electrical charge, or it does not transmit any electrical charge at all. Some scientists

FIGURE 3.5 The synapse. Information is transmitted from one neuron to another by the release of neurotransmitter molecules across the synapse.

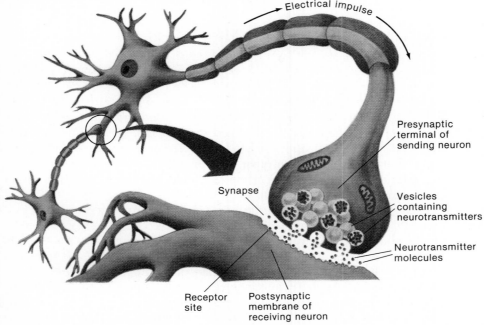

have compared the firing of a neuron to the firing of a rifle. If you pull the trigger, the rifle either fires or it does not; there is no middle ground.

A neuron can send a message by changing the pattern and rate of this firing. In one study of the visual system of the frog, for example, a particular color-sensitive neuron fired about 20 times per second when the frog looked at a blue stimulus, 7 times per second for a blue-green stimulus, and 3 times per second for a green stimulus (Muntz, 1964).

Neurotransmitters

Another way a neuron passes along information is through a **neurotransmitter**, a chemical that is released into the synapse and transmits information from one neuron to another. As shown in Figure 3.5, after the electrical impulse passes down the length of the axon it reaches an area on the axon called the *presynaptic terminal,* which stores neurotransmitters. When the electrical impulse reaches the presynaptic terminal, it causes thousands of molecules of the neurotransmitter to be released into the synapse between the axon and the next neuron. The neurotransmitter then ends its journey at the "receptor site" on the *postsynaptic membrane* of the other cell.

In the 1960s, only three different chemicals were widely recognized as neurotransmitters: acetylcholine, norepinephrine, and serotonin. Since then, an explosion of research has led to the discovery of many new neurotransmitters. In 1984, Snyder estimated the number of known transmitters to be about 30 and predicted that the final number might be around 300. The speed with which this field is changing is illustrated by the fact that, just four years before then, in the first edition of our text, the same expert estimated the number of known neurotransmitters to be "about two dozen," and he predicted that the final total "may exceed 200" (Snyder, 1980, p. 979). Given the fact that such a small proportion of possible neurotransmitters have even been identified, it is not surprising that we have a great deal to learn about their precise modes of action. Table 3.2 lists types, sites, action, and postulated functions of several important neurotransmitters.

Neurotransmitters are now believed to play a critical role in the regulation of many complex behaviors and disease processes. One recent line of research, for example, has studied the relationships between lowered brain levels of the neurotransmitter acetylcholine and the symptoms of Alzheimer's diease (see Chapter 7).

Another series of studies has focused on a class of chemicals called **endorphins,** neurotransmitters that are structurally similar to opiate drugs, such as morphine and heroin. Around 1970, scientists first identified drug receptors in the brain that responded specifically to opiates. It seemed unlikely that these receptors had evolved just in case an animal happened to consume an opium plant or a Percodan tablet. Thus, the very existence of such receptors suggested that one component in the brain's natural chemistry was a neurotransmitter that was structurally similar to morphine—an endogenous morphine substance, or endorphin. Since then, several endorphins have been found in the brain.

Because opiates are such powerful painkillers, early speculations about

synapse The microscopic space across which the axon of one neuron can stimulate the dendrite or cell body of another.

neurotransmitter A chemical released at the synapse by one neuron that influences the electrical activity of another.

endorphins Neurotransmitters that are structurally similar to opiates and may be involved in regulating pain and other psychological functions.

TABLE 3.2

Neurotransmitters

Name	Type	Brain sites of high concentration	Action	Postulated function
Enkephalin	Neuropeptide	Hypothalamus, medulla, pons	Inhibits spinal cord receptors and neurons that transmit pain messages	Analgesic (pain relief); some role in eating; reduced in Huntington's disease
B-endorphin	Neuropeptide	Hypothalamus	Inhibits spinal cord receptors and neurons that transmit pain messages	Analgesic; some role in regulating eating, body temperature, and blood pressure; modulates monoamines
ACTH (adrenocorticotropic hormone)	Neuropeptide	Hypothalamus	Activates adrenal hormones, including epinephrine and norepinephrine	Facilitates short-term memory formation; can increase attention and visual discrimination; has a suppressive effect on the immune system
Serotonin	Monoamine	Hypothalamus	Stimulates the satiety center	Stimulates eating; may be involved in depression
Dopamine	Monoamine	Hypothalamus	Stimulates the feeding center	Stimulates eating; may be involved in schizophrenia

the effects of these neurotransmitters centered around the idea that endorphins were the body's natural painkillers. Strong evidence for this hypothesis, however, would require that biochemists measure endorphin release in a specific part of the brain and show that pain is reduced when endorphins are released and not reduced when they are blocked. But as Goldstein (1980) noted, "Technology does not yet permit such measurements in the living animal, much less the conscious human."

Scientists were forced to rely on less direct tests. One common procedure involves administering other drugs, called **narcotic antagonists,** that are known to block the effects of opiates. Naloxone, for example, reverses the effects of any narcotic; it is used in emergency rooms to treat patients who have taken an overdose of heroin or morphine. Narcotic antagonists are believed to work by occupying opiate receptor sites so that the narcotic cannot affect neurons. Scientists reasoned that if naloxone blocked some form of nonchemical pain relief, this would suggest that natural opiates—endorphins—were involved in the pain relief.

Doctors have known for centuries that **placebos,** chemically inactive substances, can relieve pain by the power of suggestion. In 1978, one group of researchers (Levine, Gordon, & Fields) published data suggesting that endorphins might be the mechanism behind this mysterious effect. They studied dental patients a few hours after they had undergone oral surgery. As in many earlier studies, some people who were given a placebo reported that it eased their pain. But these researchers went on to administer naloxone and found that this drug increased the pain of those who had responded to

narcotic antagonists Drugs that are known to block the effects of opiates.

placebos Chemically inactive substances that can relieve pain by the power of suggestion.

the placebo. They concluded that the placebo worked by somehow causing the brain to release endorphins; when the naloxone reversed the effect of these natural opiates, the pain returned.

After several years of further research, endorphins remain a subject of considerable controversy. At one extreme, some scientists have speculated that endorphins play a vital role in everything from eating, sleeping, and temperature regulation to schizophrenia, obesity, and depression. At the other extreme, some have cautioned that the major lesson of this research was to remind scientists "how little we really know about the constituents of the brain" (Pert, Pert, Davis, & Bunney, 1982).

One by-product of the research on endorphins was the discovery that these neurotransmitters were sometimes found in the same neuron as other neurotransmitters. It now seems possible that two or more neurotransmitters may be released from the same axon at the same time, perhaps because "several messengers could carry more information" (Hokfelt, Johansson, & Goldstein, 1984, p. 1332). If true, this notion adds yet another layer of complexity to the problem of understanding the action of these chemicals.

We shall return to current research on neurotransmitters and behavior later in the text when we discuss mechanisms of drug action (Chapter 4); the physiology of memory (Chapter 7); and possible links among depression, mania, and levels of the neurotransmitter norepinephrine (Chapter 14).

In summary, activity within the nervous system is both electrical and chemical. While the signals that travel down axons are primarily electrical, the communication between cells is a chemical process. A synapse is the space between the axon of one neuron and the dendrite or cell body of another, and is where information is transferred electrochemically.

A typical neuron may receive information from about 1,000 other cells; some motor neurons are connected by synapses with as many as 10,000 other cells. Stimulation at some synapses increases the likelihood that the next neuron in line will transmit an electrical charge of its own; stimulation at other synapses decreases the likelihood. At any given moment, the electrical state of a neuron is determined by the activity at all of its many synapses. When you consider the fact that there are billions of neurons in the brain, and trillions of interconnections, you can begin to understand the complexity of trying to trace neural pathways through the nervous system.

The Peripheral Nervous System

central nervous system The spinal cord and the brain.

peripheral nervous system All nerve fibers outside the brain and spinal cord.

Usually, when we think of the nervous system we think of the brain. The brain is indeed the control center of our highest ideals and our basest passions. Located in the center of the body and central to all aspects of functioning, the brain, together with the spinal cord, is called the **central nervous system.** Outside the central nervous system, and reaching to the periphery of our bodies, is the **peripheral nervous system,** which consists of all the nerve fibers in the body except those in the brain and spinal cord.

The importance of the peripheral nervous system should not be underestimated. To do its work, the brain must be connected with sensory receptors, muscles, and internal organs. These connections—which transmit messages

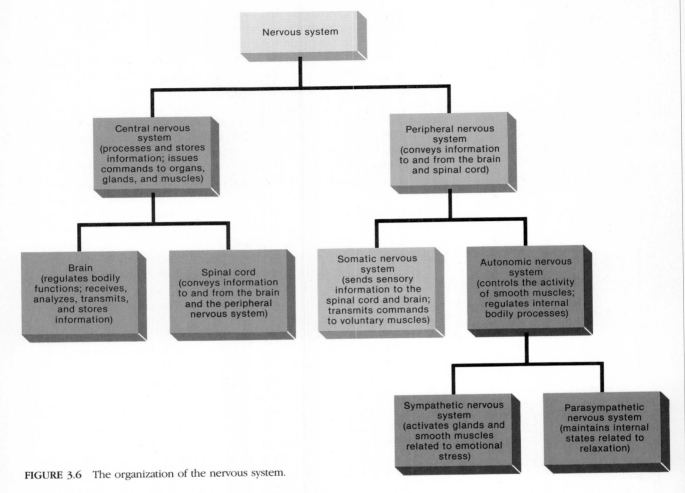

FIGURE 3.6 The organization of the nervous system.

that help us listen to the ocean's waves, climb the highest mountain, make love, and sneeze at a particular after-shave—are also a vital part of the nervous system.

One of the simplest schemes for summarizing the organization of the nervous system is diagrammed in Figure 3.6. As you can see, the large peripheral nervous system is subdivided into a somatic and an autonomic nervous system. While the most exciting current research is being conducted on the central nervous system, the somatic and autonomic portions of the peripheral nervous system play an essential role in the transmission of messages to and from the brain and spinal cord.

The Somatic Nervous System

The **somatic nervous system** connects the brain and spinal cord with sensory receptors and voluntary muscles. The neurons are divided into two major categories according to their function: afferent and efferent. **Afferent neurons**

somatic nervous system The portion of the peripheral nervous system that connects the brain and spinal cord with sensory receptors and voluntary muscles.

afferent (sensory) neurons Neurons that convey information from sensory receptors to the spinal cord and brain.

Even a sneeze involves a variety of complex nervous system processes.

(also known as **sensory neurons**) convey information from sensory receptors to the spinal cord and brain. For example, receptor cells in the skin translate feelings of pressure or cold into the electrochemical code of the nervous system. Afferent neurons then convey these messages to the spinal cord, and from there the information passes to the brain. Some details of how the receptor cells code physical stimuli are presented in Chapter 5 in the discussion of sensation. The **efferent neurons** (also known as **motor neurons**) of the somatic nervous system transmit the commands of the spinal cord and the brain to the muscles. Efferent neurons cause our fists to clench, our eyes to blink, and our fingers to do the walking through the Yellow Pages.

Thus, when your lover touches your hand, afferent neurons transmit the feeling of pressure to the brain, and efferent neurons allow you to move your own hand in reply. You are likely to be exquisitely aware of the sensations involved in this touching exchange. In contrast, we are rarely so aware of the activities of the autonomic nervous system.

The Autonomic Nervous System

The **autonomic nervous system** regulates the activity of smooth muscles and controls internal bodily processes (such as heart rate and contraction of the bladder). The primary task of the autonomic nervous system is to regulate the internal organs of the body. Ordinarily, this goes on without our awareness or conscious involvement. We do not have to decide whether to inhibit secretion of the pancreas, constrict the bronchial tubes of the lungs, or discharge stored blood from the spleen. If we had to spend our days consciously controlling all these bodily processes, we would never find time to read *War and Peace,* to watch "The Price Is Right," or to ponder the meaning of existence.

Referring again to Figure 3.6, you can see that the autonomic nervous system consists of two branches, the sympathetic and the parasympathetic. The **sympathetic nervous system** activates the glands and smooth muscles of the body in periods of emotional excitement; its nerve fibers originate in the two middle portions (thoracic and lumbar regions) of the spinal cord. The **parasympathetic nervous system** maintains appropriate internal states in times of relaxation; its nerve fibers originate at either end of the spinal cord (the brain stem and sacral regions).

Figure 3.7 illustrates the sympathetic and parasympathetic branches of the autonomic nervous system and some of their effects on the body's major organs. Note that many organs are connected to both these branches. For example, activation of the sympathetic nervous system increases heart rate, while activation of the parasympathetic nervous system lowers it; the sympathetic nervous system dilates the pupils of the eyes, and the parasympathetic nervous system constricts them. In short, these two branches oppose each other to regulate the state of the internal organs.

Walter Cannon (1927) argued that the major function of the sympathetic nervous system is to mobilize the body for an emergency, which he called the fight-or-flight reaction. When you suddenly notice a mysterious figure lurking in the shadows as you walk through a deserted neighborhood at 2 A.M., your adrenal glands secrete adrenaline, your heart beats faster, and blood

efferent (motor) neurons Neurons that transmit the commands of the spinal cord and brain to the muscles.

autonomic nervous system The portion of the peripheral nervous system that regulates the activity of smooth muscles which control internal bodily processes.

sympathetic nervous system The branch of the autonomic nervous system that activates the glands and smooth muscles of the body in periods of emotional excitement.

parasympathetic nervous system The branch of the autonomic nervous system that maintains appropriate internal states in times of relaxation.

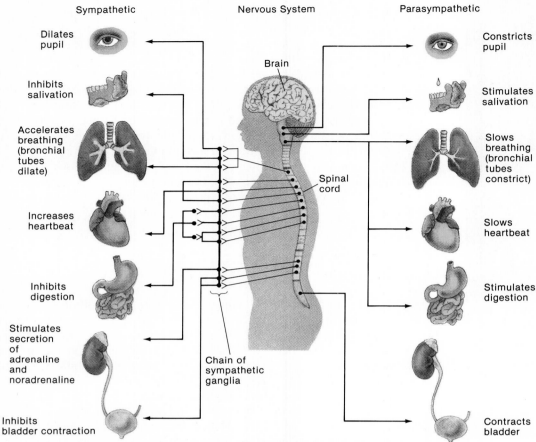

Sympathetic   Nervous System   Parasympathetic

Dilates pupil — Constricts pupil

Inhibits salivation — Stimulates salivation

Accelerates breathing (bronchial tubes dilate) — Slows breathing (bronchial tubes constrict)

Increases heartbeat — Slows heartbeat

Inhibits digestion — Stimulates digestion

Stimulates secretion of adrenaline and noradrenaline

Inhibits bladder contraction — Contracts bladder

Brain

Spinal cord

Chain of sympathetic ganglia

FIGURE 3.7 The two branches of the autonomic nervous system. The sympathetic nervous system arouses bodily processes, some of which are shown here. The parasympathetic nervous system counteracts many of these processes.

flows to your muscles and away from your skin, stomach, and intestines. All these physiological changes are designed to prepare you to deal with an emergency. For example, if you are forced to fight or to flee, you will need additional blood flowing to your muscles to supply them with oxygen and nutrients during their exertion.

When you get a little closer to the mysterious figure and identify him as an 83-year-old neighbor with insomnia, you will relax. In this case, your parasympathetic nervous system will become more active and work to restore your bodily processes to normal. The parasympathetic nervous system also dominates when you watch a dull TV program or take a nap.

Because the sympathetic and parasympathetic branches often oppose each other to maintain the equilibrium of the internal organs, they are said to be "antagonistic." However, there are exceptions to this rule. Crying, for example, is controlled strictly by the parasympathetic nervous system, and

endocrine glands Structures that secrete special chemical messengers (hormones) directly into the bloodstream.

pituitary gland The endocrine gland that controls the secretion of other endocrine glands and is itself under the control of the hypothalamus.

sweating is controlled by the sympathetic nervous system. For our purposes, it is sufficient to emphasize that the sympathetic nervous system is involved with the fight-or-flight reaction and the parasympathetic nervous system with more restful activities.

The Endocrine System

Closely related to the autonomic nervous system—although technically not a part of the nervous system at all—are the **endocrine glands**, which secrete special chemical messengers (called *hormones*) directly into the bloodstream. The most important glands of the endocrine system are the pituitary, the adrenal glands, and the gonads (see Figure 3.8).

The **pituitary gland** is located deep inside the brain, just below the hypothalamus. It is sometimes called the master gland because it controls the secretion of other endocrine glands. But it is not an independent master;

FIGURE 3.8 Major glands of the endocrine system. These glands secrete hormones that help regulate growth and behavior.

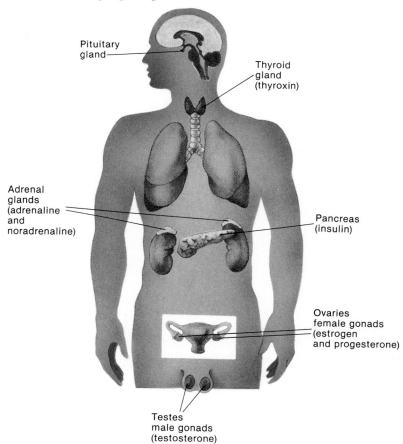

it comes under the control of the hypothalamus. Among the many chemicals secreted by the pituitary are hormones that regulate such internal functions as the reabsorption of water by the kidneys; the constriction of the arteries; and the stimulation of the thyroid, the adrenal glands, and the gonads. Still another pituitary hormone controls the growth process. If too much of this growth hormone is secreted during development, it produces a condition called giantism; too little can produce a midget.

The **adrenal glands** are two small endocrine glands that lie just above the kidneys. The two most important adrenal hormones, at least to psychologists, are adrenaline (also known as epinephrine) and noradrenaline (also known as norepinephrine). Both hormones are involved in the mobilization of the body's resources for fight or flight. Adrenaline is particularly involved in the action of the sympathetic nervous system; its effects include increased heartbeat and sweating.

Finally, the **gonads** are the sexual glands: *ovaries* in women and *testes* in men. The secretion of these glands controls the development of the reproductive organs; secondary sexual characteristics, such as the distribution of body hair; and some aspects of sexual behavior. In Chapter 10, we discuss the many physical changes triggered at puberty by the secretion of sex hormones.

The endocrine glands interact with each other and with portions of the nervous system in a series of complex circuits that ultimately regulate much of our development and behavior.

The Central Nervous System

The central nervous system, like the peripheral nervous system, can be thought of as having two major parts—in this case, the brain and the spinal cord. People can go on living if the connections between the two parts of the central nervous system are severed, but messages from the brain to the outer limbs telling them to move and sensations that start at the periphery of the body and head toward the brain cannot be transmitted. Thus, the spinal cord is not just a casual appendage of the brain; it has functions of its own that are important to normal living.

The Spinal Cord

The **spinal cord** is a long, thin column of neurons and tissue that emerges from the bottom of the brain and runs down the back inside the *spinal vertebrae,* the bony structures that protect the spinal cord from injury. There is no precise point at which the spinal cord ends and the brain begins. As we shall see in the next section, the spinal cord widens as it enters the skull and becomes the brain stem.

People whose spinal cords are damaged in an accident learn all too clearly how essential this structure is for normal body function. Since the spinal cord transmits sensory information to the brain and motor commands from the brain, a person whose spinal cord is damaged near the top can be

adrenal glands Two small endocrine glands that lie just above the kidney.

gonads Sexual glands: ovaries in women and testes in men.

spinal cord A long, thin column of neurons and tissue emerging from the bottom of the brain and running down the back next to the spinal vertebrae.

completely paralyzed and have no sensation whatever from the neck down. Oddly, however, this person will retain reflexes that do not require the brain. When the tendon of the knee is lightly tapped, a message is transmitted from sensory to motor neurons directly through the spinal cord, and the knee jerks automatically (see Figure 3.9). Thus, in the normal person, the spinal cord has two major roles: to regulate certain reflex movements and to transmit messages to and from the brain.

The Brain

The earliest recorded observation of the relationship between the brain and behavior appears in a surgical guide written about 30 centuries before Christ (Breasted, 1930). An Egyptian physician described a patient who fractured his skull and later walked with a shuffle. Thus, nearly 5,000 years ago it was noted that damage to the brain may lead to partial paralysis. But despite the astute observations of some early physicians, little or nothing was known about precisely how the brain was involved in simple motor reactions or complex thoughts about itself.

We have probably learned more about the brain in the last 100 years than in the preceding 49 centuries, and we are learning more each day. Generally, new research findings make the brain seem more complicated rather than simpler. So, as you read this section, remember that complex behaviors involve many different areas of the brain. The fact that the hypothalamus is involved with eating and the hippocampus with memory does not imply that eating and memory have nothing to do with the rest of the brain

FIGURE 3.9 Sensory neurons transmit sensory messages to motor neurons in the spinal cord that send back a motor message causing the knee to jerk.

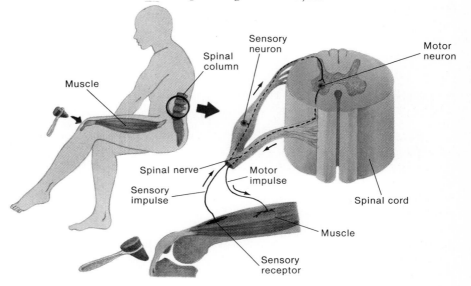

TABLE 3.3

Structures and Functions of the Brain

Name of structure	Location	Functions
Medulla[a]	First brain structure emerging from the spinal cord; part of the brain stem; connections with the autonomic nervous system	Helps regulate heart rate, breathing, and digestion; relays sensory and motor information to and from the rest of the brain.
Pons[a]	Continues out of the medulla; part of the brain stem	Involved in breathing, muscle coordination, hearing, and facial expression.
Reticular formation[a]	Continues out of the medulla, pons, and other structures; part of the brain stem	Involved in sleep, waking, alertness, and attention.
Midbrain[a]	Continues from the pons and reticular formation; part of the brain stem	Relays information from the eyes and ears to higher centers for visual and auditory processing.
Cerebellum[a]	Consists of two lobes that extend toward the back of the skull from either side of the pons	Involved in the coordination of muscle movements.
Thalamus[a]	On top of the brain stem	Is a way station for information from the eyes, ears, and skin.
Hypothalamus[a]	Between the thalamus and midbrain	Involved in eating, drinking, temperature regulation, sexual behavior, aggressive behavior; helps regulate the sympathetic nervous system and pituitary gland.
Limbic system[b]	Series of structures, including the hippocampus and amygdala, located near the border between the cerebral hemispheres and the brain stem; the hypothalamus is sometimes considered part of the limbic system	Primarily concerned with emotional behavior. "Pleasure centers" are located here. The hippocampus plays an important role in memory. The amygdala appears to be involved in aggression.
Cerebral cortex[c]	Convoluted outer layer of the human brain (organized into lobes, described below)	Is responsible for activities that make humans uniquely human—learning, remembering, analyzing, planning, performing fine-motor acts, etc.
Corpus callosum[c]	Connects the two cerebral hemispheres	Is a way station for information between the two cerebral hemispheres.
Frontal lobes[c]	Two portions of the cerebral hemispheres at the front of the brain	Primary motor projection areas at the back of the frontal lobes control muscle movements. Frontal lobes also involved in the planning and organization of actions, and may be involved in personality. Association areas involved in the organization of movement.
Parietal lobes[c]	Two portions of the cerebral hemispheres at the top rear of the brain	Somatosensory strip at the front of the parietal lobes receives input from sense organs. Association areas involved in the integration of complex sensory information.
Temporal lobes[c]	Two portions of the cerebral hemispheres, just over the ears, underneath the parietal lobes	Association areas involved in higher-level analysis of auditory information. Other areas involved in memory.
Occipital lobes[c]	Relatively small areas of the cerebral cortex at the back of the head	Association areas involved in higher-level analysis of visual information.

[a]Evolutionary status: Very primitive; found in snakes and fish; also called (along with the rest of the brain stem) the *reptilian brain.*

[b]Evolutionary status: Evolved later than the brain stem; also called the *old cortex* or *old mammalian brain;* proportionately larger in more primitive mammals than in more advanced mammals.

[c]Evolutionary status: Part of the *new cortex;* found in higher mammals; most recently evolved part of the brain.

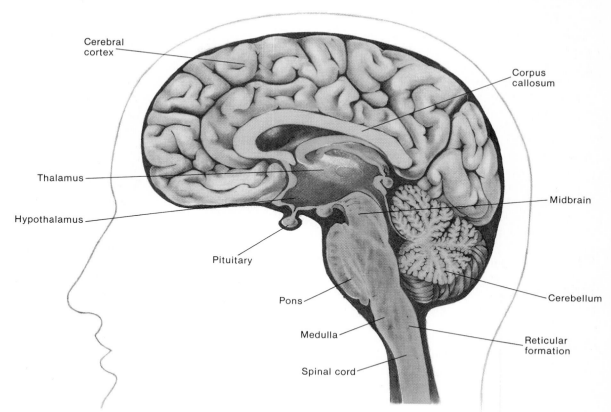

FIGURE 3.10 Major structures of the brain. The limbic system surrounds the area of the hypothalamus but is difficult to depict in a two-dimensional drawing like this.

or that the hypothalamus and hippocampus are not involved in other complex behaviors as well. Table 3.3 gives the location and functions of each structure in the brain as well as its evolutionary status (i.e., when in the course of evolution it developed). Figure 3.10 shows the major structures of the brain.

THE BRAIN STEM AND THE CEREBELLUM

The **medulla** is the first brain structure that emerges from the spinal cord as it widens upon entering the skull; it contains all the nerve fibers that connect the spinal cord to the brain. Interestingly, most of these fibers cross the medulla in such a way that, generally, the left side of the brain is connected to the right side of the body, and vice versa. As a result of this contralateral design, a person who has a stroke, say, on the right side of the brain may become paralyzed on the left side of the body. The medulla is also connected to the autonomic nervous system and helps regulate such vital functions as heart rate, breathing, and digestion. Overdoses of opiates and barbiturates can depress the vital actions of the medulla and lead to death.

Next in line is the **pons,** a structure that continues out of the medulla and also contains fibers connecting the brain and spinal cord. (The name

medulla The first brain structure that emerges from the spinal cord as it enters the skull; contains nerve fibers connecting the spinal cord to the brain.

pons A brain structure that continues out of the medulla and contains nerve fibers connecting the brain and spinal cord.

presumably came from an early anatomist who was reminded of a bridge—*pons* in Latin—by its humpbacked shape.) Passing through the pons are nerve fibers involved in breathing, muscular coordination, hearing, and facial expression, among many others.

The **reticular formation** is not a separate structure that can easily be isolated; it is a complex network of neurons and fibers that passes through the medulla, pons, and other structures. It is sometimes called the **reticular activating system**, because research has shown that the reticular formation is particularly involved in sleep, waking, alertness, and attention. Thus, if an inconsiderate roommate insists on turning the radio up while you are trying to study for a psychology exam, your ability—or inability—to concentrate on the definition of the reticular formation and ignore the "top 40" may depend on physiological processes in the reticular formation. Drugs that increase alertness, such as amphetamines, are believed to stimulate the reticular formation; drugs that decrease alertness, such as barbiturates, are believed to inhibit it.

The **midbrain** contains structures that relay some information from the eyes and ears to higher centers for visual and auditory processing. Fibers from the pons also continue through the midbrain. Taken together, the medulla, pons, reticular formation, midbrain, and closely related structures are referred to as the **brain stem**. Brain-stem structures are quite primitive in evolutionary terms. While only the highest mammals (including monkeys and humans) have a well-developed *cerebral cortex* (the thick layer of nerve cells covering the brain), even lowly snakes and fish have developed brain stems to control basic life processes, such as breathing and digestion. Although a human with extensive brain damage to the cerebral cortex may be surprisingly normal, brain-stem damage often leads to death.

Closely related to the brain stem but anatomically somewhat separate is the cerebellum, the structure removed in Flouren's classic studies in the 1820s. In appearance, it is one of the most distinctive structures in the brain. Like two very small fists, the lobes of the **cerebellum** extend out toward the back of the skull from either side of the pons; its primary known role is the coordination of muscle movements. The classic signs of drunkenness—loss of coordination and balance, staggering, and speech problems—seem to be largely due to an alcohol-induced depression of the cerebellum. Although the cerebellum does not initiate movement, its healthy functioning is essential for smooth, coordinated motion. It functions in much the same way to help fish swim, birds fly, and bank executives play golf.

THE THALAMUS, HYPOTHALAMUS, AND LIMBIC SYSTEM

The **thalamus** looks a bit like two eggs lying on their sides on top of the brain stem; it is often referred to as a way station, because so many nerve fibers meet there. Information from the eyes, the ears, and the skin (pressure, warmth, cold, and pain—see Chapter 5) passes through the thalamus on its way to be analyzed by higher processing centers in the cerebral cortex. Some analysis of sensory information also probably occurs here.

The cerebellum is involved in complex muscle coordination.

---

reticular formation (reticular activating system) A complex network of neurons and fibers that passes through the medulla, pons, and other structures and is particularly involved in sleep, waking, alertness, and attention.

midbrain A structure that relays information from the eyes and ears to higher centers for visual and auditory processing.

brain stem The part of the brain that contains such structures as the medulla, pons, reticular formation, and midbrain.

cerebellum A brain structure involved primarily in the coordination of muscle movements.

thalamus A brain structure that transmits sensory information to the cerebral cortex.

hypothalamus A brain structure lying between the thalamus and midbrain that seems to be involved in complex behaviors.

The **hypothalamus** is a much smaller structure that lies between the thalamus and the midbrain. It seems to be involved in a wide variety of complex behaviors, including eating, drinking, temperature regulation, sexual behavior, and aggressive behavior. The hypothalamus also helps to regulate the sympathetic nervous system and the pituitary gland. It is an extremely important structure; we discuss its role in eating in Chapter 11.

Some anatomists consider the hypothalamus to be part of the **limbic system,** a series of structures located near the border between the cerebral hemispheres and the brain stem (the name comes from the Latin word *limbicus,* meaning "bordering"). The limbic system is involved in the regulation of such "animal instincts" as fighting, fleeing, feeding, and reproduction.

The limbic system is sometimes called the *old cortex,* because it appeared in evolution before the *new cortex,* or neocortex. Lower animals such as fish and reptiles do not have any neocortex at all; their brains are limited to the brain stem and related structures. In mammals, the portion of the brain devoted to the cortex increases in more advanced animals. The more developed the cortex of a species, the more complex and flexible is its behavior. Thus, humans have a proportionally larger cortex than monkeys, and monkeys have a larger cortex than rabbits. Conversely, as one ascends the evolutionary scale, the proportion of limbic system (old cortex) declines. Thus, humans have a relatively smaller limbic system than monkeys, and the monkey's limbic system is proportionally smaller than the rabbit's. To some researchers, this suggests an anatomical basis for the fact that humans do not seem to be tied to instinctual drives in the same way that lower animals are: The larger neocortex dominates the primitive drives of the old cortex.

The limbic system has proved to be an especially interesting part of the brain because of its involvement in emotions, particularly in experiencing pleasure and pain. Much of the relevant research has made use of electrical stimulation techniques with laboratory animals. The notion of electrical stimulation probably makes your hair stand on end, bringing to mind electric shock therapy or, worse, electrocution. Actually, data from laboratory rats suggest that mild electrical stimulation of certain centers of the brain is sometimes more fun than eating, drinking, or copulating.

As with many major scientific discoveries, the discovery of "pleasure centers" in the limbic system was quite serendipitous. In the 1950s, two physiological psychologists, James Olds and Peter Milner (1954), were investigating the nature of "avoidance regions" in the brains of rats. When one rat behaved as if it were enjoying itself, Olds and Milner discovered that they had placed their electrode in the limbic system rather than in the reticular formation.

Subsequent research has confirmed the fact that rats appear to derive great pleasure from stimulation of centers in their limbic system. When an electric stimulator is attached to a lever so that rats can stimulate their brains by pressing the lever, they will press the lever up to 5,000 times in a single hour. Frank and Stutz (1984) claim that the evidence they review indicates that rats are more likely to stimulate their limbic systems than eat when they are hungry, drink when they are thirsty, or mate when they have been sexually deprived; that they will endure intense pain to stimulate these regions; and that they will press the lever until they drop from exhaustion. Other

limbic system   A series of structures near the border between the cerebral hemispheres and the brain stem that is involved in regulating "animal instincts."

investigators have had difficulty replicating these findings, except under extreme conditions, so we have another area of intense controversy.

THE CEREBRAL CORTEX

The **cerebral cortex** is the thick layer of nerve cells that covers the brain. In humans, the cerebral cortex contains at least 70% of the neurons in the central nervous system (Nauta & Feirtag, 1979), and it is here that we must search for the physiological basis of human nature.

We can compare the brain to a 3-pound walnut to emphasize the fact that the **cerebral hemispheres**—the two symmetrical sides of the brain—are mirror images of each other. We will have much to say about the similarities and differences in function of these two hemispheres in the next section of this chapter. In this anatomical overview, let us only note that the **corpus callosum** is a large band of nerve fibers that connects the two hemispheres of the brain.

The surface of each hemisphere of the human brain appears to be very wrinkled because it is covered with fissures, which have been described as the kinds of folds that would appear if you were to press the skin of an orange inward with a ruler (Thompson, 1975). In contrast, lower mammals, such as the rat, have a smoother and smaller cortex. This finding further supports the generalization that the greater the proportion of the brain devoted to the cerebral cortex, the more complex and flexible an animal's possible range of behavior.

FIGURE 3.11   The lobes of the cerebral cortex and primary sensory and motor areas. Damage to the primary areas produces specific deficits. For example, damage to a specific portion of the primary visual area leads to blindness in one part of the visual field.

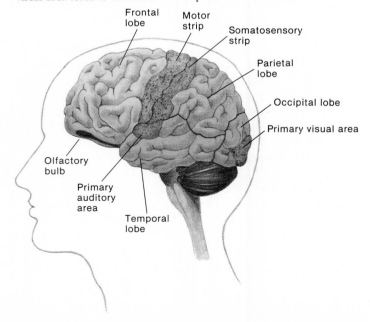

Diagnosing a Case of Brain Injury

In his 1986 book, *The Man Who Mistook His Wife for a Hat and Other Clinical Tales,* Oliver Sacks, a neurologist, describes some of his most interesting patients. In this exercise, we provide a brief clinical portrait of one patient, Mrs. S. As you read it, think back over the material you have read in Chapter 3, and decide which part of Mrs. S.'s brain has undergone damage.

Mrs. S. often complained to her nurses that they had not put dessert or coffee on her tray. When they replied that the dessert or coffee was right there, on the left side of the tray, she did not seem to understand, and did not look to the left. If someone gently turned her head so that the cookies came into sight, she would be surprised and comment, "Oh, they weren't there before." Moreover, she sometimes complained that she was not being given

enough food—because she was eating only from the right half of her plate. When she put on lipstick, it was just to the right side of her mouth. Even when people pointed out her neglect of the left side of her body, she did not seem able really to attend to and understand what was being said. Indeed, Mrs. S. seemed to have totally lost the idea of "left" in relation both to her own body and the rest of the world.

What do you think might have happened to Mrs. S.? Which portion of her brain could have been damaged? How could her medical attendants help her find the food on the left side of her tray, given that reminding her about it does not seem to work? (A discussion of this exercise appears after the "Summary" at the end of this chapter.)

---

cerebral cortex The thick layer of nerve cells that covers the brain.

cerebral hemispheres The two symmetrical sides of the brain.

corpus callosum A wide band of nerve fibers that connects the two cerebral hemispheres.

frontal lobe The major lobe at the front of the brain.

parietal lobe The major lobe at the top rear of the brain.

temporal lobe The major lobe just over the ear.

occipital lobe The major lobe at the back of the head.

primary projection areas Cortical areas of the brain that receive input from the sense organs or control the movement of particular muscle groups.

During development, the cortex of the brain grows and folds back on itself, and fissures appear on the surface. Figure 3.11 shows the two major fissures that serve as dividing landmarks to the four major lobes of the cerebral cortex. The central fissure separates the **frontal lobe**, at the front of the brain, from the **parietal lobe**, at the top rear. Just over the ears, underneath the parietal lobe and separated from it by the lateral fissure, is the **temporal lobe**. Finally, the **occipital lobe** is a relatively small area of the cerebral cortex at the back of the head.

As mentioned earlier, some basic psychological functions seem to be precisely localized in specific areas of the cortex. **Primary projection areas** receive input from the sense organs or control the movement of particular muscle groups. Figure 3.11 lists the known primary projection areas of the cerebral cortex. Lesions in these areas produce specific sensory and/or motor deficits. For example, damage to a small area in the occipital cortex would lead to blindness in only one part of the visual field; a comparable lesion in the temporal lobe would lead to a specific type of partial hearing loss. "Applying Scientific Concepts" asks you to use your new knowledge of the brain to make a diagnosis and think about intervention in a case of brain injury.

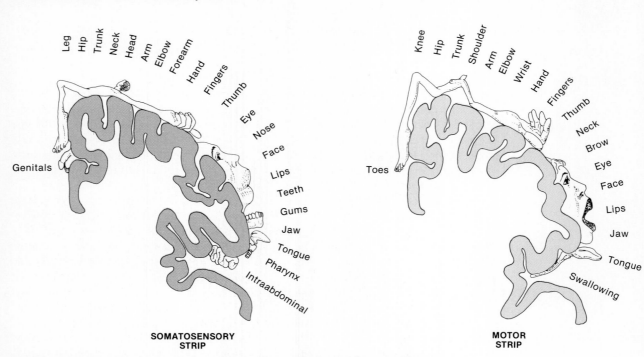

FIGURE 3.12 The somatosensory and motor strips, showing body parts drawn in proportion to the brain areas to which they are connected. For example, the lips and tongue are exaggerated on the motor strip because considerable brain tissue regulates the movement of muscles in these areas.

Another primary projection area, called the **motor strip,** lies inside the frontal lobe, in front of the central fissure. Because electrical stimulation of the motor strip of one cerebral hemisphere produces muscular movements on the opposite side of the body, it is possible to draw a detailed map of how these cortical areas are involved in movement (see Figure 3.12). Stimulation of the top end of the motor strip of the right hemisphere causes you to move your left toe; stimulation a few millimeters down provokes left ankle movement; the next spot controls the left knee; and so on.

At the front of the parietal lobe and across the central fissure from the motor strip is the **somatosensory strip.** Here, electrical stimulation produces the sensations you would feel if someone touched various parts of the opposite side of your body. Consequently, it has also been possible to map the connections to the somatosensory strip (see Figure 3.10).

Interestingly, the amount of brain tissue devoted to an area of the body is proportional to that area sensitivity, not to its size. For example, a greater area of the cerebral cortex is connected to the lips than to the shoulders, because the lips are extremely sensitive to touch and the shoulders are not. Similarly, the amount of tissue in the motor strip is related to the degree and delicacy of control we have over the movements of specific muscles. Large areas of the brain are devoted to the fingers, lips, and tongue; relatively small areas govern the shoulders, neck, and trunk.

Perhaps the most striking fact about the primary projection areas is

motor strip A primary projection area inside the frontal lobe that controls certain muscle movements.

somatosensory strip A primary projection area at the front of the parietal lobe that receives sensations from the opposite side of the body.

that they account for a relatively small proportion of the human brain. What does the rest of the cerebral cortex do? One hint comes from an analysis of the brains of other species. The proportion of the brain devoted to nonprimary cortex is higher for humans than for any other species.

The term **association areas** refers to all cortical areas that are not specifically involved with simple sensory or motor reactions. This name is based on the belief that these brain areas are involved in higher mental processes, such as forming associations. Some researchers prefer the term *silent cortex,* which makes no assumptions about the overall function of these areas but stresses the fact that electrical stimulation here does not produce obvious motor or sensory responses (the areas are "silent").

The association areas immediately adjoining primary sensory areas seem generally to be involved with the higher-level analysis of sensory information. For example, a person with brain damage to certain portions of the right occipital lobe sometimes has trouble recognizing faces. This patient is able to see and respond normally to simple visual stimuli but is not able to integrate the information into a complete perception of someone's face. Damage to portions of the temporal lobe adjoining the primary hearing areas produces a comparable auditory deficit: The person may be able to hear normally but fails to recognize the sound of running water or a ringing telephone.

Damage in the frontal lobe immediately next to primary motor areas produces an analogous deficit in the organization of movement. One example is Broca's aphasia, which involves the disorganization of speech (see Figure 3.1).

Another type of association area is involved in the integration of more complex information, often from several different senses at the same time. These are the brain areas that are believed to be involved with our most complex thoughts and actions, from deciding whether to cut class and go to the beach to trying to remember the difference between the German words *Gemeinschaft* and *Gesellschaft.*

Of all the aspects of brain organization that distinguish human beings from beasts, the most important is the development of the frontal lobes. It is therefore frustrating—though perhaps not surprising—that the frontal lobes have proved to be the most difficult area of the brain to study.

Although much controversy remains, the frontal lobes have been implicated in the planning and organization of actions. Patients with damage to the frontal lobes have special difficulty with abstract problems that require them to remain intellectually flexible, shifting from one solution strategy to another.

Personality changes have also been observed after frontal damage. This was first noted more than a century ago in the classic case of Phineas Gage, a man whose frontal lobes were severely damaged in a construction accident (see "Understanding the Scientific Method"). Later observations that frontal-lobe damage seemed to produce a calming effect on animals led for a time to the use of frontal lobotomy (in which connections from the frontal lobes to the rest of the brain were destroyed) in the treatment of mental illness, as described in the next section.

Ultimately, it is in the frontal lobes that many brain researchers expect to find the solutions to some of the mysteries of what makes us human.

---

association areas Cortical areas of the brain that are not specifically involved with simple sensory or motor reactions.

How Much Do Scientists Really Know About the Brain?

The more you read about brain research, the more impressed you will be by how much scientists still must learn. To provide a more concrete feeling for our current state of knowledge, this section will concentrate on one area of applied brain research—psychosurgery—and on one topic of more theoretical interest—cerebral asymmetry.

Psychosurgery

Psychosurgery is brain surgery aimed at changing a person's thought or behavior patterns. Though removal of a brain tumor or treatment of some other organic problem may have unintended side effects on a person's behavior, a procedure such as this is not considered psychosurgery. Only when a surgeon sets out purposely to alter a patient's psychological function do we use this term.

In 1935, Egas Moniz performed the first human **frontal lobotomy**—cutting the connections between the frontal lobes and other brain structures. The effect was equivalent to physically removing part of the frontal lobe. Animal research had suggested that this operation might calm extreme anxiety; and of the first 20 mental patients Moniz operated on, 7 were considered recovered and another 7 had improved. Other surgeons quickly became interested in the operation and began performing brain surgery to treat mental disorders on a large scale. There are no precise figures available, but the best estimate suggests that by the late 1950s over 25,000 frontal lobotomies had been performed in the United States alone (Valenstein, 1980).

One reason why so many frontal lobotomies were performed during this period is that the operation offered hope where before there had been none. The psychiatry and psychology of the 1930s and 1940s had no effective treatment for the seriously disturbed mental patient; frontal lobotomy seemed to offer a chance for improvement.

Several large-scale studies found that after frontal lobotomies, most patients were less anxious, less depressed, and generally better adjusted. But there were other, more subtle personality and intellectual changes as well. One group of psychosurgeons characterized these changes as follows:

> Patients after lobotomy always show some lack of personality depth. They are cheerful and complacent and are indifferent to the opinions and feelings of others. . . . Their goals are immediate—not remote. They can recall the past as well as ever, but it has diminished interpretive value for them, and they are not more interested in their own past emotional crises than if they had happened to someone else. They seem incapable of feeling guilt now for past misdeeds. (Robinson, Freeman, & Watts, 1951, p. 159)

When Moniz won the Nobel Prize in medicine in 1949, a *New York Times* (October 30, 1949, p. 8E) editorial provided the following glowing picture of frontal lobotomy: "The sensational operation justified itself. Hypo-

psychosurgery Brain surgery aimed at changing a person's thought or behavior patterns.

frontal lobotomy Destruction of the connections between the frontal lobes and other brain structures.

The Case Study of Phineas Gage: A Man Who Nearly Lost His Head

A *case study* is an intensive study of a single individual. A biographer might focus on the most dramatic events in a person's life; a researcher doing a case study is engaged in a more systematic search for the patterns and causes of behavior.

In a scientific sense, the study of a single individual cannot be taken as proof of any general psychological law. But a case study can provide valuable insights that can be tested on large groups. And it may provide valuable information on questions that would otherwise be impossible to study, such as how damage to the human brain affects behavior.

One of the most famous victims of accidental brain injury was a 25-year-old laborer named Phineas Gage. On September 13, 1848, Gage was blasting rock on a railroad construction project in Cavendish, Vermont. Gage's job was to pack down the explosive charge with an iron bar. In the middle of this delicate process, he was distracted and turned suddenly. The iron bar struck rock, a spark ignited the gunpowder, and the bar—roughly $3\frac{1}{2}$ feet long, 1 inch in diameter, and weighing 13 pounds—rocketed upward. It passed through Gage's left cheek, went right through the top of his head, and flew high into the air.

According to eyewitnesses, Gage was thrown to the ground and had a few minor convulsions but was up and talking within a few minutes. His men carried him to an ox cart, and the laborer sat erect for the $\frac{3}{4}$-mile ride into the village. He got out of the cart and walked up a long flight of stairs into his hotel room with a little assistance. When a physician arrived a few minutes later, Gage greeted him cheerily and proceeded to describe how he had been injured. At first, the doctor refused to believe that an iron bar could pass completely through a man's skull and leave him alive to tell the tale. But "An Irishman standing nearby said, 'Sure it was so, sir, for the bar is lying in the road below, all blood and brains' " (Bigelow, 1850, p. 16). Other eyewitnesses later provided less graphic verifications.

Although Gage bled profusely and was quite sick for a few weeks, he remained rational throughout his illness and recovered quickly (Harlow, 1848). About a year later, Gage visited Boston and was examined at the Harvard Medical School. Doctors there verified the nature of the wound. (Admittedly, a few surgeons in other cities remained skeptical and referred to the case as a "Yankee invention" [Harlow, 1868, p. 19]).

The physicians who studied this case seemed more interested in the fact that a man could have survived such a massive injury than in relatively subtle effects on behavior. But they did notice a change. Phineas Gage was described as efficient, capable, and likable before the injury. Afterward, he became restless, irreverent, and profane. He devised one wild scheme after another. Sometimes he had trouble making up his mind; at other times he became extremely stubborn and paid little

(box continues on next page)

attention to the advice of others. In the words of his physician:

> A child in his intellectual capacity and manifestations, he has the animal passions of a strong man. Previous to his injury, though untrained in the schools, he possessed a well-balanced mind, and was looked upon by those who knew him as a shrewd, smart business man, very energetic and persistent in executing all his plans of operation. In this regard his mind was radically changed, so decidedly that his friends and acquaintances said he was "no longer Gage." (Harlow, 1869, p. 14)

Gage traveled throughout New England, carrying his iron bar wherever he went. He apparently even spent a short time in a freak show (at Barnum's in New York). Four years after the injury, Gage traveled to South America to start a coach line in Chile. He became ill and returned to San Francisco in 1860. He died soon after, $12\frac{1}{2}$ years after the accident. Gage's family donated his skull and the iron bar to science, and both ended up in the Harvard Medical School museum.

The story of Phineas Gage illustrates some of the strengths and weaknesses of the case study approach. A person's life story provides a rich source of data that may suggest many more ideas than a limited scientific study that focuses on one aspect of behavior. But it is hard to know how Gage's behavior was affected by unique aspects of his personality, his experience, and the precise nature of his brain injury. This makes it very difficult to draw general conclusions about the function of the frontal lobes. It is also disconcerting that we must depend so heavily on the observational powers of Gage's physician. Perhaps if he had spoken to more of Gage's friends, for example, a different picture of the preaccident personality would have emerged.

Ultimately, it is this lack of objectivity that leads most psychologists to be cautious about case studies. Case studies can be informative, but they may also be misleading. Whenever possible, they must be supplemented by other types of research.

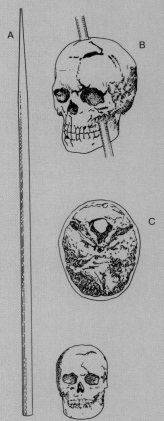

One of the physicians who treated Phineas Gage drew these sketches to show the extent of skull damage and the relative size of the iron bar that had passed through his head.

Popular beliefs about frontal lobotomy were influenced by the 1975 film *One Flew over the Cuckoo's Nest*.

chondriacs no longer thought they were going to die, would-be suicides found life acceptable, sufferers from persecution complexes forgot the machinations of imaginary conspirators."

But even in 1949, some critics were less enthusiastic. They noted that faulty operations sometimes led to physical problems, such as huge weight gain, partial paralysis, epileptic seizures, and even death. Popular beliefs about frontal lobotomy (as portrayed in the 1975 Oscar-winning film *One Flew over the Cuckoo's Nest*) seem to have been influenced greatly by this negative view. There is no question that some frontal lobotomies had tragic consequences. But while critics can cite individual cases of people whose lives were ruined by the operation, proponents of the operation can answer with individual cases of extremely successful lobotomies. One psychosurgeon described a physician who was discharged from two internships for his aggressive behavior and his delusions of being persecuted. After a frontal lobotomy, the doctor got married, established a 10-person medical clinic, and learned to fly his own plane (Valenstein, 1973).

For a more balanced picture of the effects of frontal lobotomy, we must turn not to individual cases but rather to large-scale studies. Valenstein (1973, p. 315) summarized the research on frontal lobotomies as follows: "There is certainly no grounds for either the position that all psychosurgery necessarily reduces people to a 'vegetable status' or that it has a high probability of producing miraculous cures. The truth, even if somewhat wishy-washy, lies in between these extreme positions."

In the mid-1950s, drugs became available that relieved some of the more severe symptoms of mental disorders. In the proper hands, lobotomy had always been seen as a treatment of last resort. The new, less drastic drug therapies (see Chapter 15) were a major factor in reducing the number of frontal lobotomies.

From the mid-1950s through 1980, approximately 500 psychosurgical operations were performed in the United States each year (Valenstein, 1980). During this period, many neurosurgeons turned away from frontal lobotomy and instead investigated the effects of more limited operations on structures deep inside the brain. Among the most promising of the new procedures was **cingulotomy**, an operation in which certain fibers connecting the frontal lobes to the limbic system were cut. One study of its effects (Teuber, Corkin, & Twitchell, 1976) followed 11 patients who suffered from chronic pain and depression; they had been under medical treatment for years, and all other therapies had failed. Cingulotomies cured 9 of these 11. The same operation also helped 5 people out of a group of 7 who were suffering from depression alone. Results for another 15 patients with other types of problems were more variable.

The need to understand more about psychosurgery is clear. In a later report on the effects of 85 cingulotomies, the same research group continued to support the idea that many patients were helped. But, the report also noted, "It is not understood why cingulotomy is effective in some cases and not in others, or what brain mechanisms or other factors are responsible for the improvement when it does occur" (Corkin, 1980, p. 204).

A careful reading of this conclusion reveals that this researcher is not even willing to assert that cingulotomies are effective due to physical changes

cingulotomy Brain surgery in which certain fibers connecting the frontal lobes to the limbic system are cut.

in the brain; other factors may be responsible for its success. For example, some researchers believe that these operations may suceed as a result of the **placebo effect**—medical treatments of no value in themselves sometimes seem to cure patients by the power of suggestion. Whether this is so, or whether cingulotomy works by altering specific aspects of brain function, can only be learned by further research.

Cerebral Asymmetry

The term **cerebral asymmetry** refers to differences between the two sides, or hemispheres, of the brain. Although physically they look very much alike, it is now clear that the left and right hemispheres play different roles in our behavior and mental life. The earliest evidence of this split came from studies of patients with brain damage. In 1861, when Paul Broca presented his famous cases of aphasia patients with left-hemisphere damage, he helped establish the idea that language abilities are localized on the left side of the brain. Partly because damage to the right hemisphere produces more subtle deficits, widespread recognition of its role in such areas as depth perception and spatial relationships began only around the 1930s.

It is now clear that the classical distinction between a verbal left hemisphere and a nonverbal right hemisphere applies primarily to right-handed people. The picture for the 10% of the population that is left-handed is more complex. Most of our discussion will therefore be limited to the right-handed majority; we shall conclude with a section on the special status of lefties.

SPLIT-BRAIN SURGERY

Split-brain surgery involves cutting the corpus callosum, the fibers that connect the left and right hemispheres. This operation was first tried in humans as an experimental treatment for certain epileptics whose seizures could not be effectively controlled by drugs or other treatments. This extreme procedure was a success: Severing the connection between the hemispheres of the brain did indeed reduce the incidence and severity of epileptic attacks. But Roger Sperry, Michael Gazzaniga, and their associates at the California Institute of Technology were more interested in the psychological side effects of these radical operations. How would these people fare when they literally had two separate brains in one head?

One of the first patients awoke from surgery and quipped that he had a "splitting headache." However, there is no evidence that his jokes had been funnier before the operation. All in all, split-brain patients seemed surprisingly normal. But subtle tests gradually revealed that these people now had a number of intriguing problems.

As mentioned earlier, each hemisphere is primarily connected to the opposite side of the body. For example, the right hand is connected to the left hemisphere, and the left hand is connected to the right hemisphere. The connections of the visual system are more complicated (see Figure 3.13). Both eyes are connected to both sides of the brain. But information from the left visual field (that is, the left portion of the area that each of your

placebo effect The phenomenon whereby medical treatments of no value in themselves seem to cure patients by the power of suggestion.

cerebral assymmetry Differences between the two hemispheres of the brain.

split-brain surgery Brain surgery that involves cutting the corpus callosum, surgically isolating the right and left hemispheres.

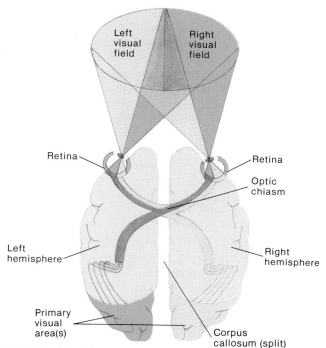

FIGURE 3.13 When a person fixates the eyes by staring at a point, information from the left visual field goes to the right hemisphere and information from the right visual field goes to the left hemisphere. In a normal person, information is quickly transferred to the opposite side via the corpus callosum. But in split-brain patients as shown here, these fibers are cut and the information is received by only one hemisphere.

eyes sees) goes to the right hemisphere; information from the right visual field goes to the left hemisphere. Under ordinary conditions, the eyes are constantly moving, so the split-brain person would get a complete picture of the world on each side of the brain.

But Gazzaniga (1967) devised a special test so that he could send visual messages to one brain hemisphere at a time. A split-brain person stared at a dot on a screen, and a visual stimulus was flashed briefly on one side of the dot or the other. If the stimulus appeared in the left visual field, the information would go to the right hemisphere; if the stimulus was flashed to the right visual field, only the left hemisphere would see it.

When a picture of a spoon was flashed at the left hemisphere, a split-brain person could easily say that she saw a spoon. But when the same picture was flashed to the right hemisphere, the split-brain patient often denied seeing anything. Yet when this person used her left hand to feel a group of objects hidden behind the screen, she was easily able to pick out the object she had seen—a spoon.

In an even more dramatic demonstration, a picture of a cigarette was flashed to the right hemisphere, and a split-brain patient picked out an ashtray with his left hand as the most closely related article in a group of 10 objects.

But the "speaking" left hemisphere of the brain was no longer connected to the left hand, so the patient could not *say* what he had picked.

These early experiments seemed to support an unambiguous distinction between the verbal left hemisphere and the nonverbal right. But, as so often happens in psychology, further research revealed that it was not quite that simple. For example, Eran Zaidel (1978) developed a new technique for presenting stimuli to the left and right visual fields through a special contact lens that moved with the eye. The earlier method of staring at a dot had allowed each hemisphere to see a stimulus only for fractions of a second. When Zaidel's new system made it possible for either hemisphere to see stimuli for much longer periods, more subtle linguistic abilities in the right hemisphere began to emerge. In one test, split-brain patients were given vocabulary questions that required choosing a picture that corresponded to a spoken word. When the pictures were presented only to the right hemisphere, people did not do as well as they did with the left. But they were able to perform at roughly the level of a 10-year-old child.

Virtually all researchers now agree that most language functions are located in the left hemisphere. But these experiments have sharpened the debate regarding exactly what role, if any, the right hemisphere plays in language. At one extreme, Gazzaniga (1983) has pointed out that few split-brain patients have shown any sign of right-hemisphere language, and that in these cases the linguistic skills varied greatly. A review of two decades of research with split-brain patients led him to the provocative conclusion that the "cognitive skills of a normal disconnected right hemisphere without language are vastly inferior to the cognitive skills of a chimpanzee" (Gazzaniga, 1983, p. 535). In response to this claim, Zaidel (1983, p. 545) argued that while "the precise limits of right hemisphere language capacity are not as yet known," there is increasing "evidence for right hemisphere involvement in normal language."

This difference of opinion is not likely to be resolved by further research on split-brain patients. Although this operation has provided valuable evidence that is highly significant from a theoretical point of view, it is performed quite rarely. To date, psychologists have had an opportunity to study only about 40 split-brain patients, and only a handful of these showed evidence of right-hemisphere language (Zaidel, 1983). Thus, future insights are more likely to come from the comparison of split-brain findings with those from other lines of evidence.

ASYMMETRIES IN THE NORMAL BRAIN

A number of different techniques have been developed to study cerebral asymmetry in the normal human brain. For example, a procedure called the Wada test has been used to localize language in patients who are about to undergo brain surgery. (This procedure is necessary to ensure that removal of diseased brain tissue does not unintentionally interfere with language.) The Wada test involves anesthetizing one hemisphere of the brain. A small tube is inserted into the carotid artery on one side of the patient's neck; when the drug sodium amytal (a barbiturate) is injected into the tube, it circulates primarily through the hemisphere on the same side of the brain.

The results of this temporary chemical ablation are quite dramatic to see. The patient is generally asked to keep both arms raised in the air and count backward from 100. Within seconds of an injection, the arm on the opposite side of the body falls limp, indicating that one side of the brain is now "asleep." If the drug has been injected into the nonspeaking hemisphere, the patient quickly resumes counting and can answer simple questions. But if the drug has reached the speaking hemisphere, the patient is not able to talk for two to five minutes. Later, the person returns to normal.

Of course, this serious surgical procedure is not used in routine research on cerebral asymmetry. Other, more indirect, tests are used for routine assessment of hemispheric functioning. EEG measurements, for example, have revealed that the electrical activity on the two sides of the brain systematically changes as a person performs different sorts of tasks. Verbal tasks, such as writing a letter or thinking of words that begin with certain letters, have been found to result in relative signs of EEG activation on the left side of the brain. Spatial tasks, such as memorizing geometric designs or pictures of people's faces, generally led to relative EEG activation on the right side of the brain.

Sensory asymmetries have also been observed. Even normal individuals have been found to respond more quickly and accurately to words and letters presented to the right visual field (left hemisphere). There is also evidence that the left visual field (right hemisphere) is superior on such tests as facial recognition and identifying the spatial position of certain figures. Under some conditions, the right ear has also proved superior at recognizing verbal stimuli and the left ear at recognizing musical chords and melodies.

Encouraged by the consistency of these results, some theorists began to speculate about the more general implications of the "logical left brain" and the "intuitive right brain." At times, these speculations have gotten out of hand, as when Marshall McLuhan argued that excessive television watching caused the children of the 1960s to become the first generation in centuries whose thinking was dominated by the right brain, and that the social upheavals of the sixties could be blamed on the conflicts between left-brained parents and right-brained children (Goleman, 1977b). Statements like this, which are based on no evidence whatsoever, are not taken seriously by brain scientists.

Nevertheless, the idea of the logical left brain and the intuitive right brain has been publicized widely. A best-seller entitled *Drawing on the Right Side of the Brain* promised to "unlock the door to the neglected right half [of the brain] and integrate both halves, so that everyone . . . can realize full artistic and creative potential" (Edwards, 1980).

Physiological researchers in this field have generally been more cautious about characterizing the functions of the two hemispheres. Although describing a verbal left hemisphere and a nonverbal right are good first approximations, a closer look at the data inevitably yields many ambiguities.

For example, consider the case of music. In support of the idea that this nonverbal stimulus would primarily involve the right hemisphere, several researchers at first reported that melodies are more easily recognized by the left ear (which is connected primarily to the right hemisphere). But later research revealed that this relationship held only for nonmusicians; trained musicians recognized melodies better through the right ear, suggesting that *they* were using the left hemisphere to process music (Bever & Chiarello, 1974). Following this line of investigation, still further research showed that the kind of musical task also made a difference. For example, in one study the left hemisphere proved superior in recognizing excerpts from unfamiliar melodies, while the right hemisphere was better at recognizing excerpts from familiar melodies (Gates & Bradshaw, 1977).

Taking these observations and many others into account, Bradshaw and Nettleton (1981) argue that the fundamental difference between the two sides of the brain involves a continuum rather than a simple dichotomy. They believe that the left hemisphere is especially involved in the sequential analysis of stimuli presented one after another, as in listening to the words of a sentence. The right hemisphere is more involved in the global, holistic response to complex stimuli, as in recognizing a face.

Research on this hypothesis and others remains very active at this time. The study of brain asymmetries has even been extended beyond humans to other species (Sherman, Galaburda, & Geschwind, 1982). In several species of birds, for example, song has been localized in the left half of the brain. And anatomical asymmetries have been found in the development of the left and right sides of the brain of chimpanzees and gorillas that parallel those characterizing the human brain.

Although the general notion of a sequential left hemisphere and a holistic right hemisphere has held up rather well, a considerable amount of additional research—and the inevitable accompanying controversy—will be necessary to explore fully the many differences in structure and function between the two sides of the brain. But there is one point on which all scientists can agree: The brain is a tremendously complex organ that is not likely to be described adequately by simple dichotomies between right and left.

HANDEDNESS

About nine out of ten people are right-handed, and the traditional distinction between a verbal left hemisphere and a nonverbal right hemisphere was based primarily on studies of righties. Apparently, the high frequency of right-handedness goes back many thousands of years: Even the people pictured in ancient Egyptian tomb paintings were predominantly right-handed.

Interestingly, left-handedness, which is more common among males than females, runs in families. According to one classic study (Rife, 1940), when both parents are lefties, about 45% of their children are also left-handed; the figure drops to 30% if only one parent is left-handed and to 8% if neither is a lefty. Although these findings do not prove that handedness is inherited, they do suggest that heritability may be an important factor.

There has been considerable progress in recent years in understanding the relationships between handedness and brain organization. For example, one might expect the brain organization of left-handed people to be the mirror image of that for right-handed people, with language on the right side of the brain rather than on the left. Although this assumption is intuitively appealing, it is also wrong. While language is sometimes found in the right hemisphere of lefties, this arrangement is less common than two other alternatives: language in the left hemisphere (the same arrangement as found for right-handers), or in both hemispheres.

The precise percentages of lefties falling into each of these three catego-ries (i.e., language in left hemisphere, right hemisphere, or both hemispheres) depends both on the technique used to assess the language competence of the hemispheres (such as the Wada test, the effects of brain damage, visual field differences, or auditory asymmetries) and on the technique used to measure handedness (such as the person's self-description versus direct obser-vation of hand use on specific laboratory tasks). In general, however, about 70% of left-handers have been found to have language in the left hemisphere, just as righties do. The remainder fall into the other two categories in roughly equal numbers: About 15% have language in the right hemisphere, and 15% have language in both hemispheres (Springer & Deutsch, 1985).

Many authors have speculated about the significance of the more complex pattern of brain organization found in lefties. For example, Fancher (1977) pointed to the left-handedness of Leonardo da Vinci, Charlie Chaplin, and Harpo Marx as evidence that the brains of lefties have a greater cognitive capacity for surprise and are thus able to see relations that escape more conventional brains. To put it kindly, speculations of this sort have no scientific basis.

More promising are studies of anatomical differences in the brains of left- and right-handed people. Wittelson (1985) studied 42 patients hospitalized for terminal cancer who generously agreed to participate in a variety of tests, including direct measures of hand preference on 12 different tasks. After these patients died, researchers performed autopsies to compare the brains of 27 who were consistently right-handed with 15 who used their left hand on some or all of the tasks. Wittelson found that the corpus callosum was 11% larger in patients who were partially or fully left-handed. This finding suggests that left-handed people have up to 25 million more nerve fibers connecting the two sides of the brain than right-handed people do. This greater anatomical link between the hemispheres helps explain the fact that cognitive functions tend to be more lateralized for right-handers (i.e., language more strictly in the left and spatial relations in the right), while left-handers more often are found to have both hemispheres involved in cognitive tasks.

Large-scale research on differences between left-handed and right-handed people is only about a decade old, and systematic theories of the physiological and psychological differences between these groups are just beginning to be explored. One of the most provocative to date was proposed by Norman Geschwind (1983, 1984), who became interested in possible relationships between handedness and medical history as a result of an accident. He had performed a number of studies of dyslexia, a learning disability that is particu-larly common in males and left-handers. While speaking to a group of dyslexics, he mentioned the possibility that the disability might be genetically linked to other disorders. After the lecture, many people came up from the audience to tell him about the medical histories of their own families. A surprisingly large number mentioned such disorders as ulcerative colitis, rheumatoid arthri-tis, lupus, and myasthenia gravis, which are known to involve the body's immune system. The immune system normally fights infection by destroying germs and foreign substances that invade the body. In the disorders just cited, the immune system attacks the body's own proteins, apparently as a result of mistakenly identifying them as foreign substances.

As a result of this observation, Geschwind and his colleagues performed several surveys of over 2,000 people. They found that left-handers were three times as likely to suffer from immune disorders as right-handers, and their relatives were twice as likely to have these disorders as the normal population. Their surveys also confirmed a finding that had been noted many times in the past: Left-handed people were far more likely than right-handers to suffer from dyslexia and other learning disabilities.

Geschwind went on to develop an ingenious theory to explain these findings and others. He argued that as the brain develops during pregnancy, an excess of male hormones, such as testosterone, can slow the development of the left hemisphere of the brain, increasing the rate of both left-handedness and learning disabilities. He also cited evidence that this surplus of male hormones has a negative effect on the development of the immune system, and thus can lead to a higher rate of immune disorders.

Other researchers have uncovered a more positive side of this theory. There is also evidence that left-handedness is linked with superior achievement in a number of areas, notably mathematics. A study at Johns Hopkins of 50,000 seventh-graders found that the mathematically gifted were more likely to be male, to be left-handed, and to have had a childhood history of allergies that involve the immune system (Kolata, 1983).

In discussing his theory, Geschwind often emphasized that it did not imply that left-handers were in any way inferior or disadvantaged. For example, Geschwind (1983, p. 32) noted: "It is my belief that the population with a genetic predisposition toward left-handedness is at no overall disadvantage compared to the right-handed population. Each group will have differing susceptibilities to different disorders." He went on to speculate that left-handers may prove to be more resistant to infections and even cancer than right-handers.

It is also important to note that despite the ingenuity of Geschwind's theory about left-handers, it must be subjected to a considerable amount of further testing. Ten years from now, his view may or may not seem valid. But it will certainly have stimulated a great deal of research to advance our knowledge about the causes and implications of handedness.

Brain Grafts

The possibility of various kinds of organ transplants—of the kidneys, liver, and even heart—has received a great deal of popular attention in recent years. The notion of transplanting brain tissue, also known as brain grafting, probably calls forth images of mad scientists, like Frankenstein, working with sinister-looking equipment in some secluded laboratory. Efforts to graft tissue in the central nervous systems of laboratory animals goes back at least to 1890 (Bjorklund & Stenevi, 1984), although it was generally assumed that neurons in the central nervous system of humans and other mammals could not regenerate after injury and that, consequently, grafts of neuronal tissue were doomed to failure. Only recently have scientists become optimistic about the possibilities of repairing damage in the central nervous system of mammals. Most typically, the research has been carried out with rats, but other species, such as mice and rabbits, have also been used.

A number of transplantation methods have been tried in the effort to graft healthy neurological tissue to damaged areas of the central nervous system. The earliest approach was to insert the graft from one animal directly into a slit near the surface of another animal's cortex. While there was some success with this method in immature rats, it did not work as well in mature animals. A more successful technique is to place the graft into a surgically prepared transplantation cavity. This procedure allows for better control over the placement of the graft and the use of larger tissue pieces (usually from the brain matter of a rat embryo).

Anders Bjorklund and Ulf Stenevi, in their 1984 review of research on intracerebral neural implants, note that the single most important factor for good survival of neural grafts is the developmental stage of the donor tissue and, to a lesser degree, the age of the recipient animal. In rats, at least, there is no strong evidence of rejection of neurological transplants by the body's immune system, leading to the possibility that the brain may be an immunologically privileged site, partly because of its protective blood-brain barrier (described in Chapter 4).

What do neurological transplants do when they are successfully grafted into a damaged area of a rat's brain? One suggestion is that the effect of the implant is to stimulate and promote a regenerative response already present in the recipient's brain as a result of the lesion. Research suggests that the transplant acts as a bridge to guide regenerating axons back to their original sites.

What does all this research with rats have to do with people? Many of the experimentally induced lesions are designed to mimic the kinds of neuro-pathological changes associated with some diseases. Research on the ability of transplants to offset the effects of these changes may ultimately improve our ability to deal with such diseases in humans. Moreover, efforts have been made to use tissue implants to offset age-related deficits in aging rats. Such research has implications for the treatment of impairments associated with human aging, including the premature senility caused by Alzheimer's disease. Research on this serious problem is beginning to show some hopeful break-throughs.

Alzheimer's Disease

What scares you most about growing old? The likely physical changes? The possible mental changes? What scares many people is the possibility of failures in memory and other cognitive processes. Such mental deterioration does not attack everybody. Only a small percentage of the population over 65 suffers from "dementia"—a severe deterioration in cognitive functioning—although others in this age group suffer from mild to moderate impairments in cognitive functioning.

Even rarer are individuals who begin experiencing serious problems in memory and other cognitive functioning at an earlier age. The term *presenile dementia* refers to individuals who begin to show a progressive deterioration in their cognitive functions in their fifties. The most well-known form of presenile dementia is Alzheimer's disease (discussed further in Chapter 7), a condition that is clinically indistinguishable from senile dementia.

Autopsies on the brains of individuals who suffered from either presenile or senile forms of the disease show a number of characteristic abnormalities. Typical are plaques on the ends of axons and "neurofibrillary tangles" (bundles of filaments accumulating within the cell bodies of neurons). These abnormalities occur primarily in the cerebral cortex and hippocampus and are thought to account for the cognitive deficits associated with Alzheimer's disease. Recent research reported by Drs. Joseph Coyle, Donald Price, and Mahlon DeLong of the Johns Hopkins School of Medicine indicates that neurons involved in the transmission of acetylcholine are particularly likely to deteriorate in Alzheimer's disease.

Recent technological advances in methods of studying the brain—for example, the development of the PET scan technique—are likely to aid in the early diagnosis of Alzheimer's and related diseases. Moreover, research on neurotransmitter systems within the brain will probably ultimately lead to important treatments for the disease. Just as the development of antibiotics proved effective in counteracting infections, so the synthesis of neurotransmitter substances may allow a breakthrough in combating the deficits in memory and cognition sustained by victims of neurological deterioration.

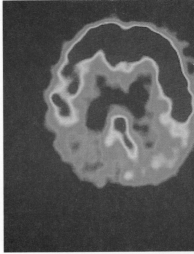

This is a PET scan of a patient with Alzheimer's disease.

Problems and Prospects

As our review of brain research draws to a close, it may leave you with somewhat mixed feelings. While the last few decades have seen an incredible explosion of knowledge in the brain sciences, it is almost impossible to avoid the frustration of thinking about how much we have yet to learn.

The way researchers describe the crudity of current methods often reflects this frustration. After reviewing numerous conclusions based on ablation studies, for example, Thompson (1975, p. 106) notes that trying to understand brain function by destroying specific structures "is like trying to determine the function of one part of a TV circuit by smashing it with a hammer and noting how the TV set misbehaves." In a similar vein, others (Margerison, St. John-Loe, & Binnie, 1967, p. 353) have described EEG interpretation of the simultaneous electrical activity of thousands of brain cells as follows: "We are like blind men trying to understand the workings of a factory by listening outside its walls."

An introductory textbook chapter, by its very nature, is likely to make current knowledge seem more definitive than it really is. Virtually every introductory psychology text, for example, gives an estimate of the number of nerve cells in the brain. Some say 10 billion, some say 13 billion, some say 15 billion. In a special *Scientific American* issue on the brain, one article (Nauta & Feirtag, 1979) accepted the estimate of 10 billion, while another (Hubel, 1979) put the number at 100 billion. Both articles explained carefully that their estimate could be off by many billions.

We must never forget how far our understanding of the brain has advanced in the three centuries or so since Gall suggested that a woman's character could be read in the pattern of bumps on her skull. But neither must we forget how far we still have to go.

The epileptic who was freed by surgery from seizures and the Parkinsonian patient whose tremors are controlled by drugs will personally testify to the value of all that researchers have learned thus far. But these accomplishments are nothing compared to what brain scientists hope someday to be able to do.

Summary

- Scientists can learn about the brain by studying victims of a **stroke** (technically known as a cerebrovascular accident).

- Strokes may lead to **aphasia**, a disturbance in the ability to speak or understand language caused by damage to the brain.

- In **expressive aphasia**, also known as Broca's aphasia, a person understands what others say but has difficulty speaking.

- In **receptive aphasia**, or Wernike's aphasia, the individual can speak fluently but has problems in understanding language.

How Scientists Study the Brain

- **Neuroanatomical studies** focus on the physical structure of the brain, spinal cord, and nervous system.

- **Ablation studies** involve surgically removing or destroying brain tissue and observing the effects on behavior of these specific brain **lesions** (wounds or injuries).

- In **electrical stimulation studies**, brain tissue is stimulated by an electric current through an **electrode** (a conductor of electrical activity that is placed in contact with biological tissue) while the effects on behavior are observed.

- **Electrical recording studies** involve measuring the normal electrical activity of the brain.

- An **electroencephalogram**, or **EEG**, is a recording of the electrical activity at the surface of the brain or on the skull.

- Another procedure, ordinarily used only with nonhumans, involves **microelectrodes**, wires small enough to record the electrical activity of a single nerve cell.

- **Chemical studies** are an invasive procedure involving introducing a chemical into the brain to determine its behavioral and physiological effects.

- **Noninvasive techniques** do not require brain surgery and can be used to study function in the normal brain.

- The most familiar noninvasive technique is the **CAT scan** (computed axial tomography, that is, X-rays taken from many different angles and analyzed by computer to generate a three-dimensional picture of the brain).

- The theory of **cerebral localization** holds that different areas of the brain are responsible for different psychological functions.

- The alternative theory, **holism**, claims that each psychological function is controlled by a wide variety of cells throughout the entire brain.

- The theory of cerebral localization derives from Gall's theory of **phrenology**, which held that the brain consisted of a number of different organs, each responsible for a particular human trait.

The Structure and Function of the Nervous System

- A **neuron** can be defined as a cell that processes and transmits information by means of electrochemical impulses.

- The **synapse** is the microscopic space across which the **axon** of one neuron can stimulate either the **dendrite** or the **cell body** of another.

- The firing of a neuron obeys the "all-or-none principle"—that is, at any given moment a neuron either transmits its maximum electrical charge or does not transmit any electrical charge at all.

- **Neurotransmitters** are the chemicals that are released into synapses to transmit information from the *presynaptic terminal* on one neuron to the receptor site on the *postsynaptic membrane* of another neuron.

- **Endorphins** are neurotransmitters that are structurally similar to opiate drugs, such as morphine and heroin.

- Opiate drugs (and endorphins) are blocked by **narcotic antagonists** such as naloxone.

- **Placebos** are chemically inactive substances that can relieve pain by the power of suggestion.

The Peripheral Nervous System

- The nervous system is organized into a **central nervous system** (the brain and spinal cord) and a **peripheral nervous system** (consisting of all the nerve fibers in the body except those in the brain and spinal cord).

- The peripheral nervous system includes a **somatic nervous system**, which connects the brain and spinal cord with sensory receptors and voluntary muscles.

- The neurons in the somatic nervous system are subdivided into **afferent neurons** (also known as **sensory neurons**), which convey information from sensory receptors to the spinal cord and brain, and **efferent neurons** (also known as **motor neurons**), which transmit the commands of the spinal cord and brain to the muscles.

- The peripheral nervous system also includes the **autonomic nervous system**, which regulates the activity of smooth muscles and controls internal bodily processes.

- The autonomic system has two divisions—the **sympathetic nervous system**, which activates the glands and smooth muscles of the body in periods of emotional excitement, and the **parasympathetic nervous system**, which maintains appropriate internal states in times of relaxation.

The Endocrine System

- Closely related to the autonomic nervous system are the **endocrine glands,** which secrete special chemical messengers (called *hormones*) directly into the bloodstream.

- The **pituitary gland** is sometimes called the master gland because it controls the secretion of other endocrine glands.

- The **adrenal glands** produce adrenaline (epinephrine) and noradrenaline (norepinephrine), hormones involved in the mobilization of the body's resources for fight or flight.

- The **gonads** are the sexual glands (*ovaries* in women and *testes* in men) whose secretions control the development of the reproductive organs, secondary sex characteristics, and some aspects of sexual behavior.

The Central Nervous System

- The **spinal cord** is a long, thin column of neurons and tissue that emerges from the bottom of the brain and runs down the back next to the protective *spinal vertebrae*.

- The **medulla** is the first brain structure that emerges from the spinal cord as it widens upon entering the skull. It contains all the nerve fibers that connect the spinal cord to the brain and helps regulate such vital functions as heart rate, breathing, and digestion.

- Next in line is the **pons**, a structure that continues out of the medulla and also contains nerve fibers connecting the brain and spinal cord. These fibers are involved in breathing, muscle coordination, hearing, and facial expression, among many other functions.

- The **reticular formation** (sometimes called the **reticular activating system** because of its role in sleep, waking, alertness, and attention) is not a separate structure that can easily be isolated; it is a complex network of neurons and fibers that passes through the medulla, pons, and other structures.

- The **midbrain** contains structures that relay some information from the eyes and ears to higher centers for visual and auditory processing.

- Taken together, the medulla, pons, reticular formation, midbrain, and closely related structures are referred to as the **brain stem**.

- Closely related to the brain stem but somewhat anatomically separated is the **cerebellum**, involved primarily in the coordination of muscle movements.

- Located on top of the brain stem, the way station known as the **thalamus** transmits and probably analyzes some sensory input.

- The **hypothalamus**, a much smaller structure lying between the thalamus and the midbrain, seems to be involved in a variety of complex behaviors and to help regulate the sympathetic nervous system and the pituitary gland.

- Located near the border between the cerebral hemispheres and the brain stem is the **limbic system** (or *old cortex*), involved in the regulation of such "animal instincts" as fighting, fleeing, feeding, and reproduction.

- The **cerebral cortex**, the thick layer of nerve cells covering the rest of the brain, contains at least 70% of the neurons in the human central nervous system.

- The two **cerebral hemispheres** (the two symmetrical sides of the brain) are connected by a large band of nerve fibers called the **corpus callosum**.

- Two major fissures divide the cerebral cortex into four major lobes: the **frontal lobe** at the front of the brain, the **parietal lobe** at the top rear, the **temporal lobe** underneath the parietal lobe, and the **occipital lobe** at the back of the head.

- **Primary projection areas** of the cortex receive input from the sense organs or control the movement of particular muscle groups.

- The **motor strip**, a primary projection area inside each frontal lobe, controls muscular movements on the opposite side of the body.

- The **somatosensory strip** at the front of each parietal lobe receives sensations from the opposite side of the body.

- **Association areas** are all cortical areas that are not specifically involved with simple sensory or motor reactions.

How Much Do Scientists Really Know About the Brain?

- **Psychosurgery** is brain surgery intended to change a person's thought or behavior patterns.

- In a **frontal lobotomy**, the connections between the frontal lobes and other brain structures are destroyed as a treatment for mental illness.

- In a **cingulotomy** certain fibers connecting the frontal lobes to the limbic system are cut to try to relieve chronic pain and depression.

- Some researchers believe that some of these operations may succeed as a result of the **placebo effect**—medical treatments of no value in themselves that seem to cure patients by the power of suggestion.

- **Cerebral asymmetry** refers to differences between the two sides, or hemispheres, of the brain.

- **Split-brain surgery** involves cutting the corpus callosum, surgically isolating the right and left hemispheres.

- Traditionally, the left hemisphere has been described as verbal, the right as nonverbal.

- Some scientists now believe that the left hemisphere is especially involved in the sequential analysis of stimuli that are presented one after another, while the right hemisphere is more involved in global holistic responses to complex stimuli.

- Brain grafts may eventually be a way of repairing damage and counteracting disease in the central nervous system.

- Alzheimer's disease is a form of "presenile dementia," a condition wherein individuals begin to show a progressive deterioration in their cognitive functions in their fifties.

Critical Thinking Exercises Discussions

Electrical Stimulation of the Brain

The type of scientific disagreement Delgado's experiment's raised among reputable experts poses a difficult challenge for the nonscientist. It is not enough simply to rely on one expert opinion; the critical consumer must look for scientific consensus among the experts. And when there is no consensus, the safest path is to remain cautious and skeptical, while waiting for a consensus to emerge.

This excerpt also raises another interesting lesson in critical thinking: It is often helpful to note the date of a particular source and see how well it has stood the test of time. This 1971 article predicted that "the next few years will bring a frightening array of refined techniques for making human beings act according to the will of the psychotechnologist." Now, approximately two decades later, it is clear that this prediction was incorrect.

A critical consumer would be wise to remain skeptical about predictions of scientific breakthroughs. The progress of science is rarely dramatic or sudden enough for magazine writers. Today's headlines about tomorrow's breakthroughs should always be viewed with caution.

Diagnosing a Case of Brain Injury

This critical thinking exercise requires you to recall facts—for example, that sensations and motor responses on each side of the body are controlled by brain centers on the opposite side of the body. It also requires you to *make inferences*—a key critical thinking skill. For example, it is clear from the case study that Mrs. S. had trouble perceiving and responding to objects on her left. You should *infer* from this information that she had suffered some sort of injury to the right side of her brain. To come to the correct inference about which portion of the right side of her brain had sustained the injury, you would need to recall—or relocate in the chapter—the information concerning the parts of the cortex responsible for various activities. As she had trouble *seeing* anything to the left, you would be correct to infer that the damage occurred in the occipital lobe, at the back of the brain.

Indeed, as Sacks reports, Mrs. S. had suffered a massive stroke affecting the deeper and back portions of her right cerebral hemisphere. The stroke altered her attention to and perception of the left side of her body and the whole left portion of her visual field.

To assist her in finding the food on the left side of her tray, Mrs. S. was given a rotating wheelchair. Then, whenever she could not find something she knew should be there, she would swivel in a circle to the right until the item came into view.

CONSCIOUSNESS

Chapter 4

At 11:14 A.M. on Tuesday, January 21, 1959, New York disc jockey Peter Tripp began a rather bizarre publicity stunt. Tripp announced that he would not sleep for the 200 hours before the official start of the annual Mothers' March on Polio (now known as the March of Dimes). For the eight days that he planned to stay awake, the 23-year-old radio celebrity would continue to broadcast his show, "Your Hits of the Week," from 5 to 8 P.M. each night on WMGM. His broadcast would originate from the armed forces recruiting booth in the middle of Times Square, so that fans would be able to watch him through the booth's large glass walls.

When he planned the stunt, Tripp approached established sleep researchers to ask for medical supervision. At first they tried to talk him out of it, but Tripp was adamant. Finally, psychiatrist Louis J. West of the University of Oklahoma agreed to supervise this attempt to set a new world record for sleep deprivation.

A team of researchers set up a laboratory in a room at the Astor Hotel, on Broadway near Times Square. They proceeded to administer every physiological and psychological test imaginable. Every few hours, they measured Tripp's blood pressure, pulse, respiration, EKG (electrocardiogram), and EEG (electroencephalogram). Blood and urine samples were sent to five laboratories for a battery of 40 tests. Psychological tests included measures of his mental ability, alertness, and vigilance.

For the next eight days, Tripp was never alone. He was in the booth for his regular program, plus a dozen or so daily bulletins reporting how he felt. At all other times, he was either with researchers at the Hotel Astor or accompanied by a doctor or nurse.

When disc jockey Peter Tripp stayed up for 200 hours, researchers were there to study the effects of sleep deprivation.

In terms of publicity, the stunt was a tremendous success. There were reports in *Time* (February 9, 1959, p. 68) and *Life* (February 9, 1959, p. 71), and even the staid *New York Times* published a short item each day reporting his progress. In terms of Tripp's physical and psychological reactions to extreme sleep deprivation, the results were more mixed. By the third day, he had begun to show serious signs of strain. He laughed uproariously at things that no one else found funny, became very upset over minor incidents, and sometimes failed to react emotionally when he should have.

As the days marched slowly on, the effects became more severe. By 100 hours, Tripp was frustrated by even the simplest psychological test. Then came visual illusions: spots of paint on a table looked like bugs, a doctor's tweed suit seemed to be made up of furry worms. One researcher's tie seemed to jump, and Tripp accused another one of dropping a hot electrode in his shoe.

After 135 hours, Dr. West prescribed Ritalin, an amphetamine-like drug, every six hours to help keep the disc jockey awake. Still the symptoms got worse. Tripp opened a drawer in the hotel, saw flames that weren't there, and came running out of the room yelling for help. He later said that he thought this fire had been set to test him.

As Tripp's paranoia mounted, he would sometimes back up against a wall and not let anyone walk behind him. He became convinced that the 200 hours were up, but that his scientist associates had turned on him and were keeping him up long past the agreed-upon limit.

Despite these frightening symptoms, Tripp managed to pull himself together for three hours each day for his show. Aside from an occasional slip, such as referring to the March of Dimes as the Red Cross, his broadcast seemed quite normal. But outside the booth, his behavior contined to deteriorate. By 150 hours, he was often disoriented and confused about where he was and even who he was. When he sat quietly, his brain waves were similar to those seen in the deepest stages of sleep.

On the morning of his final day of sleeplessness, Tripp was examined by a famous neurologist who "always insisted that patients undress and lie down on the examining table. Tripp complied, but as he gazed up at the doctor he came to the morbid conclusion that the man was actually an undertaker, there for the purpose of burying him alive. With this gruesome insight, Tripp leapt for the door with several doctors in pursuit" (Luce & Segal, 1966, p. 92).

Despite this inauspicious beginning to the last day, Tripp went on to give his final broadcast and last out the 200 hours. In fact, the scientists kept him up for one more hour for a few final tests. Then, with his EEG electrodes still taped in place, Tripp fell into a deep sleep for 13 hours and 13 minutes. The next day, Tripp held a news conference and reported that he felt fine, although a *New York Times* account appeared under the headline: "Sleepy Disk Jockey Won't Repeat Stunt" (January 30, 1959, p. 54). Scientists continued to follow Tripp and reported that his only symptom three months later seemed to be a slight depression.

Tripp's feat did not go unchallenged. In 1965, Stanford University sleep researcher William Dement read in a newspaper that a 17-year-old named Randy Gardner had completed the first 80 hours of an attempt to stay awake for 264 hours, which would earn him a place in the *Guinness Book of World Records*. Dement drove to San Diego with a colleague and a portable EEG machine. They spent the next week observing Randy and helping him stay awake.

Randy lasted the full 11 days and apparently felt much better than Peter Tripp had. In fact, he sometimes seemed more alert than the researchers, despite the fact that they did sleep. Randy spent his last night of wakefulness in a penny arcade, where he beat a comparatively well-rested Dr. Dement approximately 100 consecutive times on a baseball machine. According to Dement (1974, p. 12): "Except for a few illusions—one or two minor hallucinatory experiences—Randy demonstrated no psychotic behavior during the entire vigil, no paranoid behavior, no serious emotional change. . . . He has since been followed . . . [for several years] and appears to be completely healthy and unaffected by the experience."

It is a tribute to the human spirit that others who crave the limelight have continued to expand the frontiers of sleeplessness. According to the *Guinness Book of World Records,* the current record was set by Mrs. Maureen Weston of Peterborough, England, in a rocking chair marathon from April 14 to May 2, 1977 (18 days, 17 hours). Although she tended to hallucinate toward the end, she suffered no lasting aftereffects.

In general, healthy subjects seem to have a remarkable ability to function without sleep, leading one researcher to reach the tongue-in-cheek conclusion that the major "effect of sleep deprivation is to make the subject fall asleep" (Hartmann, 1973, p. 76). Studies of sleep, and of the sometimes bizarre mental changes that accompany sleep deprivation, are generally categorized broadly under research on states of consciousness. **Consciousness** refers to all the

consciousness All the internal mental events and responses to external stimuli of which a person is aware.

internal mental events and responses to external stimuli of which a person is aware. However, this straightforward definition ignores a number of complexities. Indeed, Natsoulas (1978) has described seven different types of definitions of consciousness proposed at various times. All these definitions refer in some way to awareness (Natsoulas, 1983).

The popularity of the study of consciousness has varied considerably during the history of psychology. At times, it has been widely accepted as the most important topic of psychology; at other times, it has been virtually ignored by researchers. Currently, the pendulum lies between these two extremes. See "Understanding the Scientific Method" for some current approaches to one popular form of consciousness—daydreaming.

As mentioned in Chapter 1, when Wundt founded the first psychology laboratory in 1879, he hoped to discover basic laws that regulated consciousness. For Wundt and many of his contemporaries, one of the most important research methods in psychology was **introspection**, the careful, rigorous, and disciplined analysis of one's own thoughts by highly trained observers.

Many of the studies that relied on introspection were based on an analogy between physical and mental science. During Wundt's time, chemists had shown that molecules were composed of combinations of elements, such as the combination of hydrogen and oxygen to form water. Some psychologists hoped to show that, similarly, all conscious experience could be reduced to a small number of basic sensations and feelings that were combined in various ways to form the "molecules" of the mind.

Unfortunately, even the most highly trained introspectionists often disagreed about the basic elements of their train of thought. Many researchers got bogged down in elaborate disputes over what people did or did not feel. When behaviorist John B. Watson published his influential paper "Psychology as the Behaviorist Views It" in 1913, psychology was ripe for a change and ready to embrace his belief that science must focus on observable stimuli and external responses (see Chapter 6). Watson believed that you can't study what you can't see, and therefore consciousness is not an appropriate topic for scientific research.

The behavioral view dominated psychology for the next half a century. It was only around 1960 that cognitive psychologists (see Chapters 7 and 8) and others began to introduce new techniques for studying thoughts and feelings that had seemed inaccessible. Many of these techniques are described in this chapter, including some modern forms of introspection.

This chapter also describes research on a number of different topics related to conscious experience. We begin with an everyday variation in consciousness—sleep and dreams—and then go on to some more unusual varieties of consciousness that are induced by special conditions or states: meditation, hypnosis, and drugs.

Sleep and Dreams

If you sleep for 8 hours each night and live to be 78 years old, you will be asleep for a total of 26 years. Thus, more of your life is likely to be devoted to sleep than to working, playing, or even worrying about your weight.

introspection The careful, rigorous, and disciplined analysis of one's own thoughts by highly trained observers.

Self-Report Techniques in the Measurement of Daydreams

Anyone who has ever spent a psychology lecture fantasizing about the student sitting in front of him knows something about daydreaming. A daydream can be defined as a shift in attention away from external stimuli and toward internal thoughts. In order to study this familiar phenomenon, psychologists must ask people to report their daydreams. Two major variations on this *self-report* type of technique have been developed: questionnaire studies, in which people are asked a predetermined series of questions about past daydreams, and introspection studies, in which people are asked to describe their daydreams as they occur.

Questionnaire studies are the most practical way to learn more about the daydreaming habits of large numbers of people. Therefore, Jerome Singer and his colleagues developed the Singer-Antrobus Imaginal Processes Inventory, a standard list of daydreams and questions about whether people ever had experienced them, the times and places they were most likely to occur, and so on. Some of the items he included were (Singer, 1975, p. 53):

As a child I imagined myself a great detective.

I picture an atomic bombing of the town I live in.

I see myself participating with wild abandon in a Roman orgy.

In one typical study that used this questionnaire, 240 people between the ages of 18 and 50 responded to these and other questions; 96% reported that they daydreamed every day (Singer & McCraven, 1961). The younger subjects reported the largest number of daydreams, and the amount of daydreaming gradually declined for each age group.

In general, studies of this sort have revealed that most daydreams include clear visual imagery of people, objects, and events, and are generally rather mundane. While some individuals have bizarre daydreams in which they murder family members or are proclaimed the Messiah, more typical themes are sexual gratification, helping others, or becoming the recipient of unusual good fortune. Overall, the most common type of daydream involves a projection of immediate practical problems into the future, particularly problems in dealing with others. Thus, daydreams may provide a mental rehearsal for future discussions, such as convincing the boss that you deserve a raise or winning an argument with a loved one.

Some studies have focused on individual

(*box continues on next page*)

differences in daydreaming by seeking statistical patterns in the responses of large numbers of subjects to the Imaginal Processes Inventory. Such studies have consistently found that most people can be categorized into one of three major styles of daydreaming: anxious-distractible, guilty-dysphoric, or positive-vivid daydreaming.

Anxious-distractible daydreamers tend to have many fleeting and loosely connected fantasies that are primarily concerned with worries and anxieties. These people take little pleasure in daydreaming and do not find it a useful resource. In contrast, the guilty-dysphoric daydreamer is likely to have high aspirations and daydream about heroic feats, but at the same time fear failure and resent others. These fantasies are likely to be full of self-doubt and self-questioning. Positive-vivid daydreaming appears to be the healthiest personal style. People who fall into this category generally enjoy their daydreams and have particularly clear imagery in them. They use daydreams to anticipate the future, solve problems, or distract themselves in boring situations.

Although the questionnaire technique makes it possible to study large numbers of people economically, it is limited by how well people remember their daydreams and other factors. In contrast, *introspection methods* ask people to report daydreams while they occur. There are several different techniques for accomplishing this purpose.

The "thinking-aloud" method requires subjects to verbalize their ongoing stream of thought continuously, sometimes while wearing headphones that interfere with their ability to listen to what they say. Somewhat similar is the "thought-sampling" method, which involves interrupting people while they are engaged in some laboratory task or going about their normal business, and asking them to report what they were just thinking about. Finally, the "key-press" method requires laboratory subjects to press a key whenever a certain type of event occurs in their stream of thought. For example, they may be asked to press the key whenever their thoughts drift from a laboratory task or when their thoughts shift from one topic to another. While this technique provides little information about daydream content, it is less vulnerable to memory gaps than thought sampling and also protects the subject's privacy to a limited extent. An added advantage of this approach is that it may cause less disruption in the normal train of thought than other methods.

These introspection techniques represent a return to one of the oldest methods in psychological research. As noted in Chapter 1, they were developed by Wilhelm Wundt and the founders of psychology around the turn of the century, but fell into disuse as a result of criticisms by John B. Watson and the behaviorists. Singer (1974, p. 23) has even proposed that psychology revive the "notion of trained introspectors."

No one is certain why people need to sleep. According to one widely held theory, the human sleep cycle had survival value during evolution (Cohen, 1979). This view holds that people who slept at night stayed out of trouble by hiding from predators and conserving energy for their more efficient daylight hours. Thus, they were more likely to survive, reproduce, and pass along their sleepiness to the next generation.

Sleep Schedules and Circadian Rhythms

Although a few unusual individuals may require as little as 45 minutes of sleep each night (Meddis, Pearson, & Langford, 1973), the average person seems to need about 7.5 hours of sleep per 24-hour day. Anthropologists have found that no culture gets by without sleep or by breaking sleep down into a shorter series of naps. Instead, even in cultures with a midday "siesta," there is an extended period of five to eight hours set aside for sleep each day. Further, the need for sleep does not seem to be determined by the cycle of light and darkness. People who live near the Arctic Circle, for example, where the sun never sets during the summer months, nevertheless sleep about 7 hours during each 24-hour period (Luce & Segal, 1966).

In a systematic study of the importance of light and other external cues in sleep, French geologist Michael Siffre lived in the French Alps for two months in a damp, chilly cave, where no sound or light could reach him. He went to sleep and arose when he felt like it, with no clocks or other clues to tell him the time. Under these isolated conditions, Siffre slept once every 24.5 hours, and his physiological body rhythms also maintained this near-normal cycle (Siffre, 1964).

Siffre's activity showed evidence of a **circadian rhythm**, a cyclical change in behavior or physiology that is repeated once every 24 hours or so. The word *circadian* comes from the Latin *circa,* "about," and *dies,* "a day." The sleep-waking cycle is the most familiar circadian rhythm, but there are many others. Body temperature, hormone secretion, psychological mood, performance, and many other variables also increase and decrease each day according to the body's clocks.

Body temperature, for example, ordinarily reaches its lowest point between 4 and 6 A.M. and begins rising before a person wakes up. It continues to go up until it peaks in midafternoon, typically between 5 and 7 P.M. Under normal conditions, people tend to work most efficiently and feel best when their body temperature hits its peak (Wilkinson, 1982). This is particularly interesting in light of the fact that those who describe themselves as "morning people" show an earlier temperature peak than evening people (Ostberg, 1973).

Most of the hormones secreted by the endocrine glands also follow a circadian rhythm. The time of day associated with maximum hormone concentration in the body varies from one hormone to the next. For example, the female hormone prolactin peaks in the middle of the night; this helps explain why twice as many pregnant women go into labor at midnight as at noon.

Like hormones, behavioral rhythms each have a cycle of their own.

circadian rhythm   A cyclical change in behavior or physiology that repeats itself once every 24 hours.

Studies of people who work shifts have consistently found that job performance is less efficient at night than during the day, and it declines markedly from around 2 to 5 A.M. Laboratory studies have revealed that efficiency on short and simple tasks (such as adding columns of numbers) is best in the afternoon, while tasks involving memory are generally performed more efficiently in the morning (Naitoh, 1982).

There are also a number of other rhythms that are related to physiology and behavior but that are not 24 hours long, such as the menstrual cycle. It is important to distinguish these well-established rhythms from the so-called biorhythms. Pseudoscientific biorhythm theories claim that human behavior is determined by three separate cycles—physical, emotional, and mental—which begin at birth. There have been a number of well-designed studies of the biorhythm theory, and they have indicated very clearly that biorhythm calculations based on the date of birth do not work (Brown, 1982). On the other hand, established circadian rhythms have been shown to have important influences on behavior, particularly when sleep schedules are disturbed by jet lag.

Jet lag refers to the discomfort or decreased efficiency caused by traveling across time zones. Its symptoms may include gastronomical distress, insomnia, headaches, irritability, and general malaise. While almost everyone feels some distress after crossing three or more time zones, some individuals are more susceptible to jet lag than others. For example, there is some evidence that people who have larger daily variations in body temperatures and certain hormones have more problems with jet lag than those with less pronounced circadian rhythms (Klein & Wegmann, 1979).

Interestingly, flying from west to east (for instance, from California to New York) takes longer to adjust to than flying in the opposite direction. In one study (Klein & Wegmann, 1979), some individuals took as many as 18 days to adjust totally to an eastbound flight that crossed six time zones. The maximum readjustment time for a westbound flight of equal duration was 8 days.

Greater jet lag after eastbound flights has been replicated in many studies. It now seems that this is just one example of a more fundamental phenomenon: Humans find it easier to delay going to sleep than to go to sleep early. When you fly westward, you gain several hours of clock time. For example, if you take a 5 P.M. flight from Washington, D.C., and arrive in San Francisco at 10 P.M., Eastern Standard Time, the local (Pacific) time will be 7 P.M. To maximize adjustment to California time, you should go to sleep near your ordinary bedtime according to the local clock. Given the time difference, this implies that you will be awake about three hours longer than usual. Most people find this delay relatively easy.

However, if you fly from San Francisco to Washington, going to bed at your regular time according to the local clock means trying to sleep three hours earlier than usual. Most people find this a more difficult adjustment, and it takes longer for all of their circadian rhythms to synchronize to the local clock.

In addition to the circadian rhythms that regulate our 24-hour patterns of activity, there are also a number of shorter rhythms within a night's sleep. Although a casual observer may see sleep as a single state, physiological

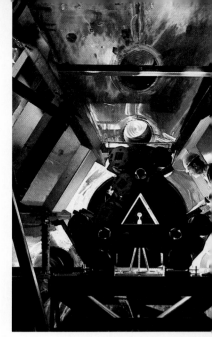

Studies of shift workers have found that job performance is less efficient at night than during the day. In a nuclear power plant, such as the one pictured here, there are potentially disastrous consequences.

jet lag Discomfort or decreased efficiency caused by traveling across time zones.

REM Rapid eye movements that occur during sleep, associated with dreaming.

researchers have found that, in fact, a night's sleep consists of a number of distinct cycles and stages.

Stages of Sleep

The modern era of sleep research began around 1950 with an accidental discovery. Eugene Aserinsky, a graduate student at the University of Chicago, was studying infant sleep patterns, carefully watching their cycles of thrashing around the crib hour after hour. During these tedious observations, he noticed that behind their closed lids, the infants' eyes were often flicking rapidly back and forth. Several similar observations were buried in the archives of sleep researchers, but Aserinsky wisely decided to pursue this phenomenon.

In 1953, Aserinsky and his mentor, Nathaniel Kleitman, reported the results in an article in *Science.* They had attached electrodes to 20 normal adults to measure the movements of their eyes as they slept. Like the infants, the adults passed through several periods of rapid eye movement (or **REM**) during each night's sleep. More important, when Aserinsky and Kleitman awakened people during this REM sleep, 20 of 27 times the sleepers reported that they had been dreaming. In contrast, when the same people were awakened during the longer periods in which their eyes were not darting back and forth (non-REM sleep), they reported dreams on only 2 of 23 occasions.

This was an extremely exciting finding for scientists, since it implied that an objective physiological technique might provide access to the subjective world of a dreamer's consciousness. Many other researchers therefore rushed to begin their own studies of sleep. These researchers quickly confirmed the idea that when people sleep, they pass through a series of separate kinds of sleep, or sleep stages. All told, five stages of sleep have been identified: four non-REM stages and REM sleep. Each stage is accompanied by a distinct pattern of physiological changes, particularly in EEG recordings.

Figure 4.1 shows a typical night's progression through the five stages. Figure 4.2 displays the brain wave patterns associated with each stage (REM sleep has brain wave patterns resembling those shown for stage 1). As you can see, when people first drift off to sleep, they are in non-REM stage 1, characterized by a slow EEG pattern that is somewhat similar to EEG patterns seen during wakeful relaxation. The sleeper then drifts slowly into deeper stages of sleep and becomes more difficult to awaken. Stage 2 (which is characterized by specific EEG changes called sleep spindles and K complexes) gives way first to stage 3 (signaled by the appearance of large, slow EEG waves called delta waves) and then to stage 4 (in which the EEG consists almost entirely of delta waves).

It is very difficult to awaken someone from stage 4 sleep. Perhaps you have had the experience of being totally out of touch with the world when someone tried to wake you up an hour or two after you fell asleep. If so, you were probably in stage 4.

Physical exhaustion seems to increase stage 4 sleep and, to a lesser extent, stage 3. For example, a study of long-distance runners found a substantial increase in stages 3 and 4 for two nights after participation in a marathon (Shapiro, Bortz, Mitchell, Bartel, & Jooste, 1981). Thus, if you exercise more

Some people are more susceptible to jet lag than others.

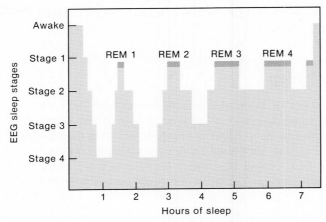

FIGURE 4.1 The progression through sleep stages over the course of a typical night's sleep. Note that stage 4 sleep occurs only during the first few hours and that REM-stage length increases as the night goes on. (The amount of REM sleep is shown by the solid-color bars.) This record shows awakening in the middle of a REM period, which would probably lead the sleeper to remember this dream.

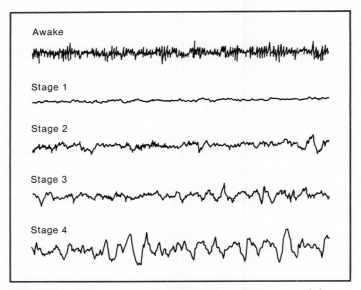

FIGURE 4.2 Brain wave patterns during the various stages of sleep.

than usual, you are likely to have a longer period of stage 4 sleep that night.

Researchers have also been able to show that sleepwalking occurs during stage 4. In their laboratory, using EEG equipment attached to a long, firmly secured cable, Jacobson and his colleagues at UCLA (1965) observed 11 sleepwalkers. They recorded over 100 incidents of sleepwalking lasting up to 7 minutes. Sometimes these sleepwalkers would shuffle into the control room where the experimenter sat with the EEG equipment. Although their eyes were wide open, they gave no sign of recognition. When later awakened,

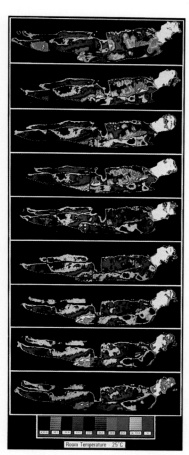

This series of thermographs shows changes in skin temperatures as a man sleeps. The color coding runs from white (hottest), through red and yellow, to blue and black (coolest). Note that the greatest changes occur in the face, chest, and hands.

the sleepwalkers usually did not remember having moved. In every case, the sleepwalking began in stage 3 or 4.

During a normal night's sleep, the typical person remains in stage 4 for perhaps 20 or 30 minutes and then begins a gradual ascent back through stages 3 and 2 to REM sleep, a cycle repeated about five times each night. In terms of brain-wave activity, REM sleep is quite similar to the non-REM stage 1 that occurs when a person first dozes off. However, people are relatively easy to awaken during non-REM Stage 1, whereas they are in the deepest sleep of the night during REM. REM sleep is often called *paradoxical sleep* because of this contrast between the EEG signs of alertness and the difficulty of awakening.

The most obvious physical change during REM sleep is, of course, the rapid darting of the eyes back and forth. Researchers measure this response with electrodes, taped on either side of the head, which detect electrical changes associated with eye movements. However, if you happen to be near someone who is dreaming, you can actually see the slight bulge of the cornea under the eyelid and its rapid movements from side to side. REM sleep is also accompanied by other changes, such as irregular breathing, twitches of the face and fingertips, a cessation of any movements in the arms, legs, and trunk, genital arousal, and increasing blood flow to the brain.

The first REM period typically occurs after more than an hour of sleep and lasts only 10 minutes or so. As the night progresses, each period of REM is likely to be a little bit longer, while stage 4 disappears in the latter part of the night (see Figure 4.1). A total of about 90 minutes will be spent in REM during an average night's sleep.

The exact pattern of sleep stages varies from person to person, and it also changes systematically as one grows older. Newborn infants sleep about 18 hours a day, spending perhaps half this time in REM sleep. The amount of sleep needed and the proportion of REM both decline rapidly during the first year of life. By one year of age, the average child sleeps about 12 hours and spends about one-third of this time in REM. The proportion of sleep devoted to REM continues to decline until it reaches about 20% for adults.

Dreams

Much of the fascination with REM sleep is caused by its association with dreaming. Although people sometimes speak as if REM sleep is identical to dreaming, the reality is a bit more complicated than that. Even in the first observations by Aserinsky and Kleitman, described above, the relationship was not perfect. In a review of 16 studies of this topic, Snyder and Scott (1971) found that dreaming was always reported more frequently after REM than after non-REM sleep. Typically, dreams were reported about 74% of the time after awakening from REM and 12% of the time after awakening from non-REM sleep. But precise estimates of the relationship varied.

Many of the differences in experimental opinion about the exact relationship can be attributed to the difficulty of deciding just what qualified as a dream. People usually will mumble something if you suddenly wake them up and ask what they were dreaming about. Most researchers specify some sort of coherent narrative as the critical characteristic of a dream, but differences in the application of *this* criterion have led to further differences of opinion about the precise relationship. In any case, it is clear that people are more likely to report a dream after being awakened from REM sleep than they are when awakened from any of the four non-REM stages.

There have been several studies of people who claim they rarely or never dreamed to see if they lack REM sleep (e.g., Goodenough, Shapiro, Holden, & Steinschriber, 1959). These self-proclaimed nondreamers not only showed the ordinary pattern of four to five REM periods per night, they also reported that they had been dreaming nearly half the times they were awakened from REM sleep. Thus, it seems clear that while some people have difficulty remembering their dreams, all people do dream.

Little is known about why everyone dreams or what dreams mean. Since earliest recorded history, people have tried to discover the meaning of their dreams. Babylonian records of dream interpretations date back to 5,000 years before Christ. Guides to the interpretations of dreams can be found in the *Odyssey*, The Talmud, the Old Testament—and at the checkout counter of your local supermarket.

Like the scholars and mystics who preceded them, psychologists have long been fascinated by this topic. In his first major book on psychoanalysis, *The Interpretation of Dreams,* Sigmund Freud argued that dreams hold the key to understanding human motivation, because they express unconscious impulses that determine behavior. Unfortunately, however, the dreamer's desires are usually disguised and hidden in cryptic symbolism. Freud and his followers have devoted considerable effort to decoding dreams according to their psychoanalytic theory.

In one dream, which Freud analyzed in his book, a young doctor dreamed that tax officials questioned his return, even though he had reported his income honestly. Freud interpreted this as a sign that the doctor unconsciously wanted to make more money; thus, his dreaming mind had created tax collectors who refused to believe how modest his income was.

As we shall see in Chapter 12, Freud believed that unconscious sexual desires were particularly important in determining behavior, and many of his examples concerned dreams that appeared innocent on the surface but that actually expressed hidden sexual urges. For example, in describing a dream in which a woman broke a candle when she tried to place it in a candlestick, Freud (1900/1953a, p. 219) referred to the "transparent symbolism" in which the candlestick stood for the male genitals, and the fact that it was broken revealed a theme of impotence.

Researchers have found Freud's theory of dreams difficult to test scientifically, in part because the interpretation of each dream requires judgment by a trained psychoanalyst. In general, there is good evidence that Freud was correct when he argued that dreams can reveal important issues in a person's life. However, they seem to do so more directly than Freud believed. In a summary of this research, Fisher and Greenburg (1977, p. 68) wrote: "There is no rationale for approaching a dream as if it were a container for a secret wish buried under layers of concealment." Thus, a person who is concerned with impotence is not more likely to dream about broken candles, but may well dream about impotence.

More recent theories of dreams tend to emphasize the possible biological role of REM in brain function. One of the more extreme biological theories holds that dreams are simply arbitrary stories the mind creates to explain or make sense out of physiological events that occur during sleep (Hobson & McCarley, 1977). For example, muscle movement is inhibited by normal brain processes during REM sleep. As a result, the dreamer may create a dream about being paralyzed or running in slow motion. According to this unromantic view, dreams of floating may "mean" merely that the inner ear is being stimulated electrically.

Another theory holds that REM sleep stimulates neural tissue and helps consolidate information in memory (Dewan, 1970). Proponents of this view explain that newborns devote more sleep to REM because so much of their experience is new.

More recently, Francis Crick (who won a Nobel Prize for his work with James Watson on the structure of DNA) and Graeme Mitchison have proposed nearly the opposite view. They argue that dreaming is designed to weaken undesirable synaptic patterns and fine-tune the brain by erasing "inappropriate modes of brain activity" produced either by the physical growth of brain cells or by experience (Crick & Mitchison, 1983, p. 112). Note that this theory too is consistent with the fact that newborns spend a greater proportion of their sleep time in REM.

The fact that so many different theories are held by various experts suggests how little is really known at this time about the function of dreams. Indeed, we don't even know whether it is correct to say that dreams have a biological or psychological function. According to Nathaniel Kleitman (1960, p. 88), one of the pioneers in the modern era of sleep research: "The low-grade cerebral activity that is dreaming may serve no significant function whatsoever."

Meditation

While sleeping and dreaming are ordinary variations in consciousness that are experienced by everyone, there are also a number of techniques used purposely by some people to induce a change in consciousness. Perhaps the simplest of these is **meditation**, which refers to a number of different techniques for internal reflection. The historical roots of these techniques can be found in religious practices that are thousands of years old.

Two Types of Meditation

In the book *On the Psychology of Meditation,* Naranjo and Ornstein (1977) distinguished between "opening-up meditation" and "concentrative meditation." In **opening-up meditation**, individuals attempt to clear their minds and "go with the flow" of experience. Chauduri (1965, p. 31) put it this way: "This approach begins with the resolve to do nothing, to think nothing, to make no effort of one's own, to relax completely. . . . Watch your ideas, feelings, and wishes fly across the firmament like a flock of birds. Let them fly freely. Just keep a watch. Don't let the birds carry you off into the clouds."

To experience this state, one might try to sit quietly outdoors and listen

meditation Any of several techniques for internal reflection.

opening-up meditation An attempt to clear one's mind and "go with the flow" of experience.

to every sound—the rustle of the wind, the chirping of birds, the profanities of a nearby group of rowdies—without paying attention to any particular sound, but rather focusing on everything at once. Obviously, this is not easy to accomplish. For example, various groups who use opening-up meditation in their practices—as do followers of Zen, Yoa, or Sufism—may spend years trying to master this skill.

The major approach to meditation involves nearly the opposite strategy. Instead of concentrating on "everything," the practitioner of **concentrative meditation** attempts to focus all attention on a single object or idea. This approach too has a long history in religion, as suggested by the following instructions for reciting "The Prayer of Jesus," given by Gregory of Sinai in the fourteenth century (quoted in Benson, Kotch, Crassweller, & Greenwood, 1977, p. 441): "Sit down alone and in silence. . . . As you breathe out, say 'Lord Jesus Christ, have mercy on me.' Say it moving your lips gently, or simply say it in your mind. Try to put all other thoughts aside." Similar techniques are employed in some of the practices of Islam, Zen, Yoga, Shintoism, Taoism, and Sufism.

In the early 1970s, a secularized American form of concentrative meditation was developed by Herbert Benson, a researcher at the Harvard Medical School. Based on several lines of research, Benson argued that many forms of meditation—from the contemplative practices of St. Augustine to Martin Luther's instructions for prayer—elicited a common physiological reaction he called the "relaxation response." This was the opposite of Walter Cannon's fight-or-flight response (see Chapter 3) and was said to be physiologically distinct from other, more casual states of relaxation.

According to Benson (1975), four basic elements are required to elicit the relaxation response: a quiet environment, a comfortable position, a mental device (such as a word repeated over and over again or a physical object on which the meditator concentrates), and a passive attitude. He particularly emphasized this last requirement; meditators should not try too hard to relax, and they should not be disturbed by thoughts that intrude on their reveries.

The following paragraphs give the essence of Benson's technique; they are the actual instructions he used in his laboratory to instruct patients and subjects (Benson et al., 1977, p. 442). Note the presence of the four elements, as well as the similarities to the "Prayer of Jesus" quoted above:

Sit quietly in a comfortable position and close your eyes.

Deeply relax all your muscles, beginning at your feet and progressing up to your face. Keep them deeply relaxed.

Breathe through your nose. Become aware of your breathing. As you breathe out, say the word one silently to yourself. For example, breathe in . . . out, one; breathe in . . . out, one; etc. Continue for 20 minutes. You may open your eyes to check the time, but do not use an alarm. When you finish, sit quietly for several minutes at first with closed eyes and later with opened eyes.

Do not worry about whether you are successful in achieving a deep level of relaxation. Maintain a passive attitude and permit relaxation to occur at its own pace. Expect other thoughts. When these distracting thoughts occur, ignore them by thinking "Oh well" and continue repeating "one." With practice the response should come with little effort. Practice the technique once or twice daily, but

concentrative meditation An attempt to focus attention on a single object or idea.

not within two hours after any meal, since the digestive processes seem to interfere with the subjective changes.

Benson originally developed this technique as a result of research he and others had performed on the relaxing effects of another concentrative technique, called *transcendental meditation,* which had been introduced in the United States in the 1960s by the Maharishi Mahesh Yogi.

The Effects of Meditation

One of the most influential scientific studies of the effects of meditation was published by Keith Wallace in 1970. Wallace himself was a practitioner of transcendental meditation. For his Ph.D. thesis at the University of California at Los Angeles, he compared the physiological states of people while they were relaxing versus meditating. Wallace concluded that meditation produced a state that differed from sleep, hypnosis, or any other relaxed state. He believed that the meditative state could be identified by a unique pattern of physiological changes, including decreased heart rate and oxygen consumption and specific EEG changes.

After earning his Ph.D., Wallace went to work in Benson's lab at Harvard, where he and others performed a series of studies that verified and extended these findings. These early studies of relaxation are all the more impressive when one considers how uncomfortable it can be to participate in physiological research of this sort. For example, Wallace, Benson, and Wilson (1971) required meditators to wear a tight-fitting mask (to measure respiration), have a needle stuck in their arm (to measure blood chemistry), and sit on a rectal thermometer (to measure body temperature). Despite the discomfort one might expect, these meditators gave evidence of a deep state of relaxation.

Wallace went on to become president of Maharishi International University, while Benson took a more secular route and proceeded to demystify meditation and develop the alternative to transcendental meditation described above. After the basic idea that meditation produces a unique form of relaxation was established, others reported success in using meditation to treat a variety of stress-related disorders, ranging from high blood pressure, insomnia, asthma, and stuttering to alcoholism, drug abuse, and psychiatric disorders (Holmes, 1984). However, when Holmes reviewed all the available studies that directly compared the physiological effects of meditation with those of sitting quietly, he found no consistent evidence that the two were physiologically distinct.

Even if Holmes's conclusion holds up under further scrutiny, it does not imply that meditation has no therapeutic value. Sitting quietly for a specified period of time each day may well be beneficial for treating a variety of stress-related problems. Moreover, the use of some ritualized form of meditation—whether it be Benson's relaxation response, transcendental meditation, or another technique—increase the likelihood that people will actually continue this practice over long periods of time, thus enhancing any therapeutic benefits that do exist. What has been seriously questioned is whether meditation per se is physiologically unique, and whether it could thus be expected to produce benefits unattainable in other ways. A similar controversy surrounds the effects of another voluntary technique to induce changes in consciousness: hypnosis.

Hypnosis

Hypnosis is a state of awareness that is induced by special techniques and that is related to changes in thought, perception, and behavior. If this definition seems a bit vague, frankly we'd be forced to agree. Is this state of awareness fundamentally different from normal waking consciousness? Exactly what qualities can induce hypnosis? And precisely what changes are associated with this state? As you will see in this section, psychologists disagree about the answers, and thus about the precise nature and definition of hypnotic states.

Origins and Characteristics

The first scientific analysis of hypnosis dates back to 1784, when King Louis XVI of France appointed a commission to investigate the activities of a physician named Franz Anton Mesmer. A few years before, Mesmer had established an unorthodox medical practice in Paris to treat disorders ranging from paralysis and blindness to ennui "produced by an overactive spleen" (Darnton, 1970, p. 4). Mesmer believed that these and other ills were caused by imbalances in the body's magnetic fields. Since he himself possessed an abnormally high amount of "magnetic fluid," Mesmer's treatments were designed to rechannel his own magnetism to cure his patients.

In a typical treatment session, up to 30 of Mesmer's patients would be seated in a heavily draped room around wooden tubs filled with water, ground glass, and iron filings. While soft music played in the background, the patients would hold onto iron bars and Mesmer would walk around the room in a lilac taffeta robe, sometimes touching a long iron wand to the diseased parts of his patient's bodies. When patients experienced seizures, as many did, they were carried by attendants into a mattress-lined room so that they would not be harmed during the convulsions.

While critics scoffed at these mystical doings, many educated Frenchmen believed that Mesmer's invisible animal magnetism was no more strange or mysterious than other recently discovered invisible forces, such as gravity and electricity. The official commission appointed to investigate Mesmer included such notables as chemist Antoine Lavoisier and American ambassador Benjamin Franklin. They performed a number of experiments before concluding that Mesmer's cures were caused not by animal magnetism, but rather by such forces as "aroused imagination."

This report probably did not make much difference to Louis XVI, since he was beheaded a few years later during the French Revolution. But it did reduce the popularity of Mesmer's cures and his theory of animal magnetism. Nevertheless, some physicians continued to experiment with procedures for inducing trances, particularly to reduce the pain of surgery. In the mid-nineteenth century, the British physician James Braid coined the term *hypnosis,* from the Greek root meaning "put to sleep," to refer to these efforts.

Today, several different techniques are used to induce a hypnotic state. One common procedure requires a seated subject to stare upward at a "target," such as a thumb tack or a spot on the ceiling. While the person stares at this object, the hypnotists speaks repetitiously in a monotone, giving suggestions of drowsiness, fatigue, and relaxation. If the person's eyes are still open after

hypnosis A state of awareness induced by special techniques and related to changes in thought, perception, and behavior.

5 to 10 minutes of instructions, the hypnotist will simply give a direct order to close them. The hypnotist will then proceed to further suggestions of relaxation, and finally to specific hypnotic tests and suggestions.

Some people are far more susceptible to hypnosis than others (Hilgard, 1965). About 5% to 10% of the population cannot be hypnotized at all, and there are great individual differences among the remainder. Hypnotic susceptibility seems to be a stable personality trait; people who score high in this trait on one occasion are likely to score high again when retested months or years later. Moreover, studies have found that identical twins resemble each other more in hypnotic suggestibility than fraternal twins do, which suggests that this trait may even be influenced by genetics. (See Chapter 13 for an explanation of how twin research can reveal differences in heritability.)

One well-known scale for measuring individual differences in this area is illustrated in Table 4.1. This test involves determining the number of sugges-

---

TABLE 4.1

The Stanford Hypnotic Susceptibility Scale
Form C

After a state of hypnosis is induced, the subject is tested on whether he or she follows the suggestions below, which are listed roughly in the order of difficulty, from *least* difficult to *most* difficult. (That is, a subject who fails on items 1 and 2 is very unlikely to complete items 10 and 11.)

1. *Arm lowering:* After a suggestion is given that an outstretched arm is getting heavier and heavier, the arm is gradually lowered.
2. *Moving hands apart:* Subject sits with arms outstretched in front; the suggestion that the hands are repelled from each other as if by magnets leads to moving them apart.
3. *Mosquito hallucination:* Suggestion that an annoying mosquito is buzzing around leads subject to shoo it away.
4. *Taste hallucination:* Subject responds to suggestion that he or she tastes first a sweet substance, and then a sour one.
5. *Arm rigidity:* Following suggestions that an arm held out straight is getting stiffer and stiffer, subject is unable to bend it.
6. *Dream:* Subject is told to have a dream about hypnosis while remaining hypnotized, and is able to relate the dream.
7. *Age regression:* Subject is told to imagine being in fifth grade and then in second grade, and is able to give realistic handwriting specimens for each age.
8. *Arm immobilization:* Following suggestions, arm becomes too heavy to lift voluntarily.
9. *Anosmia (loss of sense of smell) to ammonia:* Following suggestions, subject is unable to smell household ammonia.
10. *Hallucinated voice:* Subject answers questions raised by a suggested hallucinated voice.
11. *Negative visual hallucination:* Following suggestions, subject reports inability to see one of three small colored boxes.
12. *Posthypnotic amnesia:* Subject is unable to recall particular information after hypnosis until given a prearranged signal.

Source: Hilgard, 1977, p. 263.

tions to which the individual is susceptible while being hypnotized. Subjects who are able to reach deeper levels of hypnosis, as indicated by their reactions to suggestions listed near the end of the scale, have been said to experience a number of more dramatic hypnotic phenomena.

The possible effect of hypnosis on memory will be described in Chapter 7 when we discuss applications of psychology to the legal system—specifically in attempting to increase the accuracy of eyewitness accounts of a crime. In the next section, we shall discuss another hypnotic phenomenon—the reduction of pain.

Hypnosis and Pain

One of the first to claim that hypnosis can relieve pain was an English surgeon named James Esdaile. From 1845 to 1851, he performed about 1,000 operations in India using only hypnosis as an anesthetic. Many of his patients showed no signs of suffering during their operations and awoke with no memory of having been in pain.

Although the number of surgeons using hypnosis is very small, the scientific literature contains reports of several modern-day operations in which hypnosis was the only anesthetic. They include the removal of breast tumors, dental extractions, skin grafts, tonsillectomies, caesarean sections, and hysterectomies (Barber, 1970). Hypnosis has also helped some children to withstand painful bone marrow treatments for cancer (Hilgard & LeBaron, 1984) and has been used to reduce the suffering associated with severe burns, migraine headaches, and angina (Long, 1986).

Despite this impressive list of successes, even the strongest proponents of hypnosis do not claim that it is a panacea. In all the cases cited above, some people were helped by hypnosis and others were not. Further, hypnosis does not seem to abolish pain completely, but rather helps people to tolerate it better.

Critics have often questioned the apparent success of hypnosis in reducing pain. Several of Esdaile's contemporaries charged in British medical journals that his patients had been specially trained to show no signs of pain (Bowers, 1976). Even in modern times, some suggest that patients who have been hypnotized continue to feel pain but deny it to please a doctor who has gone to the trouble of hypnotizing them (Barber, 1970). In an attempt to resolve this controversy, many researchers have brought hypnosis into the laboratory to conduct more systematic tests of its effects on pain.

One stimulus that is used to induce pain in the laboratory is called the "cold pressor" test. Subjects who have volunteered for the test plunge their forearms into circulating ice water and keep them submerged. For the first few seconds, they simply feel cold. But then the pain begins to mount. The longer the arms remain in the ice water, the more intense the pain becomes. Within about a minute (depending on the temperature of the ice water), the pain becomes so severe that most people can't stand it anymore and withdraw their arms.

In one experiment on hypnosis and pain (Hilgard, 1969), responses on the cold pressor test were compared for 17 highly hypnotizable subjects when they were hypnotized versus not hypnotized. In the normal waking state, when the arms remained submerged, these subjects reported rapidly increasing levels of pain, typically reaching the unbearable level in about 25 seconds. When they were hypnotized but not given any instructions that the hypnosis would reduce pain, they reported only slightly less pain. But when these subjects were hypnotized and told that they would feel no pain, they were able to keep their arms submerged for 40 seconds without reporting "unbearable pain."

Other studies have shown that this suggestion works only for highly hypnotizable subjects; people whose scores are low or moderate in suggestibility do not report reduced pain in this situation. Thus, successful hypnotic pain reduction requires two factors: The person must be highly susceptible to hypnosis, and the hypnotist must explicitly suggest that the subject will feel no pain.

What of the charge that hypnotized people may simply lie about feeling no pain? These experiments provided two revealing pieces of evidence. First, there was a gradual and systematic increase in reported pain as the arms remained submerged. It seems unlikely that the subjects would have produced such an orderly progression if they had simply been lying.

On the other hand, the subjects' blood pressure was also recorded during the experiment, because increases in pain are normally accompanied by increases in blood pressure in the waking state. When pain was reported to be reduced as a result of hypnosis, these blood pressure recordings told a different story: Blood pressure was highest for the hypnotized subjects who reported no pain. One interpretation is that they were simply lying and actually did feel the pain. But other research favors a more subtle possibility: These people may have been suffering on some level, but on another level they were not consciously aware of it.

Two Theories of Hypnosis

For more than a century, psychologists have disagreed about whether hypnosis produces a unique and altered state of consciousness. **Social theories of hypnosis** claim that hypnotized people simply attempt to conform to a social role defined by the situation and the hypnotist's demands. From this perspective, hypnosis is seen as a product of a social situation rather than as an altered state of consciousness.

Proponents of the social theory have designed studies to show that any feats possible under hypnosis are also possible under normal conditions. One example of special powers often used in demonstrations is the "human-plank" trick, in which a hypnotized person remains suspended from supports placed at the back of the head and the ankles. However, Barber (1969) reported that about four out of five people can do the same thing in a normal waking state.

Other studies in this tradition have asked some people to fake being hypnotized. Orne and Evans (1965) commanded hypnotized subjects to per-

social theories of hypnosis The claim that hypnotized people simply attempt to conform to a social role defined by the hypnotist's demands.

form such bizarre acts as picking up a poisonous snake and throwing a beaker of fuming nitric acid into the face of a research assistant. Of the six hypnotized subjects in this study, five followed these suggestions. More surprisingly, six out of six people who were *pretending* to be hypnotized did the same things.

Apparently, almost everyone in the experiment assumed that it was all right to perform these outrageous acts, because psychologists would not allow anyone to get hurt in an experiment. Fortunately for the research assistant, the subjects were right: A harmless liquid had been substituted for the nitric acid, and the snake was behind a nearly invisible pane of glass. Orne later wrote (1971, p. 189): "As a clinician who worked extensively with hypnosis, I never doubted that it would be easy for me . . . to recognize those who were, in fact, simulating. It came as a complete surprise as well as a considerable blow to my fantasies of omniscience to find that [people] were able to deceive me."

Ernest Hilgard has proposed a competing point of view: the **neodissociation theory of hypnosis**, which holds that consciousness can be split into several distinct and simultaneous streams of mental activity. In hypnosis, he says, these streams can become dissociated, so that one of these streams influences thought and behavior, while another maintains conscious awareness and voluntary control. Thus, for Hilgard, hypnosis is very much a unique and altered state of consciousness.

The strongest support for neodissociation theory comes from research using a technique that seems more at home in a seance than a psychology laboratory: automatic writing. In these experiments, a hypnotized subject placed one arm in ice water and held a pencil in the other hand, poised over a pad on her lap. The subject was given the normal instructions for an experiment of this type: She would not feel any pain and would verbally rate her pain on a scale from 0 to 10. Meanwhile, the instructions continued, the other arm was to "remain out of awareness," and write down separate ratings of the same stimuli.

The first time Hilgard (1977) tried this technique, he was amazed to find that the written and verbal reports did not agree. A deeply hypnotized woman kept repeating "zero," meaning no pain, at the same time that her hand was writing larger and larger numbers: two, five, seven, nine, ten. This discrepancy led to the metaphor of the "hidden observer," which could register pain that was out of the awareness of the conscious mind. This effect has been replicated in other laboratories and is typically observed in about half of the highly hypnotizable subjects who are selected for these tests (Kihlstrom, 1985).

Neodissociation theory focuses on the theoretical significance of the hidden observer and other somewhat unusual hypnotic phenomena. Social theories tend to focus on the more common phenoma to see how many of them can be explained away without invoking special states. Although it seems likely that this controversy will not be fully resolved for some time, it is possible that each theory applies to some hypnotic states some of the time.

In summing up over two centuries of controversy over hypnosis, Goleman (1977a, p. 60) wrote: "Hypnosis has survived, and the reason is that it works— not always, not with everyone, not with everything, but well enough to make it live on."

neodissociation theory of hypnosis The claim that consciousness can be split into several distinct and simultaneous streams of mental activity.

Drugs

The final voluntary technique for altering consciousness to be discussed in this chapter is the ingestion of psychoactive drugs. A **psychoactive drug** is a chemical substance that influences behavior or subjective experience by altering responses in the nervous system. If you drink two cups of coffee to get going in the morning, the psychoactive drug caffeine increases the arousal of your brain. Some psychoactive drugs, such as caffeine and alcohol, are legal and widely used in our society. Others, such as marijuana and cocaine, are illegal and less widely used. A third category includes drugs that are prescribed by physicians, including tranquilizers, barbiturates, and amphetamines. No matter how these drugs are legally regulated, all share the power to alter behavior and emotions by changing the chemistry of the brain.

Types of Psychoactive Drugs

Thanks to the miracles of modern chemistry, Americans now use and abuse a wide variety of drugs to make themselves feel good. Table 4.2 provides an overview of major types of psychoactive drugs and their effects.

Sedatives depress the activity of the central nervous system. Alcohol, the barbiturates, and tranquilizers are examples of this category. In large doses, sedative drugs put people to sleep—sometimes permanently. In smaller doses, they may relieve anxiety and reduce inhibitions. Since reductions in anxiety and inhibitions feel good, these drugs are often used in social settings. Indeed, alcohol is so widely used in our society that many people do not even think of it as a drug. (The effects of alcohol are described in a later section of this chapter.)

Barbiturates were first synthesized from a combination of urea and malonic acid on December 4, 1862, by Dr. A. Bayer (of aspirin fame) in Munich, Germany. According to one account, the new compound took its name from "Barbara's urates," because Bayer "wished to commemorate Barbara, a person he held in affectionate regard . . . who gave him samples of urine for research purposes" (Hordern, 1968, p. 118). Barbiturates were first used clinically in 1903, and one of the most popular barbiturates, phenobarbital, was introduced in 1912. They are prescribed to this day for some types of epilepsy, as well as for sedation. Their effects are quite similar to those of alcohol, and, as a result, barbiturates are often abused as "recreational drugs."

The effects of tranquilizers, such as Valium and Librium, are milder than those of the barbiturates. When barbiturates are used to suppress anxiety, they often induce sleep; tranquilizers can reduce anxiety without putting people to sleep. They are also less dangerous than barbiturates; barbiturate overdoses can depress respiration and cause death, while this rarely or never occurs with tranquilizers.

For these reasons and others, tranquilizer use rose dramatically from 1960, the year they were introduced, to the late 1970s. According to the National Institute of Drug Abuse, around their peak, in 1977, over 3 billion Valiums and nearly 1 billion Libriums were purchased by Americans—showing that these drugs sold faster than even McDonald's hamburgers. However,

psychoactive drug A chemical substance that influences behavior or subjective experiences by altering responses in the nervous system.

sedatives Drugs that depress the activity of the central nervous system.

TABLE 4.2

An Overview of Psychoactive Drugs

Drug	Immediate effects	Psychological dependence[a]	Tolerance[b]	Physical dependence[c]
Sedatives				
Alcohol; barbiturates (e.g., Seconal, Amytal, Nembutal); methaqualone (e.g., Quaalude)	Central nervous system (CNS) depressants: relaxation, drowsiness, sometimes euphoria; impaired judgment, coordination, and emotional control	High	Yes	Yes
Tranquilizers (e.g., Valium, Librium)	Selective CNS depressants: relaxation, relief of anxiety	Moderate?	No	No
Stimulants				
Caffeine	Increased alertness, reduced fatigue	Moderate	Yes	No
Cocaine; amphetamines (e.g., Dexedrine, Benzedrine)	Increased alertness, reduced fatigue, loss of appetite, often euphoria	High	Yes	No
Antidepressants (e.g., Elavil, Parnate)	Elevates mood for severely depressed patients; used only under close medical supervision	Minimal?	No	No
Narcotics				
Opium; morphine; heroin; methadone; codeine; Demerol	CNS depressants: sedation, euphoria, pain relief, impaired intellectual function	High	Yes	Yes
Hallucinogens				
LSD; mescaline; psilocybin	Production of visual imagery, increased sensory awareness, sometimes anxiety, nausea, impaired coordination, "consciousness expansion"	Minimal	Yes (rare)	No
Cannabis (marijuana, hashish)	Relaxation, euphoria, some alteration of time perception, possible impairment of judgment and coordination	Moderate	Yes	No
Antipsychotics				
Thorazine; Serpasil; Haldol	Calm (in psychotic patients); reduction of anxiety and initiative without excessive sedation	Minimal	No	No

[a]A compulsion to use a drug for its pleasurable effects.
[b]Over time, higher doses are needed to produce similar effects.
[c]Withdrawal syndrome is experienced when drug is stopped.

Source: Based on *A Primer of Drug Action,* By R. M. Julien, copyright © 1975, by W. H. Freeman and Co. All rights reserved.

their use has since declined somewhat, due to concern among physicians that they were often prescribed inappropriately as a cure-all.

Stimulants increase the activity of the central nervous system; thus their effects are in some ways the opposite of those for sedatives. The mildest stimulant is caffeine, a drug that is present in coffee and tea, which have been popular for many centuries, and most cola drinks. Historical records suggest that tea was widely used in China by A.D. 900; an Arabian medical text from the same period suggested that coffee "was good for just about everything, including measles and reducing lust" (Ray, 1978, p. 187).

More potent stimulants found in the coca leaf have also been used for over 1,000 years. The active ingredient cocaine was chemically extracted from the coca leaf in the mid-nineteenth century, and was an ingredient in many popular elixirs and patent medicines until this use was outlawed in 1906. Its effects include increased mental awareness and decreased fatigue.

Amphetamines are a class of synthetic drugs that were discovered in the 1920s and introduced to medicine about ten years later. Although they do not resemble cocaine chemically, they have nearly identical effects on the central nervous system. The principal differences are in the duration of action; cocaine is active in the body for only a few minutes, while the effects of amphetamines typically last for hours. Before physicians became aware of the negative effects of amphetamines, they too were prescribed freely. According to one estimate, American and British soldiers in World War II used almost 150 million doses of amphetamines to defend democracy (Bloomquist, 1970).

Both cocaine and the amphetamines have been widely abused because of their energizing and euphoric effects. People often have difficulty controlling their use of these drugs, and high doses produce a schizophrenic-like syndrome characterized by paranoia and hallucinations.

A final group of stimulants are called antidepressants, because they elevate mood in severely depressed patients. This category includes drugs sold under the trade names Elavil and Parnate. Interestingly, these drugs have little effect on people who are not seriously depressed, suggesting that at least some types of depression involve a specific chemical imbalance in the brain that can be reversed by drugs (see Chapter 14).

Narcotics are opiates that relieve pain and induce sleep. Opiates include the natural products of the opium plant as well as synthetic drugs that resemble them chemically and in their pharmacological effects. Two examples of "natural" narcotics are morphine, the major active ingredient in the opium plant, and heroin, a more potent form of morphine. A number of related chemicals have been created by chemists as part of a search for a nonaddictive drug that is equally effective in relieving pain. For example, when the drug Demerol was introduced into medical practice, it was said to be nonaddicting. This turned out to be incorrect; like all other narcotics, Demerol is highly addictive.

In legal circles, the term *narcotic* is sometimes defined more broadly. Some drug control laws, for example, classify cocaine as a narcotic despite the fact that it has little in common with opiates like morphine and heroin. Virtually all pharmacologists agree that this broader definition is arbitrary and misleading, and that the term *narcotics* should be reserved for opiate drugs.

---

stimulants Drugs that increase the activity of the central nervous system.

narcotics Opiates that relieve pain and induce sleep.

Hallucinogenic drugs cause hallucinations and alter sensory perceptions. In our society, they are all illegal. Common examples include LSD, mescaline, and psilocybin. Marijuana and hashish also fall in this category, despite the fact that their effects are much milder and they cause hallucinations only in very large doses.

Finally, **antipsychotic drugs** are used to decrease the hallucinations and disordered behavior of psychotic individuals. Their use has had a dramatic impact on the nature of clinical psychology and psychiatry (see Chapter 15). Thorazine, Serpasil, and Haldol are three of the most commonly used drugs in this class.

Drug Dependence Versus Drug Addiction

Because many psychoactive drugs produce pleasurable effects, they are often used and abused in social settings. Some drugs are far more likely to be abused than others; some generalities for each class are summarized in Table 4.2. From a medical point of view, there is an important distinction between physical addiction to a drug and psychological dependence.

Drug addiction is a medical syndrome defined by physical dependence and tolerance. **Physical dependence** means that a regular user who stops taking a drug will experience a variety of physical problems. For example, a heroin addict who stops taking heroin will experience an extremely unpleasant withdrawal syndrome that includes irritability, insomnia, violent yawning, severe sneezing, nausea, diarrhea, and muscle spasms. **Tolerance** means that if a person takes the same dose of a drug day after day, it will gradually have smaller effects because the body becomes accustomed to, or tolerates, that dosage; increasingly larger doses will be required to produce the original effect.

A close look at Table 4.2 makes it clear that by this medical definition, only alcohol, the barbiturates, and the opiates are addicting drugs, for only these produce tolerance and physical dependence. That does not mean that regular users of other drugs will find them generally easy to stop. Frequent use of amphetamines, tranquilizers, or other drugs may be a hard habit to break. This more subtle potential for abuse is called **psychological dependence**, a compulsion to use a drug that is not based on physical addiction. The potential of a particular drug for producing a pattern of psychological dependence, in which people use the drug regularly despite ambivalence or attempts to quit, is hard to measure precisely. As a result, there may be some controversy over specific items in Table 4.2, such as whether Valium and Librium lead to minimal rather than moderate psychological dependence.

To provide a more complete picture of the psychological, social, and biological factors that determine drug effects and physical addiction, we shall describe two drugs: alcohol and cocaine.

Addictions: The Case of Alcohol and Cocaine

Beer and berry wine were known and used at least 6,400 years before Christ. Today, alcohol use is so firmly established in our society that two drunks in

hallucinogenic drugs Chemical substances that cause hallucinations and alter sensory perception.

antipsychotic drugs Drugs used primarily to decrease the hallucinations and disordered behavior of psychotic individuals.

drug addiction A medically defined syndrome that includes physical dependence and tolerance.

physical dependence A syndrome in which withdrawal from a drug produces physical symptoms.

tolerance A phenomenon whereby increasingly large doses of a drug are required to produce the same effects.

psychological dependence Compulsive drug use in the absence of physical need.

a bar might get into an argument about the evils of drug addiction without ever realizing that they themselves are addicted to our society's number one problem drug—alcohol.

ALCOHOL DOSES AND EFFECTS

If you go out after work and have a few drinks, your behavior will change. You may loosen up a little, act friendlier, and begin to laugh loudly at mediocre jokes. These changes are not random or accidental; they show the effects of the drug alcohol on the transmission of electrochemical impulses in the nervous system. Specifically, because alcohol is a sedative drug, it depresses activity in the central nervous system. One of the first sites affected in the brain is the reticular activating system, which is responsible for alertness, attention, and the regulation of the cerebral cortex.

The actual concentration of alcohol in the blood is determined by the amount of alcohol consumed, how fast it is consumed, and such complicating factors as the amount of food in the stomach and the type of drink. (See "Drugs and the Brain," pages 133–135.)

Low concentrations of alcohol in the blood produce relatively mild physiological and behavioral changes. Ray (1978, p. 145) describes a mild state of drunkenness as follows: "At some point we become uninhibited enough to enjoy our own charming selves and uncritical enough to accept the clods around us. . . . The reduction in concern and judgment may range from not worrying about who'll pay the bar bill . . . to being sure that you can beat the train to the crossing." Psychological variables, such as expectations, are likely to play an important role at these low levels, as described in the next section.

Higher blood levels of alcohol produce more dramatic physiological changes that are less influenced by psychological factors; once you're in a coma, it doesn't matter what your expectations were. Higher alcohol concentrations first depress sensory and motor activity, then produce staggering and a loss of muscular coordination (through depression of the cerebellum), then lead to stupor, anesthesia, coma, and finally to death.

The precise effects of a given dose of alcohol also vary from one person to the next but in general depend on sex and body weight. Alcohol is distributed throughout the body fluids, including the blood. Since heavier people have more body fluids, they take longer to reach a given blood-alcohol level. Women have proportionately more fat and less body fluids than men of the same weight and thus reach high blood-alcohol levels more quickly.

Alcohol interacts with other drugs in complex ways. A person who is taking tranquilizers or barbiturates will get drunk much more quickly than usual. Sudden and unexpected reactions between alcohol and other drugs can cause coma or death.

PSYCYHOLOGICAL FACTORS

At relatively low doses, psychological factors exert a major influence on the response to alcohol. People's expectations that alcohol will make them feel more aggressive, more relaxed, or more sexual can affect their behavior just as much as what they drink.

One study (Lang, Goeckner, Adesso, & Marlatt, 1975) examined the links between alcohol, aggression, and expectations by deceiving some experimental subjects about what they were drinking. The experimenters began by looking for a drink that could fool people; they discovered that a mixture of 1 ounce of 100-proof vodka and 5 ounces of tonic water tasted the same as plain tonic water to most people. They then divided 96 male college students who were defined as heavy social drinkers into four groups. Two groups were told the truth—that one would be drinking plain tonic and the other vodka and tonic. But the other two groups were deceived. One of these groups was told they would be drinking vodka and tonic but were actually given plain tonic; the other group was told they would be drinking plain tonic, but were given vodka and tonic.

The researchers who talked to the subjects did not know which group each one was in; this reduced the chances that the experimenters would unintentionally influence the results. (For more details, see "Understanding the Scientific Method" in Chapter 15, regarding double-blind studies.) Subjects who received vodka drank enough to produce a blood-alcohol concentration of 0.10%, which is the legal definition of drunkenness in many states. The actual dose depended on body weight; for example, a 150-pound man in this study drank 6 ounces of vodka in one hour.

To maximize the chances of observing aggression, a research assistant later provoked half of these subjects by sarcastically criticizing their performance on a complex task, asking the subject whether his attempt to solve a problem was really serious and whether he was so dumb that he had to cheat to stay in college. To measure aggression, each subject was then given an opportunity to evaluate the research assistant's performance on another task and penalize him for mistakes by giving electric shocks. (No one was actually shocked.)

The findings were clear-cut. Whether provoked or not, subjects who believed they had drunk alcohol were more aggressive. They gave longer and more intense shocks to the research assistant. The alcohol itself did not affect aggression. Those who thought they had tonic but actually drank vodka were less aggressive than those who thought they had vodka but actually drank tonic. The beliefs had greater effects than the drug.

Other studies have shown similar effects for sexual arousal. Ogden Nash expressed one common belief about alcohol and sex when he wrote

> Candy is dandy
> But liquor is quicker.

But Wilson and Lawson (1976) found that men were more likely to become aroused by erotic films when they thought they were drinking. Whether they actually received alcohol or not was again less important than their beliefs.

Attitudes and expectations have also been shown to help determine the response to other drugs, such as hallucinogens. In one typical study, subjects who said they were apprehensive before taking the drug psilocybin tended to be anxious and experience headaches and nausea after taking it; those who said they felt good about taking psilocybin were more likely to report that it put them in a pleasant mood (Metzner, Litwin, & Weil, 1965). The point here is not that psychological factors are more important than

Many experts argue that alcoholism is the nation's leading drug problem.

biological ones, or vice versa. It is that psychology and biology work together in complex ways to determine the response in any given situation.

ALCOHOLISM

How serious a problem is alcohol abuse? According to a 1982 Gallup poll, one out of every three American families reported a problem with alcohol (cited in Peele, 1984). Because of variations in definitions, estimates of the total number of alcoholics in the United States vary widely, from about 8 to 12 million Americans (Ray, 1978).

In the formal diagnostic scheme of the American Psychiatric Association (called DSM-III-R, as described in Chapter 14), "alcoholics" are defined in two different categories, depending on the seriousness of the problem. What we called "psychological dependence" corresponds roughly to "alcohol abuse"; "physical dependence" on alcohol is called "alcohol dependence." The less serious form, **alcohol abuse**, is defined by the presence of three criteria: a pattern of pathological use—for example, a need for alcohol every day or an inability to cut down or stop drinking; impairment of social or occupational function, such as absence from work or arguments with family or friends; and duration of the problem for at least one month. The more serious form, **alcohol dependence**, corresponds to the medical definition of drug addiction: a syndrome involving withdrawal symptoms and tolerance (American Psychiatric Association, 1980).

The fact that heavy drinkers develop tolerance—that is, need larger doses of the drug alcohol to produce the same effect—has been well established. It is also clear that people who are addicted to alcohol will go through a physiological withdrawal syndrome if they do not drink. This process of withdrawal usually involves several of the following: anxiety, depression, insomnia, restlessness, muscle tremors, high blood pressure, and increased body temperature. More serious cases may lead to delirium tremens (or the "DTs"), characterized by hallucinations, delirium, disorientation, and epileptic seizures. This withdrawal syndrome is medically more severe and more likely to cause death than withdrawal from heroin or other narcotic drugs.

Long-term use of large amounts of alcohol is associated with damage to the liver and the brain. Cirrhosis of the liver is often alcohol-related and is ranked among the ten leading causes of death in the United States. Chronic alcoholism can also lead to Korsakoff's disease, which leaves a person confused and disoriented as a result of brain damage similar to Wernicke's aphasia (see Chapter 3).

Alcoholism also leads to a variety of other medical problems, and not all of them afflict only the drinkers themselves. Thirty to fifty percent of the newborn infants of alcoholic mothers suffer from *fetal alcohol syndrome,* which includes growth retardation in length, weight, and head circumference; deformities of the heart, face, and fingers; mental retardation; and other problems. At this time, fetal alcohol syndrome is the third leading cause (after Down's syndrome and spinal bifida) of birth defects associated with mental retardation. It is more likely to occur with binge drinking of large amounts of alcohol during critical periods of the baby's prenatal development.

The effects on fetuses of more moderate drinking are still somewhat

alcohol abuse A pattern of pathological use of alcohol, as well as an impairment of social or occupational function, for at least one month.

alcohol dependence A syndrome involving withdrawal symptoms and tolerance.

controversial. In 1977, the National Institute on Alcohol Abuse and Alcoholism issued the following warning to pregnant women, which is still widely cited:

> While safe levels of drinking are known, it appears that a risk is established with ingestion above three ounces of absolute alcohol or 6 drinks per day. Between one and three ounces, there is uncertainty but caution is advised. Therefore, pregnant women and those likely to become pregnant should discuss their drinking habits and the potential dangers with their physicians. (U.S. Department of Health, Education, and Welfare, 1978)

In 1956, the American Medical Association defined alcoholism as a disease and began trying to treat it as a medical problem. According to this **disease model of alcoholism,** some people have an inherent weakness for alcohol that they cannot control. Thus, to be cured, an alcoholic must totally stop drinking. This view is consistent with the philosophy of Alcoholics Anonymous, a worldwide treatment organization with over 800,000 members. Alcoholics Anonymous was founded in Akron, Ohio, in 1935 by two reformed alcoholics. They believed that the susceptibility of the true alcoholic exists before the first drink is taken. Thus, the treatment program is based on the belief that "for an alcoholic, one drink is too many and a thousand not enough."

This view has become quite widely accepted; according to a 1982 Gallup poll, 79% of all Americans see alcoholism as a disease that requires medical treatment. Some psychologists, however, hold to a **social model,** which characterizes problem drinking as a complex category of behavior that may have many different causes and many different cures. One implication of the social view is that complete abstinence may not be required for every problem drinker; some alcoholics can be taught "controlled drinking" techniques and maintain their alcohol consumption within acceptable limits.

Some evidence to support the social view was found in two highly controversial studies published by the Rand Corporation. The first, which was originally published in 1976, surveyed nearly 14,000 alcoholics who had been treated at special centers set up by the federal government (Armor, Polich, & Stambul, 1978). Their major finding was rather encouraging: About 70% of those who completed treatment remained improved 6 to 18 months later.

But it was a secondary finding that got all the headlines (see "Becoming a Critical Consumer"). They reported that 22% of those treated were not abstaining but rather drinking alcohol in a controlled fashion without major problems. Critics were concerned that some alcoholics would use the Rand report as an excuse to keep drinking or begin drinking again. Many rushed to point out the flaws in the Rand study: It relied heavily on what alcoholics said about their drinking rather than direct behavioral measurements; it followed patients for just 18 months; it measured only changes in drinking rather than improvements in work life or family life.

A follow-up study tried to address some of these criticisms (Polich, Armor, & Stambul, 1981). The follow-up was extended to four years, survey reports were supplemented by breathalyzer tests, and new criteria were used to define moderate drinking. This study concluded that approximately 40% of those who were free of drinking problems four years after treatment still drank alcohol to some degree.

disease model of alcoholism The view that some individuals have an inherent uncontrollable weakness for alcohol.

social model The view that problem drinking is a complex category of behavior that may have many causes and cures.

Can Reformed Alcoholics Drink Safely?

When the Rand Foundation first reported their long-term follow-up of a group of alcoholics, the *New York Times* published an account of the results on its front page (Brody, 1976). Compare the beginning of this article with the description of the same study in the text. Do you think the excerpt is accurate or misleading? (A short discussion appears after the "Summary" at the end of this chapter.)

STUDY SUGGESTS
ALCOHOLIC, TREATED, CAN
DRINK SAFELY
Warning Is Added

A study of more than a thousand alcoholics admitted to treatment programs throughout the country suggests that a sizable percentage of alcoholics can return to normal, moderate drinking without relapsing into alcohol abuse, according to a report released yesterday by the Rand Corporation.

The finding, which runs counter to general thinking, has already aroused dissent among leading alcoholism groups, which maintain that abstinence is the only reliable form of recovery from the disorder.

Some experts have called the findings misleading and inconclusive, and dangerous to recovered alcoholics who may now think, on the basis of the study, that it is safe to drink again.

The authors of the report, however, cautioned against an assumption by alcoholics that it would be safe to resume drinking, warning that at present there is no way to distinguish between those who can safely drink and those for whom social drinking would be the first step back to alcohol abuse.

The interpretation of these findings and others remains highly controversial. In the United States, most of the emphasis in treatment is still on complete abstinence. Indeed, according to Peele (1984, p. 1342): "Today no clinician in the United States publicly speaks about the option of controlled drinking for the alcoholic." He contrasted this to the situation in Great Britain, where a 1982 survey found that 93% of treatment centers believed that controlled drinking can be beneficial for some people (Robertson & Heather, 1982).

Peele, who is one of the most outspoken critics of the disease model, went on to argue that in the United States there is a general view that people are often susceptible to uncontrollable urges. Thus, the disease model of alcoholism is "part of a larger trend in which premenstrual tension, drug use and drug withdrawal, eating junk foods, and lovesickness are presented as defenses for murder" (Peele, 1984, p. 1348). On the other side of the fence, *Time* magazine quoted one expert on this controversy as saying: "The suggestion that an alcoholic might be able to return to social drinking safely is a serious ethical problem, because at least 97% of alcoholics, if you let them drink, could die" ("New Insights into Alcoholism," 1983, p. 69).

Controversies of this sort are extremely frustrating to alcoholics, their families, and psychologists whose professional identity depends on giving the best possible advice to troubled clients. The data do indicate that getting some sort of psychological help with alcohol problems is better than getting no help at all. A review of 384 studies of psychologically oriented alcoholism treatment programs (Emrick, 1975) found few differences in the average success rate of Alcoholics Anonymous, various types of psychotherapy, and other treatments. But this review did show that patients who entered a treatment program were more likely to improve than those who did not. Psychological treatment "increases an alcoholic's chances of reducing his drinking problem" (Emrick, 1975, p. 88), but no approach offers a guaranteed cure.

COCAINE ABUSE

One of the most rapidly growing drug abuse problems in recent years is cocaine abuse. According to a survey published by the National Institute of Mental Health in 1982, 22 million Americans had tried cocaine by the early 1980s, and both initial and compulsive use was soaring. While popular myth has it that cocaine is a "safe drug," cocaine-related emergency room visits, hospitalizations, and deaths have also soared. Moreover, cocaine use is associated with a host of nonmedical problems that arise when the abuser's work and family life are sacrificed to compulsive drug use, and criminal activity becomes a way of supporting the craving.

Why do people abuse cocaine and other drugs? Theories of drug use have arisen out of three of the major psychological paradigms—the behavioral, the biological, and the psychoanalytic—and together these three theories probably help to account for many of the factors involved in drug use. Here each of the three perspectives on drug use is considered briefly, with an emphasis on its revelance to cocaine abuse.

Cocaine abuse has grown rapidly in recent years.

Charles Dackis and Mark Gold, who have conducted research and treatment programs with various types of drug addicts, offer a behavioral analysis of drug addiction (Dackis & Gold, 1985). They suggest that the feelings of euphoria that follow self-administration of cocaine are a positive reinforcer for cocaine use. Whether cocaine is administered intranasally or intravenously, the user quickly experiences a "rush" of pleasure lasting several seconds, followed by several minutes of lower-level euphoria. The sense of euphoria gradually gives way to irritability and restlessness, which act as negative reinforcers for further cocaine use—that is, they lead the user to take more cocaine to avoid the unpleasant letdown and regain the euphoria. (The nature of positive and negative reinforcement is described in more detail in Chapter 6.)

Proponents of the behavioral paradigm can point to the role of intense, if short-lived, pleasure in maintaining a cocaine habit, but we must turn to the biological paradigm to understand how cocaine operates on the brain to produce feelings of pleasure. First, the rapidity with which cocaine has its effects suggests that there are pleasure centers in the brain that respond directly and immediately to cocaine. Research with both laboratory animals and human drug users suggests that the neurotransmitter dopamine plays an important role in mediating cocaine effects. Ordinarily, when we are involved in activities that produce great pleasure (e.g., many forms of physical exercise), the neurotransmitter dopamine is released from nodes on the presynaptic neuron, acts to stimulate receptor sites on the postsynaptic neuron, and then is reabsorbed so that it is available for future use. Apparently, cocaine operates to interfere with the "re-uptake" process (Dackis & Gold, 1985). Consequently, when cocaine is abused, dopamine becomes depleted despite an increase in the number of postsynaptic neurons able to take up dopamine. Dackis and Gold speculated that cocaine euphoria may result from the powerful stimulation involved in dopamine transmission, and that acute cocaine craving stems from the depletion of synaptic dopamine.

Although the physiological effects of cocaine may help to account for its use, they do not explain why some drug abusers prefer cocaine while others prefer narcotics like heroin. Dr. Edward Khantzian, a psychiatrist at Harvard Medical School, suggests that we need to turn to the psychoanalytic model to understand why drug-dependent individuals differ in their drug preferences. Specifically, Dr. Khantzian suggests that abusers' drug of choice represents an interaction between the physical action of the drug and the dominant painful feelings with which they struggle. Drawing on clinical and research evidence, Dr. Khantzian argues that narcotic addicts prefer opiates because of their powerful soothing effects and their ability to counteract threatening and disorganizing feelings of rage and aggression. Conversely, cocaine abusers prefer this stimulant because of its ability to relieve distress associated with depression of hyperactivity.

While individuals may first try cocaine because of curiosity, peer pressure, or boredom, its short-lived euphoric effects may quickly lead to repeated use. Chronic use, in turn, involves alternating periods of acute intoxication and cocaine urges, during which users experience intense longings for the drug's effects, often accompanied by numbness of the throat, tachycardia (rapid heartbeat), and abdominal discomfort. If chronic users suddenly stop using cocaine altogether, they can expect to experience decreased energy, sleepiness, irritability, and depressed mood as part of "crashing."

Treatment of cocaine dependency often involves both biological and psychological approaches. Prescription drugs may be used to relieve the effects of cocaine withdrawal. It has also been suggested (Dackis & Gold, 1985) that it may be possible to develop drugs capable of blocking the cocaine high. Psychological interventions typically combine individual and group therapy, and are geared toward helping the client deal both with drug urges and with problems related to self-esteem and personal relationships. (Types of therapy are discussed further in Chapter 15.)

Drugs and the Brain

Although drugs differ widely in their effects and potential for abuse, in at least one way all psychoactive drugs are alike. They all act on the brain. But to act on the brain, first a chemical must get there.

When a drug is swallowed, it dissolves in the stomach fluids, is carried into the small intestine, penetrates the lining, and passes into the bloodstream. Once a drug enters the bloodstream, it circulates quickly through the entire body. It can enter most body tissues by passing through pores in the walls of the capillaries (tiny blood vessels). Ultimately, the drug is transported by the blood to appropriate sites in the brain, where it exerts its effect.

Though the route a drug follows through the body is always the same, special conditions along that route can influence a drug's effectiveness. Suppose, for example, you are celebrating the end of finals with a bottle of 1961 Mouton Rothschild (or Pagan Pink Ripple if funds are low). The alcohol molecules from the wine pass through the walls of your stomach into the small intestine, where they are absorbed into the bloodstream and travel to your brain. If your stomach is full, some molecules of the alcohol will become chemically bound to the proteins in the food. If your stomach is empty, however, the alcohol molecules will pass more quickly into the bloodstream, and you may soon find yourself standing on a table singing a medley of the Beatles' greatest hits or Madonna's latest single.

The speed of absorption may also be affected by the characteristics of a particular drug. If you consume champagne or sparkling burgundy, you will get drunk more quickly because carbonation moves alcohol more rapidly through the stomach into the small intestine and thus accelerates its flow into the blood.

When the drug actually reaches the brain, it must pass through a barrier that protects brain cells from poisonous substances. There are no pores in the capillaries of the brain. Each neuron is surrounded by a protective covering (formed of glial cells); thus, only certain types of small molecules can pass through to brain cells. This structure of the circulatory system of the brain, which makes it difficult for certain types of chemicals to pass from the blood to the neurons, is referred to as the **blood-brain barrier.**

If a drug manages to pass the blood-brain barrier, ultimately it will reach specific brain cells that are equipped with the appropriate **drug receptor,** the part of a neuron that responds to a specific type of drug. It is now thought that different types of drugs act on different drug receptors. For example, some brain cells have receptors stimulated by amphetamines; others have receptors stimulated by narcotics. After a drug reaches the appropriate receptor, it is believed to affect the transmission of nerve impulses, usually by influencing neurotransmitters.

According to Snyder (1984, p. 23): "Virtually every drug that alters mental function does so by interacting with a neurotransmitter system in the brain." As explained in Chapter 3, neurotransmitters are the chemical substances that transmit information from one neuron to another. The specific details of this process are currently the subject of a great deal of research. One advance that prompted this research came from the study of patients with Parkinson's disease, who suffer from severe muscular tremors of the limbs, hands, neck, and face. Other physiological and psychological problems appear in later stages of this progressive disease.

Within the last few decades, neurologists have discovered both the cause and cure of this disease, which afflicts 1.5 million Americans. Apparently these problems are caused by a lack of the neurotransmitter dopamine in certain structures of the brain. Dopamine neurons inhibit the action of certain muscle fibers; without this inhibitory effect, uncontrollable tremors are produced. At first, researchers gave the drug dopamine to Parkinson's patients, but it had no effect because the molecules were too large to pass through the blood-brain barrier. Currently, many cases of Parkinson's disease are treated with the drug L-dopa, a closely related chemical that is converted to dopamine

blood-brain barrier The circulatory system structures that prevent certain large molecules from reaching brain cells.

drug receptor The part of a neuron that responds to a specific type of chemical.

in the brain. As research into the nature of both drugs and neurotransmitters continues, other diseases associated with malfunctioning in the central nervous system are likely to become curable.

It is clear that drug misuse is a serious problem in contemporary American society. However, the study of drugs, like the study of hypnosis, sleep, and other aspects of consciousness, has had a number of immediate practical applications that have improved the quality of everyday life. There is every reason to suspect that the future will hold many more advances of this type.

Summary

- **Consciousness** refers to all the internal mental events and responses to external stimuli of which a person is aware.
- Wundt and others studied consciousness through the method of **introspection**—the careful, rigorous, and disciplined analysis of one's own thoughts by highly trained observers.

Sleep and Dreams

- A **circadian rhythm** is a cyclical change in behavior or physiology that is repeated once every 24 hours or so, for example, the sleep-wake cycle.
- **Jet lag**, the discomfort or decreased efficiency caused by traveling across time zones, interferes with established circadian rhythms by disturbing the sleep cycle.
- There are five stages of sleep, which are repeated throughout the night: **REM** (rapid eye movement) sleep, during which dreaming is most likely to occur, and four stages of non-REM sleep.
- REM sleep is often called *paradoxical sleep* because of the contrast between EEG signs of alertness and the difficulty of awakening.
- The evidence suggests that all people dream whether they remember it or not.
- Freud argued that dreams hold the key to understanding human motivation because they express unconscious impulses that determine behavior.
- More recent theories of dreams tend to emphasize the possible biological role of REM in brain function.

Meditation

- **Meditation** refers to a number of different techniques for internal reflection.
- In **opening-up meditation**, individuals attempt to clear their minds and "go with the flow" of experience.
- The practitioners of **concentrative meditation** attempt to focus all attention on a single object or idea.

Hypnosis

- **Hypnosis** is a state of awareness that is induced by special techniques and is related to changes in thought, perception, and behavior.
- **Social theories of hypnosis** claim that hypnotized people simply attempt to conform to a social role defined by the hypnotist's demands.
- The **neodissociation theory of hypnosis** holds that consciousness can be split into several distinct and simultaneous streams of mental activity.

Drugs

- A **psychoactive drug** is a chemical substance that influences behavior or subjective experience by altering responses in the nervous system.
- **Sedatives**—such as alcohol, the barbiturates, and tranquilizers—depress the activity of the central nervous system.
- **Stimulants**—such as caffeine, cocaine, amphetamines, and antidepressants—increase the activity of the central nervous system.
- **Narcotics**—such as morphine and heroin—are opiates that relieve pain and induce sleep.
- **Hallucinogenic drugs**—such as LSD, mescaline, psilocybin, marijuana and hashish—cause hallucinations and alter sensory perceptions.
- **Antipsychotic drugs**—such as Thorazine, Serpasil, and Haldol—are used to decrease the hallucinations and disordered behavior of psychotic individuals.
- **Drug addiction** is a medical syndrome defined by physical dependence and tolerance.
- **Physical dependence** means that a regular user who stops taking a drug will experience a variety of physical problems.
- **Tolerance** means that if a person takes the same dose of a drug day after day, it will gradually have smaller effects because the body becomes accustomed to, or tolerates, that dosage; increasingly larger doses will be required to produce the original effect.
- **Psychological dependence** is a compulsion to use a drug that is not based on physical addiction.
- **Alcohol abuse** is defined by the presence of three criteria: a pattern of pathological use—for example, a need for alcohol every day or an inability to cut down or stop drinking; impairment of social or occupational functions, such as absence from work or arguments with family or friends; and duration of the problem for at least one month.
- **Alcohol dependence,** the more serious form of alcohol abuse, corresponds to the medical definition of drug addiction: a syndrome involving withdrawal symptoms and tolerance.
- According to the **disease model of alcoholism,** some people have an inherent weakness for alcohol that they cannot control.

- According to the **social model**, problem drinking is a complex category of behavior that may have many different causes and many different cures.

- The **blood-brain barrier** refers to the structure of the circulatory system of the brain, which makes it difficult for certain types of chemicals to pass from the blood to the neurons.

- If a drug manages to pass the blood-brain barrier, ultimately it will reach the appropriate **drug receptor**—the part of a neuron that responds to the specific type of drug.

Critical Thinking Exercise Discussion

Can Reformed Alcoholics Drink Safely?

This excerpt could be used as a textbook example of good science reporting. The first paragraph is a fair summary of the major findings from the Rand study, and the following paragraphs clearly state the controversy and reservations about this finding. It is unfortunate, however, that one has to read beyond the headline "Alcoholics, Treated, Can Drink Safely" to get to the important subheading: "Warning Is Added." Thus, the critical consumer should always read beyond the headlines to get the whole story.

While acknowledging that the article may be accurate, the critical thinker also might ask whether the data gathered in the Rand Study are sufficient to support the conclusion implied in the title—that the alcoholic, when treated, can drink safely. While the Rand Study provides some support for this conclusion, the critical thinker would want to see more evidence before accepting the notion that any alcoholic, when treated, can drink safely.

This excerpt also raises some interesting questions about journalistic ethics. Suppose the experts who believe that a single drink can cause an alcoholic to relapse are correct. Then it is possible that some alcoholics who were teetering on the road to recovery and used this headline to justify having a drink would, as a result, suffer a recurrence of serious problems with alcohol.

There are legitimate questions here regarding exactly what is required in the name of journalistic accuracy versus protecting the public from itself. This debate is not about science, but rather about value judgments and the public good.

SENSATION AND PERCEPTION

Chapter 5

About 300 years ago, philosopher John Locke described an imaginary experiment that might shed light on the question of how we perceive the world. Suppose a man who had been blind from birth was suddenly able to see. Would he immediately perceive the world as we do, as though a blindfold had simply been removed? More specifically, suppose that while he was blind, the man had learned to distinguish between a cube and a globe by touch. If these objects were placed on a table before him, could he say which was which? Locke thought not. He believed that direct experience was required for learning and that the tactile sensations produced by feeling a shape would not help to interpret the visual sensations produced by looking at it.

In fact, Mother Nature has actually performed this rather macabre experiment; there are about 100 documented cases of adults who have suddenly gained sight, usually as a result of surgery. One of the most intensively studied was a man known to science as S. B. (Gregory & Wallace, 1963).

S. B. lost his sight at the age of 10 months. He adjusted well to his blindness and lived a full and active life. Sometimes he even went for bicycle rides by holding the shoulder of a friend who rode alongside on another bike. But S. B. always longed to see the world in which he lived—the flowers in his garden, the tools in his shed, and the rich colors of the morning sky. Finally, at the age of 52, he underwent an operation to restore his sight.

When the bandages were first removed from S. B.'s eyes, he turned toward the voice of his surgeon and saw only a blur. During the next few days, the images gradually sharpened. At first, S. B. was thrilled and would sit by his hospital window for hours, just watching the world go by.

S. B.'s process of recovery suggested that Locke's guess was wrong; he did learn to recognize objects more quickly if they were already known by touch. He soon learned to read a clock on the wall, apparently as a result of the fact that he had learned to tell time by feeling the hands of a pocket watch. Even more convincing, S. B. rapidly learned to recognize capital letters he had previously learned by touch. Recognition of small letters came more slowly; S. B. lacked any experience with these shapes.

In some ways S. B.'s vision was never entirely normal. Like other patients whose sight has been restored, S. B. had trouble perceiving distance and depth. Although his hospital room was several stories up, he thought the ground was only a few feet away.

Similarly, S. B. did not perceive visual illusions the way most people do. For example, if you look at the two lines in the Mueller-Lyer illusion in Figure 5.1, one line will seem longer than the other even though they are physically equal. S. B. was not fooled by this or other common illusions (see Figure 5.21); to him, the two lines looked equal.

Sadly, like many others whose sight was restored in adulthood, S. B. became rather withdrawn and depressed after the operation. He loved bright colors but found much of the world drab. He brooded over all that he had missed, and he often sat in the dark at night, not bothering to turn on the lights. The difficulty he had trusting his new sense was most obvious when he had to cross a street:

> Before the operation, he would cross alone, holding his arm or stick before him, when the traffic would subside as the waters before Christ. But after the operation it took two of us on either side to force him across a road: he was terrified as never before in his life. (Gregory, 1978, p. 197)

S. B. died a few years after the operation and never regained the contentment he had felt when he was blind.

From a theoretical point of view, the case of S. B. helped to establish the critical role that learning can play in shaping the way we perceive the world. For our discussion, it helps call attention to how much we take for granted regarding the importance of sensory processes in everyday life. To understand this role, it is useful to distinguish between two types of sensory processes. **Sensation** is the process of responding to a simple physical stimulus, such as a spot of light or a musical note. **Perception** is the more complex process of actively interpreting a pattern of stimuli as an organized mental image.

FIGURE 5.1 Do the two sections of this line look equally long? In fact, the center arrow is drawn precisely at the midpoint of the line. This is called the Mueller-Lyer illusion; like many other perceptual phenomena, it suggests that physical stimuli are actively interpreted by the human observer, sometimes incorrectly.

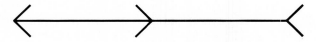

In day-to-day life, we take sensory processes for granted.

In the past, studies of sensation have been dominated by the biological paradigm; many researchers focused on the way simple stimuli affect physical structures in the sensory organs. In contrast, studies of perception have more commonly been based on a cognitive perspective, which emphasizes the active mental processes in the brain involved in interpreting patterns of stimulation. Today, it is impossible to say where sensation ends and perception begins. Some psychologists now wonder whether the field might be better off without this distinction, as almost all sensory situations involve contributions from both receptor organs and the brain. Thus the distinction between sensation and perception is best thought of not as an either/or dichotomy, but rather as a continuum.

This chapter will draw on biological, cognitive, and other perspectives as we explore the relationships between physical stimuli and the psychological sensations and perceptions they produce.

These relationships are not always as straightforward as you might expect. For example, if an electric shock doubles in physical intensity, it will feel more than 11 times stronger. This estimate comes from a precise mathematical formula that relates the psychological sensation to the actual electrical charge. Other formulas describe the relationships between the intensity of light and the sensation of brightness, between sound waves and loudness, and dozens of other sensory dimensions to the corresponding physical stimuli.

While you need not lie awake nights wondering what these formulas are, they have many practical uses. Electrical engineers who design stereo systems must understand how the physical characteristics of sound waves are related to loudness, pitch, and other sensory dimensions; and the lighting director for a play must understand the physical stimuli that are required to produce a certain psychological effect. Even food companies use these formulas in the never-ending search for the perfectly crispy cracker and the ideally spicy tomato sauce (Rice, 1978). The research area that explores these questions is called *psychophysics.*

Psychological Sensations and Physical Stimuli

Psychophysics examines the relationships between the physical attributes of stimuli (*physics*) and the psychological sensations they produce (*psycho*). The science of psychophysics may be the oldest specialty in psychology; formal experiments in this field were published several decades before Wilhelm Wundt established the first psychology laboratory in 1879.

Difference Thresholds

In 1834, physiologist Ernst Weber published several studies of the nerves that respond to muscular exertion. In one, Weber compared the sensations he felt when his finger supported two nearly identical metal weights. For example, Weber found that if he started with a metal disk weighing $14\frac{1}{2}$ ounces and then replaced it with a disk weighing $14\frac{3}{4}$ ounces, he could not tell

sensation The process of responding to a simple physical stimulus.

perception The process of actively interpreting a pattern of stimuli as an organized mental image.

psychophysics The study of the systematic relationship between the physical attributes of stimuli and the psychological sensations they produce.

them apart. But when he compared the 14½-ounce disk with another weighing 15 ounces, he was able to detect a difference between them.

Introductory psychology students who are not fans of finger weightlifting may wonder why they should care. In historical terms, Weber's study was extremely significant. Here, for the first time, a scientist looked for a systematic relationship between physical stimuli and the "subjective" world of internal sensations. Although Wilhelm Wundt is widely recognized as the world's first psychologist (see Chapter 1), some historians argue that Weber's experiments half a century earlier should be considered the first psychological research.

The type of comparison Weber invented later became a standard experimental technique in psychophysics. Researchers use the term **difference threshold** to refer to the minimum physical difference required for any two stimuli to be sensed as different from each other. Weber was the first to show that the difference threshold (which is also called the "just noticeable difference") is not an absolute quantity, but rather depends on variables like the absolute level of stimulation. Generally, the greater the level of stimulation, the greater the difference between two stimuli must be, in order for the difference to be sensed.

In the finger-weight experiment above, a difference of half an ounce produced a just noticeable difference when Weber compared weights of 14½ versus 15 ounces. But when he compared weights of 29 versus 29½ ounces, he could not tell them apart; thus, a difference of half an ounce was no longer adequate to produce a just noticeable difference. Now, he needed to go from 29 to 30 ounces before he could tell the two weights apart.

In everyday terms, your perception of difference is probably frequently based on the question: Compared to what? If you plan to buy a used car for $12,926, and the price goes up to $12,928, you will barely notice the $2 difference. But if you order a hot dog for $1.25 and are charged $3.25, the same absolute difference of $2 will be more noticeable because of the difference in proportion.

For a direct demonstration of how this principle applies to sensation, try the following test (Coren, Porac, & Ward, 1978). Take two envelopes and place one quarter in one and two quarters in the other. Hold the two envelopes by the corners, one in each hand. You should be able to feel the difference in weight. But try telling them apart under a different set of circumstances. Take a pair of shoes and place one of the envelopes in each shoe. Now hold a shoe in each hand. If you compare the weight of the two shoes, it will probably seem the same for both, despite the fact that you could detect the same absolute difference in weight when you held just the envelopes.

Weber's observations were pursued more systematically by many later researchers, who found that the difference threshold was generally proportional to the reference stimulus and that the actual value of this proportion varied from one sense to another (see Table 5.1).

By now, a great deal of practical information has been collected about the details of the relationships between physical stimuli and the sensations they produce. This information goes far beyond Weber's concept of the just noticeable difference. For example, engineers who design audio equipment rely on mathematical formulas relating perceived loudness to the amplitude of sound waves. These formulas were developed by psychological researchers

difference threshold The minimum physical difference required for any two stimuli to be sensed as different.

absolute threshold The minimum physical energy that causes a sensory system to respond.

TABLE 5.1

Some Approximate Difference Thresholds

Sensation	Difference threshold
Brightness	Two lights must differ in intensity by 8%
Pitch	Two sound waves must differ in frequency by 0.3%
Loudness	Two sound waves must differ in amplitude by 5%
Saltiness	Two solutions must differ in salt content by 8%

Source: Based on Teghtsoonian, 1971.

and have been officially accepted by the International Standards Organization (Stevens, 1962). Psychological research has also helped to determine the limits in sensitivity of each of the senses.

Absolute Thresholds

If you are sitting in the stands at a football game, you probably will not be able to hear what the players say to one another in the huddle. Some stimuli are simply too weak to be noticed. Early psychophysicists developed the concept of the **absolute threshold**, the minimum physical energy that causes a given sensory system to respond. Under ideal conditions, the human senses are extremely responsive. Table 5.2 provides one psychophysicist's everyday examples of the limits of the five major senses. These vivid analogies involve a certain amount of poetic license; in the real world, absolute thresholds are neither quite this straightforward nor quite this precise.

At first, researchers thought these thresholds would prove to be absolute. Just as your TV set will go on only if you press the power switch with a certain amount of force, so it was thought that sensory receptors went on only when they were stimulated by a particular level of physical energy.

If things were really this simple, we might expect that whenever the minimum physical energy needed to create a sensation of light in the eye was flashed, people would say they saw it. Further, a physical stimulus below the absolute threshold would never be seen. In fact, the transition is not that abrupt. When you try to spot a very dim light in the distance on a dark

TABLE 5.2

Some Approximate Absolute Thresholds

Sense modality	Absolute threshold
Light	A candle flame seen at 30 miles on a dark, clear night
Sound	The tick of a watch under quiet conditions at 20 feet
Taste	One teaspoon of sugar in two gallons of water
Smell	One drop of perfume diffused into a three-room apartment
Touch	The wing of a bee falling on the cheek from a distance of 1 cm

Note: In this table, precise psychophysical findings have been imaginatively translated into everyday terms. As the text explains, these are rough approximations.
Source: Based on Galanter, 1962, p. 96.

night, you will often find yourself unsure about whether you have seen a light or not. Similarly, when visual stimuli near the eye's lower limits of sensitivity are presented in an experiment, sometimes subjects say they see something and sometimes they do not.

There are several ways to measure absolute thresholds, and each is affected by this uncertainty in slightly different ways. In the **method of constant stimuli**, a number of stimuli of different physical intensities are presented in random order. After each trial, the subject indicates whether or not she has sensed anything. For example, in a hearing test using the method of constant stimuli, a person might listen to a series of tones of different physical intensities, such as 10 decibels, 6 decibels, 12 decibels, 14 decibels, 8 decibels, and so on; after each, she would indicate whether she had heard anything. (As explained in the section on hearing, the physical characteristic of a sound wave that is most closely related to loudness is called *sound pressure level* and is measured in decibels.)

Figure 5.2 illustrates the results of one such hypothetical test; not surprisingly, the subject's likelihood of reporting the tone gradually increases as the tone becomes louder. The S-shaped graph shown here (technically called an *ogive*) is characteristic of threshold measurements for every sensory system. For the method of constant stimuli, the absolute threshold is defined as the point at which a person senses a stimulus 50% of the time. This definition is based on convention rather than firm theoretical requirements; psychophysicists have simply agreed that this is the most sensible cutoff point. The subject in our imaginary experiment in Figure 5.2 has an auditory threshold of about 10.5 decibels for a tone of this frequency.

Other methods of measuring thresholds produce slightly different results, emphasizing the fact that these thresholds are not really absolute, and they do not reflect a fixed physical characteristic of the sensory system. Even such

FIGURE 5.2   Data from an imaginary test of the absolute threshold of hearing. This subject sometimes hears the tone at many different physical intensities; the absolute threshold is the point at which the subject senses it 50% of the time.

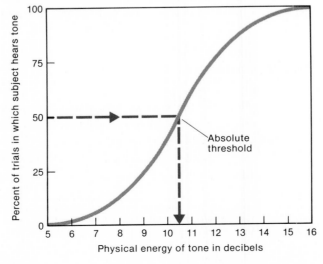

a simple task as saying whether a tone is present or absent involves a psychological decision that can be complicated by expectations, motivation, and other factors. The attempt to deal with these complications led to the development of signal-detection theory.

Signal-Detection Theory

Signal-detection theory attempts to account for both psychological and sensory factors that influence psychophysical judgments; indeed, precise mathematical procedures have been proposed to separate true sensory limits from more psychological factors.

Signal-detection theory grew out of engineers' studies of how people distinguished sensory signals from a background of random noise. (In this context, *noise* means any random disturbance of a particular process.) For example, in World War II, radar operators worked with relatively crude equipment that made it difficult to distinguish between a visual signal on a screen indicating that enemy aircraft were approaching and the random visual signals (called *noise*) caused by weather conditions or birds.

The problem of distinguishing between real and false signals can have major implications. Suppose a radar operator aboard an aircraft carrier in the Pacific saw a speck on his screen. It might have meant that a kamikaze pilot in an airplane filled with explosives was heading for his ship, planning to crash into it. Even if the operator were not entirely certain what the radar signal meant, he would pass on the information so that his own fighter planes could take off and have a closer look. In this case the price to be paid for missing the signal was extremely high; the cost of a false alarm was less serious.

But as long as we are creating a fictional problem, let's make it a bit more difficult. Suppose that the American airplanes were low on fuel. If they took off to intercept a kamikaze and found a flock of seagulls, they might not have enough fuel to stop enemy planes later. In this case, the radar operator would be more conservative. As the cost of sounding a false alarm went up, his criteria would have to change.

In less melodramatic terms, the observer in a psychophysical laboratory is faced with a similar problem. Consider a typical psychophysical experiment. On some trials a tone is sounded; on others, it is not. The subject's task is to say whether or not he heard a tone. He can make two different types of errors. False alarms occur when he says he heard a tone when in fact there was none; misses occur when he says there was no tone when in fact there was one. Signal-detection theorists have shown how the proportion of different types of errors is affected by factors such as motivation and expectations.

Table 5.3 illustrates the results from actual experiments in which subjects' expectations were manipulated by changing the likelihood of a tone's occurring on each trial. The first example in Table 5.3 shows the proportion and types of errors for a study in which a near-threshold signal was presented in 9 out of every 10 trials. In that experiment, the subject got into the habit of hearing the tone and correctly noticed its occurrence 97% of the time. However, this expectation was so strong that she often heard a tone even when there was none; the false-alarm rate was a distressing 62%. The second example

method of constant stimuli
Measuring absolute thresholds by randomly presenting subjects with stimuli of different physical intensities and asking whether they have sensed anything.

signal-detection theory Attempts to account mathematically for psychological and sensory factors that influence psychophysical judgments.

TABLE 5.3
Two Experiments in Signal Detection

Experiment 1

Faint tone is present on 9 out of every 10 trials; subject must say whether she hears a tone. Note high proportion of false alarms when signal is presented at this frequency.

		Signal Present	
		Yes	No
Subject Says Signal Present	Yes	97% correct	62% false alarms
	No	3% misses	38% correct

Experiment 2

Faint tone is present on 1 out of every 10 trials; subject must say whether she hears a tone. Note high proportion of misses under these conditions. The different error rates in experiments 1 and 2 show that expectations influence performance.

		Signal Present	
		Yes	No
Subject Says Signal Present	Yes	28% correct	4% false alarms
	No	72% misses	94% correct

Source: Galanter, 1962, p. 102.

in Table 5.3 shows that exactly the opposite occurred when a signal was presented in only 1 of every 10 trials. In that case, our psychophysical observer was nearly always right (96% of the time) when she said she heard nothing. But this mind-set was so strong that her miss rate—saying she heard nothing when the tone was really there—jumped to 72%.

Thus, expectations clearly influence the kinds of mistakes a person makes. The effects of motivation can be seen in similar experiments in which people are paid for each correct response and penalized for each error. If the penalty for false positives is high, the observer will tailor her performance to minimize them. If the penalty for false negatives is set even higher, she will work to minimize them instead. Signal-detection experiments have made it clear that you cannot eliminate error, but you can stack the deck so that one type of error is more likely to occur than another. Signal-detection theory also provides sophisticated mathematical tools for separating an observer's *sensitivity*—a true measure of the response of sense organs—from his *criterion*—the rules and guidelines he uses to decide how to label a given sensory event.

·With the development of signal-detection theory, psychophysicists have put the human being back into the equation, to take account of the cognitive processes involved in even the simplest decisions. As we go on to consider the nature of vision, hearing, and the other senses, we begin with a simpler approach by concentrating on the physical characteristics of sensory receptors. But in the final sections of this chapter, we return to the more complex world of perceptual processes influenced by motivation, expectations, and thought.

wavelength The distance from the crest of one wave to the crest of the next.

Vision

What would the world be like if the human species did not have the sense of vision? Other animals are stronger, faster, and perhaps even meaner; the success of the human species has been largely a result of its intelligence. But one can only wonder how this intelligence would have been expressed if all humans lacked the detailed knowledge of the external world provided by the visual system. Could a species without eyes build the pyramids, sail across the sea, or invent sunglasses? Of all the senses, none has been studied more intensively than sight.

Light

Each sense organ is designed to respond to a different type of physical energy. The eye, of course, responds to visible light, a particular type of electromagnetic radiation. Although physicists are still learning about the nature of light, we do know that only a few of the many types of electromagnetic radiation can be seen by the human eye.

One important physical characteristic of light is the **wavelength**—the distance from the crest of one wave of light to the crest of the next. Visible light varies from about 380 nanometers (millionths of a meter) to 760 nanometers. In contrast, X-rays are billionths of a meter long. Most of the energy that reaches the surface of the earth from the sun, however, falls within the visible spectrum. Figure 5.3 shows the portion of the spectrum to which the human eye is sensitive.

Our understanding of the visible spectrum of light dates back at least to the seventeenth century. In the summer of 1666, Sir Isaac Newton went

FIGURE 5.3 The human eye is sensitive to a small portion of the spectrum of electromagnetic radiation. Color perception is partly dependent on the wavelength of light within this range.

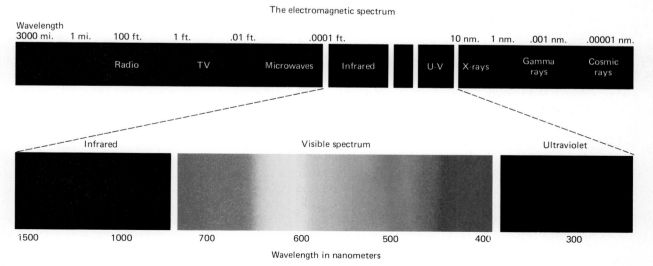

The electromagnetic spectrum

to Cambridge, England, to avoid an outbreak of the plague in London. He passed the next few months performing a series of elegant experiments that laid the foundation for modern theories of color vision. Newton cut a hole in a window shutter and directed a beam of sunlight through a triangular piece of glass called a *prism,* which separates white light into a spectrum of colors based on their wavelengths. A similar phenomenon occurs naturally when sunlight is bent by the atmosphere to produce a rainbow. Most of the time, however, psychological sensations of color are produced by more complex processes, as described later in this chapter.

The Structure of the Eye

Figure 5.4 illustrates the structure of the human eye. The outer coating of the eye is called the **sclera**, a tough covering that protects the delicate structures within. Near the front of the eye, this protective layer forms the **cornea**, the curved transparent window that helps focus light as it enters the eye. The most frequently noticed physical structure in the eye is the **iris**, a circular arrangement of muscular cells that controls the diameter of the opening that admits light. The color of the iris has no functional significance in vision.

The **pupil**, which appears black, is a hole in the center of the iris. In dim light, the iris muscles contract and increase the diameter of this hole (to about 8 millimeters) to let in more light; in bright light, the iris can decrease the diameter (to about 2 millimeters) so that less light enters. Thus, the area of the opening that admits light is about 16 times greater at the maximum opening than at the minimum.

The diameter of the pupil also changes in response to emotional arousal. It is said that Turkish rug merchants have taken advantage of this fact for centuries. When customers' pupils dilate as they look at a rug, the merchants read this as a covert sign of interest and bargain accordingly. Experienced rug buyers may wear sunglasses to hide the testimony of what researcher Eckhard Hess (1975) calls "the telltale eye." This shows that our sensory systems are influenced by other factors in addition to physical stimuli.

After light passes through the cornea and the pupil, it is filtered through a structure called the **lens**, a body of tissue that changes its shape to focus light on the retina at the back of the eye. Normally the lens is slightly flattened and is thus ideally shaped for looking at objects at a distance. But when a person looks at a stimulus near the eye, the lens assumes a more rounded shape, which brings light rays from the object into sharper focus on the retina.

If the lens does not respond properly, visual defects result. As people grow older, the lens often becomes less flexible, thus less able to focus properly. Some people become nearsighted; they can see objects nearby but may need corrective lenses to watch TV or drive, activities that require focusing on faraway objects. Others develop the opposite problem of farsightedness; they may need glasses to read or sew, because of focusing difficulties with stimuli close to the eyes. These visual problems may also result from an eyeball that is too long or too short for proper focusing. Figure 5.5 illustrates the use of corrective lenses for nearsightedness and farsightedness.

sclera   The tough outer covering that protects the delicate structures within the eye.

cornea   The curved transparent window that helps focus light as it enters the eye.

iris   A circular arrangement of muscular cells that controls the diameter of the opening that admits light into the eye.

pupil   A hole, which appears black, in the center of the iris.

lens   A body of tissue that changes its shape to focus light on the retina.

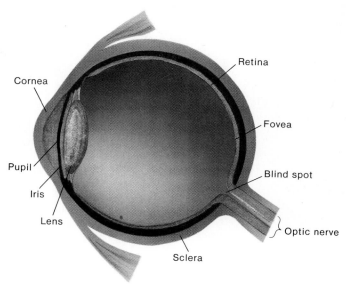

FIGURE 5.4 Major structures of the human eye.

FIGURE 5.5 When objects are not focused properly on the lens, nearsightedness or farsightedness results. Either can be corrected with lenses that refocus the image.

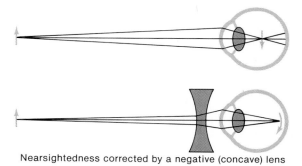

Nearsightedness corrected by a negative (concave) lens

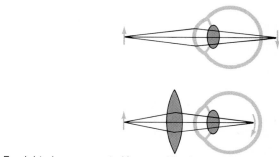

Farsightedness corrected by a positive (convex) lens

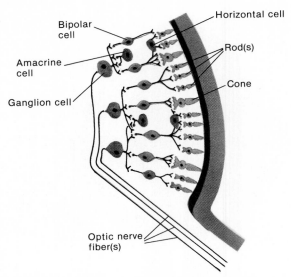

FIGURE 5.6 The layers of the retina. When light stimulates the rods and cones, signals travel through the bipolar cells to the ganglion cells, whose axons form the optic nerve. Integration is accomplished by horizontal cells, which connect rods and cones, and amacrine cells, which connect ganglion cells.

The **retina** is a light-sensitive surface at the back of the eye. It includes two types of receptor cells that respond to light energy by firing electrical impulses in the nervous system. These receptor cells are named on the basis of their shape. **Rods** are rod-shaped with cylindrical tips, and **cones** have cone-shaped tips. Rods and cones are connected to bipolar cells, the next level of the nervous system that processes visual information (see Figure 5.6). Since several rods or cones are connected to a single bipolar cell in some parts of the retina, visual information is transformed at each step of its journey to visual centers in the occipital lobe of the brain.

The 6.5 million cones in the eye are responsible for color vision. The 125 million rods in the eye are more responsive than cones in dim light, but they can only distinguish black, white, and various shades of gray. This accounts for the black-and-white appearance of visual images seen in the dim light of night.

When you want to see an object clearly in good light, you look directly at it. This causes an image of the object to be projected onto the **fovea**, a slight depression at the center of the retina. The fovea contains only cones and is more sensitive to fine visual detail than any other part of the retina. The cones are packed so tightly at the fovea that their conical tips are flattened to look like rods. But other sources of physiological evidence make it clear that not a single rod is to be found in this central portion of the retina.

The extreme visual acuity of the fovea is based on several factors, including the density of the cones and the fact that the blood vessels and nerve cells

retina A light-sensitive surface at the back of the eye.

rods Receptor cells primarily responsible for night vision.

cones Receptor cells responsible for color vision and sensitive to fine visual detail.

fovea A slight depression at the center of the retina that consists entirely of cones and is very sensitive to fine visual detail.

FIGURE 5.7 To demonstrate the blind spot, close your right eye, stare at the upper X, and move the book back and forth about 12 inches from your eye until the circle disappears. Now repeat with the lower X; at the same distance, the break in the bottom line will fall in the blind spot, and the line will appear continuous. This shows how the brain fills in information missing as a result of the blind spot.

that cover the rest of the retina are absent here. A visual image is projected more directly on the receptor cells of the fovea than on other portions of the retina. Also, each of the cones in the fovea is connected to a separate bipolar cell, allowing highly detailed information to be passed on for further processing. Outside the fovea, several rods or cones may connect to one bipolar cell, and the messages passed on represent a summary of their activity.

Not too far from the fovea is an area of the retina called the **blind spot**. The blind spot has no receptor cells, because nerve fibers are gathered here to form the **optic nerve**, which transmits information from the retina to the brain. Under normal conditions, you do not notice the blind spot, because the brain fills in this missing information, based on what is seen by both eyes as they constantly scan the visual field. But Figure 5.7 shows how easy it is to demonstrate that each of us does indeed have a blind spot.

The fact that there are only cones in the fovea makes it more sensitive under normal lighting conditions but insensitive at night. Astronomers and navigators know that if you look directly at a faint pinpoint of light at night, it seems to disappear. Thus, to see a tiny star in the distance, it is best to look slightly off to the side so that its image will be registered on the rods on the outside of the fovea.

Vision and the Brain

The process of encoding visual stimuli involves a large number of cells in the eye and brain. When a spot of light stimulates the retina, it causes an electrochemical response in a rod or cone. As noted previously, the rods and cones are connected to the bipolar cells, and the bipolar cells are connected to the retina's ganglion cells. These connections across cells allow several levels of information exchange to occur within the retina. The impulses produced by the ganglion cells are then further analyzed, transformed, and transmitted through a number of structures in the brain.

In 1981, David Hubel and Thorsten Weisel were awarded a Nobel Prize

blind spot An area in the retina near the fovea that has no receptor cells because nerve cells are gathered here to form the optic nerve.

optic nerve The structure that transmits information from the retina to the brain.

for their research tracing this pathway of visual information from eye to brain. Much of their work used the physiological technique of **single-cell recording**, which permits the recording of the electrical activity of one neuron at a time. This procedure requires brain surgery in which several very fine wires, called *microelectrodes,* are inserted into the visual cortex of laboratory animals, typically cats. In the Hubel and Weisel (1979) study, these research subjects then looked at a screen while the investigators monitored the electrical activity of one neuron at a time. The stimulus on the screen could be varied in size, shape, location, and so on to show how each cell in the visual cortex responded to different types of stimuli.

Hubel and Weisel, along with many other researchers, found that different cells in the brain respond to different sorts of stimuli. While cells in the retina often respond when the eye is stimulated by large or diffuse spots of light, neurons in higher brain centers typically respond only when light falls on a particular area on the retina or in a certain pattern.

Several decades of single-cell recordings in the visual system gradually have revealed that brain structures are organized in a hierarchy. Cells in the retina respond to the simplest classes of stimuli; cells deeper in the brain respond to more complex categories. Cells further along in the chain are called **feature detectors**, because they fire when they detect certain *features,* or patterns of stimulation. Specifically, Hubel and Weisel identified three different types of feature detectors: *simple cells, complex cells,* and *hypercomplex cells.*

In their experiments, Hubel and Weisel demonstrated that **simple cells** fire an electrical impulse when a straight-line stimulus is located in a particular place and points in a specific direction. Thus, when an animal stares at a screen, one simple cell might respond only when a horizontal line appears in the middle of the screen, while a second simple cell will respond only to a horizontal line slightly to the left of that area, and a third may respond only to a line at a 45° angle in this same area.

Simple cells feed their information to **complex cells**, which respond primarily on the basis of the line's orientation and are not as sensitive to the position on the retina. Whereas a simple cell fires for a specific vertical line, a complex cell responds to a more general category of all vertical lines. Thus, the first two simple cells we mentioned responded to horizontal lines; they might both be connected to a complex cell which would fire whenever either or both of the simple cells did.

Information from complex cells is then analyzed at a still higher level of abstraction by **hypercomplex cells**, which respond to lines only if they have the proper orientation and a particular length and width. Like the complex cells, hypercomplex cells respond regardless of the line's location on the retina.

Although virtually all researchers agree that Hubel and Weisel's work was crucial in identifying feature detectors, there is some controversy about the exact features to which these cells actually respond. For our purposes, this issue is far less important than the basic conclusion one can draw from Hubel and Weisel's work: Visual processing in the brain proceeds hierarchically, with cells later in the chain responding to increasingly complex stimuli. Thus, there is no miniature replica of a stimulus transmitted from eye to brain.

single-cell recording A technique for recording the electrical activity of one neuron at a time.

feature detectors Cells in the retina that fire when they detect certain features or patterns of stimulation.

simple cells Feature detectors that fire an electrical impulse when a straight-line stimulus is located in a particular place and points in a specific direction.

complex cells Feature detectors that receive information from simple cells and respond to a more general category of lines.

hypercomplex cells Feature detectors that receive information from complex cells and analyze it at a still higher level of abstraction.

Rather, neurons identify patterns on the basis of certain crucial features of a stimulus. Like each of the other senses, the eye transmits information in a code of its own.

Dark Adaptation

As mentioned before, visual processing begins in the retina with the firing of the receptor cells—the rods and cones. The sensitivity of these receptor cells changes in relation to the amount of light available. For example, the sensitivity of the retina gradually increases after a period in the dark, a phenomenon called **dark adaptation**. If you walk into a darkened movie theater from a well-lit lobby, your eyes will be so insensitive that you will have trouble seeing an empty seat. But if you wait a few minutes in the back of the theater, your eyes will adapt to the dark and you will be able to see quite well.

The change in sensitivity is dramatic; after 30 minutes in the dark, the retina may become 100,000 times more sensitive to light. In general, for the first 5 to 10 minutes in the dark, the cones become somewhat more sensitive. The rods adapt to the dark more slowly, reaching peak function only after 30 minutes or so. After the process of dark adaptation is complete, a weak stimulus in a dark environment may be detected only by the rods and therefore seems black and white.

Interestingly, the rods are less sensitive than the cones to certain extremes of red light. As a result, one can speed up the process of dark adaptation by limiting general illumination to long wavelengths. For example, during World War II, pilots often prepared for night missions by wearing red goggles that allowed only long-wave light to reach the retina. The fact that the rods were relatively insensitive to this red light allowed them to begin the process of dark adaptation. When the pilots took off, they removed the goggles, and the rods more quickly reached their maximum sensitivity for night vision.

Color Vision

Few people would choose to watch a TV program in black and white if a color version were just as cheap and convenient. A world without green grass, blue skies, and lavender tuxedos would seem harsh, drab, and, well, colorless.

Attempts to count the number of different colors that can be distinguished by the human eye have proved to be surprisingly complex. Psychophysicists have identified three separate dimensions that contribute to the psychological sensation of color: *hue,* which corresponds roughly to color names, such as blue or red; *saturation,* the apparent purity of the color, as in fire-engine red versus a duller grayish red; and *brightness,* how dark or light a color is. Various three-dimensional color solids have been formed to provide a concrete feeling for the way hue, saturation, and brightness define color (see Figure 5.8). The human eye can probably distinguish about 7.5 million different colors (Nickerson & Newhall, 1943), but much remains to be learned about the precise way in which the visual system accomplishes this remarkable feat.

dark adaptation The process by which the sensitivity of the retina gradually increases after a period in the dark.

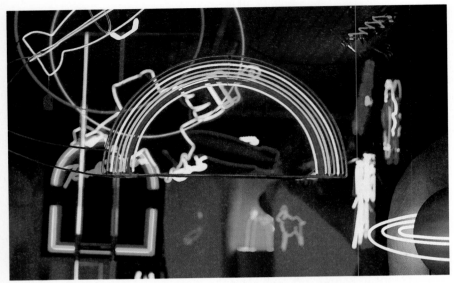

Psychological sensations of color can be broken down into several basic dimensions.

FIGURE 5.8 The color solid displays three separate dimensions involved in the perception of color: hue varies along the circumference; saturation, along the radius; and brightness, along the vertical axis. Thus, a single vertical slice shows several possible saturations and brightnesses for a single hue.

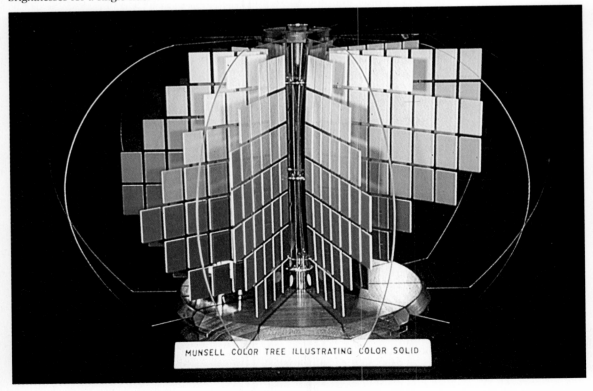

MUNSELL COLOR TREE ILLUSTRATING COLOR SOLID

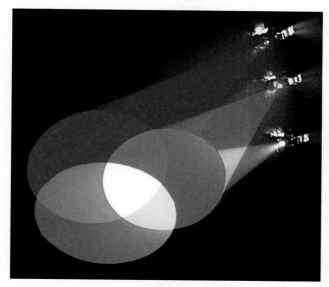

FIGURE 5.9   The effects of color mixture differ for lights and pigments. The term *additive color mixture* refers to the colors produced by mixing lights (shown on the left). Mixture of two colors produces the complement of the third, as shown in the triangular sections where the lights overlap. The term *subtractive color mixture* refers to the colors produced by mixing pigments, or to light that passes through overlapping filters (shown on the right). While additive mixtures always produce the same colors, subtractive mixtures are less predictable and may vary for different filters.

THEORIES OF COLOR VISION

Soon after Sir Isaac Newton discovered that a prism would separate a beam of sunlight into several bands of color, he used a second prism to recombine this artificial rainbow back into a single beam of white light. Newton went on to explore the basic laws of color mixture by blocking part of the spectrum before recombining the beam and seeing how various combinations produced different colors.

In 1802, Thomas Young showed that he could produce any color from the spectrum by mixing only three different colors of light: red, blue, and green. (It is important to note that Young's laws of color mixture apply only to light. The complications introduced by mixing paints or pigments are described in Figure 5.9.) Young concluded that there were three basic receptors in the retina, one for each of these primary colors. According to this theory, a sensation of yellow would be produced by simultaneously stimulating the red and the green receptors, for example, and white would result from the simultaneous stimulation of the red, green, and blue receptors. This view has come to be known as the **trichromatic theory** of color vision, from the Greek word for "three colors."

In the more than 180 years since, Young's conclusions have been challenged many times but never completely rejected. The major theoretical alternative to the trichromatic theory was proposed by Edward Hering in 1870; **opponent-processes theory** holds that each of the three separate systems in

trichromatic theory   The theory that there are separate receptors in the retina for red, blue, and green.

opponent-processes theory   The theory that there are three systems for color vision, each responding to two colors.

the retina responds not to one color but to two. This theory was proposed partly to explain certain types of color blindness, such as the fact that some people have trouble perceiving red and green but can see yellow. Since the trichromatic theory claims that yellow is a mixture of red and green, it cannot easily explain this deficit.

Also, the trichromatic theory does not provide an explanation for certain **afterimages**, sensory impressions that remain after a stimulus is taken away. One example appears in Figure 5.10; if you stare at this yellow, green, and black version of the American flag for about a minute in good light and then look at a piece of white paper, you should see the old familiar red, white, and blue version. A green image produces a red afterimage; a yellow stimulus produces a blue afterimage. The opponent-processes theory of color vision claims that there are three different visual systems that respond to red-green, blue-yellow, and black-white. The afterimages are then said to result from a kind of rebound effect—when a green stimulus stimulates the red-green system and is then withdrawn, the red portion of the system reacts.

Recent physiological recordings have shown that both the trichromatic and the opponent-processes theories are true for different portions of the visual system. Three different types of light-sensitive pigments have been identified in the cones of the human eye; the first responds primarily to blue light, the second to green, and the third to yellowish and red light. This supports the trichromatic theory. But electrical recordings from the retinal ganglion cells and other visual cells deep in the brain support the opponent-

FIGURE 5.10 Stare at the center of this oddly colored flag for about a minute and then look quickly at a white surface. You should see a negative afterimage of the familiar red, white, and blue American flag.

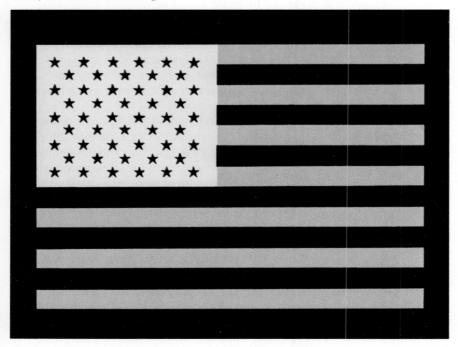

processes theory. These cells seem to code opposing colors, for example, firing rapidly when stimulated by long-wave (red) light and not firing when stimulated by short-wave (green) light. Thus, color vision consists of at least two stages. In the first stage, cones in the eye respond to three different colors. In the second stage, cells deep in the brain fire either more or less frequently, depending on the opponent pairs of colors. However, even this account is not the entire story.

Another phenomenon that emphasizes the complexity of color vision was accidentally discovered by Edwin Land (1959) when he tried to produce a high-quality instant color film for his invention, the Polaroid camera. In one experiment, Land superimposed the images of three color slides of the same scene, one taken through a red filter, one through a blue filter, and one through a green filter. When these three slides were simultaneously projected on the same screen, the colors of the original scene were reasonably well produced, as expected. But one day, the light from the blue projector was accidentally eliminated; at first neither Land nor his assistant was aware that the colors had changed, although in fact they had.

Land went on to show that the color of many natural scenes can be reproduced when photographed through only two filters (red and green) instead of the three required by the trichromatic theory of color vision. If a bowl of fruit is photographed through red and green filters, bananas will look reasonably yellow; apples, red; and oranges, orange. But images of a color test chart (like the one you might get in a paint store) photographed in the same way will not look like the original. According to Land, this experiment suggests that color perception is influenced by memory and expectations; the banana in the unusual two-filter photograph looked yellow partly because everyone knows that bananas are yellow. If this explanation holds up, it will demonstrate that an experience of color depends not just on the physical intensity and wavelengths of light nor just on photochemical changes in the retina but on a complex series of events in the brain.

COLOR BLINDNESS

The fact that some people have trouble telling the difference between colors was not widely known until the late eighteenth century. Around that time, an English chemist named John Dalton reported that he had trouble recognizing certain substances by their color. (The French word for color blindness is *daltonisme*.)

The fact that color blindness was not widely noticed in ancient times suggests that the visual defect is usually rather subtle—few people are actually blind to all color differences. The most common problem involves an inability to distinguish between red and green. Like other forms of color blindness, this deficiency has been found far more frequently among men than women.

There are a few people who are truly color-blind and see the entire world in blacks, whites, and grays. Several sources of evidence suggest that these people have few functional cones in the retina; their vision is based almost entirely on rods. People who suffer from this rare affliction are often forced to wear dark glasses because the rods are overstimulated by normal daylight.

afterimages The sensory impressions that remain after a stimulus is taken away.

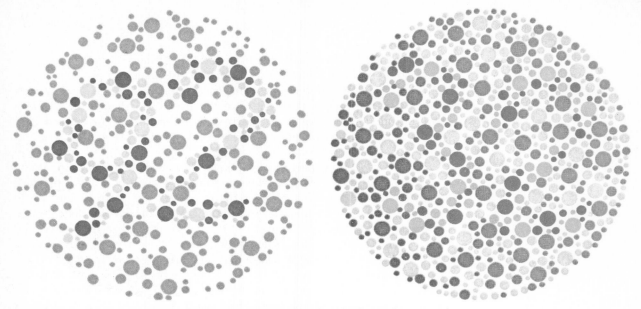

FIGURE 5.11 Two items from a 14-item test for red-green color blindness. The numerals in each plate can be distinguished from the background only by their colors. Red-green color blindness would be diagnosed if a person failed to distinguish 5 of the 14 items in the test. (The correct answers to the items here are 92 and 32.)

There are at least nine different types of color blindness, ranging from these severe deficits to various forms of color weakness, borderline problems in distinguishing reds from greens or yellows from blues. Persons who are color-blind may be unaware of this visual defect without taking special tests that force them to make fine distinctions between specific colors. One such test appears in Figure 5.11.

Hearing

Superficially, Beethoven's Fifth Symphony may appear to have little in common with the sound of an automobile screeching to a halt or the loud whine of a 3-year-old who wants another chocolate peanut butter cup. But our ability to sense each of these stimuli depends on the physiological responses of the auditory system to the mechanical energy of sound waves.

Sound Waves

Perhaps the simplest way to think of a sound wave is to imagine what happens when one strikes a tuning fork (see Figure 5.12). As the fork vibrates, it creates waves of sound as air molecules are compressed by each vibration. In general terms, the frequency of the vibration (measured in *hertz*, abbreviated Hz—the number of times per second that it vibrates; named after German physicist Heinrich Hertz) determines the **pitch** of the sound, the psychological sensation that a sound is high (for example, a note played on a piccolo) or low. Although there are some exceptions and complicating factors, high-frequency sounds are generally perceived as high in pitch. Similarly, **loudness**, the psychological dimension corresponding to the intensity of a sound, is

pitch The psychological sensation that a sound is high or low, primarily determined by the frequency of the vibrations composing a sound wave.

loudness The psychological dimension corresponding to the intensity of a sound, primarily determined by the amplitude of sound waves.

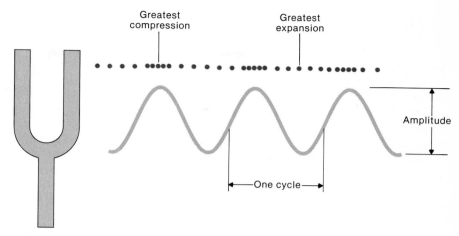

Greatest compression

Greatest expansion

Amplitude

One cycle

FIGURE 5.12 If you strike a tuning fork, its vibrations will alternately compress and expand the surrounding air, creating a sound wave.

most highly related to the amplitude, or physical height, of a sound but also depends on other factors.

Generally, **sound** can be defined as a wave motion that pulses through a material medium and is generated by physical vibrations. The "material medium" that ordinarily conducts sound waves is air. The important role air plays in conducting sound waves was first demonstrated in the seventeenth century, when physicists placed a ringing bell inside a jar and pumped out the air to create a vacuum. The sound of the ringing gradually got weaker as the air was pumped out, demonstrating that air was needed to conduct the sound waves.

Other researchers from this period estimated the speed of sound by precisely measuring the distance sound could travel in a given time period. For example, one of Galileo's students measured the time it took for an echo to reach him when he shouted at a wall from various distances. Specifically, when he stood precisely 519 feet from a wall and took precisely one second to shout the phrase "Benedicam Dominum," the echo began just as he finished shouting. This led him to estimate that the sound wave had traveled 1,018 feet in that second: 519 feet to the wall, and 519 feet back (Boring, 1942).

This estimate is quite close to modern calculations. We now know that the speed of sound varies with air temperature; at 15°C, sound travels at about 1,100 feet per second. Sound waves travel about four times faster under water and even faster than that through many solid materials (Geldard, 1972, p. 155).

FREQUENCY AND PITCH

In general terms, humans can hear sounds in the range from 20 Hz to 20,000 Hz. Animals such as cats, dogs, and rats sometimes seem terrified by police sirens because these animals are sensitive to much higher frequencies.

One of the first to demonstrate the wider range of animal hearing was Sir Francis Galton, the English researcher who was involved in the development

sound A wave motion that pulsates through a material medium and is generated by physical vibrations.

of IQ tests and genetic research (see Chapter 13). He developed a special whistle that produced sounds ranging from about 6,500 Hz to 84,000 Hz and carried it around wherever he went. Although Galton (1883) later admitted, "My experiments on insect hearing have been failures," he also reported that his impromptu studies of animals had greater success: "I have walked through the streets, and made nearly all the little dogs turn around" (p. 40).

Sound waves with higher frequencies are generally perceived as being higher in pitch. However, slight changes in the intensity of a pure tone of a single frequency may be perceived as changes in pitch rather than loudness. (A similar phenomenon is also found for other senses; increasing the brightness of a visual stimulus may change its perceived color slightly, even when wavelength is held constant.) In the real world of clashes, bangs, and country and western music, pure tones of only one frequency rarely occur. Even one key on a piano produces a complex tone characterized by one dominant frequency combined with many other sound-wave components.

AMPLITUDE AND LOUDNESS

The physical intensity of sound waves is usually expressed in terms of *decibels,* a unit of measurement developed by telephone researchers and named after Alexander Graham Bell. According to one widely used decibel scale, 0 decibels is the threshold of hearing for the average young adult. Our perception of loudness is influenced by frequency as well as intensity. Very low and very high tones must be more intense to be heard than tones in the middle of the frequency range. Thus, because the human ear is more sensitive to some frequencies than to others, the actual physical intensity of the zero point varies according to frequency. Figure 5.13 shows the physical intensity of some common sounds as measured on this scale. Obviously, sounds get louder as the number of decibels increases.

Under ideal conditions, the ear, like the eye, is about as sensitive as it

At the Bronx Zoo, children are given an opportunity to hear auditory signals roughly as a mouse would, by wearing these special ears.

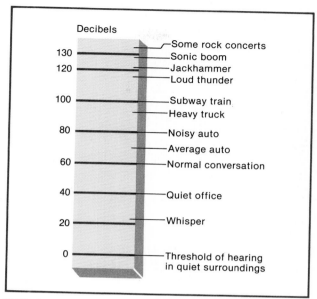

FIGURE 5.13 The decibel scale showing approximate values for familiar sounds.

possibly can be. If the eardrum were any more sensitive, we might sometimes hear the sound of blood passing through vessels in the ear (Green, 1976).

The Structure of the Ear

When most of us think of the auditory system (see Figure 5.14), we picture the external structures on either side of the head that hold up eyeglasses. In functional terms, these two folds of skin and cartilage are among the least interesting elements of the auditory system. About the only useful thing that you can do with this structure is point it in a certain direction to make a sound seem louder; the external ear is merely a funnel that transmits the vibrations of sound waves to the auditory canal. Sound waves travel from the external ear to the **eardrum** (also known as the *tympanic membrane*) via the **auditory canal**, a tube about 7 millimeters in diameter and 24 millimeters long. If the auditory canal is blocked by wax accumulations or bony growths, hearing deficits result.

The eardrum is comparable in function to the diaphragm of a microphone; it vibrates in response to sound waves. The vibrations of the eardrum are transmitted through three tiny bones in the middle ear to another membrane called the **oval window.** The names of these three bones roughly describe their appearance: The *hammer* is connected to the eardrum and vibrates with it; sound waves are then conducted to the *anvil,* which transmits these vibrations to the *stirrup* and then to the oval window. (These bones are also referred to by their original Latin names, *malleus, incus,* and *stapes.*) These bones form a system of mechanical rods and levers that alters the vibrations somewhat but accurately transmits the original message and forms the basis of normal hearing.

eardrum A tissue in the ear that vibrates in response to sound waves.

auditory canal A tube that carries sound waves from the external ear to the eardrum.

oval window A part of the cochlea that transmits sound waves from the middle ear to the basilar membrane by displacing the cochlear fluid.

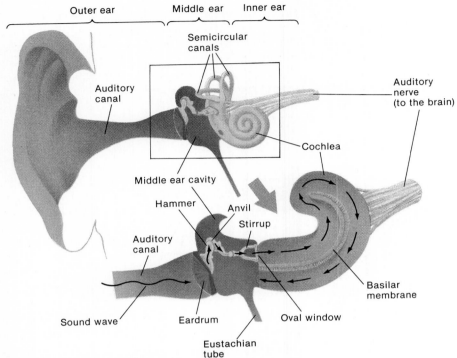

FIGURE 5.14 Major structures of the human ear.

This route of direct mechanical transmission from the eardrum to the inner ear is not the only way we hear. Even if the auditory canal is completely blocked, sound waves vibrate the entire skull and are thus transmitted to the fluids of the inner ear. This is a very inefficient route, but it does contribute to normal hearing.

If you have ever heard a tape recording of your own voice, you were probably disappointed enough to ask, "Do I really sound like that?" That is because the vibrations of the voice box are transmitted not just through air to the eardrum but also through the jawbone to the inner ear. This bone conduction route adds another dimension to the sound of the voice: low-frequency components that make the voice sound fuller are especially prominent. As a result, your own voice sounds richer to you than to anyone else.

Hearing tests also take advantage of this alternative kind of hearing to diagnose certain auditory problems. In bone conduction hearing tests, a vibrator is placed directly against a person's skull. Some people's auditory thresholds are normal when measured in this way, but they have trouble hearing through headphones. This implies that their auditory canal is blocked.

Several other ear structures are not primarily concerned with hearing. The **semicircular canals** help regulate the sense of balance and will be described later in this chapter. The **eustachian tube** runs from the middle ear cavity to the throat and is designed to equalize pressure on both sides of the eardrum. When the eustachian tube is blocked during a head cold, the eardrum may bulge or retract painfully as atmospheric pressure changes.

semicircular canals A portion of the inner ear that helps regulate the sense of balance.

eustachian tube A tube from the middle ear cavity to the throat; designed to equalize pressure on both sides of the eardrum.

As Figure 5.14 suggests, the cochlea is the major auditory portion of the inner ear. The **cochlea** is a tube 35 millimeters long, coiled about $2\frac{1}{2}$ times and resembling a snail shell. The walls of this tube are made of the hardest bone in the body. Sound waves are usually transmitted to the oval window of the cochlea through the stirrup bone. These vibrations move the fluid in the cochlea; this displaces the **basilar membrane**, which then translates these physical vibrations into a pattern of electrical activity in the nervous system. A number of different theories have been proposed to explain the precise details of this and other processes involved in hearing.

Theories of Hearing

The nineteenth-century German physiologist Herman von Helmholtz was the first to suggest that vibrations of the basilar membrane are responsible for sensations of sound, and he also proposed the first explanation of how this occurs. Helmholtz believed that the basilar membrane contained fibers that were activated much like the strings of a piano. In the simplest terms, high sounds caused the short fibers to vibrate and low sounds affected the longer ones. This became known as the **place theory of hearing**, because it suggests that different sounds activate different places on the basilar membrane. Other theorists later proposed an alternative. According to the **frequency theory of hearing**, the basilar membrane acts like the diaphragm of a microphone or a telephone; it vibrates as a whole in response to sound stimulation. According to this view, differences in the frequency of sound waves are directly coded by changes in the frequency of electrical firing in the auditory nerve.

Much of what we now know about the relative merits of these two theories is based on the work of Georg von Békésy. In one series of studies, Békésy drilled tiny holes in the cochleas of animals and human cadavers. He filled each cavity with a salt solution containing aluminun and coal particles so that he could use a microscope to observe movements of the basilar membrane. Békésy found that at very low frequencies (roughly, under 150 Hz) all portions of the basilar membrane respond at once, supporting the frequency theory. Higher frequencies, however, seemed to produce characteristic waves of basilar-membrane motion that affected some areas more than others, supporting the place theory.

Thus, just as physiological studies of color vision revealed that several processes were involved, studies of hearing have revealed that different aspects of sound are coded in different ways. Much remains to be learned about these and other processes involved in hearing the sound of a heartbeat or the voice of Bruce Springsteen.

The Other Senses

At least since Aristotle, many people have spoken of five major senses: vision, hearing, taste, smell, and touch. Psychologists accept the first four but expand the fifth, touch, to include four separate skin senses (pressure, warmth, cold, and pain) and two internal senses (balance and muscle movement).

cochlea   The major auditory portion of the inner ear.

basilar membrane   A membrane that translates physical vibrations in the ear into a pattern of electrical activity in the nervous system.

place theory of hearing   The theory that sounds of different frequencies activate different places on the basilar membrane.

frequency theory of hearing   The theory that the basilar membrane vibrates as a whole in response to sound stimulation.

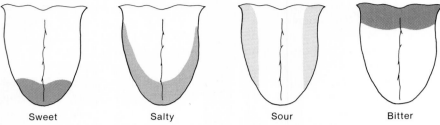

FIGURE 5.15 The tongue's areas of maximum sensitivity to four basic tastes.

Taste

A gourmet's delight in savoring veal piccata or an anchovy pizza is only partly based on the sense of taste. As anyone who has ever had a cold knows, the sense of smell is essential for appreciating a fine meal. Further, the temperature of food, its texture, and its physical appearance all contribute to the joy of eating. The actual sense of taste is rather limited, consisting of only four basic sensations: sweet, salty, sour, and bitter.

Taste buds contain the receptor cells responsible for taste sensation. As Figure 5.15 indicates, different areas of the tongue are particularly sensitive to different tastes. The tip of the tongue is most sensitive to sweet and salty tastes, for example, and the rear, to bitter. Other taste buds are located on the cheeks, lips, tonsils, and elsewhere throughout the mouth, but these areas are far less sensitive than the surface of the tongue.

Taste sensations can also be produced by some rather odd stimuli. Electrical stimulation of certain taste buds can produce either sour or soapy tastes, depending on the direction in which the current flows. Injections of certain drugs can produce sweet or bitter tastes. These demonstrations remind us that the inner world of experience does not necessarily mirror external stimulation; sensations result from electrical and chemical events in the nervous system.

There are wide variations in taste sensitivity; some of us may be "taste-blind" for specific substances. This phenomenon was discovered in 1931, when two chemists in the Du Pont laboratories accidentally spilled a substance called PTC (phenyl thiocarbamide). One chemist noted that it gave the air a bitter taste, while another noticed nothing. Further investigation revealed that thresholds to PTC vary widely; everyone can taste it sooner or later, but some people only notice high concentrations. The fact that most people do not know whether or not they are taste-blind again calls attention to the modest role of taste sensations in human affairs.

Smell

For many animals, smell plays a crucial role in locating food, enemies, and mates. Dogs, rats, and other animals have long snouts to help them follow scents on the ground. Their sense of smell is far more developed than ours; it is said that a bloodhound can track a human's scent for days, or even weeks, after the person has walked along a certain path. As primates evolved

taste buds Structures in the tongue that contain the receptor cells responsible for taste sensation.

to swing from trees, vision became more important for survival, and smell less so. In lower animals who still rely heavily on the sense of smell, the olfactory structures occupy a large proportion of the brain. In monkeys, apes, and humans, these structures are relatively reduced in size.

In insects, the smell of chemicals called **pheromones** can elicit sexual and other behavior patterns. These patterns are primitive and irresistible; if something smells like a female silkworm moth, a male silkworm will try to mate with it, even if it's only a piece of paper doused with a female silkworm pheromone called bombykol.

This kind of automatic and unthinking reaction does not occur in higher animals, but they too may respond to the odor of species-specific pheromones. A female dog in heat secretes a pheromone that powerfully attracts any male dog that smells it. Monkeys have also been found to secrete substances that seem to play a role in sexual attraction. Some studies have even raised the possibility that humans, too, secrete sexual pheromones, although the evidence to date is not conclusive (Hassett, 1978).

There are many less esoteric examples of human reliance on this forgotten sense. Many blind people, including Helen Keller, have claimed that they were able to identify friends and acquaintances by their odors. Recent experiments have shown that people who are married can identify their spouses' clothes by their odors, and parents can similarly identify the clothes of their children (Porter & Moore, 1982). Interestingly, nineteenth-century doctors sometimes diagnosed disease by the odor of their patients; yellow fever produced a butcher-shop smell, the plague produced a smell like apples, and typhoid patients smelled like freshly baked bread (Winter, 1976).

Olfactory receptor cells are located inside the top of each nasal cavity. They are stimulated by substances that are suspended in gases. Although there are many theories about how smells are sensed by the nervous system, little is certain. Attempts to categorize odors into nine basic groups (including categories of smells such as coffee, garlic, vanilla, and bed bugs), six basic groups (flowery, fruity, foul, burnt, spicy, and resinous), or four basic groups (fragrant, acid, burnt, and "goaty") all have problems accounting for some olfactory phenomena.

The Skin Senses

The actual number of different types of sensations the skin can respond to has been a matter of controversy for centuries. The best evidence now available suggests that there are four separate skin senses: pressure, warmth, cold, and pain.

Although we usually think of the skin as one type of body tissue, in fact its appearance and structure vary widely. The sole of the foot may be tough and hardened, while the skin on the inside of the arm is soft and sensitive; the skin on the elbow is stretched tight, while around some stomachs it is considerably looser; the back of the hand is covered with hair, while the palm is usually hairless. Similarly, the sensitivity of the skin to pressure— a sensation usually caused by pushing on the skin—varies from one site to another. Areas like the lips and tips of the fingers are extremely sensitive to pressure, while the kneecap, abdomen, and chest are relatively unresponsive.

pheromones In insects, smells that elicit sexual and other behavior patterns.

When the sensitivity of the skin is mapped by applying a small stimulus to one point after another, some points are found to be responsive to cold stimuli, while others are sensitive to warmth and not to cold. This is the major source of evidence for the claim that cold and warmth are separate sensations.

Paradoxically, when both warmth and cold receptors are stimulated at the same time, people experience a stinging sensation of intense heat. This can be demonstrated with a heat grill consisting of two sets of parallel pipes. If cold water is run through both pipes, they feel cold. If warm water runs through both, they feel warm. But if cold water runs through one pipe and warm water through the other, a vivid sensation of heat is produced. A person placing an arm firmly against the grill may have a hard time holding it there, even if intellectually aware that the intense heat is only an illusion.

The most complex of the skin senses is pain. Although masochists and other connoisseurs of pain can distinguish many different types—including burning pain, cutting pain, stabbing pain, and throbbing pain—all these sensations are generally considered to be variations on a single sense. And, at the risk of sounding sadistic, it is important to remember the vital function performed by pain as a signal to the brain of injury or impending injury. Individuals with spinal-cord injuries or other conditions interfering with their sense of pain are at constant risk of serious injury from excessive heat, broken glass, and other environmental hazards.

In a delightful book titled *The Puzzle of Pain,* Ronald Melzack (1973) argues that "pain perception . . . cannot be defined simply in terms of particular kinds of stimuli. Rather, it is a highly personal experience, depending on cultural learning, the meaning of the situation, and other factors that are unique to each individual" (p. 22). As one example, Melzack cites a religious ceremony practiced in remote parts of India in which a man blesses the crops while hanging on a rope from strong steel hooks embedded in his back. The exhilarated participant seems to feel no pain. Closer to home, a football player who hurts his arm in a big game is likely to experience far less discomfort than a person who gets a comparable bruise by walking into a door.

One laboratory study explored social influences on pain perception by comparing the pain thresholds of Boston homemakers from several different ethnic backgrounds (Sternbach & Tursky, 1965). These women were asked to rate the pain of electric shocks that gradually increased in intensity until they were unwilling to tolerate any more. In keeping with the attitudes from similar groups in earlier studies, the Italian-American homemakers had significantly lower pain thresholds than the others. Physiological responses differentiated the groups in other ways. For example, Yankee and Irish-American homemakers tolerated the same amount of pain, but the Yankee women were less reactive physiologically (measured by sweat-gland responses), reflecting their "phlegmatic, matter-of-fact" attitude toward pain. Like other studies, this experiment shows that learning and expectations play an important role in sensations of pain.

The best-known theory of pain perception is the **gate theory** of Melzack and Wall (1965). This theory acknowledges that the amount of pain experienced is not related in any linear way to the amount of injury inflicted on the body; indeed, football players, boxers, and survivors of other body-bruising

gate theory The theory that the amount of pain experienced is related to variables influencing the operation of neuronal gates, thus determining whether pain messages from damaged areas proceed to the brain and bring about the perception of pain.

The perception of pain depends on the context in which it occurs.

experiences report that pain from their injuries often fails to appear until minutes or hours after their trauma.

Melzack and Wall (1965) postulated that specialized axons carry information from damaged areas to the spinal cord and thence, by way of a neuronal gate, to the brain. However, a number of variables influence the operation of the neuronal gates, thus determining whether the pain messages will actually proceed to the brain and bring about the perception of pain. Immediate physical remedies (e.g., rubbing a banged shin) and deliberate redirection of one's attention appear to help close the pain gate and prevent the pain messages from passing through.

Much of the exciting research on pain perception today focuses on the role of neurotransmitters. It is known that special nerve centers in the spinal cord and brain handle sensory information concerning pain. Neurotransmitters such as serotonin, epinephrine, norepinephrine, and the endorphins may act to facilitate or interfere with the transmission of pain messages at several levels within the nervous system. As noted in Chapter 3, particular attention has been paid to the role of endorphins, the body's own naturally produced morphine-like chemicals.

There is considerable evidence that electrical stimulation of certain brain centers works to relieve pain by stimulating the production of endorphins. For example, Liebeskind and Paul (1977) have summarized a number of studies supporting the hypothesis that electrical stimulation can have an analgesic (painkilling) effect on animals without putting them to sleep. When mild currents of electricity are delivered via electrodes to portions of the reticular formation and hypothalamus, laboratory rats show no sign that they experience pain when their tails are pinched or heat is applied to their feet. The areas where electrical stimulation appears to interfere with pain sensation are often near but not identical to the "pleasure centers" identified by Olds (Chapter 3) and appear to involve different sensory systems.

Mayer and Hayes (1975) obtained direct evidence that electrical stimulation achieves its pain-interference effects in a manner similar to opiates. As mentioned in Chapter 3, it is known that naloxone interferes with the action

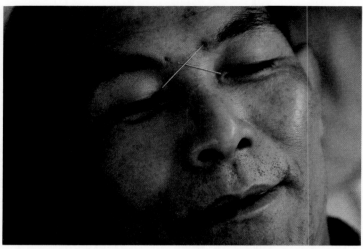

Several studies have suggested that acupuncture relieves pain by stimulating production of endorphins.

of opiates and allows the transmission of pain messages. Mayer and Hayes demonstrated that in many areas of the brain, naloxone also blocks the pain-preventive effects of electrical stimulation. Indeed, rats can develop a tolerance for electrical stimulation just as they can for morphine, so that it takes higher and higher "doses" of electrical stimulation to achieve pain-prevention effects. Moreover, rats that have become addicted to (have developed a physical dependence on) electrical stimulation to prevent them from feeling pain from aversive procedures then need much higher doses of morphine to prevent pain than rats who have not been exposed to electrical stimulation. This and other physiological theories of pain may produce rapid advances in our understanding of pain over the next few years.

Internal Bodily Sensations

The familiar senses reviewed to this point translate physical stimuli in the external world into psychological sensations. But there are several other classes of sensation that originate within the body. For example, the **visceral sense** provides feedback from internal organs and is responsible for such delights as gas pains, cramps, and pressure in the bladder.

To feel another one of your senses in action, try this experiment. Close your eyes and lift one arm. Then ask yourself how high you have raised your arm. Is it level with your shoulder? Level with your waist? Try a similar exercise with your foot. Even with your eyes closed, do you have any doubts about the location of your hand or foot? Probably not. Can you think of any circumstances when you felt "out of contact" with your hand or foot, not quite sure of its position or location? How about when you wake up at night, only to find that a hand or foot is still "fast asleep"?

visceral sense Feedback from internal organs.

Astronauts often report that motion sickness accompanies weightlessness.

A number of our senses are called "proprioceptive" because they help us "right" ourselves—that is, keep ourselves upright. For example, the **proprioceptive sense** that is concerned with your experience of the movement and positions of your body and parts of your body is the **kinesthetic sense**. Nerve receptors in your joints and tendons send messages to the somatosensory cortex (which, as you may remember from Chapter 3, is located in the brain at the front of the parietal lobes) that indicate the position of your limbs. In addition, muscle spindles (receptors in your voluntary muscles) send messages to the spinal cord and brain when your muscles are stretched; these messages contribute to your sense of movement and position.

Proper function of the kinesthetic sense is required to walk up a flight of stairs or lift a hammer. It is ironic that the first psychophysical research—Ernst Weber's experiments in 1834 on the difference thresholds for holding weights—concentrated on this minor sense.

The **vestibular sense** provides information about the pull of gravity and helps maintain balance. Major organs involved in balance are the **semicircular canals** and the **vestibular sacs** of the inner ear. Fluids within these structures move when the body rotates or the head is tilted. These fluids stimulate sensory hair cells, which trigger nerve impulses from the inner ear to the brain. Under ordinary circumstances, the vestibular sense helps you maintain an upright posture and keep your visual world in focus while you move around. However, under some circumstances, the operation of the vestibular organs can give rise to the nausea and dizziness of motion sickness. Conflicting information from the sense organs to the brain, combined with information from the vestibular organs that the environment is moving erratically, seem to be strongly implicated in motion sickness. Astronauts have undergone training in biofeedback techniques to help them deal with the severe motion sickness that can accompany weightlessness in space. An understanding of the workings of the vestibular sense is particularly important in aviation, where unusual feedback in the inner ear may deceive the normal observer. For example, blindfolded airplane passengers typically report that a plane feels as if it is tilting forward when it slows down (Clark & Graybeil, 1949). Under conditions of poor visibility, pilots must be aware of how these vestibular illusions work so that they know when the sense of balance can be trusted and when it cannot.

Clearly, our senses are essential to getting around in the world, and damage to any sense makes life more difficult. "Applying Scientific Concepts" asks you to identify which sense has been damaged in another of Dr. Sacks's patients.

Principles of Perception

Perception is the process of interpreting a pattern of stimuli as an organized whole. When you look at a photograph of your mother's face, the retina of your eye responds to a large number of spots of light and contours. But you are not aware of these elementary sensations; you simply see dear old Mom.

Some researchers have attempted to explore the biological basis of the complex process, particularly regarding visual perception. As noted earlier,

proprioceptive sense Senses reacting to movement of parts of the body, such as the muscles.

kinesthetic sense A sense of the movement and positions of the body and body parts, based on feedback from the muscles, joints, and tendons.

vestibular sense Sensations that provide information about the pull of gravity and help maintain balance.

semicircular canals A portion of the inner ear that helps regulate the sense of balance.

vestibular sacs Organs involved in the maintenance of balance.

perception The process of interpreting a pattern of stimuli as an organized whole.

Brain Injury and Sensation

In the book *The Man Who Mistook His Wife for a Hat,* neurologist Oliver Sacks (1986) described the case of Christina, "the disembodied lady." Christina was admitted to the hospital three days before an operation to remove her gallbladder and was put on an antibiotic to fight infection. The day before her operation, Christina became very unsteady on her feet; made awkward, flailing movements; and had trouble holding things in her hands.

On the day of her surgery, she was even worse. She could not stand unless she looked at her feet, and her hands "wandered" unless she kept an eye on them. When she reached out for something, her hands would miss their target, as though some essential control was gone.

A spinal tap revealed that Christina suffered from acute polyneuritis, an inflammation of specific neuronal fibers in the spinal cord and brain. This inflammation interfered with the functioning of one of Christina's sensory systems. From your reading in this chapter, you should be able to answer the question: Which of Christina's sensory systems was affected? (A discussion of this exercise appears after the "Summary" at the end of this chapter.)

David Hubel and Thorsten Wiesel charted the pathways from eye to brain by recording the electrical activity of individual cells in the visual system. The major conclusion from their research was that visual processing in the brain proceeds hierarchically, with cells later in the chain responding to increasingly complex stimuli. Thus, the eye does not transmit a miniature replica of a stimulus for the brain to "look at." Instead, cells in receptor organs and throughout the nervous system transform information into codes of their own. Science knows more about the simpler transformations early in this chain than about the complex processes in the cerebral cortex that finally determine our perceptions. While our review of sensation emphasized the biological paradigm, the discussion of perception will focus on a more cognitive perspective, analyzing the nature of perceptual experience. Many of the laws that govern human perception were first discovered by a group of German researchers known as the Gestalt psychologists.

Gestalt Principles

When Wilhelm Wundt founded the first psychology laboratory in 1879 (see Chapter 1), he hoped to discover the principles of the mental chemistry of conscious experience. Just as water is composed of hydrogen and oxygen, Wundt believed that the perception of a tree or a sausage could be broken down into basic psychological elements.

But in 1890, the German philosopher Christian von Ehrenfels argued against this kind of search for the molecules of the mind. He believed that a

proximity The Gestalt principle that stimuli which are physically close tend to be perceived as belonging together.

similarity The principle that stimuli resembling each other tend to be perceived as belonging together.

closure The principle that an incomplete pattern is often perceived as a complete whole.

figure According to the Gestalt psychologists, the object of attention, usually seen as a distinct shape in front of the ground.

Proximity

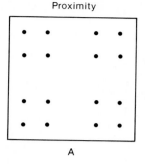

A

Similarity

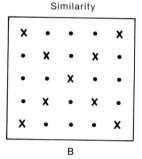

B

Closure

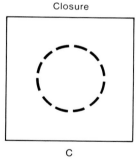

C

FIGURE 5.16 Gestalt principles. According to the principle of proximity, *A* should be perceived as four squares. According to the principle of similarity, in *B* the diagonals formed by the *X*s should be prominent. According to the principle of closure, *C* should be perceived as a circle.

perception was more than just the sum of its sensory parts. For example, if you hear a song in two different keys, every note—and thus every single elementary sensation—will be different for the two versions. Yet you hear the same melody because the relationship among the notes remains the same. What is important, then, is not the elementary constituents but the overall relationship among them. To describe this phenomenon, Ehrenfels used the German term *Gestaltqualität,* which can be roughly translated as "form quality." A number of German psychologists pursued the implications of Ehrenfel's analysis, and by the 1920s they had developed a series of observations and theories now known as Gestalt psychology.

GROUPING

In 1925, Gestalt psychologist Max Wertheimer described several major principles by which the human mind grouped stimuli into patterns (see Figure 5.16). One major principle involved **proximity**: Stimuli that are physically close together tend to be perceived as belonging together and forming a group. Another principle involved **similarity**: Stimuli that resemble one another also tend to be perceived as belonging together and forming a group. According to the principle of **closure**, an incomplete pattern is often perceived as a complete whole. In these and other ways the human mind structures the sensory world according to its own internal laws.

Since vision is our primary sense, most psychologists have emphasized the importance of Gestalt principles of grouping for visual perception. But they can be applied to other senses as well. Imagine tapping a pencil with different patterns of pauses between beats: *tap/tap . . . tap/tap . . . tap/tap* versus *tap/tap/tap . . . tap/tap/tap.* Although the physical stimuli are the same, perception is based on their grouping. According to the principle of proximity, the taps that come close together tend to be perceived as parts of the same group.

FIGURE-GROUND RELATIONSHIPS

In the normal course of perception, some objects seem to stand out from the background. For visual perception, the object of attention, or **figure**, is usually seen as a distinct shape in front of the ground; it may even seem more solid and substantial. Again, these relationships show how the human mind imposes structure on physical stimuli and perceives them in terms of patterns.

In 1915, E. Rubin emphasized this distinction by publishing perhaps the first reversible figure, in which figure and ground can be easily reversed. As you stare at Figure 5.17, notice that whether you see the faces or the vase, the figure (that is, whichever object you see) seems to have well-defined boundaries and the ground does not. You may also see the figure as nearer and more substantial.

As with the grouping principles, research and theory regarding figure-ground relationships have focused on vision, but the idea can also be applied to the other senses. When a restaurant critic tries to identify the herbs and spices in an unfamiliar chicken dish, her attention may shift from the hint of tarragon to the subtle aroma of basil, leaving the taste and odor of the chicken itself in the background. Or when a jazz fan concentrates on the classic album *Kind of Blue,* his attention may shift from Miles Davis's trumpet to John Coltrane's tenor sax to Bill Evans's piano; each instrument sometimes serves as figure and sometimes as part of the ground.

Perceptual Constancies

Other phenomena were also analyzed by Gestalt psychologists to show that the perceptual whole is different from the sum of its simple sensory parts; it is determined by the nature of the human mind. One important class of phenomena involves **perceptual constancy**, the tendency of observers to perceive an object as stable even when its sensory image changes. Here we shall concentrate on three of the most important ways in which changing objects appear the same: size, shape, and color.

FIGURE 5.17 Rubin's reversible figure can be seen as a vase or as two faces, depending on which color is perceived as figure and which as ground.

SIZE CONSTANCY

Suppose you are driving along a highway carefully observing the 55-mile-per-hour speed limit when a Toyota passes you doing 90. As this car speeds off to a fatal accident, its image on your retina will change dramatically. The Toyota image on your retina is largest when the car is right in front of you; the farther ahead it goes, the smaller the retinal image. Despite this obvious reduction in the retinal image, you do not perceive the Toyota as shrinking as it pulls away. This is an example of **size constancy**, the tendency to see objects as constant in size even when a visual image changes.

Size constancy is not perfect, as you can see by closing one eye and staring at your hand at arm's length and then bringing it toward your face. If you concentrate on this sensation, your hand may seem to get slightly larger as you move it in. But this change in perception is less dramatic than the physical increase in the size of the image on your retina.

Several factors influence size constancy, including previous experience, attention to other cues, and physiological feedback from the lens of the eye. Previous experience and knowledge of objects is probably the most important factor. We know that baseballs are not 6 feet across no matter how big an incoming pitch looks as it approaches home plate. And we know that rock singers are not 2 inches tall, no matter how small they may look from the cheap seats in the balcony. Other cues promoting size constancy in this situation would include the view of the rest of the theater and the stage in the distance as well as physiological feedback from the lens as it changed its shape to focus on the pop star in the distance. Size constancy is always based on a compromise between retinal size and other clues about the actual dimensions of an object.

SHAPE CONSTANCY

The speeding Toyota from our original example also illustrates the principle of **shape constancy**, a tendency to perceive objects as maintaining the same shape regardless of the view from different angles. If you watch the front of a car approaching in your rear-view mirror, then look at the side as

perceptual constancy The tendency of observers to perceive an object as stable when its sensory image changes.

size constancy The tendency to see objects as constant in size even when the visual image changes.

shape constancy A tendency to perceive objects as maintaining the same shape regardless of the view from different angles.

it passes you, and finally watch the rear of the car recede into the distance, you will see at least three different views of the same object. Nevertheless, you continue to perceive the Toyota as having a single shape rather than a constantly changing appearance.

Similarly, if you flip a quarter and watch it carefully, your retinal image will change from a circle to an ellipse as it flips in the air. Yet your brain will not be confused by this ever-changing image, and you will see the coin as a simple object with a constant shape. Like size constancy, shape constancy involves the brain's judgment about an object based not just on the sensory image but on all available information, including previous experience.

COLOR CONSTANCY

To most of us, lemons look yellow whether we see them in bright sunlight, in the artificial fluorescent light of a supermarket, or through colored sunglasses. **Color constancy** refers to the tendency to see objects as retaining the same color under a variety of lighting conditions. In fact, the physical stimulus does change when lighting changes. If you looked at a piece of a lemon through a long, thin tube under the three conditions described above, and you did not know what it was, you would see three different colors. Like other perceptual constancies, color constancy is based partially on learning and memory, and partially on other sensory clues (in this case, knowledge of the light source and the colors of other visible objects).

Depth Perception

The images projected on the retina are two-dimensional, like pictures printed on a page. But we live in a three-dimensional world of cube-shaped desks, cylindrical jars, and well-rounded opera stars. How are two-dimensional images transformed into a three-dimensional picture?

One of the most important factors in depth perception is **binocular disparity**, the difference between the retinal images of the two eyes. Since the pupils of the eyes are 2 to 3 inches apart, each eye registers a slightly different view of the same object.

One simple demonstration of binocular disparity involves looking at an object with one eye at a time. For example, if you hold a finger 6 inches from your face and close first the right eye and then the left, the finger seems to move. The closer your finger is to the eyes, the more it seems to move. When you open both eyes, the brain integrates these sensations into a single image. The disparity between the two retinal images helps the brain estimate distance; the closer an object, the more different it appears to the two eyes. This principle of binocular disparity has been used since the early days of photography to create three-dimensional pictures, known as stereographs (see Figure 5.18).

There are also a number of cues to depth that can be perceived by one eye alone and are thus called *monocular*. Several physiological factors, including **accommodation**, involve changes in the shape of the lens of the eye. To produce the sharpest possible image on the retina, the lens changes shape: It bulges to focus on objects close to the eye and flattens to focus on

color constancy The tendency to see an object as remaining the same color under a variety of lighting conditions.

binocular disparity The difference between the retinal image of the two eyes.

accommodation A monocular physiological factor involving changes in the shape of the lens of the eye.

FIGURE 5.18 Around the turn of the century, stereoscopes, which produced three-dimensional images by means of binocular disparity, were quite popular. These advertisements appeared in the 1906 Sears, Roebuck catalog.

Aerial perspective produces a slight blurring and tinge of blue in distant objects.

FIGURE 5.19 Interposition as a cue to distance. In the figure on the left, the king of clubs seems closest because it appears to block out the other two cards. On the right, one way to create an illusion: The king of spades is actually much closer, as suggested by its larger size. But the cards have been notched to make it seem that the king of clubs overlaps.

objects farther away. These changes are produced by the actions of tiny muscles attached to the lens; when the muscles contract for near vision, kinesthetic receptors provide feedback to the brain. Accommodation of the lens provides information about distance only for objects that are relatively close, within 3 to 4 feet of the eyes.

For objects farther away, monocular cues depend not on physiological feedback but on the physical arrangement of objects. Four of the most important monocular cues to depth are linear perspective, aerial perspective, relative size, and interposition.

Linear perspective refers to the fact that distant objects seem closer together than nearby objects. If you look down a long road or a set of railroad tracks, the two sides seem to get closer together in the distance. **Aerial perspective** refers to a slight blurring and tinge of blue in distant objects. If you look at the Rocky Mountains from downtown Denver, the mountains that are farthest away seem least clear and look somewhat blue.

The **relative size** of objects is also a monocular cue to depth; all other things being equal, larger objects are generally perceived as closer. If you see a large mountain and a small mountain in the distance, the large mountain probably seems closer. However, relative size may be overruled by other cues such as **interposition**: If one object blocks our view of another, the partially obscured object seems more distant. Therefore, if you see all of one mountain from downtown Denver and only parts of a larger mountain peeking out behind it, the smaller mountain is perceived as closer. A clever demonstration of how interposition can lead the brain to the wrong conclusion is shown in Figure 5.19. The visual system was designed to produce an accurate picture of the world, but it can be fooled.

linear perspective The tendency for distant objects to seem closer together than near objects.

aerial perspective The slight blurring and tinge of blue perceived in distant objects.

relative size The phenomenon whereby larger objects are seen as closer to the observer than smaller objects.

interposition A phenomenon whereby if one object blocks the view of another, the partially obscured object will seem more distant.

Visual Illusions

The eyes are the windows through which we see the world, and the picture they provide is generally quite accurate. But the eyes and brain are quite consistently fooled by certain stimuli, occasionally with disastrous results.

One of the most dramatic examples was an aircraft collision that occurred over New York City in 1965, in which 4 people were killed and 49 injured. An investigation by the Civil Aeronautics Board concluded that this crash was caused by the pilot's misjudgment of altitude based on a well-known visual illusion. Figure 5.20 illustrates one version of the **Poggendorf illusion:** A continuous line seems to be misplaced when it is partially obscured. In the aircraft accident, two planes emerged from a sloping cloud bank. Although the aircraft were holding steadily at altitudes of 10,000 and 11,000 feet, each pilot saw the other plane emerge from the clouds on an angle and thought they were headed for a crash. As both maneuvered to avoid an accident, they did crash. The passengers and crews were thus the victims of a complex version of the Poggendorf illusion, a phenomenon discovered more than a century before (Coren & Girgus, 1978).

Psychologists have discovered many phenomena that consistently fool the eye and brain and have studied what each has to tell us about the nature of perception. For example, some researchers have asked whether the Mueller-Lyer illusion (see Figure 5.1) is caused by basic sensory processes in the eye or higher thought processes in the brain. One line of evidence for the role of brain processes is based on the fact that if people stare at the Mueller-Lyer lines for several minutes, the difference between them gradually seems to shrink. Porac and Coren (1977) asked people to look at the figure with just one eye until the illusion decreased. Immediately afterward, these people judged the difference between the lines through their other eye. If the original adaptation took place in the eye, the other eye should not have been affected and the illusion should have seemed as large as it had at first. But this was not the case. The subjects' second eye also judged the illusion as smaller, suggesting that some adaptation had taken place in their brain. However, other sources of evidence suggest that when defects in the lens of the eye cause images to blur slightly, the magnitude of the illusion increases (Coren & Girgus, 1978). Like many other sensory and perceptual phenomena, visual illusions seem to depend on a number of different processes at various levels of the nervous system.

The Effects of Experience

One factor that appears to affect perception is experience—a fact that was not recognized in the early years of research on sensation and perception. The first psychophysical studies focused on the relationships between physical stimuli and the sensations they produced. This research often implicitly assumed that the way we see, for example, is based on the physiology of eye and brain, that it is basically the same for everyone, and that it is not particularly affected by learning. In recent years, each of these assumptions has been questioned.

Although the first researchers in this area tended to ignore the human

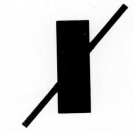

FIGURE 5.20 The Poggendorf illusion, discovered in 1860. The line is straight, although its ends seem displaced.

Poggendorf illusion A visual illusion in which a continuous line seems to be misplaced when it is partially obscured.

being who perceives a stimulus, it gradually became clear that this approach would not be able to explain many important phenomena. Perception is an active process of constructing a picture of the world, and the images that humans construct depend on more than just the receptor organ's response to a physical stimulus. Learning, beliefs, expectations, and even motivation can all play a role in what people see, hear, and sense.

Many examples that support this view have already been described in this chapter. For example, consider the opening case of S. B., the blind man whose sight was restored by surgery. If visual perception were simply based on anatomical connections between eye and brain, then once his eyes were "fixed," he should have perceived the world in exactly the same way that any other person does. But the reality of S. B.'s case was not that simple. He perceived distance and depth quite differently from most people, and he did not respond to visual illusions in the "normal" way. Thus, S. B. showed that learning is an important component in perception.

Another example of the complexity of the variables that affect sensation and perception comes from signal-detection theory. Researchers in this area have developed mathematical formulas for studying the relationships between what people expect to sense, what they are motivated to sense, and what they report sensing. Or consider Edwin Land's demonstrations that the colors we perceive can be influenced not just by physical stimuli, but also by memory and expectations.

In this section, as further examples of ways that experience can influence perception, we shall consider research in three areas: perception in other cultures, adapting to perceptual distortions, and the effects of expectations. Another relevant line of research—studies of the perceptual capabilities of newborn infants—will be described in the section on infant development in Chapter 9.

CULTURE AND PERCEPTION

One way to explore the relationship of experience to perception is to study people who have been raised in different cultures, whose experiences are quite different from ours. For example, Colin Turnbull (1961) described how cultural experiences had influenced the perceptual world of a member of the BaMbuti Pygmy tribe. Turnbull accompanied the Pygmy on his first trip out of the dense tropical rain forest of the Congo. For his entire life, this man had never seen anything farther than a few hundred feet away, because of the dense foliage in his jungle world. When Turnbull drove this man to a plain, he pointed to a herd of buffalo grazing several miles away. From that distance, the Pygmy insisted they must be insects. When the buffalo appeared to get larger, as they drove toward them, the Pygmy muttered that it was witchcraft. Like S. B., the blind man whose sight was restored, the Pygmy had never learned some of the perceptual constancies so familiar in our world.

Cultural experiences may also play a role in visual illusions. For example, some theorists have argued that the Mueller-Lyer illusion (see Figure 5.1) is based on the tendency to perceive an acute or obtuse angle on a two-dimensional page as a right angle in a three-dimensional world. They believe that this tendency is increased in Western cultures, because most people have so much experience with books and the printed page, which represent the world in two dimensions.

If this assumption is correct, people in other cultures who have had little exposure to books should be less susceptible to the Mueller-Lyer illusion. When Segal, Campbell, and Herskovits (1966) tested this hypothesis with members of the Zulu tribe in Africa, they found that Zulus were indeed less susceptible to the illusion. For our purposes, the most important implication of this finding is the simple fact that cultural experiences influence the way people perceive stimuli.

PERCEPTUAL ADAPTATION

Another way of studying the effect of experience on perception is to study how well people can adapt to new perceptual situations. One of the first and most dramatic studies of this sort was published by psychologist George Stratton in 1897. Stratton had devised a system of lenses and mirrors that reversed the visual world: Objects near the top of his visual field were now seen at the bottom, and objects actually on his right appeared on his left. For eight days, he walked around with this device over his right eye and with his left eye blindfolded.

As you might expect, the effect was quite disorienting. At first, even the simplest acts were extremely difficult. For example, when Stratton tried to pick up a pitcher that seemed to be on his left side, he actually had to reach to his right. Pouring a glass of milk became a major production, because the glass seemed to be upside down. On his first day, Stratton reported that he quickly became tired, depressed, and tense and that he avoided activity as much as he could.

By his third day of looking at this topsy-turvy world, Stratton began to adapt. He was able to write notes, despite their strange appearance, and he could walk around without bumping into every piece of furniture. By the fifth day, he had gained some confidence in his new perceptions. For the first time, he sat down in a chair without feeling it first to make sure it was really behind him. He mastered the art of putting the right shoe on the right foot by matching the shape of each foot to the appropriate shoe.

Although this adaptation was dramatic, it was never complete. For example, on the eighth and last day of the experiment, Stratton (1897) reported: "I often hesitated which hand was the appropriate one for grasping some object in view, began the movement with the wrong hand and then corrected the mistake" (p. 466).

When he removed the reversing lens, Stratton was once again disoriented. The location of objects seemed "surprising" and "bewildering," but not upside down. Thus, the aftereffects of this unusual experiment, like the original effects, were dramatic but incomplete. Stratton learned to function in the reversed perceptual world, but he never experienced it as completely normal.

In later research with devices that altered the visual world in a variety of ways, for longer periods than Stratton's eight days, some people were able to function surprisingly well. After wearing goggles that reversed right and left for several weeks, one show-off subject rode a motorcycle through the streets of Innsbruck, Austria, while wearing his goggles (Kohler, 1962). But this dramatic demonstration did not involve total reversal; it was probably a case of learning to function in a world where the rules were changed rather than totally restructuring perception.

One of the most important factors in perceptual adaptation is the opportunity for activity. In one study (Held & Bossom, 1961), people who wore prisms that displaced the world to one side were divided into two groups: Half walked freely about, while the other half were taken over the same routes in wheelchairs. Subjects who walked around gave evidence of the usual aftereffects—their world had been slightly displaced. But the passive subjects who had been wheeled about gave no signs of adaptation.

Thus, some types of experience—in this case, those involving active movement—are more influential than others. But the more important lesson from this research is again the basic idea that experience does indeed influence the perceptual world. Examples of the importance of this phenomenon in everyday perception can be seen in studies of perceptual sets.

PERCEPTUAL SETS

A **perceptual set** is a mental predisposition to perceive a stimulus in a particular way as a result of expectations or previous experience. For example, read the following words.

TAE CAT

Anyone can see that these letters spell out "THE CAT," right? But look more closely. If you examine the "H" and the "A," you will see that they are physically identical to each other. Your perception of the same stimulus as two different letters was based on your knowledge of English and the expectation that "THE" is a common word while "TAE" is not—just as you are more likely to expect "CAT" than "CHT" (Selfridge, 1955). Thus, the context or the perceptual set influenced what you saw.

Or consider the classic example in Figure 5.21. In 1930, Edwin Boring pointed out the importance of perceptual set in perceiving this ambiguous figure. The observer who expects to see an old woman will see an old woman, and one who expects to see a young woman will probably see the stimulus that way.

In a study of perceptual sets outside the laboratory, Parkinson and Rachman (1981) gave a word recognition test to a group of mothers several hours before their children underwent tonsillectomies. The anxious mothers were asked to recognize words that were spoken softly while loud music was played in the background. They proved to be more successful in recognizing words that were related to surgery (such as *infection, bleeding,* and *pain*) than they were in recognizing similar nonsurgical words (such as *inflection, breeding,* and *pine*). Thus, the anxiety-provoking situation in which these women found themselves created a perceptual set, perhaps because they were thinking about operations.

Examples like these should make it clear that human perception is an active process that can be shaped by both expectations and experience.

perceptual set A mental predisposition to perceive a stimulus in a particular way as a result of expectations or previous experience.

FIGURE 5.21 A classic example of perceptual set. The ambiguous figure in panel *A* is likely to be perceived as an old woman by viewers who see panel *B* first and as a young, attractive woman by viewers who see panel *C* first.

Extrasensory Perception

Several researchers have argued that another important category of awareness exists well outside the mainstream of accepted scientific knowledge. **Extrasensory perception** is said to provide awareness of external events without the use of known sensory receptor organs. The abbreviation *ESP* is now familiar, but few realize that the term *extrasensory perception* was invented (by J. B. Rhine) only about 50 years ago.

In the 1920s, *Scientific American* offered a $5,000 prize to anyone who could convincingly demonstrate psychic abilities. A distinguished committee appointed by the magazine was particularly impressed by the abilities of Margery Crandon, the wife of a Boston surgeon. During séances held in a dark room, the spirit of Margery's dead brother Walter seemed to take over her body. Even as a dead man, Walter was the life of the party—his spirit hurled

extrasensory perception A controversial process that may provide awareness of external events without the use of known senses.

objects around the room, impressed his fingerprints on a piece of wax, and told dirty jokes.

After observing nearly 80 séances, the committee was prepared to award Margery the prize. But when the magician Harry Houdini sat in on a séance, he declared that Margery was using tricks and the prize was never awarded. The controversy over Margery continued for nearly 10 years, until one investigator discovered the trick behind her most impressive demonstration: Walter's mysterious wax fingerprints matched those of Margery's dentist, a frequent participant in her séances. Many researchers had staked their reputations on Margery's authenticity, and psychic research nearly came to an end right then.

The lessons of this scandal led a young researcher named J. B. Rhine to take a different approach. Rhine hoped to win scientific acceptance for this controversial field by demonstrating psychic phenomena in the laboratory, following accepted scientific procedures and standards. In most of his early experiments, Rhine asked people to guess the symbols on a special deck of cards. Sometimes, another experimenter looked at each card first; this was a test of **telepathy**, thought transmission from one person to another. On other occasions, the subject tried to guess the order of the cards immediately after they had been shuffled; these were tests of **clairvoyance**, in which physical stimuli are identified without using the known senses or telepathy. Rhine also was one of the first to use the term **parapsychology** (literally, "beyond psychology") to refer to research on occult or psychic phenomena.

In a 1934 book titled *Extrasensory Perception,* Rhine reported that some subjects in his laboratory had remarkable abilities to identify the hidden cards. The decks he used consisted of 25 cards—5 copies of each of 5 different symbols. According to the statistical laws of probability, subjects who guessed at random should be right about 5 times out of every 25. But several did far better. The most successful, a ministry student named Hubert Pearce, averaged 8 correct guesses out of every 25 trials over a total of 690 times through the deck. The odds against a performance like this occurring by chance are very large. Indeed, when Rhine combined the data from his eight best subjects, the odds were $10^{1,000}$ to 1 that the results did not occur by chance. It might seem that the controversy over the existence of ESP should have ended there; in a way, it was only beginning.

Psychologists at Princeton, Brown, Colgate, Johns Hopkins, and Southern Methodist universities soon reported that they had tried to replicate Rhine's experiments but failed to locate anyone with ESP. Further confusion followed when Rhine himself tested more people; he was never again able to find such an intense concentration of psychic talent. Skeptics suggested that the early successes resulted from a lack of adequate scientific controls in the first tests. For example, some of the early decks of cards had been printed poorly, and subjects might have unconsciously noticed marks on the backs that gave hints about their identity. Rhine had another explanation. He believed that the tremendous excitement surrounding the first studies created ideal conditions for observing ESP.

In the half-century since Rhine's classic studies were published, many parapsychologists have followed in his footsteps. They now use computers and electronic devices rather than decks of cards, but subjects are still asked to predict hundreds or thousands of random events. Occasionally, some individ-

telepathy A controversial process of possible thought transmission from one person to another.

clairvoyance A controversial process by which physical stimuli may be identified without using the known senses or telepathy.

parapsychology The study of occult or psychic phenomena.

Do Scientists Believe in ESP?

In 1982, Douglas Starr published a one-page article in *Omni* magazine arguing that ESP research was becoming increasingly accepted in scientific circles. Compare the following excerpt from his article "Out of the Closet" to the survey data cited in the text. (A discussion of this comparison appears after the "Summary" at the end of this chapter.)

Not long ago any scientist who dared to declare serious interest in UFOs, parapsychology, or the Loch Ness monster found himself ostracized by the scientific priesthood. So qualified scientists stayed in the closet, pursuing their exotic investigations in private and communicating their findings among tight-knit underground networks.

Now the door seems to be opening up. Several reputable scientific groups have recently formed to investigate just those fringe subjects. The result? A new openness among scientists and some overdue respect for the study of anomalies. . . .

Don't expect too much from these tentative beginnings. You won't be studying Bigfoot in Zoology 101. But do look for a new, unsmirking willingness to study strange phenomena, even within the most scholarly of halls.

---

ual achieves a dramatic success. But whenever successful subjects have been retested, their ESP has disappeared.

This discouraging pattern has occurred even when researchers have tried to go beyond the narrow limits of card- or number-guessing tasks. In one study of dreaming (Ullman, Krippner, & Vaughan, 1973), a researcher tried to use ESP to communicate an image of a famous painting to a person who slept in another room in the same laboratory. Whenever the sleeper showed signs of rapid eye movements (a physiological indicator of dreaming; see Chapter 4), he was awakened and asked to describe his dream. Later, another experimenter studied the transcripts of the dreams and a series of eight paintings that included the one that had been "sent by ESP." This observer was asked to rank the paintings in terms of the appearance of their images in the dreams—number 1 for the painting that most resembled the dream content to number 8 for the painting with the least resemblance. For one particular subject, the correct painting was ranked in the top four for eight successive nights. The odds against this occurring by chance are 256 to 1. But when the same subject tried to repeat the performance on another occasion, there was no evidence whatsoever of ESP (Belvedere & Foulkes, 1971).

Thus, there are two major reasons why many scientists doubt whether ESP exists. The first is the possibility of experimental fraud of the sort that seemed common in the early days of psychic research. The second and far more important reason is the repeated failure of attempts to replicate any single instance of ESP.

Several surveys have been conducted to determine the general level of belief in ESP. When Wagner and Monnett (1979) surveyed college professors in both the humanities and the sciences, they found that 16% considered ESP "an established fact," and another 49% called it "a likely possibility," for a total of 65% who might be considered believers. (See "Becoming a Critical Consumer" in this chapter.)

However, McClenon (1982) found much more skepticism among a group of scientists who held leadership positions in the American Association for the Advancement of Science, perhaps the most prestigious scientific society in the United States. Among these "elite scientists," only 4% categorized ESP as an established fact, and 25% considered it a likely possibility. This gives a total proportion of 29% believers, or less than half the rate among college professors.

Interestingly, in both studies, psychologists were much more skeptical about ESP than most of their colleagues. McClenon reported that 5% of psychologists considered ESP a fact or possibility. Only experts in the history and philosophy of science and anthropology were more skeptical, with no believers in either group. The greatest acceptance of ESP was found among pharmacists and engineers.

Unfortunately, there are no reliable data that directly compare today's level of acceptance with that at any time in the past. However, given the available results and the very small number of established academic programs in ESP, even the strongest supporters of this field agree that ESP has not been accepted into the scientific mainstream. As one former president of the Parapsychological Association put it: "As an academic discipline [parapsychology] remains precarious and peripheral" (Beloff, 1977, p. 20).

Summary

- **Sensation** is the process of responding to a simple physical stimulus, such as a spot of light or a musical note.

- **Perception** is the more complex process of actively interpreting a pattern of stimuli as an organized mental image.

Psychological Sensations and Physical Stimuli

- **Psychophysics** examines the relationships between the physical attributes of stimuli and the psychological sensations they produce.

- The **difference threshold** refers to the minimum physical difference required for any two stimuli to be sensed as different.

- Early psychophysicists developed the concept of the **absolute threshold**, the minimum physical energy that causes a sensory system to respond.

- One of the methods for measuring absolute thresholds is the **method of constant stimuli**, which involves presenting a number of stimuli of different physical intensities in random order.

- **Signal-detection theory** attempts to account for both psychological and sensory factors that influence psychophysical judgments; precise mathematical procedures have been proposed to separate true sensory limits from more psychological factors.

Vision

- The eye is a sense organ that responds to visible light, a particular kind of electromagnetic radiation.
- One important physical characteristic of light is **wavelength**—the distance from the crest of one wave of light to the crest of the next.
- The outer covering of the eye is the **sclera**, a tough covering that protects the delicate structures within.
- Near the front of the eye, this protective layer forms the **cornea**, the curved transparent window that helps focus light as it enters the eye.
- The most frequently noticed physical structure of the eye is the **iris**, a circular arrangement of muscular cells that controls the diameter of the opening that admits light.
- The **pupil**, which appears black, is a hole in the center of the iris.
- After light passes through the cornea and the pupil, it is filtered through a structure called the **lens**, a body of tissue that changes its shape to focus light on the **retina**, a light-sensitive surface at the back of the eye.
- The **fovea** is a slight depression at the center of the retina that contains only **cones** (receptor cells responsible for color vision) and is more sensitive to fine visual detail than any other part of the retina.
- **Rods** are receptor cells that are more responsive than cones in dim light but can only distinguish black, white, and various shades of gray.
- Near the fovea is the **blind spot**, which has no receptor cells because nerve cells are gathered here to form the **optic nerve**, which transmits information from the retina to the brain.
- Hubel and Weisel's technique of **single-cell recording** permits the recording of the electrical activity of one neuron at a time.
- Experiments have demonstrated that there are three types of **feature detectors** (cells that fire when they detect certain *features,* or patterns of stimulation): **simple cells**, **complex cells**, and **hypercomplex cells**.
- **Dark adaptation** refers to the gradual increase in the sensitivity of the retina after a period in the dark.
- Young's **trichromatic theory** of color vision holds that there are three basic receptors in the retina, one for each of the three primary colors (red, blue, and green).
- Hering's **opponent-processes theory** holds that each of the three separate systems in the retina responds to two colors, not one.
- The trichromatic theory does not provide an explanation for certain **afterimages**, sensory impressions that remain after a stimulus is taken away.

Hearing

- Hearing depends on the physiological responses of the auditory system to the mechanical energy of sound waves.

- The **pitch** of a sound, the psychological sense that a sound is high or low, is determined by the frequency of the vibrations composing a sound wave.

- **Loudness,** the psychological dimension corresponding to the intensity of a sound, is most highly related to the amplitude or physical height of the sound waves but also depends on other factors.

- Generally, **sound** can be defined as a wave motion that pulsates through a material medium (typically air) and is generated by physical vibrations.

- Sound waves travel from the external ear to the **eardrum** (also known as the *tympanic membrane*) via a tube called the **auditory canal.**

- The vibrations of the eardrum are transmitted through three tiny bones in the middle ear (*hammer, anvil,* and *stirrup*) to another membrane called the **oval window.**

- The **semicircular canals** help regulate the sense of balance.

- The **eustachian tube** runs from the middle ear cavity to the throat and is designed to equalize pressure on both sides of the eardrum.

- The major auditory portion of the inner ear is the **cochlea.**

- Sound waves are usually transmitted to the oval window of the cochlea through the stirrup bone.

- Sound wave vibrations move the fluid in the cochlea and displace the **basilar membrane,** which then translates these physical vibrations into a pattern of electrical activity in the nervous system.

- The **place theory of hearing** suggests that different sounds activate different places on the basilar membrane.

- The **frequency theory of hearing** holds that the basilar membrane acts like the diaphragm of a microphone or telephone—that is, it vibrates as a whole in response to sound stimulation.

The Other Senses

- **Taste buds** contain the receptor cells responsible for the four major taste sensations—sweet, salty, sour, and bitter.

- In insects, the smell of chemicals called **pheromones** can elicit sexual and other behavior patterns.

- The **gate theory** of Melzack and Wall acknowledges that the amount of pain experienced is not related linearly to the amount of injury inflicted. It holds that a number of variables influence the operation of neuronal gates, thus determining whether pain messages from damaged areas will actually proceed to the brain and bring about the perception of pain.

- The **visceral sense** provides feedback from internal organs.

- **Proprioceptive senses** help us keep ourselves upright.
- The **kinesthetic sense** is concerned with the experience of the movement and positions of the body and body parts.
- The **vestibular sense** provides information about the pull of gravity and helps maintain balance.
- Major organs involved in balance are the **semicircular canals** and the **vestibular sacs** of the inner ear.

Principles of Perception

- **Perception** is the process of interpreting a pattern of stimuli as an organized whole.
- Among the Gestalt principles of perception are these: **proximity** (stimuli that are physically close together tend to be perceived as belonging together); **similarity** (stimuli that resemble each other tend to be perceived as belonging together); and **closure** (an incomplete pattern is often perceived as a complete whole). Further, the object of attention, or **figure**, is usually seen as a distinct shape in front of the ground.
- **Perceptual constancy** is the tendency of observers to perceive an object as stable even when its sensory image changes.
- Three of the most important examples of perceptual constancy are **size constancy**, **shape constancy**, and **color constancy**.
- Several factors contribute to the perception of depth, including **binocular disparity**, the difference between the retinal image of the two eyes.
- In addition to **accommodation**—a physiological factor involving changes in the shape of the lens of the eye—*monocular* cues to depth perception include **linear perspective**, **aerial perspective**, the **relative size** of objects, and **interposition**.
- Visual illusions include the **Poggendorf illusion**, in which a continuous line seems to be misplaced when it is partially obscured.
- A **perceptual set** is a mental predisposition to perceive a stimulus in a particular way as a result of expectations or previous experience.

Extrasensory Perception

- **Extrasensory perception** is said to provide awareness of external events without the use of known sensory receptor organs.
- **Telepathy** involves thought transmission from one person to another.
- In tests of **clairvoyance**, physical stimuli are to be identified without using the known senses or telepathy.
- **Parapsychology** refers to research on occult or psychic phenomena.
- There are two major reasons why many scientists doubt the existence of extrasensory perception: failure to replicate positive results and the possibility of fraud.

Critical Thinking Exercises Discussions

Brain Injury and Sensation

Sacks notes that in Christina's case, proprioceptive fibers bore the brunt of the inflammation. He explained to Christina that the sense of the body rests on three things: vision, balance organs (the vestibular system), and proprioception, which she had lost. Because of damage to the sensory roots of neurons in the brain and spinal cord, at first Christina could do nothing without monitoring her actions visually. Gradually, however, the unconscious feedback normally provided by the proprioceptive system was replaced by a sort of "visual automatism," and her reflexes gradually became more integrated and fluid.

One of the critical thinking skills that would help you solve the problem posed in this exercise involves eliminating irrelevant alternatives. The question was: Which of Christina's sensory systems was affected?" There is no indication that anything is wrong with Christina's auditory system or her sense of smell or taste. You might wonder about her visual system, as she has trouble picking up objects; however, if you read the description of her condition carefully, you will see that her problems are more visual-motor or even purely motor than strictly visual. Through a process of elimination, you should arrive at the "other senses" discussed in this chapter—specifically, the proprioceptive senses.

Do Scientists Believe in ESP?

According to one school of journalism, if two people do something, it's a trend, and if three people do something, it's a movement. The excerpt from the *Omni* article describes several scientific societies recently formed to study ESP and related phenomena. However, there is no discussion of whether new societies are formed all the time, or whether this really marks a departure from the past.

The critical consumer always looks for the empirical evidence needed to reach a firm conclusion. Thus, one might ask: How many ESP societies were formed in the last five years, and how many in the five years before that?

In the 1920s, the psychology department at Harvard was involved in several major studies of psychic phenomena. In the 1930s, J. B. Rhine's experiments were publicized to a very wide audience inside and outside the scientific community. If there is any evidence that scientists are more open-minded about ESP now than they have been for the last 60 years, it is not mentioned in this excerpt (nor elsewhere in the article itself).

LEARNING

Chapter 6

*L*iza was an eighth-grade student in a public junior high school in Kansas. Unhappy with her D average in history, she went to see the school's guidance counselor. Liza met regularly with the counselor for several weeks to talk about the problem, but these consulting sessions did not help her performance in class. Consequently, another approach was tried.

Liza was given sheets of paper containing 3 rows of 10 boxes and asked to record her study behavior in the boxes whenever she thought of it during history class. Specifically, she was told to record a "+" each time she was engaged in appropriate studying/learning behavior and a "−" each time she was not. In addition, the history teacher was asked to give Liza attention and praise whenever she appeared to be attending to her work.

Systematic observations by a visitor to the classroom revealed that Liza's study behavior improved markedly, both when she was simply observing and recording her own behavior and when she was receiving praise from her teacher for her efforts. This case study (Broden, Hall, & Mitts, 1971) is an example of the use of principles of learning to modify behavior. This chapter considers both the basic "laws of learning" studied in the research laboratory and the application of those principles to a variety of real life problems.

Children have a lot to learn and a lot of learning problems to overcome both inside and outside of the classroom. Very few 3-year-olds know how to play the tuba. A musician may take many years to learn all the complex skills involved in playing this instrument. Similarly, people have to *learn* how to barbecue spareribs, read James Joyce, and cheat on their income tax.

Learning can be defined as a relatively permanent change in behavior potential that occurs through experience. The words of this formal definition have been chosen carefully to distinguish learning from other processes. For example, *relatively permanent* excludes temporary changes in behavior that could be caused by other factors, such as fatigue. *Behavior potential* refers to the likelihood that a particular behavior will occur. The potential of shoe-tying behavior is extremely low in 2-year-olds and extremely high in most adults in shoe-wearing societies. *Experience* excludes behavioral changes caused by drugs, maturation, or other external processes. Learning is a fundamental process underlying human language, culture, and values. It is not surprising, then, that the study of learning had been one of psychology's major concerns.

What is surprising to many people is the way that psychologists have chosen to study learning. One might expect them to focus on human learning in the familiar world of the classroom or nursery. Instead, the most influential researchers established animal laboratories in which they studied the learning of pigeons, rats, monkeys, and dogs. Few people choose a career in psychology because of their interest in pigeons, yet some of the best minds in social science have devoted their lives to the study of simple learning processes in lower animals. Why?

Part of the reason can be found in the early history of psychology. As we have seen, the first psychological laboratory, established by Wilhelm Wundt in 1879, was set up to discover the laws of consciousness and the mind (see Chapter 1). To John Watson and others, these terms were vague and imprecise; their dissatisfaction led to the rise of the behavioral paradigm, which focused on observable physical stimuli and responses (thus the name, S-R psychology). Many of the pioneers in the behaviorist movement were trained in physiology, a discipline that had long used animals in laboratory research.

The practical advantages of studying lower animals are obvious. An experimenter can precisely control the environment of large numbers of animals from birth to death in a way that would never be possible with humans. Further, Charles Darwin's theory of evolution held that all animals are descended from common ancestors. Many behaviorists therefore argued that the laws of learning would be fundamentally the same throughout the animal kingdom, and that these laws could be most efficiently identified in the pure and simple world of the animal laboratory.

This emphasis on animal research does not mean that psychologists have failed to study human learning directly. According to one recent estimate (Miller, 1985), animal research is the primary topic of only about 7% of the pages published in American Psychological Association journals (the most influential group of research publications). Nevertheless, the search for fundamental laws of learning that apply across species has typically been directed at basic research findings from the animal laboratory. Despite the fact that a relatively small percentage of psychological research focuses on animal behavior, these studies have exerted a tremendous influence on the discipline of psychology.

Within the last few years, animal research has become more visible as some opponents have argued that it often violates animal rights. (Objections have been raised not just with regard to psychological research, but also

JOHN B. WATSON (1878–1958)

Watson is sometimes referred to as the father of behaviorism. He was the youngest person ever to complete the Ph.D. degree at the University of Chicago and was appointed a full professor at Johns Hopkins at the age of 29. His academic career was cut short in 1920, when his romantic involvement with graduate assistant Rosalie Rayner (with whom he studied Little Albert) led to a scandalous divorce. After he married Rayner and was forced to resign, he went to work for the J. Walter Thompson advertising agency, conducting door-to-door surveys on rubber boots. Although Watson continued to write popular articles and books on psychology, he advanced rapidly in the business world and devoted the rest of his career to advertising.

over research in medicine, physiology, biochemistry, and other areas.) There have even been several highly publicized cases of raids on laboratories in which animals have been "liberated."

Some researchers argue that the debate over animal ethics has focused on a few dramatic cases and has lost sight of the underlying issue of protecting animals. A recent report from the American Psychological Association (1986), for example, notes that even if one believes that research is a threat to animal rights, one would have to admit that it has far less impact on animal welfare than does the frequent, casual abandonment of pets.

One factor considered relevant to the debate over experimentation with animals is the extent to which animal research provides direct and indirect benefits. Therefore, as we explain the fundamental principles of learning in this chapter, we shall also include examples of the way basic learning principles discovered in the animal laboratory have been applied to human therapy. The problems treated with behavioral methods range from mundane concerns, such as stage fright and fear of meeting new people, to disabling disorders, such as schizophrenia and infantile autism. Additional examples of human applications will appear in Chapter 15, "Treating Abnormal Behavior."

We shall also cite less familiar examples of the way animal research has been of benefit to other species. For example, we shall see how insights from behavioral research have proven useful in programs for saving endangered species and for the nonviolent control of animal predators. However, it is important to remember that one cannot always predict what areas of basic research will lead to new applications. Moreover, as Tannebaum and Rowan (1985, p. 42, p. 32) have noted, "We need a much clearer understanding of the ethical issues in animal research if we are to provide the groundwork for a sensible and reasoned public policy. . . . There are no easy answers."

Attempts to understand human learning through studies of memory, language, thought, and children's reasoning are described in the next three chapters. Here, we focus on the behavioral paradigm to show how studies that began in animal laboratories have contributed to understanding the real-world behavior of humans and other species.

Classical Conditioning

Traditionally, psychologists have distinguished between two types of learning: classical conditioning and operant conditioning. Classical conditioning was so called because it was discovered first and was thus considered the classical form. It provides a model of the processes involved in many human learning situations, such as developing a fear of flying or dentists or mail carriers. As we shall see, it also explains why some people salivate whenever they drive past the golden arches of McDonald's.

learning A relatively permanent change in behavior or behavior potential that occurs through experience.

Pavlov's Discovery

Like many other scientific advances, classical conditioning was discovered by accident. Near the turn of the century, a Russian physiologist named Ivan

Petrovich Pavlov spent many years studying the digestive processes in dogs, quantifying the relationships between eating various amounts of food and the secretions of the digestive glands. But Pavlov noticed that the precise mathematical relationships he discovered occasionally broke down. Sometimes, secretions of saliva began unexpectedly when a dog saw the pan containing its food or the person bringing it or even when it heard his footsteps. Pavlov set out to study these mysterious "psychic secretions" with the same meticulous precision that had won him the Nobel Prize for his earlier physiological studies (Pavlov, 1927; Gantt, 1973).

The basic experiment began with a delicate surgical operation. A small cut was made through a dog's cheek and the duct of its salivary gland was diverted. Now the dog's saliva could be measured precisely: It flowed into a glass funnel cemented to its cheek. The dog stood in a harness while the experimenter watched through a small window in a soundproof room.

In one typical study, G. V. Anrep, a researcher in Pavlov's laboratory, struck a tuning fork about eight seconds before giving a dog "a measured dose of biscuit powder" (1920, p. 373). Not surprisingly, at first the animal salivated only when it got the food. Anrep repeated this pairing three times a day. Finally, after 10 joint presentations, Anrep tried a test: He just struck the tuning fork. Even though no food was presented, the dog secreted a few drops of saliva 18 seconds after it heard the sound. After another 20 presentations of food and sound together, the test was tried again. This time, the dog began to salivate just a few seconds after hearing the tuning fork and secreted 60 drops even though no food was presented. Because the tuning fork and the food were associated, the animal came to respond to the tuning fork the same way it responded to the food (see Figure 6.1).

Several technical terms are used to describe this learning situation. An **unconditioned stimulus (UCS)** is a stimulus that automatically elicits a natural reflex response called the **unconditioned response (UCR)**. In Anrep's study, food was the unconditioned stimulus and salivation was the unconditioned response. The word *unconditioned* emphasizes that this is a natural, inborn reflex that does not depend on learning. (Technically, the Russian word Pavlov used should have been translated as uncondition*al,* not uncondition*ed;* see Miller & Buckhout, 1973, p. 234. However, the form ending in "ed" has become so universal that we also use it here.)

A **conditioned stimulus (CS)** is a neutral stimulus that is repeatedly presented with the unconditioned stimulus until it comes to elicit the **conditioned response (CR)**, a learned response that resembles the original unconditioned response. For Anrep, striking the tuning fork was the conditioned stimulus; after learning, it came to elicit the conditioned response of salivation.

This type of learning, which later became known as **classical conditioning**, involved repeated pairing of a stimulus that naturally elicited a reflex response with a second stimulus; in time, the neutral stimulus came to elicit a response similar to the original reflex. Pavlov and his colleagues went on to investigate all the precise details of this simple learning process. They found, for example, that almost anything could become a conditioned stimulus. The sound of a metronome, the sight of a circle, the feel of a vibration on the thigh—all could easily be substituted for the tuning fork.

One important variable that affected the ease of conditioning was the

IVAN PETROVICH PAVLOV (1849–1936)

Pavlov won the Nobel Prize in 1904 for his studies of the physiology of digestion. In one of these experiments, he accidentally noticed that animals sometimes salivated in response to "psychic" stimuli such as hearing a caretaker approach with food. For the next 30 years, Pavlov studied this learning process, now known as classical conditioning. Ironically, Pavlov characterized the infant science of psychology as "completely hopeless." He insisted that his co-workers take a physiological approach; any assistant in his laboratory who used psychological terminology to describe his research was required to pay a small fine.

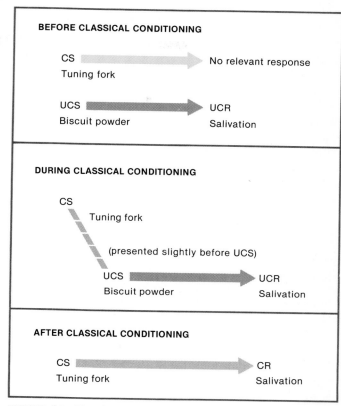

FIGURE 6.1 This diagram reflects the events in one pioneer study of classical conditioning (Anrep, 1920). CS = conditioned stimulus; CR = conditioned response; UCS = unconditioned stimulus; UCR = unconditioned response.

unconditioned stimulus A stimulus that automatically elicits a natural reflex called the *unconditioned response*.

unconditioned response A natural reflex response elicited by an unconditioned stimulus.

conditioned stimulus A neutral stimulus that is repeatedly presented with the unconditioned stimulus and gradually comes to elicit the conditioned response.

conditioned response A learned response that resembles the original unconditional response.

classical conditioning Learning involving repeated pairing of a stimulus that naturally elicits a reflex response with a second, neutral stimulus, which gradually comes to elicit a response similar to the original reflex.

time relationship between the unconditioned stimulus and the conditioned stimulus. If the unconditioned stimulus was presented before the conditioned stimulus, little or no conditioning occurred. Learning is most efficient when the conditioned stimulus begins before the unconditioned stimulus; the precise optimal timing depends on the reflex that is being conditioned.

Many American psychologists first learned of Pavlov's work through John Watson's presidential address to the American Psychological Association in 1914. Pavlov's careful experimental techniques soon caught the imagination of an entire generation of researchers, who saw an opportunity to establish psychology as a systematic scientific discipline. They proceeded to investigate a wide range of natural reflexes. Conditioned stimuli were paired with puffs of air (UCS) to elicit reflex closing of the eye (UCR); with sudden lights (UCS) to elicit contraction of the pupil of the eye (UCR); with blows to the patellar bone (UCS) to elicit knee jerks (UCR); and with electrical shocks (UCS) to elicit changes in breathing patterns (UCR).

Other researchers turned to different animals. They conditioned the responses of guinea pigs, chickens, flatworms, monkeys, rabbits, sheep, college students, and even a human fetus. In 1938, Spelt found that a loud noise—

the UCS—caused a 6½-month-old fetus to move suddenly—the UCR. A vibrating stimulus—the CS—attached to a pregnant woman's stomach was repeatedly paired with the noise until it, too, came to elicit movement by the fetus—the CR.

Taken together, these studies strongly supported the idea that classical conditioning was a fundamental type of learning that applied to many natural reflexes throughout the animal kingdom. For example, when people salivate as they pass McDonald's, it is probably a conditioned response based on a previous pairing of the golden arches (CS) with the sights and smells of a Big Mac or french fries (UCS). Scientific analysis of the principles of classical conditioning observed in the laboratory can provide insights into many examples of learning in the everyday world.

Extinction and Spontaneous Recovery

Pavlov and his co-workers went on to investigate the basic principles that governed classical conditioning. One early series of experiments studied how conditioned responses could be eliminated. A dog that had been trained to salivate for a bell heard the bell over and over but did not get any more food. Gradually, the dog took longer and longer to salivate less and less, until it finally seemed to stop. Pavlov used the term **extinction** to refer to the gradual disappearance of a learned response, in this case salivation. Classically conditioned responses are extinguished by repeatedly presenting the conditioned stimulus without the unconditioned stimulus.

But Pavlov soon found that extinction was not just a matter of simple erasure. If the dog in the original extinction experiment was returned to the laboratory the next day, it began to salivate again when it first heard the bell. This phenomenon is called **spontaneous recovery**, the reappearance, after a rest period, of a response that has been extinguished. However, it returns in a weaker form; the response may be smaller or less rapid when it reappears after extinction, and fewer trials are required to extinguish it again.

Generalization and Discrimination

In real life, stimuli often vary from one occasion to the next. Most learning would be of little value if it were linked to only one type of stimulus. If a child who was burned on a white Kenmore electric stove had to relearn this lesson on yellow stoves, gas stoves, and Hotpoint stoves, the original experience would have little significance. Pavlov studied this phenomenon by investigating the way slight changes in stimuli affect behavior. Two important concepts emerged. **Generalization** involves responding in a similar way to stimuli that resemble each other; the greater the similarity, the closer the response. The other side of the coin is **discrimination**, learning to respond only to a specific kind of stimulus. This, too, is necessary in real life. If the child was burned because there was something wrong with that particular stove, it is important that the lesson be limited to that stove alone.

G. V. Anrep (1923) began one important study of generalization by

extinction The gradual disappearance of a learned response.

spontaneous recovery The reappearance of an extinguished response after a rest period.

generalization Responding in a similar way to stimuli that resemble each other.

discrimination Learning to respond only to a specific kind of stimulus.

teaching a dog to salivate when a vibrator (CS) was applied to the dog's thigh. The dog later salivated when the vibrator was placed on his trunk, shoulder, or front paw. The farther the vibrator moved from the thigh (the original spot), the less the dog salivated. The learning had become generalized from the original conditioned stimulus to others that resembled it.

Pavlov then purposely tried to develop techniques to teach dogs to discriminate and respond only to one specific stimulus. In these experiments, two different stimuli were presented; one was always paired with the unconditioned stimulus, and the other was always presented alone. For example, a dog might be given meat every time a vibrator was placed against its thigh but never after the device was held against its shoulder. This procedure sharpened distinctions, and the dog learned to salivate only when the vibrator touched its thigh. In this way, discrimination was demonstrated in the laboratory for the first time.

Studies of generalization and discrimination can provide a unique method for asking animals questions. If Pavlov wanted to know whether dogs are color-blind, he could randomly alternate a green conditioned stimulus that was always paired with food (UCS) with a red conditioned stimulus that was never paired with food. If the dog learned to discriminate, that implied that it saw a difference between red and green. As we shall see later in this chapter, studies like this have since provided great insights into the perceptual world of lower animals and preverbal infants.

In later studies, Pavlov (1927) and his students made the discrimination problem more difficult by training dogs to distinguish between a circle and an ellipse and then presenting them with ellipses that looked more and more like circles. Finally, one poor dog couldn't stand it anymore. It began to squeal and wiggle in its harness, then bit through the tubes in the apparatus, and finally began to bark violently. These disturbed behaviors were very unusual for the docile dog, and Pavlov concluded that he had discovered the animal equivalent of human neurosis.

Pavlov was so impressed with this "experimental neurosis" that he devoted the remainder of his career to applying the principles of conditioning to psychiatry. Most of his theories were more influential in Russia than in the United States or Europe. But the idea that abnormal behavior can be caused by classical conditioning (and other types of learning) is now widely accepted.

Classical Conditioning and Human Therapy

In the history of American behaviorism, the most important demonstration that learning was involved in abnormal behavior came from John Watson's study of an infant known to several generations of psychology students as Little Albert.

LITTLE ALBERT

Watson and his colleague Rosalie Rayner (1920) wanted to show that human fears could be learned by classical conditioning. Their subject was Albert B., a "stolid and unemotional" 9-month-old child who "practically never cried." They began by confronting Little Albert with a standard series of stimuli, including a rat, a rabbit, a mask, and a burning newspaper. True to his unemotional reputation, Albert showed no fear. But when Watson made a loud noise by striking a hammer against a steel bar behind Little Albert's head, the child "started violently." After two more loud sounds, Albert "broke into a sudden crying fit."

About two months later, they began the actual conditioning. They planned to use the loud sound as an unconditioned stimulus that evoked an unconditioned response of fear (behaviorally defined by withdrawal and other responses). The conditioned stimulus was a rat, and fear was to be the conditioned response. Here are their laboratory notes from the first conditioning session:

1. White rat suddenly taken from the basket and presented to Albert. He began to reach for rat with left hand. Just as his hand touched the animal the bar was struck immediately behind his head. The infant jumped violently and fell forward, burying his face in the mattress. He did not cry, however.
2. Just as the right hand touched the rat the bar was again struck. Again the infant jumped violently, fell forward and began to whimper. In order not to disturb the child too seriously, no further tests were given for one week. (Watson & Rayner, 1920, p. 4)

Later, they continued the test with five more pairings of the rat and the sound and three presentations of the rat alone. Their description of the last trial for the day notes:

8. Rat alone. The instant the rat was shown the baby began to cry. Almost instantly, he turned sharply to the left, fell over on left side, raised himself on all fours, and began to crawl away so rapidly that he was caught with difficulty before reaching the edge of the table. (Watson & Rayner, 1920, p. 5)

Five days later, when Albert returned to the laboratory, he whimpered and withdrew from the rat. He also drew back in fear from a rabbit, a dog, a seal coat, and a Santa Claus mask, all stimuli that had not bothered the boy before. Albert's fear had generalized to a specific set of similar furry stimuli. He was still quite content to play in the experimental setting with stimuli that did not resemble the rat, such as a set of blocks.

This experiment seems unethical by current standards, and it is extremely unlikely that a study of this sort would or could be repeated by psychologists today. But in fairness to Watson and Rayner, it can be misleading to view actions taken over half a century ago by today's ethics and attitudes toward science. Watson and Rayner believed that many people would benefit from their demonstration that fears were learned and "felt that we could do [Albert] relatively little harm" (p. 2). (See "Understanding the Scientific Method" in Chapter 16 for a discussion of ethical issues in psychological research.)

They went on to propose seven techniques to help cure Little Albert's fear. Unfortunately, Albert's mother moved away with him before they had a chance to try them out. (About 50 years later, one psychologist—Murray, 1973—tried to locate Albert to see if he had any unusual fears as an adult, but he was unable to find him.)

Little Albert is shown here during the famous experiment on how human fears may be learned.

APPLICATIONS TO THERAPY

A few years after the Little Albert experiment, Mary Cover Jones (1924) tried Watson's proposed therapies on several other young children. Some of the suggestions, such as telling the child pleasant stories about the feared object, did not work at all. Others, such as watching other children play with the feared object, were more promising. The most promising was a technique called **counterconditioning**, in which relaxation is classically conditioned to stimuli that previously elicited anxiety.

Chapter 15 describes how counterconditioning has been refined by Joseph Wolpe (1958) and is now used by behavior therapists to treat a variety of human fears. As a preview of this process, consider the case of a person who has stage fright. Proponents of a behavioral model view this fear as a result of classical conditioning. As a child, this person might have felt no fear when near or on a stage (a neutral stimulus). However, ridicule appears to be an unconditioned stimulus producing fear and embarrassment (a UCR) even in young children. If the child experienced ridicule and humiliation from other children or a teacher when rehearsing for a kindergarten play, the ridicule could become associated with the stage and the whole idea of public performance. The CS could be the thought of standing in front of a group, and the CR would be a physiological fear response, including sweaty palms, nausea, and so on. (Note that in this example, the stimulus is an internal thought rather than an easily observed external behavior. Later in this chapter and others, we shall see how cognitive concepts of this sort have now been incorporated into many behavioral models.)

In treatment, the person who is afraid to give a speech or perform onstage is first taught to induce relaxation through a systematic technique

counterconditioning A process in which relaxation becomes classically conditioned to a stimulus that formerly elicited anxiety.

similar to some of the meditation techniques described in Chapter 4. Then the person is encouraged to imagine speaking in public while using this technique. The induced state of relaxation is incompatible with the physiological fear response and thus interferes with its emergence. In time, relaxation becomes classically conditioned to the thought of public speaking and later to the behavior of actually giving a speech. Thus, counterconditioning can ultimately eliminate this fear.

Another application of classical conditioning is in the treatment of *enuresis,* the medical term for bedwetting. Although this problem may seem trivial compared with the treatment of anxiety, it can be a very serious issue for the children who suffer from it. Important research on this problem began in 1938, when Mowrer and Mowrer (1938) argued that to avoid bedwetting, a sleeping child must learn to recognize the sometimes subtle cues associated with a full bladder. To accomplish this objective, they hooked up a pad that detects moisture to a bell that would ring and wake the child as soon as bedwetting began. This situation provided an effective form of classical conditioning. The sound of the bell is the UCS that produces the UCR of awakening. Through learning, the CS of internal stimuli associated with urination comes to elicit the CR of awakening in time to avoid bedwetting. Since this type of therapy was suggested in the 1930s, it has proven to be one of the most successful techniques for treating enuresis (Lovibond, 1964).

Thus, successful and widely accepted techniques for treating enuresis, anxiety, and other human problems can be traced directly to Pavlov's studies of classical conditioning in dogs. In the next section, we shall see how therapeutic techniques derived from operant conditioning have been even more widely applied.

Operant Conditioning

At about the same time that Pavlov's dogs were salivating in St. Petersburg, a New York psychologist named Edward L. Thorndike was trying to debunk popular myths about the incredible mental abilities of animals. "Dogs get lost hundreds of times and no one ever notices it," he wrote. "But let one find his way from Brooklyn to Yonkers and the fact immediately becomes a circulating anecdote" (Thorndike, 1898, p. 4). In his book *Animal Intelligence,* Thorndike described a series of experiments involving a kind of conditioning that differed from classical conditioning and that could account for many of the activities attributed to the "mental abilities" of animals.

Operant Versus Classical Conditioning

In his most famous studies, Thorndike put hungry cats in puzzle boxes with tasty morsels of fish just out of reach. Sometimes the cat had to pull a string to get out of the box and reach the fish; other times the cat had to slide a bolt or press a lever. The animals typically thrashed around for a while before discovering the solution, apparently by accident. Once they escaped and were placed back in the box, they went through this groping trial-and-error process again. Only gradually did they seem to learn the trick.

operant conditioning A type of learning in which the probability of a response changes when reinforcement or punishment is presented following that response.

**B. F. SKINNER
(1904–   )**

Skinner is probably the most famous behaviorist. He hoped to be a writer and was encouraged to pursue this path when the poet Robert Frost praised some of his college essays. In his three-volume autobiography, Skinner described the "dark year" after college graduation in which he tried to write full-time and discovered that he "had nothing to say." After reading Watson's book *Behaviorism,* Skinner went to study psychology at Harvard. His fame is based not just on his research on animal learning but also on his extensive writings on the implications of a behavioral approach.

Thorndike proposed several laws that governed the learning of his fumbling cats. The most important of these, the law of effect, emphasized the critical importance of the reward the cat got for escaping from the box (a piece of fish). The *law of effect* refers to the "stamping in" of learned connections between actions and their consequences. Specifically, actions that lead to rewards or satisfactions are more likely to be repeated, while those that fail to produce satisfying results are likely to be discontinued.

In 1938, Burrhus Frederic Skinner called attention to some of the differences between Pavlov's salivating dogs and Thorndike's puzzled cats. Salivation was *elicited*—it was a response to a specific stimulus (food). But pulling a string and manipulating a latch were not reflexes; they were *emitted* behavior, spontaneous acts that were not responses to any known stimuli. The first type of relatively passive learning became known as respondent conditioning (the animal passively responds) or classical conditioning (as in Pavlov's first, classical experiment). Such conditioning always involves new connections ultimately based on involuntary reflexes, such as salivation to a piece of food or withdrawal from pain.

In contrast, the second kind of conditioning involved more active, voluntary behavior. This more complex type of learning, in which the animal actually had to do something to gain a reward, was called operant conditioning (the animal operates on the environment) or instrumental conditioning (the act is instrumental in obtaining a reward). In **operant conditioning**, the probability of a response changes when reinforcement is presented following that response. Less formally, when a response is rewarded, it will be repeated more frequently; when punished, it will be repeated less frequently.

Both types of learning are found in the everyday world. Classical conditioning is involved in human fears and emotional reactions—for example, when you cringe (CR) at the sight of a hypodermic needle (CS) as a result of bad experiences from earlier shots. Operant conditioning may occur when a boy tells Grandma his latest joke; the likelihood of repeating the joke again increases if Grandma rewards it with a smile and decreases if she punishes it by frowning and saying, "You shouldn't tell jokes like that, dear." In similar ways, rewards and punishments influence all our voluntary behavior.

The fact that people and other animals will work for rewards is not an earth-shattering insight; it is at least as old as barter and bribery. What was new and important about the work of the early learning researchers was the development of a technology and a systematic approach to the study of how rewards and punishments shape behavior. Ultimately, this led to the formulation of precise empirical laws of learning. The single most important concept behind these laws is the idea that behavior is shaped by its consequences.

When psychology students are first exposed to the behavioral paradigm, they are often somewhat disturbed at the idea of using reinforcement and punishment to *control* human behavior. However, behaviorists are quick to point out that behavior is naturally under the control of its consequences. Some behaviors become strengthened and some become weakened not because one person rewards or punishes another, but because the behaviors themselves lead to consequences that affect the likelihood that the behavior will recur. For example, parents do not have to teach their children to walk. No grown-up has to apply the techniques of operant conditioning to encourage

Some behaviors are reinforced by natural contingencies. For example, parents do not need to use operant conditioning to teach their children to walk; walking is naturally reinforced in a normal environment.

children to abandon crawling and use their legs to perambulate. Walking has built-in consequences that bring about desired results for the child.

Similarly, parents do not have to teach children not to hit themselves on the thumb with hammers. Children can learn for themselves the contingency betweeen thumb-banging and pain, and thus the thumb-banging will cease.

Life is full of natural contingencies (connections between behaviors and consequences) such as these. Turning the doorknob when you want to go out is naturally reinforced because it leads to the opening of the door. Putting on a jacket before going out into a snowstorm is naturally reinforced because it allows you to avoid freezing to death. While it is true that parents, teachers, and law enforcement officials sometimes deliberately create contingencies to produce the behavior they want, it is also true that many behaviors develop because of natural rather than contrived contingencies.

Reinforcement and Punishment

There are two major classes of consequences that shape behavior: reinforcement and punishment. A **reinforcer** is any stimulus that, when paired with a particular behavior, increases the probability of that behavior. A **punisher** is any stimulus that, when paired with a particular behavior, decreases the probability of that behavior.

Reinforcers are further subdivided into positive and negative groups. A **positive reinforcer** is any stimulus that increases the probability of a behavior when it is presented after the behavior. In everyday language, positive reinforcers are called rewards. If you give your poor dog a bone when he barks and then he barks again, the bone probably serves as a positive reinforcer.

reinforcer Any stimulus that, when paired with a particular behavior, increases the probability of that behavior.

punisher Any stimulus that, when paired with a particular behavior, decreases the probability of that behavior.

positive reinforcer Any stimulus that increases the probability of a behavior when it is presented after the behavior.

TABLE 6.1

A General Summary of the Relationships Between Reinforcement and Punishment

	Give	*Take away*
"Pleasant" stimulus	*Positive reinforcer:* Increases probability of behavior—e.g., smile at child eating vegetables.	*Negative punisher:* Decreases probability of behavior—e.g., turn off television if child eats too much candy.
"Unpleasant" stimulus	*Positive punisher:* Decreases probability of behavior—e.g., frown at child eating too much candy.	*Negative reinforcer:* Increases probability of behavior—e.g., stop nagging if child eats vegetables.

Note: The words *pleasant* and *unpleasant* appear in quotes because these terms are used here only for purposes of simplification. See the text for more formal definitions.

But a closely related concept is a bit more confusing. A **negative reinforcer** is any stimulus that increases the probability of a behavior when it is removed after the behavior. If you get your hair cut to stop your parents' nagging, then their gripes have been an effective negative reinforcer—they led you to get your hair cut. To say this another way, the likelihood of your getting your hair cut is negatively reinforced by your parents' nagging. Or, we can say you got your hair cut (behavior) to stop the nagging (the negative reinforcer).

These relationships are summarized in Table 6.1. The most difficult idea for most people to understand is the concept of a negative reinforcer. To repeat, then, a negative reinforcer *increases* the likelihood of a certain act by ending unpleasantness; anything that *decreases* the likelihood of behavior is called a punisher.

Note that in Table 6.1, the words *pleasant* and *unpleasant* are in quotation marks. The reason is that everyday words such as these invite intuitive assumptions that can be misleading. For example, many young children would probably classify a plate of creamed spinach as an unpleasant stimulus. But for Popeye the sailor man or a vegetarian on a macrobiotic diet, creamed spinach could be a reinforcer.

Skinner was one of the first to argue that psychologists should make no assumptions about pleasantness and unpleasantness and instead let the facts speak for themselves. One empirical procedure for identifying reinforcers is called the **Premack principle**, which states that a more preferred behavior reinforces a less preferred behavior.

For example, in one study, kindergarten children were allowed to choose between several activities, including watching a movie cartoon and playing a pinball machine. Some children spent more time watching the cartoon; for them, the cartoon was a preferred activity that could serve as a reinforcer. These children learned to increase the frequency of pinball playing when segments of the cartoon were presented as a reinforcer for playing pinball. Other children, however, spent more time playing pinball when given free choice. For them, the opportunity to play pinball could be used as a reinforcer to increase the frequency of watching the cartoon. Studies like this of children, monkeys, and rats have generally verified the Premack principle (Premack, 1965).

negative reinforcer Any stimulus that increases the probability of behavior when it is removed after the behavior.

Premack principle The principle that a more preferred behavior will reinforce a less preferred behavior.

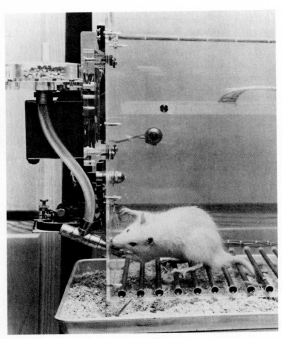

This device for studying operant conditioning is often called a *Skinner box.* When the rat presses a bar, a food pellet is delivered through an automatic feeder.

FIGURE 6.2 An early version of the Skinner box. In the late 1920s, Skinner performed a study in which rats were reinforced for running down an 8-foot alley. To save himself the trouble of replacing the food after each trial and physically lifting the rat back to the starting point, Skinner devised this long rectangular box with two parallel alleys so the rat could simply walk back to the starting point. The whole device was balanced on a fulcrum like a miniature seesaw. When the rat ran to the end, the box tipped and a mechanical device dropped a homemade food pellet. Running back to the start tipped the device again and reset it.

The fact that these relationships can get confusing and that different organisms respond to different reinforcers should serve as a reminder that intuitive terms, such as *reward* and *unpleasant,* can be misleading. The Premack principle and its revisions (Timberlake, 1980) are important because they enable researchers to identify reinforcers without making any assumptions about what an organism likes or dislikes.

Of course, most studies of animal learning rely on simple and standard reinforcers, such as food and water. Although cartoons routinely portray psychologists hovering over rats in mazes, the most common device in the animal laboratory these days is the Skinner box. In its simplest form, a *Skinner box* is a soundproof box with a lever for a rat to push or a key (a button) for a pigeon to peck and a device to deliver food (see Figure 6.2). A deluxe model may include options such as an electrified floor to deliver shocks and a series of colored lights to serve as stimuli.

As Skinner (1956) explained in his delightful article "A Case History in Scientific Method," this apparatus grew out of his attempts to develop an efficient system to deliver rewards automatically and chart the progress of animal learning (see Figure 6.2). But the efficiency of Skinner's invention created new problems. Skinner was working with eight rats at once, and each had learned how to earn about 100 reinforcements a day. Soon he was spending his weekends stamping out food pellets with a primitive pill machine. So what did Skinner do? He decided to save pellets by not reinforcing every lever press. The result, he was astonished to find, was that the rats sometimes worked even harder for fewer rewards. Thus the study of schedules of reinforcement was born.

Schedules of Reinforcement

In the real world, you are usually not rewarded every time you act in a certain way. You do not receive a paycheck every time you go to work, and you do not have a wonderful time every time you ask someone new to dinner. Instead of experiencing what psychologists call **continuous reinforcement**, in which every act is reinforced, you experience **partial reinforcement** (sometimes called intermittent reinforcement), in which some acts are reinforced and others are not. You will probably not be surprised by the fact that learning is acquired more quickly with continuous reinforcement. However, you may be surprised to learn that partial reinforcement can establish behavior patterns that are more stable and resistant to extinction than those produced by continuous reinforcement.

Pet owners often learn the power of partial reinforcement the hard way; in effect, they may unintentionally train animals to be annoying. Consider the typical actions of a pet owner whose dog hangs around the dinner table waiting for scraps. When the animal first starts rubbing dinner guests' knees and whining, it will probably be ignored or told to go away. But sooner or later, the owner may get frustrated enough to give in and feed the dog. What has the animal learned in this case? It has learned that if it makes itself a big enough pain in the knees, sooner or later it will earn a table scrap.

This behavior is difficult to extinguish. If an animal is trained to be annoying with continuous reinforcement (a reward for every annoying act), discontinuing the reward soon ends the behavior. But partial reinforcement teaches an animal to perform many irritating acts to gain a single reward. It can be difficult to get across the message that no more rewards are coming. Thus, partial reinforcement often produces persistent behavior patterns that are hard to change.

Many psychologists have studied how different patterns of reinforcement and punishment, or **schedules of reinforcement**, influence learning. There are four basic types. Two—fixed-ratio and variable-ratio—demand a certain number of responses before a reward is offered; and two—fixed-interval and variable-interval—are based on the passage of time. (Figure 6.3 illustrates response patterns under various schedules of reinforcement.)

Fixed-ratio (FR) schedules are probably the easiest to understand. An organism is rewarded for making a specific number of responses. For example, a rat on an FR25 schedule receives a pellet of food after every 25 bar presses; a pigeon on an FR12 gets a piece of grain after ever 12 key pecks. Animals on fixed-ratio schedules tend to respond rapidly so that they can get more rewards, pausing briefly after each reinforcement. Interestingly, the length of this pause is systematically related to the number of responses required— larger ratios yield longer pauses. In a natural example of a fixed-ratio scale, garment workers in turn-of-the-century sweatshops were often paid for what they accomplished, perhaps 1 or 2 cents for every 100 buttons sewn. As

continuous reinforcement The reinforcement of every response.

partial reinforcement The reinforcement of some acts but not others; sometimes called intermittent reinforcement.

schedules of reinforcement Different patterns of reinforcement and punishment that influence learning.

fixed-ratio (FR) schedules Schedules of reinforcement in which an organism is rewarded after a specific number of responses.

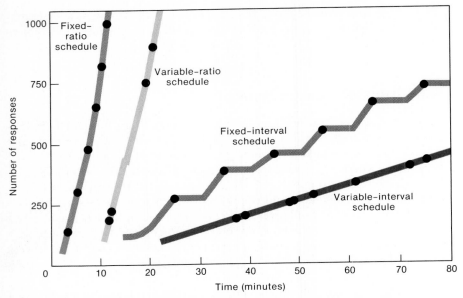

FIGURE 6.3 Response curves for pigeons being reinforced on the basis of different partial reinforcement schedules. Dark lines represent the cumulative number of key pecks. Slash marks represent the presentation of reinforcers. Fixed-ratio and variable-ratio schedules produce higher rates of responding than fixed-interval and variable-interval schedules.

labor unions grew in power, workers rejected this arrangement, perhaps because it tends to produce an unpleasantly fast pace.

Variable-ratio (VR) schedules vary the number of responses required for each reward. A pigeon on a VR10 schedule might have time to peck 8 times for the first piece of grain, 14 times for the next, then 12 times, 10 times, and 6 times. (Note that the average ratio here is 10.) Variable-ratio schedules also produce high and stable rates of response but without the pauses characteristic of fixed-ratio schedules. Casino gamblers who feed paper cups full of quarters into slot machines as fast as they can are painfully familiar with the high response rates generated by variable-ratio schedules. After all, they are reinforced with the jackpot after some average number of responses. (The average, of course, is carefully chosen to make slot-machine owners rich at the players' expense.)

Fixed-interval (FI) schedules reinforce the first response emitted after a certain amount of time elapses. A pigeon on an FI30-second schedule is reinforced for the first key peck it makes after 30 seconds is up. A lazy pigeon might simply wait 30 seconds and then peck the key once to get its dinner. Although most animals are not quite this efficient, well-trained animals on fixed-interval schedules do take a long break after each reinforcer and then gradually increase their response rate until the interval is over and they get their reinforcer. A person who gets mail every day at precisely 11 A.M. is also on a fixed-interval schedule. Somewhere around 10:30 she may start checking her mailbox for that acceptance to medical school. As 11:00 approaches, she may check more and more frequently until the first response after 11:00 is rewarded. Then there will be no more mailbox checking until the next day.

variable-ratio (VR) schedules
Schedules of reinforcement that vary the number of responses required for each reward.

fixed-interval (FI) schedules
Schedules of reinforcement that reinforce the first correct response emitted after a specific amount of time has elapsed.

Around 1900, entire immigrant families sometimes worked in "sweatshops" where they were paid low wages based on the number of garments completed. In operant terms, this would be considered a fixed-ratio schedule of reinforcement.

Finally, **variable-interval (VI) schedules** vary the time that must elapse before a response is reinforced. A VI40-second schedule might reward a rat for the first bar press after 50 seconds, then 60 seconds, 20 seconds, and 30 seconds. (The average here is 40 seconds.) Animals respond steadily without pausing on variable intervals, much as they do with variable ratios. More frequent rewards increase the rate of response. When you dial a busy number, you are on a variable-interval schedule. Sooner or later, your dialing will be reinforced by the welcome sound of a ring at the other end. If you are calling American Airlines and past experience has taught you that the lines are only busy for a few seconds at a time, you will probably dial again immediately. But if you are trying to reach your Uncle Tony, a notorious gabber, you may wait several minutes or hours before trying again.

Shaping

Studying schedules of reinforcement is fine once you have a rat that has learned to press a bar, but how do you get it to press the bar for food in the first place? One way is patience. Put a hungry rat in a Skinner box and wait for it to press the bar. Once the bar press is rewarded by food a few times, the rat will press it more frequently. But you may have a long wait. A more efficient way is to use a technique called **shaping**: teaching a complex behavior by reinforcing *successive approximations* of the desired activity. If the goal is to teach a rat to press a bar for its dinner, one first reinforces

variable-interval (VI) schedules Schedules of reinforcement that vary the amount of time that must elapse before a response is reinforced.

shaping The technique of teaching a complex behavior by reinforcing successive approximations of the desired activity.

any movement whatever toward the lever. Once this movement has been firmly established, the experimenter might reinforce only closer movements or actual touching of the bar. Gradually, the animal can be trained to touch the bar and finally to press it firmly. Thus, in shaping, a complex desired behavior is broken down into a series of simpler responses, which are taught one at a time.

Extremely sophisticated response patterns can be taught in this manner. For example, two of Skinner's students used the method of successive approximations to train animal acts (Breland & Breland, 1951), such as Priscilla the Fastidious Pig. Priscilla's behavior was gradually shaped into a complex chain that included turning on a radio, eating breakfast at a table, picking up dirty clothes and dropping them in a hamper, vacuuming the floor, and answering questions from the audience by lighting up a sign that said "yes" or "no." The biggest problem with this act was that Priscilla, being a pig, tended to eat too much and had to be replaced every four months or so for ease of shipping. Other acts developed by the Brelands included chickens that tap-danced and played tug-of-war and a calf that acted the part of a bull in a china shop.

Shaping is important because it involves a practical way of quickly teaching novel and complex behaviors. Willard (1986) has recently applied these techniques to teach pet capuchin monkeys to help quadriplegic patients whose arms and legs are paralyzed. Shaping was used to train the monkeys to respond to verbal commands. In addition, the patient was given a laser pointer that could be aimed with the teeth, projecting a harmless red dot onto any object

A nameless raccoon imitates Michael Jordan dunking a basketball, an act learned by the shaping of operant responses.

Shaping has been used to train monkeys to help quadriplegic patients whose arms and legs are paralyzed.

the patient wanted the animal to move. Again, shaping was used to train the animals to respond to the dot.

The monkeys have been taught to perform many helpful tasks, including opening and closing doors, turning lights on and off, putting tapes into a cassette deck and turning them on, and even bringing over a drink container and placing a straw in it so a patient can drink. Aside from the obvious improvements in a patient's quality of life, this assistance also serves as the basis for a special bond between these pets and their owners, which may be therapeutically beneficial in itself.

Behavior therapists have also used the method of successive approximations to teach nonverbal and retarded children to speak. They begin by reinforcing any verbal response, then reinforcing any responses that match simple words spoken by the teacher, and finally reinforcing only functional speech (Harris, 1975). The process may be long and difficult and the end results are limited by the mental abilities of the child, but it can provide hope and help where before there was none.

Extinction and Spontaneous Recovery

Many of the concepts that apply to classical conditioning also apply to operant conditioning. Among the most important are extinction, the gradual disappearance of a response, and spontaneous recovery, the reappearance, after a rest period, of a response that has been extinguished.

Skinner first observed the extinction of an operant response by accident, when his food pellet dispenser jammed on a Friday afternoon. When the food reward was discontinued, the animal gradually stopped pressing the bar. Skinner later wrote (1979, p. 95) that he was so excited by the discovery of this parallel between classical and operant conditioning that, "All that weekend I crossed streets with care . . . to protect my discovery from loss through my death." He later observed that rats also show spontaneous recovery after extinction, suddenly trying a few bar presses as if for old time's sake.

There are a number of interesting parallels between human and animal behavior during extinction. For example, one classic finding is that the form of a response becomes more variable during extinction. In one study (Notterman, 1959), rats in a Skinner box usually developed a stereotyped way of pressing the bar: a soft, efficient push. But when rewards were discontinued, they varied the response, pushing both harder and softer. In much the same way, you have probably developed a stereotyped way of writing with your pen. If you suddenly find that your pen doesn't work, you'll probably experiment—hit it sharply, strike it softly, turn it upside down, and shake it.

Another phenomenon often observed in the animal laboratory during extinction is aggression. During extinction, a rat may attack and bite the bar (Mowrer & Jones, 1943). When a pigeon's pecks are no longer rewarded, it may attack another pigeon who is just an innocent bystander (Azrin, Hutchinson, & Hake, 1966). Anyone who has ever kicked a Coke machine when it fails to deliver has experienced a similar phenomenon. Here, aggression (kicking) is elicited when the response (putting coins in the machine) is no longer reinforced (delivery of a Coke).

Generalization and Discrimination

Just as the concept of extinction applies to operant as well as classical conditioning, so the phenomena of generalization and discrimination have parallels in both types of learning. (As noted earlier, generalization involves responding in a similar way to stimuli that resemble one another; discrimination involves learning to respond to a specific kind of stimulus.)

Much of our everyday operant learning involves generalizing from one situation to the next. If you try out a joke on a friend and she rewards you with laughter, you will be encouraged to tell it again. At first, you may generalize the response of telling this joke in other situations and try it out wherever you go. When you discover that it goes over much better at the corner bar than at a church supper, you will probably learn to discriminate the types of situations in which this type of humor is appreciated. Similarly, a 3-year-old may learn that his cute trick of jumping on the sofa as if it were a trampoline is rewarded with laughter by Grandma, but not by Mom, Dad, or Uncle Tony. In this case, Grandma could technically be called a **discriminative stimulus** that signals that a particular response will be reinforced. When the discriminative stimulus (Grandma) is not present, the response (jumping on the couch) is not rewarded.

In the laboratory, a discriminative stimulus can be identified by testing an organism with a wide variety of similar stimuli to see which control the response. For example, if a pigeon is trained to peck at a yellow key, the extent to which this response generalizes to other colors can be tested by gradually changing the color of the key (by increasing or decreasing the wavelength of the light; see Chapter 5). As you can see in Figure 6.4, a pigeon trained in this way does indeed generalize and peck at other colored keys;

FIGURE 6.4 Generalization and discrimination in learning. Pigeons in the control group were reinforced for pecking at a yellow key (550 millimicrons); this response later generalized to similar colors. In discrimination training, pecks were reinforced for 550 millimicrons but not for 570 millimicrons. These pigeons later had a much higher response rate for colors near the reinforced color.

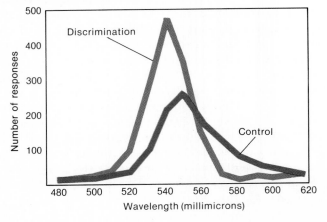

the closer the wavelength of light to the original discriminative stimulus, the more it pecks (Guttman & Kalish, 1956).

To sharpen this pigeon's distinction between yellow keys and others, a researcher can use **discrimination training**: reinforcing a particular response and extinguishing all others. In this case, the color of the key would be changed during training. Whenever it was yellow, the bird would be rewarded with a piece of grain; when the key was green, pecks would not be reinforced. The results of discrimination training are also shown in Figure 6.4; the pigeon pecks at a much higher rate for yellow lights than for other wavelengths.

Obviously, this training procedure can provide subtle information about an animal's sensory capabilities. We know that pigeons can distinguish yellow from green because they have learned to discriminate between stimuli of these colors. If they had failed to learn this discrimination, as other species have, that would suggest they were color-blind.

One particularly ingenious experiment on animals' sensory capacities (Blackwell & Schlosberg, 1943) tested rats' responses to various tones. As explained in Chapter 5, for humans the frequency of a tone (measured in hertz) is related to its pitch. Similarly, researchers have found that when a particular tone is used as a discriminative stimulus, animals generalize the response to other tones; the closer the frequency of the test tone, the greater the response.

One interesting exception involves two tones that differ from each other by a musical interval of one octave. To the human ear, tones of 5,000 Hz and 10,000 Hz sound more similar than tones of 8,000 Hz and 10,000 Hz, even though the latter pair is closer in frequency. Similarly, rats trained to respond to a 10,000-Hz tone generalized more to a 5,000-Hz tone than to an intermediate tone of 8,000 Hz. Like humans, rats seem to perceive tones an octave apart as more similar than other tones closer in frequency. This fact about their sensory world would never have been known without studies of stimulus generalization and discrimination.

Punishment

Being punished by paying a large fine, getting 40 lashes, or hearing your best friend tell you that you are a disgrace to the human race are probably not a few of your favorite things. But punishment is not supposed to be fun; it is supposed to change the way you behave (see, for example, "Understanding the Scientific Method"). Simply defined, **punishment** involves applying an aversive stimulus when an organism emits a response. The presentation of the aversive stimulus following the response reduces the likelihood that the response will be repeated. In this way, punishment is the mirror image of reinforcement, which increases the likelihood of behavior. Moreover, like reinforcement, punishment is defined by its effects on behavior. If a child stopped making pretty pictures when you praised her artistic ability, you could not claim that your priase was a positive reinforcer for her creative efforts; indeed, praise would appear to have acted as a punisher, since the efforts ceased.

While the behaviorist's definition of the term *punishment* is not synony-

discriminative stimulus A stimulus that signals that a particular response will be reinforced.

discrimination training Reinforcement of a particular response and extinction of other responses.

punishment The application of an aversive stimulus when an organism emits a response to reduce the likelihood that the response will be repeated.

mous with everyday use, unpleasant connotations still accompany the notion of using "aversive" (unpleasant) consequences to control behavior. For many years, little research was done in this area, probably because the topic is "unaesthetic and unattractive . . . tainted by association with brutality" (Walters & Grusec, 1977, p. 2). The pioneer researchers who did venture into this taboo area generally came to the conclusion that many of us would like to believe: Punishment is not an effective way to change behavior and therefore should be avoided.

In 1932, Edward Thorndike announced that punishment was not very effective in weakening learned connections. But the punishers Thorndike experimented with were quite mild. College students who failed to match a Spanish word with its English equivalent were simply told they were wrong; chicks that chose the wrong arm of a maze were confined there for 30 seconds. Despite the obvious limitations of these studies, they were widely publicized (see, for example, "Becoming a Critical Consumer") and helped lead to a period of permissive education and child rearing that is ending only now, half a century later (Walters & Grusec, 1977).

It was not until the 1950s that animal researchers seriously investigated the effects of punishment. When they did, they found that Thorndike had been wrong. Punishment clearly does decrease the frequency of behavior. These scientists then set out to analyze the precise effects of punishment, just as earlier investigators had studied the nature of reward.

One typical experiment (Camp, Raymond, & Church, 1967) examined the effects of delaying punishment. Some rats were shocked immediately after a critical lever press; others were shocked 30 seconds later. Earlier studies had made it clear that the sooner reward comes, the more effective it is (Kimble, 1961). This experiment demonstrated that when punishment is delayed, it too loses some of its power. Rats that were shocked immediately after each bar press responded less frequently than those that got a shock 30 seconds later.

Why, you might ask, did the rats continue to press the bar at all? Why didn't they just stretch out on the floor of the Skinner box and relax? If all that pressing the bar ever got them was a shock, they would have stopped. But as in most natural situations, the same response was sometimes rewarded and sometimes punished; some of the bar presses produced food for the hungry rats while others led to shock.

When does punishment work best? Among the suggestions offered in one classic review by Azrin & Holz (1966), punishment should be immediate, intense, and unavoidable. It is best to decide in advance the maximum punishment that is appropriate for a particular situation and then apply this maximum immediately. Starting with a mild punisher and gradually increasing the penalty for repeated offenses may seem more humane and it is certainly easier for the average parent, but it does not work. In the short run, mild punishers have mild effects. And in the long run, organisms adapt to punishment if its intensity is gradually increased and it loses its power to change behavior. Therefore, when Junior is caught stealing hubcaps, Dad should immediately cut off his allowance (or whatever).

While research has shown quite clearly that punishment reduces the frequency of behavior, it has also shown that harmful side effects may occur,

Experiments with a Single Subject: The Effect of Punishment on Self-Destructive Behavior

In scientific research, most psychologists study the average responses of large groups. In contrast, many learning researchers concentrate on controlling the behavior of one individual organism at a time. In the simplest case, they measure the frequency of a particular behavior during a *baseline* period of observation, then experimentally manipulate a particular variable while continuing their observations. If the frequency of behavior increases or decreases substantially during the manipulation, behavior is said to be controlled by that variable. Typically, baseline periods are alternated with experimental periods to test repeatedly the power of the manipulation. Behavior therapists use this approach to alter the frequency of troublesome behaviors.

Therapists use punishment rarely and only in extreme cases. But John, the 8-year-old subject of the experiment we discuss here (Lovaas & Simmons, 1969), had some extreme problems. Besides being severely mentally retarded, John was self-destructive. He hit himself so often that his face and head were covered with scars. Hospital staff members sometimes had to tie John's arms and legs to a bed to keep him from hurting himself. At the time this study began, John had been restrained in this way for six months.

Two behavior therapists began by trying to extinguish John's self-destructive behavior. They reasoned that busy staff members had unintentionally reinforced this bizarre behavior by paying more attention to the child when he tried to hurt himself. To extinguish this activity, they removed John's restraints and left him alone in a small hospital bedroom for 90 minutes while they watched through a one-way mirror. The results were quantified by counting the number of times John hit himself: 2,750 times during those 90 minutes. This first measurement could be considered a baseline estimate of the frequency of self-destructive behavior. Each day, John hit himself less and less frequently in his hour-and-a-half alone. By the tenth day, he had stopped completely.

Thus, the experimenters demonstrated that self-destructive behavior was subject to the laws of operant conditioning; if it was not reinforced, it would gradually disappear. But the price of extinction in this case was high. "John hit himself almost 9,000 times before he quit" (p. 146). And other self-destructive children might do themselves far more serious injury.

John's extinction did not generalize to other situations. Although he no longer hit himself in the experimental room, his behavior elsewhere in the ward was as self-destructive as ever. Extinction was clearly not the answer.

The behavior therapists reluctantly turned to punishment to see if that could control John's bizarre behavior. He got an electric shock, which felt "like a dentist drilling on an unanesthetized tooth," on his leg whenever he hit himself. This was extremely effective. After only 12 shocks, John's self-destructive behavior virtually disappeared.

But again, careful observation revealed that the effect was limited. John had stopped hitting himself when he was in the vicinity of the experimental room or when one of the experimenters was nearby, but this did not generalize to other situations. After John was shocked five more times in other settings, however, his self-destructive behavior disappeared altogether. Interestingly, once the self-destructive behavior was gone, John improved in other ways as well. For example, he spent less

(box continues on next page)

time whining and avoiding adults.

A careful application of the scientific method to John had made it clear that self-destructive behavior could be controlled like any other learned response; its frequency was decreased by either extinction or punishment. This finding was then replicated with several other self-destructive children.

Note that this type of experimentation with a single subject provides practical information. If Lovaas and Simmons had studied a large group of children and found that punishment significantly reduced the frequency of self-destructive behavior on the average, the results might have been less applicable to therapy. What works on the average does not necessarily work for every individual. Experiments with a single subject are particularly useful for identifying variables that can be used to predict and control individual behavior.

BECOMING
A CRITICAL
CONSUMER

Punishment in *Walden Two*

B. F. Skinner's novel *Walden Two* (1948) described a utopian community whose laws and regulations were derived from behavioral principles discovered in the learning laboratory. In the excerpt printed here, two characters in the novel discuss this community's attitude toward punishment. In what way does this disagree with our account of the effects of punishment? Can you explain the contradiction? (A short discussion of these issues appears after the "Summary" at the end of this chapter.)

"The old school made the amazing mistake of supposing that by removing a situation a person likes or setting up one he doesn't like—in other words by punishing him—it was possible to reduce the probability that he would behave in a given way again. That simply doesn't hold. It has been established beyond question. What is emerging at this critical stage in the evolution of society is a behavioral and cultural technology based on positive reinforcement alone. We are gradually discovering—at an untold cost in human suffering—that *in the long run punishment doesn't reduce the probability* that an act will occur. We have been so preoccupied with the contrary that we always take 'force' to mean punishment. We don't say we're using force when we send shiploads of food into a starving country, though we're displaying quite as much power as if we were sending troops and guns." . . .

"It's *temporarily effective,* that's the worst of it. That explains several thousand years of bloodshed. Even nature has been fooled. We 'instinctively' punish a person who doesn't behave as we like—we spank him if he's a child or strike him if he's a man. A nice distinction! The immediate effect of the blow teaches us to strike again. Retribution and revenge are the most natural things on earth. But in the long run the man we strike is no less likely to repeat his act."

"But he won't repeat it if we hit him hard enough," said Castle.

"He'll still tend to repeat it. He'll want to repeat it. We haven't really altered his potential behavior at all. That's the pity of it. If he doesn't repeat it in our presence, he will in the presence of someone else. Or it will be repeated in the disguise of a neurotic symptom." (p. 244)

including increased aggression and long-term emotional damage. These harm-ful effects are particularly likely when the punishment is severe and unpredict-able and thus not clearly related to particular behaviors, or when it is adminis-tered by a hostile caretaker (Walters & Grusec, 1977).

Much remains to be learned about the effects of different types of punish-ment in various situations. For example, some research suggests that physical punishment, such as spanking a child, may lead to imitation, so that the child becomes more aggressive toward other children. However, nonphysical pun-ishment, such as a verbal scolding or requiring the child to mow the lawn or stay in the house, probably does not increase aggression. More research is required to establish this point definitively and to explore the role of other factors, such as the relationship between the child and the person who administers the punishment.

Unfortunately, in the past, some psychologists made far-reaching conclu-sions that were not supported by research evidence; they argued that punish-ment should not be used on the basis of "ethical as well as scientific judgment" (Catania, 1979, p. 97). Researchers are now trying to maintain a more objective position on this emotional issue, to provide information on both the short- and long-term effects of various types of punishment.

Ultimately, practical decisions about whether society should punish a heroin addict or whether a parent should punish a misbehaving child will be based on value judgments. But psychologists must be careful not to let such value judgments cloud their research. Whether punishment works is one question; whether it should be used is quite another.

Avoidance

People do not always sit still and wait for punishment. A man may learn to leave the room when his wife loudly complains about how much he spent on a new pair of jeans; after a while, he may learn to read the early warning signs and leave the room before her tirade begins. The first situation, in which some response (leaving the room) ends an aversive stimulus that is already under way (the tirade), is called **escape**. The second situation, in which a response prevents or avoids an unpleasant stimulus before it begins, is called **avoidance**.

In one of the most important laboratory studies of avoidance, Richard Solomon, Leon Kamin, and Lyman Wynne (1953) placed dogs in a shuttle box with two compartments separated by a tall barrier. When a dog received a shock in one compartment, it could jump over the barrier to the other side and escape the shock. In a pilot study, Solomon turned on a buzzer 10 seconds before each shock began. Two dogs quickly learned to jump when they heard the buzzer and thus avoid the shock altogether. Then Solomon turned off the shock, stopped using the buzzer, and waited to see how long extinction would take. And waited some more. The psychologists gave up before the dogs did. One dog jumped 190 times, the other 490 times. Neither dog gave any indication that it would ever stop jumping; in fact, they seemed to be getting better at it.

Solomon and his colleagues proceeded to do more systematic studies with more dogs. Still no sign of extinction. Intuitively, we might say that the

escape   A response that ends an aversive stimulus that is already under way.

avoidance   A response that prevents or avoids an unpleasant stimulus before it begins.

avoidance response continues because the dog never waits around long enough to find out that the shock is gone. But even that is not the whole story. Some dogs were forced to stay in the original compartment by a glass barrier that prevented their jump. Although they now heard the buzzer, stayed in the compartment, and were not shocked 40 times, only two of nine dogs stopped jumping over the barrier after the glass was removed. The most effective procedure the experimenters found for extinguishing the dogs' response combined two different strategies. On some extinction trials, a glass barrier was present; the dog was forced to stay in the compartment and was not shocked. On other trials, the dogs were allowed to jump into the safe compartment, but they were shocked on that side.

The analogy to human fears is obvious and somewhat disturbing. Once you learn to avoid something, you may never try it again. Suppose, for example, that the electricity goes off and you're trapped in a small elevator with 17 strangers. The combination of close quarters, no lights, and no idea when— or if—you'll get out could make for a sickening or even frightening experience. In the future, you may choose to walk up 12 flights of stairs rather than take a chance on being trapped again. But as long as you keep avoiding elevators, you'll never have a chance to unlearn your fear. And even if you do go for an occasional elevator ride, that might not be enough.

Laboratory studies of animal escape and avoidance have also provided insights into possible causes of depression. In 1967, Martin Seligman accidentally discovered that, under some conditions, dogs have severe problems learning to avoid shocks. If the animals were first given a series of unavoidable shocks while they were physically restrained and then placed in a shuttle box that provided an opportunity to escape from electrical shock, these dogs never learned to jump to the other compartment. Instead, Seligman (1975) noted, when the dog first received the shock:

> It ran frantically around for about thirty seconds. But then it stopped moving; to our surprise, it lay down and quietly whined. . . . On the next trial, the dog did it again; at first it struggled a bit, and then after a few seconds, it seemed to give up and to accept the shock passively. (p. 22)

Seligman called this bizarre behavior pattern *learned helplessness,* because the dogs seemed to have learned that they were helpless; they had no control over the shocks in the earlier part of the study, and they generalized this to a later situation when it was no longer so. Other experimenters later showed comparable phenomena in a wide variety of species, including mice, rats, cats, fish, chickens, and humans.

In general terms, **learned helplessness** refers to an organism's belief, based on prior experience, that it is helpless or lacks control over a particular situation. Interestingly, there are many parallels between the behavior of humans who are depressed and animals that have learned to become helpless. For example, both groups appear passive in the face of stress, do not cope appropriately with the demands of the environment, develop eating problems, and show systematic changes in the chemistry of the brain (specifically, lower levels of the neurotransmitter norepinephrine). Many researchers now believe that human depression may be related to learned helplessness (see Chapter 14).

learned helplessness An organism's belief, based on prior experience, that it is helpless or lacks control over a particular situation.

Changing Your Own Behavior

Two of the most powerful portrayals of behavior modification in literature are George Orwell's *1984,* in which a totalitarian state maintains power by controlling the behavior of its citizens, and Anthony Burgess's *A Clockwork Orange,* whose main character is put through a torturous regimen of classical conditioning meant to rid him of his violent tendencies. Works like these have led some people to think of behaviorists as manipulative, and their work as dehumanizing and somehow sinister.

In our own society, however, behaviorists are much more likely to have written self-help books or opened clinics with precisely the opposite goal: to help people gain more control over their own lives by breaking patterns of self-destructive behavior, such as smoking or overeating.

How does this kind of behavior modification work? By understanding the contingencies that affect a particular behavior pattern, one can learn how to change the behavior itself.

For example, let us suppose you are dissatisfied with your schoolwork. Despite the best of intentions, you find yourself falling behind in your reading, having trouble getting papers done on time, and preparing inadequately for exams. What can you do? (A discussion of this exercise appears after the "Summary" at the end of this chapter.)

Operant Conditioning and Human Therapy

The principles of operant conditioning have been applied by behavior therapists in the treatment of a wide variety of human problems. At the core of **behavior therapy** is the use of reward and punishment to increase or decrease the frequency of precisely defined behaviors. Thus, one can use the techniques of operant conditioning to become, for example, more assertive, less shy, more adventurous, less phobic. See "Applying Scientific Concepts" for some advice on where to begin if you want to undertake a self-modification program.

Defining the actual target behaviors that will be changed is the first step in any application of operant conditioning to human behavior. Wanting to "be a better person" may be a fine statement for a high school yearbook, but a behavior therapist demands more specific goals. Suppose you want to have more friends. The behavior therapist might begin by translating this general desire into a more specific behavioral goal, such as going out one night a week with a new friend.

Just as researchers gradually shape the behavior of laboratory animals by rewarding one small segment of a complex behavior at a time, so a behavior therapist's program probably involves a step-by-step approach. In this case, you could start by forcing yourself to make one pleasant remark every day to a co-worker or a schoolmate.

The confirmed behavior therapist does not believe in analyzing where

behavior therapy The use of reward and punishment to increase or decrease the frequency of precisely defined behaviors.

215

a problem comes from or how deep it runs. She would probably not suggest that the reason you have trouble forming friendships is that your family moved every few years when you were a child. Beyond being skeptical about the possibility of proving this type of speculation, the behaviorist frankly does not care why you have few friends. And neither, she believes, should you. The important thing is to develop new friendships—now.

Behavior therapy also emphasizes the careful measurement of behavioral change. For example, one study of first-graders (Ward & Baker, 1968) began by asking teachers to identify problem students. But the researchers did not simply accept the teachers' classifications. Observers carefully watched these and other children in the class, 15 minutes a day, 4 days a week. After 5 weeks, they totaled the number of times each child had behaved appropriately (for example, paying attention or raising a hand before speaking) and inappropriately (such as hitting other children or blurting out comments in class).

This preliminary stage established a baseline of just how bad the troublemakers really were. The teachers were then instructed to reward the problem children with attention and praise whenever they acted appropriately and simply to ignore them when they misbehaved. Observers continued to rate classroom behavior in the same way as before. This operant conditioning was quite effective; appropriate behavior increased among the troublemakers and inappropriate behavior decreased.

Learning principles such as these have been applied in many different settings; here we focus on one of the most straightforward applications. In a **token economy**, behavior is changed by rewarding specific actions with tokens that can be exchanged for reinforcers. The first token economy was established in a special ward in Anna State Hospital in Illinois (Ayllon & Azrin, 1968). Forty-four severely disturbed female patients were chosen for this experiment. The typical patient was about 50 years old, had been diagnosed as schizophrenic (see Chapter 14), and had spent the last 16 years confined in mental institutions. Most were severely withdrawn; some had never been heard to utter a single intelligible word.

Setting up a token economy involved three stages: identifying specific behaviors to be changed, identifying effective reinforcers for the particular population, and establishing a set of rules for rewarding behavior with tokens (such as poker chips or coins) and exchanging them for rewards.

Given the extreme pathology of this group, the behaviors chosen for reinforcement were quite basic; for example, patients could earn one token by either dressing themselves, brushing their teeth, making their beds, or participating in an exercise class. Helping with work around the ward—emptying the trash, washing pots and pans, cleaning the tables and trays after a meal—earned each patient additional tokens. These could be exchanged for a wide variety of reinforcers, such as cigarettes and candy, a pass to walk around the hospital grounds, permission to attend a movie, or a more desirable dormitory assignment.

The effects on behavior were quite dramatic. Patients who had been withdrawn for years began to help around the ward to earn tokens. The average patient earned almost 500 tokens in the first 20 days of the experiment, and every person earned and spent some tokens. However, the behavior was maintained only for as long as the reinforcement was contingent on

token economy A setting in which behavior is changed by rewarding specific actions with tokens that can be exchanged for reinforcers.

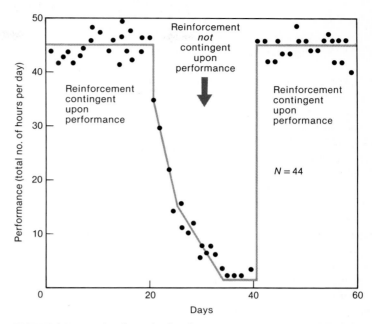

FIGURE 6.5 Results of a study of a token economy at Anna State Hospital in Illinois. Mental patients were reinforced (with tokens later exchanged for rewards) whenever they performed specific acts, such as dressing themselves. When reinforcement was suspended, performance declined.

specific actions. In the second 20 days of the experiment, patients were given a "vacation with pay" in which they were told, "We are very pleased with your work and would like you to continue working, [but] there will be no extra tokens for work" (Ayllon & Azrin, 1968, p. 243). As Figure 6.5 shows, during this period, work on the ward gradually fell off. But when tokens were once more given only after the performance of tasks, behavior improved rapidly.

Later studies revealed that token economies can dramatically alter the behavior of the mentally retarded, alcoholics, drug addicts, autistic children, and preschoolers. Research continues on the question of producing more general changes in patterns of behavior that can be transferred to other situations.

Further information on applying principles of conditioning appear in the discussion of behavior therapy in Chapter 15, and a description of the application of behavioral methods to computer-assisted instruction appears in Chapter 17.

Operant and Classical Conditioning: Similarities and Differences

To this point, we have carefully distinguished between two different learning processes, classical conditioning and operant conditioning. Classical conditioning was said to involve involuntary reflexes, such as salivation elicited by a food stimulus. In physiological terms, this learning is often linked to the autonomic nervous system (which regulates internal bodily processes—see Chapter 3). In contrast, operant conditioning was identified as a more active form of learning in which voluntary responses were shaped by reinforcement and punishment. Physiologically, it is linked to the central nervous system (the brain and spinal cord).

However, complex forms of learning are not always easy to classify in one category or the other. In the classic case of Little Albert (and as in the aversive situation described in Table 6.2) both types of learning are involved. After all, Watson struck the bar only when Albert reached out to touch the rat (see pages 195–196). Reaching is a voluntary response; the suppression of reaching through administration of an aversive stimulus (the loud noise) can be regarded as operant conditioning through punishment.

Complicating the picture further, operant and classical conditioning seem to be governed by some of the same laws. The principles of generalization, discrimination, and extinction, for example, apply equally to both.

Or consider the phenomenon of spontaneous recovery (after a rest period during extinction, a response reappears in a weaker form). This phenomenon appears during the extinction of both classical and operant responses. Might this imply that classical conditioning and operant conditioning are really two examples of one fundamental type of learning?

Some researchers have questioned the criteria that were traditionally said to distinguish the two, particularly the idea that classical conditioning involved involuntary responses (such as a dog salivating) while operant conditioning governed voluntary responses (such as a rat pressing a bar or a pigeon pecking a key). One line of relevant research considered whether key pecking was truly a voluntary response. If it was voluntary, psychologists reasoned, then the behavior of pecking a key or failing to peck a key must always be increased in frequency by reward and decreased by punishment. But Williams and Williams (1969) showed that this was not the case; under some special circumstances, pigeons would continue to peck a key even though this behavior *deprived* them of food. Thus, the Williams and Williams study suggested that key pecking may be an involuntary response.

Further evidence of the importance of inborn biological forces in determining key pecking has come from studies of the actual movements involved in this behavior. It is probably safe to conclude that as far as you and I are concerned, all key pecks are pretty much alike. But photographs of pigeons pecking a key for food rewards versus drink rewards have revealed subtle differences in different types of pecks. Pigeons peck briefly and forcefully for food rewards, as they do in eating. But when the reward is water, the pecks are soft and prolonged, as they are in drinking (Moore, 1973).

Again, the theoretical importance of this finding is the implication that pecking is a reflex that follows certain biological laws, not an arbitrary voluntary behavior that can be shaped in any way by reward. This inference, in turn, challenges the traditional distinction between operant and classical conditioning, and suggests that the two might really be different aspects of the same process.

Those who wish to argue that classical and operant conditioning are not the same can point to obvious differences between the basic learning situation in each. For example, operant conditioning requires an active response; a reward is given only if the subject emits the correct response. Classical conditioning is more passive; the unconditioned stimulus is presented after the conditioned stimulus regardless of what the subject does or does not do.

Another obvious difference between the two types of conditioning concerns the nature of what is learned. In classical conditioning, the conditioned response is quite similar to the unconditioned response; if the original reflex involves salivation, the later learning also involves salivation. But in operant conditioning, the connections seem more arbitrary: The natural response to food is to eat it, not to press a key to get more. Nevertheless, a remarkably wide variety of responses can be shaped by rewarding them appropriately.

Thus, to summarize, modern researchers recognize many important similarities between operant and classical conditioning, and they have found a number of difficulties with some of the traditional criteria for defining these types. However, there are enough differences between the two that it is still useful to distinguish between operant and classical conditioning rather than to talk about just one fundamental type of learning.

Table 6.2 illustrates the differences traditionally attributed to classical

TABLE 6.2

Key Features of Classical and Operant Conditioning

	Classical conditioning	*Operant conditioning*
	POSITIVE SITUATION: RAT IN SKINNER BOX	
Before *conditioning*	Food pellet (UCS) in rat's mouth *elicits* salivation (UCR), which is considered an *involuntary* response. Clicking noises (NS) do not elicit salivation.	Rat *emits* normal ratlike behaviors, including sniffing, scratching, moving around the experimental chamber, and poking its nose into interesting places. These behaviors are considered *voluntary*.
During *conditioning*	The click of the food box when releasing a food pellet (NS) is associated with the ingestion of the food (UCS).	Accidental touching of bar is followed by release of food pellet, which *positively reinforces* the bar touching.
After *conditioning*	The click of the food box (CS) elicits salivation (CR).	The likelihood of bar touching increases. The *behavior potential* of bar touching has been strengthened.
	AVERSIVE SITUATION: FRIENDLY CHILD BITTEN BY UNFRIENDLY DOG	
Before *conditioning*	Teeth in arm (UCS) elicit pain and fear (UCR). The emotional response of fear is considered involuntary. Sight of shaggy four-legged beastie (NS) does not elicit fear.	Child emits normal childlike behaviors, including approach to novel four-legged beasties and avoidance of circumstances that have proved painful and scary. Approach and avoidance behaviors are considered voluntary.
During *conditioning*	Sight of ferocious dog (NS) with teeth embedded in arm (UCS) is associated with pain and fear (UCR).	Child's flight from biting dog is followed by escape from painful and frightening situation. The escape *negatively reinforces* the flight because it results in the removal of the dog.
After *conditioning*	Sight of dog (CS) elicits fear and pain.	The likelihood of the child's running from the sight of dogs is strengthened, as is the likelihood that the child will avoid situations where a dog might be encountered.

Note: NS stands for neutral stimulus—a stimulus that becomes a conditioned stimulus.

and operant conditioning in two situations: (1) where there is a stimulus that acts as a positive reinforcer, and (2) where there is a stimulus that is aversive. In the first situation, a "naive" (untrained) rat in an experimental chamber (Skinner box) is being trained to press a bar. In the second situation, a small child with no previous bad experiences with canines is bitten by a neighbor's dog. Note that in both circumstances, classical and operant conditioning take place at the same time.

Biology and Learning

The studies of biological differences in the key pecks involved in eating and drinking are part of a larger trend in studying the importance of underlying biological constraints and differences between the species and the way they relate to learning. Thirty or forty years ago, behaviorists placed little emphasis on such differences. Some seemed to believe, as Lockhard (1971, p. 169) put it, that "a white rat is a simple version of a human being." But today's researchers are more aware of both similarities and differences between the species.

Species-Specific Behaviors

The definition of **species-specific behavior** is quite straightforward: patterns of behavior that are characteristic of a particular species. Attention to this topic was first prompted by **ethologists**, researchers who study the behavior patterns of each species in its natural environment.

The first ethologists were European zoologists who were interested in the behavioral implications of Darwin's theory of evolution. Just as other biologists had shown how anatomy and physiology had evolved as a result of reproductive success, the ethologists hoped to show how each species' behavior had evolved to adapt to its environment. This research was conducted in the natural environment, since ethologists believed that the artificial conditions of the laboratory could interfere with the appearance of natural forms of behavior.

For example, Konrad Lorenz (1965) studied the attachments that form between infant animals and their parents. When he hatched ducklings in incubators and presented the newborns with a variety of stimuli, he found that the ducklings became attached to the first moving object they saw after birth, whether it was a human being, a wooden decoy, or a bird of another species.

The phenomenon of a newborn animal following the first moving stimulus it encounters after birth is called **imprinting**. Once this type of learning occurs it is very difficult to change. Thus, when Lorenz himself was the first moving stimulus seen by a group of goslings, the birds continued to follow him around as if he were their mother, even when they were later given an opportunity to follow an adult female goose. In other studies, ducklings who imprinted on a wooden decoy continued to follow this unresponsive "parent" rather than a live duck to whom they were introduced at a later date.

Of course, under normal circumstances, the first moving stimulus that

species-specific behavior Behavior patterns characteristic of a particular species.

ethologists Researchers who study the behavior patterns of a particular species in its natural environment.

imprinting The phenomenon of a newborn animal following the first moving stimulus it encounters after birth.

Imprinting-type behavior has been observed in a number of species. This picture shows Sammy the squirrel with his "foster mother" cat.

a newborn duckling encounters is its mother. Imprinting thus appears to be an adaptive mechanism which ensures that newborn animals remain close to their mothers rather than wandering off into the dangerous world around them. In this way, imprinting serves an adaptive purpose that helps to ensure the survival of the species. Imprinting has been found most clearly in birds that walk or swim immediately after birth, but it has also been observed in other species, such as dogs and sheep.

Scientific knowledge about imprinting has proven useful in practical efforts to save endangered species. For example, when condor chicks have been artifically incubated in captivity as part of an effort to increase the condor population, immediately after birth they are fed by a puppet designed to look like a female adult condor. That is because researchers now know that if undisguised humans cared for the chicks, they would imprint on the human caretaker and later be unable to adapt to normal mating patterns and life in the wild (Miller, 1985).

Many other types of species-specific behavior have been observed in both natural environments and traditional learning laboratories. For example, Bolles (1970) notes that it is difficult to teach a pigeon to peck a key to avoid a shock, although a rat can quickly learn to press a bar to avoid the same situation. He argues that this is because pigeons naturally respond to a threat by flying away rather than by sitting around thinking about it.

Keller and Marion Breland (the Skinnerian animal trainers whose work with Priscilla the Pig was described earlier) also reported that they sometimes encountered unexpected difficulties that seemed to be related to species-specific behavior. For example, they described an attempt to use shaping and other operant principles to train a raccoon to pick up coins and place them in a piggy bank. Although it was a simple matter to teach the raccoon to pick them up, the animal "seemed to have a great deal of difficulty letting go of the coin. He would rub it up against the inside of the container, pull it back out, and clutch it firmly for several seconds" (Breland & Breland, 1961, p. 682). These difficulties continued until finally they gave up on the act. The Brelands concluded that their training could not overcome the raccoon's natural instinct to wash its food. (Although the coins were not edible, they had become associated with food because they were repeatedly presented with it.)

Effects of Experience on the Brain

While behaviorists emphasize environmental, experiential influences on behavior, they by no means deny that all behavior has some sort of biological basis. Without a viable biological organism, no behavior would be possible. Supporters of the biological paradigm are committed to establishing the precise biological mechanisms underlying such functions as learning, memory, sensation, and perception.

Mark Rosenzweig of the University of California at Berkeley has devoted many years of research to determining how experience affects the structure and chemistry of the nervous system and how the nervous system manages to accomplish such feats as learning and remembering. In one of his early studies with laboratory rats (Rosenzweig, Krech, & Bennett, 1958), he found a relationship between learning and concentration of acetylcholinesterase (AChE) in the brain. These results suggested that the more AChE was concentrated in the brains of the rats, the better they learned. Quite serendipitously, Rosenzweig and his colleagues also discovered that rats tested with more complicated or difficult behavioral tests showed higher levels of cortical AChE activity than rats run on simpler tasks (Rosenzweig, Krech, & Bennett, 1961). These findings suggested that AChE levels were not simply fixed by heredity but could be altered through experience.

Since this early research, Rosenzweig and his colleagues have accumulated considerable evidence concerning the effects of experience on the brains of rats. They have demonstrated, for example, that enriched experience can lead to greater brain weight, even in mature rats. Of particular interest is animal research on the effectiveness of enriched experience in promoting recovery of function after brain damage (e.g., Will, Rosenzweig, & Bennett, 1976). Applications of these basic research findings can be found in attempts to improve health and behavior by providing enriched environments for retarded children, the elderly, and victims of brain damage (Rosenzweig, 1984).

Taste Aversions

Still another line of evidence that has forced psychologists to become more aware of the interactions between biology and conditioning concerns dislikes of certain foods

One night when psychologist Martin Seligman was in graduate school, he got sick several hours after a fancy meal of filet mignon with béarnaise sauce. After that ill-fated evening, he found that his love of this sauce disappeared (Seligman & Hager, 1972); in fact, Seligman now thought that béarnaise sauce was a rather disgusting thing to put over a piece of meat.

At first glance, this looks like a straightforward case of classical conditioning. For this natural reflex, illness (the UCS) elicits vomiting (the UCR). When béarnaise sauce (the CS) is paired with illness, through learning it also comes to elicit vomiting (the CR).

However, when he thought about it, Seligman realized that his experience was inconsistent with several widely accepted laws of conditioning. The most basic was that the CS and UCS must be presented within a short time period for significant learning to occur. In this case, the béarnaise sauce (the CS) was eaten six hours before the illness (the UCS) occurred, and, therefore, traditional theory would have predicted no learning. In addition, Seligman's learning did not seem to generalize to other stimuli, as learning theory would have predicted. Although even the concept of béarnaise sauce was enough to revolt him, Seligman was not nauseated by other stimuli present when he had eaten, such as filet mignon, the white plates he ate from, or the company of his wife.

The same week that Seligman had this experience, John Garcia and Robert Koelling (1966) published an elegant experiment that had been designed to see whether the classical conditioning of sickness followed different rules than other types of classical conditioning. At the simplest level, they were able to show that when animals get sick, they instinctively seem to conclude: "It must have been something I ate."

The experiment began when thirsty rats were placed in a cage with two different water spouts. One spout delivered water that had been sweetened with saccharin. The other spout delivered normal water, but when the rat drank from it, lights flashed and clicking noises occurred. Thus, in effect, each rat had been given two different conditioned stimuli that it could associate with later events: sweet water, and what Garcia and Koelling called "bright, noisy" water.

The experimenters then divided the rats into two groups for classical conditioning: Half were exposed to X-rays, which made them sick to their stomach, and the other half received more traditional aversive training, in which the floor of the cage was electrically shocked. Several days later, each rat was deprived of water and placed in another cage with a single water spout. When rats that had been made sick were offered water flavored with saccharin, they refused to drink. Apparently, they had learned a conditioned association between illness and the sweet water, despite the fact that the illness actually occurred 12 to 24 hours after they drank the water. When rats that had been made sick were offered "bright, noisy" water, they drank freely. Apparently, the visual and auditory stimulation was not associated with illness. Rats that had previously received electrical shock rather than X-ray treatments showed the opposite pattern. They refused to drink "bright, noisy" water, since the audiovisual stimuli had become associated with shock as a result of classical conditioning. However, they did drink the sweet water freely.

Garcia and Koelling concluded that rats are biologically prepared to associate certain classes of stimuli with certain types of responses. In the entire history of rats, illness has often been associated with foods, whereas pain usually has resulted from contact with physical objects. As a result, the species has developed an innate tendency to associate illnesses with taste, and pain with sights and sounds.

Many follow-up studies verified the fact that this learning could be established with long delays between the CS and the UCS. It also became clear that if persons or animals get sick hours after eating a meal with several foods, they tend later to avoid the most novel or unusual food at the meal, as in the case of Seligman's dislike of béarnaise sauce (Logue, 1986).

Similar trends were uncovered in a questionnaire study of 517 college students who were asked whether they had ever eaten or drunk something, gotten sick later, and avoided eating the food again. About two-thirds of these subjects reported at least one such food aversion. On the average, the illness had occurred about 2.5 hours after eating, and the aversion had persisted for 5 years by the time of the study (Logue, 1986).

The principles uncovered in research on taste aversion have been applied in attempts to control predatory animals. For example, in western rangelands, there is a longstanding problem with coyotes killing grazing sheep. The traditional solution is to kill the coyotes. Gustavson and his colleagues (1974) developed a more humane approach by leaving out chunks of lamb wrapped in sheep hide and laced with a substance (lithium chloride) that would make them sick. Coyotes that ate this meat became ill and developed an aversion to eating sheep; they even stopped killing them. Although this method was later questioned by some members of the U.S. Fish and Wildlife Service (Sterner & Shumake, 1978), similar techniques have proven successful with other species (Conover, 1986).

These principles have also been shown to be relevant to the treatment of cancer patients. In 1978, Ilene Bernstein published a study of 41 children who were receiving chemotherapy treatments that made them sick. Before these treatments, some of the children were offered a serving of an unusual ice cream made with maple and black walnut flavors called Mapletoff.

Two to four weeks later, these and other children were offered a choice between playing with a game or eating Mapletoff. Those who had previously been given the ice cream before a treatment generally chose the game. In one sense, this choice seemed irrational, since many of these children could explain that it was the therapy that had made them sick, not the ice cream. Nevertheless, the ice cream had become aversive.

A control group of patients who had never seen Mapletoff before were tested to make sure that the ice cream was not inherently disgusting. When they were given the same choice, they generally chose the ice cream rather than the game, supporting the idea that the aversion was caused by association with treatment. Dr. Bernstein is currently studying ways to reduce cancer patients' food aversions by applying lessons learned from animal research to this clinical population (Miller, 1985).

Cognitive Approaches to Learning

When John B. Watson announced the birth of behaviorism in 1913, he helped found a school of thought that was to dominate American psychology for nearly half a century. According to many behaviorists, virtually all behavior resulted from classical and operant conditioning. To understand these forms of learning, behaviorists focused on the stimuli that affected an organism

cognitive psychology The study of higher mental processes in such areas as attention, perception, memory, language, imagery, and reason.

and the responses they produced. However, strict behaviorists were unwilling to speculate about the internal processes within an organism (such as memory or thought) that linked stimulus to response. This is sometimes referred to as the black-box approach. Behaviorists study what goes into the box (stimuli) and what comes out (responses) but not the nature of the box itself.

The traditional behavioral view, with its strong emphasis on the study of animal learning, began to be challenged in the 1960s as increasing numbers of psychologists turned to **cognitive psychology**, the study of higher mental processes involved in such areas as attention, perception, memory, language, imagery, and reason.

The cognitive approach differs from the behavioral approach primarily in its focus on internal mental constructs, such as *knowledge*. For example, when traditional behaviorists analyze the classical conditioning of Pavlov's dogs, they limit their discussion to observable behaviors, such as increases in the frequency of salivating. In contrast, cognitive psychologists might try to analyze what the animal knows, such as an internal mental representation of the relationship between a ringing bell and the presentation of food. This cognitive approach now dominates studies of human memory (as described in Chapter 7) and language and thought (see Chapter 8). In this chapter, we shall focus on the implications of the cognitive approach for conditioning and animal learning.

Insight Learning

Even during the most dominant periods of behaviorism, a few researchers focused on the role of internal knowledge in animal learning. For example, the German psychologist Wolfgang Köhler applied the principles of Gestalt psychology not just to perception (Chapter 5), but also to the process of learning.

From 1913 to 1920, Köhler served as director of a center for primate research on Tenerife in the Canary Islands. In his book *The Mentality of Apes,* Köhler (1925) summarized the many experiments that led him to reject Thorndike's notion that animals solve problems through a random process of trial and error. Rather, he argued, they showed evidence that they understood the problems and had insight into how they could be solved. For example, in one study a chimpanzee named Sultan was placed in a cage with a basket of fruit dangling from the ceiling out of reach. After several vain attempts to jump up and grab the fruit, Sultan solved the problem by dragging over a crate, climbing on top, and jumping from there.

Sultan and his cagemates solved one problem after another. When one box was not enough, they piled two or three; when the box was placed at the side of the cage and filled with heavy stones, they took out the stones before moving the box to a more convenient spot. They used sticks, lengths of wire, and rope to pull objects within reach of their cages; when one stick was not enough, they jammed two together; when no stick was available, they tore a branch off a tree. In fact, the chimps' ingenuity sometimes went further than planned. One chimp learned to tease innocent bystanders—including dogs, chickens, and presumably Dr. Köhler—by suddenly stabbing them

Chica the chimp uses a pole to reach for food. According to Wolfgang Köhler, this chimp and others faced with similar problems had sudden insights that produced the solutions.

with a stick whenever they passed within reach of the cage.

Köhler argued that the chimps had solved the problems by **insight**, a sudden understanding of the basic nature of the solution. He cited several sources of evidence, including the fact that chimps often discovered the solutions quite suddenly, sometimes after pausing to examine the materials. These animals were not blindly learning to associate stimuli and responses, Köhler said; they used internal thought processes to comprehend the world around them.

Learning Versus Performance

Among mainstream behaviorists, the most influential supporter of cognitive concepts was probably Edward C. Tolman. Like most of his contemporaries, Tolman had boundless optimism concerning the contributions animal research could make to the understanding of human behavior. Indeed, in 1938 (p. 34) he wrote: "I believe that everything important in psychology . . . (except perhaps matters [that] . . . involve society and words) can be investigated in essence through the continued experimental and theoretical analysis of the determiners of rat behavior at a choice point in a maze."

While it would be very difficult to find a psychologist who shared this view 50 years later, many experts are more sympathetic to Tolman's attempts to bring such commonsense notions as planning, knowledge, and purpose back into learning theory. Tolman believed that stimuli did not simply become associated with responses (S-R psychology) but rather with each other (S-S, stimulus-stimulus, psychology). According to one traditional S-R view, a rat learned to find the food in a maze by practicing a particular set of muscle movements that must always follow one another in the same sequence. Tolman believed that the rat learned more than a particular chain of stimuli and responses; it learned where the food was.

He was one of the first psychologists to distinguish clearly between *learning* (in this context, defined as what the animal knew) and *performance* (what the animal did). Thus, learning is an internal representation of knowledge, which may or may not be expressed in a particular behavioral performance.

To demonstrate the importance of this distinction, Tolman and his colleagues performed a series of experiments to show that a rat's knowledge of the maze was only expressed under certain conditions. According to many black-box behaviorists, a rat learns a path through a maze only when it receives some reward. Tolman and Honzik (1930) placed rats in a maze for 10 consecutive days, allowing them to explore it but providing no food reward. When they put food at the end of the maze on the eleventh day, the rats went straight to the goal. In fact, they made no more errors than a control group that had been rewarded with food from the beginning. Judging by their performance during the first 10 days, the unrewarded rats did not seem to have learned anything about the maze. But when provided with the proper motivation (food), the rats' performance made it clear that they had indeed learned something about the maze. Ingenious experiments like this helped move psychology away from Watson's hard-line behaviorism to include the role of the internal processes involved in thought.

insight A sudden understanding of the nature of the solution to a problem.

Expectancies

Cognitive concepts are also relevant to many contemporary studies of animal learning. One particularly influential concept is the notion of **expectancy**, an animal's knowledge or belief about reinforcement in a particular situation.

For example, Robert Rescorla has published a number of experiments showing that the learning abilities of rats are much more sophisticated than traditional models suggest. Rats seem quite capable of making complex judgments and weighing probabilities.

Rescorla based his research on earlier studies of the classical conditioning of fear. Of course, it is always risky to describe rats' reactions in terms of human emotions. But consider the following procedure. A hungry animal is first trained to press a lever at a high, steady rate to get food. Then, while the rat is pressing the bar, a tone is sounded and the rat is given an electric shock. The shock is not controlled by the bar-pressing, and no matter what the rat does, it continues to hear occasional tones and get shocks for the rest of the experiment. The rat's typical reaction to this situation is called *conditioned suppression*—an animal slows down or stops responding whenever it hears a tone that signals an oncoming shock. Note that this conditioned suppression of responses costs the hungry rat food; when it presses the bar less often, it earns fewer rewards. Speaking loosely, we might say that this irrational reaction to the tone is a sign of fear.

In Rescorla's 1968 study of the cognitive capabilities of rats, the conditional stimulus was a tone that was presented for two minutes. One group of rats was shocked 10% of the time when the tone was on and never when it was off. A second group was shocked 40% of the time whether the tone was on or off. According to traditional theory, the second group should have been more afraid of the tone because they had been shocked four times more often while it was on. In fact, however, the first group was more afraid of the tone (as measured by conditioned suppression). Intuitively, we might say that the fearful rats knew that the tone meant "maybe there will be a shock," whereas the tone provided no information for the other group. Rescorla and Wagner (1972) went on to develop complex mathematical models that successfully predicted how animals respond under various degrees of uncertainty. These results seem to imply that even the lowly rat makes internal judgments about the likelihood of various events and concludes that some stimuli mean more than others.

More recently, Colwill and Rescorla (1985) used the taste aversion paradigm to demonstrate reward expectancies during conditioning. In one part of this study, animals were given sweet water when they pressed a lever and a food pellet when they pulled a chain. Later, they were again given the sweet water when they pressed the lever, but this time were also injected with a drug that caused nausea.

Some time afterward, the responses were extinguished. The animals were placed in a cage with both a lever and a chain, but no rewards or punishments were given. They pulled the chain in the normal pattern one would expect during extinction; at first rather frequently, and then less and less when no rewards were offered. However, they very rarely pressed the lever during this extinction phase, suggesting that they had developed an

expectancy Knowledge or belief about reinforcement in a particular situation.

expectancy that the lever pressing would produce an aversive stimulus that would make them sick. Several variations on this basic experimental design led to the same conclusion: In this situation, the animals gave clear evidence of expectancies regarding future rewards.

While it has taken some time for animal researchers to design experiments that provide unequivocal evidence for expectancies, those who focus on human learning have more easily seen the effects of cognitive factors. For example, many animal experiments have shown that immediate punishment is more effective than punishment that comes long after a response (Azrin & Holz, 1966). But people are smarter than rats, and immediacy is probably not as important for the average child (Walters & Grusec, 1977). The difference is that you can explain to a 7-year-old that she has to go to bed early tonight because she called Mommy something unpleasant this morning. To understand a child's response we must explore her expectations and interpretations—in short, what she thinks.

The next three chapters describe some relevant cognitive processes. Here, our discussion of cognition concludes by introducing another form of learning, one that is based on imitation. Many examples of similar cognitive processes will be seen in Chapter 7 as we discuss the study of human memory.

Observational Learning

People do not always behave in certain ways simply because they were rewarded or punished in the past; sometimes they seem to imitate the actions of others. When your new boss takes you out for dinner at an expensive restaurant, you may not know what you're supposed to do with the third fork from the left. To learn by operant conditioning, you would have to try the fork on each new dish and watch the boss carefully to see if she frowned, indicating an incorrect guess. A more efficient and less embarrassing strategy involves learning by observation. Watch the boss carefully and use your fork when she uses hers. Anyone who has ever watched a child mimic the actions of a favorite cartoon superhero has seen a similar process at work. **Observational learning** involves modeling or copying the behavior of another.

In one of the first and most famous experiments on observational learning, Bandura, Ross, and Ross (1963) studied preschool children's reactions to observing aggression. Ninety-six 3- to 5-year-olds from the Stanford University Nursery School were divided into four groups. Three groups observed different types of aggressive models; the fourth was a control group with no special training. Each child in the first group was left in a room to play with some papers, while a stranger played with more elaborate toys at the other end of the room. After a few minutes, the adult model began to attack a 5-foot-tall inflated "Bobo doll" using "highly novel responses which are unlikely to be performed by children independently." For example, the adult model sat on the doll and repeatedly punched it in the nose, hit it on the head with a mallet, then tossed it in the air and kicked it around the room. Throughout this aggressive act, the model said things like: "Sock him in the nose," "Knock him down," "Kick him," and "Pow."

In the second experimental condition, children watched an identical

observational learning Learning by observation, which involves modeling or copying the behavior of another person.

Children often learn by observing and copying the behavior of their parents.

performance on film. The third group saw a cartoon in which Herman the Cat beat up a Bobo doll. The children in the control group did not participate in this stage of the experiment.

A few minutes later, each child (including those in the control group) was led into another room and given a set of attractive toys. But as soon as the child got involved in playing with them, the experimenter took him or her into still another room. This mild frustration was designed to increase the likelihood of aggression. The toys in the next room fell into two categories. "Aggressive toys" included a child-sized (3-foot-tall) Bobo doll, a mallet, a peg board, two dart guns, and a tether ball with a face painted on it hanging from the ceiling. "Nonaggressive toys" included a tea set, crayons, dolls, and plastic farm animals.

For the next 20 minutes, each child's behavior was carefully observed through a one-way mirror. Sure enough, the children who had watched aggressive models were more likely to engage in aggressive play. Some of them displayed virtual "carbon copies of the model's behavior." Although there were some significant differences among the groups, in general it did not seem to matter whether a child had seen a live model, a film, or a cartoon; the children in all three experimental groups were more aggressive than the children in the control group. Simply watching the actions of a model had led the children to imitate those actions.

Some of the subtleties of imitation learning began to emerge in later studies. One follow-up study (Bandura, 1965) looked at the effects of rewarding or punishing a model's act. In this experiment, nursery school children watched an adult abuse a Bobo doll on television. This time, the experimenter paired each aggressive act with a distinctive phrase, to see just how closely the child mimicked the behavior. While the model sat on the doll and punched it, he said, "Pow, right in the nose, boom, boom"; when he beat it over the head with a mallet, he said, "Sockeroo . . . stay down," and so on.

For children in the "model-rewarded" condition, the film went on to show a second adult congratulating the model for being a "strong champion" and rewarding him with popcorn, candy, Cracker Jacks, and a large glass of Seven-Up. In the "model-punished" condition, other children saw the second adult come on the scene shaking his finger and saying, "Hey there, you big bully. You quit picking on that clown" (p. 591). When the model backed up and tripped, the other adult sat on him and spanked him with a rolled-up magazine. The control group of children saw only the first part of the film.

Not surprisingly, when the children were later given their own chance to beat up a Bobo doll, the group who had seen the model punished were least likely to be aggressive themselves. (The group who saw the model rewarded were about as aggressive as the control group.) Every child was later able to repeat the distinctive phrases and tell the experimenter what the model had done in the movie. But children who had seen the model punished did not repeat this behavior themselves; in Tolman's terms, their learning was not reflected in their performance.

We shall return to some of the implications of these studies for understanding human personality in Chapter 12. In this context, observational learning is important primarily because it is a far more subtle form of learning than classical or operant conditioning. Both types of conditioning depend on direct experience with external stimuli and reinforcers. In observational learning, the organism learns through a more cognitive process that involves interpreting one's observations.

In Chapter 7, we shall see how studies of human memory have provided new insights into cognitive processes in learning.

The top row shows the aggressive behaviors displayed by an adult model. Looking down each column, note how closely children later imitated these actions.

Summary

- **Learning** can be defined as a relatively permanent change in behavior potential that occurs through experience.

Classical Conditioning

- Discovered by Ivan Pavlov, **classical conditioning** involved repeatedly pairing a stimulus, called the **unconditioned stimulus (UCS)**, that elicited a reflex response, called the **unconditioned response (UCR)**, with a previously neutral stimulus, called the **conditioned stimulus (CS)**. In time, this came to elicit a similar response, called the **conditioned response (CR)**.

- **Extinction** is the gradual disappearance of a learned response. In classical conditioning, CRs are extinguished by repeatedly presenting the CS without the UCS.

- **Spontaneous recovery** refers to the reappearance of an extinguished response after a rest period.

- **Generalization** involves responding in a similar way to stimuli that resemble each other; the greater the similarity, the closer the response.

- **Discrimination** involves learning to respond only to a specific kind of stimulus.

- **Counterconditioning** is a technique in which relaxation is classically conditioned to stimuli that previously elicited anxiety.

Operant Conditioning

- In **operant conditioning**, the probability of a response increases when reinforcement is presented and decreases when punishment is presented following that response. Traditionally, operant conditioning has been said to apply to active, voluntary processes, while classical conditioning applies to passive, involuntary reflexes.

- A **reinforcer** is any stimulus that, when paired with a particular behavior, increases the probability of that behavior. In contrast, a **punisher** is any stimulus that, when paired with a particular behavior, decreases the probability of that behavior.

- There are two types of reinforcers: **positive reinforcers** present a stimulus, and **negative reinforcers** remove a stimulus; both increase the probability of a particular behavior.

- The **Premack principle** is an empirical procedure for identifying reinforcers that states that a more preferred behavior reinforces a less preferred behavior.

- Reinforcers and punishers can be presented according to many patterns, or **schedules of reinforcement**.

- **Continuous reinforcement** involves reinforcing every single response.

- **Partial reinforcement** involves reinforcing some acts and not others.

- The four most common schedules of partial reinforcement are **fixed-ratio (FR) schedules, variable-ratio (VR) schedules, fixed-interval (FI) schedules,** and **variable-interval (VI) schedules.**

- **Shaping** involves teaching a complex behavior by reinforcing *successive approximations* of the desired activity; it is important because it is a practical and quick way to teach novel and complex behaviors.

- A **discriminative stimulus** is a stimulus that signals that a particular response will be reinforced.

- **Discrimination training** reinforces a particular response and extinguishes all others.

- **Punishment** involves applying an aversive stimulus when an organism emits a response. It reduces the likelihood that the response will be repeated.

- A situation in which some response ends an aversive stimulus that is already under way is called **escape**.

- **Avoidance** refers to a response that avoids or prevents an unpleasant stimulus. Avoidance responses are difficult to extinguish and seem to be involved in many human fears.

- Certain types of avoidance learning produce **learned helplessness,** an organism's belief that it is helpless or lacks control over a particular situation. Learned helplessness may be one cause of human depression.

- **Behavior therapy** uses reward and punishment to increase or decrease the frequency of precisely defined behaviors.

- In a **token economy,** behavior is changed by rewarding specific actions with tokens that can be exchanged for reinforcers.

- Modern researchers recognize many important similarities between operant and classical conditioning, but there are enough differences between the two that it remains useful to distinguish between them.

Biology and Learning

- **Species-specific behavior** is any pattern of behavior that is characteristic of a particular species.

- **Ethologists** are researchers who study the behavior patterns of each species in its natural environment.

- The phenomenon of a newborn animal following the first moving stimulus it encounters after birth is called **imprinting**.

- Studies of taste aversions have helped reveal how biological factors can limit learning. Animals seem to be biologically prepared to associate illness with novel tastes, even if the illness occurs several hours after eating.

Cognitive Approaches to Learning

- **Cognitive psychology** is the study of higher mental processes involved in such areas as attention, perception, memory, language, imagery, and reason.

- Some researchers argue that animals are able to solve problems using **insight**, a sudden understanding of the basic nature of the solution.

- The cognitive concept of **expectancy** refers to an animal's knowledge or belief about reinforcement in a particular situation.

- **Observational learning** involves modeling or copying the behavior of another.

Critical Thinking Exercises Discussions

Punishment in Walden Two

Skinner's opinion that punishment does not work directly contradicts the research described in the text. The explanation is simple. The novel was written in 1948, and research cited in the text was conducted after that date. When Skinner wrote his novel, most psychologists agreed that punishment was ineffective. Today, there is still a great deal of controversy about the negative effects of punishment, particularly under certain conditions described in the text. But virtually all agree that punishment does reduce the frequency of behavior.

The critical consumer should never blindly accept the opinion of an expert, no matter how famous he or she may be. It is always useful to examine the evidence behind a claim and to see whether new discoveries have challenged old beliefs.

Changing Your Own Behavior

To improve your studying, you can start by systematic observation of your study habits. Keep a log for at least a week, recording the time of day, location, and length of each study session. Note any unusual interruptions or distractions, anything that affects the quality of your studying: noise, telephone calls, hunger, fatigue.

At the end of the week, try to identify the circumstances under which you achieved the best results—and the worst. Do you work better in the daytime or at night? In your room or in the library? Alone or with others? Are the circumstances that affect your studying primarily internal (e.g., hunger, eye fatigue, loneliness) or external (noise, interruptions, temptations)?

One of the most basic strategies of thinking critically to solve a problem is to gather enough appropriate, accurate information. Until you understand the nature of the problem (in this case, what is preventing you from studying effectively), it is unlikely that you will be able to find a viable solution. By understanding the forces that influence your study habits, you can take action to eliminate those with negative effects, thus changing your studying behavior.

REMEMBERING AND FORGETTING

*A*t the age of 10, H. M. had his first epileptic seizure. By early adulthood, the disease was so severe that he could not work or lead a normal life. Despite the fact that he took a variety of anticonvulsant medicines, H. M. had a grand mal seizure in which he lost consciousness and fell into convulsions at least once a week. Less severe petit mal seizures occurred about once an hour, leaving H. M. in an almost continuous state of confusion.

Finally, in desperation, H. M. agreed to experimental surgery to destroy apparently diseased tissue in the temporal lobe of the brain, including a structure called the hippocampus. Although the operation virtually eliminated H. M.'s seizures, this success was overshadowed by an unexpected and tragic side effect—H. M. lost the ability to learn anything new. When psychologist Brenda Milner (1959, p. 49) met H. M. for the first time nearly two years later, he was quite confused and kept repeating, "It is as though I am just waking up from a dream; it seems as though it has just happened."

When his family moved to a new home after the operation, for several years H. M. was unable to learn the new address or to find his way home alone. He did not recognize his neighbors even after he had met them many times and could never remember where common household objects, such as the lawn mower or frying pans, were kept. H. M. was able to read newspapers and magazines, but he totally forgot their contents within 15 minutes. As a result, he often read the same material over and over again without ever realizing that he had seen it before.

Almost as amazing as the things H. M. could not do were the things he still could. IQ tests indicated that his intelligence had actually improved some what after the operation, probably because the frequent epileptic attacks had left him too confused and disoriented to do well on tests. In general, H. M. had a normal memory of everything that happened before the operation, although he was a bit hazy about the two years immediately before the surgery. He could briefly remember a string of digits, respond appropriately to everyday events, and reason normally; H. M. simply could not remember anything new for more than a few minutes.

To a limited extent, H. M.'s ability to remember increased as time went by. After eight years of living in the same house, he was able to draw a diagram showing how the rooms were laid out. He gradually became familiar with the two or three blocks around his home. In systematic tests, he was able to recognize the faces of some people who became famous after his operation, including Elvis Presley, Nikita Khrushchev, and John Glenn (Marslen-Wilson & Tueber, 1975).

At this writing, H. M. is about 60 years old and is still being tested by psychologists at regular intervals. To a certain extent, he has learned to cope with his disability; he apologizes frequently for not being able to remember the names of people to whom he has been introduced and uses the weather to deduce the time of the year. But his ability to learn new information remains severely limited. Even after six months of employment at a rehabilitation center for the retarded, H. M. could not describe where he worked, what he did there, or the route along which he was driven every day (Milner, Corkin, & Teuber, 1968).

H. M.'s disability has had a major impact on the practice of medicine; neurosurgeons are now reluctant to perform any operation that might involve damage to the hippocampus. But this tragic case has also led to greater understanding of the nature of human memory. For example, as we describe in detail later, H. M.'s deficits suggest that there may be at least two separate memory systems, one for storing old information (which was not damaged by the operation) and another for learning new information (which seems to involve the hippocampus).

Despite this promising beginning, we shall see that the results of biological research on memory have been rather discouraging. There have been many attempts to localize memory precisely in the brain, but no clear successes. As explained in Chapter 3, complex psychological functions such as memory seem to involve a bewildering array of changes in the central nervous system. Whether such changes can be found to account for the myriad of activities associated with memory remains to be seen.

Despite some efforts to apply the biological paradigm, studies of memory have been dominated by other theoretical paradigms. Like research on animal learning, the early history of memory research was dominated by behaviorism, and recent developments owe more to a cognitive perspective. To see how this theoretical progression applies to theories of why we forget, we must begin by describing the techniques psychologists have developed to measure precisely how much people remember under various conditions and how much they forget.

Measuring Memory

What we know about memory is linked to the methods we use to measure memory. You probably have had experiences where you could not "remember" something you really knew. For example, suppose you run into a friend accompanied by someone to whom you have recently been introduced but whose name you cannot recall, even though it's on the tip of your tongue. If your friend says, "You remember Marge," you may remember with full certainty that this is indeed the person's name. Measuring your memory of Marge's name by asking you to pull it out of your memory would have made it seem as if you had "forgotten" it entirely, yet you recognize it as the correct name when you hear it.

The Origins of Memory Research

In 1885, Hermann Ebbinghaus published a slim volume titled *On Memory*. It was his first and last book on the topic, but it had an enormous impact on the development of psychology. While earlier scholars had been content to speculate about human memory, Ebbinghaus was determined to measure it objectively.

Ebbinghaus's (1885) first problem was choosing appropriate materials to memorize. He believed that poetry or prose involved too many complicating factors:

> The content is now narrative in style, now descriptive, now reflective; it contains now a phrase that is pathetic, now one that is humorous; its metaphors are sometimes beautiful, sometimes harsh; its rhythm is sometimes smooth and sometimes rough. (p. 23)

Consequently, he invented new materials of his own, designed to be meaningless, simple, and varied: three-letter nonsense syllables like ZOK, LAR, and BEF, each consisting of a vowel between two consonants.

To discover the laws of human memory, Ebbinghaus experimented on himself. Hour after hour, day after day, year after year, Ebbinghaus memorized thousands upon thousands of lists of nonsense syllables. He compared the number of repetitions it took to learn short lists and long lists. He learned other lists, waited various periods of time, and plotted the mathematical curves of forgetting. He compared repeated learning of the same list in one day with the same amount of practice spaced over several days. Then he memorized more lists to study still other variables that might affect memory.

The care and precision of these one-man experiments is still admired by scientists today. For example, because Ebbinghaus suspected that memory might vary at different times of day, throughout 1883 and 1884 he always tested himself between 1 and 3 P.M. Recent research on biological rhythms (see Chapter 4) supports the wisdom of this course.

In one typical series of experiments, Ebbinghaus quantified how memories fade with the passage of time. In 1879 and 1880, he memorized 1,228 lists of 13 nonsense syllables. He began by reading each list aloud, at a regular pace timed by the loud ticking of a watch. After Ebbinghaus had repeated

**HERMANN EBBINGHAUS
(1850–1909)**

Ebbinghaus was one of the first to study human memory systematically, and the techniques he developed shaped the course of the next 70 years of research. After receiving a Ph.D. in philosophy at the University of Bonn, he went on to a period of private study. While supporting himself by tutoring in France and England, Ebbinghaus devoted several hours each day to studying lists of standard stimuli and later testing how well he remembered them. This lonely research led to the publication of his book *On Memory* and helped him to gain a faculty appointment in Berlin.

the list often enough to feel that he had learned it, he looked at the first nonsense syllable and tried to repeat the others from memory. When he was able to do this twice without pausing or making a mistake, he recorded the time it had taken to learn and went on to memorize five to seven more lists.

Then, Ebbinghaus would pause for a precise period of time—19 minutes, 63 minutes, 525 minutes, 1 day, 2 days, 6 days, or 31 days. When the interval was up, he would take out the original lists and memorize them again. Almost invariably, the second learning went more quickly. The actual amount of time he saved on this relearning provided a precise measure of how much he had remembered.

Figure 7.1 shows the average results of Ebbinghaus's tedious memorization of the 15,964 nonsense syllables in this experiment. As you can see, Ebbinghaus forgot more in the first hour than he did in the next month! In the 100 years since this report, many researchers have verified this systematic time course; memory drops off sharply at first, then much more slowly.

Important as this discovery was, it was probably not Ebbinghaus's greatest contribution. The first step for scientific pioneers often involves developing new methods for measuring old phenomena. Above all, Ebbinghaus showed that higher thought processes could be studied scientifically. His emphasis on carefully controlled experimental conditions and rigorous analysis of the results laid the foundation for a new science of human memory.

Relearning, Recognition, and Recall

Contemporary psychologists now distinguish between three major ways of measuring memory: recognition, recall, and relearning. Ebbinghaus relied primarily on the last of these techniques. As you saw, **relearning** studies involve learning material once, recording the time or the number of repetitions required, and relearning the same material on a second occasion. For example, Ebbinghaus's "savings scores" in Figure 7.1 were computed by measuring the time saved on the second occasion and dividing this by the original learning time.

Relearning is a sensitive procedure for measuring memory and often reveals that we know more than we realize. One of the most dramatic examples of this sensitivity appeared in a study that psychologist Harold Burtt began in the 1920s with his own son. When the boy was 15 months old, his father started reading him three short sections from Sophocles's play *Oedipus Tyrannus* in the original Greek. Burtt read each passage of 20 lines or so aloud once a day for three months. By the time the child was 3 years old, he had listened to 21 different ancient Greek selections 90 times each.

Years later, the psychologist father tested his son to see whether all that Greek had made any impression. Using the method of relearning, he was able to show that it had. At the age of 8½, the son was able to memorize the passages he had heard as an infant 30% more quickly than control passages (which he had not heard before) from the same play. Subsequent tests of different passages revealed that this dim memory continued to fade with time. At the age of 14, he relearned passages only 8% faster, and by age 18 there

relearning A comparison of the "savings" gained (e.g., measured by time or number of repetitions required) when material already learned once is learned again.

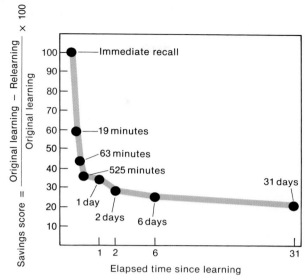

FIGURE 7.1 Ebbinghaus's forgetting curve. Note that the time saved relearning nonsense syllables declined very rapidly in the first day, then leveled off.

were no savings whatever (Burtt, 1941). In short, the relearning tests indicated that the mind of an infant records its surroundings even when it cannot make sense of them.

Most of the time, psychologists measure memory in terms of more familiar tasks. **Recognition** involves deciding whether we have encountered information before (that is, whether we recognize it). **Recall** involves remembering information spontaneously or on the basis of certain cues. Multiple-choice examinations test recognition; fill-in-the-blank examinations test recall.

You would probably find it harder to recall the year that the Magna Charta was signed than to recognize whether it was 1066, 1215, or 1492. And in general, psychologists have indeed found that recognition is easier than recall. For example, one group of researchers (Bahrick, Bahrick, & Wittlinger, 1975) investigated how well people remembered the names and faces of high school classmates anywhere from 2 weeks to 57 years after they graduated.

This particular experiment is a good example of the way many researchers are now trying to study human memory in the "real world." But leaving the laboratory has its price, and this study had to overcome a variety of complications. Some people came from larger graduating classes than others; some never opened their yearbooks and others had read them often; some people saw their old classmates frequently and others almost never did. The researchers collected data on all these factors and used a complex series of statistical corrections to minimize their effects. They also used several different tests of memory. The first was free recall; people were simply asked to write down the names of as many classmates as they could remember. Two other tests involved the recognition of names and faces. People were shown five

recognition The process of deciding whether specific information has been seen or heard before.

recall Remembering information spontaneously or on the basis of certain cues.

yearbook portraits or five names at a time and asked to pick the one from their class.

A few months after graduation, the average subject in the Bahrick et al. study could remember the names of only about 1 out of 6 classmates. This free recall dropped slowly but surely with the passing years; nearly a half-century after graduation, only 1 out of every 15 classmates came easily to mind. On the other hand, the average subject could recognize the faces of 9 out of 10 classmates a full 35 years after graduation; it made no difference whether the subjects came from large or small graduating classes. The recognition of names was almost as impressive. Up to 15 years after graduation, 90% of their classmates' names still rang a bell.

These findings provide an impressive testimonial to the staying power of human memory. The fact that people could remember the names and faces of several hundred classmates while spontaneously recalling only a few dozen supports the idea that there is a great deal more information hidden away in our minds than we may realize. Later in this chapter, we stress the distinction between storing information and retrieving it. The fact that you cannot find a book in the library does not mean that it is not there, and the fact that you cannot recall a classmate's name does not mean that this information has disappeared entirely from your mind.

Psychologists have measured relearning, recognition, and recall in many different contexts in a continuing search for the laws of human memory. In the next section we outline briefly how progress has been made over the last century on one of the most fundamental problems in this field—why people forget.

Forgetting

In Chapter 6, we saw how early behaviorists took a "black-box" approach to animal learning by focusing on external stimuli and the responses they produced while ignoring what went on inside the organism. The pioneers in memory research followed a similar path. For several decades, most of their studies were based on the notion of **associationism,** the belief that even the most complex memories are ultimately based on associations between simple ideas. From this perspective, Ebbinghaus's decision to develop a simple and pure measure of memory makes perfect sense. He assumed that once psychologists understood how associative bonds were formed between simple nonsense syllables, the same laws could be applied to more complex stimuli such as words, images, and ideas.

Through the 1950s, most researchers focused on the variables that influenced the formation of associative bonds. The experimental subject who happened to memorize a particular list was seen as a passive participant; memory was shaped by external forces. For example, many studies revealed that short lists were learned more easily than long lists. The assumption was that this external variable (the length of a list) directly influenced the strength of the bonds between stimuli, and there was little interest in how this process occurred within the human mind or whether the feelings and expectations of the memorizer made any difference.

associationism The belief that even the most complex memories are ultimately based on associations between simple ideas.

An Associative Approach: Decay Versus Interference

Given this orientation, the problem of forgetting could be restated in another way: How is the association between two verbal stimuli broken? Traditionally, researchers accepted one of two conflicting theories. Either we forget simply because the passage of time weakens the associative bond (decay theory) or forgetting results when the formation of one bond interferes with another (interference theory).

At first glance, the choosing of the "correct" theory might seem to be an easy task. Simply ask people to memorize a list, do nothing for a while, and then see whether time alone makes the memory fade. The problem is that even Zen masters find it impossible to do absolutely nothing. And anything they do in that critical waiting period between the original learning and the subsequent test may interfere with memory. This problem of logic fueled the theoretical controversy between interference and decay for several decades.

More formally, the **decay theory** holds that a physical memory trace gradually fades as time passes. Like a message drawn in sand at the beach, a physical memory first fades and then disappears altogether. In some ways, this is the simplest possible explanation of Ebbinghaus's famous forgetting curve (Figure 7.1).

By contrast, **interference theory** holds that people forget information because one memory prevents another from being recovered. For example, you may make the unfortunate mistake of calling your new boyfriend Howard when that is actually an old boyfriend's name; the old memory interferes with the new one.

In one early experiment contrasting the effects of interference and decay, Jenkins and Dallenbach (1924) asked people to memorize lists of nonsense syllables just before they went to sleep. When subjects were awakened one, two, four, or eight hours later, those who had slept longer had forgotten more. People who memorized the same lists in the morning and were tested after equal periods of staying awake had forgotten more than the sleepers at every interval. The simplest interpretation is that the passage of time does indeed cause some forgetting (by decay), but the interference of other intervening activity causes even more. However, studies of electrical activity in the brain during sleep (see Chapter 4) suggest that this period is more than just an empty period of time.

Despite continuing difficulties with performing a pure test of interference theory versus decay theory, these results and others made it clear that interference played some role in forgetting. There are two major types of interference: old learning can interfere with the memory of new learning (proactive inhibition), or new learning can interfere with the memory of old learning (retroactive inhibition). **Proactive inhibition** occurs when information is forgotten as a result of interference from material that was presented before the learning task. **Retroactive inhibition** occurs when information is forgotten as a result of interference from material that was presented after the learning task. Although this may seem confusing at first, Figure 7.2 illustrates that the difference simply depends on whether the interference comes before or after the learning task in question.

decay theory The theory that physical memory traces gradually fade as time passes.

interference theory The theory that people forget information because one memory prevents another from being recovered.

proactive inhibition The forgetting of information because of interference from material presented before the learning task.

retroactive inhibition The forgetting of information because of interference from material presented after the learning task.

Before the 1950s, memory researchers focused on the workings of retroactive inhibition. In one typical study (Melton & Irwin, 1940), subjects learned a list of nonsense syllables and then relearned it 30 minutes later. During the half-hour delay, some subjects simply rested; others were exposed to a second list of nonsense syllables from 5 to 40 times. This intervening task interfered with the memory of the first list. In fact, the relationship was quite systematic; the more times people had heard the second list, the more trouble they had remembering the first. This study demonstrates that if, for example, you memorize a list of seventeenth-century English poets and then another of eighteenth-century English poets, the second list will retroactively interfere with your memory of the first.

In 1957, Benton Underwood emphasized that interference could also work in the other direction. In a classic piece of scientific detective work, Underwood demonstrated that the more nonsense syllables a person has learned in the past, the more difficult it will be to master new ones. To demonstrate this, Underwood directly compared the performance of old pros like Ebbinghaus (who memorized literally thousands of nonsense syllables) with volunteers who were encountering stimuli like ZED, CIK, and JOP for the first time. The naive volunteers consistently performed better. In fact, on the average, people recalled their first list best, the second list second best, and so on. The more nonsense one had encountered in the past, the greater the proactive inhibition and the more forgetting. In this case, the more you know, the more likely you are to forget.

Just two years after Underwood broadened the theory of interference, Lloyd and Margaret Peterson (1959) published an influential study that rekindled interest in the possibility of memory decay. These experimenters simply read three-letter nonsense syllables aloud, waited a few seconds, and asked subjects to repeat the syllables. This sounds like an absurdly easy task. The average person could remember any syllable for seconds, minutes, or even years simply by repeating it silently while waiting. However, the Petersons prevented this type of covert rehearsal by requiring subjects to perform a distracting task while they waited. When the subjects heard the nonsense syllable, they also heard a three-digit number. They were required to count backward by threes from the number (e.g., 308, 305, 302, 299 . . .) until a

FIGURE 7.2 According to the interference theory, one memory prevents another from being recalled. The interfering information may come before or after the task in question.

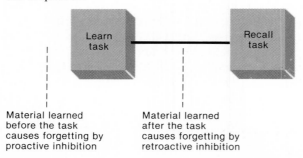

Material learned before the task causes forgetting by proactive inhibition

Material learned after the task causes forgetting by retroactive inhibition

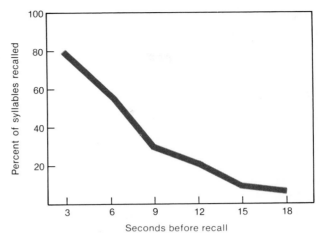

FIGURE 7.3 When rehearsal is prevented by engaging in a distracting task, memory for nonsense syllables declines rapidly. This suggests that short-term memory maintains storage for seconds rather than minutes.

light flashed on, signaling that it was time to report the original syllable.

Under these conditions, the Petersons were amazed to see how quickly memories faded. As you can see in Figure 7.3, after 3 seconds of counting backward, people correctly repeated about 80% of the syllables, after 9 seconds only 30%, and after 18 seconds less than 10%.

Since memory declined so rapidly, it seemed likely that the neglected physical trace had simply faded away. But proponents of interference theory soon came up with another explanation. According to Keppel and Underwood (1962), these memories did not fade quickly as a result of decay; rather, the Petersons' subjects confused later syllables with what had come before. To test their alternative explanation, Keppel and Underwood looked more closely at the first few trials. Using a large number of subjects, they found that when the first time people were asked to remember three letters, almost everyone did so perfectly, even after counting backward for 18 seconds. On the second trial, about one out of every five subjects forgot the letters, and by the third trial two out of every five could not remember. Proactive inhibition mounted quickly, and early learning interfered with later memory even in this simple task.

This study, like many others, shows how interference is clearly one factor in forgetting. It is also a reminder of how difficult it can be to demonstrate that the passage of time, by itself, causes memories to decay.

A Biological Approach: From Engrams to Alzheimer's Disease

Around 1915, Karl Lashley took a very different approach to the problem of understanding the nature of forgetting. He started with two assumptions. The first was that when an organism learns something new, the learning is stored in the brain. Lashley used the term **engram** to refer to the physical change in the brain responsible for memory storage. Lashley's second belief was that it would be possible to localize the engram in a particular area of the cerebral cortex.

After completing his Ph.D. at Johns Hopkins (where he studied with John Watson, the founder of behaviorism), Lashley went on to try to localize the engram by destroying particular areas in the brains of experimental animals in order to erase the memory of a task the animal had previously learned. (This is an example of the ablation technique described in Chapter 3.)

Lashley, who is widely recognized as one of the founders of physiological psychology, developed many theories and experimental procedures that are still used today. But his search was a frustrating one, and he was never able to identify or locate the physical basis of memory. Indeed, in a classic paper entitled "The Search for the Engram," Lashley (1950, p. 477) wrote, ironically: "I sometimes feel, in reviewing the evidence on the localization of the memory trace, that the necessary conclusion is that learning just is not possible."

Since then, other researchers have discovered more promising paths. In the 1960s, tremendous excitement was generated by the theory that memory is stored in RNA molecules, just as genetic information is stored in the related substance DNA. This claim was based in part on experiments in which planaria (a kind of flatworm) were classically conditioned to turn to one side in response to a flashing light. Planaria that had learned this response were sacrificed, ground up, and fed to untrained planaria. According to some researchers, after eating the meal of trained planaria, the new group learned more rapidly.

This report led to many newspaper stories about a future in which students would be able to learn psychology or astrophysics by taking a memory pill. However, attempts to replicate this finding failed, and the original RNA research was rejected by most scientists (Chapouthier, 1973). This widely publicized episode produced the unfortunate result of "a serious but only temporary setback to the young field of the neurochemistry of learning" (Thompson & Robinson, 1979, p. 432).

We are now in the midst of another explosion of research regarding the physical basis of memory in the brain. According to Woody (1986), this work has validated Lashley's first assumption; considerable evidence now supports the idea that learning produces physical changes in the brain. However, his second concept—that these changes can be localized in a physical engram—is more questionable. Researchers have found that during learning situations, many different neurons respond in a variety of ways and in many areas of the brain. Thus the simple idea that there is one type of engram in one area of the brain appears to be incorrect.

Much of the current work focuses on the role of neurotransmitters and the synapse in memory storage (Lynch & Baudry, 1984). For example, one fascinating line of research is exploring the role of the neurotransmitter acetylcholine in the memory changes seen in Alzheimer's disease, a progressive brain disorder that gradually makes individuals unable to care for themselves.

In the United States, approximately 1% of the population between the ages of 60 and 69 suffers from Alzheimer's disease; the proportion over age 80 rises to about 10% (U.S. Congress, 1984). The symptoms typically begin with periods of forgetfulness. As these become more severe, the afflicted

engram Lashley's concept of a physical change in the brain responsible for memory storage.

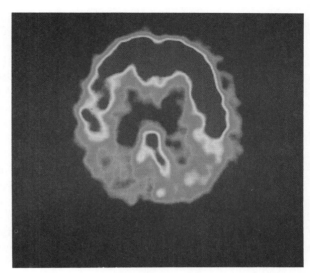

PET scans of patients like this one have revealed differences in physiological function that are associated with Alzheimer's disease.

A memory test of a patient with Alzheimer's disease.

individuals may have trouble with everyday tasks—leaving the water running, for example, or forgetting to turn off the stove. Ultimately, they may forget the names of relatives and close friends, their occupations, their birthdays, and even their own names.

Personality changes are also common, and the seriously ill may neglect their appearance and engage in inappropriate behavior. "A previously cautious businesswoman may embark on a reckless business venture. An elderly spinster may make sexual advances to strangers. A retiree may shoplift without considering the consequences . . ." (American Psychiatric Association, 1980, p. 108). The disease is generally fatal within about five years of the first appearance of symptoms.

This disorder was identified by the German neurologist Alois Alzheimer in 1860, and it has been known for many years to lead to the degeneration of brain tissue. However, it was only in 1983 that Coyle, Price and DeLong reported that people who died of Alzheimer's disease have 60% to 90% less acetylcholine in their brains than do comparable victims of other disorders. They also reported that the disease destroys neurons in a brain structure called the nucleus basalis, which supplies acetylcholine to the cortex and the hippocampus. (As you may remember, the case of H. M. described at the beginning of this chapter suggested that the hippocampus plays a critical role in memory.)

Unfortunately, attempts to treat Alzheimer's disease by increasing the supply of acetylcholine have not been successful (Wurtman, 1982). Nevertheless, this line of research promises to open up new avenues for the understanding and treatment of a disorder that is likely to pose increasing problems as Americans live longer. There is also a considerable body of promising research in progress on memory and the brain in nonhumans. However, as Farley and Alkon (1985, p. 420) noted in their review of this work, it is important to emphasize that even in the "most favorable of circumstances, considerable uncertainty still exists as to the exact mechanism of long-term information storage. The details are still very unclear." Although the biological approach to memory holds considerable promise, memory research is likely to remain dominated by a more cognitive orientation for the foreseeable future.

A Cognitive Approach:
Cue-Dependent Forgetting

Virtually all the research comparing the interference and decay theories arose from Ebbinghaus's associative tradition of verbal learning—trying to understand the way individual stimuli (usually words or nonsense syllables) were linked to responses. In the last few decades, this black-box approach has been rejected by animal-learning researchers (see Chapter 7) and by those who study human memory. It has been replaced by a more **cognitive approach** that explores the inner structure and organization of the mind and the active processes used by a learner. More specifically, many memory researchers take an **information-processing approach**, which attempts to analyze thought processes as a series of separate steps. Just as a computer reads information, transforms it, and produces output, so the human mind is seen as a device for processing information.

Cognitive psychologists distinguish between three major processes in remembering: encoding, storage, and retrieval. **Encoding** is the transformation of a physical stimulus into a form that human memory accepts. **Storage** is the retention of this memory, and **retrieval** involves recovering information from storage. Current views of forgetting stress the role of these active internal processes.

Thus, instead of focusing on whether forgetting is caused by interference or decay, many researchers are now concerned with what happens to information that is forgotten. Is it entirely lost from memory (dropped from storage) like a computer tape that has been erased? Or is it still locked away in storage but difficult to retrieve because it has been "misplaced?" This latter possibility, the failure of retrieval, is the focus of the theory of cue-dependent forgetting.

Some theorists believe that little information is ever lost from storage in long-term memory. (Short-term memory will be described in the next section.) What we lost is the ability to find, or retrieve, the information. The mind, according to this view, is like a giant reference library with books that never leave the shelves. The problem is, we often do not know where to look for a specific volume. According to Endel Tulving's (1974) theory of **cue-dependent forgetting**, forgetting is caused by a failure to retrieve information from storage due to inadequate memory cues.

Intuitively, this theory seems appealing. Every time we give someone a hint to prod memory, we acknowledge the importance of retrieval cues. Many experiments have systematically shown the difference such cues can make. In one of the simplest (Tulving & Thompson, 1971), people were asked to memorize lists of 28 words. They were generally able to remember only about 20% of the words under the specific testing conditions. But when the

---

cognitive approach The approach that explores the inner structure and organization of the mind, and the active processes used by a learner.

information-processing approach Attempts to analyze thought processes, including memory, as a series of separate steps.

encoding The transformation of a physical stimulus into the kind of code that memory accepts.

storage The retention of information.

retrieval The recovery of information from storage.

cue-dependent forgetting Tulving's notion that inadequate memory cues lead to a failure to retrieve information from storage.

first three letters of "forgotten" words were offered as a hint (for example, *gra* as a retrieval cue for *grape*), these same people remembered more than 50% of the list. Therefore, they had not lost the words from memory storage; they were just temporarily unable to retrieve them.

According to Tulving's **encoding-specificity principle**, recall improves if the same cues are present during recall as during the original learning. For example, you may have had the experience of failing to recognize a person in an unfamiliar context. This happened to a friend of ours when she saw her new gynecologist in a singles bar. She knew the man seemed familiar, but she just couldn't place him. Tulving's explanation is that this "stranger's" identity was encoded into memory in terms of particular cues. If he had worn his white lab coat—one of the cues present when she first met him—to the bar, she would have recognized him more easily. Memories are sometimes like a locked file cabinet that can be opened only with the right key.

Tulving (1974) and his colleagues have performed a series of studies demonstrating that recall can indeed be improved by providing appropriate cues. Other aspects of his theory have been questioned. For example, later in this chapter we shall question the idea that all information remains permanently stored in long-term memory. But on one point virtually all researchers now agree: Forgetting is a complex process that can be understood only by exploring the active internal workings of the mind. The next section describes the most influential model of these internal processes.

A Psychodynamic Approach: Motivated Forgetting

According to the psychodynamic paradigm, forgetting is not necessarily due to failures in biological or learning processes, but may actually be a motivated process. Freud's term for **motivated forgetting** is **repression**. The basic notion is that some events or experiences are just too painful to remember; consequently, as a defense mechanism, we "forget" them. This failure to remember the painful event is not done consciously or deliberately; rather, an unconscious repression of the memory takes place. (Defense mechanisms are discussed more fully in Chapter 12.)

Defense mechanisms such as repression help to explain many complex forms of adult behavior. For example, Freud (1901/1953b) told the story of one man whose memory was blocked by a tip-of-the-tongue phenomenon: While reciting a familiar poem, the man kept getting stuck at the words "with the white sheet," and try as he might, he simply could not remember what came next. His analyst asked him to free-associate to the expression *white sheet*. An abbreviated version of the man's train of thought went something like this: "White sheet—reminds me of a linen sheet over a corpse (pause)—now I think of a friend who died recently of heart disease—he was fat and didn't exercise enough—my grandfather died of heart disease, and I am a little chubby myself—I could die of heart disease." According to Freud, the apparently innocent forgetting of a line of a poem actually involved repression of unconscious conflicts over a fear of death.

encoding-specificity principle
Tulving's notion that recall improves if the same cues are present during recall as during the original learning.

motivated forgetting (repression)
The psychoanalytic theory that people may repress memories that are too painful for them to remember.

In another case, a man had trouble remembering the name of a business associate. His analyst later learned that his business associate had married a woman whom his patient had pursued. The loser in this war of the heart repressed the winner's name because his unconscious was protecting the conscious mind from a painful memory.

Freud provided still another example from his own life—an argument with an acquaintance over how many inns there were in a resort town where the Freud family had spent several summer vacations. Freud later had to admit that he had completely forgotten about the inn named The Hockwartner. Why? This name sounded very much like that of a doctor who competed with Freud for patients. Freud's ego defended his conscious mind from the anxiety-provoking memory of this professional rival. Even the founder of psychoanalysis was subject to repression and was a victim of hidden instinctual conflicts.

It is possible that each of these major approaches to forgetting has something useful to say about this complex process. Further insights into the process of forgetting are likely to stem from research designed to test various models of memory. The most important of the current models is described in the next section.

The Atkinson-Shiffrin Model of Memory

In 1968, Richard Atkinson and R. M. Shiffrin proposed that human memory is organized into three stages (see Figure 7.4). Our sensory impressions of the world are first held for a moment in *sensory storage*. As we shall see in the next section, this memory system holds a great deal of information but

FIGURE 7.4 A simplified diagram of the Atkinson-Shiffrin model, showing the relationships between three memory systems.

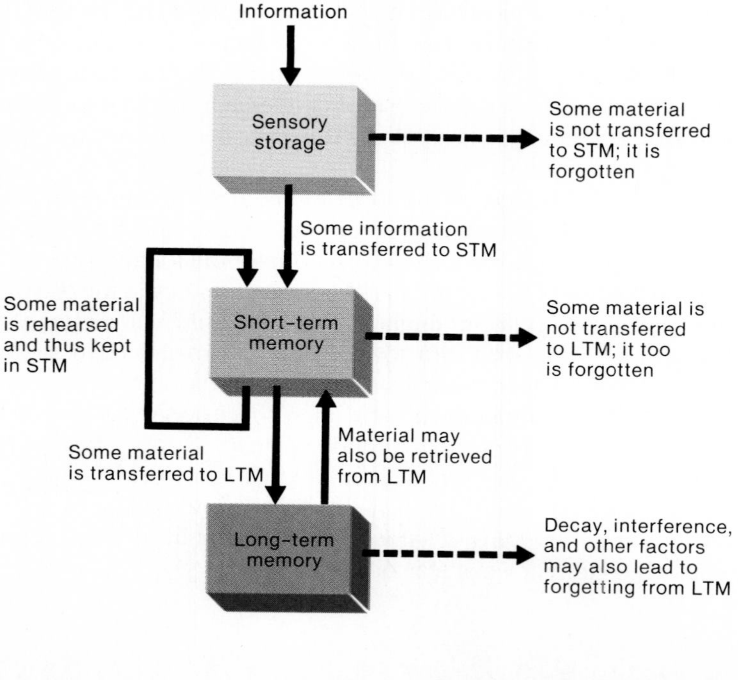

loses it within seconds. Information that is lost from sensory storage is forgotten forever, but a small amount of information is transferred to short-term memory.

Short-term memory has a limited capacity. New information displaces the old; and when an item is displaced, it too is forgotten. But information can be held in short-term memory by repeating it (this is called *rehearsal*). The longer an item is held in short-term memory, the more likely it is to be transferred into long-term memory.

Long-term memory is seen here as a storage system that can hold information almost indefinitely. However, conscious awareness of this knowledge involves transferring a memory back into short-term memory, and such factors as interference can make it difficult to retrieve some information.

To make this model more concrete, consider what happens when you flip through the Yellow Pages to find a pizzeria that will deliver at 3 A.M. Each time you read a phone number, a literal picture of what you see is held for a fraction of a second in the portion of memory called sensory storage. If you choose to dial a certain number, it is passed to a second level, called short-term memory, which will hold that information a limited period, perhaps as long as 30 seconds. But once you dial an unfamiliar phone number, it is usually forgotten. In fact, if the line is busy, you will probably have to look up the number again to redial it a few seconds later. Thus, short-term memory quickly fades away unless you rehearse the number or make some effort to retain it. If, however, you are forced to dial Pizza City 18 times before you get through, you will probably begin to remember the number. At this point the telephone number has passed into long-term memory, the major memory system, which contains everything you know about the past.

The original Atkinson-Shiffrin model was actually far more complex than this short explanation suggests. Each of the three major stages was further subdivided. For example, sensory storage included separate auditory, visual, and other components. Less common routes for memory transfer were also outlined. For example, Atkinson and Shiffrin believed that it was sometimes possible for information to bypass short-term memory, proceeding directly from sensory storage to long-term memory. For our purposes, however, it is best to concentrate on the broad outlines of the model as portrayed in Figure 7.4 and Table 7.1.

TABLE 7.1

General Characteristics of Three Stages of Memory

	Sensory Storage	*Short-term Memory*	*Long-term Memory*
Information enters by	Sensation	Attention	Rehearsal
Information is maintained by	(not maintained)	Continued attention; rehearsal	Repetition; organization
Storage capacity	Large	About 5 to 9 items	No known limits
Information is lost by	Decay	Displacement; perhaps decay	Little or no loss (?); interference makes information less accessible
Trace duration	0.25 to 2 seconds	Up to 30 seconds	Minutes to years
Retrieval	Immediate readout	Items in consciousness	Involves search process

Source: Based on Craik and Lockhart, 1972.

Evidence for Separate Memory Systems: Amnesia

The idea that short-term memory for immediate events is somehow separate and different from long-term, more permanent memories can be traced back to the 1890s in the writings of William James. But it was only in the 1960s that several lines of evidence convinced the scientific community of the importance of this distinction.

Some of this evidence came from laboratory studies of verbal learning. Other evidence came from clinical studies of people with **amnesia**—a loss of memory usually caused by damage to the brain. **Anterograde amnesia** involves an inability to remember new information for more than a few seconds. This was the problem faced by H. M., the epileptic whose hippocampus was removed. In the final stages of chronic alcoholism, patients often suffer from a similarly confused state called Korsakoff's syndrome. For both H. M. and Korsakoff's patients, short-term memory seems intact; they can remember material for up to 30 seconds. And older information that had been stored in long-term memory before the onset of disease can still be remembered. Thus, these disorders seem to involve a permanent loss of the ability to transfer information from short-term memory to long-term memory and an inability to retrieve any new information from long-term memory.

Another type of memory disorder is called **retrograde amnesia**. This involves an inability to recall events that occurred before trauma to the brain. The most common causes of retrograde amnesia are head injury, electroconvulsive shock (see Chapter 15), and carbon monoxide poisoning. Although amnesia victims who appear in soap operas often cannot even remember their names, in most cases in real life the material forgotten is quite limited. When Russell and Nathan (1946) reviewed the records of 200 people who were hospitalized for head injuries, over half of those who experienced retrograde amnesia had forgotten only the 60 seconds or so immediately preceding their accidents. This too seems easy to explain in terms of the distinction between short-term and long-term memory. Brain trauma temporarily interferes with the ability to transfer information, and the events immediately before an accident never enter long-term storage and are thus lost forever.

One particularly clever study of retrograde amnesia was made possible by the violent nature of American sports. Lynch and Yarnell (1973, p. 644) succinctly described their approach: "We waited on the football field until a player was injured, and then examined him neurologically and tested his memory status." Although they did not mention how many days they spent on the sidelines, they were able to test 6 players with concussions and compare them to a control group of 12 football players with other injuries, such as torn knee ligaments and broken noses.

The opportunity to question players within 30 seconds of their injuries revealed that retrograde amnesia was not immediately apparent in any of the six players with concussions, but it did show up later. As Lynch and Yarnell put it:

> The delayed forgetting was quite striking. One concussed player, immediately after injury, told the interviewer that he had been hit "from the front while I

amnesia A loss of memory usually caused by damage to the brain.

anterograde amnesia An inability to remember new information for more than a few seconds.

retrograde amnesia An inability to remember events that occurred before some damage to the brain.

was blocking on the punt." Questioned 5 minutes later he said, "I don't remember what happened. I don't remember what play it was or what I was doing. It was something about a punt." (p. 644)

This finding suggests that brain trauma does not immediately erase the contents of short-term memory, but interferes with their transfer to long-term memory at some later time.

Taken together, the findings from clinical studies of amnesia and laboratory studies of verbal learning were sufficient to convince many psychologists that the Atkinson-Shiffrin model was basically sound. In the final part of this section, we consider some challenges to this view. But first we shall use this model to describe some basic facts about sensory storage, short-term memory, and long-term memory.

Sensory Storage

Some people think of human memory as the equivalent of a videotape recorder, which permanently stores a literal reproduction of every event. Psychologists know that this analogy is misleading. Memory is an efficient system that does not burden itself with every insignificant detail of every stimulus we have been exposed to in our lives. Rather, the mind actively picks and chooses what we need to know by paying attention to the most relevant details. Sensory storage briefly holds a literal picture of a stimulus while this information processing takes place, giving us the time to read a sentence or hear a melody in context. Specifically, **sensory storage** maintains a vivid and complete image of sensory impressions for about 0.25 to 2 seconds. The exact duration of this image depends on the type of stimulus and the context in which it is presented.

Researchers in perception have long known that a visual image remains behind for a fraction of a second after the stimulus disappears. When a lighted cigarette is moved in a dark room, for example, you see a streak of light rather than a series of points (Woodworth, 1938). But it was not until 1960 that George Sperling provided an ingenious demonstration of just how complete this immediate image can be.

Sperling flashed visual displays briefly—for about 0.05 second—so that subjects would barely have time to see them. In some studies, the stimulus was a group of nine letters arranged in three rows like this:

Z   Q   B

M   C   W

T   K   N

sensory storage The component of memory that maintains a vivid and complete image of sensory impressions for about 0.25 to 2 seconds.

When people wrote down the letters they had seen, they could typically remember only four or five of them. Other researchers had reported similar results before and concluded that people simply could not read more than four or five letters in such a short period of time.

Sperling had another idea. He believed that the viewer registered all nine letters but that this photograph-type image faded away quickly, before the viewer had a chance to report all nine letters. To test this hypothesis, Sperling showed real ingenuity. He told his subjects that he would ask them to remember only one of the three rows—but they would not know which row until *after* the visual stimulus was turned off. Immediately after the nine letters disappeared, each person heard one of three tones. A high-pitched tone meant repeat the top line, a low tone signaled the bottom line, and the intermediate tone asked for the middle line. Under these conditions, people could report any line with almost complete accuracy. Sperling had asked his subjects to report only part of what they had seen, and the accuracy of these partial reports implied that all the original information was briefly held in memory. In effect, the subjects seemed to be reading the relevant letters back from a rapidly fading mental photograph.

Sperling was able to estimate the duration of this image by varying how long he waited after the visual stimulus to sound the tone. He found that if he waited only about half a second, people could no longer report the relevant row. Apparently, the image had already faded in that time.

Sperling's experiment and many subsequent replications left little doubt that we retain a literal image of a visual stimulus for a fraction of a second after it is presented. This visual image is sometimes referred to as **iconic memory**.

Echoic memory refers to an analogous phenomenon for the auditory system. Just as we can see a picture of a stimulus for a moment after it disappears, so we can hear a sound for a moment after it stops (Moray, Bates, & Barnett, 1965). Echoic memory seems to last a bit longer than iconic memory; auditory replicas of a stimulus may last for several seconds. This difference might be explained in terms of the function of sensory storage: to maintain a literal impression of the world long enough for us to make sense of it. It seems reasonable to suppose that auditory information such as music and speech takes longer to put into context.

Many researchers believe that other senses such as touch, taste, and smell may have separate sensory-storage systems of their own. But only time and future research will tell.

Short-term Memory

Information disappears rapidly from sensory storage. Some is forgotten and some is passed along to the next stage. **Short-term memory (STM)** stores a limited amount of information for no more than about 30 seconds. The exact duration is somewhat controversial and may depend on the type of material. To hold information in STM, we often rehearse it, as in the case of silently repeating a phone number. According to Atkinson and Shiffrin (1968), without this type of repetition, information seems to fade away from STM and is forgotten forever. When we rehearse a set of verbal items—for example, letters, numbers, or words—we are using what is called an auditory (or acoustic) code to keep the information actively in our awareness as long as it is needed.

One of the most important facts about STM is that it has a limited capacity;

iconic memory The retention in memory of a literal image of a visual stimulus for a fraction of a second after it is presented.

echoic memory The retention in memory of an auditory stimulus for a moment after it stops.

short-term memory (STM) The memory system that stores a limited amount of information for no more than about 30 seconds.

it can hold only a small amount of information at any given time. This idea can be traced back to a memory researcher named Joseph Jacobs, who wrote in 1887:

> It is obvious that there is a limit to the power of reproducing sound accurately. Anyone can say Bo after once hearing it; few could catch the name of the Greek statesman M. Papamichalopoulos without the need of a repetition. (p. 75)

And so Jacobs set out to determine the precise limits of people's ability to reproduce strings of letters and numbers without mentally rehearsing them first. When he tested students at the North London Collegiate School for Girls, he found that 8-year-olds could repeat lists of about 6.6 numbers; 13-year-olds, about 7.3 numbers; and 18-year-olds, 8.6 numbers without error. Children with higher academic standings in each class seemed able to remember more numbers.

The obvious implication that such a test might be useful in measuring intelligence was further supported by Sir Francis Galton (1887) when he showed that inmates at the Earlewood Asylum for Idiots (*idiots* was the nineteenth-century term for the mentally retarded) performed poorly on this task. When IQ tests were developed several decades later (see Chapter 13), most included a test of digit memory. People were asked to repeat four numbers, then five, then six, and so on, until they made an error. We now know that most adults can successfully remember about six words, seven letters, or eight digits (Clark & Clark, 1977).

In 1956, George Miller reviewed these observations and many others in a classic paper titled "The Magical Number Seven, Plus or Minus Two: Some Limits on Our Capacity for Processing Information." He concluded that STM can hold about seven "chunks" of information.

Miller used the word *chunk* to refer to any discrete unit of information. When you try to remember a string of letters, you usually remember each letter separately, and each thus constitutes one chunk of information. For example, if you read the following letters once, you will probably remember about seven of them:

B T R D E R R O E D R O F

But if you regrouped these same letters to spell

R O B E R T R E D F O R D

they would be much easier to remember. In this context, we could say that *Robert Redford* is a chunk. The name represents a single piece of information and we remember it as one unit, not as 13 separate letters. Similarly, it is quite difficult to remember the number

1 4 9 1 6 2 5 3 6 4 9 6 4 8 1 1 0 0

as a string of digits. But if you know that this number was formed by stringing together the squares of every integer from 1 to 10 ($1^2 = 1$; $2^2 = 4$; $3^2 = 9$; $4^2 = 16$, etc.), you are faced with only one piece of information, and the 18 digits become quite easy to commit to memory (at least if you can remember how to square the numbers from 1 to 10).

In everyday life, we often break information into chunks to make it easier to remember. You probably remember your Social Security number not as a string of nine digits (098388412) but as a series of three chunks (098–38–8412). Again, according to Miller, the capacity of short-term memory is about five to nine (that is, seven plus or minus two) chunks of information.

What happens when we try to exceed this natural limit? Our short-term memories become overloaded, and we forget. In an oversimplified way, you might think of short-term memory as a cabinet with about seven shelves; once all the shelves are filled, the only way to put something new in is to take something old out (Waugh & Norman, 1965). To remember larger amounts of information we must transfer some to long-term memory.

Long-term Memory

Can you remember what you had for dinner last Tuesday? The capital of Argentina? Your teacher in the first grade? Your mother's birthday? The number of ounces in a pound? Who played Captain Kirk in "Star Trek"? The difference between stimulus generalization and stimulus discrimination?

Long-term memory (LTM) is a relatively permanent system that stores large amounts of information for long periods of time. The storage capacity of LTM is absolutely astounding; if you tried to take an inventory of its contents, you might spend weeks simply listing all the important information and trivia stored in it. How does all that information ever fit between your ears? And what sort of incredible filing system allows you to sort through this clutter in a fraction of a second and effortlessly recover the words to the Pledge of Allegiance or the ingredients in your favorite meat loaf?

The question of how LTM is organized is far from settled, but it is currently the subject of a great deal of intensive research. One of the most influential theories is based on Endel Tulving's (1972) distinction between episodic and semantic memory.

EPISODIC VERSUS SEMANTIC MEMORY

According to Tulving, there are two types of information stored in LTM. **Episodic memory** is a record of an individual's past experiences, the episodes of daily life. For example, if Jim remembered the first time he noticed that his Aunt Emily had a faint mustache, that event would be stored in episodic memory. So would Kathie's recollection of a television talk show she saw yesterday morning regarding women's employment. Episodic memory is both specific and autobiographical.

In contrast, **semantic memory** involves more abstract knowledge of words, symbols, ideas, and the rules for relating them. For example, we know that if the Boston Red Sox are in first place on September 1, they will probably have a losing streak and fail to win the pennant. Similarly, long-term memory

long-term memory (LTM) The relatively permanent system that can store large amounts of information for long periods of time.

episodic memory A record of an individual's past experiences.

semantic memory An abstract record of words and ideas and rules for relating them.

stores the information that if the weather is cold and wet, there is a good chance the car will stall. These facts are not specific memories of particular events; rather, they are more general conclusions drawn from a variety of experiences.

So, if you remember waiting in line for $2\frac{1}{2}$ hours at the registrar's office to change a class and, when you finally got your turn, being told by the clerk that you had filled out the wrong form, these details would be stored in episodic memory. But the more general knowledge that the university registrar's office is inefficient and its employees are rude would be stored in semantic memory.

The rule-governed nature of semantic memory makes it possible to retrieve information to which you have never been exposed. If someone asks you what month comes after June in alphabetical order, you will probably be able to "remember" that it is March even if you have never seen a list of the 12 months arranged in this way.

Traditional research on verbal learning, in which people memorize lists of words or nonsense syllables, involves episodic memory; each list is remembered as a specific event in a subject's life. It was only in the 1960s that cognitive psychologists became concerned with exploring the workings of the more general system of semantic memory, which is directly involved in such ordinary activities as reading, writing, and most types of learning. Indeed, according to Tulving (1972), the term *semantic memory* was first used in a 1966 doctoral dissertation by Ross Quillian. Three years later, Quillian and Allen Collins published one of the first and most famous models of how semantic memory is organized.

One of the most amazing aspects of human memory is the ability to recover so many different types of information so quickly. Imagine how difficult it would be to find a book in the main branch of Chicago's public library if the books were not arranged according to the Dewey decimal system or some other systematic procedure. Similarly, there must be some Dewey decimal system of the mind that tells us where to look for seldom-used memories of African countries, Greek philosophers, and kinds of tropical fruits.

Collins and Quillian (1969) proposed that semantic knowledge is arranged in a network of associations. Figure 7.5 illustrates one of their most famous examples of how the meaning of different words and concepts may be arranged in human memory. In the interest of efficiency, they argued, semantic memory is organized in a hierarchy of concepts. In this example, *canary* is stored under *bird,* and *bird* is stored under *animal,* because each is a member of that larger class.

Certain key properties are stored along with each class. For example, birds have wings and can fly. Although a canary also has wings and can fly, this information is not repeated at the lower level; these properties are implied by the fact that a canary is a bird.

This theory is a good example of the way an information-processing approach tries to analyze the internal steps involved in thought. Such models are often tested by measuring whether people take more time to perform tasks that the model sees as more complex or involving more steps. Here, Collins and Quillian reasoned that if their model was correct, it should take longer to answer the question "Does a canary eat?" than to answer "Is a

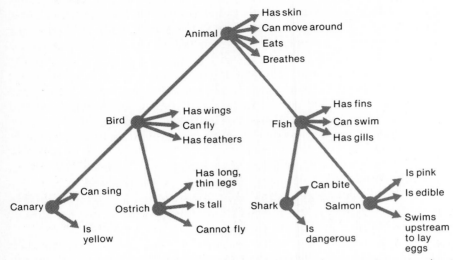

FIGURE 7.5 According to one model, information is organized in semantic memory in a hierarchy. In this example, to retrieve the fact that a canary has skin and can move around, the person who remembers must search through two levels of the hierarchy to find this information "filed under" the larger category of *animal*.

canary yellow?" The reason is that the property *yellow* is stored at the same semantic level as *canary,* and one does not have to waste time searching the memory network for it. But the concept of *eating* is stored two levels away with the more general category *animal.* Therefore, answering a question about a canary's eating requires searching through two levels of the memory network, and this should take more time.

To test this prediction, Collins and Quillian (1969) flashed various statements about canaries on a TV screen. Subjects were asked to press one button if they thought a statement was true and to press another button if they thought it was false. In general, these reaction times supported the researchers' views. For example, it took about 1.3 seconds to press a button verifying the statement "A canary can sing," in which information was stored at the same level. In the same experiment, people took about 1.35 seconds to verify the statement "A canary can fly," in which information was stored one semantic level away, with the concept *bird* (see Figure 7.5). Agreement took 1.4 seconds for "A canary has skin," information stored two semantic levels away, with the concept *animal.* Although these differences were small, they were statistically significant and supported the idea that information was organized along these general lines.

This *network model of memory* was important, because Collins's and Quillian's proposal was one of the first testable models of the way semantic information is organized in the mind. You will probably not be surprised to learn that when large numbers of psychologists tested the model, they discovered several ways in which it might be improved.

The basic problem was that many researchers found exceptions to the rules proposed by Collins and Quillian. To cite just one example, the Collins and Quillian model suggests that people should be able to verify the sentences "A robin is a bird" and "A chicken is a bird" with equal speed, since the concepts *robin* and *chicken* are each one level away from the concept *bird*. In fact, this assumption is not true: Subjects consistently verify that a robin is a bird more quickly. One explanation for this finding stems from the idea that some instances of a concept are more *typical* than others; in this case, it is assumed that a robin is a more typical bird than is a chicken. Eleanor Rosch has done interesting work on this notion of typical instances (described in Chapter 8). Here, the most important point is that the Collins and Quillian model was not sophisticated enough to account for the additional time required by subjects to identify chickens as birds.

Several other network models of semantic memory have been developed more recently. In 1975, Allen Collins revised his own model, this time in collaboration with Elizabeth Loftus. Their *spreading activation model* still holds that semantic memory is organized as a network of concepts, but it does not argue that these concepts are organized in a simple hierarchy. Thus, *bird* is not necessarily a subdivision of the concept *animal* just because this structure seems logical. According to the spreading activation model, the actual organization of concepts within human memory must be determined by empirical research rather than deduced on logical grounds.

The Collins and Loftus model, like other network models of semantic memory, emphasizes that concepts are not isolated and independent of each other, but rather bound up in a complex web of associations. The meaning of a word is thus derived from its many relationships to other concepts. Memory networks provide a basis for thinking and for placing new information into the context of what we already know.

If computer programmers tried to develop a network model of human memory on a DEC VAX or an IBM mainframe, they would probably try to conserve storage capacity by representing concepts in an efficient and logical hierarchy, just as Collins and Quillian did. But research in this area has revealed that human memory follows its own logic. Thus, as researchers continue to explore the nature of human memory networks, they must assume as little as possible and test every assumption.

STORAGE CAPACITY

Aside from the question of how information is organized in LTM, many psychologists have conducted research to try to determine its storage capacity. This issue is complicated by the distinction between storage and retrieval. When an item is stored in STM, it can usually be easily retrieved and brought into awareness. In contrast, we often have trouble retrieving information from the vast storehouse of LTM. We saw one example in the people who could recognize the names and faces of their high school classmates but not recall them.

Another example is the frustrating experience of having a name or fact "on the tip of your tongue" and just not being able to recover it. One psychologist became interested in this phenomenon when he had trouble remembering the street on which a relative lived. After guessing Congress, Corinth, and

Concord, he looked it up and discovered that the street was named Cornish. The fact that his guesses were so close to the correct answer suggested that he was not just guessing; in the tip-of-the-tongue state, he seemed to have a dim picture of the forgotten name. So he set out with another psychologist (Brown & McNeil, 1966) to see what happens when people can remember some, but not all, of stored memory.

They began by developing a list of vocabulary words that college students might know but were likely to have trouble recalling, such as *apse, nepotism, cloaca, ambergris,* and *sampan*. An experimenter read a definition of each word to a group of Harvard and Radcliffe undergraduates and asked them whether they could name the correct word. Students who experienced that tip-of-the-tongue feeling of knowing but not quite remembering the correct word were asked to describe what they could of the elusive word—its first letter, how many syllables it had, words that sounded like it, and so on.

Analysis of the resulting 233 cases of the tip-of-the-tongue feeling revealed that people could sometimes describe the first letter or other characteristics of the correct word, suggesting that there was only a partial failure of memory. Interestingly, when these subjects reported the wrong words, they made two different kinds of errors. People who were given the definition of the word *sextant,* for example, sometimes guessed words that sounded about the same (like *sexton* and *secant*) and sometimes offered words that were closer to meaning (like *compass* and *astrolabe*). Sound and meaning, then, seem to be two different features we can use to retrieve information from storage.

Since information may be stored in LTM even when it appears to have been forgotten, it is difficult to determine exactly what information—or even how much information—is held in long-term storage. This fact has helped lead some to wonder whether every piece of information that enters LTM might be held in storage. Tulving's notion of cue-dependent forgetting is in this tradition.

One study suggesting a more limited form of LTM storage examined people's ability to remember an object they had seen probably thousands of times: a United States penny (Nickerson & Adams, 1979). Figure 7.6 illustrates one part of this experiment. Before reading on, see if you can identify which of these versions is a correct illustration of a penny.

When introductory psychology students at Brown University looked at these and other choices, only about half of those who were shown an accurate drawing (*B* in Figure 7.6) believed that it was correct. Each of the other choices was considered correct by at least some students. In a series of related studies, other U.S. citizens were unable to draw a penny, accurately describe its appearance, or tell what was wrong with a series of incorrect drawings. The authors concluded that even familiar objects may be stored in LTM in an abbreviated code.

In an informal survey, Loftus and Loftus (1980) found that most people agreed with this statement:

> Everything we learn is permanently stored in the mind, although sometimes particular details are not accessible. With hypnosis, or other special techniques, these inaccessible details could eventually be recovered. (p. 410)

Acceptance of this statement was even greater among psychologists (84%)

FIGURE 7.6 Which of these is an accurate illustration of a U.S. penny?

than nonpsychologists (69%). But when they reviewed all the studies that attempted to recover long-forgotten material—such as hypnotizing witnesses to a crime or electrically stimulating the brain to elicit particular experiences—they came to a different conclusion. Observers often think they can remember long-forgotten details, but there is evidence that sometimes they reconstruct past events from partial memories, filling in the blanks with imagination and educated guesswork.

CONSTRUCTIVE MEMORY

Much of the early research on verbal learning treated memory as a passive process of learning to associate stimuli and responses. One version of this approach led to the false conclusion that the human mind is like a videotape machine that stores a complete record of every event in our lives.

A different view of the mind was proposed in 1932 by Frederick C. Bartlett. At a time when most researchers were compiling lists of nonsense syllables, Bartlett used more natural stimuli. People simply read a story and then tried to recall it hours, days, or months later. One stimulus was an old Indian tale called "The War of the Ghosts," which ended with these words:

> He told it all, and then he became quiet. When the sun rose he fell down. Something black came out his mouth. His face became contorted. The people jumped up and cried.
>
> He was dead.

Eight days after reading the original story, one typical subject recalled the event this way:

The next morning at dawn he was describing his adventures to his friends, who had gathered round him. Suddenly something black issued from his mouth, and he fell down uttering a cry. His friends closed around him, but found that he was dead.

Note how the original story was subtly altered and embroidered. For example, in the new version, his friends gathered around and it is the dead man, rather than those around him, who cried.

Six months later, another subject recalled a much more garbled account:

A voice said: "The black man is dead." And he was brought to the place where they were, and laid on the ground. And he foamed at the mouth.

These reports, and many others, led Bartlett to propose the term **constructive memory** to refer to an observer's tendency to rebuild pictures of past events from the few details remembered by filling in the details that have been forgotten. Moreover, Bartlett found that people altered these stories in predictable ways. For example, in some cases they simplified the stories by omitting many details. In others, they added new details that seemed to fit better with their prior knowledge and beliefs. Bartlett argued that knowledge for specific concepts was clustered together in memory in structures he called **schemas.** The new stories, he said, were constructed around these schemas.

Bartlett's work and his concept of memory schemas was largely ignored by his contemporaries. But when cognitive psychology began to take hold several decades later, his notion of the active learner who adds new information prompted a considerable amount of research.

A particularly vivid example of constructive memory and the way people may come to believe the details they have manufactured was provided by developmental psychologist Jean Piaget (1962) in an account of his own childhood:

One of my first memories would date, if it were true, from my second year. I can still see, most clearly, the following scene, in which I believed until I was about 15. I was sitting in my pram which my nurse was pushing in the Champs Elysées, when a man tried to kidnap me. I was held in by the strap fastened around me while my nurse bravely tried to stand between me and the thief. She received various scratches, and I can still see vaguely those on her face. Then the crowd gathered, a policeman with a short cloak and a white baton came, and the man took to his heels. I can still see the whole scene, and can even place it near the tube station. When I was about 15, my parents received a letter from my former nurse saying that she had been converted to the Salvation Army. She wanted to confess her past faults, and in particular to return the watch she had been given as a reward on this occasion. She made up the whole story, faking the scratches. I, therefore, must have heard, as a child, the account of this story, which my parents believed, and projected into the past in the form of a visual memory. (pp. 187–188)

The idea that humans sometimes construct memories around schemas is now widely accepted. One of the most practical lines of research encouraged by this view concerns the way the legal system evaluates eyewitness accounts of a crime.

constructive memory The observer's tendency to rebuild pictures of past events around the incomplete details that are remembered.

schemas Memory structures in which knowledge of specific concepts is clustered together; an important element in constructive memory.

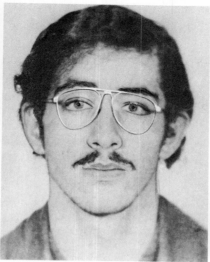

Mistaken eyewitnesses' identifications led to the arrest of Lawrence Berson (left) for several rapes and George Morales (right) for robbery. It later became clear that both men were innocent when Richard Carbone (center) was convicted of the rapes and confessed to the robbery.

EYEWITNESS TESTIMONY

In 1975, Lonnie and Sandy Sawyer were convicted of kidnapping the assistant manager of a North Carolina department store. Despite their repeated claims of innocence, the brothers were given sentences of 28 to 40 years in prison, largely on the basis of the testimony of Robert Hinson, the man who had been kidnapped. Although Hinson had only a glimpse of his kidnappers before they put on stocking masks, his identification of the Sawyers was enough to convince a jury. Private detectives pursued the case and later found one of the men who had actually committed the crime. In January 1977, the Sawyer brothers were pardoned and released after nearly two years in jail (Loftus, 1979).

What could be more impressive than having the victim of a crime point to a woman in a courtroom and say, "She's the one. I saw her do it"? When in 1973 a British government commission studied all the legal cases in England and Wales that involved a police lineup (or "identification parade," as the British call it), they found an 82% conviction rate for people who were prosecuted after being picked from a lineup. Even more impressive were the 347 cases in which people were prosecuted when the only evidence against them was the word of one or more eyewitnesses; 74% of these people were found guilty (Devlin, 1976).

In one experiment (Loftus, 1974), college students were asked to judge guilt or innocence in a fictitious case of a man accused of robbing a grocery store and murdering the owner and his 5-year-old granddaughter. On the basis of the evidence they read, only 9 of 50 jurors considered the man guilty. A second group of 50 jurors were given precisely the same case with one twist—a clerk in the store who saw the crime testified that the accused was guilty. Under these conditions, 36 of 50 people voted for conviction, showing once again that eyewitness reports are given a great deal of weight.

But the results for a third group of 50 college students were far more surprising and disturbing. These people read the original evidence and the eyewitness testimony, but they also learned that the eyewitness had been discredited. The defense attorney had proved that the eyewitness had very poor vision, had not been wearing his glasses that day, and could not possibly have seen the face of the robber from where he stood. If the jurors were totally rational and fair, they should have voted for conviction at about the same rate as the first group (9 out of 50). In fact, however, 34 of these 50 jurors voted "guilty." It was almost as if they believed that a mistaken eyewitness was better than no eyewitness at all.

These results are particularly distressing in light of the fact that other studies have consistently shown that eyewitnesses often do make mistakes. For example, on December 19, 1974, viewers of the local NBC news on Channel 4 in New York saw a short film of a staged purse snatching; the young man who committed the crime was seen running directly toward the camera for a second or so. Viewers were then shown a lineup and asked which of the six men pictured, if any, had committed the crime televised only a moment before. Over 2,000 people called a special telephone number to identify the culprit. There were seven possibilities—the purse snatcher could have been one of the six men or he might not have been in the lineup at all. If people guessed randomly, they should have been right about 1 out of 7 times, of 14.2% of the time. The results were that 14.1% picked the right man. Thus, these 2,145 eyewitnesses could have performed just as well without ever seeing the crime; the identification seemed completely random (Buckhout, 1975).

Even more disturbing than eyewitnesses' sheer inaccuracy is the fact that later information can change people's schemas and thus the memories they construct. Of particular interest to unethical lawyers is the fact that the wording of a question can influence what a witness remembers.

In one study (Loftus & Palmer, 1974), students saw various films of car crashes. Some of these eyewitnesses were asked, "About how fast were the cars going when they *smashed* each other?" They estimated the speed at an average of 40.8 miles per hour. When other eyewitnesses who saw the film were asked, "About how fast were the cars going when they *contacted* each other?" the estimate dropped to an average of 31.8 miles per hour. Other verbs produced intermediate results: *Collided* produced an average response of 39.3 miles per hour; *bumped* produced 38.1 miles per hour; and *hit* yielded 34.0 miles per hour.

A skeptic might question the precise differences in what the various groups remembered. Loftus and Palmer believed that there was a basic change in the underlying schema. If so, the subjects who said that the cars were traveling at high speeds would expect a more serious accident and thus construct a memory that included greater damage.

In a related experiment, some subjects returned to the lab one week after seeing the film. They were asked whether they had seen any broken glass lying around after the accident. Of 50 subjects who were asked about "smashing" cars, 16 said that they had seen broken glass; in fact, there was none in the film. Only 7 of 50 subjects who were asked about "hitting" cars "remembered" broken glass. The implication is that the "smashing" group thought the cars were traveling faster and therefore constructed a schema with greater damage.

Results like these suggest that lawyers who ask leading questions can manipulate not just what an eyewitness says but even what the person remembers. Other studies have shown that leading questions are even more likely to produce distorted memories if the subject is hypnotized (Sanders & Simmons, 1983). This finding is rather disturbing, given the fact that hypnosis has often been used by law enforcement agencies to elicit information from eyewitnesses, and has even been admitted as evidence in some courts (*Scientific American,* 1985).

In 1983, Dywan and Bowers reported the results of a laboratory test that cast doubt on the use of hypnosis to revive eyewitness memories. Fifty-four subjects were shown a series of 60 slides of black-and-white drawings of everyday objects and then given several memory tests. A week later, they returned to the laboratory for another memory test. At this time, half were told to relax and focus all their attention on recalling as many objects as they could; the other half were hypnotized and asked to recall.

Hypnosis produced memories of many new objects that had not been remembered a week earlier, especially among subjects who were highly suggestible. (Suggestibility was measured by the Stanford Hypnotic Susceptibility Scale, which appears as Table 4.1 in Chapter 4.) While they were hypnotized, the suggestible group described twice as many new objects as the unhypnotized controls. Unfortunately, many of the everyday objects they "remembered" were not among the original 60. Overall, the highly hypnotizable group made three times as many errors as the unhypnotized controls.

Dywan and Bowers concluded that hypnosis may not affect what people actually remember. Rather, it may simply make them less cautious about what they are willing to guess. In addition, if hypnosis makes mental images seem more vivid, people who are hypnotized may be tricked into confusing the vivid products of their imaginations with actual memories.

In 1981, Sloane reported the results of a study measuring the effects of hypnosis on eyewitnesses to a crime. In this experiment, the Los Angeles Police Department systematically compared hypnosis and other interrogation techniques in 44 consecutive witnesses and victims of crimes. Each person was randomly assigned to a particular group; half were hypnotized for their interview, and half were not. Police investigators were then given 60 days to verify the information collected in each interview. In this field study, hypnosis had no effect whatever; reports from hypnotized individuals were neither more nor less accurate than the ones elicited by normal questioning.

After reviewing these studies and many others, a panel appointed by the American Medical Association concluded that while hypnosis of eyewitnesses sometimes produces additional details, such information is often unreliable (*Scientific American,* 1985). They therefore recommended that police use of hypnosis be limited to the investigative stage rather than accepted as evidence in itself. Hypnosis, they argued, may provide new clues to a crime, but the details should always be confirmed by other sources of objective evidence.

THE ROLE OF SCHEMAS

The research with hypnotized and unhypnotized witnesses supports the idea that schemas—structural clusters of knowledge for particular concepts—

play an important role in human memory. This has been an influential notion in recent years, and many researchers have explored other applications.

For example, you may remember a study described in Chapter 2 of the way expectations can influence memory: Students who heard the fictional life story of Betty K. remembered different details depending on whether she was described as heterosexual or homosexual (Snyder & Uranowitz, 1978). The different recollections can be attributed to an active process of constructive memory, in which details were built around different schemas regarding homosexuals and heterosexuals. (Some psychologists prefer the plural form *schemata* rather than *schemas.*)

In Chapter 8, we shall describe how researchers in the field of artificial intelligence have used the concept of schemas in attempting to program a computer to perform complex tasks, such as understanding and responding appropriately to human languages like English. The notion of schemas has also proven useful in studying the unusual ability of experts in specialized fields to recall extremely specific information in their areas. For example, a biographer of Arturo Toscanini estimated that the famous conductor "knew by heart every note of every instrument of about 250 symphonic works and the words and music of about 100 operas" (Marek, 1982, p. 414). Marek cited several anecdotes to support this claim, including a story about Toscanini's efforts to have his orchestra perform a rather obscure piece (the slow movement from Joachim Riff's Quarter no. 5). When Toscanini was unable to find a score, he wrote down the entire piece from memory. Some time later, a collector found a copy and compared it to Toscanini's version; the maestro had made exactly one error. According to Horton and Mills (1984), such remarkable recall might be explained by the fact that experts have highly

Conductor Arturo Toscanini was known for his remarkable memory of symphonic scores.

Comparisons between John Dean's testimony at the Watergate hearings and tapes made by President Nixon suggest that Dean failed to remember many details. However, his central schema—the extent and nature of Nixon's involvement in the Watergate cover-up—was quite accurate.

developed schemas, which allow them to encode vast amounts of information in their areas of expertise.

One of the most interesting accounts of the possible effects of schemas is found in psychologist Ulric Neisser's analysis of the Watergate testimony of White House counsel John Dean (1981). In 1973, Dean testified before the U.S. Senate committee that was trying to determine whether President Nixon had been involved in the scheme to break into the Democratic National Committee headquarters in the Watergate housing complex for purposes of wiretapping. During his testimony, Dean recalled a conversation that had taken place nine months earlier, on September 15, 1972, between him, President Nixon, and White House Chief of Staff H. R. Haldeman. At the time Dean testified, however, neither he nor the senators knew that that conversation, as well as others, had been taped by Nixon. Later, of course, these tapes became public. The fallout from their release included President Nixon leaving office. It also afforded Neisser the rare opportunity to compare a person's memory of important events with an objective record of what actually occurred.

In his prepared testimony, Dean gave the following account:

> When I arrived at the Oval Office I found Haldeman and the President. The President asked me to sit down. Both men appeared to be in very good spirits and my reception was warm and cordial. The President then told me that Bob— referring to Haldeman—had kept him posted on my handling of the Watergate case. The President told me that I had done a good job and he appreciated how difficult a task it had been and the President was pleased that the case had stopped with Liddy. . . . (Neisser, 1981)

When Neisser compared this statement with a transcript of the tape recording of the actual meeting, he found that hardly a word of Dean's account was true (p. 147). Nixon had not asked Dean to sit down, had not said that Haldeman had kept him posted or that Dean had done a good job, and had not mentioned Liddy or the indictments.

However, Neisser goes on to explain that in this statement and other testimony, Dean generally provided an accurate account of the president's involvement in Watergate, which was, of course, the primary concern of the committee. Thus the central schema was accurately recalled, and details were constructed around it. The specific details above might have come from another schema describing what generally happens when a person enters a room: The host greets his guest warmly and asks him to sit down.

In a review of the evidence for schema theory, Alba and Hasher (1983) argue that while there is considerable evidence that such reconstructive processes influence memory in some types of situations, schemas are not likely to be involved in the retrieval of general knowledge. Similarly, according to Harry Bahrick (1984, p. 56): "There is no evidence for reconstructive change in remembering one's name . . . and thousands of other overlearned facts, rules, or meanings that constitute much of our general knowledge. These instances of literal recall are not the exception; they are the rule for overlearned memory content."

Bahrick's own research has explored natural memory phenomena— which he calls "replicative memory"—in which the information a person remembers closely matches the original content. For example, Bahrick (1984) studied how well 733 people remembered Spanish lessons weeks or years after they had learned them in school. Of these subjects, 146 were students in high school or college Spanish classes at the time of the study; 40 subjects in a control group had never taken a Spanish class and did not know the language. The others had taken Spanish courses anywhere from 1 to 50 years before the experiment.

Bahrick found that even individuals who had studied Spanish 50 years earlier and had never used it still remembered "large portions of the originally acquired information." The amount a person remembered declined most in the first 3 to 6 years after the course; after that, it remained essentially unchanged for up to 30 years before going into a final period of decline. Differences in the amount each individual remembered could be predicted from the level of original training and the grades the person received. These findings provide an example of very long-term storage of information in nearly its original form.

There is now wide agreement among psychologists that people develop both replicative and reconstructive memories in everyday life. There is still considerable controversy, however, about the exact conditions favoring one type of remembering over the other and the relative proportions of literal versus constructed memories. Thus, future research will be needed to determine how often our memories accurately encode exactly what happens, and how often we make up new facts to fit our schemas.

How to Remember

In ancient Greece and Rome, before the invention of cheap notebooks, ballpoint pens, and TelePrompTers, politicians were often forced to commit their speeches to memory. Some of the memory aids they devised are still used today. However, what the Roman orator Marcus Tullius Cicero described as the "art of memory" has begun to evolve into a science, as contemporary psychologists have developed new strategies and improved old ones.

Mnemonic Devices

Mnemonic devices are techniques for organizing information so that it can be remembered more easily. One of the simplest mnemonic devices involves rhyming, as in "*I* before *e* except after *c*" and "Thirty days hath September, April, June, and November." Because these rhymes place information in a context and give it structure, they help many people remember what would otherwise be isolated facts.

Similarly, acronyms provide structure by taking the first letter of a series of words and forming a single item. The acronym ROY G. BIV, for example, has helped generations of students remember the order of the color spectrum: red, orange, yellow, green, blue, indigo, violet. This strategy is an example of converting several chunks of information into a single chunk to reduce the load on memory.

mnemonic devices Techniques for organizing information so that it can be remembered more easily.

method of loci Visualizing images of a list of things to be memorized and mentally placing them in an orderly arrangement of locations.

Less familiar to most people is a mnemonic device invented by the ancient Greek poet Simonedes. According to legend, Simonedes was called outside a banquet one evening moments before the roof of the hall caved in. All the other guests were crushed to death; their bodies were mangled beyond recognition. As the sole survivor, Simonedes had to identify the corpses by remembering where each victim had been sitting. This grisly experience gave Simonedes an idea for improving memory. The **method of loci** (*loci* is Latin for "places") involves visualizing images of the things to be memorized in an orderly arrangement of locations (see Figure 7.7).

Suppose you want to remember the following shopping list: pecan pie, potato chips, chocolate fudge cookies, and Diet Pepsi. Using the method of loci, you would begin with a series of familiar places. You might, for example, visualize walking around your living room—from the couch to the rocking chair to the fireplace to the TV. You would then proceed to associate a vivid picture of each item from your shopping list with one of these locations: a pecan pie on the couch, the rocking chair covered with potato chips, a bag of chocolate fudge cookies in the fireplace, and a can of Diet Pepsi on top of your TV. When you get to the store, you can simply take a mental stroll through your living room and look at each image.

In one systematic test of the effectiveness of the method of loci (Ross & Lawrence, 1968), college students memorized a list of 40 nouns by visualizing each at a specific campus location. Immediately after, the students were able to remember an average of 38 items in the correct order; a day later, they still remembered 34. This performance is astounding, especially when com-

FIGURE 7.7   These woodcuts come from a sixteenth-century text describing how the method of loci can be used to improve memory. On the left are the sample loci at an abbey; on the right are the objects to be remembered by picturing them at specific locations on the abbey grounds.

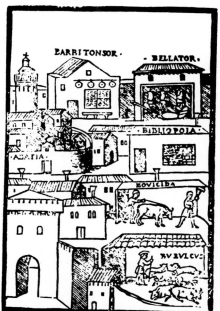 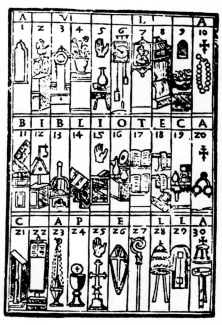

pared with the results of experiments in which people tried to master lists without the help of such memory aids.

Other research investigated the effectiveness of various strategies for using the method of loci. Many memory experts claim that the most effective memory images are bizarre ones (see "Becoming a Critical Consumer"). Following this theory, you would be most likely to remember the pie if you imagined some bizarre image, such as a 6-foot pecan pie reading a newspaper while reclining comfortably on the couch. However, several direct tests of this claim have failed to find evidence that it is true (Bower, 1970). One study (Wollen, Weber, & Lowry, 1972) asked students to memorize pairs of easily imagined words, such as *elephant, sofa,* and *cigar.* One group saw the stimuli in ordinary drawings; the other group saw the objects pictured in much more bizarre and imaginative drawings. Both groups remembered the objects equally well.

On the other hand, this same study verified another claim of memory experts: Two objects are easier to remember together if their images interact in the mental picture. For example, *elephant* and *sofa* are easier to associate if one pictures an elephant actually sitting on a sofa. Drawings that illustrated two interacting images did indeed lead to better memory for the word pairs. Thus, this systematic study helped reveal which claims of memory experts are accurate and which are myths.

Organization and Meaning

The success of these and other mnemonic devices calls attention to the underlying importance of meaning and organization to effective memory. Since Ebbinghaus, memory researchers have observed that it is easier to memorize meaningful material, such as a story or poem, than a meaningless list of digits or nonsense syllables. In fact, some nonsense syllables are easier to remember than others simply because they seem more meaningful. DOZ, LIF, and RUF remind us of English words and are generally remembered better than less familiar-sounding syllables such as GIW, ZOJ, and JYQ (McGeoch, 1930).

It took longer for memory researchers to recognize explicitly the importance of organization. In one classic experiment (Bousfield, 1953), people memorized lists of 60 words from 4 categories of 15 words each. For example, the category *animals* included *baboon, zebra, camel,* and *giraffe;* the category *professions* included *milkman, florist, dentist,* and *waiter.* Although the words were presented in random order, people recalled them in distinct clusters based on the categories. Memory imposed organization on the unstructured material.

Later investigations were able to show that knowledge of categories or an underlying organization actually helped memory. One of the more elaborate tests (Bower, Clark, Lesgold, & Winzenz, 1969) involved memorizing lists of apparently unrelated words such as *cookie, germ, tiger, cheese, yellow, bear, tan, hot, moth, wheat, cat, net, cow, cage, cool, mouse, bread, butterfly, milk, field, sun, trap.* Not surprisingly, high school students who were given this type of list had trouble memorizing all the words. But others from the same

BECOMING A
CRITICAL
CONSUMER

A Bizarre Route to a Better Memory

There are many books that promise to help people improve their memories. In one highly respected guide, Harry Lorayne and Jerry Lucas (1974) described some of the strategies they have used to improve their own memories. As you read the following passage, evaluate its recommendations in light of the study of Wollen, Weber, & Lowry (1972) described in the text. Is the recommended strategy based on systematic research? (A discussion of this strategy appears after the "Summary" at the end of this chapter.)

> In Order to Remember Any New Piece of Information, It Must Be Associated to Something You Already Know or Remember in Some Ridiculous Way. . . . [This] will force the Original Awareness that's necessary to remember anything, it will force you to concentrate and use your imagination as you never have before, and it will force you to form associations consciously.

Assume you wanted to memorize [an association between the words *airplane* and *tree*]. . . . All you need to do is to form a ridiculous picture, or image, in your mind's eye—an association between those two things.

There are two steps involved. First you need a ridiculous—impossible, crazy, illogical, absurd—picture or image to associate the two items. What you don't want is a logical or sensible picture.

An example of a logical picture might be: an airplane parked near a tree. Though unlikely, that is not ridiculous, it is possible—therefore, it probably won't work. A ridiculous or impossible picture might be: A gigantic tree is flying instead of an airplane, or an airplane is growing instead of a tree, or airplines are growing on trees, or millions of trees (as passengers) are boarding airplanes. These are crazy, impossible pictures. Now, select one of these pictures, or one you thought of yourself, and see it in your mind's eye. (pp. 25–26)

classes learned these words in the more organized form illustrated in Figure 7.8. Although their performance was not perfect, the group exposed to the organized list did remember significantly more words.

Most books on how to study emphasize the practical importance of understanding the overall meaning and content of materials. For example, consider the SQ3R study method described in Chapter 1. The first step in this process is to conduct a survey to identify the critical concepts in a book or chapter. This is a way of organizing material in advance so that it will be easier to remember.

Several researchers have shown that supplying an informational schema that organizes material in advance can improve comprehension and memory, particularly for ambiguous materials. For example, Bransford and Johnson (1973) asked people to remember several ambiguous "procedures." Subjects who were helped to develop organizing schemas in advance remembered this material far better than others who were not.

To see why, read the following paragraph from the Bransford and Johnson

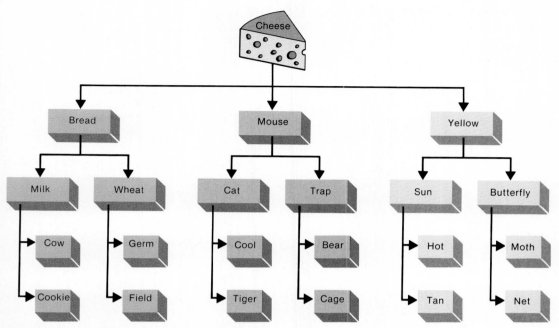

FIGURE 7.8 Organization aids memory. In one study, people who saw these words organized in this way later remembered them far better than others who saw the same words in an unorganized list.

study to see how many details you can remember when you don't know what the "procedure" is and therefore lack a memory schema to organize the material.

> The procedure actually is quite simple. First you arrange things into different groups. Of course, one pile may be sufficient, depending on how much there is to do. If you have to go somewhere else due to lack of facilities, that's the next step. Otherwise, you're pretty well set. It is important not to overdo things. That is, it is better to do too few things at once than too many. In the short run, this may not seem important, but complications can easily arise. A mistake can be expensive as well. At first, the whole procedure will seem complicated. Soon, however, it will become just another fact of life. It is difficult to foresee an end to the necessity of this task in the immediate future, but then one can never tell. After the procedure is completed, one arranges the materials into different groups again, and then they can be put in their appropriate places. Eventually, they will be used once more, and the whole cycle will have to be repeated; however, that is a part of life. (p. 400)

People who were not given hints about the underlying meaning found this passage quite difficult to remember. But others, who were told that this referred to washing clothes, had far less trouble. If you reread the paragraph with this organizing principle in mind, you too will probably find it much easier to understand and remember. An opportunity to test your memory under a different set of circumstances can be found in "Applying Scientific Concepts."

Testing Your Memory

To gain the most from this exercise, follow each of the steps below in sequence. Do not move on to a new step until you have completed the instructions in the preceding one. (A discussion of this exercise appears after the "Summary" at the end of this chapter.)

1. Try to think of what you were doing exactly six months ago today. For example, if today is October 23, think back to April 23. What were you doing on that day? Before you read beyond this sentence, get a piece of paper and write down everything you can recall from that date six months ago.

2. If you differ from politicians who seem to remember everything when interviewed about previous events, and find yourself having difficulty recalling what you did, said, heard, and saw six months ago, give your memory a boost by asking yourself the following questions:

   What were you doing in general that month (work, vacation, school, etc.)?

   Were there any important personal events that took place around that time (e.g., birthdays, job interviews, exams, engagements, breakups)?

   What day of the week was the date in question? (To find out, use a general calendar rather than a personal diary, which might tell you specifics about the day.)

   What activity did you typically engage in on that day of the week in that month?

   As you ask yourself these questions, try to add to your list of recollections from that day.

3. Finally, identify the key concepts from this chapter that apply to the preceding questions. For example, what memory system were you using? Did the questions asked in step 2 help you recall additional information? If so, why? Do you think you have recalled everything you experienced that day? If not, what concepts help you account for why you remember some things but not others? Do you think you have literal recall of events, or does your description of that day illustrate other important attributes of memory? Be specific.

Practice

No matter how effective one's study techniques, in the final analysis memorization and understanding always require the effort of practice—and the more practice, the better. Memory researchers use the word **overlearning** to refer to practice beyond the point of mastery. In terms of traditional memory experiments, persons who read and rehearse a list beyond the point where they repeat it without error have overlearned the material. Many experiments have shown that overlearned material is remembered longer and better than information that is barely mastered. It is particularly helpful when one wants to remember material for days or weeks rather than minutes or hours.

overlearning   Practice beyond the point of mastery.

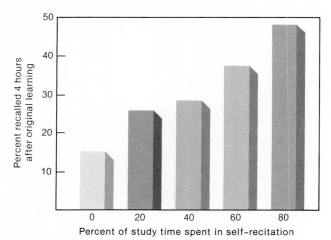

FIGURE 7.9   Reciting material aloud improves recall. In this experiment, subjects who spent a larger proportion of study time reciting aloud remembered material better four hours later.

Of course, overlearning eventually reaches a point of diminishing returns. You probably would not gain much by rehearsing the spelling of your last name; this material is already firmly established in your memory. Deciding just how much practice is enough can sometimes be difficult. But it is probably safe to assume that most students who do poorly in school have studied too little rather than too much.

The type of practice also makes a difference. About 70 years ago, A. I. Gates (1917) demonstrated the advantages of active recitation. Figure 7.9 compares the performance of several groups of students who spent the same amount of time studying but devoted different proportions of their time to reciting material aloud. As you can see, the more they recited aloud, the more they remembered.

Robinson (1970) cited Gates's finding when he developed the SQ3R method, which included steps of reading, reciting, and reviewing. On the basis of this study and others, many experts provide the following advice: If you have three hours to study a chapter that takes one hour to read carefully, you should probably read it once and use the remaining time to ask yourself questions and rehearse the answers.

The more actively you participate in this process, the more effective it is likely to be. Relating new ideas to known information, organizing material in personally relevant ways, and forming images can all be useful strategies. Asking yourself questions also provides immediate feedback that can help you identify the material that needs the most work. It also encourages deeper levels of processing in which you try to understand the material instead of just repeating it by rote. Last but not least, active study techniques make it difficult to fall asleep.

Summary

Measuring Memory

- Hermann Ebbinghaus, the first scholar to study memory objectively, used nonsense syllables in his experiments.
- Contemporary psychologists distinguish among three different ways of measuring memory.
- **Relearning** involves learning material for a second time so that researchers can compare the time or effort it took to learn material the first time with the second, later time.
- **Recognition** involves deciding whether specific information has been seen or heard before.
- **Recall** involves remembering information spontaneously or on the basis of certain cues.

Forgetting

- **Associationism** is the belief that even the most complex memories are ultimately based on associations between simple ideas.
- According to the **decay theory** of forgetting, physical memory traces gradually fade with the passage of time.
- The **interference theory**, which holds that people forget information because one memory prevents another from being recovered, is supported by more evidence than the decay theory.
- **Proactive inhibition** occurs when interference comes from material presented before the learning task.
- **Retroactive inhibition** occurs when interference comes from material presented after the learning task.
- A biological approach to forgetting can be found in Lashley's concept of the **engram**, a physical change in the brain responsible for memory storage.
- A **cognitive approach** to human memory explores the inner structure and organization of the mind, and the active processes used by a learner.
- Many cognitive researchers take an **information-processing approach**, which attempts to analyze thought processes, including memory, as a series of separate steps.
- Cognitive psychologists distinguish between three major processes in memory.
- **Encoding** is the transformation of a physical stimulus into the kind of code that memory accepts.
- **Storage** is the retention of this memory.
- **Retrieval** is the recovery of the memory from storage.
- According to Tulving's information-processing theory of **cue-dependent for-**

getting, inadequate memory cues lead to a failure to retrieve information from storage.

- Tulving's **encoding-specificity principle** holds that recall improves if the same cues are present during recall as during the original learning.

- According to psychodynamic theory, some forgetting is **motivated**; for example, when an event is too painful to remember, **repression** of the memory takes place.

The Atkinson-Shiffrin Model of Memory

- **Amnesia,** usually caused by damage to the brain, means a loss of memory.

- **Anterograde amnesia** involves an inability to remember new information for more than a few seconds.

- **Retrograde amnesia** involves an inability to remember events that occurred before damage to the brain.

- **Sensory storage** maintains a vivid and complete image of sensory impressions for about 0.25 to 2 seconds.

- Sperling's research demonstrated that we retain a literal image, sometimes called **iconic memory,** of a visual stimulus for a fraction of a second after it is presented.

- **Echoic memory** refers to an analogous phenomenon in the auditory system—that is, the ability to hear a sound for a moment after it stops.

- **Short-term memory (STM)** stores a limited amount of information for no more than about 30 seconds.

- **Long-term memory (LTM)** is a relatively permanent system that can store large amounts of information for long periods of time. It includes **episodic memory**—a record of an individual's past experiences—and **semantic memory**—a more abstract record of words, symbols, ideas, and rules for relating them.

- **Constructive memory** refers to an observer's tendency to rebuild pictures of past events around the incomplete details that are remembered.

- **Schemas,** memory structures in which knowledge of specific concepts is clustered together, are an important element in constructive memory.

- Partly as a result of this process, eyewitness memories of a crime or some other event are often extremely inaccurate.

How to Remember

- **Mnemonic devices** are techniques for organizing information so that it can be remembered more easily.

- One such technique, the **method of loci,** involves visualizing images of the things to be memorized and mentally placing them in an orderly arrangement of locations.

- Other common mnemonic devices include rhyming and acronyms.
- Other techniques for improving memory include focusing explicitly on meaning, reciting material actively, and **overlearning**—practicing material beyond the point of mastery.

Critical Thinking Exercises
Discussions

A Bizarre Route to a Better Memory

This strategy probably sounds convincing; many memory experts agree that bizarre interacting images improve memory. But when Wollen and his colleagues tested this idea, they found that bizarre images did *not* improve memory. Although an expert may know that a particular strategy seems to work for him or her, it takes systematic research to learn which elements of the strategy are truly vital to success and which are based on habit or superstition. Thus, the critical thinker will not accept a statement simply because it seems plausible, but rather he will use higher standards of scientific validity.

Testing Your Memory

Recollection of what one was doing six months ago clearly involves the long-term memory system; moreover, it is episodic memory specifically that is being tested when one is asked about events in one's life. The questions asked to help in the retrieval of memories are useful because they also call on semantic memory—the store of information that includes guidelines as to what one does on weekdays versus weekends, when in school or on vacation, etc. Some events may be recalled more readily than others, because their significance led them to be processed at a deeper level. It is likely that the recollection shows the results of constructive memory rather than a literal recall of events.

The critical thinking skills involved in this exercise include identifying and focusing on the relevant concepts and ignoring irrelevant ones. Initially, this task was facilitated by explicit use of the term *memory system* in the first question. That term gave you a clue as to where to look for the relevant information (i.e., in the material on memory systems). The other questions were more open-ended and required you to rely more on your own problem-solving skills to find the answers. Your approach probably involved comparing the information on memory in the text with the kind of information you needed to supply in order to answer the questions.

THOUGHT AND LANGUAGE

Chapter 8

 $\mathcal{S}$ lips of the tongue in which sounds are misplaced are called *spoonerisms,* after the Reverend William Spooner, an Oxford dean who was famous for errors of this sort. On one notorious occasion, Spooner meant to refer to "the dear old queen" and instead mentioned "the queer old dean." On another, he wanted to say to a student, "You have missed all my history lectures . . . in fact, you have wasted the whole term." What Spooner actually said was, "You have hissed all my mystery lectures . . . in fact, you have tasted the whole worm."

Although there is some question whether Spooner himself made these errors intentionally, there is no doubt that people sometimes transform words and phrases by accident. Recordings of radio and television bloopers often include spoonerisms, such as an announcer's introduction of President Herbert Hoover as Hoobert Heever. Psychologists and linguists see errors of this sort as more than a chance for a cheap laugh; slips of the tongue may provide valuable clues about the way we use language and thus about the workings of the human mind. (In Chapter 12, we review another approach: Sigmund Freud's contention that these errors may also reveal powerful unconscious forces that shape our behavior.)

Slips of the tongue seem to follow certain rules. For example, when new words are formed by an English-speaking person, they always conform to characteristics of English. When a nervous bridegroom says, "With this wing, I thee red," his statement almost sounds as though it makes sense; the error produces other English words.

Even when people form nonwords, they follow certain rules. You may say "stips of the lung" by accident, but you will not say "tlips of the sung."

Although you could repeat this phrase easily enough, speakers of English know that words do not begin with *tl*. Other languages do begin words with this sound; some Indian tribes in America's Northwest, for example, speak a language called Tlingit, which allows this combination. Along the same lines, you will never hear an English-speaking person accidentally create the word *nga*. English words do not begin with *ng*, although, as Fromkin (1973) notes, " 'nga' . . . is a perfectly good word in the Twi language of the Ashanti in western Africa" (p. 111). In short, when people make errors speaking a certain language, they continue to follow its specific rules.

More complex errors also provide insights into the general question of the organization of human speech. Consider the man who meant to say, "On the verge of a nervous breakdown," and instead said, "On the nerve of a vergeous breakdown." Note that this error involves two words that are separated by *of a*. According to one simplistic model of human language, a speaker associates each individual word with the next rather than thinking through a phrase or sentence in advance. But this slip of the tongue involves a reversal of the sounds in two words that are not next to each other but are separated by others. Therefore, it seems reasonable to assume that the phrase *verge of a nervous breakdown* had been held in memory before it was uttered, and the confusion entered at that point.

In general, researchers have found that slips of the tongue resemble the intended word or phrase in either sound or meaning. This suggests that our "mental dictionaries" may be organized along these lines and that the speaker who makes a mistake has retrieved a word that is stored nearby in the network of words that sound alike or share similar meanings.

This analysis may remind you of the information-processing approach described in Chapter 7. While some psychologists have studied the active internal processes involved in the storage and retrieval of memory, others have used similar concepts to explore such topics as problem solving, concept formation, decision making, and language. Thus, even an apparently trivial phenomenon like a slip of the tongue can provide insight into the rules that govern speech. In this chapter, we provide an overview of what is known about these rules and the active internal processes involved in thought and language.

The Origins of Cognitive Psychology

The same historical forces that shaped psychology's approach to learning and memory also affected studies of language and thought. One of the most influential approaches was John B. Watson's attempt to remove all reference to internal processes from the science of behavior. Common sense tells us that people can perform internal thought processes, such as multiplying 4 by 30, without emitting an observable response. In his extreme version of behaviorism, Watson (1930) was not willing to grant even this simple point. Thinking, he said, was simply a case of subvocal speech in which an external stimulus (such as the command "multiply 4 times 30") produced an overt behavioral response (here, activating the muscles of the speech apparatus slightly for the answer—120).

human engineering The application of scientific principles to the design of equipment and machines that maximize human efficiency.

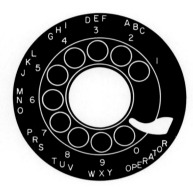

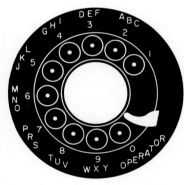

FIGURE 8.1 Before World War II, the printing inside the holes of a telephone dial was difficult to see from certain angles. A 1947 experimental model with the numbers outside the holes led to slower dialing by about 1 second per call; with 500 million calls per day, that adds up to over 139,000 hours of extra hookup time and considerable money. Human engineers proposed a simple solution for the 1949 model. They placed a white dot in the center of each hole. People could aim at these dots while the dial spun, and this reduced dialing to the original time.

Philosopher Herbert Feigl mocked this radical proposal when he said that Watson "made up his windpipe that he had no mind." But many psychologists took it seriously; one even allowed himself to be temporarily paralyzed by curare to see if that would affect his thought processes (Smith, Brown, Tolman, & Goodman, 1947). The behaviorist theory was not supported. Despite the fact that this brave soul could not move a single muscle (or even breathe without the help of a respirator), he was able to observe, understand, and think about the events that went on around him.

This study was just one small piece of a much larger puzzle. Over the last few decades, the interests of American psychology have shifted from a behavioral emphasis on the isolation of stimuli and responses to a more cognitive approach that analyzes the nature of thought. This change in the dominant scientific paradigm (see Chapter 2) resulted from the joint effect of many lines of research described throughout this text, such as Köhler's and Tolman's studies of animal learning (see Chapter 6), Atkinson's and Shiffrin's model of human memory (see Chapter 7), Chomsky's analysis of human language (described here in Chapter 8), and Jean Piaget's observations of children's intelligence (see Chapter 9). In these cases and others, scientists have focused on the active internal process involved in thinking.

Another important force in the shift to a cognitive approach was far less theoretical. In the 1940s, psychologists were called out of their laboratories to help solve some of the practical problems involved in waging World War II. Sophisticated new devices like radar and aircraft made heavy demands on their operators, and human errors often had disastrous consequences. Many psychologists therefore turned away from the "pure" problems faced by rats negotiating a maze and focused instead on how skilled radar operators and pilots could avoid mistakes in moments of stress. These new questions inevitably led psychologists to reconsider issues, such as attention and decision making, that had been ignored by strict behaviorists.

This work led to the emergence of the field of **human engineering**, which applies scientific principles to the design of equipment and machines to maximize human efficiency. In Chapter 1, we described one example: an airplane with a history of crashes caused by the design of the cockpit controls. Figure 8.1 provides another example; human engineers at Bell Laboratories helped develop telephone dials that human callers could use most efficiently. These practical examples underline the value of a cognitive approach that analyzes how quickly people can process and respond to different forms of information.

In Chapter 6, we defined cognitive psychology as the study of higher mental processes involved in such areas as attention, perception, memory, language, imagery, and reasoning. In all these areas, cognitive psychologists focus on knowledge. How do people gain knowledge about the world around them? How is knowledge coded and stored in the human mind? How do people retrieve knowledge when they need it and transform it so that it applies to new situations? How is knowledge related to what people actually do?

As the cognitive influence has grown in psychology, these concerns have become intertwined with psychologists' approaches to virtually all the topics covered in this text. In this chapter, we will focus on two of the most central research areas in cognitive psychology: thought and language.

Concept Formation

In studying cognitive processes, one of the most important concepts is the concept of a concept. In other words, concepts are important; they summarize past knowledge and help us deal efficiently with the world.

A **concept** is a mental category of objects or events, grouped on the basis of certain common features. A person who was unable to form concepts would be forced to deal with every unfamiliar object or event as if it were entirely new and never encountered before.

Suppose, for example, that as you enter a friend's home for the first time, a large, brown, four-legged animal jumps up on you and tries to lick your face. If you lacked the concept *dog,* you might be quite alarmed and try to defend yourself by kicking the animal in the head. But in fact our previous experience allows you to categorize the animal under the concept *pet dog* and respond appropriately by playfully wrestling with the animal or by telling your friend please to prevent this disgusting creature from licking your face.

Concepts not only help to predict future events; they also summarize past knowledge. For example, we noted in Chapter 5 that the human eye can distinguish among as many as 7.5 million different colors. Imagine how confusing it would be if these many gradations were not summarized under a few basic concepts, such as *red, yellow,* and *blue.*

The first major studies of human concepts focused on the rules people use to identify concepts. Bruner, Goodnow, and Austin (1956) presented a series of problems like those listed in Figure 8.2 to see whether people found some types of concepts more difficult to identify than others. For instance, to be an example of a **conjunctive concept,** an item must possess two attributes at the same time. The concept *red square* is conjunctive; to belong, an item must be both red and square. In contrast, to belong to a **disjunctive concept,** an item may possess one or both of two attributes, such as red or square. Disjunctive concepts are more difficult to learn; this example would include red squares, green squares, and red circles, but not green triangles. The examples become even more complex if a judgment is made on more than two dimensions (such as big, red, or square).

Studies of the rules people use to identify such concepts in the laboratory provided many insights into the nature of logical reasoning processes. However, in the 1970s, several researchers argued that in the real world, concepts are rarely as well defined as these laboratory examples. Eleanor Rosch (1975) noted that some items are more *typical,* or better examples of a concept, than others. For example, the concept *furniture* includes some items that are typical and easily agreed upon, such as chairs, beds, and tables. But the boundaries of this concept can become rather fuzzy. Is an ashtray furniture? Or a vase? Or drapes?

Rosch found that there is a clear consensus on which members of a category are typical and which are not. When a group of subjects independently rated how typical certain examples were, the agreement was quite high. For example, a robin is a typical bird, a chicken is not; murder is a typical crime, vagrancy is not; and an apple is a typical fruit, but a fig is not.

These differences in typicality may determine how information is stored

concept A mental category of objects or events grouped on the basis of common features.

conjunctive concept An item that possesses two attributes at the same time.

disjunctive concept An item that possesses either one or both of two attributes.

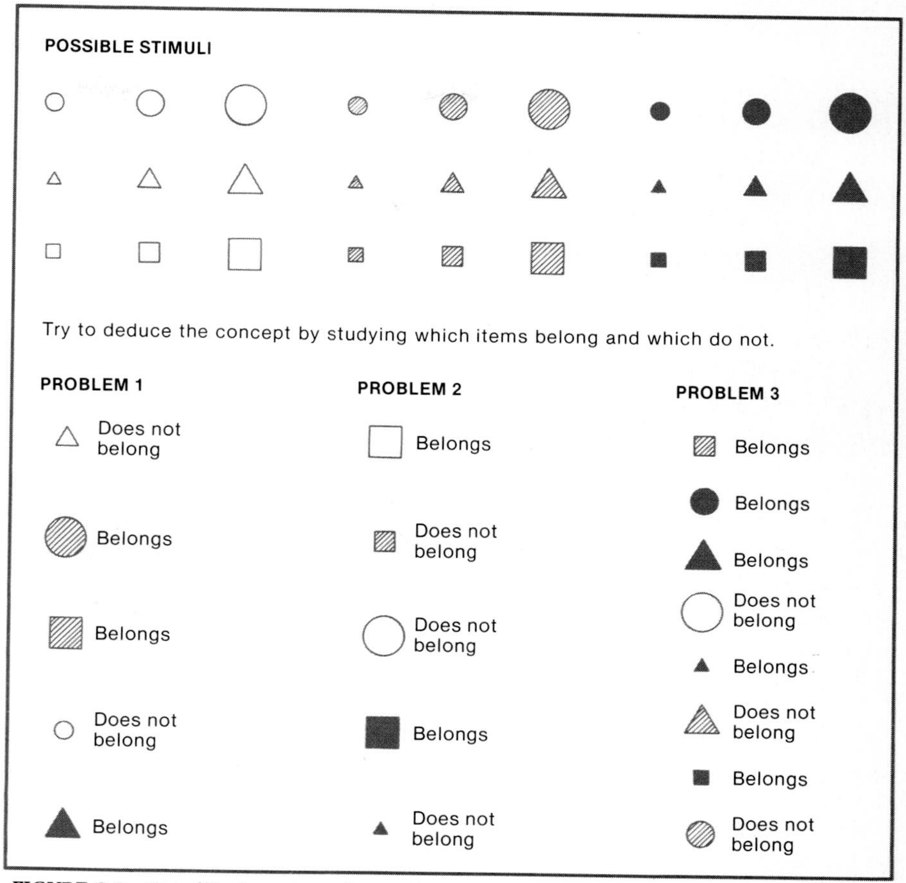

POSSIBLE STIMULI

Try to deduce the concept by studying which items belong and which do not.

PROBLEM 1

△ Does not belong

◎ Belongs

▨ Belongs

○ Does not belong

▲ Belongs

PROBLEM 2

□ Belongs

▨ Does not belong

○ Does not belong

■ Belongs

▲ Does not belong

PROBLEM 3

▨ Belongs

● Belongs

▲ Belongs

○ Does not belong

▲ Belongs

◸ Does not belong

■ Belongs

◎ Does not belong

FIGURE 8.2 Simplified version of a concept-identification experiment. For each problem, try to identify the concept that is based on a particular value for one or more of the three dimensions: size (small, medium, large), color (light, medium, dark), and shape (circle, triangle, square). See footnote on page 282 for answers.

in long-term memory. For example, people take longer to answer the question "Is a chicken a bird?" than to answer "Is a robin a bird?" Experiments that require people to identify diagrams, stick figures, and dot patterns lead to the same conclusion. More typical instances are easier to recognize as belonging to a concept.

Such findings concerning concepts suggest that similar chunks of information may be stored together in the network of semantic memory (see Chapter 7), overlapping each other according to their similarity. At the center of this network is the "pure concept"; a bird, for example, is defined by certain characteristics, such as wings and feathers. All the many kinds of birds are stored in the same network, with atypical birds like chickens, penguins, and ostriches at the outer fringes.

In addition, the information we use often fits into more than just one category. In such cases, we can create a new concept to organize complex information. One type of organizing concept is the **goal-derived concept**, a

goal-derived concept A specialized concept created to help a person reach a specific target.

Which is the best example of a bird? For most people, a robin is a more "typical" example of the concept *bird* than a chicken or an ostrich. This difference seems to be related to the way information is stored in long-term memory.

specialized concept created to help a person reach a specific target. For example, suppose you set yourself a goal to lose 5 pounds before your birthday, four weeks from now. You might create a concept of "food I should eat while dieting." This concept would probably include salad and milk but exclude Black Forest cake and rocky road ice cream.

Goal-derived concepts are different from the simple-object concepts discussed earlier because of their complexity and because different criteria are used to decide what is included. In the previous example of the natural concept of a bird, similarity is the major criterion for including or excluding an organism. But similarity is not a major factor for goal-derived concepts (Barsalou, 1981). After all, ice cream and milk are more similar to each other than salad and milk are, yet milk is included as a "food to eat," while ice cream and cake are not. Thus, including an object in a goal-derived concept

Answers to Figure 8.2: 1. A simple concept—large size.   2. A conjunctive concept—large size and square shape.   3. A disjunctive concept—dark color or square shape.

is dependent on its value in some relevant dimension (e.g., calories) and on how often the object has been included in the concept before.

Another way people determine which objects fit into a concept is by using probabilities based on past experiences. Rips and Handte (1984) asked people if a 5-inch round object was more likely to be a coin or a pizza. Most people guessed that it would be a pizza. Actually, 5 inches is bigger than large coins and smaller than a typical pizza. The reason people guessed pizza was that even though a 5-inch pizza would be a very small one, pizzas vary in size more than coins do. Also, we know from experience that very large coins would be difficult to use and therefore are unlikely to exist. So, pizza is a better bet for the unknown object.

Although most people guessed that the object was a pizza, not everyone did. Agreement among people is typically high when they are identifying examples of pure concepts, but there is less agreement at the outer fringes. The existence of the fuzzy boundaries of categories is a reminder that concepts can be subjective. In an extreme example of an abstract category, one person may interpret "roughing it on vacation" to mean hiking through a virginal forest, eating only wild berries, and sleeping on pine cones. To another, it may mean getting a motel room with no room service and a black-and-white television. Clearly, abstract concepts like this can depend on a whole lifetime of learning. And such concepts may have an important influence on how we make decisions.

Decision Making

We are constantly faced with choices, from relatively minor ones (like what flavor of ice cream to have for dessert or what movie to see) to major ones (like what occupation to pursue or when to get married). The process of **decision making** involves evaluating choices and picking the best one. There are a number of conceptual tools that help us in this process.

Heuristics

Just think about all the choices you faced this morning. When your alarm went off, you had to decide whether to get up or to sleep for 10 more minutes. You may even have decided to turn off the alarm altogether and skip your first class. When you got up, you had to decide what to wear. Selecting one's wardrobe often involves several small decisions (for example, which shirt to put on, whether to wear jeans or not, what kind of shoes to wear). Then you had to decide whether to eat breakfast, and if so, what to eat. If you picked eggs, you then needed to decide how to prepare them— scrambled, fried, boiled. Given this large number of choices so early in the morning, it is amazing that we ever manage to leave the house.

Decision making is facilitated by the use of **heuristics**, general rules of thumb, usually derived from experience, that guide our thoughts and give us a basis for making choices. For example, you might have a heuristic to decide what shoes to wear: If it's hot and dry outside, wear sandals; if it's

decision making The process of evaluating choices and picking the best one.

heuristics General rules of thumb that can influence decision making.

snowing, wear boots; otherwise, wear sneakers. Or you may have guidelines for breakfast: Eat cornflakes on weekdays; eggs or pancakes on weekends. Then you no longer have to check the refrigerator and cabinets deciding what to eat for breakfast each morning (unless you decided not to go shopping last week and you're out of cornflakes).

Studies of the thought processes involved in decision making have focused on specific heuristics that influence decisions. For example, people often try to minimize risks. If given a choice between purchasing a $5 raffle ticket with a 5 percent probability of winning $100 and a $5 raffle ticket with a 10 percent probability of winning $100, you would no doubt choose the second; it is less risky. However, if you had to drive 30 miles to buy the second raffle ticket, while you could get the first one across the street, then you might change your mind. Thus, factors such as convenience or cost of travel might also influence your choice. Typically, decisions are based on our tolerance for risks, intuition about probable outcomes, and willingness to accept costs or losses.

Heuristics help us make decisions more quickly and improve our efficiency. But sometimes they cause us to make bad decisions, because we don't take the time to consider alternatives or to think about the underlying problem. Although common sense tells us that people make rational choices that are consistent with the information available, research does not always support this.

Decision Frames

Reserach by Tversky and Kahneman (1981) showed that the way a problem is presented has a major influence on the decision made; just changing the way a problem is phrased can affect people's decisions. Consider the following example (Tversky and Kahneman, 1981, p. 453).

Imagine that the United States is preparing for the outbreak of an unusual Asian disease, which is expected to kill 600 people. Two programs to fight the disease have been proposed:

Program A: 200 people will be saved.

Program B: There is a $\frac{1}{3}$ probability that 600 people will be saved and a $\frac{2}{3}$ probability that no one will be saved.

Which program would you choose? If you said program A, then you're like the subjects in Tversky and Kahneman's study; about 75 percent of them chose A. Apparently, the certainty of saving 200 lives is more attractive than the risk of losing everyone. Where human life is at stake, no one wants to take risks.

Research subjects were then asked to consider two other programs to deal with the disease:

Program C: 400 people will die.

Program D: There is a $\frac{1}{3}$ probability that nobody will die and a $\frac{2}{3}$ probability that 600 people will die.

Which program would you choose? If you picked D this time, you're in the majority. Almost four out of five subjects chose this option. When the programs are presented this way in terms of losses, then even a 1 in 3 chance of saving everyone seems preferable to the certain deaths of 400 people.

But let's look at the four programs more closely. Programs A and C are really identical. Out of 600 people, 200 would be saved and 400 would die. Programs B and D are also the same. The probability is $\frac{2}{3}$ that all 600 will die.

Tversky and Kahneman (1981) used the term **decision frames** to refer to people's conceptions of the acts, outcomes, and contingencies associated with a particular choice. In the problem above, the only difference is in the way the outcomes are framed. For A and B, emphasis is on the number of lives *saved;* for C and D, emphasis in on the number of lives *lost.* This shift in emphasis is enough to make most people change their minds about which program is better.

Thus, people aren't always consistent. Very often, decisions are affected by the way the problem is formulated. Of course, people are rarely aware of this. It would be too time-consuming to analyze every problem for all possible consequences or to rethink the wording of different choices. So people typically work with the information as it is presented.

Consider another example. Suppose you pull into a gas station and ask for 10 gallons of gas. You decide to pay by credit card, since you only have $15 in cash. The attendant tells you the gas costs $10, but if you pay with cash, you will get a discount and the gas will cost $9.25. You decide to charge it anyway. You then drive off with your full tank, feeling fine. You don't care about the cash discount.

The next week you go back for gas again. This time, the attendant tells you that the 10 gallons cost $9.25, but if you want to use your credit card, there will be a surcharge and the cost will be $10. You decide to charge the gas, because you're short of cash again. But this week you drive off annoyed, feeling that the gas station overcharged you 75 cents. Even though you paid the same amount each time—$10—somehow, paying a surcharge is more bothersome than passing up a discount. This is another example of the influence of framing on our decisions and reactions.

We all have this type of reaction at one time or another. Even if the consequences are the same, our reactions are affected by the way we perceive the problem. Losses are seen as worse than gains. Therefore, people are more willing to pass up a discount than to accept a surcharge. Sophisticated advertisers know how to frame their ads to ensure positive reactions. They avoid talking about surcharges, since they seem like penalties. Instead, they typically use eye-catching terms like "spectacular sale" or "incredible discounts." We all know that $99.99 is really $100 (after all, what's a penny when you're spending that much money?), but somehow seeing $99.99 is easier to accept.

Researchers have demonstrated framing effects in doctor-patient situations as well. Suppose a patient with a serious disease is told that surgery might help the illness. Of course, no surgery is without risks, and a patient has to make a decision about how to proceed. When the doctor describes the outcome in terms of survival rates—say a 70 percent chance of surviving—

decision frames Conceptions of the acts, outcomes, and contingencies associated with a particular choice.

then patients are more likely to go ahead with surgery than when the outcome is described in terms of mortality rates—in this example, a 30 percent chance of dying. Just a switch in the doctor's emphasis, without any distortion of information, can influence the patient's decision.

Kahneman and Tversky (1984) provided the following example to illustrate how people prefer costs rather than losses. A man joined an expensive tennis club and then developed tennis elbow. He continued to play, despite severe pain, in order to get his money's worth. One assumes he wouldn't have continued to play if there had been no membership fee. But how can playing in pain improve his situation? When the man plays in pain, he continues to perceive the membership fee as a cost. If he stopped playing altogether, he would have to see the fee as a total loss. Perhaps he is the type of person for whom a loss is so unpleasant that he would rather play in pain. In this way, we use framing to fool ourselves.

Understanding how people make decisions provides insight into human thought. As we have seen, decision making is a complex process that involves integrating our past experiences, values, and preferences. The language used to describe our choices also plays an important role in influencing our decisions.

Problem Solving

Everyday life is as full of problems to solve as decisions to make. How do we get into the car when we've locked the keys in and ourselves out? How can we get a wrinkle out of a shirt without an iron? How can we get that somebody special to notice us when we're too shy even to say hello? What makes some people so clever at solving problems when others have trouble figuring out how to get out of bed in the morning?

The Gestalt Approach

The first social scientists to examine systematically the processes involved in solving a problem were a group of German researchers now known as Gestalt psychologists. In Chapter 5, we described the Gestalt approach to perception: The human mind imposes order and structure by grouping stimuli according to such principles as proximity, similarity, and closure. In like manner, Gestalt studies of thought focused on how the human mind imposes structure on a problem by understanding how its elements are related to one another.

One of the problems Gestalt psychologists asked their subjects to solve has since become a classic brainteaser. Take six matchsticks or toothpicks of equal length and try to arrange them into four equilateral triangles with each side equal to one stick. If you try to find the answer by pushing six matches around the table top, you are likely to come to the conclusion that there must be some mistake; any idiot can see that six sticks can only form two equilateral triangles.

Figure 8.3 illustrates another classic Gestalt problem. This, too, is likely to confuse and frustrate the average puzzle solver; repeated attempts may make it seem that there is no solution.

FIGURE 8.3 One of the classic Gestalt problems: Connect all nine dots using only four lines and without lifting your pencil. Solution appears in Figure 8.4.

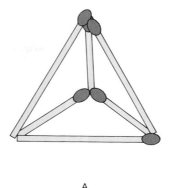
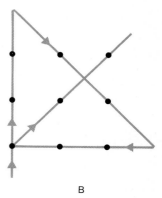

A   B

FIGURE 8.4 Solutions to the six-matchstick problem (A) and the nine-dot problem (B). Both are examples of productive thinking and require a reorganization of the elements—considering the possibility of a three-dimensional solution (A) or going beyond the boundaries (B).

If you are the type who would rather turn ahead to the answers than work up a sweat trying to solve these problems yourself, go directly to the solutions (in Figure 8.4). There you will see two examples of what Gestalt psychologists called the principle of **reorganization**—solving a problem by perceiving new relationships among its elements.

On the other hand, if you are a good sport who will valiantly push matchsticks around for 15 minutes before turning to the answer, your first reaction to the solution in Figure 8.4 may be to grumble about psychologists and cheap tricks. But you will have the last laugh if your experience helps you remember that simple assumptions (such as the idea that the matches must be arranged in two dimensions) can stand in the way of creative thinking.

Many great inventions can be traced to the Gestalt principle of reorganization. For example, in the nineteenth century, numerous attempts to design a sewing machine failed because people accepted the simple assumption that a needle has a point at one end and an eye at the other. Sewing machines that tried to pass a needle completely through the fabric for each stitch were very cumbersome and hard to design. But in 1846, Elias Howe invented the sewing machine by placing the eye of the needle in its point; in Gestalt terms, he had reorganized the elements of the problem.

Gestalt psychologists distinguished between two major types of thinking—productive and reproductive. **Productive thinking** solves problems by producing a new organization, as in the preceding examples. It is similar to what Wolfgang Köhler called *insight* in his studies of chimpanzees who reached fruit by standing on a crate or reaching with a stick (see Chapter 6). In contrast, **reproductive thinking** applies past solutions to new problems; it reproduces habits that worked in the past. Many researchers emphasized the value of productive thinking and demonstrated how old habits can interfere with solutions.

For example, Abraham Luchins (1942) studied how people solved a series of water-jug problems such as the following: A person is given three jugs of different sizes. Jug *A* holds 5 quarts, jug *B* holds 40 quarts, and jug *C*

reorganization The Gestalt term for solving a problem by perceiving new relationships among its elements.

productive thinking The Gestalt principle of solving problems by producing a new organization.

reproductive thinking (set effect) The Gestalt principle of applying past solutions to new problems.

Elias Howe's invention of the sewing machine provides an example of the Gestalt principle of problem solving by reorganization.

holds 18 quarts. Measure out 28 quarts by filling the jugs completely as often as you like and pouring the water from one jug to another. The solution is quite straightforward. Fill jug *A* twice and pour it into jug *B;* then fill jug *C* and pour it into jug *B.* This gives $5 + 5 + 18 = 28$ quarts. After you understand this example, try to solve the problems in Table 8.1. Complete as many as you can before you read on.

If you are like Luchins's subjects, you will probably discover that most of these problems can be solved with the formula $B - 2C - A$. That is, fill jug *B,* pour it into jug *C* twice, and pour it into jug *A* once. This leaves the desired quantity in jug *B;* for example, in problem 1, $127 - 3 - 3 - 21 = 100$. However, you may have trouble with problem 8 because $B - 2C - A$ does not work in this one case; 64% of Luchins's subjects fell into this trap and failed to solve problem 8 even though it involved a simpler approach ($A - C;$ fill jug *A* and pour it into jug *C;* the amount remaining in jug *A* is the desired quantity).

Further, some of the problems in Table 8.1 can be solved in more than one way. For example, for problems 7 and 9, simply adding the contents of jugs *A* and *C* is the simplest solution. However, problems 7 and 9 can also be solved with the more complex formula used for problems 1 through

functional fixedness The failure to see that an object may have more functions than its usual ones.

TABLE 8.1

Luchins's Water-Jug Problems

Problem number	Given containers of these sizes			Measure out this much water
	A	B	C	
1	21	127	3	100
2	14	163	25	99
3	18	43	10	5
4	9	42	6	21
5	20	59	4	31
6	23	49	3	20
7	15	39	3	18
8	28	76	3	25
9	18	48	4	22
10	14	36	8	6

5: $B - 2C - A$. Luchins found that the majority of his subjects (81%) used this familiar formula on problems 6, 7, 9, and 10, even though there were simpler solutions.

Psychologists use the term **set effect** to describe this tendency to solve problems in terms of old habits and assumptions, even when they no longer apply. In Gestalt terms, the set effect produces reproductive thinking when a problem demands productive thinking.

The term **functional fixedness** refers to one type of set effect, that is, the failure to see that an object may have functions (uses) other than its usual ones. If you need to pound a nail and don't have a hammer, functional

The mental processes involved in chess are related to general strategies people use in problem solving.

fixedness would keep you from thinking of the heel of a shoe or a rock as a hammering tool.

Luchins's study and others like it provided fascinating insights into the processes involved in solving certain types of problems. But this knowledge was like a small island in a vast sea of ignorance. The Gestalt psychologists were not able to develop a complete scientific theory that applied to all human problems—from how to start the car on a cold, rainy morning to how to avoid nuclear war. Many psychologists have been discouraged by the complexity of these issues; and there has been far less research on problem solving than on related issues, such as memory and language. However, the rise of a new theoretical approach has helped revive psychology's interest in this important topic.

Creativity

The Gestalt distinction between productive and reproductive thinking is similar to a number of other distinctions made by investigators interested in human cognition. For example, J. P. Guilford, who was part of a World War II team responsible for selecting aircraft crews, distinguished between divergent and convergent mental operations. In his complex model of the structure of human intelligence (Guilford, 1959), **convergent thinking** refers to the process by which individuals arrive at a correct answer to a problem by remembering past learning or by deducing through the application of logical rules. Guilford, who worked for a time in a psychological clinic testing children, noted that most intelligence tests measure convergent thinking and that such operations constitute only a very limited aspect of human intellect.

While doing well in school typically requires successful convergent thinking, Guilford argued that divergent thinking was more essential to the process of creativity. **Divergent thinking** refers to the ability to generate alternatives, to envision possibilities. Questions such as "How many uses can you think of for a Kleenex?" or "What are all the things this design could be?" are designed to tap divergent thinking.

In a classic study with fifth-grade children, Wallach and Kogan (1965) administered IQ tests as measures of intelligence and divergent-thinking tasks (such as those mentioned above) as measures of creativity. On the basis of these test scores, they were able to identify four groups of children: high intelligence/low creativity, low intelligence/high creativity, low intelligence/low creativity, and high intelligence/high creativity. On the basis of observations of the children, personality test results, and teacher interviews, Wallach and Kogan argued that schools should do more to foster divergent thinking and not just emphasize convergent thinking.

Another related point of view can be found in Cattell's (1971) distinction between crystallized and fluid intelligence. **Crystallized intelligence** refers to general information and knowledge. **Fluid intelligence** refers to the ability to perceive, encode, and reason about information. There is some evidence that fluid intelligence but not crystallized intelligence declines in the elderly.

A number of researchers, such as Wallach and Kogan (1965), have differentiated between creativity and intelligence, linking creativity to divergent, productive, and fluid intellectual processes. Current cognitive researchers typically

convergent thinking The process of answering a problem correctly by remembering it from past learning or by deriving it deductively from the application of logical rules.

divergent thinking The ability to generate alternatives, to envision possibilities.

crystallized intelligence General information and knowledge.

fluid intelligence The ability to perceive, encode, and reason information.

Analyzing Reasoning Tasks

This chapter provides sample items from a variety of tests of cognitive and linguistic processes. In this exercise, you are given several more test items. Your task is to solve the problems and decide what kinds of reasoning abilities or cognitive processes are involved. Use as many new concepts (an important term in this chapter) as you can to describe the type of reasoning or cognitive process each item taps.

1. Choose the correct response to fill in the blank.

   Sugar:sweet::Lemon: _____ (a) yellow, (b) sour, (c) fruit, (d) squeeze, (e) tea

2. Name as many uses as you can for an inner tube.

3. Read the example below of a successful military strategy in operation. Then decide how you would deal with the second dilemma—the X-ray problem—described.

   A fortress was located in the center of the country. Many roads radiated out from the fortress. A general wanted to capture the fortress with his army. The general wanted to prevent mines on the roads from destroying his army and neighboring villages. As a result the entire army could not attack the fortress along one road. However, the entire army was needed to capture the fortress. So an attack by one small group would not succeed. The general therefore divided his army into several small groups. He positioned the small groups at the heads of the different roads. The small groups simultaneously converged on the fortress. In this way the army captured the fortress. (Gick & Holyoak, 1980, p. 311)

   Suppose you are a doctor faced with a patient who has a malignant tumor in his stomach. It is impossible to operate on the patient, but unless the tumor is destroyed the patient will die. There is a kind of ray that can be used to destroy the tumor. If the rays reach the tumor all at once at a sufficient high intensity, the tumor will be destroyed. Unfortunately, at this intensity the healthy tissue that the rays pass through on the way to the tumor will also be destroyed. At lower intensities the rays are harmless to healthy tissue, but they will not affect the tumor either. What type of procedure might be used to destroy the tumor with the rays, and at the same time avoid destroying the healthy tissue? (Gick & Holyoak, 1980, pp. 307–308)

see such a dichotomization of abilities as an oversimplification—as did earlier researchers, such as Guilford (1954). Robert Steinberg (1985), for example, argues that creative individuals must be able to work with a rather substantial knowledge base, which would consist of the products of crystallized, reproductive intelligence. Creativity would then consist of a productive, fluid transfer of information to and from this knowledge base. Steinberg also admits that a substantial knowledge base is no guarantee of creativity. Like other aspects of human cognition, creativity appears to be extremely complex, and we are only beginning to understand it. (In "Applying Scientific Concepts," you are asked to analyze items from a number of different tests and decide what kinds of cognition abilities are being assessed.)

The Information-Processing Approach

As noted in Chapter 7, the **information-processing approach** attempts to analyze thought processes as a series of separate steps. Partly as a result of the computer revolution, this theoretical approach to memory, thought, and language has become so common and so influential that students sometimes mistakenly equate it with the more general area of cognitive psychology. The two are not the same. Cognitive psychology consists of a series of general questions concerning the way observers gain knowledge and use it; the information-processing approach provides one particular set of answers to these questions.

Probably the best-known information-processing model of problem solving is summarized in a series of computer programs called the General Problem Solver, originally developed by Allen Newell and Herbert Simon (1972). The Newell and Simon model began by noting that any problem can be seen as the difference between some initial state (*A*) and a desired goal (*B*). For example, in Luchins's water-jug problem, the initial state *A* involves three jugs with fixed capacities and an unlimited amount of water, while the goal *B* is some particular amount of water. Solving the problem, then, consists of a series of steps, operations, and transformations to get from *A* to *B*.

To discover the actual steps that human problem solvers take, Newell and Simon first used themselves as subjects. They tried to trace the sequence of their own thoughts as they played chess, cracked a code, or solved other problems. Then they asked other subjects to do the same—to think out loud, giving a running commentary as they worked through the problems. The systematic steps these people consciously reported were used to develop a computer program that would solve the same problem in the same way. This is called **computer simulation**, imitating some behavior or process (here, problem solving) on a computer.

This computer model of problem solving can be tested in a fairly straightforward manner: Give another problem to the person and the computer and see whether they go through basically the same steps and reach the same conclusion. If so, it seems reasonable to conclude that the person and the computer have used similar strategies.

One of Newell's and Simon's conclusions after reviewing how people thought aloud was that problem solvers systematically pursue one line of thought at a time. Ordinarily, this is not a process of trial and error; rather it is guided by general rules called algorithms and heuristics. As noted before, a heuristic is a general solution strategy. **Algorithms** are procedures or formulas that guarantee the solution to a given problem. To find the area of a rectangle, for instance, multiply the length by the width; this formula invariably provides the area.

As an example, one important heuristic, called **means-end analysis**, tries to solve problems by repeatedly comparing the current state of affairs with the final goal state and taking steps to reduce the difference between the two. Suppose you have a job interview tomorrow and want to be sure you will create a good impression. If you try to solve this problem by means-end analysis, the process might go something like this. What is one way to create a good impression? Be well groomed. What do you need to be well groomed? Nice clothes. Where do you find clothes? In the bureau drawer.

information-processing approach Attempts to analyze thought processes as a series of separate steps.

computer simulation A technique for imitating behaviors or processes, such as problem solving, on a computer.

algorithms Procedures or formulas that guarantee a solution to a problem.

means-end analysis Solving problems by repeatedly comparing current affairs with the final goal state and taking steps to reduce the differences between the two.

But it's empty. Where else can you find clothes? In a tangled heap on the floor of the closet. But they are filthy and smell like something other than lemon-fresh Fab. How can you make them clean? Wash them at a laundromat. But that would take hours. Where else can you find clean clothes? In your roommate's drawer. But your roommate would rather pour Jell-O on your record collection than lend you a shirt. How can you convince your roommate to let you borrow nice clothes? . . . And so on through a step-by-step process that gradually brings you closer to the final goal.

To see whether human beings really do solve problems with this type of means-end analysis, Atwood and Polson (1976) programmed a computer to solve a Luchins-type water-jug problem using this strategy. They then asked 250 college students to solve the same problem. The performance of the computer was found to be similar to that of the humans. They started with the same steps, took about the same number of moves to solve the problem, and made the same type of errors. Thus, computer simulation supported this information-processing model of thought. Note, however, that its scope was limited; another type of problem would require a new computer program and, possibly, a different heuristic or algorithm.

Newell and Simon had originally set out to discover fundamental laws of human reasoning that could be used to program computers to perform many different kinds of tasks. However, experiments with the General Problem Solver convinced them that general techniques, such as means-end analysis, were not adequate to solve most complex problems.

In the 1970s, many researchers reacted to these limitations by turning their attention to more narrowly defined problems and applications (Hayes-Roth, Waterman, and Lenat, 1983). This work forms the foundation for an area of computer science known as *artificial intelligence.*

Artificial Intelligence

According to a committee of experts that met in 1983 to review progress in this field, **artificial intelligence** includes efforts to understand the general nature of human intelligence and to program computers to perform tasks that require reasoning and perception (Waltz, 1982). There is a fundamental difference between these two goals. A researcher could make great progress in the task of understanding human intelligence without discovering a single thing that could be applied in computer programming. Conversely, one might succeed in programming a computer to formulate mathematical theorems, play chess, or hold a conversation without gaining any insights into the way the same operations are performed by the human brain.

The history of research in artificial intelligence has involved a gradual shift in emphasis between these two goals. Pioneers in this area, such as Newell and Simon, were primarily interested in using computers to understand human intelligence. In recent years, there has been a gradual shift to a practical emphasis on programming computers to perform complex tasks.

Thus, many of today's most influential researchers in this field are not concerned with creating models of human cognition; they simply want to program a computer to play chess or translate a language in the most efficient

artificial intelligence The field that includes efforts to program computers to perform tasks that require reasoning and perception.

possible way. Just as aerospace engineers design planes that do not necessarily imitate the flight of birds, so computer scientists may program machines using strategies that are very different from those a human would employ to solve the same problem.

EXPERT SYSTEMS

Expert systems are computer programs that apply knowledge in a specific area so that the computer can function as effectively as a human expert. These programs include both specific factual knowledge about an area and rules for reasoning based on that information.

One of the first successful expert systems was a program called MYCIN, which was designed at Stanford University to help physicians diagnose and treat infectious diseases (Shortliffe, 1976). The program provided advice to physicians by engaging them in a conversation like the one shown in Table 8.2. Basically, the computer asks the physician a series of questions about a

---

TABLE 8.2

Sample Dialogue with MYCIN

The program MYCIN was designed by artificial-intelligence researchers to help diagnose and treat certain types of infectious diseases. The following was adapted from a sample interaction with MYCIN.

Computer: Patient's name: (first-last)?
Doctor: Fred Smith.
Computer: Sex?
Doctor: Male.
Computer: Age?
Doctor: 55.
Computer: Have you been able to obtain positive cultures from a site at which Fred Smith has an infection?
Doctor: Yes.
Computer: What is the infection?
Doctor: Primary-bacteremia.
Computer: Please give the date and approximate time when the signs or symptoms of the primary-bacteremia first appeared (mo/da/yr).
Doctor: May 5, 1975.
Computer: The most recent positive culture associated with the primary-bacteremia will be referred to as Culture-1. From what site was the specimen for Culture-1 taken?
Doctor: Blood.
Computer: Please give the date and time when this blood culture (Culture-1) was obtained (mo/da/yr).
Doctor: May 9, 1975.
Computer: The first significant organism from this blood culture (Culture-1) will be referred to as Organism-1. Enter the identity of Organism-1.
Doctor: Unknown.
Computer: Is Organism-1 a rod or coccus (ec)?

Doctor: Rod.
Computer: What is the gram stain of Organism-1?
Doctor: Gramneg.
Computer: Have there been POSITIVE cultures from sites that are NOT associated with infections about which you are seeking advice?
Doctor: No.
Computer: Did Organism-1 grow aerobically?
Doctor: Yes.
Computer: Did Organism-1 grow anaerobically?
Doctor: Yes.
Computer: Does Fred Smith have a clinically significant allergic reaction to any antimicrobial agent?
Doctor: No.
Computer: What is Fred Smith's weight in kilograms (or pounds)?
Doctor: 70 kilograms.
Computer: My preferred therapy recommendation is as follows:

GIVE: GENTAMICIN.
DOSE: 119 mg (1.7 mg/kg) q8h IV [or IM] for 10 days.
COMMENTS: Modify dose in renal failure.

AND

GIVE: CLINDAMYCIN.
DOSE: 595 mg (8.5 mg/kg) q6h IV [or IM] for 14 days.
COMMENTS: If diarrhea or other GI symptoms develop, patient should be evaluated for possible pseudomembranous colitis.

Source: Davis, Buchanan, & Shortliffe, 1984, pp. 103–104.

patient's history, the patient's condition, and the results of laboratory tests. It then suggests a tentative diagnosis of the cause of the condition and therapy that could be used to treat it.

Physicians who use MYCIN to help them make decisions have several options if they disagree with the computer. If they do not understand how the computer reached a conclusion, they can type in a command asking the program to explain its line of reasoning. If they still disagree, they can tell the computer simply to reject that conclusion and report its next best guess.

The MYCIN program includes over 400 if/then rules regarding relevant diseases. For example, rule 209 in MYCIN states that if a blood culture shows evidence that an organism entered through the GI tract and there is a significant disease, and that "the patient is a compromised host," then therapy should be given for bacteroid organisms (Fagan, Shortliffe, & Buchanan, 1983, p. 244). These rules were derived through intensive interviews designed to discover the implicit and explicit rules of thumb, or heuristics, that specialists in bacteriology and meningitis used to make diagnoses.

Although MYCIN was originally designed for research rather than wide-scale use in the field, several related programs are now being used in routine medical practice. For example, a program called PUFF is being used to interpret the results of tests of pulmonary function at the Pacific Medical Center (Aikins, Kunz, Shortliffe, & Fallat, 1984). In clinical evaluation studies (Yu, Buchanan, Shortliffe, Wraith, Davis, Scott, & Cohen, 1979), MYCIN diagnosed disorders and prescribed treatments nearly as well as specialists in these diseases, and with far greater accuracy than general practitioners.

Many other expert systems are also being used in a variety of commercial settings. Another successful program, called PROSPECTOR, was developed in cooperation with the U.S. Geological Survey to help geologists explore for minerals. In 1982, a company that used PROSPECTOR to explore for molybdenum in the Cascades (in the state of Washington) found a deposit of this ore at a site that had been ignored by the company's human experts. In fact, the site was being used to dump waste from a nearby dig. The value of this deposit has been estimated as high as $100 million (Feigenbaum & McCorduck, 1983). With potential payoffs this large, it is not surprising that many firms have begun to explore the potential of expert systems for solving their commercial problems.

UNDERSTANDING NATURAL LANGUAGE

Another artificial intelligence research area where science and commerce have met is in programs designed to respond appropriately to requests phrased in everyday English (Hassett, 1984). Ironically, artificial intelligence researchers were more optimistic about this area 40 years ago than they are today. In the 1950s (which is roughly equivalent to the stone age for computer scientists), many programs were written to translate documents from one natural language to another. Their approach was quite straightforward. A Russian-to-English computer translation program, for example, simply looked up each Russian word in a bilingual dictionary and rearranged the English equivalents into a sensible sentence.

Unfortunately, these literal translations often left much to be desired.

expert systems Computer programs that apply knowledge in a specific area so that the computer can function as effectively as a human expert.

According to one often-repeated story, when the Biblical phrase "The spirit is willing but the flesh is weak" was translated from Russian, it became: "The wine is agreeable but the meat is spoiled." Another computer program was said to have translated the advertising slogan "Coke adds life" into the Chinese equivalent of "Coke brings your ancestors back from the grave."

Failures like this convinced most computer scientists that natural-language software needed to analyze not just the words in a message, but also its underlying context and meaning. As in the area of expert systems, researchers therefore began to lower their sights and construct more limited programs designed to understand language only about a very specific topic. One early program could discuss only baseball; another answered conversational requests about lunar rock samples. These and other programs were quite impressive within their limited domains, but they were unable to discuss anything else.

Several practical products were built upon this foundation. The first to achieve success was a program called INTELLECT, which was designed to solve a problem that had been created, ironically, by the very success of the computer revolution. As computers had become more widely used in business in the 1960s and 1970s, companies increasingly relied on them for filing away information about everything from accounting to personnel records. But once the data sets were filed away, they could often be retrieved only by programmers who were familiar with the computer's mysterious ways.

INTELLECT was designed to avoid the expense and annoyance of teaching large numbers of employees to understand the computer's language. Instead, the computer would learn enough English to answer user requests. For example, suppose that the user typed in a question to the computer, such as "How many of our salespeople earn more than $40,000 per year?" INTELLECT "understood" this request by applying a standard set of rules for analyzing syntax and a lexicon, or dictionary, that defined English words and phrases in terms of the computer's own query language. The dictionary included common English words and stems, such as *is, greater,* and *less,* as well as a special list of words tailored for the individual business. Thus, a company whose computer contained information on salespeople would include *salespeople* and *salesperson* in its vocabulary, as well as synonyms, such as *sales representative* and *sales rep.* INTELLECT can answer routine requests with a high degree of accuracy. Its conversational powers are quite impressive—as long as users limit themselves to questions within the realm of its vocabulary.

Other researchers sought to develop more sophisticated "knowledge-based" natural-language programs that could understand a broader range of statements within a particular context. To illustrate the point that understanding natural language often requires a vast storehouse of related knowledge, Abelson (1981, p. 715) gave the following example.

> John was feeling very hungry as he entered the restaurant. He settled himself at a table and noticed that the waiter was nearby. Suddenly, however, he realized that he'd forgotten his reading glasses.

The average reader will know why John might be disturbed; he needs his glasses to read the menu. Notice, however, that a menu was never mentioned in this passage. For a computer to be able to respond sensibly to simple questions about this story, it needs to be told more than just the meaning of individual words; the computer must be told about restaurants.

In Chapter 7 we introduced the notion of a schema as a cluster of knowledge regarding a particular concept. In these terms, the human reader has a schema about restaurants and the computer does not. The solution then is obvious. To understand narratives, a computer must be provided with relevant schemas of its own.

Schank and Abelson (1977) used the term **script** to refer to a schema that summarizes general knowledge about particular situations. They then programmed specific scripts into a computer to allow it to understand the restaurant scenario and other simple situations. For example, one artificial-intelligence program along these lines was capable of reading items from the United Press International news wire and writing short summaries. It accomplished this by programming more than 30 separate scripts for such categories as earthquakes, military invasions, and diplomatic actions.

The large number of scripts that might be required to enable a computer to write a book report on *Crime and Punishment* or to engage in a written form of cocktail-party chitchat fills programmers with awe for the complexity of the human information-processing system. Interpretation becomes even more complicated when a message is spoken rather than typed into the computer. In principle, programming a computer to transcribe the spoken word sounds like a time-consuming task but not a conceptually difficult one. After all, words are composed of a limited number of distinctive sounds. If you could find some electronic whiz to build a circuit that could recognize these several dozen sounds, a typewriter could easily be hooked up to spell out each word. Of course, the computer might have trouble transcribing unusual spellings or telling the difference between words like *wait* and *weight,* but all in all this sounds like a task that the massive resources of a major corporation like IBM or Digital could solve without a great deal of fuss.

However, as we shall see, human speech is an imperfect signal filled with ambiguity. Listeners actively perceive speech on the basis of a large number of implicit grammatical rules, expectations, and pieces of knowledge stored in memory. In the last few years, there have been tremendous advances in voice recognition devices that can recognize a limited vocabulary of words. However, typically they must be "trained" to recognize each speaker's voice and accent, and they are far more accurate with isolated words that are pronounced one at a time than they are with continuous speech.

Predictions about the future achievements of artificial-intelligence technology are a risky business. But of one fact we can be sure: Future studies of artificial intelligence and computer simulation will stimulate research not just on microchips and software packages but also on the workings of the most amazing device of all—the human mind.

script A schema that summarizes general knowledge about particular situations.

analogical reasoning Reasoning that involves judging, categorizing, or developing an argument about something new based on its similarity to something familiar.

Analogical Reasoning

While computer simulations of intelligence may still seem fairly esoteric, other issues of interest to cognitive psychologists—for example, analogical reasoning—are of obvious everyday relevance. **Analogical reasoning** involves judging, categorizing, or developing an argument about something new on the basis of its similarity to something familiar. Reasoning by analogy is something people do often. If you don't want to eat brussels sprouts because they smell like cabbage and you hate cabbage, your decision is rooted in an analogical connection between brussels sprouts and cabbage. If you oppose a government policy because it reminds you of the type of policy-making that led the country into the war in Vietnam, you are again reasoning analogically. If you tell your mom that nagging you about studying is going to lead to the same kind of rebellion your sister showed in response to curfews, your argument rests in an analogy.

Robert Sternberg of Yale University developed a preliminary theory of intelligence that rests heavily on the role of analogical reasoning. In his research program, he has used a variety of analogical problems of the form $A:B::C:D$ (read A is to B as C is to D). Some samples of his analogies can be found in Table 8.3.

In evaluating subjects' performance, Sternberg considers such variables as accuracy, rationale given for response, and reaction time. (For more on the use of reaction time as a variable in cognitive experiments, see "Understanding the Scientific Method.") Sternberg interprets his findings as supporting the notion that intelligence consists of specialized components. The components used in analogical reasoning are **encoding** (identifying attributes and values of each term of the problem), **inference** (discovering the rule relating A to B), **mapping** (discovering the rule relating A to C), **application** (generating a rule to produce and evaluate D), and **preparation-response** (preparing for and monitoring the solution process and translating the solution into a response). Whether such components really represent fundamental cognitive units is the type of issue not likely to be resolved in the near future.

Linguistics

Most of the time, we take our astounding language abilities for granted. Yet it is hard to imagine what human society would be like without language. Communicating simple thoughts, such as "pass the salt" and "I love blue eyes," could become major undertakings. Although we would all save money on our telephone bills, a world without language would almost certainly be far more primitive. Without language, how could one generation tell the next how to build a bridge, treat a broken leg, or bake moist and tender Toll House cookies?

Orators and philosophers have studied the nature of language at least since the ancient Greeks. But in the last few decades, two separate disciplines have arisen to study language from somewhat different perspectives. One discipline is **linguistics**, the study of the fundamental nature and structure of human language. It is concerned with language in the abstract, such as the way words can be combined in English to form an acceptable sentence. The other discipline is **psycholinguistics**, the study of how people actually speak and use language. For example, a psycholinguist might study the way children learn to speak for the first time in the hope of discovering fundamental principles of language use. A linguist, on the other hand, would be more concerned

TABLE 8.3

Verbal Analog Problem (Analogies)

feline:canine::cat:	_____
lose:win::liability:	_____
hand:foot::finger:	_____
dime:10::nickel:	_____
attorney:law::doctor:	_____
merchant:sell::customer:	_____

Source: Sternberg, 1977.

encoding Identifying attributes and values of each term of the problem $A:B::C:D$.

inference Discovering the rule relating A to B.

mapping Discovering the rule relating A to C.

application Generating a rule to produce and evaluate D.

preparation-response Preparing for and monitoring the solution process and translating the solution into a response.

linguistics The study of the fundamental nature and structure of human language.

psycholinguistics The study of how people actually speak and use language.

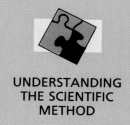

The Measurement of Reaction Time in Cognitive Psychology Experiments

Given the disillusionment with introspection as a means of analyzing the workings of the mind, cognitive psychologists have attempted to develop more objective and precise measures of mental activity. One common approach to a variety of questions in cognitive psychology involves measurement of subjects' *reaction time* to particular tasks. For example, in the reaction time method, subjects may be presented with a word and asked to press one of two buttons to indicate whether that word does or does not belong to a set of words they have just memorized. Or subjects may be presented with statements like: "A fish can swim," "A striped bass can swim," and "A peacock can swim," and asked to press one of two buttons to indicate whether the statement is true or false. Variations in reaction time to different types of statements are presumed to reveal something about the neurological basis of cognitive processes.

In one experiment by Cooper and Shepard (1982), subjects were asked to discriminate between normal and backward images of letters, presented in one of six orientations shown in the figure. The experimenters note that any one of the stimuli pictures in the figure can be identified almost immediately as some version of the letter "R." However, it seems to take at least a small amount of additional time to determine whether the particular letter is normal or backward—especially if it is markedly tipped. For this task, subjects were instructed to indicate whether each stimulus was normal or backward (regardless of its orientation) as rapidly as they could, without making errors, by pressing the appropriate button

(*box continues on next page*)

with the nature of linguistic rules than with the way children learn them or violate them.

The differences between those two specialties can be understood in terms of a fundamental distinction, drawn by linguist Noam Chomsky, between competence and performance. **Linguistic competence** is abstract knowledge of a language; **linguistic performance** involves applying this knowledge to speaking and listening. Psycholinguists tend to concentrate on performance, while linguists focus on competence. It is a bit like choosing to understand the game of Monopoly by concentrating on its formal rules, as a linguist might, or by observing how people play the game, as a psycholinguist might—noting which rules they follow religiously and which seem less important. (Note that this is also similar to Tolman's distinction between a rat's learning a cognitive map of a maze versus the animal's performance; see Chapter 6.)

Each type of research provides valuable clues about the nature of human

linguistic competence Abstract knowledge of a language.

linguistic performance Applying one's knowledge of language to speaking and listening.

on the response box. Try this task yourself, and see if the judgment appears to take slightly longer in some cases than others (although you won't be able to see your results in microseconds). If there are differences, what do you think is responsible—something about the stimulus, something in the way your brain works, a combination of both?

Cooper and Shepard (1982) interpreted their reaction time results, in combination with subjects' introspective reports, as supporting the notion that subjects made each judgment by mentally rotating the stimulus figure so that it could be compared with an upright normal or reversed figure. Further, the data indicated that this "mental rotation" could be carried out successfully no faster than about 60 degrees per second.

What is the significance of findings from studies using the reaction time method to study cognitive processes? Cognitive psychologists, particularly those interested in information processing, hope that the analysis of reaction time data from a broad range of cognitive tasks may eventually provide a precise picture of the mental operations involved in solving a variety of problems. Their precise calculations of the microseconds required to perform simple mental tasks may give us a window into the workings of the brain as it performs its task.

In the Cooper and Shepard (1982) experiment, subjects were presented with letters in different orientations and asked to identify each letter as normal or backward by pressing a button as rapidly as possible. This figure shows the letter "R" in each of its possible orientations.

THE SIX ORIENTATIONS

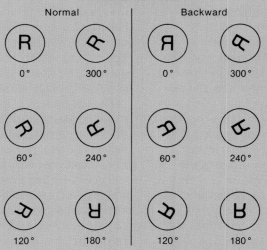

language. The usefulness of both approaches is one more example of how complex human behavior is best understood by viewing it from several perspectives.

The Grammatical Components of Language

One of the most amazing features of human language is the fact that each of us is capable of creating an infinite number of sentences. Similarly, there is no limit on the combinations of words that we can understand. It is relatively easy to produce a sentence that is unique. Consider the following statement: "With the crisis over AIDS, a new sexual revolution has replaced the old one, and questions about love and sex once again abound across college campuses." Although there is no way to be entirely certain, it seems likely that no one on the face of the earth has ever before strung these specific

grammar The complete system of rules that relates sounds to meanings for a specific language.

phonology The study of the rules governing the use of sounds in a specific language.

phonemes The distinct sounds that make a difference in a particular language.

words together in precisely this way. Yet we had no trouble writing this sentence, and you have no trouble understanding it. (You will probably also have no trouble concluding that the statement is false.)

Given our ability to use language in infinitely novel ways, linguists have come to the conclusion that each of us must master some fundamental principles that we use to generate sentences. Taken together, all these rules form the grammar of a language. When most of us think of the word *grammar,* we picture an English teacher sternly reminding students that nice boys and girls don't say "ain't." But for a linguist, **grammar** is the complete system of rules that relates sounds to meanings for a specific language. In this section, we consider the three main branches of grammar: *phonology,* the study of sounds; *syntax,* the way words combine to form sentences; and *semantics,* the meaning of words and sentences.

PHONOLOGY

Phonology refers to the rules that govern the use of sounds in a specific language. Every language contains a limited number of **phonemes,** the distinct sounds that make a difference in meaning in a particular language. By one count, English contains 41 phonemes; or distinct perceptual units. Although there are only 26 letters in English, the same letter may stand for several different sounds. For example, if you place your fingers over your Adam's apple and say the word *sounds,* you will notice that the *s* at the end of the word vibrates the vocal cords—it is therefore called a voiced consonant— while the *s* at the beginning produces no vocal-cord vibration—it is called voiceless. Figure 8.5 illustrates the major vocal tract structures when we form the sounds for *p, t,* and *k.*

The human vocal apparatus is capable of producing many more sounds than the limited set English speakers use—perhaps several hundred of them. Other languages use roughly 20 to 60 phonemes, often making distinctions that English speakers do not or failing to make distinctions that English speakers

FIGURE 8.5 When we talk, air from the lungs is forced through the larynx, mouth, teeth, lips, and sometimes the nose. Different speech sounds are produced by varying the shape of this system. This illustration shows the position of major vocal-tract structures for the English consonants *p, t,* and *k.*

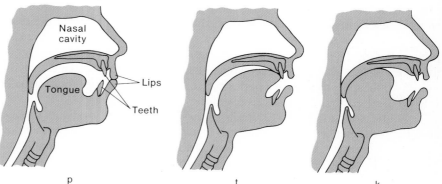

p   t   k

consider important. For example, the two words *keep cool* may seem to begin with the same sound. But there is a subtle difference between those two hard sounds. For the *k* in *keep,* the tongue touches the roof of the mouth farther toward the back of the oral cavity than it does for the *c* in *cool.* You may have difficulty specifying the precise placement of the tongue in the mouth for these two sounds, but if you listen closely enough you should be able to tell them apart.

While English treats these sounds as interchangeable versions of the same phoneme, Arabic does not. In Arabic, the word *kalb,* meaning "dog," begins with the sound of *k* in *keep.* The spoken word *qalb,* meaning "heart," sounds different only because it begins with the sound of *c* in *cool.* Such differences between the basic phonemes of various languages are one of the major obstacles faced by those who want to perfect their pronunciation of a foreign tongue. Native Japanese speakers may say *read* instead of *lead* because in Japanese *r* and *l* are interchangeable versions of the same phoneme.

Phonology is concerned not just with a list of acceptable sounds, but also with the rules by which they are combined. For example, you intuitively know that *kpax* and *gdoller* are not English words; each violates certain phonological rules in our language by requiring an unfamiliar pattern of lip and tongue movements. These letter combinations, however, would be perfectly acceptable words in Russian or Czechoslovakian, languages that have different phonological rules.

SYNTAX

Syntax (from Greek roots meaning "arranging together") refers to the rules that specify the way words can be combined to form sentences. On the simplest level, the rules of syntax specify which strings of words form acceptable sentences and which do not. Intuitively, we know that the statement "Bob Barker was my favorite game-show host" is grammatically correct. In contrast, there is clearly something wrong with the statement "Bob Barker was favorite game-show host my." We may have difficulty stating the precise grammatical rule this violates, but a native speaker of English has no problem recognizing that this string of words is not a well-formed sentence.

Beginning in the 1950s, Noam Chomsky developed an influential theory that attempted to make intuitive rules like this explicit. He hoped to lay the groundwork for a detailed grammar that would be capable of generating every string of words that a person who spoke English would recognize as a well-formed sentence. At the same time, this grammar should never generate a string of words that would not be an acceptable sentence. Thus, Chomsky proposed a model of linguistic competence, the abstract nature of language— the word strings that form acceptable sentences. He did not claim that his model would apply to linguistic performance, that is, that people would actually rely on these particular processes when they spoke or listened.

At the simplest level, Chomsky's (1965) theory analyzed the **surface structure** of sentences, the actual words in a sentence and the relations among them. In some ways, Chomsky's analysis of the surface structure is similar to the exercises schoolchildren perform in grammar classes. The basic idea involves breaking a sentence down into its component parts. For example, the sentence

syntax The way words combine to form sentences.

surface structure According to Chomsky, the actual words in a sentence and the relations among them.

> The dachshund bit the bus driver.

might be broken down into

> (The dachshund) (bit) (the bus driver).

Chomsky saw language as organized into a hierarchy, from the highest level—a sentence—to the lowest level—an individual noun, verb, or adjective. It is important to note that the parts of the surface structure of a sentence are not interchangeable. If we were to reverse the two noun phrases, it becomes

> The bus driver bit the dachshund.

Reporters everywhere would recognize this sentence as far more newsworthy than the original version.

Chomsky tried to specify the actual rules that were capable of generating the surface structure of the original sentence. One rule is that a noun phrase consists of an article, sometimes an adjective, and then a noun or another noun phrase. Sentences with more complex structures than our example require additional rules. For our purposes, it is not necessary to remember the details of the many possible rules. What is important is Chomsky's goal—to develop a complete, logical system capable of generating every sentence that is grammatically correct.

However, Chomsky also noted that the surface structure of a sentence was only part of the story. For example, consider the following two sentences:

> The dachshund bit the bus driver.

> The bus driver was bitten by the dachshund.

These sentences are obviously similar; grammatically aware readers will recognize the first as the active voice and the second as the passive voice. The surface structures of these two sentences—the order of the words and the relationships among them—are quite different, yet at the level of meaning they are practically the same.

Chomsky (1957) therefore introduced the notion of **deep structure**, the underlying organization and intent of sentences. In the case of a simple sentence in the active voice, such as

> The dachshund bit the bus driver.

the surface and deep structure are exactly the same. But for the passive voice, the surface structure is

> The bus driver was bitten by the dachshund.

and the deep structure is the simpler:

> The dachshund bit the bus driver.

deep structure According to Chomsky, the underlying organization and intent of sentences.

Two sentences with different surface structures (active and passive voice) can have the same deep structure (here, the active voice).

Noam Chomsky's influential views of language were developed as a model of linguistic competence—the abstract nature of language. But psycholinguists wondered whether it might also apply to linguistic performance—the actual processes people use in speaking and listening. Thus, Chomsky's model stimulated serious research on the problem of language comprehension; that is, what are the processes you use to understand this text or to comprehend Joe Garagiola's description of the World Series?

One of the first studies inspired by Chomsky's theory examined whether the structure of syntax helped people understand and remember linguistic stimuli; in other words, did normal listeners seem to use surface structure in some way? To avoid the complications produced by word meaning, Epstein (1961) developed a series of nonsense stimuli. Some, like Lewis Carroll's poem "Jabberwocky," were made to appear to conform to English syntax. For example, one of Epstein's stimuli read

A haky deebs reciled the dison tofently um flutest pav.

The glers un cligs wur seping un vasing a rad moovly.

Although few of the words make sense, this seems to read like an English sentence in which *haky* is an adjective, *deebs* a noun, *recile* a verb, and so on. Other nonsense strings removed the punctuation, capitals, and grammatical endings:

haky deeb um flut recile pav tofent dison

clig sep wur rad un moov gler un vas

People were able to learn the first set of stimuli far more easily than the second, despite the fact that the first list is somewhat longer. Syntax provided a structure that helped people remember, even when it was arbitrarily applied to meaningless syllables and words. This finding seemed consistent with Chomsky's strong emphasis on the importance of syntax.

Other early studies also supported the idea that Chomsky's model of linguistic competence might describe linguistic performance as well. For example, in Chomsky's system, a simple statement in the active voice requires no transformation to uncover its deep structure. A statement in the passive voice, however, must be transformed. Thus, if people actually use deep structures to understand a sentence, the active voice should be comprehended more quickly than the passive, because it does not require this time-consuming transformation.

In one test of this prediction, Gough (1965) asked people to read a sentence and then look at a picture. Sometimes the sentence accurately described the picture and sometimes it did not. The subjects in this experiment were asked to decide as quickly as possible whether the sentence and picture were consistent. Gough found that people responded more quickly when the statements were in the active, rather than the passive, voice, supporting the idea that people might actually analyze deep structures in order to comprehend a sentence.

Not surprisingly, however, later researchers found that things were not always this straightforward. To cite just one example, Olson and Filby (1972) found that in some cases the passive voice is easier to understand than the active voice. When people were told a story about a truck and then shown a picture of a car hitting it, they were able to verify the passive sentence:

The truck was hit by the car.

more quickly than the active one:

The car hit the truck.

This finding suggests that context (in this case, hearing a story) also plays a large role in human speech comprehension. This was one of many studies that made psycholinguists reconsider their optimism about Chomsky's model and think more seriously about the role of factors other than syntax; particularly semantics.

The word *mother* conjures up emotional connotations that go far beyond its literal definition.

SEMANTICS

Semantics refers to the rules governing the meaning of sentences, words, or morphemes. A **morpheme** is the smallest unit of speech that has meaning; it would be a word or a part of a word. For example, the words *slip, sense,* and *squeal* are all morphemes. Many prefixes and suffixes that change the meaning of a word are also morphemes. The word *slips* contains two morphemes: *slip* is one, and the *s* that makes it a plural is the other. Similarly, the words *nonsense* and *squealed* each contain two morphemes (*non-sense* and *squeal-ed*).

The meaning of morphemes and words in a given language is generally based on arbitrary symbols. There is no particular reason why the word *green* refers to a color midway between the blue and yellow. This color could have just as easily been named *orange* or *justice* or *Harold*. However, centuries of usage by English speakers have given the word *green* a certain meaning.

But semantics involves far more than just a mental dictionary that specifies the meaning of every morpheme in the English language. A word like *dictator* or *housewife* may conjure up emotional associations that go far beyond its literal dictionary definition.

Further, the interpretation of a statement may involve knowledge that goes far beyond the words themselves. The sentence "That doesn't sound right" may mean different things to a musician playing a tune for the first time, a doctor listening to a patient breathe, and an auditor reviewing your income tax returns. As a result of the fact that so many factors can affect meaning, semantics is probably the most complex area in linguistics.

Comprehending Language

In the last few years, many psycholinguists have focused on the role of context, schemas, and outside knowledge in comprehension. To paraphrase a sentence properly, we often need to understand a great deal about the context in which it was uttered. If a man says to his boss, "I am not paid enough," he probably means, "Please give me a raise." But if the same man tells his teenaged

semantics The rules governing the meaning of sentences, words, or morphemes.

morpheme The smallest unit of speech that has meaning; it may be a word or part of a word.

daughter, "I am not paid enough," when she asks for a new car, he means, "I can't afford it." In this case, comprehending a statement properly depends on far more than the syntax of the sentence or even the literal meanings of the individual words. If you did not know that bosses decide how much to pay their employees or that cars are expensive, you might interpret these sentences differently.

CONTEXT AND SCHEMAS

The role of context and schemas in comprehension is well illustrated in a study by Rumelhart. In this study, subjects heard a story that began

> Mary heard the ice-cream truck coming down the street. She remembered her birthday money, and ran into the house. (Hunt, 1982, p. 117)

When he questioned the listeners, they explained easily that Mary is a little girl who wants ice cream and that she went into the house to get money to buy some. These facts are obvious, but they are not stated in the story. Comprehension is based not just on words and their meanings but on schemas that fill in the gaps of what is mutually understood.

Both the study and the conclusion may sound familiar because of their resemblance to Roger Schank's work on scripts and artificial intelligence. In the late 1970s, several cognitive psychologists—including Rumelhart, Schank, and others—proposed ambitious models of the way knowledge is stored in long-term memory and how it is involved in the everyday comprehension of language. The details are controversial, as psycholinguists are just beginning to test their specific predictions. For our purposes, however, the similarities are more important than the differences between these models. All portray the listener as an active participant in the comprehension process who brings to the situation knowledge that allows understanding of not just the specific words in a statement but also the larger message it was intended to convey.

SPEECH PERCEPTION

The notion of an active listener becomes even more critical when one considers the further problems posed by the spoken word. Your ear probably does not distinguish differences in the sound of the letter *b* in the words *bill, ball, bull, able,* and *rob.* Yet careful acoustic analysis would reveal that each of these *b*'s has a slightly different sound. Add to this the complications of different speakers wtih different accents, some talking with their mouths full of roast beef and others whispering sweet nothings, and you may begin to wonder how we ever understand another human being.

Further, listeners sometimes make distinctions that speakers do not. In the normal course of conversation, the statements " 'Why choose,' she said" and " 'White shoes,' she said" are pronounced in precisely the same way. Although you as a listener will have little trouble knowing which phrase was meant in a certain context, if you had nothing to go on but the physical sounds of speech, you would never be able to tell these phrases apart.

In normal conversation, the quality of pronunciation is very low. This was most vividly demonstrated in a study (Pollack & Pickett, 1964) in which people were simply asked to repeat isolated words that were spliced from tape-recorded conversations. Astoundingly, fewer than half of these individual words were intelligible; listeners correctly identified single words only 47% of the time. The researchers went on to show that this result was not limited to conversational English. When people tried to identify single words from a tape of a person reading, they were correct 55% of the time. When the passages were read quickly, only 41% of the words were correctly identified.

Note that there was nothing unusual about the readings or conversations used in this study. When people listened to the entire tapes under normal conditions, they had no trouble understanding what was said with almost 100% accuracy. The researchers also asked people to identify two words in a row, three words, four words, and so on. The longer the stretch of speech, the more accurately listeners were able to identify the words. These findings again suggest that a person listening to the speech does not passively respond to a series of sounds. Rather, the listener actively uses clues from the context to fill in gaps in an imperfect auditory stimulus.

Additional support for this active picture of the listener comes from a study of the kinds of errors people make when they misunderstand what others say (Garnes & Bond, 1975). In virtually every case, mistakes involved substituting a similar word that served the same grammatical function: "Warpping service" was heard as "wrecking service," for example, and "get some sealing tape" was heard as "get some ceiling paint." It is almost as though the listener has an implicit idea of what should come next; after hearing "get some," the listener expects a noun and possibly an adjective. Ambiguous sounds are then perceived as conforming to this pattern.

Normal speech is at best an imperfect signal filled with ambiguity. Yet despite sloppy pronunciation, we usually hear it properly and make few mistakes. The listener starts out with certain implicit syntactic and semantic rules and actively perceives speech in terms of these expectations.

Some researchers believe that cultural expectations also influence the way we comprehend language. If you have ever traveled in another country or if you have friends who grew up outside the United States, you may be aware that sometimes you "hear" things differently. What may seem harmless to you may be an insult to them and vice versa.

Language and Thought

From the time Western anthropologists first began to study other cultures, they noted that the languages these people spoke often had little in common with the familiar European languages descended from Latin and Greek. A linguist named Benjamin Lee Whorf argued that these differences were so fundamental that they could actually change the way a person perceived the world. This idea became known as the **linguistic-relativity hypothesis**—the notion that language determines the content of thought or the way a person perceives the world.

Whorf (1956) cites the example of an Eskimo language that has three different words for referring to snow—one for falling snow, another for slushy

linguistic-relativity hypothesis The theory that language determines thought content or perception of the world.

snow, and a third for snow packed hard as ice. These extra categories, Whorf argued, lead the Eskimo actually to perceive a snowy world in a different way from a resident of South Dakota, who has only a single basic word. And both an Eskimo and a South Dakotan would perceive the scene differently from an Aztec, for Aztecs have only one word stem to refer to snow, ice, and cold.

This is a provocative idea, but one that is difficult to test. After all, the way we learn another individual's thoughts is by asking a question. We already know that an Eskimo will use several different words for snow in the answer. But how can we go beyond that to determine whether the Eskimo actually thinks in a different way?

No one would be surprised to learn that Eskimos know more about snow than Aztecs; after all, how many Aztecs live in igloos? The Eskimo's greater experience with snow is bound to give them more knowledge about it. And greater knowledge is often expressed in a more discriminating vocabulary. For example, English-speaking skiers also have several words for snow—such as *powder* and *corn*—because these distinctions are important to them. There is bit of a chicken-and-egg problem here; which comes first, the difference in language or the difference in perception?

The most intensive tests of this idea have considered the question of color perception. Do languages that divide the color spectrum differently actually lead to differences in color perception? In one study, Heider and Olivier (1972) compared the ability to remember colors for English speakers and for members of a primitive tribe from Indonesian New Guinea named the Dani. The Dani language has only two words for identifying colors; one refers roughly to light colors, the other to dark colors. In this study, each person was shown a colored chip for 5 seconds; 30 seconds later, the subjects were asked to pick out the chip they had seen from among 40 different colored chips. Both the English speakers and the Dani made many mistakes on this task, but the pattern of errors suggested that they perceived the color spectrum in the same way. If the linguistic-relativity hypothesis were correct, one might predict that people would be most likely to confuse two similar colors that they called by the same name; if similar colors had different names, they could be linguistically coded into two different categories. But this was not the case; labeling did not seem to affect the confusion among colors.

Even though the strong claim that language *determines* thought is not supported by the most careful research to date, there is evidence for a weaker version of the linguistic-relativity hypothesis: The words a person uses can certainly have some influence on thought processes. One typical study of this phenomenon examined the use of pronouns like *he* and *his* as neutral terms that may refer to either men or women (Moulton, Robinson, & Elias, 1978). When feminists proposed substituting expressions like *he or she* in neutral contexts, some writers argued that they were being overly sensitive, as if English speakers automatically assume that in some contexts *he* can refer to males or females.

In one study of the implications of using masculine pronouns, men and women were asked to make up stories about themes like this: "In a large coeducational institution, the average student will feel isolated in ———————— introductory courses." The blank was filled with *his, their,* and *his*

One Eskimo language has three different words for the English concept *snow*. Does this difference imply that speakers of the two languages perceive snow differently?

or her for three different groups. The researchers then noted whether the students wrote about male or female characters. The results appear in Figure 8.6; the actual pronoun used had a pronounced effect on the sex of the fictional characters. There is no question that language and thought are linked; the challenge for future research will be to specify the precise nature of these interrelationships.

At the same time that some psycholinguists have extended the boundaries of research on the nature of language with studies like these, others have gone even further to ask whether language is truly unique to the human species, or whether it can also be found elsewhere in the animal kingdom.

At least since the time when Clever Hans tapped his foot to answer Herr von Osten's questions (see Chapter 2), psychologists have been fascinated by the idea of teaching animals to "talk." Several early researchers took this goal quite literally. In her delightful book *The Ape in Our House,* Cathy Hayes (1951) described how she and her husband valiantly tried to teach a chimpanzee to hold a reasonable conversation.

They treated Viki the chimp like their own child. Viki wore diapers, followed her "mother" around the house, and for several years was generally treated as though she were merely an ugly person. In some ways, Viki behaved like any mischievous child. She could open windows, turn on lights, wash her face, listen to the radio, and scribble on walls. On the other hand, she never did master toilet training, she had an unsettling habit of biting the Hayes' visitors, and she was a whiz at swinging from trees. More to the point, after six years of intensive psychological training and motherly love, poor, slow-learning Viki could only mutter a few simple words like *mama, papa,* and *cup.*

In 1969, Allen and Beatrice Gardner published a groundbreaking report. They had actually taught a chimp to communicate with humans! In retrospect, the insight that made this achievement possible seems quite simple. Chimpan-

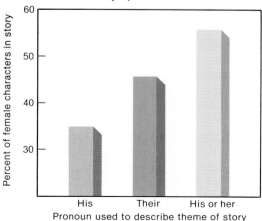

FIGURE 8.6 Sexist pronouns produced sexist stories. When the pronoun *his* was used to describe the theme of a composition, fewer people wrote about female characters than when the more neutral terms *their* or *his or her* were employed.

Viki the chimp was raised by Cathy and Keith Haye as if she were a normal child. Viki never learned to "speak" more than a few words, but she did learn to light cigarettes.

zees have trouble talking because their mouths and vocal apparatus are not designed to speak. Like some people, however, monkeys frequently gesture with their hands. The Gardners therefore decided to teach a chimpanzee American Sign Language, a linguistic system used by the deaf. While some deaf people use hand signals to spell out words, letter by letter, American Sign Language uses signs to represent entire words. To say *always,* for example, you would rotate your arm at the elbow while holding your hand in a fist with the index finger pointed forward. The sign for *flower* intuitively seems closer to its source—all five fingertips are held together and touched first to one nostril and then to the other, as if sniffing a flower.

The female chimpanzee the Gardners chose to study was born in the wild. When Washoe moved to her new family at the University of Nevada in June 1966, she was about a year old. Reasoning that Washoe would be most likely to speak if she were raised in a pleasant environment with lots of things to talk about, the Gardners built a home for Washoe in a trailer in their backyard. She was constantly surrounded by friendly humans who chattered away in sign language with her and with one another.

For the first few months, Washoe lived the lazy life of the typical infant. Most of her time was devoted to sleeping, crawling, and having her diaper changed. But as she grew, she gradually began to imitate the signs of her human friends and to respond to their encouragement and guidance.

About a year after the project began, the Gardners established a firm criterion for deciding when Washoe was using a sign properly. Three different people had to notice an appropriate use of a sign, and Washoe had to use the sign appropriately without prompting at least once a day for 15 consecutive days. By this criterion, Washoe had mastered 30 signs at the time of the initial report, 22 months into her training (Gardner & Gardner, 1969). Some of the signs Washoe used were quite concrete, including *flower, brush, hat,* and *toothbrush.* Others represented more abstract concepts, such as *hurry, more, sorry,* and *funny.*

Washoe's use of some signs seemed to be based on imitation. For example, she was one of the few chimpanzees in the world who was required to brush her teeth after every meal. Whenever she brushed, the adults around her frequently repeated the sign for *toothbrush.* In the tenth month of her training, Washoe wandered into the bathroom on a visit to the Gardner home. To their infinite delight, she climbed up on the counter, saw a mug full of toothbrushes, and, for the first time, spontaneously signed *toothbrush.*

Washoe's acquisition of the sign for *funny* was somewhat less direct; the Gardners saw it as the chimpanzee equivalent of an infant's babbling. One day while Washoe was fooling around with her psychologist playmates, she happened to press the tip of her index finger to her nose and snort. The American Sign Language symbol for *funny* involves pressing the index and second fingers to the tip of the nose, without the simian snort. But, amid much giggling, the trainer imitated Washoe's action. Washoe repeated the sign, then her trainer did, then Washoe did, and so on. Later, Washoe's trainers repeated the sign whenever they began to laugh and smile. "Eventually," the Gardners reported, "Washoe came to use the 'funny' sign spontaneously in roughly appropriate situations" (p. 667). There were, however, occasional disagreements about what was appropriate. On at least one occasion, Washoe giggled and signed *funny* after urinating on one of her trainers (Linden, 1974). The trainer did not agree.

After a while, Washoe began to combine signs into strings such as "gimme tickle" (*gimme* was a single sign for "give me"), "gimme drink, please," and "please open, hurry." Later reports placed Washoe's vocabulary at 160 signs (Fleming, 1974).

The Gardners and others saw these phrases as evidence that Washoe was mastering basic rules of syntax. But others were far more skeptical about precisely what Washoe had learned. One of the most vocal critics was Herbert Terrace, who studied an animal of his own, whimsically named Nim Chimpsky. Like Washoe, Nim was raised somewhat as a human child would be. (There are some slight cultural differences. Since he was raised in the Bronx, in New York City, Nim slept in a loft bed and commuted to classes at Columbia University.) But there was at least one important respect in which Nim differed from Washoe; Terrace and his colleagues attempted to record literally every statement Nim ever made. Within two years, they noted over 20,000 statements of two or more signs.

As Terrace tells the story in his book *Nim* (1979), at first he and his co-workers were amazed by the chimp's linguistic abilities. But when they later reviewed videotapes of Nim's learning sessions, they began to suspect that the chimp was just imitating his teachers and responding to their prompting. He was not forming novel utterances the way young children do when they learn language.

For example, Nim tended to form long "sentences" by almost randomly stringing together symbols that roughly applied to a given context, such as "You me sweet drink give me." When children speak in sentences this long, they seem to choose and arrange words far more carefully to convey meaning, such as "Johnny's mother poured me some Kool-Aid."

Although, compared to humans, the linguistic capabilities of chimpanzees are limited, efforts to teach chimps language have resulted in some remarkable achievements.

Terrace's charges led to more countercharges. In a review of the book *Nim,* Beatrice Gardner (1981) charged that Nim's upbringing was not comparable to Washoe's; Nim was largely restricted to a "windowless cell," for example, and trained by over 60 different teachers, many of whom lacked sign language competence themselves.

Both the controversy and the research have continued. The Gardners have supplemented their naturalistic methods with more controlled tests, and some researchers (e.g., Premack, 1986) have extended the work on animal language to a more general consideration of cognitive abilities in animals, especially chimps.

In one of their experimental studies, the Gardners (1984) conducted systematic vocabulary testing with Washoe and four other chimps. Two experimenters watched as each chimp saw a series of slides that were projected in such a way that only the animals could see them. The slides included many examples of each concept that was tested. For example, the category "soda pop" was tested with slides of a large bottle of Schweppes tonic, a different-shaped and smaller bottle of Canada Dry ginger ale, and two cans of Pepsi. Under these conditions, the chimps still showed that they recognized the concepts and could name them in sign language.

While the debate has gotten rather heated at times [see, for example, Patterson, Patterson, & Brentari (1987), Bernstein (1987), Kent (1987), and Terrace (1987)], several conclusions are quite clear. Chimpanzees are capable of far more elaborate forms of communication than most scientists previously believed. Nevertheless, compared to humans, their linguistic abilities are quite limited; no chimpanzee has been able to reproduce the achievements of the average 3-year-old child.

The issue for future research, then, is not whether apes are different from people or what the "correct" definition of language is. The more interesting questions involve specifying *exactly how* apes are different from people and how each species can use words and symbols to communicate.

Language Development

The more you learn about the complexity of the processes involved in adult language comprehension and production, the more amazed you will be by the fact that children are able to learn to speak so quickly. Indeed, in one expert's opinion (Moskowitz, 1978), in the first few years of life, the average child is able to accomplish more than "ten linguists working full time for 10 years to analyze the structure of the English language" (p. 92).

This rapid and efficient learning is tied to the child's growing cognitive abilities. English children, French children, Russian children, and others all seem to learn their native tongues in similar ways, moving through comparable stages at roughly the same pace. Understanding the process of language development can lead to fundamental insights into the nature of human linguistic abilities.

Infancy: From Sounds to Words

The sounds a baby makes in the first weeks after birth seem to be reflexive. A father may read a message into his child's shrill cry—"It's time for a fresh diaper" or "Tommy is hungry again"—but most of the communication seems to be in the eye or the ear of the beholder. Nevertheless, even in this "prelinguistic period," it is likely that important foundations for language development are being established. While unable to vocalize a wide range of sounds themselves, infants typically are ushered into a world characterized by communicative interaction. They may not be able to talk, but others certainly talk to them.

Imagine yourself meeting a baby or small child. What would you say, and how would you say it? Adults and even other children tend to talk "baby talk" to infants—using high-pitched vocal levels and regular, singsong rhythms. While some adults may find baby talk undignified and even silly, there is evidence that babies like it. For example, in a study by Fernald (1981), 4-month-old babies listened to tapes of female voices talking either with or without the characteristic baby-talk intonations. Babies could "select" the tape they wanted to hear by turning their heads in the direction of one or the other speaker. They preferred hearing baby talk. Thus, even in everyday life, it is possible that small babies "tune into" and derive pleasure from baby talk, and that their attention to baby talk helps prepare them for later verbal interactions.

By the third or fourth month, the vocal tract has matured to become capable of speech sounds, and the infant begins to **babble**—to produce speechlike sounds, usually alternating consonant and vowel sounds such as *babababa* or *googoogoogoo*. Proud parents often claim that their child is desperately

babble To produce speechlike sounds that involve the alternation of consonant and vowel sounds.

trying to communicate some profound message through this string of syllables. Most psychologists disagree. Nonetheless, the parents' pleasure in engaging their infant in early "conversations" probably contributes to the child's langauge development. Consider the following "dialogue" between a mother and her infant daughter:

MOTHER	BABY
	(smiles)
Oh, what a nice little smile!	
Yes, isn't that nice?	
There.	
There's a nice little smile.	(burps)
What a nice wind as well!	
Yes, that's better, isn't it?	
Yes.	
Yes.	
Yes!	(vocalizes)
There's a nice noise.	

Notice how the mother speaks in short, simple utterances and responds to her daughter's actions. Such parental responsiveness may help the child learn about conversational turn taking—although both children and adults are sometimes notoriously unsuccessful at remembering to give others a chance to express competing points of view.

Interestingly, babbling infants seem to produce phonemes (speech sounds) from all the world's languages. Adult speakers of English may find it difficult to form some of the harsh consonants of German, the changing pitch of Vietnamese, or the hard clicks found in certain African languages. The babbling infant in any culture, having not yet learned these limitations, seems to make all these sounds and more. The American infant who babbles an African-type click that she has almost certainly never heard thus seems to be responding to some biological program for exercising the speech apparatus. Further evidence that babbling is a built-in stage of language development comes from the observation that deaf children—who cannot hear their own sounds—began babbling around the normal age (Lenneberg, Rebelsky, & Nichols, 1965).

Sooner or later, a child's meaningless babble shades over into the long-awaited first word. This historic moment may be difficult to pinpoint. Before babies correctly use adult words, they may begin to communicate with more primitive sounds. For example, six of the first seven "words" used by one intensively studied American child bore little resemblance to English (McNeill, 1970). At the age of 6 months, the child began to say *uh* whenever he tried to address people, distant objects, or "escaped" toys. A month later, his vocabulary doubled; the new word, *dididi*, seemed to reflect disapproval when he said it loudly and contentment when he repeated it softly. During the tenth month, he added five new sounds: *Nenene* involved scolding; *u!* was used to call squirrels; *piti* seemed to mean "interesting"; *deh* was an interjection something like *uh;* and *mama* seemed to refer not to his mother but rather to food.

Most children seem to follow this pattern of deliberate efforts to communicate even before they begin to use "real" speech. Scoville (1983) has identified several characteristics of the intentional communication that typically begins to emerge around 9 months of age:

1. The child gestures and makes eye contact with the adult.
2. The child uses particular sounds and intonation patterns consistently (e.g., *dididi* for disapproval).
3. The child persists in attempting to communicate if not understood.

At about the same age, children show evidence of a receptive language ability that surpasses their expressive ability. That is, they demonstrate understanding of words like *no* and *bye-bye,* even if they can't say these words themselves.

The first words that seem clearly based on adult models tend to appear between the ages of 10 and 13 months (deVilliers & deVilliers, 1978). Most often, they are simple sounds that alternate consonants and vowels. Countless mothers have been thrilled when Junior's first word was *mama* and his second was *papa*. Beyond the selective perception that may be involved, this choice probably has at least as much to do with the child's vocal capabilities as with his fondness for Mom and Dad. There is not a single documented case of an infant whose first three words were *iambic, pentameter,* and *onomatopoeia*. That is not because children lack interest in poetry but rather because these words are complex and hard to pronounce.

Consonant sounds like *m, p,* and *d* are easily produced by closing the front of the mouth. The sound of the vowel *a* is produced at the rear of the mouth by opening the oral cavity completely. This contrast makes words like *mama, papa,* and *dada* easy to pronounce. It is probably no accident that words like these have come to refer to parents in many of the world's languages.

By the age of 18 months, most children have a vocabulary of dozens of words. In one study of 18 children, Nelson (1973) found that some children had a vocabulary of 50 words as early as 15 months, while others did not have this large a vocabulary until they were 2 years old. The words these toddlers actually used suggested that they actively chose to talk about things that interested them rather than passively imitate the words used most by the adults around them. Nelson did not observe a single child who could say *diaper, mittens,* or *pants,* despite the fact that they had almost certainly heard these words repeated many times. Instead, they talked about such fascinating categories as foods (juice, milk, and cookies were the most common), animals (such as dog, cat, and duck), and toys (including ball and blocks).

Childhood: From Words to Sentences

It is easy enough to list the things children say; it is much harder to decide what they mean. When a child points at the household pet and says, "doggie," does she really mean, "This is a dog"? When she reaches out to her mother after dinner and cutely says "cookie, cookie," does she really mean, "Mother, I certainly would appreciate it if you would bring me another one of those tasty Oreos"? A **holophrase** is a single word a young child seems to use to express an entire message. Some question remains about just what messages young children intend to send and how much is inferred by the listener.

One line of research has examined this question by trying to determine whether young children use different intonations—as adults do—for statements, questions, and emphasis. For example, Menyuk and Bernholtz (1969) tape-recorded several different versions of the same word uttered in different contexts by one child between the ages of 18 and 20 months. They found that questions and statements could be identified with 80% accuracy by adults who simply listened to the tapes without any information about the situation in which the child used the words. This study suggests that there are real differences in intonation and supports the idea that children who utter holophrases do have some larger message in mind. Although this study is not the final word, it suggests that further research may be able to provide some insights into the abilities and intentions of even very young children.

Around the age of 2, children begin to put words together into two-word sentences like "see doggie," "book there," and "my candy." Like holophrastic speech, the two-word message seems to be a stage of speech development that appears at roughly the same time in many different cultures. American children may say "more milk," while Germans say "mehr milch" and Russians say "yeshche moloko," but in each culture toddlers begin expressing their thoughts in two-word sentences somewhere around the age of 2 (Slobin, 1971).

During this period, children use a shortened style called **telegraphic speech**, avoiding "unnecessary" words, such as articles, prepositions, and adjectives, and using only words that communicate the essence of their message. The term *telegraphic speech* calls attention to the fact that young children usually simplify their messages as much as possible. Since long messages cost more than short ones, few telegrams begin with idle chat: "As I was walking past the grocery store today, I thought of you. . . ." Instead, the message in a telegram is likely to be stripped to the bare essentials: "Lost all money. Send cash" or "Met another man. Goodbye." Similarly, a young child will not say, "May I please have a piece of Duncan Hines double fudge layer cake?" but rather, "Have cake?" or "I have cake?" Again, telegraphic speech has been observed not only in studies of English but also in studies of other languages.

Throughout the preschool years, children make certain systematic errors that reveal a great deal about their language use. In English, most verbs form the past tense by adding *ed* to the present tense, as in *walked, talked,* and *asked*. But a number of irregular verbs do not follow this rule; the past tense is not related to the present in any obvious way in *go/went* or *break/broke*. Interestingly, some children learn the irregular form early in development and may form such telegraphic sentences as "Daddy went" and "It broke."

Their parents may be alarmed when these children later discover the *ed* rule and start saying things like "Daddy goed" and "It breaked." However,

holophrase A single word used by young children to express an entire message.

telegraphic speech A form of speech characteristic of children that consists of shortened sentences.

Studies of the precise words children use as they learn to speak can reveal underlying rules of language organization.

this is a normal phenomenon in language development called **overregularization**, in which children force every utterance to conform to the regular rules of grammar, even when it means making an error. Similarly, children often overregularize the formation of English plurals, and say things like *foots, mans,* and *mouses.* After children have firmly mastered these rules, they are able to go back and learn the exceptions.

The phenomenon of overregularization is strong evidence that language acquisition involves more than a simple process of imitation learning. Four-year-olds do not talk about *foots* and *mouses* because they are repeating words they have heard elsewhere; rather, they seem to be applying a general rule that they have deduced regarding the English language. Such rules resist gentle efforts at correction, as shown in the following conversation recorded by Jean Berko Gleason (1967):

> CHILD: My teacher holded the baby rabbits and we patted them.
> MOTHER: Did you say your teacher held the baby rabbits?
> CHILD: Yes.
> MOTHER: What did you say she did?
> CHILD: She holded the baby rabbits and we patted them.
> MOTHER: Did you say she held them tightly?
> CHILD: No, she holded them loosely.

overregularization The tendency of children to force every utterance to conform to the regular rules of grammar, even when it means making an error.

Despite Mom's efforts to prod the child to say *held,* he continued to repeat the incorrect form *holded.* The appeal of the overregularized rule seems to be stronger than any desire to imitate.

Children's tendency to overregularize is just one of the ways in which they are creative and not strictly imitative in their language development. They also tend to invent words as needed to fill in gaps in their vocabularies. Clark (1981) noted that preschoolers often created verbs from nouns—as when one child, not yet 4, commented that she was crackering her soup. Twins, moreover, may invent a "mini language" of their own to communicate with each other.

School Age: From Oral to Written Language

Learning to read and write are extremely difficult processes. Even if you have been fluent in your native language for many years, it is likely that there are still times when you struggle to decipher a difficult passage in one of your textbooks or agonize over writing a coherent and stylistically elegant term paper. Indeed, the evolution of written language is a relatively recent phenomenon in the history of humanity; a scarce 5,000 years ago, written language was little more than a set of pictographic symbols representing a limited number of objects and actions (Gelb, 1952).

For children in most societies, learning to read is made difficult by the lack of a one-to-one correspondence between sounds and letters. When children are learning their letters, they are subjected to a massive deception when they are taught that "*a* is for apple" and "*e* is for elephant," as if the sound of the letter was always the same as the sound in the particular word. In reality, *a* and *e* can "say" many different sounds or make no sound at all: Think of the *a* in *late* and *alone,* the *e* in *eel* and *bone.* When you think of all the different ways that dipthongs like *ou* can be pronounced, it is not surprising that when you are mastering new vocabulary in some of your college courses, you are not always sure how a word should be pronounced.

Mapping sounds on letters is only part of the complex task of reading. Eyes must be trained to move in the right direction, and words must be imbued with meaning. (If you know how to pronounce the letters in a foreign language, you may be able to recite passages without the slightest idea of what they mean. Such recitation without meaning is not really reading, either for you or for children mastering the reading process in their native language.)

For most children, the process of mastering written language is a long one, beginning in infancy with the child's first baby book. As adults and older children read to the child, tell stories, and play alphabet games, they are teaching the child something about reading and writing. Research by Chomsky (1972) and Snow (1983) reveals that being read to in the home is the single largest factor in the child's learning to read. Moreover, television programs like "Sesame Street," designed to encourage early skill development in children, have had an important impact. Five-year-old children are now much better at naming letters, colors, and numbers than 5-year-olds of the pre-"Sesame Street" era (Wolf, Bally, & Morris, 1984).

Chall (1983) has identified a number of stages in the process of learning to read. In the prereading stage, which lasts until around age 6, children typically learn letter and number discrimination, recognition, and scanning, as well as acquiring the ability to recognize their own names and a few other words. In stage 1 (the first and second grade), children generally focus on decoding single words and simple stories. Comprehension lags behind decoding, but meaningful word groups are read faster than isolated words. By stage 2 (starting midway through the second grade and continuing into the fourth grade), reading becomes more fluent and the child is more concerned with understanding the meaning of what is read. This shift from the decoding of single words to the comprehension of increasingly complex material continues through later stages. By stage 5 (college level and beyond), a whole new set of cognitive goals typically becomes integrated into reading development. Now conceptual integration, critical judgment, and new thinking—all so important to the mastering of new fields like psychology—become emphasized.

Theories of Language Development

A number of theories have been formulated to account for the child's acquisition of language. Noam Chomsky, whose work in psycholinguistics has already been mentioned, takes a biological approach to language development, which he sees as having a genetic foundation. Chomsky (1979) theorizes that through evolution human brains have developed a *language acquistion device (LAD)*. Despite surface differences, all human language can be seen to share a single underlying structure—the universal grammar. Given a minimally acceptable environment, Chomsky holds, language development, like sexual maturation, will emerge naturally as children grow.

Not surprisingly, behaviorists have a very different view of language development. Skinner (1957), for example, maintains that language behavior, like other behaviors, is a product of reinforcement. Because mothers typically engage in "conversations" with their babies while taking care of them, the mother's speech becomes reinforcing. (The fact that babies increasingly turned their heads toward the "baby-talk speaker" in the experiment described earlier is direct evidence of the reinforcing value of baby talk.) As babies mature and produce babbling sounds that are more and more similar to the loving words they hear, their own vocalizations can take on a reinforcing quality. Finally, when babies actually begin to talk, Skinner holds, adults reinforce their efforts with attention and approval.

Supporters of a cognitive point of view acknowledge that both heredity and experience play a role in language development; however, they also emphasize the importance of the child's *active* interaction with the social environment. As Jean Berko Gleason (developer of the well-known Wug Test for assessing children's mastery of syntax) and Sandra Weintraub point out, children cannot acquire language merely through simple exposure to it as passive listeners (Gleason & Weintraub, 1978).

Jerome Bruner (1978), a noted cognitive psychologist, argues that Chomsky's LAD theory is wrong, because it fails to recognize how dependent language acquisition is on the parent-child interaction. The behavioral view fails, Bruner argues, because it does not recognize that the child learns to communicate (e.g., through gestures and vocalizations) before learning to talk. Talking, like the earlier forms of communication, is a functional tool used by children to master their environments. With the development of language, children have an increasingly effective means for achieving their goals, expressing their needs and feelings, satisfying their curiosity, and so forth. "Mommy read the bunny book now," conveys a much more precise meaning to the child's mother than gesturing at the bookcase and crying.

All these theoretical perspectives have generated a good deal of research that has contributed to our understanding of language development and its connections with cognition. Although the precise relationships of language and thought are still a matter of controversy, it seems clear that they are closely related from early in life. In the long run, it is likely that research on both thought and language will be crucial to our understanding of that elusive concept, the human mind.

Summary

The Origins of Cognitive Psychology

- Experts in the field of **human engineering** apply scientific principles to the design of equipment and machines to maximize human efficiency.

Concept Formation

- A **concept** is a mental category of objects or events, grouped on the basis of common features.
- To be an example of a **conjunctive concept**, an item must possess two attributes at the same time.
- To be an example of a **disjunctive concept**, an item may possess either one or both of two attributes.
- A **goal-derived concept** is a specialized concept created to help somebody reach a specific target.

Decision Making

- **Decision making** involves evaluating choices and picking the best one.
- **Heuristics,** or general rules of thumb, can influence decision making.
- **Decision frames**—conceptions of the acts, outcomes, and contingencies associated with a particular choice—also influence decision making.
- Studies indicate that people prefer costs to losses.

Problem Solving

- Gestalt psychologists identified the principle of **reorganization**, solving a problem by perceiving new relationships among its elements.

- The Gestalt principle of **productive thinking** refers to solving problems by producing a new organization.

- **Reproductive thinking** (also known as the **set effect**) involves applying past solutions to new problems.

- **Functional fixedness** is a type of set effect involving the failure to see that an object may have more functions than its usual ones.

- **Convergent thinking** is the process by which individuals achieve a correct answer to a problem by remembering it from past learning or by deriving it deductively from the application of logical rules.

- **Divergent thinking** is the ability to generate alternatives, to envision possibilities.

- **Crystallized intelligence** refers to general information and knowledge.

- **Fluid intelligence** refers to the ability to perceive, encode, and reason about information.

- The **information-processing approach** attempts to analyze thought processes as a series of separate steps.

- **Computer simulation** involves imitating behaviors or processes, such as problem solving, on a computer.

- In addition to heuristics, or general rules of thumb, problem solving is typically guided by **algorithms**, procedures or formulas that guarantee solution to a problem.

- One important heuristic, called **means-end analysis**, tries to solve problems by repeatedly comparing the current state of affairs with the final goal state and taking steps to reduce the differences between the two.

- The field of **artificial intelligence** includes efforts to understand the general nature of human intelligence and to program computers to perform tasks that require reasoning and perception.

- **Expert systems** are computer programs that apply knowledge in a specific area so that the computer can function as effectively as a human expert.

- MYCIN is an expert system designed to help physicians diagnose and treat infectious diseases.

- Computer programs have also been developed to understand natural language and answer questions in specified areas. For example, businesses can work with the INTELLECT program to answer questions about their company data sets.

- A **script**—a schema that summarizes general knowledge about particular situations—can be programmed into a computer to allow it to understand and communicate about simple events.

- **Analogical reasoning** involves judging, categorizing, or developing an argument about something new on the basis of its similarity to something familiar.

- The components used in analogical reasoning are **encoding** (identifying attributes and values of each term of the problem, e.g., $A:B::C:D$), **inference** (discovering the rule relating A to B), **mapping** (discovering the rule relating

A to *C*), **application** (generating a rule to produce and evaluate *D*), and **preparation-response** (preparing for and monitoring the solution process and translating the solution into a response).

Linguistics

- **Linguistics** is the study of the fundamental nature and structure of human language.
- **Psycholinguistics** is the study of how people actually speak and use language.
- **Linguistic competence** is abstract knowledge of a language.
- **Linguistic performance** involves applying this knowledge to speaking and listening.
- **Grammar** is the complete system of rules that relates sounds to meanings for a specific language.
- Grammar has three main components—phonology, syntax, and semantics.
- **Phonology** is the study of the rules governing the use of sounds in a specific language.
- **Phonemes** are the distinct sounds that make a difference in meaning in a particular language.
- **Syntax** is the way words combine to form sentences.
- In his model of linguistic competence, Chomsky proposed that sentences have both a **surface structure** (the actual words in a sentence and the relations among them) and a **deep structure** (the underlying organization and intent of sentences).
- **Semantics** refers to the rules governing the meaning of sentences, words, or morphemes.
- A **morpheme** is the smallest unit of speech that has meaning; it may be a word or part of a word.
- A **linguistic-relativity hypothesis** holds that language determines the content of thought or the way a person perceives the world.

Language Development

- By the age of 3 or 4 months, infants begin to **babble**, that is, to produce speechlike sounds.
- First words appear between the ages of 10 and 13 months.
- A **holophrase** is a single word used by a young child to express an entire message.
- Around the age of 2 children use **telegraphic speech**, avoiding "unnecessary" words such as articles, prepositions, and adjectives, and using only words that communicate the essence of their message.
- A normal phenomenon in preschool language development is **overregularization**, in which children force every utterance to conform to the regular rules of grammar, even when it means making an error.

Critical Thinking Exercise Discussion

Analyzing Reasoning Tasks

1. The first item is an example of an analogy; it calls for *analogical reasoning,* described in the chapter as a type of problem solving technique. You probably solved this problem without even being aware of the critical thinking strategy you used. In this case, a critical thinker would analyze the relationship between the first two words and use that understanding to choose the correct term to complete the second pair. This is a form of *convergent thinking.* First, look at "sugar" and "sweet" and analyze their relationship: Sugar is sweet. Then you look at "lemon," and, because you know you are looking for its taste, you easily pick the correct answer, "sour."

2. The second item calls for *divergent thinking.* There is no single correct solution to this problem. (Such items are often found on creativity tests.) Among the uses one might envision for an inner tube are such common ones as a flotation device or a swing. Other uses might be as a planter, a base for a low table, or a means of packing something large and breakable. The point is that this kind of freewheeling thinking often is the key to solving certain kinds of problems. For example, your available options for solving a problem may be limited, as when you have inadequate tools on hand or no electricity. Or an answer may remain elusive, as when your best efforts to solve a math problem simply do not work. In this case, the most effective critical thinking strategy may be to stop looking so closely at the method you have been using to solve the problem and to consider an alternative conceptualization of the problem—that is, look at it in a new way.

3. The third item calls for the application of a *heuristic.* The military problem is analogous to the radiation problem and thus allows you to conceive of a solution (attacking the problem from many angles) that might otherwise elude you. (The correct solution to the radiation problem is to bombard the tumor with rays from many different angles at once.)

INFANCY AND CHILDHOOD

Chapter 9

*W*hy does a stork stand on one leg?
If he lifted up the other one, he would fall down.

Somewhere around the age of 7, I (JH) devoted several months of my life to this joke. I told it to my mother, my father, my sister, my brother, my aunts, and my uncles. I told it to my friends, my relatives' friends, my friends' relatives, the mailman, the butcher. And then I told them all again. And again.

At this very moment, second-graders all over America are driving their families crazy with similar riddles:

Why did the moron throw butter out the window?
To see the butterfly.

What's big and green and has a trunk?
An unripe elephant.

How do you catch a rabbit?
Hide in the bushes and make noises like a carrot.

In response to this onslaught of riddles, patient parents everywhere reassure themselves that "it's only a stage" and hope that the next stage won't be worse.

The commonsense notion that a certain pattern of behavior is only a stage calls attention to an obvious fact: People change as they grow older. But exactly how do they change? And how do they remain the same? Do all children pass through similar stages at more or less the same rate? What causes a specific change?

These are just a few of the questions asked by the field of **developmental**

developmental psychology The study of human physical, intellectual, and emotional changes from infancy to old age.

psychology—the study of how and why people change physically, intellectually, and emotionally as they grow from infancy to old age. Developmental psychologists have investigated all the traditional topics in psychology—from learning and memory to personality and motivation. Their many diverse studies have one thing in common: an emphasis on the process of development, on change and continuity throughout the life span.

Consider, for example, the development of humor. While humor is not one of the central issues of the field and relatively few psychologists have studied it, a brief review of the development of humor can provide insights into the way researchers compare the abilities of children at different ages.

As you might expect, it is difficult to pinpoint the precise age at which humor begins. In one thorough study of infant laughter, Sroufe and Wunsch (1972) asked mothers to try to amuse their 4- to 12-month-old infants in 33 different ways. The least funny stimuli involved sounds like Mom's falsetto imitation of Mickey Mouse saying, "Hi, baby, how are you?" and parental horse sounds. The 4-month-olds laughed most for coochie-coochie-coo games, like four quick kisses on a bare stomach. The 1-year-olds preferred more complex social interactions, such as a silent version of peek-a-boo. Overall, children laughed more as they grew, and they increasingly came to appreciate more complex stimuli.

But this appreciation comes slowly. A 4-year-old's idea of a comedy routine may simply be to point to his nose and say, "Here's my ears." If an adult smiles cooperatively, he is likely to follow that by pointing to his cute little behind and saying, "Here's my eyes." And so on.

In a study designed to trace the gradual development of sophistication in humor, Schultz and Horibe (1974, p. 14) told jokes like this to elementary school children:

> Doctor, doctor, come at once! Our baby swallowed a fountain pen!
> I will be right over. What are you doing in the meantime?
> Using a pencil.

Most children thought this was reasonably funny. To see just what was funny about it, the researchers created another "joke," which was just as silly but lacked a sensible punchline:

> Doctor, doctor, come at once! Our baby swallowed a rubber band!
> I will be right over. What are you doing in the meantime?
> Using a pencil.

You might be reluctant to classify this new anecdote as a joke. Children from the third, fifth, and seventh grades agreed; it simply was not funny. But first-graders did not seem to care what the baby had swallowed; to them, both versions of the joke were funny.

To rule out the possibility that first-graders will chuckle at absolutely anything, Schultz and Horibe developed a third version, which they told to still another group:

> Doctor, doctor, come at once! Our baby swallowed a fountain pen!
> I will be right over. What are you doing in the meantime?
> We don't know what to do.

Even first-graders knew this was not funny. Their definition of humor seemed to demand incongruity; if it's silly, it's funny. For older children, humor required something more. Silliness must have a point to be amusing and a joke has to "make sense," as it did in the original form.

Patterns of change like this are quite common throughout development. As children grow, they increasingly come to see the world as adults do. This is no surprise. But one of the things that makes developmental psychology such a fascinating field is the way it charts these step-by-step changes to reveal what people feel, think, and do at different ages.

Many students find development more interesting than any other topic in psychology and are amazed to learn that it was only in the nineteenth century that scientists began to record and analyze the changes that occur in childhood. In 1877, Charles Darwin published one of the first systematic accounts of human development: a diary detailing the growth of his son William—his reflexes, his sensory abilities, and the gradual appearance of more complex traits. From this baby biography we may learn, for example, that William Darwin first laughed at the age of 53 days, a sound proudly recorded by the father of evolutionary theory as "a little bleating noise."

In 1878, one year after Darwin published these observations, Harvard University granted the first American Ph.D. in psychology to G. Stanley Hall. Hall is often referred to as the first developmental psychologist; he conducted nearly 200 surveys of children's behavior, attitudes, and beliefs. But despite Hall's tremendous energy and enthusiasm, few of his contemporaries studied children, and developmental psychology remained outside the mainstream of psychological research. In 1907, Wilhelm Wundt wrote that experimental studies of children were doomed to be "wholly untrustworthy on account of the great number of sources of error" (p. 336).

For the first few decades of this century, developmental psychology was an isolated field studied by just a few scattered experts like Jean Piaget. The dominant figures of the time—including Sigmund Freud and John B. Watson—had some strong opinions about childhood, but little data. Among social scientists, only those who studied intelligence and IQ directly observed large numbers of children.

The entire field of psychology grew rapidly after World War II (see Chapters 15 and 16), and for the first time large numbers of researchers began to explore the dramatic changes that occur in the first few years of life. Much of this research focused on the way heredity and environment interact in determining behavioral development.

Heredity: Behavioral Genetics

The idea that human characteristics can be passed by heredity from parent to child can be traced back at least to ancient Greece. Four centuries before the birth of Christ, Plato wrote in *The Republic* that in an ideal society, young men who distinguished themselves in war or other pursuits should be rewarded with "the most ample liberty of lying with women," so that they could have many children and thus pass on their desirable characteristics to the largest possible number.

Similarly, for many centuries farmers have systematically mated male and female animals and plants to try to produce desirable offspring. However, until recently the rules that breeders relied on to form these unions were a confusing mass of contradictions. As one commentator put it, the first rule of breeding was "like produces like" and the second was "like does not always produce like" (Lush, 1951, p. 496). This confusion began to clear up after a monk named Gregor Johann Mendel published his theory of heredity in 1867, based on his experiments with pea plants.

Mendel's work became widely recognized around the turn of the century, and the science of **genetics**—the study of the transmission of inherited characteristics—has developed rapidly ever since. However, human beings are difficult organisms for geneticists to study. Humans may pause 20 or 30 years between generations, they do not have many children; they cannot be raised in controlled environments; and they cannot be forced to mate with specific people to see what happens.

It took years for biological research on genetics to have a major impact on psychology. The behaviorists who dominated psychological research in the first part of the twentieth century emphasized environmental influences on behavior. In one of the more extreme statements of this view, behaviorist John B. Watson (1930) boasted:

> Give me a dozen healthy infants, well-formed, and my own specified world to bring them up in and I will guarantee to take any one at random and train him to become any type of specialist I might select—doctor, lawyer, artist, merchant-chief, and yes, even begger-man and thief—regardless of his talents, penchants, tendencies, abilities, vocations, and race of his ancestors. I am going beyond my facts and I admit it, but so have the advocates of the contrary and they have been doing it for many thousands of years. (p. 82)

However, later psychologists took a more moderate view, and many became interested in **behavioral genetics**, the study of the inheritance of behavioral characteristics. Behavioral geneticists have made important contributions to our understanding of the capacities and potentials that individuals bring to their experiences by virtue of their evolutionary heritage—that is, by being born to human parents rather than to orangutans, platypuses, or Gila monsters. For example, research on inbred strains of animals and studies using selective breeding of animals have provided useful information on the ways **genotypes**, the genetic composition of the individual, are expressed when environmental features are held constant. Research on twins and other types of family studies have also yielded valuable insights into the contribution of genotype and environment to development.

Genes and Chromosomes

Genes are the physical structures that transmit characteristics from parent to child. If you have your father's short nose and your mother's short temper, this resemblance may be partially based on the fact that from the moment of conception, you developed according to a blueprint provided by your parents' genes.

Genes are composed of complex molecules of a substance called deoxyri-

genetics The study of the transmission of inherited characteristics.

behavioral genetics The study of the inheritance of behavioral characteristics.

genotypes The genetic composition of an individual.

genes Physical structures that transmit characteristics from parent to child.

chromosomes Long, thin structures in the nucleus of every cell that contain many genes.

bonucleic acid (DNA). Through a complicated code involving the precise order of four chemicals (the organic bases adenine, guanine, cytosine, and thymine), DNA determines the production of proteins (including enzymes) in the cells of the body. The precise way in which this genetic blueprint influences physical and behavioral development is just beginning to be understood.

Genes are so small that, given the limits of present technology, they cannot be seen. However, we can see **chromosomes**—long, thin structures in the nucleus of every cell that contain hundreds of thousands of genes. Almost every cell in the human body ordinarily has 46 chromosomes arranged in 23 pairs. In contrast, frogs have 26 chromosomes; chimpanzees, 48; and chickens, 78. But human reproductive cells—the mother's egg and the father's sperm—have only 23 chromosomes. When egg and sperm combine in conception, the fertilized egg begins life with the requisite 23 pairs, half of each pair contributed by Mom and half by Dad.

The specific chromosomes a child receives from each parent are chosen at random. As a result, according to the laws of probability, two children with the same mother and father will have about half their genes in common. More complex calculations can reveal the genetic similarity between any two relatives, from half sisters to second cousins. In general, the more closely related two people are biologically, the more closely they resemble each other genetically.

You may conclude that height is inherited if you notice that very few jockeys have children who are tall enough to play professional basketball. The behavioral geneticist goes beyond this to seek mathematical relationships that summarize basic laws of heredity.

Except for the reproductive cells, every cell in the human body contains 46 chromosomes. The twenty-third pair determines an individual's sex; in this photograph, the sex is female. Chromosomes were first observed in 1951 when a laboratory technician accidentally washed some slides in the wrong cleanser and the chromosomes became swollen enough to be seen through a microscope.

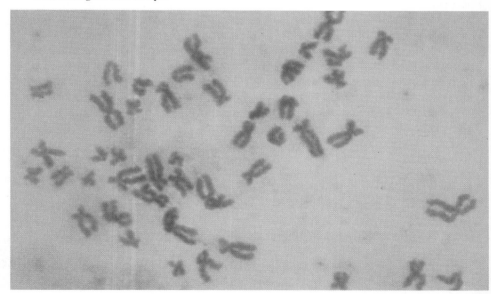

Methods in Human Genetics

The first scientist to study human behavioral genetics systematically was Francis Galton, an English cousin of Charles Darwin. In 1869, Galton published *Hereditary Genius,* which summarized his study of nearly 1,000 eminent judges, politicans, military commanders, scientists, artists, religious leaders, and scholars. Because there were at that time no objective measures of intelligence or achievement, Galton (p. 37) developed his own scale of reputation as "a leader of opinion, of an originator, or a man to whom the world deliberately acknowledges itself largely indebted." A careful statistical analysis of the relatives of eminent men found that they were much more likely than the average person to achieve eminence themselves. Indeed, the closer the genetic relationship to an eminent man, the more one was likely to achieve.

Galton was aware that people in the same family not only share similar genes but are also ordinarily raised in similar environments. The resemblances he found could have been caused by heredity, by environment, or by both. Galton cited several arguments to support his idea that eminence resulted from "hereditary genius." For example, he noted that many men had risen to achievement from humble families. Further, he found that the biological sons of eminent men were more successful than the adopted relatives of Roman Catholic popes, despite the fact that these adopted children were given many advantages.

Since Galton, the measurement of human abilities has advanced considerably, and mathematical tools of analysis have also become far more sophisticated. By today's standards, Galton's studies prove little or nothing about the inheritance of genius. But his pioneer research did help to establish two of the most important techniques in human behavioral genetics—the study of twins and the study of adopted children.

The rationale of adoptive studies is quite straightforward. If a characteristic is primarily based on heredity, children should resemble their biological parents even if they never knew them. However, if environment is the key to a particular trait, children should come to resemble the adoptive parents who raised them.

More common than adoptive studies are comparisons of the behavioral characteristics of twins. About 1 out of every 87 white births in North America is a twin birth. Thus, 2 out of every 88 babies, or about 2.3% of the white population, are twins. Interestingly, North American blacks have a somewhat higher proportion of twin births—1 in every 73.

Indentical twins are called **monozygotic** because they develop from the division of a single fertilized egg (zygote) and thus have precisely the same genes. Fraternal twins are called **dizygotic** because they develop from two different eggs that happen to be fertilized by two different sperm at the same time. They are often male and female, whereas monozygotic twins, being identical, must always be of the same sex. Dizygotic twins are no more similar genetically than any other two siblings; that is, they share about half their genes.

To geneticists, the most interesting cases are those rare individuals who were separated from an identical twin at birth. Although few in number, these people are great in significance; they represent a kind of natural experiment in which heredity is held constant while the environment is varied.

SIR FRANCIS GALTON (1822–1911)

Few people have made such a variety of contributions to science as Sir Francis Galton. A cousin of Charles Darwin, Galton was independently wealthy; for his entire adult life, he simply followed his curiosity wherever it led. As a meteorologist, Galton developed several techniques now used in weather forecasting. As a criminologist, he pioneered the study of fingerprints for criminal investigations. As a statistician, Galton helped lay the mathematical groundwork that led to the development of the correlation coefficient. As a social scientist, Galton invented the questionnaire: in 1874, he sent 200 British scientists a long list of questions covering everything from their religious beliefs to their hat sizes. But Galton is best remembered by psychologists for his pioneering studies of behavioral genetics and individual differences in intelligence.

TABLE 9.1

Resemblance Between Twins

	Correlation between identical twins	Correlation between fraternal twins
General ability	.86	.62
Personality scales	.50	.28
Self-concepts	.34	.10
Ideals, goals, and vocational interests	.37	.20

Source: Based on Loehlin and Nichols, 1976, p. 87.

A review of all the published cases of monozygotic twins raised apart found only 95 pairs that were adequately reported. The results showed striking "similarities in many dimensions, including physical characteristics as disparate as height and the pattern of tooth decay; temperament and personality; mannerisms, such as a firm or limp handshake; smoking and drinking habits; tastes in food; and special aptitudes and interests, especially in the arts or in athletics"(Farber, 1981, p. 59). Other similarities included weight, blood pressure, EEG, voice characteristics, and even symptoms of anxiety, such as nail biting and headaches.

Fascinating as these results are, they must be considered provocative rather than conclusive. Many of the twins had met before they were studied, and some were even raised in different branches of the same family. Thus, in some cases they shared the same environment, and their resemblances may not depend on heredity alone (see Taylor, 1980, and Bouchard, 1983, for a debate on this issue).

A much larger body of research compares the degree of resemblance between identical and fraternal twins (e.g., Lykken, 1982). Typically, these studies assume that pairs of twins who grow up in the same family are exposed to similar environments whether they are monozygotic or dizygotic. Thus, if identical twins generally resemble each other more in terms of some characteristic, it seems reasonable to conclude that heredity played a part.

One typical study of this sort (Loehlin & Nichols, 1976). studied 850 sets of same-sex twins who took the National Merit Scholarship Test in 1962. In addition to taking this standard test of academic ability, each set of twins and their parents filled out several questionnaires regarding their personalities and interests. Table 9.1 shows some of the basic results.

Note that in each category, the correlation between identical twins was greater than the correlation between fraternal twins (see "Appendix" for more details on correlations). Since each pair of twins was raised in a similar environment, it seems reasonable to conclude that the greater resemblance of identical twins was based on their genes.

However, also note that even the identical twins are never precisely the same; if every pair of scores were a perfect match, those correlations would be 1.0—but they are not. Since two people with identical genes never end up precisely the same, it is obvious that the environment shapes their differences. These data suggest the reasonable conclusion that complex human abilities are determined by *both* heredity and environment. In this particular case, the researchers (p. 90) concluded that "genes and environment carry roughly equal weight" in accounting for these traits.

monozygotic twins Twins that develop from the division of a single fertilized egg (also called identical twins).

dizygotic twins Twins that develop from two different fertilized eggs (also called fraternal twins).

In the next section, we consider the role heredity and environment play in determining physical growth. We shall return to the issue of quantifying heritability later in this book when we discuss research on the roles of heredity and environment in intelligence (Chapter 13) and in mental disorders, such as schizophrenia (Chapter 14).

Physical Development

Developmental psychologists use the word **maturation** to refer to sequences of growth and internal bodily changes that are primarily determined by biological timing. Environmental factors such as health and nutrition can affect the rate of maturation, but the limits are set by biology. No matter how well a 3-month-old child is fed and taken care of, she will not weigh 60 pounds or walk across a room. This biological pacing of an orderly process of physical growth begins the moment a human being is conceived.

Prenatal Development

During sexual intercoure, the male releases approximately 400 million sperm cells into the female reproductive tract. If this occurs during the ovulatory phase of the menstrual cycle, a sperm cell may unite with a female's egg, or ovum, causing pregnancy. The fertilized egg, called a **zygote**, begins to develop immediately. This tiny cell is only about $\frac{1}{175}$ inch in diameter at conception; over the next months, it will divide, and divide, and divide again until a human being is formed. About one week after the egg is fertilized, it becomes firmly attached to the wall of the uterus.

The developing organism is called an **embryo** during the next stage of rapid development, which lasts roughly from the second to the eighth week of pregnancy. By the fourth week of pregnancy, the embryo is $\frac{1}{5}$ inch long and has begun to develop a heart, a brain, a gastrointestinal tract, and other primitive organs. By the eighth or ninth week, the embryo is about 1 inch long and has developed human features; face, mouth, arms, and legs are clearly recognizable.

From the time bone cells begin to develop, about eight weeks after conception, the developing organism is called a **fetus**. Dramatic development continues throughout the fetal period. Around 16 to 18 weeks, the mother is likely to feel the first fetal movements. A fetus born prematurely at the age of 24 weeks can open and close its eyes, cry, and hiccup. Normal development, however, takes about 40 weeks from conception to birth.

The timing of these changes throughout the prenatal period is partly determined by the organism's genes and partly by the mother's condition. If the mother contracts certain diseases during pregnancy, the illness may interfere with development, particularly if the problem occurs during the weeks immediately following conception. In one study of mothers who had German measles (Michaels & Mellin, 1960), maternal illness during the first month of pregnancy produced abnormalities in 47% of the offspring, versus 7% for mothers who had the same illness in the third month of pregnancy.

Many drugs are also known to increase the risk of birth defects. Pregnant

maturation Sequences of growth and internal bodily changes that are primarily determined by biological timing.

zygote A fertilized egg.

embryo A prenatal organism from 2 to 8 weeks old.

fetus A prenatal organism from 8 weeks to birth.

mothers who use narcotics, barbiturates, or even some prescription drugs, such as certain antibiotics, are more likely to have abnormal infants. There is even evidence that smoking cigarettes or drinking moderate amounts of alcohol during pregnancy may interfere with fetal growth. For obvious reasons, many researchers are now trying to learn the precise effects of these and other, more subtle prenatal influences.

From Infancy to Childhood

A newborn baby enters the world covered with a white lubricating liquid that helps ease its passage through the birth canal. The skull consists of somewhat flexible cartilage, which may be somewhat misshapen by compression, and the rest of the body may look somewhat the worse for wear. In 1891, G. Stanley Hall described his overall impression of the newborn in terms of its "monotonous and dismal cry, with its red, shriveled, parboiled skin . . . squinting, cross-eyed, pot-bellied, and bowlegged. . . ." Fortunately, most parents find that their own children are gorgeous exceptions to this unattractive rule.

Within a few weeks, infants begin to fill out; even neutral observers see them as roly-poly bundles of joy. Physical growth is not a simple matter of increasing size; as Figure 9.1 shows, body proportions change dramatically during development. Before birth, the head grows faster than any other part of the body. In the first year of life, the trunk of the body grows fastest. From then until adolescence, the legs grow fastest.

Interestingly, big babies do not necessarily grow up to be oversized adults; the correlation between infant size and adult size is quite low. The fast pattern of infant growth begins to slow down around the age of 3 into a slower, more predictable course. Height at age 3 is a good predictor of how tall the child will grow up to be. The next sudden increase in physical growth occurs in adolescence, a period that will be described in Chapter 10. These

FIGURE 9.1 As the human body grows, it changes in size and proportion. The decrease in the relative size of the head is particularly dramatic during the prenatal period and infancy.

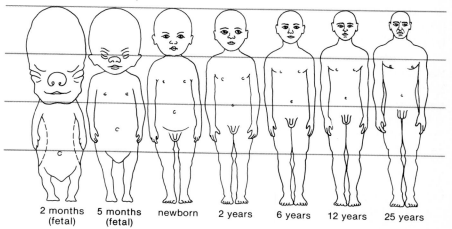

| 2 months (fetal) | 5 months (fetal) | newborn | 2 years | 6 years | 12 years | 25 years |

processes of physical growth and maturation help provide the infant and child with ever-increasing abilities to deal with the external world. Perhaps the most obvious changes in ability involve motor activities.

Motor Development

The newborn baby enters the world with a number of **reflexes**, involuntary acts automatically elicited by certain stimuli. For example, newborn babies close their eyes when stimulated by bright light and move their limbs away from sources of pain. Some of these reflexes are clearly linked to survival, as is the case with breastfeeding being aided by the *rooting reflex:* A newborn baby turns toward any object, such as a finger or a nipple, that gently stimulates the corner of its mouth. Like many other reflexes, this reaction tends to disappear as a child grows older.

At birth, the child's behavior is largely controlled by subcortical structures deep within the brain (see Chapter 3). As the child grows, the cortex develops and voluntary control of behavior becomes possible. Doctors monitor the changes in these and other reflexes as one clue to patterns of development in the brain.

To chart the course of motor development, some researchers have followed the progress of large groups of children to establish **norms**, standard figures that describe the performance of the average person. Pediatricians and psychologists use such norms to help locate problems in development for specific children.

The widely used Denver Developmental Screening Test (Frankenburg & Dodds, 1967) was developed from tests in Denver, Colorado, of 1,036 normal children between the ages of 2 weeks and 6½ years. One section of the test measures gross motor movements, while another section is concerned with finer muscle control. Figure 9.2 lists the age ranges for the first appearance of several typical abilities in each category. It is important to remember that norms like this simply reflect the average performance of large numbers of babies. Although the average baby begins walking around 12 months, 25% of all babies start before 11.3 months and 10% start after 14.3 months. And despite the hopes and fears of parents, the actual date does not predict later development. The child who first walks at 10 months will not necessarily grow up to win the Boston Marathon, and the one who begins walking at 14 months will not necessarily be slow to develop in other ways.

Of course, at some point extreme slowness in development does suggest that there may be a problem. In the Denver Developmental Screening Test, a child who lags behind 90% of the children of the same age on two different motor skills will generally be referred for further tests to see whether there is some underlying problem. But the range of ages in Figure 9.2 demonstrates that normal development is far more variable than some anxious parents suspect.

These sequences of behavior are primarily determined by maturation. A child's nervous system and muscles must develop to a certain point before complex behavior becomes possible. No matter how well they are raised, 2-week-old infants will not sit up by themselves, 3-month-old babies will not

reflexes Involuntary acts automatically elicited by certain stimuli.

norms Standard figures that describe the performance of the average person in relation to some larger group.

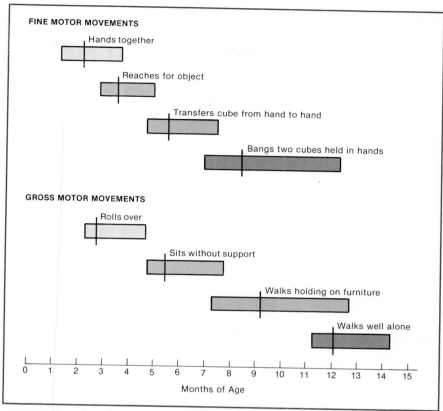

FIGURE 9.2 Infants develop motor control at different rates. This chart illustrates norms for typical motor movements from the Denver Developmental Screening Test. Of all infants, 25% have mastered the particular movement by the age at the left side of the bar, 50% by the age at the mark on the bar, and 90% by the age indicated by the right end of the bar. Note that many different patterns of development fall within the normal range.

walk, and 2-year-old children will not discuss the state of the economy. However, throughout this text we have emphasized that behavior is determined by the interaction between heredity and environment. In the case of motor development, for example, one group of researchers has shown how specific training can speed the process of maturation (Zelazo, Zelazo, & Kolb, 1972).

Week-old babies have two simple reflexes that resemble walking. The *placing reflex* causes a baby to try to place a foot on any surface the foot comes in contact with; if the upper surface of the foot touches the edge of a table, the child will move to step on it. The *stepping reflex* mimics a standing motion until feet touch and the knees bend; a child carefully bounced up and down under these conditions will probably straighten both legs as if to stand, although they are not nearly strong enough to support the baby's weight.

Zelazo and his colleagues taught mothers special exercises to elicit the placing and stepping reflexes from their newborn babies. The exercise continued for 12 minutes each day, from the age of 1 week to 8 weeks. This practice was effective in increasing the number of walking responses in tests throughout this period. Normally, these reflexes, like many others, disappear around the age of 8 weeks. But for these infants, the early practice made a long-term difference. The children who had practiced the reflexes took their first real steps at the age of 10 months; infants in three control groups started walking significantly later, at ages ranging from about 11½ to 12½ months.

None of the infants in this study walked before the ninth month, which suggests that very young babies are not physically capable of this action. But the fact that special practice produced walking two months earlier than normal reminds us that although biology sets certain limits, environmental factors can affect the actual rate of maturation.

Motor development continues through childhood as children become stronger, faster, and better coordinated. When a 2-year-old throws a ball, she is likely to jerk her arm while standing firmly facing the target. By the age of 4, the same child may have developed an overhand throwing motion that involves shifting her weight in the adult manner. For the complex skills of later childhood, just as for the simple motor actions of the toddler, physical maturation provides the basic abilities that make certain actions possible, while practice and experience can refine the skills and increase the child's expertise.

While physical changes in the developing infant and child are obvious to the eye, many other changes take place that are not so apparent to the casual observer. Indeed, the infant's abilities in such areas as perception were long inaccessible even to scientific observations. Consequently, people greatly underestimated the extent to which infants could see and hear and respond in predictable ways to their sensory experience.

Perceptual Development

In 1890, William James wrote: "The baby, assailed by eyes, ears, nose, skin and entrails at once, feels it all as one great blooming, buzzing confusion" (p. 488). This famous claim was repeated so often in the succeeding century that many people seemed to accept the notion of the disorienting perceptual world of the infant simply because they had heard it so many times. The truth is that James's analysis was a guess—an educated guess based on the best evidence available at that time, but still only a guess.

Since then, psychologists have learned a great deal about the way infants see, hear, and feel. In general, they have found that infant perception is far more structured and orderly than James believed. Many of these discoveries have been quite recent. In 1979, one enthusiastic researcher (Leslie B. Cohen) wrote that "more has been learned about infant perception in the past 15 or 20 years than in all previous years" (p. 894). He traced this progress back to work begun by Robert Fantz in the 1950s.

Testing Infant Perception

The basic problem in testing infant perception is obvious: How can you ask newborn infants what they feel or hear? Fantz (1961) proposed the first experimental solution. Present babies with two visual stimuli and measure how long they look at each. If the babies look at both stimuli for the same amount of time, either they cannot tell the difference between them, or they do not prefer one over the other. But if a child consistently stares at one stimulus, he does notice a difference and prefers to look at that one.

In his earliest studies Fantz (1961) placed infants in a specially constructed "looking chamber." The child lay comfortably in a crib, staring at two visual stimuli directly above her. An experimenter looked through a peephole overhead and watched the baby's eyes. When the baby looked at one stimulus or the other, a tiny image was reflected in her eyes, and the observer simply recorded the amount of time the child looked at each. This relatively simple and inexpensive procedure made it possible for the first time to quantify precisely how much an infant preferred to look at a particular object.

In one set of early studies, Fantz found that infants spent more time looking at patterned surfaces than plain ones. He used this fact to test infants' abilities to distinguish between lines. Fantz compared babies' responses to plain gray cards and to black-and-white striped cards. When the stimuli were placed 10 inches from their eyes, 1-month-old infants preferred to look at stripes ⅛ inch wide or wider. If the stripes were made any thinner, the infants would look equally at a plain gray card, suggesting that they could not tell the stimuli apart. By the age of 6 months, most babies spent more time looking at stripes as narrow as ¹⁄₆₄ inch. Although the precise details have been questioned by later investigators, many researchers have verified that visual acuity improves dramatically in the first few months of life. Studies are now being conducted on the feasibility of adapting this procedure to diagnose visual problems in infants (L. B. Cohen, 1979).

Fantz was able to demonstrate that while the newborn's visual abilities are quite crude compared to those of an adult, it is undeniably true that a child comes into the world with the ability to distinguish a number of basic patterns. In later research, Fantz (1961) turned to the perception of human faces. Reasoning that an innate ability to perceive faces would be useful for a newborn child, Fantz compared infants' reactions to three flat objects the size and shape of a head. One had a human face painted on it, the second had a scrambled version of the same features (with eyes, nose, and mouth scattered randomly), and the third simply had a black patch at one end equal to the total of all the facial features. From about 2 weeks to 5½ months of age, infants consistently looked more at the real face than at the scrambled features; they ignored the black patch almost entirely, presumably because they found it less interesting.

This result and others like it led Frantz to argue that infants enter the world with an innate ability to distinguish certain types of patterns that will help them deal with their new environment. While not all researchers go this far, it is now quite clear that infants' perceptual abilities are far more sophisticated than many parents ever suspected. In one study (see L. B. Cohen, 1979), for example, 4-month-old infants were simultaneously shown two films, one of a quickly bouncing toy kangaroo and another with a donkey bouncing at a slower rate. When the infants heard a sound track that was timed to the bouncing in one film or the other, they spent more time watching the film that went with that particular sound. Clearly, as early as 4 months, infants have the ability to coordinate visual and auditory information.

Depth Perception

About the same time that Fantz developed his visual-preference test, Eleanor Gibson developed a way to test infant depth perception. She was particularly concerned with whether such abilities are innate or learned. Are children naturally able to perceive depth, or must they learn the hard way by falling from high places?

Gibson invented a device called a *visual cliff* to test infant depth perception. This apparatus consisted of a piece of heavy glass divided in the middle by a narrow board; on one side of the board, a piece of checked cloth was placed flush against the glass, giving this "shallow" side an appearance of solidity. On the other side, the same type of cloth was placed on the floor a foot or more below the glass, thus presenting the appearance of a visual cliff.

In the original experiment, Gibson tested 36 infants between the ages of 6 and 14 months. Each child was placed in the center of the board, and his mother alternately called to him from the shallow side and the deep side. Nine of the infants stayed firmly on the board no matter where Mom called from. Of the 27 infants who were willing to move, only 3 were foolhardy enough to crawl across the glass suspended over the floor. The other 24 infants seemed to recognize the signs of depth and crawled only across the shallow side. Some stopped and stared down through the glass over the visual cliff and then backed away. Others patted the glass suspiciously but still refused to venture across; getting to Mom simply wasn't worth the risk of falling (Gibson & Walk, 1960).

In this test of a child's depth perception, a piece of glass is suspended over a "visual cliff."

**ELEANOR GIBSON
(1910–   )**

Gibson is best known for her work on the development of depth perception in infants. According to one source (Gregory, 1978), her classic studies of the "visual cliff" were partly inspired by the concern she felt during a picnic on the rim of the Grand Canyon— she worried whether her young child could tell that it was a very long way down to the bottom.

Gibson went to graduate school at Yale University in the 1930s, a time when there was tremendous bias against women who wanted to pursue professional careers. In an autobiographical article (Gibson, 1980), she described a meeting at which she informed one of Yale's most prestigious professors that she had come to graduate school to study with him. In reply, the famous researcher "stood up, walked to the door, held it open, and said, 'I have no women in my laboratory' " (p. 246). Despite such barriers, and the demands of raising a family, Eleanor Gibson completed her Ph.D. and went on to conduct research in a wide variety of areas, including the development of reading and linguistic skills.

Of course, one cannot argue from this that depth perception is innate; the youngest child in the experiment had already had 6 months of experience in living. And later studies suggested that some experience in crawling was necessary to make a proper distinction. One study (Scarr & Salapatek, 1970) found that 7-month-old infants used depth cues to avoid edges on a visual cliff only if they had begun crawling by that age.

There is now a large body of evidence that dramatic changes in infants' reactions to the visual cliff occur between 5 and 9 months of age. The 9-month-olds are less willing to crawl over the glass, and they have higher heart rates in response to the situation.

However, some controversy remains about the interpretation of these changes (Richards & Rader, 1983). According to Bertenthal and Campos (1984, p. 288), "Contrary to popular belief, this developmental shift occurs too late to provide much novel information about the development of depth perception." Instead, these authors argue, this experimental procedure is more useful in providing insights into the development of fear. They note that at around the same age, infants also show the first signs of becoming afraid of strangers, new toys, and animals, and of being separated from their parents.

Another report from the same group emphasized that when a child first learns to crawl, this achievement gives the infant a new experience of mastery over the environment. They believe that the appearance of crawling may have broad implications not only for perceptual development, but also for the development of cognition and emotions (Bertenthal, Campos, & Barrett, 1984).

Perceptual Abilities of the Newborn

Since the pioneer studies of Fantz and Gibson, many different techniques have been invented to ask babies sophisticated questions about how they perceive the world. Some of the most exciting work has involved the development of techniques for testing the abilities present immediately after birth, before the child has had much opportunity to learn.

In 1969 two researchers at Brown University (Siqueland & DeLuca) reported that young infants can learn to suck a pacifier harder to produce a reward. Just as a rat will press a bar or a pigeon will peck a key to produce food, an infant can learn to suck harder to produce a reinforcer such as an auditory stimulus.

In one study, researchers used this technique to test the ability of 3-day-old babies to recognize their mothers' voices (DeCasper & Fifer, 1980). Each mother tape-recorded a lengthy selection from Dr. Seuss's *To Think That I Saw It on Mulberry Street.* Later, the ten babies wore tiny headphones while they sucked on a pacifier that held a pressure-sensitive electronic device. After the infants adapted to this rather odd situation, their normal sucking pattern was recorded for five minutes. Then for 20 minutes, five of the infants heard their own mother's voice when they sucked faster than normal and heard another woman's voice when they sucked more slowly. This relationship was reversed for the other five infant subjects. Slow sucking produced their own mother's voice and fast sucking produced the stranger's voice.

Sure enough, eight of the ten infants changed their sucking pattern so that it produced their own mother's voice. These particular newborn infants had spent their first three days of life in a hospital nursery, and none had had more than 12 hours of contact after birth with their mothers. Yet almost all showed a clear-cut preference for their own mothers' voices. Had they learned to recognize their mothers' voices during their 12 hours of contact since birth, or was their preference based on prenatal experience?

To answer this question, DeCasper and Prescott (1984) followed the same procedure as in their earlier study, except that this time they used the fathers' voices. They reasoned that if contact after birth was the source of the infants' preferences for mothers' voices, then infants should also show a preference for fathers' voices.

The fathers were encouraged to talk to their children as much as possible before testing. The procedure was virtually identical to the one in the study above: The fathers recorded the same Dr. Seuss passage, and six 2-day-old infants heard the voices of their own father or another man's voice. Fast sucking produced the father's voice for half the infants; slow sucking produced the father's voice for the other half.

In contrast to the infants who showed clear preferences for their mothers' voices, these six infants showed no preferences at all for their own fathers' voices. Thus, experience after birth does not lead to a clear-cut voice preference in newborns. The results suggest that early voice preferences are probably more closely related to prenatal experience.

Interestingly, recordings of sounds in the uterus document the opportunity for infants to hear voices before birth. Low-frequency sounds, which include male voices, are masked by background noise so there is little opportunity for infants to hear their fathers' voices before birth. And, of course, the father does not carry the baby around in his abdomen for nine months. While the preference for mothers' voices over fathers' has great theoretical significance, it probably has little impact on development. About two weeks after birth, infants begin to show a preference for their own fathers' voices over those of other males (Hulsebus, 1981).

Even younger infants were tested in a study of responses to crying (Martin & Clark, 1982). Forty newborn infants were tested at an average age of 18 hours; each sometimes heard a tape recording of another newborn crying and sometimes heard a tape recording of himself or herself crying. Astoundingly, these produced different reactions. In response to the cry of another newborn child, infants cried along. But when each heard a recording of his or her own cries, the child actually stopped crying.

Of course, there is no way of knowing what went through these little minds—whether the children were fascinated by hearing their own voices, for example, and stopped their crying to listen. But we do know that they responded differently; it is clear that they could distinguish between the two cries just 18 hours after birth. Similar studies of vision and the other senses increasingly seem to support the notion that some perceptual abilities are present at birth and do not depend on learning.

These perceptual abilities are some of the building blocks from which a child gradually constructs a cognitive view of the world. Other researchers have focused on this larger problem of cognitive development: how children's thought processes change as they grow.

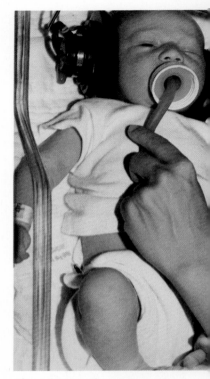

This infant can change the pattern of auditory stimuli presented on the headphones by changing the pattern of sucking on the pacifier. This procedure has helped psychologists to explore the auditory world of very young infants.

epistemology The philosophical study of the nature of knowledge and how we come to know about the world.

Cognitive Development

Some of the major issues of cognitive development have already been encountered in our discussion of language acquisition (see Chapter 8). Here we concentrate on the theories of Jean Piaget, one of the most influential figures in the history of psychology.

These days, many developmental psychologists study statistical patterns of behavior in large groups of subjects, sometimes with the help of elaborate tests and procedures. Piaget preferred a different approach. He observed children's behavior in naturalistic settings, taking detailed notes hour after hour. Sometimes he asked the children questions, and sometimes he developed special tests of their abilities. But above all, he never stopped observing. Indeed, many of Piaget's books and articles describe his detailed observations of his own three children—Jacqueline, Lucienne, and Lauren.

These unorthodox methods gradually led Piaget to develop a highly influential theory of cognitive development that focused on the organization of intelligence and how it changes as the child grows. For Piaget, an 8-year-old boy is not a miniature adult, a shorter and dumber version of his father. Rather, the child perceives the world in a fundamentally different way from his parents because of the very nature of his thought processes. By studying the growth of intelligence, Piaget hoped to establish a biological basis for **epistemology**—the philosophical study of the nature of knowledge—that is, how we come to know about the world.

Piaget's Theory

Jean Piaget focused on the active processes a child uses to learn about the world. The young infant must experiment to learn basic lessons, such as the fact that his arms and legs are attached to him and under his direct control and his mother's breast is not. The process of discovery continues through adolescence, when the child learns how to deal with the realm of hypothetical possibilities. Along this path from infancy to adolescence, there are several important shifts in the way children think. For Piaget, intellectual growth was not just a matter of adding one skill to another; it was far more complex and far more interesting, involving several different ways of understanding the world.

These cognitive differences were summarized in four major stages of development, as outlined in Table 9.2. It is important to emphasize that the ages given to identify the stages throughout this section are only approximations. Each child develops at a slightly different rate. While psychologists who study IQ are concerned with such differences among individuals, Piaget focused on the underlying processes that are common to all. The exact timing for a given individual depends on the interaction of maturation and experience. Further, moving from one stage to the next is a gradual process—a child does not suddenly enter what Piaget called the concrete operational stage on her seventh birthday. However, Piaget did believe that these stages must always occur in the same order.

**JEAN PIAGET
(1896–1980)**

Piaget was one of the most influential figures in the history of developmental psychology. Born in Switzerland, he published his first article, a description of an albino sparrow for a natural history magazine, at the age of 10. After completing a Ph.D. in biology, he accepted a position at the Binet Laboratory in Paris developing items for IQ tests. While most IQ researchers were interested in developing standardized items for accessing intelligence, Piaget became fascinated by the errors children made and discovered that children of the same age frequently made the same kinds of mistakes. Piaget gradually came to the conclusion that young children are not just "dumber" than adults; rather, they actually think in different ways. He rejected the idea of using rigid test questions and began to experiment instead with flexible and free-flowing interviews, following the natural thought processes of his young subjects. Piaget hoped to establish a biological basis for *epistemology,* the philosophical study of the nature of knowledge—that is, how we come to know about the world.

TABLE 9.2

Piaget's Stages of Cognitive Development

Stage	Approximate age	Characteristics
Sensorimotor	Birth to 2 years	Child learns to distinguish self from external objects; lacks symbolic thought—lives entirely in the present; gradually develops a sense of cause and effect and object permanence (objects continue to exist even when they are not physically present).
Preoperational	2 to 7 years	Child begins to develop symbolic thought—words, play, gestures, and mental images begin to represent external objects; remains *egocentric*—unable to take the viewpoint of another.
Concrete-operational	7 to 11 years	Child becomes capable of logical thought but only about concrete, observable objects; is gradually able to *conserve,* that is, recognize that certain basic properties of objects remain constant even when appearances change.
Formal-operational	Begins at 11 years or later	Child can solve abstract problems; logically takes different factors into account and can systematically test hypotheses; is concerned with the future and hypothetical possibilities.

THE SENSORIMOTOR STAGE

In the **sensorimotor stage**, which lasts roughly for the first two years of life, infants gradually discover the relationships between sensations and their motor acts. During this period, the child develops a primitive sense of identity, differentiating herself from the rest of the world, and begins to understand cause and effect.

Piaget's choice of the term *sensorimotor* emphasized his belief that in this stage the child learns directly from sensations and motor actions. More abstract types of thought do not appear until later.

A newborn baby's behavior is largely a matter of reflex. Her eye closes when you touch it; her knee flexes when you prick her foot; and if you put a nipple in her mouth, she begins to suck. But almost immediately after birth, the child begins to adapt her behavior to the demands of the environment. She will begin to adjust her sucking, for example, to make her mother's milk flow at the ideal rate. As the infant becomes capable of more complex behavior, this active process of experimenting on the world grows more elaborate.

Perhaps the most important development in the sensorimotor stage is the achievement of **object permanence**: the awareness that objects continue to exist even when they are not present to be seen, touched, or sensed. This is such a basic level of intellectual achievement that it is often hard for adults to comprehend it fully. Unless you have ingested large quantities of drugs or become enchanted by the paradoxes of Zen Buddhism, you probably take it for granted that objects continue to exist in your absence. If you put a pen in a drawer, you do not doubt that there is now a pen in a drawer, even though you can no longer see or touch it. Similarly, you are willing to accept the fact that the Statue of Liberty sits on an island in New York Harbor even if it's been years since you've been there and seen it. But, for a 6-month-old infant, out of sight is quite literally out of mind.

In early infancy, a child responds only to what he can sense directly. He will stare at his mother's face as she looks down into the crib, but if

sensorimotor stage According to Piaget, the stage from birth to age 2 when infants discover the relationship between their own sensations and motor acts.

object permanence According to Piaget, the awareness that objects continue to exist even when they are not present to be seen, touched, or sensed.

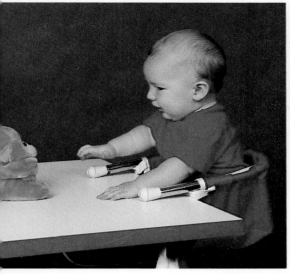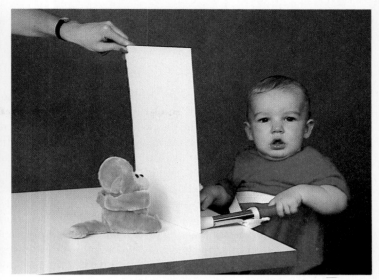

In a study of object permanence, this infant first stares intently at a toy monkey, but then seems unaware of its existence when it is blocked from view.

Mom suddenly moves away, the child will casually look in another direction as if she had never been there. Piaget studied this phenomenon by manipulating objects in front of his own children and observing their reactions. When Piaget dropped a paper ball into his son's crib, at first the infant did not react at all. But at the age of 6 months, he began to look for the ball after it dropped. The infant had become more aware of the existence of the object. Still, he looked only in front of him, where the ball had originally been. When Piaget's daughter was 10½ months old, he played a game in which he took a toy from Jacqueline's hands and placed it under the left side of her mattress. Each time he did this, the child watched his movements and retrieved the toy. But when Piaget slowly moved the toy to the right until Jacqueline could no longer see it, she immediately looked again under the mattress on the left. Piaget concluded that his 10½-month-old daughter had not yet developed a full understanding of object permanence.

In a test of Jacqueline's abilities at 18 months, Piaget put a coin in his hand, placed the hand under a blanket, and then withdrew it. Jacqueline showed how far she had advanced by first opening her father's hand and then, when she found that the coin was not there, looking under the blanket until she found it. Around the age of 12 months, most children master the concept of object permanence; they understand that objects continue to exist even after they have disappeared from their view.

One of the continuing themes in cognitive development that Piaget identified is called *egocentrism*. Although in normal English usage this word implies selfishness, Piaget defined it in a different way. **Egocentrism** involves the child's failure to take into account the perspective of another person. At first, the child is intellectually centered around herself (or her ego) and fails to realize that other people may perceive the same events in a different way. Intellectual growth involves gradually becoming less egocentric. The first milestone in this process comes near the end of the sensorimotor stage, when the child becomes fully aware of the distinction between her own body and external physical objects. Egocentrism continues to decline throughout the next period of Piaget's scheme of development, the preoperational stage.

egocentrism According to Piaget, the child's failure to take into account the perspective of another person.

THE PREOPERATIONAL STAGE

Symbolic thought first appears in the **preoperational stage** of development, as the 2- to 7-year-old child gradually learns to use speech, play, gestures, and mental images to represent the world. The infant in the sensorimotor stage can deal only with objects that are physically present; the toddler in the preoperational stage is able to manipulate mental symbols and therefore deal with the world on a somewhat more abstract level.

But the young child's ability to deal with abstract information is quite limited; this stage is called *preoperational* because of the child's inability to perform the mental transformations that Piaget called *operations*. The term is borrowed from mathematics, which recognizes certain operations, such as addition and subtraction, for specifying the relationship between numbers. For Piaget, **operations** were mental actions that reorganize one's views of the world. For example, an adult who has put a hat on can mentally reverse this action and imagine never having done it. A child in the preoperational stage is not capable of mentally performing this logical operation.

The preoperational child remains egocentric, unable adequately to take others' perspectives into account. These limitations can be seen in the way children use language. In one of his first psychological investigations, Piaget (1926/1960) observed two 6-year-old schoolchildren in Geneva. For about a month, he followed them around in a progressive school and wrote down everything each said. While adults use language primarily to communicate with one another, Piaget found that about 35% to 40% of these children's statements did not involve the transmission of information.

For example, when one child sat down alone at a table, he said to himself aloud, "I want to do that drawing there. . . . I want to draw something, I do. I shall need a big piece of paper to do that" (Piaget, 1960, p. 37). Monologues of this sort sometimes went on at great length, despite the fact that from the child's point of view no one was there to listen to him.

A similar type of egocentric ongoing commentary often occurred when several children played together. In fact, Piaget noted, the children often became so absorbed in their own idiosyncratic conversations with themselves that they paid little attention to the comments of their playmates. The proportion of a child's speech that conforms to this egocentric pattern declines over the course of the preoperational stage.

In a more systematic study of how youngsters use language to communicate, Piaget asked children to repeat a story he had told them. Again, the younger children often failed to communicate. They reported events in the wrong order, left out key details, referred to characters without naming them, and often confused cause-and-effect relationships. For example, in repeating a story about a fairy who turned children into swans, one young subject said, "There was a fairy, wicked fairy. They turned themselves into swans" (Piaget, 1960, pp. 126–127). In this example, the child clearly fails to take the perspective of his audience into account. Although he may know who "they" were, he does not fill in the gaps in the story for the listener. As a result, the imprecise use of the pronoun *they* muddles the whole story and makes it almost impossible to understand.

This type of egocentrism is familiar to anyone who has ever tried to get a straight story from a 5-year-old. An amusing anecdote about life at the

preoperational stage According to Piaget, the stage from age 2 to 7 when symbolic thought first appears.

operations According to Piaget, the mental actions that organize a person's view of the world.

playground may make little sense unless the listener repeatedly asks for more details about who, what, when, where, and why. Only as children grow older do they begin to take another person's knowledge and perspective into account and thus communicate more effectively. This sort of egocentric speech points to the most fundamental characteristic of the preoperational period—the lack of logical operations and symbolic thought.

THE CONCRETE-OPERATIONAL STAGE

During the **concrete-operational stage** (roughly ages 7 to 11), the child becomes capable of logical thought but only regarding concrete, observable objects. In Piaget's terms, the child becomes capable of performing operations, mental actions that reorganize the world. Later, during the formal-operational stage, the adolescent is able to perform mental operations on more abstract stimuli, such as words and mathematical symbols.

The best-known landmark between the preoperational thought of the young child and the concrete-operational ability of the school-aged youngster involves mastery of **conservation**: the recognition that certain basic properties of objects (such as volume and number) remain constant even when appearances change.

For example, in a typical test of the conservation of liquid, young children are shown two identical containers filled with the same amount of water. After the child agrees that the two containers hold the same amount, the liquid from one container is poured into another that is taller and thinner than the original. Of course, the water rises to a higher level in this thinner container.

Typically, 4-year-olds think that the simple act of pouring has changed the amount of liquid. They may argue that there is more water because it rose higher or less water because the container is thinner, but clearly they feel there has been a change. In contrast, 5- and 6-year-olds often have mixed reactions. They may have trouble deciding, or they may think that the amount of liquid remains constant even when its appearance has changed.

Closely related to conservation is the mental operation of **reversibility**, in which a person can think of a transformation that would restore the orignial condition. For example, addition and subtraction are logical opposites; the operation of adding $3 + 4 = 7$ can be reversed and the original situation can be restored by subtracting: $7 - 4 = 3$. In the conservation-of-liquid task, older children understand that pouring has not changed the amount of liquid in part because the action is reversible. You can always pour the liquid back to restore the original situation. Nonconservers are fooled by appearances, by irrelevant transformations that make things look or feel different.

Earlier, we referred to the ability to conserve as one landmark that separates the preoperational from the concrete-operational child. However, the picture is complicated by the fact that there are several types of conservation, and they do not all appear at the same time. For example, to test conservation of weight, children might be shown on a scale that two balls of clay balance each other perfectly and weigh the same amount. After they watch the experimenter roll one ball of clay into the shape of a long, fat sausage, the children are asked whether the sausage and ball still weigh the same. In-

In a test of Piaget's concept of conservation, a child points to the container that he believes contains more liquid.

concrete-operational stage
According to Piaget, the stage from age 7 to 11 when a child becomes capable of logical thought regarding observable actions.

conservation According to Piaget, the recognition that certain basic properties of objects remain constant even when appearances change.

reversibility According to Piaget, a mental operation in which a person can imagine a transformation that would restore an original condition.

terestingly, many children who have mastered the conservation of liquid are not able to conserve in this situation; they believe that the change in shape yielded a change in weight. Conservation of weight seems to be a more subtle concept than conservation of liquid, and it typically appears a year or two later in development.

The fact that a young child may be able to conserve in one situation but not in another emphasizes the concreteness of thought between the ages of 7 and 11. Reasoning seems closely tied to specific situations and objects.

THE FORMAL-OPERATIONAL STAGE

The highest stage of intellectual achievement discussed by Piaget appears in early adolescence. (Though it could easily be described in Chapter 10, which discusses postchildhood development, for continuity we shall consider it here.) In the **formal-operational stage**, which can begin as early as the age of 11, the child is capable of solving abstract problems and dealing with hypothetical possibilities. The formal-operational thinker tests hypotheses as a scientist might, considering all the alternatives and efficiently looking for a way to choose among them (see "Applying Scientific Concepts").

Many of the experiments Piaget devised to test formal-operational thinking involved problems from the chemistry or physics laboratory. In one typical study, adolescents were given five containers filled with clear liquid—four "test chemicals" and one "indicator." When the proper combination of one or more test chemicals was added to the indicator, it turned yellow. The adolescents were faced with the problem of finding the proper combination of test chemicals.

Preoperational children given this problem simply mix chemicals randomly; concrete-operational children are more systematic but generally fail to consider all the possible combinations. Only children in the formal-operational stage consider all the alternatives and systematically vary one factor at a time in their search for the correct combination. They often write down all the results and draw general conclusions about each chemical.

While Piaget's earlier stages of intellectual development have been accepted by most developmental psychologists, the formal-operational stage has proved far more controversial. Some people seem to arrive at these strategies only at the age of 15 or 17, and some never master them at all. Even among college students, success on different types of formal-operational tasks seems to vary as a function of college major—with students most likely to show a capacity for formal-operational reasoning only on tasks with which they have some familiarity (White & Ferstenberg, 1978). As a result of this limitation and others, Piaget (1972) withdrew his earlier claims that the formal-operational stage naturally occurs in every culture without any special training.

Evaluating Piaget's Contribution

Among psychologists, there is a vast range of opinion about the ultimate value of Piaget's complex views. But on one point there can be no argument:

formal-operational stage
According to Piaget, the stage (which can begin as early as age 11) when a person becomes capable of solving abstract problems and dealing with hypothetical possibilities.

The Pendulum Problem

Piaget used what he called "clinical interviews" to assess children's cognitive processes. Typically, he would present a child with a problem, such as figuring out how to create a yellow liquid from five different chemicals. Since Piaget believed that children's reasoning about these problems provided the key to their mental operations, he would listen carefully as the child worked toward a solution.

One of the problems Piaget devised for adolescents and young adults was called the "pendulum problem." Use your powers of imagery (see Chapter 8) to visualize a simple pendulum. For example, you could picture a structure like the one used in the game Hangman, with a weighted string hanging from it. Now imagine this pendulum swinging back and forth, first slowly, then rapidly. Try to answer the question that Piaget asked of his subjects: "What factor or factors determine how fast the pendulum swings back and forth?"

A child at Piaget's stage of concrete operations would probably need to experiment with an actual pendulum even to try to answer this question. An individual at Piaget's stage of formal operations would not necessarily be able to reach the correct answer without this kind of physical experimentation. But the formal-operational person could formulate a set of hypotheses and devise a plan for testing them systematically. (A discussion of the strategy involved in solving the pendulum problem appears after the "Summary" at the end of this chapter.)

Jean Piaget has had a tremendous impact on the ways developmental psychologists have tried to understand children's thought processes.

Some of this influence has been quite direct. For example, literally hundreds of studies have explored the appearance of conservation. This is considered an important landmark in cognitive development because the conserving child can, for the first time, reverse a physical action in his or her head (mentally pouring the liquid back into the original container). On a broader scale, the concrete-operational child has mastered the ability to imagine future actions and their consequences.

Some of the most interesting research on conservation has focused on the possibility of teaching preoperational children to conserve. According to a strict interpretation of Piaget's theory, this should not be possible. Ordinarily, a 5-year-old lacks both the mental capacity and sufficient active experience to conserve; ordinarily the 4-year-old simply does not have the mental capacity to conserve.

In one early study (Smedslund, 1961), 5- to 7-year-old children were first tested to see whether they conserved weight. Nonconservers were children who claimed that the weight of a ball of clay had changed after it was rolled or flattened. These children were then given specific instructions to conserve. They were repeatedly shown that changing the shape of the clay ball did not change its weight on a scale. After sufficient training, these children began to conserve; when the ball was flattened, they now said that its weight had not changed.

But Smedslund was not content with this demonstration; he devised several clever tests to see whether the children really understood. In one subsequent test, when he flattened a clay ball, he secretly removed a piece of it. Now the flat piece of clay really *did* weigh less. Children who had been trained to conserve were not surprised or upset when the scale proved that the two pieces of clay were now different. In contrast, many of the children who were true conservers on the initial test suspected foul play. One suggested diplomatically, "We must have lost some clay on the floor," and a more direct child said, "I think you have taken away some of the clay."

Smedslund concluded that although preoperational children could be trained to imitate conservation responses, they did not really understand what they were doing. Other researchers took this as a challenge and developed increasingly sophisticated techniques for teaching children to conserve. For example, Botvin and Murray (1975) put first-grade children in groups of five, each group consisting of two conservers and three nonconservers. Each child was asked several conservation questions, and the other children listened to the answers. Then the children talked about the problem as a group and agreed on one answer. Most nonconservers learned to conserve from participating in these groups; just being exposed to the reasoning of conservers seemed to help the nonconservers understand the problem.

Still other researchers have examined the conservation problem from the child's perspective to see how children might interpret the questions they are asked. Typically, a child first is asked if two things—say two balls of clay—are equal. After the child says Yes, the experimenter tells the child, "Watch this," and then changes the shape of one ball by flattening it. Children may think that the experimenter intended to make a change, and thus may answer No when asked the second question, "Are these two still the same?" They may be responding to the whole situation, which suggests a change, and not just to the specific question.

To test this possibility, Rose and Blank (1974) decided to omit the traditional first question in conservation tests ("Are these two equal?") Instead, they simply rearranged the objects and then asked 6-year-old children if the two objects were equal. These children made fewer errors when asked only one question. Further, when given standard conservation tests the following week, these children still made fewer errors than 6-year-olds typically make. Maybe children do pay attention to the overall situation.

This finding led to still more controversy. Researchers scurried back to their bookshelves to find out *exactly* what Piaget has said about the matter. They found that Piaget's own proposals contained a certain amount of ambiguity.

Similar events occured when large numbers of experimenters tested other aspects of Piaget's theory. This led at first to disillusionment and later to an attempt to find something better. John Flavell (1982), one of the most influential researchers in this field, summarized Piaget's current status in this way:

Piaget's stage theory has made an enormous—indeed unmatched—contribution to the field of cognitive development. . . . Like all theories of great reach and significance, however, it has problems that gradually come to light as years and years of thinking and research get done on it. Thus, some of us now think that the theory may in varying degrees be unclear, incorrect, and incomplete. (p. 2)

In the 1980s, researchers have continued to study this theory, developing "neo-Piagetian" alternatives to try to develop a more complete and accurate picture of children's cognitive growth. Research by one Piagetian scholar, John H. Flavell of Stanford University, has mapped the long, slow process by which children master the distinction between appearance and reality (Flavell, 1986). One of the more interesting trends in this new research involves the relationship between a child's cognitive abilities and larger understanding of the social world.

Social Cognition

Traditionally, studies of cognitive development have focused on how children understand physical objects and the relations among them. Recently, many developmental researchers have turned to the study of **social cognition**: the understanding of the social world, including other people's behavior, thoughts, and feelings.

For example, Berndt (1981) studied children's ideas of what friends are and how they should treat one another. In several studies comparing kindergarten children with third- and sixth-graders, he asked questions like, "How do you know that someone is your friend?" and "What would make you decide not to be friends with someone anymore?" The children's answers revealed systematic changes in the way children define friendship.

Some social scientists believe that intimacy and trust are two of the more important characteristics of adult friendship. Sixth-grade children often mentioned these features, saying such things as, "We can talk freely to one another," "I can tell secrets to her," or simply, "I can trust him." In contrast, younger children rarely mentioned intimacy or trust. Other defining features of friendship showed less change. Children of all ages, for example, often mentioned physical association, such as, "I sleep over at his house sometimes," or "She calls me all the time."

Developmental trends of this sort seem to be related to the child's growing cognitive capabilities. Younger children define friendship in terms of obvious surface characteristics like association, just as their understanding of physical objects is based on superficial appearances. In the concrete-operational stage, they begin to understand that an object—like water poured from one glass to another—can remain the same despite changes in appearance. At roughly the same age, their definition of friendship begins to reflect a deeper level of understanding; it is based not just on obvious features like physical association, but also more subtle notions, such as trust and intimacy.

Studies of social cognition are almost inevitably more complicated by cultural differences than studies of nonsocial cognition. In some cultures, for example, intimacy is not considered a vital part of adult friendship. Children

social cognition   Understanding of the social world, including other people's behavior, thoughts, and feelings.

In one series of studies on social cognition, children were asked questions about the way they related to their friends.

raised in these cultures would therefore be expected to have a different pattern of social cognitive development regarding intimacy issues. In contrast, the way children perceive glasses of liquid would be far less likely to vary from one culture to the next. Despite such difficulties, many researchers are now beginning to study social cognition in the hope that it will provide new information about the child's changing world.

Harvard psychologist Robert Selman has formulated the best-known theory of stages in the development of social cognition. Working in the tradition of Piaget, Selman (e.g., Selman & Byrne, 1974; Selman, 1980) has identified four levels (called Level 0, 1, 2, and 3) in the development of children's ability to take the role of another person. With each new level of maturity, the child achieves a better understanding of the perspectives of others.

At Selman's Level 0, the level of *egocentric role taking,* the child cannot differentiate among different points of view. Children at this level typically fail to recognize that others may see a situation differently than they themselves do.

At Selman's Level 1, children are characterized by *subjective role taking.* They realize that others may interpret the same social situation differently than they do, but they cannot really put themselves in the shoes of the other.

At Level 2, children become capable of *self-reflective role taking.* They realize that other people have their own values and goals and can see themselves from the other's point of view. Finally, at Level 3, they become capable of *mutual role taking.* At this level, they can differentiate their own perspective from that of the average member of a group. Moreover, they can imagine how a third person might make judgments on both their own and another's point of view.

How do these abstract concepts translate into children's real-life orientations to their social world? Ben, when he was a Level 1 child, was afraid of the big, bad wolf and could not imagine that his brother, Jeff, felt unafraid when hearing the classic children's story. For Ben, at this age, scary was scary, and there were no other possibilities.

When he reached Level 1, Ben had become a child who worshipped his big brother, Jeff. For Ben, Jeff was the perfect boy, to be followed and imitated. However, Ben did not recognize and could not have imagined that Jeff felt annoyed at Ben's constant presence and aping of his behavior.

When Ben became self-reflective (Level 2), he realized that Jeff would see him as a pest if he became too intrusive; that is, he could comprehend Jeff's perspective on his behavior. However, even at this level, Ben was not able to understand his parents' amusement when watching his interactions with Jeff.

By the time he reached Level 3, Ben could understand that his parents sometimes saw things differently than either he or his brother did, and that other brothers could be either similar to or different from himself and his brother in important ways. He had reached a level of social cognitive maturity that allowed him to conceptualize several different viewpoints at the same time, to evaluate potential similarities and differences in perspectives, and to understand that two different perspectives could be analyzed from a third point of view.

In a study of children aged 4, 6, 8, and 10, Selman and Byrne (1974) found that most of the 4- and 6-year-olds were at Level 1. Selman did not find a majority of children at Level 2 until the age of 8, and even among the 10-year-olds, Level 2 was the predominant level.

Judgments about the morality of particular behaviors is considered another important aspect of social cognition. Lawrence Kohlberg utilized Piaget's cognitive developmental perspective to approach the question of how children's thinking about morality changes over time. Because Kohlberg's theory extends the analysis of social cognition into the adolescent and adult years, we consider it in detail in Chapter 10.

Personality and Social Development

While some researchers have concentrated on the growth of intellectual and perceptual abilities, others have been more concerned with the formation of personality. As we shall see in Chapter 12, **personality** can be defined as an individual's characteristic pattern of thought, behavior, and emotions. From the pioneer theories of Sigmund Freud to the present day, many personality psychologists have argued that lifelong patterns of behavior may be established in childhood. Here, we focus on several lines of research that specifically examined the effects of early experience and predisposition.

Temperament

personality An individual's characteristic pattern of thought, behavior, and emotions.

From the moment of birth, each child gives signs of individuality. One infant sleeps peacefully while another tosses and turns. One child quickly and easily accepts an irregular feeding schedule; another will eat only when he is good and ready. One child fusses the second her diaper is wet; another barely seems to notice. **Temperament** refers to an underlying energy level or other factor that helps produce a consistent style of responding in many different situations.

Mothers have observed such differences for centuries. However, some psychologists questioned the idea that individual differences were present at birth. In Chapter 6, for example, we quoted John B. Watson's famous claim that he could train any child to become a doctor, lawyer, or thief. Many behaviorists argued that mothers' perceptions of consistency were exaggerated (see Chapter 12) and that real individual differences appear only after the infant had an opportunity to learn certain behavior patterns.

Many researchers have therefore tried to see whether temperament differences are present at birth or only appear later in development. One such study compared the behavior of 24 Chinese and 24 Caucasian infants immediately after they were born (Freedman, 1979). Caucasian babies cried longer and harder and had more trouble adapting to changes in position. When their noses were pressed briefly with a cloth, the Caucasian babies turned away or swiped at the cloth with their hands; the Chinese infants simply lay still and calmly breathed through their mouths. This researcher hesitantly summarized these and other observations by saying: "It was as if the old stereotypes of the calm, inscrutable Chinese and the excitable, emotionally changeable Caucasian were appearing spontaneously in the first 48 hours of life" (p. 38). This finding seems to support the biological paradigm that emphasizes the effects of innate predispositions.

The New York Longitudinal Study is an ongoing attempt to determine whether early differences like this have long-term implications for personality development. Alexander Thomas, Stella Chess, and Herbert Birch (1970) and their colleagues began by studying 141 newborn infants from middle-class families in New York. At first, they interviewed the parents at regular intervals concerning factual details about how the children behaved in specific situations (see "Understanding The Scientific Method" for details).

Gradually they found that some personality traits tended to go together to form three more general personality types, which they called *easy, difficult,* and *slow to warm up*. For example, infants who had a generally positive mood also tended to be rhythmic (have regular patterns of sleeping and eating), to approach new situations, and to adapt to changes in the environment. About 40% of the children fell into this category; they were easy because their good moods, regular schedules, and easy adaptability made them a pleasure to raise.

Another 10% of the children were difficult because they acted in almost exactly the opposite way. They were generally in a bad mood, had irregular eating and sleeping habits, adapted to new situations slowly, withdrew from new people, and generally reacted intensely. The 15% in the slow-to-warm-up group were generally inactive, adapted slowly, withdrew at first from new people or objects, and were usually in slightly negative moods. (The remaining 35% of the children had a mixture of traits and did not fall easily into any of these three basic personality types.)

Interpretation of the consistency of these traits through childhood is

temperament An underlying energy level or other factor that helps produce a consistent style of responding in many different situations.

Longitudinal Research: Studies That Can Last a Lifetime

Longitudinal studies involve the repeated observation of the same individuals over a long period of time, sometimes through their entire life. Such cradle-to-grave observation provides valuable information about development that cannot be gained in any other way. But it also means that a study can take 80, 90, or even 100 years to complete.

The New York Longitudinal Study began in 1956. The major focus of this study was to trace the evolution of temperament. Can adult personality be predicted from the behavior of a newborn infant? Thomas, Chess, and Birch (1970) began with 141 infants; most of the original subjects, now in their twenties, still participate at regular intervals. In the early stages, most of the data came from regular interviews with the parents—every three months for the first year and a half, then every six months until the age of 5, then once a year.

The results of these interviews led the researchers to focus on nine basic dimensions of personality: activity level, rhythmicity, distractability, approach-withdrawal, adaptability, attention span and persistence, intensity of reaction, threshold of responsiveness, and quality of mood.

Later, these characteristics were assessed by Thomas and Chess (1977) through standard questionnaires. For example, mothers were asked which of the following three statements best applied to their infants:

With interruptions of milk or solid feedings, as for burping, is:

(a) Generally happy, smiles;
(b) Variable responses; or
(c) Generally cries with these interruptions (p. 213).

Choice *a* was classified as a sign of a positive mood; choice *c* reflected a negative mood. The overall response to a number of similar items provided a general score for the infant's quality of mood.

(box continues on next page)

quite complicated, in part because each child interacts in a different family. The relationship between mother and father influences the way a particular type of child is treated. In addition, developmental psychologists have become increasingly aware that influence is not a one-way street—children also shape parents' behavior. And there may be individual differences in parental response. One mother of a difficult child may try to become more understanding, while another could be affected by the same personality pattern in the opposite way and become a harsher disciplinarian.

After taking these and other complications into account, Thomas and Chess (1977) concluded that the personality differences found in infancy did indeed influence the behavior patterns of later years. As these researchers have followed the same children into adolescence and early adulthood, they have shown that infants with difficult temperaments are more likely to develop

Another questionnaire assessed the same characteristics for the 3- to 7-year-old child. Parents were asked to rate a series of statements, for example, "When playing with other children, my child argues with them," on a 7-point scale (Thomas & Chess, 1977, p. 242). If a parent said this was hardly ever true, that indicated a generally positive mood. But if it was almost always true, the child was at the negative end of the scale. Again, the average response to a number of items gave an overall rating of positive or negative mood.

By computing correlation coefficients (see "Understanding the Scientific Method" in the Appendix) between each child's scores at different ages, Thomas and Chess (1977) were able to prove that some personality characteristics were reasonably stable. For example, the correlations between mood quality at age 1 and age 2 ($r = .45$) and age 1 and age 3 ($r = .25$) were statistically significant; the predictions from age 1 to age 4 ($r = .10$) or from age 1 to age 5 ($r = .08$) were less reliable. The clearest evidence of personality stability was found over relatively short periods of time. This finding is consistent with other longitudinal studies of personality development.

An inherent problem for all developmental research on the stability of character traits becomes particularly obvious in longitudinal studies. How does one equate the different behavioral patterns observed at different ages? In the example given here, is it really legitimate to consider an infant's fussiness during feeding as somehow parallel to a 7-year-old's argumentativeness? This gradually became a problem for the New York Longitudinal Study; as the children entered adolescence and adulthood, it became increasingly difficult to analyze their personalities in terms of standard reactions to a limited number of situations.

This is only one of the conceptual and practical hurdles that longitudinal researchers face. These studies are expensive and time-consuming; it takes a special kind of commitment for psychologists to begin a study that they can't possibly live to complete. Still, despite the difficulties, several major longitudinal studies that plan to follow people for their entire lives are now in progress (see Chapter 10). It is a measure of psychology's youth that no large-scale study of this sort has ever followed a complete group from birth to death.

into children with behavior problems that include being disruptive in school and aggressive with other children.

Thomas, Chess and Korn (1982) provide two possible explanations for this pattern. First, mothers of these children often feel that they are to blame for their children's behavior. The mother's self-doubts about her competence as a parent can lead to a poor mother-child relationship, with a negative effect on the child. Second, pressures to conform may be overwhelming for children with difficult temperaments. Young children are expected to adapt to routines and schedules (such as sleeping and eating at regular times) and to social situations (such as starting school and staying with unfamiliar babysitters). While these pressures for behavior change are hard on all children, they are particularly stressful for children with difficult temperaments. For example, an easy child might be unhappy about staying with a new babysitter but cope silently, perhaps by snuggling up with a favorite blanket or by trying to make friends with the babysitter. But the child with a more difficult temperament may respond by crying, yelling at the babysitter, or withdrawing—behaviors that are socially unacceptable and that may result in negative consequences for the child.

Of course, not all children with difficult temperaments develop problems, and simply knowing the temperament of children when they are young does not allow you to predict their later development accurately. Indeed, Thomas and Chess (1984) more recently reported that only about one-third of the differences in adult behavior can be explained by childhood factors. The environment and interactions with other people also play major roles in affecting development.

While some of the Thomas and Chess subjects showed striking stability in development between childhood and adulthood, others had undergone dramatic changes. Some of these changes were due to life situations and uncontrollable events. One girl, for example, had a potential for behavioral problems but did fine in childhood because of positive relationships with her parents, especially her father. However, when this girl was 13, her father died suddenly. Her mother was overwhelmed by the situation and was unable to maintain a good relationship with her daughter. The girl subsequently developed severe behavior problems, including antisocial behavior (Thomas, Chess, & Korn, 1982).

One key to positive family situations is a parent's acceptance of each child's temperament.

Another difficult child in the Thomas and Chess sample had parents who were intolerant of her behavior. Her father expected her to adapt quickly to new situations and was openly critical of her inability to adapt. Her mother didn't know how to deal with her at all. In early childhood the girl developed serious behavior problems, and the prospects for improvement seemed bleak. Then, when she was about 9 years old, the girl suddenly began to show talent in music and drama. Her teachers and other adults were quite impressed with her, and ultimately her own parents became impressed. They considered these talents to be valuable and started to interpret their daughter's behavior differently. In the past, an outburst was considered a sign of a "rotten kid"; now it was viewed as "artistic temperament." The family situation improved greatly, and the girl's psychological problems disappeared by adolescence (Thomas, Chess, & Korn, 1982).

Clearly, while temperament is important, it does not explain everything. Development is affected by "goodness of fit"—that is, by the match between parents' expectations and styles and the child's style. If parents are in tune with their child's behavior and are able to accept whatever temperament their child has, then the family situation will be much more positive. On the other hand, as Thomas and Chess (1984) point out, if children experience a lot of parental conflict by age 3, they are more likely to have poor adjustment in early adulthood, regardless of temperament. Thus, adult character is shaped by a complex interaction between early predispostions and a lifetime of experience. Moreover, as is shown by the two classic lines of research reviewed in the remainder of this section, ongoing personality development may be influenced by early experiences.

Monkeys and Motherly Love

One of the first studies of the effects of infant experience on later development focused on the nature of motherly love. Because it would be unethical to deprive human infants of their mothers for the purposes of an experiment, Harry Harlow decided to begin by studying motherhood among rhesus monkeys.

Before Harlow's research, many psychologists had speculated that infants' love for their mothers could be learned by associating the mothers' physical characteristics with the reduction of biological tensions, such as hunger and thirst. Psychoanalytic followers of Sigmund Freud particularly emphasized the importance of breast-feeding—the child's first form of gratification—in forming an attachment between mother and child. Harlow (1959) decided to test this idea by comparing monkeys raised by two artificial, or surrogate, mothers. One was a wire cylinder with a crude face and a single nipple supplying milk; the other was an identical cylinder wrapped in terry cloth to make it softer and more comfortable.

In the first experiment, eight newborn rhesus monkeys were placed in cages with two surrogate mothers. Half received milk through the wire mother, and half through the cloth-covered parent. All eight monkeys drank about the same amount of milk and gained weight normally. If the parental bond was based on this feeding, each monkey should have become attached to the mother that fed it. However, the monkeys given milk through the wire cylinder left as soon as they finished eating and went over to cling to the terry-cloth parent. All eight infant monkeys clung to the terry-cloth mother 12 to 18 hours each day. Bodily contact and comfort seemed to be more important factors than feeding in establishing a bond of affection.

Later tests provided an impressive demonstration of the security these infant monkeys felt when they clung to the terry-cloth mother. Into the peaceful world of the monkey cage Harlow introduced a windup teddy bear beating a drum. The poor infants were obviously scared silly. Each monkey rushed over to the cloth mother and hung on for dear life. After a period of rubbing against "Mom" for reassurance, the infant monkeys seemed much calmer; they turned to look at the toy and sometimes even climbed down to approach it.

Less stressful circumstances elicited a similar response. When a motherless monkey was placed in a large cage filled with unfamiliar objects, it ran over to the cloth mother, climbed up, and rubbed against it reassuringly. Again, a few moments of this physical contact seemed to calm the infant. The monkey would climb down after a while and begin to explore the cage, returning frequently to the cloth mother to give it a brief, assuring hug.

Although the surrogate mothers were quite satisfactory in some ways, their monkey children did not grow up to be completely normal. Many of these primates were abusive or indifferent to other monkeys, and virtually all of them grew up to have sexual problems (Harlow & Harlow, 1969).

Even more disturbed behavior was seen in control groups of monkeys who were raised in total social isolation, without monkey playmates or artificial mothers. They spent many hours clutching themselves and rocking back and forth aimlessly, acting in a way that reminded Harlow of some emotionally disturbed children. Their interactions with other monkeys ranged from inap-

critical period According to Harlow, a fixed interval during which key events relating to motherly love had to occur for normal development to follow.

propriate to bizarre. Sometimes they simply ignored other animals, and sometimes they behaved very aggressively. On some disturbing occasions, the isolated monkeys even self-destructively bit their own hands, arms, and legs.

After many attempts to rehabilitate these isolated monkeys had failed, Harlow (1971) concluded that contact comfort between mother and child was an essential ingredient for normal primate development. Further, he believed that this bond had to be formed in the first few months of life. Borrowing a concept from ethological studies of animal behavior, Harlow spoke of a **critical period** for motherly love, a fixed interval during which key events had to occur if normal development was to follow.

During the 1950s and 1960s, many psychologists were influenced by this idea. However, several lines of research later questioned the importance of such critical periods in the development of higher primates. Harlow himself later discovered that the problems of isolated monkeys could be reversed by "monkey therapists"—playful young infants who interacted with the older monkeys without threatening them (Suomi & Harlow, 1972). Other researchers have discovered that closely related species of monkeys were not as dramatically affected as the rhesus monkeys used in Harlow's studies (Sackett, Ruppenthal, Fahrenbruch, & Holm, 1981).

More to the point for those who are primarily interested in human development, studies of human children who have unfortunately been raised in isolation indicated that even severe problems may be reversed with proper attention in later childhood. (See "A New Perspective on Early Experience?" later in this chapter.)

When a monkey in Harlow's study was frightened by a toy teddy bear, he retreated to the warm and cuddly terry-cloth-covered "mother" rather than the uncomfortable wire "mother."

Human Attachment

Another influential theory involving the possible role of critical periods in human development was developed by psychiatrist John Bowlby. In his 1969 book *Attachment and Loss,* Bowlby argued that the basis for motherly love has been built into the human species by millions of years of evolution. Unlike newborn animals of some species, the human infant is entirely helpless; to ensure the survival of the species, human infants must be cared for by adults. According to Bowlby, babies are genetically programmed to cling to an adult, usually the mother; and the mother, in turn, is programmed to respond to the child's needs. Attachment, an emotional bond of love between mother and child, is the natural result.

While evolutionary explanations of this sort are difficult to test scientifically, other aspects of Bowlby's work did generate a great deal of research. Moreover, he set the stage for much of this research by focusing attention on symptoms of emotional loss expressed by infants in the absence of an attachment relationship. Indeed, much of the research on attachment has concentrated on expressions of anxiety in infants and children when separated from their mothers. Bowlby argued that at first an infant's grasping, clinging, and crying are not directed at a specific individual; only by the age of 6 months has the infant clearly learned to recognize the primary caretaker. This can often be seen in the differences in the responses of 6-month-old infants to their mother and to other adults.

Stranger anxiety refers to a phase in which infants seem anxious when strangers are nearby. They may cry, fret, or try to move away. Such behavior is likely to increase if a stranger comes too close or the mother moves away. Stranger anxiety typically appears around the age of 6 months, peaks at 8 or 9 months, and disappears around 15 months. While it may be difficult for you to think of anxiety as a *positive* developmental achievement, stranger anxiety is considered evidence of the infant's ability to recognize caretakers.

A closely related phenomenon is **separation anxiety**—a more profound distress whenever a child is separated from its mother or primary caretaker. This occurs slightly later in development, beginning around 8 to 12 months and ending between the ages of 2 and 2½. At this age, children actively try to prevent their caretakers from leaving by clinging, crying pitifully, or even blocking the door. Parents who want to avoid this trauma often sneak out of the room.

Many researchers have brought Bowlby's concepts into the laboratory to quantify stranger anxiety and separation anxiety. One typical series of studies (Ainsworth & Bell, 1970) observed the response of 1-year-old babies when they were left in a room with various adults. When mother and child were in a room together, the infant seemed quite content; there was very little crying and a great deal of exploratory behavior: crawling around and looking at and handling everything in the room. When a stranger replaced Mom or when the baby was left alone, the child spent much less time exploring and much more time crying. When both mother and a stranger were in the room together, the response was intermediate—the child cried more than when only the mother was present but less than when only the stranger was present.

In addition to these average differences in response to various situations,

stranger anxiety The phase in infancy when children seem anxious around strangers, and may cry, fret, or try to move away.

separation anxiety Profound distress occurring when a child is separated from the mother or primary caretaker.

there are important and consistent individual differences in children's overall anxieties. Children who are *securely attached* explore confidently when mother is present, become distressed when she leaves, but calm down quickly when she returns. *Insecurely attached* children are usually fussy even with the mother present and, when she returns, show ambivalence, such as asking to be picked up and then struggling to get down. In a less common type of insecure attachment, some infants pay little attention to their mothers and are not particularly upset when they leave (Sroufe & Waters, 1977).

Secure attachment is most likely to occur when mothers are sensitive, accepting, cooperative, sociable, accessible, and positive during the child's first year. There is also some evidence that the child can influence parental responsiveness and thus influence the form of attachment. Research on this question is just beginning, but early results suggest that insecurely attached infants are more likely to have behavior problems during the preschool period. Bretherton (1985) describes how 3- to 5-year-old children with insecure attachments were not able to get along well with other children in nursery school. They were often hostile, inept, and socially isolated. Securely attached children, on the other hand, were more curious about their environment and about other children, were more empathic, and were generally more socially competent.

Erickson, Sroufe, and Egeland (1985) studied 96 infants at ages 12 months and 18 months to determine whether they were securely or insecurely attached to their mothers. Several years later, they studied the same children around the age of 5 to see how well they got along in nursery school. They found that insecurely attached children were much more likely to have behavior problems in school. Of 16 insecurely attached children, 14 exhibited problems (88%), as compared with only 7 of 22 securely attached children (32%).

What types of behavioral problems did these insecurely attached children have? A number of them were disobedient, inconsiderate of others (e.g., taking a toy they wanted, regardless of who was using it), and more likely to fight with other children. Other insecurely attached children exhibited behaviors at the opposite extreme—they were withdrawn and showed no interest in playing with anyone or anything. Overall, these children were lacking in the social skills necessary to get along with others. Teachers described them as impulsive and hostile.

This study suggests that the type of attachment during infancy can indeed be a good predictor of later behavior. But it is important to note that not all children fit the predicted pattern: There were several securely attached children who had behavior problems in preschool, while some insecurely attached children did fine.

Rather than ignore this discrepancy, Erickson and her associates decided to look at additional characteristics of the mother-child relationship. They found two possible reasons why some children did not fit the predicted patterns. First, insecurely attached children who had no behavioral problems in preschool were generally above average in intelligence. This may have helped them cope with the new demands of the school setting. For example, they may have learned quickly which behaviors were acceptable to teachers and other children and which weren't, and then behaved accordingly.

On the other hand, some mothers of children who were securely attached in infancy had trouble supporting and encouraging their children as they grew up. While these mothers were insensitive to the needs of their infants, they had problems coping with the changing needs of their children over time. For example, when the children were given a specific task, such as putting together a puzzle, these mothers had trouble telling the children what they should do. In contrast, mothers of preschoolers who had no behavior problems were warm and supportive and provided structure for completing the puzzle task.

Research on various forms of attachment and on the "symptoms" of attachment are not limited to the United States. For example, laboratory studies of stranger anxiety and separation anxiety have now been performed on infants who were raised in a number of different cultures, ranging from an Israeli kibbutz to an African tribe. As Figure 9.3 indicates, the appearance of stranger anxiety was surprisingly regular.

The fact that separation anxiety peaks around the age of 1 year in so many cultural settings led Jerome Kagan and his colleagues (Kagan, Kearsely, & Zelazo, 1978) to argue that this fear is based on the natural emergence of certain cognitive skills. It is only around the age of about 8 months that most infants become cognitively mature enough to understand that Mama may be somewhere else. This separation confuses and upsets the child, who is not yet old enough to test hypotheses about where she went. One factor involved in the disappearance of separation anxiety is the 18-month-old child's ability to crawl or walk around and, under some circumstances, actually find the mother.

Bowlby's original theory singled out the mother as the primary figure in these early dramas. He believed that the mother is naturally disposed to behave in certain ways (cuddling an infant during feeding, for example) and that motherly love cannot be replaced by the father or any other adult. You

Several studies have found that the children of warm and supportive mothers have fewer behavioral problems as they grow up.

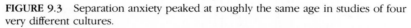

FIGURE 9.3 Separation anxiety peaked at roughly the same age in studies of four very different cultures.

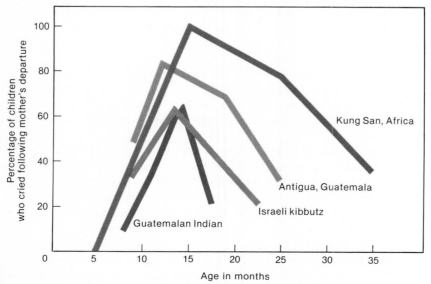

might guess that this would be a controversial assertion in a society in which more and more mothers of young children are working outside the home. Many researchers have investigated Bowlby's claim, and most have rejected his exclusive reliance on the mother.

It is now clear that infants often react as strongly to separation from their fathers as they do to separation from their mothers. A parent's sensitivity to the young child is critical to the formation of a secure attachment. If both the mother and father are sensitive to the infant, the child will form a secure attachment to each of them. Interestingly, if one parent is sensitive and the other is not, the infant may form a secure attachment to one parent and an insecure attachment to the other. Also, attachment relationships can change. An insecure attachment is not always permanent; changes in the parent-child relationship can result in a more secure attachment. Moreover, as we saw above, development reflects more than just the attachment bond. A child's intelligence, combined with experiences with other people and other environments, can foster normal social development. One issue that has stimulated considerable controversy in the United States concerns the impact of day care on children. In the last section of this chapter we will examine recent research regarding day-care centers and whether or not they affect the attachment bond between mother and child. First we will consider the more general issue of child-rearing practices and their effects on children.

Child Rearing

According to one estimate, nearly 5 million how-to-parent books are sold every year in the United States. Surveys suggest that nearly all American parents read some of these books and articles. People are particularly likely to rely on this type of advice when they are from small families (and thus have little experience with other children) and are isolated from their own parents. The fact that American families are becoming smaller and more mobile suggests that expert advice will become more popular in the future (Clark-Stewart, 1978). (See "Becoming a Critical Consumer" for an excerpt from one of the most popular guidebooks for parents.)

Historical Trends

Many practices that would now be classified as criminal child abuse were commonplace throughout most of recorded history. In the civilizations of ancient Greece and Rome, parents simply abandoned unwanted children— usually girls—and allowed them to die. Until the eighteenth century, nearly every Western society practiced swaddling: tightly wrapping young infants so they could not move and would be less likely to bother adults. According to Lloyd de Mause (1974), beatings, sexual abuse, and even the murder of children were frequent occurrences at least through the Middle Ages.

Beginning around the sixteenth century, families became smaller and more mobile, and children began to contribute economically to their success. This led to a new concern with effective child-rearing practices. The dominant

Ask Doctor Spock

The most famous guidebook for parents is Dr. Benjamin Spock's *Baby and Child Care,* which has sold over 28 million copies since it was first published in 1946. Along with medical advice on measles and mumps and practical hints on diapers and diet, this book has much to say about personality and emotional development. As you read the following short selection, consider how much evidence is cited and whether it supports or contradicts the material presented in this chapter. (A short discussion of these issues appears after the "Summary" at the end of this chapter.)

Whether children will grow up to be lifelong optimists or pessimists, whether warmly loving or cool, whether trustful or suspicious, will depend to a considerable extent on the attitudes of the individuals who have taken responsibility for a major portion of their care in the first two years. Therefore, the personalities of parents and caregivers are of great importance.

One person acts toward children as if they were basically bad, always doubting them, always scolding them. Such children grow up doubting themselves, full of guilt. A person with more than average hostility finds a dozen excuses every hour for venting it on a child; and the child acquires a corresponding hostility. Other people have the itch to dominate children and unfortunately they can succeed.

In the first year, a baby has to depend mainly on the attentiveness, intuition, and helpfulness of adults to get her the things that she needs and craves. If the adults are too insensitive or indifferent to serve (within sensible limits—they shouldn't be submissive slaves) she will become somewhat apathetic or depressed. (pp. 38–39)

---

educational philosophy of this period held that children were weak, impulsive creatures; only strict discipline could transform them into moral adults.

The dramatic difference from current attitudes can also be seen in the large numbers of parents who sent their children away to be raised by servants. Breast-feeding was considered a vulgar annoyance, and because bottled formula had not yet been invented, infants were often sent away to wet nurses who breast-fed the children. In 1780, the police chief of Paris estimated that 17,000 of the 21,000 infants born in that city each year were sent away to live with wet nurses in the countryside (Maccoby, 1980).

In the nineteenth century, the emphasis on beating the bad impulses out of children decreased, and parents began to try to learn the most effective ways to socialize their children. With the advent of scientific psychology, a large number of experts began to offer advice.

One of the first guidebooks for parents was written by none other than behaviorist John B. Watson. His 1928 book, *Psychological Care of Infant and Child,* was an odd mix of scientific fact and unscientific speculation. Watson believed that too much love can make a child "totally unable to cope with the world it must live in" (p. 44). He therefore offered the following unsentimental advice:

> Treat [children] as though they were young adults. Dress them, bathe them with care and circumspection. Let your behavior always be objective and kindly firm. Never hug and kiss them, never let them sit on your lap. If you must, kiss them once on the forehead when they say good night." (pp. 81–82)

A more permissive approach became popular in the 1930s. In its more extreme versions, this philosophy held that the child is naturally able to choose the best course and that the parent's job is to help the child achieve its full potential by providing love and support. Discipline should be avoided for fear of producing emotional problems or other harmful effects. Consider, for example, one mother's description of the schools her 6-year-old daughter attended in the 1970s: "LuAnn liked the school in California best—the only rules were no chemical additives in the food and no [sex] in the hallways" (quoted in Kessen, 1979, p. 815). Recent evidence suggests that the pendulum is now swinging back from liberalism and that today's parents are less likely to be permissive, believing that a moderate use of punishment is sometimes appropriate (Walters & Grusec, 1977).

These historical changes in expert opinion may leave parents wondering just how useful current advice books are. To some extent, it is probably unreasonable to ask for an entirely objective approach to child rearing; expert advice will always reflect the ethics and goals of a specific culture. Despite such reservations, social scientists continue to believe that knowledge is better than ignorance and that studying the effects of different ways of rearing children can help to reveal how early experiences shape later development.

At least since Freud, many psychologists have believed that childhood experiences can establish lifelong behavior patterns. Freud himself argued that the first five years of life determined the general outlines of adult personality. Taken to its logical extreme, this theory implied that adults had to be extremely careful how they dealt with children in those first critical years. Fortunately, recent research seems to be reducing this burden. The effects of early experience may not be so overwhelming after all. Some of the most interesting research supporting this more moderate position concerns the effects of day care.

Effects of Day Care

As more and more American women have entered the labor force to pursue careers, day-care centers to take care of young children have become increasingly common. In one of the most thorough studies of this subject (Kagan, Kearsely, & Zelazo, 1978), researchers actually set up an elaborate day-care center for 33 infants. Beginning at the age of 3½ to 5½ months, the children lived at this day-care center from 8 A.M. to 5 P.M., five days a week, until they were 2½ years old. Standard laboratory tests of emotional and intellectual development were used to compare the progress of these children with a control group raised at home.

In one standard test of emotional development, experimenters observed each child's reaction to being separated from his or her mother. Once the child began to play happily with the toys in the laboratory, the mother simply left the room for two minutes while an observer reported any incidents of fretting or crying. There were no significant differences between day-care children and those raised at home. The developmental course of separation anxiety in both groups of children was nearly identical to that observed in other cultures.

Day-care and home-raised children were compared on a variety of tests of intellectual development. For example, at the age of 20 months they were given a simple vocabulary test in which they had to pair pictures with words. Each child was asked to pick out the fork from the pictures of a knife, a fork, and a spoon and to choose the apple from pictures of an apple, an orange, and a banana. Here, too, there were no differences between the two groups of children.

In fact, 19 standard tests of attentiveness, sensitivity to discrepancy, fearfulness, language, memory, social behavior, and attachment to the mother failed to reveal any major differences between children raised by mothers at home and those reared in a day-care center. Informal observations and discussions with parents also failed to reveal any differences.

Although this study was well planned and carefully done, we have to be cautious about generalizing from the results of just one study. To get a broader perspective on the effects of day care, Belsky and Steinberg (1978) reviewed over 40 studies to see if there were any consistent differences between children raised at home and those raised in day-care centers. (See also Belsky, Lerner, and Spanier, 1984.) When middle-class children in day care were compared with home-reared children on intellectual development, there were no differences. However, economically disadvantaged children who were in day care were more advanced intellectually than disadvantaged children at home. Thus, sometimes a group setting designed to enrich a child's experiences can be more intellectually stimulating than the child's home.

Belsky and Steinberg (1978) also looked at the effects of day care on emotional development and on the attachment relationship. Most of the studies reviewed had uncovered no differences between the two groups of children. However, a more recent study by Vaughn, Deane, and Waters (1985) reported that children who started day care before age 1 were more likely to develop insecure attachments. For those who started day care after age 1, there were no effects on attachment.

In the Belsky and Steinberg review, the most consistent differences between day-care and home-reared children were in their social development. Overall, children in day care were more oriented toward peers. In one study, 19 three- and four-year-old children who had been in day care for more than two years were compared with 19 children who had been in day care only four months. Rated on nine behavior scales, the two groups of children differed on three: Day-care children were more physically and verbally advanced, they were less cooperative with adults, and they were more physically active. Another study of these same children found that those who had just begun day care spent more time interacting with adults than with children.

Overall, given the large number of behaviors that researchers have exam-

Many studies have compared children raised in day-care centers with those raised at home.

ined, the differences between day-care and home-care children are strikingly small. Of course, critics could always charge that other tests of other behaviors, or more sensitive measures, might show differences. It is just not logically possible to demonstrate conclusively that day care is always as good as home care.

We shall have to wait until day-care children grow up to study possible long-term effects of their early experience. Further, it is important to note that most studies of the effects of day care take place in centers that are of good quality. As we saw above, Kagan and his associates actually set up their own center, with low child-caretaker ratios and well-trained child-care workers. Unfortunately, more than 60% of centers in the United States are considered to be only fair to poor in quality (Belsky & Steinberg, 1978). Thus, we need to find out specifically whether poor-quality day care has harmful effects.

After reviewing all the studies conducted to that point, one researcher (Etaugh, 1980) conservatively concluded that the available evidence "does not warrant the sweeping conclusion that nonmaternal care is not harmful to young children. The evidence does permit the more cautious conclusion that high-quality nonmaternal care has not been found to have negative effects on the development of preschool children" (p. 316).

A New Perspective on Early Experience?

If day-care children do grow up to be just as happy and emotionally well adjusted as children reared at home by their mothers, this might suggest that Bowlby overemphasized the importance of the mother-infant bond. It might even suggest that the first few years of life could be no more critical than any other period of development.

This idea goes against traditional wisdom. At least since Freud, developmental psychologists have emphasized the importance of childhood experiences in determining adult personality. The traditional view may place a heavy burden on anxious parents. For example, Burton White (1975) wrote: "Sometimes when I present my views about the importance of the first three years of life I notice sad looks coming over the faces of parents . . . followed by the questions, 'Is it all over after three? Is there nothing further I can do to be useful?' " (p. 257). Although he mentions several qualifications, White goes on to say that "Answering these questions is rather difficult for me because *to some extent* I really believe that it *is* too late after age three."

However, White (1975) does have a number of suggestions for ways in which parents can provide the best learning environment for their young children. First, he says, they should design the living quarters so that the child is protected from dangers and is free to explore. For example, a child should be able to pull pots and pans from a kitchen cabinet without finding a knife in the same place. Second, parents should be available as consultants for their children. In this role, they can provide assistance if needed and can talk to the child about whatever is going on (like why pots make such a loud noise when dropped on the floor). Finally, White suggests that parents provide authority. They should set clear limits, but at the same time be free with praise and warmth.

While many researchers agree that these three child-rearing guidelines are reasonable, they consider White's emphasis on the first three years as the critical time in development to be rather extreme. In recent years many researchers have moved away from this pessimistic emphasis on early experiences.

One source of evidence that children may be more adaptable than previously believed comes from the victims of neglect in infancy. One classic case study (Davis, 1947) followed the later progress of a child who had been isolated with her deaf-mute mother until the age of 6 and deprived of any other human contact. The girl was later able to learn to speak and interact with other people surprisingly well.

Similarly, a study of adopted children who were refugees from war-torn areas of Greece and Korea found that they developed normally. Despite their having many emotional problems when they arrived in the United States and stress due to the need to adapt to a new language and a new culture, most of these children were emotionally and physically healthy when they were reexamined six years later (Rathbun, McLaughlin, Bennett, & Garland, 1965).

Other systematic studies of neglected children who were removed from their homes by court order, of children who were raised in poverty in rural Guatemala, and of other infants deprived in various ways (Clarke & Clarke, 1976) all point in the same direction: Children seem quite resilient. The first few years of life may prove to be no more important—or less important—than any other period of development.

According to this optimistic view, if a child is deprived during the first few years of life, the resulting problems can be corrected by later improving the quality of care. Most developmental psychologists now believe that human beings are surprisingly flexible and that each of us can continue to change and to grow for as long as we live.

Summary

Heredity: Behavioral Genetics

- **Developmental psychology** is the study of how and why people change physically, intellectually, and emotionally as they grow from infancy to old age.
- **Behavioral genetics**, the study of the inheritance of *behavioral* characteristics, is a subfield of the science of **genetics**, which studies the transmission of inherited characteristics.
- Some researchers in the field of behavioral genetics study the way **genotypes**, the genetic composition of the individual, are expressed when environmental features are held constant.
- **Genes** are the physical structures that transmit characteristics from parent to child.
- **Chromosomes** are long, thin structures in the nucleus of every cell that contain hundreds or thousands of genes.
- Identical twins are called **monozygotic** because they develop from the division of a single fertilized egg (zygote) and thus have precisely the same genes.
- Fraternal twins are called **dizygotic** because they develop from two different eggs that happen to be fertilized by two different sperm at the same time.

Physical Development

- **Maturation** refers to sequences of growth and internal bodily changes that are primarily determined by biological factors.
- Prenatally, the fertilized egg, called a **zygote**, begins to develop immediately.
- The developing organism is called an **embryo** during the next stage of development, from about the second to the eighth week of pregnancy.
- From the time bone cells begin to develop, about eight weeks after conception, the developing organism is called a **fetus**.
- The newborn baby enters the world with a number of **reflexes**, involuntary acts automatically elicited by certain stimuli.
- **Norms**, standard figures that describe the performance of the average person, can be used to chart the course of a baby's motor development.
- Researchers in infant perceptual development study the way infants see, hear, and feel.
- A device called a *visual cliff* has been used to test infant depth perception.

Cognitive Development

- Piaget studied cognitive development (the growth of intelligence) to establish a biological basis for **epistemology**, the philosophical study of the nature of knowledge.

- Piaget suggested that in the **sensorimotor stage**, which lasts roughly the first two years of life, infants gradually discover the relationships between sensations and their motor acts.

- During the sensorimotor stage, infants achieve **object permanence**: the awareness that objects continue to exist even when they are not present to be seen, touched, or sensed.

- **Egocentrism**, which involves the child's failure to take into account the perspective of another person, is high in the sensorimotor stage but declines throughout the next (preoperational) stage.

- Symbolic thought first appears in the **preoperational stage**, from roughly 2 to 7 years, as the child gradually learns to use speech, play, gestures, and mental images to represent the world.

- **Operations** are the mental actions that reorganize one's views of the world.

- During the **concrete-operational** stage (roughly ages 7 to 11), the child becomes capable of logical thought but only regarding concrete, observable objects.

- The best-known landmark of concrete-operational ability is **conservation**: the recognition that certain basic properties of objects (such as number and volume) remain constant even when appearances change.

- Closely linked to conservation is the mental operation of **reversibility**, in which a person can think of a transformation that would restore an original condition.

- In the **formal-operational stage**, which can begin as early as age 11, the child is capable of solving abstract problems and dealing with hypothetical possibilities.

Personality and Social Development

- **Social cognition** refers to the understanding of the social world, including other people's behavior, thoughts, and feelings.

- **Personality** can be defined as an individual's characteristic pattern of thought, behavior, and emotions.

- One aspect of personality is **temperament**, the underlying energy level or other factor that helps produce a consistent style of responding in many different situations.

- From their studies of early differences in temperament, Thomas, Chess, and Birch identified three general personality types: easy, difficult, and slow to warm up.

- On the basis of research with infant rhesus monkeys, Harlow proposed that there is a **critical period** for motherly love, a fixed interval during which key events had to occur if normal development was to follow.

- **Stranger anxiety** refers to a phase in which infants seem anxious when strangers are nearby.

- **Separation anxiety** is a more profound distress whenever a child is separated from its mother or primary caretaker.

- Laboratory studies of human attachment have revealed two attachment patterns in human babies: secure attachment and insecure attachment.

Critical Thinking Exercises Discussions

The Pendulum Problem

This chapter's application of scientific concepts focuses on Piaget's pendulum problem (what variable or variables determine how fast a pendulum swings back and forth). Piaget formulated this problem to help illustrate the difference between concrete- and formal-operational thinking skills. Formal operations are critical thinking skills *par excellence;* they allow individuals to think critically about a broad range of problems, even in areas with which they are unfamiliar.

. The critical thinking skills most salient to the pendulum process involve a *systematic* testing of hypotheses about the variables affecting the pendulum's speed. The key strategy of the formal-operational thinker is to hold everything constant except the variable being tested at each step of the problem-solving process. Students who actually employ this systematic procedure while testing their hypotheses should be able to discover that the sole variable responsible for the speed of the pendulum's movement is length of the string.

Ask Doctor Spock

If you read this material closely, you noticed that Dr. Spock did not cite any evidence to support these conclusions. To a developmental psychologist, the idea that *all* children who are frequently scolded will grow up to be guilty seems far too simplistic. Similarly, the notion that hostile caretakers produce hostile children would only be totally accepted if it were backed by systematic research. The critical thinker will consider only the hard facts and will disregard unsupported conclusions, no matter how logical they appear.

While this popular guidebook on child care may provide accurate advice on medical matters, many of its psychological claims seem to be based on common sense or casual observations. As we have stressed throughout this text, the critical consumer must always remember that common sense can lead to incorrect conclusions.

ADOLESCENCE AND ADULTHOOD

Chapter 10

*I*n our society, it is difficult to understand truly the problems and feelings of people in a different age group. The 18-year-old who is just beginning college will probably find it impossible to explain the hopes and fears of this new world to her 12-year-old brother. But the same college student, in turn, may find it very difficult to imagine herself as a 35-year-old mother of two children, forced to stay at a job she doesn't like in order to support her family. Similarly, the 63-year-old man who fears retirement may get little real sympathy and understanding from his co-workers, even if they are only a few years younger. Thus, one may face many "generation gaps" in the journey through life.

In the preface to his book *The Seasons of a Man's Life,* researcher Daniel Levinson (1978) eloquently described one implication of this ignorance about other age groups:

> The most distressing fear in early childhood is that there is no life after youth. Young adults often feel that to pass 30 is to be "over the hill," and they are given little beyond hollow clichés to provide a fuller sense of the actual problems and possibilities of adult life at different ages. The middle years, they imagine, will bring triviality and meaningless comfort at best, stagnation and hopelessness at worst. . . .

> Adults hope that life begins at 40—but the great anxiety is that it ends there. The result of this pervasive dread about middle age is almost complete silence about the experiences of being adult. The concrete character of adult life is one of the best-kept secrets of our society. (p. IX)

Until quite recently, social scientists have offered little to help us understand the way people in our society change as they grow older. Most developmental psychologists have concentrated on the dramatic changes that occur in the first few years of life. Relatively few have focused on adolescence or old age, and fewer still have studied the changes that occur through adulthood and middle age. If you had taken an introductory psychology course in 1960 or 1970, your textbook probably would not have included a chapter like this one, describing development in adolescence and adulthood. Only recently have large numbers of researchers begun to study development as a lifelong process extending from the cradle to the grave.

Many developmental psychologists are currently exploring these new frontiers to discover how we change and how we remain the same over the full life cycle. Since wide-scale research is just beginning, there are many gaps in our knowledge. As a result, it is difficult to provide an overview of the physical, perceptual, cognitive, and personality changes associated with each phase of later development, as we did for childhood in Chapter 9. Instead, this chapter focuses on some of the most influential topics and lines of research in this rapidly growing area.

Most studies of adolescence and adulthood are also limited in another way. While researchers in such areas as learning, memory, sensation, and perception try to find general laws that apply to all human beings, many of the developmental changes described in this chapter probably apply only to certain types of technologically sophisticated twentieth-century Western societies. In prehistoric times, for example, few people lived to the age of 40; those who managed to survive into their thirties were therefore perceived as wise elders (Lerner, 1976). Thirty-five-year-old Americans are rarely viewed in this way today. Developmental processes found in our culture do not necessarily apply to other times and other places.

Erikson's "Eight Ages of Man"

Erik Erikson was one of the first and most influential theorists to chart the course of development over the entire life span. Erikson took a psychoanalytic approach, building on the foundations laid by Sigmund Freud's theory of four psychosexual stages of development (see Chapter 12). Erikson stressed the importance of cultural influences on development and outlined eight **psychosocial stages**, periods during which all individuals must confront a common crisis, caused in part by the new demands posed by different phases of life. The individual who resolves such a crisis improperly will, according to Erikson, have later problems as a result. The first four are similar to Freud's oral, anal, phallic, and genital stages; the last four were added by Erikson to provide a fuller account of the entire life cycle. Here is an outline of what Erikson called the "eight ages of man."

1. *Trust versus mistrust.* In the first year of life, infants must gradually learn to trust their mothers or other caretakers to satisfy their basic needs. This can help lead to a more general sense of trust in society and in themselves.

psychosocial stages According to Erikson, the periods when people must face certain crises caused, in part, by new demands posed at different phases of life.

**ERIK ERIKSON
(1902–   )**

Erikson is best known for his psychoanalytic theory of the "eight ages of man." In early adulthood, he wandered through Europe trying to earn a living as an artist. He took a job teaching art at a school founded by Anna Freud, a famous analyst in her own right and also the daughter of Sigmund Freud. She was impressed by Erikson's ability to work with children and invited him to enter the Vienna Psychoanalytic Institute. When Hitler's forces threatened to overrun Europe, Erikson fled to the United States to work as a therapist and continue his education. In a long and distinguished career, Erikson published records of his investigations ranging from psychoanalytic biographies of Martin Luther and Mahatma Gandhi to anthropological studies of the Sioux and Yurok Indians.

2. *Autonomy versus shame and doubt.* The second year brings a new source of conflict between children's growing independence and their need to depend on adults. As they become capable of walking and talking, children are faced for the first time with important distinctions between good and bad and yes and no. Parental firmness and consistency can lead to a sense of autonomy, but too much criticism can burden children with a lifelong sense of shame and self-doubt.

3. *Initiative versus guilt.* In the third or fourth year, toddlers begin to play at being adults. They can initiate their own activities to a greater extent than before. Conscience begins to develop, as children measure themselves against external standards. If parents are overly harsh and restrictive, children may lose the desire to initiate new activities and instead be overwhelmed by guilt.

4. *Industry versus inferiority.* From the age of 6 or 7 to puberty, schoolchildren are faced with the task of learning what their culture expects of them and how to achieve it. One danger of this stage is that children may conclude that their own status or skills are inadequate; this can sometimes establish a lifelong pattern of feeling of inferiority. More often, children learn to become industrious and productive members of society.

5. *Identity versus identity confusion.* Around puberty, dramatic physical and emotional changes lead adolescents to question their own identity, to wonder who they really are. Failure to integrate all the different roles each person must fill can lead to identity confusion, with no firm sense of self.

6. *Intimacy versus isolation.* The major challenge of young adulthood involves commitment to relationships and to a career. The people who are secure in their own identity can make the compromises necessary for an intimate partnership with another person. The alternative is to remain isolated from others. The isolated person may have many affairs, or even a single long-term relationship, but always avoids true emotional closeness.

7. *Generativity versus stagnation.* In middle age, the major crisis involves a sense of making a contribution to society; *generativity* is a concern for establishing and guiding the next generation. It may be expressed in a variety of ways of giving to others, whether it be to our own children or to careers and activities designed to help younger people find their place in society. The generative person leads a productive life that can serve as a model for the next generation. The other side of the coin is *stagnation*—a selfish concern with one's own goals that can lead middle-aged people to become insensitive to the needs of others or to live in the past.

8. *Integrity versus despair.* Finally, in old age, some people achieve integration; they look back over life with a true long-term perspective and a sense of satisfaction, accepting the bad as well as the good. For those with a sense of integrity, death loses some of its final sting. Others despair that there is no time left to pursue new paths; they face death with bitterness and regrets.

Like many other psychoanalytic theories, Erikson's conclusions were based on his clinical experience rather than on empirical data from a series of systematic tests. Nevertheless, many professionals who deal with problems of adult adjustment have found this scheme very useful. To this day, it remains one of the most complete accounts of the entire life cycle; most developmental psychologists have focused on one specific aspect or period of development rather than trying to develop a coherent view of the life span.

Critics wonder whether these 8 stages are really the best way of subdividing the life cycle. Might there really be 6 ages, or 7, or 23? Only future research can tell. Erikson is important to psychology not because he provided the final answers about the human life cycle, but because he was one of the first to ask the questions. And, as you will see in this chapter's description of the identity and intimacy crises, some of Erikson's ideas have stimulated research that has begun to help us specify more precisely how individuals change as they grow older.

Male-Female Differences

Psychologists are people who live and work in a specific society, and their research will almost inevitably reflect some of the current biases of their culture. In the 1960s and 1970s, many Americans became interested in "women's issues." In 1972, a new division of the American Psychological Association devoting itself exclusively to the psychology of women was formed. Many researchers began to examine issues that had long been ignored by this male-dominated profession. One of the early targets of such researchers was Erikson's theory of development. Feminists like Rae Carlson and Carol Gilligan argued that Erikson's theory, like several other theories formulated by men, was really a theory of male development rather than of human development. According to the feminists, these male theories emphasized such "male" concerns as identity, autonomy, and impartial justice at the expense of such "female" concerns as intimacy, caring, and compassion. Moreover, they suggest, Erikson was simply incorrect in assuming that the identity crisis must always be resolved before the intimacy crisis; indeed, they argue, women—and perhaps men, too—may work through both of these life issues simultaneously, or even reverse their order (Franz & White, 1985).

A good deal of valuable research has grown out of such feminist concerns. Much of the research has been directed at determining the extent to which men and women differ and the causes of any sex differences. Other research has been directed at identifying sexual stereotypes— the unquestioned assumptions that people hold about men and women. In this whole area, it has proved difficult to separate stereotype from reality.

Sexual Stereotypes

In our society, males and females have traditionally been thought to differ in a number of important ways. In one typical study of sexual stereotyping (Rosenkrantz, Vogel, Bee, Broverman, & Broverman, 1968), the average subject

Tradition has defined different roles for males and females in our society.

described men as more competent, skillful, assertive, and aggressive than women. As a group, women were seen as warmer and more emotionally expressive than men. One does not have to look far to find additional evidence for the existence of such stereotypes.

When a feminist group from New Jersey called Women on Words and Images analyzed 134 children's readers, they found that most of the fictional characters were male, whether the stories were about children, adults, or even animals. Boys were characterized as curious, clever, and adventurous; girls, as fearful and incompetent. The adult males portrayed in these books held 147 different jobs, ranging from astronauts and cowboys to clowns. The career options for females were more limited—only 26 different occupations, including such impractical choices as circus fat lady and witch. An updated survey of books published after 1972 found some changes but still an overwhelming male bias (Tavris & Offir, 1977).

Some psychologists claim that all this propaganda takes a heavy toll on female self-esteem. In one often-quoted study (Goldberg, 1968), college women were asked to rate short articles on their persuasive impact, profundity, professional competence, and other criteria. Some of the articles were consistently rated higher when these female students thought they had been written by men. In another study (Pheterson, Kiesler, & Goldberg, 1971), two groups of women judged the quality of several paintings. Some of the paintings were rated more highly when the artist was thought to be a male rather than a female.

The major lesson of these studies—that women often underrate the works of other females—has been widely publicized. Some of the more subtle feelings however, have often been ignored. For example, paintings by male artists were rated more highly only when they were described as "attempts" or "entries"; paintings described as prizewinners were equally valued whether the artist was said to be male or female.

Further, some later studies failed to replicate the original finding. When a group of students from the University of California at Berkeley were given a task similar to Goldberg's original procedure, women did not seem biased against other women (Isaacs, 1981). The author argued that this finding reflected the effects of women's liberation; in the few years between the two studies, the bias had been reduced. These complications serve as another reminder of the fact that complex beliefs and behavior patterns are affected by culture, and findings from one time and place may or may not apply to another.

In any case, people's beliefs about differences between the sexes can affect their perceptions and behavior from the moment of birth, when the obstetrician announces, "It's a boy" or "It's a girl." In one classic study (Rubin, Provenzano, & Luria, 1974), fathers were asked to describe their first babies almost immediately after they were born; mothers were asked the same questions within 24 hours of birth. Despite the fact that objective hospital records showed that the baby boys and girls in this study were almost identical in terms of color, muscle tone, reflex responses, and even weight and length, the parents described them differently. Baby girls were perceived as softer, finer-featured, smaller, and less attentive. The fathers were particularly susceptible to this type of selective perception and the tendency to describe sons and daughters differently. Other studies have shown that as children grow, fathers pressure their children to behave in "sex-appropriate" ways, such as encouraging boys to play with toy armies and girls to play with dollhouses (Maccoby, 1980).

No one knows whether these pressures will be reduced as society's expectations for little boys and little girls change. Indeed, we do not even know for certain whether such differences in adult behavior lead to any lasting differences in behavior between boys and girls. The task of identifying stable sex differences has proved extremely difficult.

Research on Sex Differences

In 1974, Eleanor Maccoby and Carol Jacklin published a careful review of over 2,000 studies of the differences between males and females. Many common sexual stereotypes turned out to be myths. For example, girls are not more sociable than boys, they are not more suggestible, and they do not have lower self-esteem. Maccoby and Jacklin did, however, find evidence that by adolescence clear differences have emerged between the sexes in four main areas: verbal ability, visual-spatial ability, mathematical ability, and aggressiveness.

Girls seem to mature more rapidly in terms of verbal skills. From the preschool years through early adolescence, the sexes seem equal in this respect. But beginning around age 11 and continuing at least through high school, girls become more verbal. They have larger vocabularies, are more fluent, and score higher in reading comprehension and creative writing.

In contrast, adolescent boys do better on visual-spatial tasks such as reading maps, solving mazes, and locating hidden geometric patterns. Similarly, greater male facility with mathematical problems also becomes established in adolescence. But since many mathematical problems involve verbal abilities, the relative standings of the sexes may vary for some types of problems.

Finally, cultural stereotypes about aggression have some basis in fact. Boys are more aggressive than girls, on the average, both physically and verbally. This difference has been observed in many cultures, and it appears much earlier in development than other sex differences. Greater male aggression can be observed in children as young as 2 or 2½. This male-female difference applies to indirect measures of aggression, such as mock fighting and fantasy, as well as direct measures. At least until their early twenties, men remain more aggressive than women; few statistics are available for older adults.

Recent research on sex differences in adults has focused considerable attention on issues of emotionality and expressiveness. There is evidence from a number of studies (e.g., Rubin, 1976) that women are more open in expressing their feelings than men and that inexpressiveness in husbands is a source of frustration for wives. Some investigators note that anger is one emotion that men often express quite freely (Gelles, 1972). In general, there is support for the view that women are both more in tune with a wider range of feelings than men and readier to talk about their feelings with "intimate others."

When faced with such information concerning possible sex differences, many people are likely to ask, "So what?" That is, are any differences between the sexes large enough to have any important impact on life in a complex technological society?

One answer comes from an analysis of the cognitive differences mentioned earlier—girls' greater verbal skills and boys' greater abilities in mathematics and visual-spatial tasks like map reading. When Janet Hyde (1981) reanalyzed 53 of the studies from Maccoby and Jacklin's original 1974 review, she found that while sex differences were quite consistent, they were also rather small. (In technical terms, they ranged from .24 to .52 standard deviations.)

After noting how small the average sex differences were, Hyde was particularly concerned with the possibility of misinterpretation. For example, a guidance counselor would be very wrong to conclude that young girls should not try to become engineers or computer programmers because females lack mathematical ability. This fear led Hyde to wonder whether such differences should even be mentioned in introductory textbooks. "At the very least," she cautioned, it is "important to stress how small the differences are and how unwise it would be to apply them in counseling a given individual" (1981, p. 897).

In Chapter 13, we emphasize that the average performance of a particular group (such as women) does *not* apply to every individual. To cite one simple commonsense example, men are taller than women, but many women are taller than some men. Similarly, sex differences in aggression and certain cognitive abilities are quite consistent on the average, but there are many individual exceptions.

Sources of Sex Differences

While there is no final agreement as to which sex differences are "real" and not just cultural stereotypes, social scientists argue about the sources of the sex differences in which they believe. One of the most common arguments concerns whether particular differences are caused by nature or nurture. (See Chapter 9 regarding the interaction of biology and environment and the difficulty in distinguishing between the effects of each on the individual.)

In the case of aggression, Maccoby and Jacklin (1974) argue that "the sex difference has a biological foundation" (p. 242). They were careful to note that there is clear evidence that aggression is affected by learning; nevertheless, they believed that males inherited a tendency to react more aggressively. They cited four separate lines of evidence for this belief: Males are more aggressive than females in all known human societies; sex differences in aggression appear early in life; similar sex differences are found in apes and other primates; and higher levels of male sex hormones can induce aggression.

Each of these assertions was challenged in a review by Todd Tieger (1980) and subsequently defended again by Maccoby and Jacklin (1980). The details of these arguments and counterarguments quickly became rather involved, concerning both the quality of the original research and the various authors' interpretations. For example, Tieger summarized the results of 23 comparisons of male and female children between the ages of 2 and 6 and concluded that there is no consistent difference in the level of aggressiveness at this tender age (although he did concede that after the age of 6, males are more aggressive). Maccoby and Jacklin (1980) countered with a fuller tabulation of 38 experimental comparisons that led to the opposite conclusion—even among preschoolers, males are more aggressive than females.

For now, it seems safe to conclude only that there may be a biological foundation for male aggressiveness. This issue has tremendous theoretical significance, and it is likely to take considerable time and effort to resolve. Moreover, as noted in Chapter 9, most developmental psychologists assume there is always an interaction between biological and environmental factors in the development of behavior.

The whole issue of sex differences is far from resolved. While developmental psychologists are typically interested in identifying universal developmental principles that apply to all human beings, some feminist researchers insist that males and females follow different developmental pathways through life. In our review of selected areas of research on adolescent and adult development, we indicate some of the sex differences that have been found. However, readers should keep in mind that an understanding of the nature of these sex differences—for example, how "real" they are, what their implications and causes are—requires an ongoing research effort.

Adolescence

Scientific studies of the teenage years are usually traced back to G. Stanley Hall's 1905 text *Adolescence,* which described "a period of storm and stress" in which "every step of the upward way is strewn with the wreckage of the body, mind, and morals" (p. xiii). This notion of *Sturm und Drang* (German for "storm and stress") is quite consistent with many popular stereotypes. American teenagers are often portrayed by the mass media as moody, rebellious, alternately energetic and lazy, and overly influenced by peer groups that bring them into conflict with parental values. Moreover, some psychologists have suggested that the combination of a developmental crisis over identity and the new intellectual abilities that come with formal-operational thinking (see Chapter 9) can propel many adolescents into conflicts with their parents (White & Speisman, 1977).

However, systematic research has provided a far more ambiguous picture. One study of the families of middle-class American adolescents (Bandura & Walters, 1959), suggested that adolescence is no more stressful than childhood or adulthood. This research found that the average adolescent accepted most parental values quite fully and associated with other adolescents who also shared these beliefs.

Historical, economic, and social forces can also influence the course of teenage development. Michael Katz (1975) studied how industrialization changed life patterns in Hamilton, Ontario, in the middle of the nineteenth century. In 1851, more than half of all 13- to 16-year-old boys in Hamilton did not work or attend school. Presumably, this large group of idle youth spent much of their time roaming the streets and giving teenagers a bad name. By 1871, as a result of increased opportunities for education and employment, less than 30% of the same group fell in this category. During the same 20-year period, the median age for leaving home rose from 17 to 22 for males. Clearly, these shifting social patterns influenced the activities of adolescents and the way they were perceived by society.

Studies of cultures that are quite different from ours and studies of subtle changes within a culture caused by historical forces suggest that the precise details of adolescent development do not remain constant. It seems likely that some individuals in any society will experience adolescence as a period of storm and stress. The exact proportion, and thus the accuracy of the general description of adolescence as a particulary stressful period, will vary from time to time and place to place.

However, there are some constant themes that influence the development of adolescents in every culture. The most obvious ones involve the physical changes that occur during this period.

Physical Development

The most obvious physical changes in adolescence are associated with **puberty**—the period when sexual maturation begins. Technically, puberty begins with the enlargement of the prostate gland and seminal vesicles in males and enlargement of the ovaries in females. The actual age at which these changes occur is determined by the action of many different hormones—substances secreted into the bloodstream by the pituitary and other endocrine glands (see Chapter 3). For example, at puberty the adrenal cortex, ovaries, and testes dramatically increase the secretion of the sex hormones known collectively as *androgens* (male hormones) and *estrogens* (female hormones). Both males and females have androgens and estrogens in the bloodstream; the sexes are distinguished by their relative proportions. Androgens dominate male biochemistry, estrogens are particularly plentiful in females.

The first sign of sexual development in girls is usually a slight increase in breast size and the appearance of pubic hair. This is followed by a **growth spurt**, a sudden increase in the rate of growth for both height and weight, and by the first menstrual period. Further breast growth, increases in the amount of pubic hair, and changes in the female sex organs go on for the next few years.

On the average, puberty begins about two years later for boys than for girls. The first sign of male puberty is an increase in the rate of growth of the testes and the scrotum. For males too, this early development is followed by a growth spurt in height and weight. Pubic hair usually begins to appear at the onset of puberty, while facial and body hair grow about two years later. The larynx, or Adam's apple, becomes much larger late in puberty, and the vocal cords inside the larynx double in length. When this change occurs abruptly, boys may have trouble controlling the vocal cords, and their voices "crack."

The precise timing of these events varies widely. Testicular growth in boys may begin as early as 9½ or as late as 13½ and still be in the normal range. For girls, the age at onset of menstruation can range from 10 to 16½. Thus, normal adolescents can mature sexually at many different ages. The

puberty The period when sexual maturation begins.

growth spurt A sudden increase in the rate of growth for both height and weight.

growth spurt usually occurs at the age of about 11 for girls and 13 for boys, although it, too, can occur over a wide range. This sudden growth can be a source of awkwardness and embarrassment. The head, hands, and feet tend to grow first, producing gawky adolescents whose bodies seem out of proportion by adult standards. The dramatic physical changes of adolescence often confuse teenagers, who are also undergoing cognitive changes that lead them to be preoccupied with their bodies, their selves, their families and friends, their values. (See Chapter 9 for a description of Piaget's formal-operational stage of cognitive development, which begins around puberty.)

Adolescents are often preoccupied with their physical appearance.

Moral Development

Adolescence is a period of physical, emotional, and cognitive change. The growing intellectual sophistication of teenagers coupled with the demand that they suddenly make important decisions about such issues as careers, relationships, and sexuality helps lead adolescents to ask questions not just about their own identities but also about moral standards, to begin to decide for themselves what is really right and what is really wrong.

One of the most influential techniques for studying the development of values and morals was developed by Lawrence Kohlberg for his doctoral dissertation in 1958. Building on earlier work by Jean Piaget, Kohlberg showed how the growth of cognitive abilities made it possible for adolescents to reason about moral values in increasingly sophisticated ways. Higher stages of morality could emerge only after thought became more logical, structured, and personalized.

It is important to emphazise Kohlberg's commitment to the cognitive paradigm; he was primarily concerned with the process of moral reasoning—how people decide what is moral and what is not. We begin with an overview of this influential cognitive approach before turning to the behavioral question of what people actually do.

KOHLBERG'S STAGES OF MORAL REASONING

For his Ph.D. thesis Kohlberg asked boys between the ages of 10 and 16 to resolve nine moral dilemmas. Here is the most famous one:

> In Europe, a woman was near death from a rare form of cancer. There was one drug that doctors thought might save her, a form of radium that a druggist in the same town had recently discovered. The druggist was charging $2,000, ten times what the drug cost him to make. The sick woman's husband, Heinz, went to everyone he knew to borrow the money, but he could only get together about half of what the drug cost. He told the druggist that his wife was dying and asked him to sell it cheaper or let him pay later. But the druggist said, "No." So Heinz got desperate and broke into the man's store to steal the drug for his wife.
>
> Should the husband have done that? Why?

Kohlberg was not particularly interested in whether each subject thought the husband should steal the drug; he argued that judgment depends too

TABLE 10.1

Kohlberg's Six Stages of Moral Reasoning

Orientation	Characteristics
PRECONVENTIONAL LEVEL	
Stage 1 Punishment and obedience orientation	Obeys rules to avoid punishment
Stage 2 Marketplace orientation	Seeks rewards, or having favors returned
CONVENTIONAL LEVEL	
Stage 3 Good-boy orientation	Conforms to avoid disapproval by others
Stage 4 Law-and-order orientation	Conforms to avoid blame by legitimate authorities
POSTCONVENTIONAL LEVEL	
Stage 5 Social contract, legalistic orientation	Obeys rules for approval by others concerned with the welfare of the community
Stage 6 Universal ethical principle orientation	Acts on basis of own abstract ethical principles, freely chosen

much on a person's religious or ethical upbringing. Instead, he analyzed the way each boy came to a decision—what sorts of factors were involved in actually making a choice.

The results led Kohlberg to distinguish between three levels of moral reasoning, which the boys seemed to progress through as they grew older. Each level consisted of two separate stages, for a total of six stages in the development of moral reasoning (see Table 10.1).

At the lowest level, some boys were said to be at the **preconventional level** of moral reasoning—they accepted parents' or society's commands because they wanted to gain rewards and avoid punishments. In other words, they simply responded to external rules. Most of the time, this type of reasoning was characteristic of children in Piaget's concrete-operational stage. For example, Kohlberg (1975) cites the response of one 10-year-old boy to Heinz's dilemma over the drug that could cure his wife:

"Why shouldn't you steal from a store?"

"It's not good to steal from the store. It's against the law. Someone could see you and call the police." (p. 36)

The preconventional level consisted of two separate stages. In the first, as seen in the quote, children simply try to avoid being punished for doing something bad. In the second, some notion of other people's needs enters the picture, but only at the most fundamental level of making a deal: "You scratch my back and I'll scratch yours." For example, a child might choose

preconventional level According to Kohlberg, a level of moral reasoning in which people accept society's commands primarily to gain rewards and avoid punishment.

not to reveal another person's secret so that later on the other person will not reveal the child's.

Next comes the **conventional level** of moral reasoning, at which a person accepts the standards of the family, society, or some other group. These conventional views are completely adopted as one's own. This type of reasoning can first appear in adolescence, with the emergence of Piaget's formal-operational thought. To illustrate this level, Kohlberg (1975) quoted the more sophisticated response to Heinz's dilemma of the same boy at the age of 17:

> "Why shouldn't you steal from a store?"
>
> "It's a matter of law. It's one of our rules that we are trying to help protect everyone, protect property, not just to protect the store. It's something that's needed in our society. It we didn't have these laws, people would steal, they wouldn't have to work for a living and our whole society would get out of kilter." (p. 36)

The first stage of the conventional level is often called the good-boy orientation, a stage of conformity to what most people expect of a good person. For the first time, judgments are based on people's intentions—whether they meant well. The second stage (reflected in the quote) is called the law-and-order orientation, because it involves an active support of society's laws and rules in the interest of maintaining social stability. Here, good intentions are not enough; rules must be obeyed because they provide the basis for an orderly society.

Finally, the highest level of moral reasoning is called the **postconventional level** because it involves the application of the universal principles of right and wrong, which are more fundamental than the laws of any specific society. At this more abstract level, each person must follow his or her own conscience, regardless of what society says. This type of reasoning becomes possible only in the advanced stages of formal-operational thought, and many adults never reach the postconventional level. As an example of this type of reasoning, Kohlberg (1975) quotes one more time from the same male subject, this time at the age of 24:

> "Why shouldn't someone steal from a store?"
>
> "It's violating another person's right, in this case to property."
>
> "Does the law enter in?"
>
> "Well, the law in most cases is based on what is morally right, so it's not a separate subject, it's a consideration."
>
> "What does "morality" or "morally right" mean to you?"
>
> "Recognizing the right of other individuals, first to life and then to do as he pleases as long as it doesn't interfere with somebody else's rights." (p. 36)

Here, too, there are two stages. In the first, what is right depends on a consensus reached by a society of people who may hold somewhat different values. Laws can change as society's idea of what is good changes. Finally, at the most advanced stage in Kohlberg's original scheme, judgments are based

conventional level According to Kohlberg, a level of moral reasoning in which society's standards are totally adopted as one's own.

postconventional level According to Kohlberg, a level of moral reasoning that involves applying universal principles of right and wrong that are more fundamental than the laws of any specific society.

on abstract universal ethical principles, such as the golden rule: Do unto others as you would have them do unto you.

Kohlberg argues that as a person grows, these six stages always appear in the same order. Not everyone goes through all six, but Kohlberg says that the stages always appear in the same order, no one will go through the postconventional level before the conventional, or the law-and-order stage before the good-boy stage. Studies of the growth of moral development among adolescents in other cultures, such as Mexico and Taiwan, are often cited to support the idea that this theory is not limited to the United States; the six stages are said to be universal.

Thus, Kohlberg believes that moral reasoning is linked to age; as people grow, their increasing cognitive capabilities make it possible for them to take increasingly sophisticated moral stands. But the fact that someone is intelligent enough to understand ethical principles does not necessarily mean that person will apply them. It is what logicians call a necessary, but not sufficient, condition.

Kohlberg has found that most children under 9, some adolescents, and many adolescent and adult criminals have preconventional morality. Conventional morality is the most common stage for adolescents and adults; only a few achieve the highest level of postconventional morality.

EVALUATING KOHLBERG'S THEORY

Many psychologists have challenged specific aspects of Kohlberg's theory and methods. Some have critized Kohlberg's actual test of nine moral dilemmas; others have questioned whether every person really moves through these stages, one after another, in every culture.

On a more fundamental level, psychologists who prefer the behavioral paradigm (see Chapter 1) wonder about the links between moral reasoning and moral action. When Blasi (1980) reviewed studies relating moral reasoning to delinquency, honesty, altruism, resistance to conformity, and other types of moral behavior, he found that the relationships are often rather complex.

As any priest can tell you, the fact that people know that something is right does not necessarily mean that they will do it. In one study (Hassett, 1981), adults were asked to predict their behavior in a number of everyday ethical dilemmas, such as whether to return extra change to a grocery clerk. In many cases, people said that keeping the change would be wrong, but they would do it anyway. On a list of eight mundane ethical dilemmas of this sort (including driving away without leaving a note after scratching a parked car and buying a stolen color TV set), two out of three respondents predicted that in at least one case, they would act in a way that they themselves considered wrong. This finding and others suggest one important question for future studies of moral behavior: Under what conditions are people most likely to choose a course of action they consider wrong?

Among researchers who prefer Kohlberg's cognitive approach, another question that is attracting increasing attention involves possible differences between male and female conceptions of morality. The original proposal of six stages of moral reasoning was based on a study of males. Later research found that when these criteria were applied to women's responses, most reflected a stage-three concern with approval by others. Carol Gilligan (1982) argues that while men may conceive of morality in terms of abstract ethical principles, women are more concerned with the immediate goal of not hurting the people around them. Women's judgments of morality are thus more closely tied to feelings of empathy and compassion for others than those of men.

Much remains to be learned about possible differences between male and female conceptions of morality. However, the simple fact that psychologists have begun to explore this question is a sign of progress toward more sophisticated theories of human behavior.

Personality Development: Identity

The same cognitive development processes that are associated with advances in moral reasoning also appear to be involved in adolescents' preoccupations with who they are. The suddenness of the physical changes of puberty combined with a new intellectual sophistication may result in the adolescent's experiencing considerable confusion over his or her identity. While *identity crisis* is now a familiar expression, it entered the language only a few decades ago. Psychoanalyst Erik Erikson and his co-workers invented the term during World War II to describe the psychiatric disturbance of some soldiers who seemed to lose their sense of personal identity as a result of the stress of combat. Later, Erikson extended the expression **identity crisis** to include "severely conflicted young people whose sense of confusion is due . . . to a war within themselves" (Erikson, 1963, p. 17).

Many psychologists believe that the most fundamental problem of adolescents in our society is to answer the question: "Who am I?" Erikson included the crisis of establishing a strong sense of personal identity as one of his eight basic stages of development. Thus, according to Erikson, adolescents are particularly concerned with finding their own personal spot in adult society and must begin a long and painful process of assessing personal strengths and weaknesses to help set realistic goals. All people want to meet their potential and carve out the best possible life for themselves. At the same time, adolescents are concerned with remaining true to their ideals. The alternative is *identity confusion,* a failure to integrate perceptions of oneself into a coherent whole.

Our society frees adolescents from most responsibilities so that they have time to experiment with different types of relationships with people of both sexes, with different ways of acting and talking, even with political ideologies and philosophies of life. According to Erikson, crushes, infatuations, and puppy love are also involved with the identity crisis: Adolescents try to gain insights into their own character partly by seeing themselves idealized through the eyes of others. Even the clannishness and coolness of adolescents who form tight social groups and cliques is seen by Erikson as a step in the search for identity—teenagers help one another through this insecure period by providing stereotypes of acceptable behavior that set their group apart from others.

Researchers who have studied the process of achieving identity have distinguished between four different states in dealing with these issues. Some

identity crisis The crisis of establishing a strong sense of personal identity.

people are referred to as *identity achievers* because they have completed a period of decision making and have accepted certain occupational and ideological goals. A second group are called *foreclosures;* they too have accepted certain goals, but they seem to have adopted them directly from their parents, without going through a period of crisis or decision making. *Identity diffusions* are those who have no clear goals, whether or not they went through a period of crisis. Finally, people who are actively trying to set their own occupational or ideological goals are called *moratoriums;* they are in an identity crisis.

Many studies have been done contrasting the characteristics of adolescents in each of these groups. For example, moratoriums are the most anxious of the four groups, as might be expected from the fact that they are facing an identity crisis. Further, both identity achievers and moratoriums seem to be more independent and to take more responsibility for their actions than adolescents in the foreclosure or identity-diffusion categories.

Several studies have suggested that the ages 18 to 21 are a very important period for establishing identity, particularly for people who attend college. Interestingly, foreclosures tend to be most satisfied with their college experience, perhaps because it helps them progress toward unambiguous occupational goals. Moratoriums are the least satisfied with their college experiences and tend to change their majors more than any other group (Marcia, 1980).

Other studies of these groups bear more directly on Erikson's idea that people must achieve a sense of identity before they become capable of intimate relationships. One study that graded the depth and mutual basis of adolescents' interpersonal relationships found that identity achievers and moratoriums achieved the most intimacy. Foreclosures were more likely to have "stereotyped relationships" that lacked depth, and identity diffusions were often isolated from other people (Orlofsky, Marcia, & Lesser, 1973). It is particularly interesting that foreclosures, who have a strong sense of identity, lack intimate relationships. The greater intimacy of the moratoriums, who were actually experiencing identity crises, suggests that simply achieving identity is not the only factor in intimacy; other personal characteristics may be more important for deep relationships.

Adolescence is now recognized as a major developmental period, a time of important physical, cognitive, moral, and psychosocial change. It is often seen as a time of transition—but transition to what? What is the nature of the period that follows adolescence? Are there more important changes, or is adulthood a time of stability and consolidation?

Adulthood

If the self-appointed experts are to be believed, American society worships youth. But it is only in adulthood that most people become fully productive and achieve their career goals. Adulthood can bring a new perspective on life, as a middle-aged woman noted:

It is as if I'm looking at a three-way mirror. In one mirror I see part of myself in my mother who is growing old, and part of her in me. In the other mirror,

I see part of myself in my daughter. I have had some dramatic insights, just from looking in those mirrors. . . . . It is a set of revelations that I suppose can only come when you are in the middle of three generations. (Neugarten, 1975, p. 383)

Social scientists are just beginning to collect data on the perspective provided by adulthood and the many other issues in adult development, from family life and relationships to work, leisure, and retirement. In this introduction, we focus on three of the most promising lines of research: stages of adult development, personality mechanisms associated with healthy adjustment, and sexuality.

Personality Development: Intimacy

According to Erikson's "eight ages of man," the most important issue in young adulthood is intimacy versus isolation. As a developmental task, **intimacy** includes the challenge of making a commitment to another person and developing and maintaining a mature relationship. As researchers in this area note, we have many relationships with other people, but few of these qualify as truly intimate.

Psychologists have identified three major features that characterize intimate relationships: interdependence, emotional attachment, and sharing and caring. Interdependence refers to the fact that two people rely on each other, and each one's behavior is affected by the other. Emotional attachment refers to the special affection or love for another person that one doesn't feel for most other people. Finally, an intimate relationship lets a person share feelings and problems with someone, and gives him or her a chance to care for and help this special person (Brehm, 1985).

The emphasis on these three features varies for different people and changes over time. For example, a newly married couple may not be particularly interdependent. Moreover, differing needs of the husband and wife for sharing feelings and problems may have an impact on the marital adjustment of the young couple (White et al., 1986). Nevertheless, interdependence is likely to increase after the couple has been together for 5 or 10 or 20 years.

To understand how the need for intimacy relates to other aspects of psychological development, McAdams and Valliant (1982) rated stories that men had made up when they were 30 years old. In analyzing the stories, he looked for themes that are associated with intimacy, such as a concern for responsibility and commitment and a desire to share feelings with another person. He then correlated these scores to the same men's overall adjustment 17 years later. McAdams found that those with a high need for intimacy at age 30 reported more satisfaction with their marriages and their jobs at age 47.

McAdams also conducted a survey of 1,200 men and women to see how intimacy needs related to general functioning. People who had a high need for intimacy were generally happier, more secure, and had a better feeling of well-being than those who had low scores on intimacy. This finding further supported the notion that a high need for intimacy has positive effects.

Researchers working in the Eriksonian tradition have approached intimacy the same way they have approached identity, that is, by identifying the

intimacy The challenge of making a commitment to another person and developing and maintaining a mature relationship.

Psychologists have identified three major features of intimate relationships: interdependence, emotional attachment, and sharing and caring.

statuses into which individuals may fall. Orlofsky (e.g., Orlofsky, Marcia & Lesser, 1973) has suggested that there are five basic intimacy statuses: intimate, preintimate, stereotyped relationships, isolate, and pseudointimate. These statuses are defined by the nature of relationships with both sexes: Are they open and honest? Is there mutual care and respect? Are differences dealt with equitably? Are sexual attitudes and behavior mature?

Bill is an example of an *intimate* individual. He works at developing mutual relationships and has a number of close friends with whom he discusses personal matters. He has a satisfying sexual relationship with his long-time girlfriend, whom he considers to be one of his best and closest friends. He is able to be open and honest in his feelings toward her, admitting to anger as well as affection. He is looking forward to getting married someday, although he is not completely sure that this is the woman he will marry. He is highly self-aware and has a genuine interest in and concern for others.

Mark is *preintimate*. He has had some dating experience, but he has never had a really intimate love relationship with a woman. He has had women friends as well as a number of close friendships with other men. He has several characteristics—openness, responsibility, mutuality, and a respect for the independence of others—that make him ready for an intimate relationship. However, he still feels conflict and ambivalence about entering into a committed and intimate sexual relationship with a woman.

Jonathan is in the status that Orlofsky calls *stereotyped relationships*. Jonathan is a rather immature young man whose relationships are fairly superficial. He has a number of friends with whom he does things, such as going to ball games, but these relationships lack depth. Jonathan is a playboy who dates regularly, enjoys sex, and is constantly "on the make." Unlike intimate and preintimate individuals, he has little self-awareness and treats others principally as objects.

Michael is what Orlofsky would call an *isolate*. He has had few enduring personal relationships and seldom initiates social contacts. He hardly ever dates and never sees the same girl more than two or three times. He is anxious, immature, and lacks assertiveness and social skills. He seems to be afraid to enter into a sexual relationship with a woman and is reluctant to expose his thoughts and feelings to anybody. He considers himself, and is considered by others, to be a loner.

Ralph is *pseudointimate*. He has entered into a commitment with his fiancée, Joanne, but this relationship, like his relationships with male friends, lacks depth. He does not like to talk much about his feelings with anybody, and he constantly insists that if Joanne really loved him, she would not always be pushing him to open up. He is looking forward to marrying her because she is attractive, comes from a "good background," and is likely to be a good hostess at the business functions he foresees as part of his professional future. He thinks sex is fine, but it has already become fairly routinized for him.

The research that generated Orlofsky's five intimacy statuses was conducted with college males. As is so often the case, other researchers have come along to suggest that Orlofsky's system needs revision if it is to be relevant to females. Two additional intimacy statuses have been identified that are seen as particularly relevant to women: committed merger and uncommitted merger. Individuals in both of these merger statuses have love relationships characterized by neediness and dependency rather than mature choice. As in the intimate status, individuals in *committed mergers* have established long-term, committed, heterosexual relationships. Like individuals in the preintimate, isolate, and stereotyped relationships statuses, people in *uncommitted mergers* are not committed to any long-term relationship.

Sheila is a good example of the committed-merger status. She appears to have little identity apart from her live-in boyfriend. Her involvement in this relationship is deep and intense to the point of desperation. She will do anything to maintain the relationship with her boyfriend and tries to capitalize on her sexual wiles to keep him interested in her. He often seems indifferent to her efforts to please him and has even been abusive to her. Despite his callousness, she is convinced that she can never be happy unless they get married.

Rhoda falls into the uncommitted-merger status. She is quick to "fall in love" and enter into a sexual relationship, but she also quickly becomes disappointed and is apt to end relationships abruptly. Whenever she is in a relationship, she is jealous of everybody who is friendly with her partner. She is torn by issues of dependency and autonomy, security and entrapment. Although not without some sensitivity and insight, she is currently too caught up in her own needs and anxieties to get to know and appreciate any man as an individual.

Much of the research on intimacy has been designed to explore the relationship between identity status and intimacy status. The findings often make good sense in terms of Erikson's theory. That is, studies using the identity-status and intimacy-status measures generally support the hypothesized relationship between identity resolution and maturity of interpersonal relationships. There is also evidence that preintimate and intimate individuals, who have achieved some depth of communication with their partners, are more accurate in predicting their partners' responses to a personality and attitude inventory than individuals in active but superficial relationships (pseudointimate and stereotyped). In turn, pseudointimate and stereotyped individuals are more accurate in their "partner perception" (knowledge of partner's view of self) than isolates.

What kinds of experiences lead individuals to become intimate, isolate, pseudointimate, and so on? To answer this question, Orlofsky (1978) examined college men's intimacy statuses in relation to their scores on a test measuring degree of resolution of earlier Eriksonian stages (trust, autonomy, initiative, industry, and identity). The findings supported Erikson's view that positive resolution of earlier developmental issues is a partial prerequisite for intimacy development in young adults. For example, isolates scored lower than all other groups on trust. On the autonomy scale, intimates and preintimates scored highest, followed by pseudointimates and stereotyped men, with isolates lowest. Orlofsky suggests that the interpersonal problems of isolate individuals may be traced to difficulties encountered in the earliest developmental stages. Fortunately, Erikson believes that difficulties in mastering the crises of each developmental stage can be overcome—although therapy may be needed for individuals with a long string of defeats in achieving trust, autonomy, initiative, and so forth. (In this chapter, "Applying Scientific Concepts" provides an opportunity for you to speculate on the intimacy status of some literary characters as well as people you know.)

While Erikson's theory has stimulated considerable research on the adolescent identity crisis and the young adult intimacy crisis, it has not had a corresponding impact on the middle- and old-age concerns of generativity and integrity. For an empirically based view of development across the adult years, we need to turn to the work of Daniel Levinson. There has also been much recent work on marriage and divorce, which helps round out our view of the challenges of life during the adult years.

Stages of Adult Personality Development

One of the most careful and systematic studies of life changes in adulthood began when Daniel Levinson (1978) and his colleagues at Yale interviewed four groups of men between the ages of 35 and 45, carefully chosen to represent a range of American life-styles: ten hourly workers in industry, ten business executives, ten university biologists, and ten novelists. For example, to secure a representative group of executives, the Levinson group first considered all major companies located within a 50-mile radius of New Haven, Connecticut, where the research was conducted. They chose two different companies— one an old and established manufacturer and the other a rapidly growing technology firm—secured a list of all managers, and chose ten for maximum diversity. All ten agreed to take part. (Compare this careful procedure to that for the best-seller *Passages,* as described in "Becoming a Critical Consumer.")

The major data involved 10 to 20 hours of detailed biographical interviews with each man. The interviews were spread out over several months and included standard psychological tests like the Thematic Apperception Test,

Intimacy and Literary Characters

As explained in this chapter, Erik Erikson characterized young adulthood as a time of crisis over the issue of intimacy versus isolation. Orlofsky extended this notion to identify several possible outcomes of this crisis, which he called "intimacy statuses." Ideally, one should be able to describe any adult—real-life or fictional—in terms of one of these categories.

You will recall that the statuses are defined by the dimensions of commitment and depth, including such characteristics as openness, honesty, empathy, and sharing. Intimate individuals have deep interpersonal relationships with both men and women, and they are involved in an enduring, committed heterosexual relationship. Preintimates also have deep relationships but have not yet made a commitment to a lasting heterosexual relationship. Pseudointimates have entered into a somewhat permanent heterosexual relationship, but all their relationships lack depth. The stereotyped-relationships individual has superficial and conventional relationships with others. The isolate has achieved neither depth nor commitment in any relationship.

Following the steps below, apply these categories to the following literary characters: Romeo, Casanova, and Scrooge. Then follow the same steps to categorize three people you know. (A discussion of this exercise appears after the "Summary" at the end of this chapter.)

First, decide which intimacy status best applies to each character. Then try a more systematic test: Rate each character on his interpersonal relationships using two 7-point scales—from 1 (very low commitment) to 7 (very high commitment), and from 1 (very low depth) to 7 (very high depth). Does this test lead to the same conclusions as the first, more general method of categorizing?

Passages

In the influential best-seller *Passages,* journalist Gail Sheehy (1976) described a series of "predictable crises" that American adults face as they grow from the "trying twenties" to the "deadline decade." These stages of adult development were identified primarily on the basis of Sheehy's interviews of 115 people between the ages of 18 and 55. As you read the following paragraphs from Sheehy's account of her sample and method, decide whether it seems reasonable to conclude that the general trends she described actually apply to most middle-class Americans. (A discussion of this issue of generalizability appears after the "Summary" at the end of this chapter.)

The people I chose to study belong to America's "pacesetter group"—healthy motivated people who either began in or have entered the middle class. . . . The men include lawyers, doctors, chief executives and middle managers, ministers, professors, politicians, and students, as well as men in the arts, the media, the sciences, and those who run their own small business. I sought out top-achieving women as well and also followed the steps of many traditional nurturing women. . . .

Although many of my respondents were raised in small towns, the urban centers to which they have gravitated include New York, Los Angeles, Washington, San Francisco, Chicago, Detroit, Boston, New Haven and Dayton, Ohio. (pp. 20–21)

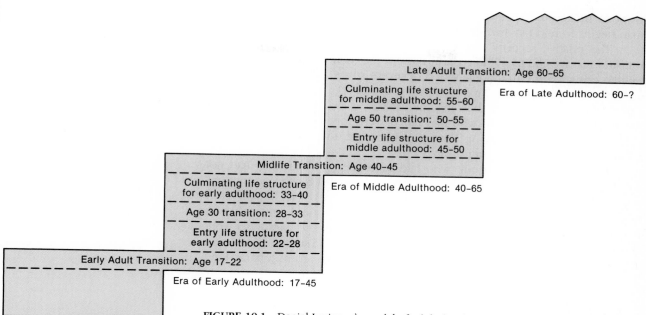

Late Adult Transition: Age 60–65

Era of Late Adulthood: 60–?

Culminating life structure for middle adulthood: 55–60

Age 50 transition: 50–55

Entry life structure for middle adulthood: 45–50

Midlife Transition: Age 40–45

Era of Middle Adulthood: 40–65

Culminating life structure for early adulthood: 33–40

Age 30 transition: 28–33

Entry life structure for early adulthood: 22–28

Early Adult Transition: Age 17–22

Era of Early Adulthood: 17–45

Era of Preadulthood: 0–22

FIGURE 10.1   Daniel Levinson's model of adult development. Levinson divides the life cycle into four major eras that are separated by periods of transition.

in which the men were asked to make up stories about ambiguous pictures (see Chapter 11). In addition, whenever possible, researchers interviewed the men's wives, studied the companies for which they worked, and conducted follow-up interviews two years later.

Levinson was surprised to find that all the men seemed to face very similar problems at specific ages. Of course, he did not discover that every man faced precisely the same crisis the day he turned 39. But every man did seem to go through the same stages, in the same order, and within a surprisingly narrow age range.

Figure 10.1 illustrates Levinson's scheme of adult development. Note that he distinguished among four major periods: the eras of preadulthood (ages 0–22), early adulthood (ages 17–45), middle adulthood (ages 40–65), and late adulthood (age 60 on). The clear boundaries between the three adult phases were quite a surprise to these researchers. They were also impressed with the orderly progression between reasonably stable periods of life, in which men worked toward clear goals, and the emotional turmoil of the period of transition between stages.

The first major period of early adulthood extends roughly from ages 22 to 28, a stage Levinson called "entering the adult world." In this phase, the novice adult must explore all the possibilities open to him and begin to put down roots, establishing a stable life structure. During the "age 30 transition," life decisions seem less tentative and more serious. Suddenly, the person feels that he is playing for keeps. This is a period of fine-tuning to meet the goals of adulthood; it is likely to be far less stressful than the transition at the beginning (age 17) or end (age 40) of early adulthood. In the later thirties, men begin "settling down," working toward the goals they established in early years. They strive to develop competence in their chosen field and work to build a better life. The novice period of adulthood ends as each man begins to find his own place in society.

The relative security of these years is threatened during the midlife transition at ages 40 to 45. For about 80% of the men Levinson studied, the **midlife crisis** was a tumultuous period of severe stress, a time of new doubts and new decisions. For example, before the age of 40, the ten novelists were simply concerned with establishing themselves as professional authors. In the midlife transition, those who had failed were forced to admit that they probably would never make it. Now, in middle age, they saw themselves as failures who had to begin over again.

But even the larger group who had succeeded felt that they had not accomplished enough; thus, the business executives who got the promotions they had been working for discovered that their success was flawed. They were forced to face realistically a future in which they would never serve as chairman of the board for General Motors or IBM. Successful biologists wondered about a future that did not include a Nobel Prize; and successful laborers realized that they would probably be trapped in their current jobs as long as they worked.

At the end of this period of intense questioning and self-doubt, most men entered middle adulthood around the age of 45 with a new sense of finality. For better or worse, their lives had taken shape. In some cases, this meant that they had made peace with their marriages and occupations and were able to enjoy what they had to the fullest. Not everyone was this fortunate, however, and for others, middle adulthood was a period of decline.

In the 1980s, Levinson has expanded his research program to include interviews with 45 women (Levinson, in press). Moreover, several of his graduate students have applied his perspective on the life course to a variety of other men and women, including historical figures. Information from these additional sources has not altered the basic stage description just presented. Indeed, Levinson (1986, p. 12) reports that he knows of no systematic evidence disconfirming the hypothesis that there is an underlying order of the sort he has described in the human life course. While his effort to derive his depiction of adult developmental phases from a rich and solid data base makes his contribution an important one, more of the details of his methods and findings will have to be published and reviewed before his model can attain wide-scale acceptance.

Successful Adjustment

Other researchers have investigated American adulthood without outlining clearly defined stages of this sort. For example, after noting that medical and psychiatric research almost always focused on disease, philanthropist William T. Grant established a fund in 1937 for a "systematic inquiry into the kinds of people who are well and do well." The Grant study began by choosing 268 undergraduates from the Harvard classes of 1939 through 1944 on the basis of their superior physical and mental health. The latest major report on the Grant study, George Vaillant's 1977 book, *Adaptation to Life,* reports how 95 of these men have fared through the years.

midlife crisis A period of severe stress, a questioning of goals and progress that occurs roughly between ages 40 and 45.

Now in their seventies, the subjects included best-selling novelists, recognized scholars, and successful executives, physicians, teachers, and judges. One of the original subjects was described as "a man destined to play a role in every child's history book . . . pointlessly murdered before he reached his prime" (p. 366); at least one reviewer concluded from this remark that one subject in Grant's study was John F. Kennedy, a member of the Harvard class of 1940 (Muson, 1977). This was hardly a representative sample of the American population—but it was never meant to be one. The intent of the Grant study was reflected in the subtitle of Vaillant's book: *How the Best and the Brightest Came of Age*.

While they were still in college, the men took part in about 20 hours of psychiatric interviews, medical examinations, and psychological tests. At this time, one investigator traveled around the country to interview all their parents about family histories and early experiences. After graduation, the men regularly filled out questionnaires, at first every year and later every other year. Around 1950 and again around 1970, many of the men were interviewed once more. All told, the investigators had several hundred pages of information about each man's medical and psychiatric history as it developed over 30 years.

One key set of findings related physical and mental health to the way each man characteristically coped with conflict and stress. The Grant study was strongly influenced by Freud's psychoanalytic perspective, and Vaillant was particularly interested in the long-term effects of using different types of **defense mechanisms** to defend the ego from excessive anxiety by unconsciously denying, distorting, or falsifying reality (see Chapter 12).

Vaillant classified some defense mechanisms as immature. Although they are normal up to about the age of 15, in adults they are a sign of inadequate adjustment. One immature defense mechanism was *passive-aggressive behavior,* expressing anger and hostility indirectly or ineffectively. For example, one man in the Grant study had a chronic history of lateness and procrastination; when something annoyed him, he simply put it off. He was separated from his wife for many years, but he never divorced her and would not admit overt conflict. He dealt with his hostility passively, by not doing anything.

In contrast, suppression was classified as a mature defense mechanism, a healthy way for an adult to deal with stress. *Suppression* involves a conscious decision to postpone attention to sources of conflict. For example, in World War II one subject in the Grant study became so angry at his superior officer that he wanted to hit him. He forced himself to think of other things and later discussed his anger with another officer. In another example, just before getting married, one man was so anxious that he refused to answer a questionnaire item about marriage; later on, at a more relaxed time, he was willing to discuss this anxiety.

Vaillant identified six major defense mechanisms that he classified as mature and another six that were immature. He then collected about 20 short descriptions of key conflicts in each subject's life and how the person dealt with them. In most cases, two mental health workers independently used these descriptions to rate the characteristic defense mechanisms of each subject without any other knowledge of the man. Vaillant then went on to compare 25 men who used mostly mature defense mechanisms with 31 whose

defense mechanisms Mental processes for protecting the ego from excessive anxiety by unconsciously denying, distorting, or falsifying reality.

TABLE 10.2

Comparisons of Grant Study Subjects Who Used Mature or Immature
Defense Mechanisms

	Percent mature *(N = 25)*	*Percent immature* *(N = 31)*
"Happiness" (top third)	68	16
Income over $20,000 per year	88	48
Job meets ambition for self	92	58
Active public service outside job	56	29
Rich friendship pattern	64	6
Marriage in least harmonious quartile or divorced	28	61
Ever diagnosed mentally ill	0	55
Emotional problems in childhood	20	45
Recent health poor by objective exam	0	36
Subjective health consistently judged "excellent" since college	68	48

Source: Vaillant, 1977, p. 87.

responses were characteristically immature. As you can see in Table 10.2, men who characteristically responded to stress in a mature way were more successful in their careers, had more satisfying friendships and marriages, were physically sick less often, and seemed better adjusted psychologically. Mature defense mechanisms seemed to help people do well in life.

The Grant study went on to dig deeper into these men's histories to find the causes and correlates of adjustment. As these men continue to develop into old age and finally die, this landmark longitudinal study will continue to provide clues to complex processes of being a success in twentieth-century America.

Sexual Relationships

Although there have been a number of excellent studies of the physiology of human sexual response and of sexual problems (Masters & Johnson, 1970), at this time there is no fully accurate source of data on sexual behavior. The major surveys to date are discussed in "Understanding the Scientific Method." As explained there, although sexual behavior has changed dramatically in the United States in recent decades, some of the most important insights into this subject come from a series of surveys that began nearly half a century ago at the University of Indiana under the direction of Alfred Kinsey.

Perhaps the most important lesson of the Kinsey surveys was the tremendous variability of human sexual response. As we shall see, average figures do show that sexual activity is related to age. But these average figures must always be considered in the perspective of wide individual differences. One of Kinsey's co-workers (Pomeroy, 1972) summarized the problem this way: "The smallest person in our society . . . might be 25 inches high, and the tallest 8 feet, or a variation of one to 10. . . . This is the normal kind of range. But in sex behavior . . . the range can be one to 10,000. People have difficulty understanding this fact. For example, roughly 10% of women never

Surveys of Sexual Behavior

Surveys gather information about the attitudes and behaviors of a specific population by asking people questions. Because it is impractical to ask every person in a large group (such as U.S. voters) to answer questionnaires, survey results are ordinarily based on a smaller group called a *sample*.

Many people think that larger samples lead to more accurate survey results. This is not necessarily true. For example, in the early days of public opinion polling, *Literary Digest* magazine polled voters about the 1936 presidential election by sending 10 million postcards to people listed in telephone directories and auto registration lists. Over 2 million people replied, and overwhelmingly they picked Alf Landon as the next president of the United States.

They were wrong. In the middle of the Great Depression, people with phones and cars were far wealthier than the average person and were likely to vote Republican. Their opinions did not reflect those of the majority of American voters, who elected Franklin D. Roosevelt by a landslide.

This outcome was correctly predicted by a novice pollster named George Gallup, who had surveyed a mere 312,551 people. The reason this smaller group provided more accurate results was that Gallup had carefully chosen a *stratified random sample* in which subjects were chosen in proportion to their frequency in the general population. (Advances in sampling techniques have substantially reduced the size required for accurate results; many national surveys now test fewer than 2,000 people.)

Sexual behavior and attitudes may be one of the most difficult topics to do a survey on, because this information is so personal and so private. Ironically, the best information we have comes from a survey that was concluded more than three decades ago.

The Kinsey Report was the popular name for a series of studies published by Alfred C. Kinsey and his associates at Indiana University's Institute for Sexual Research (Kinsey, Pomeroy, & Martin, 1948; Kinsey, Pomeroy, Martin, & Gebhard, 1953). Starting in 1938, some 18,000 volunteers were recruited and questioned about their sexual behavior. Each interview lasted several hours and included up to 521 standard questions covering everything from a person's socioeconomic background to his or her sexual experiences alone, with others of both sexes, and even with lower animals.

An elaborate code was used to protect people's confidentiality, and the nine project interviewers were trained never to seem shocked or to express value

(box continues on next page)

judgments. For example, they did not ask if people had ever engaged in a particular activity; they asked when such activity first began. One measure of their success in establishing the right tone is the fact that fewer than 10 of the 18,000 people who allowed themselves to be interviewed by this group refused to give a complete sexual history (Pomeroy, 1972).

There are a number of obvious problems with the Kinsey data. The sample did not accurately reflect the American population, and ultimately it relied on the reports of volunteers, who might well differ from people who refused to cooperate. But as one text stated, "Unfortunately . . . there is no better information available" (Katchadourian & Lunde, 1975, p. 180).

According to the same text, the next best survey of sexual behavior was one sponsored by the Playboy Foundation in the early 1970s (Hunt, 1974). This survey was based on questionnaires completed in private by a representative sample of 2,026 people who were chosen on the basis of age, education, race, marital status, and other characteristics to match the U.S. population as a whole. Unfortunately, only one out of every five people who were originally contacted agreed to participate. This heavy reliance on volunteers and the fact that published reports omitted many important details about procedures makes the quality of this sample a distant second to the Kinsey reports.

More reliable information is available for some more limited questions about sexual behavior. For example, Kanter and Zelnick (1972) studied a representative sample of 15- to 19-year-old women living in the continental United States; 91% of these respondents (versus 20% in the Playboy survey) agreed to be interviewed. This study provided excellent information, but only on the topic of heterosexual intercourse among adolescent females.

At the other end of the continuum, some widely publicized sex surveys are virtually impossible to generalize to any larger group. For example, for *The Hite Report,* writer Shere Hite (1976) distributed 100,000 questionnaires through such sources as chapters of the National Organization for Women, abortion rights groups, and university women's centers. Advertisements were placed in *The Village Voice* and *Mademoiselle, Brides,* and *Ms.* magazines; *Oui* magazine printed the questionnaire in its entirety. Only 3,019 questionnaires were returned, each with essay answers to 50 questions such as "Do you think sex is in any way political?" and "How do you masturbate? Please give a detailed description. . . ." While the detailed revelations this book contained were entertaining enough to make it a best-seller, you don't need a Ph.D. in methodology to suspect that the Hite survey results do not apply to the U.S. population as a whole.

A survey's results are only as good as the sample it is based on. Applying the strictest criteria, no adequate survey of human sexual behavior has yet been published.

have orgasm, but it is possible for a woman to have 50 to 75 orgasms in 20 minutes. The range is tremendous" (p. 467).

Men, too, show tremendous variability. One middle-aged man in the Kinsey sample claimed to have had only one orgasm in his life; another reported averaging 30 orgasms per week over the last 30 years. Both men were in good physical health and seemed perfectly normal in every respect. Thus, the averages presented here do not apply to every person and should not be seen as standards for normal activity. And if you assume that all other people have sexual needs and desires similar to your own, you are wrong. The sexual differences between people are much more impressive than the similarities.

With those reservations firmly in mind, it is interesting to note that Kinsey found that sex was differentially related to age for males and females. As Figure 10.2 indicates, sexual activity for men peaks in adolescence and early adulthood and then begins a gradual decline. Women show a different pattern of sexual activity, increasing gradually from puberty to about the age of 30, then maintaining this peak for a full decade while male rates are declining. Although sexual activity does decline through later adulthood on the average for both sexes, some individuals maintain vigorous sex lives through old age. In general, people who are sexually active early in life maintain this pattern of activity as they grow older. To gain more insight into the nature and course of human sexuality, let us consider age trends for several specific forms of activity.

FIGURE 10.2 The relationship between age and sexual activity. Note that male activity peaks earlier in life and declines more rapidly.

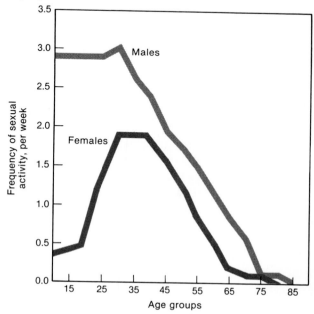

Alfred Kinsey is shown here interviewing one of the subjects in his famous survey of sexual behavior.

MASTURBATION

For many people, the first sexual activity consists of self-stimulation. Ordinarily, deliberate masturbation does not become common until the early teens. Here, Kinsey and his colleagues found some fascinating differences between the sexes. Some 92% of all men and 58% of all women had masturbated to orgasm at some time in their lives. As for other forms of sexual activity, male and female age trends were different. Almost every man who would ever masturbate in his life had done so by the time he reached the age of 20; by this age only one out of three females had ever masturbated. According to more recent data (Hunt, 1974), both boys and girls now begin masturbating at an earlier age than they did in Kinsey's day.

As with other forms of sexual behavior, the variability of masturbation was far more impressive than any general population of trends. Some men never masturbated or did so only once or twice in their entire lives; others averaged two or three orgasms every day over a period of many years.

HETEROSEXUAL INTERCOURSE

One of the most dramatic changes resulting from the "sexual revolution" of the last few decades has been the increase in the frequency of premarital sexual intercourse. However, even in his interviews in the 1930s and 1940s,

Kinsey found that half the women in his sample were not virgins when they married. The figures for men were highly dependent on education and social class. Virtually all the men (98%) who quit school before the eighth grade had tried premarital sex; the figure for college-educated men was much lower (68%). Kinsey's data also suggested that even several decades ago America was gradually becoming more permissive about women having sex before marriage.

Some of the most reliable information about more recent rates of premarital sex comes from a series of national surveys of teenage American women (Zelnick & Kanter, 1980). Table 10.3 presents a summary of their findings for the age at which unmarried women first experienced premarital sex in surveys they conducted in 1971, 1976, and 1979. Even over this short period, the changes were obvious—in each survey year, more women were experiencing premarital intercourse at younger ages. The changes are even more dramatic when compared with the data collected by Kinsey in the 1940s. According to Kinsey and his colleagues (1953), 20% of white American females had had premarital sex by the age of 20 (Kinsey collected little information on blacks). In 1979, the comparable figure for unmarried white 19-year-olds was 65%.

Through the early 1980s, virtually every major sex survey supported the idea that premarital sex was becoming more and more common, particularly in women. However, by the mid-eighties, there were some signs of change. For example, Meg Gerrard, a psychologist at Iowa State University, found that college women from the 1983–1984 academic year had returned to approximately the same level of sexual behavior and contraceptive use as women from the 1973–1974 year—a level that was lower than what was characteristic of a comparable sample of women in 1978–1979. Moreover, sexual attitudes in the 1983–1984 group were more conservative than in either of the two previous samples.

Gerrard (1987) suggests that the sexually permissive attitudes of the mid-1970s were seen by many women as a sexual mandate; that is, everyone was expected to be sexually active. She speculates that by 1983, young women with negative emotional reactions to sex were, as in earlier times, able to act on their feelings and resist being pressured into premature and unprotected sexual activity. At the same time, women who were emotionally ready to become sexually active were able to prepare for sexual intercourse and use effective contraception.

TABLE 10.3

Percentage of Unmarried Women in the United States Who Have Had Premarital Sexual Intercourse

By the age of	*1971*	*1976*	*1979*
15	14%	19%	23%
16	21	29	38
17	26	43	49
18	40	51	57
19	46	60	69

Source: Zelnick & Kanter, 1980.

Regarding marital sex, it was no surprise that the Kinsey surveys found that virtually every married couple had tried sex at least once. But when husbands and wives were asked independently how often they had sex, women consistently gave higher estimates. Kinsey et al. (1953) believed that some women objected to frequent intercourse and therefore overestimated its rate, while many men wanted to have more sex and therefore underestimated its rate (p. 349).

The frequency of intercourse decreases as a married couple gets older. According to Kinsey, the youngest group (16 to 25 years old) had sex about 2½ times each week (median frequency); by the age of 60, this had declined to once every 12 days. More recent data from Hunt's 1974 survey suggest that married people are now having sex more often and are experimenting more. Married couples in the 1970s were more likely to try different sexual positions and more likely to have oral sex than the couples questioned by Kinsey in the 1940s.

Despite such liberating trends, many young adults still have unrealistic ideas about the effects of aging on sexual activity. According to one survey at a midwestern university, most college students believe that their parents have intercourse no more than once a month, never have oral sex, and never had sex before they were married. About one out of every four students believed that if their parents had sex at all during the last year, it happened only once. In fact, some students were offended by the very idea of a questionnaire on parental sexuality. One wrote, "Whoever thinks about their parents' sexual relations, except perverts?" (Pocs, Godow, Tolone, & Walsh, 1977, p. 54). No one knows whether these students would be willing to admit that other people's parents have sex after 40. But even the outdated Kinsey figures make it clear that college students have some quaint ideas about their parents' sexual habits.

These students might be even more upset to learn of their parents' infidelities. According to Kinsey, by the age of 40, half of all husbands and one out of four wives had had at least one extramarital affair. The Hunt survey of sex in the early 1970s found about the same rate of infidelity for men as Kinsey had but noted that married women were gradually catching up in the infidelity department—their rate, too, now seems to be gradually approaching 50%.

HOMOSEXUALITY

In 1951, Clellan Ford and Frank Beach conducted a worldwide survey of sexual practices in primitive societies that had been studied by anthropologists. Information on homosexuality was available for 76 studies; in 26 of these, adult homosexuality was "totally absent, rare, or carried on only in secrecy" (p. 129). But in the majority of cases, homosexual activities were socially acceptable for some members of the community. Sometimes, puberty rites included homosexual activity; in other cases, specific males who were believed to have magical powers were raised to live as women. Still other societies considered homosexuality a normal form of activity for unmarried men and young boys. (Anthropological reports provided little information about female homosexuality.)

Recent studies of homosexual couples have revealed the error of many common myths about homosexuality.

One of the most sensitive, controversial areas in the original Kinsey survey was homosexuality. Perhaps the most widely disbelieved figure in the Kinsey volumes was the report that 37% of all American males had had at least one homosexual orgasm by the age of 45. But the data showed that not all these men were equally homosexual; some had had exactly one experience with another man and a lifelong pattern of lovemaking with women, while others were exclusively involved with other males.

As with masturbation, premarital sex, and extramarital sex, the proportion of women involved in homosexual activity was much lower. Only 13% had had a homosexual orgasm by age 45 (versus 37% of the men). About three to four times as many men as women were exclusively homosexual; the best guess currently puts these figures at 2% to 4% for American males and 0.5% to 1% for American females. Similar proportions of homosexuals have been found in surveys of other countries, such as Germany and Sweden (Katchadourian & Lunde, 1980).

As one might expect, there is considerable controversy over the developmental forces that cause homosexuality. Some of the most recent and best evidence comes from an elaborate study of 979 male and female homosexuals who lived in the San Francisco Bay area in 1969 and 1970 (Bell, Weinberg, & Hammersmith, 1981). While earlier studies of homosexuality often concentrated on individuals who sought psychiatric help, this sample was recruited through the gay community and was carefully chosen to include representative proportions of people according to age, race, education, and so on.

Each person was interviewed about his or her childhood, adolescence, and sexual history for three to five hours. The homosexuals' responses were compared with the answers given by a control group of 477 heterosexuals to the same questions. The results revealed the fallacy of several widely accepted myths.

For example, many people believe that lesbians turn to other women because of disappointing or traumatic early experiences with men. In fact, there were few differences between the early heterosexual histories of lesbians and other women. Similarly, Freud's notion that male homosexuality is caused by a dominating mother and a weak or detached father had little basis in fact.

What these researchers did find was that homosexuals reported a lifelong pattern of gender nonconformity. At least for exclusive homosexuals (as opposed to bisexuals), there were signs of nonconformity long before puberty— little boys who had little interest in masculine activities like baseball and little girls who were tomboys. Of course, many tomboys and males who hate baseball grow up to be heterosexual. But these early signs sometimes indicate an unwillingness or inability to accept traditional sex roles. These authors suspect that the roots of exclusive homosexuality lie in biological factors present as early as birth.

This is sure to be a controversial view, particularly since it is inferred from the reports of adults rather than direct observation of children or actual biological differences. As pointed out in Chapter 7, human memory often reconstructs the past to fit certain beliefs or schemas; whether these subjects were distorting the memories of childhood remains to be seen. But one thing is sure: Before the issue is settled there will be many more studies of the way each person comes to choose a sexual path.

AIDS

With the advent of the 1980s, a health problem emerged that had enormous implications for sexual behavior—Acquired Immune Deficiency Syndrome (AIDS). Transmitted through the sharing of bodily fluids, AIDS could be contracted, it soon became known, through sharing intravenous needles, blood transfusions, and sexual intercourse, particularly anal intercourse between homosexual men.

Government data published in 1985 revealed that most AIDS patients were gay or bisexual men, or intravenous drug users. A new homophobia (fear of homosexuality) emerged (Johnson, 1987), and some anti-gay groups scapegoated homosexuals as carriers of the "gay plague." Moreover, because of some sensationalism in the popular media, many Americans at low risk for contracting AIDS (e.g., exclusive heterosexuals) nevertheless developed considerable anxiety over the possibility of becoming infected with the disease.

While there is some debate as to whether AIDS is truly a new problem, it certainly did not enter public consciousness before the early 1980s. In 1981, 261 cases of AIDS were reported. By April 1985, 10,000 cases had been reported, with the number of new cases doubling each year [Centers for

The AIDS epidemic seems to be having a major impact on patterns of sexual behavior.

Disease Control (CDC), 1985]. In the first nine months of 1987 alone, 13,000 new cases were reported (CDC, 1987). While the deadliness of the disease makes it frightening for whatever age group it strikes, the fact that 90% of adults with AIDS are only 20–49 years old probably increases its frightfulness.

With the increase in incidence of AIDS, there has also been increased research, not just into causes and medical treatment but also into its psychological effects—both on its victims and the public at large (see Grant & Anns, 1988). There is some evidence that monogamy is back in fashion, that singles are delaying longer before entering into a sexual relationship with a new partner, and that many women are insisting that their partners use condoms (Stevens, 1987; Dunning, 1986). However, there is also evidence that on college campuses, at least, there is more talk than preventative action when it comes to AIDS (Kantrowitz, 1987).

Psychological research with AIDS patients is complicated by the enormous ethical issues related to privacy (see Melton & Gray, 1988). However, by the 1990s, much more is likely to be known about AIDS and its effects on individuals and relationships.

Marriage and Divorce

Marriage and parenthood traditionally have been considered appropriate developmental achievements for adults. Getting married and having children is the "normal and healthy" course for grown-ups. Increasingly, however, as we shall see, divorce is also becoming a normal part of adult life.

MARRIAGE

Traditionally, Americans have been quite marriage-oriented. By the time adults reach their forties, 93% of all men and 95% of all women have been married at least once (*World Almanac,* 1987). Americans are not marrying as young as they used to. In 1960, the average age of first marriage was 22.8 for men and 20.3 for women. By 1986, it was 25.7 for men and 23.1 for women (*Information Please Almanac,* 1988). And if at first a marriage doesn't succeed, most people are willing to try and try again. Five out of six divorced men remarry, as do three out of four divorced women.

Psychologists have found a number of benefits to being married. Overall, married people are healthier, live longer, and are happier than those who are not married. Of course, these are group averages that don't apply to all individuals. Not surprisingly, those with happy marriages report more positive effects.

Several studies have explored how individuals perceive their marriages. For example, among the questions Campbell (1981) asked a sample of married people were:

1. How often do you disagree with your (wife-husband) about how much money to spend on various things?
2. How well do you think your (wife-husband) understands you—your feelings, your likes and dislikes, and any problems you may have?
3. How well do you understand your (wife-husband)?
4. How much companionship do you and your (wife-husband) have—how often do you do things together? (p. 83)

Men and women gave similar answers to questions 1, 3, and 4. For example, about 60% of men and women said rarely or never to question 1. But there was a large discrepancy between the sexes in their perceptions of question 2. While 55% of men felt their wives understood them very well, only 42% of women felt this way about their husbands.

Campbell also found that people reported different perceptions of marriage over the course of the life span. Overall, the happiest people were young, married women without children and older married men with grown children. Young married couples indicated a good deal of satisfaction with marriage, as did couples in their fifties and older. However, people in their thirties and forties indicated a drop in marital satisfaction.

Campbell offers two explanations for this decrease in satisfaction. First, in contrast to the beginning period of a marriage, when couples have relatively few responsibilities, couples in their 30s and 40s are highly stressed. This is the time when children are small, expenses are high, and career pressures are strong. No doubt these difficulties are reflected in the marital relationship, and couples report less satisfaction. By the time couples reach their fifties, the children are grown and on their own, job pressures are often reduced, and life is more tranquil. A married couple can begin enjoying their relationship again.

Second, Campbell suggests that people might gradually lower their expectations about their marriage partner. Youthful idealism gives way to realism, and marriage partners come to accept that neither of them is perfect. The

In the United States, over 93% of all men and 95% of all women are married before the age of 40.

resulting acceptance of a mate often results in a greater sense of satisfaction and more positive feelings about the marriage.

Thus, a person's level of satisfaction with an intimate marriage relationship is not constant but changes over the course of adulthood. A relationship that starts off as a dream can deteriorate into a nightmare as circumstances change. Several decades ago, married couples often stayed together through such problem periods "for better or for worse." These days, they are more likely to seek a divorce.

DIVORCE

In the last 20 years, the divorce rate in the United States has more than doubled (Brehm, 1985). Information from the 1987 *World Almanac* revealed that for every ten marriages taking place there were five divorces. This does not mean that half of all marriages will end in divorce. In any year, divorcing couples range from those who have been married only a few months to those who have been married for over 50 years. Nevertheless, as Table 10.4 indicates, the divorce rate has increased steadily since the turn of the century while the marriage rate has remained more stable.

A number of explanations have been offered for this change. On the societal level, the stigma that used to be associated with divorce is virtually gone. In addition, the legal system is much more manageable; many states have "no-fault" divorces, and the time period for obtaining a divorce has been shortened.

On the individual level, changed social roles for men and women have given adults greater options. For example, decades ago women sometimes stayed in an unhappy marriage because of financial dependency. Now, many women work outside the home and are able to support themselves. Further, couples have fewer children than in the past. As a result, there is more opportu-

In the last 20 years, the divorce rate in the United States has more than doubled.

TABLE 10.4

Marriages, Divorces, and Rates in the United States

Year	Marriages[a] Number	Rate	Divorces[b] Number	Rate	Year	Marriages[a] Number	Rate	Divorces[b] Number	Rate
1895	620,000	8.9	40,387	0.6	1945	1,612,992	12.2	485,000	3.5[c]
1900	709,000	9.3	55,751	0.7	1950	1,667,231	11.1	385,144	2.6
1905	842,000	10.0	67,976	0.8	1955	1,531,000	9.3	377,000	2.3
1910	948,166	10.3	83,045	0.9	1960	1,523,000	8.5	393,000	2.2
1915	1,007,595	10.0	104,298	1.0	1965	1,800,000	9.3	479,000	2.5
1920	1,274,476	12.0	170,505	1.6	1970	2,158,802	10.6	708,000	3.5
1925	1,188,334	10.3	175,449	1.5	1975	2,152,662	10.0	1,036,000	4.8
1930	1,126,856	9.2	195,961	1.6	1980	2,413,000	10.6	1,182,000	5.2
1935	1,327,000	10.4	218,000	1.7	1984	2,487,000	10.5	1,155,000	4.9
1940	1,595,879	12.1	264,000	2.0	1985	2,425,000	10.2	1,187,000	5.0

Note: Data refer only to events occurring within the United States, including Alaska and Hawaii, beginning with 1960. Rates per 1,000 population.

[a] Includes estimates and marriage licenses for some states for all years.
[b] Includes reported annulments.
[c] Divorce rates for 1945 based on population including armed forces overseas.
Source: National Center for Health Statistics, U.S. Department of Health and Human Services.

nity to evaluate the marital relationship and to decide that the marriage isn't working well. Despite its increased acceptance and frequency, there is evidence that divorce remains a very difficult life experience. For example, Bloom, Asher, and White (1978) compared divorced or separated individuals with those who were married, never married, or widowed. They found that the divorced-separated group of men and women had higher rates of suicide, alcohol abuse, car accidents, and psychiatric problems.

One of the most extensive studies of the effects of divorce was conducted by Wallerstein and Kelly (1980). They studied 60 families and their 131 children, ages 3 to 18, over a five-year period. Through extensive interviews and question-naires, they acquired detailed information about the divorce process.

They began by examining the reasons why couples divorced. Typically, one partner wanted to end the marriage much more than the other. In three-quarters of these families, women took the initiative on the divorce; about half of these husbands were very much opposed to ending the marriage.

Partners who wanted the divorce did so for different reasons. Some sought a rational solution to a difficult situation. For example, Mrs. N. was married to a man who wasn't home four or five nights a week and who was typically drunk the other nights. He was routinely abusive to his family. Although his wife was unhappy with the situation, she stayed married to him for ten years because of financial concerns and fear of living alone. When she finally couldn't stand it anymore, she filed for divorce. Her husband was strongly opposed. Initially, he refused to leave the house, and then he refused to provide adequate support for his children. In this case, Mrs. N. viewed divorce as the most reasonable course of action.

Other times, divorce occurred in couples where marital discontent was not especially great but where a stressful experience unrelated to the marriage had occurred. In the case of Mrs. K., shortly after her mother died, she decided to seek a divorce from her husband, a mild-mannered, family-oriented man. She felt he hadn't been sympathetic enough about her mother's death. He pleaded with her to reconsider; the children cried and tried to persuade their mother to stay in the marriage, but she went through with the divorce. When interviewed four years later, she realized that it had been a mistake. "I wish I could marry him again," she told the researchers. "It was a terrible mistake, but there is nothing to do now. I have ruined the lives of four people" (Wallerstein & Kelly, 1980, p. 20).

Some divorces occurred impulsively, with little thought to the conse-quences. This type often results when one partner discovers an extramarital affair of the other partner. As a way to punish the spouse, and as a reaction to anger and jealousy, the offended husband or wife will threaten to end the marriage. Often the spouse really hopes to win back the straying partner, but this tactic rarely works.

Immediately after a divorce, there are changes in the economic situation of the parents. Women who gain custody of children are typically poorer than they were before. Often the families move to less expensive housing, and children are forced to change schools. But the greatest changes are emo-tional. Adults are clearly stressed, with feelings of failure, humiliation, anger, and sadness.

More than 80% of the divorced people in Wallerstein and Kelly's study were angry and bitter toward their spouses. There was at least one angry partner in virtually every family. Interestingly, the intensity of anger was greater among women. Arguments about money, support for the children, and visiting arrangements were quite frequent.

In addition to anger, more than one-third of the adults in this study experienced some depression. Even the spouses who had initiated the divorce were often depressed. Depressed individuals are typically more withdrawn and distanced from other people. As a result, these parents spent less time with their children at a time when the children needed them more. These children reported feeling lonely and abandoned.

Of course, not all the reports were negative. A number of adults felt that the divorce offered freedom and a chance for a fresh start in life. This was especially common among women who left a bad marriage in which their self-esteem was constantly threatened. It was also the case when men had divorced to marry someone else.

In previous generations, parents often believed that they should stay in an unhappy marriage for the sake of the children. Today, the prevailing view is that if the adults are unhappy, the children will be, too, and that it is better to end a bad marriage. But children themselves do not report this. In marriages where parents reported great discord and conflict, children were not necessarily unhappy.

While divorced adults often had a difficult period after the marriage broke up, for children and adolescents the marital breakup was a major disruption in their lives. They were extremely frightened, upset, alone, and worried about their futures. They felt overwhelmed by the changes. Fewer than 10% of the children were relieved to see their parents' marriage end, even when there had been physical abuse in the family. Moreover, changes in parents' moods and behaviors were quite disruptive to children.

Eighteen months after their original study, Wallerstein and Kelly did follow-up interviews with parents and children. Overall, both women and men were accepting the divorce and were adjusting to new life-styles. Anger and bitterness had declined. Still, the partners were not quite finished with the emotional trauma of divorce. The major problems that remained were depression, loneliness, and anger. While the number of men and women who were depressed was about equal, the intensity was much greater in women: Almost half were at least moderately depressed, and some were suicidal. They felt overwhelmed by the responsibilities of daily living and were upset that life hadn't improved enough after the divorce. Almost two-thirds of the women and two-fifths of the men reported loneliness; social life was a disappointment to many of these people.

For other parents, positive changes were evident. For women in particular, there was likely to be an increase in self-esteem. Eighteen months after the divorce, relationships with children were stabilizing, and parents were taking seriously the chance to start life anew. Many children were also doing much better in this follow-up study: About half were adjusting appropriately. But about 25% of the children were not doing well in school and were having social problems.

Wallerstein and Kelly's (1980) final follow-up occurred after five years. Generally, both adults and children were doing much better. More than half the adults described their divorces as beneficial and felt that they had improved their lives. Mrs. C.'s comments reflect the positive changes: "When I look back, I wish I had gotten out earlier, before things were so desperate, and didn't wait until the breaking point. . . . My divorce was a necessity—it was sad and painful. But it turned out well for me" (Wallerstein & Kelly, 1980, p. 187).

There was a small group of adults, approximately one-fifth, who still viewed the divorce as negative. Another fifth had mixed feelings, realizing that their marriages hadn't been all bad. But for a majority of people, life had restabilized, and the negative effects of the divorce had decreased.

Children were also doing better after five years. Some had reevaluated their parents' decision to divorce and had decided that it had been, in fact, the right thing to do, despite their initial opposition. But for children whose parents had not adjusted well to the divorce, life was still difficult.

Like many life experiences, divorce is not an event but a process. Social and psychological changes occur during the transition period and afterward. The initial breakup is stressful to parents and children alike. The transition period can be a time of healing and rebuilding or a time of anger and frustration. Individual responses to the disruption and changes that result from divorce determine whether the final outcome will be psychologically beneficial or harmful.

Old Age

In 1900, only 4% of the population of the United States was 65 years old or older; currently this proportion is over 10%. One reason that our society seems to be growing older is the dramatic increase in *life expectancy,* the number of years the average person lives. In 1900, life expectancy was about 47 years; by 1984, this figure had increased to 75 years.

However, these average figures are quite deceiving. In 1900, a far larger proportion of the population died in infancy and childhood, thus substantially lowering the average age of death. The life expectancy of people who survived into adulthood has not changed very much in this century. In 1900, a 65-year-old could expect, on the average, to live to the age of 77; in 1988, the average 65-year-old would survive to 81.8 years. Thus, the life span of adults has been surprisingly constant; what has changed in the last 100 years is the proportion of the population that has survived into old age.

As the proportion of elderly people in our society continues to grow, developmental psychologists are likely to focus increasingly on their special abilities and problems. The scientific study of the elderly is called **gerontology** (from the Greek root *geron,* meaning "old man").

A Period of Cognitive Decline?

One problem that has fascinated gerontologists involves the common belief that old age is a time of decreasing physical and mental abilities. Folklore has it that as each of us grows older, we can expect to grow progressively less intelligent than the younger generation. But systematic tests of cognitive

gerontology The scientific study of the elderly.

As the number of elderly people continues to grow, developmental psychologists are becoming increasingly concerned with understanding the factors associated with positive adjustment to old age.

decline in adulthood have revealed just how complex the relationships between age and abilities can be.

The first studies of this topic were quite consistent. When large groups of people took the Wechsler Adult Intelligence Scale and other IQ tests (see Chapter 13), older groups almost invariably made more mistakes, on the average. Depending on the precise nature of the specific IQ test, this intellectual decline might begin as early as age 35. In any case, pronounced drops in test scores were observed in the sixties and beyond.

Beginning in the 1950s, however, K. Warner Schaie and his colleagues began to question this view. They pointed out that virtually all the studies showing IQ decline used the **cross-sectional method**—they compared groups of different ages at one point in time. Schaie believed that longitudinal studies tracing the progress of specific individuals over many years might reveal a different pattern (see Chapter 9, "Understanding the Scientific Method," pages 353–354).

In 1956, Schaie began a major study of IQ change that combined elements of the longitudinal and cross-sectional approaches. He administered an IQ test called the Primary Mental Abilities Test to 500 adults ranging in age from 20 to 70. Analysis of these cross-sectional results yielded the typical pattern of apparent declines of intelligence scores beginning around middle age. But Schaie proceeded to follow these 500 people through adulthood. In 1963, 7 years after his first study, he was able to retest 302 of the original group. In 1970, 14 years after the original test, he measured IQ in 161 of the original subjects. (We shall see later that this gradual reduction in sample size created certain problems for interpretation of the results.)

Analysis of the longitudinal data from the 7-year and 14-year follow-ups yielded a different picture. The individuals who were tested several times showed much smaller and more gradual changes. Many intellectual abilities did not decline at all before the age of 60, and subsequent decreases were quite minor. Figure 10.3 illustrates the results for tests of verbal meaning, the ability to understand ideas expressed in words.

Schaie explains this contradiction by pointing to the importance of differences between **cohorts**, groups of people who were born at roughly the same time. For example, the youngest cohorts were 20 to 25 years old in 1956, when Schaie's study began. They were born during the Great Depression and were children during World War II. The oldest cohorts in Schaie's study were 64 to 70 in 1956, born near the end of the nineteenth century. Compared to the younger subjects, they probably received less education and less adequate medical care in childhood and grew up in larger families and in more rural areas. These social and cultural differences, along with other factors, seemed to affect scores on certain tests. And these differences between cohorts were enough to bias the results of cross-sectional studies.

This does not mean that cross-sectional studies have no place in developmental psychology. As pointed out earlier, longitudinal studies are costly and take a long time to complete. For other types of behavior, cohort differences may be less dramatic and less likely to bias cross-sectional studies. And longitudinal studies have methodological problems of their own. Botwinick (1979), for example, has called attention to the problem of decreasing sample size in the study by Schaie and Labouvie-Vief (1974). As you may remember, Schaie started out with 500 subjects but 14 years later could find only 161 of them.

cross-sectional method An analytical research approach that compares groups of different ages at one point in time.

cohorts Groups of people born at approximately the same time.

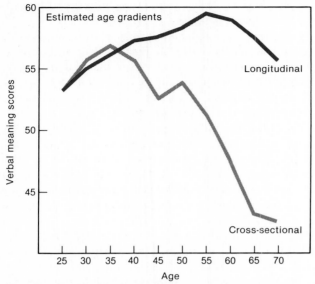

FIGURE 10.3 The relationship between age and test scores of the ability to understand verbally expressed ideas. Cross-sectional studies seemed to show that this ability declined rapidly beginning as early as age 35. But longitudinal studies, which followed individuals through life, suggest that the decline is far smaller and only begins around the age of 55.

Several studies have shown that people who do poorly on IQ tests are less likely to be available for follow-up studies. One reason that this is so is a phenomenon called *terminal drop*. IQ tends to decline in the five years or so preceding death, perhaps as a result of a general decline in health and physical abilities. People who are ill thus may show greater IQ decline; when they fail to reappear for follow-up studies, the average for the remaining healthy group may be misleading (Riegel & Riegel, 1972).

The overall conclusion is a familiar one for psychologists. The study of behavior poses many hard questions and few easy answers. The best answers are likely to emerge from converging data from several different sources. In this context, cross-sectional studies probably overestimate declines in cognitive function in old age, while longitudinal studies may underestimate these changes. Botwinick (1979) concludes that for such cognitive skills as verbal abilities, the decline with age is probably small and does not begin before the age of 50 or 60. Other intellectual skills, particularly those that require fast responses on nonverbal problems (such as timed IQ tests in which people are asked to arrange several pictures to form a coherent story) decline earlier in life and more rapidly.

Improving the Quality of Life

Some gerontologists are now becoming less concerned with cataloging the effects of the aging process and more concerned with how our society can best deal with the problems of senior citizens. Some have found evidence that our society may actually be causing some of these problems. Judith Rodin and Ellen Langer (1977) studied 91 nursing-home residents between the ages of 65 and 90. One group was given special instructions designed to increase personal responsibility for caring for themselves and increasing the quality of life in the nursing home. In short, they were encouraged to take active control of their lives. For example, as part of the study each elderly person in this group was given a present of a plant, which they chose for themselves and which they agreed to take care of. A control group consisted of elderly patients who were allowed to conform to the nursing-home routine in the more traditional, passive way. For example, these patients were told that the staff would take care of their plants.

The experimental group that was encouraged to seize control of their own lives later scored dramatically higher than the passive group on tests of alertness, active participation, and general well-being. These positive effects persisted even 18 months later; nurses rated the experimental group as happier, more vigorous, and more sociable. The authors explained the importance of this sense of personal control in terms of the link between depression and learned helplessness (see Chapter 14).

While some researchers seek new ways to increase the quality of life in old age, others are exploring a much more difficult problem: promoting a realistic acceptance of the inevitability of death.

Death and Dying

In the fall of 1965, four students from the Chicago Theological Seminary approached psychiatrist Elisabeth Kübler-Ross for help on a research project on dying. As Kübler-Ross later described this meeting (1969): "We . . . decided that the best possible way we could study death was by asking terminally ill patients to be our teachers" (p. 22). But when she approached other doctors in the hospitals in which she worked, the reactions varied from stunned disbelief to avoidance. No one wanted to admit that some patients were dying; death was a taboo topic in the world of medicine.

When Kübler-Ross finally found volunteers, however, they were eager to talk about their feelings. In 1969, she published the book *On Death and Dying,* summarizing some of her interviews with over 200 dying patients. Kübler-Ross was not the first to do research on this topic; her own bibliography listed over 180 professional books and articles relevant to this research. But this psychiatrist's sensitive writing on what people felt as they approached death became a best-seller and helped to break down some of the traditional taboos.

Kübler-Ross believed that people who learned they were dying go through predictable emotional reactions that can be broken down into five stages. The first is *denial*—patients simply refuse to believe that they are dying. In one extreme case, a 28-year-old woman who "fell apart" when she learned that she was dying from a liver disease began to feel better when a neighbor told her that there was always hope and urged her to visit a local faith healer. The visit was a "success," and the woman proclaimed herself cured. She stopped following the diet that she needed to stay alive, because she insisted that she was well. She soon needed to be hospitalized. She remained a difficult patient, often refusing to eat properly or take her medication. It was only after several weeks of treatment that she began to accept the reality of her condition and to prepare herself for death.

According to Kübler-Ross, most patients pass from denial to a second stage of *anger,* in which they experience rage, envy, and resentment and ask over and over again, "Why me?" At this stage, patients often alienate family, friends, and the hospital staff. Doctors are criticized for the diets and drugs they prescribe. When a nurse straightens the bed, she is criticized for never leaving the patient alone; when she leaves, the patient is likely to call her back to arrange the bed more comfortably. An innocent TV commercial showing healthy young people having a good time can send the patient into a rage because it reminds him how painful even the simplest movements have become. He snaps at his family and sooner or later they snap back, increasing his anger still further.

As the rage begins to wear itself out, the dying person moves into a third stage of trying to *bargain* with God or fate. The question shifts from "Why me?" to "Why now?" Dying patients react like children who believe that they can get whatever they want for Christmas as long as they remain on their best behavior. Some patients promise their organs to science if the doctor can keep them alive just a little longer; others offer God a life of dedication to His work if only He will let them live. But this self-delusion usually does not last long, and the patient soon moves into a fourth stage of *depression.*

At first, the depression may revolve around mundane matters, such as how to take care of one's children or how to pay for a lengthy hospital stay. Relatives and friends usually react to such worries by urging the patients to look at the brighter side—the children have many happy years left, and sooner or later bills will be paid. This is followed by mourning, in which patients prepare for death by letting go of their attachment to life. For example, one man regretted the fact that he was always away from home trying to make a living when his daughter was young. Now it was too late to spend time with her—she was fully grown and had her own friends and her own life. When people go through this stage of grieving for all the dreams that were never fulfilled and all the hopes that will never be met, the best help others can offer may be just to sit silently with the loved ones, letting them detach themselves from life.

In the fifth and final stage before death, many patients come to *accept* their fate. Patients who do not die suddenly have time to work through the progression of emotions, from denial to anger to hope to depression. Now, as life draws to a close, they seem too tired for further upset. Void of emotion, and withdrawn from those around them, they seem to accept the inevitable withdrawal that death will bring.

Kübler-Ross's scheme in intuitively appealing and seems to correspond to many people's experiences. But researchers have remained skeptical about this well-known theory. It is difficult to prove or disprove; so many feelings and behaviors are subject to interpretation. Almost everyone who is confined in a hospital will sometimes become angry or depressed. Kübler-Ross never specified precisely how a psychologist could know when this indicated that the patient was in a specific stage. And she did not provide objective evidence that most of her patients went through each of the five stages in precisely this order.

Other researchers who studied the terminally ill have come to rather different conclusions. One study (Kastenbaum & Weisman, 1972) distinguished between two reactions to death. Some patients, like Kübler-Ross's, seemed to accept death and withdrew from most activities. But others continued to live active lives until the very end. They did not seem to fear death and continued to start new activities and new relationships even though they knew they were dying.

Clearly, more research is needed to understand the complex emotional experiences of people who know they are going to die. The contribution of Kübler-Ross and other pioneers, then, is just a beginning that helped break down the barriers preventing discussion of this taboo topic.

A new public awareness of the inevitability of death may help our society deal more intelligently and humanely with the terminally ill. One sign of such change is the establishment of special institutions called **hospices**, which are specifically designed to meet the needs of the dying. The most famous facility of this sort is St. Christopher's Hospice in London, England. Dealing primarily with cancer patients, St. Christopher's tries to relieve pain as much as possible and to provide maximum contact with loved ones. Various mixtures of drugs help relieve pain while allowing patients to remain alert. Paid staff and volunteers work to provide a loving and caring atmosphere rather than the sterile and impersonal one so commonly found in hospitals. Visiting hours are extremely liberal, to allow family and friends to spend as much time as possible with their loved ones.

The first American hospice was established in New Haven, Connecticut, in 1974; by 1985, there were more than 1600 hospice programs in the United States (McCann & Hill, 1985). Psychologists are now working with the 50,000 patients who enter these programs each year to deal with the inevitability of death and make the most of the time left to them. In this way, and in many others, psychology's studies of the lifelong process of growth and development are being applied to promote the most productive lives possible.

Summary

Erikson's "Eight Ages of Man"

- According to psychoanalyst Erik Erikson, each of us passes through eight distinct **psychosocial stages**, periods of life when we must face certain crises.

- Erikson identifies eight psychosocial crises associated with the eight psychosocial stages: trust versus mistrust in infancy; autonomy versus shame in the second year; initiative versus guilt in the third or fourth year; industry versus inferiority in late childhood; identity versus identity confusion in adolescence; intimacy versus isolation in young adulthood; generativity versus stagnation in middle age; and integrity versus despair in old age.

hospices Institutions that are specifically designed to meet the needs of dying patients.

Male-Female Differences

- Sexual stereotypes are the unquestioned assumptions that people hold about boys and girls, men and women, solely on the basis of their gender.

- Studies of male-female differences have generated a good deal of controversy.

- The most widely accepted review of all the research to date concluded that by adolescence, there are several major sex differences that emerge: girls develop verbal skills more rapidly, while boys excel on visual-spatial and mathematical tasks.

- Another stable sex difference appears much earlier in development: Boys are physically and verbally more aggressive than girls.

Adolescence

- Beginning with G. Stanley Hall, many psychologists characterized adolescence as a period of great storm and stress.

- Later researchers have shown how the precise character of this period depends on cultural and historical factors.

- **Puberty** is the time when sexual maturation begins.

- In addition to changes in the structure and function of sex organs, puberty is characterized by a **growth spurt,** a sudden increase in the rate of growth for both height and weight. The precise timing of these changes varies over a wide normal range.

- Lawrence Kohlberg focused attention on the way adolescents' growing cognitive capacities enable them to reason about morality in increasingly sophisticated ways.

- Kohlberg distinguished six major stages of moral development, two at each of three levels.

- At Kohlberg's **preconventional level** of moral reasoning, people accept society's commands primarily to gain rewards and avoid punishments.

- At the **conventional level,** society's standards are totally adopted as one's own.

- At the **postconventional level,** moral reasoning involves applying universal principles of right and wrong that are more fundamental than the laws of any specific society.

- Kohlberg has been criticized for his cognitive focus on the way people think about morality rather than on what they actually do and for developing a theory that applies more to males than to females.

- Erikson coined the term **identity crisis** to include loss of a sense of personal identity in combat soldiers and the sense of confusion that could be found in severely conflicted young people who were experiencing a war within themselves.

Adulthood

- Erikson holds that the developmental task of young adulthood is **intimacy,** which involves the challenge of making a commitment to another person and developing and maintaining a mature relationship.

- Orlofsky has identified five basic intimacy statuses: intimate, preintimate, stereotyped relationships, isolate, and pseudointimate.

- The statuses of committed and uncommitted merger have been added to this list.

- In his study of middle-aged men, Levinson found several distinct stages of adult development.

- Around the age of 30, a transition occurs as men settle down to pursue adult goals.

- Between the ages of 40 and 45, Levinson holds, many men experience a **midlife crisis**, a stressful period of questioning their goals and progress.

- The Grant study includes a longitudinal follow-up of 95 men who graduated from Harvard between 1939 and 1944.

- Valliant's investigation of Grant study participants focused on their use of **defense mechanisms**—mechanisms for defending the ego from excessive anxiety by unconsciously denying, distorting, or falsifying reality.

- Men in the Grant study who typically responded to stress with mature defense mechanisms, such as suppression, were more successful in their careers, more satisfied with their marriages and friendships, and physically healthier.

- Americans are very marriage-oriented, and psychologists have found a number of benefits to being married.

- Research by Wallerstein and Kelly reveals that the process of adjusting to divorce can be lengthy.

- Studies of human sexual activity have emphasized the tremendous variability of response.

- On the average, male sexual activity peaks in adolescence and early adulthood; female sexual activity rises more gradually from puberty and peaks in the thirties.

- The causes of homosexuality are not fully understood.

- According to one controversial study, adult homosexuals often report a pattern of lifelong gender nonconformity. The researchers interpreted this as a sign of a biological predisposition, but other explanations are also possible.

Old Age

- The proportion of the population that is over 65 has been steadily increasing.

- One key problem in **gerontology**, the scientific study of the elderly, concerns the possibility of cognitive decline in old age.

- Studies using the **cross-sectional method**, in which groups of different ages are compared at one point in time, have generally found that IQ declines in adulthood, perhaps beginning as early as the age of 35.

- Longitudinal studies, however, have found much smaller cognitive declines, beginning much later in adulthood.

- One reason for the discrepancy in cross-sectional and longitudinal findings involves differences between **cohorts,** groups of people who are born at roughly the same time.

- According the Kübler-Ross, people typically go through five stages when they learn they are dying: denial, anger, bargaining, depression, and acceptance.

- While researchers have challenged the idea that every patient moves through all five stages in precisely this order, the scheme was useful in breaking down the taboos against studying dying.

- One sign of change is the increasing acceptance of **hospices**—institutions specifically designed to meet the needs of patients who are dying.

Critical Thinking Exercises
Discussions

Intimacy and Literary Characters

For this chapter's exercise in applying scientific concepts, you were asked to apply Orlofsky's intimacy statuses to three well-known literary characters: Romeo, Casanova, and Scrooge. Romeo should probably be considered preintimate—having made a good start with Juliet on the development of a fairly deep relationship, characterized, as far as we can tell, by considerable openness, honesty, empathy, and sharing. Moreover, while one might argue that he had also become involved in an enduring, committed heterosexual relationship with her, the newness and youngness of their love, combined with the lack of opportunity to test the durability of the relationship, make the preintimate status more appropriate than the intimate status.

Casanova should probably be categorized as pseudointimate. Although he enjoyed many sexual encounters with women, he did not enter into committed relationships, and his encounters lacked depth.

At the beginning of Dickens' classic Christmas tale, Scrooge is certainly the classic example of an isolate. He has no close, committed relationships. As the story unfolds, it becomes clear through his encounter with the ghost of Christmas past that he had once participated in a relationship that was at least at the preintimate level. Moreover, by the end of the story, he would appear to be preintimate in relation to his nephew's family—moving toward achieving some depth and commitment of a nonheterosexual variety.

This exercise required the use of such critical thinking skills as discrimination and generalization. It was important to discriminate among the defining characteristics of each of the intimacy statuses and then to generalize the meaning of the statuses to new characters. The process also involved keeping several different defining characteristics (e.g., depth of closeness, degree of commitment) in mind, while matching what is known about the literary individuals against these characteristics.

Passages

What is *not* said in this account is far more significant than what is said. To assess the validity of Sheehy's research, the critical consumer will focus on the precise details of her methods. For example, how did she choose the actual people who were interviewed? Journalists often find people to write about simply by "asking around" among friends and acquaintances; was this highly biased technique used here? Further, what was the exact procedure used for interviews? Did each begin with the same core group of questions? And what criteria did Sheehy use to identify the general characteristics of a particular period of life?

These are the kinds of questions scientists consider when they evaluate the validity of a particular study. A talented journalist like Sheehy can provide insights into individual lives that are far more intense and fascinating than one usually encounters in scientific reports. But general conclusions about all Americans or another specific population are likely to be valid only when they are based on proper methods of scientific research.

MOTIVATION AND EMOTION

Chapter 11

Why did Sir Thomas More choose to die as a martyr rather than compromise his religious principles? Why did Elvis Presley sometimes give Cadillacs to perfect strangers? Why did the King of England abdicate in 1936, giving up his throne to marry the woman he loved? Why did Adolf Hitler order the execution of over 6 million Jews? And why did Henry Marshall try to get his 3-year-old son a place in the *Guinness Book of World Records* by having the child do more than 1,000 push-ups in two hours (*Boston Globe*, June 18, 1980, p. 4)?

According to "common sense," the answers to questions like these about human motivation may be quite straightforward—simply ask the people involved. Thomas More and Elvis may not have much to say, but people who are alive, alert, and reasonably verbal can usually explain their own actions. Or can they?

In an influential paper titled "Telling More Than We Can Know," Richard Nisbett and Timothy Wilson (1977) cited dozens of studies showing how little insight people have into the causes of their own behavior. When subjects were questioned in classic studies of how people react to emergencies, how first impressions influence later judgments, how people solve problems, and how drugs affect behavior, they consistently failed to notice or to admit the influence of critical variables. The subjects almost always gave reasons for what they did. But the reasons they offered were often the wrong ones, explanations that were shown by other research to be factually incorrect.

For example, in one simple study, shoppers were asked to evaluate the quality of four pairs of nylon stockings. In fact, the stockings were identical, but when people looked at the four pairs side by side, they overwhelmingly chose the pair that was placed on the right end. While effects like this are familiar to psychologists, none of the shoppers said that the position of the articles had anything to do with their choices. Indeed, when the experimenters asked directly whether the placement of the articles might affect preference, "virtually all subjects denied it, usually with a worried glance at the interviewer, suggesting that they felt either that they had misunderstood the question or were dealing with a madman" (Nisbett & Wilson, 1977, p. 244).

This research does not imply that we never have any insight into the underlying reasons for our actions. But it does suggest that psychologists must probe beneath the surface to understand the tangled forces that motivate human behavior.

Although speculation about the underlying causes of behavior probably dates back to the first cave woman who wondered why her husband was late for dinner, "systematic investigations of . . . motivational behavior are almost unbelievably recent" (Brown, 1979, p. 231). Scientific theories of motivation began to appear only about a century ago; widespread experimentation in this area began around the 1920s. It should come as no surprise that there is still considerable controversy over many basic issues.

Even the definition of motivation has proved difficult to specify in an abstract form that satisfies every psychologist. For our purposes, **motivation** involves the forces that influence the strength or direction of behavior. *Physiological motives* direct behavior toward such basic goals as food, water, and sex. *Social motives* direct behavior toward more complex goals, such as acceptance from others, independence, or recognition of one's achievements. In either case, studies of motivation explore how and why behavior is directed toward a certain goal.

Closely related to the concept of motives is that of **emotions**, physical reactions that are experienced as strong feelings. Common sense classifies feelings such as anger, fear, and joy as emotions and distinguishes them from such motivational forces as hunger, thirst, and a need for achievement. However, psychologists have found it difficult to pinpoint the formal or theoretical differences between motivation and emotion.

The American Psychological Association has no division devoted to motivation and emotion, and very few psychologists identify themselves exclusively with this area. Rather, these are general problems faced by psychologists working in many different specialties.

As this chapter reviews what is known about motivation and emotion, it will become clear that psychology is not yet in a position to provide final answers to questions like those posed about the motivations of Elvis Presley and Henry Marshall. It is, however, able to provide insights into questions that are more limited in scope but every bit as fascinating and provocative.

Models of Motivation

The idea that motivation involves the forces that influence behavior implies a hidden assumption: The way you act is determined, at least in part, by internal and external forces. In its more extreme versions, philosophers call

motivation The forces that influence the strength or direction of behavior.

emotions Physical reactions that are experienced as strong feelings.

this idea **determinism**, that every event is the inevitable product of a series of natural forces. A strict determinist would argue that human choice is an illusion. You may think that you have the power to decide whether you should break up with your boyfriend or whether to eat vanilla or chocolate mint chip ice cream. However, a determinist would say you have no choice at all—that every act is determined by what comes before.

While the roots of this deterministic view can be traced back to the ancient Greek philosopher Democritus, the history of human thought has been dominated by the opposite view of **free will**, that people are free to choose what they will do. Free will does not imply that human behavior is totally independent of outside stimuli and internal desires, only that each of us has the power to choose what we will do.

Different psychologists hold a variety of views on this ancient controversy. At one extreme, B. F. Skinner and some behaviorists believe that science can ultimately discover a set of laws that will fully predict every human act. At the other extreme, Abraham Maslow and some humanistic psychologists argue that people do have control over their actions and that a complete scientific account of human behavior will never be possible. The debate over determinism versus free will has gone on for several thousand years, and it would be presumptuous for psychologists to expect to have the final word in this controversy. However, it is worth noting that if human behavior is totally unpredictable and capricious, the search for systematic relationships must fail. Therefore, every scientific account of human motivation inevitably implies some acceptance of the deterministic view.

General Theories: From Instincts to Incentives

When psychologists first attempted to specify the forces that determined the direction and intensity of behavior, most sought a single general theory that could account for every type of motivation. The first candidate involved the concept of **instincts**, or inborn forces that direct an organism toward a certain goal. Note that this is quite similar to our earlier definition of motivation; the key difference is the notion that instincts are unlearned and present at birth, part of the biological heritage of a species.

For example, in 1890 William James argued that human beings were born with the following instincts: locomotion, vocalization, imitation, rivalry, pugnacity, sympathy, hurting, fear, acquisitiveness, constructiveness, play, curiosity, sociability, secretiveness, cleanliness, modesty, love, jealousy, and parental love. Unfortunately, James cited little systematic evidence that any of these forces were truly inborn; his list was based largely on arguments about the evolutionary advantage of these traits and observations of his own children.

Other psychologists developed lists of their own, and by 1923 one critic of this concept counted several thousand different instincts that social scientists had invoked to explain every imaginable type of behavior (Tolman, 1923).

One major problem with the indiscriminate use of the word *instinct* was that there were no firm criteria for deciding whether a particular instinct was innate, or universal, or anything else. Another problem was that some

determinism The idea that every event is the inevitable product of a series of natural forces.

free will The idea that people are free to choose what they will do.

instincts Inborn forces that direct an organism toward a certain goal.

researchers seemed to feel that they had explained behavior simply by labeling it instinctive. Thus, a woman who spent all day cleaning her gun collection was expressing her cleanliness instinct; a man who read 20 volumes of the *Encyclopaedia Britannica* from cover to cover was expressing his curiosity instinct. Critics noted that these "instincts" did not explain anything, they simply provided a label such as "cleanliness" or "curiosity" for the actual behaviors observed.

As a result of these arguments and others, most psychologists abandoned the idea that all motivation could be explained by a general theory of instincts. Beginning around the 1920s, they substituted the notions of needs and drives. A **need** is a physiological requirement of the organism, such as a need for food, water, or oxygen. This is distinguished from a **drive**, a motivational force that incites an organism to action. Ordinarily, needs and drives are parallel; a physiological need for food is expressed in the behavioral drive that leads an animal to seek it out. In some cases, however, the distinction is an important one. A woman who is starving may have an overwhelming need for food, but she may become so weak that she has little behavioral drive to search for nourishment.

For learning theorists such as Clark Hull, the concept of drive played a central role in explaining all behavior. According to the behavioral paradigm, which dominated American psychology at least until the 1950s, all behavior was based on learning, and all learning was motivated by the organism's attempt to satisfy such drives as hunger, thirst, and sex. According to some theorists, even the most complex forms of behavior could ultimately be traced back to the influence of these few basic biological drives. For example, Tolman (1942) argued that a hungry infant learns to demand food assertively by crying or whining. Depending on which responses actually succeed in reducing hunger, these assertive behaviors can develop into personality patterns that motivate such complex activities as verbal aggression or learning to manipulate others.

Given the perspective provided by several decades of research, this attempt to reduce all human motivation to a few basic drives now seems far too simplistic. Even the simplest forms of animal learning cannot be fully explained by the push of internal needs and drives. To cite just one example, Guttman (1953) found that rats would press a bar more frequently for sugar water than plain water. These animals were influenced not just by internal states but also by external stimuli called **incentives**—external stimuli that influence the probability of behavior. Humans too are motivated by external incentives: A hot fudge sundae can be an incentive to eat even when the internal hunger drive is relatively weak.

Other complications for drive theory arose as psychologists became increasingly concerned with the role of cognitive processes and thought in motivation. In the last few decades, the gradual shift among researchers toward an emphasis on the active internal cognitive processes involved in such areas as perception, learning, memory, and thought has affected the study of motivation and emotion as well. For example, according to Schachter and Singer's cognitive theory of emotion (described later), the way people perceive and interpret situations in which they find themselves determines the actual emotions they feel.

**WILLIAM JAMES
(1842–1910)**

One of the founders of the science of psychology, and the older brother of the novelist Henry James, William James was raised by wealthy parents who provided a rather unorthodox education as the family traveled through England, Switzerland, France, and Germany. After graduating from medical school, James accepted a position teaching physiology at Harvard. In 1875, he taught the first course in an American university that focused on psychology and founded the first American psychology laboratory. In 1890, he published *Principles of Psychology,* the first textbook in this infant field. Although this book cited no empirical research whatsoever, James's literary insights into psychological phenomena still continue to fascinate contemporary psychologists.

Psychological thinking has evolved significantly in its first century. Around 1900, psychologists saw human behavior as mindlessly driven by inborn instincts. Today the picture seems far more complex. Human beings actively interpret the world and react to both internal drives and external incentives.

Current Directions

These days, most researchers believe that motivation and emotion are too complex to be explained by any single theory. Most of this chapter focuses on individual motives, such as hunger and the need for achievement, each on its own terms. It is important to note, however, that an influential minority of scientists rejects this fragmented approach. In Chapter 12, we consider how Freud's instinct theory and Malsow's notion of a hierarchy of needs suggest general principles that might account for many different motives. Here, we introduce a more recent and more modest theory of motivation, Solomon's notion of opponent processes.

OPPONENT-PROCESS THEORY

In the fifth century B.C., Plato noted the paradoxical relations between pleasure and pain: "Whenever the one is found, the other follows up behind." Consider the often repeated story about the man who had a habit of hitting his head against a wall because it felt so good when he stopped. Or consider the common report by marathon runners of the incredible high they experience after "passing through the wall" of nearly unbearable physical pain.

Richard Solomon (1980) drew on these observations and others to develop his **opponent-process theory**, which holds that many acquired motives arise from the interplay of two opposing processes in the brain, such as pleasure in response to pain or pain in response to pleasure. Addictions are also explained by this theory, and Solomon believes that such acquired motives as love, social attachments, thrill seeking, and the needs for achievement, power, and affiliation all follow the same empirical laws as addictions.

When a person first takes an addictive drug such as heroin, a peak of euphoria (the "rush") is followed by a gradual decline and later a minor craving. A second dose of the drug produces a smaller amount of pleasure and a greater unpleasant craving. By the time a person is addicted, the drug is sought to avoid the pain of withdrawal rather than to produce the pleasure of a rush.

Solomon also argues that this sequence of events is based on structures in the brain that are automatically triggered to reduce any intense feeling. Hence, the rush of pleasure from that first dose of heroin triggers an opponent process to reduce its intensity. After several repetitions, the opponent process increases in strength until it provides the motivational force.

Similarly, he argues, love begins with a wave of euphoria. But over time, the euphoria when the loved one is present is replaced by unpleasant feelings when the loved one is absent. The driving force has shifted from pleasure to pain and has created a kind of addiction to another human being.

At this writing, it seems fair to describe the notion of opponent processes

need An organism's physiological requirement, such as food, water, or oxygen.

drive A motivational force that incites an organism to action.

incentives External stimuli that increase the likelihood of behavior.

opponent-process theory The theory that many acquired motives arise from the interplay of two opposing processes in the brain, such as pleasure in response to pain.

According to the opponent-process theory of motivation, a person's first experience in a physically risky situation is likely to be terrifying. But this fear elicits an opponent process in the brain that produces a feeling of euphoria several minutes later. If the behavior is repeated, the fear decreases and the euphoria increases in length and intensity.

of motivation as a provocative theory that has received some experimental support. Only time and future research can tell whether it will prove to be of enduring value in understanding the nature of motivation.

ANALYSIS OF INDIVIDUAL MOTIVES

Again, Solomon's attempt to develop a general theory of motivation goes against the trend; most modern researchers focus on the workings of an individual motive rather than seeking general principles that apply to all drives or all acquired motives.

Even motives that seem to be closely related are often controlled by different mechanisms and respond to different variables. The most obvious example is the fact that hunger is far more complex than thirst, even though the two intuitively seem to be closely linked. Water intake is regulated within very narrow boundaries, whereas food intake is far more variable and sensitive to external conditions. Richard Thompson (1975) wryly noted one implication of this difference: "Many people are too fat but we never hear of someone being too wet" (p. 308). Because water intake is so closely attuned to the body's needs, a person can survive only a few days without liquids. But the same person can live for weeks or months without food, surviving on stored energy. This sort of difference has encouraged many researchers to consider each individual motive separately and on its own terms.

At this time, there is no single list of human motives that is accepted by all psychologists. Most agree, however, that motives can be divided into two major classes, *physiological motives* and *social motives*. Other names are sometimes used (such as basic or inborn versus derived or acquired motives), and there is sometimes disagreement over the precise definitions and boundaries of each concept. Nevertheless, the broad division into physiological and social categories is widely accepted.

Of the physiological motives, the three that have been studied most intensively are hunger, thirst, and sex. Most of this research has been conducted by experimental and physiological psychologists who seek to understand the bodily mechanisms involved, often by performing surgery on lower animals.

In contrast, the social motives seem more distinctly human, such as the need for achievement, for power, or for self-esteem. These have typically been studied by personality psychologists, who analyze the most complex forms of human behavior. The contrast between these two broad classes should become clearer as we describe each type and focus on research for representative examples.

Physiological Motives

Physiological motives are internal bodily states that direct an organism's behavior toward a goal. Virtually every list of physiological motives begins with hunger, thirst, and sex. While hunger and thirst are intimately involved with personal survival, there is not a single documented case of a person who died from lack of sex. However, sex is required for the survival of the species. (See Chapter 10 for a discussion of research on human sexuality.)

Other motives involved with survival include the need for oxygen and maintenance of a constant body temperature. Needs for sleep, elimination of wastes, and avoidance of pain are also commonly cited as physiological motives.

More controversial is the issue of whether curiosity is a physiological motive. In the 1950s, at a time when drive theory held that all behavior could be traced back to physical tensions, such as hunger, researchers reported that monkeys will manipulate puzzles and latches with no reward except their apparent satisfaction in solving them. Later studies revealed that the same is true of other species, and some argued that this proved that curiosity (or perhaps manipulation or mastery) was a basic inborn drive.

Maternal behavior also seems to be partly inborn, at least for lower animals. (Although liberated authors sometimes prefer the term *parental behavior* so that fathers will not feel left out, among lower animals the female of the species is responsible for nearly all care of the young.) In rats, injections of certain hormones have been shown to increase maternal activity. However, in apes and humans, experience seems to play a far larger role in parental practices than biology. Thus, the higher one proceeds on the evolutionary scale, the less influence hormones have on maternal behavior.

Some researchers argue that aggression is also an inborn physiological motive (Lorenz, 1966), but that claim is extremely controversial. Social-learning researchers have repeatedly shown that aggression is modified by learning

physiological motives Internal bodily states that direct an organism's behavior toward such goals as food, water, and sex.

(see Chapter 6). No one knows whether it could be abolished from the human species under the proper conditions.

To gain more insight into the nature of physiological motivation, we now focus on one motive that has been studied in some detail—hunger.

Hunger

Large animals that eat low-calorie foods—cows that survive on a diet of grass, for example—must eat almost continuously to gain sufficient nourishment. In contrast, humans eat meals. Much of the research on hunger has focused on the bodily mechanics of eating meals. Why do we start eating, and why do we stop?

At least for most Americans, food is readily available almost all the time. If you are reading this at home, you are probably only steps away from potato chips and wheat germ, Pepsi and milk, Hershey bars and alfalfa sprouts. What internal force makes you suddenly being thinking about these foods when it's time for lunch? And after you begin eating, how does your body know when it has had enough?

It is easy to demonstrate that visual sensations arise in the eye, but where does hunger begin? Many early studies focused on this question of localizing the origins of hunger. Being no fools, researchers began by looking at the stomach.

ATTEMPTS TO LOCALIZE HUNGER

Near the turn of the century, Harvard Medical School physiologist Walter Cannon attempted to demonstrate that hunger was caused by stomach contractions. Unfortunately, at that time the only way to measure stomach contractions involved swallowing a balloon attached to a long air hose. Once the balloon was in the stomach, it could be partially inflated; when the stomach contracted, it would squeeze the balloon, forcing out a certain amount of air, which could be measured on a pressure gauge attached to the hose (see Figure 11.1). The whole experience is rather unpleasant and has a tendency to reduce hunger.

Perhaps demonstrating the wisdom that led to his appointment at Harvard, Cannon decided that he himself would read the pressure gauges while someone else swallowed the balloon. That unappetizing task was left to his research assistant, A. L. Washburn.

It took Washburn several weeks of valiant practice to get used to feeling a tube in his throat and the partially inflated balloon in his stomach; then, the experiment began. Washburn skipped breakfast and lunch each day, came to the laboratory around 2 P.M., swallowed the balloon, and sat quietly while his stomach contractions were measured. Whenever Washburn felt hungry, he pressed a telegraph key, which made a mark on the physiological record. Just as Cannon had predicted, stomach contractions tended to peak right before Washburn felt hungry. These investigators concluded that a psychological sensation of hunger was caused by a definite physiological event, a stomach contraction (Cannon & Washburn, 1912).

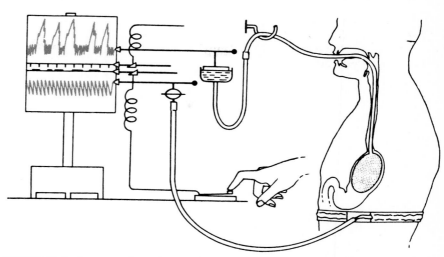

FIGURE 11.1 In one early study of hunger, a research assistant swallowed a balloon and pressed a telegraph key whenever he felt hungry. Stomach contractions were measured by changes in the pressure on the balloon. Although studies using this unappetizing procedure found that stomach contractions tended to peak with subjective feelings of hunger, this conclusion was later challenged by other types of evidence.

Several sources of evidence led later researchers to reject this simplistic theory of hunger. Cutting the nerves that deliver information about stomach contractions to the brain has surprisingly little effect on human or animal hunger. Even humans whose stomachs have been completely removed continue to experience hunger pangs, and animals with no stomachs contined to work for food. Clearly, something other than stomach contractions produces hunger for these individuals.

There is evidence that a full stomach sends to the brain signals that play a role in ending a meal, but they constitute only one factor in the regulation of hunger. Another important part of the story involves the processing of these signals in the brain. According to one theory of brain function, the *ventromedial hypothalamus*—an area in the front and central portions of the hypothalamus (see Chapter 3)—was said to be a "satiety center" that signaled animals when to stop eating. The *lateral hypothalamus*—an area on the sides of this structure—was said to be a "feeding center" that sent signals to start eating.

The evidence for the involvement of these structures in eating goes back to the turn of the century, when a Viennese physician named Alfred Frölich observed that people with tumors of the pituitary gland often became obese. Later physicians showed that it was a smaller structure next to the pituitary—the hypothalamus—that actually regulated hunger. Several decades of experimentation followed before researchers agreed on the precise site. Destruction of the ventromedial hypothalamus led to such gross overeating that animals ultimately doubled or even tripled their normal weight. This finding led to the idea that the ventromedial hypothalamus told animals when to stop eating; when it was damaged or destroyed, the animal no longer knew when to stop (Hetherington & Ranson, 1942).

After surgical destruction of a portion of the brain called
the ventromedial hypothalamus, this rat overate until it was
about three times its normal weight.

A few years later, researchers discovered that destruction of the lateral
hypothalamus produced the opposite effect (Anand & Brobeck, 1951). If the
damaged area was large enough, a rat would starve to death even if it was
sitting on a mountain of food.

From this evidence arose a relatively simple theory localizing hunger
in the brain: The lateral hypothalamus turns hunger on; the ventromedial
hypothalamus turns hunger off. Not surprisingly, later researchers found that
this model was far too simplistic. For example, rats whose ventromedial hypo-
thalami were destroyed ate more if food were freely available but ate less if
they had to work for it by pressing a bar or lifting a heavy lid. When food
was mixed with the unpleasant taste of quinine, these rats also ate less than
normal ones; but when it was mixed with sugar, they ate far more than
usual (Teitelbaum, 1955). Obviously, the ventromedial hypothalamus is involved not just with stopping eating but also with sensitivity to external cues.

Similarly, a rat whose lateral hypothalamus was destroyed would sometimes resume eating. If such rats were forcibly tube fed for several weeks,
they later began to eat again, especially if they were tempted by a treat like
eggnog (Teitelbaum & Epstein, 1962).

These findings and others challenged the idea that hunger is a single
phenomenon that can be precisely localized in the body and the brain. Eating

involves a number of different processes that interact to produce weight gain. For example, one line of research later suggested that rats with ventromedial lesions get fat even when they eat the same amount as a control group of normal rats. Thus, the ventromedial hypothalamus may be involved with food metabolism, particularly the proportion of nutrients that are stored as fat (Friedman & Stricker, 1976).

Other researchers have been examining the effects of drugs and neuro-transmitters in the hypothalamus, including epinephrine and serotonin. For example, when researchers injected epinephrine into animals' brains, the animals overate; when they injected serotonin, they underate. This helps explain why certain drugs, like tricyclic antidepressants, cause weight gain in patients. Drugs like amphetamines, which concentrate in the hypothalamus, have the opposite effect—they suppress appetite (Kolata, 1982).

Continuing studies of the effects of drugs on appetite, along with increasingly sophisticated methods for destroying precise areas of brain tissue and measuring a range of behavioral effects, will provide new information about the many different processes involved in eating and how these processes are regulated by the brain.

OTHER VARIABLES THAT INFLUENCE EATING

When researchers abandoned the idea of localizing the "hunger drive" in a single spot, they went on to investigate the many factors that influence eating in different situations. Among the physiological factors that have been shown to be involved are body temperature, blood-sugar levels, and fat deposits.

Psychological variables have also been shown to influence human eating. From a social-learning perspective, modeling has proven important: College students ate their lunch faster in the presence of another person who ate quickly and ate more when their companion ate more (Rosenthal & McSweeney, 1979). Another series of studies has shown that the external cues associated with food affect obese individuals more than those of normal weight. For example, in 1964, psychologist Albert Stunkard found that stomach contractions were more closely related to feelings of hunger for normal-weight individuals than for obese subjects. Specifically, on 71% of the occasions that normal-weight people reported feeling hungry, their stomachs were contracting; the corresponding figure for obese people was 48% (Stunkard & Koch, 1964).

These results suggest that normal-weight people may eat when their bodies tell them to, while obese people eat for other reasons. In a direct test of this notion, Schachter, Goldman, and Gordon (1968) manipulated internal hunger sensations by comparing some subjects who had eaten recently with others who had not. The prediction was that normal-weight people would eat less when their stomachs were full, while obese people would be less affected by these internal signals.

Men in the normal-weight category were about the average weight for people their height; obese subjects were on the average 20% overweight according to the norms published by the Metropolitan Life Insurance Company. The Columbia undergraduates who participated in this study thought they were volunteering for a taste-testing experiment and agreed to skip one meal just before their appointments. Subjects in the full-stomach condition were

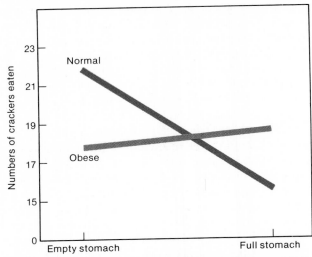

FIGURE 11.2 In this study, obese subjects ate the same amount whether or not they had eaten recently. In contrast, normal-weight subjects ate less when they had just eaten. Along with other evidence, this suggests that normal-weight people eat when internal bodily sensations signal hunger, while obese people are more responsive to external cues.

offered two large roast beef sandwiches and a glass of water when they arrived; those in the empty-stomach condition got only a warm hello. Then both groups were given crackers to eat. Of course, these men had no idea that eating a roast beef sandwich was a key step in the experiment. Figure 11.2 shows that obese subjects ate about the same number of crackers whether their stomachs were relatively empty or full; normal-weight men ate significantly fewer crackers when their stomachs were full.

Schachter concluded that normal-weight people eat when internal bodily sensations signal hunger, while the obese eat in response to external, food-relevant cues. This interpretation was further supported by a long series of creative experiments and natural observations. In a typical follow-up study (Schachter & Gross, 1968), obese and normal-weight subjects filled out questionnaires and sat quietly for an hour of boring physiological tests. The study always began at 5 P.M. and ended at 6 P.M. But a large clock on the wall facing the subjects was altered to run fast for one group and slow for another. When the experimenter brought in a stack of questionnaires near the end of the session, he was casually munching on some Wheat Thins. He left the box behind and invited the subject to eat as much as he liked.

Once again, all the questionnaires and physiological measures were an elaborate ruse. The question was, how many Wheat Thins would obese and normal-weight people eat? As predicted, they found that normal-weight people ate the same amount whether the clock was running fast or slow, whereas obese people ate more when external cues told them that it was dinner time (that is, when the clock ran fast and suggested that it was 6:10 rather than 5:25).

Many investigators have replicated the finding that obese people are, on the average, more responsive to external cues. But this does not mean that every obese person responds to external food cues and every normal-weight person to internal ones. Both internally oriented and externally oriented individuals can be found in any weight category (Rodin, 1981). This distinction is one factor in obesity; but we see in the next section that there are also many others.

Human Obesity: Causes and Cures

There is no precise border between obesity and normal weight. The tables in every diet book showing the "ideal" weight for men and women of various heights are largely based on the averages found in insurance company records for millions of individuals. **Obesity** is often defined as at least 15% to 20% over these ideal weights; depending on the precise definition, some 20 million to 40 million Americans are obese.

Many experts believe that charts of ideal weight are misleading (Mayer, 1968). A 5-foot 10-inch, 190-pound linebacker for the Cincinnati Bengals football team could be all muscle, while a dentist of the same height and weight could be all fat. A better definition of obesity, therefore, might rely on the proportion of body fat. A rough estimate of this proportion can be made by measuring the thickness of skin folds, as when you place your hands above your hips on either side and pinch the skin folds known colloquially as "love handles."

It is widely agreed that three major factors determine body weight: the amount and type of food eaten, the amount of energy expended in physical activity, and the storage of fat in cellular tissue. The relations between these factors are complex and probably differ from one person to the next.

Body fat is stored in the form of adipose tissue, or fat cells. Weight gaining can result from an increase in the number of fat cells in the body or an increase in the average size of existing fat cells. Many researchers believe that the number of fat cells is particularly critical. This remains relatively constant over the life span. Some research suggests that excessive eating can increase the number of fat cells, particularly during the first few months of life (Knittle, 1975). If this finding is verified, attention to proper diet during this critical period can have lifelong implications.

Another theory of obesity emphasizes the importance of **set points**, the body's internal levels for regulating body weight. The set point is like a thermostat; if weight drops below the acceptable level, the body will take steps to bring it back up. For example, if your set point is 150 pounds and you drop down to 140, your metabolism may actually slow down and your appetite increase so that ultimately your weight returns to 150. If your weight goes above the set level, then your body will make adjustments to bring it back down. This theory helps explain why so many dieters ultimately return to their original weights (Keesey & Powley, 1986).

The set point theory also explains why weight loss is not always consistent for dieters. Many people find that when they do go on a diet, the first few weeks are very encouraging, as they quickly shed the excess pounds and their love handles get a little closer to their hips. But at some point they get a rude shock when they stick to the diet and nothing happens.

Set point theorists say that the body adapts to a diet by slowing down

obesity The condition of being at least 15% to 20% over one's ideal body weight.

set points The body's internal levels for regulating body weight.

metabolism. Consequently, the dieter uses less energy to do the same things—such as sleeping, watching TV, and going back to sleep again. This slower metabolism means that the dieter will burn off less fat and lose fewer pounds. The body also tries to increase hunger to get back to the set weight. Thus it is impossible to always predict weight loss just from knowing the amount of decreased food intake.

The set point also varies among individuals. For example, why is it sometimes different in individuals who are the same age and height? Heredity seems to play a role. Studies of twins found that identical twins raised in different homes had weights that were more similar than those of fraternal twins raised in the same home (Bray, 1981).

Before you despair about ever losing weight, however, keep in mind that the set point theory has not yet been adequately tested. And even if it is eventually validated, set points are not fixed for life. For example, they change with hormonal variation, drugs, and diet. Exercise can be particularly effective, since it can affect metabolic rate and reduce appetite.

While we wait for psychologists to settle the controversy over set points, what should we do when we start feeling chubby? Nearly 400 years before Christ was born, Socrates warned the overweight: "Beware of those foods that tempt you to eat when you are not hungry and those liquors that tempt you to drink when you are not thirsty."

The wisdom of this common sense has been verified in many studies. In one such study (Sclafani & Springer, 1976), rats that were given unlimited access to the standard boring laboratory menu (Purina Rat Chow and water) maintained relatively constant weights. But another group of rats who were permitted to nibble away at chocolate chip cookies, salami, cheese, marshmallows, milk chocolate, and peanut butter gradually got fatter and fatter. Thus, even rats get chubby when exposed to the external incentives found in any American supermarket.

Unfortunately, there is no simple way to lose weight. To keep the American preoccupation with effortless weight loss in perspective, it is worth noting that fad diets have been with us for more than a century. In the 1860s and 1870s, many Americans went on the Banting Diet, trying to lose weight by eating fewer carbohydrates. This basic principle has been reincarnated in countless forms in the last few decades, including the Calories Don't Count Diet, the DuPont Diet, the Air Force Diet, the Mayo Clinic Diet, the Drinking Man's Diet, the Stillman Diet, the Boston Police Diet, and the Atkins Diet Revolution (Goldbeck & Goldbeck, 1975). In the month that you read this, some magazine will almost certainly headline a "new miracle" diet that will make the same basic recommendations.

Low-carbohydrate diets like these do promote in the early stages the sort of rapid weight loss that encourages people to continue. But, like all diets, they are difficult to maintain for long periods. Further, some forms of the diet actually lack adequate nutrition and may be harmful to health.

Almost any weight-loss diet will help people shed pounds, at least temporarily. People who are unsophisticated about social science may be genuinely enthusiastic about a diet they have seen work for specific individuals. Researchers who have conducted carefully controlled outcome studies of the long-term effects of weight-loss programs are far more cautious. New miracle diets are rarely new—and never miracles. Nevertheless, people do succeed in losing weight. In a study of 40 adults who had been obese at some time and had actively tried to lose weight, Schachter (1982) found that about two out of three were no longer obese.

Many psychologists now recommend behavior modification programs for weight control (Stunkard, 1979). Typically, these begin by requiring people to keep detailed records for several days of everything they eat and the situations in which it is eaten. Some people are so appalled by the number of potato chips they consume while watching TV that they immediately plan to reform. One possibility is to avoid situations associated with overeating; watching less TV may help our potato chip addict trim down. Another strategy is to replace snacking with another pleasurable activity.

Increasing the frequency of exercise is also an important ingredient in most successful weight-loss programs. However, all behavioral programs demand effort and commitment over an extended period of time.

Psychologists now believe that they will never find a single cause for obesity, nor a single cure. Rodin (1981) put it this way: "The plump baby, the chubby adolescent boy, the woman who gets fatter after pregnancy, the overweight business executive—all have fatness in common—but it is doubtful that the cause or natural history of their fatness is the same" (p. 382). Researchers are now searching for ways to tailor weight-loss programs to individual needs to improve people's chances of maintaining the healthy weight levels they desire.

Other Eating Disorders:
Anorexia Nervosa and Bulimia

Clinical psychologists—and much of the American public—are familiar with two unhealthy patterns of behavior that involve disturbances in eating: anorexia nervosa and bulimia.

Anorexia nervosa is a syndrome characterized by the refusal to eat enough food to maintain or gain weight, a fear of becoming fat, and significant weight loss. While the term *anorexia nervosa* literally means "nervous loss of appetite," in fact anorexics are often hungry; they starve themselves because of fear of gaining weight. Many anorexics are preoccupied with food: They think about it constantly, read cookbooks, and even prepare elaborate meals for friends. But their own dinner might consist of a leaf of lettuce, a carrot, and an ounce of chicken.

Anorexics often have distorted body images. Despite protruding bones, they see themselves as too fat and continue to diet. They may also engage in excessive physical activity to increase weight loss.

Severe weight loss has a number of negative effects, including chemical imbalances that affect major organs. As a result, anorexia is life-threatening. Although most cases consist of a single episode with full recovery, follow-up studies "indicate mortality rates between 15% and 21%" (American Psychiatric Association, 1980, p. 68).

Anorexia is much more common in women than in men; the ratio is about 20 females for every male. Typically, anorexia begins during adolescence, with as many as 1 in every 250 adolescent females affected.

There are several explanations for this disorder. One focuses on the

anorexia nervosa A syndrome characterized by the refusal to eat enough food to maintain or gain weight, a fear of becoming fat, and significant weight loss.

adolescent girl's conflict about her sexuality and fear of growing up. By starving herself, she enables her body to return to a prepubescent appearance. In fact, menstruation ceases in many anorexics, the breasts shrink, and the body takes on a boylike appearance. So, at least temporarily, the issue of sexuality is avoided.

A second, environmental explanation ties fear of being fat to our society's admiration for thin women. Think about the ads you've seen on television and in magazines. How often are the women even the slightest bit overweight? Models and celebrities are likely to be painfully thin. To an impressionable adolescent girl, being overweight or even average weight may seem undesirable. An adolescent girl might acquire an image of the beautiful, successful woman as one who has no noticeable body fat, and she might want to look the same way.

A third explanation focuses on family conflicts and views anorexia as a girl's attempt to have some control over her life. Many anorexics are "good girls"—they do well in school, are cooperative and well-behaved, and are often perfectionists. They may feel that they have no choices, that they are being controlled by the desires and demands of others. Choosing not to eat is a way to regain control over something in their lives.

Treating anorexia is often difficult, in part because the young women suffering from it don't always recognize that they have a serious problem. It is also often difficult to change the distorted body image. Typical therapy involves helping the patient to gain weight in order to prevent physical deterioration that can lead to death. Hospitalization, including intravenous feeding, is sometimes necessary. Efforts are made to reinforce eating and weight gain. Research is currently under way to identify the underlying causes of this serious eating disorder and to evaluate preventive therapies that will arrest the syndrome of self-starvation.

A related eating disorder is **bulimia**. Instead of starving, bulimics engage in "binge" eating and then force themselves to vomit. A binge might include a quart of cherry vanilla ice cream, two giant-size bags of potato chips, a pizza, and a gallon of Diet Pepsi. Bulimics also use laxatives and diuretics to rid themelves of food they have eaten and fluids they are retaining.

Binge eating itself is relatively common in our society. Between 13% and 67% of college students report that they occasionally binge (Polivy & Herman, 1985). What characterizes bulimia is the frequency of bingeing—an average of once a week or more—and the self-induced vomiting. Some bulimics report bingeing and purging 30 times in a week.

Like anorexics, bulimics are primarily women who fear getting fat and are unduly concerned with their body size. In fact, many anorexics show symptoms of bulimia; they sometimes binge and purge. But unlike women with anorexia, bulimic women rarely have low body weights, because they eat enough food to maintain normal weight. Some are even overweight. Since the binge-purge behavior is done secretly, many bulimics go unrecognized. These individuals often feel guilty and hide their disorder from friends and family.

Physiological effects include nutritional imbalances, damage along the digestive tract, and dehydration. Without treatment, the bulimic individual is unlikely to end the syndrome. Unfortunately, our understanding of this disorder is incomplete, and no single treatment is consistently effective.

bulimia A condition in which people engage in "binge" eating and then force themselves to vomit.

It is ironic that while many people in the world are starving, others are going to extreme efforts to avoid eating, either to reduce weight or because of eating disorders. Both the lack of and overabundance of food can lead to life-threatening problems and psychologists are continuing the search for interventions that can help individuals deal with these difficulties.

Social Motives

Social motives are forces, such as autonomy or affiliation, that direct human behavior toward certain patterns of relationships with other people. Several decades ago, social motives were often referred to as "derived," because many investigators believed that they were learned by association with more basic motives like hunger, as in the case of the child who learns to be assertive to get food and later becomes assertive in other respects. Today, these motives are often referred to more neutrally as "acquired," implying that social motives are learned but not necessarily derived directly from physiological drives.

There is no universally accepted list of social motives. Perhaps the most influential attempt to catalog social motives grew out of Henry Murray's 1938 book, *Explorations in Personality*. After intensively studying a small group of individuals, Murray proposed a list of human needs that included achievement (to accomplish difficult tasks), affiliation (to gain affection from friends), autonomy (independence), exhibition (to make an impression on others), understanding (intellectually asking questions), dominance, order, play, nurturance, deference, and ten others. He believed that complex human behavior could best be understood by studying the interplay of these social motives within a particular individual.

Later investigators focused on some of these motives more than others. The most intensively studied of all was the need for achievement.

The Need for Achievement

Because he was influenced by the psychoanalytic paradigm (see Chapter 12), Henry Murray believed that many social motives were unconscious and thus could be measured only indirectly. In the **Thematic Apperception Test (TAT)**, people were asked to use their creative imaginations to make up stories about a series of ambiguous pictures. There were no right or wrong answers on the TAT. Rather, the fantasies people produced were analyzed to reveal the hidden forces that motivated their behavior. Data from this test helped Murray develop his original list of 20 human needs. (See "Applying Scientific Concepts.")

To test the idea that such fantasies really did provide a valid measure (see Chapter 13) of motivation, John Atkinson and David McClelland (1948) began by manipulating the hunger drive to see whether this change in motivation would actually influence people's TAT stories. They started with hunger rather than one of the social motives because, in practical terms, it is much easier to increase hunger than to increase the need for autonomy or order.

In this study, sailors at a U.S. Navy submarine training school were not allowed to eat for 1 hour, 4 hours, or 16 hours. The relative hunger of these

social motives Forces, such as autonomy and affiliation, that direct human behavior toward certain patterns of relationships with other people.

Thematic Apperception Test (TAT) A test in which a person is asked to make up stories about a series of ambiguous pictures; used to reveal the hidden forces that motivate behavior.

In the Thematic Apperception Test, people are asked to tell stories about ambiguous pictures like this one.

three groups was indeed reflected in the stories they told about ambiguous pictures.

Encouraged by this success, McClelland and his co-workers went on to the more difficult task of manipulating social motivation and seeing whether this change influenced the stories people told. Once again, they drew on the work of Henry Murray and chose to study the **need for achievement** (sometimes abbreviated as *nAch*), which involves the attempt to excel and surpass others and to accomplish difficult tasks as rapidly and independently as possible. Again, the choice was partly a practical one; people could be deprived of achievement by creating a situation in which they were almost certain to fail.

In the original study (McClelland, Clark, Roby, & Atkinson, 1949), students at Wesleyan University were given a series of short writing tests that they were told "directly indicate a person's general level of intelligence . . . [and] demonstrate whether or not the person is suited to be a leader" (p. 244). These students expected success, because they were told that Wesleyan students generally did well on this particular test. But when the subjects in this group received their own grades, each person was told that his score was quite low compared with other Wesleyan students. Several control groups took

need for achievement (nAch) The attempt to excel and surpass others and to accomplish difficult tasks as rapidly and independently as possible.

Scoring Political Speeches

The study of motive patterns begun by Henry Murray now extends far beyond the TAT. One of the most interesting applications involves scoring the motives of political leaders "from a distance." Building on the earlier work of Henry Murray and David McClelland, David Winter (1980) has developed scoring systems that allow him to quantify the motivation reflected in the speeches of political leaders or candidates.

Winter has concentrated on three motives: the need for achievement (discussed in this chapter); the need for power (i.e., concern with getting and maintaining power); and the need for affiliation (i.e., concern with seeking the security of friendship).

Basically, Winter's procedure involves looking for verbal "images" that reflect the motives. For example, statements are scored as displaying the need for power if they are concerned with impact on others, arousal of strong emotions in others through inherently powerful actions, and preoccupation with one's reputation. Statements are scored as displaying the need for affiliation if they show a concern with establishing, maintaining, or restoring warm and friendly relationships or with

participating in friendly, convivial activity. Finally, the statements are coded as showing need for achievement when they show concern with standards of excellence, unique accomplishments, long-term involvements, and success in competition.

Provided below are verbatim quotations from the speeches of three American presidents. Use the preceding guidelines to code each excerpt for its predominant motive. (A discussion of the coding and scoring of these quotations appears after the "Summary" at the end of the chapter.)

> We are beginning to wipe out the line that divides the practical from the ideal; and in so doing we are fashioning an instrument of unimagined power for the establishment of a morally better world.
> —Franklin Delano Roosevelt

> [We must be prepared] in order to prevent other nations from taking advantage of us and of our inability to defend our interests and assert our rights with a strong hand.
> —William Howard Taft

> The physical configuration of the earth has separated us from all the Old World, but the common brotherhood of man, the highest law of all our being, has united us through inseparable bonds with all humanity.
> —Calvin Coolidge

the same test under less threatening circumstances. A relaxed group, for example, were told that the questions were being perfected for use in a new psychological test; their scores on this pilot version were meaningless.

As in the hunger experiment, this change in motivation was followed by administration of part of the Thematic Apperception Test. The students were asked to write stories about four ambiguous pictures. This time, the stories were scored for the appearance of achievement-related imagery. As the scoring system evolved, three main themes came to be recognized as signs of a need for achievement: competition with a standard of excellence, unique accomplishments, and pursuit of a long-term goal. For example, competition with a standard of excellence could be seen from stories in which a student worried about an exam or a surgeon had to work quickly and accurately. Other stories mentioned unique accomplishments such as inventions and artistic creations. Still other students revealed their needs for achievement by telling stories about a long-term goal, such as becoming a doctor or a successful businessman.

As expected, achievement imagery was far more common among those who thought they had failed. Just as hungry men had fantasized about food, so men who were "deprived of achievement" showed an increase in achievement imagery. This experiment supported the basic validity of TAT stories as a measure of this complex social motive.

Later studies revealed that the need for achievement is related to many different behavior patterns. For example, people who are high in the need for achievement work harder at laboratory tasks, learn faster, do their best work when it counts for the record, resist social pressure, are more active in community activities, and get better grades in high school (McClelland, 1958). They also tend to choose moderate risks rather than high-risk or no-risk situations, since this seems to maximize their chances for the greatest success.

In one demonstration of this last phenomenon, McClelland (1958) studied the way 5-year-old children played a game tossing rings onto a peg on the floor. The children were allowed to stand as close to the peg as they liked. Children who had previously been classified as high in the need for achievement tended to stand at an intermediate distance so that the game was challenging

FIGURE 11.3   In a ring-toss game, subjects who were high in the need for achievement and low in test anxiety were more likely to stand about 8 to 11 feet from the ring, a distance that makes success challenging but not impossible. People who were low in the need for achievement and high in test anxiety were more likely to stand either very close to the ring or very far away.

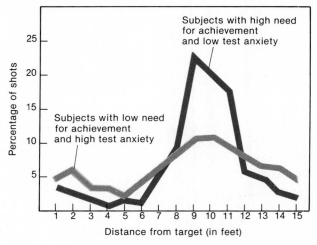

but not impossible. In contrast, children who were low in the need for achievement sometimes stood so close that they virtually could not fail or so far away that they could not succeed. Figure 11.3 illustrates the same pattern of results for a group of college students (Atkinson & Litwin, 1960).

While there have been demonstrations of this sort to show that the need for achievement predicts behavior on a wide variety of laboratory tasks, perhaps the most impressive evidence of the usefulness of this concept comes from studies of its relationship to real-life behavior. One long-term study examined the relationship between 55 college sophomores' scores in the need for achievement between 1947 and 1951 and the jobs these same men held in 1961, some 10 to 14 years later. McClelland (1965) divided the later occupations into two categories: *entrepreneurial* positions, in which the men had more individual responsibility for initiating action and greater risk (such as real estate and insurance sales, or operating one's own company), and *nonentrepreneurial* positions, with less responsibility and risk (such as credit managers and appraisers). Those who were high in the need for achievement in college were indeed more likely to end up in entrepreneurial jobs, just as one might predict. Of course, the need for achievement is only one of many factors involved in employment, so the relationship was far from perfect. In business jobs, 67% of the entrepreneurs were high in the need for achievement, versus 35% of the nonentrepreneurs. Nevertheless, it seems astounding that the result of a short test, in which college students simply made up stories describing the ambiguous pictures in the Thematic Apperception Test, could help predict their occupations a decade later.

McClelland went on to try to change people's behavior by increasing their needs for achievement. Four- to six-week training programs were designed to teach people what the need for achievement is and how it is measured. In one study (McClelland & Winter, 1971), 50 businessmen from a small city in India were instructed how to set specific business goals, taught to communicate with other businessmen, and encouraged to try to increase their own need for achievement. Studies of the behavior of these businessmen two years later revealed that they were far more active than a control group of businessmen from a neighboring Indian city. Those who had taken the short course had participated more in community development efforts, started more new businesses, invested more money in expanding their business, and employed more workers.

McClelland (1978) readily admits that "it is difficult to be certain of causation in field studies of this sort" (p. 205). Other economic and social differences between the two locations might have played some role, for example, or the simple act of participating in a special program may have been more important than its focus on the need for achievement. But this study is extremely encouraging for future research on the role of the need for achievement in real-life success.

Since real-life behavior probably most often involves combinations of motives rather than individual motives that work alone, future research is likely to achieve even greater success by concentrating on patterns of motivation. For example, in the study of college students' performance in the ring-toss game (see Figure 11.3), the most accurate predictions were achieved by also considering how anxious each individual felt about tests. Subjects who had high achievement motivation and low test anxiety were the most likely of all to stand at an intermediate distance from the peg, thus making the task somewhat risky. Interestingly, the real-life implications of this pattern have also been documented. College freshmen who score high in the need for achievement and low in test anxiety also tend to choose major subjects of intermediate difficulty rather than majors that are considered very difficult or very easy (Isaacson, 1964). With sufficient information about an individual's pattern of social motives, future researchers may be able to predict behaviors years or even decades before they occur.

Fear of Success

Fascinating as the early studies of achievement motivation were, they shared one critical shortcoming: The predominantly male researchers had devoted almost all their attention to men. In 1958, John W. Atkinson edited *Motives in Fantasy, Action and Society,* an 800-page summary of findings, theories, and speculation about achievement motivation; women were mentioned only in one footnote.

In 1965, Matina Horner began to collect the data for her doctoral dissertation on sex differences in achievement motivation. As part of the study, 88 men who were taking introductory psychology at the University of Michigan were asked to write several stories, beginning with sentences like the following: "After first term finals, John finds himself at the top of his medical school class." A typical male subject described John as dedicated and conscientious and concluded: "John continues working hard and eventually graduates at the top of his class" (Horner, 1969, p. 36). But when 89 women in the same class were asked to tell stories about what "Anne" felt when she was at the top of her medical school class, the answers were far less straightforward. Many involved themes of social rejection, such as: "Anne is an acne-faced bookworm," and: "Everyone hates and envies her." Other responses stressed doubts and guilt about succeeding, such as the story that ended: "Anne will finally have a nervous breakdown and quit medical school and marry a successful young doctor." Still other women expressed their conflict by distorting the story: "Anne is a code name for a nonexistent person created by med students. They take turns writing exams for Anne" (Horner, 1969, p. 38).

Horner concluded that some people have a **fear of success**—they are afraid that doing well in competitive situations will have negative consequences, such as unpopularity. Using a standard system to analyze each story, she found that 65% of the women's stories were characterized by fear of success. Only 9% of the men showed this same ambivalence. Horner linked this sex difference to American stereotypes that teach young girls that doing better than men is not ladylike.

She also found that fear of success seemed to affect performance in some situations. Subjects were given a variety of simple verbal tasks, such as seeing how many words they could form from the letters in the word *generation.* Sometimes students worked alone; other times they sat in a large classroom with males and females on opposite sides of the room. Women who were low in fear of success did better in the latter situation, which Horner referred

fear of success The fear that doing well in competitive situations will have negative consequences.

Although the original research on fear of success seemed to suggest that many women might do poorly in competitive environments such as medical schools, later studies revealed that fear of success is equally common in men and women.

to as "mixed sex competition." But women who scored high on fear of success did better when they worked by themselves. This suggested that fear of success can interfere with doing well in some types of competitive situations.

Horner's research became well known as a result of widespread publicity about its possible significance for the women's movement (*Ms.*, Spring 1972; *Time*, July 15, 1974). It is not uncommon to hear people talking, even today, about women's career conflicts that are caused by fear of success.

However, psychologists were not willing to accept such sweeping conclusions on the basis of a single study, and many went on to conduct investigations of their own. In 1977, David Tresemer reviewed 42 studies comparing over 6,000 men and women on a variety of measures of fear of success. Most of this research, like Horner's original study, concentrated on white American college students. But there were also surveys of many other groups, including high school students, Harvard Law School graduates, and executives of the Atlantic Richfield Company. Taken together, these studies made it quite clear that fear of success is just as common among American men as it is among American women.

Some of the most interesting follow-ups were direct descendants of Horner's thesis. A direct replication of Horner's methods (Hoffman, 1974; see "Understanding the Scientific Method") concluded that, at least in 1971, University of Michigan male undergraduates feared success just as much as females did.

Interestingly, the same researcher followed up the actual subjects Horner had studied in her doctoral dissertation. In the intervening years, 14 women from the original sample had gotten pregnant at a time when they were on the verge of advancing in their careers or at a time when their achievements threatened to outstrip their husbands'. Of these 14 women, 13 had been diagnosed as fearing success when they were in college. Here again, a short and simple test of social motivation in college seemed to predict important life choices years later.

Continuing research on the fear of success has revealed several layers of complexity. For example, it is often hard to tell whether a person who does not try is afraid of success or failure. Further, being a homemaker might be very satisfying for one woman and a sign of failure for another.

The recognition of such complications is a sign of the maturity of this research and its promise for the future. Like other physiological and social motives, fear of success does not act alone but rather provides another piece in the complex puzzle of human behavior. It is not a "women's problem"; it is a human problem.

Emotion

The topic of emotion has been a difficult one to study scientifically. Some psychologists have become so frustrated by this subject that they have argued—often quite angrily—that "emotion" is not a useful scientific concept at all.

Emotion is the spice of life—indeed, the very stuff of it. The emotion of love inspired Shah Jehan to build the Taj Mahal as a monument to his wife, and hatred and anger lay behind Auschwitz and the atrocities of World War II. If psychology is ever to understand the lustful, spiteful, idealistic world of human behavior, it must explain how we feel the things we do.

According to *Webster's* dictionary, *emotions* involve "strong feelings (as of love, hate, desire, or fear) . . . manifest in neuromuscular, respiratory, cardiovascular, hormonal, and other bodily changes." Psychologists too have emphasized the role of internal bodily changes in emotion and have attempted to chart its complex interactions between brain and body. The two oldest theories of emotion, the James-Lange and the Cannon-Bard, agree that there is an interaction, but they disagree on whether the fundamental source of emotional feelings lies in the body or the brain.

Early Theories of Emotion

Near the end of the nineteenth century, Harvard psychologist William James and Danish researcher Carl Lange each independently proposed a theory that seems to deny our everyday experience of emotions. According to common assumption, we laugh because we are happy and cry because we are sad. What came to be known as the **James-Lange theory** turned this view around. According to this theory, an event in the environment automatically stimulates a particular pattern of bodily changes. The brain then recognizes this pattern as belonging to a specific emotion and proceeds to label it. Thus, the feeling and experience of emotion comes second, while a direct physiological response comes first.

James-Lange theory The theory that an event automatically triggers a particular pattern of bodily changes, and that the brain then identifies each emotion on the basis of a particular physiological pattern.

Replication: Are Women Afraid to Succeed?

In the history of science, one of the most important checks on the accuracy of research has been replication—repeating a study to see if it yields the same result. There are several major types of replication, each with slightly different goals and slightly different procedures (Lykken, 1968). In a *literal replication,* an experimenter tries to repeat a study as precisely as possible. In a *constructive replication,* the experimenter changes the procedure in systematic ways to gain further insight into the result. As we shall see below, a single replication can include both literal and constructive aspects.

As noted in this chapter, Matina Horner, in her doctoral dissertation (1969), found that more women (65%) than men (9%) showed signs of fear of success when they wrote stories about a person of the same sex who had finished first in a medical school class. Because of the tremendous interest in the implications of this study and the controversy generated by it, in 1971 Lois Wladis Hoffman tried to replicate it.

She followed Horner's procedures as closely as possible. Once again, the subjects were students at the University of Michigan who were required to participate in an experiment as part of their introductory psychology course. Even apparently trivial features of the experiment were repeated, for example, "data were collected in two evening sessions; the date was at the same point in the term. . . . The room and the seating arrangements were the same. The male experimenter was chosen because he seemed to several persons who knew both of them to be a 1971 equivalent of the experimenter in the earlier study. The questionnaire books and instructions were identical. . . . The coders were personally trained by Horner to the exact coding procedures that she had used in the earlier study [to quantify fear of success]" (Hoffman, 1974, pp. 354–355).

This slavish attention to duplicating every detail was designed to ensure that any difference in the results could be attributed to the one major factor that *had*

(box continues on next page)

Consider the following example: The sight of a stranger in a dark alley may elicit pounding of the heart and sweaty hands. The brain notes these physiological changes and others from the internal organs and realizes, so quickly that we are not aware of any delay, "if my body is reacting this way, I must be afraid!" Implicit in the James-Lange theory is the idea that each emotion is physiologically distinct. If the brain decides when the body is angry and when it is afraid by performing an inventory of physiological changes, these two emotions must be characterized by distinct patterns of physiological activity.

Physiologist Walter Cannon rejected this view. As we noted in Chapter 3, Cannon was the first to discuss the activation of the sympathetic nervous system in "fight or flight." He believed that all strong emotions produced a single pattern of physiological arousal—including increased heart rate, se-

changed: The original study was conducted in 1965, the replication in 1971. If popular stereotypes of women's liberation were correct, the intervening six years had seen dramatic changes in the way American women perceived their roles in society. And any such changes should be especially obvious in a young, highly educated group like college students.

A total of 92 students participated in a literal replication that reproduced every detail of Horner's study. Another 116 subjects took part in several constructive replications in which one key aspect of the original procedure was changed. For example, 24 women were asked to write a story that began, "After first term finals, Anne finds that she is the top child psychology graduate student." Since medicine is traditionally a male-dominated field in the United States and child psychology is not, this cue was designed to see whether the nature of the profession was an important variable.

This minor change and others like it did not make any difference. Some 65% of the women still scored high in fear of success. But Hoffman's figure for 1971 men was 77%. Although the 1971 difference between the sexes did not quite achieve statistical significance, men actually showed more fear of success than women did. This replication seems to show that the cultural changes in the late 1960s had made men more ambivalent about success rather than making women less so.

But this conclusion was placed in doubt by still more research. It is extremely difficult to reproduce an experiment exactly. When Hoffman (1977) reanalyzed the original stories written for Horner in 1965, she found that her system for measuring fear of success was *not* the same as the original, despite her many attempts to make it the same. In the original study, 8 men out of 71 were classified as having a fear of success; when the same 71 stories were reanalyzed, 39 men showed this fear.

This careful series of replications and reanalyses led to two major conclusions: Fear of success is indeed a common phenomenon, but one that is quite difficult to measure precisely, and American women do not fear success more than men do. These careful follow-ups also make it clear that replication can distinguish between legitimate findings and those based on faulty procedures or random variation. Thus, replication is a critical step in the scientist's search for truth.

cretion of the hormone adrenaline, reduced blood flow near the surface of the skin, and increased sweating—which prepared the organism to deal with an emergency.

Cannon firmly rejected James's notion of a separate physiological pattern for each emotion. Instead, he saw the key to emotional experience in the brain. For William James, the brain recognized an emotion simply by passively checking which internal organs were on and which were off. For Cannon, the brain played a much more important role. Electrical and chemical changes in the brain (in the area he called the optic thalamus) simultaneously produced bodily changes and emotional experience. Because this view was supported by a series of experiments performed by Philip Bard, this became known as the **Cannon-Bard theory** of emotion. The basic assumptions of common sense,

Cannon-Bard theory The theory that the brain responds to external events, simultaneously producing both physiological and emotional experiences.

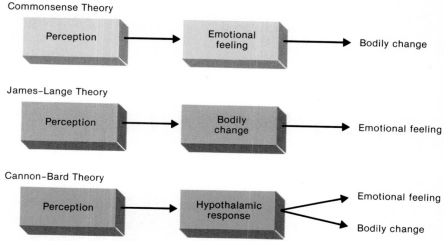

Commonsense Theory

Perception → Emotional feeling → Bodily change

James–Lange Theory

Perception → Bodily change → Emotional feeling

Cannon–Bard Theory

Perception → Hypothalamic response → Emotional feeling / Bodily change

FIGURE 11.4 Three theories of emotion.

the James-Lange theory, and the Cannon-Bard theory are outlined in Figure 11.4.

To support his theory, Cannon (1927) cited evidence that signals from the peripheral organs were not a necessary ingredient in the experience of emotion. Specifically, when internal feedback was cut off by surgically destroying the fibers that connected the sympathetic nervous system to the brain in dogs and cats, the experimental animals still gave behavioral signs of emotion. For example, cats continued to show all the normal signs of feline rage when confronted with a barking dog.

Hohmann (1966) challenged this conclusion in a study of 25 patients with spinal-cord injuries. For these unfortunate victims, Mother Nature and human carelessness had performed cruel experiments in which certain nerve fibers were severed accidentally. Some patients had damaged relatively low portions of the spinal cord, so feedback from internal organs still reached the brain through the higher, undamaged sections. Others, whose damage was closer to the brain, received little or no information from internal organs.

Hohmann (1966) asked these patients to remember an emotional incident that occurred before the injury and to compare it to one that occurred afterward. Interestingly, he found that the loss of internal sensations did indeed reduce emotional feeling. As one subject put it:

> [Now] it's sort of cold anger. Sometimes I act angry when I see some injustice. I yell and cuss and raise hell, because if you don't do it sometimes, I've learned people will take advantage of you, but it just doesn't have the heat to it that it used to. It's a mental kind of anger. (Quoted in Schachter, 1971, p. 50)

Even more convincing than such testimonials was Hohmann's evidence that the less feedback patients had from internal organs, the more their emotional experience was reduced.

This evidence suggests that Cannon was wrong when he claimed that bodily responses are only a side effect of emotion and have no role in our feelings. However, some of his other claims were quite influential, particularly the idea that all strong emotions produce a single pattern of physiological arousal.

Arousal

As noted earlier, if the James-Lange theory is correct, each emotion must produce a different pattern of physiological activity so that it can be recognized by the brain. While researchers have been able to identify such differences between anger and fear (Ax, 1953), in general most emotions seem to be accompanied by a more general pattern of **arousal** in which several physiological systems are activated at the same time, including higher heart rate, sweat gland activity, and electrical activity of the brain. Several theories have been proposed to explain the significance of arousal in motivation and emotion.

Low levels of arousal characterize periods of drowsiness or sleep, although a few purists maintain that the *lowest* level of arousal is death. Higher levels of arousal are characterized by high activation or stress (see Chapter 17). Extreme emotions, such as panic, also produce high arousal. According to an influential theory called the **Yerkes-Dodson law**, there is an *optimal level*, or most desirable amount, of arousal for activity; too little or too much arousal produces inferior performance. For example, most people would agree that if a student stays up all night to study and comes to a final exam half asleep, this low level of arousal is likely to result in a reduced grade. However, the person who gets a full night of rest and then drinks 16 cups

FIGURE 11.5 The relationship between arousal and performance according to the Yerkes-Dodson law. This theory holds that there is an optimal (or ideal) level of arousal for the most efficient performance of any task. Too little or too much arousal will produce inferior performance.

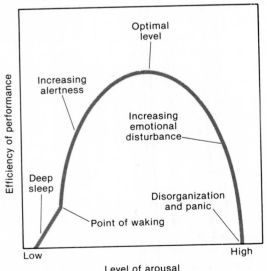

According to the Yerkes-Dobson law, individuals will perform particular activities best at some optimal level of arousal.

arousal A general pattern in which several physiological systems are activated simultaneously, including heart rate, sweat gland activity, and electrical activity of the brain.

Yerkes-Dodson law The theory that there is an optimal level of arousal for any activity; too much or too little arousal produces inferior performance.

Schachter and Singer's cognitive theory The theory that emotional response to a particular situation depends on the individual's perception and interpretation of that situation, and that the emotion's intensity depends on the degree of physiological arousal.

of coffee to increase concentration is also likely to do poorly—in this case because too much arousal interferes with performance. Figure 11.5 summarizes the Yerkes-Dodson law in a form that is sometimes called the inverted-*U* relationship between arousal and performance (that is, the graph looks like the letter *U* upside down).

The actual ideal amount of arousal may be different for a tennis match and a chess game or may vary from one person to another. But according to this theory, any individual will perform a particular task best at some optimal level of arousal.

While this notion has been influential and has generated a large body of research, it is not without problems. Psychophysiologists have found that different measures of arousal do not always vary together; increases in blood pressure are often associated with decreases in EEG arousal, for example, and some drugs produce behavioral arousal and EEG signs of relaxation (Lacey, 1967). The notion that there is one single variable called arousal is at best only a first approximation. But this notion has proved useful in research in many areas, including the topic of lie detection.

Cognitive Approaches

Despite the fact that lie detection is closely related to arousal theories of motivation, this work has had little influence on the study of emotion. Within the scientific mainstream, current views have combined the best of past theories with a more cognitive orientation.

Stanley Schachter and Jerome Singer (1962) combined William James's idea that bodily reactions are an important element in emotional experience and Cannon's notion of arousal with a cognitive emphasis on the individual's thoughts and interpretations. According to **Schachter and Singer's cognitive theory**, the specific emotion individuals experience depends on how they perceive and interpret their situation, while its intensity is determined by the degree of physiological arousal. Thus, a woman whose sympathetic nervous system is aroused might feel happy if she is at a party but angry if the same physiological response occurs during an argument.

To test this theory, Schachter and Singer (1962) decided to produce arousal artificially and then place people in situations that might elicit different emotions. Male psychology students at the University of Minnesota were recruited for a study of how the "vitamin compound Suproxin" influenced vision. In fact, no visual tests were planned, and the injection the men received was either a harmless placebo (salt water) or epinephrine, a drug that activates the sympathetic nervous system. The effects of epinephrine (also known as adrenaline) include increases in heart rate and blood pressure, decreased blood flow to the skin, and increases in blood sugar and lactic acid. The injection produced essentially the same physical reaction that you might have if you were frightened suddenly and adrenaline was secreted into your bloodstream by the adrenal glands (see Chapter 3).

One group of subjects—called "epinephrine informed"—were warned that Suproxin had certain side effects, including shaky hands, a pounding heart, and a flushed face. Another group—called "epinephrine ignorant"—

received no such warning. There were several control groups; the most important received placebo injections.

Schachter and Singer then set up situations in which people were likely to label their experience as "happy" or "angry." They predicted that epinephrine-ignorant subjects would experience the strongest emotions because they would attribute their physical reactions to the situations. Epinephrine-informed subjects would have another explanation for their pounding hearts ("it's only a side effect of the drug") and would therefore not experience such intense emotions. Similarly, the placebo group would not experience intense emotions because the salt-water injections would not produce physiological arousal.

To induce happiness, a research assistant posing as another participant joined the first subject while they "waited for the drug to take effect" and proceeded to make a fool of himself according to a prearranged script—flying a paper airplane, using a rubber band as a slingshot, building a tower out of manila folders and knocking it down with the slingshot, and so on.

In the anger-inducing condition, the stooge continually complained about a five-page questionnaire the two subjects were supposed to fill out while they waited. Since the questions were designed to grow increasingly personal and insulting, he had plenty to grumble about. For example, question 25 asked each subject to list one person in his family who "does not wash or bathe regularly," "seems to need psychiatric care," and so on. After saying "I'll be damned if I fill out number 25," the stooge angrily crossed out the item.

The stooge's anger peaked for question 28: "How many times each week do you have sexual intercourse?" At this point he ripped up the questionnaire, threw the pieces on the floor, and stomped out of the room. Had he stayed around, he could have read eight more offensive questions, ending with: "With how many men (other than your father) has your mother had extramarital relationships? Four and under _____; Five–Nine _____; Ten and over _____."

The subjects' emotional reactions were measured in two different ways. Throughout the stooge's act, an observer watched through a one-way mirror and systematically coded how much each subject went along with the stooge. In addition, after the routine was finished, the experimenter returned with a series of questionnaires that included items asking people to rate their anger, happiness, and physical symptoms. Once these were finished, the researcher announced that the experiment was over and explained the deception in detail. (See "Understanding the Scientific Method" in Chapter 16 for a discussion of the ethical issues involved in this type of deception.) Schachter and Singer reported that subjects who had been correctly informed about the drug's effects were relatively uneffected by the stooge's behavior. However, subjects who had been misinformed or uninformed were strongly influenced by the stooge acting euphoric or angry and reported feelings of euphoria or anger depending on what the stooge had done.

After reviewing the results of this experiment and others like it, Schachter and Singer concluded that their cognitive theory of emotion was basically correct. However, other researchers were later unable to replicate some of their specific findings (Marshall & Zimbardo, 1979), and many questions have been raised about their original interpretations. Despite these complications, the research had an important impact on the way psychologists viewed emotions.

Schachter and Singer's most important conclusion was that cognitive interpretations affect emotional experience and behavior. There is now a large body of research supporting this view. One example comes from a series of studies performed by Richard Lazarus and his colleagues in which reactions to a very arousing stimulus are manipulated by providing people with different cognitive attitudes. The stimulus was chosen for its stressfulness: A film showing an Australian aborigine puberty rite—a circumcision performed with a stone knife—in graphic detail and living color.

To influence the way viewers reacted to this film, several sound tracks were developed. One tried to maximize stress by emphasizing the trauma produced by the procedure ("Several men . . . hold the boy so that he cannot escape"); another denied the painfulness ("The words of encouragement offered by the older men have their effect"); a third sound track produced a more detached and intellectual perspective ("The surgical technique, while crude, is very carefully followed"). Physiological measurements of the arousal produced by these and other versions revealed that subjects who heard the denial or intellectualization sound track did indeed respond less than those who heard the more stressful commentary (Speisman, Lazarus, Davidson, & Mordkoff, 1964).

In an article entitled "The Schachter Theory of Emotion: Two Decades Later," Reisenzein (1983) summarized the specific points that were supported or challenged by later research. For example, Zillmann (1971) found that autonomic arousal often continues after an arousing situation, such as physical exercise, is over. In some cases, this "leftover arousal" may intensify an emotional experience.

For example, studies have shown that when people are still slightly aroused from physical exercise, an unpleasant situation will make them angrier and more aggressive than it otherwise would. Similarly, after sexual arousal there is evidence for a heightened response to such diverse situations as aggression and enjoyment of music (Leventhal & Tomarken, 1986). Apparently, people attribute all the arousal they feel to the second situation, even though some of it is actually left over from the first.

Several related phenomena have also been observed under carefully arranged situations. While these subtle details are critical for the researchers who are seeking a full understanding of cognitive factors in emotion, for our purposes a much simpler conclusion will suffice. In general, later research has supported Schachter and Singer's idea that the way people interpret a situation can affect their emotional response.

Lie Detection

Physiological tests to determine whether a person is telling the truth have a long history. In ancient times, the Chinese required a man accused of a crime to chew a mouthful of dried rice; if he could spit it out, he was judged innocent. In retrospect, this test of guilt was crudely based on a physiological fact: When the sympathetic nervous system is activated by stress, salivation decreases. If the man was guilty, he would be anxious and his mouth would be dry; he would find it difficult to swallow or to spit. Unfortunately, the test ignores the fact that the innocent man might also be scared spitless.

The modern era of lie detection began around 1890 when an Italian criminologist named Cesare Lombroso claimed that he could tell when a criminal suspect was lying by measuring his blood pressure while he was being interrogated. About 30 years later, Leonarde Keeler quit his job with the Berkeley, California, police department to manufacture Keeler *polygraphs,* devices that simultaneously recorded breathing, relative blood pressure, and the electrical activity of the skin (an indirect measure of sweat gland activity). Most lie detectors are modern versions of Keeler's primitive machine.

Traditionally, psychologists have had little to do with the lie detection business. The field of polygraphy—a term most professionals prefer to the popular term *lie detection*—was founded by men with experience in the police and the military. These skilled interrogators often saw academic research as an ivory-tower science that had little to say about a real world full of criminals and liars. Physiological researchers, in turn, saw polygraphers as businessmen who were more interested in selling their own lie detection tests than in objectively evaluating their accuracy. The relationship between psychology and commercial polygraphy was one of distrust founded on ignorance.

Lie detection is big business. Estimates of the number of polygraph examinations given in the United States each year range from several hundred thousand to several million. Contrary to popular belief, most of these examinations are conducted not for the police but in the world of business. A woman who has applied for an executive position in a department store may be tested to see if she has ever been in trouble, or all the employees at the local Burger King may be grilled to see who's been pocketing the money that should have ended up in the cash register.

The legal status of lie detection is somewhat ambiguous. Some states regulate polygraphy; in other states you could become a professional lie detector simply by placing your name in the Yellow Pages. Ordinarily, polygraph examinations are not permitted as evidence in a court of law. But exceptions have been made. And when suspects confess as a result of a polygraph test, their statements can usually be held against them.

Typically, a criminal lie detection test begins with an interview covering the subject's history and background. Before the machine is connected, the interrogator and subject agree on about ten questions that can be answered simply yes or no. Some questions are emotionally neutral, some are control questions designed to elicit an emotional response (for example, "Have you ever hurt someone?"), and some are relevant to the crime in question. If the questions are designed properly, a person who is innocent should have the largest physiological response to the irrelevant emotional questions; a guilty person's largest physiological response should be to the questions that relate specifically to the crime.

No single physiological response always signals a lie. Rather, the polygrapher looks for signs of general emotional arousal associated with activation of the sympathetic nervous system—irregular breathing, high blood pressure, and electrical signs of increased sweating. The actual decision about whether

As this man takes a lie detector test, a cuff around his arm measures blood pressure, and a tube around his chest measures breathing. Electrodes on his fingertips also measure his sweat-gland activity.

a particular pattern of responses indicates arousal is based on a complex interaction of the three measures and has not been specified precisely. For this reason, polygraph reading is usually treated as an art rather than a science. Further, most professional polygraphers prefer to base their final verdict on all the evidence available (including the conduct of the suspect during the interview) rather than strictly on physiological responses. Thus, polygraph examination is not a simple and unambiguous physiological test; it is a complex type of interrogation.

There have been many tests of the validity of lie detection, in both the laboratory and the real world. In one study, Kleinmutz and Szucho (1984) reanalyzed the polygraph records of 100 people who had been investigated by a commercial polygraph firm in connection with some crime. Half of these subjects had later confessed to the crime. The other half were considered innocent, since someone else had come forward and confessed to the crime.

The polygraph records were evaluated by six apprentice polygraphers who had just completed their training. There was considerable disagreement among these polygraphers as to who was innocent and who was guilty; the correlations among their ratings ranged from .45 to .61. (See Appendix for explanation of correlation coefficients.) The relationship between the polygraphers' opinions and the independent judgments of guilt or innocence of the case was also rather weak. These correlations ranged from .45 to .55.

Even more distressing was the fact that in this study, on the average, 37% of the innocent subjects were judged guilty by the polygraphers. Some of the polygraphers had been far more accurate than others; the best judge misclassified only 18% of the subjects, while the worst misclassified half.

Kleinmutz and Szucho (1984, p. 774) concluded that "the technique is not only highly fallible, it is also highly fakeable." They cite the story of a man who was convicted of murder, largely on the basis of polygraph tests, and later exonerated. While in prison, he took up the study of polygraphy as a hobby and coached a number of fellow prisoners on how to beat the test. His fellow prisoners were given lie detector exams on drug charges and other violations of prison rules, which they had freely confessed to the coach. After only 20 minutes of coaching, 23 of 27 prisoners succeeded in beating the test.

In 1983, the U.S. Congress conducted hearings regarding the validity of lie detection and commissioned a review of the entire scientific literature. Saxe, Dougherty, and Cross (1985) found that only 10 of the 250 studies they reviewed met their criteria for adequacy. They involved real crimes and some independent criterion of guilt, usually a confession.

Over the ten studies, polygraph tests of guilt or innocence were more accurate than chance, but there were many errors. The percentage of guilty subjects falsely judged innocent ranged from 0% to 25% in different studies. The variation between studies was higher for innocent people judged guilty; from 0% to 75% fell victim to this error. Other types of errors also varied greatly from study to study.

Overall, these figures suggest that the test has some validity; polygraph determinations of guilt and innocence are substantially more accurate than the flip of a coin. But errors are also quite common, particularly for people who are in fact innocent.

These conclusions were also consistent with reviewers' analysis of laboratory studies of mock crimes and with the analyses of earlier reviewers. A properly conducted polygraph examination can indeed help distinguish a liar from someone who tells the truth. However, although there is still controversy about exactly how often errors are made, there is no question that even the best polygraphers do make mistakes. And in the hands of an unskilled operator, the lie detector may be a real menace to civil liberty. (See "Becoming a Critical Consumer.")

Psychologists must continue to do research to establish the conditions in which lie detection works best and to estimate the reasonable likelihood of its success. Ultimately, however, others will have to decide on the place of lie detection in our society—how good is good enough?

Facial Expressions

Even before William James proposed his first theory of emotion, Charles Darwin started a research tradition that continues to the present day. In 1872, he published *The Expression of the Emotions in Man and Animals,* a book that extended his theory of evolution to the study of postures, gestures, and facial expressions. For example, Darwin noted that such widely different species as cats, dogs, monkeys, rats, and humans have been known to defecate and urinate when they are afraid. He wished to show the continuity of emotional

Should Lie Detectors Be Used on Defense Workers?

In a 1985 interview (*U.S. News & World Report*, p. 44) General Richard Stilwell (retired), Deputy Under Secretary in the U.S. Department of Defense, argued that lie detector tests should be required for all Defense Department employees with access to classified information. When asked why polygraphs should be administered to such employees, General Stilwell asserted that lie detectors could help prevent unauthorized release of information that "could jeopardize lives or lose the U.S. an important strategic advantage." In answer to several follow-up questions, General Stilwell made a number of assertions about lie detection. Compare these comments with the material on lie detection in this chapter. (A discussion of this comparison appears after the "Summary" at the end of this chapter.) As you make the comparison, ask yourself this question: Does the evidence in the chapter provide strong support for the assertions made by General Stilwell?

Q: Don't polygraphs often give incorrect results, indicating a person is lying when he is merely nervous?
A: They are not 100 percent valid. But they accurately record three physiological reactions to questions. . . .
Q: Can't some people learn to control their reactions and "beat the machine"?
A: That may happen but very rarely. We give these tests to employees who work 10 hours or more a day. It's inconceivable that they could also be undergoing rigorous training to control three reactions simultaneously.

expression across species to support his theory that all animals are descended from common ancestors. Darwin believed that some common emotional expressions are innate, that they are biologically wired into the human species.

Of course, the meanings of some nonverbal gestures are simply a matter of convention and vary from one society to the next (see Chapter 16). When Americans disagree, they sometimes wag their heads from side to side to say no; Bulgarians use the same movement to say yes. Tibetans stick out their tongue to say hello, and in parts of Greece the thumbs-up gesture Americans use to signify approval has an obscene meaning that we associate with the middle finger (Ekman, 1975). But cross-cultural similarities in facial expressions of emotion do support Darwin's idea that some expressions are innate. In one study (Ekman, Sorenson, & Friesen, 1969), researchers sorted through over 3,000 pictures to choose faces that seemed to represent one of six basic emotions: happiness, sadness, fear, anger, surprise, and disgust. They chose 30 photographs of Caucasian children and adults whose faces seemed to unambiguously communicate one of these six emotions.

In the original study, these photographs were shown to college students in the United States, Brazil, and Japan. Each observer was given the list of six emotions and asked which emotion was expressed by each face. Table 11.1 lists the results, along with those of later experiments in Argentina and Chile. As you can see, the agreement is not perfect. But what is? This table does show a remarkable degree of consistency; apparently the meaning of an American's happy face would be quite clear in Japan, Argentina, Chile, and Brazil. Similar studies found comparable results from other groups in England, France, Germany, Greece, Hawaii, Sweden, Turkey, and several African nations (Izard, 1971).

Despite this impressive cross-cultural consistency, some critics were still not satisfied. Since the mass media have made our planet a small world, they reasoned that Greeks and Swedes might have learned to read American expressions by watching reruns of "Kojak" and the "Mary Tyler Moore Show." To rule out this possibility, Ekman and Friesen (1971) conducted studies of the most isolated group they could find—members of the Fore culture in the southeast highlands of New Guinea.

This primitive group was "discovered by civilization" only 12 years before the study was conducted. The 189 adults and 130 children who participated in the experiment had never seen a movie, spoke neither English nor pidgin, had not lived in a Western settlement or government town, and had never worked for a Caucasian. They were the most isolated members of an isolated culture. A special task was developed to avoid difficulties in translation. Adults were to pick one of three Caucasian faces that fit the emotion expressed in a particular story. For example, the fear story began: "She is sitting in her house all alone, and there is no one else in the village. There is no knife, axe, or bow and arrow in the house. A wild pig is standing in the door of the house, and the woman is looking at the pig and is very afraid of it." The sadness story said simply: "His child has died, and he feels very sad" (Ekman & Friesen, 1971, p. 126).

TABLE 11.1

Cultural Interpretations of the Facial Expressions of Six Emotions

Photograph judged						
Judgment	HAPPINESS	DISGUST	SURPRISE	SADNESS	ANGER	FEAR
Culture			*Percent who agreed with judgment*			
99 Americans	97	92	95	84	67	85
40 Brazilians	95	97	87	59	90	67
119 Chileans	95	92	93	88	94	68
168 Argentinians	98	92	95	78	90	54
29 Japanese	100	90	100	62	90	66

Both children and adults in the Fore culture were able to pick out the appropriate Western face. (For example, 92% of the Fore adults picked a smiling face when they heard the happiness story.) There was one interesting exception: These people could not tell the difference between Western faces that represented surprise and fear. One possible explanation is that in the Fore culture, fearful events are almost always also surprising, like the wild pig that suddenly appeared in the empty village.

Interestingly, other studies of facial expression support a modified version of the James-Lange theory. According to Silvan Tomkins (1962), feedback from facial muscles can influence emotional experience. For a do-it-yourself demonstration of this theory, try setting your face in a big, broad, stupid grin and see if it doesn't make you feel just a little happy. In a more systematic test of this notion, people who received mild electric shocks found that they experienced more pain when they allowed the pain to show in their faces than when they maintained more stoic expressions (Colby, Lanzetta, & Kleck, 1977). It is possible that people purposely ignored the shock to achieve stoic expressions and that the direction of attention is the critical factor.

Recent findings point to other subtleties in the link between facial expression and subjective feeling. For example, the link between expression and subjective feeling appears to be stronger when people spontaneously make faces than when they pose for a viewer. In a study by Kraut (1982), people sniffed 12 different odors while an experimenter recorded their facial expressions. At first, subjects simply sniffed and issued their verdicts. Later, these same people were asked to make faces that would communicate the quality of the odor to a viewer. Kraut found that the association between facial expression and subjective judgments about the odors was stronger in the spontaneous trial than in the communication trial. Two related findings shed light on the results of this experiment.

First, there is a great deal of evidence that spontaneous facial expressions and voluntarily induced facial expressions use two different neurological pathways. People who have suffered certain kinds of neurological damage are unable to produce more than a lopsided grin when asked to smile, yet they smile normally if someone tells a joke about golfing and they are genuinely amused. Patients with Parkinson's disease show the opposite problem: They can produce a perfect smile on command, but cannot produce spontaneous emotional expressions. Finally, patients with a third type of neurological damage suffer from spells of involuntary weeping or laughing, despite the fact that they do not feel the corresponding emotion (Rinn, 1984).

The second finding is that careful analyses of posed facial expressions reveal that they are not identical to natural expressions. Both timing and the coordination of different parts of the face (eyes, mouth, etc.) are noticeably "off" in posed expressions (Ekman & Friesen, 1975).

Perhaps fake smiles do not trigger the correct neuronal pathway for spontaneous emotions. Therefore, the smilers do not feel as happy as if they had genuinely beamed at something that pleased them. Putting on a happy face may make you feel better, but it is not as good as the real thing.

Another interesting trend in this research involved physiological recordings of facial muscles to reveal slight changes in expression that cannot be seen by the naked eye. For example, when subjects are instructed to think happy thoughts, changes in the rate of electrical activity in the depressor muscle near the chin can be detected by physiological recording devices even when a person does not seem to be smiling. Similar recordings also revealed that when depressed persons are asked to "imagine a typical day," their facial muscles reveal subtle signs of sadness (Schwartz, Fair, Salt, Mandel, & Klerman, 1976). Although we are far away from a physiological technology that allows us to read people's minds, perhaps we will soon discover new physiological procedures that will help us to read their faces.

Summary

- **Motivation** involves the forces that influence the strength or direction of behavior.
- The topic of motivation is closely related to the study of **emotions**, physical reactions that are experienced as strong feelings, such as happiness, fear, and anger.

Models of Motivation

- Early theories of motivation debated the relative merits of **determinism**, in which every event is seen as the inevitable product of a series of natural forces, versus **free will**, which assumes that people are free to choose what they will do.
- Around 1900, psychologists emphasized the importance of **instincts**, inborn forces that direct an organism toward a certain goal.
- According to a later theoretical formulation, **needs** are physiological requirements of the organism, while **drives** are motivational forces that incite an organism to action.
- More recently, theories of motivation have recognized the importance of **incentives**, external stimuli that increase the likelihood of behavior.
- According to Solomon's **opponent-process theory**, many acquired motives arise from the interplay of two opposing processes in the brain, such as pleasure in response to pain, and vice versa.
- These days, most researchers have moved away from general theories of this sort and concentrate instead on the analysis of individual motives.

Physiological Motives

- **Physiological motives** are internal bodily states that direct an organism's behavior toward a goal, such as food, water, or sex.
- Early studies of hunger tried to localize its origins, first in the stomach and later in the hypothalamus.
- Researchers now know that many other processes are involved in hunger, including body temperature, fat deposits, blood-sugar levels, and the responsiveness of obese people to external cues.

- Body weight is determined by the interactions between three major factors: the amount and type of food eaten, the amount of energy expended in physical activity, and the storage of fat in cellular tissue. The relations among these factors may vary in different individuals.

- **Obsesity** can be defined as at least 15% to 20% over one's ideal weight.

- One theory of obesity emphasizes the importance of **set points**, the body's internal levels for regulating body weight.

- **Anorexia nervosa** is a syndrome characterized by the refusal to eat enough food to maintain or gain weight, a fear of becoming fat, and significant weight loss.

- A related eating disorder is **bulimia**, a condition in which people engage in "binge" eating and then force themselves to vomit.

Social Motives

- **Social motives** are forces, such as autonomy and affiliation, that direct human behavior toward certain patterns of relationships with other people.

- In the **Thematic Apperception Test (TAT)**, people are asked to make up stories about a series of ambiguous pictures.

- The results of a TAT test can identify people with a high **need for achievement**, who attempt to excel and surpass others and to accomplish difficult tasks as rapidly and independently as possible.

- In the late 1960s, some studies suggested that women are more likely than men to have a **fear of success**. They are afraid that doing well in competitive situations will have negative consequences, such as unpopularity.

- Later studies revealed that fear of success characterized as many men as women.

Emotion

- According to the **James-Lange theory** of emotion, an event can automatically trigger a particular bodily response. The feeling of emotion is based on the brain's later identification of the physiological response.

- In contrast, the **Cannon-Bard theory** held that the brain responded to external events, simultaneously producing both physiological responses and emotional experience.

- Most emotions are accompanied by a general pattern of **arousal** in which several physiological systems are activated at the same time, including higher heart rate, sweat gland activity, and electrical activity of the brain.

- According to the **Yerkes-Dodson law**, there is an *optimal level* (most desirable amount) of arousal for any activity; too little or too much arousal interferes with performance.

- According to **Schachter and Singer's cognitive theory** of emotions, the intensity of emotional experience is determined by the degree of arousal of the sympathetic nervous system, but the actual emotion is determined by the perception of the situation.

- Most psychologists now believe that cognitive factors have a major influence on emotional experience.

- Tests of lie detection assume that deception will produce a pattern of physiological arousal, including irregular breathing, high blood pressure, and increased sweat-gland activity.

- Studies of facial expressions have identified six basic emotions that are expressed the same way in virtually every culture: happiness, sadness, anger, fear, surprise, and disgust.

Critical Thinking Exercises Discussions

Scoring Political Speeches

The quotations in this exercise were among the most straightforward examples analyzed by David Winter and Abigail Stewart (1977) in a study assessing the motive patterns of political leaders. The first quotation, from a speech by President Roosevelt, was scored as reflecting the need for achievement. The second, from President Taft, was scored as reflecting the need for power. Finally, the third quotation, from a speech by President Coolidge, was scored as reflecting the need for affiliation. Other studies (such as Winter, 1980; Winter & Stewart, 1977) have shown that more sophisticated ratings of this type correlate highly with experts' ratings of important political dispositions and style, as well as with actual political actions and outcomes.

The process of coding qualitative material, such as speeches, always involves *categorizing* information. Categorization is a key critical thinking skill that is essential to the scientific method. It involves several component skills highlighted in previous thinking exercises: identifying the defining characteristics of a concept or category, discriminating among related concepts, and extending what is known about categories to new items so as to categorize the new items correctly.

Should Lie Detectors Be Used on Defense Workers?

The research results reported in this chapter estimate the success rate of lie detection at considerably less than 100%. For example, Saxe, Dougherty, and Cross (1985) found that the percent of subjects falsely judged innocent ranged from 0% to 25% in various studies, while the proportion falsely judged guilty ranged from 0% to 75%. In addition, Kleinmutz and Szucho (1984, p. 744) are quoted as concluding that lie detection is "not only highly fallible, but also highly fakeable." They cited one study in which 27 convicts were trained to "beat the polygraph." Twenty-three of them succeeded after just 20 minutes of training.

A systematic comparison of different sets of information is itself an important critical thinking skill. While General Stilwell acknowledges that polygraphs are not 100% valid, he does not provide any precise figures as to potential invalidity. If polygraphs led to correct judgments 99% or even 90% of the time, they might be considered sufficiently valid for making employment decisions. However, when you look at the actual data reported by Saxe et al., you see that polygraphs have led to incorrect inferences concerning guilt in as many as 75% of research subjects. Moreover, while General Stilwell says it is "inconceivable" that employees could train to beat the polygraph, Kleinmutz and Szucho report data indicating that convicts can be trained rather quickly and easily to beat the machine.

One of the reasons that scientific knowledge progresses over time is that scientists don't assume that all the facts about an issue have been discovered just because some expert claims to know the answers. That is, scientists do not turn off their critical thinking abilities just because somebody with credentials tells them something. Instead, they examine the available data to see if the weight of the relevant empirical evidence supports or fails to support the assertions being presented. In General Stilwell's case, the objective evidence does not provide strong support for his claims.

PERSONALITY

Chapter 12

*T*he first eleven chapters of this book have focused on the search for general laws of behavior and experience. For example, we described how the memory of the average eyewitness distorts the details of a crime and how the typical infant lacks a sense of object permanence. In each case, researchers have tried to establish principles that apply generally to all people. However, intuitively we believe that people are not all alike—that Aunt Jane is far more extraverted than Aunt Edna, and that because the local butcher tells so many meat jokes he has a better-than-average sense of humor.

Consider the case of two hypothetical students who fail their first psychology exam. One might be so upset that he would cut his next class, skip lunch, and feel sick to his stomach for the next several days. He might even wonder whether he should forget about college and go directly to a $40,000-per-year job selling used cars. Another student could react quite differently; she might glance quickly at the *F* on her way to the cafeteria and then sit down to a lunch of extra-hot curried chicken while telling jokes about balding psychology teachers, as if she didn't have a care in the world.

Studies of personality raise two basic questions about these hypothetical cases. Do different reactions in this specific situation give insight into a general pattern of individual behavior? If so, what causes these individual differences? The first question is the more fundamental one. Would the man with the upset stomach react the same way to an *F* in art history, an inability to repair a broken window, and a bad job evaluation from his boss? For if he reacts to each of these situations in entirely different ways, it would not be legitimate to characterize him as insecure or easily upset on the basis of a single observation.

In general, personality psychologists argue that there are consistent patterns of differences among people. Indeed, **personality** may be defined as an individual's characteristic pattern of thought, behavior, and emotions. Recently, some psychologists have argued that the consistency of these patterns may be an illusion caused by biases in the way people perceive one another (see "Of Persons and Situations" later in this chapter).

But it is the second question we raised, on the causes of the complex behavior patterns of a specific individual, that has historically attracted the most attention. In other words, why do we do the things we do? This is a broad question indeed; it almost seems arrogant for a psychologist to try to answer it. After all, one might argue that the entire history of literature and a good part of philosophy reflect an attempt to solve the puzzle of human character. From Homer's attempt to understand Odysseus to Shakespeare's characterization of Julius Caesar and Carolyn Keene's insights into Nancy Drew, writers have tried to understand and explain specific personalities.

The complexity of the subject matter of personality makes it one of the most fascinating topics in psychology. But it is also one of the most frustrating, because psychologists have not agreed on a single, unified, complete, and coherent view. We have encountered such theoretical conflicts before, as in the clash between behavioral and cognitive views of learning or memory. But in the case of personality, all five major paradigms (see Chapter 1) have had some impact. There are psychoanalytic theories of personality, behavioral theories, humanistic theories, cognitive theories, and even biological theories. To add to the complications, many theorists have drawn on ideas from more than one paradigm. For example, the social-learning theory combines behavioral and cognitive principles.

This chapter is organized around the four most influential approaches to personality: psychoanalytic, social-learning, humanistic, and trait. Although many different theorists belong to each of these schools, each section here focuses on the thought of one major figure: Sigmund Freud for psychoanalysis, Albert Bandura for social learning, Abraham Maslow for the humanistic school, and Gordon Allport for traits. These are not the only theorists associated with each view, and not all psychologists would agree that these four figures are the best representatives of these schools. This approach is designed simply to provide a concrete example of each view in order to lay the groundwork for understanding the broader differences. The chapter ends with a description of current trends in personality research.

It would be more convenient for textbook writers and less confusing for students if one particular approach to personality had triumphed, had been proved right, and the other approaches had been proved wrong. But this is not the case. An accurate introduction to this field must portray several approaches to personality that sometimes contradict one another and sometimes go off in entirely different directions to explore phenomena that others ignore.

The Psychoanalytic Approach

The **psychoanalytic approach** to personality emphasizes the importance of unconscious forces and biological instincts in shaping complex human behav-

personality An individual's characteristic pattern of thought, behavior, and emotions.

psychoanalytic approach A theory of personality that stresses the importance of unconscious conflicts and biological instincts in the determination of complex human behavior.

**SIGMUND FREUD
(1856–1939)**

One of the most important figures in the history of psychology and psychiatry, Freud was born in Freiburg, Moravia (now part of Czechoslovakia). After graduating with a medical degree from the University of Vienna in 1881, Freud began a career in physiological research. However, financial pressures forced him to practice medicine. Freud chose to specialize in the treatment of emotional and nervous disorders and experimented with hypnosis and other cures. His work with Josef Breuer on Anna O. and other cases helped establish some of the basic principles of psychoanalysis. Freud's first major book describing the foundations of this new system was *The Interpretation of Dreams,* published in 1900. Only 600 copies were printed, and it took eight years to sell them all. But Freud began to gain international recognition after he gave a series of lectures at Clark University in 1909. For the next 30 years, he continued to develop his monumental theories of psychoanalysis. Since his death, scholars have written countless books and articles painstakingly exploring the possible implications of every event in Freud's life—from his bed-wetting at the age of 2 to the remote possibility that he had an affair with his sister-in-law.

ior. This school of thought was founded by Sigmund Freud, one of the most controversial and influential figures in the history of psychology.

After receiving his medical degree from the University of Vienna in 1881, Freud decided to specialize in the treatment of mental disorders. At that time, physicians knew little about the nature of mental illness, and many of Freud's ideas about the normal personality grew out of his pioneering work with disturbed individuals. We begin with an account of a woman known to medical science as Anna O., one of the first and most famous patients whose illness helped shape the thinking of the young Dr. Freud.

The Case of Anna O.

On the surface, Anna O. seemed to have everything a young woman could ask for. She was intelligent, charming, witty, and beautiful. But at the age of 21, she was referred to a Viennese doctor named Josef Breuer for treatment of a severe chronic cough she had developed while caring for her ailing father. Various specialists had been unable to find anything physically wrong with Anna; Breuer diagnosed her as a victim of hysterical neurosis, a nervous disorder that medical science had many theories about but few techniques for curing.

When Anna's father died in 1881, her symptoms multiplied. Anna refused to eat and became physically weak. She lost feeling in her hands and feet, became partially paralyzed, and suffered from visual disturbances. Her speech became bizarre; she sometimes left so many words out of a sentence that she did not make any sense. For a period of two weeks, Anna became totally mute; no matter how hard she tried, she could not speak at all. Anna even showed signs of developing two different personalities—one depressed and anxious, the other excited and given to bizarre outbursts in which she threw things at people and suffered from frightening visual hallucinations.

Breuer found the loss of feeling in Anna's hands and feet particularly interesting from a medical point of view. About that time, physicians had discovered that the symptom of *glove anesthesia*—in which feeling was lost in the entire hand (roughly, the area that might be covered by a glove)— could not possibly have a physical basis (see Figure 12.1). Anatomically, the nerves responsible for feeling in the hand also control other areas in the arm; thus, if these nerves were damaged, the loss of feeling could not be limited just to the hand. The obvious conclusion: A patient who reported glove anesthesia suffered from a psychological disorder rather than a purely physical one. This does not imply that Anna O. was faking her disease, only that its causes were buried in her psyche.

Breuer gradually discovered that when Anna O. told him in detail of her hallucinations and fantasies, her condition slowly began to improve. Thus did doctor and patient stumble upon the solution of the "talking cure." The progress of this therapy convinced Breuer that Anna's symptoms were not the random products of an irrational mind. Rather, each symptom had developed as a result of particular events in Anna's life and expressed a hidden emotional logic.

For example, some of Anna's visual problems were traced back to a long and difficult evening by her dying father's bedside. When her father suddenly asked what time it was, Anna found that the tears in her eyes prevented her from seeing the watch clearly. She valiantly tried to keep from crying so that her father would not be upset by her tears. This attempt to strangle such powerful emotions was buried in her unconscious mind and later led to the physical symptoms of visual problems. When Anna consciously remembered this event and described it over the course of many sessions to Breuer, her vision slowly improved.

Aristotle had used the Greek word *katharsis* to describe the emotional release an audience felt during a tragic drama. When Breuer and Freud (1893/1955) described the case of Anna O. in their book *Case Studies in Hysteria,* they used the term **catharsis** to refer to the relief of symptoms of mental illness by bringing unconscious emotional conflicts into conscious awareness.

Perhaps because of his own emotional conflicts regarding the beautiful young Anna O., Breuer did not pursue the study of hysterical neurosis (Pollock, 1968). But Sigmund Freud went on to work with many other patients to develop new therapeutic techniques for producing catharsis (see Chapter 15). He also explored the workings of unconscious impulses in dreams, in everyday behavior, and even in his own life. In fact, beginning in the summer of 1897, Freud reserved the last half hour of each day for an analysis of his own thoughts and conflicts (Jones, 1953). He continued this practice until he died in 1939.

Over the course of more than half a century of thinking and writing about psychoanalysis, Freud gradually developed an extremely detailed theory about the causes of human behavior. Although we can only hint at its richness and complexity here, the next section of this chapter describes some of Freud's basic concepts.

**ANNA O.
(1859–1936)**

Anna O. was one of the most famous patients analyzed by Freud. "Anna's" real name was Bertha Pappenheim; after her recovery she became famous as a pioneer social worker and militant feminist.

FIGURE 12.1 Figure *A* shows the areas of the hand and arm connected to three major nerves. Figure *B* shows the area of sensation lost in glove anesthesia. Damage to the nerves that convey sensations from the hand would also eliminate sensation from the arm. Therefore, loss of sensation in the hand alone must have a psychological rather than a physiological cause.

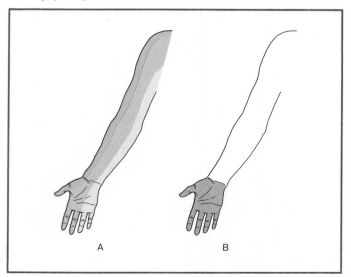

A   B

Instincts

In the nineteenth century, many scientists believed that every action and reaction in the physical world was completely determined by the operation of the forces of nature. If science could uncover these natural laws, they believed, it would be able to predict every event. Freud tried to extend this model by specifying the psychic forces that determined human behavior.

Freud focused on **instincts**, which he defined as the inborn mental representations of physical needs. Ultimately, he traced all human behavior back to the expression of instincts. Freud never compiled a complete list of human instincts, but he did gradually come to the conclusion that they fell into two major classes—life instincts (*eros*) and death instincts (*thanatos*).

The **life instincts** help the individual, and the species, to survive. The most obvious examples are hunger, thirst, and sex. The sexual instinct was the one Freud devoted the most attention to, particularly in his early writings.

For Freud, sex was not a single instinct but involved a number of different types of impulses. He distinguished several **erogenous zones**, areas of the body that are sensitive to feelings of both irritation and pleasure. As we shall see, the major erogenous zones are the mouth, the anus, and the sex organs. Freud's definition of sex was far broader than the everyday meaning of the term.

In opposition to sex and the other life instincts stand another group called **death instincts**, whose workings can be summarized in Freud's (1920/1955) famous statement that "the goal of all life is death" (p. 38). Freud added the notion of an unconscious death wish to his theory partly in an attempt to explain the tragic destruction he saw in World War I. When aggressive drives are directed inward, they can produce depression or even suicide. When these self-destructive forces are blocked, they may be turned outward and produce violence toward other people.

The motivational force of instincts is based on a process of tension reduction; for example, the hunger instincts gradually build up psychic tension, which is reduced when a person eats. But this tension reduction can sometimes take place in ways that are not at all obvious. The word **displacement** refers to a process by which instinctual energy is rechanneled from one object to another. Displacement is one of the most important concepts in psychoanalysis, because it explains complex forms of adult behavior in terms of basic biological urges.

For example, Freud (1910/1957) argued that Leonardo da Vinci painted Madonnas partly because he had been separated from his mother at an early age. The instinctual energy built up by da Vinci's unconscious desire for motherly love was rechanneled into painting portraits of the mother of Christ. This particular type of displacement, in which instinctual energy is rechanneled into higher cultural goals, is called *sublimation*.

In some special circumstances, it is possible to glimpse the mysterious workings of unconscious instincts. For example, during sleep the censor of the conscious mind relaxes, and unconscious material may force its way into the content of dreams, sometimes in a disguised form.

In *The Interpretation of Dreams*, Freud (1900/1953a) gave many examples of the way instinctual forces can be displaced and otherwise transformed in

catharsis According to Freud, the relief of symptoms of mental illness by bringing unconscious emotional conflicts into conscious awareness.

instincts According to Freud, the inborn mental representations of physical needs.

life instincts According to Freud, instincts (e.g., hunger, thirst, and sex) that help the individual and the species to survive.

erogenous zones According to Freud, areas of the body that are highly sensitive to feelings of both irritation and pleasure.

death instincts According to Freud, a major class of instincts that includes aggressive and self-destructive forces.

displacement According to Freud, the process by which instinctual energy is rechanneled from one object to another.

Freud argued that interest in vigorous contact sports is related to unconscious aggressive instincts.

dreams. For instance, Freud reported a dream he had the night before his father's funeral. It included a scene in a barber shop with a posted sign that said, "You are requested to close an eye." Freud had arranged a simple ceremony for the funeral, in keeping with his father's wishes. He interpreted the barber-shop dream as a reflection of his guilt; the sign asked relatives who would have preferred a more elaborate ceremony to "close an eye"—overlook the inadequacy of the arrangements.

For Freud, things are usually not what they seem. The conscious mind is at best only dimly aware of the workings of instinctual forces. Indeed, our unconscious can purposely deceive our conscious mind to protect us from the knowledge and the consequences of our animal instincts. As a result, even our strongest beliefs about our own actions are often based on error and self-deception.

The Organization of Personality

According to Freud, the human personality is organized into three interrelated elements: the id, the ego, and the superego. When he described personality in this way, Freud was not referring to physical structures in the brain but to different psychic processes that interact with one another to produce behavior and personality.

The **id** is a primitive force of innate biological instincts. It is the first and most basic aspect of personality, consisting of both life and death instincts, which are present at birth. All these instincts chaotically seek one goal—immediate satisfaction. As noted earlier, Freud proposed a tension-reduction model of personality: Instincts automatically build up a state of tension that

id According to Freud, an aspect of personality composed of innate biological instincts that seek immediate satisfaction.

must be discharged to achieve satisfaction. An infant deprived of food, even for a short time, experiences a buildup of tension from the hunger instinct; an infant who is deprived of oral stimulation experiences increased tension of this "sexual" drive.

The id operates according to what Freud considered the most basic law of life—the **pleasure principle**, in which the id reduces instinctual tension and returns the organism to a comfortable state. For some primitive responses of the newborn infant, tension can be reduced by reflex. For example, a sneeze reduces irritation of the nose. But most of the infant's instinctual desires cannot be met so quickly and automatically. No matter how much a mother may pamper her infant, there will be times when the child must wait to be fed and instinctual tension will build up. This kind of frustration stimulates the psychological development of the id and activates an unconscious attempt to reduce tension by forming a mental picture of a desired object, in this case perhaps the mother's breast or a Big Mac. Obviously, a mental image of food is not enough. A person whose id never developed any further would not be able to survive.

As a result of this frustration, a force begins to develop out of the id that is able to cope with the real world and protect the organism from harm. The **ego** distinguishes between the subjective world of the mind and the objective world of physical reality. It is governed by the **reality principle**, which means it tries to delay the discharge of instinctual energy until an appropriate object is present. Instead of conjuring up an image of food, the ego forces the id to wait for tension reduction until food is actually present. This does not mean that the pleasure principle is forgotten. The ego wants to satisfy instinctual urges just as much as the id does; it simply learns to go about doing so in a productive, realistic way.

The ego is often referred to as the "executive" of personality, because it makes the hard decisions that balance the needs of the id against the demands of reality on the one hand and the demands of the superego on the other. The **superego** is the aspect of personality that represents moral ideals and strives for perfection rather than pleasure. The superego develops from the ego partly as a result of learning. When the Oedipus complex (described in the next section) is resolved, children internalize their parents' standards and thus form a picture of what their society sees as good and bad.

The superego acts to inhibit the impulses of the id, including sexual and aggressive instincts. It strives for perfection and tries to persuade the ego to pursue moralistic goals. Like the id, the superego fails to distinguish between subjective and objective reality. Bad thoughts may be punished as severely as bad actions. The superego controls various rewards and punishments; it can make you feel warm inside when you are good or upset your stomach when you are bad.

Psychosexual Stages

One of Freud's most influential ideas was the notion that adult personality was shaped by experiences in early childhood (see also Chapter 9). In particular, he proposed several distinct **psychosexual stages**—periods during which

pleasure principle According to Freud, the tendency of the id to reduce instinctual tension and return the organism to a comfortable state.

ego According to Freud, an aspect of personality that develops from the id to distinguish between the subjective world of the mind and the objective world of physical reality.

reality principle The principle governing the ego's effort to delay energy discharge until an appropriate object is present.

superego According to Freud, an aspect of personality that represents moral ideals and strives to perfection rather than pleasure.

psychosexual stages According to Freud, developmental periods emphasizing sexual instincts associated with different erogenous zones.

sexual instincts associated with different erogenous zones are particularly important. Each stage presents certain developmental challenges that must be resolved to achieve healthy adult adjustments. A poorly adjusted individual sometimes becomes *fixated* when he or she fails to resolve the problems of a certain psychosexual stage and, as a result, fails to continue developing normally through later stages. In Freud's view, critical events in any psychosexual stage can determine lifelong patterns of behavior. (See Table 12.1 for a summary of the childhood psychosexual stages and adult characteristics associated with fixations at or regressions to each stage.)

The first year of life is called the **oral stage** because infants derive satisfaction primarily through the mouth—sucking, biting, swallowing, and so on. If instinctual tension is not appropriately discharged through oral satisfaction, the child may become fixated. For example, a child who is weaned too early to get enough sucking gratification may continue to seek oral gratification later in life by smoking or drinking. Problems with infant biting may be displaced and transformed into adult aggression. More generally, fixation at the oral stage can lead to later problems of dependency and trust, since the young infant depends so totally on others for the satisfaction of instinctual impulses.

The beginning of toilet training, usually in the second year of life, is the child's first contact with external authority. For the first time the child is expected to control biological urges. This period of development is called the **anal stage**, since the child's major source of irritation and gratification involves processes of elimination. Here too, Freud said, early conflicts may have important long-term consequences. If the parents are too strict about toilet training, the child may resist authority by withholding feces and becoming constipated. This pattern of response may generalize later to other behaviors, and the adult may be stubborn, stingy, or extremely fastidious—symbolically, always holding back. On the other hand, children may resist by intentionally

TABLE 12.1

Freud's Stages of Psychosexual Development

Stage	Age	Childhood characteristics	Characteristics of adult fixated at or regressing to stage
Oral	0 to 12–18 months	Major gratifications from sucking, biting, eating	Excessive interest in oral activities (e.g., eating, smoking, talking); optimistic; dependent; generous; sarcastic; demanding
Anal	12–18 months to 3 years	Major gratifications from expelling and withholding feces; first major confrontation between self and social controls	Unusual orderliness, punctuality, rigidity; extreme cleanliness or sloppiness; obstinate; rebellious
Phallic	3 to 5–6 years	Interest in and pleasure from genitals; Oedipal conflict; development of identification with same-sex parent	Strong competitiveness, especially with individuals of the same sex; problems with people in authority; proud, vain, self-assured or timid, bashful
Latency Period	5–6 years to puberty	No new bodily sources of gratification	
Genital	Puberty on	Reemergence of sexual interests and aggressive feelings	

Freud was one of the first to emphasize the link between a child's relationships with parents and later patterns of adult behavior.

soiling themselves to get back at their parents. Persons who become fixated at the anal stage may grow up to be messy, irresponsible, wasteful, and extravagant.

The **phallic stage** extends roughly from the ages of 3 to 6, when the child first becomes fully aware of the genital differences between males and females. This knowledge helps produce great affection for the parent of the opposite sex and a sense of jealousy and rivalry with the parent of the same sex.

For boys, this issue is called the *Oedipus complex,* after the ancient Greek king Oedipus of Thebes, who unwittingly killed his father and married his mother. According to Freud, the young boy becomes anxious that his father will discover his rivalry and severely punish him. The Oedipus conflict is successfully resolved when the boy realizes that he can never possess his mother and tries instead to be like, or *identify* with, his father, adopting his values, beliefs, and habits. The superego is sometimes called the "heir to the Oedipus complex" because this process of identification is a crucial step in adopting the parents' moral values. Adult attitudes toward people in authority and the opposite sex are also said to be largely determined by the resolution of the Oedipus conflict. Freud had less to say about female children, who come to adopt their mothers' values through a similar process of identification.

The **latency period** begins around the age of 6. Here, according to Freud, children of both sexes are less concerned with psychosexual conflicts and more involved in refining ego processes for dealing with the environment.

Finally, the **genital stage** begins around puberty, when the physical changes of adolescence reawaken sexual urges. As long as a person has not become fixated in one of the earlier stages of development, mature heterosexual

oral stage According to Freud, the psychosexual stage, lasting for the first year of life, when the infant derives satisfaction primarily through the mouth.

anal stage According to Freud, the psychosexual stage, beginning around age 2, when the child's major source of irritation and gratification involves processes of elimination.

phallic stage According to Freud, the psychosexual stage from age 3 to 6 when a child first becomes fully aware of male-female genital differences.

latency period According to Freud, the psychosexual stage, beginning around the age of 6, when no new psychosexual conflicts emerge.

genital stage According to Freud, the last stage of psychosexual development, beginning around puberty, and characterized by the reawakening of sexual urges.

impulses emerge in the genital stage of adolescence and adulthood. Obviously, this is the longest stage, but it is the one least discussed by Freud because he believed that early childhood events were more likely to influence adjustment.

Defense Mechanisms

Freud believed that much of our behavior expresses the conflict between the unacceptable sexual and aggressive impulses of the id and the restraining influences of the ego and superego. But the desires of the id are powerful forces that can never be completely denied. When a child learns that society forbids the expression of these instincts, the very existence of these feelings may become a source of great anxiety, even if they are never expressed in action.

One way the ego reduces such anxiety is through the use of **defense mechanisms**—unconscious processes that work to deny, distort, or falsify reality. Two common defense mechanisms are displacement, defined earlier in this chapter, and **repression**, which involves reducing anxiety by preventing an anxiety-producing situation, feeling, or memory from becoming conscious (see also Chapter 7). Freudians believe that these and other defense mechanisms operate, often in joint fashion, to protect the ego from being overwhelmed by anxiety. (Also see Chapter 10.)

Sometimes when a loss or experience is simply too horrendous to bear, the individual psyche (the ego, to be specific) responds by simply *denying* the existence of the loss or experience. As a defense mechanism, **denial** involves a refusal on the part of individuals to believe that something terrible has happened or that they are experiencing some unacceptable emotion. For example, someone might be unable to accept the reality of a loved one's death or the loss of the family home through war or natural disaster. At a more everyday level, a person might find it impossible to accept feelings of hatred and rage toward a family member, even if they are momentary.

Sometimes when people unconsciously begin to feel an emotion that is unacceptable to their ego (because such emotions are "bad" and therefore anxiety-producing), the emotion becomes translated into its opposite. Children who are taught that it is bad or sinful to hate their siblings, parents, or others, for example, experience anxiety if something happens to stimulate feelings of hatred. While in such cases human defenses might act simply to repress or deny feelings of hatred, sometimes these emotions become distorted, and the individuals convince themselves that they are really feeling love. The unconscious process by which an emotion becomes translated into its opposite is called **reaction formation**.

Another defense mechanism that allows individuals to avoid conscious recognition of unacceptable impulses or feelings is **projection**, which involves attributing those impulses or feelings to somebody else. For example, a wife who has come to despise her husband but cannot accept such a strong negative feeling in herself, may accuse him, with great conviction, of despising her. Or a man who is lusting after his neighbor's wife may believe that his own wife is planning to cheat on him.

defense mechanism According to Freud, an unconscious denial, distortion, or falsification of reality to protect the ego from excessive anxiety.

repression According to Freud, a defense mechanism that reduces anxiety by preventing an anxiety-producing object or feeling from becoming conscious.

denial The refusal to believe that something terrible has happened or that one is experiencing an unacceptable emotion.

reaction formation The unconscious process by which an emotion becomes translated into its opposite.

projection Attributing unacceptable impulses or feelings to somebody else.

Defense Mechanisms in Action

Freud's notion of defense mechanisms can be quite useful in understanding complex human behavior. While you should not expect to be able to apply psychoanalytic theory on the basis of a single psychology course, the following exercise is designed to get you thinking along these lines. (A discussion of this exercise appears after the "Summary" at the end of this chapter.)

Read each of the following scenarios and indentify the specific defense mechanism that best applies:

1. Michael showers his new baby sister with hugs and kisses and repeatedly asserts how much he loves her. However, unconsciously he is very jealous of the new arrival.
2. Five years ago, after a big blow-up, Mary's brother stopped speaking to her. However, Mary tells everyone how close she is to her brother. Indeed, she has convinced herself that she has more contact with her brother than most siblings who live so far apart.
3. Cheryl is filled with rage when her mother refuses to buy her an expensive new outfit to add to the costly wardrobe already bursting from her closet. Weeping dramatically, Cheryl screams at her mother, "You are a mean and hateful person. How can you hate me like this when I love you so much?"
4. Joanne is furious at her teacher when she fails her first psychology test. Back at the dorm she tells her roommate she doesn't care about the stupid test. She then picks a fight over what time they should eat supper.
5. Jana says that she writes her best poetry after she has abstained from sexual intimacy for an extended period of time.
6. David considers himself to be a model of maturity. However, when he doesn't get his way, he stamps his feet, pounds his fists, and goes into a full-blown temper tantrum.

Adults who bite their fingernails or chew the erasers off pencils when they are anxious illustrate the defense mechanism of **regression**—a retreat to behaviors that proved satisfying in earlier stages of psychosexual development. Smoking, overindulging in alcoholic beverages, and talking baby talk to oneself or other people are examples of regression, as are footstamping and temper tantrums. (See "Applying Scientific Concepts" for an exercise on defense mechanisms.)

Some defense mechanisms are seen as more adaptive and less primitive than others, because they involve less distortion of reality. The most successful defense mechanism is **sublimation**, which alters unacceptable impulses into completely acceptable and even admired social behaviors. According to Freudians, creative activities like painting, sculpting, and writing music are sublimations of the sexual drive, and vigorous contact sports and even careers like surgery are sublimations of the aggressive drive.

regression A retreat to behaviors that proved satisfying in earlier stages of psychosexual development.

sublimation A successful defense mechanism that alters unacceptable impulses into completely acceptable and even admired social behaviors.

Evaluating Freud's Contribution

No one in psychology is more controversial than Sigmund Freud. At one extreme, orthodox psychoanalysts read Freud the way biblical scholars read the Old Testament, agonizing over hidden meanings and debating the interpretation of every adverb. At the other extreme, many experimental psychologists dismiss Freud with a wave of the hand. Freud was no scientist, they say; he was merely the creator of a muddled system of untestable ideas.

Freud believed that creative activities like sculpting are sublimations of the sexual drive.

The roots of this controversy may lie partly in Freud's own ambivalence toward traditional scientific methods. Freud was originally trained as a physiologist and began his career totally committed to nineteenth-century ideals of science. But after years of studying human behavior, he became convinced that the mind was so complex that psychology might never become an exact science. Because small shifts in instinctual energy can have dramatic effects on behavior, Freud (1920/1955) believed that it is often impossible to predict what people will do in advance; thus it became possible to explain behavior only after the fact. This idea is almost a kind of scientific heresy; if a scientist is never willing to make predictions that can be tested against the facts, how can an incorrect theory ever be disproved? Skeptics felt that Freud's approach was a little like that of racetrack experts who claim to know why every horse won and lost but never test themselves by betting on a race.

Some researchers did go on to test Freud's ideas, but many psychoanalysts were not particularly concerned with the results. In the preface to a book that reviews over 2,000 separate tests of Freud's theory and therapy, Seymour Fisher and Roger Greenberg (1977) told the following story to illustrate how little Freud himself might care about such an attempt.

> One psychologist who wrote to Freud to cheer him with the news that he had been able to find scientific laboratory support for one of his major ideas, was chagrined to receive in return a hostile letter informing him that psychoanalysis did not need outside validation. (p. ix)

For Freud, and for many others, the proof of psychoanalysis did not lie in simpleminded lab tests but rather in the internal consistency of the theory and its ability to explain patients' lives.

Indeed, many psychoanalysts would argue that it is impossible to make an informed judgment about this theory on the basis of a brief account like the one provided here. An overview of Freud of 5 or 10 or even 100 pages can acquaint the reader with some of his vocabulary and perhaps provide some feeling for the flavor of psychoanalytic explorations of unconscious motives, but such a short account inevitably misses the rich, detailed observations that provide evidence for the theory's validity.

On the other side of the fence, opponents argue that this type of thinking makes psychoanalysis seem more like a religion than a testable science— either you have the true Freudian faith or you don't. No theory can be exempted from the normal rules of scientific testing, according to these skeptics, not even Sigmund Freud's. So, many researchers have set out to test specific psychoanalytic claims.

For example, one study (Sears, Whiting, Nowlis, & Sears, 1953) asked mothers how severely they had weaned their infants from breast-feeding and examined correlations with character traits observed during the preschool years. They found that children who were weaned more severely were, on the average, somewhat more dependent. After reviewing this study and 30 others like it, Fisher and Greenberg (1977) concluded that the available data do indeed support Freud's idea that dependency in adulthood is linked to early infant oral experiences.

After reviewing over 2,000 studies testing a wide variety of Freudian assertions, Fisher and Greenberg (1977) concluded:

> When we added up the totals resulting from our search, balancing the positive against the negative, we found that Freud has fared rather well. But like all theorists, he has proved in the long run to have far from a perfect score. He seems to have been right about a respectable number of issues, but he was also wrong about some important things. (p. 395)

But this brief introduction has told only part of the story of psychoanalysis. Our focus on Freud alone provides an opportunity to explore his views in greater depth than we might have if we reviewed the work of four or five major psychoanalysts. However, it runs the risk of leaving the impression that psychoanalytic theory is synonymous with Freudian theory. Nothing could be further from the truth.

Freud was fascinated by the irrational side of human nature and the immense potential power of unconscious instinctual impulses. It was left to those who came later to develop a more complete picture of the ego as the true executive of personality, able to function on its own and fully capable of dealing with reality.

The most influential developments in psychoanalytic thought after Freud are generally summarized in the term **ego psychology**, which refers to psychoanalytic theories that propose an autonomous ego with its own reality-based processes that can be independent of purely instinctual aims. For example, Robert White (1963) argues that the ego can motivate behavior on the basis of such intellectual processes as exploration, manipulation, and effective competence. Similarly, in Chapter 10 we saw how Erik Erikson revised Freud's psychosexual stages to discuss the motivational significance of ego-based issues, such as forming an identity in adolescence and choosing between integrity and despair in old age.

Many other theorists—including Carl Jung, Alfred Adler, Karen Horney, Erich Fromm, and Anna Freud—have enriched psychoanalytic thought and extended its boundaries. Whatever one thinks about the ultimate validity of Sigmund Freud's ideas, there can be no doubt that he founded one of our century's most influential schools of thought about the nature of being human. (See Table 12.2 for a summary of the theoretical contributions of several well-known "neo-Freudians.")

ego psychology Psychoanalytic theories that propose the existence of an autonomous ego with its own reality-based processes that can be independent of purely instinctual aims.

social-learning approach A theory that emphasizes internal cognitive processes as important factors in determining behavior.

The Social-Learning Approach

While the psychoanalytic approach grew out of medical attempts to treat disturbed patients, the roots of social-learning theory lie in behaviorism and the animal-learning laboratory. The **social-learning approach** sees personality

TABLE 12.2
Neo-Freudians

Name	Dates of sample publications	Major theoretical assumptions
Alfred Adler	1927; 1939	Individuals have two major motives: a drive for power or superiority (need to be as excellent or perfect as possible) and a social interest (desire to help construct best possible society).
Erich Fromm	1941; 1956	Historically, as individuals have become freer and more independent, they have become more isolated and have developed an unconscious need for unity.
Karen Horney	1939; 1950	The individual's primary need, growing out of an early "basic anxiety" (i.e., a childhood fear of being alone and vulnerable) is for security.
Harry Stack Sullivan	1953	People's personalities reflect the relationships they have with significant others. Personality development takes place through stages characterized by particular interpersonal relationships and by progress toward greater socialization.
Heinz Kohut	1971; 1978	Positive childhood experiences lead to development of an autonomous self (stable, effective, and vigorous). Negative experiences can lead to development of narcissistic disorders (where one's attachment to self is too strong, too weak, or unrealistic).

as a pattern of learned responses produced in part by a history of rewards and punishments and in part by more cognitive processes, such as observational learning.

As we explained in Chapter 6, for the first half of the twentieth century, American psychology was dominated by attempts to provide a scientific account of the learning process. Behaviorists typically assumed that virtually all behavior was learned, including the most complex patterns of human behavior, which we call "personality." They concentrated on the search for fundamental laws of learning that specified the relations between changes in the environment and changes in behavior.

In our review of animal learning, we saw how researchers began with simple models in which external stimuli elicited individual responses (S-R psychology). We also saw how they gradually came to emphasize the importance of internal cognitive processes. Here we consider how theoretical approaches to personality have developed along similar lines.

From Radical Behaviorism to Social Learning

While most behaviorists have concentrated on fundamental learning processes in lower species, a few have tried to show how the same principles apply to complex human behavior and personality.

For example, B. F. Skinner (1953) argues that psychologists should concentrate on a **functional analysis** that specifies the external variables regulating behavior. Behavior is the dependent variable for Skinner, and science is the search for the independent variables that cause it to change. To put it another way, behavior is a function of certain changes in the environment. Thus,

functional analysis Specification of the external variables that regulate behavior.

scientists should not try to construct elaborate theoretical models (as Freud did) to understand the origins of behavior. Rather, they should focus on a more limited and pragmatic search for external causes that enable them to predict and control behavior.

Skinner particularly objects to attempts to explain behavior in terms of internal traits and conditions. Consider one simple example. When someone asks why your roommate hasn't studied for her courses this semester, you might reply, "Because she's lazy." But how do you know she's lazy? The answer is simple: She hasn't studied this semester. Intuitively, laziness may seem to explain her failure to study, but in fact it is nothing more than a label for the behavior you have observed. Skinner would suggest a functional analysis of this behavior to explore the variables that regulate study activities, including stimuli, such as the presence of friends who want to chat, and reinforcers, such as good grades.

The study of personality, then, would consist of a functional analysis of external events that shape a certain pattern of behavior. The macho behavior of a college football player, for example, might result from certain rewards and punishments. If the middle linebacker opened beer bottles with his teeth and spoke only in four-letter words, he might be rewarded by the approval of his peers. If, however, the same player cut football practice to go see Mikhail Baryshnikov dance in the ballet *Swan Lake,* he might be punished by his teammates' remarks questioning his virility.

Familiar concepts from the learning laboratory play a large role in such behavioral analyses of personality. For example, when our macho football player went home to visit his mother, he might have a very different pattern of behavior. He would never utter a single four-letter word, because although obscenity may be reinforced in the locker room, it is punished around the family dinner table.

In his later writings, Skinner (1974) describes a position called **radical behaviorism**, which accepts the existence of internal events, such as thoughts and ideas, but continues to emphasize the relationships between environmental events and observable behavior. While grudgingly admitting that people do have internal sensations of hunger, for example, Skinner continued to maintain that the act of seeking food is usually best understood by focusing on the external conditions that precede it, such as being deprived of food. The feeling of hunger itself, he says, is an unimportant by-product of external conditions.

In contrast, *social-learning theory* holds that internal cognitive processes are an important factor in determining behavior, along with other types of learning. Skinner's accounts of human behavior tended to emphasize learning by doing, in which specific acts were rewarded or punished. In contrast, social-learning theory claims that much of our learning is vicarious; we imitate models and learn symbolically about skilled actions (for example, by reading about them or hearing them explained).

In Chapter 6, we described some of Albert Bandura's classic studies of observational learning in which young children imitated an adult model's aggressive acts. As noted, a large number of factors influence observational learning; for example, imitation is less likely when a model is punished for his acts. To account for the many relationships observed to date, Bandura (1977) proposed a model of observational learning that emphasizes the impor-

radical behaviorism A position that accepts the existence of internal cognitive processes but emphasizes the relationships between environmental events and observable behavior.

tance of such internal processes as attention, memory, and motivation. When people learn by observing, they do not form simple bonds between stimuli and responses; rather, they form symbolic images of an act and make judgments about it.

While a radical behaviorist might concentrate on the objective features of a reward or punishment (for example, how big it is in physical terms), a social-learning theorist might focus instead on its subjective characteristics (how big it seems to this learner). Further, radical behaviorism tends to see the individual as a relatively passive responder to a series of external events; social-learning theory sees the learner as a more active agent who can actually change the environment and the way it is perceived. For example, a person who is rude can cause others to act in a hostile manner. Thus, the environment in which we live is partly of our own making.

In summary, social-learning theory stresses the importance of active internal cognitive processes in learning, while radical behaviorism does not. For our purposes, the similarities between these two approaches are greater than the differences—both see personality as a complex pattern of learned behaviors. Thus, an adequate theory of personality must focus on the learning process.

Self-efficacy

One of the most important internal factors studied by social-learning theorists in recent years involves expectations of **self-efficacy**—belief in one's own competence or ability to achieve a goal through certain actions. Albert Bandura (1977) distinguishes self-efficacy expectations about one's own behavior from more general beliefs that certain courses of action have certain consequences for most people, which he calls *outcome expectations*. For example, you might have the outcome expectation that most people need to study at least two hours every day to get an *A* in organic chemistry. However, if you have a low self-efficacy expectation in this regard, you might be convinced that *your* only hope for an *A* in organic chemistry would involve bribery or a clerical error.

Bandura believes that such feelings play a key role in how quickly and how well a person will learn a specific task. His first major study of self-efficacy compared several types of therapy for snake phobias (Bandura, Adams, & Beyer, 1977). (As explained in Chapter 14, *phobias* involve excessive and inappropriate fears of objects and events.) While many ordinary people may be reluctant to handle the red-tailed boa constrictors used in this study, the 33 subjects in this experiment had such extreme feelings that they were afraid to participate in ordinary activities like gardening for fear they would see a snake.

The subjects participated in a behavioral test of their willingness to approach a snake in a glass cage and also provided self-efficacy ratings—estimates of the probability that they would be willing to touch a snake or approach it in various other specific ways. Since these subjects had been chosen because of their fear of snakes, these preliminary ratings of behavior and self-efficacy were generally rather low.

**ALBERT BANDURA
(1925–   )**

Bandura helped found the social-learning approach, which extended the behavioral analysis of learning to include cognitive factors and observational learning. Bandura's parents were wheat farmers in Alberta, Canada; he was raised in the small town of Mundare and attended a high school that had only 20 students. Bandura received a doctorate in clinical psychology from the University of Iowa in 1952, moved to Stanford University a year later, and has remained there for his entire professional career.

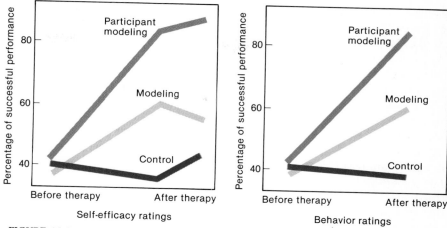

FIGURE 12.2 In a study of therapies designed to overcome a fear of snakes, participant modeling produced the largest changes in behavior and self-efficacy ratings.

The subjects were then divided into three groups: participant modeling, modeling, and control. The subjects in the participant-modeling group were the most active. They were gradually encouraged to watch, and then actually touch, a rosy boa constrictor.

At first, they simply watched through a window while an experimenter handled the snake. Then they came into the room and watched the experimenter and the snake from a distance. Then, they were asked to come closer and put their hands near the snake's head. Those people who just couldn't bring themselves to do it began by wearing gloves and touching the experimenter's hand while she touched the snake. Others worked at first with a smaller baby boa constrictor. In each case, subjects gradually got to the point where they could touch and hold the snake. Indeed, by the end of therapy session, which typically took about 90 minutes, many subjects were actually able to hold the snake without any help from the therapist and even allow the reptiles to slither over their bodies.

Treatment for the modeling group was more passive. Each subject simply watched the therapist perform a similar set of actions for precisely the same length of time as the participant-modeling subjects. The control groups received no treatment at all.

All three groups were tested a week later with another type of snake (a corn snake 90 centimeters long) and asked to provide further ratings of self-efficacy. The major results are summarized in Figure 12.2. As you can see, participant modeling resulted in the largest changes in both self-efficacy and behavior ratings. Modeling produced smaller improvements in both. And the control group apparently still felt that the best place for a snake was far, far away.

All the subjects who had received therapy in this experiment reported that they were now able to participate in activities like picnicking, gardening, and swimming, which they had previously avoided because of their dread of snakes. Some of them also seemed to have gained a more general sense of

self-efficacy The belief in one's own competence or ability to achieve a goal through certain actions.

self-efficacy. As one person put it: "I have a greater self-confidence. When something comes up that is new or unknown to me, I feel, 'Well, I could handle that' " (Bandura, Adams, & Beyer, 1977, p. 136).

Interestingly, the self-efficacy ratings closely paralleled the average behavior changes for the groups and for the individuals within each group. For example, the participant-modeling subjects who actually approached and handled the snake after therapy also had the greatest feelings of self-efficacy. Bandura argues that the participant-modeling procedure was more effective than modeling alone because actual accomplishments are one of the most important sources of efficacy information.

Eastman and Marzillier (1984) proposed another explanation for Bandura's findings. They argued that outcome expectations may have as much to do with a person's behavior as estimates of self-efficacy. For example, they argued, a man who is afraid to fly will not refuse to board a plane because of doubts about his own efficacy. Rather, the key issue is his belief that airplanes crash, taking those foolish enough to board them to a fiery death. So, the expected outcome—coming to resemble burnt toast—accounts for the person's behavior, rather than doubts about his ability to sit out the flight.

Bandura (1984) replied that it is precisely fear of not being able to sit out the flight without crying, shrieking, or otherwise making a fool of oneself that keeps phobics off planes. To support his argument, he pointed out that everyone knows planes crash, and most people fly anyway. As further evidence, he cited the case of the patient who was able to fly once she had demonstrated to herself that she could keep her cool on board, even though she was still afraid that the plane would crash.

This, of course, is only one isolated case history. More solid evidence about the relative importance of self-efficacy and outcome expectations in predicting behavior comes from a study done by Lee (1984). In this research, 40 female undergraduates at the University of Adelaide in Australia were asked to predict their reactions to seven situations that dictated an assertive response. For example: "You have four essays due in a two-week period, and there's really no way you can get them all done in time. . . . you really need an extension, and you decide to go and see a tutor about it. When you go into her room, she says, 'Hello. How's the essay going?' " (Lee, 1984, p. 40).

First, she provided a general description of this situation and six others like it, and asked students how positive or negative the outcome would be if they responded assertively. Then she asked them to rate their ability to respond assertively in each situation, regardless of the outcome. Finally, Lee had each subject listen to a taped description, like that above, which ended with a direct verbal challenge to the listener. Subjects were instructed to answer the tape back, as they would a person in real life. These responses were then rated for assertiveness.

Lee found that *both* self-efficacy and outcome expectations were significantly related to the assertiveness of responses, though perceived self-efficacy correlated more highly with assertiveness than did outcome expectation.

Other investigators have gone beyond the laboratory to see whether self-efficacy affects behavior in the real world. They have accumulated evidence that perceived self-efficacy does indeed predict a wide range of behaviors, from quitting smoking, to managing pain, to adhering to medical treatments (O'Leary, 1985). So, as in the case of the little engine that could, it seems that believing in your own ability has a lot to do with successful performance.

It also seems that people who doubt their ability don't try. Betz and Hackett (1981) found that a group of female undergraduates reported low self-efficacy for traditionally male occupations, such as engineering and mathematics, even though their verbal and mathematical achievement scores were equivalent to those in a male control group. Their perceived range of career options was correspondingly limited, focusing primarily on traditionally female occupations, such as teaching. The males in this study saw themselves as equally competent to perform jobs traditionally associated with both sexes.

Thus, research on self-efficacy has now gone far beyond its original focus on phobia. These studies provide an excellent example of the way social-learning theorists are now investigating personality and behavior.

The Humanistic Approach

The **humanistic approach** to personality emphasizes positive human qualities, such as freedom to pursue rational and spiritual goals. Humanistic approaches to personality have been called psychology's "third force," because they provide an alternative to psychoanalysis and behaviorism, the two major schools of thought that have long dominated the field. Freud saw human behavior as a product of hidden irrational instinctual forces, and the early behaviorists pictured humans as machines that mindlessly responded to rewards and punishments. But humanistic psychology paints a much more optimistic picture, one that is much closer to the commonsense notion that we command our own fate. As noted in Chapter 11, while other paradigms are largely deterministic, humanism emphasizes the role of free will.

Among the many influential psychologists who are known as humanists, two names stand out—Carl Rogers and Abraham Maslow. Since Rogers is better known for his innovations in psychotherapy than for his theory of personality, we discuss his views in Chapter 15.

Abraham Maslow criticized traditional psychology for taking a negative, pessimistic, and limited view of human behavior. He argued that this lopsided picture was partly a result of the limitations of research methods. "It is tempting, if the only tool you have is a hammer," he wrote, "to treat everything as if it were a nail" (Maslow, 1966, p. 15). This statement implies that because Freud began by studying people with emotional problems, he ended up with a rather warped view of normal human behavior. Similarly, because behaviorists laid the foundations of their view in the animal-learning laboratory, they failed to consider adequately the qualities that distinguish humans from the beasts. As a corrective, Maslow himself turned to the study of healthy, normal individuals.

According to Maslow, normal human behavior is motivated by a **hierarchy of needs**, a series of biological and psychological requirements that must be satisfied in a certain order. As Figure 12.3 suggests, the most basic category includes **physiological needs**, such as hunger and thirst. These needs are more urgent than any others and take precedence over everything else. How-

humanistic approach A theory of personality that emphasizes human qualities, such as the freedom to pursue rational and spiritual goals.

hierarchy of needs According to Maslow, a series of biological and psychological needs that motivate normal human behavior and must be satisfied in a certain order.

physiological needs The first set of needs in Maslow's hierarchy (e.g., hunger, thirst).

FIGURE 12.3 Maslow believed that human behavior was motivated by a hierarchy of needs that must be satisfied in a certain order, beginning with physiological needs, such as hunger and thirst.

ABRAHAM MASLOW (1908–1970)

Maslow was one of the most influential of the humanistic psychologists. As a student at City College, in New York, the day Maslow first learned of John B. Watson's work he was so excited by the promise of behaviorism that he danced down Fifth Avenue. But after working for several years on behavioral research, Maslow gradually became disillusioned with this approach. He was profoundly disturbed by the tragedy of World War II and later described how it influenced him to try "to prove that human beings are capable of something grander than war and prejudice and hatred" (Hall, 1968, p. 55).

ever, in our society, physiological needs are routinely satisfied for most people and are consequently not a major factor in shaping our most important decisions. The next category involves **safety needs** for physical security and freedom from pain or fear. The power of the safety needs may be particularly obvious in high-crime neighborhoods, where people are forced to stay home at night or take other actions to protect their physical security.

Next in importance are the **belongingness and love needs**, to feel accepted and wanted by family, friends, and others. Then come **esteem needs**, to be valued by others and to have respect for ourselves (self-esteem). Some seek esteem by seeking fame or dominance over others; some attempt to find appreciation in more modest ways. It is only after all four of these categories are met that a final set of motives come into play. **Self-actualization needs** involve the attempt to use all our talents to achieve our potentials.

According to Maslow's conception of the need hierarchy, then, self-actualization needs ordinarily motivate behavior only after all the lower needs are satisfied. If you have not eaten in three days (physiological need), you will probably spend little time worrying about whether your friends really like you (belongingness and love needs). Similarly, if you feel that you are a worthless excuse for a human being (esteem needs), you will not focus your energy on making the best possible use of your talents (self-actualization needs).

Since Maslow was most interested in healthy adjustment and the positive side of human nature, he decided to focus his research on self-actualization. The problems were immense. How could he know, for example, whether a particular pattern of behavior was motivated by self-actualization needs or by a need for esteem or belongingness? The complexity and uncertainty surrounding this issue would have caused many researchers to abandon the subject. In response to this challenge, Maslow (1954) wrote:

This kind of research is in principle so difficult . . . that if we were to wait for conventionally reliable data, we would have to wait forever. It seems that the

Two of the people Maslow classified as self-actualized were Albert Einstein and Eleanor Roosevelt.

only manly thing to do is not to fear mistakes, to plunge in, to do the best that one can, hoping to learn enough from blunders to correct them eventually. (p. 199)

He plunged in by studying friends, acquaintances, and historical figures who seemed to use the full range of their abilities and who were free of psychological problems. Ultimately, Maslow (1970) was able to find only 18 fully self-actualized people; half were acquaintances and contemporaries, and the rest were historical figures (Abraham Lincoln, Thomas Jefferson, Albert Einstein, Eleanor Roosevelt, Jane Addams, William James, Albert Schweitzer, Aldous Huxley, and Baruch Spinoza).

Maslow's observations of these 18 individuals and others who approached this ideal revealed 15 major characteristics that self-actualized people had in common (see Table 12.3). For one thing, they are accepting—of themselves, of others, and of the world in general. Instead of being crippled by guilt, shame, and anxiety, they have learned to accept the world and human nature as they are. Further, while many of us are obsessed with our own personal problems, the self-actualized person usually takes a larger view and has a mission in life. A somewhat more surprising characteristic of self-actualized people is the fact that they all seem to enjoy a certain amount of solitude and privacy. By being somewhat aloof and reserved at times, they are able to maintain perspective and dignity.

One of the most enviable characteristics of the self-actualized person is the ability to appreciate the everyday pleasures of the world. The smell of a flower or a visit from an old friend can be a source of infinite wonder, amazement, and joy. While most of us easily become rather jaded, the self-actualized person can appreciate the thousandth baby she sees as much as the first.

Maslow also noted that the self-actualized person frequently has **peak experiences**, mystical feelings of happiness, peace, and contentment that are difficult to describe. Many different activities can lead to a peak experience—

safety needs The second set of needs in Maslow's hierarchy (e.g., physical security, freedom from pain or fear).

belongingness and love needs The third set of needs in Maslow's hierarchy (e.g., to feel accepted and wanted by family, friends, and others).

esteem needs The fourth set of needs in Maslow's hierarchy (e.g., to be valued by others and to have respect for ourselves).

self-actualization needs The highest level of needs in Maslow's hierarchy—involve the attempt to use all one's talents to achieve one's potentials.

peak experiences According to Maslow, mystical feelings of happiness, peace, and contentment that a self-actualized person frequently experiences.

sex, listening to music, watching a sunset, religious meditation. What all peak experiences have in common is a feeling of ecstasy, peace, and losing oneself in a feeling of oneness with the universe: All is well with the world, and life makes sense. While almost everyone has an occasional peak experience, such occurrences are far more common for self-actualized people.

In his last book, *The Farther Reaches of Human Nature* (1971), Maslow described how people can strive to become self-actualizing. Among his suggestions: We should learn to be completely honest, to take responsibility for our own actions, to become autonomous, and to trust our own instincts and act on them. Although few people ever achieve full self-actualization, those who do are different from the rest of us in degree rather than in kind. Virtually every human being occasionally has a peak experience; the goal is to progress toward self-actualization so that such feelings may come more frequently.

Maslow's emphasis on free will seems more consistent with our everyday experience than the deterministic views of the psychoanalysts or behaviorists. But because his theory grapples so directly with difficult problems of human values, much of Maslow's writing seems to be rather culture-bound. Some of the traits he admires in self-actualizers—honesty, independence, spontaneity—have a distinctly American ring. Indeed, critics argued that the flaw in these studies of self-actualized people is the fact that the ultimate criterion from being included in this category was whether Abraham Maslow thought a given person was admirable. Maslow was fully aware of this difficulty and noted that any study of well-adjusted people will almost inevitably be criticized for its definition of adjustment. He felt that the issue was so important that researchers had no choice but to go ahead and study it as best they could.

Like other global theories of personality, Maslow's notion of the need hierarchy has been difficult to evaluate in traditional scientific terms (Wahba & Bridwell, 1976). It should be seen as a useful first step rather than a firmly established set of facts. But whatever the failings of the details of this theory, Abraham Maslow and other humanistic psychologists have posed an important challenge to social science researchers: to learn more about the positive side of the human experience.

TABLE 12.3

Characteristics of the Self-actualized Person

1. An ability to perceive the world realistically and accurately
2. An acceptance of self and others
3. Spontaneity
4. A focus on problems outside the self
5. A need for privacy
6. A relative independence from the environment
7. Continued freshness of appreciating life
8. Peak experiences of oneness with the universe
9. A genuine identification with and sympathy for the human race
10. Deep personal relationships
11. A democratic belief that all humans are equal
12. A definite sense of right and wrong
13. A sense of humor that is not hostile
14. Creativity
15. A resistance to cultural conformity

Another criticism of Maslow's work on self-actualization is that his criteria for self-actualizing were quite subjective. Everett Shostrum (1963, 1974; Shostrum, Knapp, & Knapp, 1976) responded to this criticism by developing an objective test designed to measure adherence to values and behaviors related to self-actualization. The Personal Orientation Inventory consists of 150 items that require respondents to choose which of two statements applies to them more consistently. For example, a respondent may have to choose between the statements "I consider most people to be friendly" and "I consider most people to be unfriendly." Subscales of the test measure characteristics that Maslow attributed to self-actualizing people, such as flexibility in applying principles to one's life, sensitivity to one's own needs and feelings, and the ability to form meaningful, close relations with others. While the development of an objective test does not guarantee reliable and valid measurement (see Chapter 13) of self-actualization, it has stimulated some interesting research. For example, Mathes, Zevon, Roter, and Joerger (1982) have found that women (but not men) who report peak experiences tend to score slightly higher on Shostrum's Personal Orientation Inventory than women (and men) not reporting peak experiences.

Type and Trait Approaches

The earliest stages of a new science are often concerned with trying to establish a scheme for fitting the world into neat and orderly categories. Some of the first biologists, for example, proposed a taxonomy of the many species of plant and animal life. Similarly, some students of human nature have proposed various **type theories** of personality that sort people into separate personality categories or types.

The first personality theory involved just such an attempt. About 400 years before Christ, the Greek physician Hippocrates tried to classify human temperament into four basic types: choleric (irritable and hot-tempered), melancholic (sad or depressed), sanguine (optimistic or hopeful), and phlegmatic (calm or apathetic). Hippocrates also suggested that these basic differences in character and temperament were related to differences in body chemistry. The sanguine person, for example, had too much blood, while the choleric person had too much bile.

The biochemical details now seem quaint, but the basic typology has weathered 24 centuries rather well. The four temperaments are represented in many famous works of art and serve as the basis for such literary classics as Robert Burton's *Anatomy of Melancholy,* published in 1621. Pioneer psychologist Wilhelm Wundt tried to explain the four types in terms of two key underlying personality dimensions: weak versus strong emotions and slow versus quick reactions. In this scheme, choleric people were quick reactors with strong emotions, and melancholic people were slow reactors with weak emotions. When Pavlov found that some dogs were easier to condition than others, he proposed four basic canine personalities that were also closely related to Hippocrates's temperaments.

Theories of character types like these are appealing partly because they seem so simple and straightforward. But as personality psychologist Gordon Allport (1961) put it, "The doctrine is as elastic as the platform of a political

type theory An approach to personality that sorts people into separate personality categories or types.

party. One may see in it what one wants to see" (p. 39). And in its very simplicity lies the seeds of its downfall, because, Allport went on to note, "Our phlegmatic friends, we know, have choleric moments and our sanguine friends may show threads of melancholy" (p. 39). Thus, a categorization of all the complexity of human behavior into a few basic personality types is likely to have more intuitive appeal than scientific value.

Nevertheless, type theories of personality do have a role to play in a science of human behavior, as is demonstrated in the discussion later in this chapter of the relationship between personality patterns and heart disease.

Closely related to the notion of discrete character types is the more modest idea of describing personality in terms of **traits**, predispositions to respond to a variety of situations in similar ways. While personality types are either-or propositions, personality traits are continuous and allow more subtle distinctions (for example, a person may be very aggressive, fairly aggressive, slightly aggressive, or not at all aggressive).

We often use the concept of personality traits in commonsense descriptions of the people around us. When we say that Abraham Lincoln was more straightforward than Richard Nixon or that John Kennedy was more charismatic than Millard Fillmore, we are describing presidential character in terms of personality traits. Because personality can be described as the product of many different traits, this approach allows a much more complex classification than does a simple typology. Thus, you might describe a friend as slightly hostile, quite extraverted, reasonably stable, and totally dependable.

Allport's Research

Traits bring order into the chaos of dealing with the complexity of personality by focusing attention on the consistency of behavior. Theorist Gordon Allport saw traits as the best "unit of analysis" for understanding personality. For Allport, traits are the sources of the underlying unity of behavior; they can make a variety of stimuli and responses seem equivalent from a psychological point of view. Figure 12.4 illustrates how this could apply for the trait of introversion. Such widely different situations as waiting in line for the bus, going to a party, sitting in a college class, shopping for groceries, and going to Grandma's house may evoke a similar pattern of behavior. In all these situations, the trait of introversion can be seen in similar responses—remaining quiet with other people, not talking to strangers, doing things alone and avoiding groups whenever possible, and making few friends. Allport emphasized the importance of an underlying personality structure that can be inferred from characteristic patterns of behavior.

He also distinguished between several different kinds of traits that differ in their influence on behavior. For example, *central traits* are highly characteristic personality patterns that often influence behavior and are therefore relatively easy to observe. Allport believed that most personalities could be fairly summarized in five to ten central traits. *Secondary traits* are less pervasive patterns of behavior that can be seen only under specific conditions. Other trait theorists use different names for these concepts, but most agree with the fundamental idea that not all traits are created equal; some are more powerful determinants of behavior than others.

GORDON ALLPORT (1897–1967)

Allport is known not only as one of the most influential proponents of the trait approach to personality but also for his pioneer research on topics ranging from prejudice, attitudes, and values to the psychology of rumor. The son of a country doctor from Montezuma, Indiana, Allport decided to major in psychology in college to follow the example of his older brother. At the age of 23, he managed to arrange a private meeting with Sigmund Freud during a visit to Vienna. When Freud sat silently for several minutes, Allport finally began the meeting by telling about a 4-year-old boy he had seen on the streetcar on the way over who didn't want to sit near any passengers because they were too dirty. Freud hesitated and said kindly, "And was that little boy you?" Allport was amazed that Freud ignored the more obvious explanation that Allport was merely being sociable—relating an anecdote he thought Freud might find interesting. Much of Allport's professional career was devoted to developing theoretical alternatives to Freudian psychoanalysis.

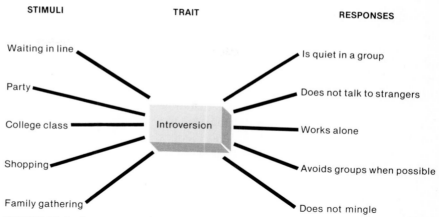

STIMULI   TRAIT   RESPONSES

Waiting in line
Party
College class
Shopping
Family gathering

Introversion

Is quiet in a group
Does not talk to strangers
Works alone
Avoids groups when possible
Does not mingle

FIGURE 12.4   Some personality theorists see traits as the source of consistent behavior. This diagram shows how a wide variety of stimuli may evoke similar patterns of behavior through a single underlying trait.

Allport also drew a distinction between *common traits,* which characterize most people, and *individual traits* (or personal dispositions), which apply uniquely to a single person. While most personality theorists concentrated on the search for general laws that apply to all people, Allport also emphasized the study of specific individuals as unique human beings. Indeed, he formally defined two distinct approaches to psychological science: The **nomothetic approach** attempts to understand the behavior and experience of people in general or of the average case, while the **idiographic approach** attempts to understand the behavior and experience of a single individual.

One example of Allport's idiographic approach was his detailed study of a woman whom he called Jenny Masterson. The analysis was based on 301 letters Jenny wrote between the ages of 58 and 70 in which the lonely woman described her life to a young couple she had met through her son.

Jenny Masterson was born in 1868. Her parents were Irish Protestants who migrated to Canada when Jenny was 5 years old. When her father died, 18-year-old Jenny left school to work as a telegrapher to support her younger brothers and sisters. At the age of 27, she infuriated her family by marrying a divorced man. He died two years later, leaving her estranged from her family and with an infant son to support. For the next 17 years, Jenny devoted every waking moment to caring for her son Ross. She continued to support him through his college years at Princeton. Ross enlisted in the ambulance corps during World War I and returned from the war disillusioned and disoriented. He married secretly and fought constantly with his mother. Many of Jenny's letters describe her continuing arguments with her son and her lonely life in late middle age.

In a systematic analysis of Jenny's personality, Allport (1965) asked 36 people to read the letters and describe her characteristic traits. Although these judges mentioned a total of 198 trait terms, many were synonymous or closely related. Indeed, "nearly all" the judges agreed that Jenny's character revolved around eight central traits; she was suspicious, self-centered, independent, dramatic-intense, artistic, aggressive, morbid, and sentimental. The judges

traits   Predispositions to respond to a variety of situations in similar ways.

nomothetic approach   An approach to personality that attempts to understand the behavior and experience of people in general or the average case.

idiographic approach   An approach to personality that attempts to understand the behavior and experience of a single individual.

also identified 13 less important themes that could be considered secondary traits, including intelligence, wittiness, and whimsicality.

Though this was not a particularly flattering portrait, it was quite a consistent one. Indeed, other studies using different techniques to analyze the letters came to surprisingly similar conclusions. Jeffrey Paige, a student of Allport's, used a computer to count the number of repetitions in 56 of Jenny's letters of words falling into 3,000 categories. Elaborate statistical analysis of these word counts revealed eight underlying character traits that were generally similar to those mentioned by the clinical judges.

Allport's idiographic analysis of individual cases like Jenny's has had a tremendous theoretical impact on the development of trait concepts. However, most researchers now take a nomothetic approach and investigate the average predictive value of particular traits for large groups. One example is described in the next section—the involvement of androgyny in sex-role behavior. First, however, we review recent challenges to the trait approach and to the very idea of studying personality patterns.

Current Issues in Personality Research

Most textbooks in personality are organized around major theorists and schools of thought, just as this chapter is. From this, you might get the impression that if you were an ambitious young psychologist, you would want to develop a personality theory of your own so that your name would go down in history as future generations of psychologists debated the merits of your approach.

In fact, however, personality psychologists are moving in a different direction in the late twentieth century. We mentioned in Chapter 6 that the global theories of learning that once dominated experimental psychology have not been abandoned. Researchers are instead setting more modest goals and trying to ask one small question at a time. The same thing has happened in personality psychology.

The major theories described up to this point have shaped the direction of the field and have provided the theoretical foundations for many studies. But in recent years personality psychologists have come to believe that we will not be able to explain the infinite complexity of every individual person through one master theory. Instead, researchers are increasingly focusing on more limited and more manageable problems, such as personality differences between women and men or the relation of specific traits to heart disease.

Of Persons and Situations

MISCHEL'S CHALLENGE

In 1968, Walter Mischel published *Personality and Assessment,* a book that seemed to attack the very essence of personality theory by suggesting that the relationship between personality trait labels and actual behavior is a weak one at best. To cite just one example, many trait theorists have discussed the way people relate to such diverse authority figures as parents, bosses, and peers. According to this view, some people are rebels and some follow authority meekly. If rebelliousness really is a generalized personality trait, then children who resist their fathers should grow up to resist the boss and give traffic cops a hard time. Burwen and Campbell (1957) studied the relationship among many different measures of the way Air Force men related to authority figures. They found that the correlations were relatively low. This study did not support the idea that people who are rebellious in one situation are also rebellious in another.

In general, Mischel found that correlations between behavior and personality traits rarely exceeded .30. While a correlation coefficient of .30 may be statistically significant and does indicate that there is *some* relationship between two variables, it is not strong enough accurately to predict individual behavior. (For a further discussion of correlation coefficients, see "Understanding the Scientific Method" in Chapter 13.)

Mischel further argued that social-learning theory could explain why personality traits are such poor predictors of behavior. In essence, he said that a person's behavior in a given situation is shaped by rewards and punishments in that particular situation. One person may seem introverted at parties but quite extraverted with family; another may be introverted at home but extraverted at parties. It all depends on what each individual was reinforced for doing in the past, personal expectations, and the motivating force of particular rewards. From this point of view, it is not surprising that people do not always act consistently from one situation to the next.

Yet common sense tells us that however low psychologists' correlations may be, behavior is reasonably consistent from one situation to the next. We assume this whenever we contrast the characteristics of a social friend with another who is aggressive and a third who is shy. But, according to this point of view, common sense is quite wrong. Consistency may lie in the eye of the beholder.

As explained in Chapter 2, commonsense explanations of behavior are often systematically incorrect because of the limitations of the human observer. The most important of these limitations, at least in this context, has become known as the **fundamental attribution error**—observers consistently underestimate the power of situational forces that influence other people's behavior and overestimate the importance of personal dispositions (Nisbett & Ross, 1980).

In one series of studies of the fundmental attribution error (Jones, 1979), observers read essays and listened to speeches that strongly supported a certain political view—favoring or opposing the legalization of marijuana, for example, or criticizing or supporting Fidel Castro's leadership of Cuba. In each case, the observers were told that the speaker or author had been required to take this particular stand by a debate coach, political science instructor, or psychology experimenter. Nevertheless, observers consistently believed that the speeches and essays expressed the true beliefs of their authors. In other words, they tended to ignore the strong situational constraints of the requirement to take a certain position and to attribute the differences in content to the personal beliefs of the authors.

In our culture, people seem to believe that character is the most important determinant of behavior. Much of our mythology and literature, from Henry

fundamental attribution error The idea that observers consistently underestimate external influences on other people's behavior and overestimate the importance of personal dispositions.

Fielding to Horatio Alger, supports the idea that personal traits and abilities can triumph over the accidental circumstances of our birth. It is therefore not surprising that as children grow up in our culture, they increasingly come to believe in the importance of personality traits for explaining behavior (Ross, Turiel, Josephson, & Lepper, 1978). It will be important for future researchers to see whether people in less individually oriented cultures— such as the People's Republic of China—fall victim to the fundamental attribution error or whether their different world view leads them to perceive their comrades' behavior in an entirely different light.

In any case, Mischel (1968) not only cited evidence for a lack of consistency in personality traits across situations, he also argued that our commonsense impressions of personality consistency may be quite wrong. His book sparked a major controversy that continues to the present time.

THE CONSISTENCY OF PERSONALITY

Researchers were quick to respond to this challenge. Some pointed to problems in the data Mischel himself had cited. For example, the study of attitudes toward authority cited earlier involved 155 Air Force men whose attitudes toward the testing itself left much to be desired. The original authors (Burwen & Campbell, 1957) admitted their subjects showed signs of "perfunctory compliance and occasional humorous sabotage of the test purpose" (p. 24).

Beyond such point-by-point rebuttals of Miscel's argument, many took his challenge seriously enough to reexamine the direction of personality research. Daryl Bem and Andrea Allen (1974) returned to Allport's idiographic view that some traits may be relevant only to certain individuals. They argued that each of us acts consistently, but only in terms of some traits. They tested this idea by asking 64 undergraduates to rate their own friendliness. Each person was also asked, "How much do you vary from one situation to another in how friendly and outgoing you are?" (p. 512). Later, they found a strong relationship among different measures of friendliness, but only for people who described themselves as consistent on this trait. The correlations between how actively each person participated in a group discussion and how long it took him to strike up a conversation with a stranger was .73 for those who described themselves as consistent on friendliness and .30 for those who did not. Again, a given trait may not be equally relevant for all people.

A different type of response to Mischel's challenge has come from personality psychologists who emphasized the importance of the interaction between traits and situations. According to Norman Endler (1977), two people who get the same score on a psychological test of anxiety may become anxious in very different situations. On the basis of responses to questionnaires, Endler found that some people are frightened by social situations (such as going out on a blind date), while others fear physical danger (such as climbing a mountain). Physiological measurements of anxiety later verified this dichotomy. People who feared physical danger had higher heart rates when they took part in a study that involved a risk of electrical shock; those whose anxiety was related to social factors had higher heart rates before taking a test, presumably because they feared being evaluated. Clearly, it is not enough to say that a person is usually anxious; one must also specify the situations in which this trait is most likely to be seen.

Still another line of research generated by Mischel's book argued that the problem is a methodological one. According to this view, some researchers failed to see the consistency of behavior because they relied too heavily on isolated observations. Many studies compared a person's responses on one questionnaire with a single behavioral test. Seymour Epstein (1979) has shown that when questionnaires are repeated time after time and behavioral observations are made day after day, greater consistency emerges. In one study, college students filled out personality tests before every psychology class for a whole semester. At the same time, the instructor secretly rated them on such behavior as coming to class late, forgetting to bring pencils to fill out computerized forms, and erasing mistakes on the answer sheets.

This averaging technique revealed many substantial correlations. One group showed a strong relationship between feelings of confusion, tension, and powerlessness, and failing to turn in papers, coming late to class, and erasing mistakes. Over the course of a semester, it became clear that at times these students were living in a fog of disorganized carelessness. This would not have been apparent if Epstein had simply measured each student's attitude and behavior on a single day; the pattern emerged only because he averaged his students' daily ratings over several months.

A decade after publishing the work that sparked this controversy, Walter Mischel (1979) wrote: "My intentions in writing that book were not to undo personality, but to defend individuality and the uniqueness of each person" (p. 740). Whatever Mischel's original intentions were, the resulting debate helped psychologists concentrate on the complex relationships between personality traits and situational determinants of behavior. This continues to be one important theme in current personality research.

Androgyny

Another line of personality research was inspired in the early 1970s by apparent changes in American society's view of the appropriate roles for men and women. According to traditional psychological tests, masculinity involved an instrumental orientation, focusing cognitively on getting a job done; femininity was usually defined as more expressive, involving an emotional concern for other people. When Sandra Bem (1974) asked college students to rate the "desirability in American society" of 400 personality traits "for a man" and "for a woman," she came up with lists of words that both males and females agreed applied mostly to one sex. The male list included words like *aggressive, ambitious, competitive,* and *independent;* females were characterized as *affectionate, compassionate, loyal,* and *tender.*

In the past, most psychologists had thought of masculinity and femininity as opposite ends of the same continuum; a person could be masculine or feminine, but not both. Bem rejected this idea and added a third category: A person could be classified as masculine, feminine, or androgynous. The word *androgynous* is derived from two Greek roots, *andro,* meaning "man," and *gynē,* meaning "woman." **Androgyny** was defined as a personality pattern

androgyny   A personality pattern that combines traditionally masculine and feminine traits in the same person.

that combined traditionally masculine and feminine traits in the same person.

Using precise statistical definitions of all three categories, Bem gave her questionnaire to 723 Stanford University undergraduates in 1973. The results were that 34% of the men and 27% of the women were classified as androgynous. They described themselves by checking off about the same number of masculine and feminine traits.

Right from the start, androgyny was a value-laden concept. Bem (1975) explicitly argued that being androgynous was better than being masculine or feminine: "It is our general hypothesis that a nonandrogynous sex role can seriously restrict the range of behaviors available to an individual as he or she moves from situation to situation" (p. 634). She contended that androgynous people are more adaptable to a wide range of situations.

In this study, masculine, feminine, and androgynous people were given an opportunity to play with a kitten (a female task) and to act as a nonconformist (a male task). Both feminine and androgynous males did indeed get more involved with the kitten and enjoyed it more than masculine men did. On the conformity task, masculine and androgynous people were more likely to resist group pressure than those who were classifed as feminine. The androgynous people seemed more flexible than those who conformed to traditional sexual stereotypes.

The concept of androgyny became popular among researchers, and many studies appeared attesting to the value of this liberated approach to sex roles. In one of the more extreme examples of the early enthusiasm over this personality trait, Alexandra Kaplan (1976) argued that psychotherapists should encourage women to become androgynous (see "Becoming a Critical Consumer").

Others saw the relation between androgyny and mental health in more complex terms. One study of 20- to 59-year-old women (Hoffman & Fidell, 1979) found that androgynous women were no less neurotic or less likely to visit a doctor than masculine or feminine women. While feminine women had lower self-esteem than androgynous women, they also expressed greater satisfaction with their housework activities. Along with other studies (Lenney, 1979), this finding suggests that androgynous women may adapt better to some types of situations and feminine women to others.

Although Bem was the first to use the word *androgyny* to describe a personality trait, she was not the only psychologist who studied sex role changes in the last decade. In their studies with the Personal Attributes Questionnaire, Janet Spence and Robert Helmreich (1978) found that masculinity and femininity were separate dimensions. While Bem (1974) believed that American sex roles were best described by three categories (masculine, feminine, and androgynous), Spence and Helmreich added a fourth, *undifferentiated*. They distinguished between people who scored high in both masculinity and femininity (androgynous) and those who scored low in both traits (undifferentiated). And, indeed, when Bem (1977) went back to reanalyze some of her earlier data by dividing her androgynous subjects into these two subgroups, she found that this more sophisticated approach did permit her to improve some of her predictions. People who scored high in both masculinity and femininity, for example, were more likely to play with the kitten than undifferentiated subjects who scored low in both traits.

Androgyny

When psychological concepts are described in the popular media, they sometimes seem exaggerated or even distorted. Consider the following example from a *Cosmopolitan* article on androgyny (Dalby, 1986). Try to find one or two specific claims in this excerpt that you think a scientist would be likely to question. (A discussion of this issue appears after the "Summary" at the end of this chapter.)

> No question that the gender revolution is upon us, and you may find it either exhilarating or upsetting. . . . Americans simply take it for granted that men are men and women are women in some true-to-nature sense. And that's why androgyny makes such a powerful statement: It shocks our sense of reality by blending what has traditionally been considered not only separate but opposite. . . . Indeed, the androgynous image proclaims freedom from society's stereotyped sex roles. . . .

Any kindergarten teacher knows that there are developmental differences between boys and girls. Recent evidence even suggests a somewhat different emphasis in the way the right and left hemispheres of the brain process information in males and females. Yet far from proving some irreducible difference between women and men, research on gender always comes up with the same basic profile: The traits overlap. Society demands that we be male or female, but it appears that nature is androgynous!

Androgyny may shift its expression, but it will always be with us. And because it whispers of unlimited sexual possibilities and symbolizes an ultimate fusion of opposites, it will continue to have mystique and power. We may not know how many angels can dance on the head of a pin, but you can bet if there *are* angels, they are probably androgynous. (pp. 199, 200, 201)

Since the early 1980s, Bem has revised her theory to emphasize the importance of *gender schema* in the development of sex roles. Borrowing from cognitive developmental theory, Bem (1983) defines **gender schema** as cognitive structures that sort attributes and behaviors into masculine and feminine categories. Thus, when a woman describes "pink," "empathic," and "enjoys sunsets and symphonies" as feminine and "blue," "independent and secure," and "enjoys computers" as masculine, we are seeing her gender schema at work.

Borrowing from social-learning theory, Bem (1983) argues that through socialization, children learn what attributes are linked by society to each sex and thus to themselves. Bem points out that adults in the child's world rarely comment on how strong a little girl is becoming or how nurturant a little boy is becoming. Because there is a strong need within the developing individual for cognitive consistency, children develop self-concepts that are consistent with their other cognitive schemata and thus can develop self-concepts that

gender schema The cognitive structures that sort attributes and behaviors into masculine and feminine categories.

491

are sex-typed. Here we can see how an internal (developmental) factor (the need for cognitive consistency) prompts individuals to change their behavior so that it conforms to cultural definitions of maleness and femaleness. "Thus do cultural myths become self-fulfilling prophecies, and thus, according to gender schema theory, do we arrive at the phenomenon known as sex typing" (Bem, 1983, p. 605).

In a study of this notion, Bem (1981) first used her Sex Role Inventory to classify individuals as sex-typed (i.e., describing themselves in traditionally masculine or feminine terms) or non-sex-typed (i.e., describing themselves in androgynous terms). She found that sex-typed individuals are much more likely to process information about themselves and others in terms of gender. For sex-typed individuals, everything they do—how they eat, how they dress, what they like, where they go—reflects on their masculinity or femininity. Some fathers refuse to change diapers because they see such activities as "feminine." Some women won't change the oil in the car because they see such an undertaking as "masculine." In both cases, Bem would say, cognitive schema have led sex-typed individuals to view tasks in sex-typed ways and to change their behavior accordingly.

When a new theoretical concept is suddenly embraced by a large number of other researchers, an initial wave of enthusiasm is usually followed by an increasing awareness of the complexity of the underlying issues and of the difficulty of precise measurement. And so it was with the explosion of androgyny research. Personality psychologists have become more sophisticated about measuring androgyny, about what this concept can teach us about how Americans currently define sex roles, and about larger issues such as stereotyping and prejudice in general (Lenney, 1979).

As the line between traditional sex roles has become blurred, psychologists have begun to study androgynous personality patterns.

Type A Behavior and Heart Disease

The third and final line of research to be described here built upon the clinical observations of two physicians. When cardiologists Meyer Friedman and Ray Rosenman began treating heart attack patients, they offered the standard medical advice: Smoke less; exercise more; and eat less red meat, butter, eggs, and other foods high in the chemical cholesterol (which many scientists believe contributes to blockage of the arteries). But as they continued their research and medical practice, they gradually became convinced that they were ignoring one of the most important factors in heart disease—stress.

General observations of their patients suggested to Friedman and Rosenman that many heart attack victims were very competitive and always in a hurry. They called this personality syndrome **Type A behavior**. In the most general terms, they provided the following list of questions people can ask themselves to see whether they are Type A:

> Do you have a habit of explosively accentuating key words in your ordinary speech . . . and finishing your sentences in a burst of speed?

> Do you always move, walk, eat rapidly?

> Do you feel (and openly show) impatience with the rate at which most events take place?

Type A behavior A personality pattern characterized by competitiveness and the tendency to be always in a rush.

Do you get unduly irritated at delay—when the car in front of you seems to slow you up, when you have to wait in line, or wait to be seated in a restaurant?

Does it bother you to watch someone else perform a task you know you can do faster?

Do you often try to do two things at once (dictate while driving or read business papers while you eat)?

Do you almost always feel vaguely guilty when you relax and do absolutely nothing for several days (even several hours)? (Friedman & Rosenman, 1974, cover)

For each question, a yes answer is a sign of Type A behavior; a no answer suggests the more relaxed Type B pattern.

The most thorough study of the Type A syndrome began in 1960 (Rosenman, Brand, Jenkins, Friedman, Straus, & Wurm, 1975). The subjects were 3,154 men between the ages of 39 and 59 who had no signs of heart disease at the beginning of the study. On the basis of standardized interviews about their attitudes toward stress and competition, about half the men were classified as Type A and half as Type B. Researchers also collected data on such variables as medical history, exercise habits, smoking, and blood pressure.

For the next 8½ years, doctors kept track of each man's medical history and gave him an annual physical. None of the physicians who were doing these checkups knew which men were Type A and which were Type B. (This minimized the possibility of experimenter bias.) During the time of the study, 50 men died of cardiovascular disease; 34 of them were Type A and 16 were Type B. Another 257 men were diagnosed as suffering from heart disease; 178 were Type A and 79 were Type B. Since the original group consisted of roughly half of each type, statistical analysis of these figures indicated that Type A men were indeed more likely to develop a heart ailment and to die from it.

Elaborate statistical procedures were used to demonstrate that Type A behavior led directly to heart attacks (Rosenman, Brand, Shultz, & Friedman, 1976). Other factors, such as cigarette smoking, high cholesterol levels, and high blood pressure, also increased the likelihood of heart disease. However, a Type A man was more likely to have a heart attack than a Type B man even if neither of them smoked, had high blood pressure, or had a high cholesterol level.

In our society, women are less likely to develop heart disease than men. Research has also shown that women are less likely to have the Type A behavior pattern. Many possible explanations have been offered, ranging from hormonal and physiological differences between the sexes to differences in the traditional roles of men and women. After the relationship between Type A behavior and heart disease was established, an obvious question arose: As more and more women entered the business world, would they experience more heart disease?

A number of studies by Suzanne Haynes and her colleagues suggest that the answer may be yes. Haynes (1984) found that women with the Type A behavior pattern who worked in business and the professions were just as likely to develop heart disease as their Type A male colleagues. Type A employed women are four times as likely to develop heart disease than Type B employed women (Haynes, 1984). The comparison with Type B housewives is even more striking; here the relative risk of developing heart disease is seven times greater for Type A employed women.

However, the severity of the disease is still greater for men. Women who develop coronary heart disease more frequently develop the chest pain syndrome known as angina pectoris, while men are more likely to experience a life-threatening heart attack. The reasons are still not entirely understood, but there has been speculation that this difference is related to the fact that muscle cells—including those in the heart, which are involved in a heart attack—multiply more rapidly in men.

A related question, which is also now a focus of intensive research, involves helping Type A people change their behavior in order to improve their health. In one study (Roskies, Spevack, Surkis, Cohen, & Gilman, 1978), 27 executives who seemed to conform to the Type A pattern participated in psychotherapy for 1½ hours every Monday night for 14 weeks. Half talked to therapists about how their competive striving was rooted in their early lives; the others were trained in standard methods of relaxation and learned to avoid the situations that created the most stress for them.

Of the 27 executives, 25 finished the program. In the short run, the two forms of psychotherapy were almost equally effective. Both groups had lower blood pressure and lower cholesterol levels after treatment. They also reported an increased feeling of emotional satisfaction and less sense of time pressure. However, a follow-up study found that the group that had received training in techniques for stress management and relaxation showed greater positive effects six months later (Roskies, Kearney, Spevack, Surkis, Cohen, & Gilman, 1979).

After reviewing several studies of this topic, Hart (1984, p. 134) concluded that "brief psychologically based interventions may cause reductions in certain types of Type A behaviors and that behavioral programs with a stress-management component may be most effective."

The key question, of course, is whether such changes actually reduce the risk of heart attacks. This question was addressed in a five-year study of over 1,000 men called the Recurrent Coronary Prevention Project (Friedman & Ulmer, 1984). All the participants had experienced a heart attack before being recruited for the study. The researchers chose to focus on this group since they were at high risk for another heart attack and thus provided an opportunity to evaluate treatment procedures.

These patients were divided into three groups. One group consisted of 150 men who volunteered for yearly physical checkups but were unwilling to participate in counseling sessions aimed at changing their behavior; this was the control group. The remainder received regular counseling from cardiologists and mental-health professionals on how to avoid a heart attack.

They were randomly divided into two groups that received different types of advice. A group of 270 were given standard medical counseling. They were told that "figuratively speaking, they were carrying . . . a 'bomb' inside [which] . . . would probably never explode, but only if they avoided lighting one or more of several fuses" (Friedman & Ulmer, 1984, p. 136).

These dangerous activities, or fuses, included eating meals rich in vegetable or animal fat, participating in severe physical exercise, ingesting caffeine or alcohol, visiting high altitudes, and being exposed to cold for prolonged periods.

This was another control group, to be compared with the final group of 592 men. These patients received the standard medical advice above but were also given counseling to reduce classic Type A behavior patterns. The sessions focused particularly on reducing the sense of time urgency and "free-floating hostility." This latter trait can be seen clearly in the response of one participant to a questionnarie item asking him about this characteristic:

> I do not believe that I have excess hostility; this is due in part to the fact that my intellectual, physical, cultural, and hereditary attributes surpass those of 98 percent of the bastards I have to deal with. Furthermore, those dome-head, fitness freak, goody-goody types that make up the alleged 2 percent are no doubt faggots anyway, whom I could beat out in a second if I weren't so damn busy fighting every minute to keep that 98 percent from trying to walk over me. (Friedman & Ulmer, 1984, p. 216)

Although the counseling did not seem to work wonders with this particular subject, overall it was a success. Analysis of both interviews and questionnaires revealed that the group that received couseling about modifying their Type A behavior succeeded; that is, the intensity of these behaviors decreased approximately 30%.

More important, there was also a statistically significant drop in the recurrence of heart attacks. In each of the two control groups, there were about 6 heart attacks per 100 men each year. In contrast, for those who had received Type A counseling, there were only 3 heart attacks per 100 men each year. The study had originally been planned to continue this analysis for five years. However, after three years, the advantages of Type A counseling had been demonstrated so clearly and convincingly that the researchers offered this therapy to the patients in the two control groups.

This example shows how basic research on personality processes can lead to applications that are of great benefit to society. Thus, the age of great, sweeping theories of personality like Freud's is past. Most researchers now agree that it is simply not possible to understand all the richness and complexity of human behavior within one theoretical scheme. But the process of chipping away at the problem, one small piece at a time, is a fascinating one that offers the promise of many new insights and applications.

Summary

- **Personality** may be defined as an individual's characteristic pattern of thought, behavior, and emotions.

- Personality researchers have focused on two basic questions: How consistent are individual differences in behavior? What causes individual differences?

The Psychoanalytic Approach

- The **psychoanalytic approach** to personality emphasizes the importance of unconscious forces and biological instincts in shaping complex human behavior.

- **Catharsis** refers to the relief from symptoms of mental illness that follows from bringing unconscious conflicts into conscious awareness.

- Freud traced all behavior back to **instincts**, which he defined as the inborn mental representations of physical needs.

- **Life instincts**, including hunger, thirst, and sex, help the individual and the species to survive.

- **Erogenous zones** are areas of the body that are sensitive to both irritation and pleasurable feelings.

- **Death instincts**, such as aggressive and self-destructive forces, are the other major class of instincts in Freud's theory.

- **Displacement** refers to a process by which instinctual energy is rechanneled from one object to another.

- The conscious mind is usually unaware of the way instinctual energy is transformed and displaced, though we can glimpse the work of the unconscious mind in dreams and free association.

- According to Freud, the human personality is organized into three interrelated structures: id, ego, and superego.

- The **id** is a primitive force of inborn biological urges.

- The id operates according to the **pleasure principle**; that is, it reduces instinctual tension and returns the organism to a comfortable state.

- The **ego** develops from the id to distinguish between the subjective world of the mind and the objective world of physical reality.

- The ego is governed by the **reality principle**, which means that it tries to delay the discharge of instinctual energy until an appropriate object is present.

- The **superego** is the aspect of personality that represents moral ideals and strives for perfection rather than pleasure. It develops partly from restrictions on id impulses that come from parents and authority figures.

- Freud emphasized the importance of childhood experiences in shaping adult personality.

- He described four distinct **psychosexual stages** of development—periods emphasizing sexual instincts associated with different erogenous zones.

- The first year of life is called the **oral stage**, because infants derive satisfaction primarily through the mouth.

- The second period of development is called the **anal stage**, since the child's major source of irritation and gratification involves processes of elimination.

- The **phallic stage** extends roughly from the ages of 3 to 6, when the child first becomes aware of the genital differences between males and females.

- The **latency period**, beginning around age 6 and extending to puberty, is a period when children are less concerned with psychosexual conflicts and more involved in refining ego processes for dealing with the environment.

- The **genital stage** begins around puberty, when the physical changes of adolescence reawaken sexual urges.

- **Defense mechanisms** deny, distort, or falsify reality to protect the ego from excessive anxiety.

- **Repression** prevents an anxiety-producing object or feeling from becoming conscious.

- **Denial** involves a refusal on the part of individuals to believe that something terrible has happened or that they are experiencing some unacceptable emotion.

- **Reaction formation** is the unconscious process by which an emotion becomes translated into its opposite, as hate into love.

- **Projection** involves attributing unacceptable impulses or feelings to somebody else.

- **Regression** is a retreat to behaviors that proved satisfying in earlier stages of psychosexual development.

- **Sublimation**, the most successful defense mechanism, alters unacceptable impulses into completely acceptable and even admired social behaviors.

- Even today, many of Freud's assertions remain controversial. While some reject his views entirely, others favor closely related theories called **ego psychology**, which proposes an independent ego with its own reality-based processes.

The Social-Learning Approach

- The **social-learning approach** sees personality as a pattern of learned responses produced in part by a history of rewards and punishments and in part by more cognitive processes, such as observational learning.

- Social-learning theory has its roots in behaviorism.

- Skinner argued that behaviorists should focus on a **functional analysis** of behavior that specifies the external variables causing an organism to behave in a certain way.

- In his later writings, Skinner describes a position called **radical behaviorism**, which accepts the existence of internal events, such as thoughts and ideas, but continues to emphasize the relationship between environmental events and observable behavior.

- Albert Bandura stressed the importance of observational learning, in which people form symbolic images of an act and make judgments about it.

- Bandura has studied the consequences of an individual's expectation of **self-efficacy**, a belief in one's own competence or ability to achieve certain goals through certain actions.

The Humanistic Approach

- The **humanistic approach** to personality emphasizes such positive human qualities as the freedom to pursue rational and spiritual goals.

- According to Abraham Maslow, normal human behavior is motivated by a **hierarchy of needs**, a series of biological requirements that must be satisfied in the following order: **physiological needs** (e.g., hunger, thirst), **safety needs** (physical security), **belongingness and love needs** (being accepted or desired by others), **esteem needs** (being valued by others, having self-respect), and **self-actualization needs** (using all talents to achieve full potential).

- According to Maslow, the self-actualized person frequently has **peak experiences,** mystical feelings of happiness, peace, and contentment that are difficult to describe.

Type and Trait Approaches

- **Type theories** of personality sort people into separate personality categories or types.

- Closely related to type theories is the idea of describing personality in terms of **traits**, predispositions to respond to a variety of situations in similar ways.

- Gordon Allport saw traits as the fundamental source of personality unity, but he distinguished between two different approaches to the study of individual differences.

- The **nomothetic approach** attempts to understand the behavior and experience of people in general or of the average case.

- The **idiographic approach** attempts to understand the behavior and experience of a single individual.

Current Issues in Personality Research

- Current personality research tends to avoid global theories and focus instead on more modest problems. For example, Walter Mischel's charge that adult behavior is not particularly consistent from one situation to the next has led to considerable controversy.

- Bem and Allen have shown that a given trait may be relevant only for people who describe themselves as consistent in that trait.

- The **fundamental attribution error** refers to the tendency to underestimate the power of the situational forces that influence other people's behavior and to overestimate the importance of their personal dispositions.

- A line of research begun by Sandra Bem has investigated the implications of **androgyny**, a personality pattern that combines traditionally masculine and feminine traits in the same person.

- More recently, Bem has focused on **gender schema**, the cognitive structures that sort attributes and behaviors into masculine and feminine categories.

- **Type A behavior** refers to a personality pattern characterized by competitiveness and the tendency to be always in a rush.

- Numerous studies have shown that Type A individuals are more susceptible to cardiovascular disease and heart attacks.

Critical Thinking Exercises Discussions

Defense Mechanisms in Action

In each of these cases, repression is the operant defense mechanism. That is, the character is not aware of his or her primary feeling or conflicts. Other defense mechanisms that can be identified are: reaction formation (1), denial (2), projection (3), displacement (4), sublimation (5), and regression (6).

This application of scientific concepts is an example of coding. It required you to master several critical thinking skills—that is, identifying the defining characteristics of each defense mechanism, differentiating among the different defense mechanisms, and focusing on the relevant information in each brief case study in order to identify the relevant defense mechanism. A correct generalization of the meaning of each defense mechanism meant recognizing that repression was present in each case, along with other mechanisms that varied across the specific examples.

Androgyny

A critical consumer always looks for the evidence behind sweeping generalizations. In this excerpt, it is simply not there.

For example, consider the claim that "Nature is androgynous. . . ." Not only is there no evidence cited, but it is hard to imagine precisely what this means. How would the world be different if nature were not androgynous? How could you test the idea that nature is androgynous?

What about the statement: "Androgyny may shift its expression, but it will always be with us"? How could anyone possibly prove that androgyny will always be around? And how could a scientist decide that a particular phenomenon proved that androgyny was shifting its expression?

There are a number of other questionable claims in this excerpt. You will not need a Ph.D. in psychology to guess that most scientists would be uncomfortable with the claim that "if there *are* angels, they are probably androgynous."

A critical consumer looks for the scientific test that lies behind every assertion. In this case, a close look suggests that these statements simply could not be tested.

MEASURING INTELLIGENCE AND PERSONALITY

Chapter 13

More than 2,000 years before the birth of Christ, the emperor of China instituted a system of formal examinations to determine whether particular public officials were capable of continuing in office. Later, the Chinese developed the first "civil service" exams to choose government workers. For example, in 1115 B.C., job candidates had to demonstrate proficiency in music, archery, horsemanship, writing, arithmetic, and the ceremonies of public and private life (DuBois, 1970). Thus, the first known tests in the history of the human race were designed to choose people for jobs on the basis of their knowledge and abilities rather than on the basis of favoritism or accidents of birth, as practiced in many other societies.

The first psychological tests were designed with similar goals in mind. Alfred Binet developed the first intelligence test in 1905 for the objective identification of mentally retarded schoolchildren who required special schooling. The first personality test was devised by Robert Woodworth for the U.S. Army during World War I to identify draftees who would be unable to function psychologically under the stress of combat.

Today, hundreds of psychological tests are routinely adminstered to millions of Americans every year; indeed, every person who reads this text has almost certainly taken a number of them. Ordinarily, testing starts in grade school with standardized tests of achievement and IQ. The SAT may have helped determine the college you attend, and if you go on to graduate or professional school, your future may depend in part on your scores from an alphabet soup of tests including the GMAT, GRE, LSAT, and MCAT.

If you go to see a counselor or clinical psychologist, you may take the Rorschach, the Thematic Apperception Test, the Bender-Gestalt, or the Minne-

The Scholastic Aptitude Test for college admission was developed in 1926 by some of the same psychologists who had developed the first group IQ tests for the U.S. Army during World War I.

sota Multiphasic Personality Inventory. If you see a job counselor, you may take the Kuder Occupational Interest Survey or the Strong-Campbell Interest Inventory. If you apply for a job at a large corporation, you may take the Personnel Tests for Industry; and if you go to work for the United States government, you may take the Professional and Administrative Career Examination.

All these tests grew out of attempts to measure people's strengths and weaknesses fairly and objectively. But any type of evaluation is likely to involve problems, and from the beginning tests have been questioned by psychologists and nonpsychologists alike. Some of the questions raised by critics are serious and legitimate; several of these are discussed in the final section of this chapter. But too frequently, attacks on tests have been based on misconceptions and fallacies. Throughout this book, we have seen that trusting common sense can lead to some mistaken conclusions; this is particularly true regarding the interpretation of psychological test scores. Therefore, most of this chapter focuses on the basic principles of testing and measurement so that you, the consumer, can become more sophisticated about how psychological tests are designed to meet specific goals.

Basic Concepts of Measurement

The most important criteria by which psychologists judge any test are two technical characteristics called reliability and validity. In general terms, a **reliable** test is consistent and reproducible. A test is a kind of measuring device, and an unreliable test that gives inconsistent results is of little value.

reliable Consistent and reproducible.

Suppose, for example, that you bought a new tape measure to check your height. If the first measurement was 5 feet 10½ inches, a second measurement read 5 feet 8¾ inches, and a third read 6 feet, this inconsistency (or unreliability) would mean that something was wrong with your new tape measure.

However, even if the tape measure were totally consistent, it could still be wrong. It might give you a reading of 7 feet 2 inches time after time, but if you know you are about 5 feet 4 inches tall, you will be suspicious. Reliability is a necessary, but not a sufficient, condition for good measurement.

If a psychological test is not reliable, there is no need to go any further. But if a test is reliable, we must also ask whether it is **valid**—whether it accurately measures what it is supposed to measure. This is much harder to determine than consistency, so our discussion of specific types of validity is more complex than our discussion of reliability. Examples of the different types of reliability and validity can be found in Table 13.1.

Reliability

Measuring the reliability of a psychological test is relatively straightforward. One simply compares two independent scores achieved by the same individual on the test. More specifically, pairs of independent scores are collected for a large number of people, and the researcher simply computes the correlation coefficient (see "Appendix") between the two sets of scores.

If the two scores are identical for each individual, the correlation would be 1.0 and the test would be considered totally reliable. Psychologists expect the reliability of most tests to be around .9 or perhaps .8, since there is usually some slight error or variation in scores. This is to be expected even in physical measurements. If you weigh yourself every morning for a week, you will probably find that these measurements are not all precisely the same, because your weight varies slightly from day to day. Your psychological state may also vary from one test administration to another.

To cite just one example, the reliability for the verbal aptitude section of the College Entrance Examination Board's Scholastic Aptitude Test is .89; the reliability of the mathematics section is .88 (Wallace, 1972). These figures suggest that people who take the test a second time often get a slightly different score, but only a small fraction of them score much higher or much lower than they did the first time.

There are different types of reliability, depending on how the two independent scores are collected. For example, **test-retest reliability** is the correlation between pairs of test scores based on repeating precisely the same test on two different occasions. In many cases, however, this technique is not appropriate. For example, once you have taken a particular math test, the answers may come easier the second time around. In this case, a researcher might compute **alternate-form reliability**—the correlation between pairs of test scores achieved by the same person on two different forms (or sets of questions) testing the same material. There are also other forms of reliability; each provides a systematic measurement of consistency or stability over time.

Again, no matter how this characteristic is measured, unreliable test scores are of little scientific value. In some cases, a particular psychological

valid Accurately measuring a particular trait.

test-retest reliability The correlation between two different scores achieved by the same individual on the same test on two different occasions.

alternate-form reliability The correlation between two different scores achieved by the same individual on two different forms of the test.

TABLE 13.1

Definitions and Examples of Different Types of Reliability and Validity

Type	Definition	Example of a good test	Example of a poor test
Test-retest reliability	The correlation between scores on the same test taken on two different occasions	A sophomore French class takes a practice SAT language exam twice—once at the beginning of April and again at the end of May. The correlation between the two sets of scores is .90.	Students in a general psychology course take an exam being developed by one of their classmates to assess likability. The correlation between the scores they get the first time they take the test and the second time they take the test is .21.
Alternate-form reliability	The correlation between pairs of test scores achieved by the same people on two different forms of the same test	Students take a "practice test" in psychology before the real final exam. The two tests are designed to measure the exact same material, with minor changes in the wording of questions. The correlation between the two sets of scores is 91.	A graduate student develops alternate forms of a test for assertiveness. When the same group of subjects takes both forms of the test, there is no correlation between their two sets of scores. Some students who score as assertive on Form A score as unassertive on Form B, while others score as assertive on both forms. Similarly, some students who score as unassertive on Form A score as assertive on Form B, while others score as unassertive on both.
Criterion validity	Comparison of performance on a test with some external and independent measure, or criterion, of what the test is supposed to predict	Scores on SAT examinations taken in high school correlate significantly with grade point average in the first year of college.	All students passing the sample driving provided by the Ace Driving School for Adolescent Daredevils flunk the official test required by the Department of Motor Vehicles.
Content validity	Direct measurement of relevant knowledge and abilities related to a particular skill that has been analyzed systematically to produce the test	Students' knowledge of general psychology is assessed through a test that covers the material in the textbook and lectures.	Students' knowledge of general psychology is assessed through a test developed by the teacher on the basis of his rather shaky memory of what was talked about during the last few weeks of class.
Construct validity	Evidence that the trait or ability measured by a test is systematically related to a larger pattern of behavior that makes conceptual sense	Individuals who score high on a test for altruism show that they are always ready to help others, regularly give to charities, and frequently do volunteer work.	High scores on a test for altruism are obtained by a group of juvenile delinquents known for their frequent acts of selfishness.

test has been discredited when researchers showed it was unreliable. For example, some early scoring systems for the Rorschach test (a projective test of personality described later in this chapter) were shown to be unreliable and were therefore abandoned.

Validity

The validity of a test is far more difficult to determine or define. Again, there are several types. Let us begin with the most straightforward approach—**criterion validity**, which compares performance on a test with some external and independent measure, or criterion, of what the test is supposed to predict.

For example, a test called the Computer Programmer Aptitude Battery has been designed to identify job applicants who are likely to become effective programmers. One can imagine several external criteria that could be used to evaluate the validity of this test, such as supervisors' ratings of later job performance or the time taken to complete a specific programming assignment. In one study of the validity of this test (Perry, 1967b), 114 newly hired computer programmers were given the test before their training began. The external criterion of validity was the grade they received in their job training course. The correlations between the training course grades and scores on two subscales of the Computer Programmer Aptitude Battery were around .6, suggesting that it did indeed have criterion validity. Thus, the test is useful for companies who want to identify the strongest candidates in advance. In contrast, college grades were not highly correlated with performance in the training course and thus were of little predictive value for identifying the potential of applicants.

Note that while correlations of about .9 are expected for reliability, a correlation of .6 is considered adequate evidence of criterion validity. It is extremely difficult, or perhaps even impossible, to measure in advance all the factors that might be related to an external criterion. Performance in the computer training course, for example, was probably affected by applicants' motivation, how much they liked the teacher, how much stress they were under at home, and a wide variety of other factors that the Computer Programmer Aptitude Battery did not even try to measure.

Of course, this analysis assumes that the criterion itself is reliable and relevant. If grades in the computer training course were assigned on the basis of participation in class rather than ability to solve programming problems, or based on how much the teacher liked each student, this criterion would have little value.

If the criterion was adequate, the observed coefficient of .6 implies that this particular company would be wise to use the Computer Programmer Aptitude Battery to screen job candidates. Job decisions based strictly on this test alone will sometimes be wrong; if the test were a perfect predictor of performance, the validity coefficient would have been 1.0. However, wise use of these test scores can increase the likelihood of the best decisions.

As this example suggests, the validity of a test is always evaluated for some specific application. The Computer Programmer Aptitude Battery is a valid predictor of programming performance (at least by this criterion), but it would probably not be able to predict who would be the best Fuller Brush salesperson or bus driver.

criterion validity A comparison of performance on a test with some external and independent measure, or criterion, of what the test is supposed to predict.

A test may have criterion validity even if the questions it asks seem to be totally irrelevant. For example, it is theoretically possible that people who say they drink Pepsi for breakfast, are uncomfortable talking to strangers, and wear clothes that do not fit well make better computer programmers than stylish, coffee-drinking extraverts. On a superficial level, these three questions do not seem to have anything to do with performance as a computer programmer. But if they predict later performance, they have criterion validity.

A different approach to defining validity stresses the relevance of the content of a test. **Content validity** involves a systematic analysis of a particular skill followed by the design of test items that directly measure relevant knowledge and abilities. The key term here is *systematic analysis*. A test of French grammar would have high content validity only if one started by compiling a list of specifications of the key points in the field. This could be done by reviewing the content of courses and textbooks in French grammar and consulting experts in the language. The final list of specifications would then serve as the basis for drawing up actual test items.

The third major approach to validity is a bit more more theoretical. A test has **construct validity** if the trait it measures is systematically related to a larger pattern of behavior that makes conceptual sense. For example, suppose a woman got high scores on a test of anxiety under three different conditions: when she took a math test she was unprepared for, when she went out on a date with someone new, and when she went skydiving. In this case, the theoretical construct of anxiety seems to explain this pattern of scores. But, as this example suggests, construct validity is a bit more subtle than criterion validity or content validity.

Whether a test approaches the problem of validity in terms of external criteria, test content, or a theoretical construct, it is important to remember that psychologists insist that any test meet certain technical specifications to prove its worth. Intuitive analyses of the superficial characteristics of a test are often misleading.

Human Variation and the Normal Curve

Reliability and validity are the two most important characteristics of any test. There are a number of other basic principles and concepts, however, that are useful to understand the nature of psychological tests.

Test scores quantify individual differences by assigning numbers to different personal characteristics, such as intelligence and extraversion. To understand the rationale of tests, one must learn something about mathematical approaches to human variation.

The nineteenth-century Belgian scientist Adolphe Quetelet was the first to note that many human physical characteristics fell into similar patterns. Figure 13.1 illustrates one example. In 1939, the height of every man in England who was called up for military service was measured. The graph shows that the average height of these 91,163 men was about 5 feet 7½ inches. More important, the distribution of heights was arranged systematically around the average value; that is, the farther one gets from 5 feet 7½ inches, the fewer men there are.

More specifically, height conformed to a **normal distribution**, a particular

content validity A systematic analysis of a particular skill and the design of test items that measure all relevant knowledge.

construct validity A larger pattern of conceptually meaningful relationships.

normal distribution A particular mathematical distribution in which cases are symmetrically arranged around the average.

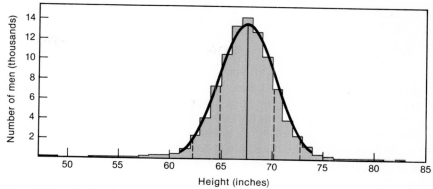

Figure 13.1 The heights of 91,163 Englishmen who were called up for military service in 1939. The solid lines show the actual number for each height; the dotted line represents a normal distribution. (Also see Figure 3.2.)

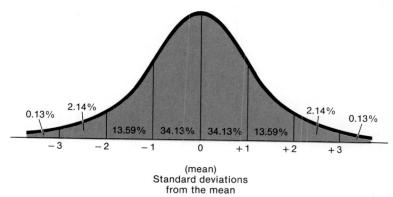

Figure 13.2 The normal distribution. Note that roughly 68% of all cases fall within one standard deviation of the mean; roughly 95% within two standard deviations; and 99.7% within three standard deviations.

mathematical distribution in which cases are symmetrically arranged around the average. Figure 13.2 illustrates the form of the normal distribution. As you can see, the normal distribution curve is symmetrical; the left and right sides are mirror images of each other.

The central value of the normal distribution is the **mean**, or arithmetic average. The shape of a particular normal curve is also determined by the **standard deviation**, a mathematical measure of the amount of variability, spread, or dispersion of a particular set of scores. (See "Appendix.")

In Figure 13.1, the mean height is 67.5 inches and the standard deviation is 2.6 inches. Referring to Figure 13.2, the normal distribution implies that about 68% of all men should fall within one standard deviation of the mean. To put it another way, 68% of all English military recruits were between 64.9 inches (67.5 − 2.6) and 70.1 inches (67.5 + 2.6) tall. Again referring to the Figure 13.2 summary of characteristics of the normal curve, note that about 95% of all values fall within two standard deviations of the mean. In this case, that implies that 95 out of every 100 English recruits were between 62.3 inches [67.5 − (2.6 × 2)] and 72.7 inches [67.5 + (2.6 × 2)] tall. Because

mean The arithmetic average.

standard deviation A mathematical measure of the amount of variability, spread, or dispersion of a particular set of scores.

the normal curve is a particular mathematical distribution that can be specified quite precisely, one can determine exactly how many cases fall within a particular range.

The normal distribution is useful not just for describing such physical characteristics as height, weight, and chest size, but also for psychological characteristics, such as intelligence. The first tests of IQ often found that scores were distributed roughly according to a normal distribution.

There is some controversy about whether this distribution tells us something about the nature of intelligence or something about the tests psychologists use to measure it. Whatever the implications, the fact is that IQ scores conform roughly to a normal distribution and that researchers have found that the normal curve is useful for describing the distribution of many psychological characteristics.

Commonsense Errors in Evaluating Tests

Before describing how reliability, validity, and the normal curve apply to tests of human personality and intelligence, it is useful to spell out some of the implications of these concepts in understanding tests. In part because psychological tests are so familiar, people often evaluate them in terms of commonsense criteria. But, as we have seen throughout this text, arguments that are intuitively appealing are sometimes quite wrong. Here, we focus on three common errors of common sense: relying on the appearances of a test, placing too much emphasis on criticisms of individual items, and assuming that population predictions apply to every individual.

RELYING ON FACE VALIDITY

Psychologists use the term **face validity** to refer to what a test *appears* to measure. Superficial appearances are a weak basis for evaluating a test, and in some cases they can be quite misleading.

Consider an analogy from another field. Many medical examinations have little face validity. If you lived in the fifteenth century, when little was known about the biochemistry of pregnancy, a pregnancy test based on analyzing chemicals in the urine might have seemed magical or even laughable. But that is not the point. If such a test had been available, it could have proved its value by successfully predicting childbirth. This test would have had little face validity but high criterion validity.

Similarly, the items on a personality test may be useful even if they are not related to personality in any obvious way. Art Buchwald poked fun at the superficial appearance of some psychological tests with a satirical personality inventory that included the following true-or-false questions:

Most of the time I go to sleep without saying goodbye.

A wide necktie is a sign of disease.

Frantic screams make me nervous.

When I was a child, I was an imaginary playmate.

face validity Superficial appearance that a test seems to measure what it is supposed to measure.

If you have ever taken a true-or-false personality test, these items may seem funny. In fact, they are funny. But it would be unfortunate if a satire like this led you to believe that test questions that seem odd, or even silly, are signs of a useless test. For test items, as for used cars, looks can be deceiving. The question of validity should be tied to performance, not to superficial appearances.

OVEREMPHASIS ON INDIVIDUAL ITEMS

Judgments about validity should always be based on the overall performance of an entire test. A second error commonsense critics often make is singling out an individual item for intuitive analysis. For example, journalists are fond of taking one question from the SAT and asking rhetorically whether it is really necessary for a student to be able, say, to define *hirsute* to do well in college.

Aside from the fact that this argument appeals to face validity rather than criterion validity, it makes the additional mistake of assuming that one or two questions will make much difference. Good tests usually consist of many items; they work by the sheer weight of numbers. A person with a large vocabulary might not happen to know the definition of one particular word but probably could identify the meanings of most of the other words on the test. The individual skills needed to answer a large number of specific items tend to balance one another out.

In a well-constructed test, a poor item is easy to locate because it is probably not systematically related to the total score. Suppose you constructed a test of 43 vocabulary items and added the irrelevant question, "How many miles is it from Chicago to St. Louis?" You would almost certainly find that, on the average, people who knew that *hirsute* means "hairy" would score higher on other vocabulary items than those who defined it incorrectly. But there probably would not be much difference in vocabulary scores among those who got the Chicago–St. Louis item right or wrong. Because it tapped a different type of knowledge, it would be poorly correlated with the total score. To an expert in testing, the results would stick out like a sore thumb.

Even if the mileage question were kept in the vocabulary test, it would not make much difference. It is only one item of many; it would simply decrease the validity of the test slightly.

INDIVIDUAL VERSUS GROUP PREDICTIONS

A third error that people sometimes make when they evaluate tests is assuming that group predictions apply to every individual. Tests are like the actuarial tables used by life insurance companies to predict the death rate; they are extremely effective in predicting probabilities for large groups but fail in many individual cases.

For example, if your father is a 50-year-old business executive who has high blood pressure and smokes two packs of cigarettes every day, he will have to pay high rates for his life insurance because actuarial tables predict that he is likely to die sooner than a healthy 25-year-old nonsmoker. If he lives to be 100, the life insurance company will not throw away its charts.

Some smokers with high blood pressure live to be 100, but they are the exceptions to the rule.

The same is true for test scores. It is possible that a high school senior who gets 300 on the SATs will go on to be the class valedictorian. Anything is possible. But this event is not likely. If you were to collect the SAT scores of 500 valedictorians at major colleges each year, few would have scores as low as 300.

Tests predict probabilities for large groups; they do not determine the future course for every individual. Indeed, test makers can predict just how often they will be wrong by examining validity coefficients. A test with a criterion validity of .8 will be right far more often than a test with a criterion validity of .5; this greater predictive power is exactly what the magnitude of the correlation tells us.

Critics of IQ tests often cite cases of individuals who did far better in school than their IQ scores might seem to predict. These cases come as no surprise to people who understand the nature of tests; the predictions they make are extremely accurate for large groups but less accurate for individuals.

Experienced clinicians assign far less value to a single test score than does the proverbial man in the street. That is one reason that IQ scores and other results are often withheld from the people who take the tests. If one child in a family is told that his IQ is 118 and his older sister's is 123, he may conclude that he is the slow one in the family and start to act the part. A psychologist would know that a difference of 5 points is very likely to result from random variation and is of little or no practical significance. (If the difference were 30 points, however, it probably would have practical implications.)

In summary, people who do not understand the nature of psychological tests often misinterpret them. It is only by learning more about the nature of tests that you can make informed judgments about them.

When interpreting tests, it is important to remember that group predictions do not apply to every individual. For example, as a group, smokers die younger than nonsmokers. However, this does not imply that every smoker will die younger than every nonsmoker.

Intelligence Tests

The nature of intelligence tests has changed over time, and the history of their evolution can enrich your understanding of them. Moreover, even today there are controversies over intelligence tests and what they measure.

Measuring Intelligence

Sir Francis Galton was probably the first scientist to try systematically to measure differences in human intellectual ability. After completing his studies of eminent Englishmen (see Chapter 9), he looked for a more precise index of ability. Galton assumed that people with good eyesight and hearing, fast motor reactions, and other basic abilities would also prove to be superior in reasoning power. It is a testimonial to Galton's own intelligence that he thought of a profitable way to test this hypothesis. He set up an exhibit of tests in a London museum and invited people to see how their mental and physical abilities

mental age A particular group's average performance level on an intelligence test.

compared with those of other people; 9,337 visitors paid 4 pence each for this privilege. Unfortunately, later analysis of these and other studies did not support Galton's idea that reasoning power was associated with sensory and motor skills.

THE FIRST IQ TESTS

The roots of modern ideas of measuring intelligence can be traced back to a practical problem. After the French government passed a law in 1881 requiring every child to go to school, teachers soon found that some children seemed totally unable to master the curriculum. In 1904, the minister of public instruction appointed a special committee to look into the problem of identifying retarded students who needed special instruction. One of its members, a psychologist named Alfred Binet, devised a special test to screen students so that "no child suspected of retardation would be . . . put in a special school without having taken . . . [an] examination showing that . . . he could not profit, at least moderately, from the teaching in the regular school" (quoted in DuBois, 1970, p. 34).

In collaboration with Theodore Simon, Binet published this first modern intelligence test in 1905. It consisted of 30 different tests that a trained examiner could quickly administer to an individual child. Virtually all of these tasks had been studied before by Binet and others; what was new was the idea of combining information from a wide variety of tasks to determine a child's mental age. **Mental age** was defined by the average performance of a large number of children who were actually that old.

For example, Figure 13.3 shows one of the items from Binet's 1905 scale. A boy with a mental age of at least 3 could point to a simple object in

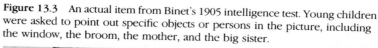

Figure 13.3   An actual item from Binet's 1905 intelligence test. Young children were asked to point out specific objects or persons in the picture, including the window, the broom, the mother, and the big sister.

this picture and could also repeat two digits, tell his family name, and perform other specified intellectual tasks. This definition was based on Binet's systematic observation that average 3-year-olds could perform these tasks but younger children generally could not. A person with a mental age of 8 could count backward from 20 to 0 and could repeat five digits. A mental age of 12 or more was indicated by an ability to compose a sentence using three given words (such as *Paris, gutter,* and *fortune*) and perform other specific tasks. These are actual examples from the 1911 revision of Binet's scale; similar items are used in present-day tests of children's intelligence.

The idea of computing an **intelligence quotient** (or **IQ**) came from a German psychologist named William Stern. He argued that a 5-year-old with a mental age of 4 was more retarded than a 13-year-old with a mental age of 12. In other words, it is not the difference between mental and chronological age that provides the best index of development but the ratio:

$$\text{Intelligence quotient (IQ)} = \frac{\text{mental age}}{\text{chronological age}} \times 100$$

Chronological age is determined by the date of birth; the ratio is multiplied by 100 simply for convenience, so that IQ can be expressed without decimals. Using this formula, the average child's IQ is 100; slower children have IQs below 100, and brighter-than-average children will have IQs over 100.

Many psychologists around the world tried Binet's test and published revisions based on their own data regarding which items successfully distinguished children of different chronological ages. Items shown to be ineffective were replaced with better questions. The most famous revision was published by Lewis Terman at Stanford University in 1916. This scale, now known as the **Stanford-Binet**, underwent further major revisions in 1937 and 1960. Although hundreds of other tests have been published, the Stanford-Binet is still one of the most frequently used tests for assessing the intelligence of an individual child.

When similar tests were later developed for adults, the idea of an intelligence quotient based on mental age no longer applied. There is little or no difference between the reasoning power of 20-year-olds and 40-year-olds. The term IQ was still used, however, and adult scores were standardized in terms of the normal distribution. The IQ of the average adult was defined as 100; once the standard deviation of a particular adult IQ test is specified, it is possible to determine where any other score stands in relation to the total adult population.

After Binet, the next major step in the development of psychological tests involved instruments that could be administered to a large group of people at the same time. Like the notion of IQ, group testing grew out of a practical problem. When millions of men were drafted in World War I, the U.S. Army needed to screen out quickly any retarded individuals who could not function as soldiers. A group of psychologists developed the Army Alpha Test to measure the IQ of soldiers who could read English and the Army Beta Test for those who could not. Alpha was largely composed of verbal and numerical tests, such as vocabulary and arithmetic problems; Beta items focused on such tasks as mazes, counting cubes, and noting missing parts of

**ALFRED BINET
(1857–1911)**

Binet wrote a doctoral dissertation on the nervous system of insects, but later he became interested in the measurement of human intelligence. In 1904 he was appointed to a commission that sought a reliable way to identify retarded children early in their school careers so that they could receive special instruction. A year later, Binet and Theodore Simon published the first systematic test of intelligence. The scale was an immediate success; revisions in 1908 and 1911 were quickly accepted around the world. At the time of his death, Binet was trying to develop an intelligence test that could be administered to an entire group rather than to one individual at a time.

familiar pictures. Within two years, more than 1.7 million men took these tests in the first mass-testing program in history.

Encouraged by the success of the army tests, psychologists went on to develop a large number of tests for industry and education after the war ended. Indeed, some historians believe that the success of the army testing program changed the course of American psychology; an academic discipline focusing on basic research turned into a profession with strong applied interests (DuBois, 1970).

IQ AND INTELLIGENCE

As more and more IQ tests were developed, critics became increasingly concerned with a fundamental question. Did IQ tests really measure intelligence? One problem with this question is that people sometimes disagree over the definition of the word *intelligence*. For example, a study of "lay people"—such as commuters, supermarket shoppers, and people chosen from the phone book (Sternberg, Conway, Ketron, & Bernstein, 1981)—found some specific disagreements. One subject in this study said an intelligent person is "fun to be with"; another said an intelligent person "bores people." Clearly, no measure of intelligence can satisfy such contradictory criteria.

Nevertheless, there was general agreement. The characteristics these lay people listed in definitions of intelligence included the skills measured in IQ tests, such as good vocabulary, verbal fluency, and an ability to see the connections between ideas. But they also included interpersonal characteristics, such as "sensitivity to other people's needs and desires" and "gets along well with others." Traditional IQ tests have not attempted to measure this type of "street smarts." Thus, while there is a close relationship between IQ and everyday definitions of intelligence, there may also be some important differences. Intuitively, it is easy to identify individuals with great intellectual abilities who do not relate well to other people. Only future research can tell whether these individuals represent the exceptions or the rule—that is, whether interpersonal skills are independent from more intellectual forms of intelligence.

Most of the research to date on the nature of intelligence has focused on the relationships among performance on various intellectual tasks. For example, if people who score high in verbal ability also generally do well on tests of mathematical ability, it seems reasonable to conclude that both reflect the same underlying dimension of general intelligence. If, on the other hand, the correlation between verbal and mathematical ability is typically low, these intellectual skills are probably independent of each other and represent two different types of intelligence.

Early researchers were impressed by the high correlations between different ways of measuring intelligence. Around the turn of the century, Charles Spearman concluded that IQ tests measure one general intelligence factor (called g). Other researchers later developed new statistical techniques that challenged this view. After analyzing the performance of hundreds of subjects on a variety of mental tests, L. L. Thurstone concluded that there are seven relatively independent primary mental abilities: verbal comprehension, word fluency, number, space, memory, perceptual speed, and reasoning. Thurstone

intelligence quotient (IQ)   Mental age divided by chronological age times 100.

Stanford-Binet   One of the most frequently used tests for assessing the intelligence of an individual child.

argued that IQ tests that assign a single score of intelligence are too simplistic. One person with an IQ of 120 might have a very good memory, while another person with the same score might have an average memory but above-average word fluency.

The question of whether intelligence is best thought of as one general ability or several separate abilities revolves around sophisticated mathematical analyses of test results; it remains controversial (Carroll & Horn, 1981). For our purposes, however, this theoretical issue may be less important than some of the practical questions considered in the next section: What kinds of performance can be predicted from the results of the most common tests of IQ?

The Wechsler Adult Intelligence Scale

At first, tests of adult IQ simply consisted of more difficult versions of items developed for schoolchildren. In 1939, David Wechsler published an IQ test that had been specifically designed with adult interests and abilities in mind. Wechsler's test became the most widely used instrument for assessing the IQ of adults on a one-to-one basis; more than 3,000 articles have been published on its use (Anastasi, 1982).

The scale was revised in 1955 and again in 1981; reliability, validity, and other technical characteristics were improved by replacing items that failed to meet certain statistical criteria. The revisions also updated the test's content so that it could accurately reflect the knowledge and interests of subsequent generations. For example, the 1981 edition (called the **Wechsler Adult Intelligence Scale-Revised**, or **WAIS-R**) eliminated some items that seemed implicitly racist or sexist.

The WAIS-R consists of two major parts, a verbal scale and a performance scale. The verbal scale consists of six subtests that ask different types of questions; another five subtests make up the performance scale (see Table 13.2). Thus, the WAIS-R includes 11 different categories of questions to test a wide range of intellectual skills and to identify people who don't know—or don't care—about one particular type of question. Under ordinary conditions, the total score an individual receives on the verbal scale is closely related to the total score on the performance scale. For people with little education or verbal facility, however, these two approaches may provide different estimates of IQ.

Actual IQ scores on the WAIS-R are based on the performance of a representative sample of 1,880 Americans tested between 1976 and 1980 (see Figure 13.4). The proportions of subjects were matched to the 1970 census in terms of sex, age, race, geographic region, occupation, education, and urban or rural residence. Tables are provided for the examiner to convert a particular number of correct answers into a normally distributed IQ score, with a mean of 100 and a standard deviation of 15. The actual conversion formula depends on the age of the person taking the test. For example, if a 65-year-old and a 22-year-old got all the same questions right, the 65-year-old would have a higher IQ. The reason is that performance declines somewhat as a person grows older (see Chapter 10), so a 65-year-old would be farther

Wechsler Adult Intelligence Scale-Revised (WAIS-R) Six verbal and five performance scales; considered a reliable and valid test of IQ.

TABLE 13.2

Subtests of the Wechsler Adult Intelligence Scale

Subtests	*Typical items*
Verbal	
Information	At what temperature does water freeze?
Comprehension	Why are traffic lights needed?
Arithmetic	A car goes 50 miles in one hour. Traveling at the same speed, how far could it go in 15 minutes?
Similarities	In what way are oranges and apples alike?
Digit span	Repeat the following numbers: 7, 4, 3, 6, 2, 6, 5, 1.
Vocabulary	What does *autumn* mean?
Performance	
Digit symbol	Given a key that lists a symbol (such as ⊥ or ∧) for each digit from 1 to 9, write the symbol for each number that appears on a long list.
Object assembly	A small jigsaw puzzle of a familiar object.
Block design	Arrange a set of blocks (with different designs on each side) so that they reproduce a specified pattern.
Picture completion	What is missing from this picture?

Picture arrangement Arrange these pictures in the proper order to tell a logical story:

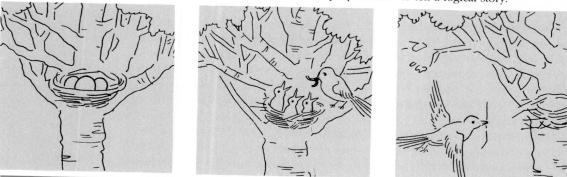

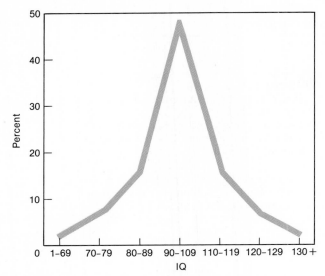

Figure 13.4 The actual distribution of IQs for a recent standardization sample of the WAIS-R. There were 1,880 adults chosen to represent the United States population in sex, age, race, and other characteristics. Note the similarity to the normal distribution shown in Figure 13.2.

above the average for that age group than a 22-year-old with the same score.

Extensive tests were done to ensure the reliability of the WAIS-R. For example, test-retest reliability was assessed by giving people the WAIS-R on two different occasions (two to seven weeks apart). These correlations were around .95, indicating that the WAIS-R is a highly reliable instrument.

As you might expect, the validity of the WAIS-R is far more difficult to assess. Wechsler (1958) argues for its content validity (as noted earlier, this is based on the systematic analysis of relevant abilities) because the 11 subtests were chosen to sample all the different components of intelligence that have proved important in clinical practice. From another perspective, he argues that the fact that the WAIS-R is highly correlated (typically around .8) with other tests of IQ suggests construct validity (based on the test's theoretical relation to other behaviors). Further, the fact that scores on the 11 subtests generally correlate with each other (typically, correlations between pairs of tests range from .3 to .8) supports the idea that they all measure the same underlying construct—intelligence.

The strongest argument for the validity of the WAIS-R probably involves criterion validity (its ability to predict external behavior). Countless studies have shown that a wide variety of IQ tests, including the WAIS-R, predict performance in school (see "Understanding the Scientific Method"). Correlations are typically on the order of .5 and tend to be higher for objective achievement tests than for course grades. (Other evidence suggests that course grades reflect more than just intelligence, particularly in elementary school. All other things being equal, teachers tend to give higher grades to socially outgoing students, those who put in extra effort, and girls.) IQ scores also correlate highly (typically .6 to .8) with ratings of intelligence by both teachers

Correlations and Causality: IQ and School Grades

As explained in the "Appendix," a *correlation coefficient* is a mathematical expression of the relationship between two variables. The absolute value of a correlation coefficient varies from 0 (no relationship) to 1 (one variable predicts another perfectly), while the sign of the correlation (plus or minus) indicates the direction of the relationship. But even after a correlation between two variables has been computed, there is still the question of what it means.

When an investigator finds that there is a correlation between education and income, for example, intuitively the implication seems clear: If you stay in school longer, you are likely to make more money. This "obvious" conclusion may be quite wrong, for one simple reason—correlations do not necessarily imply causal relationships.

Statistics teachers are fond of describing correlations where the lack of causality is easy to see. For example, Fuerst (1979) notes that around 1950 someone discovered that there was a correlation of +.90 between the number of babies born in Stockholm, Sweden, each year and the number of storks' nests in the city. Does that mean that storks really do bring babies? Of course not.

However, it is possible to imagine a causal basis of the correlation that most of us could accept. The extra storks in the city may have been noisy as they left their nests early in the morning to find food, leaving the rudely awakened human inhabitants with extra time to make babies. More likely, both more storks and more babies were caused by a third factor—as Stockholm grew during these years, there were more houses for storks to nest on and people to live in.

A significant correlation between *A* and *B* can be explained at least three ways— *A* causes *B*, *B* causes *A*, and changes in both *A* and *B* are caused by something else. For example, Vane (1966) found that grammar school IQ scores correlated significantly ($r = .56$) with the average grades of 272 students at a Long Island, New York, high school; dozens of other studies have reported similar correlations between IQ and grades.

The implication seems obvious. Having a high IQ improves your chances of doing well in school. It may seem obvious, but it is not necessarily correct. Perhaps the grades are the more fundamental variable; doing well in courses increases knowledge and helps a person get more items right on an IQ test. Or perhaps it is some third, unmeasured variable that accounts for success on IQ tests and high school grades. Maybe exposure to educational games at the age of 3 is the key to later academic success, and children who watched *Sesame Street* are more likely to do well on IQ tests and school tests. All these explanations—high IQ causes high grades, high grades cause high IQ, and both are caused by something else—are equally plausible explanations of the correlation.

That does not mean that causal relationships can never be uncovered. Experimental studies can prove causality, and sophisticated analyses of some kinds of correlational data can suggest it. In the study described here, the fact that the IQ scores were measured several years before the grades suggests that IQ is the more basic factor.

The most important point for the introductory student is that simple correlations do not prove causal relationships, no matter how obvious the links may seem intuitively.

and students. People with high IQs also tend to go further in school and work in more demanding occupations with higher income and prestige (Matarazzo, 1972; Jensen, 1980).

Psychologists still do not agree on exactly what IQ means in theoretical terms, so there is some controversy over the precise implications of IQ scores. But all three approaches to validity—content, construct, and criterion—suggest that the WAIS-R measures at least one kind of intelligence that is systematically related to a number of behaviors.

Genetics and IQ

The considerable amount of debate that has gone on over the nature of intelligence and how it is measured seems calm and civilized compared with the controversies that have arisen over psychologists' attempts to study the relative role of heredity and environment in determining IQ. Unfortunately, the emotion surrounding this issue often has made it difficult to get to the heart of the complex technical problem of estimating hereditary and environmental influences on IQ, or on any other trait, for that matter. Before considering the specifics of IQ, then, let us return to the basic issues surrounding behavioral genetics, which were introduced in Chapter 9.

THE CONCEPT OF HERITABILITY

Heritability is a mathematical estimate of the relative importance of genetics and environment in determining a particular trait for a specific population. For our purposes, the technical details of how it is computed are not important. However, it is important to understand what it means to say that intelligence or extraversion or schizophrenia has a high heritability for a particular group. There are two points to remember: Heritability estimates are always limited to a particular group; and a trait that is highly heritable is not necessarily fixed at birth and impossible to change.

Genes provide a biochemical blueprint for development. But many other factors affect development, and the way genes are expressed always depends to some extent on the environment. Suppose, for the sake of argument, that a tendency toward obesity is partially inherited. A person with the obesity genes could gain weight if he just sat near chocolate, while another individual with another set of genes could stay thin even if she lived entirely on potato chips and pecan pie. These genetic predispositions will be expressed only if these two people are raised in an environment in which fattening food is freely available. If both are unfortunate enough to be born in a time of famine, the genetic differences might never be expressed, and both children could be extremely thin.

The fact that the environment affects the way genes are expressed implies that one can never totally isolate nature from nurture. This is the reason psychologists think it is naive and misleading to ask such a question as: Is intelligence inherited? The answer is that it depends on the group you study and the environment in which they were raised.

Imagine two different studies of our obesity example, both using the

heritability A mathematical estimate of the relative importance of genetics and environment in determining a particular trait for a specific population.

same technique of comparing adopted children's weight with that of their biological and adoptive parents. A study of middle-class American children would probably find that adopted children were more likely to resemble their biological parents and conclude that obesity was influenced by genetics. But suppose the study was replicated precisely in a society in which lower-class children suffered from poor nutrition and inadequate food but upper-class children overate. For this group, children would probably resemble their adoptive parents' weight, since this population had such a wide variety of eating habits. These studies would come up with two different estimates for the heritability of the same trait, and each would be correct for a different group.

Human characteristics are always determined by a mixture of heredity and environment. The relative importance of nature and nurture varies from one group to another. Further, even when a trait is largely inherited in a given group, that does not mean it can never be changed. Quite the contrary. Understanding the genetic basis of a phenomenon may make it easier to control.

The best example of this comes from research on a rare disease called phenylketonuria—PKU, for short. Children with PKU seem normal at birth, but their intellectual and motor development soon slows down. One-third never learn to walk and two-thirds never learn to talk. Doctors now know that PKU is caused by a genetic disorder that results in the lack of a liver enzyme involved in the digestion of a specific protein (phenylalanine) found in milk and other foods. The undisgested protein becomes toxic and attacks nerve cells, causing progressive mental retardation. Once PKU children are identified, they can be put on a diet that includes very little of the culprit protein, and they will then develop normally. Since the mid-1960s, routine blood tests on newborn babies have identified over 1,000 American infants who had this disease, and dietary treatment has saved them from becoming mentally retarded. In this case, knowledge of genetic factors actually made it possible to change the course of a very serious disease.

Thus, biological effects on behavior are neither separate nor independent from psychological factors. This complex interdependence should be kept firmly in mind as we review the evidence regarding inheritance and IQ.

INDIVIDUAL DIFFERENCES

In 1963, a classic article summarized all the evidence then available regarding IQ resemblances among biological and adoptive relatives (Erlenmeyer-Kimling & Jarvik, 1963). More than 30,000 pairs of people had participated in 52 studies in eight countries over two generations. Despite the wide range of samples and methods, the overall results proved to be quite consistent. The more closely two people were biologically related, the more similar their IQs. These data suggested that genetic factors strongly influenced individual differences in IQ. But over the next two decades, this conclusion was repeatedly challenged and criticized as other investigators reexamined the original data and conducted investigations of their own.

In the course of this painstaking reanalysis, evidence emerged that one of the most famous investigators, Sir Cyril Burt, had actually falsified data in his attempt to prove that IQ was inherited (Hearnshaw, 1979). There have been few documented cases of scientific fraud of this sort, and the seriousness of this incident suggests that the debate over the genetics of IQ was no ordinary academic controversy.

On a more positive note, the fact that so much attention has now been devoted to the reanalysis of these data increases scientific confidence in the conclusions that finally emerged. In 1980, Robert Plomin and J. C. De Fries compared results from studies published in the 1970s analyzing 9,300 pairs of relatives with the earlier review of 30,000 pairs. They found that the later studies typically produced somewhat lower estimates of heritability, perhaps as a result of methodological improvements or of differences in the populations studied. However, even these newer, more conservative results "nonetheless implicate genes as the major systematic force influencing the development of individual differences in IQ" (p. 21).

One line of data supporting this conclusion compared IQ resemblance among identical and fraternal twins. According to Plomin and De Fries's summary of the data, identical twins who are raised in the same family are more closely related in IQ (correlation = .86) than fraternal twins of the same sex who are raised together (correlation = .62). (See "Appendix.") Since the major difference between these twin pairs is that identical (monozygotic) twins are genetically identical, while fraternal (dizygotic) twins are no more closely related than any pair of siblings, most psychologists interpret these data to mean that genetic forces are particularly powerful.

The most interesting twins, from a theoretical point of view, are identical twins who are raised in different families, for they represent an experiment in nature in which two individuals with the same genes are exposed to different environments. Such cases are extremely rare, and only three studies have withstood careful scrutiny. Juel-Nielsen (1965) found a correlation of .62 between the IQs of 12 pairs of monozygotic twins raised apart; Newman, Freeman, and Holzinger (1937) reported a correlation of .67 for 19 pairs of twins; and Shields (1962) found a correlation of .77 for 40 pairs of separated identical twins. Although these studies too have been criticized, the fact that these correlations are generally higher than those found for fraternal twins raised together provides further support for the powerful effects of genes on IQ.

Another line of evidence for the genetic hypothesis comes from studies of adopted children. The correlation between IQs of biological parent and child who are separated by adoption is .31, while the correlation between adoptive parent and child is .15. This finding is consistent with other evidence that the more closely two people are related biologically, the closer their IQs are likely to be (see Figure 13.5).

Another review of this literature came to the following conclusion: "Within populations of European origin, both the genotype and the environment demonstrably influence IQ, the former tending under present conditions to account for more of the individual variation in IQ than does the latter" (Loehlin, Lindzey, & Spuhler, 1975, p. 233). If the phrasing seems cautious, it is purposely so. Since the vast majority of studies to date have focused on samples of European origin, the authors limit their conclusion to that group "under present conditions." Behavioral geneticists stress such limitations because their findings are so often misunderstood.

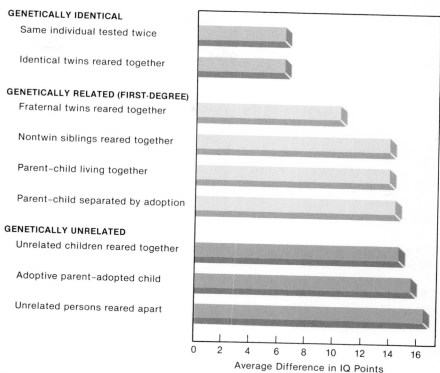

GENETICALLY IDENTICAL
Same individual tested twice

Identical twins reared together

GENETICALLY RELATED (FIRST-DEGREE)
Fraternal twins reared together

Nontwin siblings reared together

Parent–child living together

Parent–child separated by adoption

GENETICALLY UNRELATED
Unrelated children reared together

Adoptive parent–adopted child

Unrelated persons reared apart

Average Difference in IQ Points

Figure 13.5 Summary of data from over 18,000 people regarding similarity between various types of relatives. These data suggest that both genes and environment influence IQ.

IMPLICATIONS OF HERITABILITY

Again, it is important to remember that the relative importance of nature and nurture is always defined for a specific group. Further, high heritability within a particular group does not imply that a trait cannot be changed, and human characteristics are always determined by both heredity and environment.

The issue of specificity of heritability to a particular group has caused considerable confusion. Much of the fuel for the controversy over the genetics of IQ came from a 1969 article by Arthur Jensen. At that time, most psychologists accepted the findings from numerous studies that showed that, on the average, American whites scored somewhat higher on IQ tests than American blacks. However, most believed that these differences reflected the limitations of the test or environmental influences on IQ. Jensen was one of the first to raise the possibility that genetic factors might be involved in this racial difference.

It is important to emphasize that the origin of differences *between* groups is logically separate from the question of whether individual differences in IQ *within* a particular population are strongly influenced by genetics. As noted above, there is a great deal of evidence that IQ is highly heritable within the American white population. But this conclusion may not apply to other groups. According to one school of thought, American blacks have often been raised in educationally disadvantaged environments, so they are unable to express their genetic potential. If this were so, estimates of the heritability of IQ within the black population would be lower than similar estimates within the white population. There have been direct tests of this idea, but to date the results have been inconsistent and inconclusive (Loehlin, Lindzey, & Spuhler, 1975; Mackenzie, 1984).

The related question of the origin of differences between groups is even more complex and controversial. To try to get some distance from the emotional issue of race, consider an example of genetics in agriculture. Imagine an Arizona parsley farmer who uses the same seed to plant two different plots of land. One plot is fertilized and watered regularly, the other neglected. Some parsley plants within each field will be taller and sturdier than others, based on the genetic characteristics of individual seeds. But overall, the plants in the plot that was well watered and taken care of will be taller and healthier than those in the neglected field. Thus, the differences *between* these plots of land are the result of environmental variation while, at the same time, the differences *within* each plot are determined largely by genetics.

Analogously, the fact that IQ is strongly influenced by genes for American whites does *not* imply that any differences in IQ between blacks and whites are also based on genetics. There are scientific methods that can reveal the source of group differences, but the convictions of those who debate this topic have often exceeded the quality of their evidence. The details of this controversy are extremely complex and confusing, but the most reasonable conclusion is extremely simple: At this point, no one knows the cause of black-white IQ differences.

In any case, we must remember that a genetic trait is not fixed for life at the moment of birth. We described earlier the example of PKU, a genetic disorder that leads to mental retardation when untreated but the effects of which are relatively minor when treated properly. In that example, understanding the genetic basis of a characteristic actually made it easier to change.

And there is no doubt whatever that the environment plays an important role in determining IQ. The simple fact that monozygotic twins have different IQs proves that the environment has an impact. Studies of adopted children have shown that higher socioeconomic status can raise IQ. For example, Scarr and Weinberg (1976) studied 130 black and interracial children who were adopted by economically advantaged white families in Minnesota. If genetics were the only factor in determining intelligence, these children would have been expected to have IQs somewhat below average, around 90. In fact, the mean IQ of this group was 106, testifying to the importance of the conditions under which children are raised. Children who had been adopted within the first year of life had even higher IQs.

Additional support for the role of a stimulating environment in the nurturance of intelligence comes from research by a group of French psychologists. Schiff and his associates (1978) studied a group of poor mothers who had given up one baby for adoption while keeping and raising at least one other child. The results indicated that the average IQ of the children adopted into upper-middle-class homes was about 110, while the average IQ of the half-siblings raised by impoverished biological mothers was 95. This IQ difference suggests that the more stimulating homes of the adopted children gave

An intellectually stimulating environment can increase intelligence.

them an intellectual advantage over their biologically related but environmentally deprived half-siblings.

Much of the research on the influence of environment on intellectual development does not involve IQ testing at all, because the research subjects are rats. In one illustrative study, Greenough (1975) studied the brains of rats raised under either enriched or impoverished conditions. Microscopic analyses revealed that the neurons of the rats raised under the enriched conditions had developed more regions for synaptic connections than the deprived rats. Such findings suggest, at least in lower animals, that the environment can have a direct impact on the biological basis for intelligence—the brain itself.

It is unfortunate that the high heritability of IQ is so often misunderstood. It does not imply that differences between groups are genetic nor that IQ can never be changed. However, it may imply that the best way to deal with human diversity is to try to understand it fully in order to help each individual achieve as much as possible.

Mental Retardation

As noted earlier, the first IQ tests were designed in part to identify children whose limited intellectual ability would create special problems in their schooling. From the start, however, those who invented IQ measurements worried that a diagnosis of retardation could not be made on the basis of an IQ score alone. Binet and Simon wrote that IQ diagnosis "is not automatic, like a scale in a railroad station, on which it is necessary only to step for the machine to emit a ticket with our weight printed on it. . . . The results of our examination have no value if separated from all comment; they must be interpreted" (quoted in DuBois, 1970, p. 39).

Similarly, the current guidelines for the diagnosis of mental retardation (American Psychiatric Association, 1980) stress that this label should be based not just on an IQ score but also on a clinical judgment that a person is intellectually unable to function in society without some special help. Unfortunately, human judgment is sometimes wrong and some individuals have been falsely diagnosed as mentally retarded. In the past, diagnosis has been particularly troublesome for blind, deaf, and verbally limited children who may lack the physical skills to respond appropriately on many intelligence tests.

A critical consumer of psychology will remain somewhat skeptical of a diagnosis of mental retardation, for fear that the label itself may become a self-fulfilling prophecy. Unfortunately, children who believe they are retarded may develop low expectations for themselves. However, this caution about an individual's diagnosis is not meant to imply that all mental retardation is in the eye of the beholder; the vast majority of people who are diagnosed as mentally retarded suffer from a serious intellectual deficit that interferes with their ability to function adequately in our society.

The current diagnostic system distinguishes four levels of retardation: mild, IQ 50 to 70; moderate, IQ 35 to 49; severe, IQ 20 to 34; and profound, IQ below 20. Most researchers believe that cases of moderate, severe, and profound retardation are usually caused by identifiable biological problems, while the much more common diagnosis of mild retardation is usually a result of environmental factors summarized by the label *cultural-familial retardation.*

Cultural-familial retardation involves a family pattern of mild mental retardation with no evidence of organic brain damage. About four out of five mentally retarded people fall into the mild category, and the overwhelming majority of these cases fall into the cultural-familial group. This pattern is rarely found in middle-class or upper-class children; it is limited to people who grow up in homes that are socially, economically, and culturally disadvantaged.

People in this group are often called "educable" because they can develop adequate social and communication skills with special training. Mild retardation often is diagnosed only in late childhood, when problems with reading, writing, and arithmetic become prominent. In nonindustrialized societies that do not emphasize these skills, mild retardation might go unnoticed.

In contrast, the more severe categories of mental retardation are equally common among all social classes and ordinarily seem to be caused by biological and organic problems. People who fall into the moderate group (about 12% of the retarded population) are considered "trainable." Although they are unlikely to pass the second-grade level in academic subjects, they can learn to care for themselves with some supervision. Severe mental retardation (about 7% of the retarded) interferes with motor development and speech. People in this category can learn simple work tasks if they are closely supervised. Profound mental retardation (less than 1% of the retarded) is so severe that people must live in a highly structured environment with aid and supervision.

Among the biological causes of the more severe forms of retardation, the most common and best understood is **Down's syndrome**, first described

cultural-familial retardation A family pattern of mild mental retardation with no evidence of organic brain damage.

Down's syndrome A biologically caused, severe form of mental retardation characterized by certain physical abnormalities. (Formerly called *mongolism.*)

by British physician Langdon Down in 1866. Down used the term *mongolism* to refer to the physical abnormalities that accompany this condition, including slanting eyes; a flat face and nose; a large, protruding tongue; stubby fingers; and sparse, straight hair. About 1 out of every 660 births produces a Down's syndrome child; the IQ of such a child rarely exceeds 50.

In 1959, physicians discovered that Down's syndrome is caused by a chromosomal abnormality. As noted in Chapter 9, every cell in the human body ordinarily contains 46 chromosomes (structures composed of genes). The Down's syndrome child has an extra, forty-seventh chromosome because of an abnormality in the mother's egg. The risk of this problem increases dramatically as a woman gets older. For mothers under the age of 30, only about 1 in 1,500 births produce a Down's syndrome child; for mothers over 45, the risk is 1 in 65. The possible importance of the father's age is not fully understood.

In recent years, a new diagnostic procedure has been developed that can diagnose Down's syndrome—and many other conditions—before birth. In *amniocentesis,* fluid is withdrawn from the amnion, the sac surrounding the fetus. If chromosomal abnormalities are detected, the mother then has the option of terminating the pregnancy with an abortion.

Moderate, severe, and profound retardation can also be caused by a variety of other biological problems. Along with genetic disorders, these include infectious diseases, such as syphilis; traumatic events before birth, such as malnutrition or certain types of poisoning; and traumatic events during or following birth, such as head injury or deprivation of oxygen.

Society's attitudes toward mental retardation have undergone many changes since the problem was identified by the French physician Edouard Sequin in the nineteenth century. Sequin optimistically believed that special

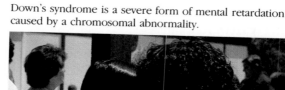

Down's syndrome is a severe form of mental retardation caused by a chromosomal abnormality.

training of the muscles and senses could overcome the limitations of the retarded. Unfortunately, this was not the case. Institutions that started out as training centers gradually evolved into warehouses in which the unfortunate victims of retardation were segregated from society.

It was only in the 1960s and 1970s that the American public became aware of the dismal and dehumanizing condition of these underfinanced and understaffed institutions. The lack of intellectual stimulation often limited the development of retarded individuals. A number of recent laws and court cases have begun to protect the human rights of retarded citizens. It remains to be seen whether our society is willing to make a serious commitment of money and resources to ensure that every victim of retardation is given an opportunity to live up to his or her full potential.

Personality Tests

Like tests of intelligence, the first systematic instruments for measuring personality grew out of practical concerns. During World War I, Robert Woodworth attempted to develop a questionnaire to help locate individuals who might develop a psychiatric condition then known as "shell shock," emotional problems that would interfere with their ability to function as soldiers. Woodworth began with a questionnaire listing symptoms commonly reported by psychiatric patients and tested this survey on groups of normal and disturbed individuals.

In Chapter 12, we discussed the difficulty of defining personality and the controversy over the significance of particular personality traits. It should come as no surprise that there are a number of approaches to assessing personality, each with its own strengths and weaknesses. Here, we focus on two major types of tests—personality inventories and projective tests.

Personality Inventories

A **personality inventory** is a standard list of questions about an individual's behavior and feelings that assesses personality traits. Personality inventories are sometimes called paper-and-pencil tests because they can be administered simply by giving a person a piece of paper with the printed list of standard questions, which can be answered in pencil.

The first personality inventory was Woodworth's list of 116 yes-or-no questions, including:

Do you usually sleep well?

As a child, did you like to play alone better than to play with other children?

Has your family always treated you right?

Do you get tired of people quickly?

The war ended before Woodworth had a chance to collect sufficient data to evaluate the test's validity. But this pioneer effort did encourage other psychologists to try to develop systematic and ojective devices for assessing both normal and abnormal personality traits.

personality inventory A standard list of questions about an individual's behavior and feelings, to assess personality traits.

One of the first personality tests was a questionnaire designed to screen soldiers who might develop "shell shock" and, therefore, be unable to perform under the stress of combat.

BASIC CONCEPTS

Some personality inventories were designed to measure a single trait, such as anxiety or extraversion. Others, like the MMPI (described here) measure several traits at the same time. Further, some personality inventories follow Woodworth's lead in trying to assess abnormal traits that may be associated with mental illness (see Chapter 14). Others focus on normal personality traits and types, such as androgyny and Type A behavior (see Chapter 12).

Since personality inventories consist of lists of multiple-choice questions, they are easy to administer and score. The objective scores a person achieves can then be related to other criteria to establish the test's reliability and validity. Literally hundreds of personality inventories have been developed to measure normal and abnormal personality traits. To provide more insight into the actual workings of such a test, let us concentrate on the personality inventory that has generated the largest body of research. According to one count (Buros, 1978), over 5,000 different research reports have been published regarding the uses and characteristics of a test called the MMPI.

THE MINNESOTA MULTIPHASIC PERSONALITY INVENTORY

The name *Minnesota Multiphasic Personality Inventory* is such a mouthful that even jargon-loving psychologists refer to it by the abbreviation MMPI. But each of the words in this fearsome title says something about the popular test, which was published in 1942.

The original authors of the MMPI, S. R. Hathaway and J. C. McKinley, began their research at the University of Minnesota in the 1930s. The word *Minnesota* in the title reminds us that the original scoring system, which is still widely used, was based on a sample of about 1,500 normal subjects and 800 psychiatric patients from a single geographical location in and around Minneapolis, Minnesota.

The word *multiphasic* was chosen to emphasize the authors' attempt to include a large and varied group of items that could give insight into many different patterns of behavior. Before that time, most scales were constructed with a single purpose in mind, like Woodworth's test to predict shell shock. But Hathaway and McKinley proposed a single questionnaire that would assess many different personality traits at the same time, and thus be multiphasic.

Finally, of course, the test was a *personality inventory*—a standard list of questions that any individual could answer. The authors began with over 1,000 items chosen from clinical experience, psychiatry textbooks, and previously published scales. After several revisions, they agreed on a list of 550 short, simple, clear statements to which individuals were asked to respond "true," "false," or "cannot say." Here are four examples:

I get angry sometimes.

I think most people would lie to get ahead.

Once in a while I put off until tomorrow what I ought to do today.

Someone has been trying to poison me.

Since the MMPI was multiphasic, each test taker was assigned separate scores on 13 subscales that measured different aspects of personality. For example, there were separate measures of depression, hypochondriasis, paranoia, and masculinity-femininity. Instead of describing one personality trait with a single number, the MMPI yields a profile of interrelated scores.

The items that composed each scale were chosen strictly in terms of their criterion validity—their actual ability to distinguish between particular groups. For example, responses on the MMPI by a group of paranoid psychiatric patients (who had delusions of being persecuted) in the University of Minnesota hospitals were compared with responses from a "normal" group that included hospital visitors and medical patients. Only when there was a statistically significant difference between these groups was an item included on the paranoid scale.

Sometimes, the results of this empirical procedure were quite close to common sense. For example, two of the four sample statements given earlier actually appear on the paranoid scale. Take a moment to review these four, see whether you can pick the two statements that identified paranoids, and predict how these patients would answer each item. If you guessed that paranoids are more likely to say "true" to "someone has been trying to poison me," you are quite right.

The answer to the other question, however, may not be so obvious. If you are like most people, you probably guessed that a paranoid person would say it's true that most people would lie to get ahead. Indeed, this item on the MMPI was borrowed from an earlier psychological test that had graded "true" as a paranoid response on the basis of its face validity—this looked like something a paranoid person would say. In fact, however, researchers who studied the actual responses of a group of paranoid patients found exactly the opposite. Paranoids were more likely to say this statement was false (Meehl & Hathaway, 1946). This finding provides still another example of the way commonsense or intuitive analyses of test items can be misleading. The original MMPI scores were always empirically defined by the actual responses of a particular group of people.

As a further guarantee that MMPI scores would provide useful information, the authors included several subscales to check for unusual response patterns. For example, the lie scale included 15 items that involved admitting faults that probably apply to almost everyone. Two of the four sample statements come from the lie scale: "I get angry sometimes" and "Once in a while I put off until tomorrow what I ought to do today." If you answered false to both of these questions and to 13 other items like them, you are either Saint Theresa of Avila or a liar. The authors of the MMPI were willing to bet on the latter, that people who admitted few minor faults were probably lying to make themselves look good. When a person gets a high score on the lie scale, all results from that particular MMPI are viewed skeptically.

Perhaps the greatest strength of the MMPI is the fact that it has been used by so many different investigators in such a wide variety of settings. About 300 new scales have been formed from MMPI items, and information on criterion validity is available for many of them. The shortcomings of the original standardization sample have been corrected in some later versions.

In clinical practice, the MMPI is often administered to individuals who seek psychological therapy or counseling. Interpretation of a particular profile of 13 scores is more difficult than their names suggest. For example, a person with a high score on the schizophrenia scale is not necessarily schizophrenic; it is the overall pattern of scores that provides insight, and subscales cannot be isolated from one another.

Figure 13.6 illustrates the MMPI profile of one 34-year-old man who sought psychiatric help. The first four scales (?, L, F, K) refer to response

Figure 13.6   The MMPI profile of a 34-year-old male psychiatric patient. The ?, L, F, and K scores reflect response style and are all within the normal range (50 = mean, 10 = standard deviation of normal standardization sample). Scales 1 to 9 are clinical scales; the most elevated score appears on scale 2, depression. Excerpts from a computer analysis of this profile follow:

> This patient shows a personality pattern which occurs frequently among persons who seek psychiatric treatment. Feelings of inadequacy, sexual conflict, and rigidity are accompanied by a loss of efficiency, initiative, and self-confidence. Insomnia is likely to occur along with chronic anxiety, fatigue, and tension. He may have suicidal thoughts. In the clinical picture, depression is a dominant feature. Psychiatric patients with this pattern are likely to be diagnosed as depressives or anxiety reactions. The basic characteristics are resistant to change and will tend to remain stable with time. Among medical patients with this pattern, a large number are seriously depressed, and others show some depression, along with fatigue and exhaustion. There are few spontaneous recoveries, although the intensity of the symptoms may be cyclic. . . .

> This person may be hesitant to become involved in social relationships. He is sensitive, reserved, and somewhat uneasy, especially in new and unfamiliar situations. He may compensate by unusual conscientiousness in his work and other responsibilities.

> Some aspects of this patient's test pattern are somewhat similar to those of psychiatric patients. Appropriate professional evaluation is recommended. (Dahlstrom et al., 1972, pp. 295, 314)

Although not a substitute for the clinician's professional judgment and skill, the MMPI can be a useful adjunct in the diagnosis and management of emotional disorders. The report is for professional use only and should not be shown or given to the patient.

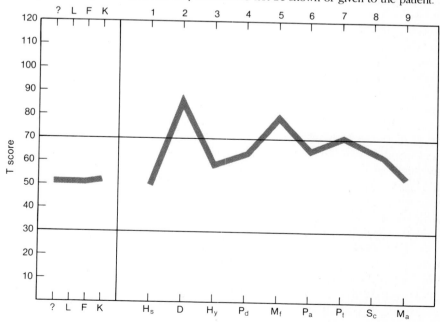

style (for example, L is the lie-scale score); the numbers 1 to 9 refer to the nine major clinical scales. All scores have been standardized (in terms of the original normal sample of about 700 persons), with a mean of 50 and a standard deviation of 10. For example, this individual's score of 88 on scale 2 (depression) is nearly 4 standard deviations above the mean and thus extremely high (see the normal curve in Figure 13.2).

Again, interpretation of this profile depends on the interrelationships of the scores on all 13 scales. Many books have been published to help clinicians interpret MMPI results. For example, in 1951 Hathaway and Meehl published *An Atlas for the Clinical Use of the MMPI,* which included MMPI profiles and case histories of 968 patients with a wide variety of problems.

A number of computerized scoring systems for the MMPI have also been developed in recent years. These systems vary widely in the detail and kind of information they provide. Figure 13.6 also provides a computer-generated interpretation of this particular profile. Even a thorough report like this one, however, should not be considered as a final basis for making decisions about this individual. The MMPI is a tool that a clinician often finds useful, but only he or she can decide exactly how to use it in a particular case.

Projective Tests

While personality inventories like the MMPI were designed to be objective and easy to administer and score, an entirely different type of test was published in 1921 by a Swiss psychiatrist named Hermann Rorschach. Rorschach had been trained in Freudian psychoanalysis and sought a test that could help reveal unconscious impulses by forcing the test takers to use their imagination. He developed a set of ambiguous inkblots and asked people what each blot represented or reminded them of. There were no "right" answers; the ambiguous stimulus was designed as a sort of screen onto which a person could project inner conflicts, fears, and desires. One of the more optimistic accounts of this technique (Frank, 1939) referred to the projective approach as an "X-ray of the personality" because it provided a glimpse of the inner workings of the mind.

BASIC CONCEPTS

Rorschach's inkblots were among the first **projective tests** in which a person projects inner feelings and conflicts by responding to an ambiguous stimulus, such as a picture or an inkblot. Another example was mentioned in Chapter 13: the Thematic Apperception Test (TAT), in which people are asked to make up stories about ambiguous pictures. The stories are then analyzed for themes of a need for achievement and other normal personality traits.

The ambiguous stimulus need not be a picture or an inkblot. In the Draw-a-Person Test, people are asked to do just that, and the features of the individuals they draw are systematically analyzed. Other projective tests asks individuals to say the first thing that comes to mind in response to certain words, or to complete such sentences as: "What worries me . . ." or "My mother always. . . ."

projective test An individual's projection of inner feelings and conflict by responding to an ambiguous stimulus, such as a picture or an inkblot.

HERMANN RORSCHACH (1884–1922)

Rorschach's father was an art teacher in Zurich, Switzerland; in his childhood, the younger Rorschach's nickname was *Klex,* meaning "painter" or "inkblot." After studying psychiatry with Eugen Bleuler, Rorschach began to experiment with mental patients' perceptions of inkblots. Encouraged by the test's apparent ability to distinguish among different types of patients, he published a book in 1921 describing his research. Because of space limitations, the printer would include only 10 of the 15 cards Rorschach had studied; the printer also changed their size and color. The Rorschach test consists of the 10 altered cards. Rorschach died a year after his book was published, long before his technique became widely known.

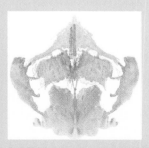

One of the cards from the Rorschach inkblot test.

As with personality inventories, a large number of projective tests have been developed to measure both normal and abnormal personality traits. Again let us focus on the test that has generated the largest body of research, Hermann Rorschach's original inkblots.

THE RORSCHACH TEST

The stimuli of the most famous projective test consist of ten symmetrical inkblots, half of them black and white and half colored. One inkblot is presented at a time and the ten are always shown in the same order. The person is asked what each blot could represent or "what it reminds you of." The examiner records these responses verbatim, as well as other factors, such as the time a person takes to respond and any emotional expressions. After all ten cards have been reviewed in this manner, the examiner asks further questions about the details of each response.

There are a number of different scoring systems for interpreting subjects' responses. Traditionally, most clinicians did not focus on the content of a response—it did not matter whether a particular inkblot was seen as a bat, a butterfly, or two fat clowns dancing the Hucklebuck. Perceptual characteristics of the response were generally considered more important. For example, Rorschach thought that the mention of movement (as in the dancing clowns) suggested imaginative and creative impulses, while reference to color reflected an active emotional life. Other scoring systems consider not just the characteristics of individual responses but also their interrelationships. Graduate students in clinical psychology may study techniques of Rorschach interpretation for several years.

The first research published in the United States on the Rorschach test appeared in 1930. The test gradually gained in popularity, particularly during World War II. At one time, studies of this test completely dominated the field of psychological testing. Many of the reports were unfavorable. Aspects of many scoring systems were so subjective that results did not meet acceptable standards of reliability; two clinicians might interpret the same test in entirely different ways. When reliable scoring systems were used, the results often proved invalid; research often failed to verify theoretical claims that certain types of responses were linked to particular personality traits (Zubin, Eron, & Schumer, 1965).

One reason that the Rorschach had gained such popularity despite its shortcomings was the fact that in actual clinical practice, interpretations were often based not just on the inkblot responses but also on other sources of information, such as case histories. Some clinicians used inkblot responses to "verify" their own biases and stereotypes, showing that even the experts are subject to observational errors.

In one study, two researchers interpreted Rorschach tests administered before the Nuremberg trials to 16 Nazi war criminals, including Adolf Eichmann and Hermann Göring. They knew who the test takers were and concluded that these infamous men were quite different from normal people; among other things, that they were depressed, violent, and preoccupied with status (Miale & Selzer, 1976). However, another researcher provided the same Rorschach responses to experts who did not know their origin. One thought that the responses came from a cross section of middle-class Americans; another thought they might be from clergymen (Harrower, 1976). The judgment of disturbance in the Rorschach records of Nazis seemed to be based on external opinions that had little to do with the actual test responses. Similarly, a clinical psychologist who had interviewed a client for many hours might find it difficult to interpret Rorschach responses in a vacuum, as if no other information were available regarding this individual.

Despite such criticisms and problems, the Rorschach test continues to be widely used. In 1970, long after research that attacked the Rorschach had peaked, a survey of 251 clinical settings found that although its popularity had declined somewhat, 91% of the clinics still used the Rorschach in some cases (Lubin, Wallis, & Paine, 1971).

Although efforts are still under way to establish reliable and valid scoring systems of the type originally outlined by Rorschach, many clinicians now see the Rorschach as a type of standardized interview. People who are reluctant to reveal their inner feelings may be somewhat more open when responding to these ambiguous stimuli. Here, the content of responses—what people actually say—is seen as more important than the perception of movement, color, or other traditional aspects.

To see the potential value of this clinical approach, consider the following brief excerpt from the Rorschach test of a 25-year-old woman who had been hospitalized after a suicide attempt:

> Psychologist: What do you see in this card?
>
> Client: Two monkeys—warming their hands over a fire.
>
> Psychologist: What does that remind you of?
>
> Client: My parents.
>
> Psychologist: In what way?
>
> Client: Just the word *monkeys*. The stupidest thing they ever did was to get married. . . . [The] fire they're warming their hands over is their children burning." (Aronow & Reznikoff, 1976, p. 286)

This powerful response was buried among a large number of unemotional mundane responses. But as long as people continue to respond to the ambiguous inkblots of the Rorschach test with statements that seem to be so revealing, it is likely that projective tests will continue to play an important role in clinical practice and personality research. In his discussion of the use of Rorschach and other projective tests, Kline (1987) concludes that such techniques can be extremely useful in "elucidating the unconscious" (p. 379).

Uses and Abuses of Psychological Tests

The results of psychological tests may help determine the classes a schoolchild takes, the colleges to which a student is admitted, or the job a person is offered. In the ideal world, psychological test results would provide objective information to help make fair and rational decisions. But in case you haven't noticed, we do not live in an ideal world. Before the ink was dry on the first psychological tests, controversies began over their use. Let us examine two of these continuing debates, to show how these problems often defy simple solutions.

Interpreting Test Results

Because of concern over the complexity of the ethical issues involved in the appropriate interpretation of psychological tests, the American Psychological Association has developed several sets of ethical standards for the profession, which are revised at regular intervals (London & Bray, 1980).

Trained psychologists are familiar with the extent to which a single test score can be influenced by such external factors as fatigue, illness, or motivation; they would be very reluctant to use a test score as the sole basis for any important decision. In fact, in some cases, a clinician who administers an IQ test may be less interested in the IQ score itself than in the way a person takes the test. Self-confidence, persistence, concentration, and other personality characteristics may be assessed in this situation, albeit somewhat intuitively.

Because of their keen awareness of the limitations of test scores, psychologists have traditionally taken the position that, in many situations, scores should not be revealed, even to the person who took the test. However, others consider this position paternalistic and feel that people have the right to know their own scores.

One of the more extreme instances of this concern led the New York State Legislature to enact a truth-in-testing law in 1980, which permitted students to obtain a copy of their answers on the Scholastic Aptitude Test. In 1981, the test's publishers voluntarily extended this practice to the entire country.

One positive effect occurred almost immediately when one student successfully argued that one of his geometry answers, which had been marked wrong, was actually correct. His alternate interpretation led to changes in thousands of scores on a particular version of the PSAT, a preliminary version of the SAT. Since the National Merit Scholarship committee screened applicants on the basis of PSAT scores, 200 additional individuals became National Merit semifinalists after their scores were changed on this one question. As a result of this error and one other, the publishers of the SAT developed new procedures for checking their own answers on solid geometry questions.

On the other hand, this same truth-in-testing law led to certain problems. In the past, test companies have determined individual items that correlate best with later performance. As a result, they could increase the predictive value of a test by reusing only the most efficient items. However, once a particular question is published, it is no longer a fair test of general knowledge, since some individuals may study the actual item. Since it costs companies money to develop larger pools of new items, one unintended result of truth-in-testing laws is that "students might expect to pay a higher fee to take a less valid test" (Kaplan, 1982, p. 22). The new truth-in-testing laws obviously have both positive and negative effects, and the controversy over their value is likely to continue for some time.

Cultural Bias

One of the most controversial issues in psychological testing involves the possible effects of cultural bias, particularly on tests of intelligence. From the outset, it is important to distinguish between the technical characteristics of a test and its political uses. Test bias can be defined in a number of ways; here, we shall use the term **cultural bias** to refer to a statistical difference in the validity of a test for different cultural groups. For example, if white children's scores on a particular IQ test predicted their high school grades but black children's scores did not, that test would be culturally biased in that situation. Note that this definition is based strictly on the actual performance of the test, not on the political or social consequences of using the same criterion for blacks and whites.

This technical issue of cultural bias must be kept separate from the moral and political issue of **fairness**, the justice (or injustice) of using a particular test to select individuals. In a diverse society like the United States, there may be sharp disagreements about what is fair. Psychologists have no special insights or competence regarding fairness, and in a democracy these value judgments must ultimately be made not by social scientists but by all concerned citizens.

A surprisingly large number of psychologists have proved that they are fallible humans by blurring the distinction between fairness and cultural bias, and sometimes even bending the facts, to try to provide scientific support for their political beliefs. For example, IQ data collected by the U.S. Army in World War I provided some information on differences between ethnic groups. This was later cited to support laws setting immigration quotas. It is embarrassing to read technical reports written by some of the leading researchers in the 1920s about the "menace of race deterioration" and the "genuine intellectual superiority of the Nordic [Northern European] group" (quoted in Kamin, 1974, pp. 20–21). In today's political climate, it is easy to see the error of these arguments for racial superiority; clearly, some of these IQ pioneers failed to remain scientific and objective. But it is more difficult to criticize researchers who cite faulty evidence that could be used to support policies that most Americans now believe to be totally just (see "Becoming a Critical Consumer").

TABLE 13.3

IQ and Achievement in Four Cultural Groups

Cultural group	Number of children	Correlation between WISC-R IQ and	
		Reading achievement	Math achievement
Anglo	250	.59	.55
Black	222	.64	.52
Mexican-American	215	.55	.52
Papago Indian[a]	223	.45	.41

[a] The smaller correlations for Papago Indians imply that the test is culturally biased regarding this group (Reschly & Sabers, 1979). See text for a discussion of the implications for policy.

**BECOMING
A CRITICAL
CONSUMER**

Does This IQ Question
Discriminate Against Minorities?

There has been a tremendous amount of controversy over the question of discrimination in IQ tests. This issue involves some complex technical questions as well as value judgments. Popular attempts to analyze the bias in IQ tests have sometimes led to conclusions that may seem convincing but are in fact based on faulty arguments.

In the CBS-TV documentary "The IQ Myth," Dan Rather presents the argument that questions on IQ tests are based on the experiences of the average American child, both in and outside of school. Rather comments that "average" means "middle-class" and notes that it is economic class that creates the main dividing line on IQ scores. That is, he explains, middle-class children tend to do well on IQ tests, regardless of their ethnic or racial background, probably because they are the group toward which the tests are directed. By contrast, lower-class children—

including poor whites, blacks, and Chicanos—all tend to do poorly. Rather goes on to comment that IQ tests are slanted against the social and cultural background of lower-class children. In support of this argument, Rather introduces Dr. Robert Williams of Washington University in St. Louis, a psychologist who has been calling public attention to this built-in cultural bias. Williams cites a biased test item from the Wechsler individual IQ test: "What is the thing you do if a boy or girl much smaller than yourself starts to fight with you?" Williams notes that the child is scored correct "only if he says he will not fight back," but Williams maintains that "in black communities, a child is told that if another child hits him, he should hit back."

See if you can spot the error in this argument. (A short discussion appears after the "Summary" at the end of this chapter.)

To sharpen the distinction between cultural bias and fairness, consider the results of a study comparing the performance of schoolchildren from different ethnic groups in one Arizona county (Reschly & Sabers, 1979). The Wechsler Intelligence Scale for Children–Revised (WISC-R) was used to predict scores on standardized tests of scholastic achievement in math and reading for 910 first- to ninth-graders from four ethnic groups. Table 13.3 shows that the correlations between IQ and achievement were similar for Anglo, black, and Mexican-American children. But the criterion validity was significantly lower for Indian schoolchildren from the Papago tribe. The WISC-R was culturally biased in its predictions of achievement because it was not equally valid for all four groups.

Does that mean that its predictions were unfair? It all depends on your point of view. A closer analysis of the original data from all schoolchildren revealed that the validity coefficient was lower for the Indian group because high-IQ Indian pupils did not do as well in achievement as the WISC-R predicted they should. Suppose, then, that WISC-R IQ scores were used to select children for scholarship classes in these Arizona schools. This application of the test would be culturally biased in favor of Indian pupils, selecting more of them

cultural bias A statistical difference in the validity of a test for different cultural groups.

fairness The justice (or injustice) of using a particular psychological test to select individuals.

535

Understanding Intelligence

Presented below are nine statements about intelligence and personality. Compare what is said in each statement with what you have learned in this chapter, and decide whether each of the statements is true or false. (A short discussion appears after the "Summary" at the end of this chapter.)

1. Children's IQ scores have very little relationship with how well they do in school.
2. All people are created equal in capacity for achievement.
3. Very bright children tend to be physically weaker and more illness-prone than children of average intelligence.
4. A high forehead is a sign of intelligence.
5. Dull children often become bright adults.
6. Most people have only the intelligence of a moron.
7. Very bright children tend to be less well emotionally adjusted than children of average intelligence.
8. The unstructured interview is the most valid method for assessing someone's personality.
9. The average college student is usually more successful in later life than the superior student.

on the basis of IQ than it would on the basis of achievement. Is that fair? One person might argue that given the long history of oppression of American Indians, justice is served by using the test and increasing their chances of getting a better education. Another might reply that the past is the past, and tests must be found that choose children with equal predictive power without regard to race, religion, or creed.

A policy decision regarding the fairness of a test is entirely separate from the technical question of cultural bias. In this case, we have a test that has been proved to be culturally biased. But some people could argue that it is still a fair basis for selection. People might argue that, in this case, a test that is not culturally biased is unfair.

It is impossible to provide a complete understanding of cultural bias and related issues without going into many complex statistical details regarding the assessment of reliability and validity. Further, different definitions of test bias lead to different conclusions. The issues are so complex that one must be skeptical of any simple solution.

Obviously, our conclusion here cannot provide a complete resolution of this controversial set of issues. But it can emphasize the most important point of all: Psychologists must collect the facts about exactly what a particular test can and cannot do, and society as a whole can then decide how and when the test should be used. There are no simple answers that apply to every case. But there are scientific procedures we can follow to collect the best possible information to make rational policy decisions. As Cronbach

(1975) put it, "Sound policy is not for tests or against tests; what matters is how tests are used" (p. 1). (To determine how much you have learned about psychological tests and related issues, see "Applying Scientific Concepts.")

Summary

- Most psychological tests grew out of attempts to measure objectively people's strengths and weaknesses. Despite the fact that millions of psychological tests are administered every year, many people have misconceptions about the goals and design of tests.

Basic Concepts of Measurement

- A **reliable** test is consistent and reproducible.
- A **valid** test accurately measures what it is supposed to measure.
- There are several different ways of measuring reliability, including **test-retest reliability**, the correlation between two different scores achieved by the same individual on the same test on different occasions.
- **Alternate-form reliability** is the correlation between two different scores achieved by the same individual on two different forms of the test.
- Validity is much more difficult to assess than reliability.
- There are three major approaches to validity: criterion, content, and construct.
- **Criterion validity** compares performance on the test with some external and independent measure, or criterion, of what the test is supposed to predict.
- **Content validity** involves a systematic analysis of a particular skill and the design of test items that measure all relevant knowledge.
- **Construct validity** involves a larger pattern of conceptually meaningful relationships.
- Many physical and psychological characteristics conform to a **normal distribution,** a particular mathematical apportionment in which individual cases are symmetrically arranged around the average.
- The **mean** is the central value, or arithmetic average, of a normal distribution.
- The **standard deviation** is a mathematical measure of the amount of variability, spread, or dispersion of a particular set of scores.
- Several commonsense errors must be avoided when one interprets test scores. Observers should not rely on the **face validity** (superficial appearance of a test), place too much emphasis on criticisms of individual items, or assume that population predictions will apply to every single individual.

Intelligence Tests

- Early scales of intelligence defined the **intelligence quotient (IQ)** as **mental**

age, the average performance level for a particular group, divided by chronological age times 100.

- The **Stanford-Binet**, developed by Alfred Binet and revised by Lewis Terman, is still one of the most frequently used tests for assessing the intelligence of an individual child.

- Later, adult IQ scores were defined in terms of a normal distribution with a mean of 100 and a standard deviation of about 15 (depending on the specific test).

- Although there is some theoretical controversy over the precise nature of intelligence, strong arguments can be made for criterion, content, and construct validity of the most common IQ tests.

- The **Wechsler Adult Intelligence Scale-Revised**, or **WAIS-R**, includes six verbal and five performance scales. A large body of evidence supports the idea that it is a reliable and valid test of IQ.

- **Heritability** is a mathematical estimate of the relative importance of genetics and environment in determining a particular trait for a specific population.

- There is strong evidence that genetic factors account for a larger proportion of individual variation in IQ than environmental factors within populations of European origin.

- At this time, differences in IQ between groups cannot be attributed to genetic factors.

- The fact that genes account for a high proportion of the variation in IQ does not imply that IQ is fixed at birth; many studies have shown that improved environments can raise IQ.

- Mild retardation (IQ between 50 and 70) usually results from a family pattern called **cultural-familial retardation**, with no evidence of brain damage.

- More severe deficits, such as **Down's syndrome**, are usually biological in origin.

- Severe deficits are usually subdivided into three levels, based partly on the ability to function independently: moderate, IQ 35 to 49; severe, IQ 20 to 34; and profound, IQ below 20.

Personality Tests

- A **personality inventory** is a standard list of questions about an individual's behavior and feelings, designed to assess personality traits.

- The most widely researched personality inventory is the *Minnesota Multiphasic Personality Inventory* (MMPI), a test with 13 personality subscales originally based on the performance of criterion groups.

- In a **projective test**, a person projects inner feelings and conflicts by responding to an ambiguous stimulus, such as a picture or an inkblot.

- The most famous projective test is the Rorschach inkblot test, a series of ten inkblots to which a patient reacts.

Uses and Abuses of Psychological Tests

- The term **cultural bias** can be defined as a statistical difference in the validity of a test for different cultural groups.

- Cultural bias is a technical term that must be kept separate from the moral and political issue of **fairness**, the justice of using a particular test to select individuals. Arguments over these and related issues often become extremely emotional and confuse political desires with technical facts.

Critical Thinking Exercises
Discussions

Does This IQ Question Discriminate Against Minorities?

Intuitively, it may seem that this IQ question discriminates against American blacks who are taught to fight back. But throughout this chapter we have emphasized the fact that intuition can be misleading. In a study that directly compared WISC results for 163 white and 111 black Georgia schoolchildren, there was no evidence that this item discriminated against blacks (Miele, 1979). In fact, when the items were ranked in their order of difficulty, it turned out that this was one of the easier questions for black children and one of the harder ones for white children.

The critical consumer must always try to understand the technical issues involved in scientific measurement and avoid facile explanations based on common sense.

Understanding Intelligence

All the items were taken from Vaughan's Test of Common Beliefs (Vaughan, 1977). According to Vaughan, all of them are false. In your reading of Chapter 13, you will not have found any support for these statements; nevertheless, you may have agreed with some of the statements because they fit with popular opinions you have heard. While it is sometimes difficult to abandon popular myths, the scientist relies on objective, empirical evidence as the only acceptable basis for the truth or falsity of statements.

As you reread each of the statements, you might use your critical thinking skills to ask a number of questions about each one. For example: what unstated assumption(s) might underlie each assertion? What kinds of argument might be made in support of each assertion, and what are the weaknesses in those arguments? Your conclusion should be that the unstated assumptions, like the assertions themselves, are not supported by any of the empirical evidence reported in the text.

DIAGNOSING ABNORMAL BEHAVIOR

Chapter 14

*I*n a lecture at the Heidelberg Medical School around 1890, Professor Emil Kraepelin described the case of a 35-year-old woman who had started to develop problems in her mid-twenties, soon after her husband died. The young widow became nervous, slept badly, and began to hear voices of people talking loudly in her bedroom at night. She became convinced that people from Frankfurt, the German town in which she had formerly lived, were trying to steal her money and persecute her.

Gradually, her condition got worse until she was committed to a mental asylum. There, the widow decided that the other patients were the people from Frankfurt who were out to get her. She also "noticed poison in the food, heard voices, and felt influences" (Kraepelin, 1912, p. 160). When she was released from the asylum after a year, she accused her former doctors of having mutilated her and abused government officials for failing to protect her. Finally, she was admitted to another hospital.

When Kraepelin brought the woman before his medical school class, she seemed normal at first. She was able to answer questions about her background and knew the date, the year, and where she was. But the professor pointed out that from the start, there was something odd about the woman's manner: "She does not look at her questioner, and speaks in a low and peculiar, sugary, affected tone."

When the physician first asked how she felt, she said that she was quite well. On further probing, however, the widow began to discuss bizarre ideas of persecution: "For many years she has heard voices, which insult her and cast suspicion on her chastity. They mention a number of names she knows, and tell her that she will be stripped and abused. The voices are very distinct, and, in her opinion, they must be carried by a telescope or a machine from her home. Her thoughts are dictated to her; she is obliged to think them, and hears them repeated after her." In her own words, she was also "persecuted by a secret insect from the District Office."

The woman also reported a variety of physical complaints: "Her 'mother parts' are turned inside out, and people send a pain through her back, lay ice-water on her heart, squeeze her neck, injure her spine, and violate her." On cross-questioning, she could not say exactly who was subjecting her to this abuse. Sometimes, it was the doctors who mutilated her at the previous hospital; at other times, it was the people from her hometown.

Perhaps even odder than the woman's complaints was the way she reported them: "without showing much emotion," a manner clinicians call *flattened affect,* meaning with little variation in affective (emotional) response. At other times, her affect seems inappropriate, as when the patient "describes her morbid experiences again with secret satisfaction and even with an erotic bias."

At times, her speech became totally irrational, as the patient referred to herself as "a picture of misery in angel's form" and a "defrauded mamma and housewife of sense of order." She sometimes invented words, such as "flail-wise, utterance-wise, and terror-wise."

After being admitted to the hospital, she was generally apathetic and socially withdrawn. She spent her days sitting idly around and would have little to do with other patients or the staff. Her only occupations were to repeat her complaints day after day "without showing much excitement" and to write "long-winded letters full of senseless and unvarying abuse about the persecution from which she suffered."

In Professor Kraepelin's opinion, this poor woman had little chance of ever recovering. He used the Latin term *dementia praecox* to refer to her condition because this label emphasized the symptoms he considered most fundamental—a progressive intellectual deterioration (*dementia*) that began early in life (*praecox*). Kraepelin is generally considered the father of the first coherent system for diagnosing abnormal behavior, and the term *dementia praecox* was used until the 1940s (Arieti, 1974).

To a mental-health worker in the 1980s, one of the most remarkable facts about this case is how familiar it seems. While the woman's prospects for improvement would be far better today than they were a century ago, anyone who has ever worked in a mental hospital has met many patients with similar symptoms. Today, the widow's illness would be diagnosed as "schizophrenia, paranoid type, chronic" (Spitzer, Skodol, Gibbon, & Williams, 1981).

Schizophrenia is one of the most dramatic categories of abnormal behavior, but it is not the most common one. The most frequent disorders—alcohol and drug abuse, anxiety, and depression—are far more ordinary and mundane than the bizarre problems of Kraepelin's patient. And the large number of people involved leaves no doubt that abnormal behavior represents a problem of staggering proportions for our society. In this chapter, we focus on defining abnormality and diagnosing its many forms. In Chapter 15, we consider the problem of treatment—what can be done for those among us who suffer from these problems.

EMIL KRAEPELIN (1855–1926)

Kraepelin proposed the first widely used system for classifying mental disorders into separate diseases. He was trained as a physician in Germany and early in his career worked with Wilhelm Wundt at Leipzig. Kraepelin collected literally thousands of case histories of patients in mental asylums. He examined their early life experiences and their current symptoms to look for similar patterns and a few basic disease processes. Kraepelin's general approach to psychiatry was strongly influenced by nineteenth-century biology and the medical model. He was rather fatalistic about mental illness, believing that many diseases were caused by inherent constitutional factors and could never be cured.

Understanding Abnormal Behavior

It may be relatively easy to see the difference between the abnormal behavior of a severely disturbed individual like Kraepelin's widowed patient and the normal behavior patterns of most of your friends and relatives. But clearly distinguishing the normal from the abnormal is not always this straightforward.

What Is Abnormal?

Suppose a housewife drinks half a bottle of gin every day to help her through the tedium of her daily chores. Is that normal? What about a man who refuses to drive a car because he's afraid of having an accident? What about a girl who is so obsessed with slenderness that she practically starves herself? Is she normal?

There are no easy answers or simple criteria that can be applied to these specific cases. But we can discuss four general approaches to defining abnormality, each of which sheds light on these issues from a different angle: statistical definitions, violations of cultural norms, deviations from ideal mental health, and failure to function adequately.

STATISTICAL DEFINITION

By definition, the word *abnormal* means "deviating from the norm or the average." When we say that Kareem Abdul Jabbar is abnormally tall, we are basing this observation on the fact that the average height for adult males is far below 7 feet.

The same logic could be applied to any human characteristic that can be quantified. We simply compute the average value for a particular trait—such as intelligence or personal ratings of satisfaction with life—and define abnormality as a substantial deviation from this average. For example, in Chapter 13 we discussed how IQ tests have been developed that assign the value 100 to average intelligence. On this scale, a mentally retarded child who had an IQ of 50 would be considered abnormal.

However, if we use nothing but the simplest statistical criteria, an intelligent child with an IQ of 150 would be considered equally abnormal. Without some system for distinguishing between desirable and undesirable deviations, the statistical model seems to imply that being just like everyone else is always best. If the statistical definition were taken to its logical extreme, it would suggest that people who are unusually satisfied with their lives, for example, or people whose ethical standards are higher than the rest of ours would be considered abnormal. Perhaps these model citizens would even be considered candidates for treatment that would make them less satisfied and less moral.

The question of deciding which deviations from the norm are desirable and which are undesirable is not the only problem with a strictly statistical approach. Americans are involved in a wide variety of socially undesirable behavior patterns ranging from mild depression to child abuse. If you could add up all the numbers, it would become clear that as many as one out of every two Americans falls into at least one of these categories. Behavior patterns that characterize half the population cannot be considered abnormal on statistical grounds alone.

VIOLATION OF CULTURAL NORMS

A second approach defines abnormality in terms of violations of *cultural norms,* the rules of a culture for what is right and what is wrong. If the newly elected mayor of Billings, Montana, worked in his office from precisely 2:37 A.M. to 10:37 A.M. every day, his work habits would be considered odd. If the mayor always wore the same pink linen suit and bright blue tie, and lunched every day on a thermos full of cornflakes mixed with white wine, he would probably be considered downright abnormal. This mayor might have trouble getting reelected even if he ran the town quite effectively, simply because he violated cultural norms.

One problem with using cultural norms to define abnormality is that they vary so much from time to time and place to place. Several decades ago, among natives of the Trobriand Islands in the Pacific, when a man died his sons were expected to clean his bones and distribute them to relatives to wear as ornaments. A Trobriand widow who wore her former husband's jawbone on a necklace would be considered perfectly normal (Malinowski, 1929). In Twin Falls, Idaho, that same behavior would seem more than a little bizarre.

In some cases, violating cultural norms is a sign of abnormal behavior. However, violation of one set of norms simply may indicate conformity to another set of rules.

Defining abnormality as any violation of cultural norms ultimately implies that only conformists are normal. A woman who pursued a career as a business executive in 1937 refused to accept the 1930s cultural norms that a woman's place was in the home. Does this mean that she should have received psychological therapy to restore her normality?

Like the statistical definition of normality, the notion of violating cultural norms has relevance to many cases of labeling behavior as abnormal, but it cannot serve as a complete and acceptable definition by itself.

DEVIATION FROM IDEAL MENTAL HEALTH

A third approach involves defining normality as some ideal pattern of behavior and feeling—which may or may not be statistically common—then defining abnormality as a deviation from this ideal. A number of ideals have been proposed. For example, Jahoda (1958) stressed the importance of insight into one's own motivations, resistance to stress, autonomy, competence, accurate perception of reality, and self-actualization. Lists like this tend to be difficult to apply to a specific individual. For example, exactly what constitutes a healthy level of autonomy and independence? Further, the criteria are so demanding that virtually everyone is considered abnormal to some degree. After all, Maslow's studies of several thousand people located only a small number whom he considered self-actualized (see Chapter 12).

Just as cultural norms are limited to a certain time and a certain place, lists of ideal characteristics depend on society's value judgments. For example, Jahoda's definitions of autonomy and independent choice might be rejected by a communal society that emphasized group cooperation rather than individual choice. Nevertheless, notions of ideal characteristics have had some influence on the mental-health field, particularly for the many affluent Americans who have gone into psychotherapy not because they were overwhelmed by their problems but rather because they wanted to realize their full human potential.

FAILURE TO FUNCTION ADEQUATELY

Of the four approaches to abnormality described here, this last criterion is the closest to common sense and is perhaps the most useful single approach. It assumes that every human being should achieve a sense of personal well-being and make some contribution to a larger social group. Specifically, we would say that individuals fail to function adequately and are therefore abnormal if they experience great personal distress, disturb others, or are unable to care for themselves in society.

A troubled saleswoman may seem fine to her co-workers if she meets all her quotas. But if she is deeply unhappy with her job and a victim of chronic and overwhelming anxiety, we would say that this high level of personal distress makes her at least somewhat abnormal. On the other hand, a highly disturbed individual who tries to assassinate a rock star may experience no personal distress whatever. Nevertheless, the fact that this person is a threat to other individuals constitutes a failure to function in society. Finally, some people may present no danger to anyone but themselves. A man who is so obsessed with dirt that he must clean his apartment compulsively for 12 hours each day would be considered abnormal because this ritualistic behavior interferes with his ability to care for himself or contribute to society.

Given the differences in the four major approaches to defining abnormality, it should come as no surprise that there is sometimes controversy over whether particular patterns of behavior should be considered abnormal. Some theorists have taken the extreme position that the line between normality and abnormality is entirely arbitrary and a matter of convention. However, there is cross-cultural evidence that some patterns of behavior that are considered highly disturbed in our culture are also labeled abnormal in primitive non-Western societies very different from our own (see "Understanding the Scientific Method"). Consequently, most psychologists believe that the label *abnormal* is not entirely arbitrary.

From Witch Hunts to the Medical Model

To some extent, a culture's conception of abnormal behavior always reflects its larger beliefs about human nature and humanity's place in the cosmos. In ancient times, when earthquakes, eclipses, and outbreaks of disease were seen as messages from the gods, abnormal behavior was often taken as a sign of possession by demons or evil spirits.

The Old Testament, for example, recounts some bizarre behavior on the part of King Saul in the eleventh century B.C. In one incident, he stripped off all his clothes in a public place; in another, Saul tried to kill his son Jonathan. The Bible attributes these actions to an evil spirit (1 Sam. 16). Modern commentators believe that Saul may have been mentally ill (Coleman, Butcher, & Carson, 1980); Saul has been tentatively diagnosed as suffering from a bipolar affective disorder, also known as manic-depressive psychosis.

Similarly, in the Middle Ages abnormal behavior was sometimes taken as a sign of possession by a devil or evil spirit who must be driven from the body. In the witch hunts of the fifteenth, sixteenth, and seventeenth centuries, as many as 100,000 people were executed for this reason. Some historians have cited tales of flying to secret meetings with the devil and similar confessions as evidence that most "witches" were actually mentally ill (Zilboorg & Henry, 1941). While critics have challenged this idea, there can be no doubt that superstitious cultures interpreted abnormal behavior very differently from the way we do.

The roots of the twentieth century's scientific approach can be traced back at least as far as Hippocrates, the Greek physician who looked for natural causes of mental illness 400 years before the birth of Christ. In an empirical study of epilepsy, Hippocrates noted, "If you cut open the head, you will find the brain humid, full of sweat and smelling badly. And in this way you may see that it is not a god which injured the body, but disease" (quoted in Zilboorg & Henry, 1941, p. 44).

Even during the witchcraft trials of the Middle Ages, some physicians called for a more rational approach, treating the emotionally disturbed as victims of illness rather than sinners in league with the devil. Many of these theories of mental illness now seem quaint, as in the case of the Swiss physician

Cross-cultural Studies: Abnormal Behavior Among the Eskimos and the Yoruba

In a cross-cultural study, patterns of behavior and experience from different cultural settings are compared. Few psychologists use this method extensively; such comparisons are usually performed by anthropologists. Nevertheless, cross-cultural studies can provide important insights into the way a particular environment shapes behavior.

Evidence of this sort is particularly relevant to attempts to define abnormal behavior in terms of the violation of cultural norms. Some researchers believe that the line between mental illness and normality is arbitrarily drawn by each society to enforce its own beliefs. This notion is closely related to several theories discussed in this chapter, notably Thomas Szasz's book *The Myth of Mental Illness.* An even more extreme version of this view claims that behavior that our society condemns as mentally ill is actually rewarded by other societies. For example, shamans, or witch doctors, in primitive cultures often hear voices and behave in ways that we might label schizophrenic, yet they are valued members of society who play an important role in their culture (Silverman, 1967).

To evaluate such claims, anthropologist Jane Murphy analyzed mental-health data from two field studies she carried out in non-Western cultures. She spent one year living among Yupik-speaking Eskimos on an island in the Bering Sea and another year living with the Yoruba tribe in Nigeria. Her actual data came from interviews with key informants and healers and from her observations of daily life in these dramatically different settings.

The major question Murphy asked was whether these cultures had a word or a category that corresponded roughly to Western notions of madness or abnormal behavior. Both cultures did. The Eskimo word *nuthkavihak* referred to a complex pattern of behavior that included talking to oneself, believing that one was an animal, refusing to eat or talk, making strange gestures, and threatening others. Similarly, the Yoruba word *were* referred to hearing voices, laughing inappropriately, talking all the time or not at all, and so on.

(box continues on next page)

Paracelsus's (1493–1541) theory that madness was caused by the movements of the stars and the moon. But the notion that abnormal behavior was a type of illness gradually evolved into today's medical model.

According to the **medical model**, abnormal behavior is caused by physical disease. In 1883, Emil Kraepelin published his influential *Textbook of Psychiatry,* in which he argued that abnormal behavior was based on dysfunction in the brain and proposed the first comprehensive system for classifying mental disorders. We have already introduced one of his most important categories, dementia praecox. For Kraepelin, this was a disease analogous to the measles or the mumps and was thus best understood by studying its symptoms, course, causes (or, in medical terminology, its *etiology*), and treatment. According

medical model A theoretical model of abnormal behavior that argues that abnormality is caused by physical disease.

547

Interestingly, both patterns of behavior were treated by village healers; they were perceived as a kind of illness.

Murphy also questioned the claim that shamans, or witch doctors, would be labeled mad in their own culture. She found that both cultures distinguished the state of madness (hearing voices and so on) that is part of a shaman's religious or healing ceremony from the chronic state of madness that characterizes the *nuthkavihak* or *were*. The shaman can consciously control the state, according to the Eskimos, while the *nuthkavihak* cannot. Indeed, of the 18 Eskimos who had played the shaman's role at some time in their lives, none was considered *nuthkavihak* by other tribe members.

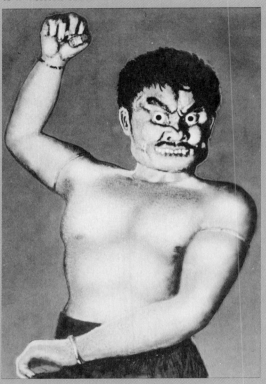

Shamans (roughly, medicine men) in primitive cultures sometimes act in ways that may seem mad or insane to a Western observer.

Murphy also noted that percentages for the frequency of *nuthkavihak* and *were* behaviors were roughly the same as prevalence figures for schizophrenia in comparable studies of Sweden and Canada. Overall, she concluded that mental illness is not an arbitrary category defined idiosyncratically by each culture but rather that "symptoms of mental illness are manifestations of a type of affliction shared by virtually all mankind" (Murphy, 1976, p. 1,027).

Anthropological field studies of this sort must, by their very nature, rely on the perceptiveness of individual observers. They are thus unusually susceptible to the criticism of observer bias. Nevertheless, they do provide valuable information about human nature and the range of behaviors in vastly different cultural settings.

to the medical model, dementia praecox was to be diagnosed on the basis of a specific set of symptoms, and all cases of this disease could be expected to develop in the same predictable course, with about the same chance of recovery. It was assumed that it was caused by a particular organic problem, although the actual etiology of this and other mental illnesses was not yet known. Finally, it was assumed that all cases of dementia praecox would respond to the same form of treatment, once a cure was discovered.

Around the turn of the century, researchers did indeed discover an organic basis for several syndromes of abnormal behavior, most notably *general paresis,* a gradual breakdown of mental and physical function that was proved to be an advanced case of the venereal disease syphilis. In 1906, August von

Wassermann developed a blood test that could diagnose syphilis before its most dramatic symptoms appeared, and in 1917, Julius Wagner von Jauregg discovered a partial cure. This was the first time in history that medical science was able to prove the link between a mental disorder and a physical disease; many believed that bodily cures for all mental disease would soon be found. There were other dramatic discoveries during this period into the nature of such problems as senility and mental retardation. But the medical model's promise of early cures was never fulfilled, and researchers do not yet fully understand the causes of such common disorders as schizophrenia and depression.

Throughout the twentieth century, some mental-health professionals have rejected the medical model completely. For example, in his 1961 book *The Myth of Mental Illness,* psychiatrist Thomas Szasz argued that most behaviors that are considered symptoms of illness are merely deviations from society's norms. He prefers the expression "problems in living" and argues that the illness label encourages us to think that people are not responsible for their actions. We may tend to consider a sexual criminal a sick man who cannot help himself rather than an adult who should take full responsibility for his choices.

Despite these and other criticisms, medical notions have shaped most approaches to abnormal behavior throughout the twentieth century. As Brendan Maher (1966) has noted, the very words we use in everyday discussions of deviant behavior reveal this medical orientation: clinicians *diagnose* mental *illness* on the basis of its *symptoms* and treat *patients* in mental *hospitals* and *therapies* that are designed to *cure* them. Therefore, our overview of abnormal behavior focuses on the most basic goal of the medical model: diagnosing separate diseases on the basis of their symptoms.

In the Middle Ages, many people believed that mental illness was caused by evil spirits. In this fifteenth-century painting, St. Catherine of Siena is pictured driving a satanic imp from the head of a disturbed woman.

The Controversy over Classification

The classification of abnormal behavior into discrete categories is a major part of the current mental-health system. When one person is diagnosed as schizophrenic and another is diagnosed as phobic, these labels have important consequences for the way these people are treated. (Schizophrenia, phobia, and other diagnostic categories are defined later.) But some critics of the current system argue that labels like schizophrenia do more harm than good.

Criticisms of Diagnostic Labels

Some mental-health workers emphasize that diagnosis can be dehumanizing; instead of perceiving John Smith as a unique and complex individual, we dismiss him simply as a schizophrenic. Such labels may also become self-fulfilling (see Chapter 2); individuals diagnosed as schizophrenic may have trouble getting a job, for example, or may even perceive themselves as sick and act differently as a result.

To support the argument that labels are misleading, critics of psychiatric diagnosis often cite a study by David Rosenhan (1973) in which people who had no history of psychiatric problems were admitted to mental hospitals. Eight pseudopatients—Rosenhan himself, four other mental-health professionals, a housewife, a painter, and a pediatrician—went to the admissions offices of different mental hospitals and falsely reported that they had been hearing voices. Except for hiding their true identities, these pseudopatients answered all other questions about their experiences and backgrounds truthfully.

All were admitted to the mental hospitals, and almost all were diagnosed as schizophrenic. (There were 12 admissions, since some patients went to more than one hospital. Eleven were diagnosed as schizophrenic; the twelfth was labeled a manic-depressive psychotic.) After they were admitted, the pseudopatients acted normally and no longer reported hearing voices. Yet they were hospitalized for an average of 19 days (the shortest stay was 7 days, the longest 52 days). In that time, not one single staff member accused a pseudopatient of faking symptoms. Many observers interpreted this as a damning indictment of psychiatric diagnosis.

Others, however, questioned the basic rationale of Rosenhan's study. One provided the following analogy (Kety, 1974): If you swallowed a quart of blood, then went to an emergency room vomiting blood, you would probably be diagnosed as having a bleeding peptic ulcer. The fact that a physician failed to notice your deception would not imply that medical science is unable to diagnose an ulcer. Another critic (Spitzer, 1976) noted that when Rosenhan's pseudopatients were released, their diagnoses were qualified with the phrase "in remission," implying that they no longer showed signs of illness. This is an unusual diagnostic label and implies that the psychiatrists knew there was something different about the pseudopatients.

Rosenhan's (1973) study probably says more about the nature of United States mental hospitals than it does about psychiatric diagnosis. Due to understaffing, paperwork, and other factors, doctors and nurses spend little time with patients. In the hospitals in this study, staff members spent virtually all their time in a glassed-in area that the patients called "the cage." Systematic measurements revealed that attendants spent 89% of their workday with other staff members inside the cage. Pseudopatients were not able to measure the amount of time nurses and doctors spent with patients because it "was too brief" (Rosenhan, 1973, p. 254). Instead, they simply counted the number of times senior staff members emerged from the cage—about ten times per eight-hour shift for nurses, about seven times for doctors.

Interestingly, the only people who spent a lot of time with the pseudopatients—namely, the real patients—did notice that something was wrong. In three of the wards, the pseudopatients kept track of exactly how many of their fellow patients voiced suspicions. Some 35 of the 118 real patients actually approached the experimenters, saying things like, "You're not crazy. You're a journalist or a professor. . . . You're checking up on the hospital" (Rosenhan, 1973, p. 252). Ironically, then, Rosenhan's study might be interpreted as showing that there really is "something different" about people who are mentally ill.

However Rosenhan's study is interpreted, there is no doubt that psychiatric classification is a critical part of the current mental-health system. In the view of most professionals, any disadvantages of classification are outweighed by its advantages in promoting the understanding and treatment of abnormal behavior. If every patient is treated as an entirely new and unique case, it is difficult to predict how to treat any new patient. Classifying a person as a manic-depressive, for example, will probably lead a psychiatrist to prescribe the drug lithium rather than another drug. Diagnosis is useful not only for finding the most effective treatment for a particular individual but also for research into the nature of specific illnesses. By starting with a group of patients who have certain well-defined symptoms in common, researchers may be able to identify the cause and cure of a distinct mental illness. For these and other reasons, considerable attention has been devoted to developing a complete and comprehensive system for classifying mental illness.

The Rationale of DSM-III and DSM-III-R

Throughout the first half of the twentieth century, no single system for classifying all types of abnormal behavior was universally accepted. In 1952, the American Psychiatric Association filled this gap by publishing its *Diagnostic and Statistical Manual* (DSM). This complete and official list of syndromes of abnormal behavior was based on a scheme developed for the U.S. Army in World War II. Advances in theory and research have led to two major revisions of this influential system. The second version (DSM-II) was published in 1968. The ***Diagnostic and Statistical Manual,*** Third Edition (DSM-III), was adopted by the American Psychiatric Association in 1980, and the **DSM-III-R** (Revision) was published in 1987.

To be scientifically acceptable, any system for classifying abnormal behavior must meet the same basic criteria as a psychological test: It must be reliable and valid (see Chapter 13). Briefly, the *reliability* of a test score or a diagnosis is a measure of its consistency across repeated measurements; *validity* involves the more difficult issue of estimating the accuracy of a particular measurement.

Before one can ask whether a diagnosis is valid, it must first be shown to be reliable. If clinicians cannot agree on the disorder of a specific patient,

---

***Diagnostic and Statistical Manual, Third Edition, Revised* (DSM-III-R)** A complete, official list of syndromes of abnormal behavior designed to improve diagnosis in terms of reliability and validity.

their different opinions cannot possibly all be correct. Therefore, the most fundamental problem for any diagnostic scheme is to establish reliability. One reason psychiatrists decided to revise DSM-II was that research revealed that its diagnostic categories were not sufficiently reliable (Spitzer & Fleiss, 1974); the single most important goal of the architects of DSM-III was to develop a more reliable system.

They attempted to accomplish this by specifying the criteria for each diagnosis precisely and in great detail. The value of this approach was demonstrated in an elaborate set of field trials conducted while DSM-III was being developed. A total of 12,667 patients were evaluated by 550 different clinicians using early drafts of DSM-III. In one pretest of DSM-III reliability, 770 patients were diagnosed by two different clinicians who interviewed them independently. When their diagnoses were compared, the agreement between judges (one form of reliability) was generally higher than had previously been found for DSM-I and DSM-II (American Psychiatric Association, 1980).

That does not mean that every patient received a single label from both clinicians; abnormal behavior takes a wide variety of forms, and some cannot easily be fit into any diagnostic scheme. However, the agreement was quite good for most diagnostic categories.

This improved reliability does not guarantee the validity of diagnosis, but it does make it possible. Several other changes were also introduced into DSM-III in the hope of increasing validity. Categories were redefined in the light of research findings, and theoretical constructs of questionable value were eliminated.

For example, the most important and most controversial change in DSM-III eliminated neurosis as a major diagnostic category. At least since Freud, clinicians have defined **neurosis** as an enduring set of symptoms that bother an individual or interfere with healthy functioning while the person remains in contact with reality. Traditionally, this was distinguished from the more dramatic impairment of **psychosis**, a serious mental disorder involving obvious disturbances in thought, emotion, and behavior. As one old psychiatric joke put it: "A psychotic thinks that two plus two equals five. A neurotic knows that two plus two equals four, but it really bothers him." While this whimsical distinction should not be taken too literally, it does convey the flavor of an important difference in the degree and kind of disturbance.

Freud's category of psychoneurosis included a number of different behavioral symptoms, ranging from excessive fears, or phobias (defined more formally later), to physical symptoms of hysteria, such as *glove anesthesia,* a loss of feeling in the hand that is not based on physical damage. (See the description of Freud's case of Anna O. in Chapter 12.) Although phobias and hysterias may superficially seem to have little in common, Freud believed that both were caused by similar unconscious conflicts in which anxiety led to the maladaptive use of defense mechanisms.

Some clinicians question Freud's theory of neurosis, and no definitive proof of its validity has been uncovered by research. The DSM-III and DSM-III-R classifications pay more attention to concrete behavior and less to unverified theory. Therefore, the major category of neurosis was eliminated, and phobia and hysteria (now called "conversion disorder") are no longer grouped together.

neurosis An enduring set of symptoms that bother an individual or interfere with healthy functioning while the person remains in contact with reality.

psychosis A serious mental disorder involving obvious disturbances in thought, emotion, and behavior.

Another difference from earlier systems is that in DSM-III and DSM-III-R, a complete diagnosis of an individual includes the systematic evaluation of five different dimensions of behavior, called *axes*. For example, the problem of a businessman who was afraid to fly might have been diagnosed under DSM-II as simply "phobic neurosis." The DSM-III-R diagnosis might look something like this:

Axis I (Psychiatric Syndrome): Simple phobia
Axis II (For adults, Personality Disorders): Narcissistic personality disorder
Axis III (Physical Disorders): High blood pressure
Axis IV (Severity of Stress in Past Year): Moderate; began new job
Axis V (Highest Level of Functioning in Past Year): Very good

Even without understanding all the details, you can see that this assessment of five separate axes provides a more detailed picture of the person's condition than the older approach of a single label. (The terms *phobia* and *narcissistic personality disorder* are explained later in this chapter.)

Like other changes in DSM-III, the introduction of five separate axes was designed to make diagnosis as specific and unambiguous as possible. But, as you might anticipate, this new system did not satisfy everyone, and critics attacked everything from its political and economic implications to its basic philosophy.

Axes I, II, and III call for evaluation of the client's current condition. For example, Axis I records the client's specific psychological disorder. Selection is made from 16 major categories, including the 11 listed in Table 14.1. Axis II records any personality disorder that may occur with the Axis I diagnosis. If the client has a medical disorder, it is recorded on Axis III. Attention can then be given to the need for medication. For Axis IV, the clinician estimates the severity of life stresses related to the Axis I diagnosis. Finally, Axis V calls for an estimate of the client's highest level of adaptive functioning in social, occupational, and recreational activities over the past year. This rating, from 1 (superior) to 7 (grossly impaired), is intended to guide the therapist in making a prognosis (prediction) concerning the client's potential for recovery from the disorder.

A number of research findings led to the fine-tuning of some of the DSM-III categories. A full revision, under the name DSM-IV, is currently scheduled for publication in 1993. The interim revision, DSM-III-R, has already begun stimulating new controversies.

Perhaps the most significant change in DSM-III-R concerns its treatment of homosexuality. In DSM-II, homosexuality had been considered a form of pathology in and of itself. DSM-III took the more moderate view that those who were content with homosexuality were psychologically healthy. However, it still maintained a diagnosis called "ego dystonic homosexuality," referring to "a sustained pattern of overt homosexual arousal that the individual explicitly states has been unwanted and a persistent source of distress" (American Psychiatric Association, 1980, p. 281). Critics argued that this category represented a kind of discrimination against homosexuals, since there was no corresponding category for "ego dystonic heterosexuality."

DSM-III-R thus is not the ultimate system for classifying abnormal behavior, but it is the official system now used for everything from hospital files

TABLE 14.1

The Range of Abnormal Behavior—A Partial List of DSM-III-R Categories

Diagnosis	General description	Example
Disorders usually first evident in infancy, childhood, or adolescence	A wide variety of developmental problems ranging from mental retardation (see Chapter 13) to attention deficit disorder with hyperactivity (see Chapter 9) to excessive sleepwalking or stuttering. The major common feature of these problems is appearance before adulthood.	*Anorexia nervosa:* An eating disorder characterized by serious weight loss, intense fear of becoming obese, and refusal to eat enough to maintain normal body weight. Particularly common among adolescent females. Most cases involve a single episode with complete recovery, but anorexia sometimes leads to death by starvation.
Organic mental disorders	Psychological or behavioral abnormalities known to be associated with brain dysfunction. Range from transitory drug-induced states of inebriation to chronic brain disease.	*Senile dementia:* Degeneration of brain tissue that produces a gradual loss in intellectual abilities, such as memory and judgment; may also produce personality changes. Occurs in 2% to 4% of the population over the age of 65.
Substance-use disorders	Undesirable behavioral changes associated with the regular use of such drugs as alcohol, heroin, barbiturates, and marijuana.	*Alcohol dependence:* Physical addiction to alcohol, including tolerance (increasingly larger doses are needed to produce same effect) and withdrawal (physical symptoms occur when the drug is stopped) (see Chapter 4).
Schizophrenic disorders	Serious disturbances of thought, perception, and emotion. By definition, these must involve deterioration from a previous, more adequate state and must be maintained for at least six months before the age of 45.	*Process schizophrenia:* The young widow who "noticed poison in her food," described at the beginning of this chapter.
Affective disorders	Prolonged and fundamental disturbances of mood and emotion, including severe depression and mania.	*Mania:* Euphoria associated with hyperactivity, distractibility, loud and rapid speech, inflated self-esteem, and a decreased need for sleep.
Anxiety disorders	Anxiety so severe that it interferes with the normal ability to function in everyday life.	*Social phobias:* Fear of situations in which one might be observed by others, such as eating in public.
Somatoform disorders	Physical symptoms (such as pain or stomach distress) that seem to be based on psychological conflicts rather than an organic disease.	*Glove anesthesia:* Loss of sensation in the hand caused by psychological conflicts (see Chapter 12).
Dissociative disorders	Sudden, temporary, and dramatic changes in memory, identity, and other complex psychological functions.	*Multiple personality:* An extremely rare syndrome in which a single individual is dominated by several distinct personalities at different points in time. One such case was popularized in the book and movie *Sybil.*
Psychosexual disorders	Problems in sexual function or adjustment that are related to psychological factors.	*Fetishism:* A disorder in which nonliving objects (such as shoes or underwear) are the preferred or only source of sexual excitement.
Psychological factors affecting physical condition	Diseases or physical conditions in which psychological problems play an important role.	*High blood pressure:* In most cases caused by psychological stress (see Chapter 17).
Personality disorders	Inflexible patterns of behavior and enduring personality traits that interfere with social or occupational functioning or cause personal distress.	*Narcissistic personality disorder:* A grandiose sense of self-importance that leads a person constantly to seek admiration and become preoccupied with success.

to insurance claims; consequently, the remainder of this chapter is organized in terms of its categories.

DSM-III-R accepts the medical model's notion that there are separate mental diseases, each with its own symptoms, course, cause, and treatment. It lists 16 major categories of disorders and over 200 subcategories. Obviously, an introductory chapter of this sort cannot begin to cover them all. However, to provide a concrete feeling for the wide range of possible abnormal behavior patterns, Table 14.1 lists the most important categories.

The Prevalence of DSM-III Disorders

The specificity of diagnoses in DSM-III has helped to provide some new insights into an old question: How widespread are various types of mental disorders? This is a critical issue not just for theoretical reasons, but also for planning and implementing mental-health services for those in need.

As part of a report for the President's Commission on Mental Health, Dohrenwend, Dohrenwend, Gould, Link, Neugebauer, and Wunsch-Hitig (1980) summarized the findings of over 80 studies performed since the turn of the century to answer this question. Unfortunately, these studies provided conflicting estimates of the overall level of mental illness in the U.S. population and offered little information on the relative frequencies of specific disorders.

As a result, the National Institute of Mental Health commissioned the Epidemiologic Catchment Area (ECA) program to provide basic data on the question of numbers. The first set of results from the ECA study were published in 1984 (Myers et al., 1984; Robins et al., 1984). Based on over 10,000 interviews conducted in three metropolitan areas—Baltimore, Maryland; St. Louis, Missouri; and New Haven, Connecticut—these studies provided two types of estimates of the frequency of 13 DSM-III disorders. Both were based on **prevalence** rates, which give the percentage of the population suffering from each disorder at a particular time. Separate estimates were provided for six-month prevalence (the percentage of people who reported the disorder in the six months preceding the interview) and for lifetime prevalence (the percentage of people who reported the disorder at any time in their lives). Table 14.2 summarizes the prevalence rates for the most common DSM-III disorders.

Some of these results were quite surprising. Prior to this survey, for example, many clinicians believed that depression was the most common mental disorder. Indeed, the last edition of this introductory psychology text included a table summarizing the best information then available; it cited depression as the most common disorder in the United States. However, according to the ECA study results shown in Table 14.2, alcohol abuse or dependence is most common, followed closely by phobia (a type of anxiety).

This study also provided some fascinating insights into sex differences in abnormal behavior. Virtually all previous surveys had found that women reported a higher rate of abnormal behavior than men. However, in the ECA study there were no major sex differences in the total amount of disorder at any of the three sites.

There were, however, major differences in the types of disorders: Men were significantly more likely than women to report alcohol abuse or dependence as well as antisocial personality disorder at all three of the sites. At

Alcohol abuse and dependence are the most common types of abnormal behavior in the United States.

prevalence The percentage of people who report a particular disorder within a given time period.

TABLE 14.2

Prevalence Rates of Most Common DSM-III Disorders[a]

Disorder	Six-month prevalence (%)[b]	Lifetime prevalence (%)[b]
Total, all disorders	18.0	32.6
Alcohol abuse/dependence	5.0	13.6
Phobia	8.2	13.5
Drug abuse/dependence	2.0	5.6
Major depressive episode	3.0	5.3
Dysthymia (neurotic depression)	3.0	3.0
Antisocial personality disorder	0.9	2.7
Obsessive-compulsive disorder	1.6	2.5
Panic disorder	0.8	1.4
Schizophrenia	1.0	1.2
Cognitive impairment (severe)	1.2	1.2
Manic episode	0.6	0.9

[a] Average rates, across three sites in an Epidemiologic Catchment Area (ECA) study.

[b] Figures do not sum to column totals since some individuals may be included in several categories.

Source: Based on Robins et al., 1984, and Myers et al., 1984.

two of the three sites, men were also more likely to report drug abuse or dependence. In contrast, women at all three sites reported higher rates of major depressive episodes and several types of phobias.

In explaining the discrepancy from earlier studies, Robins et al. (1984, p. 953) noted that in earlier surveys, "Symptoms of the male-predominant diagnoses, such as alcoholism, drug dependence, and antisocial personality, were little inquired about. Questions about them were omitted because they were thought likely to lead to poor rapport, and unlikely to be answered positively in any case because of respondent embarrassment."

All told, the ECA study ultimately will interview over 20,000 people. Each person will be interviewed on two separate occasions a year apart. In addition to the original three sites, later reports will also include information collected in North Carolina and California, and it will cover institutionalized populations as well as the general population. This body of data will undoubtedly present a clearer picture than ever before of the extent and severity of mental disorders in the United States.

The remainder of this chapter provides a more detailed picture of four broad categories of abnormal behavior, including personality disorders, anxiety disorders, affective disorders, and schizophrenic disorders. They are presented in a rough progression from the most ordinary and least pathological category—personality disorders—to perhaps the most frightening and bizarre syndrome of all—schizophrenia.

Personality Disorders

A **personality disorder** is an inflexible behavior pattern or enduring personality trait that significantly interferes with a person's occupation or social life or causes personal distress. Note that this definition stresses disturbance of one's

personality disorder An inflexible behavior pattern or enduring personality trait that significantly interferes with a person's occupation or social life or causes personal distress.

feelings or relationships with others; only when a trait causes a problem is it considered a personality disorder.

DSM-III distinguishes among 12 different types of personality disorders. Although some of the terms sound familiar—such as paranoid, dependent, or histrionic personality disorders—each is defined by a specific list of behavioral symptoms. For example, the term **antisocial personality disorder** refers to a behavior pattern of violating the rights of others that begins before the age of 15 and interferes with adult responsibilities, such as holding a job. More specifically, this diagnosis demands at least four of the following nine habitual patterns of behavior after the age of 18: problems with the law, aggressiveness, failure to plan ahead, lying, recklessness, ignoring financial obligations, inability to hold a job, inability to maintain an enduring sexual relationship, and irresponsibility as a parent. DSM-III-R further defines each of these nine patterns, as well as other criteria that a person must meet to be diagnosed as having an antisocial personality disorder.

People with personality disorders generally function reasonably well in society and often seek therapy only when faced with another problem, such as a crisis in the family or a criminal conviction. Compared with other more serious forms of abnormal behavior, very little is known about the causes or effective treatment of personality disorders.

To provide a more concrete understanding of this category, consider the case of one man with a **narcissistic personality disorder**, a grandiose sense of uniqueness or self-importance that leads a person to seek admiration constantly and to become preoccupied with fantasies of success.

A Case History:
Narcissistic Personality Disorder

Peter, a graduate student in English literature, believed that his Ph.D. thesis would provide a revolutionary breakthrough in his field. For some reason, Peter's mentor failed to recognize his brilliance, so he had trouble getting past the third chapter. He blamed his professor for his difficulties and complained that his mentor should help more by doing some of the research. Peter resented other students who made faster progress through his program and referred to them as "dull drones" who were jealous of his brilliance and creativity.

Peter also had trouble relating to friends and lovers. He often became infatuated with women, but soon after actually getting involved he realized that this person failed to meet his high personal standards. Before he had sex with a woman for the first time, he would have powerful and persistent fantasies about her; afterward, each woman seemed dumb, clinging, and physically repugnant (Spitzer, Skodol, Gibbon, & Williams, 1981, p. 52).

Peter had many narcissistic traits: an exaggerated sense of the importance of his thesis, a feeling that he was entitled to more help from his mentor, and a pattern of first overidealizing and then devaluing women. His relationships with male friends were equally shallow and transitory. Because these traits interfered with his work at school and his social life, Peter was given the diagnosis of narcissistic personality disorder. This leads to the question

antisocial personality disorder   A behavior pattern of violating others' rights that begins before age 15 and interferes with adult responsibilities.

narcissistic personality disorder   A grandiose sense of uniqueness or self-importance that leads a person to seek admiration constantly and to become preoccupied with fantasies of success.

of etiology: How did Peter develop this unpleasant and socially maladaptive pattern of behavior?

Causes of Narcissism

Much remains to be learned about the causes of abnormal behavior; therefore, when we discuss the etiology of any syndrome we shall present several different lines of theory and research. Each explanation will be based on the five theoretical paradigms introduced in Chapter 1 (psychoanalytic, behavioral, humanist, cognitive, and biological). On the simplest level, the psychoanalytic approach looks for causes in unconscious conflicts rooted in childhood. The behavioral approach seeks environmental causes and cures based on learning. The humanistic approach emphasizes self-fulfillment in the present. The cognitive approach analyzes errors in thought and interpretation of reality. Finally, the biological approach seeks physical causes of mental disease. We shall also consider social-learning theory, which combines elements of the behavioral and cognitive approaches (see Chapter 12).

As noted throughout this text, human behavior is so complex that it is often useful to consider it from several theoretical perspectives to get a complete picture. But instead of providing five or six accounts of the etiology of each syndrome, we shall focus on two or three that have proved particularly useful for understanding that category of behavior. For narcissistic personality disorders, this implies contrasting psychoanalytic and social-learning views.

A PSYCHOANALYTIC VIEW

In recent years, many psychoanalysts have developed new theories regarding the development of narcissism; one of the most influential was proposed by Otto Kernberg (1975). According to Kernberg, although Peter gives a surface impression of being extremely confident or even in love with himself, his outward demeanor masks powerful feelings of self-hatred; unconsciously, Peter sees himself as unworthy and unlovable.

As explained in Chapter 12, psychoanalysts believe that the unconscious can deceive the conscious mind to protect the ego against threatening impulses. In this case, on a conscious level Peter seeks recognition for his revolutionary Ph.D. thesis. But on an unconscious level, he may actually have a low opinion of his own work.

Kernberg's theory of narcissism, like other psychoanalytic theories, seeks the origins of these unconscious conflicts in childhood. Among his own narcissistic patients, Kernberg often found a mother or parent figure who seemed well adjusted to the outside world but who was cold, indifferent, or spitefully aggressive toward the child. Although we do not know the facts of Peter's childhood, Kernberg would hypothesize that such a person frustrated Peter's needs for comfort and emotional support during the oral stage of development. Thus, as an infant Peter failed to develop the healthy relationship with his mother that could provide a foundation for intimate social relationships later in life.

The early rejection by his mother produced an insatiable appetite for emotional nourishment. As an adult, Peter approaches other people with the idea that they too will fail to meet his needs. The attempts to degrade and devalue the women in his life could be Peter's way of frustrating other people so that they will not be able to frustrate him.

A SOCIAL-LEARNING VIEW

Other explanations of narcissism have also been proposed. According to one social-learning theory (Millon, 1981), Peter's parents may have seen him as "God's gift to mankind"; by indulging Peter's every whim, they made him believe that he could receive without giving and that every minor action deserved praise. According to this view, Peter's inflated sense of his own worth was a natural outgrowth of the way his parents indiscriminately rewarded every act. He came to feel that he was entitled to gratification and that other people were as solicitous as his own parents; to get what he wanted, Peter had only to ask for it. These patterns of behavior were further maintained by self-reinforcement. While most people have to learn to please others to gain the reward of approval, the narcissist can be reinforced by fantasizing about his own superior qualities; he does not need other people to the same extent.

Note that there are some points of agreement between the psychoanalytic and social-learning theories. Both predict, for example, that a child without any brothers or sisters would be more likely to become narcissistic, but they would invoke different explanations. In any case, at this time the etiology of narcissism has been the topic of more theory than research. Only when future researchers collect more data contrasting narcissists to other groups will we have a better idea of which perspective provides more useful insights.

Anxiety Disorders

In an **anxiety disorder**, severe anxiety interferes with the normal ability to function in everyday life. This interference can take several forms. In a **generalized anxiety disorder**, a person chronically suffers from intense anxiety and tension that do not appear to be related to any particular situation or stimulus. A more limited version, called **panic disorder**, involves unpredictable and repeated attacks of anxiety and panic. The symptoms may include shortness of breath, chest pain, dizziness, feelings of unreality, trembling, sweating, and faintness; again, these attacks are not related to any specific stimulus.

Another type of anxiety disorder is a bit more removed from the common-sense definition of nervousness. An **obsessive-compulsive disorder** involves persistent, repetitive thoughts that cannot be controlled (such as the thought of killing one's brother) or behavior patterns that are constantly repeated in a kind of ritual (such as washing one's hands over and over). Of course, everyone has thoughts and behavior patterns that are repeated; psychologists use the term *obsessive-compulsive disorder* only if they become so extreme that they cause personal distress or interfere with normal function. Although in everyday language we might speak of a person with a compulsion to drive fast cars or eat anchovy pizzas, in DSM-III-R a true compulsion is perceived

anxiety disorder A condition in which severe anxiety interferes with the normal ability to function in everyday life.

generalized anxiety disorder Chronic, intense anxiety and tension that do not seem related to any particular situation or stimulus.

panic disorder Unpredictable, repeated attacks of anxiety and panic.

obsessive-compulsive disorder Persistent, repetitive thoughts that cannot be controlled or behavior patterns that are repeated ritualistically.

Agoraphobics fear crowded public places, and often restrict their activities until they are afraid to leave home.

as senseless, an external force that cannot be resisted but provides no joy. Because theory and research suggest that the ritualistic thoughts and behaviors are linked to anxiety, this rather rare condition is classified with the anxiety disorders.

Perhaps the most common type of anxiety disorder is a **phobia**, a persistent and irrational fear of a specific object, activity, or situation. Vocabulary buffs may like to list the many English words that add the suffix *phobia* (from the Greek, "to fear") to a prefix for a particular feared object. These range from the familiar (for example, *claustrophobia,* for a fear of closed places) to the ridiculous (for example, *ergasiophobia,* for a fear of work). DSM-III recognizes only three major categories. **Social phobia** refers to a fear of situations in which one might be observed by others, such as speaking or eating in public. **Agoraphobia** refers to a fear of public places, such as crowds, tunnels, or public transportation; typically, the result is that the agoraphobic restricts activities until he or she is afraid to leave home. All other phobias, whether to animals, heights, closed spaces, or gym clothes, are called **simple phobias**.

Table 14.3 summarizes the results of one survey of the frequency of different types of fears. Note that the everyday objects and situations most people fear—snakes, heights, flying, the dentist—differ from the sources of phobias that are strong enough to interfere with everyday life—illness, storms, death, and public places. To get a feeling for this last and most common category, consider the story of one woman who was afraid to leave her house.

A Case History: Agoraphobia

Lisa was a 28-year-old homemaker who sought professional help because she was afraid that her anxiety attacks would interfere with the care of her three young children. About a year earlier, she began to experience periods

phobia A persistent and irrational fear of a specific object, activity, or situation.

social phobia A fear of situations in which one might be observed by others.

agoraphobia A fear of public places.

simple phobias Specific fears.

TABLE 14.3

The Most Common Fears

Mild fears		Intense fears		Phobias		Phobias so severe that people sought professional help[a]
Source	Frequency (%)	Source	Frequency (%)	Source	Frequency (%)	
Snakes	39	Snakes	25	Illness	3	Public places
Heights	31	Heights	12	Storms	1	Illness
Storms	21	Flying	11	Animals	1	Death
Flying	20	Enclosures	5	Public places	0.6	Crowds
Dentist	20	Illness	3	Death	0.5	Animals

[a] Estimates of frequency in the general population are not available; listed in order of relative frequency among patients.

Note: Fears are listed in order of their frequency; percentage estimates are based on a survey of a representative sample of the population of Burlington, Vermont. Totals may exceed 100% because some people report two or more fears.

Source: Agras, Sylvester, & Oliveau, 1969, p. 152.

of nervousness in which she suddenly felt light-headed and dizzy, breathed rapidly, trembled, and felt strange and detached. Although Lisa had led an active and outgoing life before the first attack, she gradually began to restrict her activities so that she would not have an attack in public or someplace where she could not get help. For the last six months, Lisa had been comfortable leaving home only if she was accompanied by her husband or mother. When she was forced to go to a supermarket or department store, she tried to stay near the exits. She canceled her usual summer vacation because she wouldn't feel safe so far from home. Shortly before deciding to see a therapist, Lisa had asked her mother to stay with her whenever the children were home; she was worried about what would happen if there was an accident and she was not able to help because of an anxiety attack. Both Lisa and her family were confused and disturbed by these sudden odd feelings and behavior patterns (Spitzer et al., 1981, p. 268).

A year before Lisa sought help, she had all the symptoms of a panic disorder—the sudden onset of extreme signs of anxiety from no apparent cause. Like many other patients with a panic disorder, Lisa soon developed more complex problems. She began to avoid places where such attacks might occur in public. The gradual restriction of her activities, coupled with the recurrent attacks, leads to the DSM-III-R diagnosis of agoraphobia with panic attacks.

Causes of Phobias

As with other victims of mental disorders, Lisa's problems can be seen in terms of several theoretical paradigms. Two of the most influential views of phobia come from psychoanalytic and social-learning theory.

A PSYCHOANALYTIC VIEW

For Freud, a phobia was the surface expression of a much deeper conflict. All the anxiety disorders are caused by unconscious conflicts between id, ego, and superego processes. The sexual and aggressive impulses of the id seek expression in behavior and the conscious mind. But the reality processes of the ego and the ideals of the superego oppose this expression and work to repress the impulse back into the unconscious. The final product of this unconscious conflict is intense anxiety that the id impulse will not be successfully repressed—a fear that it will force its way into the conscious mind and even lead a person to lose control.

It is impossible to understand the nature of Lisa's unconscious conflicts without knowing more about her childhood and current situation. However, since the welfare of her children seems to be one focus of the anxiety, one possibility is that they are the target of her unconscious impulses. Perhaps on rainy days, when all three children are cooped up in a small space, they act so bratty that Lisa has an unconscious desire to run away or even hurt them. According to the ideals of her superego, Lisa cannot admit these feelings even to herself. The panic attack occurred when this impulse first threatened to become conscious.

To a psychoanalyst, the fact that Lisa developed agoraphobia, rather than some other type of phobia, is no accident. Unconsciously, she fears running away and leaving the children behind. As a result, leaving her house even for a short time becomes a source of anxiety. If the unconscious aggressive impulse breaks through, she may never return.

A SOCIAL-LEARNING VIEW

The roots of social-learning theories of phobia go back at least to John B. Watson's attempt to teach Little Albert to fear a rat by pairing movements toward the rat with a loud, frightening sound. Later learning theories stressed the role of internal cognitive processes in learning fear. In one study (Bandura & Rosenthal, 1966), subjects watched as a model apparently received a painful electrical shock whenever a buzzer was sounded. This produced observational learning; over time, these people began to experience physiological signs of anxiety whenever they heard the buzzer. Whether learned by classical conditioning or observational learning, fears may be generalized to other situations and lead to avoidance responses—actions designed to prevent the occurrence of an aversive stimulus (see Chapter 6).

In Lisa's case, it is easy to imagine a social-learning explanation of her problems. Some stimulus triggered the first anxiety attack. While it might be interesting to know what that initial stimulus was, ultimately that is less important than the continuing learning process it set into motion. At first, Lisa avoided public situations that were similar to the stimuli present at her first attack. This avoidance was designed to prevent the unpleasant symptoms from occurring again. But over time, the stimuli generalized further and further, until Lisa was avoiding any stimulus outside her familiar home base. Thus, for the social-learning theorist, Lisa's agoraphobia is a case of learning to be afraid.

As with other psychological disorders, it is not yet known whether psychoanalytic theory, social-learning theory, another approach, or some mixture of approaches presents the best explanation for anxiety disorders. However, we shall see in Chapter 15 that social-learning theory has developed some particularly effective techniques for treating phobias like Lisa's.

Affective Disorders

Affective disorders involve a prolonged and fundamental disturbance of mood and emotion. Technically, they are also defined by the presence of certain symptoms of depression or mania. Of course, everyone is depressed from time to time, and it can sometimes be difficult to distinguish normal from abnormal depression. But clinicians define **depression** as a persistent and prominent loss of interest or pleasure in almost all ordinary activities, associated with such symptoms as disturbances in eating or sleeping habits, decreased energy, feelings of worthlessness or guilt, difficulty in concentrating, and recurrent thoughts of suicide or death. On the other side of the coin is **mania,** a feeling of euphoria and enthusiasm (sometimes alternating with irritability) that is associated with such symptoms as hyperactivity, loud and rapid speech, inflated self-esteem, decreased need for sleep, and distractibility.

As early as the first century, physicians were aware that mania was often linked to depression and that the two might even be different manifestations of the same underlying disease. Many people experience severe depressions without mania, but most who have a manic episode "will eventually have a major depressive episode" (American Psychiatric Association, 1980, p. 216).

In DSM-III-R, the two major categories of affective disorders are **bipolar disorder** (formerly called manic-depressive psychosis), in which manic and depressive episodes alternate, and **major depression**, in which severe depression appears alone. Each is defined precisely in terms of a list of specific symptoms. Manic episodes usually begin suddenly and end suddenly. They last a few days to a few months, and a person's first manic episode usually occurs before the age of 30. In contrast, major depression may appear at any age, and the symptoms may begin gradually or suddenly. When mania and depression alternate in a bipolar disorder, they are usually separated by periods of at least several months in which the person's mood is relatively normal.

Estimates of the prevalence of bipolar disorder range from 0.4% to 1.2% of the population, and it occurs equally in women and men. Major depression is far more common, particularly for women (Nolen-Hoeksema, 1987). Around 20% of all women have a major depressive episode sometime in their lives, versus 10% of all men (American Psychiatric Association, 1980). At one time, critics argued that this discrepancy between the sexes reflected the bias of male mental-health professionals, that the same percentage of men and women experienced major depressive episodes but that women were more likely to be labeled depressed. There is now a large body of evidence that this is not true. No matter what definition is used, more women experience depression than men (NIMH, 1981; Weissman & Paykel, 1974). No one is certain of the reason, although theories have ranged from feminist assertions that this is a by-product of unhealthy women's roles in our society to biological theories involving female hormone levels.

Depression may also come in milder forms. For example, your Aunt Tessie may complain that she always becomes depressed during the winter. If so, she has a condition that occurs often enough to appear in DSM-III-R: seasonal affective disorder (SAD). **Seasonal affective disorder** involves recurrent winter depression characterized by oversleeping, overeating, a craving for

affective disorders Conditions characterized by a prolonged and fundamental disturbance of mood and emotion.

depression A loss of pleasure in ordinary activities, associated with such symptoms as disturbances in eating or sleeping and decreased energy.

mania A feeling of euphoria, associated with such symptoms as loud and rapid speech, inflated self-esteem, and hyperactivity.

bipolar disorder A condition in which manic and depressive episodes alternate.

major depression A severe depression that appears without a history of mania.

seasonal affective disorder A recurrent winter depression characterized by oversleeping, overeating, a craving for carbohydrates, and frequent sluggishness.

carbohydrates, and frequent sluggishness. One speculation is that reduced levels of light contribute to this disorder, perhaps through the buildup of melatonin, a neurotransmitter hormone (Rosenthal, Sack, Carpenter, Parry, Mendelson, & Wehr, 1985).

Again, it is important to emphasize that both depression and mania are experienced by everyone, and the line between normal and abnormal may sometimes be hard to draw. But in more severe cases, there is little doubt that something is wrong. Consider, for example, the case of an actual patient whom we shall call John.

A Case History: Bipolar Disorder

At the age of 54, John suddenly became restless and talkative. He began to send checks to friends, and even to perfect strangers, who he said "might be in need." He was soon suspended from his office job because he was "overwrought." A few days later, he was admitted to a private mental hospital (Noyes & Kolb, 1963, p. 309).

On his arrival, John gave $5 to one patient and $1 to another. He talked quickly, loudly, and constantly. He promised several patients that he would have them released. Whenever a doctor entered the ward, John greeted him effusively, slapped him on the back or shook his hand warmly, and talked and talked. He became attracted to one woman physician and nearly drove *her* mad with his "familiar, ill-mannered, and obtrusive attentions." John was so affable that he became obnoxious, and other patients began to resent his interference in their affairs; on two separate occasions, other patients actually punched him in the face.

John was constantly and incessantly active and mischievous. He drew pictures of the doctors and nurses on his arms and wrote music on the toilet paper. He painted the face of another manic patient with Mercurochrome and played the ward piano incessantly whenever he was permitted.

At times, however, this euphoric mood seemed to shatter. In the middle of an interview, he would begin to sob audibly and bury his face in his arms. When he was first admitted, he pretended to commit suicide by poisoning himself with mercury, then drew a skull and crossbones on the wall in his room.

Interestingly, John's psychiatric history revealed three previous episodes of serious depression, lasting about six months each, at the ages of 35, 41, and 47. During his manic periods, he showed many of the classic symptoms, including excessive talkativeness and activity, a decreased need for sleep, and an inflated sense of self-esteem. In DSM-III-R, this patient would be diagnosed as having a bipolar disorder. More specifically, his diagnosis at the time of his hospitalization would include the adjective *mixed* to refer to the fact that he alternated quickly between periods of mania and depression.

Causes of Depression and Mania

Research on the causes of affective disorders has focused more on depression than mania, perhaps because depression occurs far more frequently. The cognitive and social-learning theories described in this section refer only to John's depressive episodes; however, our discussion of biological theories will return to the issue of the causes of mania.

A COGNITIVE VIEW

Psychiatrist Aaron Beck's therapeutic experiences with large numbers of depressed patients led him to conclude that depression is caused by logical errors of thought that produce excessive self-blame. This is called a **cognitive theory of depression**, because it emphasizes the critical role thoughts may play in causing the disorder.

One error that Beck's patients often made when they evaluated themselves was that they *overgeneralized* from single events. For example, when John went out on one unpleasant date, he might conclude that he would never find the woman of his dreams. A related error, called *magnification,* involved exaggerating trivial occurrences. For example, if John saw a single pimple on his nose, he might decide that his face was so severely scarred that he would only find work in a freak show. In extreme cases, the logic of depressed patients may become totally distorted by *arbitrary inferences.* For example, if John invited three friends to a baseball game that was rained out, he might conclude that he was worthless because he couldn't even pick a clear day to go out with his friends. The common theme underlying all these errors in logic is blaming oneself and feeling guilty or worthless at times when these feelings are inappropriate.

There is considerable evidence that depressed people do indeed describe their world in precisely the ways that Beck (1967) outlined. However, we have noted many times that correlations like this do not prove causality (see Chapter 13, "Understanding the Scientific Method"). Other theorists have argued that both feelings of depression and logical errors of thought could be caused by a third factor, such as a biochemical imbalance (as described later). While Beck's theory has been useful in the treatment of depression, no one has yet been able to prove that cognitive errors actually *cause* depression.

A SOCIAL-LEARNING VIEW

In Chapter 6, we introduced Martin Seligman's theory that a sense of **learned helplessness**, an organism's belief that it lacks control over a situation, can lead to depression. The animal laboratory research described there grew out of the behavioral paradigm and an attempt to understand the external stimuli that control certain forms of passive behavior. Seligman (1975) soon noticed many parallels between the behavior of animals who learned to be helpless and depressed humans. Both groups passively fail to cope with environmental demands; both develop eating problems; and, in both groups, levels of the neurotransmitter norepinephrine are decreased in the brain.

When researchers tried to apply this behavioral model from the animal laboratory to the real problems of human patients, however, they found that cognitive factors also seemed to play an important role. A new model of depression was therefore proposed that considered not just the feeling of lack of control but also the way people interpreted these feelings. Drawing

Judy Garland had a long history of depressive episodes and emotional problems. She died in 1969 after an accidental overdose of barbiturates.

cognitive theory of depression The idea that depression is caused by logical errors of thought that produce excessive self-blame.

learned helplessness A belief based on experience that people lack control over their lives or situations.

on attribution theory (see Chapter 16), this model distinguished several kinds of conclusions a person can draw when facing failure. Its causes can be perceived as internal or external, long-term or short-term, and global or specific. Table 14.4 gives an example of the way these three types of attributions might interact if a woman interpreted the fact that a particular man rejected her. Depression is most likely to occur when attributions are global, long-term, and internal, again giving one a feeling of helplessness or lack of control.

According to Seligman, John's periods of depression could have resulted from learning that he was not in control of his life. Specifically, John probably attributed any failures in his life to internal faults that were global, long-term personality traits.

A BIOLOGICAL VIEW

Since the 1950s, a number of drugs have been introduced that have proven extremely useful in treating depression, mania, and other mental disorders (see Chapter 15). During this same period, there has been an explosion of research using new techniques for studying brain chemistry and psychobiology (see Chapter 3). Taken together, these facts have led many researchers to explore the role of biological factors in abnormal behavior.

A great deal of this attention has focused on the effects of several different neurotransmitters on depression and mania. One of the most influential theories holds that the neurotransmitter norepinephrine plays a particularly critical role in regulating these disorders. Too much norepinephrine at certain sites in the brain is said to produce mania; too little produces depression (Schildkraut, 1965).

Several different lines of evidence support this view (DePue and Evans, 1981). A number of drugs that increase norepinephrine levels (including monoamine oxidase inhibitors and tricyclics) have been proven effective in reducing depression. Conversely, the natural salt lithium carbonate decreases the symptoms of mania as well as levels of norepinephrine.

In animal research, a number of other drugs that decrease norepinephrine levels (such as reserpine) have produced lethargy and lack of interest in the environment. A similar effect was found in humans when the drug reserpine was used to treat high blood pressure. This drug was effective, but it also

TABLE 14.4

Possible Interpretations of Personal Failure
(*Conclusions a Woman Might Draw after Being Rejected by Her Boyfriend*)

	Internal		*External*	
	Long-term	*Short-term*	*Long-term*	*Short-term*
Global	I'm ugly.	Maybe I have bad breath.	Men hate intelligent women like me.	In that mood, a man would reject Ms. Right.
Specific	Duane thinks I'm ugly.	Duane thinks I have bad breath.	Duane hates intelligent women like me.	Duane was in such a bad mood he would have rejected Ms. Right.

Source: Based on Abramson, Seligman, & Teasdale, 1978, p. 57.

Do We Know "The Facts About Manic Depression"?

On the basis of what you have learned in this chapter about abnormal behavior, evaluate the claims in the following excerpt from an article in *Glamour* magazine (Bodger, 1986). (A discussion of these claims appears after the "Summary" at the end of this chapter.)

> We all experience life's ups and downs, but for the approximately two million Americans who suffer from manic depression, those peaks and valleys can take on life-or-death importance. Although the exact nature of the psychosis remains a mystery, progress is being made not only in treatment methods, but in learning who is susceptible even before the symptoms first arise. . . .
>
> Although hereditary factors have long been suspected to cause the chemical abnormality that results in manic depression, only recently has a possible genetic marker been detected. It is this inherited defect, found in skin cells, that some researchers hope will provide the answer to predicting the likelihood of the disorder, eliminating years of confusing torment for its victims—and for their friends. (p. 155)

decreased norepinephrine levels and produced serious depression as a side effect in about 15% of those who took it. Its use was largely discontinued as a result.

The evidence pointing to a correlation between neurotransmitters and manic depression is impressive but incomplete. To test this theory further, it would be extremely useful to compare the actual levels of neurotransmitters, such as norepinephrine, in the brains of depressed versus normal persons. However, given the limits of current technology, this is simply not possible.

Thus, while there is considerable evidence supporting the idea that brain chemistry is intimately related to mood, more research will be required to understand the complex links. If low norepinephrine levels are indeed shown to cause depression (as opposed to simply being a by-product of it), then the case of John's manic and depressive symptoms might be partially understood as a problem in the chemistry of his brain.

However, it is important to emphasize that even if this biological theory is completely correct, psychological factors can still be important. As noted, events that produce a feeling of learned helplessness have been shown to lower brain levels of the neurotransmitter norepinephrine. Human behavior is best understood by considering how biological and psychological factors work together and by examining behavior from several theoretical perspectives. (Consider the extent to which this maxim is acknowledged in the excerpt in "Becoming a Critical Consumer.")

Schizophrenic Disorders

In 1908, a professor of psychiatry at the University of Zurich named Eugen Bleuler argued that Kraepelin had defined the disease dementia praecox too narrowly, and as a result the diagnosis excluded too many patients with similar symptoms. He argued that the disease did not always lead to irreversible intellectual deterioration (and thus was not true dementia), and it did not always begin early in life (and thus was not praecox). Bleuler proposed a broader definition and a new name for this disorder—**schizophrenia** (from the Greek *schizein,* "to split," and *phren,* "mind"). This term has often been misunderstood. A schizophrenic is not a person with multiple personalities. (As noted in Table 14.1, multiple personality is an extremely rare form of dissociative disorder.) The splitting of the mind that Bleuler referred to is far more disabling and far more common; it involves a fragmentation of thought, perception, emotion, and other psychological processes.

Bleuler's definition was so broad that he even included a category of latent schizophrenia, for people who showed only subtle symptoms. The controversy over precisely where schizophrenia ends and other disorders begin has continued to the present day.

Traditionally, clinicians in the United States leaned toward Bleuler's more inclusive concept of the disorder, and schizophrenia was sometimes called a "wastebasket diagnosis"; a disturbed patient who was hard to classify precisely would probably be diagnosed as schizophrenic. In contrast, European mental-health workers generally used the term more sparingly.

As a result, studies of the prevalence of schizophrenia usually found that it was more common in the United States than in Europe. This reflects a difference in diagnostic practices rather than a true difference in the prevalence of the disorder. When researchers directly compared the diagnoses of specific mental patients by different clinicians, for example, they found that many individuals who were called schizophrenic by New York psychiatrists would have been classified as manic-depressives or neurotics by London psychiatrists (Cooper, Kendell, Gurland, Sharpe, Copeland, & Simon, 1972).

Thus, questions about how common schizophrenia is depend on precisely how the term is defined. According to DSM-III, studies using narrow definitions of the term in Europe and Asia have found lifetime prevalence rates between 0.2% and 1%. American studies using broader definitions generally report higher rates. As a rough approximation we might say that 1 out of every 100 people in the world will become schizophrenic at some point in their lives.

A closely related issue concerns the existence of distinct subcategories or types of schizophrenia. One approach divides schizophrenia into two major categories, process and reactive. *Process schizophrenics* generally have a history of poor adjustment beginning in childhood and a low probability for recovery. This gradual deterioration suggests that some fundamental process in the brain has gone awry. This category is similar to Kraepelin's original notion of dementia praecox. In contrast, *reactive schizophrenics* have relatively normal childhood histories and a rapid onset of more severe symptoms, and their chances of returning to normal function are greater. They suffer from what laypersons call a "nervous breakdown," which often appears to be a reaction to severe stress. This generalization does not imply that every patient with a

schizophrenia Serious disturbance of thought, emotion, and perception, persisting at least six months and starting before age 45.

long history of problems has no chance to recover; it does imply that those who are correctly diagnosed as process schizophrenics have a poor prognosis.

No one knows whether these and other differences in symptoms result from fundamentally different disease processes. This makes schizophrenia a difficult topic to study. One can hardly find the cause of a disease when no one is even sure which patients have it. Some researchers emphasize this ambiguity by using the plural term *the schizophrenias* rather than the singular *schizophrenia,* which seems to imply that all victims suffer from the same disease.

According to DSM-III, the diagnostic label **schizophrenic disorder** is reserved for people who develop serious disturbances of thought, perception, and emotion for a period of at least six months before the age of 45 and who have deteriorated from a previous, more adequate level of functioning. The detail of this definition is quite purposeful. For example, the requirement of six months' duration is meant to exclude transient psychotic episodes; the mention of deterioration excludes individuals who are born with severe mental disturbances from which they never recover.

Schizophrenia usually begins with a phase of gradual deterioration, including such symptoms as social isolation and withdrawal, severe impairment in the ability to function as a wage earner, student, or homemaker, severe decline in personal hygiene and grooming, and extremely peculiar behavior, such as talking aloud to oneself in public or collecting garbage. This is followed by an active phase characterized by psychotic disturbances of thought, perception, and emotion. In most cases, active phases of the illness alternate with calmer periods characterized by the less dramatic symptoms. According to DSM-III (American Psychiatric Association, 1980, p. 185), complete recovery is "so rare . . . that some clinicians would question the diagnosis."

We began this chapter with Kraepelin's case history of a widow who would now be classified as suffering from a schizophrenic disorder. But not one of her symptoms would apply to every schizophrenic. Indeed, the symptoms seen in the active phase of the disease are so dramatic, so varied, and so fundamental that it is difficult to characterize them systematically.

There is even evidence that the particular symptoms of schizophrenia that are most prevalent vary cross-culturally. A World Health Organization survey (1973, 1981) revealed that the incidence of schizophrenia did not vary across nine selected countries, but patterns of symptomology did. Even within the United States, Irish-American schizophrenics have been found to show less hostility and acting out but more fixed delusions than Italian-American schizophrenics (Opler, 1967). Moreover, one study (Abebimpe, Chu, Klein, & Lange, 1982) of 273 schizophrenics in Missouri revealed that black patients showed more severe symptoms than white patients. Specifically, the black schizophrenics exhibited more angry outbursts, more impulsivity, more strongly antisocial behavior, greater disorientation and confusion, and more severe hallucinatory behavior than the white schizophrenics.

The Symptoms of Schizophrenia

Because the schizophrenia label includes such a wide and diffuse array of problems, in this section we survey the many possible symptoms of schizophre-

schizophrenic disorder   Serious disturbances of thought, perception, and emotion that persist for at least six months prior to age 45 in people who have deteriorated from a more adequate level of functioning.

nia in terms of their effect on thought, perception, emotion, and other psychological processes.

DISORDERS OF THOUGHT

Thought disorders can be subdivided into disturbances of *form* (the *way* people think) and disturbances of *content* (*what* people think).

Perhaps the most classic disturbance in the schizophrenic form of thought involves *loose associations,* in which the person shifts quickly from one subject to another and fails to form complete and coherent thoughts. Consider, for example, this excerpt from a letter written by a patient of Dr. Bleuler's (1911):

> Dear Mother:
>
> I am writing on paper. The pen which I am using is from a factory called "Perry & Co." This factory is in England. I assume this. Behind the name of Perry Co. the city of London is inscribed; but not the city. The city of London is in England. I know this from my school-days. Then, I always liked geography. My last teacher in that subject was Professor August A. He was a man with black eyes. I also like black eyes. There are also blue and gray eyes and other sorts, too. I have heard it said that snakes have green eyes. All people have eyes. There are some too, who are blind. These blind people are led about by a boy. (p. 17)

In this paragraph the reader can follow the shifts from one topic to another. But when associations become too loose, the result is incoherence, as can be seen in a sample of the speech of another patient:

> I am the nun. If that's enough, you are still his. That is a brave cavalier, take him as your husband. Karoline, you well know, though you are my Lord, you were just a dream. If you are the dove-cote, Mrs. K. is still beset by fear. Otherwise I am not so exact in eating. Handle the gravy carefully. Where is the paintbrush? Where are you, Herman? (p. 21)

The monologue continued in the same vein, jumping from one topic to the next, abruptly and without any apparent logic or plan.

Many other disturbances in the form of thought have been observed. Logic may be twisted by some personal law, as in the case of a schizophrenic patient who learned that his girlfriend had become pregnant. Since the patient had not had intercourse with her, he concluded that the conception was immaculate. This led to the further conclusion that his girlfriend must be the Virgin Mary and he must be God (Rosen & Gregory, 1965).

Along with disturbances in the form of thought come disturbances in its actual content, particularly **delusions**, or false beliefs. These may involve persecution, religion, grandeur, and other issues. Whatever the theme, schizophrenic delusions tend to be bizarre, fragmented, or patently absurd. (In contrast, the delusions of patients with paranoid disorders and other psychoses may be quite coherent and logical.)

One of Bleuler's (1911) patients, for example, reported that he was being poisoned with "hydrochloric acid, hair-bread, and urine." Another com-

delusions False beliefs, typically about being persecuted.

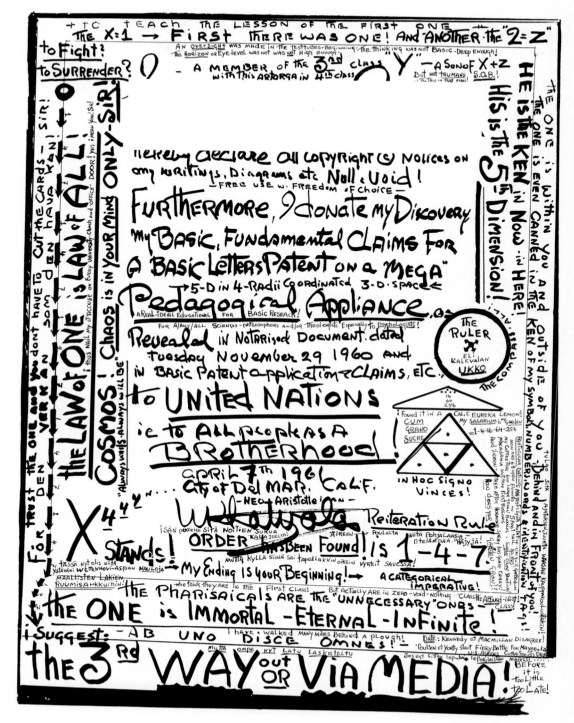

A letter written by a schizophrenic shows many signs of thought disorders.

plained of "human beings in her fingers who want to kill her and drink her blood." A third patient believed that if he stayed in the mental asylum "more than one year and 87 weeks, his father will have a leg torn off" (p. 119).

Delusions of grandeur are equally bizarre. One 20-year-old schizophrenic believed that he was responsible for every invention of the last 50 years and "he also possesses a remedy against spinal cord diseases. He can fly; and refuses food because he receives manna from heaven" (Bleuler, 1911, p. 120). For another, more religiously inclined schizophrenic, "A brilliant star arose which led him from his bed to the toilet and back again three times" (p. 121).

To an outsider, these beliefs may seem incredible or even laughable. To the victim of schizophrenia, such disorders of thought are all too real. They can be frightening manifestations of an entire world gone mad.

DISORDERS OF PERCEPTION

In schizophrenia, the most common perceptual disorders involve auditory hallucinations, particularly voices coming from inside the head that threaten, curse, or provide a running commentary on a patient's behavior. Among Bleuler's (1911) examples:

> While getting ready in the morning a patient hears "Now she is combing her hair," "Now she is getting dressed"; sometimes in a nagging tone, sometimes scornfully, sometimes with critical comments. . . . [Another reports,] When I stop speaking, then the voices repeat what I have just said. . . . [A third] patient hears his leg talking . . . the voices come from various places under the skin, and constantly call out: "Don't let me out," "Don't cut it open." (pp. 98–100)

Hallucinations of the other senses are also reported, but they are less frequent. Tactile hallucinations may involve electrical, tingling, or burning sensations. Parts of the body may seem too large or small, or the body may seem so depersonalized that it feels like a machine.

DISORDERS OF EMOTION

Schizophrenia also disrupts emotional responsiveness, leading to what clinicians call *flattened affect* (a drastic reduction in the intensity of emotional experience) or *inappropriate affect.*

Bleuler (1911) provided an eerie portrait of the drab, emotionless atmosphere of a mental asylum at the turn of the century:

> [The patients] sit about the institutions to which they are confined with expressionless faces, hunched up, the image of indifference. They permit themselves to be dressed and undressed like automatons, to be led from their customary place of inactivity to the mess-hall, and back again without expressing any sign of satisfaction or dissatisfaction. . . . During a fire in the hospital, a number of patients had to be led out of the threatened ward; they themselves would never have moved from their places; they would have allowed themselves to be suffocated or burnt without showing an affective response. (p. 40)

When emotion is shown, it may seem quite inappropriate to the situation. For example:

> A patient . . . broke out into loud laughter at the news of her brother's death, because she was so pleased at receiving letters with black borders; but the loss of the brother did not seem to arouse any feeling. (p. 52)

The English artist Louis Wain was known for his portrayals of cats in human situations, such as the tea party in the first painting in this series. In the 1920s, he developed schizophrenia and spent most of the remaining years of his life in mental institutions. This series of paintings shows how his portrayals of cats became more and more bizarre as the disease progressed.

DISORDERS OF OTHER PSYCHOLOGICAL PROCESSES

DSM-III lists a number of other schizophrenic symptoms that are less central than the disorders of thought, perception, and emotion. There is almost always a disturbance in goal-directed activity that significantly interferes with everyday life; patients may be paralyzed by ambivalence regarding even such commonplace activities as getting dressed in the morning. There is sometimes a total loss of identity, as a schizophrenic comes to believe that he or she is controlled by an outside force. There is a tendency to become preoccupied with fantasies and withdraw from other people.

Finally, bizarre motor actions characterize a severe form of schizophrenia called **catatonia.** A catatonic patient may maintain a rigid posture and resist efforts to be moved or may engage in purposeless repetitive movements, such as rocking back and forth, for long periods of time.

Remember, no one symptom occurs in every schizophrenic. But, as the many examples in this section suggest, schizophrenic disorders are severe conditions that can dramatically interfere with or entirely destroy an individual's ability to function in the world. Fortunately, as we see in the next chapter, many of the most frightening schizophrenic symptoms can be reduced by drug therapy. The portrait painted here is of the untreated disease, as observed in Bleuler's asylum before the discovery of antipsychotic medications.

Causes of Schizophrenia

In recent years, it has become quite clear that biological predispositions play an important role in the development of schizophrenia. The most compelling evidence comes from studies of behavioral genetics. Other important research centers on "high risk" children—that is, children of schizophrenic parents.

A BIOLOGICAL VIEW

As noted in Chapter 9, one important technique for studying the inheritance of human characteristics compares the resemblance of identical (monozygotic) and fraternal (dizygotic) twins. In the case of a continuous characteristic like IQ, we defined resemblance in terms of the correlation between twins' IQ scores. However, schizophrenia is considered discontinuous—a person is either schizophrenic or not. *Resemblance* is then defined as the **concordance rate,** the percentage of twins (or other pairs) that share the same trait. If two twins are schizophrenic, they are said to be concordant for that trait; if one twin is schizophrenic and the other is not, they are discordant.

Perhaps the most difficult part of conducting a twin study of the genetics of schizophrenia is finding a large enough number of schizophrenic twins to participate. In one classic study, Gottesman and Shields (1972) reviewed the history of every patient treated at two London mental hospitals between 1948 and 1964—a total of over 45,000 people. They found 57 schizophrenics with twins who could be located and who agreed to participate in the study.

Given the controversy over the clinical diagnosis of schizophrenia, these researchers considered several definitions of schizophrenia. The strictest and

A catatonic schizophrenic may remain in the same odd position for minutes or hours.

catatonia A severe form of schizophrenia characterized by a rigid posture or purposeless repetitive movements.

concordance rate The percentage of twins (or other pairs) that share the same trait.

most straightforward demanded that a person had been hospitalized and diagnosed as schizophrenic. By this conservative criterion, the concordance rate for monozygotic twins was 42%; for dizygotic twins, 9%. Although the mathematical details need not concern us here, this dramatic difference suggests that schizophrenia is highly heritable.

This conclusion is quite consistent with results from the other ten major twin studies of schizophrenia (Rosenthal, 1971). Although precise concordance rates vary from one sample to the next, depending in part on the definition of schizophrenia, monozygotic twins consistently had a higher concordance rate than dizygotic twins, and the monozygotic concordance rate was always less than 100%.

This last point has important implications. If schizophrenia were entirely determined by genetics, two people with the same genes—such as monozygotic twins—would always be concordant for this trait. It is apparent from these studies that what one inherits is not the disease itself but rather a susceptibility or a predisposition to become schizophrenic.

Skeptics may ask whether the environments of monozygotic twins are more identical and whether this could account for the consistency. As in other areas of behavioral genetics, one answer could come from monozygotic twins who were separated at birth. In 10 of the 16 such cases reported to date, both twins were schizophrenic (a concordance rate of 62.5%).

Given the fact that this study and many others indicate that genetic predispositions do indeed play a role in the development of schizophrenia, one of the most interesting questions for future research is this: Why do some children of schizophrenic parents become schizophrenic themselves, while others do not?

CHILDREN AT RISK

One way to discover why only some children of schizophrenics develop later problems would be to interview adults who were raised by schizophrenic parents. But we know that human memory often reconstructs the past to fit present beliefs (see Chapter 7) and that people are often unaware of the forces that motivate their behavior (see Chapters 1, 11, and 12). One partial solution is a longitudinal follow-up of a large group of people with a high risk of becoming schizophrenic. Although such studies are expensive and take decades to complete, this research design potentially offers so much insight that several studies of this sort are now in progress.

The first and most famous longitudinal study of the high-risk children of schizophrenic parents is still in progress; it was begun by Sarnoff Mednick and Fini Schulsinger in 1962. Around 1960, Mednick had been forced to cancel a similar study of Michigan mental patients when he found that as many as half of his subjects moved every year, making it extremely difficult to test this group repeatedly over several decades. The combination of excellent psychiatric records, low mobility, and a small geographical area made Denmark a more promising place for this type of research.

Mednick and Schulsinger began by identifying women who were hospitalized as process schizophrenics who had children between the ages of 10 and 18. Social workers then went to the homes in which these youngsters

Diagnosing Psychological Disorders

Many students take their first psychology course so that they can understand themselves and others better; indeed, many psychologists have embarked on their careers for similar reasons. "Understanding" often seems to mean having some sort of label to apply to behavior that is confusing. As we have tried to indicate in this chapter, labeling can be dangerous; for example, it can lead to various kinds of self-fulfilling prophecies. We do not want you to become a labeler; however, it is legitimate for you to want to learn to use diagnostic labels appropriately. Therefore, in this exercise we are providing you with several case histories and asking you to decide which of the diagnostic categories you have studied applies best to each. (A discussion of this exercise appears after the "Summary" at the end of this chapter.)

1. Andrew drops out of college and starts wandering the streets, convinced that the CIA has bugged his television set and is listening to all his thoughts. In college, this intrusiveness was particularly upsetting to Andrew because the CIA took his thoughts and broadcast them through all the radios and television sets in the dormitory. Andrew realizes that the CIA wants to have him crucified because he is Christ—as signified by the ABC network (Andrew Became Christ).
2. Bobby, a college freshman, is getting further and further behind in his work because all the rituals he follows interfere with his studying. Afraid that his roommate is full of germs, Bobby scrubs the whole bathroom three times every time his roommate uses it; washes his sheets and blankets every morning and night; and vacuums the floor between the desks every time his roommate leaves the room.
3. Carla begins feeling trapped whenever she is in a small or crowded place. She becomes afraid that she will suffocate and die whenever she is in an elevator or a busy cafeteria. These fears become so overwhelming that she will not go anywhere without her roommate.
4. Dotty expected to be class valedictorian when she graduated from college—after all, she knows she is the smartest and the most likely to succeed of anybody in her class. When somebody else was chosen, she proclaimed to everybody the injustice of it all, going on and on about her own talents and about the inadequacies of the student chosen and of all the other competitors.
5. Ethel is a homemaker whose husband is very successful in his career. She has become very unhappy about her life and feels guilty that she has no goals or ambitions. She lacks energy even to do housework and pays no attention to the children when they get home from school. Sometimes she breaks down into uncontrollable sobbing.

were living and enlisted the cooperation of 207 children of schizophrenic mothers for a study of the "effects of a nervous breakdown." Another 104 children, whose parents and grandparents had no psychiatric history, were also recruited as the control group. They were carefully matched on such variables as sex, age, social class, and the number of years spent in foster homes. Extensive interviews, physiological tests, and psychological tests have been conducted with each subject at regular intervals since 1962 (Mednick, 1966).

The high-risk children have indeed had more problems as they have grown up. By 1974, 8 of the high-risk children had died of suicide, accidents, or other causes; all of the control group were still alive. More important, 15 of the high-risk group were themselves diagnosed as schizophrenic, versus only 1 member of the control group. An additional 55 from the high-risk group were diagnosed as suffering from milder "borderline" schizophrenic deficits; only 4 from the control group fell into this category. Similar differences were seen for other forms of psychopathology (Schulsinger, 1976).

Analyses are still continuing to identify variables that predicted the adjustment of specific groups. For example, one report (Mednick, 1970) compared two subgroups of the high-risk children: those who were disturbed as adolescents and those who were better adjusted. Interestingly, those who became disturbed in the teenage years were more likely to have had medical problems when they were born. These complications included prematurity, long labor, and a variety of other problems that may have deprived their brains of an adequate oxygen supply at birth.

It will probably be several decades before this study is complete. The continuing follow-up of this group, and others like it, may help to identify factors that cause a child with a genetic predisposition to schizophrenia actually to become schizophrenic. Perhaps the clinical psychology of the future will include preventive therapy, with specific steps that a parent can take to decrease the likelihood that a child will develop schizophrenia or other mental disorders.

(To evaluate the extent to which you have mastered the basic elements of the diagnostic categories presented in this chapter, try your hand at "Applying Scientific Concepts.")

Summary

Understanding Abnormal Behavior

- Abnormal behavior may be defined according to four different approaches: statistical definitions, violations of cultural norms, deviations from ideal mental health, and failure to function adequately. Each approach has certain advantages and disadvantages; none is adequate by itself.

- According to the **medical model**, abnormal behavior is caused by physical disease. This approach has proved useful in understanding some disorders, such as general paresis, but does not seem adequate to account for all types of abnormal behavior.

The Controversy over Classification

- The leading classification scheme for abnormal behavior is the ***Diagnostic and Statistical Manual,*** third edition (DSM-III), approved by the American Psychiatric Association in 1980, and its 1987 revision, the **DSM-III-R.** The DSM-III and DSM-III-R were designed to improve psychiatric diagnosis in terms of reliability and validity.

- A **neurosis** is an enduring set of symptoms that bother an individual or interfere with healthy functioning while the person remains in contact with reality.

- A **psychosis** is a serious mental disorder involving obvious disturbances in thought, emotion, and behavior.

- **Prevalence** refers to the percentage of people who report a particular disorder within a given time period.

Personality Disorders

- A **personality disorder** is an inflexible behavior pattern or enduring personality trait that significantly interferes with a person's occupation or social life or causes personal distress.

- **Antisocial personality disorder** refers to a behavior pattern of violating the rights of others that begins before the age of 15 and interferes with adult responsibilities, such as holding a job.

- A **narcissistic personality disorder** involves a grandiose sense of uniqueness or self-importance.

Anxiety Disorders

- In an **anxiety disorder**, severe anxiety interferes with the normal ability to function in everyday life.

- In a **generalized anxiety disorder,** a person chronically suffers from intense anxiety and tension that do not appear to be related to any particular situation or stimulus.

- **Panic disorders** involve unpredictable and repeated attacks of anxiety and panic.

- **Obsessive-compulsive disorders** involve persistent, repetitive thoughts that cannot be controlled or behavior patterns that are repeated ritualistically.

- A **phobia** is a persistent and irrational fear of a specific object, activity, or situation.

- **Social phobia** refers to a fear of situations in which one might be observed by others, such as speaking or eating in public.

- **Agoraphobia** involves a fear of public places that often leads a person to restrict activities to the point of being afraid to leave home.

- **Simple phobias** are specific fears—for example, of animals, heights, or closed spaces.

- According to psychoanalysts, a phobia involves the displacement of unacceptable id impulses onto a neutral object. Social-learning theorists see phobias as fears that are learned by classical conditioning and observational learning.

Affective Disorders

- **Affective disorders** involve a prolonged and fundamental disturbance of mood and emotion.

- They may involve **depression**—a loss of pleasure in everyday activities, associated with such symptoms as disturbances in eating or sleeping and decreased energy.

- They may also involve **mania**—a feeling of euphoria associated with such symptoms as loud and rapid speech, inflated self-esteem, and hyperactivity.

- Episodes of depression alternate with mania in **bipolar disorder** or appear alone as **major depression**.

- **Seasonal affective disorder** involves recurrent winter depression characterized by oversleeping, overeating, a craving for carbohydrates, and frequent sluggishness.

- Psychiatrist Aaron Beck proposed **cognitive theory** that depression is caused by logical errors of thought that produce self-blame.

- A social-learning theory holds that depression is caused by **learned helplessness**—a belief based on experience that people lack control over their lives or situations.

- According to one biological theory, when brain levels of the neurotransmitter norepinephrine are too low, depression occurs; when they are too high, mania is the result.

Schizophrenic Disorders

- There is a great deal of controversy over the precise definition of **schizophrenia**, but roughly 1 out of every 100 people in the world is schizophrenic.

- There is an important distinction between *process schizophrenics,* who have a history of poor adjustment and a poor prognosis, and *reactive schizophrenics,* who have a more rapid onset of severe symptoms and a greater likelihood of recovery.

- The term **schizophrenic disorder** refers to serious disturbances of thought, emotion, and perception that persist for at least six months in people under the age of 45 who have deteriorated from a previous, more adequate level of function.

- The major symptoms of schizophrenia include disorders of the *form* of thought.

- These disorders include *loose associations*—ideas shifting quickly from one idea to another.

- There may also be disorders in the *content* of thought, such as **delusions**—false beliefs, typically about being persecuted.

- Also prominent are disorders of perception, such as auditory hallucinations.

- There may also be disorders of emotion, such as *flattened affect* or *inappropriate affect*.

- Other symptoms of schizophrenia include ambivalence and disturbance of motor activity.

- **Catatonia** is a severe form of schizophrenia characterized by a rigid posture or purposeless repetitive movements.

- **Concordance rates** refer to the percentage of twins (or other pairs) that share a particular trait—for example, schizophrenia.

- Studies of identical versus fraternal twins strongly suggest that a predisposition to develop schizophrenia is inherited. Studies of high-risk children born to schizophrenic mothers are now in progress to try to identify specific factors that cause a schizophrenic breakdown.

Critical Thinking Exercises Discussions

Do We Know "The Facts About Manic Depression"?

This chapter examined three different views of depression, including one theory (the biological) that also attempted to account for mania. The exerpt makes no attempt to acknowledge the existence of competing explanations of manic depression, and the critical thinker is thus at the disadvantage of not having complete information on hand. Further, the assertion is made that manic depression is *caused* by a chemical abnormality. You know from your reading that it is not a *fact* that manic depression is caused by a chemical abnormality; this is but one interpretation of some of the available data (which are not reviewed in the article). There are other explanations as well, and your text makes it clear that factors other than the biological ones cannot be ignored.

The critical thinker will read the assertions in this excerpt with a degree of skepticism, noting that they are based on limited data rather than on full, scientific research.

Diagnosing Psychological Disorders

The primary diagnosis for each of the case histories (unless there was other information that changed the picture) would be:

1. Schizophrenia
2. Obsessive-compulsive disorder
3. Agoraphobia
4. Narcissistic personality disorder
5. Depression

Some of the relevant critical thinking skills should be familiar to you by now, for example, the ability to identify defining characteristics of a concept and generalize them to new situations. Another relevant critical thinking skill involves the ability to recognize when there is insufficient evidence to arrive at a conclusion. In this case, you did well if you were tentative in your application of concepts and recognized that if you were a clinician, you would want more information before arriving at a diagnosis. These case histories, like the ones in the chapter, are simplified abstractions designed to highlight particular behaviors. Real-life diagnoses are seldom as easy to make as implied by these case studies.

TREATING ABNORMAL BEHAVIOR

Chapter 15

On June 23, 1900, 24-year-old Clifford Beers tried to kill himself. Six years earlier, while attending college at Yale, Beers had become obsessed with the idea that he would be disabled by epilepsy, as his older brother had been. This fear remained secret until, filled with despair, he jumped from a fourth-story window at his home. However, instead of being killed on the concrete pavement 30 feet below, he landed feet first on a small patch of soft earth a few inches away.

Beers was rushed to a hospital, where he began to experience delusions of being persecuted. The hospital became a prison, and the hot bandages applied to his feet became tortures designed to elicit confessions for unknown crimes. Voices inside his head accused him vaguely. Then, suddenly, Beers felt he was trapped on an ocean liner that was sinking because he had accidentally left a porthole open.

These hideous delusions continued after he was sent home. Beers was convinced that he was under surveillance, surrounded by sinister actors who played the parts of his relatives. His family reluctantly decided to send him to a private mental asylum, beginning a journey through several institutions that was later chronicled in his autobiography *A Mind That Found Itself* (Beers, 1908).

For the next two years, Beers remained haunted by delusions and profoundly depressed. Except for an occasional curse or complaint, he never spoke a word. The medical staff ignored Beers, save for an occasional crude attempt to force him to speak. For example, one doctor tried to force Beers to speak by pulling him out of bed and requiring him to stand on his injured feet. This cruelly incompetent "therapy" had no effect. In a second institution, for more than a year Beers's only interaction with a mental-health professional was an occasional "Good morning" from the doctor. The staff saw that he ate three times a day, bathed regularly, and exercised by walking around the grounds in a column of men "which greatly resembled a 'chain gang.'" Meanwhile, Beers silently plotted ways to kill himself when imaginary detectives would come to take him to court for crimes he had not committed.

Ever so slowly, the patient emerged from his depression. But the pendulum swung too far, and Beers suddenly became manic and overexcited. Delusions of persecution were replaced by grandiose schemes. Beers interpreted several trifling incidents as signs that God wanted him to reform the mental-health system. He slept only two or three hours a night and wrote rambling letters on strips of manila wrapping paper 20 to 30 feet long. Then he decided to investigate rumors of serious abuse on the wards reserved for violent patients by having himself transferred there.

Beers's wish was granted after he physically assaulted an attendant. He found himself locked in a small room where the only furniture was a bed screwed to the floor. Lacking paper, he wrote long messages on the walls with a lead pencil he had hidden in his clothes and sharpened with his teeth. Frustrated by the imprisonment, he used a shoe to break a glass bulb suspended from the 12-foot ceiling. Two attendants rushed into the room, threw Beers on the bed, and "choked me so severely that I could feel my eyes starting from their sockets." After several additional incidents, Beers was tied in a straitjacket that the physician vindictively tightened until "within one hour . . . I was suffering pain as intense as any I ever endured." Although he screamed, moaned, and cried, the jacket was not loosened to make him more comfortable until the next morning, 12 hours later.

Beers was moved to a small cell with little ventilation, padded walls, and only a filthy mattress on the floor. The room was often so cold he could see his breath. For three weeks, Beers was held in this room, tied into his straitjacket for about half of each day. At night, he was not even able to arrange the blankets over his body because his arms were tied.

These brutalizing experiences continued after he was transferred to another mental hospital. But, despite the incompetent actions of the staff, Beers gradually recovered. In September 1903, he was released from the hospital. What had begun as a scheme conceived in mania gradually developed into his life work as Beers began a campaign for mental-health reform. Clifford Beers's influential autobiography, upon which this account was based, was published in 1908. In 1909, Beers formed the National Committee for Mental Hygiene to raise the standard of care for mental patients and promote research on mental illness. By the time he died in 1943, the mental hygiene movement had helped improve psychiatric treatment around the world (Deutsch, 1949).

For the contemporary reader, *A Mind That Found Itself* provides fascinating insights into mental-health care, or the lack of it, in America at the turn of the century. Brutality was not uncommon, and insensitivity and incompetence were everywhere. Patients were perceived as helpless victims of a natural disease process; the institution's role was merely to keep the patients from harming themselves or others for as long as they remained ill.

It is hard to predict exactly how a contemporary Clifford Beers would fare if he had similar manic and depressive episodes in the late twentieth

**CLIFFORD BEERS
(1876–1943)**

Beers suffered from mental illness as a young man and was hospitalized for several years. In *A Mind That Found Itself,* he provided a vivid account of living conditions in U.S. mental institutions around the turn of the century.

century. Unfortunately, even today the adequacy of care varies from one institution to the next, partly because of inadequate funding at some facilities. However, the hospital stay of today's patient would surely be shorter and of a far different character.

The most obvious difference in contemporary psychiatry is the widespread use of drugs that reduce psychotic symptoms. For example, today Beers would probably be given carefully regulated doses of the natural salt lithium carbonate to calm his manic symptoms. While modern psychiatric drugs do not cure mental illness as effectively as antibiotics can kill some infections, they do substantially relieve the behavior, thoughts, and feelings associated with mental illness.

If Beers did have to remain hospitalized for an extended period, today's institutions would have proved far more pleasant; the sort of brutality Beers encountered is now extremely rare. One of the three asylums to which Beers was committed was "considered one of the best of its kind in the country" (Beers, 1908, p. 68). A comparable institution today would probably have numerous classes, therapy sessions, and rehabilitation activities designed to encourage patients to take responsibility for their own actions and prepare for the transition back to normal life.

Thus, mental patients are considerably better off today than they once were. To appreciate just how much better off, one must go back in history, beyond the experiences of Clifford Beers at the beginning of the twentieth century, to consider the treatment of abnormal behavior throughout recorded history.

A Brief History of Treatment

In ancient times, madness was often attributed to possession by evil spirits. Many treatments of mental illness therefore involved superstitious practices designed to drive the devils out of the body. One medieval English text suggested the following cure: "In case a man be lunatic, take a skin of a [porpoise], work it into a whip, and [whip] the man therewith; soon he will be well. Amen" (Zilboorg & Henry, 1941, p. 140). Other religious treatments were less painful; Christian monks established humane asylums for the care of the mentally ill as early as the sixth century.

The Rise and Fall of Moral Therapy

Unfortunately, history has recorded numerous cases of abuse of the mentally ill. In 1547, King Henry VIII decreed that Bethlehem Hospital in London should be entirely devoted to the confinement of the mentally ill. But this institution provided no treatment; "lunatics" were simply placed in cells that lacked heat, light, and sanitation. Some of these unfortunate individuals were chained in dungeons, whipped, beaten, and ridiculed. Medical therapy was simple and the same for everyone: "Bleeding of all patients in April, purges and 'vomits' of surviving patients in May, and once again bleeding all patients in October" (Reisman, 1966, p. 10).

The center photograph shows the Fools' Tower in nineteenth-century Vienna. All of the surrounding pictures show devices used in the "treatment" of the mentally ill during this period. The enormous machine in the middle of the top row was used to swing lunatics until they quieted down. Sometimes troublesome inmates also were locked in the "English coffin," seen at the left in the second row, or the huge wheel, in the third row.

The popular name of this famous institution was Bedlam, which was adopted into English to refer to a place of uproar and confusion. In the eighteenth century, Bedlam was one of the most popular tourist attractions in the city of London. While the visitor to the Tower of London or Westminster Abbey saw only historic sites, presumably at Bedlam one could watch real live lunatics act crazy and strain against their chains.

A more humane approach to treatment was favored by Philippe Pinel, a French physician who argued that mental patients were human beings who were entitled to compassion and dignity. In 1793, in the midst of the French Revolution, Pinel was placed in charge of a large mental asylum in Paris called La Bicêtre. His first official act was to order the chains removed from a small number of patients.

In some cases, the effects were quite dramatic. One man had been locked in chains ten years earlier after taking part in a drunken brawl. Pinel approached this "lunatic" and said "give me your hand, you are a reasonable man, and if you behave well I shall take you in my employment" (Zilboorg

moral therapy The treatment of mental disorders by kindness, understanding, and a pleasant environment.

psychiatry The medical specialty concerned with mental illness.

**DOROTHEA DIX
(1802–1877)**

Dix crusaded for the rights of the mentally ill in the United States, Canada, and Scotland. She worked as a Boston schoolteacher, but tuberculosis forced her to retire at the age of 39. Dix then took a job teaching Sunday school to female prisoners and became aware of the gruesome conditions in many primitive institutions. She then began to tour prisons, asylums, and poorhouses to collect evidence regarding mistreatment of the insane. Her campaign led directly to the founding of 32 mental hospitals and helped establish public awareness of the problems of the mentally ill.

& Henry, 1941, p. 323). The man became calm, even docile, and was later hired as Pinel's bodyguard. The favor was returned when this patient saved Pinel from a mob that wanted to lynch him for suspected antirevolutionary acts.

Encouraged by his success, Pinel experimented with a number of reforms. Sunny rooms replaced dungeons, and patients were permitted to wander around the grounds and exercise regularly. Staff members spent many hours talking to patients about their problems, offering both comfort and advice. Under these more positive conditions, some patients recovered and were released; others became calmer and easier to deal with. In addition, Pinel kept notes about his conversations with patients and his observations of their behavior. These were the first systematic case histories of mental patients.

Pinel's work helped to establish **moral therapy**, the treatment of mental disorders by kindness, understanding, and a pleasant environment. Moral therapy was practiced widely in European and American mental institutions early in the nineteenth century; current evidence suggests that it helped many patients achieve more adequate adjustment (Bockhoven, 1963).

In the United States, one of the leading figures in the movement for a humane approach to mental illness was a New England schoolteacher named Dorothea Dix. Dix documented and publicized many cases of disturbed individuals who had been abused, such as Abram Simmons, a man who was imprisoned in an 8-square-foot vault for several years in a small Rhode Island town. No light or fresh air could make its way into this stone prison; in the winter, its walls were covered with half an inch of frost. Her campaign led to greater public awareness of mistreatment of the mentally ill and the establishment of many state-supported mental hospitals.

Ironically, the very success of Dorothea Dix's movement helped lead to the decline of moral therapy. When large state hospitals were built in secluded areas, mental patients were segregated from society. According to United States Census figures, the number of insane patients in hospitals and asylums rose from 2,561 in 1840 to 74,028 in 1890. (This rate of growth was about eight times faster than the increase in the general population.) The rapid rise in the number of mental patients led to overcrowding and chaotic conditions in many hospitals; the personal attention demanded by moral therapy was no longer possible. Asylums once more assumed a custodial role, simply caring for the physical needs of those who could not care for themselves.

The Growth of the Helping Professions

Traditionally, the care of the mentally ill was supervised by physicians. However, **psychiatry**, the medical specialty concerned with mental illness, was often learned by trial and error. Before the second half of the nineteenth century, medical schools barely mentioned mental illness in their formal training.

In 1844, a group of 13 physicians formed the Association of Medical Superintendents of American Institutions for the Insane, which was renamed the American Psychiatric Association in 1921. The 13 original members quickly formed themselves into 16 committees to study such issues as moral treatment, the restraint of patients, the prevention of suicide, and the construction of mental hospitals. Throughout the nineteenth century, practical issues regarding the administration of overcrowded and underfinanced asylums often seemed more pressing than theoretical questions regarding the causes and cures of insanity. Further, psychiatry was practiced almost exclusively within the walls of mental asylums (Deutsch, 1949).

All this began to change after a Viennese neurologist and private practitioner named Sigmund Freud introduced a number of new techniques for treating emotional illness (see Chapter 12). In the early 1900s, psychiatrists began to work in clinics and private practices to treat a wide range of mental and behavioral problems.

Other professional groups also became involved in mental-health services during this period. Of greatest interest to us here is the field of **clinical psychology**—the application of psychological principles and research to the understanding and treatment of mental illness. Although pioneer work in this field began around 1900, the profession grew slowly before World War II. The psychologists who did specialize in clinical practice during this period were employed primarily to administer tests of personality and intelligence rather than as psychotherapists, and before 1947 there was not one single training program that granted degrees specifically in clinical psychology.

The demands of World War II forced many psychologists to develop clinical skills. About one out of every four American psychologists served in the military. In 1944 alone, they administered 60 million psychological tests to 20 million soldiers and civilians. In addition, many psychologists were required to perform therapy with patients for the first time (Garfield, 1965).

In 1946, the Veterans Administration (VA) provided extensive financial support for the training of new clinical psychologists to help care for the 40,000 veterans who were patients in neuropsychiatric VA hospitals. From this point, the profession grew rapidly. Twenty-two graduate programs in clinical psychology were established in 1947 to meet the demands of the Veterans Administration, and by December of 1986 the number of programs approved by the American Psychological Association had grown to 214 (Howard et al., 1986).

Other new specialties gained in influence during this period, notably **counseling psychology**, a specialty closely related to clinical psychology that emphasizes problems in normal adjustment, such as marital or school problems, rather than abnormal function.

Table 15.1 summarizes the major professional groups that currently work in mental-health settings. In actual practice, the lines between the roles of these specialties are often blurred. It is easy to distinguish a psychiatrist from a clinical psychologist or a psychiatric social worker on the basis of training, but all three may perform similar tasks in a particular mental-health setting.

The growth of these professions in the United States reflected fundamental changes in society's perception of the nature of mental health and government's role in fostering it. In 1854, President Franklin Pierce vetoed a bill sponsored by Dorothea Dix for federal support of a mental hospital; Pierce claimed that the federal government should not be concerned with the life conditions of individuals. In contrast, in 1963, President John Kennedy signed the Community Mental Health Centers Act, which provided massive financial support to achieve two goals: the treatment of severe mental illness within the community and the prevention of future mental illness.

clinical psychology The application of psychological principles and research to the understanding and treatment of mental illness.

counseling psychology A specialty that emphasizes normal adjustment rather than abnormal function.

TABLE 15.1

Major Groups of Mental Health Professionals

	Typical training	*Typical clinical tasks*
Psychiatrists	4 years of college 4 years of medical school (M.D. degree) 3 or 4 years of internship and psychiatric residency	Diagnosing and assessing abnormal behavior; providing psychotherapy; giving medical treatment and prescribing drugs
Clinical psychologists	4 years of college 4 to 6 years of graduate study of psychology (Ph.D. or Psy.D. degree)	Diagnosing and assessing abnormal behavior; providing psychotherapy
Counseling psychologists	4 years of college 4 to 6 years of graduate study of counseling (Ph.D. or Ed.D. degree)	Providing counseling and psychotherapy for normal problems of adjustment, such as marital problems and vocational guidance
Psychiatric social workers	4 years of college 2 years of graduate study of social work (M.S.W. degree)	Assessing social needs of psychiatric patients (work, education, etc.); providing psychotherapy
Psychiatric nurses	4 years of college (B.S. in nursing) 2 years of graduate study of psychiatric nursing (M.A. degree)	Supervising daily care of hospitalized psychiatric patients; providing psychotherapy
Paraprofessionals	Limited short-term training; college degree not necessarily required	Performing specific tasks, such as telephone counseling for suicide prevention or direct care of psychiatric patients

The fact that so many young men had been rejected from military service in World War II because of psychiatric problems had helped make the country more aware of the widespread prevalence of mental disorders. Then, in the early 1950s, psychiatry discovered several new drugs that treated psychotic behavior and thought disorders, resulting in the release of thousands of patients from mental institutions. This, in turn, created a new need for continuing programs and more trained professionals to help these individuals adjust to life within the community.

Thus, a century ago psychiatry was primarily concerned with caring for extremely disturbed individuals. Today, psychiatry, psychology, and related professions, (e.g., human service worker) play a much larger role in society, providing therapy and counseling for a wide range of problems in living. In 1957, a survey of a representative sample of the United States revealed that about three out of every ten people had sought help at some time from mental-health professionals; by 1976, this number had grown to nearly six out of every ten (Veroff, Kulka, & Douvan, 1981). The most common and most important treatment offered to these many people was some form of counseling or psychotherapy.

Psychotherapy

People have probably sought advice from one another ever since they first started living in groups. But psychotherapy involves more than just a casual conversation between two friends or the advice a bartender gives to a regular customer. In **psychotherapy,** a trained professional employs systematic psychological procedures to help a client change troublesome thoughts, feelings, and behavior patterns.

The actual systematic procedures may vary from therapist to therapist and from client to client. Some psychotherapeutic techniques have been employed with hundreds of thousands of patients over many years. Others are relatively new, relatively untested, and sometimes even faddish.

In this short overview, it would not be useful to try to list all the many variations of psychotherapeutic technique. Instead, we focus on four theoretical paradigms in psychology (originally described in Chapter 1) to see how each has led to the development of different techniques for treating abnormal behavior: psychoanalytic, behavioral, cognitive, and humanistic. The biological approach, the fifth and final theoretical orientation described in Chapter 1, is examined separately because techniques like psychosurgery and drug therapy are not forms of psychotherapy.

Psychoanalytic Therapy

The first patient to undergo psychotherapy might have been Anna O., a young woman whose emotional conflicts produced a variety of physical symptoms (see Chapter 12). In treating this patient, Josef Breuer laid the groundwork for the "talking cure"; when Anna talked about the roots of her psychological problems, her physical symptoms began to disappear. Starting from this observation, Sigmund Freud went on to develop the theory of psychoanalysis.

FREUDIAN ANALYSIS

As explained earlier, Freud believed that anxiety, neurosis, and other adult personality patterns are determined by unconscious conflicts regarding biological instincts and that early childhood experiences are particularly influential in establishing lifelong patterns of behavior.

In Freudian analysis, the treatment of inappropriate behavior patterns is based on the therapeutic power of **insight.** Once the unconscious forces that motivate behavior are consciously understood, a person can deal with reality more effectively. Insight is not simply an intellectual process; it also involves reliving intense emotional experiences. Repressed thoughts and feelings do not emerge suddenly to produce dramatic cures. Instead, psychoanalysis involves a long and repetitious process of seeing that the same underlying themes can account for behavior in many different situations. Gradually, over a period of years, the patient learns to face reality and deal with it effectively rather than unconsciously deny and distort it.

The most important therapeutic technique used throughout this long process is **free association,** in which the patient relaxes and reports every single thought as it comes to mind. Under ordinary conditions, the ego acts as a kind of editor, preventing threatening unconscious impulses from becoming conscious. In free association, the idea is to circumvent this unconscious editing by reporting every single thought, no matter how trivial or indiscreet

psychotherapy The application, by a professional, of systematic psychological precedures to help a client change troublesome thoughts, feelings, and behavior patterns.

insight The conscious understanding of the unconscious forces that motivate behavior.

free association A therapeutic technique in which a patient relaxes and reports every single thought as it comes to mind.

resistance An unconscious attempt to avoid therapeutic insights into motivation.

transference Strong positive or negative feelings toward the therapist originating in the patient's early experiences.

it might seem. Indeed, Freud (1913/1958) specifically instructed his own patients as follows:

> You will be tempted to say to yourself that this [thought] or that is irrelevant here, or is quite unimportant, or nonsensical, so that there is no need to say it. You must never give in to these criticisms, but must say it in spite of them—indeed, you must say it precisely because you have an aversion to doing so. (p. 135)

Since Freud believed that restraints on the unconscious are loosened during sleep, patients in analysis are also encouraged to report their dreams. Unconscious conflicts may be revealed in symbolic form in dreams, as in the case of Freud's own dream about his father's funeral (see Chapter 12). In analyzing a patient's dreams, a psychoanalyst differentiates between the *manifest content* (what the patient remembers of the dream) and the *latent content* (the underlying unconscious meanings).

Any aversion or reluctance to discuss a particular dream could be a sign of **resistance,** an unconscious attempt to avoid therapeutic insights into motivation. Similarly, when patients refuse to free-associate, it may mean that they are being defensive about important conflicts. In the same way, patients who are habitually late for therapy, miss an appointment, or refuse to pay their bills are seen as resisting the entire psychoanalytic enterprise because it may uncover threatening thoughts and feelings that have long been hidden in the unconscious mind.

As therapy progresses, the patient's relationship with the therapist becomes an important tool and a sign of progress. The term **transference** refers

Here is a glimpse of Sigmund Freud's office and the first psychoanalytic couch.

to some of the patient's strong positive or negative feelings toward the therapist. Freud defined this term very precisely to refer only to a repetition of emotions originally directed toward parent figures during the Oedipal period (see Chapter 12). The course of psychoanalysis expresses themes determined in childhood: A woman who hated her father may transfer these feelings to the analyst and come to hate him.

The therapist can help patients understand these and other reactions through **interpretation,** in which the analyst gradually guides patients to an understanding of their thoughts and behavior. For example, if the woman who hated her father becomes very angry at the analyst, he may ask whether she wishes she could direct this anger at her own father. Such interpretations are most likely to help only when the patient is ready for this insight; premature interpretation merely produces resistance, and the patient will deny the connection, often quite vehemently.

This is one reason why Freud believed that psychoanalysis was a long and gradual process; years of intensive therapy could be required to overcome the defenses a patient had built up. In classical Freudian analysis, the patient could expect to continue psychotherapy two to five times each week for several years. Throughout this period, the analyst's role was passive. At each session, the patient would lie on a couch and free-associate and report dreams for about an hour. The analyst typically sat behind the patient, to avoid giving unintentional nonverbal cues, such as nodding in encouragement or frowning at a particular theme. Interpretations were offered only when the patient appeared ready for them.

A CASE HISTORY

To get a more concrete feeling for the process of psychoanalysis, consider the case of Jim, a 37-year-old unemployed and unmarried man who came to a psychotherapist for vocational counseling. Even in the first session, "the analyst listened, doing little talking, prompting him with short, open-ended sentences" (Fine, 1973, p. 26). The analyst suggested that Jim's problems were deep-seated and that he should undergo psychoanalysis. At first Jim objected strongly, claiming that he had no serious problems. This resistance gradually lessened, and Jim agreed to come twice a week for a two-month trial period.

As Jim free-associated, it gradually became clear that he had a long history of aimlessness, drifting from job to job and dropping out from one college after another without ever completing his degree. Jim was also rather withdrawn socially; his first sexual relationship came at the age of 27 in a single homosexual experience with an older man. At the time he entered therapy, Jim's only interests in life were masturbating and going to the movies.

At this point the analyst called attention to the discrepancy between Jim's limited forms of amusement and his claim that he had no serious problems. Jim agreed that this was a type of resistance and began to seek the root of his problems. He gradually focused on his lifelong battles with his dominating mother. Jim's mother had constantly criticized him in childhood and sometimes had beaten him severely. He fought back by withdrawing; one of the "greatest

interpretation The process by which the psychoanalyst gradually guides patients to an understanding of their thoughts and behavior.

victories" of his childhood was learning not to cry when his mother beat him with a strap. Early in therapy, Jim transferred this resentment to the therapist and threatened to withdraw from therapy whenever he disliked a particular interpretation.

When Jim achieved the insight that withdrawal was a lifelong pattern based on early experiences with his mother, he began to change. He gradually saw a pattern in his adult relationships of rejecting women to gain revenge on the female sex and his mother. Over the course of two years of intensive psychoanalysis, he slowly developed a healthy relationship with a woman he had known for years. He married the woman and successfully terminated psychotherapy.

CONTEMPORARY ANALYSIS

As noted in Chapter 12, among psychoanalysts who later revised Freud's theory, the most influential group were the *ego psychologists,* who emphasized the autonomy of the ego and its reality-based processes. Erikson, Jung, Adler, and others proposed a number of changes in Freud's classical analytic technique.

Freud's therapy had been designed to bring unconscious material into consciousness so that repressed conflicts could be resolved. Later forms of analytic therapy were developed with a somewhat different goal in mind: to promote the development and functioning of the ego in all areas of life (Kutash, 1983). The classical techniques devised to reveal unconscious conflicts—free association and dream analysis—play a less central role in contemporary analysis. Contemporary analysts also devote a great deal of attention to the way personality may be shaped by the external environment as well as internal conflicts.

On a practical basis, one of the most important sets of changes in psychoanalytic therapy is the attempt to make it more efficient. Few waitresses or college professors could afford to spend the time or money for years of classical psychoanalysis; it was generally limited to a wealthy minority. Many modifications have therefore been proposed to speed up the process.

While classical analysts often insisted on four or five therapy sessions each week, the contemporary analyst is more flexible in fitting the schedule to a patient's needs and abilities. In classical analysis, the patient typically lay on a couch while the therapist remained out of sight and the lights were dimmed to promote concentration on the inner chain of free associations. In contemporary analysis, patient and analyst sit face to face and carry on a more normal conversation. Freud believed that interpretation could not begin until transference was established; contemporary analysts argue that some types of interpretation are useful even at first analytic sessions. Thus, the contemporary analyst actively intervenes to direct discussion along the most productive path rather than waiting passively for insight to occur at its own pace.

These and other changes in technique are related to changes in the psychoanalytic-patient population. Classical analysis was often limited to neurotic patients; in contemporary terminology, patients with anxiety disorders and somatoform disorders were thought to be most likely to benefit. Contemporary analysis can serve a far wider range of problems, including narcissistic and other personality disorders (see Chapter 14).

According to one recent survey of clinical psychologists, Freudian and contemporary analytic techniques are still among the most widely practiced forms of psychotherapy. However, between 1961 and 1982 the proportion who identified themselves as psychoanalysts had dropped from 41% to 14% (Smith, 1982). Much of this decline could be attributed to the growth of an alternative set of approaches known as behavior therapy.

Behavior Therapy

Behavior therapy or **behavior modification**, is a type of psychotherapy that applies scientific principles to alter observable behaviors through learning. Chapter 6 also described several basic principles of the behavioral approach: Focus on observable behaviors; identify the variables that control a problem behavior in the present; manipulate these relevant variables; and measure the behavioral effects of any intervention.

The roots of the behavioral approach are as old as humankind. Even the Old Testament includes many examples, beginning with Adam and Eve's punishment for eating the forbidden fruit. But large-scale, systematic study of behavior therapy began only around 1960.

The two types of behavior therapy described in Chapter 6—token economies and the reduction of self-destructive behavior through punishment—were straightforward applications of operant conditioning. As behavior therapy has grown in influence, there has been increasing recognition of the importance of internal cognitive factors and observational learning. The two techniques described here—systematic desensitization to reduce fear and self-control procedures for altering one's own behavior—both recognize the way internal thoughts and feelings can influence external behavior.

SYSTEMATIC DESENSITIZATION

Systematic desensitization is a form of behavior therapy that reduces fear by requiring an anxious person to imagine increasingly threatening situations while remaining deeply relaxed. The therapy involves three steps: relaxation training, development of an anxiety hierarchy, and the actual desensitization. Relaxation therapy, the first step, is probably the simplest; as noted in Chapter 4, there are a number of forms of meditation and training that can help people to learn systematically to relax. Many therapists use a technique called *progressive muscle relaxation* (Jacobson, 1938), in which various muscles in the arms, in the legs, and throughout the body are tensed and then relaxed.

The second step involves constructing an *anxiety hierarchy,* a list of situations that provoke fear for that person, organized from the least threatening to the most threatening. Each anxiety hierarchy is based on some theme that evokes fear, such as traveling, giving a speech, or failing at work. Table 15.2 lists an actual anxiety hierarchy constructed in behavior therapy for a client who had an excessive fear of being criticized. Note that the order of

behavior therapy (behavior modification) The application of scientific principles to alter observable behavior through learning.

systematic desensitization A process that requires an anxious person to imagine increasingly threatening situations while remaining deeply relaxed.

TABLE 15.2

An Anxiety Hierarchy

In behavior therapy, a 23-year-old nurse who suffered from extreme anxiety constructed this list of situations that evoked fear. They all refer to a common theme regarding fear of criticism and are arranged from the least threatening stimulus to the most threatening.

1. Your mother reminds you that you have not yet sent a thank-you letter to a relative from whom you received a gift.
2. Your uncle wonders out loud why you don't visit him more often.
3. Your mother notes that you haven't been to church with her in quite a while.
4. Your mother comments that it has been a long time since you have visited your grandmother.
5. Your mother criticizes a friend: She just makes herself at home!
6. Your stepfather says that he can't understand how anyone could be so stupid as to be a Catholic.
7. You return an overdue book to the library; the librarian looks at you critically.
8. A physician making rounds discovers a baby in convulsions. He comments to a colleague: "You see what I mean about having to make rounds."
9. Bill [her fiancé] looks over your shoulder as you are writing, and comments that it doesn't look very neat.
10. Bill comments that you are too heavy in the waist and should exercise.
11. Bill criticizes you for being quiet on a double date.
12. You are at a party given by one of Bill's friends. You mispronounce a word and Bill corrects you.
13. Your mother comes into a room and finds you smoking.

Source: Lang, 1965, p. 217.

these situations reflects this particular person's fears; another individual might place similar events in a different order.

In the actual *desensitization,* the client imagines each item on the list, beginning with the least threatening situation, while trying to remain relaxed. For example, after practice imagining the first item on her list, this young woman was able to think about her mother criticizing her for not sending a thank-you note without feeling anxious. Training proceeded until she could feel relaxed while imagining any of the 13 situations in the anxiety hierarchy. This learning generalized to everyday life, and her fears about criticism were reduced. For this client, training on a separate anxiety hierarchy regarding fears of travel was even more successful; after several months of therapy she bought a car, drove freely around the city, and even went on a long vacation with friends.

According to Joseph Wolpe (1958), the therapist who developed this procedure, systematic desensitization involves a process of **counterconditioning,** in which relaxation becomes classically conditioned to the same stimuli that once elicited anxiety. Because the states of relaxation and fear are physiologically incompatible, through repeated practice, relaxation can take the place of fear. While others disagree about the underlying process, there is a large body of evidence that systematic desensitization is an effective way to change a wide range of behaviors, from snake and insect phobias to lack of assertiveness and anxiety about dating (Rimm & Masters, 1979).

counterconditioning A process in which relaxation becomes classically conditioned to a stimulus that formerly elicited anxiety.

SELF-CONTOL

Behavior therapy techniques for **self-control** provide clients with active coping strategies to deal with specific problems. While the person who undergoes systematic desensitization learns new behaviors rather passively, self-control programs require very active commitment and participation on the patient's part. Indeed, in some cases, one might be able to develop a self-control program with little or no help from a therapist by following behavioral principles regarding self-control.

For example, Williams and Long (1983) described a model for self-control that consists of six steps:

1. Select a goal.
2. Monitor target behaviors.
3. Alter setting events.
4. Establish effective consequences.
5. Focus on contingencies.
6. Use covert control.

Williams and Long's book outlines the most important elements for each step and shows how the model can be applied to such problems as losing weight, quitting smoking, developing athletic skills, or managing anxiety.

Let us consider one example. A student who wanted to improve her study habits would start by selecting a concrete and achievable goal; a college student who had not cracked a book since *Winnie the Pooh* might start with a modest goal, such as studying for 15 minutes every afternoon. The second step consists of monitoring the target behavior—in this case, studying—for some reasonable period of time. Detailed records could include the starting time, finishing time, place, and emotional state on each study occasion for a week. Baseline estimates of this sort are often surprising; many people have misconceptions about their own habits. These techniques are examples of the first principle of behavior therapy: Focus clearly on concrete, observable behaviors.

Setting events are the types of situations that promote or interfere with the target behavior. Detailed records might reveal that in the library, this student spent all her time people-watching, but that she could study for long periods in the privacy of her room. The conclusion is obvious: She should plan to study in her room, perhaps at the same time each day. Note that if one follows these instructions, it is possible to identify the variables that control a problem behavior.

Establishing effective consequences could mean reinforcing the desired behavior. This student might decide that she is not allowed to watch her favorite soap opera or telephone her boyfriend until the 15 minutes of study are completed. Once this behavior is established, she could gradually increase the study time, reinforcing for only 30 minutes of study, then 45 minutes, and so on. In this way, she could manipulate relevant variables and apply the operant principle of shaping (see Chapter 6).

To maintain this learning, she should focus on the contingencies—tape today's assignment to her pillow, so she can't avoid looking at it if she's

self-control Active coping strategies used by an individual to deal with personal problems.

tempted to rest her eyes for a few hours. Anything that would make her more aware of her specific new commitment to study could help.

Finally, covert control involves using thoughts and images to alter behavior. For example, the student might allow herself to fantasize about a loved one only after completing a certain study assignment. Or she might reduce some of the anxiety associated with studying by trying some relaxation exercises. Cognitive strategies like these have become an increasingly used strategy, not just in self-control programs, but in behavior therapy in general.

Cognitive Therapy

Cognitive therapy traces the roots of emotional and behavioral problems to particular thought patterns; psychotherapy therefore aims to change the way people think. This idea can be traced back at least 2,000 years to the philosopher Epictetus, who wrote, "Men are disturbed not by things, but by the view which they take of them." Shakespeare expressed this notion more gracefully in *Hamlet:* "There is nothing either good or bad but thinking makes it so."

Cognitive approaches first began to have a major impact on psychotherapy in the 1950s, when Albert Ellis developed a system called **rational-emotive therapy**. According to Ellis, many psychological problems are caused by irrational thoughts that a particular event is awful, horrible, or catastrophic. These "foolish thoughts" can lead to feelings of "worthlessness, guilt, anxiety, depression, rage and inertia" that can drive a person "to whine and rant and to live less enjoyably" (Ellis, 1973, p. 200).

For example, imagine the cognitive processes involved in a typical dating-rejection scenario. A young man spends several days building up his courage, then telephones the woman of his dreams to invite her to a Wednesday-night-all-you-can-eat fish fry at the local Howard Johnson's. She replies coolly that on Wednesday nights she always washes her hair. Stung by this rejection, our hero thinks to himself, "What a tragedy. This woman has turned me down. I'm worthless. I'll probably spend the rest of my life at Howard Johnson's alone."

A rational-emotive therapist would point out the irrational nature and self-defeating effects of these thoughts. Perhaps the woman really enjoys Wednesday hair washes. And even if this was an excuse and she did think our hero was an ugly fool, so what? That doesn't mean she's right. Unhappiness is caused not by her beliefs but by the young man's beliefs about himself. It is his irrational conclusion of worthlessness that produces the crippling fear that he will never find someone to share his flounder with.

The role of the therapist, then, is to teach a person "how to accept reality even when it is pretty grim" (Ellis, 1973, p. 182). Some cognitive therapists take a very active and aggressive approach to correcting irrational thought patterns. While the humanist Carl Rogers believes that the client is the only expert on his or her own problems, Albert Ellis believes that the therapist is the expert who can efficiently identify irrational thoughts and tell a person how to act.

Ellis tries to provide emotional support by regarding the total person in a positive and supportive light. But the rational-emotive therapist does not hesitate to criticize faulty thought patterns.

cognitive therapy A form of psychotherapy that concentrates on changing thought patterns.

rational-emotive therapy A cognitive approach to therapy in which people are taught actively to avoid irrational thoughts that unpleasant events are catastrophic.

Other cognitive approaches to therapy have been mentioned earlier in this text, such as Aaron Beck's cognitive theory that depression is caused by logical errors of thought that produce self-blame (see Chapter 14). Just as cognitive approaches to basic research have become increasingly influential in recent years (see Chapters 7 and 8), so cognitive approaches to therapy have also grown in impact.

Some psychologists now use the term *cognitive behavior therapy* to include Ellis's approach, covert behavior therapies, and a variety of other techniques. Though there may be some doubt about whether cognitive and behavior therapies belong in the same category, there is no doubt that they are currently attracting a great deal of theoretical and research attention. According to one recent survey of trends in psychotherapy, cognitive behavior therapy is "one of the strongest, if not the strongest theoretical influence today" (Smith, 1982, p. 808).

Humanistic Therapy

In Chapter 12, we noted that the humanistic approach to personality emphasizes positive human qualities, such as the ability freely to pursue rational and spiritual goals. Similarly, **humanistic therapy** assumes that people who seek help in psychotherapy have the freedom and the capacity to choose their own goals and to fulfill their human potential. While the psychoanalyst tries to guide the patient to gain insight into motivation, and the behavior therapist attempts to modify the patient's behavior, the humanistic approach seeks a genuine encounter in which two human beings try to understand each other.

Humanistic therapy, first proposed in the early 1940s by Carl Rogers, has strongly influenced the development of psychotherapy to the present day. Rogers called his approach *client-centered therapy*. His use of the word *client* rather than *patient* emphasizes the essential dignity of the person who seeks help. Rogers also sometimes used the word *facilitator* instead of *therapist* to emphasize that clients are the real experts on themselves. The professional's goal is to facilitate progress, to make it easier for clients to find their own solutions.

Rogers's technique is also called **nondirective therapy** because, unlike many other therapists, he refused to tell people what to do or what to think. Instead of directing, Rogers tried to clarify feelings by rephrasing clients' statements and repeatedly asking the clients what they really believed and felt. This process usually focused on the present, rather than seeking the source of people's problems in childhood or the past.

At first, some people may be frustrated when the psychotherapist refuses to offer expert advice. In 1964, Carl Rogers was filmed in a half-hour interview with a divorced woman named Gloria who sought advice on what to tell her 9-year-old daughter about her own relationships with men. In this film (*Three Approaches to Psychotherapy*), Gloria repeatedly asks what she should do, and Rogers repeatedly asks Gloria what *she* thinks. Finally, after several direct questions, Rogers replies: "I feel that this is the kind of very private thing that I couldn't possibly answer for you. But I sure as anything will try to help you work toward your own answer" (Meador & Rogers, 1973,

CARL ROGERS (1902–1987)

Rogers developed humanistic psychotherapy and had a major influence on current approaches to mental health. He was raised in a religious fundamentalist atmosphere, which was opposed to such activities as smoking, drinking, playing cards, or expressing interest in sex. In a short autobiography, Rogers even recalled a "slight feeling of wickedness when I had my first bottle of (soda) 'pop' " (Rogers, 1961, p. 5).

He attended the University of Wisconsin to major in agriculture but switched first to religious studies and then to psychology. A strong believer in the basic goodness of every human being, Rogers went on to develop a "client-centered" approach to psychotherapy to provide a supportive atmosphere in which each person could find his or her own answers to any problem.

Humanistic therapists stress genuineness, unconditional positive regard, and empathy.

p. 161). Although it may seem frustrating at first, in the final analysis many people come to accept nondirective therapy that forces them to look inside themselves for the answers.

Rogers believed that to encourage personal growth, the psychotherapist must adopt three related attitudes: genuineness, unconditional positive regard, and empathy.

Genuineness refers to a real human relationship in which the therapist honestly expresses his own feelings. According to Rogers, if a therapist tries to manufacture phony concern or hide his or her own beliefs, ultimately this dishonesty can impede true personal growth. For example, at one point in their filmed encounter, Gloria says, "All of a sudden while I was talking to you, I thought, 'Gee, how nice I can talk to you and I want you to approve of me and I respect you, but I miss that my father couldn't talk to me like you are.' I mean, I'd like to say, 'Gee, I'd like you for my father.' " A psychoanalyst would not be able to resist analyzing this statement as a sign of transference. But Rogers does not interpret the statement in terms of some abstract theoretical system; rather, he treats this as a legitimate human expression of emotion and responds without pretense, "You look to me like a pretty nice daughter" (Meador & Rogers, 1973, p. 161).

Along with genuineness, Rogers insisted that a therapist must express *unconditional positive regard* by caring about all clients as persons, totally accepting them and their ability to solve their own problems. The therapist should not judge clients' worth by their behavior. Instead, he or she should recognize the essential dignity of each person and believe that the client is able to choose the best path. One therapist, who used this approach at a community center in a troubled Brooklyn neighborhood, described the challenge this way: "You try not to judge, because inevitably judging is rejecting"

humanistic therapy Therapy in which the therapist guides clients to find their own solutions.

nondirective therapy A type of humanistic therapy in which the therapist refuses to tell the client what to do or think.

(*Time,* 1985, p. 25). At times, this may be difficult. An observer noted that: "[These therapists] certainly don't love every one of their clients. It's hard to love wife batterers and child molesters. But they have this basic, nonjudgmental quality of acceptance" (*Time,* 1985, p. 23).

Finally, the therapist should have *empathy,* the ability to perceive the world as the client does. This should not be confused with sympathy. The therapist who says, "I'm sorry you feel insecure," may genuinely express a kind feeling, but that is not empathy. Empathy involves an attempt to "get inside the client's head" to try to understand fully why the client lacks security.

These three attitudes are very closely interrelated. To maintain a deep empathy for the moment-to-moment changes in another person's feelings, the therapist must accept and value the client; that is, empathy is best built on a foundation of unconditional positive regard. And the attitude of genuineness is the most basic of all, because a meaningful relationship demands that these feelings be honest and real.

An Eclectic Approach

A survey of the actual practices of clinical and counseling psychologists indicates that 41% of all clinicians do not identify themselves with a single theoretical orientation (Garfield & Kurtz, 1976; Smith, 1982). Instead, they take an **eclectic approach,** choosing different therapeutic techniques to meet the needs of different clients. An eclectic therapist might use systematic desensitization to treat a person with a phobia and client-centered psychotherapy to help a depressed executive find joy in his work. In fact, several different techniques might be used with the same patient to resolve different problems.

Along with various forms of psychotherapy that fall easily under one of the four theoretical orientations described here, eclectic therapists also employ "mixed models" that cut across theoretical boundaries. For example, there are many different types of **group therapy,** in which one or more therapists meet with several patients at the same time. Group therapy first became popular during World War II for a very practical reason: There were simply not enough therapists available to treat all the psychological casualties of wartime. However, many experienced therapists came to believe that group therapy had a number of advantages beyond efficiency. Patients provided their own form of therapy, subjecting one another to social pressures, learning how to interact effectively, and comforting one another with the knowledge that other people face similar problems.

Group therapy has grown rapidly in popularity and influence over the last few decades, and many different forms of group therapy have been developed. **Sensitivity training groups** (sometimes called T-groups) promote personal growth by encouraging participants to focus on their immediate relationships with others in the group. Their goals and techniques are closely related to the humanistic paradigm. A more behavioral approach is taken in **assertiveness training groups,** in which therapists demonstrate specific ways of standing up for one's rights and participants practice these behaviors. Many other types of group therapy are eclectic combinations that borrow techniques from several theoretical paradigms.

eclectic approach The use of different psychotherapeutic techniques to meet the needs of different clients.

group therapy Psychotherapy in which one or more therapists meet with several patients at the same time.

sensitivity training groups A form of group therapy that attempts to promote personal growth by encouraging participants to focus on their immediate relationships with others in the group.

assertiveness training groups A behavioral form of group therapy in which therapists demonstrate specific ways of standing up for one's rights and participants practice these behaviors.

Under the proper conditions, group therapy with several patients and one or more therapists can provide increased social support and other advantages over individual psychotherapy.

Another recent development is the growth of **family therapy**, in which all the members of a family meet together for psychotherapy. A family may enter therapy because one member appears to have behavioral or emotional problems, but family therapists often find that this problem is caused by, or aggravated by, patterns of interaction among all family members. Here, the goal is to improve the workings of the family unit as well as the functioning of individual members.

One of the key interests of family therapy is how family members handle issues of closeness and distance. Some family members may seek and offer closeness, reassurance, and support; others may emphasize separateness, independence, and autonomy. Struggles over the balance between these orientations is seen by some family therapists as one of the most important issues in marital and family relationships (e.g., Napier, 1978) and therefore one of the key issues to be addressed by the therapist.

In describing what family therapists do, Warburton and Alexander (1985) have described five phases to the therapist's work:

1. Create expectations for positive change within the family—for example, by establishing one's credibility as a therapist.
2. Gain understanding of the family—for example, by seeking and analyzing information about the family from family members.
3. Create a context for new definitions of the family—for example, by using relationship skills and interpersonal sensitivity.
4. Produce change—for example, by teaching family members better communication skills, time-out procedures, and relaxation techniques.

family therapy Group psychotherapy for all the members of a family.

5. Assist the family in maintaining the change in a way that is independent of the therapist's input—for example, by determining the appropriate time for termination of therapy and supporting the family's ability to operate independently of the therapist.

Think of your own family. You can probably recall conflicts you have had with your mom or dad over matters of independence. Perhaps you wanted more autonomy than they were willing to allow, or maybe they pushed you for greater independence than you felt ready to assume. Or there may have been disagreements between your parents over issues of closeness. Perhaps your mom argued that your dad should spend more time with the family or vice versa. Typically, such problems are worked through without the aid of a therapist; but sometimes it helps to have an objective outside person available to assist family members in addressing the issues.

Like other psychotherapies, the family therapy category can be further broken down into several theoretical approaches. Our point here is to emphasize that there are many different kinds of psychotherapy that clinicians use to treat different problems. Given this tremendous diversity, it is not surprising that the question of evaluating psychotherapy has proved to be complex and controversial.

Is Psychotherapy Effective?

For the first decades after Freud "invented" psychotherapy, few questioned its value or effectiveness. Therapists observed that many patients seemed to improve, and patients too seemed satisfied with the results. But in 1952, Hans Eysenck published a controversial article in which he argued that psychotherapy was "unsupported by any scientifically acceptable evidence" (p. 323).

Eysenck's basic idea was that many of the problems that bring people to therapy will disappear with the simple passage of time. Along with this type of spontaneous recovery, many psychotherapy patients may be helped by the power of suggestion or a placebo effect (see "Understanding the Scientific Method"). The fact that a therapy seems effective to both patients and doctors does not necessarily imply that it *is* effective (see "Becoming a Critical Consumer").

Previous studies had often claimed that psychotherapy worked because 50% or 60% or 70% of a particular group of patients improved by some criterion. Eysenck argued that such statistics could not prove anything until they were compared with the improvement rate for a control group of similar patients who did not undergo psychotherapy.

Eysenck located two studies of neurotics who did not receive any psychotherapy but whose problems were assessed over the course of several years. By his count, 72% of these people were classified as improved, much improved, or cured after one or two years in which they received no professional treatment. In other words, the ordinary steps people take to solve their problems—talking to friends, going on a vacation, or buying a hot tub—

Double-Blind Studies: Testing Drugs to Treat Schizophrenia

Throughout this text, we emphasize the fact that bias and expectations can influence observations of behavior. In medicine, this is seen in the *placebo effect:* A patient's condition may improve as a result of the expectation that a particular treatment would work rather than as a result of the treatment itself.

In the centuries before medicine became a modern science, folk healers and physicians treated diseases they did not understand with drugs made of crocodile dung, swine's teeth, flyspecks, powder of precious stones, and human perspiration (Shapiro, 1971). Despite the fact that these and other ingredients had no inherent medicinal value, the placebo effect kept physicians in business as some patients improved after swallowing these bizarre concoctions.

Modern drugs may also benefit from the placebo effect in that many patients will improve even if a drug has no specific effect on the illness for which it is prescribed. To compensate for this phenomenon, the actual therapeutic power of a drug is generally tested in a *double-blind study* in which the effects of expectations are minimized by keeping both subjects and experimenters ignorant of the precise treatment being tested. Some patients in a double-blind study of a drug would receive a placebo, while others would receive the drug to be tested; neither the patients nor their immediate physicians would know which drug they had received. Sometimes, for practical reasons, it is only possible to perform a single-blind study, in which patients do not know which drug they receive but their doctors do.

One of the most convincing studies of drug treatment of schizophrenia was a double-blind test comparing the drug Thorazine to a placebo (Cole, 1964). (Two chemically related drugs were also analyzed in this study. Their results were virtually identical to those for Thorazine. For simplicity's sake, however, we ignore them in this discussion.)

The patients in this study were newly admitted schizophrenics in nine different mental institutions. Each new patient was assigned a code number and was given drugs that came in number-coded containers several times a day for the next six weeks. All the pills looked the same, and the doctors and nurses who treated a particular patient did not know whether that person was receiving Thorazine or lactose, a sugar pill that served as the placebo.

At regular intervals, doctors, nurses, and ward attendants rated the behavior of each patient. Questionnaires and interviews permitted the assessment of 21 specific symptoms. In addition, each patient was regularly rated by staff members on a scale from 1 to 7 on the following general questions: "Considering your total clinical experience, how mentally ill is this patient at this time?" and "Compared to his condition at admission to the project, how much has he changed?"

The results were clear and unambiguous: 75% of the patients taking Thorazine were rated "much improved" or "very much improved," versus 23% of the placebo group. The placebo did seem to have some effect, but the Thorazine effect was much stronger. After six weeks of treatment, 16% of the schizophrenics who had received Thorazine were judged "normal," and another 30% were considered only "borderline mentally ill."

For 13 of the 21 specific symptoms measured in this study, the Thorazine

(box continues on next page)

group improved significantly more than the placebo group. For example, patients who received Thorazine were less confused, took better care of their physical needs, participated more in social activities, were less agitated and tense, had fewer auditory hallucinations and ideas of persecution, and had more coherent speech.

This experiment provided conclusive proof that Thorazine was effective in treating a broad range of schizophrenic symptoms. Double-blind studies of this sort can provide the most powerful test of the effectiveness of any new drug or medical treatment.

BECOMING A CRITICAL CONSUMER

Would You Believe Reincarnation Therapy?

One of the most difficult problems in evaluating the effects of psychotherapy is the fact that almost every type of therapy can point to the testimonials of patients who have been "cured." As you read the following account of one extremely unusual type of therapy, try to answer the following question: Does this patient's recovery prove the value of this unorthodox approach? (For an answer, see the discussion after the "Summary" at the end of this chapter.)

Nancy S., 33, a California writer, always had trouble finishing books and articles. But unlike most authors bedeviled by blocks, she now knows where her troubles began: in the 17th century. During a session with . . . a Los Angeles therapist, she had a vision of herself as a woman on trial in America in 1677 for heresy and trying to hide an incriminating diary from her inquisitors. Three hundred years later she was still "hiding the book." But no more. After . . . therapy she says: "I seem to have very little problem finishing up things now, as if the pattern were erased."

[Nancy S.] is one of many devotees of a growing fad known as "past-lives therapy." Essentially, its practitioners take a conventional Freudian idea—that much adult behavior is unconsciously guided by early traumas—and apply it to the concept of reincarnation. Although the treatment has had a following in the U.S. and Europe for at least 15 years, more and more Americans are experimenting with the notion that their psychological problems arose during previous existences as, say, Shinto priests, Roman guards, citizens of Atlantis or even another planet. (*Time,* October 3, 1977, p. 53)

were quite effective. Time may not heal all wounds, but in Eysenck's survey it helped 72% of them.

In contrast, the recovery rates in 24 studies of 8,053 neurotics who received psychotherapy were distressingly low. Eysenck computed recovery rates of 64% for eclectic psychotherapy and only 47% for psychoanalysis. Although noting several qualifications, Eysenck's conclusion was quite provocative: "There thus appears to be an inverse correlation between recovery and psychotherapy; the more psychotherapy, the smaller the recovery rate" (1952, p. 322).

Many psychotherapists were not thrilled to be told that all their professional efforts had been either ineffective or harmful. A lively controversy began, and it took nearly three full decades for the smoke to clear. Although Eysenck's criticisms are still quoted by critics of psychotherapy, most experts now agree that his conclusions have been disproved. A later review of the studies cited by Eysenck (Bergin, 1971) argued that he had underestimated the recovery rate among psychoanalytic patients and made a number of errors. More important, a large body of subsequent research (partly generated by Eysenck's challenge) indicates that psychotherapy does have positive effects.

One widely cited study (Sloane, Staples, Cristol, Yorkston, & Whipple, 1975) compared the effects of psychoanalysis and behavior therapy with improvement in a control group of people who were assessed in interviews and placed on a waiting list for later therapy but never received any treatment. The patients were 90 people who came to the Temple University Outpatient Clinic with a typical range of complaints. The therapists were all highly experienced and recognized as experts in either psychoanalysis or behavior therapy. Patients were divided into three groups of 30, matched for age, sex, and the severity of their problems, and randomly assigned to psychoanalysis, behavior therapy, or the waiting-list control group.

After four months, all three groups were assessed on a number of standard tests (such as the MMPI) and in interviews. Perhaps the most straightforward criterion for improvement was based on an interview by another clinician who did not know the patient or which group each belonged to. In the judgment of these unbiased observers, 80% of the psychoanalytic patients improved or recovered, along with 80% of the behavior therapy patients and 48% of the no-treatment group. Thus, the precise type of treatment did not seem to matter, but psychotherapy did make a difference for many individuals, at least over this time period.

Of course, no single study, no matter how well designed and executed, could be expected to resolve an issue of this complexity. The most compelling conclusions to date come from a review by Mary Lee Smith, Gene Glass, and Thomas Miller (1980) of 475 different studies that compare the effects of psychotherapy with a control group of some type. The criteria for improvement in these studies included ratings by both patients and clinicians of such characteristics as self-esteem, anxiety, and social competence, as well as more objective behavioral and physiological variables. Since many studies included more than one criterion of improvement, a total of 1,776 outcome measures were considered in this review.

Their overall conclusion was clear and unambiguous:

The evidence overwhelmingly supports the efficacy of psychotherapy. . . . Psychotherapy benefits people of all ages as reliably as schooling educates them, medicine cures them, or business turns a profit. (Smith, Glass, & Miller, p. 183)

These researchers also addressed the question of possible differences in the effects of psychoanalysis, behavior modification, client-centered therapy, and other approaches. They reported that all produced beneficial changes and asserted that the similarities between various schools of therapy are more important that the differences.

Given the long history of controversy surrounding the worth of psychotherapy, it is not surprising that others continued to disagree. Some questioned the conclusion that all therapies are equivalent. For example, Stiles, Shapiro, and Elliott (1986) argued that more detailed analysis of what occurs during therapy might reveal differences that are masked when one looks only at general-outcome measures. For example, patients with phobias might find behavioral or cognitive therapy more helpful than humanistic therapy. However, while calling for more research, they conclude (p. 175), "Although we know that psychotherapy works, we do not clearly understand how it works. Differently labeled therapies have demonstrably different behavioral contents, yet appear to have equivalent outcomes."

On a more fundamental level, Prioleau, Murdock, and Brody (1983) argued that Smith, Glass, and Miller's review had been rather indiscriminate in lumping together all the studies of this complex phenomenon, including many that were seriously flawed. They argued that the most revealing studies were those that directly compared psychotherapy with some type of "placebo treatment," such as a pill that had no medicinal value or a group discussion that was not aimed at therapy. They also excluded studies of behavior therapy, since they felt this therapy was fundamentally different from the more traditional "talking cures."

They reexamined the 475 studies considered by Smith, Glass, and Miller and found that only 32 met their far more stringent criteria. They reached the considerably more negative conclusion that psychotherapy was no more beneficial than placebo treatments. As Prioleau and her colleagues (1983, p. 284) summed it up: "Thirty years after Eysenck (1952) first raised the issue of the effectiveness of psychotherapy . . . and after about 500 outcome studies have been reviewed, we are still not aware of a single convincing demonstration that the benefits of psychotherapy exceed those of placebos for real patients."

When this article was published in the journal *The Behavioral and Brain Sciences,* it was accompanied by 23 commentaries by noted experts in the field, including Eysenck and Smith, Glass, and Miller. Unfortunately, it seemed that the major consensus was that there was still no consensus. A neutral observer of the controversy at that time would have most likely concluded that if psychotherapy does have important positive effects, these effects are hard to demonstrate in a way that would satisfy every skeptic. Perhaps a clearer picture would emerge if researchers focused more on the specific problem of what clients with what types of problems are best treated with what therapies.

electroconvulsive therapy A treatment for severe mental illness, usually depression, in which an electric current is passed through the brain.

Biological Therapies

An entirely different approach to treatment is based on a biological model that stresses the importance of brain processes in abnormal behavior. In Chapter 3, we discussed one such therapeutic technique: psychosurgery to alter thought and behavior patterns. Here we describe two other biological therapies—electroconvulsive therapy and drugs.

Electroconvulsive Therapy

Almost as controversial as psychosurgery is the concept of **electroconvulsive therapy,** a treatment for severe mental illness (particularly depression) in which an electric current is passed through the brain to produce a convulsion. In the 1930s, several researchers believed that schizophrenia and epilepsy were mutually exclusive diseases. Thus, they reasoned, the artificial induction of an epileptic-type seizure could relieve mental illness. Scientists now know that this theory is wrong. However, despite the disproof of its theoretical basis, and the lack of a widely accepted theory explaining why electroconvulsive therapy *should* work, it does seem to help some types of patients.

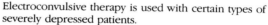
Electroconvulsive therapy is used with certain types of severely depressed patients.

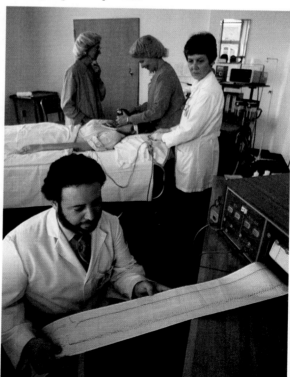

These days the patient is anesthetized and given various muscle-relaxing drugs to minimize the physical effects of the seizure. Electroconvulsive therapy typically begins by placing two electrodes on the right side of the head (the idea is to stimulate the right cerebral hemisphere because it is less involved in speech; electrodes might be applied to the left side of the head for left-handed patients whose right hemisphere controls language—see Chapter 3). An electric current of about 100 volts is then passed through the electrodes for a few fractions of a second to produce an epileptic-type convulsion. Typically, about ten treatments are given over a period of several weeks.

Later, the patient remembers nothing about the shock or the convulsion. After regaining consciousness, the person is likely to be somewhat confused and disoriented. There is also some loss of memory, particularly for events minutes before and after the treatment.

The controversy over electroconvulsive therapy was partly based on the side effects of more primitive techniques used in its early days. Anesthesia and drug treatment have now substantially reduced the risk of bruises and bone fractures, and electrical stimulation of only the nondominant hemisphere has reduced memory loss.

A review of 60 studies that evaluated the effects of electroconvulsive therapy (Scovern & Kilmann, 1980) concluded that it is the most effective treatment available for certain types of severely depressed patients, including those with bipolar disorders or a major depressive episode in late middle age. It is particularly useful for suicidal patients because it acts very quickly and thus reduces the risk that they will harm themselves. Its effects on some other conditions are more controversial, although it is now clear that electroconvulsive therapy is *not* useful in the treatment of anxiety or personality disorders.

According to the report of a special committee appointed by the American Psychiatric Association (1978) to study electroconvulsive therapy, a survey in the mid-1970s revealed that about two out of three American psychiatrists favored the use of electroconvulsive therapy with some patients, while the remaining third were generally opposed. However, only 2% of these psychiatrists felt that electroconvulsive therapy should never be used with any patient. After reviewing all available research data, this committee concluded that electroconvulsive therapy is an appropriate treatment for several specific patient groups, including severely depressed suicidal individuals who are a threat to themselves and violent patients who are a threat to others. In general, the committee recommended that electroconvulsive therapy be considered a treatment of last resort that should be attempted only when drugs do not work or cannot be used for medical reasons.

Drug Therapy

Of all the changes that have occurred in the treatment of mental illness over the past century, the single most influential event may have been the "drug revolution" that began in the mid-1950s. For nearly 100 years before that time, the number of patients in U.S. public mental institutions had slowly and steadily increased, at a rate of about 2% a year. In 1956, shortly after

TABLE 15.3

Drugs Commonly Prescribed for Mental Disorders

Mental disorder	*Drug type*	*Chemical group (common trade names)*
Schizophrenia	Antipsychotic	Phenothiazines (Thorazine, Stelazine, Mellaril)
		Butyrophenones (Haldol)
		Thioxanthenes (Taractan)
Depression	Antidepressant	MAO inhibitors (Nardil, Parnate)
		Tricyclics (Tofranil, Elavil)
Manic depression (some cases)	Mood regulators	Lithium carbonate (Lithium)
Anxiety	Tranquilizers	Dicarbamates (Miltown, Equanil, Soma)
		Benzodiazepines (Valium, Librium, Dalmane)

Note: Drugs listed here may also be prescribed for other conditions and purposes.

effective drugs became widely available, the patient population declined for the first time in modern history.

Despite the fact that the number of people being admitted to mental hospitals has risen steadily over the past decades, their average stay has shortened considerably. Consequently, the total number of patients confined in mental hospitals at any given time has declined dramatically since effective drugs were introduced into psychiatric practice.

Table 15.3 lists the major categories of drugs currently used to treat mental disorders. In this short overview, we discuss the first type of drug therapy to have a major impact: phenothiazine treatment of schizophrenia.

Although phenothiazines were first synthesized in 1883, it was only in 1952 that a French researcher reported that one member of the phenothiazine family, a drug now sold under the trade name Thorazine, reduced psychotic symptoms. The effects were so immediate and so dramatic that within a few years phenothiazine drugs were being used throughout the world to treat psychosis, particularly schizophrenia.

Phenothiazine drugs have wide-ranging effects; they reduce hallucinations, delusions, confusion, agitation, irritability, hostility, indifference, social withdrawal, and other psychotic symptoms. Their efficacy has been repeatedly demonstrated under the most carefully controlled conditions (see "Understanding the Scientific Method"). The widespread use of phenothiazines and related drugs has changed the very nature of mental institutions around the world. Physical restraint and straitjackets for violent patients were no longer necessary, and institutions were no longer expected to house most severely disturbed patients until they died.

However, the drug revolution has not abolished mental illness, and it has created some new problems of its own. Some patients are not helped by available drugs, and others improve only marginally. Many patients must continue to take the drug indefinitely to prevent the reappearance of psychotic symptoms. Even when the drug is maintained, relapses occur in about one out of every three patients (Davis, Gosenfeld, & Tsai, 1976). This is preferable

phenothiazine drugs A group of antipsychotic drugs that reduce hallucinations, delusions, confusion, agitation, social withdrawal, and other psychotic symptoms.

to the two out of three patients who relapse when taking placebos, but it indicates that many setbacks will occur with any form of treatment.

These figures also highlight our ignorance in another way. The one-third of patients who do *not* relapse when they take placebos obviously do not need to continue taking powerful drugs. However, there is currently no precise way to tell which patients need to continue taking antipsychotic drugs and which can get along without them.

On a theoretical level, the success of drug treatments has led many investigators to search for physiological causes and correlates of mental illness. As explained in Chapter 4, many drugs are believed to affect the brain and the body by influencing the action of neurotransmitters. There are several separate lines of indirect evidence that phenothiazines work by blocking drug receptors for the neurotransmitter dopamine (Berger, 1978). Since the technology does not yet exist for precisely charting neurotransmitter chemistry in the living human brain, this hypothesis must remain somewhat tentative.

You may remember that a lack of dopamine in the brain produces Parkinson's disease, a syndrome involving severe muscular tremors of the limbs, hands, neck, and face. Since phenothiazines block dopamine receptors, they often produce as a side effect muscle problems that resemble Parkinson's disease.

After long-term treatment with phenothiazines and chemically related drugs, about 15% of patients develop a similar syndrome called **tardive dyskinesia**, which produces frequent and involuntary muscle movements including lip-smacking, sucking, and chin-wagging motions. Aside from the social embarrassment, this syndrome can interfere with speech and eating.

Research continues with other drugs that can reduce psychotic symptoms without producing tardive dyskinesia. In the meantime, physicians must weigh the relative costs and benefits of phenothiazine treatment for each individual patient.

Motor problems are the most obvious side effect of phenothiazines, but these drugs may also lead to such disagreeable symptoms as grogginess, constipation, and dryness of the mouth. These side effects contribute to patients' unwillingness to continue to take the drugs on a long-term basis. Many patients now stay in mental hospitals until their psychotic symptoms have been controlled by drugs, then stop taking medication after they leave the institution, and eventually they are forced to return once more to the hospital. This revolving door effect is one of the most fundamental problems faced by mental-health workers who hope to help former patients establish themselves in their local communities.

Community Psychology

Beginning in the mid-1960s, a large number of psychologists became involved in trying to bring mental-health services directly into the community. This effort was not limited to serving the needs of former mental patients after their release; it included the potential to help every individual in our society to cope more effectively with a wide variety of problems in living. Before the community psychology movement, most clinical psychologists limited their

tardive dyskinesia A syndrome of involuntary muscle movements that occurs after long-term treatment with phenothiazines and chemically related drugs.

community psychologists Psychologists who have attempted to make mental-health services available to every U.S. citizen on a local level.

activities to diagnosing mental disorders and to treating problems with psychotherapy. But community psychologists assumed a far broader role: They established telephone hotlines to prevent suicide; they trained paraprofessionals to intervene in family crises; they evaluated correctional systems for prison and parole; they even organized rent strikes and demonstrations for public assistance. Thus, **community psychologists** have attempted to make mental-health services available to every person in their local communities.

The radical new approaches of community psychology, and its political activism, made this wide-ranging movement quite controversial. Here, we can only briefly describe three of the most important goals of this approach: providing mental-health services in local communities, training paraprofessionals, and preventing mental illness.

Mental-Health Services in Local Communities

In 1963, the Community Mental Health Centers Act provided federal funding for establishing one comprehensive mental-health care center for every community of 75,000 to 200,000 people in the United States. These centers were designed so that every citizen could receive mental-health care without leaving the community in which he or she lived and worked. Services were to include short-term hospitalization, therapy available on a walk-in basis, and 24-hour-a-day emergency services, such as counseling and suicide prevention.

This federal support and the new emphasis on a mental-health presence in the community helped lead to the development of many novel programs. For example, a number of rape crisis centers have been established to provide help for victims of sexual assaults. Professional and paraprofessional staff members, including some volunteers who have themselves been victims of rape,

Community centers provide support to battered women through professional therapists and paraprofessional staff.

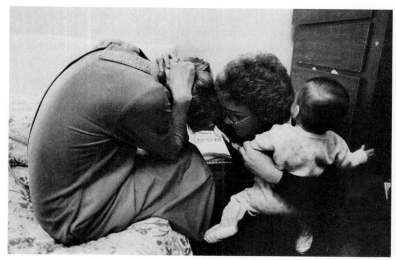

may accompany a woman to the hospital and the police station to provide medical and legal advice as well as emotional support.

But despite some notable success stories, community mental-health centers have generally failed to live up to their original promise. One very practical problem is money. The original idea was that these centers would become self-supporting, largely through insurance payments for patient services. But most of the people who came for help were poor and lacked the insurance or the personal funds to pay for the services they needed. Also, government support was reduced as national priorities shifted. By the mid-1970s, community mental-health centers were supposed to be established to meet the needs of the entire United States; in fact, centers were available to serve only about 40% of the U.S. population. Many of these were inadequately staffed and supported (Bassuk & Gerson, 1978).

One result of the failure of community mental-health centers is that former mental patients often face very unpleasant living conditions. Because of their psychiatric illnesses, they may lack the ability to obtain appropriate care. Sometimes they show up looking for help at hospital emergency rooms, but they often outnumber the available beds. An increasing number of deinstitutionalized mental patients reside in nursing homes (Shadish, 1984). Ironically, the environment of many nursing homes is similar to the institutions from which patients were released. Other individuals live in any available housing, and some remain homeless altogether.

In 1978, for example, about 40,000 chronically mentally ill patients lived in New York City. Only 424 of these lived in true halfway houses that provided a transition from the hospital to city life; about another 2,000 could be cared for in sheltered workshops. The remainder had been "dumped" by city agencies into whatever housing was available (Koenig, 1978).

In recent years, a number of efforts have been initiated to help the homeless mentally ill. The State Comprehensive Mental Health Services Plan Act of 1986, for example, authorized federal grants to states to establish community-based systems of care for the chronically mentally ill, and the Urgent Relief for the Homeless Act of 1987 authorized federal grants to states for mental-health services and for transitional housing for the homeless (Melton & Garrison, 1987).

Despite such efforts, providing mental-health services in local communities, while sound in theory, remains an elusive reality. Adequate financial support could improve matters considerably, but a true integration of mental patients into local communities would also require changes in social attitudes and the public's perception of mental illness. In the meantime, some experts have begun to wonder publicly whether certain chronic groups might be better off living in humane mental asylums.

Paraprofessionals

One chronic problem faced by community psychology is that there simply are not enough trained professionals to work with all the people who need help. One economical solution is to rely on **paraprofessionals**, mental-health workers with more limited training to perform specific tasks.

paraprofessionals Mental-health workers with limited training to perform specific tasks.

The de-institutionalization of mental patients has contributed to the problem of homelessness in many urban areas.

In one study (Lick & Heffler, 1977), college students were trained to teach certain relaxation techniques that have proved useful in the treatment of insomnia. One group of patients were taught the techniques by these paraprofessionals, while a second group of patients were taught the same techniques by a clinical psychologist. In this study, the professional and parapro-fessional therapists were equally successful in helping insomniacs to improve their sleep.

Some paraprofessionals have received far more intensive training to perform more complex tasks. Margaret Rioch (1967) supervised a carefully selected group of women who had given up their jobs after marriage for two years of training in mental-health counseling. Elaborate training of this sort may be almost as intensive as a professional-degree program.

Many community mental-health centers have recruited and trained local residents to perform interviews, home visits, and counseling. Because these paraprofessionals have an intimate knowledge of local problems, they may be particularly sensitive to the needs of clients. Further, studies of observational learning have revealed that models are perceived as more believable and relevant when they resemble learners in age and background (Rosenthal & Bandura, 1978).

A review of 42 studies that directly compared the effectiveness of professional and paraprofessional helpers found that the paraprofessionals consistently achieved well-defined clinical results that were equal to those of professionals, and in some cases even better (Durlak, 1979).

The issue of why paraprofessionals sometimes produce better results is a provocative one for research. Perhaps it results from their greater resemblance to patients, or a more careful selection of people whose personality traits are suited to a particular task, or greater enthusiasm and interest on the part of the paraprofessional. Whatever the answer proves to be, it may have important implications for the future training of mental-health professionals as well as the training of their assistants.

Prevention

By far the most ambitious goal of community psychology is the prevention of future cases of mental illness. This idea was first championed by none other than Clifford Beers, the turn-of-the-century mental patient whose experiences were described at the beginning of this chapter. The National Committee for Mental Hygiene, founded by Beers, was inspired partly by the victories of medical science over such diseases as typhoid and tuberculosis. They hoped to discover an analogous form of mental "inoculation" that could prevent people from becoming mentally ill in the first place.

In the 1960s, this goal was adopted by the community psychology movement. Several levels of prevention are possible. One type of program attempts to locate individuals who have a high risk of developing a disorder and then quickly provide help at an early stage. For example, the Primary Mental Health Project used various screening procedures to identify elementary school children with behavioral and educational problems. Paraprofessionals then worked with these children to develop new skills. The behavior of the children did indeed improve as a result (Cowen & Schochet, 1973).

Although there have been some successful programs at this level, the ultimate goal of community psychology is even more ambitious: to reduce the frequency of mental illness in society and, ultimately, eliminate it altogether. Many believe that such prevention must begin with political programs that will change the very nature of society and produce more equitable opportunities for all citizens.

Critics have charged that "community psychology's greatest failure is in the area where it sought its greatest success: primary prevention" (Bernstein & Nietzel, 1980, p. 459). The reason is not surprising to anyone who has studied abnormal psychology: At this time, psychologists simply do not know enough about mental illness and its causes to effectively prevent future cases from developing.

Depending on personal preference, one may choose cynically to emphasize the current failure or optimistically to view this challenge as a tremendous opportunity for future research. In either case, if you decide to go on to a career in mental health, there undoubtedly will be times when you are frustrated by the limitations of current knowledge and wish that psychology and psychiatry knew more. At such moments, it may be useful to remember the horrifying experiences of Clifford Beers in one of the best mental asylums in the United States in the year 1900. Today's institutions and therapies are certainly not perfect, but they are a tremendous improvement over some of the practices and beliefs that were common just a few decades ago.

Summary

A Brief History of Treatment

- At the end of the eighteenth century, Philippe Pinel proposed **moral therapy**, which treated mental disorders through kindness, understanding, and a pleasant environment.

- Ironically, following Pinel, calls for reform of the mental-health abuses led to hospitalization of more patients, and overcrowding led to chaotic conditions under which therapy was replaced by custodial care.

- Throughout the twentieth century, several groups of professionals have specialized in the treatment of mental disorders.

- **Psychiatry** is the medical specialty concerned with mental illness.

- In **clinical psychology** professionals are trained in psychological principles and research and apply this knowledge to the treatment of mental illness.

- **Counseling psychology** is a specialty closely related to clinical psychology that emphasizes problems in normal adjustment rather than abnormal function.

Psychotherapy

- In **psychotherapy**, a trained professional employs systematic psychological procedures to help a client change troublesome thoughts, feelings, and behavior patterns.

- Classical Freudian analysis attempts to provide **insight** into the unconscious forces that motivate behavior, in the belief that once these conflicts become conscious, a person can deal more effectively with reality.

- The most important therapeutic technique in Freudian analysis is **free association**, in which a patient reports every single thought as it comes to mind.

- **Resistance** is a patient's unconscious attempt to avoid therapeutic insights into motivation.

- **Transference** refers to some of the patient's strong positive or negative feelings toward the therapist—viewed by Freud as a repetition of emotions originally directed toward parent figures during the Oedipal period.

- **Interpretation** is the process by which the analyst gradually guides patients into an understanding of their thoughts and behavior.

- Contemporary analysis involves a more active role for the therapist and places more emphasis on external constraints and ego development.

- **Behavior therapy**, or **behavior modification**, applies scientific principles to alter observable behavior through learning.

- One example is **systematic desensitization**, which required an anxious person to imagine increasingly threatening situations while remaining deeply relaxed.

- In **counterconditioning,** relaxation becomes classically conditioned to the same stimuli that once elicited anxiety.

- Another application of behavior therapy teaches clients **self-control** by providing them with active coping strategies to deal with specific problems.

- **Cognitive therapy** tries to solve human problems by changing people's thought patterns.

- One example of cognitive therapy is Albert Ellis's system of **rational-emotive therapy,** which tries to teach people actively to avoid irrational thoughts that unpleasant events are tragic or catastrophic.

- **Humanistic therapy** seeks a genuine human encounter in which a therapist can help clients find their own solutions.

- For example, in Carl Rogers's **nondirective therapy,** the therapist refuses to tell the client what to do and instead tries to clarify the client's own feelings. This approach involves genuineness, unconditional positive regard, and empathy.

- Many therapists take an **eclectic approach** in which different therapeutic techniques are used to meet the needs of different clients.

- In **group therapy,** one or more therapists meet with several patients at the same time.

- In **sensitivity training groups,** sometimes called T-groups, therapists promote personal growth by encouraging participants to focus on their immediate relationships with others in the group.

- In **assertiveness training groups,** therapists demonstrate specific ways of standing up for one's rights, and participants practice these behaviors.

- In **family therapy,** all members of a family meet in a group for simultaneous counseling.

- Beginning in the 1950s, some researchers questioned whether people who received psychotherapy were more likely to improve than control groups who simply waited for their problems to be resolved. According to one extensive review of 475 different outcome studies, psychotherapy is indeed quite effective in changing behavior. However, there do not appear to be important differences in the effectiveness of different types of psychotherapy.

Biological Therapies

- In one biological treatment called **electroconvulsive therapy,** an electric current is passed through the brain to produce a convulsion and relieve depression and other mental disorders.

- Beginning in the mid 1950s, drug treatment substantially decreased the patient population in mental institutions.

- **Phenothiazine drugs** and other antipsychotic drugs reduce such psychotic symptoms as hallucinations, delusions, confusion, agitation, and social withdrawal. However, they do not "cure" mental illness; many patients must continue to take maintenance doses indefinitely. Unfortunately, many of the drugs produce serious side effects.

- **Tardive dyskinesia**, characterized by frequent involuntary muscle movements, appears in about 15% of long-term users of phenothiazines and chemically related drugs.

Community Psychology

- **Community psychologists** have attempted to make mental-health services available to every U.S. citizen on a local level.

- **Paraprofessionals** are mental-health workers with limited training to perform specific tasks. Outcome studies have revealed that in some settings, paraprofessionals are at least as effective as professional therapists.

Critical Thinking Exercise Discussion

Would You Believe Reincarnation Therapy?

The answer is no. The positive effect on the woman whose writer's block was removed could equally well be accounted for by the placebo effect, expectations, or the simple passage of time.

Past-lives therapy is likely to strike many people as so outrageous that they will be skeptical of this patient's claims. But would you be equally skeptical if a friend told you that his anxiety was cured by taking massive doses of vitamin E or if you saw a celebrity on TV who said her therapist had cured her of alcoholism?

As noted in the text, systematic research has revealed that psychotherapy has positive effects. But the critical consumer is skeptical of the conclusions of a small number of satisfied customers. Such testimonials may only prove, as an expert said in the same *Time* article, "Suckers are born every minute and customers can be found for anything."

SOCIAL PSYCHOLOGY

Chapter 16

On March 13, 1964, Kitty Genovese arrived home from work about 3:20 A.M. She parked her red Fiat in a lot about 100 feet from her apartment house in a quiet residential neighborhood in Queens, New York. As she walked toward her door, she noticed a man suspiciously standing in her path. She stopped, turned, and first walked, then ran, toward a streetlight. The man chased her and caught up quickly. He jumped on her back and stabbed her four times.

Genovese screamed, "Oh, my God, he stabbed me! Please help me! Please help me!" Several lights went on in the 10-story apartment building opposite the scene of the attack. One neighbor opened a window on one of the upper floors and yelled down, "Let that girl alone!"

The assailant hurried back to his car, and Genovese staggered away. But, the attacker later reported, "I had a feeling this man would close his window and go back to sleep, and sure enough he did."

Moments after the first stabbing, Genovese had only managed to round the corner a few yards away. The attacker quickly caught up and stabbed her again. Genovese screamed, "I'm dying. I'm dying." Again windows were opened and lights went on. This time, the assailant went to his car and drove away.

Genovese crawled to the entryway of her apartment house but didn't have the strength to open the door. A few minutes later the man returned for a third attack. He looked for his victim through the windows of a coffee shop and a railroad station and tried the doors of several apartment houses. Finally, he found Genovese lying on the floor. He stabbed her again until she was quiet, then sexually molested her. During this final fatal attack, the killer later reported that he "heard the upstairs door open at least twice, maybe three times."

Finally, 30 minutes after the first attack, a neighbor called the police. They arrived within minutes, but Kitty Genovese was dead and the killer had escaped.

The police later concluded that parts of the attack had been witnessed by at least 38 neighbors. The man who actually called the police later explained that he had done so only after telephoning a friend for advice and then going to the apartment of another neighbor to convince her to call so that he wouldn't get involved (Gansberg, 1964, p. 38; *Time,* June 26, 1964, p. 22).

The tragic story of the death of Kitty Genovese became a national scandal as the experts debated the reasons for her neighbors' callous indifference. Some editorial writers saw the event as a sign of alienation or moral decay; others claimed that it proved that urban life had dehumanizing effects. One group of experts—social psychologists—avoided such facile explanations and empty slogans; instead, they set out to perform systematic studies (described later in this chapter) to identify the causes of this disturbing event.

Why did social psychologists consider the Kitty Genovese case to fall into their domain of expertise? **Social psychology** studies the way people respond to other human beings and how they interact with one another. The focus is generally on individuals and how they are affected by particular social situations.

As this definition implies, the problems studied by social psychologists are also of interest to experts in other fields, particularly sociology. In general, sociologists take a somewhat different approach, studying groups, such as the family or a political party, as self-contained units.

The first research in social psychology was published in 1898, when Norman Triplett reported several studies suggesting that people performed a task better when they were in direct competition with others than when they worked alone. The first social psychology texts appeared about ten years later, but much of this early work was speculative rather than empirical in nature.

In World War II, many psychologists began to do research on practical questions in applied social psychology, such as how to motivate groups to work together, how to identify potential leaders, and how to influence public opinion and morale. This research on social processes generated tremendous enthusiasm and stimulated interest in the field of social psychology.

As we have emphasized throughout this text, human behavior and experience are complex issues. This complexity will become even more evident in this chapter as we consider social psychologists' attempts to understand how people interact with each other. We will discuss social psychological research under three main headings: cognition, influence, and relationships.

The study of social cognition and the way we understand the world has become very prominent in the last few years as part of the more general trend in psychology toward an interest in cognitive phenomena. Because this research has been so broadly influential, some topics in social cognition have been covered elsewhere in this text. For example, Chapter 2 described how expectations can influence the way we perceive other people and how

social psychology The study of the way people respond to other human beings and how they interact with one another.

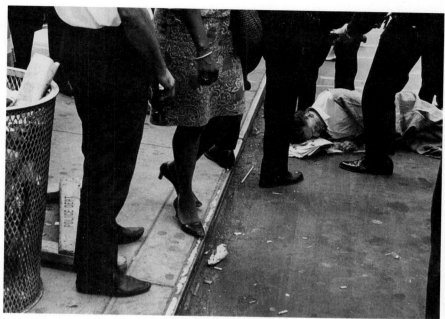

One topic studied by social psychologists is the way people respond to each other in a contemporary urban environment.

these perceptions can in turn affect behavior through self-fulfilling prophecies. In this chapter, we provide a theoretical context for understanding these phenomena in greater detail.

There has also been keen interest in social influences on human interaction. This area first became prominent in the 1940s and 1950s when research was done to determine how propaganda changes attitudes. Social psychologists have used this information as a foundation for trying to understand how people influence one another's attitudes and behavior to conform to social norms or obey the orders of an authority figure.

The chapter concludes with an overview of some of the processes involved in social relationships. This discussion examines studies of the factors involved in intimate relationships—both platonic and sexual; of altruism and aggression in human relationships; and finally of the way people behave in social groups.

Our review of research on this wide range of topics shows how social psychology is beginning the 1990s with a renewed respect for the complexity of social behavior and a continuing commitment to a systematic and empirical approach.

Social Cognition

social cognition The process of interpreting and understanding human behavior and feelings.

Social cognition is the process of interpreting and understanding human behavior and feelings. It includes our attempts to try to bring order into a confusing world by inferring motivation from behavior, that is, by trying to interpret the actions of the people we meet. In this way, we form perceptions and develop informal theories about others, and even about ourselves.

When we discussed the process of perceiving physical objects in Chapter 5, we saw how the human brain actively constructs a coherent mental image from incomplete and sometimes ambiguous information. Similarly, social perception and social cognition are active mental processes that involve making inferences and drawing conclusions.

But social perception is more complicated than object perception, because the observer is called on to draw many more conclusions: What is the person feeling? What are her intentions? What is she really like? Are her actions based on inner traits ("That's the way she is") or on the social situation ("I'd do the same thing in her shoes")?

Suppose you are a college freshman meeting your roommate for the first time. No doubt you will form a quick impression based on the immediate information you receive—for example, whether she comes from California or New York; acts friendly and warm or aloof and unpleasant; is dressed in a way that would please your mother or shock your wildest friend. Even her college major—art, pre-law, nursing, psychology—may influence your initial impression.

We all have a need to understand other people and to predict how they will act. In the case of your new roommate, your judgment about what kind of person she is will affect the way you interact with her. As our previous discussion of self-fulfilling prophecies (see Chapter 2) implies about situations like this one, if you decide that your roommate is a nice person and that you probably have a lot in common, you will be more likely to be friendly and helpful. On the other hand, if you find her rude and unpleasant, you might treat her in a similar manner. Thus, perceptions are likely to influence your treatment of her and, in turn, her treatment of you. Social psychologists who have studied the factors that influence judgments of this sort have developed a number of **attribution theories** that explain how people interpret and understand behavior in social situations.

Attribution Theory

In 1958, Fritz Heider provided the first theoretical framework for explaining how we make attributions about the behavior of others. In the book *The Psychology of Interpersonal Relations,* he explored the way people use common sense to try to understand and explain the events of everyday life. For Heider, the ordinary person was a "naive psychologist," collecting as much information as possible about causes for behavior and then arriving at logical conclusions.

When we make judgments about the behavior of others, Heider believed, we first determine the relative importance of internal or personal factors versus external or environmental factors. For example, if the new waiter at your favorite restaurant is extremely friendly, you might decide he is a cheerful person (internal) or that he has just received a great tip from someone (external).

Or suppose that a friend of yours is a marathon runner. With your encouragement, she has entered the world-famous Boise, Idaho, marathon

attribution theories Social-perception theories that describe how people interpret and explain behavior in everyday life.

Attribution theory explains how people interpret everyday events such as winning or losing a race.

and you are there to cheer her on. At the 24-mile mark, only 2 miles short of finishing, she drops out. How do you interpret this behavior?

Using Heider's dichotomy between internal and external factors, you would make judgments about both factors. On the internal side, you know your friend was highly motivated. You also know she has the ability, since you've seen her run marathon distances before. Maybe she just didn't exert herself enough. But you also consider the external factors: The temperature was almost 90 degrees that day, and the humidity was high; in fact, many good runners were dropping out all along the route. So you decide that the circumstances for this marathon weren't right.

Much of our behavior is affected by both internal and external factors. But when we make judgments about others, we rely on the factors that seem most important at the time. When the heat is unbearable, you will consider the weather important; when it is pleasantly cool, you are unlikely to focus on this factor.

Other theorists have extended Heider's ideas. Jones and Davis (1965) developed the model of **correspondent inferences**, which holds that we try to explain the behavior of others by finding correspondences between what we see of their behavior and what we infer about their intentions. Thus, we assume that both the behavior and the intentions represent underlying qualities or dispositions in the other persons. We "explain" the behavior by assuming that it corresponds to these inner qualities.

Suppose you have been waiting in line at a movie theater for 30 minutes to see *Rocky XII*. As the line finally starts to move, you see a couple break into line a few feet in front of you. You will probably decide that they are impatient and pushy, and perhaps deserve the death penalty. When you get to the popcorn line and see them again, you will probably expect them to further prove their subhuman status by pushing ahead again. Thus, you infer that their behavior in line reflects a basic disposition and that their future actions will correspond to this disposition.

According to Jones and Davis, when observers try to identify these underlying qualities, they are particularly likely to focus on *noncommon effects*. If behavior in a situation is normal, we learn less about people than we would if their behavior was unusual. In the example above, you had no basis for making inferences about the people who waited in line with you. But the people who behaved differently, who acted in an uncommon fashion, gave you more information for making inferences about them. Other cues we use to obtain information about people include our prior expectations, the social role of the person, how socially acceptable and appropriate the behavior is, and whether it is done by choice.

Harold Kelley (1967) further expanded attribution theory to explain how people decide whether behavior is due to internal or external causes. He used the term **covariation principle** to refer to the fact that people assume causal relationships between events and behaviors that occur together, or "covary." Thus, if you see a person start sneezing whenever there is a cat in the room and stop sneezing whenever the cat leaves, you will assume that the behavior (sneezing) covaries with the event (location of the cat).

Kelley also identified the **discounting principle**, which says that behavior is not attributed to a cause if there are more plausible alternatives. For example,

correspondent inferences A model holding that people try to explain behavior by finding correspondences between what is seen of behavior and what is inferred about intentions.

covariation principle The fact that people assume causal relationships between events and behaviors that occur together, or "covary."

discounting principle The fact that behavior is not attributed to a cause if there are more plausible alternatives.

suppose everyone in your accounting class gets an A on the first exam. You might wonder if, by some strange coincidence, you are in a class of very bright people. But you also have heard rumors that this professor always makes the first exam easy. So you discount the internal explanation (high intelligence) in favor of the external one (easy exam).

As we saw in Chapter 2, commonsense analyses often lead to incorrect results. Our personal biases and beliefs interfere with accurate judgments. Research has consistently demonstrated the frequency of the **fundamental attribution error**: Observers consistently underestimate the power of external forces that influence others' behavior and overestimate the importance of internal personal dispositions. (See Chapter 12.)

The fundamental attribution error is most common when we are explaining the behavior of other people. When it comes to evaluating our own behavior, however, we are likely to attribute successes to internal dispositions and failures to external factors. Thus, when we perceive ourselves, we are more likely to blame outside situations for problems and take credit for successes. The general tendency to see ourselves favorably is called the **self-serving bias**. For example, when students get exams back, those who have done poorly are likely to criticize the test. Those who have done well assume the exam was a good one and take personal credit for getting a good grade (Davis & Stephan, 1980).

In another study of how strong this effect is in a real-world setting, Lau and Russell (1980) analyzed newspaper accounts of baseball and football games for the attributions of coaches, players, and fans. They too found evidence for the self-serving bias: Winners were more likely to attribute their wins to internal factors, while losers talked about external factors more often. For example, after the Dodgers lost one game to the Yankees, Dodger Ron Cey was quoted as saying: "I think we've hit the ball all right. But I think we're unlucky" (Lau & Russell, 1980, p. 32).

This overview of attributions and errors in social cognition is relevant to some of the Chapter 2 material on common sense. There, we saw that expectations and bias often influence perception, as in the case of the Dartmouth and Princeton fans who saw the same football game in very different ways. Stereotypes can also change what people remember, as when the childhood of the fictional character Betty K. was described as tranquil by people who thought she was heterosexual and stormy by people who thought she was homosexual. People also tend to be overly influenced by vivid, concrete information, as in the example of the smoker who was convinced that cigarettes are not dangerous because he knew one three-pack-a-day man who lived to be 86.

Another common error results from the **expectancy bias effect**. People with different expectations about someone else may observe the same behavior, and yet they will interpret the actions to match their initial expectations. For example, Darley and Gross (1983) showed Princeton University students a videotape of a fourth-grade girl performing an academic task. Some were led to believe she was from a lower-class background, and others thought she was middle class. Then they were asked to rate her ability. Those who had been told that the child was from a lower-class background gave lower ratings on ability than those who were told the child came from a middle-class home.

fundamental attribution error The tendency to underestimate the power of external forces that influence others' behavior and overestimate the importance of internal dispositions.

self-serving bias The general tendency to see ourselves favorably.

expectancy bias effect The tendency of people with different expectations about someone else to interpret the same behavior differently to match their initial expectations.

By gaining an understanding of these phenomena and of attribution theory, we may begin to improve our social perceptions and avoid the most common pitfalls of common sense.

Research on attribution theory has provided useful information about how we interpret the behavior of others and ourselves. Their findings reinforce a theme that we introduced at the beginning of the book: Common sense can sometimes lead to errors of judgment.

Impressions

The final topic in our brief review of social cognition concerns the way we form or modify our impressions of others. Research indicates that we often form impressions of people on the basis of small fragments of data. In one classic study (Kelley, 1950), college students were given brief written descriptions of a guest instructor before he began teaching. Half the written statements described the man as a "rather cold" person, while the other half said that he was "very warm." These casually constructed first impressions strongly influenced the way students evaluated his teaching. Although both groups sat through the same class, those who had been told that the teacher would be warm rated him as less formal and more considerate, sociable, popular, and humorous. More important, they actually treated him differently: 56% of the students who expected a warm teacher participated in class discussions, versus 32% of those who expected him to be cold.

The two men pictured below provide another example of how our impressions of others can affect our treatment of them. Which man would you lend $100 to? Most people would probably pick the man in the suit and tie, because he looks more respectable and reliable. Of course, he may have

How important is physical appearance? For instance, which man would you lend money to?

Reading Body Language

Several guidelines are available to reading the nonverbal messages unconsciously sent by body language. As you read this short selection from *How to Read a Person Like a Book* (Nierenberg & Calero, 1972), evaluate the quality of the evidence on which the claims are based. Should you believe it? (A brief discussion appears after the "Summary" at the end of this chapter.)

> We have observed in our recordings that quite frequently during the stage of the negotiation when issues are being presented and discussed or when a heated argument is taking place, one or both of the negotiators have their legs crossed. . . . We observed that the number of negotiations where settlements were reached increased greatly when both negotiators have uncrossed their legs and moved toward each other. In our recordings of such confrontations, we cannot recall one situation that resulted in a settlement where even one of the negotiators still had his legs crossed. Individuals who cross their legs seem to be the ones who give you the most competition and need the greatest amount of attention. In further verification, we discussed the crossed-leg, leaning-away position with numerous salesmen. None could recall being able to close a sale with the prospect in that position. If crossed legs are coupled with crossed arms, you really have an adversary. (pp. 49–50)

put on a tie because he is posing as an insurance salesman to cheat a 69-year-old widow out of her life savings. And the other fellow may actually be a suburban dentist with three children who likes to sit around in an undershirt sipping beer on weekends. In reality, the two photos show the same man in different situations. Despite the fact that impressions can be quite misleading, they often influence the way we treat people and the way they treat us in return.

PHYSICAL APPEARANCE

Although the cliché warns us not to judge a book by its cover, research suggests that much of the time we do judge others primarily by their physical appearance. For example, people who wear glasses are frequently considered more intelligent, reliable, and industrious than those who don't wear them (Manz & Lueck, 1968). Similarly, obese teenaged girls were judged to be less disciplined and more self-indulgent than girls of normal weight (De Jong, 1977). In another study, bearded college students were perceived as more masculine, mature, self-confident, dominant, courageous, and liberal (Pellegrini, 1973)—not to mention hairier.

One factor that is especially influential in shaping impressions is physical attractiveness. In one typical study (Dion, Berscheid, & Walster, 1972), college students were asked to rate the personal characteristics of photographs of people who had been classified by other judges as physically attractive, unattractive, or average. The attractive people were perceived as happier, more successful, having a better personality, and more likely to get married.

This bias against "uglies" extends to children. In one study (Dion, 1972), women were asked to evaluate the actions of various children who had misbehaved. In some cases, the written account was accompanied by a photograph of an attractive child; other adults read the same account but saw a picture of a less attractive child. The women tended to make excuses for the attractive children and blame the unattractive ones.

Although this positive bias for physically attractive people has now been observed by many researchers, there is one fascinating exception: It may not apply to American blacks. In a study of 662 elementary school children, Muruyama and Miller (1981) found that among whites and Mexican-Americans, physically attractive children (identified by raters who did not know them) were indeed likely to be rated more favorably by interviewers, teachers, parents, and peers. But this was not true for black children; physical attractiveness did not lead to higher ratings on other qualities. These cultural differences could also be seen in the children's concepts of themselves; self-esteem was highest among the most physically attractive children for whites and Mexican-Americans but not for blacks. If this finding is replicated, it may provide fascinating insights into cultural differences between these groups. In the next section, a comparable difference in the nonverbal behavior of blacks and whites serves to remind us of the complexity of social stimuli; they never act in a vacuum but always derive their meaning from a particular context.

NONVERBAL BEHAVIOR

Ordinarily, our conscious communication with other people is based on language. But nonverbal cues help to form impressions; how close another person stands or whether she looks you in the eye, lightly touches your arm, gestures, or maintains a certain posture.

Although some authors have published dictionaries of body language describing what many different postures and gestures "really mean" (see "Becoming a Critical Consumer"), these systems are more often based on creative imagination than on factual research. Like words themselves, nonverbal cues may have many different meanings depending on the precise context.

One form of nonverbal behavior that has been extensively studied involves gaze and eye contact. In a number of situations, people who avert their gaze and fail to look others in the eye are perceived as more formal, nervous, or less friendly (LeCompte & Rosenfeld, 1971). But in religious confession and some types of psychotherapy, eye contact may be avoided to minimize embarrassment.

The impression created by eye contact may depend not just on the physical situation but also on what is being said. During interviews about pleasant matters, interviewers who looked the subject right in the eye received more positive ratings. But when the same interviewers raised unpleasant topics, more eye contact led to less positive ratings (Ellsworth & Carlsmith, 1968).

Further, the meaning of eye contact can vary for different social groups

Gazing into another's eyes is often a nonverbal sign of attraction, as in this scene from the film *Fatal Attraction.*

and sometimes can create misunderstandings. LaFrance and Mayo (1976) compared the gaze patterns in conversations between two white people or two black people in such natural settings as cafeterias, fast-food outlets, and airport waiting rooms. They found that whites tended to look at their conversational partner as they listened, while blacks tended to look away while listening.

Some disturbing implications of this cultural difference emerged when they went on to film an extended conversation between a black graduate student and a white corporation executive. As in earlier studies, the white person tended to look at his partner when he listened and look away when he spoke. But the black participant did just the opposite. As a result, when the white speaker paused and looked directly at the black, this nonverbal cue to take over the conversation was sometimes misinterpreted and both remained silent. Similarly, when the black speaker paused and stared at his partner, sometimes both began to speak at once. In this case, cultural differences in the meaning of nonverbal cues produced some uncomfortable moments that interfered with communication.

In an unusual study of nonverbal behavior in the real world, Mullen et al. (1986) examined the facial expressions of network newscasters (Peter Jennings, Dan Rather, and Tom Brokaw) during their coverage of Reagan's and Mondale's 1984 presidential campaigns. They found one important difference: Peter Jennings had more positive facial expressions when talking about Reagan. A few months later, the researchers surveyed people in different parts of the United States to find out whom they had voted for and which network news show they had watched most often (if any). They found that those who had watched Peter Jennings on ABC were more likely to have voted for Reagan. Whether Jennings himself or his positive expressions influenced voters' choices is not clear. However, the study provides a vivid example of the important issues raised by social cognition research and the implication that we need to pay more attention to the way we form our opinions and beliefs.

Social Influence

What is the best way to persuade a friend to accompany you to a Swedish film about alienation instead of going bowling? How can you convince a potential employer that you are the best woman for the job? How do advertisers motivate us to buy a particular brand of snow tires?

One of the most important themes in social psychology is the study of how people influence one another. Much of this research has focused on the nature of attitudes—how they are first formed and how they can later be changed.

Attitudes

An **attitude** can be defined as a relatively lasting tendency to react to a person, object, or event in a particular way. This reaction includes three major components: cognitive, affective, and behavioral tendencies. The *cognitive component* involves intellectual beliefs, such as the idea that a mango is a tropical fruit. The *affective component* involves emotional evaluations, as when you like tropical fruit. Finally, an attitude involves a *behavioral component,* such as being likely to order the mango cocktail in a fruit bar.

All three components—cognitive, affective, and behavioral—must be present in an attitude. In contrast, psychologists use the word *belief* to refer to information that does not have affective implications. For example, the conclusion that the human eye can distinguish between 7.5 million different colors (see Chapter 5) is a belief. Whether this belief is factually correct or not, most people are not likely to get too upset if someone else came along to argue that the eye can really only see 6.4 million different colors.

The relationships of the three components of attitudes can be quite complex. Social psychologists have been particularly interested in the extent to which behavior can be predicted from emotional feelings and cognitive beliefs.

One of the first researchers to tackle this problem was a psychologist named LaPiere (1934), who was interested in the nature of prejudice. In the 1930s, many Americans were prejudiced against Orientals. When LaPiere went on a cross-country tour with a Chinese couple during this period, he kept notes about the service at 66 hotels and 184 restaurants they went to. During the entire vacation, only one establishment refused to serve the Chinese couple. But when LaPiere sent a questionnaire to these very same hotels and restaurants, 92% of the 128 places that responded said that they would not serve Chinese guests. Clearly, there was a tremendous discrepancy between intolerant attitudes and tolerant behavior.

Psychologists now know that the strength of the relationship between verbal attitudes and overt behavior varies with such factors as the strength

attitude A relatively lasting tendency to react to a person, object, or event in a particular way.

of the attitude, its relevance in a particular situation, and the length of time between the attitude and behavior measurements. For example, Davidson and Jaccard (1979) interviewed 244 married women about their attitudes toward birth control, then interviewed them again two years later about their own behavior. Actual use of birth control pills was only very weakly correlated (see Chapter 2) with general attitudes toward birth control ($r = .08$). However, the correlation was much higher when the question asked specifically about attitudes toward birth control pills ($r = .32$). And an even more specific question about using birth control pills during the next two years was most strongly correlated with behavior ($r = .57$). Thus, when questions were phrased so that they related specifically to the particular behavior, the relationship was quite strong.

Among the types of attitudes that have interested social psychologists most profoundly are biased attitudes, or prejudices (prejudgments based on little or no information about something). Social psychologists have studied **prejudices**—specifically hostile, negative feelings toward individuals based solely on their group membership—toward a variety of groups, including various racial and ethnic groups, females, the elderly, and the handicapped.

One group of researchers from the University of California at Berkeley (Adorno, Frenkel-Brunswik, Levinson, & Sanford, 1950) began an important study of prejudice in the 1940s. One of their principal goals was to understand the pervasiveness of the anti-Semitism that emerged in Nazi Germany. How, they wondered, could the masses of people in Germany tolerate the extermination of their fellow citizens? And could the same thing happen in the United States? Through the years, considerable evidence has amassed (Cherry & Byrne,

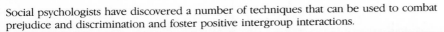

Social psychologists have discovered a number of techniques that can be used to combat prejudice and discrimination and foster positive intergroup interactions.

1976) demonstrating that strongly held prejudices are a characteristic of the *authoritarian personality* (Adorno et al., 1950). Authoritarian individuals see the world in terms of black-white, good-bad, we-they. They have strongly antidemocratic feelings and opinions and are characterized by strongly conservative political, economic, and social convictions. Research results indicate that they also tend to be highly prejudiced in general and anti-Semitic in particular.

Another approach to prejudice views prejudices as reflections of social norms and people's tendency to form groups on the basis of perceived similarity (van den Berghe, 1981). One implication of this link between social norms and prejudices is that if norms can be changed, it may be possible to reduce prejudices. For example, segregation of public schools on the basis of race was made illegal by the famous *Brown v. Board of Education of Topeka* (1954) Supreme Court case. That decision was followed, in turn, by at least some attitudinal change among whites who developed a more favorable attitude toward blacks (Middleton, 1976). Deliberate efforts to have Chicano, black, and white elementary school students cooperate on assignments have also been somewhat successful in producing positive intergroup interactions.

Persuasion and Attitude Change

Social psychologists' interest in bringing about change is not limited to the effort to modify social norms. Considerable emphasis has also been placed on the process of attitude change. Four centuries before Christ, Aristotle identified three ways an effective speaker could be persuasive: by convincing his listeners he was credible, by stirring the emotions of his audience, or by the speech itself. When social psychologists began systematically to study attitude change nearly 24 centuries later, they focused on these same three factors: the *source,* the *audience,* and the *message.*

The most influential figure in pioneer research on persuasion was Carl Hovland, a psychologist who was assigned during World War II to study ways to maintain military morale. Table 16.1 provides an overview of the major factors Hovland and later researchers (Zimbardo, Ebbeson, & Maslach, 1977; Middlebrook, 1980) found to be important. Here, we focus on some typical studies to provide a concrete feeling for the nature of this research.

FEAR-INDUCING MESSAGES

In everyday life, people often try to persuade others by inducing fear. The minister who tells the congregation that sinners will burn in hell, the parent who threatens to cut off a child's allowance, and the drug agency that tells us that crack kills all assume that these fears will affect attitudes and behaviors.

Not surprisingly, researchers have learned that the effects of a threatening message depend in part on other variables. In one study (Dabbs & Leventhal, 1966), several groups of college students were warned about the seriousness of tetanus and urged to get inoculations. Subjects in the high-fear condition heard vivid, explicit, and frightening descriptions of the disease. A milder

prejudices Prejudgments based on little or no information about something.

TABLE 16.1

How to Be Convincing

The following general guidelines are based on a large body of systematic research on the process of attitude change (Zimbardo, Ebbesen, & Maslach, 1977; Middlebrook, 1980). As explained in the text, more precise predictions are possible from the interactions between several variables.

For maximum effect, the *source* of a message should:

1. Be perceived as having expertise (relevant knowledge and judgment).
2. Be perceived as trustworthy (unbiased).
3. Be perceived as likable and powerful.
4. Begin by expressing views that agree with those of the audience.

For maximum effect, the *message* should:

1. Repeat important arguments.
2. Invoke fear only if explicit action is recommended that is guaranteed to reduce unpleasant consequences.
3. Support a position that is *moderately* different from that of the audience.

For maximum effect, the message should be tailored to the *audience*.

1. Present only one side of an argument if the audience is basically in agreement and will not soon hear a speaker for the other side; present both sides of the argument if the audience disagrees substantially with the speaker or will soon hear the other side from someone else.
2. Simple messages are more likely to convince audience members low in self-esteem; complex messages are more likely to convince audience members high in self-esteem.
3. Draw explicit conclusions for most audiences; if the audience is very intelligent, let them draw their own conclusions.
4. Direct arguments at the reasons this particular audience holds an attitude.

description of the physical problems produced low fear for another group. The results were extremely clear-cut: The high-fear message produced more attitude change regarding tetanus shots, and more people from the high-fear group actually went to the college health service and received inoculations.

However, other studies have revealed that if the message unintentionally produces a feeling of vulnerability, people may be "paralyzed by fear" and actually be less likely to change their attitudes or take action to cope with the threat (Leventhal, 1970). To be effective, a threatening message must provide strong evidence that very unpleasant consequences are likely, as well as concrete recommendations for action that will almost certainly avoid these consequences. In other words, if a fire-and-brimstone preacher overdoes it and makes people feel that they are almost certainly going to hell, many may become worse sinners as a result.

AUDIENCE SELF-ESTEEM

One of the most important personality characteristics known to be related to persuasion is **self-esteem**, the value one places on one's own worth. According to McGuire (1968), because people with low self-esteem are less confident of their own abilities, they tend to yield more easily to other people's arguments.

self-esteem The value one places on one's own worth.

Mark Waters was a chain smoker. Wonder who'll get his office?

This advertisement is based on fear. Research suggests that this particular ad should be effective because it explains one cause of lung cancer and offers a concrete solution: Stop smoking.

On the other hand, people with high self-esteem have been shown to be more interested in the external world and therefore more attentive to complex messages and more capable of understanding them. If this reasoning is correct, simple messages should produce more attitude change for people who are low in self-esteem, while complicated messages should produce more attitude change for people who are high in self-esteem.

To test this idea, Nisbett and Gordon (1967) administered a test of self-esteem to 152 undergraduates and then provided them with a number of statements about health. Some statements were simple and direct claims that did not cite supporting evidence. Others were more complicated and included a great deal of documentation that was rather involved. These complex messages did indeed produce the greatest attitude change for the high–self-esteem group. In contrast, the simpler messages were most influential for people whose self-esteem was somewhat lower.

Cognitive Dissonance

While some social psychologists have studied the influence of characteristics of the source, message, and audience, others have developed more general theories of attitude change. Leon Festinger's (1957) theory of cognitive dissonance has been particularly influential, in part because its predictions often contradict common sense.

For example, suppose two teenagers are hired one summer by a large suburban cinema complex to scrape bubble gum off the bottom of the theater seats. One teenager earns $3 an hour for this menial task, but the other is a nephew of the owner and is paid $12 an hour for the same work. If neither worker knows what the other earns, who will have a higher opinion of his summer job? The $12-an-hour employee will be more content with his work, your common sense probably replies without hesitation. Wrong, wrong, wrong says Festinger's theory. In a few pages, we shall see why.

Festinger uses the expression **cognitive dissonance** to refer to a contradiction (dissonance) between two different thoughts (cognitions) or between thought and behavior. He further argues that people find such contradictions unpleasant; therefore, when faced with a logical conflict, a person will try to reduce the cognitive dissonance by changing attitudes or behavior.

Consider the cognitive dissonance faced by a woman who smokes a pack of cigarettes every day even though she knows cigarettes cause heart disease, lung cancer, and bad breath. Unless this woman is suicidal and enjoys bad breath, she is faced with a logical discrepancy between the attitude "Cigarettes are harmful" and the behavior "I smoke cigarettes." There are two major ways to reduce the unpleasantness associated with this cognitive dissonance: Change the behavior or change the attitude.

Quitting smoking may seem the most rational course, but it is so difficult that many people will reduce the cognitive dissonance by changing the attitude. They may seek out information that questions the negative effects of smoking, or they may argue that "I could be hit by a bus tomorrow," so it's more important to eat, smoke, and be merry in the meantime.

In one of the first studies of cognitive dissonance, Festinger, Riecken, and Schachter (1956) followed the progress of a small religious cult that had predicted that much of the world would be destroyed by earthquakes, tidal waves, and floods on December 21. This claim was based on messages a suburban housewife named Marian Keech had received from superior beings from the planet Clarion. Cynics that they were, these social psychologists assumed that the world would still be intact on December 22. But they joined the cult anyway to study the massive cognitive dissonance that would result when this prophecy failed.

In the early evening on December 21, a group of about 15 believers met in Mrs. Keech's home to wait for a flying saucer that would arrive at

cognitive dissonance A contradiction between a thought and behavior or between two different thoughts.

midnight to transport the faithful to Clarion, or possibly Venus. While a skeptical Mr. Keech slept soundly through the night, Mrs. Keech and the others followed the instructions they had received from the aliens. Since metal is not allowed on flying saucers, they removed all metal buttons, clasps, buckles, and zippers from their clothing. Just to be on the safe side, one man even threw away the aluminum foil wrapper from his gum. After everyone had memorized the secret password needed to enter the flying saucer ("I left my hat at home"), they sat around to wait.

Midnight came and went without any sign from the aliens. After several hours of unbearable tension, Mrs. Keech finally received another message at 4:45 A.M.: God had decided to spare the earth because of the faith of this special group. There would be no flood and no flying saucer.

Intuitively, one might expect the others to slink quietly home and hope their neighbors would forget the prediction. But instead this message marked the beginning of a new phase for the group. Previously, they had tried to avoid all publicity; now they called reporters and agreed to television interviews to let everyone know of their victory and to seek new members. Festinger and his colleagues explained this surprising reaction by their theory of cognitive dissonance. A member who abandoned the sect would be faced by a massive contradiction; some had even quit their jobs or squandered their savings in anticipation of leaving the Earth. But this dissonance could be reduced by the new explanation and bolstered by the support of other members of the small group "whose faith had saved the world."

A freshman who hopes to join the marching band at Georgia's Young-Harris High School is initiated by having an egg cracked over her head. According to the theory of cognitive dissonance, this unpleasant experience should increase her later commitment to the marching band.

In a more systematic study of cognitive dissonance, Festinger and Carlsmith (1959) required subjects to perform such dull tasks as removing spools from a tray, placing them back, removing them again, and so on for an hour. Afterwards, a control group of one-third of the subjects was simply asked to rate the interest value of these "measures of performance"; as expected, their ratings suggested that the experiment was duller than watching vanilla ice cream melt.

The remaining people were asked to tell a waiting subject that the experiment they had just completed was "exciting and fun." The researcher claimed that his assistant had failed to show up to provide this positive introduction and that he was willing to pay for the help. Half the subjects were paid $1 for describing the deadly dull task as exciting; the other half were paid $20. After giving their little pep talks, all of these subjects were later asked for an honest rating of just how exciting removing all those spools had really been. According to the theory of cognitive dissonance, describing a dull experiment as exciting involved a logical contradiction that people will find unpleasant. The people who were given $20, however, had a rational explanation for the lie: They were well paid. In contrast, those who earned only $1 did not have a logical excuse. In order to reduce their dissonance, Festinger predicted that the low-paid subjects would justify the "exciting" description by convincing themselves that it was not a complete lie; the experiment was not really *that* boring.

The results confirmed this prediction: People who had been paid $1 later described the study more favorably than those who had been paid $20. Festinger argued that these results supported a more general proposition: The less justification one has for behavior, the more favorably it will be perceived. The implication for the two teenagers described at the beginning of this section is obvious. The worker who is paid only $3 an hour to remove chewed gum will have less external justification for the job than the person who is paid $12 an hour. Thus, the poorly paid worker will experience greater dissonance; one way to reduce it is to develop a more favorable attitude toward his work. (See Figure 16.1.)

In another study that led to the same conclusion, college women went through mild or severe initiations to join a discussion group about sexual behavior. The severe initiation consisted of an "embarrassment test" that involved reading aloud 12 obscene words, which "nice" girls didn't use when the study was conducted, and also two vivid sex scenes from novels; the mild initiation involved reading far less offensive material. The actual group the women were allowed to join after "passing this test" was a dull, dry, banal discussion of a book on sex-related habits of lower animals in which participants spoke haltingly, contradicted themselves and one another, and "in general conducted one of the most worthless and uninteresting discussions imaginable" (Aronson & Mills, 1959, p. 179).

As expected, those who went through a mild initiation or none at all later rated the discussion as stupid and boring; those who went through the more severe initiation consistently gave the discussion higher ratings. Thus, the theory of cognitive dissonance has important implications for fraternities, sororities, and social groups everywhere: The more foolish and insignificant

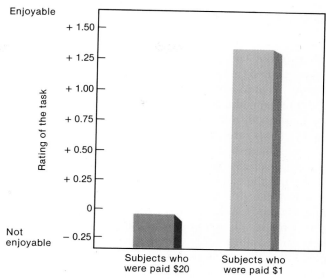

FIGURE 16.1 In Festinger and Carlsmith's classic study of cognitive dissonance (1959), subjects who were paid only $1 to describe a boring task as interesting later rated the task more favorably than did those who had been paid $20.

a group, the more severe an initiation may be required to make people think that membership is worthwhile.

In an extension of dissonance theory, Axsom and Cooper (1985) wondered whether people who wanted to lose weight would be more successful if they put extra effort into reaching their goal by obtaining therapy. They argued that if people put a lot of time and effort into an activity, they might be more committed to following it through. These researchers advertised in newspapers to recruit subjects for a study "concerning possible methods of weight reduction" (p. 152). Some of the subjects participated in high-effort activities, such as reciting rhymes and reading a story while their own voices were played back a few seconds later. Low-effort subjects read for shorter periods of time.

At the beginning of the study, the average subject was about 17 pounds overweight. After three weeks and five days of these therapy sessions, the high-effort subjects had lost an average of almost 2 pounds, while the low-effort subjects lost only a pound. The long-term pattern of greater weight loss for the high-effort group was even more striking: After six months, they had lost an average of 8½ pounds, compared to less than 1 pound for the low-effort subjects. This difference held up even after a full year.

Putting time and effort into boring tasks seemed to increase the subjects' motivation to lose weight. In an attempt to justify their efforts, they made the goal of weight loss more desirable. Thus, an effectively designed weight-loss program ideally would be expensive, time-consuming, and boring. It is interesting to note that, intentional or not, many weight loss programs apparently share these characteristics.

Self-perception Theory

While virtually all social psychologists agree that insufficient justification for an act produces more favorable attitudes, some have questioned the idea that this is caused by cognitive dissonance. Daryl Bem (1965) suggested an alternative view: According to **self-perception theory**, if we are unsure of our feelings about something, we may simply note our behavior and then assume that our attitudes match it.

Thus, subjects who are paid $20 to exaggerate their interest in an experiment will conclude that the money caused them to tell this lie. But if there is no convincing external cause—as in the case of the subjects who were paid only $1 to tell the same lie—they will attribute the action to internal causes. They may decide, for example, that they must have liked the experiment at least a little or they would not have told the lie. To summarize, we are most likely to perceive our actions as consistent with our beliefs when there is minimal external justification.

Self-perception theory also helps explain a phenomenon that is familiar to most good salespeople: the **foot-in-the-door technique**. People who comply with a small request are more likely to go along with a larger one, compared with people who are asked only to comply with the larger one.

For example, suppose someone knocks at your door and asks for a small donation to the local Little League team. If you agree to this small donation, it increases the chances that you will agree to a more demanding request, such as helping to complete the collection for your neighborhood.

According to self-perception theory, we infer our attitudes from our actions. Thus, after donating to the fund, we assume that we care about the cause. Agreeing to the larger request to collect is then in accordance with our self-perceptions.

Self-perception theory goes a step further and provides a new way of looking at rewards. Suppose you decide to begin reading Homer's *Odyssey* on a free weekend, and then, on Monday, your Greek literature teacher announces that anyone who reads Homer will receive extra credit. Intuitively, you might think this news would increase your motivation to finish the book. But self-perception theorists argue that when people are rewarded for doing something they already enjoy doing, they may start to think they are doing it just for the reward. This phenomenon is called the **overjustification effect**. In your case, therefore, when you finish *The Odyssey,* you might assume you did so because of the extra credit. What started out as pleasure has turned into work, resulting in a corresponding decrease in internal interest.

If the reward is unanticipated, however, then internal interest does not drop. Suppose your teacher had announced the extra credit after you finished the book; in that case, you would have still believed you read it because of personal desire. Our self-perception is thus influenced by whether we think we did something because we really wanted to and were fortunate enough to receive an unexpected reward after the fact, or whether we think we did something because of an external reward.

Research to evaluate the relative merits of self-perception theory, cognitive dissonance, and other alternatives has made it clear that each type of theory is useful in explaining certain types of behavior. Self-perception theory

self-perception theory The idea that people with uncertain feelings about something simply note their behavior and assume their attitudes match it.

foot-in-the-door technique The idea that people who comply with a small request are more likely to go along with a larger one than people asked to comply only with the larger one.

overjustification effect The idea that rewarding people for doing something they already enjoy may make them think they are doing it just for the reward.

conformity Behavior motivated by pressure from other members of a group.

seems especially applicable to vague, ambiguous, and minor attitudes; cognitive dissonance seems to apply to more controversial issues in which a person feels committed to a particular point of view by choice. Given the fact that there are so many different types of attitudes and so many ways to try to change them, it is not surprising that several processes are involved. The question for future research is not to decide which theory is "right" but rather what are the situations in which a particular theory will apply?

Conformity

While some psychologists have focused on social influences on attitudes, others have studied the way social groups directly influence behavior through con-formity. **Conformity** refers to behavior motivated by pressure from other members of a group.

In 1951, Solomon Asch published an elegant study of the extent to which judgment could be influenced by social pressure from the members of a group. He devised a simple and unambiguous task for his experimental groups: They would be shown cards displaying four lines of various lengths and simply be asked to pick out the two lines that were equally long, as in Figure 16.2. This comparison would be performed by each member of a group of seven to nine people; each person would take a moment to look at the cards, then announce his decision aloud so that it could be recorded by an experimenter.

All but one of the group members were confederates who had been hired to behave in a certain way. On 5 of the 12 sets of lines used in this

FIGURE 16.2 Stimuli similar to those from Asch's study of conformity. The line in *A* is obviously equal in length to the middle line in *B*. But when other group members said that it matched one of the other lines, subjects often conformed to the majority view.

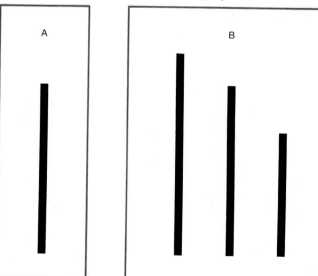

A   B   C

These are actual photos of Asch's experiment. The sixth man from the left in photograph A was the subject. In photo B, the subject learned forward to look at the cards when all other group members agreed on an obviously incorrect response. In photo C, this particular subject resisted the group pressure and gave the correct answer.

experiment, they provided the correct answer. But on the other 7 trials, all the confederates chose the same wrong answer. The actual subject was carefully seated at the end of the group, so that he heard everyone else agreeing on the wrong answer before it got to his turn. Asch's question was this: Would the subject have the backbone to give the answer that was obviously correct, or would he simply go along with the crowd and provide the same wrong answer everyone agreed with?

Of the 217 trials in which the group chose the wrong answer, the subject went along with this incorrect opinion on 72 trials. Subjects fidgeted, looked bewildered, smiled foolishly, and even walked over to look more closely at the lines, but in the end they went along with the group's clearly incorrect opinion about 33% of the time.

Asch also noted that some of his subjects seemed far more susceptible to this social influence than others. Only 6 of the 31 participants gave the right answer on every trial, no matter what the group thought. At the other extreme, 2 subjects gave in on all 7 trials and repeatedly agreed with the majority opinion even when it was quite clearly wrong.

Asch and other researchers went on to specify the precise conditions that produced the greatest conformity. Unanimity was one important factor; when just one other group member gave the right answer, the percentage of answers conforming to the majority opinion dropped dramatically (Asch, 1951). Ambiguity was another critical variable; when the test lines were closer in length, the subject was even more likely to accept the judgment of others.

The way we perceive the situation also makes a difference. If we find the group appealing, we are more likely to go along with a wrong answer. Group size is another important factor. If the group has at least three members, people are much more likely to conform to a unanimous response. Interestingly, including more than five people does not increase the group effect. Finally, if our behavior will be observed, we are more likely to conform. (This last finding supports the wisdom of secret ballots.)

There has been a considerable amount of attention devoted to the question of whether some groups are more likely to conform than others. After

Research supports the wisdom of secret ballots, since people are less likely to conform to group norms when they are not being observed.

reviewing this literature, Eagly and Carli (1981) concluded that women tend to conform more than men, especially in laboratory studies. This difference was most noticeable in situations where responses were observed by others. Perhaps women are more sensitive to the reactions of others and therefore are more reluctant than men to differ from other members of the group. Or perhaps women go along because men are more dominant and influential in the groups studied (Eagly, 1983).

Of course, the way we interpret conformity reflects our underlying values. In the United States, conformity is sometimes perceived as unimaginative and dull. Other cultures place a high value on conformity. In reality, if we could not count on people going along with basic rules, we would be faced with great confusion. Think about how many rules we follow when we are driving, for example. Most of us stop for red lights, stop signs, and school buses. Anyone who has ever driven in Boston, a city legendary for its traffic snarls, is familiar with the chaos that results when large numbers of drivers decide not to conform. Thus, some conformity to basic social rules make daily life more predictable and less difficult.

Obedience

obedience Following the suggestions or orders of another person even when one prefers not to.

Conformity, which involves following implicit or traditional rules, can be distinguished from **obedience**, in which people follow the suggestions or orders of another person even when they prefer not to. Stanley Milgram (1963) described the societal problems obedience can cause as follows:

From 1933–45 millions of innocent persons were systematically slaughtered on command. Gas chambers were built, death camps were guarded, daily quotas of corpses were produced with the same efficiency as the manufacture of appliances. These inhumane policies may have originated in the mind of a single person, but they could only be carried out on a massive scale if a very large number of persons obeyed orders. (p. 371)

To bring obedience into the laboratory, Milgram told subjects that they were participating in a study of the effects of punishment on learning. The learner was a 47-year-old accountant who was really an accomplice of the experimenter. Through a rigged drawing, each subject who reported to the laboratory was "randomly" assigned to the role of the "teacher" who would administer electric shocks to punish mistakes the learner made on a memory task. The front panel of the shock generator had a series of 30 switches for increasingly intense shocks, as shown in Figure 16.3. Each time the learner made an error, the teacher was to administer a stronger shock.

In fact, of course, the study was not really concerned with punishment or memory, and the learner received no shocks at all. Instead, errors were made in a prearranged sequence to see how many shocks these subjects would administer. The victim was out of sight in another room, and in later versions of the study, as the shocks increased in intensity he began to complain: grunting aloud at 75 volts, shouting that it was becoming painful at 120 volts, then at 150 volts crying out, "Experimenter, get me out of here! I won't be in the experiment any more! I refuse to go on!" (Milgram, 1974, p. 23)

If the subject who was delivering the shocks stopped, the experimenter told him sternly to continue. If he did continue, the victim's response would increase to an agonized scream at 270 volts; at 300 volts the victim refused to provide any more answers.

Under these conditions, how far do you think the average person would go? Take a moment to look back to Figure 16.3 and predict which switch would be the maximum shock delivered by the typical subject.

When Milgram (1974) asked a group of 39 psychiatrists this question, the average prediction was that people would stop around 120 volts. Separate groups of college students and middle-class adults made similar predictions;

FIGURE 16.3 Diagram of the shock generator in Milgram's study of obedience. Subjects were required to administer increasingly stronger shocks when a "learner" made mistakes on a memory task. If the "learner" complained about the shocks, at what point would you refuse to give any more shocks?

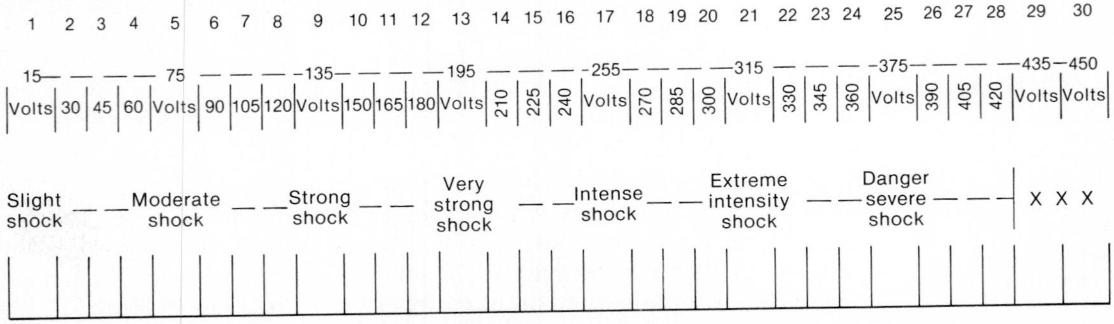

Here are four scenes from Milgram's study of obedience: the shock generator (upper left); the "victim" was strapped into his chair (upper right); a subject received a sample shock (lower left); a subject refused to continue administering shocks (lower right).

even the most cynical respondents believed that the average person would stop at 300 volts. When asked how many people would go all the way to 450 volts, the psychiatrists said that only about 1 person out of 1,000 would deliver this maximum shock.

In his first study with 40 adult men, every single one of them went beyond the average prediction of 120 volts. At 300 volts, 5 subjects refused further cooperation; no one stopped before that point. Fully 26 out of the 40 subjects, or 65%, went all the way to the end and delivered the 450-volt shock. These subjects showed considerable conflict and anxiety, and they did not seem to take sadistic pleasure in the suffering of the mild-mannered learner they had met a few moments before. But the firmness of the experimenter's repeated commands was enough to motivate most subjects to administer shocks they believed dangerous. After all, they were "just following orders." (Some of the ethical implications of this study are described in "Understanding the Scientific Method.")

This basic pattern of results was repeated in other studies of over 1,000 subjects at several universities. Some factors were found to lower obedience, such as being placed in the same room with the learner or being inspired to feel personal responsibility.

Even aside from these qualifications, the results of any psychological study should be generalized cautiously. Other social psychologists have focused on the way people sometimes resist social pressure. For example, people are likely to rebel when they feel that social pressure is so strong that they are losing their freedom. Just think how you would feel if your roommate announced that the TV in your room could not be turned on during the week. Even if you did not like any of the weekday shows, you would be tempted to watch just to demonstrate your freedom.

In one study of the way people in groups react to a threatened loss of freedom, researchers invited citizens in a midwestern town to a hotel conference center to discuss community standards (Gamson, Fireman, & Rytina, 1982). After the townspeople arrived, they were falsely told that an oil company was videotaping the group discussion. The researchers went on to explain that a local station manager had publicly opposed high gas prices and that the oil company was taking legal action against the station. The unsuspecting subjects were asked to speak against the station manager and to allow the taped discussions to be used in court. Then the researchers left the people alone to see how they would react.

When these midwesterners thought their freedom was being threatened, they rebelled. They strongly defended the station and refused to give in to the demands of the oil company. Some groups even made plans to call the Better Business Bureau to report the oil company; others decided to tell their story to a newspaper.

Thus, Asch's and Milgram's results do not mean that people are like sheep, just waiting for someone to lead them astray. They do suggest, as Milgram (1974) put it, that under some conditions, "ordinary people, simply doing their jobs, and without any particular hostility on their part, can become agents in a terrible destructive process" (p. 6). The challenge for social psychology is to specify the types of situations in which this destructive pattern is most likely to appear.

Social Relationships

The final section of this chapter considers the way people relate to one another both in intimate relationships and in larger social groups. One of the most basic questions in this area concerns the factors that influence attraction.

Attraction

When people describe how they became involved with their friends or lovers, they often refer to "love at first sight" or a kind of "natural chemistry" that attracted them. According to social psychologists, the truth is often far duller. For example, after reviewing several studies of how married couples first met, Kephart (1961) concluded:

Ethical Issues in Psychological Research: The Case of the Obedient Subjects

Diana Baumrind (1974) argued that the rights and feelings of Milgram's subjects in the obedience study had been abused. She believed that people who had administered high levels of shock would have trouble justifying their actions and as a result would lose respect for themselves and lose the ability to trust authority figures. In Baumrind's opinion, a deceptive procedure as emotionally charged as Milgram's would be ethically justified only if it provided clear and immediate benefits to humanity, such as a cure for cancer.

Milgram (1974) replied that he had taken several steps to protect the welfare of his subjects. After the experiment was concluded, each subject was given a complete explanation of the nature and purpose of the research and was reassured that many others had administered high levels of shock to the learner. At this time, subjects were also given an opportunity to work through their feelings. Fully 92% of the original subjects later returned a questionnaire that was mailed to them; 84% of these said they were glad they had participated in the study. A year after the study had ended, a psychiatrist interviewed 40 subjects whom he judged to have the greatest risk of experiencing long-term effects. In his professional judgment, none of these subjects showed signs of having been harmed by the experiment.

Some critics were not satisfied by this reply and continued to debate the ethical values of Milgram's procedure. This was not the first debate among psychologists over the ethics of a research project, but it did help stimulate widespread discussion within the profession about a variety of ethical issues, and the American Psychological Association (APA) appointed a committee to review these problems. After several years of study and consultation, in 1973 the APA adopted a list of ten ethical principles to regulate research with human participants. (Other principles have also been adopted to regulate animal research.)

(box continues on next page)

Cherished notions about romantic love notwithstanding, it appears that when all is said and done, the "one and only" may have a better than 50–50 chance of living within walking distance! (p. 269)

And indeed, many researchers have found that one of the most important factors in both liking and loving is sheer physical proximity.

PROXIMITY

People who have lived their whole lives in St. Louis, Missouri, are not likely to have many friends in Albuquerque, New Mexico. But on a far more immediate level, you are likely to be most friendly with people who live or work nearby. For example, department store clerks are more likely to become

According to these principles, participation in an experiment must be totally voluntary, and subjects must be aware of their right to withdraw from any study at any time. Before a study begins, each subject should sign a statement of informed consent that outlines the nature of the study and the agreements between experimenter and subject. Subjects must be protected from physical and mental discomfort, harm, and danger, and procedures that are likely to cause serious and lasting harm are never permitted.

Psychologists who violate any of the ten principles outlined in this document can be suspended or expelled from the APA after a complaint is investigated by its Committee on Scientific and Professional Ethics. In addition, universities and research institutions now have committees of their own to review the implications of research proposals, and only ethically acceptable research is allowed to proceed. The United States government requires this type of review for all federally funded programs.

However, the existence of these guidelines and procedures does not imply that debate over the ethics of research is now a thing of the past. The question of deceiving subjects has been particularly complex. According to one principle of the APA (1973) code:

> Openness and honesty are essential characteristics of the relationship between investigator and research participant. When the methodological requirements of a study necessitate concealment or deception, the investigator is required to ensure the participant's understanding of the reasons for this action and to restore the quality of the relationship with the investigator. (p. 1)

The problem is that even with the best of intentions, psychologists may disagree about when deception is required and what steps will actually restore the quality of the relationship. The APA's code of conduct is only 2 pages long, but it was published with over 100 pages of commentary and explanations to show how it applies in specific cases.

Human societies have debated the relative merits of various ethical codes for several thousand years. It is not surprising that psychologists sometimes disagree about whether a particular experimental procedure is right or wrong. In the final analysis, we psychologists can promise only to debate ethical issues openly as they arise and to try our best to choose the right course.

---

friendly with a salesperson who works right next to them than to a person who works a few feet farther away (Gullahorn, 1952).

Perhaps the most convincing evidence regarding proximity comes from a classic study of friendships in housing for married graduate students at the Massachusetts Institute of Technology (Festinger, Schachter, & Back, 1950). Since students were randomly assigned apartments as they became available, researchers simply asked each resident to name the three people in the building whom they saw most frequently on a social basis. Next-door neighbors were named most often, then people two doors away, three doors away, and so on (see Figure 16.4).

Interestingly, seemingly minor physical features of the housing had a major impact on the social lives of its occupants. People whose apartments were next to mailboxes, entrances, and stairways came into contact with a larger number of residents and formed more friendships. Further, the building was designed in such a way that the doors of a few apartments opened on the opposite side of the building from all the others; presumably, the architect felt that this produced a more attractive exterior. The couples assigned to these apartments rarely came into contact with other residents and became socially isolated. This study was one of the first to suggest that architectural design could have a major impact on social relationships (see Chapter 17).

Another demonstration of the power of proximity came from a study of 44 men who went through a training program for the Maryland State Police (Segal, 1974). Here, the single most important factor in predicting friendships was their place in alphabetical order! Men whose last names were close in the alphabet sat near each other in classes and were assigned nearby rooms in the barracks. This physical proximity was a better predictor of who became friends than religious or ethnic background, age, marital status, parents' education, leisure activities, or a variety of other common interests and attitudes.

Although in some situations proximity can intensify hostile feelings, it more often leads to attraction. The reasons are not entirely understood, but they may be related to the fact that familiarity seems to increase liking (rather than contempt, as the proverb would have us believe). Further, other sources of evidence suggest that most human interactions are rewarding. As a result, the more frequent contact brought on by physical proximity is likely to produce positive feelings (Berscheid & Walster, 1978).

SIMILARITY

The possible importance of another factor in human attraction is mentioned in two contradictory clichés: "Opposites attract"; but, "Birds of a feather

Research has shown that friendships are more likely to flourish between people who live or work close to one another.

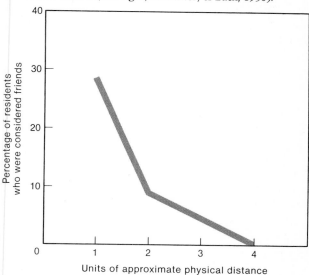

FIGURE 16.4 In a classic study of friendship in graduate student housing, the most important factor was physical proximity. The closer two people's apartments were, the more likely they were to become friends (Festinger, Schachter, & Back, 1950).

flock together." Social psychological research has supported the idea that similarity promotes friendship, but little evidence has been found for the idea that people who are very different from each other are likely to end up together.

Theodore Newcomb (1961) studied male college students who lived in a cooperative house at the University of Michigan. Attitudes and values were first measured before the students came to school; friendship patterns and attitude changes were monitored throughout the semester. In the first few weeks, physical proximity was the only factor that correlated with friendships. But as these men had more opportunity to get to know one another, similar attitudes played an increasingly large role in the friendships they formed.

Donn Byrne (1971) has established the precise effects of similarity in a careful series of laboratory studies. To eliminate the complications introduced by such variables as physical appearance, chance encounters, mannerisms, and personality, he developed a procedure based on evaluating a "phantom other." After filling out a series of questionnaires describing his own attitudes, the typical subject in these studies read questionnaires filled out by "a stranger" and predicted how much he would like this person. In fact, the questionnaires were completed by the experimenter to construct a "phantom other" who resembled the subject in very specific ways. Similar studies have been performed in several countries, with such varied groups as elementary school children, surgical patients, Job Corps trainees, and alcoholics. The results have been remarkably consistent: The more similar a stranger's attitudes, the more a person expects to like him or her.

Byrne explains this relationship in terms of reinforcement theory: It is rewarding to have someone agree with you. Therefore, the more someone agrees with your attitudes (specifically, the higher the proportion of agreement), the more that stranger will reinforce you and the greater will be your attraction. When other complications are eliminated in the controlled world of the "phantom other," there is a direct numerical relationship between the degree of attraction and the proportion of shared attitudes (Clore & Byrne, 1974).

Attempts to evalute the idea that opposites attract have been less promising. Some researchers (Winch, 1958) have claimed that people seek mates to fulfill complementary needs (for example, a dominant male looks for submissive females). However, most studies have failed to support this idea. Nevertheless, according to one review of the literature (Berscheid & Walster, 1978), the notion of complementary needs "sounds so reasonable" that "psychologists are reluctant to abandon the hypothesis" (p. 80).

Perhaps future research will demonstrate that under some conditions, opposites do indeed attract. In any case, there is little doubt that similarity of attitudes and values is a far more potent factor in human attraction.

Intimate Relationships

You cannot have an intimate relationship with someone you have never met. Thus, variables that influence initial attraction are relevant to deeper relationships, as in the case of the large number of married couples who lived within walking distance before they met. However, several researchers have noted that as a relationship develops, different factors grow in importance.

self-disclosure The degree to which people are willing to reveal information about themselves.

romantic love Intense and passionate love.

companionate love A deep and enduring bond, often marked by a strong sense of intimacy and closeness.

For example, as our review of first impressions might suggest, in the early stages of a potential sexual relationship, people tend to choose partners on the basis of physical attractiveness (Walster, Aronson, Abrahams, & Rottman, 1966). However, studies of couples who are engaged or "going steady" have found that these couples tend to be matched on physical attractiveness; external ratings of the beauty of the two partners are highly correlated. There is even some evidence that couples who are mismatched in this respect are more likely to break up; a beauty and a beast may be attracted to each other in some cases, but it is less likely to last than a more even match (Hill, Rubin, & Peplau, 1976).

It was only in the 1970s that social psychologists began to study the nature of intimate relationships between friends and lovers. One of the most interesting issues explored in this research regards **self-disclosure**, the degree to which people are willing to reveal information about themselves and their feelings. Table 16.2 lists one scale for assessing self-disclosure in various relationships.

Several studies have shown that self-disclosure is often regulated by *reciprocity;* people tend to match each other's levels of self-disclosure. The development of an intimate relationship is usually a process of revealing oneself little by little. Violation of this norm may lead to negative feelings. In one study, people observed a videotaped conversation between two actresses. In some cases, the women purposely mismatched the level of self-disclosure: One described such intimate matters as her mother's nervous breakdown, while the other limited her conversation to the problems of commuting and her college courses. When others rated the two women in the tape, they were best liked when they both had the same degree of self-disclosure at either a high or low level of intimacy. When they were mismatched, the woman who disclosed little was perceived as cold; the woman who bared her soul was seen as maladjusted.

In self-disclosure, as in so many other aspects of life, timing may be critical. In a similar study, a male confederate of the experimenter revealed that his girlfriend was pregnant near the beginning or near the end of a staged conversation. The person who revealed this intimate information was rated more highly when the disclosure came near the end of the conversation, perhaps because too much too soon can make a person seem nondiscriminating and thus reduce the value of the disclosure (Wortman, Adesman, Herman, & Greenberg, 1976).

Other researchers have gone still further in the difficult task of measuring liking and loving. For example, Walster and Walster (1978) distinguished between two different types of love: romantic love and companionate love. **Romantic love** is the type we often see on TV or in old movies—intense and passionate. Two people in love are absorbed in each other. They feel anxious when separated and are often jealous of their partner's attention to others. Your first crush was probably like this—a searing flame of emotion that adults like to dismiss with the term "puppy love." Given its intensity, romantic love often burns out rather quickly.

Romantic love may be followed by a deeper, more enduring bond called **companionate love.** Since it is not marked by high intensity, this type of love is more likely to last over years and decades. Instead of searing passion, there is often a strong sense of intimacy and closeness.

Companionate love is deeper and more enduring than romantic love.

TABLE 16.2

Measuring Self-disclosure

Check off the topics you would be willing to discuss with three specific people you know.

A casual acquaintance	An intimate friend of your sex	An intimate friend of the opposite sex	Value	
_____	_____	_____	2.85	1. Whether or not I have ever gone to a church other than my own
_____	_____	_____	5.91	2. The number of children I want to have after I am married
_____	_____	_____	10.02	3. How frequently I like to engage in sexual activity
_____	_____	_____	3.09	4. Whether I would rather live in an apartment or a house after getting married
_____	_____	_____	9.31	5. What birth control methods I would use in marriage
_____	_____	_____	8.56	6. What I do to attract a member of the opposite sex whom I like
_____	_____	_____	5.28	7. How often I go on dates
_____	_____	_____	8.56	8. Times that I have lied to my girlfriend or boyfriend
_____	_____	_____	7.00	9. My feelings about discussing sex with my friends
_____	_____	_____	9.50	10. How I might feel (or actually felt) if I saw my father hit my mother
_____	_____	_____	5.39	11. The degree of independence and freedom from family rules that I have (had) while living at home
_____	_____	_____	2.89	12. How often my family gets together
_____	_____	_____	5.83	13. Who my favorite relatives (aunts, uncles, and so on) are and why
_____	_____	_____	6.36	14. How I feel about getting old
_____	_____	_____	6.88	15. The parts of my body I am most ashamed for anyone to see
_____	_____	_____	4.75	16. My feelings about lending money
_____	_____	_____	6.88	17. My most pressing need for money right now (outstanding debts, major purchases that are needed or desired)
_____	_____	_____	7.17	18. How much I spend for my clothes
_____	_____	_____	3.08	19. Laws that I would like to see put into effect
_____	_____	_____	8.94	20. Whether or not I have ever cried as an adult when I was sad
_____	_____	_____	5.33	21. How angry I get when people hurt me
_____	_____	_____	3.44	22. What animals make me nervous
_____	_____	_____	9.37	23. What it takes to hurt my feelings deeply
_____	_____	_____	8.25	24. What I am most afraid of
_____	_____	_____	7.29	25. How I really feel about the people I work for or with
_____	_____	_____	8.85	26. The kinds of things I do that I don't want people to watch

Scoring instructions: The values listed next to each topic were based on judges' ratings of intimacy; high values reflect greater intimacy. The degree of self-disclosure for each person is the average value for the statements you have checked off. For example, if you checked off only statements 12, 16, 19, and 22 for a casual acquaintance, the self-disclosure score would be the average of the values of these four statements $[(2.89 + 4.75 + 3.08 + 3.44) \div 4 = 3.54]$. In all probability, your lowest score will be for the casual acquaintance. More interesting is the comparison between the two intimate friends: Which has a higher score for self-disclosure?

Source: Taylor & Altman, 1966.

Berscheid (1982) argues that good love relationships are marked by calm, relatively flat emotions when things are going well. Only when there are major interruptions, such as a divorce or death, does the depth and intensity of this love become noticeable.

While some social psychologists have studied factors like these that influence the relationships formed between lovers and friends, more commonly they have focused on larger social groups. One particularly interesting topic has been the study of the behavior of larger social groups, such as that of the unresponsive neighbors of the young crime victim whose case was described at the beginning of this chapter.

Altruism

After analyzing the details of the Kitty Genovese case, social psychologists John Darley and Bibb Latané (1968) came up with several possible explanations for her neighbors' failure to call the police. According to the most promising theory, one important factor was **diffusion of responsibility**: When many observers are present during an emergency but cannot directly observe one another, each can rationalize doing nothing by assuming that someone else must be taking action. The social responsibility to help someone in trouble is diffused across the entire group. The larger the group, the less responsibility any particular individual will feel, and the more slowly he or she will react.

Darley and Latané (1968) devised an experiment to test this prediction by observing people's reactions to an artificially staged emergency. The subjects were college students who were told that they were participating in a group discussion of personal problems associated with school. To avoid embarrassment and preserve anonymity, they were told, the discussion would be held over an intercom system, each participant isolated in a separate room with a microphone that would be turned on for only two minutes at a time. Some subjects were told that there were five others in the group, some were told that there were two others, and some were told that they were discussing their problems with only one other person.

In fact, all the other "participants" were prerecorded tapes that were played through the intercom. The first "participant" hesitantly admitted that he was prone to epileptic-type seizures when he was under stress. Subjects in the two-person groups were then given two minutes to describe their own problems; those in larger groups heard one or four more voices before they got their turn. On the second round of discussion, the first tape-recorded voice grew first louder, then incoherent, as he said he was actually having a seizure and needed help.

The independent variable (see Chapter 2) was the size of the group; one dependent variable was the number of people who left the isolation room within six minutes to look for help for the seizure victim. Just as Darley and Latané had predicted, larger groups led to more diffusion of responsibility and less help. As Figure 16.5 shows, only 31% of those in the six-person group (who thought that five other people were present) tried to help by the end of the two-minute seizure, compared to 62% for the three-person group and 85% for the two-person discussion.

Interestingly, the people who failed to help did not seem apathetic,

---

diffusion of responsibility A phenomenon that occurs when the social responsibility to help someone in trouble is diffused across a group of observers.

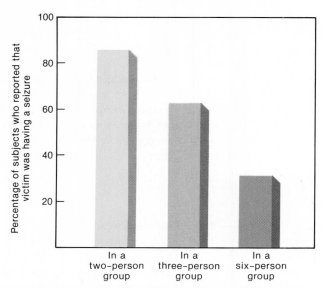

FIGURE 16.5 In a study of diffusion of responsibility, subjects were less likely to report an apparent epileptic seizure when they thought it was witnessed by others.

callous, or indifferent. "If anything, they seemed more emotionally aroused than did the subjects who reported the emergency" (Darley & Latané, 1968, p. 382). The authors argued that these observers were caught in a conflict between their own guilt and shame at doing nothing and the fear of making fools of themselves and ruining the experiment by overreacting.

Latané and Darley (1970) later provided a more complete account of several separate decisions an observer must make before coming to a victim's aid: The bystander must notice the event and interpret it as an emergency, feel personal responsibility for acting, and possess the proper skills and resources to act. In a series of experiments involving different sorts of emergencies, they found little support for the idea that there is "safety in numbers." Larger groups, it seemed, were less likely to help for several different reasons.

Along with the diffusion of responsibility, two other processes were involved in the social inhibition of helping. **Audience inhibition** refers to the fact that a bystander runs the risk of embarrassment by trying to help in a situation that turns out not to be an emergency. If you see someone lying on the beach gasping for breath and you immediately begin mouth-to-mouth resuscitation, you will feel pretty silly if a crowd gathers and learns that your "victim" was just breathing heavily after a long swim.

Another factor is **social influence:** In trying to decide whether an ambiguous event is indeed an emergency, a bystander tends to follow the reactions of other people. If you see a well-dressed man staggering as he walks down the street and holding one hand on his chest, he could be having a heart attack, or he could be feeling the aftereffects of a four-martini business lunch. If other people calmly step around the staggering executive, you are likely to decide that they are correct in assuming that the man does not need help, and ignore him.

audience inhibition A process in which bystanders risk embarrassment if they decide to help in a situation that turns out not to be an emergency.

social influence A bystander's tendency to follow the reactions of other people during an ambiguous event.

These social effects on the perception of an ambiguous situation were dramatically demonstrated in another study with a phony emergency. As college students sat in a waiting room filling out questionnaires, a stream of smoke began to puff through a wall vent. Subjects who were alone in the room typically went to the vent, sniffed around, and then left to find someone to report the problem to.

But some people were left in the room with two other subjects who were actually hired by the experimenter to remain calm throughout this false emergency. Fully 90% of the people who were left with these passive confeder-ates stayed in the waiting room as it filled up with smoke, "doggedly working on the questionnaire and waving the fumes away from their faces. They coughed, rubbed their eyes, and opened the window—but they did not report the smoke" (Latané & Darley, 1968, p. 218).

When questioned later, these passive subjects gave a variety of explana-tions for the smoke—it might have been steam or air-conditioning vapors, or, in the eyes of two particularly imaginative subjects, a "truth gas" that would make them answer the questionnaire honestly. But all agreed that the smoke did not come from a fire and thus was nothing to worry about. The presence of other people produced audience inhibition and social influence that led these subjects to decide that the ambiguous situation was not a threat.

Later research verified that these effects were quite general and easily observed in many different settings. In 48 separate studies of over 6,000 individ-uals, groups consistently helped less than a single person (Latané & Nida, 1981). This large body of research also enabled social psychologists to identify factors that increased—and decreased—helping behavior. For example, by-standers were more likely to help in an emergency when the situation was less ambiguous or when others at the scene affirmed the seriousness of the situation and the desirability of taking action.

Another factor that has been shown to increase the likelihood that a person will help is mood, especially whether a person is happy or sad. This factor has been shown to play a role not just in response to emergencies, but also in more ordinary situations.

Suppose a classmate asks you for a favor: She is ill and needs someone to accompany her to the doctor. There is really not anything in it for you; she will be graduating in a couple weeks, and you don't expect to see her again. Do you think your mood would have an effect on your decision to help her or not?

Manucia, Baumann, and Cialdini (1984) designed a study to answer this question. They recruited psychology students to participate in a study suppos-edly about mood and memory. Half of the subjects were given a drug named "Mnemoxine" (actually a placebo—flat tonic water), with simple instructions that it should produce only a dryness of the mouth that would disappear in about 45 minutes. The other half were told that for this 45-minute period, the drug would cause them to remain in whatever mood they were in when they took it. For example, if subjects felt happy when they took the drug, this feeling would persist for about 45 minutes. Then the subjects discussed a happy, sad, or neutral event to put them into a specific mood.

The researchers then asked the subjects to volunteer to make phone calls to blood donors. Although the precise relationships between mood and helping behavior were somewhat complex, both happy and sad subjects helped more than the neutral ones.

Thus, happy people seem to like helping others, perhaps because their sense of well-being leads them to want to share their happiness. Sad people also like to help others, and helping seems to improve their moods. Interestingly, when sad people think that nothing they do for others will change their mood, then they are no longer likely to help.

Another factor that influences altruistic behavior is empathy, the ability to put yourself in someone else's shoes or to feel their distress. Empathic people are more likely to help others and behave altruistically (Batson, O'Quinn, Fultz, Vanderplas, & Isenr, 1983).

Is it possible to increase altruistic behavior? Yes, if you involve individuals in the situation and make them feel more responsible. For example, personal appeals are often helpful. If someone approaches you in person to ask for help, you are more likely to assist because your anonymity is reduced.

Modeling is another way to increase altruism. Several studies have found that if people see someone else help another person or contribute to a charity, they are more likely to do the same thing (e.g., Bryan & Test, 1967).

One way to increase altruistic behavior is to involve individuals in the situation and make them feel more responsible.

Of course, people, are not always kind to others. In fact, they sometimes harm others intentionally. Our next section deals with this type of aggressive behavior.

Aggression

Any physical or verbal behavior that is intended to hurt someone is considered **aggression**. Whether aggression is an instinctive human drive or is simply a learned behavior has been debated for many years. Certainly aggression is common among animals (Lorenz, 1967), and it has survival value for many species. But whether human aggression reflects biological drives or learned behavior is not an easy question to answer.

Many observers have noted strong sex differences in aggression. Even among preschool children, boys show more aggressive behavior—such as fighting, throwing toys, hitting other children—than girls do (Maccoby & Jacklin, 1980). And adolescent males are five times more likely to be arrested for violent crimes than are adolescent females (Parke & Slaby, 1983).

Social psychologists have focused on ways in which we learn aggressive behaviors and on situations that encourage people to act aggressively. In Chapter 6 we described Bandura's classic research showing how children copied the aggressive behavior of particular models. Bandura (1977) believes that we can learn aggressive behaviors by observing them in other people and seeing the consequences. Opportunities for such observations in everyday life abound. We are all exposed to aggressive models each day—in our families, at work or school, and through the mass media, especially television.

Television is a major source of information about aggressive behavior. Studies have consistently shown that violent TV leads to aggressive behavior, at least among children and adolescents (Rubinstein, 1983). It is difficult to prove causality, and certainly most people do not immediately beat up someone just because they saw it on TV. But when so many studies, using different procedures, conclude that television promotes aggression, one has to take the finding seriously.

Virtually every household in the United States has at least one TV, and more than half own two or more. On the average, children watch over three hours per day, and some watch a lot more. Few parents restrict either the amount of TV or the specific shows their children watch. Moreover, while prime-time TV often contains violence, children's cartoons typically contain the highest levels of violence of all television shows (Gerbner, Gross, Morgan, & Signorielli, 1980). These facts are rather disturbing, given the data that watching violence on televion leads to increased aggressiveness and decreased sensitivity to violence.

A number of other factors have also been found to lead to aggressive behavior, including noise, heat, and crowded conditions. Even being around weapons can increase a person's aggressive behavior. In one study, for example, Berkowitz and LePage (1967) gave college students electric shocks (supposedly administered by a fellow student). They then allowed the students to administer shocks back to the student. For some of the subjects, a 12-gauge shotgun and a .38-caliber revolver were on the table near the shock instruments.

aggression Any physical or verbal behavior that is intended to hurt someone.

They found that subjects who had weapons in view gave more electric shocks to their fellow students than did those who had no weapons in view. Thus, simply seeing weapons may increase a peron's aggressive behavior. By identifying situations that encourage aggression, such as this one, social psychologists provide us with the opportunity to reduce aggressive behavior by making changes in the environment.

Group Processes

Whenever people do something in the presence of others, their performance is affected. As noted at the beginning of this chapter, this phenomenon was first demonstrated by Norman Triplett in 1898. In the first publication in social psychology, Triplett analyzed thousands of performances from the 1897 bicycle racing season of the League of American Wheelmen. He found that average performance was considerably faster when two or more men raced around the course together than when individual cyclists tried to beat the clock. Triplett went on to develop a laboratory device that timed how quickly a person could turn a fishing reel. Most of the 40 children he tested did best when they were in direct competition with one another. Since then, social psychologists have gone on to perform thousands of studies of human behavior in groups and in the presence of others.

The phenomenon Triplett discovered was called **social facilitation**—an improvement in performance associated with the presence of other people. However, later studies indicated that this effect occurred only under some conditions. In fact, the presence of observers sometimes actually slowed people down.

Social psychologists were puzzled; how could the presence of other people sometimes enhance performance and other times hinder it? In 1965, Robert Zajonc reviewed this literature and explained the contradiction. Social facilitation occurred in the performance of tasks that had already been mastered; new learning occurred more slowly if others were present.

Were you ever called to the blackboard in school to compute a math problem in front of your class? You might remember some of your feelings at the time: tension, excitement, a pounding heart, and other signs of arousal. According to Zajonc, if you had mastered the math procedure, then being in front of the class would improve your performance. But if you were not sure of the procedure, then it is likely that being observed made you perform more poorly.

One recent study of this phenomenon examined the performance of students who were shooting pool in a student union. First, researchers observed from the sidelines to classify good players (who made about 70% of their shots) and poor players (who made about 35% of their shots). Four observers then approached the pool table to watch. These observations supported Zajonc's view. Good pool players did even better while they were being watched (up to 80% of shots), while poor players did worse (down to 25%) (Michaels, Blommel, Brocato, Linkous, & Rowe, 1982).

Social facilitation shows how the presence of others affects the performance of an individual. Other factors come into play when several people

social facilitation An improvement in performance when other people are present.

work together toward a group goal. Researchers have found that people often put forth less effort when working in a group than when working alone. This has been called the **social loafing effect**.

Several explanations have been offered to explain social loafing. Perhaps we feel we can hide in the group; no one can identify our specific contribution, so we do not bother to perform as best we can. Another possibility is that we think others are not working very hard, so we see no reason why we should be any different. After all, no one wants to work hard, watch others do very little, and then see everyone get equal credit. By reducing your own efforts to match those of other group members, you keep an equal split of the work (Jackson & Harkins, 1985). However, if you know your work will be individually identified, then the social loafing effect disappears (Williams, Harkins, & Latané, 1981).

So it seems that groups can have powerful influences on our behavior. Sometimes group members behave in ways they never would individually. The group vandalism, riots, and mob behavior that sometimes occurs at rock concerts all result from the decreased inhibitions of group members. This loss of normal restraints in groups is called **deindividuation**. Think about what happens when you are part of a group. You feel less personally responsible for what happens, and you also feel unidentifiable. So you are more likely to go along with actions you might never consider by yourself.

Mann (1981) studied 21 dramatic instances of deindividuation, such as cases in which a person threatened to jump off a bridge, while the crowd observing shouted, "Jump." He found that if it was daylight and the crowd was small, the group did not encourage the person to jump. Only when the crowd was large or it was dark enough for people to be anonymous did group members jeer. Somehow, if we think everyone is doing something we normally would not do, we are more likely to do the same thing. It is easy to get caught up in the group behavior and lose our self-awareness.

What happens when groups are asked to make important decisions? Beginning in the 1930s, many social psychologists became interested in the processes involved when groups reach decisions and the relative merits of individual versus group decision making. Their methods ranged from laboratory studies of groups formed strictly for the purposes of an experiment to more naturalistic studies of already existing juries and committees.

In one of the most naturalistic investigations to date, Irving Janis (1972) studied historical documents to reconstruct President John F. Kennedy's ill-fated decision based on the advice of Robert McNamara and other trusted colleagues, to send a group of CIA-trained Cuban exiles to invade Cuba at the Bay of Pigs in 1961. The invasion was a colossal failure from start to finish. Janis later cited it as a prime example of **groupthink**—the suspension of critical thought that can lead to poor decisions when highly cohesive groups become preoccupied with seeking unanimity. Janis identified several symptoms of groupthink, including an illusion of invulnerability produced by high morale, an illusion of morality produced by shared values, and an illusion of unanimity produced by members' reluctance to express nonconformist doubts.

But at other times groups perform better than individuals. Certainly the ideas of three people about an issue can be more insightful than the ideas of only one person. Janis (1982) argues that groups are especially likely

social loafing effect   The tendency to work less hard in a group than alone.

deindividuation   The loss of normal restraints that sometimes occurs in groups.

groupthink   The suspension of critical thought in highly cohesive groups that become preoccupied with seeking unanimity.

to be useful if members are aware of potential problems, such as the dangers of groupthink.

Another line of research has examined the relationships between groups that can lead to cooperation or conflict. In one classic field study (Sherif, Harvey, White, Hood, & Sherif, 1961), researchers divided boys at a summer camp into two groups. The Eagles and the Rattlers, as the groups later nicknamed themselves, lived in separate cabins, and their major contact came in contests that pitted the two groups against each other, including baseball games and a tug-of-war. By minimizing contact and emphasizing competition rather than mutual enjoyment, the investigators developed a strong differentiation between the *in-group* (the group a particular boy belonged to) and the *out-group* (the other). Mutual hostility was seen when the boys were asked to describe members of the out-group; more than half used terms like *weak, sneaky,* and *stinkers.* Occasional acts of hostility occurred, as when the Eagles burned the Rattlers' flag after they had lost an athletic event.

To reconcile the groups, the investigators first provided an opportunity for pleasant interactions by having them go to movies and other events together. This was a dismal failure; the Eagles and the Rattlers called each other names and threw paper plates around the room. Appeals to ethical values and good sense were equally unsuccessful. Finally, the researchers discovered a tactic that worked: They created common crises. In one instance, a rag "got stuck" in the water line to the camp; when the two groups were forced to work together to solve this mutual problem and other problems, the level of hostility was gradually reduced.

Later studies supported the idea that common goals can bring together the warring factions of a larger group. Nevertheless, the ease with which these groups of 11- and 12-year-olds formed themselves into in-groups and out-groups was quite disturbing. Many social psychologists have built upon this foundation to study how prejudice, stereotyping, and discrimination arise in the real world and what can be done about them. Although there are no simple answers, the application of that knowledge could make a difference to the future of society.

Summary

- **Social psychology** studies the way people respond to other human beings and how they interact with one another.

Social Cognition

- **Social cognition** is the process of interpreting and understanding human behavior and feelings.

- **Attribution theories** explain how people interpret and understand behavior in social situations.

- Heider argued that people are "naive psychologists" who try to collect as much information as possible about the causes of behavior and then arrive at logical conclusions.

- One extension of this theory is the model of **correspondent inferences**, which holds that people try to explain the behavior of others by finding correspondence between what is seen of their behavior and what is inferred about their intentions. The assumption is that both the behavior and the intentions represent underlying qualities or dispositions in the other persons.

- In his expansion of attribution theory, Harold Kelley used the term **covariation principle** to refer to the fact that people assume causal relationships between events and behaviors that occur together, or "covary."

- Kelley's **discounting principle** says that behavior is not attributed to a cause if there are more plausible alternatives.

- According to the **fundamental attribution error**, observers consistently underestimate the power of external forces that influence others' behavior and overestimate the importance of internal personal dispositions.

- The **self-serving bias** is the general tendency to see ourselves favorably.

- Another common error results from the **expectancy bias effect**; that is, people with different expectations about someone else may observe the same behavior yet interpret the actions differently to match their initial expectations.

Social Influence

- An **attitude** is a relatively lasting tendency to react to a person, object, or event in a particular way. This reaction includes cognitive, affective, and behavioral tendencies.

- **Prejudices** are prejudgments based on little or no information about something.

- Three major classes of variables can influence attitude change: the *source,* the *message,* and the *audience.*

- **Self-esteem**, the value one places on one's own worth, is related to the extent to which people succumb to persuasive messages.

- According to Leon Festinger's theory of **cognitive dissonance**, a contradiction between two different thoughts or between a thought and behavior is unpleasant, so people try to reduce cognitive dissonance by changing the attitude or the behavior.

- Festinger's theory leads to several predictions that contradict common sense, such as the idea that the less justification a person has for a particular act, the more favorably he or she will evaluate the behavior.

- This general proposition of cognitive dissonance has been verified in many different contexts, but some researchers have challenged Festinger's interpretation.

- According to Daryl Bem, these results can be explained by a **self-perception theory**, which suggests that if we are unsure of our feelings about something, we simply note our own behavior and then assume that our attitudes match it.

- Self-perception theory helps explain the **foot-in-the-door technique**, whereby people who comply with a small request are more likely to go along with a larger one, compared with people who are asked only to comply with the larger one.

- According to the **overjustification effect,** if you reward people for doing something they already enjoy doing, they may start to think they are doing it just for the reward.

- **Conformity** refers to behavior motivated by pressure from other members of a group.

- Solomon Asch demonstrated the power of conformity when people agreed to perceptual errors simply because they were accepted by other group members.

- **Obedience** involves following the suggestions or orders of another person even when one prefers not to.

- Stanley Milgram showed how easily people will obey orders in a dramatic and controversial study in which subjects thought they were administering painful and dangerous shocks to a stranger as part of a "study of learning."

Social Relationships

- **Self-disclosure** is regarded as the degree to which people are willing to reveal information about themselves and their feelings.

- **Romantic love** is the type we often see on TV or in old movies—intense and passionate.

- **Companionate love** is a deeper, more enduring bond, often marked by a strong sense of intimacy and closeness.

- **Diffusion of responsibility** occurs when the social responsibility to help someone in trouble is diffused across a group of observers.

- **Audience inhibition** refers to the possible embarrassment of bystanders if they decide to help in a situation that turns out not to be an emergency.

- **Social influence** refers to a bystander's tendency to follow the reactions of other people during an ambiguous event.

- **Aggression** includes any physical or verbal behavior that is intended to hurt someone.

- **Social facilitation** refers to an improvement in performance when other people are present. It occurs more readily with tasks that have already been mastered.

- The **social loafing effect** often occurs when people are working in a group rather than alone. The effect disappears when it is known that individual work will be identified.

- **Deindividuation** is the loss of normal restraints that sometimes occurs in groups; people feel less personally responsible and less identifiable.

- **Groupthink** is the suspension of critical thought that can lead to poor decisions when highly cohesive groups become preoccupied with seeking unanimity.

Critical Thinking Exercise
Discussion

Reading Body Language

The critical thinker will note that the "evidence" cited for these claims consists of casual observations that are questionable and will look instead for scientifically based proof that crossed legs is a direct indicator of one's attitude during negotiations. Chapter 2 describes some of the errors of untrained observers, including selective attention, selective memory, and self-fulfilling prophecies.

As explained in the text, systematic studies of behavior have revealed that the meaning of nonverbal communication is determined by the situation, the cultural context, and other variables. Schemes like this that promise to reveal the "real meaning" of a particular posture or gesture are far too simpleminded to be accurate.

APPLIED PSYCHOLOGY

Chapter 17

*M*any psychologists study *basic* psychological issues because they want to contribute to the knowledge base of their field. Such psychologists find basic problems intrinsically fascinating, aside from any applications they may have to human dilemmas. Other psychologists are more interested in *applied* issues. These psychologists want to apply basic psychological knowledge to a range of human problems in order to help alleviate them. One technological innovation that has proved useful to basic and applied researchers alike is the computer.

It looked like a computer terminal, but the show on the screen had more in common with a TV movie than it did with any software package I (JH) had used before. I was still tapping my foot to the theme music when I saw a picture of an office door with the sign "Richard Benjamin—Vice President for Marketing," and the words "Go right in. Mr. Benjamin is expecting you."

I touched the computer screen to go on, and saw a film of a well-dressed executive who looked me in the eye and said: "I've thought it over and I'm ready to make you an offer." He paused for a moment to look sincere, then continued: "I'll be honest, we're a company in trouble." Despite a booming market for the type of equipment they sold, Findley Machines had failed to meet its sales projections for the last two quarters. Dick confided that I was just the sort of person who was needed to turn things around. I accepted the position and a few moments later saw my own office door: "Jim Hassett—Associate Vice President for Sales."

My first days on the job were as confusing in this computer game as they would have been in real life. I was introduced to a string of fellow executives whose greetings ranged from pleasantness to veiled hostility. My favorite was Karen Nicholson, of Customer Relations, who stopped on her way down the hall to whisper: "I hope you're ready to be the next sacrificial victim in our soap opera here at Findley."

My chair was hardly warm when I got my first phone message from Harriet Dorfman; she wanted to discuss her promotion as soon as possible. A short time later, while I was trying to sort out some conflicting opinions about whether the Findley Sales Support group needed to be reorganized, Harriet stepped into my office uninvited and said that while she knew I must be very busy, my predecessor had promised to promote her and action was now overdue.

This was one of ten "decision points" I would face in this simulation. For each, I was given four choices: keep the status quo, make a change, collect more information from several sources, or put the decision on hold. Since I felt that evaluating Harriet's promotion was less urgent than other problems I faced, I postponed a decision.

As the game went on, I met with Dick Benjamin over racquetball to discuss Findley's discount policy, dealt with Paul Bukowski's urgent phone call giving me 24 hours to stop the sales staff from disturbing his engineers with technical questions, and investigated the charges of a bright young salesman who quit because his regional sales manager was incompetent. Through it all, I got increasingly urgent phone calls and memos from Harriet Dorfman. Finally, after she threatened to bring in her lawyer, I sent Harriet to a management training program and made her promotion contingent on her performance there.

After I had finished all ten decisions, Dick Benjamin called me in for a performance evaluation. I was feeling rather pleased with myself, since my changes in Findley policy had increased sales from $40 million to $48 million, which was quite close to the $50 million sales goal. But I knew I was in trouble when Dick began: "I did say that this job would be a challenge." He proceeded to explain that while there were many positive aspects to my performance, he had decided that I was not the right person to serve as associate vice-president of sales. I was so stunned that I missed the details of his offer to transfer me to another department.

I still don't understand exactly why I lost my job. All right, my decisions on credit policy and report distribution could have been better. And maybe I should have spent less time with my spreadsheets and more time playing racquetball with Dick. But there was a job to be done, and I did it. I had solved long-standing problems in technical training and sales support, and we had turned the corner on sales.

To be perfectly honest, I'm still a little bitter over the way I was treated at Findley. Nevertheless, I must admit that this was the most fun I've ever had with a computer.

The program described above is an example of computer-based training, an approach to employee training that is becoming increasingly popular both in private industry and among government agencies (Hassett & Dukes, 1986). The example just given was designed by a group of applied psychologists, programmers, scriptwriters, and others at the Digital Equipment Corporation to help managers explore the complexities of making decisions in the business world.

On the surface, computer-based training may seem to be more closely related to high technology than to psychology. But later in this chapter, we show how these programs have been shaped by psychological research on learning. We also explain how the simulation strategy used in this program is related to cognitive theory and how it differs from computer-based training, which is more behaviorally oriented.

In Chapter 1, we introduced the area of applied psychology, which uses scientific principles and knowledge to solve concrete problems in the real world. As shown in Figure 1.1, the largest number of applied psychologists work in the areas of clinical and counseling psychology, which were discussed in Chapters 14 and 15. In this chapter, we focus on applied work in three other areas that have become increasingly important in recent years: industrial/organizational psychology, environmental psychology, and health psychology.

Industrial/Organizational Psychology

Industrial/organizational psychology studies human behavior and experience in the workplace. As a science, its goal is to acquire systematic knowledge about people's experience on the job and about the ways in which people interact with machines. As a profession, it attempts to apply that knowledge to solving problems in the real world, such as increasing worker motivation, preventing accidents, improving communication within an organization, and developing nondiscriminatory hiring practices (McCormack & Ilgen, 1980).

Areas of Research and Practice

The many activities that industrial/organizational psychologists engage in—as researchers, as managers, and as consultants to industry—can be divided into three major subfields: industrial psychology, organizational psychology, and human factors engineering. While these areas are easy to distinguish in theory, in practice there is some overlap among them.

Industrial psychology is the study of individual workers, their abilities, and the way these abilities relate to job performance. Traditionally, industrial psychologists have been particularly concerned with selecting personnel and predicting which applicants are most likely to succeed at a job. This area had its roots in the successful use of IQ tests to screen soldiers in World War I (see Chapter 13). This success led to the development of a number of tests to predict other types of job performance in industry.

In addition to personnel selection, industrial psychologists are also involved in such areas as personnel evaluation and training. Thus, they might analyze the skills, behaviors, and decisions involved in a particular job. For example, industrial psychologists who work for the military have conducted studies of the skills pilots need to accelerate a plane to climbing speed in order to attack another plane. The results of these job analyses have been used to design training programs to teach pilots these skills (Gilmer, 1966).

By the late 1920s, the field of industrial psychology had widened to include not only the study of individual differences that predict job performance

---

industrial/organizational psychology The study of human behavior and experience in the workplace.

industrial psychology The study of individual workers, their abilities, and the way these abilities relate to job performance.

Organizational psychologists have found that job satisfaction increases when people are responsible for producing a product rather than performing just a single step.

but also such concerns as worker motivation, group dynamics, communications, and leadership. These and related topics are now considered the domain of a separate subfield called organizational psychology.

Organizational psychology studies human interaction in the workplace. In a typical study performed by organizational psychologists, Ford (1975) and his co-workers at AT&T found that clerks who compiled telephone directories reported far greater job satisfaction when allowed to produce their own books from start to finish. Previously, each worker performed one step of the procedure over and over on a kind of production line. With this system, people were far less interested in their work than when responsible for all the steps in making a single book of which they could be proud.

The third subfield within industrial/organizational psychology is **human factors engineering**, which studies the way people interact with machines and the physical work environment (Chapanis, 1975). This area is also sometimes called *engineering psychology* or *ergonomics*. Its goal is to design machines, tools, and environments with human needs and limitations in mind. For example, in Chapter 8 we described how human factors engineers helped design a telephone that is easier to dial, thus increasing speed and reducing dialing errors.

Although it is difficult to summarize nearly a century of achievement in a field as diverse as industrial/organizational psychology, two trends stand out. First, in the early days, the field was mainly employer-oriented, addressing such needs as the selection of efficient workers. Today there is as much concern for the needs of workers as there is for those of employers. More important, industrial/organizational psychologists now recognize the complex

organizational psychology The study of human interaction in the workplace.

human factors engineering The study of the way people interact with machines and the physical work environment.

ways in which workers' and employers' interests intermesh. The Ford (1975) study is a good illustration: Changing the way telephone books are produced not only made the clerks happier, it also made them more productive and thus saved AT&T money.

The second trend has been away from strictly pragmatic problem-solving approaches toward more sophisticated theory and more rigorous research. This second trend is particularly visible in the area of personnel selection.

Predicting Job Performance

In the early days of industrial psychology, employers typically had a relatively informal approach to personnel selection. As Guion (1976, p. 778) put it: "One man once expressed his employment policy in these words, 'We hire only the kind of people I wouldn't mind having my daughter work beside.' Translated, he meant clean, well-groomed men and women whose manners, language, and moral attitudes were 'nice.' " While such a policy may have protected his daughter's sensibilities, as Guion points out, the qualities this industrialist looked for probably had very little to do with successful performance of a particular job.

Today's approach is more sophisticated. Psychologists begin identifying attributes or characteristics that appear to be related to a particular job. Next, they develop a test for those characteristics. Finally, they attempt to validate the test to see whether it really does predict success in that job.

In Chapter 13, we distinguished between three major types of validity: criterion, content, and construct. For the purpose of personnel selection, criterion validity is most relevant, because it involves correlating test scores with some independent measure of behavior—in this case, job performance.

There are two methods for establishing the criterion validity of a personnel test. In a *predictive validity* study, psychologists administer the test to a group of newly hired employees. At a later date, the test scores are compared with some measure of job performance, such as supervisors' ratings or success in a training program.

For example, Chapter 13 described a study by Perry (1967b) in which 114 new employees took a test called the Computer Programmer Aptitude Battery before starting their training. Later, these test scores were compared with the grades the employees received in the training course. The correlation between grades and scores on two subscales of the test were around .60, which suggests that it was reasonably successful in predicting success in the training course.

The second technique is referred to as a *concurrent validity* study, because test scores are obtained at the same time as performance measures. Here, a group of employees who have been on the job for some time take the test. Then, their scores are correlated with performance measures that are already available. If the test is valid, it should discriminate between good workers and poor ones.

In one such study, Campion (1972) developed a number of tests of the skills of 34 maintenance mechanics, such as installing and repairing a motor. He also asked supervisors to rate these mechanics on their work.

Campion found significant correlations between scores on the test and supervisors' ratings of how well the mechanics used tools (.66), how accurately they worked (.42), and their overall mechanical ability (.46).

Studies of predictive and concurrent validity have helped industrial/organizational psychologists identify a number of useful predictors of job success. Just as important, these studies have sometimes revealed that a test that intuitively seemed to be useful for screening candidates was not, in fact, a good predictor of performance.

In this brief introduction, we focus on six general types of tests that have been widely used in industry: cognitive tests, tests of motor skills, tests of job-specific skills, personality tests, biographical questionnaires, and interviews. Our goal is to give some feeling for the range of instruments that have been used to try to predict job performance and to provide an overview of the kinds of tests that have been found most useful in various situations.

COGNITIVE TESTS

Cognitive tests are designed to measure intelligence and other mental abilities. Traditionally, most have been paper-and-pencil tests rather than behavioral measures of performance.

As we saw in Chapter 13, the history of these tests goes back at least to the turn of the century, with Binet's attempts to measure IQ to predict children's classroom learning. In that chapter we also mentioned the controversy over the nature of intelligence. Some researchers hold that intelligence is a single trait, and that a person who is very bright in one area, such as vocabulary, will also be bright in others, such as math.

Others argue that there are different types of intelligence that are independent of each other. For example, we mentioned L. L. Thurstone's conclusion that there are seven relatively independent primary mental abilities: spatial verbalization, perceptual speed, number facility, verbal comprehension, word fluency, memory, and inductive reasoning.

Many industrial psychologists favor this notion of separate cognitive abilities; however, there is considerable controversy as to the nature of these abilities and their relation to job performance. Hundreds of different cognitive tests have been designed to measure mental abilities, and thousands of studies have been developed to relate them to performance in various settings.

For example, McCormack and Ilgen (1980) used a test of mental adaptability to predict success in supervisory positions. The test was administered to 70 newly promoted employees of a rubber company at the beginning of a training program. Six months later, approximately 25% of these employees had either quit, been fired, demoted, or transferred, presumably because they could not handle the position. How well did the test predict who would survive and who would leave? Quite well: Ninety-five percent of those who obtained a score of 15 or better on the test were still on the job, while nearly half of those who scored between 5 and 9 were gone. None of those who got a 4 or less survived.

After reviewing literally thousands of studies of this sort, Hunter and Hunter (1984), reported that for entry-level jobs, cognitive tests predict job performance better than any other type of predictor. By their estimate, the

cognitive tests Tests designed to measure intelligence and other mental abilities.

use of cognitive tests to screen job applicants saves employers millions of dollars by locating suitable candidates and thus improving productivity.

TESTS OF MOTOR SKILLS

Motor skills tests evaluate a worker's speed, coordination, or precision in using his or her muscles. Intuitively, these skills seem to be quite important for such occupations as typists, watchmakers, and brain surgeons.

Psychologists have found that there are roughly 11 independent motor skills. They are independent in the sense that people who do well in one of these skills do not necessarily do well in others. (That is, scores on tests of these different skills are poorly correlated with each other.) Three of the most important motor skills are *reaction time,* the speed with which a person responds to a stimulus; *finger dexterity,* which refers to the ability to handle small objects; and *multilimb coordination,* the ability to move two or more limbs at the same time (Dunnette, 1976).

One well-known motor skills test, called the Purdue Pegboard, measures dexterity by requiring people to place small pegs into holes along a board. In 1961, Wolins and MacKinney used this test in a study of 27 women who were employed to pack mail-order handcraft-kit components into envelopes and boxes. The workers' Purdue Pegboard scores proved to be related to the supervisor's ratings of job performance.

Dunnette (1976) has argued that tests that sample complex motor skills (similar to those used on the job) predict performance better than tests of simple abilities (such as finger dexterity). According to this view, an actual typing test should predict secretarial skill better than a test like the Purdue Pegboard; it might also keep secretaries from jumping to conclusions about psychologists and their wacky tests.

TESTS OF JOB-SPECIFIC SKILLS

Tests that require the worker to demonstrate skill in performing a task very similar to the tasks actually required on the job are called **tests of job-specific skills**, or work sample tests. These range from typing tests to the road test you had to pass in order to get your driver's license. They focus on motor skills or more complex verbal/cognitive skills.

The In-Basket test, for example, is an ingenious simulation of a task performed by managers every day as they shovel through their overloaded in-baskets and decide what to do about various memos, reports, requests, and proposals. Meyer (1970) used this test to predict managerial performance. In this study, 81 managers at General Electric received identical baskets containing 38 items. Among them were: a complaint from a worker who thought he had gotten "a pretty raw deal"; a request for production figures; and a "strictly confidential" letter (which the secretary had already opened "by mistake") discussing a plant closing.

Subjects had two hours to get through as much of the material as possible. Then they described in writing what action they had taken on each item and why. These descriptions were scored by judges for the content of the behavior, including what subjects did about each item, and the style of the behavior,

motor skills tests Tests that evaluate workers' speed, coordination, or precision in using their muscles.

tests of job-specific skills Tests that require skills in performing a task very similar to skills required on the job.

Tests of job-specific skills, such as the In-Basket test, include tasks that closely resemble those actually performed on the job.

such as whether or not a final decision was reached. In addition, scorers rated each subject's overall performance. This overall score correlated moderately with higher-level managers' ratings of how well these subjects actually handled planning and administrative tasks.

In general, tests of job-specific motor skills, such as typing tests, predict on-the-job performance better than tests of job-related verbal skills, such as the In-Basket test. On the average, the correlation for job-specific motor tests is about .62, which is quite high for this type of research (Asher & Sciarrino, 1974).

PERSONALITY AND INTEREST INVENTORIES

Some industrial psychologists have tried to predict job performance by using personality tests or paper-and-pencil inventories of people's interests. The intuitive rationale is that individual differences in personality and interests are related to success in different types of jobs. Thus, outgoing people may make good salespersons and introverted people good monks, while people who are interested in adventure and foreign travel might do as well as CIA agents.

In Chapter 13, we distinguished between two major types of personality tests. Projective tests, like the Rorschach and the TAT, are designed to reveal inner feelings and conflicts. Industrial psychologists have used them mainly to predict success among executives. Personality inventories, like the MMPI, assess traits through questionnaires. Industrial psychologists have used these more frequently, perhaps because they are easier to administer and interpret than projective tests. One questionnaire that has proven particularly popular is the California Personality Inventory (CPI), an adaptation of the MMPI for use among normal adults. The CPI measures such traits as dominance, sociability, tolerance, sense of well-being, and flexibility.

Interest inventories typically ask about a person's preference for, or interest in, various activities, tasks, hobbies, and so on. One well-known test of this sort, the Strong Vocational Interest Blank, is often used by guidance counselors to help people choose a satisfying career. The test has been administered to large groups of people in various professions, including doctors, lawyers, and chicken farmers.

Thus, an individual's interest profile can be compared with those of others who work in a variety of different jobs. The assumption is that if you enjoy the same things on and off the job as biologists typically do, you will probably be happier and more successful as a biologist than as an architect or doctor.

However, in terms of actually predicting job performance, personality and interest inventories have not proven particularly accurate or helpful. Asher and Sciarrino (1974) reviewed a large number of studies and reported that only 12% of the studies correlating personality test scores with job performance yielded a correlation coefficient of .50 or higher.

The relationship between the Strong Vocational Interest Blank and job performance was even weaker. Hunter and Hunter's review (1984) found an average correlation of .10 between Strong scores and supervisor ratings of job performance. In fact, it had the worst record of all the predictors they reviewed.

Why do personality and interest inventories do such a poor job of predicting performance? One possibility is that they too often measure global qualities that are not specifically related to any one job. Some industrial psychologists have therefore turned to the study of single traits that seem likely to be related to job performance. For example, recently a number of studies have been done regarding the measurement of one aspect of personality that has obvious relevance for personnel selection: honesty.

In measuring this trait, two major problems must be overcome. First, since dishonest job applicants may well lie when asked such questions as, "Compared to other people, how honest are you?" the test for honesty must be reliable and valid. Second, in order to tell whether the test accurately distinguishes honest people from those likely to rob the company blind, test scores have to be compared with some measure of on-the-job behavior. And while it is clear that employees do steal, it is often difficult to catch them at it. Fortunately, there have been some imaginative attempts to get around these problems (see Sackett & Harris, 1984).

For example, Jones and Terris (1981) administered an honesty test called the London House Personnel Selection Inventory to 80 Salvation Army "kettlers," the people who stand on street corners at Christmastime ringing their bells and soliciting donations. They compared the test scores with the average daily intake of money, taking into account that some locations typically produced a better "take" than others.

Jones and Terris found that kettlers who scored in the "honest" range on the inventory took in an average of $81.00 a day, while kettlers who failed the test took in an average of only $62.77 a day. The researchers concluded that those who scored low on the honesty test were dipping into the kettle. Critics have noted, however, that it is also possible that they were simply taking unauthorized coffee breaks or that their low take was due to some factor unrelated to honesty, such as low physical attractiveness (Sackett & Harris, 1984).

On the basis of all the studies they reviewed, Sackett and Harris concluded that while people who are caught stealing typically have gotten low scores on various honesty tests, the vast majority of those who failed the tests were *not* later caught stealing or even suspected of it. This implies that using the tests to screen prospective employees would be unwise and unfair. Yet, they also noted that despite the fact that honesty is a very difficult trait to research, studies do show consistently positive correlations between honesty tests and various behavioral measures. Sackett and Harris, along with many other industrial psychologists, believe that this is an important area that deserves additional study.

BIOGRAPHICAL DATA

You have probably been asked to provide biographical data nearly every time you have applied for a job. Biographical forms or questionnaires may inquire about your education, marital status, work experience, health, and even leisure activities.

Biographical items often have high "face validity"; that is, they intuitively seem to be related to the ability to do a particular job. For example, if you applied for a teaching position at a university, your prospective employer would want to know whether you had an advanced degree.

Nonetheless, it is often important to establish that such items also have high criterion validity. For example, years ago many employers were interested in marital status, because they assumed that a young man who was married would be more "settled" and conscientious than one who was single. While this assumption seems reasonable, it is no more than an intuitive guess. In order to know whether marital status was a valid predictor of job performance, it would be necessary to separate employees into two groups on the basis of some measure of conscientiousness, such as the number of times an employee is late for work. If it turned out that the conscientious (on-time) group tended to be married and the unconscientious (tardy) group single, there would be some grounds for concluding that marital status is a valid predictor.

By doing studies of this sort, a number of investigators have discovered connections between job performance and various kinds of biographical information. For example, Morrison and her co-workers (1962) administered a 484-item biographical questionnaire to 418 petroleum research scientists. They also obtained three measures of job performance: supervisor's ratings of creativity, ratings of overall performance, and the number of patent disclosures submitted over a five-year period. They then performed a *factor analysis,* a mathematical procedure that examines the pattern of correlations among a large number of scores or items and indicates which items tend to cluster in groups.

Morrison and her co-workers discovered a number of systematic relation-

Organizational psychologists have attempted to devise a number of honesty tests that could screen employees before they are assigned to such tasks as loading an automatic teller machine.

ships between biographical data and performance. While some of those biographical items (e.g., preferring to work on one's own) seem intuitively to match our image of the creative inventor, many of them (e.g., soliciting funds for charity) do not. Nevertheless, according to Hunter and Hunter (1984), biographical data are second only to tests of cognitive ability in predicting job performance.

INTERVIEWS

Interestingly, job interviews have the poorest record of any predictor. Many studies have shown that interviews lack both reliability and validity: Different interviewers tend to disagree in their evaluations of the same people, and evaluations tend to have a poor record as predictors of job success. Why, then, does virtually every employer still rely on some kind of interview to make hiring decisions?

One reason, as Bingham (1949) pointed out, is that interviews serve many purposes aside from the purpose of personnel selection. An interviewer typically answers a prospective employee's questions about the job and tries to "sell" the firm to the applicant. In addition, it may be that interviewing is a fine art at which some individuals excel. This would imply that some interviewers' conclusions are valid and some are not, a hypothesis that is difficult to test.

There have been some reports of success in using interviews to predict job performance. Interestingly, these have come mainly from research done in what are called assessment centers, places set up by many large corporations where employees are assessed for managerial potential. These centers typically employ a range of tests, simulation exercises, and interviews in order to select people who would make good managers. The interviews done in these centers are usually longer and more in-depth than those used elsewhere. For example, Grant and Bray (1969) reported results of interviews done at AT&T's assessment center. Subjects were 81 college graduates and 122 nongraduates, all of them managers in their twenties and thirties. The study looked at whether or not information obtained in interviews would predict progress in management, as measured by salary increases.

The interviews were conducted by psychologists who were given biographical information about the subjects in order to identify areas to probe. Interviews lasted up to two hours and covered such topics as work goals, attitudes on social issues, and hobbies. After being transcribed, each interview was rated by two independent judges for 18 variables, including personal impact—forcefulness, tolerance of uncertainty, and inner work standards.

Analysis of the results indicated that the scoring procedure was reliable; that is, the two judges tended to agree on their ratings. There was also evidence that the interviews served as valid predictors of progress in management, as measured by salary increases. Five variables were particularly good predictors: Managers who had made progress had a wide range of interests, believed in the primacy of work, had a need for advancement, did not feel a need for the approval of their superiors, and did not yearn for security.

In another line of research, investigators have looked at what are called *process issues*—that is, factors that influence the process of evaluating an applicant. For example, in Chapter 16 we described some of the social psychological research supporting the idea that first impressions are important. Similarly, industrial psychologists have found that interviewers seem to form an overall impression of an applicant quite early in the interview and that additional information tends to be interpreted on the basis of this first impression.

In addition, the impression an applicant makes on an interviewer may depend in part on the contrast between that applicant and the one directly before or after him or her. A mediocre candidate may look very promising following a truly awful one, and that same mediocre candidate may later appear less appealing if the interviewer subsequently has talked to someone who seems a paragon of all the virtues the company deems most essential. Finally, interviewers do seem to have a preconceived image of the "ideal" person for the job against which they measure each candidate (McCormack & Ilgen, 1980).

This research contains an implicit warning for employers: Those who rely solely on interviews for choosing job applicants may make some costly errors. In combination with the results of the job performance research described above, this study suggests that employers would be wise to place more emphasis on cognitive tests, biographical questionnaires, tests of job-specific skills, or tests of motor skills, depending on the requirements of a particular job.

Industrial psychologists have generally found that if such testing were discontinued for some reason and the government was forced to use other methods for choosing new employees, it would cost an additional $3.12 billion per year in lost productivity. With amounts like this at stake, it is easy to see why both government agencies and private industry are interested in sponsoring research and applying its results to the selection of new personnel.

Similar economic factors lie behind research in other areas of industrial/ organizational psychology. Training programs for new and old employees derive from such factors.

Personnel Training

Whenever individuals are hired for a job or change jobs within an organization, they are likely to require training to understand the nature of the new job and the skills it requires. This topic is assuming greater importance as new technology changes the way America does business.

In the next two decades, several million jobs in U.S. industry may be eliminated as a result of factory automation. All these displaced workers will need to be retrained. The evolution of office automation also creates a new need in this area. According to one estimate, "Employers will have to retrain office workers five to eight times during their career in the near future" (Wexley, 1984, p. 520).

As a result, many industrial psychologists now specialize in the area of **personnel training**, which can be defined as an organization's program to teach employees job-related behaviors. Naturally, many of the principles developed by educational psychology for use in schools are relevant to industrial training programs. But there are also some interesting differences. As Romiszowski (1981) put it: " 'Training' is akin to following a tightly fenced

personnel training An organization's program to teach employees job-related behaviors.

path, in order to reach a predetermined goal at the end of it. 'Education' is to wander freely in the fields to left and right of this path—preferably with a map" (p. 3).

This area has been strongly influenced by the behavioral approach to learning theory. Many training programs begin with a **task analysis** to determine the precise skills and behaviors required to perform a particular job. This analysis leads to the definition of a target audience and precise behavioral objectives for each training program.

For example, a program designed to teach clerical personnel to use new word-processing equipment might limit the target audience to: *employees with a typing speed of at least 40 words per minute and with some previous experience with word processors.* Those who did not have any previous experience would probably be required first to enroll in another training program to cover general principles. A typical behavioral objective for such a program might be: *After completing this training, the student will be able to use WordPerfect 4.1 software on the IBM-PC computer to type and print memos and letters.*

Note how specific these statements are. The student is not going to learn about word processing in general; he or she is going to learn to use a particular word-processing program called WordPerfect 4.1 on particular hardware and for a particular purpose. The behavioral objective helps the person who is designing the course to decide exactly what information must be covered and what can be excluded. For example, a general course on WordPerfect 4.1 might cover special procedures to generate footnotes. However, footnotes would probably not be covered in this course, since they are rarely used in memos and letters.

The philosophy behind this behavioral approach was stated succinctly by R. F. Mager in his influential book, *Preparing Instructional Objectives* (1975): "If you don't know where you're going, you're likely to end up someplace else." The behavioral model is most easily applied to concrete tasks, such as learning to repair equipment or use a new computer system.

After the target audience and behavioral objectives of a training course have been determined, the instructional designer is likely to perform a *media analysis* to determine the most appropriate medium for presenting instruction, such as classroom training, a pamphlet or book, a videotape, or some combination of media.

Industrial programs are increasingly turning to **computer-based training** programs, which use computers to deliver instruction in job-related skills. This trend has been fueled by the fact that computers are cheaper, more powerful, and more widely available than ever before. [These same factors have also led to increasing use of educational software in the nation's schools (Hassett, 1984).]

Surveys have revealed that companies use the computer for employee training primarily because it saves money by reducing training time (Hassett & Dukes, 1986). One key reason is the fact that computer-based training is "self-paced": that is, the computer can jump ahead for the student who has mastered the material or move slowly for the student who has trouble with a particular concept. The computer never gets angry or impatient with the slow student, and it never holds back the quick learner.

task analysis An analysis that determines the precise skills and behaviors required to perform a particular task.

computer-based training Programs that use computers to deliver instruction in job-related skills.

This air traffic controller is practicing job-related tasks with a computer-based simulation.

In a review of 30 studies comparing the time students took to master material in computer-based training courses versus traditional classroom training, Orlansky and String (1981) found a median time savings of 30% for the computer-based approach. Other researchers have consistently replicated the fact that computer-based training takes less time than more traditional approaches (Wexley, 1984).

Many computer-based training programs are designed to provide drill and practice in motor skills or simple concepts. For example, when a consumer buys a microcomputer, it often comes with a disk that gives a tutorial and practice exercises in such basic topics as how to use the keyboard, printer, and disks. Each lesson presents information on the screen and requires the user to practice typing in commands required for simple operations. A correct answer is immediately rewarded with a statement such as, "Good! You would now have identical files on each disk." A wrong answer produces more detailed instructions and another chance to practice the correct response.

The instructional principles behind this interaction are quite similar to those described by B. F. Skinner (1954) for his "teaching machine." This device presented instruction and questions on a paper tape, which the student moved to see a few sentences at a time. The student wrote answers on a second tape and then turned the teaching tape to the next "frame" to see whether the answers were correct.

Today's computer-based training courses permit more sophisticated feedback than Skinner's teaching machine, because the computer can be programmed to respond with specific explanations for many different possible errors. But the emphasis on frequent questions, small steps, and immediate feedback is the same.

A different approach to computer-based training is found in programs like the "Decision Point" course described at the beginning of this chapter. This open-ended discovery approach has been strongly influenced by cognitive theories of learning, which place less emphasis on specific behavioral goals and more emphasis on restructuring knowledge with new conceptual insights. For example, "Decision Point" designers Jo-Anne Wyer and Charles Findley described their goal as creating a learning experience that would go "far beyond the event itself, being continually reanalyzed by the learner until it is incorporated into a new way of looking at the world" (quoted in Hassett & Dukes, 1986, p. 28).

Although there is some controversy as to the relative merits of these and other approaches, there seems to be a surprising consensus that computer-based training will play an important role in industrial psychology in the future. Indeed, Snelbecker (1981) has compared the current explosion of growth in computerized education to several key events that have shaped psychology's history. For example, the need to classify military personnel during World War I stimulated the development of psychological tests; the War on Poverty and Operation Head Start programs led to increased research and understanding of child development. In the same way, he argues, the widespread use of microcomputers in education may stimulate research that will lead not only to better computer-based training, but also to a better understanding of how people learn.

This interplay between theory and practice is one of the most exciting aspects of applied psychology. As we shall see, it is not limited to industrial/organizational psychology; it is also apparent in the other areas described in this chapter: environmental psychology and health psychology.

Environmental Psychology

Environmental psychology is the study of the interrelationships between human behavior and the physical settings of everyday life. Thus, an environmental psychologist might study the effects of air pollution on depression, or temperature changes on job performance, or the effects of noisy environments on cognitive efficiency, or the way the design of an office or living space affects the occupants' feelings and behavior.

This area of psychological research is relatively new, having grown in importance during the 1970s and 1980s as our society became increasingly concerned with the physical environments humans have created and the possible negative effects. Although there has been some basic laboratory research on these issues, in many cases the environmental psychologist prefers to work in the field in order to study behavior in its natural settings. As we shall see, the results of some of these studies are now being used to change the physical environment so that it is more likely to produce positive effects on behavior and perception.

In this section, we focus on three of the issues that have been studied

environmental psychology The study of the interrelationships between social behavior and the physical settings of everyday life.

most intensively by environmental psychologists: the effects of crowding; how architectural design influences behavior; and the effects of noise, particularly on children.

Crowding

In 1975, the world population passed 4 billion. If it continues to grow at the present rate, there will be 8 billion human beings packed on our planet by the year 2010 (Freedman, Sears, & Carlsmith, 1981). Although there are signs that the rate of population growth is beginning to slow, it is likely that the world of tomorrow will be more crowded than today.

There seems to be a widespread perception that this crowding helped create many of the problems of our troubled world. When two psychologists reviewed popular articles listed in the *Readers' Guide to Periodical Literature* over a ten-year period, they found writers who blamed crowding for everything from disease and pollution to crime, war, mental illness, drug addiction, and the breakdown of the family (Zlutnick & Altman, 1972). Many of these articles helped substantiate their claims by describing a classic study by John Calhoun that showed how overcrowding can lead to chaotic conditions in a rat colony.

Calhoun (1962) had devised a special environment by dividing a 10-by-14-foot room into four pens set off from each other by an electrified fence, with ramps for the rats to move from one pen to another. By his estimate, about 48 rats could live in this room comfortably. But Calhoun allowed the population to grow to 80 rats so that he might observe the effects of overcrowding.

Two of the four pens were purposely constructed with fewer connecting ramps and other features to make them less accessible. Each of these two pens was usually taken over by a dominant male rat and his harem of six or seven females; most of the remaining rats would congregate in one of the more central and accessible pens; as many as 60 rats might jam themselves into one pen to eat, although other pens were accessible. Calhoun used the term **behavioral sink** to refer to the pattern of bizarre and antisocial behavior that occurred in the overcrowded pens. Female rats had trouble reproducing and failed to care for the offspring that did survive. Male disturbances included sexual deviation, cannibalism, wild overactivity, and total social withdrawal.

While some experts quickly claimed that overcrowded human slums produced similar "behavioral sinks," those who studied Calhoun's procedures warned that it was not legitimate to generalize from a specially designed rat colony to the real world of human cities. Direct studies of human environments led to very different conclusions. For example, Freedman, Heshka, and Levy (1975) examined the correlations between the crime rate in 97 cities and the population per square mile as well as other possibly relevant variables, such as income, education, and race. Even if they had found that crime and population density were correlated, that would not prove that crowding *causes* crime (see "Understanding the Scientific Method" in Chapter 13), only that the two variables were somehow related. As it turned out, this qualification proved unnecessary. A careful statistical analysis revealed that, by itself, population density was not particularly related to crime. Sociological studies of this

behavioral sink A pattern of bizarre and antisocial behavior that may occur in an overcrowded environment.

sort generally have found very few negative effects that are directly related to crowding.

Laboratory studies in which groups are confined in small rooms under crowded conditions have been somewhat less consistent. Some studies report that crowded conditions can lead to poorer performance on difficult tasks, increase later frustration and hostility, raise blood pressure, and sometimes even produce aggression (Sherrod, 1982).

Many environmental psychologists now believe that it is important to distinguish between population density—as measured by the number of square feet per person in a given situation—and the psychological perception of crowding (Stokols, 1972; Fisher, Bell, & Baum, 1984). People may feel quite comfortable if they are jammed into a small space at a concert, football game, or party. But precisely that same amount of space per person may feel more crowded on a bus ride or while waiting in line for a license.

Interesting real-life research on crowding has been conducted in Chicago. In their first study, Galle, Gove, and McPherson (1972) analyzed data on mortality, fertility, public assistance, delinquency, and psychiatry admission rates in relation to population density (measured by the number of inhabitants per acre). All the measures of social pathology were related to population density regardless of social class or ethnicity. A follow-up study (Cox, Hughes, & Galle, 1979) involving intensive interviews revealed that even the subjective experience of crowding was related to poor mental and physical health, inadequate child care, psychological and physical withdrawal, and poor social relationships in the home. On the other hand, other field studies in high-density cities like Hong Kong, one of the most densely populated cities in the world, show few negative effects attributable to housing density (Mitchell, 1982).

Perceptions of crowding depend not just on the physical space available per person but also on the setting in which crowding occurs.

While issues of crowding and density in a college dormitory may not seem to have the same social significance as urban crowding, there is evidence that they are greatly relevant to the student's experience. Hughes (1983) studied one college campus where some of the residences originally designed as doubles were converted to triples. Residents of the triples had lower self-esteem and greater likelihood of social, emotional, and intellectual problems than residents of regular doubles. These findings are consistent with those of other studies showing that students living in crowded conditions show lower academic performance (Russell & Ward, 1982).

There are several major theories regarding the way the psychological perception of crowding can sometimes produce stress and negative effects. One of the most influential theories is that crowding can reduce people's feeling of control by restricting their movement and forcing them to interact with other people (Cohen & Sherrod, 1978). This idea is related to Martin Seligman's notion of *learned helplessness*—that when people lack a feeling of control, they give up easily when frustrated and become depressed (see Chapter 14). Some environmental psychologists have applied this theory to help architects design living spaces that maximize feelings of control and thus increase the satisfaction of the people who live in them.

Architectural Design

According to an old architects' joke, "A doctor can bury his mistakes, but an architect can only advise his clients to plant ivy." To some, this may suggest that old architects are not very funny. But it does call attention to the fact that architects have traditionally been primarily concerned with exterior appearance and that buildings last a very long time. In the past, architects who were concerned with the way the interior design of a building might influence social behavior had only their own intuition as a guide.

To fill this gap in knowledge, environmental psychologists are now systematically investigating the way different sorts of living spaces affect human interaction. Studies have been performed on a wide range of physical environments, including offices, apartment buildings, classrooms, dormitories, and prisons.

One of the first and most influential series of studies in environmental psychology concerned the Pruitt-Igoe Housing Project in St. Louis. When its 33 high rises were built in the 1950s, there was tremendous optimism about the fact that this subsidized housing made it possible for nearly 12,000 people to live in apartments they otherwise could not have afforded. But within a few years, vandalism and crime had turned this project into an urban nightmare. The problems were so severe that, in 1972, the city gave up and demolished many of the buildings.

Oscar Newman (1972) was one of several social scientists who studied Pruitt-Igoe to try to determine where it had gone wrong. He argued that its poor architectural design contributed to the problems of crime and vandalism. For example, each of the 11 stories in each high rise had a central elevator shaft and long corridors. This type of design tends to isolate apartment dwellers and minimize interactions between neighbors.

Smaller buildings with garden apartments have been shown to give people more of a sense of "home" and ownership of the common space near their apartments. In a high rise with no common areas, an apartment dweller's sense of ownership does not extend to the other end of the corridor. The person who lives in a high rise may not even know the other people who live on the same floor and thus will not recognize troublemakers who do not belong there. In the smaller building, residents will challenge unfamiliar outsiders and try to prevent vandalism. In large, impersonal high rises, this behavior is less likely to occur.

Although later researchers challenged the idea that the design of high rises is an important determinant of crime in housing projects (McCarthy & Saegert, 1979), this research prompted many social scientists to become interested in the question of how architectural design can influence behavior. For example, several studies have compared the psychological effects of living in different kinds of college dormitories.

Baum and Valins (1977) studied incoming freshman at the State University of New York at Stony Brook. Each student was randomly assigned to either a traditional corridor dormitory (with an arrangement similar to that at Pruitt-Igoe) or to a dorm arranged into suites. As shown in Figure 17.1, each corridor consisted of 17 double bedrooms, a bathroom, and a lounge; the suites grouped 3 bedrooms with a bath and a lounge. The actual number of square feet per

FIGURE 17.1 Floor plans for corridor and suite-style dormitories studied in Baum and Valins's (1977) explorations of the effects of architecture on behavior.

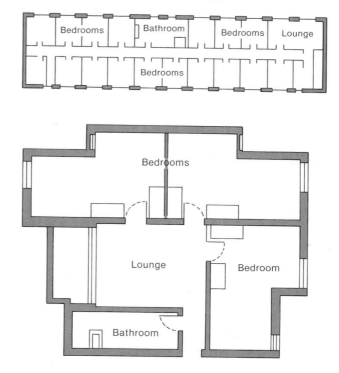

person was almost identical for these two types of dormitories; however, as you might guess, the psychological sensation of crowding was not.

On a series of questionnaires, people who lived on the corridor dorm reported feeling more crowded and less satisfied with college life; they also reported more negative feelings about other students who lived in their dorm. Other questions revealed that corridor residents felt less control over their personal lives; they were more often forced into inconvenient or unwanted interactions with others, and over the course of the seven weeks of living in the dorm they increasingly agreed with statements like: "It is not worthwhile trying to change things."

These feelings of helplessness and alienation were not limited to life in the dormitory itself. When corridor residents came to a psychology experiment, they sat farther away from others in the waiting room and looked at them less than students who lived in the suite dormitories. Finally, corridor residents performed more competitively on a laboratory task, even when a cooperative approach would have been more productive (Baum, Aiello, & Calesnick, 1978).

A later study revealed how minor changes in the use of physical space could improve the quality of life in a corridor dorm (Baum & Davis, 1980). The dormitory floor chosen for study had 27 single and double bedrooms arranged along a corridor. The design change could not have been simpler: 3 bedrooms in the middle of the floor were converted into a lounge. This arrangement effectively divided the corridor in half; instead of housing a single group of 43 students, the same floor now seemed to house two separate groups of 19 and 20 students. The attitudes and behavior of students living on the redesigned corridor were then compared with others who lived on an unmodified corridor in the same dorm and with a third group of students living in a dorm designed to house about 20 students along a short corridor.

In general, students who lived on the unmodified long corridor were least satisfied with their housing; they reported feeling more crowded, had fewer friends in their dorm, and described dormitory life as more hectic and less controllable. As in the earlier study, over the course of several weeks, long-corridor residents increasingly agreed with general statements of helplessness like: "It is often not worth the effort to try to change the way things are."

In this study, an experimenter who was not aware of these predicted effects periodically observed behavior on the three dormitory floors. As the semester wore on, fewer groups of people were observed talking to each other on the long-corridor floor, and fewer doors were left open to encourage contact. Effects were also observed on laboratory behavior. Long-corridor residents acted more withdrawn than the short-corridor groups: They sat farther away from others in a waiting room, looked at others less often, and later reported feeling more uncomfortable during this period.

In this study and others, researchers noted that not all people responded in exactly the same way; some individuals seemed to be more seriously affected than others by their living conditions. Later research therefore explored the origins and nature of these individual differences.

One group (Baum, Calesnick, Davis, & Gatchel, 1982) believed that part of the answer lay in a personality trait called "screening," which measures how people respond to excessive information (Mehrabian, 1977). When "screeners" are confronted with many stimuli that demand their attention, they try to determine the priority of various stimuli and deal with the most important ones first. In contrast, "nonscreeners" are less discriminating; they try to attend to each stimulus as it appears.

These researchers believed that screening was an adaptive style of coping with the excessive demands of crowded dormitories and that students with this personal trait would show fewer negative effects of dormitory life. They tested 214 freshmen who had been randomly assigned to long- and short-corridor dormitories. Just as they had predicted, screeners who lived in the long-corridor dorms seemed less bothered by the situation.

Thus, environmental psychologists are now exploring not just the average effects of different types of settings, but also the reasons why some people adapt better than others to the stresses created by perceptions of crowding or other unpleasant stimuli, such as excessive noise.

Noise

On July 27, 1968, Biovanni Gatto just couldn't take it anymore. According to a report from United Press International in Palermo, Italy, the 44-year-old man "attempted suicide with an overdose of drugs . . . because his eleven children made too much noise while he was watching the Olympic Games on television" (Berland, 1971, p. 49). Few people react this melodramatically to the stresses of everyday life. But society seems increasingly aware of noise pollution, and researchers are trying to determine how harmful chronic noise really is.

According to the government's Council on Environmental Quality (1980), half the population of the United States may be exposed to environmental noise levels that are high enough to interfere with normal activities, such as sleeping, listening, and speaking. Over 20 million people may be exposed to such high levels of noise, for such a long period of time, that they could experience hearing damage as a result.

The most obvious effect of prolonged exposure to loud noise is deafness. This phenomenon was noted as early as the nineteenth century, when doctors reported that many weavers in noisy textile mills gradually lost their hearing. According to one conservative estimate, people who are exposed to noise levels over 80 decibels for eight hours each day will have some permanent loss of hearing. The time course of the loss depends on both the individual and the type of noise (Green, 1976).

The Occupational Safety and Health Administration (OSHA) (1971) has set standards for acceptable levels of noise in American industry. Depending on the dominant frequency of the noise, the maximum levels range from 85 to 100 decibels.

Interestingly, sound levels at rock concerts and nightclubs often exceed these recommendations. In one study of rock musicians (Kryter, 1970), temporary partial losses of hearing were found immediately after a performance. When these same musicians were tested at other times, the hearing loss was less serious but still noticeable.

Excessive noise levels can produce harmful physical and psychological effects.

While the extreme noise levels that can cause deafness are now reasonably well understood, there is still a great deal of controversy about more subtle effects of somewhat lower noise levels. Laboratory studies have revealed that the effects of noise on performance vary from one situation to the next. Even very loud noises often do not affect performance on simple tasks (like pressing a button as quickly as possible after a light comes on). In fact, performance on very boring tasks may actually improve in a noisy environment, possibly because the racket keeps subjects awake and alert. Performances on more complex tasks (such as multiplying long strings of numbers) and those that require a high degree of attention (such as watching carefully for a specific light) are more likely to suffer under noisy conditions. Unexpected noises over which the subject has no control are particularly likely to disrupt performance (Glass & Singer, 1972).

Early psychological studies of noise were primarily concerned with its effects on industrial and military performance and concentrated on the kinds of simple tasks described above. But in recent years, many psychologists have begun to study the long-term effects of living in noisy cities and have turned to more complex behaviors. For example, several social psychologists have found that people are less friendly and helpful in noisy environments. In one field study (Mathews & Canon, 1975), a student wearing a cast on his arm dropped a pile of books and papers. Under low-noise conditions (about 50 decibels), 80% of those who passed by offered to help. But when a noisy lawn mower was running nearby (increasing the background noise to 87 decibels), only 15% of those who passed by were this helpful.

One of the most disturbing studies of chronic urban noise (Cohen, Glass & Singer, 1973) considered its effects on elementary school children who lived in the Bridge Apartments in New York City—four high rises that were built directly over the Cross Bronx Expressway, a heavily traveled road that leads to the George Washington Bridge. The design of these apartment towers unintentionally produced an echo-chamber effect that magnified sounds from the highway underneath and made them very noisy places in which to live. In this study, average readings taken outside the buildings at ground level were about 84 decibels, near the border of sound levels that OSHA would consider unacceptable if they occurred in a factory.

This experiment analyzed the abilities of elementary school children who lived in these noisy apartments. Fifty-four children were given a special test of auditory discrimination. Each child listened to 40 tape-recorded pairs of words and was asked whether the two words were the same or different. Ten of the word pairs were identical; the other 30 were only slightly different, such as *gear/beer* and *cope/coke*. For the 34 children who had lived in the Bridge Apartments for at least four years, there was a significant correlation ($r = .48$) between the floor they lived on and their score on the discrimination test. Even though the children took this test in school under identical conditions, those who lived in the noisier apartments on the lower floors made more mistakes.

Interestingly, the 20 children who had lived there three years or less did not show this relationship. A separate series of statistical tests verified that the longer the children had lived in the Bridge Apartments, the more trouble they had making these auditory discriminations. After ruling out a number of other explanations (such as the possibility of mild carbon monoxide poisoning from automobile fumes on the lower floors), these researchers suggested that children in the noisier apartments learned to pay less attention to auditory cues. This ability helped them to adapt to their apartments, but it also gave them less practice distinguishing speech sounds.

Later research has generally supported these findings. For example, Bronzaft and McCarthy (1975) studied second-, fourth-, and sixth-graders in a school located next to an elevated train line. In the classrooms facing the tracks, the average noise level was 59 decibels; when a train passed by every five minutes or so, this level rose to 89 decibels. Children in these classrooms had lower reading achievement scores than their classmates whose schoolrooms were on the "quiet" side of the building.

Similarly, a study that compared reading achievement at New York City schools located at various distances from airports found that the more aircraft noise the children were exposed to, the lower their average reading achievement (Green, Pasternack, & Shore, 1982). After reviewing the entire literature on this topic, DeJoy (1983, p. 191) concluded that "deficits in reading achievement and cognitive task performance have been reported in a number of studies, involving different noise sources and populations of children."

Fortunately, there is some evidence that these effects are not permanent. In a follow-up study of the school located next to the train tracks, Bronzaft (1981) looked at achievement scores after steps were taken to reduce the train noise. (These included inserting special rubber pads next to the rails and installing acoustic tiles in the classrooms.) A year later, achievement scores were the same in classrooms on both sides of the building (that is, the children who initially scored low now scored on a par with children in the "quiet" rooms).

Thus, environmental psychology began as a result of studies on the effects of environmental stresses, such as noise. Once these stressors were identified, it went one step further to apply this knowledge to try to improve the situation and people's ability to cope with it. Finally, the researchers evaluated their intervention to verify that it did indeed make a difference.

This same progression from basic understanding to changing the situation and evaluating the results will be seen in the final topic in this chapter: health psychology.

Health Psychology

The field of **health psychology** is concerned with the relationships between behavior, health, and illness. This area includes basic research on these issues and the application of its findings to change people's behavior in order to prevent or cure disease.

The success of twentieth-century science in diagnosing and treating certain types of diseases has actually changed the pattern of disease and thus is changing the principal problems faced by most physicians. In 1900, the three most common causes of death in the United States were influenza, pneumonia, and tuberculosis. Today, the three leading causes of death are heart disease, cancer, and strokes (Sexton, 1979). Thus, while doctors at the turn of the

health psychology The field concerned with the relationships between behavior, health, and illness.

century struggled primarily with contagious diseases, today's major medical problems may be more closely related to behaviors, such as smoking, eating the right foods, and dealing with stress. As a result, physicians are becoming increasingly involved in trying to change the way people live rather than focusing on how they die.

Although social scientists have studied the relationships between behavior and health for many years, it was only in the 1970s that researchers defined this area as a separate discipline (Schwartz & Weiss, 1977). At first, health psychology was called *behavioral medicine,* a term some psychologists prefer and continue to use. However, many feel that "behavioral medicine" conjures up images of hospitals and severe illnesses. They prefer the name health psychology, because it calls attention to the positive role that behavior and experience can play in promoting health.

Our review of this exciting new area begins with one of the classic issues: stress, its relation to health and various techniques for reducing it. We conclude with a discussion of the role psychology can play in preventing disease before it occurs.

Stress and Illness

Stress involves a perception of threat to physical or psychological well-being and the individual's reaction to that threat.

One of the first researchers to explore the consequences of stress was Hans Selye. In 1936, he reported that animals responded to a variety of stressors, ranging from extreme cold to injection of a small amount of poison, with the same physiological pattern. Selye called this physiological response to stress the **general adaptational syndrome** and divided it into three stages: alarm, resistance, and exhaustion.

The *alarm stage* began at the first sign of stress, as the animal's body tried to defend itself by mobilizing the endocrine glands. In particular, the adrenal glands became enlarged and secreted higher levels of the hormone adrenaline into the bloodstream. This in turn led to a variety of physiological changes, including a breakdown of some tissue into energy-giving sugars.

After several days of stress, the animal would adapt and its body chemistry would return to normal. This *resistance stage* was only temporary, however. If the stress continued, the adrenal glands again became enlarged and lost their stores of adrenal hormones. In this final stage—*exhaustion*—the endocrine glands, the kidneys, and other internal organs were damaged, and the animal ultimately died.

Inspired by these findings, many researchers went on systematically to expose animals to various types of stressful stimuli and to chart their precise physiological responses. But scientists who chose to study human responses to stress were forced to rely on a clumsier method, letting Mother Nature choose the people who would be subjected to the greatest physical and emotional strain.

At first, human stress research focused on a group of illnesses known as psychosomatic disorders. In everyday language, the term *psychosomatic* is often used incorrectly to refer to imaginary diseases. If you feel sick to your

stress A perception of threat to physical or psychological well-being and the reaction to that threat.

general adaptational syndrome According to Selye, a physiological response to stress that is divided into three stages: alarm, resistance, and exhaustion.

stomach before your final examination in Zen Accounting, a friend may tell you smugly, "It's only psychosomatic," as though there were nothing really wrong with you, almost as though it were your own fault that you threw up. In fact, however, a **psychosomatic disease** is a real physical illness that is partly caused by psychological factors. The most common psychosomatic disorders are ulcers, high blood pressure, migraine or tension headaches, asthma, and a variety of skin conditions such as eczema, hives, and psoriasis.

Countless studies have shown that people under stress are particularly vulnerable to these problems. For example, when London was bombed by the Germans at the beginning of World War II, the number of people who came to London hospitals with ulcers increased substantially (Stewart & Wisner, 1942). High-stress jobs can also lead to physical problems. In the early 1970s, air traffic controllers were twice as likely to have ulcers and four times as likely to have high blood pressure as comparable groups of pilots (Cobb & Rose, 1973). Psychologists have known for some time that stress can trigger psychosomatic disorders. More recent is the idea that stress can trigger other diseases as well.

One of the most important lines of research that led to this new view began in 1967 when Thomas Holmes and Richard Rahe published the **Social Readjustment Rating Scale** to measure normal life stress. Holmes and Rahe listed 43 events that they believed were particularly likely to cause stress for the average American adult. They then asked 394 people to rate each event according to the amount and intensity of readjustment it required. The death of a spouse was considered the most stressful event and was given an average rating of 100 "life-change units." This event was rated twice as stressful as getting married (rated 50) and about four times as stressful as beginning or ending school (rated 26). Any person could now be assigned a life-stress score simply by adding the point values of all the events that had occurred in a certain period of time, usually the last 6 or 12 months.

Despite the fact that these were only average scores and that any individual might rate specific stressors somewhat differently, many researchers have shown that the higher a person's score on the Social Readjustment Rating Scale, the more likely he or she is to get sick. For example, Rahe (1972) studied the illnesses of sailors in the U.S. Navy. Before beginning a cruise, each man completed the Social Readjustment Rating Scale, describing how much stress he had been under in the last six months. When the ship returned to port six to eight months later, Rahe simply counted the number of times each sailor had reported to the sick bay with objective signs of a new illness. He then divided the men into four groups on the basis of their life-stress scores and found an orderly and statistically significant progression in the frequency of illness (see Figure 17.2). Stress seemed to increase the risk not only of psychosomatic problems, such as hives and asthma, but also of all sorts of physical diseases.

Some researchers went on to develop alternative questionnaires that were specially suited to the life experiences of different groups. Table 17.1 illustrates the College Schedule of Recent Experience, the questionnaire likely to be relevant for readers of this text. Certainly, major life changes, like leaving home for the first time or being fired from a job, are quite stressful. But less dramatic events can also be stressful, especially if they occur continuously.

psychosomatic disease   A physical illness that is partly caused by psychological factors.

Social Readjustment Rating Scale   A measurement of normal life stress.

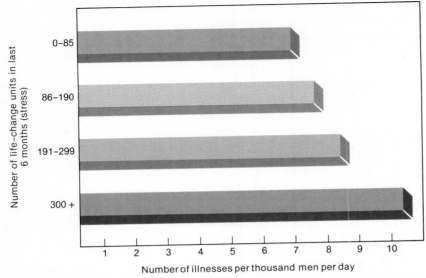

FIGURE 17.2 During a six-month U.S. Navy cruise, sailors who had experienced more stress in the previous six months were more likely to become ill.

For example, being stuck in a traffic jam in the morning can leave you tense for the whole day.

Delongis, Coyne, Dakof, Folkman, and Lazarus (1982) developed a questionnaire to measure how stressful such everyday stressors are. The 117 items on the Hassles Scale included having unexpected company, owing money to someone, worrying about weight, misplacing things, and being too busy. (Table 17.2 lists 37 of these items.) They found that the more hassles a person reported, the more likely the person was to have some health problems. Interestingly, hassles were even more highly correlated with physical and mental health than were major life events (Kanner, Coyne, Schaefer, & Lazarus, 1981). They also measured uplifts, such as relating well with family members and friends, eating out, and meeting responsibilities. Though they had expected to find that these uplifts counterbalanced the effects of stress, there was little evidence that positive events had any impact on health (Lazarus, 1981).

Thus, even if your stress score on Table 17.1 is low, that does not mean you have not been stressed. We all have days that make us tense and exhausted; yet when we think about the day, we can not point to any specific event that caused the stress. More likely, small annoyances have accumulated: the co-worker who refused to turn her radio down; the fact that they put onions on your hamburger at lunch, even though you told them not to; or the fool who cut into the lane ahead of you while everyone else waited their turn. Although these events may seem minor, they still can be stressful enough to affect health.

Overall, a large number of studies using a variety of scales have shown that people who have recently experienced a great deal of stress are more likely to develop minor medical complaints as well as heart disease, tuberculosis, leukemia, diabetes, and multiple sclerosis. They are also more likely to have accidents or to injure themselves in athletic competition (Rabkin & Struening, 1976).

TABLE 17.1

The College Schedule of Recent Experience

To quantify the stress you have been subjected to lately, multiply the value for each event by the number of times it occurred in the past year (up to a maximum of 4) and add all values. In the original study, scores below 347 were considered to fall in the low-stress category, and scores above 1,435 were classified as high stress.

Event	*Numerical value*
(1) Entered college	50
(2) Married	77
(3) Trouble with your boss	38
(4) Held a job while attending school	43
(5) Experienced the death of a spouse	87
(6) Major change in sleeping habits	34
(7) Experienced the death of a close family member	77
(8) Major change in eating habits	30
(9) Change in or choice of major field of study	41
(10) Revision of personal habits	45
(11) Experienced the death of a close friend	68
(12) Found guilty of minor violations of the law	22
(13) Had an outstanding personal achievement	40
(14) Experienced pregnancy or fathered a pregnancy	68
(15) Major change in health or behavior of family member	56
(16) Had sexual difficulties	58
(17) Had trouble with in-laws	42
(18) Major change in number of family get-togethers	26
(19) Major change in financial state	53
(20) Gained a new family member	50
(21) Change in residence or living conditions	42
(22) Major conflict or change in values	50
(23) Major change in church activities	36
(24) Marital reconciliation with your mate	58
(25) Fired from work	62
(26) Were divorced	76
(27) Changed to a different line of work	50
(28) Major change in number of arguments with spouse	50
(29) Major change in responsibilities at work	47
(30) Had your spouse begin or cease work outside the home	41
(31) Major change in working hours or conditions	42
(32) Marital separation from mate	74
(33) Major change in type and/or amount of recreation	37
(34) Major change in use of drugs	52
(35) Took on a mortgage or loan of less than $10,000	52
(36) Major personal injury or illness	65
(37) Major change in use of alcohol	46
(38) Major change in social activitites	43
(39) Major change in amount of participation in school activities	38
(40) Major change in amount of independence and responsibility	49
(41) Took a trip or a vacation	33
(42) Engaged to be married	54
(43) Changed to a new school	50
(44) Changed dating habits	41
(45) Trouble with school administration	44
(46) Broke or had broken a marital engagement or a steady relationship	60
(47) Major change in self-concept or self-awareness	57

Source: Marx, Garrity, & Bowers, 1975, p. 97.

TABLE 17.2

The Hassles Scale

Directions: Hassles are irritants that can range from minor annoyances to fairly major pressures, problems, or difficulties. They can occur few or many times. Listed below are a number of ways in which a person can feel hassled. First, circle the hassles that have happened to you in the past month. Then look at the numbers on the right of the items you circled. Indicate how SEVERE each of the *circled* hassles has been for you in the past month by circling 1 (somewhat severe), 2 (moderately severe), or 3 (extremely severe). If a hassle did not occur in the last month do NOT circle it. Calculate your score by adding together all the numbers you circled. The higher your score, the more hassles you have experienced in the last month—and the more likely you are to be experiencing some health problems.

Hassles	Severity			Hassles	Severity		
(1) Misplacing or losing things	1	2	3	(20) Decisions about having children	1	2	3
(2) Troublesome neighbors	1	2	3	(21) Nonfamily members living in your house	1	2	3
(3) Social obligations	1	2	3				
(4) Inconsiderate smokers	1	2	3	(22) Care for pet	1	2	3
(5) Troubling thoughts about your future	1	2	3	(23) Planning meals	1	2	3
				(24) Concerned about the meaning of life	1	2	3
(6) Thoughts about death	1	2	3	(25) Trouble relaxing	1	2	3
(7) Health of a family member	1	2	3	(26) Trouble making decisions	1	2	3
(8) Not enough money for clothing	1	2	3	(27) Problems getting along with fellow workers	1	2	3
(9) Not enough money for housing	1	2	3				
(10) Concerns about owing money	1	2	3	(28) Customers or clients give you a hard time	1	2	3
(11) Concerns about getting credit	1	2	3				
(12) Concerns about money for emergencies	1	2	3	(29) Home maintenance (inside)	1	2	3
				(30) Concerns about job security	1	2	3
(13) Someone owes you money	1	2	3	(31) Concerns about retirement	1	2	3
(14) Financial responsibility for someone who doesn't live with you	1	2	3	(32) Laid off or out of work	1	2	3
				(33) Don't like current work duties	1	2	3
(15) Cutting down on electricity, water, etc.	1	2	3	(34) Don't like fellow workers	1	2	3
				(35) Not enough money for basic necessities	1	2	3
(16) Smoking too much	1	2	3				
(17) Use of alcohol	1	2	3	(36) Not enough money for food	1	2	3
(18) Personal use of drugs	1	2	3	(37) Too many interruptions	1	2	3
(19) Too many responsibilities	1	2	3				

Source: Kanner, Coyne, Schaefer, & Lazarus, 1981, Appendix.

Are Women Under More Stress Than They Used to Be?

A number of assertions were made in a 1978 article in the *Boston Globe* entitled, "What's new for women? Stress." In this article, Connie Berman suggested that in recent years more and more women were smoking because of stress and tension-filled situations. Quoting a spokesperson for the American Cancer Society, Berman suggested that career women were smoking more because of the stress-inducing demands of their jobs and that homemakers were smoking more because of the anxiety generated by criticisms that women should do more than be homemakers.

Berman also reported that women were drinking more. She acknowledged that the majority of the nation's 5 million alcoholics were homemakers, but also noted that an increasing number of alcoholics are women working outside the home. After noting that women tend to drink because of their confusion over sex roles, inferiority complexes, insecurity about their femininity, and life crises, Berman concluded:

> It is quite possible that the women's movement may have triggered these feelings in some cases: career women feel pressured to get ahead and prove their mettle; housewives who don't work feel compelled to find work. (p. 25)

What other interpretations can you think of for the facts presented? Do the assertions seem firmly based on hard evidence? (A discussion appears after the "Summary" at the end of this chapter.)

Critics have been quick to point out that the fact that life stress *correlates* with physical disease does not necessarily mean that life stress *causes* physical disease. It is possible that people under stress smoke more, drink more, sleep less, eat poorly, or act in other ways that increase the risk of medical problems. In other words, it remains to be seen whether stress causes disease directly or if the link is more subtle. (See "Becoming a Critical Consumer" for a consideration of this link in women.)

Further, it is important to emphasize that while the relationship between stress and illness is quite consistent, it is rather modest in size. (The typical correlation is about .30; see the "Appendix" for an explanation.) Stress is one of a large number of factors involved in physical disease; many people who are not particularly stressed get sick, and many others go through very stressful periods and remain healthy.

This finding leads directly to a fascinating question of individual differences: Why do some people get sick when they are stressed while others do not?

Individual Differences
in the Stress Response

It is a fact of life that people experience stress for different reasons. What you perceive as stressful may not bother your best friend at all, while you may not even notice a situation that drives him wild. As Lazarus, DeLongis, Folkman, and Gruen (1985) point out, external events do not cause stress; our reactions to a situation or our personal appraisal of it is what matters.

The fact that you got onions on your hamburger after specifically requesting none may have been enough to make you fantasize about mass homicide of all the incompetents on the face of the earth. Someone else might just shrug off the same event as a natural mistake that is easy to make in the rush of lunchtime crowds.

Naturally, some events will be perceived as stressful by almost anyone. For example, it is hard to be blasé if you are a passenger on a hijacked plane. But even in this type of extreme situation, some people will be more upset than others.

COPING MECHANISMS

One reason for these individual differences derives from the coping mechanisms people employ during difficult situations. These mechanisms can have an important impact on stress. Some people have personal characteristics that enable them to deal with stressful situations and that ultimately protect them from negative effects on health. For example, some people are able to

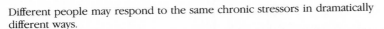

Different people may respond to the same chronic stressors in dramatically different ways.

look on the bright side of things; if the ballgame is canceled because of rain, they might say that now they can go bowling instead.

Another adaptive personal characteristic is flexibility. If Saturday night plans fall through, flexible people just come up with alternatives. Those who are less flexible might become upset or angry and spend the evening doing nothing. Such a reaction is more likely to be detrimental to health. Flexibility helps in coping with stress by giving alternative ways of responding (Gore, 1985).

Fatalism is another personal characteristic that affects coping. If you just accept a situation, saying there is nothing you can do, you are less likely to feel in control and the stress will be greater. For example, suppose you have just been told that your apartment building has been sold and you must move out within a month. If you are fatalistic, you will probably accept the situation, rather miserably, and start looking for a new apartment. But this is not always the most adaptive approach. You might instead decide to contact the new owner to see if your lease can be renewed. Fatalism can lead to inaction because of an unwillingness to seek solutions to reduce stress. Of course, if you explore all possibilities and still have to move, then flexibility will be an asset.

Being able to predict when stressful events will occur is another factor that can reduce the negative effects of stress. With predictability, at least we can prepare for a stressful event, using whatever coping mechanisms we have.

Suppose you have to give a presentation to your history class on the Battle of Manassas in the Civil War. You are nervous about it, because you wonder what your classmates will think if you lose your train of thought in the middle of the speech and start to drool. And, of course, you would not mind impressing your professor and getting a decent grade. You know the date of the presentation, so the event is predictable. To feel in control, you practice your talk ahead of time. All these preparations will help you deal with the stress, and the predictability of the event will reduce the stress.

Thus, we can explain some individual differences in response to stress by understanding ways in which people react to and cope with stress. But inner resources alone are not always enough to handle stress successfully.

SOCIAL SUPPORT

Sharing problems with a friend or family member can be enormously helpful in reducing the effects of stress, even if the stressful situation remains unchanged. Having support from others can buffer us against the negative effects of stress.

We all have those days when everything goes wrong from the time you put your shoes on the wrong feet to the moment you burn your dinner. At the end of the day, you want to tell someone about everything that went wrong in order to vent your frustration and maybe even regain a sense of humor. In other words, you want someone with whom you can share your concerns.

Social support refers to the resources that other people provide. The effects of such support can be quite positive on our mental and physical

social support The resources that other people provide.

Social support can increase both physical and psychological well-being.

health as well as on our overall sense of well-being (Cohen & Syme, 1985). Social support helps in two ways. First, it can give a person an enhanced sense of worth, which contributes to health regardless of stress level. Second, support can provide a buffering effect that helps one deal with specific stressful events.

Typically, when external events seem overwhelming, people not only experience lack of control over their lives, they are also likely to have lower self-esteem and a diminished sense of effectiveness. For example, if a couple has been going together for two years and then one day the woman decides to break it off, the man is likely to experience rejection, unhappiness, loneliness, and a loss of self-confidence. But if he has a good friend to talk to, someone who can assure him that he is still the great guy he always was, then he has a source of encouragement while dealing with the breakup. Support from others can counter doubts about ability, worthiness, and performance by providing information as well as social companionship.

Of course, self-esteem doesn't always decrease when one faces a stressful situation. It is most likely to drop when people believe that their incompetence caused the difficult situation in the first place. Consider how two different men might react to losing their jobs. The first man thinks his inability to find work is due to his incompetence, and his self-esteem drops as his job search remains unsuccessful; he feels worthless. The second man is in the same situation; he too cannot find a job. But he blames the national economy for his joblessness. Since he does not feel personally responsible, his unemployment will not affect his sense of self-worth or cause as much stress.

Researchers have used questionnaires and interviews to measure social support. For example, Sarason and Sarason (1984) asked people to list others who were available to turn to in times of stress and to report how satisfied they were with the support. Their Social Support Questionnaire included the following items: "Whom can you really count on to listen to you when you need to talk?"; "Whom could you really count on to help you out in a crisis situation, even though they would have to go out of their way to do so?"; and "Whom can you count on to console you when you are very upset?" People who had a high number of support persons and were satisfied with the support these people provided had a more optimistic view of life, higher self-esteem, and more desirable experiences than those who were low in social support.

Numerous studies have shown that the effects of stress are greater when there is no social support. One group of researchers (Nuckolls, Cassel, & Kaplan, 1972) studied pregnant women. They found that 91% of those who had high-stress scores, poor opinions of themselves, and little help from relatives and friends had complications in later pregnancy or childbirth. Only 33% of those who were equally stressed but in a better sociopsychological position had similar complications. Life stress by itself did not predict medical problems; neither did lack of sociopsychological supports. But when the two factors came together, health problems were likely to result.

In another study of nearly 4,000 Japanese-American men, researchers found that low social affiliation (for example, few memberships in groups) was related to the incidence of coronary heart disease (Joseph & Syme, 1981, cited in Berkman, 1984). Similarly, when angina rates were examined for 10,000 Israeli men, those with more family support reported less angina pain (Medalie & Goldbourt, 1976).

Even mortality is affected when social support is lacking. Over a nine-year period, Berkman et al. (1984) conducted a large-scale study of death rates among a group of nearly 7,000 men and women in California. For each individual, the researchers obtained information about marriages, contact with close friends and relatives, and church and other group memberships. They found that people who had the fewest community ties were actually more likely to die than those who had strong community ties. This was true regardless of physical health at the beginning of the nine-year period.

For many people, a major source of social support is their marital partner—and the most stressful event on Holmes and Rahe's original Social Readjustment Scale is the death of a spouse. The death itself, often preceded by a period of illness, is, of course, a major stress. But, in addition, the surviving spouse suffers the loss of a primary source of social support. This may explain why the incidence of illness for new widows and widowers is quite high.

Yet even under these difficult circumstances, sharing problems with others can be helpful. Pennebaker and O'Heeron (1984) studied spouses of suicide and accident death victims. They found that subjects who kept their grief to themselves were more likely to have health problems than those who talked to others.

As with all correlational research, we must be careful in interpreting the results of these studies in terms of cause-and-effect relationships. It is clear that there is a strong connection between social support and health. However, we cannot be as certain about the underlying cause. Having people to share problems with and to help during difficult times is indeed likely to reduce stress. But it also may be true that people who seek out social support are those who are better at coping. (As we saw above, people with good support systems have higher self-esteem. It is plausible that because of their confidence in themselves, they make friends more easily.) Thus, we need to be cautious in interpreting the findings of social-support research.

Further, although the correlations between support and health are statistically significant (see Chapter 2), they are not especially high, often in the .20 to .30 range (Sarason & Sarason, 1984). As is so often the case, additional research will be required to identify other factors and to determine whether programs that increase social supports might have a positive impact on health. In the meantime, a number of more direct procedures are being used to control and reduce stress.

Reducing Stress

Psychologists and physicians are often called on to help people reduce stress, and in this text we have already discussed a number of possible techniques. These include psychotherapy and counseling (see Chapter 15), and meditation and anxiety-reducing drugs (see Chapter 4). Another technique that has proven useful in recent years is biofeedback.

BIOFEEDBACK

The basic principle of biofeedback is simple: Feedback makes certain types of learning possible. Imagine trying to learn to play the electric guitar if you always wore earplugs when you practiced. Without the feedback of hearing your mistakes, you would never be able to learn to play a recognizable version of "The Star-Spangled Banner." Or imagine trying to learn to throw darts while blindfolded. If you never knew whether you had hit the bull's-eye or an innocent bystander, how could you ever improve your aim?

Our bodies are not designed to allow us to be consciously aware of subtle feedback about internal physiological states. At this moment, you do not know precisely how fast your heart is beating, what your blood pressure is, or how tense the muscles in your forehead are. However, if you were given this information, you could learn to control these physiological processes to some extent.

Biofeedback involves learning to control physiological states on the basis of precise physiological information (feedback). For example, suppose your heart beats about 80 times per minute (or once every three-fourths of a second) and you want to learn to slow it down. You could be connected to a machine that measures precisely the time interval between the beats of your heart. Whenever two beats were more than three-fourths of a second apart, a light would go on, telling you that your average heart rate was now lower than 80 beats per minute. If you sat quietly watching the machine and concentrating on whatever thoughts seemed to make the light go on more frequently, you could gradually learn to keep the light on and thus make your heart rate go down. Precisely how would you do this? It's hard to say.

biofeedback The technique of learning to control physiological states on the basis of precise physiological data.

When researcher David Shapiro (1973) asked a person in one of his experiments how he had lowered his heart rate, the subject asked in return, "How do you move your arm?"

However people do it, subjects in biofeedback experiments have learned to control a wide variety of physiological processes. They have raised and lowered their heart rates and their blood pressures and precisely regulated the level of tension in many different muscles. They have changed the rhythms of their brain waves (as measured by EEG; see Chapter 3) and changed the diameter of their blood vessels.

Such remarkable feats have led many researchers to investigate whether biofeedback can be used to help patients suffering from various diseases (Olton & Noonberg, 1980). Some epileptics, for example, have been able to learn to control a specific type of EEG rhythm that is associated with seizures (a 12- to 14-cycle-per-second wave that appears over the motor cortex) and have had fewer seizures as a result. Biofeedback has also been successfully used in some cases to help people regain use of muscles that were damaged by accident or disease.

When you feel anxious or under stress, you may tense many muscles in the body, including the frontalis muscle in your forehead. Biofeedback training to reduce this muscle tension has been used to treat many types of disorders, including insomnia, chronic anxiety, certain types of headaches, asthma, and high blood pressure.

At this point, it is clear that biofeedback therapy has helped some people learn to relax and overcome some of the effects of stress. What is not so clear is what makes biofeedback therapy work. Some skeptics believe that the biofeedback may be less important than factors such as the patient's commitment to getting better and active involvement with the therapist. Some of these issues can be seen more clearly by focusing on the treatment of one of the most common stress-related disorders: high blood pressure.

TREATING HIGH BLOOD PRESSURE

Blood pressure is the force exerted as blood moves away from the heart, pushing against the artery walls. One factor that can raise blood pressure is psychological stress; visiting the dentist, taking an examination, thinking about how much money you had to borrow to go to college, even drinking a cup of coffee (a mild stimulant) will increase blood pressure temporarily. When blood pressure goes up and stays above normal levels, this medical condition is called **high blood pressure**, or **hypertension**.

About one out of every three American adults has high blood pressure. It is particularly common among blacks, older people, and those with a family history of hypertension. Hypertension is called "the silent killer," because it usually produces neither pain nor any other symptoms or warnings before causing severe damage to the cardiovascular system or other organs. But a killer it is. It is a primary cause of stroke (blood vessel damage in the brain) and, like smoking and high cholesterol levels, increases the risk of heart attack and coronary artery disease.

Most serious cases of hypertension require drug therapy to return blood pressure to safer levels. However, there is no drug that can cure hypertension

blood pressure The force exerted as blood moves away from the heart, pushing against the artery walls.

high blood pressure (hypertension) Consistently elevated levels of blood pressure.

permanently; if a patient stops taking the pills, his or her blood pressure will rise again.

This is where health psychology comes into the picture. Patients with definite hypertension must take drugs every day for the rest of their lives. But 50% or more of all hypertensives fail to take their pills. There are many possible reasons: They may not understand the treatment, they may find it too expensive or too much trouble, or they may be bothered by side effects.

One study of an inner-city hypertension clinic found a dropout rate of 42%. Researchers discovered that part of the problem was the inefficient way the clinic was run. The average waiting time to see a doctor was 2½ hours, and the patient was likely to see a different physician at each visit. Simply by cutting down the waiting time and assigning each patient to a specific doctor, the clinic cut its dropout rate to 4% (Wingerson, 1977). Future improvements in twentieth-century medicine may have more to do with restoring the personal touch than with inventing ever more sophisticated machines and treatments.

Behavioral medicine has also proposed alternate techniques for treating high blood pressure without pills. These include blood pressure biofeedback, electromyographic (EMG) biofeedback for reducing tension in the frontalis muscle in the forehead, relaxation training, and meditation. Because all these techniques produce similar effects (Agras & Jacob, 1979) and biofeedback requires physiological measurement devices whereas the other techniques do not, it seems likely that meditation and relaxation will be more widely practiced. (See Chapter 4 for more information about meditation and relaxation training.)

How do biofeedback and meditation compare with more traditional medical treatments? According to one review (Jacob, Kraemer, & Agras, 1977), relaxation reduces blood pressure far more than placebos do (indicating that relaxation involves more than the power of suggestion) and even compares favorably with some drugs. This report also notes that regular practice is necessary for the development and maintenance of the treatment effect, which builds up gradually over a period of several months.

This idea of regular practice over an extended period of time is the one great weakness of biofeedback treatment. Even in the very first study of blood pressure biofeedback, there were hints that the effects did not always last after the subjects left the laboratory. Psychologist Gary Schwartz noticed that one man had a puzzling pattern of successes and failures. Five days a week, this hypertensive client faithfully attended training sessions, collecting $35 from the researcher every Friday as a reward for his success in lowering his systolic pressure. When he returned each Monday morning, however, he again had a high blood pressure reading. After several weeks of this, Schwartz took the patient aside and asked for an explanation. It seemed that on Saturday nights the man took his biofeedback earnings to the racetrack, gambled, and lost both his money and his controlled level of blood pressure.

Thus, over the long term, the clinical usefulness of most forms of medical treatment depend not just on their physical effects, but also on the psychological issue of people's compliance with the doctor's orders. This same issue lies at the core of some of the most interesting work in health psychology: trying to prevent disease by encouraging people to change their behavior.

Preventing Disease

Many chronic diseases stem from life-styles. For example, there is a large body of evidence that coronary heart disease is related to improper diet and lack of exercise. Other problems result from alcohol abuse, drug abuse, and cigarette smoking. Yet, despite increasing awareness in our society of the harmful effects of these behaviors, many people continue to drink to excess, take drugs, and smoke cigarettes.

Why is it so hard for people to change to more healthful life-styles? One reason is the lack of immediacy: If a business executive gives up Bloody Mary breakfasts, it may have no noticeable effect on that person's present health—and make breakfast a lot more boring. Or consider your own feelings if you go with a friend to an ice cream parlor. When you are surrounded by all that hot fudge, it's hard to concentrate on the negative health effects of being overweight. Thus, the effort and inconvenience involved in acquiring more healthful habits are discouraging to many people.

There may also be negative pressures from society. Although our society

Applied psychologists are exploring ways to help people develop habits that promote good health.

has become more conscious of the value of exercise and good nutrition, we still do not always make it easy for people to follow health-promoting lifestyles. For example, few workers have the opportunity or time for exercise during the workday; just as few people have easy daily access to healthier foods. Even elementary school children are losing recess time in response to parental pressures that they spend more time in the classroom.

Stress can also be an indirect cause of unhealthy habits. People who are stressed are more likely to engage in unhealthful behavior, like smoking or drinking excessively. How many students who are dieting have ordered a double pizza with extra cheese the night before a big exam? How many overworked salespeople have decided that their schedule simply does not allow time for exercise?

Researchers in health psychology are therefore trying to determine the most effective ways of helping people modify their behavior to promote health. One of their greatest challenges is in the area of smoking.

Smoking is the most preventable reason for death and illness in the United States (Krantz, Grunberg, & Baum, 1985). Even children are aware of the dangers of smoking. In fact, between ages 4 and 11, many children try to convince their parents to give up smoking, fearing that their parents will get sick. But when these children reach adolescence, they are among the many thousands of people who begin smoking each year. All told, approximately 54 million Americans still smoke, despite awareness of the high risk for developing cancer, coronary heart disease, emphysema, and bronchitis.

Why do people decide to start smoking? Many are modeling the behavior of someone they admire, such as family members or media figures. Cigarette advertisements often portray smokers as beautiful, vigorous, and desirable men and women, and some people may begin smoking to try to acquire such an image.

Social pressure is another important factor, especially among adolescents. Being the only nonsmoker in a group can be difficult; peers may pressure a friend to try one cigarette. Adolescent rebellion sometimes contributes to the decision to smoke, particularly if an adolescent is ordered not to smoke. Finally, many people who begin smoking either misunderstand the risks or deny that anything bad will ever happen to them.

Once a pattern of smoking is established, it is very difficult to stop. No doubt you know people who have tried many times to stop smoking, perhaps even succeeded for a while, but then began smoking again. Clearly, smoking is not an easy habit to give up. Some people complain that they gain weight when they stop smoking; others say that they can no longer enjoy coffee after dinner.

Systematic approaches to help people stop smoking include hypnotism, behavior modification, and group support. While many people do stop while they are in a specific program, more than 50% to 75% return to smoking within a year after the program ends (Krantz et al., 1985). Many researchers have therefore focused their attention on preventing smoking in the first place.

Evans et al. (1981) conducted a three-year intervention program to prevent smoking in adolescents. Several thousand junior high students were shown films dealing with the dangers of smoking and the problems of peer pressure. To increase the likelihood that these films would be effective, Evans, Raines, and Hanselka (1984) used feedback from students to modify them. They held discussions with seventh-graders to learn their perceptions of why teens smoke, who is likely to smoke and when, and what kinds of people smokers and nonsmokers are. These students also reacted to hypothetical situations in which someone offered them a cigarette.

Based on these discussions, Evans et al. (1984) developed role-playing scripts to portray real-life situations. For example, one segment shows how to deal with pressure from friends. When offered a cigarette, this teenager stalls, making an excuse like, "Not today. I have this real sore throat" (Evans et al., 1984, p. 293).

The films also made students aware of the immediate negative effects on health that stem from smoking. The researchers reasoned that adolescents ignore warnings about possible long-term health problems, such as cancer, because these problems have no current impact on their lives. So the films focused instead on immediate effects, such as changes in carbon monoxide levels in the blood. The aim of the program was to reduce the number of students who would begin smoking.

While the program did not prevent smoking among all students, it did have an effect. At the end of the eighth grade, students who had seen all the movies had a lower percentage of smokers (5.5%) than various control groups who had seen only one or none of the movies (11%). By the end of the ninth grade, the difference remained between the groups, although the total proportion of smokers unfortunately went up (to 9.5% for the experimental group versus 14.2% for the controls). It is disappointing that the program could not have been more successful, but every teenager who did not begin smoking benefited from this research.

Generally, results from intervention studies are encouraging; they seem to prevent smoking in a significant number of people. Public health campaigns to educate people about the risks of smoking have also been effective in reducing tobacco use (Krantz et al., 1985).

While none of us can eliminate all unhealthy behavior from our lives, we can take charge of our own actions and decide how we will react to unavoidable stress. Understanding reasons for unhealthy behavior and learning how to eliminate it is a major challenge not only for applied psychology, but for every one of us.

Summary

Industrial/Organizational Psychology

- **Industrial/organizational psychology** studies human behavior and experience in the workplace.

- The subfield of **industrial psychology** studies individual workers, their abilities, and the way these abilities relate to job performance.

- **Organizational psychology** studies human interaction in the workplace.
- The subfield of **human factors engineering** studies the way people interact with machines and the physical work environment.
- **Cognitive tests** are designed to measure intelligence and other mental abilities.
- **Motor skills tests** evaluate workers' speed, coordination, or precision in using their muscles.
- **Tests of job-specific skills**, or work sample tests, require the worker to demonstrate skill in performing a task very similar to the tasks actually required on the job.
- **Personnel training** involves an organization's program to teach employees job-related behaviors.
- A **task analysis** determines the precise skills and behaviors required to perform a particular job.
- **Computer-based training** programs use computers to deliver instruction in job-related skills.

Environmental Psychology

- **Environmental psychology** is the study of the interrelationships between human behavior and the physical settings of everyday life.
- The term **behavioral sink** refers to the pattern of bizarre and antisocial behavior that occurs in a pen overcrowded with rats.

Health Psychology

- **Health psychology** is concerned with the relationships between behavior, health, and illness.
- **Stress** involves a perception of threat to physical or psychological well-being and the individual's response to that threat.
- The **general adaptational syndrome** is a physiological response to stress that is divided into three stages: alarm, resistance, and exhaustion.
- A **psychosomatic disease** is a real physical illness that is partly caused by psychological factors.
- The **Social Readjustment Rating Scale** measures normal life stress.
- **Social support** refers to the resources that other people provide.
- **Biofeedback** involves learning to control physiological states on the basis of precise physiological information (feedback).
- **Blood pressure** is the force exerted as blood moves away from the heart, pushing against the artery walls.
- **High blood pressure**, or **hypertension**, is the medical term used when blood pressure goes up and stays above normal levels.

Critical Thinking Exercise
Discussion

Are Women Under More Stress
Than They Used to Be?

The author of this article seems to believe that the women's movement is making women sick. The critical thinker will always look for the factual evidence that lies behind a conclusion.

In this excerpt, there is no exploration of alternative explanations for increased smoking among women. How does the American Cancer Society expert *know* that this is a corollary of stress? Even while noting that alcoholism is still higher among housewives than working women, the author connects alcohol abuse with women's liberation. Thus, whether women work or stay home, any misuse of alcohol seems linked somehow to the women's movement.

APPENDIX: STATISTICS

Somewhere in the world there may be a college that does not require psychology majors to learn something about statistics. But we've never heard of it, and you probably don't go there.

Statistics is a vital ingredient in any psychology curriculum. The reason should be obvious to anyone who has read a chapter or two of this book: Statistical analysis provides powerful tools for evaluating claims about behavior. This type of evaluation and critical analysis lies at the very heart of the scientific method.

When psychologists systematically study behavior or experience, they typically begin by quantifying such variables as learning, color perception, aggression, or introversion. For example, in his pioneer studies of human memory, Hermann Ebbinghaus began by counting the number of nonsense syllables he was able to remember after various intervals (see Chapter 7). Mathematical procedures were then required to summarize his data and specify the time course for this memory task.

Some people break into a cold sweat when they hear the word *statistics* and may require treatment if asked to compute the probability of a coin coming up tails. This type of math anxiety can lead a student who would like to major in psychology to concentrate on Sanskrit or medieval agriculture instead, simply to avoid a course requirement in statistics.

But, as with most fears, the imagination is usually worse than the reality. Anyone who has ever played cards or tried to decide whether to trust a meteorologist's forecast has applied intuitive notions of statistics and probability.

This appendix is designed to review some basic concepts of statistical reasoning and to reassure the worriers that statistics is quite straightforward. True, statistical calculations can get involved at times. But even people who have trouble balancing their checkbooks can learn to compute a standard deviation or a correlation coefficient if they just take the calculations one small step at a time.

Descriptive Statistics

Descriptive statistics provide techniques for summarizing groups of numbers. Several examples are explained throughout this book, ranging from arithmetic averages to correlation coefficients. Here, we review several basic techniques for summarizing a set of data.

THE FREQUENCY DISTRIBUTION

Suppose a test of reading comprehension is given to the entire fifth-grade class at Wayne Newton Memorial Elementary School. The test has 25 multiple-choice questions, and scores could theoretically range from 0 to 25 correct. The scores for the 22 girls in the class are as follows: 18, 19, 16, 21, 17, 20, 20, 19, 22, 21, 19, 19, 18, 17, 21, 20, 19, 18, 18, 20, 17, 19. How would you characterize the performance of this group?

To make sense out of this confusing list, a statistician might begin by grouping the scores into a **frequency distribution**, which summarizes the number of scores that fall into different intervals or segments. The simplest frequency distri-

TABLE A.1

Frequency Distribution of
Reading Comprehension Scores
for 22 Fifth-Grade Girls

Test score	Number of students
22	1
21	3
20	4
19	6
18	4
17	3
16	1

bution for the fifth-grade girls would simply count the number of students who had earned each score, as shown in Table A.1.

This summary table obviously presents a far clearer picture of the group's performance than the original list. Clearer still are graphic representations of the frequency distribution. Figure A.1 shows a *frequency histogram* of the scores in which each frequency is represented by a bar. Alternatively, each value could be represented by a point on a graph in a *frequency polygon*, as shown in Figure A.2. These two graphs summarize the same information.

To keep this example simple, each interval in Table A.1 consists of a single score. But if you wanted to draw a frequency histogram summarizing the distribution of income in the United States, it would be very confusing to have a separate category for each individual income; people who earned $15,127.64, $15,127.65, and $15,127.66 would be placed in three different categories. Therefore, frequency distributions often classify cases together into larger classes or intervals. Categories of income might be $0 to $10,000, $10,001 to $20,000, $20,001 to $30,000, and so on. The precise intervals would depend on the researcher's interests and data.

Many frequency polygons and histograms appear

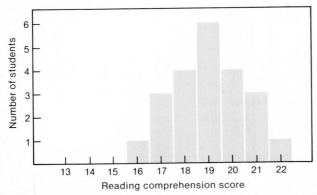

FIGURE A.1 Frequency histogram of reading comprehension scores for 22 fifth-grade girls.

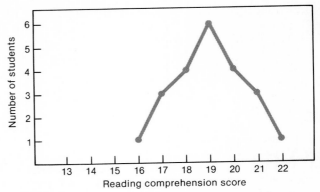

FIGURE A.2 Frequency polygon of reading comprehension scores for 22 fifth-grade girls.

throughout this book. For example, Figure 13.5 is a frequency polygon of the distribution of IQ in a representative sample of the U.S. population. Figure 17.2 is a frequency histogram of the number of illnesses reported by groups of men who had experienced differing levels of stress in the preceding six months.

Frequency distributions, polygons, and histograms can be very informative, but they are only the first step in a statistical description. To describe a set of data more succinctly, statisticians compute summary statistics of two sorts: measures of central tendency and measures of variability.

MEASURES OF CENTRAL TENDENCY

Three different statistics are commonly used to measure the central tendency of a distribution: the *mean*, the *median*, and the *mode*.

The **mean** is the arithmetic average of a group of numbers, computed by summing the values and dividing by the number of values. If we added the 22 scores in Table A.1, the sum would be 418; dividing by 22 yields a mean score of 19.

The **median** is the middle number in a set of values that has been arranged from the smallest to the largest. Thus, to find the median in the series 10, 2, 4, 8, 6, begin by ranking the numbers in order: 2, 4, 6, 8, 10. The middle number, or median, can be identified easily as 6 because there is an odd number of values (five) in this series; two of the numbers are larger and two are smaller.

The median is slightly more difficult to compute if there is an even number of values, as in the series 2, 4, 6, 8. In this case, the median is the average of the two central values:

$$\frac{4 + 6}{2} = 5$$

The same procedure can be used to identify the median of our fifth-graders' reading scores. When the scores are ranked in order, the series reads: 16, 17, 17, 17, 18, 18, 18, 18, 19, 19, 19, 19, 19, 19, 20, 20, 20, 20, 21, 21, 21, 22. The computation of the median is often more complex when the central value is repeated, but in this case it is the average of the two values:

$$\frac{19 + 19}{2} = 19$$

Finally, the **mode** is the value that occurs most frequently in a set of numbers. Since six students scored 19 on our test, and no other score occurred more frequently, the mode is 19.

Thus, in this hypothetical sample, the mean, median, and mode are identical. In the section that follows on "Types of Frequency Distributions," we shall see that this often occurs in symmetrical distributions like this one.

MEASURES OF VARIABILITY

Two very different distributions can easily have the same measure of central tendency. Consider two hypothetical families with a mean income of $20,000. In one, three adult brothers work as police officers and earn $19,000, $20,000, and $21,000 per year. In the other family, two adult males work only occasional odd jobs and earn $2,000 and $3,000, respectively. The third brother owns a health and diet spa and earns $55,000. Clearly, the mean income of $20,000 has very different implications for the two families. Statisticians therefore characterize distributions not just by their central tendencies but also by their spread, or variability.

The simplest such statistic is the **range**, or difference between the highest and lowest values in a distribution. For our three police officers, the range in income is

$$\$21,000 - \$19,000 = \$2,000$$

Similarly, the family of the prosperous spa owner has an income range of $53,000, and the fifth-grade girls' reading scores have a range of 6 points.

More frequently, statisticians compute a more revealing figure called the **standard deviation**, which is a particular mathematical measure of the amount of variability, spread, or dispersion in the scores of a distribution. More formally,

$$\text{Standard deviation} = \sqrt{\frac{\text{sum of diff}^2}{N}}$$

where   diff = difference between each score and the mean
N = number of values

Thus, to compute the standard deviation of a set of scores, compute the mean, subtract each score from the mean, and square each of these differences. Then add these squared differences and divide by the number of scores. The square root of this value is the standard deviation.

While this formula may seem intimidating at first, in fact the computations are quite straightforward. Consider how this formula could be applied to the reading comprehension scores in Table A.1:

Score	Difference from mean (Mean = 19)	Difference squared
22	+3	9
21	+2	4
21	+2	4
21	+2	4
20	+1	1
20	+1	1
20	+1	1
20	+1	1
19	0	0
19	0	0
19	0	0
19	0	0
19	0	0
19	0	0
18	−1	1
18	−1	1
18	−1	1
18	−1	1
17	−2	4
17	−2	4
17	−2	4
16	−3	9
Sum of diff^2 =		50

$$\text{Standard deviation} = \sqrt{\frac{\text{sum of diff}^2}{N}}$$
$$= \sqrt{\frac{50}{22}}$$
$$= \sqrt{2.27}$$
$$= 1.51$$

This formula can be used to compute the standard deviation of any distribution. As this example suggests, the calculations are more likely to be tedious than to be confusing or mysterious.

TYPES OF FREQUENCY DISTRIBUTIONS

The hypothetical reading scores we have focused on to this point provide an example of a **symmetrical distribution** in which the same number of values are equally distributed on either side of the central point and the mean, median, and mode are identical or close together. The most important

TABLE A.2
Frequency Distribution of
Reading Comprehension Scores
for 22 Fifth-Grade Boys

Test score	Number of students
20	2
19	2
18	6
17	4
16	3
15	2
14	2
13	1

symmetrical distribution for psychology was described in Chapter 13; many physical and psychological characteristics conform to a *normal distribution,* as illustrated in Figure 13.2.

However, many measurements conform to a **skewed distribution,** which is asymmetrical, with more scores falling at one end than at the other. Consider other hypothetical data: the reading comprehension scores for 22 fifth-grade boys shown in Table A.2. As you can see in the frequency histogram for this distribution (Figure A.3), these scores are not evenly distributed around a central point.

This distribution is said to be *skewed to the left* because the most deviant scores (that is, those farthest from the central tendency) fall to the left. The mirror image of this distribution, with the most deviant scores to the right of the central tendency, would be *skewed to the right.*

In symmetrical distribution, the mean, the median, and mode fall close together. Indeed, for the data in Table A.1, they were identical. However, these three measures of central tendency have different values for the skewed distribution of the boys' scores in Table A.2.

Confusion over the differences between the mean, median, and mode of skewed distributions may lead to many

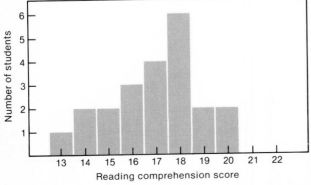

FIGURE A.3 Frequency histogram of reading comprehension scores for 22 fifth-grade boys.

misunderstandings. Consider, for example, how the mean and median could be used to describe the skewed distribution of salaries in a four-person firm that stuffs pimientos inside cocktail olives. The three laborers who do all the stuffing earn $10,000, $14,000, and $16,000. But the owner-president of the firm pays himself $40,000 annually to drop by once a week, check the pimiento inventory, and make sure that "Everything is under control."

This distribution of salaries is skewed to the right, with a mean of $20,000 and a median of $15,000. These two figures provide different types of information. A stockholder in the company who wants to monitor the total payroll would probably be more interested in the $20,000 mean, while a labor organizer who wondered whether the workers were underpaid would learn more from the $15,000 median.

To see how misleading these figures can be, suppose that the company prospers. The president attributes this success to the fact that he always keeps the right number of pimientos in the warehouse and gives himself a raise to $60,000 per year. If the salaries of the three workers remained unchanged, the mean salary in this firm would increase to $25,000. In his annual report to the stockholders, the president might cite this 25% increase in average salary to prove that the firm rewards productivity. But the laborers would probably argue that this figure proves nothing of the sort. The more relevant figures, they might say, are the median income (which held constant at $15,000) and the income range (which increased from $30,000 to $50,000, showing a widening gap between labor and management).

Examples of this sort are sometimes cited to show that "You can prove anything with statistics." People who hate math may argue that since statistical calculations can be misleading, they can safely be ignored. In fact, the real lesson of this example is precisely the opposite: You can prove anything with statistics only to people who do not understand statistics. Thus, to avoid being misled, an educated person must become sophisticated about the appropriate uses of statistics to describe data and to infer conclusions. This is particularly vital when one discusses statistical methods for measuring the relationships, or correlation, between two variables.

THE CORRELATION COEFFICIENT
A **correlation coefficient** is a precise statistical expression of the relationship between two variables.

Consider the question of how closely twins resemble each other. It is easy to say in general terms that most twins seem pretty much alike, but it is much more difficult to specify how much is "pretty much." Quantification is essential for psychology to advance as a science.

The absolute value of a correlation coefficient is always between 0 and 1. If a correlation coefficient is 0, the two variables are unrelated; if it is 1, one variable predicts another perfectly, with no exceptions. Such perfect relationships are hard to find in this imperfect world; most correlation coefficients are somewhere between 0 and 1. The closer they are to 1, the stronger the relationship between two variables.

As an additional complication, every correlation coefficient is preceded by a + or a − sign. The sign of a correlation coefficient indicates the direction of the relationship. In *positive correlations,* high values on one variable (for example twin *A*'s score) are associated with high values on another variable (twin *B*'s score). In some cases, high values on one variable are associated with low values on another; these are *negative correlations.*

Imagine computing the correlation coefficient between the average temperature of each week in winter and the amount paid for fuel oil that week. Low temperatures mean high heat bills; high temperatures mean low heat bills. Thus, the correlation would be negative. Similarly, there is often a negative correlation between psychological variables, such as when high levels of math anxiety are associated with low scores on math tests. The important thing to remember is that the sign indicates only the direction of the relationship, not its magnitude. Correlation coefficients of +.47 and −.47 represent relationships of equal strength. The difference is that +.47 means that high scores for one variable are associated with high scores for another, while −.47 implies that high scores for one are associated with low scores for the other.

Geneticists use correlation coefficients to compare the resemblances between identical and fraternal twins. In Chapter 9, for example, we described several findings from a study of 850 pairs of twins who took the National Merit Scholarship Test (Loehlin & Nichols, 1976). To understand these results fully, you need to understand what correlation coefficients mean.

Consider a graph summarizing the scores on a math test in which each dot on the graph represents the scores of one pair of twins. Suppose we had four pairs of twins with these scores: *A* 5, 5; *B* 6, 6; *C* 9, 9; *D* 6, 7. The graph would look like the one in Figure A.4. Note that the dots fall more or less on a straight line. If you knew one twin's score, you could use this straight line to predict the score of the other. High correlations imply more accurate predictions.

Loehlin and Nichols compared the mathematics scores of 216 pairs of identical male twins on the National Merit Test. If they had summarized all the data on a graph, it would have looked something like the graph in Figure A.5. Even a casual glance makes it clear that the twins' scores were correlated; when one twin did well in math, the other also tended to get a high score. Loehlin and Nichols went on to compute a correlation coefficient of +.74, indicating a strong relationship.

The math scores from the 135 pairs of fraternal male twins in this study looked something like the graph in Figure A.6. These scores still seem to be related, but not as strongly

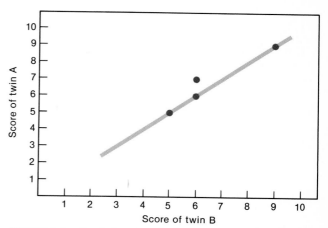

FIGURE A.4 Graph showing a high correlation between scores in a small set of twins.

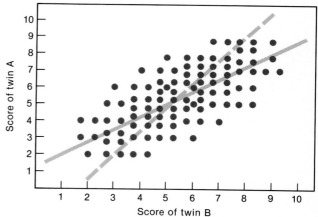

FIGURE A.5 Typical scores for a correlation of approximately +0.7.

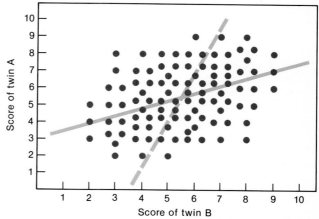

FIGURE A.6 Typical scores for a correlation of approximately +0.4.

as those of the identical twins. The lower correlation coefficient of +.41 between fraternal male twins' math scores implies that the prediction from one twin's score to the other is less accurate; thus, they are spread out more. The actual correlation coefficients provide a precise estimate of the relative accuracy of the predictions from one identical twin to the other or from one fraternal twin to the other. (As explained in Chapter 9, the difference observed here implies that genetic factors influenced performance on this test.)

Of course, psychologists are interested in the relationships among many pairs of variables aside from twins' scores on a particular test. Correlation coefficients have been computed to study the relationships between income and education, frustration and aggression, extraversion and sexual activity, anxiety and test performance, and countless other pairs of variables. In each case, the basic interpretation of the correlation coefficient is the same; absolute values close to 0 imply little or no relationship; absolute values close to 1 imply a very strong relationship.

Even when this is clear, people often misinterpret correlations. In Chapter 13, we explained why strong correlations do not necessarily imply that one variable causes another. For example, the simple fact that people who are anxious about taking tests do more poorly does not mean that anxiety necessarily interferes with performance. It could imply that people who begin to do poorly worry more. See "Understanding the Scientific Method" in Chapter 13 for a discussion of how correlations should be interpreted.

Inferential Statistics

Inferential statistics are techniques for drawing conclusions (or making inferences) from a particular set of data. The basic concepts of inferential statistics are described in "Understanding the Scientific Method" exercises throughout this book.

For example, in Chapter 10 the discussion of "Surveys of Sexual Behavior" distinguished between a *population* (the full group of people that a researcher hopes to understand or generalize to) and a *sample* (the small subgroup of a population that actually participates in a given study). For obvious reasons, researchers can never study the entire population if they want to generalize to such large groups as human females or even U.S. citizens who weigh more than 300 pounds. Inferential statistics are therefore used to reach accurate conclusions about large populations on the basis of studies of relatively small samples. As explained in Chapter 10, only samples that accurately represent relevant features of the population lead to trustworthy conclusions.

Another key concept was explained in Chapter 2: *Tests of statistical significance* determine whether a particular mathematical result is likely to have occurred by chance. The vast majority of the empirical results described in this text were statistically analyzed and found to meet predetermined levels of significance.

For example, many psychological studies are designed to compare the mean scores of two or more groups that differ in terms of key variables. The Chapter 2 "Understanding the Scientific Method" exercise described Rosenthal and Jacobson's (1968) study of teacher expectations. In one analysis, inferential statistics compared the mean change in IQ in an experimental group of first-graders (whose teachers had been told to expect a sudden burst of intellectual growth) with the mean IQ change in a control group (whose teachers had been given no special expectations). As explained there, a *t* test revealed that there was a statistically significant difference between these two means, thus supporting the more general conclusion that expectations made a difference in this situation.

The details of the calculations involved in *t* tests and other inferential statistics can be found in any introductory statistics test. Learning more about them may not be everyone's idea of a good time, but this experience is essential for anyone who wants to understand the nature of current research in psychology.

Summary

- **Descriptive statistics** are techniques for summarizing groups of numbers. For example, a **frequency distribution** summarizes the number of scores that fall into different intervals. Graphically, this may be summarized by bars in a *frequency histogram* or by points in a *frequency polygon*.

- There are three major measures of central tendency. The **mean** is the arithmetic average of a group of numbers. The **median** is the middle number in a set of values that has been arranged from the smallest to the largest. The **mode** is the value that occurs most frequently in a set of numbers.

- Two major measures of variability are the range and the standard deviation. The **range** is the difference between the highest and lowest values in a distribution. The **standard deviation** is a particular mathematical measure of the amount of variability, spread, or dispersion in the scores of a distribution, based on the squared differences of each score from the mean. The *normal distribution* is one example of a **symmetrical distribution** in which the same number of values are equally distributed on either side of the central point. In a **skewed distribution**, more scores fall at one end than at the other.

- A **correlation coefficient** is a precise statistical expression of the relationship between two variables.

- **Inferential statistics** provides techniques for drawing conclusions (or making inferences) from a particular set of data. For example, *tests of statistical significance* determine whether a particular result is likely to have occurred by chance.

GLOSSARY

ablation studies Studies in which surgical removal or destruction of brain tissue is followed by observation of the effects on behavior.

absolute threshold The minimum physical energy that causes a sensory system to respond.

accommodation A monocular physiological factor involving changes in the shape of the eye's lens.

adrenal glands Two small endocrine glands that lie just above the kidney.

aerial perspective The slight blurring and tinge of blue perceived in distant objects.

affective disorders Conditions characterized by a prolonged and fundamental disturbance of mood and emotion.

afferent (sensory) neurons Neurons that convey information from sensory receptors to the spinal cord and brain.

afterimages The sensory impressions that remain after a stimulus is taken away.

aggression Any physical or verbal behavior that is intended to hurt someone.

agoraphobia A fear of public places.

alcohol abuse A pattern of pathological use of alcohol, as well as an impairment of social or occupational function, for at least one month.

alcohol dependence A syndrome involving withdrawal symptoms and tolerance.

algorithms Procedures or formulas that guarantee solutions to a problem.

alternate-form reliability The correlation between two different scores achieved by the same individual on two different forms of a test.

amnesia Loss of memory usually caused by brain damage.

analogical reasoning Judging, categorizing, or developing an argument about something new based on its similarity to something familiar.

anal stage According to Freud, the psychosexual stage, beginning around age 2, when the child's major source of irritation and gratification involves the process of elimination.

androgyny A personality pattern that combines traditionally masculine and feminine traits in the same person.

anorexia nervosa A syndrome characterized by the refusal to eat enough food to maintain or gain weight, a fear of becoming fat, and significant weight loss.

anterograde amnesia An inability to remember new information for more than a few seconds.

antipsychotic drugs Drugs used primarily to decrease the hallucinations and disordered behavior of psychotic individuals.

antisocial personality disorder A behavior pattern of violating others' rights that begins before age 15 and interferes with adult responsibilities.

anxiety disorder A condition in which severe anxiety interferes with the normal ability to function in everyday life.

aphasia A disturbance in the ability to speak or understand language caused by damage to the brain.

application According to Sternberg, the generation of a rule to produce and evaluate the missing item in an analogy.

applied research The application of scientific principles and knowledge to solve specific problems.

arousal A general pattern in which several physiological systems are activated simultaneously, including heart rate, sweat-gland activity, and electrical activity of the brain.

artificial intelligence The field that includes efforts to program computers to perform tasks that require reasoning and perception.

assertiveness training groups A behavioral form of group therapy in which therapists demonstrate specific ways of standing up for one's rights and participants practice these behaviors.

association areas Cortical areas of the brain that are not specifically involved with simple sensory or motor reactions.

associationism The belief that even the most complex memories are ultimately based on associations between simple ideas.

attitude A relatively lasting tendency to react to a person, object, or event in a particular way.

attribution theories Social-perception theories that describe how people interpret and explain behavior in everyday life.

audience inhibition A process in which bystanders risk embarrassment if they decide to help in a situation that turns out not to be an emergency.

auditory canal A tube that carries sound waves from the external ear to the eardrum.

autonomic nervous system The portion of the peripheral nervous system that regulates the activity of smooth muscles that control internal bodily processes.

avoidance A response that prevents or avoids an unpleasant stimulus before it begins.

axon The part of a neuron that transmits electrical impulses to other neurons.

babble To produce speechlike sounds that involve the alternation of consonant and vowel sounds.

basic research The use of scientific method to try to understand fundamental laws of the mind and behavior.

basilar membrane A membrane that translates physical vibrations in the ear into a pattern of electrical activity in the nervous system.

behavioral approach A paradigm that focuses on the systematic study of observable behavior.

behavioral genetics The study of the inheritance of behavioral characteristics.

behavioral sink The pattern of bizarre and antisocial behavior that may occur in an overcrowded environment.

behavior therapy (behavior modification) The application of scientific principles to alter observable behavior through learning.

belongingness and love needs The third set of needs in Maslow's hierarchy; that is, to feel accepted and wanted by family, friends, and others.

binocular disparity The difference between the retinal images of the two eyes.

biofeedback The technique of learning to control physiological states on the basis of precise physiological data.

biological approach A paradigm that analyzes the physiological events associated with behavior and experience.

bipolar disorder A condition in which manic and depressive episodes alternate.

blind spot An area in the retina near the fovea that has no receptor cells because nerve cells are gathered here to form the optic nerve.

blood-brain barrier The circulatory-system structures that prevent certain large molecules from reaching the brain.

blood pressure The force exerted as blood moves away from the heart, pushing against the artery walls.

brain stem The part of the brain that contains such structures as the medulla, pons, reticular formation, and midbrain.

bulimia A condition in which people engage in binge eating and then force themselves to vomit.

Cannon-Bard theory The theory that the brain responds to external events, simultaneously producing both physiological and emotional experiences.

case history A detailed description of the life experiences and behavior patterns of a single person.

catatonia A severe form of schizophrenia characterized by a rigid posture or purposeless, repetitive movements.

catharsis According to Freud, the relief of symptoms of mental illness by bringing unconscious emotional conflicts into conscious awareness.

CAT scan A technique in which X-rays taken from many different angles are analyzed by computer to generate a three-dimensional picture of the brain.

cell body The central part of the neuron.

central nervous system The spinal cord and the brain.

cerebellum A brain structure involved primarily in the coordination of muscle movements.

cerebral asymmetry Differences between the two hemispheres of the brain.

cerebral cortex The thick layer of nerve cells that covers the brain.

cerebral hemispheres The two symmetrical sides of the brain.

chemical studies Procedures involving introducing a chemical into the brain to determine its behavioral and physiological effects.

chromosomes Long, thin structures in the nucleus of every cell that contain many genes.

cingulotomy Brain surgery in which certain fibers connecting the frontal lobes to the limbic system are cut.

circadian rhythm A cyclical change in behavior or physiology that repeats itself once every 24 hours.

clairvoyance A controversial process by which physical stimuli may be identified without using the known senses or telepathy.

classical conditioning Learning involving repeated pairing of a stimulus that naturally elicits a reflex response with a second, neutral stimulus that gradually comes to elicit a response similar to the original reflex.

clinical psychology The application of psychological principles and research to the understanding and treatment of mental illness.

closure The principle that an incomplete pattern is often perceived as a complete whole.

cochlea The major auditory portion of the inner ear.

cognitive approach The approach that explores the inner structure and organization of the mind, and the active process used by a learner.

cognitive dissonance A contradiction between a thought and a behavior or between two different thoughts.

cognitive psychology The study of higher mental processes in such areas as attention, perception, memory, language, imagery, and reason.

cognitive tests Tests designed to measure intelligence and other mental abilities.

cognitive theory of depression The idea that depression is caused by logical errors of thought that produce excessive self-blame.

cognitive therapy A form of psychotherapy that concentrates on changing thought patterns.

cohorts Groups of people born at approximately the same time.

color constancy The tendency to see an object as remaining the same color under a variety of lighting conditions.

community psychologists Psychologists who have attempted to make mental-health services available to every U.S. resident on a local level.

companionate love A deep and enduring bond, often marked by a strong sense of intimacy and closeness.

complex cells Feature detectors that receive information from simple cells and respond to a more general category of lines.

computer-based training Programs that use computers to deliver instruction in job-related skills.

computer simulation A technique for imitating behaviors or processes, such as problem solving, on a computer.

concentrative meditation An attempt to focus attention on a single object or idea.

concept A mental category of objects or events grouped on the basis of common features.

concordance rate The percentage of twins or other pairs that share the same trait.

concrete-operational stage According to Piaget, the stage from age 7 to 11 when a child becomes capable of logical thought regarding observable actions.

conditioned response A learned response that resembles the original unconditional response.

conditioned stimulus A neutral stimulus that is repeatedly presented with the unconditioned stimulus, and gradually comes to elicit the conditioned response.

cones Receptor cells responsible for color vision and sensitive to fine visual detail.

conformity Behavior motivated by pressure from other members of a group.

conjunctive concept An item that possesses two attributes at the same time.

consciousness All the internal mental events and responses to external stimuli of which a person is aware.

conservation According to Piaget, the recognition that certain basic properties of objects remain constant even when appearances change.

constructive memory The observer's tendency to rebuild pictures of past events around the incomplete details that are remembered.

construct validity A larger pattern of conceptually meaningful relationships.

content validity A systematic analysis of a particular skill and the design of test items that measure all relevant knowledge.

continuous reinforcement The reinforcement of every response.

control condition The part of an experiment lacking special treatments or manipulations, allowing a basis for comparison with the experimental condition.

conventional level According to Kohlberg, a level of moral reasoning in which society's standards are totally adopted as one's own.

convergent thinking The process of answering a problem correctly by remembering it from past learning, or by deriving it deductively from the application of logical rules.

cornea The curved transparent window that helps focus light as it enters the eye.

corpus callosum A wide band of nerve fibers that connects the two cerebral hemispheres.

correlation coefficient A precise statistical expression of the relationship between two variables.

correspondent inferences A model holding that people try to explain behavior by finding correspondences between what is seen of behavior, and what is inferred about intentions.

counseling psychology A specialty that emphasizes normal adjustment rather than abnormal function.

counterconditioning A process in which relaxation becomes classically conditioned to a stimulus that formerly elicited anxiety.

covariation principle According to Kelley, the fact that people assume causal relationships between events and behaviors that occur together, or covary.

criterion validity A comparison of performance on a test with some external and independent measure, or criterion, of what the test is supposed to predict.

critical period According to Harlow, a fixed interval during which key events relating to motherly love had to occur for normal development to follow.

cross-sectional method An analytical research approach that compares groups of different ages at one time.

crystallized intelligence General information and knowledge.

cue-dependent forgetting Tolving's notion that inadequate memory cues lead to a failure to retrieve information from storage.

cultural bias A statistical difference in the validity of a test for different cultural groups.

cultural-familial retardation A family pattern of mild mental retardation with no evidence of organic brain damage.

dark adaptation The process by which the sensitivity of the retina gradually increases after a period in the dark.

death instincts According to Freud, a major class of instincts that includes aggressive and self-destructive forces.

decay theory The theory that physical memory traces gradually fade as time passes.

decision frames Conceptions of the acts, outcomes, and contingencies associated with a particular choice.

decision making The process of evaluating choices and picking the best one.

deep structure According to Chomsky, the underlying organization and intent of sentences.

defense mechanism According to Freud, an unconscious denial, distortion, or falsification of reality to protect the ego from excessive anxiety.

deindividuation The loss of normal restraints that sometimes occurs in groups.

delusions False beliefs, typically about being persecuted.

dendrite The part of a neuron that usually receives electrical and chemical messages from other neurons.

denial The refusal to believe that something terrible has happened, or that one is experiencing an unacceptable emotion.

dependent variable The factor that is affected by an experimenter's manipulation.

depression Loss of pleasure in ordinary activities associated with such symptoms as disturbances in eating, sleeping, and decreased energy.

descriptive statistics Techniques for summarizing groups of numbers.

determinism The idea that every event is the inevitable product of a series of natural forces.

developmental psychologists Psychologists who study the physical, intellectual, and emotional changes associated with aging.

developmental psychology The study of human physical, intellectual, and emotional changes from infancy to old age.

***Diagnostic and Statistical Manual,* Third Edition, Revised (DSM-III-R)** A complete, official list of syndromes of abnormal behavior, designed to improve diagnosis in terms of reliability and validity.

difference threshold The minimum physical difference required for any two stimuli to be sensed as different.

diffusion of responsibility A phenomenon that occurs when the social responsibility to help someone in trouble is diffused across a group of observers.

discounting principle According to Kelley, the fact that behavior is not attributed to a cause if there are more plausible alternatives.

discrimination Learning to respond only to a specific kind of stimulus.

discrimination training Reinforcement of a particular response and extinction of other responses.

discriminative stimulus A technique that signals that a particular response will be reinforced.

disease model of alcoholism The view that some individuals have an inherent uncontrollable weakness for alcohol.

disjunctive concept An item that possesses either one or both of two attributes.

displacement According to Freud, the process by which instinctual energy is rechanneled from one object to another.

divergent thinking The ability to generate alternatives, to envision possibilities.

dizygotic twins Twins that develop from two different fertilized eggs; also called *fraternal twins.*

Down's syndrome A biologically caused, severe form of mental retardation characterized by certain physical abnormalities; formerly called *mongolism.*

drive A motivational force that incites an organism to action.

drug addiction A medically defined syndrome that includes physical dependence and tolerance.

drug receptor The part of a neuron that responds to a specific type of chemical.

eardrum A tissue in the ear that vibrates in response to sound waves.

echoic memory The retention in memory of an auditory stimulus for a moment after it stops.

eclectic approach The use of different psychotherapeutic techniques to meet the needs of different clients.

educational psychologists Psychologists who work within school systems to find ways of increasing teacher effectiveness.

efferent (motor) neurons Neurons that transmit the commands of the spinal cord and brain to the brain.

ego According to Freud, an aspect of personality that develops from the id to distinguish between the subjective world of the mind and the objective world of physical reality.

egocentrism According to Piaget, the child's failure to take into account the perspective of another person.

ego psychology Psychoanalytic theories that propose the existence of an autonomous ego with its own reality-based processes that can be independent of purely instinctual aims.

electrical recording studies Studies that measure the normal electrical activity of the brain.

electrical stimulation studies Studies in which brain tissue is stimulated by an electrical current while the effects on behavior are observed.

electroconvulsive therapy A treatment for severe mental

illness, usually depression, in which an electric current is passed through the brain.

electrode An electrical conductor that is placed in contact with biological tissue.

electroencephalogram (EEG) A recording of electrical activity at the surface of the brain or on the skull.

embryo A prenatal organism from 2 to 8 weeks old.

emotions Physical reactions that are experienced as strong feelings.

encoding The transformation of a physical stimulus into the kind of code that memory accepts.

encoding-specificity principle Tulving's notion that recall improves if the same cues are present during recall as during the original learning.

endocrine glands Structures that secrete special chemical messengers (hormones) directly into the bloodstream.

endorphins Neurotransmitters that are structurally similar to morphine and may be involved in regulating pain and other psychological functions.

engram Lashley's concept of physical change in the brain responsible for memory storage.

environmental psychology The study of the interrelationships between social behavior and the physical settings of everyday life.

episodic memory A record of an individual's past experiences.

epistemology The philosophical study of the nature of knowledge, and how we come to know about the world.

erogenous zones According to Freud, areas of the body that are highly sensitive to feelings of both irritation and pleasure.

escape A response that ends an aversive stimulus that is already underway.

esteem needs The fourth set of needs in Maslow's hierarchy; that is, to be valued by others and to have respect for ourselves.

ethologists Researchers who study the behavior patterns of a particular species in its natural environment.

eustachian tube A tube from the middle-ear cavity to the throat; designed to equalize pressure on both sides of the eardrum.

expectancy Knowledge or belief about reinforcement in a particular situation.

expectancy bias effect The tendency of people with difference expectations about someone else to interpret the same behavior differently in order to match their initial expectations.

experiment A scientific study that attempts to establish a causal link between two variables by manipulating the independent variable and observing changes in the other.

experimental condition The manipulation of the independent variable to test its effect.

experimental psychologists Basic researchers who typically conduct laboratory studies in such areas as learning, human memory, and sensation and perception.

expert systems Computer programs that apply knowledge in a specific area so that the computer can function as effectively as a human expert.

expressive aphasia Difficulty in speaking resulting from tissue damage in Broca's area.

extinction The gradual disappearance of a learned response.

extrasensory perception A controversial process that may provide awareness of external events without the use of known senses.

face validity Superficial appearance that a test seems to measure what it is supposed to measure.

fairness The justice (or injustice) of using a particular psychological test to select individuals.

family therapy Group psychotherapy for all members of a family.

fear of success The fear that doing well in competitive situations will have negative consequences.

feature detectors Cells in the retina that fire when they detect certain features or patterns of stimulation.

fetus A prenatal organism from 8 weeks to birth.

figure According to the Gestalt psychologists, the object of attention, usually seen as a distinct shape in front of the ground.

fixed-interval (FI) schedules Schedules of reinforcement that reward the first correct response emitted after a specific amount of time has elapsed.

fixed-ratio (FR) schedules Schedules of reinforcement in which an organism is rewarded after a specific number of responses.

fluid intelligence The ability to perceive, encode, and reason information.

foot-in-the-door technique The idea that people who comply with a small request are more likely to go along with a larger one than people asked to comply only with the larger one.

formal-operational stage According to Piaget, the stage—which can begin as early as age 11—when a person becomes capable of solving abstract problems and dealing with hypothetical possibilities.

fovea A slight depression at the center of the retina that consists entirely of cones, and is very sensitive to fine visual detail.

free association In psychoanalysis, a therapeutic technique in which a patient relaxes and reports every single thought as it comes to mind.

free will The idea that people are free to choose what they will do.

frequency distribution Summarizes the number of scores that fall into different intervals.

frequency theory of hearing The theory that the basilar membrane vibrates as a whole in response to sound stimulation.

frontal lobe The major lobe at the front of the brain.

frontal lobotomy Destruction of the connections between the frontal lobes and other brain structures.

functional analysis Specification of the external variables that regulate behavior.

functional fixedness The failure to see that an object may have more functions than its usual ones.

fundamental attribution error The idea that observers consistently underestimate external influences on other people's behavior, and overestimate the importance of personal disposition.

gate theory The theory that the amount of pain experienced is related to variables influencing the operation of neuronal gates, thus determining whether pain messages from damaged areas proceed to the brain and bring about the perception of pain.

gender schema The cognitive structures that sort attributes and behaviors into masculine and feminine categories.

general adaptation syndrome (GAS) According to Selye, a physiological response to stress that is divided into three stages: alarm, resistance, and exhaustion.

generalization Responding in a similar way to stimuli that resemble each other.

generalized anxiety disorder Chronic, intense anxiety that does not seem related to any particular situation or stimulus.

genes Physical structures that transmit characteristics from parent to child.

genetics The study of the transmission of inherited characteristics.

genital stage According to Freud, the last stage of psychosexual development, beginning around puberty and characterized by the reawakening of sexual urges.

genotype The genetic composition of an individual.

gerontology The scientific study of the elderly.

goal-derived concept A specialized concept created to help a person reach a specific target.

gonads Sexual glands: ovaries in women, testes in men.

grammar The complete system of rules that relates sounds to meanings for a specific language.

group therapy Psychotherapy in which one or more therapists meet with several patients at the same time.

groupthink The suspension of critical thought in highly cohesive groups that become preoccupied with seeking unanimity.

growth spurt A sudden increase in the rate of growth for both height and weight.

hallucinogenic drugs Chemical substances that cause hallucinations and alter sensory perception.

health psychologists Specialists who apply a psychological perspective to stress-related diseases or other physical disorders.

health psychology The field concerned with the relationships among behavior, health, and illness.

heritability A mathematical estimate of the relative importance of genetics and environment in determining a particular trait for a specific population.

heuristics General rules of thumb that can influence decision making.

hierarchy of needs According to Maslow, a series of biological and physiological needs that motivates normal human behavior and must be satisfied in a certain order.

high blood pressure (hypertension) Consistently elevated levels of blood pressure.

holism The theory that each psychological function is controlled by a wide variety of cells throughout the entire brain.

holophrase A single word used by young children to express an entire message.

hospices Institutions that are specifically designed to meet the needs of dying patients.

human engineering The application of scientific principles to the design of equipment and machines that maximize efficiency.

human factors engineering The study of the way people interact with machines and the physical work environment.

humanistic approach A paradigm that is concerned with human values, subjective experience, and the uniqueness of each individual.

humanistic therapy Therapy in which the therapist guides the clients to find their own solutions.

hypercomplex cells Feature detectors that receive information from complex cells and analyze it at a still higher level of abstraction.

hypnosis A state of awareness induced by special techniques and related to changes in thought, perception, and behavior.

hypothalamus A brain structure lying between the thalamus and midbrain that seems to be involved in complex behaviors.

iconic memory The retention of memory of a literal image of a visual stimulus for a fraction of a second after it is presented.

id According to Freud, an aspect of personality composed of innate biological instincts that seek immediate satisfaction.

identity crisis The crisis of establishing a strong sense of personal identity.

idiographic approach An approach to personality that attempts to understand the behavior and experience of a single individual.

imprinting The phenomenon of a newborn animal following the first moving stimulus it encounters after birth.

incentives External stimuli that increase the likelihood of behavior.

independent variable   The factor in an experiment that the experimenter manipulates.

industrial/organizational psychology   The study of human behavior and experience in the workplace.

industrial/organizational psychologists   Psychologists who apply research findings to the work world.

industrial psychology   The study of individual workers, their abilities, and the way these abilities relate to job performance.

inference   Discovering the rule relating *A* to *B*.

inferential statistics   Techniques for drawing conclusions (or making inferences) from a particular set of data.

information-processing approach   Attempts to analyze thought processes, including memory, as a series of separate steps.

insight   In psychoanalysis, the conscious understanding of the unconscious forces that motivate behavior.

instincts   According to Freud, the inborn mental representations of physical needs.

intelligence quotient (IQ)   Mental age divided by chronological age times 100.

interference theory   The theory that people forget information because one memory prevents another from being recovered.

interposition   A phenomenon whereby if one object blocks the view of another, the partially obscured object will seem more distant.

interpretation   The process by which the psychoanalyst gradually guides the patients to an understanding of their thoughts and behavior.

interviews   Systematic discussions of a person's experiences and feelings.

intimacy   The challenge of making a commitment to another person, and developing and maintaining a mature relationship.

introspection   The careful, rigorous, and disciplined analysis of one's own thoughts by highly trained observers.

iris   A circular arrangement of muscular cells that controls the diameter of the opening that admits light into the eye.

James-Lange theory   The theory that an event automatically triggers a particular pattern of bodily changes, and that the brain then identifies each emotion on the basis of a particular physiological pattern.

jet lag   Discomfort or decreased efficiency caused by traveling across time zones.

kinesthetic sense   A sense of the movement and positions of the body and body parts, based on feedback from the muscles, joints, and tendons.

latency period   According to Freud, the psychosexual stage, beginning around the age of 6, when no new psychosexual conflicts emerge.

learned helplessness   An organism's belief, based on prior experience, that it is helpless or lacks control over a particular situation.

learning   A relatively permanent change in behavior or behavior potential that occurs through experience.

lens   A body of tissue that changes its shape to focus light on the retina.

lesions   Wounds or injuries.

life instincts   According to Freud, instincts that help the individual and the species to survive (e.g., hunger, thirst, and sex).

limbic system   A series of structures near the border between the cerebral hemispheres and the brain stem that is involved in regulating "animal instincts."

linear perspective   The tendency for distant objects to seem closer together than near objects.

linguistic competence   Abstract knowledge of a language.

linguistic performance   Applying one's knowledge of language to speaking and listening.

linguistic-relativity hypothesis   The theory that language determines thought content or perception of the world.

linguistics   The study of the fundamental nature and structure of human language.

localization   The theory that different areas of the brain are responsible for different psychological functions.

long-term memory (LTM)   The relatively permanent system that can store large amounts of information for long periods of time.

loudness   The psychological dimension corresponding to the intensity of a sound, primarily determined by the amplitude of sound waves.

major depression   A severe depression that appears without a history of mania.

mania   A feeling of euphoria associated with such symptoms as loud and rapid speech, inflated self-esteem, and hyperactivity.

mapping   Discovering the rule relating *A* to *C*.

maturation   Sequences of growth and internal bodily changes that are primarily determined by biological timing.

mean   The arithmetic average of a group of numbers.

means-end analysis   Solving problems by repeatedly comparing current affairs with the final goal state, and taking steps to reduce the differences between the two.

median   The middle number in a set of values that has been arranged from the smallest to the largest.

medical model   A theoretical model of abnormal behavior that argues that abnormality is caused by physical disease.

meditation   Any of several techniques for internal reflection.

medulla   The first brain structure that emerges from the spinal cord as it enters the skull; it contains nerve fibers connecting the spinal cord to the brain.

mental age A particular group's average performance level on an intelligence test.

method of constant stimuli Measuring absolute thresholds by randomly presenting subjects with stimuli of different physical intensities, and asking whether they have sensed anything.

method of loci Visualizing images of a list of things to be memorized, and mentally placing them in an orderly arrangements of locations.

microelectrodes Wires small enough to record the electrical activity of a single nerve cell.

midbrain A structure that relays information from the eyes and ears to higher centers for visual and auditory processing.

midlife crisis A period of severe stress, a questioning of goals and progress that occurs roughly between ages 40 and 45.

mnemonic devices Techniques for organizing information so that it can be remembered more easily.

mode The value that occurs most frequently in a set of numbers.

monozygotic twins Twins that develop from the division of a single fertilized egg; also called *identical twins.*

moral therapy The treatment of mental disorders by kindness, understanding, and a pleasant environment.

morpheme The smallest unit of speech that has meaning; it may be a word or part of a word.

motivated forgetting (repression) The psychoanalytic theory that people may repress memories that are too painful for them to remember.

motivation The forces that influence the strength or direction of behavior.

motor skills tests Tests that evaluate workers' speed, coordination, or precision in using their muscles.

motor strip A primary projection area inside the frontal lobe that controls certain muscle movements.

narcissistic personality disorder A grandiose sense of uniqueness or self-importance that leads a person to seek admiration constantly, and to become preoccupied with fantasies.

narcotic antagonists Drugs that are known to block the effects of opiates.

narcotics Opiates that relieve pain and induce sleep.

need An organism's physiological requirement, such as for food, water, or oxygen.

need for achievement (nAch) The attempt to excel and surpass others, and to accomplish difficult tasks as rapidly and independently as possible.

negative reinforcer Any stimulus that increases the probability of a behavior when it is removed after the behavior.

neodissociation theory of hypnosis The claim that consciousness can be split into several distinct and simultaneous streams of mental activity.

neuroanatomical studies Studies that focus on the physical structure of the brain, spinal cord, and nervous system.

neuron An individual nerve cell, the fundamental building block of the nervous system.

neurosis An enduring set of symptoms that bothers an individual or interferes with healthy functioning while the person remains in contact with reality.

neurotransmitter A chemical released at the synapse by one neuron that influences the electrical activity of another.

nomothetic approach An approach to personality that attempts to understand behavior and experience of people in general, or of the average case.

nondirective therapy A type of humanistic therapy in which the therapist refuses to tell the client what to do or think.

noninvasive techniques Nonsurgical techniques for studying functions in the normal brain.

normal distribution A particular mathematical distribution in which cases are symmetrically arranged around the average.

norms Standard figures that describe the performance of the average person in relation to some larger group.

obedience Following the suggestions or orders of another person even when one prefers not to.

obesity The condition of being at least 15 to 20% over one's ideal body weight.

object permanence According to Piaget, the awareness that objects continue to exist even when they are not present to be seen, touched, or sensed.

observational learning Learning by observation, which involves modeling or copying the behavior of another person.

obsessive-compulsive disorder Persistent and repetitive thoughts that cannot be controlled, or behavior patterns that are repeated ritualistically.

occipital lobe The major lobe at the back of the head.

opening-up meditation An attempt to clear one's mind and "go with the flow" of an experience.

operant conditioning A type of learning in which the probability of a response changes when reinforcement or punishment is presented following that response.

operations According to Piaget, the mental actions that organize a person's view of the world.

opponent-processes theory of color vision The theory that there are three systems for color vision, each responding to two colors.

opponent-process theory of motivation The theory that many acquired motives arise from the interplay of two opposing processes in the brain, such as pleasure in response to pain.

optic nerve The structure that transmits information from the retina to the brain.

oral stage According to Freud, the psychosexual stage, lasting for the first year of life, when the infant derives satisfaction primarily through the mouth.

organizational psychology The study of human interaction in the workplace.

oval window A part of the cochlea that transmits sound waves from the middle ear to the basilar membrane by displacing cochlear fluid.

overjustification effect The idea that rewarding people for doing something they already enjoy may make them think they are doing it just for the reward.

overlearn To practice beyond the point of mastery.

overregularization The tendency of children to force every utterance to conform to the regular rules of grammar, even when it means making an error.

panic disorder Unpredictable, repeated attacks of anxiety and panic.

paradigm A common set of beliefs and assumptions shared by a particular group of scientists.

paraprofessionals Mental-health workers with limited training to perform specific tasks.

parapsychology The study of occult or psychic phenomena.

parasympathetic nervous system The branch of the autonomic nervous system that maintains appropriate internal states in times of relaxation.

parietal lobe The major lobe at the top rear of the brain.

partial reinforcement The reinforcement of some acts but not others; sometimes called *intermittent reinforcement.*

peak experiences According to Maslow, mystical feelings of happiness, peace, and contentment that a self-actualized person frequently experiences.

perception The process of interpreting a pattern of stimuli as an organized whole.

perceptual constancy The tendency of observers to perceive an object as stable even when its sensory image changes.

perceptual set A mental predisposition to perceive a stimulus in a particular way as a result of expectations or previous experience.

peripheral nervous system All nerve fibers outside the brain and spinal cord.

personality An individual's characteristic pattern of thought, behavior, and emotions.

personality disorder An inflexible behavior pattern or enduring personality trait that significantly interferes with a person's occupation or social life, or causes personal distress.

personality inventory A standard list of questions about an individual's behavior and feelings to assess personality traits.

personality psychologists Psychologists who focus on the problem of individual differences and how they develop.

personnel training An organization's program to teach employees job-related behaviors.

phallic stage According to Freud, the psychosexual stage from age 3 to 6 when a child first becomes aware of male-female genital differences.

phenothiazine drugs A group of antipsychotic drugs that reduces hallucinations, delusions, confusion, agitation, social withdrawal, and other psychotic symptoms.

pheromones In insects, smells that elicit sexual and other behavior patterns.

phobia A persistent and irrational fear of a specific object, activity, or situation.

phonemes The distinct sounds that make a difference in a particular language.

phonology The study of the rules governing the use of sounds in a specific language.

phrenology The outdated theory that the brain consists of several different organs, each responsible for a particular human trait.

physical dependence A syndrome in which withdrawal from a drug produces physical symptoms.

physiological motives Internal bodily states that direct an organism's behavior toward such goals as food, water, and sex.

physiological needs The first set of needs in Maslow's hierarchy (e.g., hunger, thirst).

physiological psychologists Psychologists who study the biological bases of behavior.

pitch The psychological sensation that a sound is high or low, primarily determined by the frequency of the vibrations composing a sound wave.

pituitary gland The endocrine gland that controls the secretion of other endocrine glands and is itself under the control of the hypothalamus.

place theory of hearing The theory that sounds of different frequencies activate different places on the basilar membrane.

placebo effect The phenomenon whereby medical treatments of no value in themselves seem to cure patients by the power of suggestion.

placebos Chemically inactive substances that can relieve pain by the power of suggestion.

pleasure principle According to Freud, the tendency of the id to reduce instinctual tension and return the organism to a comfortable state.

Poggendorf illusion A visual illusion in which a continuous line seems to be misplaced when it is partially obscured.

pons The brain structure that continues out of the medulla and contains nerve fibers connecting the brain and spinal cord.

positive reinforcer Any stimulus that increases the probability of a behavior when it is presented after the behavior.

postconventional level According to Kohlberg, a level of moral reasoning that involves applying universal principles of right and wrong that are more fundamental than the laws of any specific society.

preconventional level According to Kohlberg, a level of moral reasoning in which people accept society's commands primarily to gain rewards and avoid punishment.

prejudices Prejudgments based on little or no information about something.

Premack principle The principle that a more-preferred behavior will reinforce a less-preferred behavior.

preoperational stage According to Piaget, the stage from age 2 to 7 when symbolic thought first appears.

preparation-response Preparing for and monitoring the solution process, and translating the solution into a response.

prevalence The percentage of people who report a particular disorder within a given time period.

primary projection areas Cortical areas of the brain that receive input from the sense organs or control movement of particular muscle groups.

proactive inhibition The forgetting of information because of interference from material presented before the learning task.

productive thinking The Gestalt principle of solving problems by producing a new organization.

projection Attributing unacceptable impulses or feelings to somebody else.

projective test An individual's projection of inner feelings and conflict by responding to an ambiguous stimulus, such as a picture or an inkblot.

proprioceptive sense Senses reacting to movement of parts of the body, such as the muscles.

proximity The Gestalt principle that stimuli that are physically close tend to be perceived as belonging together.

psychiatrists Licensed physicians who specialize in the treatment of mental and emotional problems.

psychiatry The medical specialty concerned with mental illness.

psychoactive drug A chemical substance that influences behavior or subjective experiences by altering responses in the nervous system.

psychoanalytic approach A theory of personality that stresses the importance of unconscious conflicts and biological instincts in the determination of complex human behavior.

psycholinguistics The study of how people actually speak and use language.

psychological dependence Compulsive drug use in the absence of physical need.

psychology The scientific study of behavior and mental process.

psychophysics The study of systematic relationships between the physical attributes of stimuli and the psychological sensations they produce.

psychosexual stages According to Freud, developmental periods emphasizing sexual instincts associated with erogenous zones.

psychosis A serious mental disorder involving obvious disturbances in thought, emotion, and behavior.

psychosocial stages According to Erikson, the periods when people must face certain crises caused in part by new demands posed at different phases of life.

psychosomatic disease A physical illness that is partly caused by psychological factors.

psychosurgery Brain surgery aimed at changing a person's thought or behavior patterns.

psychotherapy The application, by a professional, of systematic psychological procedures to help a client change troublesome thoughts, feelings, and behavior patterns.

puberty The period when sexual maturation begins.

punisher Any stimulus that when paired with a particular behavior decreases the probability of that behavior.

punishment The application of an aversive stimulus when an organism emits a response in order to reduce the likelihood that the response will be repeated.

pupil A hole which appears black in the center of the iris.

questionnaires Written lists of questions to which people are asked to respond.

radical behaviorism A position that accepts the existence of internal cognitive processes but emphasizes the relationships between environmental events and observable behavior.

range The difference between the highest and lowest values in a distribution.

rational-emotive therapy A cognitive approach to therapy in which people are taught actively to avoid irrational thoughts that unpleasant events are catastrophic.

reaction formation The unconscious process by which an emotion becomes translated into its opposite.

reality principle The principle governing the ego's effort to delay energy discharge until an appropriate object is present.

recall Remembering information spontaneously or on the basis of certain cues.

receptive aphasia Difficulty in understanding language resulting from tissue damage in Wernike's area.

recognition The process of deciding whether specific information has been seen or heard before.

reflexes Involuntary acts automatically elicited by certain stimuli.

regression A retreat to behaviors that proved satisfying in earlier stages of psychosexual development.

reinforcer Any stimulus that when paired with a particular behavior increases the probability of that behavior.

relative size The phenomenon whereby larger objects are seen as closer to the observer than smaller ones.

relearning A comparison of the "savings" gained (e.g., measured by time or number of repetitions required) when material already learned once is learned again.

reliable Consistent and reproducible.

REM Rapid eye movements that occur during sleep associated with dreaming.

reorganization The term for solving a problem by perceiving new relationships among its elements.

replications Repetitions of a study to see whether similar results are found.

representative sample A group in which subjects are systematically chosen to represent a larger population.

repression According to Freud, a defense mechanism that reduces anxiety by preventing an anxiety-producing object or feeling from becoming conscious.

reproductive thinking (set effect) The Gestalt principle of applying past solutions to new problems.

resistance In psychoanalysis, an unconscious attempt to avoid therapeutic insights into motivation.

reticular formation (reticular activating system) A complex network of neurons and fibers that passes through the medulla, pons, and other structures, and is particularly involved in sleep, waking, alertness, and attention.

retina A light-sensitive surface at the back of the eye.

retrieval The recovery of information from storage.

retroactive inhibition The forgetting of information because of interference from material presented after the learning task.

retrograde amnesia An inability to remember events that occurred before some damage to the brain.

reversibility According to Piaget, a mental operation in which a person can imagine a transformation that would restore an original condition.

rods Receptor cells primarily responsible for night vision.

romantic love Intense and passionate love.

safety needs The second set of needs in Maslow's hierarchy; that is, the need for physical security and freedom from pain or fear.

Schachter and Singer's cognitive theory The theory that emotional responses to a particular situation depend on the individual's perception and interpretation of that situation, and that the emotion's intensity depends on the degree of physiological arousal.

schedules of reinforcement Different patterns of reinforcement and punishment that influence learning.

schemas Memory structures in which knowledge of specific concepts is clustered together; an important element in constructive memory.

schizophrenia Serious disturbances of thought, perception, and emotion that persist for at least six months prior to the age of 45 in people who have deteriorated from a more adequate level of functioning.

school psychologists Psychologists who provide advice and guidance in the school system.

sclera The tough outer covering that protects the delicate structures within the eye.

script A schema that summarizes general knowledge about particular situations.

seasonal affective disorder A recurrent winter depression characterized by oversleeping, overeating, a craving for carbohydrates, and frequent sluggishness.

sedatives Drugs that depress the activity of the central nervous system.

self-actualization needs The highest level of needs in Maslow's hierarchy involves the attempt to use all one's talents to achieve one's potential.

self-control Active coping strategies used by an individual to deal with personal problems.

self-disclosure The degree to which people are willing to reveal information about themselves.

self-efficacy One's belief in one's own competence or ability to achieve a goal through certain actions.

self-esteem The value one places on one's own worth.

self-fulfilling prophecies Expectations that come true partly because people believe they will.

self-perception theory The idea that people with uncertain feelings about something simply note their behavior and assume their attitudes to match it.

self-serving bias The general tendency to see ourselves favorably.

semantic memory An abstract record of words, and ideas and rules for relating them.

semantics The rules governing the meaning of sentences, words, or morphemes.

semicircular canals A portion of the inner ear that helps regulate the sense of balance.

sensation The process of responding to a simple physical stimulus.

sensitivity training groups A form of group therapy that attempts to promote personal growth by encouraging participants to focus on their immediate relationships with others in the group.

sensorimotor stage According to Piaget, the stage from birth to age 2 when infants discover the relationship between their own sensations and motor acts.

sensory storage The component of memory that maintains a vivid and complete image of sensory impressions for about 0.25 to 2 seconds.

separation anxiety Profound distress occurring when a child is separated from the mother or primary caretaker.

set points　The body's internal levels for regulating body weight.

shape constancy　A tendency to perceive objects as maintaining the same shape regardless of the view from different angles.

shaping　The technique of teaching a complex behavior by reinforcing successive approximations of the desired activity.

short-term memory (STM)　The memory system that stores a limited amount of information for no more than about 30 seconds.

signal-detection theory　Attempts to account mathematically for psychological and sensory factors that influence psychophysical judgments.

similarity　The principle that stimuli resembling each other tend to be perceived as belonging together.

simple cells　Feature detectors that fire an electrical impulse when a straight-line stimulus is located in a particular place and points in a specific direction.

simple phobias　Specific fears.

single-cell recording　A technique for recording the electrical activity of one neuron at a time.

size constancy　The tendency to see objects as constant in size even when the visual image changes.

skewed distribution　More scores fall at one end than at the other end of a central point.

social cognition　The process of interpreting and understanding human behavior and feelings.

social facilitation　An improvement of performance when other people are present.

social influence　A bystander's tendency to follow the reactions of other people during an ambiguous event.

social-learning approach　A theory that emphasizes internal cognitive processes as important factors in determining behavior.

social loafing effect　The tendency to work less hard in a group than alone.

social model　The view that problem drinking is a complex category of behavior that may have many causes and cures.

social motives　Forces such as autonomy and affiliation that direct human behavior toward certain patterns of relationships with other people.

social phobia　A fear of situations in which one might be observed by others.

social psychology　The study of the way people respond to other human beings, and how they interact with one another.

Social Readjustment Rating Scale　A measurement of normal life stress.

social support　The resources that other people provide.

social theories of hypnosis　The claim that hypnotized people simply attempt to conform to a social role demanded by the hypnotist's demands.

somatic nervous system　The portion of the peripheral nervous system that connects the brain and spinal cord with sensory receptors and voluntary muscles.

somatosensory strip　A primary projection area at the front of the parietal lobe that receives sensations from the opposite side of the body.

sound　A wave motion that pulsates through a material medium, and is generated by physical vibrations.

species-specific behavior　Behavior patterns characteristic of a particular species.

spinal cord　A long, thin column of neurons and tissues emerging from the bottom of the brain and running down the back next to the spinal vertebrae.

split-brain surgery　Brain surgery that involves the cutting of the corpus callosum, surgically isolating the right and left hemispheres.

spontaneous recovery　The reappearance of an extinguished response after a rest period.

SQ3R method　A method for efficient study consisting of five steps: survey, question, read, recite, and review.

standard deviation　A mathematical measure of the amount of variability, spread, or dispersion of a particular set of scores.

Stanford-Binet　One of the most frequently used tests for assessing the intelligence of an individual child.

statistically significant　Unlikely to have occurred by chance according to some predetermined criterion, usually a probability of less than .05.

stimulants　Drugs that increase the activity of the central nervous system.

storage　The retention of information.

stranger anxiety　The phase in infancy when children seem anxious around strangers and may cry, fret, or try to move away.

stress　A perception of threat to physical or psychological well-being and the reaction to that threat.

stroke　A cerebrovascular accident that occurs when a blood vessel is blocked or broken and brain tissue is damaged.

sublimation　A successful defense mechanism that alters unacceptable impulses into completely acceptable and even admired social behaviors.

superego　According to Freud, an aspect of personality that represents the moral ideals, and strives to perfection rather than pleasure.

surface structure　According to Chomsky, the actual words in a sentence and the relations among them.

surveys　Summaries of information drawn from many interviews or questionnaires in order to measure the behavior of large groups of people.

symmetrical distribution　The same number of values are equally distributed on either side of the central point.

sympathetic nervous system　The branch of the autonomic nervous system that activates the glands and smooth muscles of the body in periods of emotional excitement.

synapse The microscopic space across which the axon of one neuron can stimulate the dendrite or cell body of another.

syntax The way words combine to form sentences.

systematic desensitization A process that requires an anxious person to imagine increasingly threatening situations while remaining deeply relaxed.

systematic observation The careful observation, recording, and analysis of behavior.

tardive dyskinesia A syndrome of involuntary muscle movements that occurs after long-term treatment with phenothiazines and other chemically related drugs.

task analysis An analysis that determines the precise skills and behaviors required to perform a particular task.

taste buds Structures in the tongue that contain the receptor cells responsible for taste sensation.

telegraphic speech A form of speech characteristic of children that consists of shortened sentences.

telepathy A controversial process of possible thought transmission from one person to another.

temperament An underlying energy level or other factor that helps produce a consistent style of responding in many different situations.

temporal lobe The major lobe just over the ear.

test-retest reliability The correlation between two different scores achieved by the same individual on the same test on two different occasions.

tests of job-specific skills Tests that require skills in performing a task very similar to skills required on the job.

thalamus A structure that transmits sensory information to the cerebral cortex.

Thematic Apperception Test (TAT) A test in which a person is asked to make up stories about a series of ambiguous pictures; used to reveal the hidden forces that motivate behavior.

token economy A setting in which behavior is changed by rewarding specific actions with tokens that can be exchanged for reinforcers.

tolerance A phenomenon in which increasingly large doses of a drug are required to produce the same effects.

traits Predispositions to respond to a variety of situations in similar ways.

transference In psychoanalysis, a patient's inappropriately strong positive or negative feelings toward the therapist.

trichromatic theory The theory that there are separate receptors in the retina for red, blue, and green.

Type A behavior A personality pattern characterized by competitiveness and the tendency to be always in a rush.

type theory An approach to personality that sorts people into separate personality categories or types.

unconditioned response A natural reflex response elicited by an unconditioned stimulus.

unconditioned stimulus A stimulus that automatically elicits a natural reflex called the unconditioned response.

valid Accurately measuring a particular trait.

variable-interval (VI) schedules Schedules of reinforcement that vary the amount of time that must elapse before a response is reinforced.

variable-ratio (VR) schedules Schedules of reinforcement that vary the number of responses required for each reward.

vestibular sacs Organs involved in the maintenance of balance.

vestibular sense Sensations that provide information about the pull of gravity and help maintain balance.

visceral sense Feedback from internal organs.

wavelength The distance from the crest of one wave to the crest of the next.

Wechsler Adult Intelligence Scale-Revised (WAIS-R) Six verbal and five performance scales, considered a reliable and valid test of IQ.

Yerkes-Dodson law The theory that there is an optimal level of arousal for any activity; too much or too little arousal produces inferior performance.

zygote A fertilized egg.

BIBLIOGRAPHY

ABEBIMPE, V. R., CHU, C. C., KLEIN, H. E., & LANGE, M. H. (1982). Racial and geographic differences in the psychopathology of schizophrenia. *American Journal of Psychiatry, 139,* 888–891.

ABELSON, R. P. (1981). Psychological status of the script concept. *American Psychologist, 36,* 715–729.

ABRAMSON, L. Y., SELIGMAN, M. E. P., & TEASDALE, J. D. (1978). Learned helplessness in humans: Critique and reformation. *Journal of Abnormal Psychology, 87,* 49–74.

ADORNO, T., FRENKEL-BRUNSWICK, E., LEVINSON, D., & SANFORD, R. (1950). *The authoritarian personality.* New York: Harper & Row.

AGRAS, S., & JACOB, R. (1979). In O. F. Pomerleau & J. P. Brady (Eds.), *Behavioral medicine: Theory and practice.* Baltimore: Williams & Wilkins.

AGRAS, S., SYLVESTER, D., & OLIVEAU, D. (1969). The epidemiology of common fears and phobias. *Comprehensive Psychiatry, 10,* 151–156.

AIKINS, J. S. (1983). Prototypical knowledge for expert systems. *Artificial Intelligence, 20,* 163–210.

AIKINS, J. S., KUNZ, J. C., SHORTLIFFE, E. H., & FALLAT, R. J. (1984). PUFF: An expert system for interpretation of pulmonary function data. In W. J. Clancey & E. H. Shortliffe (Eds.), *Readings in medical intelligence: The first decade.* New York: Addison-Wesley.

AINSWORTH, M. D., & BELL, S. M. (1970). Attachment, exploration, and separation: Illustrated by the behavior of one-year olds in a strange situation. *Child Development, 41,* 49–67.

ALBA, J. W., & HASHER, L. (1983). Is memory schematic? *Psychological Bulletin, 93,* 203–231.

ALLPORT, G. (1961). *Pattern and growth in personality.* New York: Holt, Rinehart and Winston.

ALLPORT, G. W. (1965). *Letter from Jenny.* New York: Harcourt Brace Jovanovich.

American Psychiatric Association. (1978). *Electroconvulsive therapy.* Washington, DC: Author.

American Psychiatric Association. (1980). *Diagnostic and statistical manual of mental disorders* (3d. ed.). Washington, DC: Author.

American Psychological Association. (1973). *Ethical principles of psychologists.* Washington, DC: Author.

American Psychological Association. (1986). APA-Accredited doctoral programs in professional psychology: 1986. *American Psychologist, 41,* 1357–1363.

American Psychological Association. (1986). *Survey of the use of animals in behavioral research in U.S. universities.* Washington, DC: Author.

ANAND, B. K., & BROBECK, J. R. (1951). Hypothalamic control of food intake in rats and cats. *Yale Journal of Biological Medicine, 24,* 123–140.

ANASTASI, A. (1982). *Psychological testing* (5th ed.). New York: Macmillan.

ANREP, G. V. (1920). Pitch discrimination in the dog. *Journal of Physiology, 53,* 367–385.

ANREP, G. V. (1923). The irradiation of conditioned reflexes. *Proceedings of the Royal Society B, 94,* 404–426.

ANTROBUS, J. L., ANTROBUS, J. S., & SINGER, J. L. (1964). Experiments accompanying daydreaming, visual imagery, and thought suppression. *Journal of Abnormal and Social Psychology, 69,* 244–252.

ARIETI, S. (1974). *Interpretation of schizophrenia.* New York: Basic Books.

ARKES, H. R., WORTMAN, R. L., SAVILLE, P. D. & HARKNESS, A. R. (1981). Hindsight bias among physicians weighing the likelihood of diagnoses. *Journal of Applied Psychology, 66,* 252–254.

ARMOR, D. J., POLICH, J. M., & STAMBUL, H. B. (1978). *Alcoholism and treatment.* New York: Wiley.

ARONOW, E., & REZNIKOFF, M. (1976). *Rorschach content interpretation.* New York: Grune & Stratton.

ARONSON, E., & MILLS, J. (1959). The effects of severity of initiation on liking for a group. *Journal of Abnormal Psychology, 59,* 177–181.

ASCH, S. E. (1951). Effects of group pressure upon the modification and distortion of judgement. In H. Guetzkon (Ed.), *Groups, leadership, and men.* Pittsburgh: Carnegie.

ASERINSKY, E., & KLEITMAN, N. (1953). Regularly occurring

periods of eye motility and concomitant phenomena during sleep. *Science, 118,* 273–274.

ASHER, J. J. & SCIARRINO, J. A. (1974). Realistic work sample tests: A review. *Personnel Psychology, 27,* 519–533.

ATKINSON, J. W., & LITWIN, G. H. (1960). Achievement motive and test anxiety conceived as motive to approach success and motive to avoid failure. *Journal of Abnormal and Social Psychology, 60,* 52–63.

ATKINSON, J. W., & McCLELLAND, D. C. (1948). The effect of different intensities of hunger on thematic apperception. *Journal of Experimental Psychology, 38,* 643–658.

ATKINSON, R. C., & SHIFFRIN, R. M. (1968). Human memory: A proposed system and its control processes. In K. W. Spence & J. T. Spence (Eds.), *The psychology of learning and motivation: Advances in research and theory* (Vol. 2). New York: Academic Press.

ATWOOD, M. E., & POLSON, P. G. (1976). A process model for water jug problems. *Cognitive Psychology, 8,* 191–216.

AX, A. F. (1953). The physiological differentiation between anger and fear in humans. *Psychosomatic Medicine, 15,* 433–442.

AXSOM, D., & COOPER, J. (1985). Cognitive dissonance and psychotherapy: The role of effort justification in inducing weight loss. *Journal of Experimental Social Psychology, 21,* 149–160.

AYLLON, T., & AZRIN, N. (1968). *The token economy.* Englewood Cliffs, NJ: Prentice-Hall.

AZRIN, N. H., & HOLZ, W. C. (1966). Punishment. In W. K. Honig (Ed.), *Operant behavior: Areas of research and application.* Englewood Cliffs, NJ: Prentice-Hall.

AZRIN, N. H., HUTCHINSON, R. R., & HAKE, D. F. (1966). Extinction-induced aggression. *Journal of the Experimental Analysis of Behavior, 9,* 191–204.

BACKIS, C. A., & GOLD, M. S. (1985). New concepts in cocaine addiction: The dopamine depletion hypothesis. *Neuroscience & Biobehavioral Review, 9,* 469–477.

BAHRICK, H. (1984). Replicative, constructive, and reconstructive aspects of memory: Implications for human and animal research. *Physiological Psychology, 12,* 53–58.

BAHRICK, H. P., BAHRICK, P. D., & WITTLINGER, R. P. (1975). Fifty years of memory for names and faces: A cross-sectional approach. *Journal of Experimental Psychology: General, 104,* 54–75.

BAKER, J. P., & CHRIST, J. L. (1971). Teacher expectancies: A review of the literature. In J. D. Elashoff & R. E. Snow (Eds.), *Pygmalion reconsidered.* Worthington, OH: Charles A. Jones.

BANDURA, A. (1965). Influence of models' reinforcement contingencies on the acquisition of imitative responses. *Journal of Personality and Social Psychology, 1,* 589–595.

BANDURA, A. (1977). *Social learning theory.* Englewood Cliffs, NJ: Prentice-Hall.

BANDURA, A. (1984). Recycling misconceptions of perceived self-efficacy. *Cognitive Therapy and Research, 8*(3), 231–255.

BANDURA, A., ADAMS, N. E., & BEYER, J. (1977). Cognitive processes mediating behavioral change. *Journal of Personality and Social Psychology, 35,* 125–139.

BANDURA, A., & ROSENTHAL, T. L. (1966). Vicarious classical conditioning as a function of arousal level. *Journal of Personality and Social Psychology, 3,* 54–62.

BANDURA, A., ROSS, D., & ROSS, S. (1963). Imitation of film mediated aggressive models. *Journal of Abnormal and Social Psychology, 66,* 3–11.

BANDURA, A., & WALTERS, R. H. (1959). *Adolescent aggression.* New York: Ronald Press.

BARBER, T. X. (1969). *Hypnosis: A scientific approach.* New York: Van Nostrand.

BARBER, T. X. (1970). *LSD, marijuana, yoga, and hypnosis.* Chicago: Aldine.

BARCHAS, J. D., AKIL, H., ELLIOT, G. R., HOLMAN, R. B., & WATSON, S. J. (1978). Behavioral neurochemistry: Neuroregulators and behavioral states. *Science, 200,* 964–973.

BARSALOU, L. W. (1981). *The determinants of graded structure in categories.* Ph.D. thesis. Stanford University, Stanford, California.

BARTLETT, F. C. (1932). *Remembering: A study in experimental and social psychology.* London: Cambridge University Press.

BASSUK, E. L., & GERSON, S. (1978). Deinstitutionalization and mental health services. *Scientific American, 238,* 46–53.

BATSON, C. D., O'QUIN, K., FULTZ, J., VANDERPLAS, M., & ISEN, A. M. (1983). Influence of self-reported distress and empathy on egoistic versus altruistic motivation to help. *Journal of Personality and Social Psychology, 45,* 706–718.

BAUM, A., AIELLO, J. R., & CALESNICK, L. E. (1978). Crowding and personal control: Social density and the development of learned helplessness. *Journal of Personality and Social Psychology, 36,* 1000–1011.

BAUM, A., & DAVIS, G. E. (1980). Reducing the stress of high-density living: An architectural intervention. *Journal of Personality and Social Psychology, 38,* 471–481.

BAUM, A., DAVIS, G. E., CALESNICK, L. E., & GATCHEL, R. J. (1982). Individual differences in coping with crowding: Stimulus screening and social overload. *Journal of Personality and Social Psychology, 43,* 821–830.

BAUM, A., & VALINS, S. (1977). *Architecture and social behavior: Psychological studies in social density.* Hillsdale, NJ: Erlbaum.

BAUMRIND, D. (1964). Some thoughts on ethics of research: After reading Milgram's "Behavioral study of obedience." *American Psychologist, 19,* 421–423.

BECK, A. T. (1967). *Depression: Clinical, experimental and theoretical aspects.* New York: Harper & Row.

BEERS, C. W. (1908). *A mind that found itself: An autobiography.* Garden City, NY: Doubleday.

BELL, A. P., WEINBERG, M. S., & HAMMERSMITH, S. K. (1981). *Sexual preference.* Bloomington: Indiana University Press.

BELOFF, J. (1977). Historical overview. In B. B. Wolman (Ed.), *Handbook of parapsychology.* New York: Van Nostrand Reinhold.

BELSKY, J., LERNER, R. M., & SPANIER, G. B. (1984). *The child in the family.* Reading, MA: Addison-Wesley.

BELSKY, J., & STEINBERG, L. D. (1978). The effects of day care: A critical review. *Child Development, 49,* 929–949.

BELVEDERE, E., & FOULKES, D. (1971). Telepathy and dreams: A failure to replicate. *Perceptual and Motor Skills, 33,* 783–789.

BEM, D. J. (1965). An experimental analysis of self-persuasion. *Journal of Experimental Social Psychology, 1,* 199–218.

BEM, D. J., & ALLEN, A. (1974). On predicting some of the people some of the time: The search for cross-situational consistencies in behavior. *Psychological Review, 81,* 506–520.

BEM, S. L. (1974). The measurement of psychological androgyny. *Journal of Consulting and Clinical Psychology, 42,* 153–162.

BEM, S. L. (1975). Sex-role adaptability: One consequence of psychological androgyny. *Journal of Personality and Social Psychology, 31,* 634–643.

BEM, S. L. (1977). On the utility of alternative procedures for assessing psychological androgyny. *Journal of Consulting and Clinical Psychology, 45,* 196–205.

BEM, S. L. (1981). Gender scheme theory: A cognitive account of sex typing. *Psychological Review, 88,* 354–364.

BEM, S. L. (1983). Gender scheme theory and its implications for child development—Raising gender-aschematic children in a gender-schematic society. *Signs, 8,* 598–616.

BENJAMIN, L. T., CAVELL, T. A., & SHALLENBERGER, W. R. (1984). Staying with initial answers on objective tests: Is it a myth? *Teaching of Psychology, 11,* 133–141.

BENSON, H. (1975). *The relaxation response.* New York: Avon Books.

BENSON, H., KOTCH, J. B., CRASSWELLER, K. D., & GREENWOOD, M. M. (1977). Historical and clinical considerations of the relaxation response. *American Scientist, 65,* 441–443.

BERGER, P. A. (1978). Medical treatment of mental illness. *Science, 200,* 974–981.

BERGIN, A. E. (1971). The evaluation of therapeutic outcomes. In A. E. Bergin & S. L. Garfield (Eds.), *Handbook of psychotherapy and behavior change: An empirical analysis.* New York: Wiley.

BERKMAN, L. F. (1984). Assessing the physical health effects of social networks and social support. *Annual Review of Public Health, 5,* 413–432.

BERKOWITZ, L., & LePAGE, A. (1967). Weapons as aggression-eliciting stimuli. *Journal of Personality and Social Psychology, 7,* 202–207.

BERLAND, T. (1971). *The fight for quiet.* Englewood Cliffs, NJ: Prentice-Hall.

BERNDT, T. J. (1981). Relations between social cognition, non-social cognition, and social behavior: The case of friendship. In J. H. Flavell & L. D. Ross (Eds.), *Social-cognitive development: Frontiers and possible futures.* New York: Cambridge University Press.

BERNSTEIN, D. A., & NIETZEL, M. T. (1980). *Introduction to clinical psychology.* New York: McGraw-Hill.

BERNSTEIN, E. (1987). Response to Terrace. *American Psychologist, 42,* 272–273.

BERNSTEIN, I. L. (1978). Learned taste aversions in children receiving chemotherapy. *Science, 200,* 1302–1303.

BERSCHEID, E. (1982). Attraction and emotions in interpersonal relationships. In M. S. Clark and S. T. Fiske (Eds.), *Affect and cognition: The 17th Annual Carnegie Symposium on Cognition.* Hillsdale, NJ: Erlbaum.

BERSCHEID, E., & WALSTER, E. H. (1978). *Interpersonal attraction* (2nd ed.). Reading, MA: Addison-Wesley.

BERTENTHAL, B. I., & CAMPOS, J. J. (1984). A reexamination of fear and its determinants on the visual cliff. *Psychophysiology, 21,* 413–417.

BERTENTHAL, B. I., CAMPOS, J. J., & BARRETT, K. C. (1984). Self-produced locomotion: An organizer of emotional, cognitive, and social development in infancy. In R. Emde & R. Harmon (Eds.), *Continuities and discontinuities in development* (pp. 175–210). New York: Plenum Press.

BETZ, N. E., & HACKETT, G. (1981). The relationship of career-related self-efficacy expectations to perceived career options in college women and men. *Review of Counseling Psychology, 28*(5), 399–410.

BEVER, T. G., & CHIARELLO, R. J. (1974). Cerebral dominance in musicians and nonmusicians. *Science, 185,* 137–139.

BIGELOW, H. J. (1850). Dr. Harlow's case of recovery from the passage of an iron bar through the head. *American Journal of the Medical Sciences, 39,* 14–22.

BINGHAM, W. V. (1949). Today and yesterday. *Personnel Psychology, 2,* 267–275.

BJORKLUND, A., & STENEVI, U. (1984). Intracerebral neural implants: Neuronal replacement and reconstruction of damaged circuities. *Annual Review of Neuroscience, 7,* 279–308.

BLACKWELL, H. R., & SCHLOSBERG, H. (1943). Octave generalization, pitch discrimination, and loudness thresholds

in the white rat. *Journal of Experimental Psychology,
33,* 407–419.

BLASI, A. (1980). Bridging moral cognition and moral action: A critical review of the literature. *Psychological Bulletin, 88,* 1–45.

BLEULER, E. (1950). *Dementia praecox or the group of schizophrenics* (J. Zinkin, trans.). New York: International Universities Press.

BLOCK, T. C., & BALLOUN, J. L. (1967). Behavioral receptivity to dissonant information. *Journal of Personality and Social Psychology, 6,* 413–428.

BLOOM, B., ASHER, S. J., & WHITE, S. W. (1978). Marital disruption as a stressor: A review and analysis. *Psychological Bulletin, 85,* 867–894.

BLOOMQUIST, E. R. (1970). The use and abuse of stimulants. In W. G. Clark and J. del Giudice (Eds.), *Principles of psychopharmacology.* New York: Academic Press.

BOCKHOVEN, J. S. (1963). *Moral treatment in american psychiatry.* New York: Springer-Verlag.

BOLLES, R. C. (1970). Species-specific defense reactions and avoidance learning. *Psychological Review, 77,* 32–48.

BORGIDA, E., & NISBETT, R. (1977). The differential impact of abstract vs. concrete information on decisions. *Journal of Applied Social Psychology, 3,* 258–271.

BORING, E. G. (1942). *Sensation and perception in the history of experimental psychology.* Englewood Cliffs, NJ: Prentice-Hall.

BORING, E. G. (1950). *A history of experimental psychology* (2nd ed.). Englewood Cliffs, NJ: Prentice-Hall.

BOTVIN, G. J., & MURRAY, F. B. (1975). The efficacy of peer modeling and social conflict in the acquisition of conservation. *Child Development, 46,* 796–799.

BOTWINICK, J. (1979). Intellectual abilities. In J. E. Birren & K. W. Schaie (Eds.), *Handbook of the psychology of aging.* New York: Van Nostrand Reinhold.

BOUCHARD, T. J. (1984). Twins reared apart and together: What they tell us about human diversity. In S. Fox, *The chemical and biological bases of individuality* (pp. 147–184). New York: Plenum.

BOUSFIELD, W. A. (1953). The occurrence of clustering in the recall of randomly arranged associates. *Journal of General Psychology, 49,* 229–240.

BOWER, G. H. (1970). Analysis of mnemonic device. *American Scientist, 58,* 496–510.

BOWER, G. H., CLARK, M. C., LESGOLD, A. M., & WINZENZ, D. (1969). Hierarchical retrieval schemes in recall of categorized word lists. *Journal of Verbal Learning and Verbal Behavior, 8,* 323–343.

BOWERS, K. S. (1976). *Hypnosis for the seriously curious.* Monterey, CA: Brooks/Cole.

BRADSHAW, J. L., & NETTLETON, N. C. (1981). The nature of hemispheric specialization in man. *Behavioral and Brain Sciences, 4,* 51–91.

BRANSFORD, J. D., & JOHNSON, M. K. (1973). Considerations of some problems of comprehension. In W. G. Chase (Ed.), *Visual information processing.* New York: Academic Press.

BREASTED, J. H. (Ed.). (1930). *The Edwin Smith surgical papyrus* (Vol. 1). Chicago: University of Chicago Press.

BREHM, S. S. (1985). *Intimate relationships.* New York: Random House.

BRELAND, K., & BRELAND, M. (1951). A field of applied animal psychology. *American Psychologist, 6,* 202–204.

BRELAND, K., & BRELAND, M. (1961). The misbehavior of organisms. *American Psychologist, 16,* 681–684.

BRENNAN, J. G. (1942). *Thomas Mann's world.* New York: Columbia University Press.

BRETHERTON, I. (1985). Attachment theory: Retrospect and prospect. In I. Bretherton and E. Waters (Eds.), *Growing points of attachment theory and research. Child Development Monographs, 50* (Serial No. 209), 1–2.

BREUER, J., & FREUD, S. (1955). Case studies in hysteria. In J. Strachey (Ed.), *The standard edition of the complete psychological works of Sigmund Freud* (Vol. 2). London: Hogarth Press. (Original works published 1893–1895.)

BRODEN, M., HALL, R. V., & MITTS, B. (1971). The effect of self-recording on the classroom behavior of two eighth-grade students. *Journal of Applied Behavior Analysis, 4*(3), 191–199.

BRODY, J. (1976, June 10). Study suggests alcoholic, treated, can drink safely. *New York Times,* p. 1.

BRONZAFT, A. L. (1981). The effect of a noise abatement program on reading ability. *Journal of Environmental Psychology, 1,* 215–222.

BRONZAFT, A. L., & McCARTHY, D. P. (1975). The effects of elevated train noise on reading ability. *Environmental Behavior, 7,* 517–527.

BROTHERS, J. (1978). *How to get whatever you want out of life.* New York: Simon & Schuster.

BROWN v. BOARD OF EDUCATION OF TOPEKA (1954). 98F. Supp. 797 (1951), 347 U.S. 438 (1954), 349 U.S. 294.

BROWN, F. M. (1982). Rhythmicity as an emerging variable for psychology. In F. M. Brown & R. C. Graeber (Eds.), *Rhythmic aspects of behavior.* Hillsdale, NJ: Erlbaum.

BROWN, J. S. (1979). Motivation. In E. Hearst (Ed.), *The first century of experimental psychology.* Hillsdale, NJ: Erlbaum.

BROWN, R., & McNEILL, D. (1966). The "tip of the tongue" phenomenon. *Journal of Verbal Learning and Verbal Behavior, 5,* 325–337.

BRUNER, J. S. (1978). Learning how to do things with words. In J. S. Bruner & A. Garton (Eds.), *Human growth and development.* Oxford: Clarendon.

BRUNER, J. S. (1978). From communication to language: A psychological perspective. In I. Markova (Ed.), *The social context of language.* London: Wiley.

BRUNER, J. S., GOODNOW, J., & AUSTIN, G. A. (1956). *A study of thinking.* New York: Wiley.

BRYAN, J. H., & TEST, M. A. (1967). Models and helping: Naturalistic studies in aiding behavior. *Journal of Personality and Social Psychology, 6,* 400–407.

BUCKHOUT, R. (1975). Nearly 2000 witnesses can be wrong. *Social Action and the Law, 2,* 7.

BUROS, O. K. (Ed.). (1978). *The eighth mental measurements yearbook.* Lincoln: University of Nebraska, Buros Institute of Mental Measurements.

BURTT, H. E. (1941). An experimental study of early childhood memory: Final report. *Journal of Genetic Psychology, 58,* 435–439.

BURWEN, L. S., & CAMPBELL, D. T. (1957). The generality of attitudes toward authority and non-authority figures. *Journal of Abnormal and Social Psychology, 54,* 24–31.

BUTWIN, I. J., & SIEGLER, J. C. (1980). Intellectual ability among the elderly: Simultaneous cross-sectional and longitudinal comparisons. *Developmental Psychology, 16,* 49–53.

BYRNE, D. (1971). *The attraction paradigm.* New York: Academic Press.

CALHOUN, J. B. (1962). Population density and social pathology. *Scientific American, 206,* 139–146.

CAMP, D. S., RAYMOND, G. A., & CHURCH, R. M. (1967). Temporal relationship between response and punishment. *Journal of Experimental Psychology, 74,* 114–123.

CAMPBELL, A. (1981). *The sense of well-being in America.* New York: McGraw-Hill.

CAMPBELL, S. (1982–1983, Winter). The "monster" tree-trunk of Loch Ness. *Skeptical Inquirer,* pp. 42–46.

CAMPION, J. E. (1972). Work sampling for personnel selection. *Journal of Applied Psychology, 56,* 40–44.

CANNON, W. B. (1927). The James-Lange theory of emotions: A critical examination and an alternative theory. *American Journal of Psychology, 39,* 106–124.

CANNON, W. B., & WASHBURN, A. L. (1912). An explanation of hunger. *American Journal of Physiology, 29,* 441–454.

CARMAN, R. A., & ADAMS, W. R. (1972). *Study skills: A student's guide for survival.* New York: Wiley.

CARROLL, J. B. & HORN, J. L. (1981). On the scientific basis of ability testing. *American Psychologist, 36,* 1012–1020.

CASTAIGNE, P., LHERMITTE, F., SIGNORET, J. L., & ABELANET, R. (1980). Déscription et étude scannographique du cerveau de Leborgne (la découverte de Broca). *Revue Neurologique, 136,* 563–583.

CATANIA, A. C. (1979). *Learning.* Englewood Cliffs, NJ: Prentice-Hall.

CATTELL, R. B. (1971). *Abilities: Their structure, growth, and action.* Boston: Houghton Mifflin.

CENTERS FOR DISEASE CONTROL (1985). Update: Acquired Immune Deficiency Syndrome, United States. *Morbidity and Mortality Weekly Report, 34,* 245–248.

CENTERS FOR DISEASE CONTROL (1987). Summary: Cases specified certifiable diseases, United States. *Morbidity and Mortality Weekly Report, 46,* 604.

CHALL, J. S. (1983). *Stages of reading development.* New York: McGraw-Hill.

CHAPANIS, A. (1975). Interactive human communication. *Scientific American, 232,* 36–42.

CHAPOUTHIER, G. (1973). Behavioral studies of the molecular basis of memory. In J. A. Deutsch (Ed.), *The physiological basis of memory.* New York: Academic Press.

CHAUDURI, H. (1965). *Philosophy of meditation.* New York: Philosophical Library.

CHERRY, F., & BYRNE, D. (1976). Authoritarianism. In. T. Blasi (Ed.), *Personality variables in social behavior.* Hillsdale, NJ: Erlbaum.

CHOMSKY, C. (1972). Write now, read later. In C. B. Cazden (Ed.), *Language and early childhood education.* Washington, DC: National Association for the Education of Young Children, 119–126.

CHOMSKY, N. (1957). *Syntactic structures.* The Hague: Mouton.

CHOMSKY, N. (1965). *Aspects of the theory of syntax.* Cambridge, MA: M.I.T. Press.

CHOMSKY, N. (1979). *Language and responsibility.* New York: Pantheon.

CLARK, B., & GRAYBEIL, A. (1949). Linear acceleration and deceleration as factors influencing nonvisual orientation during flight. *Journal of Aviation Medicine, 20,* 92–101.

CLARK, E. V. (1981). Lexical innovations: How children learn to create new words. In W. Deutsch (Ed.), *The child's construction of language* (pp. 299–328). London: Academic Press.

CLARK, H. H., & CLARK, E. V. (1977). *Psychology and language.* New York: Harcourt Brace Jovanovich.

CLARK-STEWART, K. A. (1978). Popular primers for parents. *American Psychologist, 33,* 359–369.

CLARKE, A. M., & CLARKE, A. D. (1976). *Early experience: Myth and evidence.* New York: Free Press.

CLORE, G. L., & BYRNE, D. (1974). A reinforcement-affect model of attraction. In T. L. Huston (Ed.), *Foundations of interpersonal attraction.* New York: Academic Press.

COBB, S., & ROSE, R. M. (1973). Hypertension, peptic ulcers, and diabetes in air traffic controllers. *Journal of the American Medical Association, 15,* 489–492.

COHEN, D. B. (1979). *Sleep and dreams: Origin, nature and functions.* Elmsford, NY: Pergamon Press.

COHEN, L. B. (1979). Our developing knowledge of infant perception and cognition. *American Psychologist, 34,* 894–899.

COHEN, S., GLASS, D. C., & SINGER, J. E. (1973). Apartment noise, auditory discrimination and reading ability in children. *Journal of Experimental Social Psychology, 9,* 407–422.

COHEN, S., & SHERROD, D. R. (1978). When density matters: Environmental control as a determinant of crowding effects in laboratory and residential settings. *Journal of Population: Behavioral, Social, and Environmental Issues, 1,* 189–202.

COHEN, S., & SYME, S. L. (1985). Issues in the study and application of social support. In S. Cohen and S. L. Syme (Eds.), *Social support and health.* New York: Academic Press.

COLBY, C. Z., LANZETTA, J. T., & KLECK, R. E. (1977). Effects of the expression of pain on autonomic and pain tolerance responses to subject-controlled pain. *Psychophysiology, 14,* 537–540.

COLE, J. O. (1964). Phenothiazine treatment in acute schizophrenia. *Archives of General Psychiatry, 10,* 246–261.

COLEMAN, J. C., BUTCHER, J. N., & CARSON, R. C (1980). *Abnormal Psychology and Modern Life* (6h ed.). Glenview, IL: Scott, Foresman.

COLLINS, A. M., & LOFTUS, E. F. (1975). A spreading-activation theory of semantic processing. *Psychological Review, 82,* 407–428.

COLLINS, A. M., & QUILLIAN, M. R. (1969). Retrieval time from semantic memory. *Journal of Verbal Learning and Verbal Behavior, 8,* 240–247.

COLWILL, R. M., & RESCORLA, R. A. (1985). Post-conditioning devaluation of a reinforcer affects instrumental responding. *Journal of Experimental Psychology: Animal Behavior Processes, 11,* 120–132.

CONOVER, M. R. (1986). Alleviating nuisance Canada goose problems through methiocarb-induced aversive conditioning. *Journal of Wildlife Management.* [Cited in N. E. Miller, The value of behavioral research on animals. *American Psychologist, 40,* 423–440.]

COOPER, J. E., KENDELL, R. E., GURLAND, B. J., SHARPE, L., COPELAND, J. R. M., & SIMON, R. (1972). *Psychiatric diagnosis in New York and London.* London: Oxford University Press.

COREN, S., & GIRGUS, J. S. (1978). *Seeing is deceiving: The psychology of visual illusions.* Hillsdale, NJ: Erlbaum.

COREN, S., PORAC, C., & WARD, L. M. (1978). *Sensation and perception.* New York: Academic Press.

CORKIN, S. (1980). A perspective study on cingulotomy. In E. S. Valenstein (Ed.), *The psychosurgery debate.* San Francisco: Freeman.

COWEN, E. L., & SCHOCHET, B. B. (1973). Referral and outcome differences between terminating and nonterminating children seen by nonprofessionals in a school mental health project. *American Journal of Community Psychology, 1,* 103–112.

COWLES, M., & DAVIS, C. (1982). On the origins of the .05 level of significance. *American Psychologist, 37,* 553–558.

COYLE, J. T., PRICE, D. L., & DELONG, M. R. (1983). Alzheimer's disease: A disorder of cortical cholinergic innervation. *Science, 219,* 1184–1190.

CRAIK, F. I. M., & LOCKHART, R. S. (1972). Levels of processing: A framework for memory research. *Journal of Verbal Learning and Verbal Behavior, 11,* 671–684.

CRICHTON, M. (1970). *Five patients: The hospital explained.* New York: Knopf.

CRICK, F., & MITCHISON, G. (1983). The function of dream sleep. *Nature, 304,* 11–114.

CRONBACH, L. J. (1975). Five decades of public controversy over mental testing. *American Psychologist, 30,* 1–14.

DABBS, J. M., & LEVENTHAL, H. (1966). Effects of varying the recommendations in a fear-arousing communication. *Journal of Personality and Social Psychology, 4,* 525–531.

DACKIS, C. A., & GOLD, M. S. (1985). New concepts in cocaine addiction: The dopamine depletion hypothesis. *Neuroscience and Biobehavioral Review, 9,* 469–477.

DAHLSTROM, W. G., ET. AL. (1972). *An MMPI handbook* (Vol. 1, rev. ed.). Minneapolis: University of Minnesota Press.

DALBY, L. (1986, January). Androgyny: Yes Ma'am, a woman can be more like a man! *Cosmopolitan,* pp. 198–201.

DAMASIO, A. R., & GESCHWIND, N. (1984). The neural basis of language. *Annual Review of Neuroscience, 7,* 127–147.

DARLEY, J. M., & GROSS, P. H. (1983). A hypothesis-confirming bias in labeling effects. *Journal of Personality and Social Psychology, 44,* 20–33.

DARLEY, J., & LATANÉ, B. (1968). Bystander intervention in emergencies: Diffusion of responsibility. *Journal of Personality and Social Psychology, 8,* 377–383.

DARNTON, R. (1970). *Mesmerism and the age of enlightenment in France.* New York: Schocken.

DAVIDSON, A. R., & JACCARD, J. J. (1979). Variables that moderate the attitude-behavior relation: Results of a longitudinal survey. *Journal of Personality and Social Psychology, 37,* 1364–1376.

DAVIS, J. M., GOSENFELD, L., & TSAI, C. C. (1976). Maintenance antipsychotic drugs to prevent relapse: A reply to Tobias and MacDonald. *Psychological Bulletin, 83,* 431–447.

DAVIS, K. (1947). Final note on a case of extreme isolation. *American Journal of Sociology, 52,* 432–437.

DAVIS, M. H., & STEPHAN, W. G. (1980). *Journal of Applied Social Psychology, 10,* 235–248.

DAVIS, R., BUCHANAN, B. G., & SHORTLIFFE, E. H. (1984). Production rules as a representation for a knowledge-based consultation program. In W. J. Clancey & E. H. Shortliffe (Eds.), *Readings in medical artificial intelligence: The first decade.* New York: Addison-Wesley.

DeCASPER, A. J., & FIFER, W. P. (1980). Of human bonding: Newborns prefer their mothers' voices. *Science, 208,* 1174–1176.

DeCASPER, A. J., & PRESCOTT, P. A. (1984). Human newborn's perception of male voices: Preference, discrimination, and reinforcing value. *Developmental Psychobiology, 17,* 481–491.

DE JONG, W. (1977). *The stigma of obesity: The consequences of naive assumptions concerning the causes of physical deviance.* Unpublished doctoral dissertation, Stanford University.

DEJOY, D. M. (1983). Environmental noise and children: Review of recent findings. *Journal of Auditory Research, 23*(3), 181–194.

DELONGIS, A., COYNE, J. C., DAKOF, G., FOLKMAN, S., & LAZARUS, R. S. (1982). Relationship of daily hassles, uplifts, and major life events to health status. *Health Psychology, 1,* 119–136.

DE MAUSE, L. (Ed.). (1974). *The history of childhood.* New York: Psychohistory Press.

DEMENT, W. C. (1974). *Some must watch while some must sleep.* New York: Norton.

DEPUE, R. A., & EVANS, R. (1981). The psychobiology of depressive disorders: From pathophysiology to predisposition. In Brendan A. Maher and Winifred B. Maher (Eds.), *Progress in experimental personality research,* (Vol. 10). New York: Academic Press.

DEUTSCH, A. (1949). *The mentally ill in America* (2nd ed.). New York: Columbia University Press.

DEVALOIS, R. L., & DEVALOIS, K. K. (1980). Spatial vision. *Annual Review of Psychology, 31,* 309–341.

DE VILLIERS, J. G., & DE VILLIERS, P. A. (1978). *Language acquisition.* Cambridge, MA: Harvard University Press.

DEVLIN, HON. LORD PATRICK (CHAIR) (1976). *Report to the Secretary of State for the Home Department of the Departmental Committee on Evidence of Identification in Criminal Cases.* London: Her Majesty's Stationery Office.

DEWAN, E. (1970). The programming (P) hypothesis for REM sleep. In E. Hartmann (Ed.), *Sleep and dreaming.* Boston: Little, Brown.

DION, K. (1972). Physical attractiveness and evaluations of children's transgressions. *Journal of Personality and Social Psychology, 24,* 207–213.

DION, K., BERSCHEID, E., & WALSTER, E. (1972). What is beautiful is good. *Journal of Personality and Sexual Psychology, 24,* 285.

DOHRENWEND, B. P., DOHRENWEND, B. S., GOULD, M. S., LINK, B., NEUGEBAUER, R., & WUNSCH-HITIG, R. (1988). *Mental illness in the United States: Epidemiological estimates.* New York: Praeger.

DUBOIS, P. H. (1970). *A history of psychological testing.* Boston: Allyn & Bacon.

DUNNETTE, M. D. (1976). Aptitudes, abilities, and skills. *Handbook of industrial and organizational psychology.* Skokie, IL: Rand McNally.

DUNNING, J. (1986, November 3). Women and AIDS: Discussing precautions. *The New York Times.*

DURLAK, J. A. (1979). Comparative effectiveness of paraprofessional helpers. *Psychological Bulletin, 86,* 80–92.

DYWAN, J., & BOWERS, K. S. (1983). The use of hypnosis to enhance recall. *Science, 222,* 184–185.

EAGLY, A. H. (1983). Gender and social influence: A social psychological analysis. *American Psychologist, 38,* 971–981.

EAGLY, A. H., & CARLI, L. L. (1981). Sex of researchers and sex-typed communications as determinants of sex differences in influenceability: A meta-analysis of social influence studies. *Psychological Bulletin, 90,* 1–20.

EASTMAN, C., & MARZILLI, J. S. (1984). Theoretical and methodological difficulties in Bandura self-efficacy theory. *Cognitive Therapy and Research, 8,* 213–229.

EBBINGHAUS, H. (1885). *On memory* (H. A. Ruger & C. E. Bussenves, Trans.). New York: Teachers College, Columbia University.

EDDINGTON, A. G. (1974). A new tabulation of statistical procedure used in APA journals. *American Psychologist, 29,* 25–26.

EDEN, D., & SHANI, A. B. (1982). Pygmalion goes to boot camp: Expectancy, leadership, and trainee performance. *Journal of Applied Psychology, 67,* 194–199.

EDWARDS, B. (1980). *Drawing on the right side of the brain.* Boston: Houghton Mifflin.

EKMAN, D., & FRIESEN, W. V. (1975). *Unmasking the face.* Englewood Cliffs, NJ: Prentice-Hall.

EKMAN, P. (1975, September). Face muscles talk every language. *Psychology Today,* pp. 35–39.

EKMAN, P., & FRIESEN, W. V. (1971). Constants across cultures in the face and emotion. *Journal of Personality and Social Psychology, 17,* 124–129.

EKMAN, P., SORENSON, E. R., & FRIESEN, W. V. (1969). Pancultural elements in facial displays of emotion. *Science, 164,* 86–88.

ELASHOFF, J. D., & SNOW, R. E. (Eds.) (1971). *Pygmalion reconsidered.* Worthington, OH: Charles A. Jones.

ELLIS, A. (1973). Rational-emotive therapy. In R. Corsini (Ed.), *Current psychotherapies.* Ithaca, IL: F. E. Peacock.

ELLSWORTH, P. C., & CARLSMITH, J. M. (1968). Effects of eye contact and verbal content on affective response to dyadic interaction. *Journal of Personality and Social Psychology, 10,* 15–20.

EMRICK, C. D. (1975). A review of psychologically oriented treatment of alcoholism. *Journal of Studies on Alcohol, 36,* 88–108.

ENDLER, N. S. (1977). The role of person-by-situation interactions in personality theory. In D. Magnusson & N. S. Endler (Eds.), *Personality at the crossroads: Current issues in interactional psychology.* New York: Halsted Press.

ENGLISH, H. B., WELBORN, E. L., & KILLIAN, C. D. (1934). Studies in substance memorization. *Journal of General Psychology, 11,* 233–259.

EPSTEIN, S. (1979). The stability of behavior: I. On predicting most of the people much of the time. *Journal of Personality and Social Psychology, 37,* 1097–1125.

EPSTEIN, W. (1961). The influence of syntactical structure

on learning. *American Journal of Psychology, 74,* 80–85.

ERICKSON, M. F., SROUFE, L. A., & EGELAND, B. (1985). The relationship between quality of attachment and behavior problems in preschool in a high-risk sample. In I. Bretherton and E. Waters (Eds.), Growing points of attachment theory and research. *Child Development Monographs, 50* (Serial No. 209), 1–2.

ERIKSON, E. (1963). *Childhood and society* (2nd ed.). New York: Norton.

ERLENMEYER-KIMLING, L., & JARVIK, L. F. (1963). Genetics and intelligence: A review. *Science, 142,* 1477–1478.

ETAUGH, C. (1980). Effects of nonmaternal care on children. *American Psychologist, 35,* 309–319.

EVANS, R. I., RAINES, B. E., & HANSELKA, L. (1984). Developing data-based communications in social psychological research: Adolescent smoking prevention. *Journal of Applied Social Psychology, 14,* 289–295.

EVANS, R. I., ROZELLE, R. M., MAXWELL, S. E., RAINES, B. E., DILL, C. A., GUTHRIE, T. J., HENDERSON, A. H., & HILL, P. C. (1981). Social modeling in families to deter smoking in adolescents: Results of a three-year field investigation. *Journal of Applied Psychology, 66,* 399–414.

EYSENCK, H. J. (1952). The effects of psychotherapy: An evaluation. *Journal of Consulting Psychology, 16,* 319–324.

FAGAN, L. M., SHORTLIFFE, E. H., & BUCHANAN, B. G. (1984). Computer-based medical decision making: From MYCIN to VM. In W. J. Clancey & E. H. Shortliffe (Eds.), *Readings in medical artificial intelligence: The first decade.* New York: Addison-Wesley.

FANCHER, R. E. (1979). *Pioneers of psychology.* New York: Norton.

FANTZ, R. L. (1961). The origin of form perception. *Scientific American, 204,* 66–73.

FARBER, S. L. (1981, January). Telltale behavior of twins. *Psychology Today,* pp. 58–62, 79–80.

FARLEY, J., & AIKEN, D. L. (1985). Cellular mechanisms of learning, memory and information-storage. *Annual Review of Psychology, 36,* 419–494.

FEIGENBAUM, E. A., & McCORDUCK, P. (1983). *The fifth generation.* New York: Addison-Wesley.

FENSTERHEIM, H., & BAER, J. (1975). *Don't say yes when you want to say no.* New York: Dell.

FERNALD, D. (1981). *Four-month olds prefer to listen to "motherese."* Paper presented at a meeting of the Society for Research in Child Development.

FESTINGER, L. (1957). *A theory of cognitive dissonance.* Stanford, CA: Stanford University Press.

FESTINGER, L., & CARLSMITH, J. M. (1959). Cognitive consequences of forced compliance. *Journal of Abnormal and Social Psychology, 58,* 203–210.

FESTINGER, L., RIECKEN, H. W., & SCHACHTER, S. (1956). *When prophecy fails.* Minneapolis: University of Minnesota Press.

FESTINGER, L., SCHACHTER, S., & BACK, K. (1950). *Social pressures in informal groups: A study of a housing community.* New York: Harper & Row.

FINE, L. J. (1973). Psychodrama. In R. Corsini (Ed.), *Current psychotherapies.* Itasca, IL: F. E. Peacock.

FISHER, J. D., BELL, P. A., & BAUM, A. S. (1984). *Environmental psychology* (2nd ed.). New York: Holt, Rinehart and Winston.

FISHER, S., & GREENBERG, R. P. (1977). *The scientific credibility of Freud's theories and therapy.* New York: Basic Books.

FLAVELL, J. (1982). On cognitive development. *Child Development, 53,* 1–10.

FLAVELL, J. H. (1986). Development of childhood knowledge about the appearance-reality distinction. Distinguished Scientific Contributions Award Address. *American Psychologist, 41,* 418–425.

FLEMING, J. D. (1974, January). Field report: The state of the apes. *Psychology Today,* pp. 31–46.

FLETCHER, G. J. O. (1984). Psychology and common sense. *American Psychologist, 39,* 203–213.

FORD, C. S., & BEACH, F. A. (1951). *Patterns of sexual behavior.* New York: Harper & Row.

FORD, R. N. (1975). *Organizational behavior and industrial psychology.* New York: University Press.

FOX, J. L. (1984). PET scan controversy aired. *Science, 224,* 143–144.

FRANK, L. K. (1939). Projective methods for the study of personality. *Journal of Personality, 8,* 389–413.

FRANK, R. A., & STUTZ, R. M. (1984). Self-deprivation. *Psychological Bulletin, 66,* 384–393.

FRANKENBURG, W. K., & DODDS, J. B. (1967). The Denver Developmental Screening Test. *Journal of Pediatrics, 71,* 181–191.

FRANZ, C., & WHITE, K. (1985). Individuation and attachment in personality development: Extending Erikson's theory. In A. Stewart & B. Lykes (Eds.), *Gender and personality.* Durham, NC: Duke University Press.

FREEDMAN, D. G. (1979, January). Ethnic differences in babies. *Human Nature,* pp. 36–43.

FREEDMAN, J. L., HESHKA, S., & LEVY, A. (1975). Population density and pathology: Is there a relationship? *Journal of Experimental Social Psychology, 11,* 539–552.

FREEDMAN, J. L., SEARS, D. O., & CARLSMITH, J. M. (1981). *Social psychology* (4th ed.). Englewood Cliffs, NJ: Prentice-Hall.

FREUD, S. (1953a). The interpretation of dreams. In J. Strachey (Ed. and Trans.), *The standard edition of the complete psychological works of Sigmund Freud* (Vols. 4 and 5). London: Hogarth Press. (Original work published 1900.)

FREUD, S. (1953b). The psychopathology of everyday life. In J. Strachey (Ed. and Trans.), *The standard edition of the complete psychological works of Sigmund Freud* (Vol. 6). London: Hogarth Press. (Original work published 1901.)

FREUD, S. (1955). Beyond the pleasure principle. In J. Strachey

(Ed. and Trans.), *The standard edition of the complete psychological works of Sigmund Freud* (Vol. 17). London: Hogarth Press. (Original work published 1920.)

FREUD, S. (1957). Leonardo da Vinci: A study in psychosexuality. In J. Strachey (Ed. and Trans.), *The standard edition of the complete psychological works of Sigmund Freud* (Vol. 11). London: Hogarth Press. (Original work published 1910.)

FREUD, S. (1958). On beginning the treatment. In J. Strachey (Ed. and Trans.), *The standard edition of the complete psychological works of Sigmund Freud* (Vol. 12). New York: Norton. (Original work published 1913.)

FRIEDMAN, M., & ROSENMAN, R. H. (1974). *Type A behavior and your heart.* Greenwich, CT: Fawcett.

FRIEDMAN, M. I., & STRICKER, E. M. (1976). The physiological psychology of hunger: A physiological perspective. *Psychological Review, 83,* 409–431.

FRIEDMAN, M., & ULMER, D. (1984). *Treating type A behavior and your heart.* New York: Alfred A. Knopf.

FROMKIN, V. A. (1973). Slips of the tongue. *Scientific American, 229,* 110–117.

FUERST, R. E. (1979, March). Inference peddling. *Psychology Today.* pp. 92–96.

GALANTER, E. (1962). Contemporary psychophysics. In R. Brown et al. (Eds.), *New directions in psychology I.* New York: Holt, Rinehart and Winston.

GALLE, O. R., GOVE, W. R., & McPHERSON, J. M. (1972). Population density and pathology: What are the relationships for man? *Science, 176,* 385–389.

GALTON, F. (1869). *Hereditary genius: An inquiry into its laws and consequences.* London: Macmillan.

GALTON, F. (1883). *Inquiries into human faculty and its development.* London: Macmillan.

GALTON, F. (1887). Supplementary notes on "prehension" in idiots. *Mind, 12,* 79.

GAMSON, W. B., FIREMAN, B., & RYTINA, S. (1982). *Encounters with unjust authority.* Hornwood, IL: Dorsey Press.

GANSBERG, M. (1964). 37 who saw murder didn't call the police. *The New York Times,* pp. 38–39.

GANTT, W. H. (1973). Reminiscences of Pavlov. *Journal of the Experimental Analysis of Behavior, 20,* 131–136.

GARCIA, J., & KOELLING, R. A. (1966). The relation of cue to consequence in avoidance learning. *Psychosomatic Science, 4,* 123–124.

GARDNER, A. R., & GARDNER, B. T. (1969). Teaching sign language to a chimpanzee. *Science, 165,* 664–672.

GARDNER, R. A., & GARDNER, B. T. (1984). A vocabulary test for chimpanzees (Pan troglodytes). *Journal of Comparative Psychology, 98,* 381–404.

GARDNER, B. T. (1981). Project Nim: Who taught whom? *Contemporary Psychology, 26,* 425–426.

GARDNER, H. (1974). *The shattered mind.* New York: Random House.

GARFIELD, S. L. (1965). Historical tradition. In B. B. Wolman (Ed.), *Handbook of clinical psychology.* New York: McGraw-Hill.

GARFIELD, S. L., & KURTZ, R. (1976). Clinical psychologists in the 1970's. *American Psychologist, 31,* 1–9.

GARNES, S., & BOND, Z. S. (1975). *Slips of the ear: Errors in perception of casual speech.* In Papers from the Eleventh Regional Meeting, Chicago Linguistic Society, 214–255.

GATES, A. (1917). Recitation as a factor in memorizing. *Archives in Psychology, 40.*

GATES, A., & BRADSHAW, J. L. (1977). The role of the cerebral hemispheres in music. *Brain & Language, 4,* 403–431.

GAZZANIGA, M. S. (1967). The split brain in man. *Scientific American, 217,* 24–29.

GAZZANIGA, M. S. (1983). Right hemisphere language following brain bisection: A 20-year perspective. *American Psychologist, 38,* 525–537.

GELB, I. C. (1952). *A study of writing.* Chicago: The University of Chicago Press.

GELDARD, F. A. (1972). *The human senses* (2nd ed.). New York: Wiley.

GELLES, R. J. (1974). *The violent home: A study in physical aggression between husbands and wives.* Beverly Hills, CA: Sage.

GERBNER, G., GROSS, L., MORGAN, M., & SIGNORIELLI, N. (1980). The mainstreaming of America. *Journal of Communication, 30,* 12–29.

GERRARD, M. (1987). Sex, sex guilt, and contraceptive use revisited: The 1980s. *Journal of Personality and Social Psychology, 52,* 975–980.

GESCHWIND, N. (1983). Biological associations of left-handedness. *Annals of Dyslexia, 33,* 29–40.

GESCHWIND, N. (1984). The biology of cerebral dominance: Implications for cognition. *Cognition, 17,* 193–208.

GHISELLI, E. E. (1966). *The validity of occupational aptitude tests.* New York: Wiley.

GIBSON, E. J. (1980). In G. Lindzey (Ed.), *A history of psychology in autobiography* (Vol. 7). San Francisco: Freeman.

GIBSON, E. J., & WALK, R. D. (1960). The "visual cliff." *Scientific American, 202,* 65–71.

GICK, M. L., & HOLYOAK, K. J. (1980). Analogical problem solving. *Cognitive Psychology, 12,* 306–355.

GILLIGAN, C. (1982). *In a different voice: Psychological theory and women's development.* Cambridge, MA: Harvard University Press.

GILMER, B. H. (1966). *Industrial psychology.* New York: McGraw-Hill.

GLASS, D. C., & SINGER, J. E. (1972). *Urban stress: Experiments on noise and social stressors.* New York: Academic Press.

GLEASON, J. (1967). Do children imitate? *Proceedings of the International Conference on Oral Education of the Deaf, 2,* 1441–1448.

GOL, A. (1967). Relief of pain by electrical stimulation of the septal area. *Journal of Neurological Sciences, 5,* 115–120.

GOLDBECK, N., & GOLDBECK, D. (1975). *The dieter's companion.* New York: Signet.

GOLDBERG, P. (1968). Are women prejudiced against women? *Trans-action, 5,* 28–30.

GOLDSTEIN, A. (1980). *Endorphins as pain regulators—reality or fantasy?* Speech presented to the American Pain Society.

GOLEMAN, D. (1977a). *The varieties of meditative experience.* New York: Dutton.

GOLEMAN, D. (1977b, October). Split-brain psychology: Fad of the year. *Psychology Today, 11,* pp. 89–90.

GOLEMAN, D. (1986, July 22). Psychologists pursue the irrational aspects of love. *New York Times,* p. C1.

GOODENOUGH, D., SHAPIRO, A., HOLDEN, M., & STEINSCHRIBER, L. (1959). A comparison of "dreamers" and "non-dreamers." *Journal of Abnormal and Social Psychology, 59,* 295–302.

GORE, S. (1985). Social support and styles of coping with stress. In S. Cohen & S. L. Syme (Eds.), *Social support and health.* New York: Academic Press.

GOTTESMAN, I., & SHIELDS, J. (1972). *Schizophrenia and genetics: A twin study vantage point.* New York: Academic Press.

GOTTMAN, J., NOTARIUS, C., GONSO, J., & MARKMAN, H. (1976). *A couple's guide to communication.* Champaign, IL: Research Press.

GOUGH, P. B. (1965). Grammatical transformations and speed of understanding. *Journal of Verbal Learning and Verbal Behavior, 4,* 107–111.

GOVE, W. R., HUGHES, M., & GALLE, O. R. (1979). Overcrowding in the home. *American Sociological Review, 44,* 59–80.

GRANT, D., & ANNS, M. (1988). Counseling AIDS antibody-positive clients: Reaction and treatment. *American Psychologist, 43,* 72–74.

GRANT, D. L., & BRAY, D. W. (1969). Contributions of the interview to assessment of management potential. *Journal of Applied Psychology, 53,* 24–34.

GREEN, D. M. (1976). *An introduction to hearing.* Hillsdale, NJ: Erlbaum.

GREEN, K. B., PASTERNACK, B. S., & SHORE, R. E. (1982). Effects of aircraft noise on reading ability of school-age children. *Archives of Environmental Health, 37,* 24–31.

GREENOUGH, W. T. (1975). Experimental modification of the developing brain. *American Scientist, 63*(1), 37–46.

GREGORY, R. L. (1978). *Eye and brain* (3rd ed.). New York: McGraw-Hill.

GREGORY, R. L., & WALLACE, J. G. (1963). Recovery from early blindness: A case study. *Experimental Psychology Society Monograph No. 2,* Cambridge, MA.

GUILFORD, J. (1954). Traits of creativity. In H. Anderson (Ed.), *Creativity and its cultivation.* New York: Harper & Row.

GUILFORD, J. (1959). Three faces of intellect. *American Psychologist, 14,* 469–479.

GUION, R. M. (1976). Recruiting, selection, and job placement. In M. Dunnette (Ed.), *Handbook of industrial and organizational psychology* (pp. 777–828). Chicago: Rand McNally.

GULLAHORN, J. (1952). Distance and friendship as factors in the gross interaction matrix. *Sociometry, 15,* 123–134.

GUSTAVSON, C. R., GARCIA, J., HANKINS, W. G., & RUSINIAK, K. W. (1974). Coyote predation control by aversive conditioning. *Science, 184,* 581–583.

GUTTMAN, N. (1953). Operant conditioning, extinction, and periodic reinforcement. *Journal of Experimental Psychology, 46,* 213–224.

GUTTMAN, N., & KALISH, H. I. (1956). Discriminability and stimulus generalization. *Journal of Experimental Psychology, 51,* 71–88.

HALL, M. H. (1968, July). A conversation with Abraham Maslow. *Psychology Today,* pp. 35–37, 54–57.

HARLOW, H. F. (1959). Love in infant monkeys. *Scientific American, 200,* 68–74.

HARLOW, H. F. (1971). *Learning to love.* New York: Ballantine Books.

HARLOW, H. F., & HARLOW, M. (1969). Effects of various mother-infant relationships on Rhesus monkey behaviors. In B. M. Foss (Ed.), *Determinants of infant behavior* (Vol. 4). London: Methuen.

HARLOW, J. M. (1868). Passage of an iron bar through the head. *Boston Medical and Surgical Journal, 39,* 390–393.

HARLOW, J. M. (1869). Recovery from the passage of an iron bar through the head. *Massachusetts Medical Society Publication, 2,* 329–347.

HARRIS, S. L. (1975). Teaching language to nonverbal children, with emphasis on problems of generalization. *Psychological Bulletin, 82,* 565–580.

HARROWER, M. (1976, July). Were Hitler's henchmen mad? *Psychology Today,* pp. 76–80.

HART, K. E. (1984). Anxiety management training and anger control for Type A individuals. *Journal of Behavioral and Experimental Psychiatry, 15,* 133–139.

HARTMANN, E. L. (1973). *The functions of sleep.* New Haven, CT: Yale University Press.

HASSETT, J. (1978). *A primer of psychophysiology.* San Francisco: Freeman.

HASSETT, J. (1981, November). But that would be wrong. . . . *Psychology Today,* pp. 34–50.

HASSETT, J. (1984). Hacking in plain English. *Psychology Today, 18*(6), 38–45.

HASSETT, J., & DUKES, S. (1986). The new employee trainer: A floppy disk. *Psychology Today, 20,* 30–36.

HASTORF, A. H., & CANTRIL, H. (1954). They saw a game: A case study. *Journal of Abnormal and Social Psychology, 49,* 129–134.

HAYES, C. (1951). *The ape in our house.* New York: Harper & Row.

HAYES-ROTH, F., WATERMAN, D., & LENAT, D. (Eds.). (1983). *Building expert systems.* Reading, MA: Addison-Wesley.

HAYNES, S. G. (1984). Type A behavior, employment status, and coronary heart disease in women. *Behavioral Medicine Update, 6,* 11–15.

HEARNSHAW, L. S. (1979). *Cyril Burt, psychologist.* Ithaca, NY: Cornell University Press.

HEIDER, E. R., & OLIVER, D. C. (1972). The structure of the color space in naming and memory for two languages. *Cognitive Psychology, 3,* 337–354.

HEIDER, F. (1958). *The psychology of interpersonal relations.* New York: Wiley.

HELD, R., & BOSSOM, J. (1961). Neonatal deprivation and adult rearrangement: Complementary techniques for analyzing plastic sensory-motor coordinations. *Journal of Comparative and Physiological Psychology, 54,* 33–37.

HESS, E. (1975). *The tell-tale eye.* New York: Van Nostrand Reinhold.

HETHERINGTON, A. W., & RANSON, S. W. (1942). The spontaneous activity and food intake of rats with hypothalamic lesions. *American Journal of Physiology, 136,* 609–617.

HILGARD, E. R. (1965). *Hypnotic susceptibility.* New York: Harcourt Brace Jovanovich.

HILGARD, E. R. (1977). *Divided consciousness: Multiple controls in human thought and action.* New York: Wiley.

HILGARD, E. R., & HILGARD, J. R. (1983). *Hypnosis in the relief of pain* (rev. ed.). Los Altos, CA: Kaufmann.

HILGARD, J. R., & LeBARON, S. (1984). *Hypnosis in the treatment of pain and anxiety in children with cancer: A clinical and quantitative investigation.* Los Altos, CA: Kaufmann.

HILL, C. T., RUBIN, Z., & PEPLAU, L. A. (1976). Breakups before marriage: The end of 103 affairs. *Journal of Social Issues, 32,* 147–168.

HITE, S. (1976). *The Hite report.* New York: Dell.

HOBSON, J. A., & McCARLEY, R. W. (1977). The brain as a dream state generator: An activation-synthesis hypothesis of the dream process. *American Journal of Psychiatry, 134,* 1335–1348.

HOFFMAN, F. J. (1945). *Freudianism and the literary mind.* Baton Rouge, LA: State University Press.

HOFFMAN, L. W. (1974). Fear of success in males and females: 1965 and 1971. *Journal of Consulting and Clinical Psychology, 42,* 353–358.

HOFFMAN, L. W. (1977). Fear of success in 1965 and 1974: A follow-up study. *Journal of Consulting and Clinical Psychology, 45,* 310–321.

HOHMANN, G. W. (1966). Some effects of spinal cord lesions on experienced emotional feelings. *Psychophysiology, 3,* 143–156.

HOKFELT, T., JOHANSSON, O., & GOLDSTEIN, M. (1984). Chemical anatomy of the brain. *Science, 225,* 1326–1333.

HOLMES, D. S. (1984). Meditation and somatic arousal reducation: A review of the experimental evidence. *American Psychologist, 39,* 1–10.

HORDERN, A. (1968). The barbiturates. In C. R. B. Joyce (Ed.), *Psychopharmacology: Dimensions and perspectives.* Philadelphia: Lippincott.

HORNER, M. (1969, November). Fail: Bright women. *Psychology Today,* pp. 36–38, 62.

HORTON, D. L., & MILLS-BERGFELD, C. (1984). Human learning and memory. *Annual Review of Psychology, 35,* 361–394.

HOWARD, K. I., KOPTA, S. M., KRAUSE, M. S., & ORLINSKY, D. F. (1986). The dose effect relationship in psychotherapy. *American Psychologist, 41,* 159–164.

HUBEL, D. H. (1979). The brain. *Scientific American, 241,* 44–53.

HUBEL, D. H., & WEISEL, T. N. (1979). Brain mechanisms of vision. *Scientific American, 241,* 150–163.

HUGHES, W. A. (1983). Effects of living accommodations of high proximity on the self-perceptions of college students residing in university housing facilities. *Psychological Reports, 53,* 1013–1014.

HULSEBUS, R. C. (1981, March). *Father discrimination two weeks after birth.* Paper presented at Southeastern Psychology Association Meeting, Atlanta, GA. (Cited in DeCasper.)

HUNT, M. (1974). *Sexual behavior in the 1970's.* Chicago: Playboy Press.

HUNT, M. (1982). *The universe within.* New York: Simon & Schuster.

HUNTER, J. E. & HUNTER, R. F. (1984). Validity and utility of alternative predictors of job performance. *Psychological Bulletin, 96,* 72–98.

HYDE, J. S. (1981). How large are cognitive gender differences? *American Psychologist, 36,* 892–901.

INGVAR, D. H., & LASSEN, N. A. (Eds.). (1975). *Brain work: The coupling of function, metabolism, and blood flow in the brain.* Stockholm: Munksgaard.

ISAACS, M. B. (1981). Sex role stereotyping and the evaluation of the performance of women: Changing trends. *Psychology of Women Quarterly, 6,* 187–195.

ISAACSON, R. L. (1964). Relation between N achievement, test anxiety, and curricular choices. *Journal of Abnormal and Social Psychology, 68,* 447–452.

IZARD, C. E. (1971). *The face of emotion.* Englewood Cliffs, NJ: Prentice-Hall.

JACKSON, J. M., & HARKINS, S. G. (1985). Equity in effort: An explanation of the social loafing effect. *Journal of Personality and Social Psychology, 49,* 1199–1206.

JACOB, R. G., KRAEMER, H. C., & AGRAS, W. S. (1977). Relaxation therapy in the treatment of hypertension: A review. *Archives of General Psychiatry, 34,* 1417–1427.

JACOBS, J. (1887). Experiments on "prehension." *Mind, 12,* 75–79.

JACOBSON, A., KALES, A., LEHMANN, D., & ZWEIZIG, J. R. (1965). Somnambulism: All night EEG studies. *Science, 148,* 975–977.

JACOBSON, E. (1938). *Progressive relaxation.* Chicago: University of Chicago Press.

JAHODA, M. (1958). *Current concepts on positive mental health.* New York: Basic Books.

JAMES, W. (1890). *The principles of psychology.* New York: Holt, Rinehart and Winston.

JANIS, I. (1972). *Victims of groupthink: A psychological study of foreign-policy decisions and fiascoes.* Boston: Houghton Mifflin.

JENKINS, J. G., & DALLENBACH, K. M. (1924). Oblivescence during sleep and waking. *American Journal of Psychology, 35,* 605–612.

JENSEN, A. (1980). *Bias in mental testing.* New York: Free Press.

JEPSON, C., KRANTZ, D. H., & NISBETT, R. E. (1983). Inductive reasoning: Competence or skill. *The Behavioral and Brain Sciences, 3,* 494–501.

JOHNSON, D. (1987, April 24). Fear of AIDS stirs new attacks on homosexuals. *The New York Times.*

JONES, E. (1953–1957). *The life and work of Sigmund Freud* (3 vols). New York: Basic Books.

JONES, E. E. (1979). The rocky road from acts to dispositions. *American Psychologist, 34,* 107–117.

JONES, E. E., & DAVIS, K. E. (1965). From acts to dispositions: The attribution process in person perception. In L. Berkowitz (Ed.), *Advances in experimental social psychology* (Vol. 2). New York: Academic Press.

JONES, J., & TERRIS, W. (1981). *Predictive validation of a dishonesty test that measures theft proneness.* Paper presented at the XVIII Interamerican Congress of Psychology, Santo Domingo, The Dominican Republic.

JONES, M. C. (1924). The elimination of children's fears. *Journal of Experimental Psychology, 7,* 382–390.

JONES, R. A. (1977). *Self-fulfilling prophecies.* Hillsdale, NJ: Erlbaum.

JOSEPH, J. G., & SYME, S. L. (1981). *Risk factor status, social isolation, and CHD.* Paper presented at 21st Conference on Cardiovascular Disease Epidemiology, American Heart Association, San Antonio, TX (cited in Berkman, 1984).

JOY, D. M. (1983). Environmental noise and children: Review of recent findings. *The Journal of Auditory Research, 23,* 181–194.

JUEL-NIELSON, N. (1965). Individual and environment: A psychiatric-psychological investigation of monozygotic twins reared apart. *Acta Psychiatrical Scandinavia, 183,* 152–292.

KAGAN, J., KEARSELY, R. B., & ZELAZO, P. R. (1978). *Infancy: Its place in human development.* Cambridge, MA: Harvard University Press.

KAHNEMAN, D., & TVERSKY, A. (1984). Choices, values, and frames. *American Psychologist, 39,* 341–350.

KAMIN, L. J. (1974). *The science and politics of IQ.* Hillsdale, NJ: Erlbaum.

KANNER, A. D., COYNE, J. C., SCHAEFER, C., & LAZARUS, R. S. (1981). Comparisons of two modes of stress measurement: Daily hassles and uplifts versus major life events. *Journal of Behavioral Medicine, 4,* 1–39.

KANTER, J. F., & ZELNICK, M. (1972, October). Sexual experience of young unmarried women in the United States. *Family Planning Perspectives,* pp. 9–18.

KANTROWITZ, B. (1987, April 1). The year of living dangerously. *Newsweek on Campus,* pp. 12–21.

KAPLAN, A. G. (1976). Androgyny as a model of mental health for women: From theory to therapy. In A. G. Kaplan & J. P. Bean (Eds.), *Beyond sex-role stereo-types.* Boston: Little, Brown.

KAPLAN, R. M. (1982). Nader's raid on the testing industry. *American Psychologist, 37,* 15–23.

KASTENBAUM, R., & WEISMAN, A. D. (1972). The psychological autopsy as a research procedure in gerontology. In D. P. Dent, R. Kastenbaum, & S. Sherwood (Eds.), *Research planning and action for the elderly.* New York: Behavioral Publications.

KATCHADOURIAN, H. A., & LUNDE, D. T. (1975). *Fundamentals of human sexuality.* New York: Holt, Rinehart and Winston.

KATCHADOURIAN, H. A., & LUNDE, D. T. (1980). *Biological aspects of human sexuality* (2nd ed.). New York: Holt, Rinehart and Winston.

KATZ, M. (1975). *The people of Hamilton, Canada West: Family and class in a mid-nineteenth-century city.* Cambridge, MA: Harvard University Press.

KAUSLER, D. H., & HAKAMI, M. K. (1983). Memory for activities: Adult age differences and intentionality. *Developmental Psychology, 19*(6), 889–894.

KEESEY, R. E., & POWLEY, T. L. (1986). The regulation of body weight. In M. R. Rosenzweig and L. W. Porter (Eds.), *Annual Review of Psychology,* Vol. 37. Palo Alto, CA.: Annual Reviews, Inc.

KELLEY, H. (1970). The warm-cold variable in first impressions of persons. *Journal of Personality, 18,* 431–439.

KENT, T. C. (1987). Comment on Terrace. *American Psychologist, 42,* 273.

KEPHART, W. M. (1961). *The family, society, and the individual.* Boston: Houghton Mifflin.

KEPPEL, G., & UNDERWOOD, B. J. (1962). Proactive inhibition in short-term retention of single items. *Journal of Verbal Learning and Verbal Behavior, 1,* 153–161.

KERNBERG, O. F. (1975). *Borderline conditions and pathological narcissism.* New York: Aronson.

KESSEN, W. (1979). The American child and other cultural inventions. *American Psychologist, 34,* 815–820.

KETY, S. S. (1974). From rationalization to reason. *American Journal of Psychiatry, 131,* 957–963.

KHANTZIAN, E. J. (1985). The self-medication hypothesis of addictive disorders: Focus on heroin and cocaine dependence. *The American Journal of Psychiatry, 142,* 1259–1264.

KIHLSTROM, J. F. (1985). Hypnosis. *Annual Review of Psychology, 36,* 385–418.

KIHLSTROM, J. F. (1985). Hypnotic misrecall. *Scientific American, 252,* 73.

KIMBLE, G. A. (1961). *Hilgard and Marquis' conditioning and learning.* Englewood Cliffs, NJ: Prentice-Hall.

KINSEY, A. C., POMEROY, W. B., & MARTIN, C. E. (1948). *Sexual behavior in the human male.* Philadelphia: Saunders.

KINSEY, A C., POMEROY, W. B., MARTIN, C. E., & GEBHARD, P. H. (1953). *Sexual behavior in the human female.* Philadelphia: Saunders.

KLEIN, K. E., & WEGMANN, H. M. (1979). Circadian rhythms in air operations. In A. N. Nicholson (Ed.), *Sleep, wakefulness and circadian rhythms* (Vol. 105). Neuilly-sur-Seine, France: NATO Advisory Group for Aerospace Research and Development.

KLEINMUTZ, B., & SZUCHO, J. J. (1984). Lie detection in ancient and modern times: A call for contemporary scientific study. *American Psychology, 39*(7), 766–776.

KLEITMAN, N. (1960, November). Patterns of dreaming. *Scientific American, 203,* 82.

KLINE, P. (1987). The experimental study of the psychoanalytic unconscious. *Personality and Social Psychology Bulletin, 13,* 363–378.

KNITTLE, J. L. (1975). Early influences on the development of adipose tissue. In G. A. Brag (Ed.), *Obesity in perspective.* Washington, DC: U.S. Government Printing Office.

KOENIG, P. (1978, May 21). The problem that can't be tranquilized. *The New York Times Magazine,* pp. 15–17, 44–50, 58.

KOHLBERG, L. (1975). Moral stages and moralization. In T. Lickona (Ed.), *Moral development and behavior: Theory, research and social issues.* New York: Holt, Rinehart and Winston.

KOHLER, I. (1962). Experiments with goggles. *Scientific American, 206,* 62–73.

KOHLER, W. (1925). *The mentality of apes* (E. Winter, Trans.). New York: Harcourt Brace Jovanovich.

KOLATA, G. (1982). Brain receptors for appetite discovered. *Science, 218,* 460–461.

KOLATA, G. (1983). Math genius may have hormonal basis. *Science, 222,* 1312.

KRAEPELIN, E. (1902). *Clinical psychiatry: A textbook for physicians* (A. Diffendorf, Trans.). New York: Macmillan. (Original work published 1883.)

KRAEPELIN, E. (1912). *Lectures on Clinical Psychiatry* (2nd ed.) (T. Johnstone, Trans.). London: Bailliere, Tindall & Cox.

KRANTZ, D. S., GRUNBERG, N. E., & BAUM, A. (1985). Health psychology. In M. R. Rosenzweig and L. W. Porter (Eds.), *Annual Review of Psychology, 1985.* Palo Alto, CA: Annual Reviews, Inc.

KRAUT, R. E. (1982). Social presence, facial feedback, and emotion. *Journal of Personality and Social Psychology, 42,* 853–863.

KRYTER, K. D. (1970). *The effects of noise on man.* New York: Academic Press.

KÜBLER-ROSS, E. (1969). *On death and dying.* New York: Macmillan.

KUHN, T. S. (1970). *The structure of scientific revolutions.* Chicago: University of Chicago Press.

KUTASH, S. B. (1983). Modified psychoanalytic therapies. In B. B. Wolman (Ed.), *The therapist's handbook: Treatment methods of mental disorders* (2nd ed.). New York: Van Nostrand Reinhold.

L'ABATE, L. (1985). Descriptive and explanatory levels in family therapy: Distance, defeats and dependence. In L. L'Abate (Ed.). *The handbook of family psychology and therapy* (Vol. 2), pp. 1218–1248. Homewood, IL: Dorsey.

LACEY, J. I. (1967). Somatic response patterning and stress: Some revisions of activation theory. In M. H. Apley & R. Trumbull (Eds.), *Psychological stress.* Englewood Cliffs, NJ: Prentice-Hall.

LACHMAN, R., LACHMAN, J. L., & BUTTERFIELD, E. C. (1979). *Cognitive psychology and information processing: An introduction.* Hillsdale, NJ: Erlbaum.

LaFRANCE, M., & MAYO, C. (1976). Racial differences in gaze behavior during conversations: Two systematic observational studies. *Journal of Personality and Social Psychology, 33,* 547–552.

LAMAL, P. A. (1979). College students' common beliefs about psychology. *Teaching of Psychology, 6,* 155–158.

LAND, E. H. (1959). The retinex theory of color vision. *Scientific American, 200,* 84–99.

LANG, A. R., GOECKNER, D. J., ADESSO, V. J., & MARLATT, G. A. (1975). Effects of alcohol on aggression in male social drinkers. *Journal of Abnormal Psychology, 84,* 508–518.

LANG, P. J. (1965). Behavior therapy with a case of anorexia nervosa. In L. P. Ullman & C. Krasner (Eds.), *Case studies in behavior modification.* New York: Holt, Rinehart, and Winston.

LaPIERE, R. (1934). Attitudes versus actions. *Social Forces, 13,* 230–237.

LASHLEY, K. S. (1950). In search of the engram. *Symposium of the Society for Experimental Biology, 4,* 454–482.

LATANÉ, B., & DARLEY, J. M. (1968). Group inhibition of bystander intervention in emergencies. *Journal of Personality and Social Psychology, 10,* 215–221.

LATANÉ, B., & DARLEY, J. M. (1970). *The unresponsive bystander: Why doesn't he help?* Englewood Cliffs, NJ: Prentice-Hall.

LATANÉ, B., & NIDA, S. (1981). Ten years of research on group size and helping. *Psychological Bulletin, 89,* 308–324.

LAU, R. R., & RUSSELL, D. (1980). Attributions in the sports pages. *Journal of Personality and Social Psychology, 39,* 29–38.

LAWRENCE, B., & SCOVILLE, R. (1984). Dyadic specificity in prelinguistic communication. *Bulletin of the British Psychological Society, 37,* A32–A33.

LAZARUS, R. S. (1981, July). Little hassles can be hazardous to health. *Psychology Today,* pp. 58–62.

LAZARUS, R. S., DeLONGIS, A., FOLKMAN, S., & GRUEN, R. (1985). Stress and adaptational outcomes. *American Psychologist, 40,* 770–779.

LeCOMPTE, W., & ROSENFELD, H. (1971). Effects of minimal eye contact in the instruction period on impressions of the experimenter. *Journal of Experimental Social Psychology, 7,* 211–220ff.

LEE, C. (1984). Accuracy of self-efficacy and outcome expectations in predicting performance in a simulated assertiveness task. *Cognitive Therapy and Research, 8*(1), 37–48.

LENNEBERG, E. H., REBELSKY, F. G., & NICHOLS, I. A. (1965). The vocalizations of infants born to deaf and hearing parents. *Human Development, 8,* 23–37.

LENNEY, E. (1979). Concluding comments on androgyny: Some intimations of its mature development. *Sex Roles, 5,* 829–840.

LERNER, M. (1976). When, why and where people die. In E. S. Schneidman (Ed.), *Death: Current perspectives.* Palo Alto, CA: Mayfield.

LERNER, M. J. (1980). *The belief in a just world: A fundamental delusion.* New York: Plenum.

LEVENTHAL, H. (1970). Findings and theory of the study of fear communications. In L. Berkowitz (Ed.), *Advances in experimental social psychology* (Vol. 5). New York: Academic Press.

LEVENTHAL, H., & TOMARKEN, A. J. (1986). Emotion: Today's problems. *American Review of Psychology, 37,* 565–610.

LEVINE, J. D., GORDON, N. C., & FIELDS, H. L. (1978). The mechanism of placebo analgesia. *Lancet, II,* 654–657.

LEVINSON, D. (1978). *The seasons of a man's life.* New York: Knopf.

LEVINSON, D. J. (1986). A conception of adult development. *American Psychologist, 41,* 3–13.

LEVINSON, D. J. (in press). *The seasons of a woman's life.* New York: Knopf.

LICK, J. F., & HEFFLER, D. (1977). Relaxation training and attention placebo in the treatment of severe insomnia. *Journal of Consulting and Clinical Psychology, 45,* 153–161.

LIEBESKIND, J., & PAUL, L. (1977). Psychological and physiological mechanisms of pain. *Annual Review of Psychology, 28,* 41–60.

LINDEN, E. (1974). *Apes, men, and language.* New York: Saturday Review Press.

LOCKARD, R. B. (1971). Reflections on the fall of comparative psychology, *American Psychologist, 26,* 168–179.

LOEHLIN, J. C., LINDZEY, G., & SPUHLER, J. N. (1975). *Race differences in intelligence.* San Francisco: Freeman.

LOEHLIN, J. C., & NICHOLS, R. C. (1976). *Heredity, environment, and personality: A study of 850 sets of twins.* Austin, TX: University of Texas Press.

LOFTUS, E. F. (1974, December). Reconstructing memory: The incredible eyewitness. *Psychology Today,* pp. 116–119.

LOFTUS, E. F. (1979). *Eyewitness testimony.* Cambridge, MA: Harvard University Press.

LOFTUS, E. F., & LOFTUS, G. R. (1980). On the permanence of stored information in the human brain. *American Psychologist, 35,* 405–420.

LOFTUS, E. F., & PALMER, J. C. (1974). Reconstruction of automobile destruction: An example of the interaction between language and memory. *Journal of Verbal Learning and Verbal Behavior, 13,* 585–589.

LOGUE, A. W. (1986). *The psychology of eating and drinking.* San Francisco: Freeman.

LONDON, M., & BRAY, D. W. (1980). Ethical issues in testing and evaluation for personnel decision. *American Psychologist, 35,* 890–901.

LONG, P. (1986, January). Medical mesmerism. *Psychology Today,* pp. 28–29.

LORAYNE, H., & LUCAS, J. (1974). *The memory book.* Briarcliff Manor, NY: Stein & Day.

LORENZ, K. (1965). *Evolution and the modification of behavior.* Chicago: University of Chicago Press.

LORENZ, K. (1966). *On aggression.* New York: Harcourt Brace Jovanovich.

LOVAAS, O. I., & SIMMONS, J. Q. (1969). Manipulation of self-destruction in three retarded children. *Journal of Applied Behavior Analysis, 2,* 143–157.

LOVIBOND, S. H. (1964). *Conditioning and enuresis.* Elmsford, NY: Pergamon Press.

LUBIN, B., WALLIS, R. R., & PAINE, C. (1971). Patterns of psychological test usage in the United States: 1935–1969. *Professional Psychology, 2,* 70–74.

LUCE, G., & SEGAL, J. (1966). *Sleep.* New York: Lancer Books.

LUCHINS, A. S. (1942). Mechanization in problem-solving: The effect of Einstellung. *Psychological Monographs, 54* (Whole no. 248).

LUSH, J. L. (1951). Genetics and animal breeding. In L. C. Dunn (Ed.), *Genetics in the twentieth century.* New York: Macmillan.

LYKKEN, D. T. (1968). Statistical significance in psychological research. *Psychological Bulletin, 70,* 151–159.

LYNCH, G., & BAUDRY, M. (1984). The biochemistry of memory: A new and specific hypothesis. *Science, 224,* 1057–1064.

LYNCH, S., & YARNELL, P. R. (1973). Retrograde amnesia: Delayed forgetting after concussion. *American Journal of Psychology, 86,* 643–645.

MACCOBY, E. E. (1980). *Social development: Psychological growth and the parent-child relationship.* New York: Harcourt Brace Jovanovich.

MACCOBY, E. E., & JACKLIN, C. N. (1974). *The psychology of sex differences.* Stanford, CA: Stanford University Press.

MACCOBY, E. E., & JACKLIN, C. N. (1980). Sex differences in aggression: A rejoinder and reprise. *Child Development, 51,* 964–980.

MACKENZIE, B. (1984). Explaining race difference in IQ—the logic, the methodology and the evidence. *American Psychologist, 39,* 1214–1233.

MAGER, R. F. (1962). *Preparing objectives for programmed instruction.* Reprinted (1975) as *Preparing instructional objectives.* Belmont, CA: Fearon.

MAHER, B. A. (1966). *Principles of psychopathology: An experimental approach.* New York: McGraw-Hill.

MALINOWSKI, B. (1929). *The sexual life of savages in northwestern Melanesia.* New York: Harcourt Brace Jovanovich.

MANN, L. (1981). The baiting crowd in episodes of threatened suicide. *Journal of Personality and Social Psychology, 41,* 703–709.

MANUCIA, G. K., BAUMANN, D. J., & CIALDINI, R. B. (1984). Mood influences on helping: Direct effects or side effects? *Journal of Personality and Social Psychology, 46,* 357–364.

MANZ, W., & LUECK, H. (1968). Influence of wearing glasses on personality ratings: Cross-cultural validation of an old experiment. *Perceptual and Motor Skills, 27,* 704.

MARCIA, J. E. (1980). Identity in adolescence. In J. Adelson (Ed.), *Handbook of adolescent psychology.* New York: Wiley.

MAREK, G. R. (1975). *Toscanini.* London: Vision Press.

MARGERISON, J. H., ST. JOHN-LOE, P., & BINNIE, C. D. (1967). Electroencephalography. In P. H. Venables & I. Martin (Eds.), *A manual of psychophysiological methods.* New York: Wiley.

MARSHALL, G. D., & ZIMBARDO, P. G. (1979). Affective consequences of inadequately explained physiological arousal. *Journal of Personality and Social Psychology, 37,* 970–988.

MARSLEN-WILSON, W. D., & TEUBER, H. L. (1975). Memory for remote events in anterograde amnesia: Recognition of public figures from news photographs. *Neuropsychologia, 13,* 353–364.

MARTIN, G. B., & CLARK, R. D. (1982). Distress crying in neonates: Species and peer specificity. *Developmental Psychology, 18,* 3–9.

MARX, M. B., GARRITY, T. F., & BOWERS, F. R. (1975). The influence of recent life history on the health of college freshmen. *Journal of Psychosomatic Research, 19,* 87–98.

MASLOW, A. (1954). *Motivation and personality.* New York: Harper & Row.

MASLOW, A. H. (1966). *The psychology of science; A reconnaissance.* New York: Harper & Row.

MASLOW, A. (1971). *The farther reaches of human nature.* Baltimore: Penguin Books.

MASTERS, W. H., & JOHNSON, V. E. (1970). *Human sexual inadequacy.* Boston: Little, Brown.

MATARAZZO, J. D. (1972). *Wechsler's measurement and appraisal of adult intelligence* (5th ed.). Baltimore: Williams & Wilkins.

MATHES, E. W., ZEVON, M. A., ROTOR, P. M., & JOERGER, S. M. (1982). Peak experience tendencies—scale development and theory testing. *Journal of Humanistic Psychology, 22,* 92–108.

MATHEWS, K. E., & CANON, L. K. (1975). Environmental noise-level as a determinant of helping-behavior. *Journal of Personality and Social Psychology, 32,* 571–577.

MAYER, D. J., & HAYES, R. L. (1975). Stimulation produced by analgesia: Development of tolerance and cross-tolerance to morphine. *Science, 188,* 941–943.

MAYER, J. (1968). *Overweight: Causes, cost and control.* Englewood Cliffs, NJ: Prentice-Hall.

MCADAMS, D. P., & VALLIANT, G. E. (1982). Intimacy motivation and psychosocial adjustment: A longitudinal study. *Journal of Personality Assessment, 46,* 586–593.

MCCANN, B. A., & HILL, K. L. (1985). The hospice project. In K. Gardmer (Ed.), *Quality of care for the terminally ill: An examination of the issues.* Chicago: Joint Commission on Accreditation of Hospitals.

MCCARTHY, D., & SAEGERT, S. (1978). Residential density, social overload, and social withdrawal. *Human Ecology, 6*(3), 253–272.

MCCARTNEY, K. (1984). Effect of quality day care environment on children's language development. *Developmental Psychology, 20*(2), 244–260.

MCCLELLAND, D. C. (1958). Risk-taking in children with high and low need for achievement. In J. W. Atkinson (Ed.), *Motives in fantasy, action, and society.* New York: Van Nostrand Reinhold.

MCCLELLAND, D. C. (1965). Achievement and entrepreneurship: A longitudinal study. *Journal of Personality and Social Psychology, 1,* 389–392.

MCCLELLAND, D. C. (1978). Managing motivation to expand human freedom. *American Psychologist, 33,* 201–210.

MCCLELLAND, D. C., CLARK, R. A., ROBY, T. B., & ATKINSON, J. W. (1949). The effect of the need for achievement on thematic apperception. *Journal of Experimental Psychology, 37,* 242–255.

MCCLELLAND, D. C., & WINTER, D. G. (1971). *Motivating economic achievement.* New York: Free Press.

MCCLENON, J. (1982). A survey of elite scientists: Their attitudes toward ESP and parapsychology. *Journal of Parapsychology, 46,* 127–152.

MCCORMACK, E. J. & ILGEN, D. R. (1980). *Industrial Psychology.* Englewood Cliffs, NJ: Prentice-Hall.

MCGEOCH, J. A. (1930). The influence of associative value

upon the difficulty of nonsense-syllable lists. *Journal of Genetic Psychology, 37,* 421–426.

McGuire, W. J. (1968). Personality and susceptibility to social influence. In E. F. Borgatta & W. W. Lambert (Eds.), *Handbook of personality theory and research.* Skokie, IL: Rand McNally.

McNeill, D. (1970). *The acquisition of language.* New York: Harper & Row.

Meador, B. D., & Rogers, C. R. (1973). Person-centered therapy. In R. Corsini (Ed.), *Current psychotherapies.* Itasca, IL: F. E. Peacock.

Medalie, J., & Goldbourt, V. (1976). Angina pectoris among 10,000 men: II. Psychosocial and other risk factors as evidenced by a multivariate analysis of a five year incidence study. *American Journal of Medicine, 60,* 910–921.

Meddis, R., Pearson, A. J. D., & Langford, G. (1973). An extreme case of healthy insomnia. *Electroencephalography and Clinical Neurophysiology, 35,* 213–244.

Mednick, S. A. (1966). A longitudinal study of children with a high risk for schizophrenia. *Mental Hygiene, 50,* 522–535.

Mednick, S. A. (1970). Breakdown in individuals at high risk for schizophrenia: Possible predispositional perinatal factors. *Mental Hygiene, 54,* 50–62.

Meehl, P. E., & Hathaway, S. R. (1946). The K factor as a suppressor variable in the MMPI. *Journal of Applied Psychology, 30,* 525–564.

Mehrabian, A. (1977). A questionnaire measure of individual differences in stimulus screening and associated differences in arousability. *Environmental Psychology and Nonverbal Behavior, 1,* 89–103.

Melton, G. B., & Garrison, E. G. (1987). Fear, prejudice, and neglect: Discrimination against mentally disabled persons. *American Psychologist, 42,* 1007–1026.

Melton, G. B., & Gray, J. N. (1988). Ethical dilemmas in AIDS research: Individual privacy and public health. *American Psychologist, 43,* 60–64.

Melton, A. W., & Irwin, J. McQ. (1940). The influence of degree of interpolated learning on retroactive inhibition and the overt transfer of specific responses. *American Journal of Psychology, 53,* 173–203.

Melzack, R. (1973). *The puzzle of pain.* New York: Basic Books.

Melzack, R., & Wall, P. S. (1965). Pain mechanisms: A new theory. *Science, 150,* 971–979.

Menyuk, P., & Bernholtz, N. (1969). Prosodic features and children's language production. *Quarterly Progress Report* (Research Laboratory of Electronics, M.I.T.), *93,* 216–219.

Meskin, B., & Singer, J. L. (1974). Reflective thought and laterality of eye movements. *Journal of Personality and Social Psychology, 30,* 64–71.

Metzner, R., Litwin, G., & Weil, G. M. (1965). The relation of expectation and mood to psilocybin reactions: A questionnaire study. *Psychedelic Review, 5,* 3–39.

Meyer, H. H. (1970). The validity of the In-Basket Test as a measure of managerial personnel performance. *Personnel Psychology, 23,* 297–307.

Miale, F. R., & Selzer, M. (1976). *The Nuremberg mind.* New York: Quadrangle.

Michaels, J. W., Blommel, J. M., Brocato, R. M., Linkous, R. A., & Rowe, J. S. (1982). Social facilitation and inhibition in a natural setting. *Replications in Social Psychology, 2,* 21–24.

Michaels, R. H., & Mellin, G. W. (1960). Prospective experience with maternal rubella and the associated congenital malformations. *Pediatrics, 26,* 200–209.

Middlebrook, P. N. (1980). *Social psychology and modern life.* New York: Knopf.

Middleton, R. (1976). Regional differences in prejudice. *American Sociological Review, 41,* 94–119.

Miele, F. (1979). Cultural bias in the WISC. *Intelligence, 3,* 1949–164.

Milgram, S. (1963). Behavioral study of obedience. *Journal of Abnormal Psychology, 67,* 371–378.

Milgram, S. (1964). Issues in the study of obedience: A reply to Baumrind. *American Psychologist, 19,* 848–852.

Milgram, S. (1974). *Obedience to authority: An experimental view.* New York: Harper & Row.

Miller, G. (1956). The magical number seven, plus or minus two: Some limits on our capacity for processing information. *Psychological Review, 63,* 81–97.

Miller, G. A., & Buckhout, R. (1973). *Psychology: The science of mental life* (2nd ed.). New York: Harper & Row.

Miller, N. E. (1985). The value of behavioral research on animals. *American Psychologist, 40,* 423–440.

Millon, T. (1981). *Disorders of personality; DSM III: Axis II.* New York: Wiley.

Milner, B. (1959). The memory defect in bilateral hippocampal lesions. *Psychiatric Research Reports of the American Psychiatric Association, 11,* 43–52.

Milner, B., Corkin, S., & Teuber, H. L. (1968). Further analysis of the hippocampal amnesic syndrome: 14-year follow-up study of H.M. *Neuropsychologia, 6,* 215–234.

Mischel, W. (1968). *Personality and assessment.* New York: Wiley.

Mischel, W. (1979). On the interface of cognition and personality. *American Psychologist, 34,* 740–745.

Mitchell, T. R. (1982). *People in organizations: An introduction to organizational behavior* (2nd ed.). New York: McGraw-Hill.

Moore, B. R. (1973). The role of directed Pavlovian reactions in simple instrumental learning in the pigeon. In R. A. Hinde & J. S. Hinde (Eds.), *Constraints on learning.* London: Academic Press.

Moray, N., Bates, A., & Barnett, T. (1965). Experiments on

the four-eared man. *Journal of the Acoustical Society of America, 38,* 196–201.

MORRISON, R. F., OWENS, W. A., GLENNON, J. R., & ALBRIGHT, L. E. (1962). Factored life history antecedents of industrial research performance. *Journal of Applied Psychology, 46,* 281–284.

MOSKOWITZ, B. A. (1978). The acquisition of language. *Scientific American, 239,* 92–108.

MOULTON, J., ROBINSON, G. M., & ELIAS, C. (1978). Psychology in action: Sex bias in language use. *American Psychologist, 33,* 1032–1036.

MOWRER, O. H., & JONES, H. M. (1943). Extinction and behavior variability as functions of effortfulness of task. *Journal of Experimental Psychology, 33,* 369–385.

MOWRER, O. H., & MOWRER, W. M. (1938). Enuresis—A method for its study and treatment. *American Journal of Orthopsychiatry, 8,* 436–459.

MULLEN, B., FUTRELL, D., STAIRS, D., TICE, D. M., DAVIDSON, K. E., Riordan, C. A., Kennedy, J. G., Baumeister, R. F., Radloff, C. E., Goethals, G. R., & Rosenfeld, P. (1986). Newscasters' facial expressions and voting behavior of viewers: Can a smile elect a president? *Journal of Personality and Social Psychology, 51,* 291–295.

MUNTZ, W. R. A. (1964). Vision in frogs. *Scientific American, 210,* 110–119.

MURPHY, J. M. (1976). Psychiatric labeling in cross-cultural perspective. *Science, 191,* 1019–1028.

MURRAY, F. (1973). In search of Albert. *Professional Psychology, 4,* 5.

MURRAY, F. S. (1980). Estimation of performance levels by students in introductory psychology. *Teaching of Psychology, 7,* 61–62.

MURUYAMA, G., & MILLER, N. (1981). Physical attractiveness and personality. In B. A. Maher (Ed.), *Progress in experimental personality research.* New York: Academic Press.

MUSON, H. (1977, September). The lessons of the Grant Study. *Psychology Today,* pp. 42, 48–49.

MYERS, J. K., WEISSMAN, M. M., TISCHLER, G. L., HOLZER, C. E., LEAF, P. J., ORVASCHEL, H., ANTHONY, J. C., BOYD, J. H., BURKE, J. D., KRAMER, M., & STOLTZMAN, R. (1984). Six-month prevalence of psychiatric disorders in three communities. *Archives of General Psychiatry, 41,* 959–967.

NAITOH, P. (1982). Chronobiologic approach for optimizing human performance. In F. M. Brown & R. C. Graeber (Eds.), *Rhythmic aspects of behavior.* Hillsdale, NJ: Erlbaum.

NAPIER, A. Y. (1978). The rejection–intrusion pattern: A central family dynamic. *Journal of Marital Family Therapy, 4*(1), 5–12.

NARANJO, C., & ORNSTEIN, R. E. (1977). *On the psychology of meditation.* Baltimore: Penguin Books.

NATSOULAS, T. (1978). Consciousness. *American Psychologist, 33,* 906–914.

NATSOULAS, T. (1983). Addendum to consciousness. *American Psychologist, 38,* 121–122.

NAUTA, W. J. H., & FEIRTAG, M. (1979). The organization of the brain. *Scientific American, 241,* 88–111.

NELSON, K. (1973). Structure and strategy in learning to talk. *Monographs of the Society of Research in Child Development, 38* (*Nos. 1 and 2*).

NEUGARTEN, B. L. (1975). Adult personality: Toward a psychology of the life cycle. In W. C. Sze (Ed.), *Human life cycle.* New York: Aronson.

NEWCOMB, T. (1961). *The acquaintance process.* New York: Holt, Rinehart and Winston.

NEWELL, A., & SIMON, H. A. (1972). *Human problem solving.* Englewood Cliffs, NJ: Prentice-Hall.

NEWMAN, H. H., FREEMAN, F. N., & HOLZINGER, K. J. (1937). *Twins: A study of heredity and environment.* Chicago: University of Chicago Press.

NICKERSON, D., & NEWHALL, S. M. (1943). A psychological color solid. *Journal of the Optical Society of America, 33,* 419–422.

NICKERSON, R. S., & ADAMS, M. J. (1979). Long-term memory for a common object. *Cognitive Psychology, 11,* 287–307.

NIERENBERG, G. I., & CALERO, H. H. (1972). *How to read a person like a book.* New York: Cornerstone Library.

NISBETT, R., & ROSS, L. (1980). *Human inference: Strategies and shortcomings of social judgment.* Englewood Cliffs, NJ: Prentice-Hall.

NISBETT, R., & WILSON, T. D. (1977). Telling more than we can know: Verbal reports on mental processes. *Psychological Review, 84,* 231–259.

NISBETT, R. E., BORGIDA, E., CRANDALL, R., & REED, H. (1976). Popular induction: Information is not always informative. In J. S. Carroll & J. W. Payne (Eds.), *Cognition and social behavior.* Hillsdale, NJ: Erlbaum.

NISBETT, R. E., & GORDON, A. (1967). Self-esteem and susceptibility to social influence. *Journal of Personality and Social Psychology, 5,* 268–276.

NISBETT, R. R., & KUNDA, Z. (1985). Perception of social distributions. *Journal of Personality and Social Psychology, 48,* 297–311.

NOLEN-HOEKSEMA, S. (1987). Sex differences in unipolar depression: Evidence and theory. *Psychological Bulletin, 101,* 259–282.

NOTTERMAN, J. M. (1959). Force emission during bar pressing. *Journal of Experimental Psychology, 58,* 341–347.

NOYES, A. P., & KOLB, L. C. (1963). *Modern clinical psychiatry* (6th ed.). Philadelphia: Saunders.

NUCKOLLS, K. B., CASSEL, J., & KAPLAN, B. H. (1972). Psychosocial assets, life crisis and the prognosis of pregnancy. *American Journal of Epidemiology, 95,* 431–441.

OCCUPATIONAL SAFETY AND HEALTH ADMINISTRATION (1971). Occupational safety and health standards. *Federal Register, 36,* 105.

OLDS, J., & MILNER, P. (1954). Positive reinforcement produced by electrical stimulation of septal area and other regions of rat brain. *Journal of Comparative Physiological Psychology, 47,* 419–427.

O'LEARY, A. (1984). Self-efficacy and health. *Behavioral Research and Therapy, 23,* 437–451.

OLSON, D. R., & FILBY, N. (1972). On the comprehension of active and passive sentences. *Cognitive Psychology, 3,* 361–381.

OLTON, D. S., & NOONBERG, A. R. (1980). *Biofeedback: Clinical applications in behavioral medicine.* Englewood Cliffs, NJ: Prentice-Hall.

OPLER, M. K. (1967). *Culture and social psychiatry.* New York: Atherton Press.

ORLANSKY, J., & STRING, J. (1981). Computer-based instruction for military training. *Defense Management Journal, 18,* 46–54.

ORLOFSKY, J. L. (1978). The relationship between intimacy status and antecedent personality components. *Adolescence, 8,* 420–441.

ORLOFSKY, J. L., MARCIA, J. E., & LESSER, I. M. (1973). Ego identity status and the intimacy vs. isolation crisis of young adulthood. *Journal of Personality and Social Psychology, 27,* 211–219.

ORNE, M. T. (1971). The simulation of hypnosis: Why, how, and what it means. *International Journal of Clinical and Experimental Hypnosis, 19,* 183–210.

ORNE, M. T., & EVANS, F. J. (1965). Social control in the psychological experiment: Antisocial behavior and hypnosis. *Journal of Personality and Social Psychology, 1,* 189–200.

OSTBERG, O. (1973). Circadian rhythms of food intake and oral temperature in "morning" and "evening" groups of individuals. *Ergonomics, 16,* 203–209.

PARKE, R. D., & SLABY, R. G. (1983). The development of aggression. In P. H. Mussen (Ed.), *Handbook of child psychology* (Vol. 4, 4th ed.). New York: Wiley.

PARKINSON, L., & RACHMAN, S. (1981). Intrusive thoughts: The effects of an uncontrived stress. *Advances in Behavior Research and Therapy, 3,* 111–118.

PATTERSON, F. G., PATTERSON, C. H., & BRENTARI, D. K. (1987). Language in child, chimp, and gorilla. *American Psychologist, 42,* 270–273.

PAUK, W. (1974). *How to study in college* (2nd ed.). Boston: Houghton Mifflin.

PAVLOV, I. P. (1927). *Conditioned reflexes* (G. V. Anrep, Trans.). London: Oxford University Press.

PEELE, S. (1984). The cultural context of psychological approaches to alcoholism: Can we control the effects of alcohol? *American Psychologist, 39,* 1337–1351.

PELLEGRINI, R. (1973). Impressions of male personality as a function of beardedness. *Psychology, 10,* 29.

PENNEBAKER, J. W., & O'HEERON, R. C. (1984). Confiding in others and illness rate among spouses of suicide and accident death victims. *Journal of Abnormal Psychology, 93,* 473–476.

PERRY, D. K. (1967a). *Tests for improvement of programmer trainee selection.* (SDC Technical Memorandum 3570.) System Development Corporation.

PERRY, D. K. (1967b). *Evaluation of tests for improvement of programmer trainee selection.* (SDC Technical Memorandum 3570.) System Development Corporation.

PERT, A., PERT, C. B., DAVIS, G. D., & BUNNEY, W. E. (1982). Opiate peptides and brain function. In H. M. van Praag (Ed.), *Handbook of biological psychiatry* (Vol. 2). New York: Dekker.

PETERSON, L. R., & PETERSON, M. J. (1959). Short-term retention of individual verbal items. *Journal of Experimental Psychology, 58,* 193–198.

PFUNGST, O. (1911). *Clever Hans.* New York: Holt, Rinehart and Winston.

PHETERSON, G. I., KIESLER, S. B., & GOLDBERG, P. A. (1971). Evaluation of the performance of women as a function of their sex, achievement, and personal history. *Journal of Personality and Social Psychology, 19,* 114–119.

PIAGET, J. (1954). *The construction of reality in the child* (M. Cook, Trans.). New York: Basic Books.

PIAGET, J. (1960) *The child's conception of the world.* Totowa, NJ: Littlefield, Adams. (Original work published 1926.)

PIAGET, J. (1962). Play, dreams and imitation in childhood. New York: Norton.

PIAGET, J. (1972). Intellectual evolution from adolescence to adulthood. *Human Development, 15,* 1–21.

PLOMIN, R., & DEFRIES, J. C. (1980). Genetics and intelligence: Recent data. *Intelligence, 4,* 15–24.

POCS, O., GODOW, A., TOLONE, W. L., & WALSH, R. H. (1977, June). Is there sex after 40? *Psychology Today,* pp. 54–56, 87.

POLICH, J. M., ARMOR, D. J., & STAMBUL, H. B. (1981). *The course of alcoholism: Four years after treatment.* New York: Wiley.

POLIVY, J., AND HERMAN, C. P. (1985). Dieting and binging. *American Psychologist, 40,* 193–201.

POLLACK, I., & PICKETT, J. M. (1964). Intelligibility of excerpts from fluent speech: Auditory vs. structural context. *Journal of Verbal Learning and Verbal Behavior, 3,* 79–84.

POLLOCK, G. H. (1968). The possible significance of childhood object loss in the Josef Breuer–Bertha Pappenheim (Anna O.)–Sigmund Freud relationship: I. Josef Breuer. *Journal of the American Psychoanalytic Association, 16,* 711–739.

POMEROY, W. B. (1972). *Kinsey and the Institute for Sex Research.* New York: Harper & Row.

POPE, K. S. (1978). How gender, posture, and solitude influence the stream of consciousness. In K. S. Pope and J. L. Singer (Eds.), *The stream of consciousness: Scientific investigations into the flow of human experience* (pp. 259–299). New York: Plenum.

PORAC, C., & COREN, S. (1977). The assessment of motor control in sighting dominance using an illusion decrement procedure. *Perception and Psychophysics, 21,* 341–346.

PORTER, R. H., & MOORE, J. D. (1982). Human kin recognition by olfactory cues. *Physiology and Behavior, 27,* 493–495.

PREMACK, D. (1965). Reinforcement theory. In M. R. Jones (Ed.), *Nebraska symposium on motivation: 1965.* Lincoln: University of Nebraska Press.

PRIOLEAU, L., MURDOCK, M., & BRODY, N. (1983). An analysis of psychotherapy versus placebo studies. *Behavioral and Brain Sciences, 6,* 275–285.

RABKIN, J. B., & STRUENING, E. L. (1976). Life events, stress, and illness. *Science, 194,* 1013–1020.

RAHE, R. H. (1972). Subjects' recent life changes and their near-future illness in susceptibility. *Advances in Psychosomatic Medicine, 8,* 2–19.

RAMSEY, P. H., RAMSEY, P. P., & BARNES, M. J. (1987). Effects of student confidence and item difficulty on test score gains due to answer changing. *Teaching of Psychology, 14,* 206–210.

RATHBUN, C., McLAUGHLIN, H., BENNETT, I., & GARLAND, J. A. (1965). Later adjustment of children following radical separation from family and culture. *American Journal of Orthopsychiatry, 35,* 604–609.

RAY, O. (1978). *Drugs, society, and human beavior* (2nd ed.). St. Louis: Mosby.

REGIER, D. A., MYERS, J. K., KRAMER, M., ROBINS, L. N., BLAZER, D. G., HOUGH, R. L., EATON, W. W., & LOCKE, B. I. (1984). The NIMH epidemiologic catchment area program. *Archives of General Psychiatry, 41,* 934–941.

REISENZEIN, R. (1983). The Schachter theory of emotion: Two decades later. *Psychological Bulletin, 94,* 239–264.

REISMAN, J. M. (1966). *The development of clinical psychology.* Englewood Cliffs, NJ: Prentice-Hall.

RENSBERGER, B. (1971, September 12). Can a pill be mightier than the sword? *The New York Times.*

RESCHLY, D. J., & SABERS, D. L. (1979). An examination of bias in predicting MAT scores from WISC-R scores for four ethnic-racial groups. *Journal of Educational Measurement, 16,* 1–9.

RESCORLA, R. A. (1968). Pavlovian conditioned fear in Sidman avoidance learning. *Journal of Comparative and Physiological Psychology, 65,* 55–60.

RESCORLA, R. A., & WAGNER, A. R. (1972). A theory of Pavlovian conditioning: Variations in the effectiveness of reinforcement and non-reinforcement. In A. H. Black &

W. F. Prokasy (Eds.), *Classical conditioning II.* Englewood Cliffs, NJ: Prentice-Hall.

RHINE, J. B. (1934). *Extrasensory perception.* Boston: Boston Society for Psychic Research.

RICE, B. (1978, June). The new truth machines. *Psychology Today,* pp. 61–78.

RICHARDS, J., & RADER, N. (1983). Affective, behavioral, and avoidance responses on the visual cliff: Effects of crawling onset age, crawling experience, and testing age. *Psychophysiology, 20,* 633–642.

RIEGEL, K. F., & RIEGEL, R. M. (1972). Development, drop, and death. *Developmental Psychology, 6,* 306–319.

RIFE, D. C. (1940). Handedness, with special reference to twins. *Genetics, 25,* 178–186.

RIMM, D. C., & MASTERS, J. C. (1979). *Behavior therapy: Techniques and empirical findings* (2nd ed.). New York: Academic Press.

RINN, W. E., (1984). The neuropsychology of facial expression: A review of ten neurological and psychological mechanisms for producing facial expression. *Psychological Bulletin, 95*(1), 52–77.

RIOCH, M. J. (1967). Pilot projects in training mental health counselors. In E. L. Cowen, E. A. Gardner, & M. Zax (Eds.), *Emerging approaches to mental health problems.* Englewood Cliffs, NJ: Prentice-Hall.

RIPS, L. J., & HANDTE, J. (1984). Classification without similarity. Unpublished manuscript, University of Chicago.

ROBERTSON, I. H., & HEATHER, N. (1982). A survey of controlled drinking treatment in Britain. *British Journal on Alcohol and Alcoholism, 17,* 102–105.

ROBINS, L. N., HELZER, J. E., WEISSMAN, M. M., ORVASCHEL, H., GRUENBERG, E., BURKE, J. D., & REGIER, D. A. (1984). Lifetime prevalence of specific psychiatric disorders in three sites. *Archives of General Psychiatry, 41,* 949–958.

ROBINSON, F. P. (1970). *Effective study* (4th ed.). New York: Harper & Row.

ROBINSON, M. F., FREEMAN, W., & WATTS, J. W. (1951). Personality changes after psychosurgery. In N. Bigelow (Ed.), *Proceedings of the First Research Conference on Psychosurgery, 1949* (pp. 159–162). Bethesda, Md: National Institutes of Health, U.S. Public Health Service, Publication No. 16.

RODIN, J. (1981). Current status of the internal-external hypothesis for obesity. *American Psychologist, 36,* 361–372.

RODIN, J., & LANGER, E. (1977). Long-term effects of a control-relevant intervention with the institutionalized aged. *Journal of Personality and Social Psychology, 35,* 897–902.

ROGERS, C. R. (1961). *On becoming a person.* Boston: Houghton Mifflin.

ROMISZOWSKI, A. J. (1981). *Designing instructional systems.* New York: Nichols Publishing.

ROSCH, E. (1975). Cognitive representation of semantic categories. *Journal of Experimental Psychology: General, 104,* 192–233.

ROSE, S. A., & BLANK, J. (1974). The potency of context in children's cognition: An illustration through conservation. *Child Development, 45,* 499–502.

ROSEN, E., & GREGORY, I. (1965). *Abnormal psychology.* Philadelphia: Saunders.

ROSEN, P. L. (1972). *The Supreme Court and social science.* Urbana: University of Illinois Press.

ROSENHAN, D. L. (1973). On being sane in insane places. *Science, 179,* 250–258.

ROSENHAN, D. L. (1973). Reply to letters to the editor. *Science, 180,* 250–258.

ROSENKRANTZ, P., VOGEL, S., BEE, H., BROVERMAN, I., & BROVERMAN, D. J. (1968). Sex role stereotypes and self-conceptions of college students. *Journal of Consulting and Clinical Psychology, 32,* 287–295.

ROSENMAN, R. H., BRAND, R. J., JENKINS, D., FRIEDMAN, M., STRAUS, R., & WURM, M. (1975). Coronary heart disease in the Western collaborative group study. *Journal of the American Medical Association, 233,* 872–877.

ROSENMAN, R. H., BRAND, R. J., SHULTZ, R. I., & FRIEDMAN, M. (1976). Multivariate prediction of coronary heart disease during the 8.5-year follow-up in the Western collaborative group study. *American Journal of Cardiology, 37,* 903–910.

ROSENTHAL, B., & MCSWEENEY, F. K. (1979). Modeling influences on eating behavior. *Addictive Behavior, 4,* 205–214.

ROSENTHAL, D. (1971). *Genetics of psychopathology.* New York: McGraw-Hill.

ROSENTHAL, N. E., SACK, D. A., CARPENTER, C. J., PARRY, B. L., MENDELSON, W. B., & WEHR, T. A. (1985). Antidepressant effects of light in seasonal affective disorder. *American Journal of Psychiatry, 146,* 163–170.

ROSENTHAL, R., & JACOBSON, L. (1968). *Pygmalion in the classroom.* New York: Holt, Rinehart and Winston.

ROSENTHAL, R., & RUBIN, D. (1978). Interpersonal expectancy effects: The first 345 studies. *Behavioral and Brain Sciences, 3,* 377–415.

ROSENTHAL, T. L., & BANDURA, A. (1978). Psychological modeling: Theory and practice. In S. L. Garfield & A. E. Bergin (Eds.), *Handbook of psychotherapy and behavior change: An empirical analysis* (2nd ed.). New York: Wiley.

ROSENZWEIG, M. R. (1984). Experience, memory, and the brain. *American Psychologist, 39,* 365–376.

ROSENZWEIG, M. R., KRECH, D., & BENNETT, E. L. (1958). Brain enzymes and adaptive behavior. In Ciba Foundation Symposium on *Neurological basis of behavior* (pp. 337–355). London: J. E. A. Churchill.

ROSENZWEIG, M. R., KRECH, D., & BENNETT, E. L. (1961). Heredity, environment, brain chemistry and learning. In *Current trends in psychological theory* (pp. 87–110). Pittsburgh, PA: University of Pittsburgh Press.

ROSKIES, E., KEARNEY, H., SPEVACK, M., SURKIS, A., COHEN, C., & GILMAN, S. (1979). Generalizability and durability of treatment effects in an intervention program for coronary-prone (Type A) managers. *Journal of Behavioral Medicine, 2,* 195–207.

ROSKIES, E., SPEVACK, M., SURKIS, A., COHEN, C., & GILMAN, S. (1978). Changing the coronary-prone (Type A) behavior pattern in a nonclinical population. *Journal of Behavioral Medicine, 1,* 201–216.

ROSS, J., & LAWRENCE, K. A. (1968). Some observations on memory artifice. *Psychonomic Science, 13,* 107–108.

ROSS, L., TURIEL, E., JOSEPHSON, J., & LEPPER, M. R. (1978). *Developmental perspectives on the fundamental attribution error.* Unpublished manuscript, Stanford University.

ROTTER, J. B. (1966). Generalized expectancies for internal versus external control of reinforcement. *Psychological Monographs, 80,* 1.

RUBINSTEIN, E. A. (1983). Television and behavior: Research conclusions of the 1982 NIMH Report and their policy implications. *American Psychologist, 38,* 820–825.

RUBIN, J. Z., PROVENZANO, F. J., & LURIA, Z. (1974). The eye of the beholder: Parents' view on sex of newborns. *American Journal of Orthopsychiatry, 44,* 512–519.

RUBIN, L. B. (1976). *Worlds of pain.* New York: Basic Books.

RUBOVITS, P. C., & MAEHR, M. L. (1971). Pygmalion analyzed: Toward an explanation of the Rosenthal-Jacobson findings. *Journal of Personality and Social Psychology, 19,* 197–203.

RUMBAUGH, D. M. (Ed.). (1977). *Language learning by a chimpanzee: The Lana project.* New York: Academic Press.

RUSSELL, J. A., & WARD, L. M. (1982). Environmental psychology. *Annual Review of Psychology, 33,* 651–688.

RUSSELL, W. R., & NATHAN, P. W. (1946). Traumatic amnesia. *Brain, 69,* 280–300.

SACKETT, G. P., RUPPENTHAL, G. C., FAHRENBRUCH, C. E., & HOLM, R. A. (1981). Social isolation rearing effects in monkeys vary with genotype. *Developmental Psychology, 17,* 313–318.

SACKETT, P. R. & HARRIS, M. M. (1984). Honesty testing for personnel selection: A review and critique. *Personnel Psychology, 37,* 221–245.

SACKS, OLIVER (1987). *The man who mistook his wife for a hat.* New York: Harper & Row.

SANDERS, G. S., & SIMMONS, W. L. (1983). Use of hypnosis to enhance eyewitness accuracy: Does it work? *Journal of Applied Psychology, 68,* 70–77.

SARASON, I. G., & SARASON, B. R. (1984). Life changes, moderators of stress, and health. In A. Baum, S. E. Taylor, & J. E. Singer (Eds.), *Handbook of psychology and health: Vol. IV. Social psychological aspects of health.* Hillsdale, N.J.: Erlbaum.

SAXE, L., DOUGHERTY, D., & CROSS, T. (1985). The validity of polygraph testing. *American Psychologist, 40,* 355–366.

SCARR, S., & SALAPATEK, P. (1970). Patterns of fear development during infancy. *Merrill-Palmer Quarterly, 16,* 53–90.

SCARR, S., & WEINBERG, R. A. (1976). IQ test performance of black children adopted by white families. *American Psychologist, 31,* 726–739.

SCHACHTER, S. (1982). Recidivism and self-cure of smoking and obesity. *American Psychologist, 37,* 436–444.

SCHACHTER, S. (1971). *Emotion, obesity, and crime.* New York: Academic Press.

SCHACHTER, S., GOLDMAN, R., & GORDON, A. (1968). The effects of fear, food deprivation, and obesity on eating. *Journal of Personality and Social Psychology, 10,* 91–97.

SCHACHTER, S., & GROSS, L. (1968). Manipulated time and eating behavior. *Journal of Personality and Social Psychology, 10,* 98–106.

SCHACHTER, S., & SINGER, J. E. (1962). Cognitive, social, and physiological determinants of emotional state. *Psychological Review, 69,* 379–399.

SCHACHTER, S. (1982). Recidivism and self-cure of smoking and obesity. *American Psychologist, 37,* 436–444.

SCHAIE, K. W. (1984). The Seattle longitudinal: A 21-year exploration in the development of psychometric intelligence. In K. W. Schaie (Ed.), *Longitudinal studies of adult psychological development.* New York: Guilford Press.

SCHAIE, K. W., & LABOUVIE-VIEF, G. (1974). Generational versus ontogenetic components of change in adult cognitive behavior: A fourteen-year cross-sectional study. *Developmental Psychology, 10,* 305–320.

SCHANK, R. C., & ABELSON, R. P. (1977). *Scripts, plans, goals, and understanding.* Hillsdale, NJ: Erlbaum.

SCHIFF, N., DUYME, M., DUMARET, A., STEWART, J., TOMKIEWICZ, S., & FEINGOLD, J. (1978). Intellectual status of working-class children adopted early into upper-middle-class families. *Science, 200,* 1503–1504.

SCHILDKRAUT, J. (1978). The biochemistry of affective disorders: A brief summary. In M. Lipton, A. DiMascio, & K. Killan (Eds.), *Psychopharmacology: A generation of progress* (pp. 1223–1234). New York: Raven.

SCHULSINGER, H. (1976). A ten-year follow-up of children with schizophrenic mothers. *Acta Psychiatrical Scandinavia, 63,* 371–386.

SCHULTZ, T., & HORIBE, F. (1974). Development of the appreciation of verbal jokes. *Developmental Psychology, 10,* 13–20.

SCHWARTZ, G. E., FAIR, P. L., SALT, P., MANDEL, M. R., & KLERMAN, G. L. (1976). Facial muscle patterning to affective imagery in depressed and nondepressed subjects. *Science, 192,* 489–491.

SCHWARTZ, G. E., & WEISS, S. (1977). What is behavioral medicine? *Psychosomatic Medicine, 36,* 377–381.

SCLAFANI, A., & SPRINGER, D. (1976). Dietary obesity in adult rats: Similarities to hypothalamic and human obesity syndromes. *Physiology and Behavior, 17,* 461–471.

SCOVERN, A. W., & KILMANN, P. R. (1980). Status of electroconvulsive therapy: Review of the outcome literature. *Psychological Bulletin, 87,* 260–303.

SCOVILLE, R. (1983). Development of the intent to communicate: The eye of the beholder. In L. Feagans, C. Garvey, & R. Golinkoff (Eds.), *The origins and growth of communication.* New York: Holt, Rinehart and Winston.

SEARS, R. R., WHITING, J. W. M., NOWLIS, V., & SEARS, P. S. (1953). Some child-rearing antecedents of aggression and dependency in young children. *Genetic Psychology Monographs, 47,* 135–234.

SEGAL, M. H., CAMPBELL, D. T., & HERSKOVITS, M. J. (1966). *The influence of culture on visual perception.* Indianapolis: Bobbs-Merrill.

SEGAL, M. W. (1974). Alphabet and attraction: An unobstrusive measure of the effect of propinquity in a field setting. *Journal of Personality and Social Psychology, 30,* 654–657.

SELFRIDGE, O. G. (1955). Pattern recognition and modern computers. *Proceedings of the Western Joint Computer Conference.* New York: Institute of Electrical and Electronics Engineers.

SELIGMAN, M. E. P. (1975). *Helplessness: On depression, development, and death.* San Francisco: Freeman.

SELIGMAN, M. E. P., & HAGER, J. L. (Eds.). (1972). *Biological boundaries of learning.* Englewood Cliffs, NJ: Prentice-Hall.

SELMAN, R. L. (1980). *The growth of interpersonal understanding.* New York: Academic Press.

SELMAN, R. L., & BYRNE, D. (1974). A structural-developmental analyses of levels of role-taking in middle childhood. *Child Development, 45,* 803–806.

SEXTON, M. M. (1979). Behavioral epidemiology. In O. F. Pomerleau & J. P. Brady (Eds.), *Behavioral medicine: Theory and practice.* Baltimore: Williams & Wilkins.

SHADISH, W. R., JR. (1984). Lessons from the implementation of deinstitutionalization. *American Psychologist, 39,* 725–738.

SHAPIRO, A. K. (1971). Placebo effects in medicine, psychotherapy and psychoanalysis. In A. E. Bergin & S. L. Garfield (Eds.), *Handbook of psychotherapy and behavior change: An empirical analysis.* New York: Wiley.

SHAPIRO, C. M., BORTZ, R., MITCHELL, D., BARTEL, P., & JOOSTE, P. (1981). Slow-wave sleep: A recovery period after exercise. *Science, 214,* 1353–1354.

SHAPIRO, D. (1973). Preface. In D. Shapiro, T. X. Barber, L. V. Di Cara, J. Kamiya, N. E. Miller, & J. Stoyva (Eds.), *Biofeedback and self-control.* Chicago: Aldine.

SHEEHY, G. (1976). *Passages: Predictable crises of adult life.* New York: Dutton.

SHEPARD, R. N., & COOPER, L. A. (1982). *Mental images and their transformations.* Cambridge, MA: MIT Press.

SHERIF, M., HARVEY, D., WHITE, B., HOOD, W., & SHERIF, C. (1961). *Intergroup conflict and cooperation: The Robber's Cave experiment.* Norman: Institute of Group Relations, University of Oklahoma.

SHERMAN, G. F., GALABURDA, A. M., & GESCHWIND, N. (1982). *Trends in neurosciences, 5,* 429–431.

SHIELDS, J. (1962). *Monozygotic twins.* New York: Oxford University Press.

SHORTLIFFE, E. H. (1976). *Computer-based medical consultations: MYCIN.* New York: American Elsevier.

SHOSTRUM, E. L. (1963). *Personal Orientation Inventory.* San Diego: EDITS/Educational & Industrial Testing Service.

SHOSTRUM, E. L. (1974). *Manual for the Personal Orientation Inventory.* San Diego: EDITS/Educational & Industrial Testing Service.

SHOSTRUM, E. L., KNAPP, L. F., & KNAPP, R. R. (1976). *Actualizing therapy: Foundations for a scientific ethic.* San Diego: EDITS/Educational & Industrial Testing Service.

SIFFRE, M. (1964). *Beyond time* (H. Briffault, Ed. & Trans.). New York: McGraw-Hill.

SILVERMAN, J. (1967). Shamans and acute schizophrenia. *American Anthropologist, 69,* 21–31.

SINGER, J. L. (1975). *The inner world of daydreaming.* New York: Harper & Row.

SINGER, J. L., & McCRAVEN, V. J. (1961). Some characteristics of adult daydreaming. *Journal of Psychology, 51,* 151–164.

SIQUELAND, E. R., & DE LUCIA, C. A. (1969). Visual reinforcement of nonnutritive sucking in human infants. *Science, 165,* 1144–1146.

SKINNER, B. F. (1948). *Walden two.* New York: Macmillan.

SKINNER, B. F. (1953). *Science and human behavior.* New York: Macmillan.

SKINNER, B. F. (1954). The science of learning and the art of teaching. *Harvard Educational Review, 24,* 86–97.

SKINNER, B. F. (1956). A case history in scientific method. *American Psychologist, 11,* 221–233.

SKINNER, B. F. (1957). *Verbal behavior.* New York: Appleton-Century-Crofts.

SKINNER, B. F. (1974). *About behaviorism.* New York: Knopf.

SKINNER, B. F. (1979). *The shaping of a behaviorist.* New York: Knopf.

SKINNER, N. F. (1983). Switching answers on multiple-choice questions: Shrewdness or shibboleth? *Teaching of Psychology, 10,* 220–222.

SLOANE, M. C. (1981). A comparison of hypnosis vs. waking state and visual vs. non-visual recall instructions for witness/victim memory retrieval in actual major crimes. Ph.D. thesis. Florida State University, Tallahassee.

SLOANE, R. B., STAPLES, F. R., CRISTOL, A. H., YORKSTON, N. J., & Whipple, K. (1975). *Psychoanalysis versus behavior therapy.* Cambridge, MA: Harvard University Press.

SLOBIN, D. I. (1971). *Psycholinquistics.* Glenview, IL: Scott, Foresman.

SMEDSLUND, J. (1961). The acquisition of conversation of substance and weight in children. *Scandinavian Journal of Psychology, 2,* 11–20.

SMITH, M. L., GLASS, G. V., & MILLER, T. I. (1980). *The benefits of psychotherapy.* Baltimore: Johns Hopkins University Press.

SMITH, S. (1982). Trends in counseling and psychotherapy. *American Psychologist, 37,* 802–809.

SMITH, S. M., BROWN, H. Q., TOMAN, J. E. P., & GOODMAN, L. S. (1947). The lack of cerebral effects of d-tubercurarine. *Anesthesiology, 8,* 1–14.

SNELBECKER, G. E. (1981). Impact of computers and electronic technology on the teaching methodologies and the learning process. *Journal of Children in Contemporary Society, 19*(1), 43–53.

SNOW, C. E. (1983). Saying it again: The role of expanded and deferred imitations in language acquisition. In K. E. Nelson (Ed.), *Children's language* (vol. 4). Hillsdale, NJ: Erlbaum.

SNYDER, F., & SCOTT, J. (1972). The psychophysiology of sleep. In N. S. Greenfield & R. A. Sternbach (Eds.), *Handbook of psychophysiology.* New York: Holt, Rinehart and Winston.

SNYDER, M. (1982, July). Self-fulfilling stereotypes. *Psychology Today,* pp. 60–67.

SNYDER, M., & URANOWITZ, S. W. (1978). Reconstructing the past: Some cognitive consequences of person perception. *Journal of Personality and Social Psychology, 36,* 941–950.

SNYDER, S. H. (1980). Brain peptides as neurotransmitters. *Science, 209,* 976–983.

SNYDER, S. H. (1984). Drug and neurotransmitter receptors in the brain. *Science, 224,* 22–31.

SOLOMON, H., SOLOMON, L. Z., ARNONE, M. M., MAUR, B. J., REDA, R. M., & ROTHER, E. O. (1981). Anonymity and helping. *Journal of Social Psychology, 113,* 37–43.

SOLOMON, R. L. (1980). The opponent-process theory of acquired motivation: The costs of pleasure and the benefits of pain. *American Psychologist, 35,* 691–712.

SOLOMON, R. L., KAMIN, L. J., & WYNNE, L. C. (1953). Traumatic avoidance learning: The outcomes of several extinction procedures with dogs. *Journal of Abnormal and Social Psychology, 48,* 291–302.

SPEISMAN, J. C., LAZARUS, R. S., DAVIDSON, L., & MORDKOFF, A. (1964). Experimental reduction of psychological stress based on ego defense theory. *Journal of Abnormal and Social Psychology, 68,* 359–380.

SPELT, D. K. (1938). Conditioned responses in the human fetus in utero. *Psychological Bulletin, 35,* 712–713.

SPENCE, J. T., & HELMREICH, R. L. (1978). *Masculinity and*

feminity: Their psychological dimensions, correlates and antecedents. Austin: University of Texas Press.

SPITZER, R. L. (1976). On pseudoscience in science, logic in remission, and psychiatric diagnosis: A critique of Rosenhan's "On being sane in insane places." *Journal of Abnormal Psychology, 84,* 442–452.

SPITZER, R. L., & FLEISS, J. L. (1974). A reanalysis of the reliability of psychiatric diagnosis. *British Journal of Psychiatry, 125,* 341–347.

SPITZER, R. L., SKODOL, A. E., GIBBON, M., & WILLIAMS, J. B. W. (1981). *DSM III case book.* Washington, D.C.: American Psychiatric Association.

SPOCK, B. (1946). *Baby and child care.* New York: Pocket Books.

SPRINGER, S. P., & DEUTSCH, G. (1985). *Left brain, right brain.* (2nd ed.). San Francisco: Freeman.

SROUFE, L. A., & WATERS, E. (1977). Attachment as an organization construct. *Child Development, 48,* 1184–1199.

SROUFE, L. A., & WUNSCH, J. C. (1972). The development of laughter in the first year of life. *Child Development, 43,* 1326–1344.

STARKER, S. (1978). Dreams and waking fantasy. In K. S. Pope and J. L. Singer (Eds.), *The stream of consciousness: Scientific investigations into the flow of human experience* (pp. 302–319). New York: Plenum.

STARR, D. (1982, December). Out of the closet. *Omni,* p. 41.

STERNBACH, R. A., & TURSKY, B. (1965). Ethnic differences among housewives in psychophysical and skin potential responses to electric shock. *Psychophysiology, 1,* 241.

STERNBERG, R. J. (1985). Implicit theories of intelligence, creativity, and wisdom. *Journal of Personality and Social Psychology, 49,* 607–627.

STERNBERG, R. J., CONWAY, B. E., KETRON, J. L., & BERNSTEIN, M. (1981). People's conception of intelligence. *Journal of Personality and Social Psychology, 41,* 37–55.

STERNBERG, R. S. (1977). *Intelligence, information processing and analogical reasoning: The componential analysis of human abilities.* Hillsdale, NJ: Erlbaum.

STERNER, R. T., & SHUMAKE, S. S. (1978). Bait-induced prey aversions in predators: Some methodological issues. *Behavioral Biology, 22,* 565–566.

STEVENS, S. S. (1962). The surprising simplicity of sensory metrics. *American Psychologist, 17,* 29–39.

STEVENS, W. K. (1987, February 17). Fear of AIDS brings explicit advice to campus, caution to the singles bar. *The New York Times.*

STEWART, D. N., & WISNER, D. M. DE R. (1942). Incidence of perforated peptic ulcer during the period of heavy air raids. *Lancet, 1,* 259–261.

STILES, W. B., SHAPIRO, D. A., & ELLIOTT, R. (1986). Are all therapies equivalent? *American Psychologist, 41,* 165–180.

STOKOLS, D. (1972). On the distinction between density and crowding: Some implications for future research. *Psychological Review, 79,* 275–278.

STRATTON, G. M. (1897). Vision without inversion of the retinal image. *Psychological Review, 4,* 341–481.

STUNKARD, A. J. (1979). Behavioral medicine and beyond: The example of obesity. In O. F. Pomerleau & J. P. Brady (Eds.), *Behavioral medicine: Theory and practice.* Baltimore: Williams & Wilkins.

STUNKARD, A. J., & KOCH, C. (1964). The interpretation of gastric motility: I. Apparent bias in the reports of hunger by obese persons. *Archives of General Psychiatry, 11,* 74–82.

SUOMI, S. J., & HARLOW, H. F. (1972). Social rehabilitation of isolate-reared monkeys. *Developmental Psychology, 6,* 487–496.

SZASZ, T. (1961). *The myth of mental illness.* New York: Harper & Row.

TANKE, E. D., & TANKE, T. J. (1979). Getting off a slippery slope: Social science in the judicial process. *American Psychologist, 34,* 1130–1138.

TANNENBAUM, J. & ROWAN, A. N. (1985, October). Rethinking the morality of animal research. *Hastings Center Report,* pp. 32–43.

TAVRIS, C., & OFFIR, C. (1977). *The longest war.* New York: Harcourt Brace Jovanovich.

TAYLOR, D. A., & ALTMAN, I. (1966). *Intimacy-scaled stimuli for use in research on interpersonal exchange.* San Diego: Naval Medical Research Institute.

TEGHTSOONIAN, M. (1971). On the experiments of Stevens' Law and the constant in Exman's Law. *Psychological Review, 78,* 71–80.

TEITELBAUM, P. (1955). Sensory control of hypothalamic hyperphagia. *Journal of Comparative and Physiological Psychology, 43,* 156–163.

TEITELBAUM, P., & EPSTEIN, A. N. (1962). The lateral hypothalamic syndrome: Recovery of feeding and drinking after lateral hypothalamic lesions. *Psychological Review, 69,* 74–90.

TERRACE, H. (1979). *Nim: A chimpanzee who learned sign language.* New York: Knopf.

TERRACE, R. S. (1987). Reply to Bernstein and Kent. *American Psychologist, 42,* 273.

TEUBER, H., CORKIN, S., & TWITCHELL, T. E. (1976). A study of cingulotomy in man. In *Psychosurgery* (Report of the National Commission for the Protection of Human Subjects of Biomedical and Behavioral Research). Washington, DC: U.S. Government Printing Office.

THOMAS, A., & CHESS, S. (1977). *Temperament and development.* New York: Brunner/Mazel.

THOMAS, A., & CHESS, S. (1984). Genesis and evolution of behavioral disorders: From infancy to early adult life. *American Journal of Psychiatry, 141,* 1–9.

THOMAS, A., CHESS, S., & BIRCH, H. G. (1970). The origin of personality. *Scientific American, 223,* 102–109.

THOMAS, A., CHESS, S., AND KORN, S. J. (1982). The reality of difficult temperament. *Merrill-Palmer Quarterly, 28,* 1–20.

THOMPSON, R. F. (1975). *Introduction to physiological psychology.* New York: Harper & Row.

THOMPSON, R. F., & ROBINSON, D. N. (1979). Physiological psychology. In E. Hearst (Ed.), *The first century of experimental psychology.* Hillsdale, NJ: Erlbaum.

THORNDIKE, E. L. (1898). Animal intelligence. An experimental study of the associative processes in animals. *Psychological Review, Monograph Supplement, 2,* 1–109.

THORNDIKE, R. L. (1968). Review of *Pygmalion in the classroom. American Educational Research Journal, 5,* 708–711.

TIEGER, T. (1980). On the biological basis of sex differences in aggression. *Child Development, 51,* 943–963.

TIMBERLAKE, W. (1980). A molar equilibrium theory of learned performance. In G. H. Bower (Ed.), *The psychology of learning and motivation* (Vol. 14). New York: Academic Press.

TOLMAN, E. C. (1923). The nature of instinct. *Psychological Bulletin, 20,* 200–216.

TOLMAN, E. C. (1938). The determiners of behavior at a choice point. *Psychological Review, 45,* 1–41.

TOLMAN, E. C. (1942). *Drives toward war.* Englewood Cliffs, NJ: Prentice-Hall.

TOLMAN, E. C., & HONZIK, C. H. (1930). Introduction and removal of reward, and maze performance in rats. *University of California Publications in Psychology, 4,* 257–275.

TOMKINS, S. S. (1962). *Affect imagery consciousness: Vol. 1. The positive effects.* New York: Springer-Verlag.

TULVING, E. (1972). Episodic and semantic memory. In E. Tulving & W. Donaldson (Eds.), *Organization of memory.* New York: Academic Press.

TULVING, E. (1974). Cue-dependent forgetting. *American Scientist, 62,* 74–82.

TULVING, E., & THOMPSON, D. M. (1971). Retrieval processes in recognition memory. *Journal of Experimental Psychology, 87,* 116–124.

TURNBULL, C. (1961). Some observations regarding the experiences and behavior of the BaMbuti Pygmies. *American Journal of Psychology, 74,* 304–308.

TVERSKY, A., & KAHNEMAN, D. (1981). The framing of decisions and the psychology of choice. *Science, 211,* 453–458.

ULLMAN, M., KRIPPNER, S., & VAUGHAN, A. (1973). *Dream telepathy.* New York: Macmillan.

UNDERWOOD, B. J. (1957). Interference and forgetting. *Psychological Review, 64,* 49–60.

U.S. CONGRESS, SELECT COMMITTEE ON AGING AND COMMITTEE ON ENERGY AND COMMERCE, NINETY-EIGHTH CONGRESS. (1984). *Alzheimer's disease.* Washington, DC: U.S. Government Printing Office.

U.S. DEPARTMENT OF HEALTH, EDUCATION, AND WELFARE. (1978). *Alcohol and health: Third special report to the U.S.* *Congress.* Washington, DC: U.S. Government Printing Office.

VAILLANT, G. E. (1977). *Adaptation to life.* Boston: Little, Brown.

VALENSTEIN, E. S. (1973). *Brain control: A critical examination of brain stimulation and psychosurgery.* New York: Wiley.

VALENSTEIN, E. S. (1980). Historical perspective. In E. S. Valenstein (Ed.), *The psychosurgery debate.* San Francisco: Freeman.

VAN DEN BERGHE, P. L. (1981). *The ethnic phenomenon.* New York: Elsevier.

VANDENBOS, G. R., DELEON, P. H., & PALLAK, M. S. (1982). An alternative to traditional medical care for the terminally ill. *American Psychologist, 11,* 1245–1248.

VANE, J. R. (1966). Relation of early school achievement to high school achievement when race, intelligence, and socioeconomic factors are equated. *Psychology in the Schools, 3,* 124–129.

VAUGHAN, E. D. (1977). Misconceptions about psychology among introductory psychology students. *Teaching of Psychology, 4,* 138–141.

VAUGHN, B. E., DEANE, K. E., & WATERS, E. (1985). The impact of out-of-home care on child-mother attachment quality: Another look at some enduring questions. In I. Bretherton and E. Waters (Eds.), Growing points of attachment theory and research. *Child Development Monographs, 50,* Ser. No. 209, 1–2.

VEROFF, J., KULKA, R. A., & DOUVAN, E. (1981). *Mental health in America.* New York: Basic Books.

WAGNER, M. W., & MONNET, M. (1979, December). Attitudes of college professors toward extra-sensory perception. *Zetetic Scholar,* pp. 7–16.

WAHBA, M. A., & BRIDWELL, L. G. (1976). Maslow reconsidered. *Organizational Behavior and Human Performance, 15,* 212–240.

WALLACE, R. K. (1970). Physiological effects of transcendental meditation. *Science, 167,* 1751–1754.

WALLACE, R. K., BENSON, H., & WILSON, A. F. (1971). A wakeful hypometabolic physiological state. *American Journal of Physiology, 221,* 795–799.

WALLACE, W. L. (1972). Review of the Scholastic Aptitude Test. In O. K. Buros (Ed.), *The seventh mental measurements yearbook.* Lincoln: University of Nebraska, Buros Institute of Mental Measurements.

WALLACH, M. A., & KOGAN, N. (1965). *Modes of thinking in young children.* New York: Holt, Rinehart and Winston.

WALLERSTEIN, J. S., AND KELLY, J. B. (1980). *Surviving the breakup: How children and parents cope with divorce.* New York: Basic Books.

WALSTER, E., ARONSON, V., ABRAHAMS, D., & ROTTMAN, L. (1966). Importance of physical attractiveness in dating behavior. *Journal of Personality and Social Behavior, 4,* 508–516.

WALSTER, E., AND WALSTER, G. W. (1978). *A new look at love.* Reading, MA: Addison-Wesley.

WALTERS, G. C., & GRUSEC, J. E. (1977). *Punishment.* San Francisco: Freeman.

WALTZ, D. L. (1982). Artifical intelligence. *Scientific American, 247,* 118–133.

WARBURTON, J. R., & ALEXANDER, J. F. (1985). The family therapist: What does one do? In L'Abate, L. (Ed.), *The handbook of family psychology and therapy* (Vol. 2) (pp. 1218–1248). Homewood, IL: Dorsey Press.

WARD, M. H., & BAKER, B. L. (1968). Reinforcement therapy in the classroom. *Journal of Applied Behavior Analysis, 1,* 323–328.

WATSON, G., & GLASER, E. M. (1952). *Critical thinking appraisal.* Yonkers-on-Hudson, NY: World Book.

WATSON, J. B. (1928). *Psychological care of infant and child.* New York: Norton.

WATSON, J. B. (1930). *Behaviorism* (rev. ed.). New York: Norton.

WATSON, J. B., & RAYNER, R. (1920). Conditioned emotional reactions. *Journal of Experimental Psychology, 3,* 1–14.

WAUGH, N., & NORMAN, D. A. (1965). Primary memory. *Psychological Review, 72,* 89–104.

WECHSLER, D. (1958). *The measurement and appraisal of adult intelligence.* Baltimore: Williams & Wilkins.

WEISSMAN, M., & PAYKEL, E. (1974). *The depressed woman.* Chicago: University of Chicago Press.

WEXLEY, K. N. (1984). Personnel training-review. *Annual Review of Psychology, 35,* 519–551.

WHITE, B. L. (1975). *The first three years of life.* Englewood Cliffs, NJ: Prentice-Hall.

WHITE, K. M., & FERSTENBERG, A. (1978). Professional specialization and formal operations: The balance task. *Journal of Genetic Psychology, 133,* 97–104.

WHITE, K. M., & SPEISMAN, J. C. (1977). *Adolescence.* Monterey, CA: Brooks/Cole Publishing Company.

WHITE, K. M., SPEISMAN, J. C., JACKSON, D., BARTIS, S., & COSTOS, D. (1986). Intimacy maturity and its correlates in young married couples. *Journal of Personality and Social Psychology, 50* (1), 152–162.

WHITE, R. W. (1963). Ego reality in psychoanalytic theory: A proposal regarding independent ego energies. *Psychological Issues, 3,* 1–210.

WHORF, B. L. (1956). Science and linguistics. In J. B. Carroll (Ed.), *Language, thought and reality: Selected writings of Benjamin Lee Whorf.* Cambridge, MA: M.I.T. Press.

WILKINSON, R. T. (1982). The relationship between body temperature and performance across circadian phase shifts. In F. M. Brown & R. C. Graeber (Eds.), *Rhythmic aspects of behavior.* Hillsdale, NJ: Erlbaum.

WILL, B. E., ROSENZWEIG, M. R., & BENNETT, E. L. (1976). Effects of differential environments on recovery from neonatal brain lesions, measured by problem-solving scores and brain dimensions. *Physiology and Behavior, 16,* 603–611.

WILLARD, M. J. (1986). The psychosocial impact of using Capu-

chin monkeys as aides for quadriplegics. *Einstein Quarterly Journal of Biology and Medicine.* [Cited in N. E. Miller, The value of behavioral research on animals. *American Psychologist, 40,* 423–440.]

WILLIAMS, D. R., & WILLIAMS, H. (1969). Automaintenance in the pigeon: Sustained pecking despite contingent nonreinforcement. *Journal of the Experimental Analysis of Behavior, 12,* 511–520.

WILLIAMS, K., HARKINS, S., & LATANÉ, B. (1981). Identifiability as a deterrent to social loafing: Two cheering experiences. *Journal of Personality and Social Psychology, 40,* 303–311.

WILLIAMS, R. L., & LONG, J. D. (1983). *Toward a self-managed lifestyle* (3rd ed.). Boston: Houghton Mifflin.

WILSON, G. T., & LAWSON, D. M. (1976). Expectancies, alcohol, and sexual arousal in male social drinkers. *Journal of Abnormal Psychology, 85,* 587–594.

WINCH, R. F. (1958). *Mate selection: A study of complementary needs.* New York: Harper & Row.

WINGERSON, L. (1977). Hypertension compliance. *Medical World News, 18,* 20–28.

WINTER, D. G. (1980). Measuring the motives of southern Africa political leaders at a distance. *Political Psychology, 2*(2), 75–85.

WINTER, D. G. & STEWART, A. J. (1977). Content analysis as a method of studying political leaders. In M. G. Hermann (Ed.), *A psychological examination of political leaders.* New York: Free Press.

WINTER, R. (1976). *The smell book: Scents, sex and society.* Philadelphia: Lippincott.

WITTELSON, S. F. (1985). The brain connection: The corpus callosum is larger in left-handers. *Science, 229,* 665–668.

WITTNER, D. (1972, May 26). A boy who shut everyone out. *Life,* pp. 32–35.

WOLF, M., BALLY, H., & MORRIS, R. (1984). *Automaticity, retrieval processes, and reading: A longitudinal investigation of average and impaired readers.* Manuscript submitted for publication.

WOLF, M., BALLY, H., & MORRIS, R. (1986). Automaticity, retrieval processes, and reading: A longitudinal study in average and impaired readers. *Child Development, 57,* 988–1000.

WOLLEN, K. A., WEBER, A., & LOWRY, D. H. (1972). Bizarreness versus interaction of mental images as determinants of learning. *Cognitive Psychology, 3,* 518–523.

WOLPE, J. (1958). *Psychotherapy by reciprocal inhibition.* Stanford, CA: Stanford University Press.

WOODWORTH, R. S. (1938). *Experimental psychology.* New York: Holt, Rinehart and Winston.

WOODY, C. D. (1986). Understanding the cellular basis of memory and learning. *Annual Review of Psychology, 37,* 433–494.

WORLD HEALTH ORGANIZATION. (1973). *Report on the international pilot study of schizophrenia* (Vol. 1). Geneva: Author.

WORLD HEALTH ORGANIZATION. (1981). *Current state of diagnosis and classification in the mental health field.* Geneva: Author.

WORTMAN, C. B., ADESMAN, P., HERMAN, E., & GREENBERG, R. (1976). Self-disclosure: An attributional perspective. *Journal of Personality and Social Psychology, 33,* 184–191.

WUNDT, W. (1907). [*Outlines of psychology*] (C. H. Judd, Trans.). New York: Stechert.

WURTMAN, R. J. (1982). Nutrients that modify brain function. *Scientific American,* 50–59.

YU, V. L., BUCHANAN, B. G., SHORTLIFFE, E. H., WRAITH, S. M., DAVIS, R., SCOTT, A. C., & COHEN, S. N. (1979). Evaluating the performance of a computer-based consultant. *Computer Programs in Biomedicine, 9,* 95–102.

ZAIDEL, E. (1978). The split and half brains as models of congenital language disability (NINCDS Monograph No. 22, U.S. Public Health Service Publication No. 79-440). Washington, DC: U.S. Government Printing Office.

ZAIDEL, E. (1983). A response to Gazzaniga: Language in the right hemisphere, convergent perspectives. *American Psychologist, 38,* 542–546.

ZAJONC, R. B. (1965). Social facilitation. *Science, 149,* 260–274.

ZELAZO, P. R., ZELAZO, N. A., & KOLB, S. (1972). Walking in the newborn. *Science, 176,* 314–315.

ZELNICK, M., & KANTER, J. F. (1980). Sexual activity, contraceptive use and pregnancy among metropolitan-area teenagers: 1971–1979. *Family Planning Perspectives, 12,* 230–237.

ZILBOORG, G., & HENRY, G. W. (1941). *A history of medical psychology.* New York: Norton.

ZILLMANN, D. (1971). Excitation transfer in communication-mediated aggressive behavior. *Journal of Experimental Social Psychology, 7,* 419–434.

ZIMBARDO, P. G., EBBESEN, E. B., & MASLACH, C. (1977). *Influencing attitudes and changing behavior* (2nd ed.). Reading, MA: Addison-Wesley.

ZLUTNICK, S., & ALTMAN, I. (1972). Crowding and human behavior. In J. F. Wohlwill & D. H. Carson (Eds.), *Environment and the social sciences: Perspectives and applications.* Washington, DC: American Psychological Association.

ZUBIN, J., ERON, L. D., & SCHUMER, F. (1965). *An experimental approach to projective techniques.* New York: Wiley.

CREDITS

TEXT AND TABLES

Chapter 2   Page 32, from Nisbett, R. E., Borgida, E., Crandall, R., & Reed, H. (1976). Popular induction: Information is not always informative. In J. S. Carroll & J. W. Payne (Eds.), *Cognition and social behavior* (p. 129)., Hillsdale, NJ: Lawrence Erlbaum Associates; p. 46, from *Blooming by deception.* Copyright 1968 Time Inc. All rights reserved. Reprinted by permission from TIME.

Chapter 3   Page 52, from *The shattered mind,* by Howard Gardner. Copyright 1974 by Alfred A. Knopf, Inc.; p. 64, Can the pill be mightier than the sword?, by Boyce Rensberger. From *The New York Times,* September 12, 1971. Copyright © 1971 by The New York Times Company. Reprinted by permission.

Chapter 4   Pages 116–117, as cited in Teaching yourself to relax, by James Hassett. In *Psychology Today* (August 1978). Reprinted by permission of the author; p. 119 (Table 4.1), from *Divided consciousness: Multiple controls in human thought and action,* by Ernest Hilgard. Copyright © 1977. Reprinted by permission of John Wiley and Sons, Inc.; p. 122, Orne, M. T. The simulation of hypnosis: Why, how and what it means. *International Journal of Clinical and Experimental Hypnosis,* 1971, *19,* 183–210. Reprinted by permission; p. 124 (Table 4.2), from *A primer of drug action,* 3rd edition, by R. M. Julien. Copyright © 1981 by W. H. Freeman and Company. All rights reserved; p. 131, Study suggests alcoholic treated, can drink safely, by Jane E. Brody. From *The New York Times,* June 10, 1976. Copyright © 1976 by The New York Times Company. Reprinted by permission.

Chapter 5   Page 143 (Table 5.2) and p. 146 (Table 5.3), from Contemporary psychophysics, by E. Galanter. In R. Brown et al. (Eds.), *New directions in psychology I.* Copyright 1962 by Holt, Rinehart and Winston. Used by permission of the author; p. 182, Continuum: Out of the closet, by Douglas Starr. Copyright 1982 by *Omni* magazine and reprinted with the permission of Omni Publications International, Ltd.

Chapter 6   Page 212, Reprinted with permission of Macmillan Publishing Company from *Walden two,* by B. F. Skinner. Copyright 1948 by B. F. Skinner; renewed 1976 by B. F. Skinner.

Chapter 7   Page 249 (Table 7.1), from Levels of processing: A framework for memory research, by F. Craik and R. Lockhart. In *Journal of Verbal Learning and Verbal Behavior,* Vol. 11. Copyright 1972 by Academic Press.

Chapter 8   Page 289 (Table 8.1), from Mechanization in problem solving: The effect of Einstellung, by A. Luchins. In *Psychological Monographs,* Vol. 54. Copyright 1942 by the American Psychological Association; p. 294 (Table 8.2), from Production rules as a representation for a knowledge based consultation program, by R. Davis, B. Buchannan, and E. Shortliffe. In *Artificial Intelligence,* Vol. 8. Copyright 1977 by Elsevier Science Publishers; p. 298 (Table 8.3), Sternberg, R. J. (1977). *Intelligence, information processing, and analogical reasoning: The componential analysis of human abilities* (pp. 113, 223). Hillsdale, NJ: Lawrence Erlbaum Associates; pp. 299–300, from Cooper and Shepard (Chapter 3) in *Visual information processing,* W. G. Chase (Ed.). Copyright 1973 by Academic Press.

Chapter 9   Page 331 (Table 9.1), from John C. Loehlin and Robert C. Nichols, *Heredity, environment and personality: A study of 850 sets of twins,* p. 87. Copyright © 1976 by John C. Loehlin and Robert C. Nichols. By permission of the authors and The University of Texas Press; pp. 348–349, On cognitive development, by J. Falvell. In *Child Development,* Vol. 53. Copyright © 1952 by The Society for Research in Child Development, Inc.; p. 362, from *Baby and child care,* by Benjamin Spock, M.D. Copyright © 1945, 1946, 1957, 1958 by Benjamin Spock, M.D. Reprinted by permission of Pocket Books, a division of Simon & Schuster, Inc.

Chapter 10   Pages 380–382, from Moral stages and moralization, by L. Kohlberg (1958, 1975). In T. Likona (Ed.), *Moral development and behavior: Theory, research and social issues.* Copyright © 1976 by Holt, Rinehart and Winston. Used by permission of the authors; p. 390, from *Passages: Predictable crises of adult life,* by Gail Sheehy. Copyright © 1974, 1976 by Gail Sheehy. Reprinted by permission of the publisher, E. P. Dutton, a division of NAL Penguin, Inc.

Chapter 11   Pages 443–444, from Fear of success in males and females: 1965 & 1971, by L. W. Hoffman. In *Journal of Consulting and Clinical Psychology,* Vol. 42. Copyright 1974 by the American Psychological Association; p. 453, from Use lie detector tests on defense workers? In *U.S. News and World Report,* February 25, 1985. Reprinted with permission; pp. 453–454 (Table 11.1), adapted from Ekman and Freiser, *Journal of Personality and Social Psychology* (p. 127). Copyright 1971 by the American Psychological Association. Used by permission of the authors.

Chapter 12   Page 491, from Androgyny: Yes ma'am, a woman can be more like a man, by K. Dalby. In *Cosmopolitan* (January 1986).

FIGURES AND ILLUSTRATIONS

Culver Pictures; p. 206, Animal Behavior Enterprises, Ltd.; p. 207, Ira Wyman/Sygma-Paris; p. 208, adapted from Discrimination training effects on stimulus generalization gradient for spectrum stimuli, by H. Hanson, *Science,* Vol. 125 (May 1957): 888–890; p. 221, Oxford Scientific Films, G. I. Bernard/Animals Animals; p. 225, from *The mentality of apes,* by Wölfgang Köhler. Copyright © 1976 by Routledge and Kegan Paul PLC. Reprinted by permission; p. 229, Carol Lee/The Picture Cube; p. 230, Courtesy Albert Bandura, Stanford University.

Chapter 7 Page 235, Hank Morgan/Rainbow; p. 237, The Bettman Archive; p. 243 (Fig. 7.3), adapted from Short-term retention of individual verbal items (Figure 2), by Lloyd and Margaret Peterson. In *Journal of Experimental Psychology,* Vol. 58. Copyright 1959; p. 245, Dan McCoy/Rainbow; p. 256 (Fig. 7.5), from Retrieval line from semantic memory, by A. Collins and H. Quillian. In *Journal of Verbal Learning and Verbal Behavior,* Vol. 8. Copyright 1969 by Academic Press; p. 259 (Fig. 7.6), from Long-term memory for a common object, by R. Nickerson and M. Adams. In *Cognitive Psychology,* Vol. 11. Copyright 1979 by Academic Press; p. 261, New York Times Pictures, published in *Scientific American* (December 1974); p. 264, The Granger Collection, New York; p. 265, UPI; p. 271 (Fig. 7.8), from Hierarchical retrieval scheme in recall of categorized word lists, by G. Bower. In *Journal of Verbal Learning and Verbal Behavior,* Vol. 8. Copyright 1969 by Academic Press.

Chapter 8 Page 277, Timothy Eagan/Woodfin Camp; p. 279 (Fig. 8.1), Lachman, R., Lachman, J. L., & Butterfield, E. C. (1979). *Cognitive psychology and information processing: An introduction* (p. 242). Hillsdale, NJ: Lawrence Erlbaum Associates; p. 282 (left), Alan G. Nelson/Animals Animals; (middle), Richard Kolar/Animals Animals; (right), Oxford Scientific Film/Animals Animals; p. 288, The Bettman Archive; p. 289, Timothy Eagan/Woodfin Camp; p. 305, Grace Angeline/DPI; p. 308, Bill Strode/Black Star; p. 309 (Fig. 8.6), from Sex bias in language use, by J. Moulton, G. Robinson, and C. Elias. In *American Psychologist,* Vol. 33. Copyright 1978 by the American Psychological Association; p. 310, copyright © 1951 by Catherine Hayes. Reprinted by permission of McIntosh and Otis, Inc.; p. 312, Bill Nation/Sygma; p. 317, Barbara Kirk/International Stock Photography.

Chapter 9 Page 325, Sandra Lousada/Woodfin Camp; p. 329, M. Abbey/Photo Researchers; p. 330, The Granger Collection, New York; p. 338, Enrico Ferorelli/DOT; p. 339, Cornell University; p. 340, Professor Anthony J. DeCasper, University of North Carolina; p. 341, The Bettman Archive; p. 343, Doug Goodman/Monkmeyer; p. 345, Forsyth/Monkmeyer; p. 350, Miro Vintoniv/Stock, Boston; p. 355, Gabe Palmer/Mug Shots; p. 357, Harry F. Harlow/University of Wisconsin Primate Laboratory; p. 360, David Lissey/Click, Chicago; p. 365, Bill Stanton/International Stock Photography.

Chapter 10 Page 371, Lenore Weber/Omni-Photo Communications; p. 373, United Press International; p. 375, Ann Hagen Griffiths/Omni-Photo Communications; p. 380, Jeffrey Meyers/Stock, Boston; p. 387, Lenore Weber/Omni-Photo Communications; p. 391 (Fig. 10.1), from *The seasons of a man's life,* by Daniel J. Levinson et. al. Copyright © 1978 by Daniel J. Levinson. Reprinted by permission of Alfred A. Knopf, Inc.; p. 397 (Fig. 10.2), adapted from *Sexual behavior in the human male,* by A. Kinsey, W. Pomeroy, C. Martin, and P. Gebhardo. Copyright 1948 and 1953 by W. B. Saunders. Reprinted by permission of the Kinsey Institute for Research in Sex, Gender, and Reproduction, Inc.; p. 398, photo by Dellenback,

courtesy of the Kinsey Institute, Indiana University; p. 401, Bettye Lane/Photo Researchers; p. 403, James D. Wilson/Woodfin Camp; p. 404, Peter Pearson/Click, Chicago; p. 405, J. Albertson/The Picture Cube; p. 409, Michael Grecco/Stock, Boston; p. 410 (Fig. 10.3), from Generational versus ontogenetic components of change in adult cognitive behavior: A fourteen-year cross sequential study, by Schaie and Strother. In *Psychological Bulletin,* Vol. 70. Copyright 1968 by the American Psychological Association.

Chapter 11 Page 419, Johan Elbers/Sygma; p. 422, The Granger Collection, New York; p. 424 (left), Johan Elbers/Sygma; (right), Dario Perla/International Stock Photography; p. 428, courtesy Dr. Neal E. Miller, Rockefeller University; p. 430 (Fig. 11.2), from *Emotion, obesity and crime,* by Stanley Schachter. Copyright 1971 by Academic Press. Used by permission of the author; p. 436, reprinted by permission of the publisher from Henry A. Murray, *Thematic apperception test,* Cambridge, MA: Harvard University Press, copyright © 1943 by the President and Fellows of Harvard College, © 1971 by Henry A. Murray; p. 438 (Fig. 11.3), adapted from Achievement motive and test anxiety conceived as motive to approach success and motive to avoid failure, by J. W. Atkinson and G. H. Litwin. In *Journal of Abnormal and Social Psychology,* Vol. 60. Copyright 1960 by the American Psychological Association; p. 441, Barbara Alper/Stock, Boston; p. 447, John Kelly/The Image Bank; p. 451, Kenneth Karp/Omni-Photo Communications; p. 454, by permission of Dr. Paul Ekman, University of California, San Francisco, Dr. Silvan Tomkins and Edward Gallob.

Chapter 12 Page 461, Robert McElroy/Woodfin Camp; p. 463, The Granger Collection, New York; p. 464, The Granger Collection, New York; p. 466, Bob Daemmrich/Stock, Boston; p. 469, Peter Southwick/Stock, Boston; p. 472, Robert McElroy/Woodfin Camp; p. 476, Courtesy Dr. Albert Bandura, Stanford University; p. 477 (Fig. 12.2), from Cognitive processes mediating behavioral change, by A. Bandura, N. E. Adams and J. Beyer. In *Journal of Personality and Social Psychology,* Vol. 35. Copyright 1977 by the American Psychological Association; p. 480, The Bettman Archive; p. 481 (left), Courtesy of the Archives, California Institute of Technology; (right), Sam Falk/Monkmeyer Press Photo Service; p. 484, Howard University News Office; p. 492, Owen Franken/Stock, Boston.

Chapter 13 Page 501, Bob Harris/Educational Testing Service; p. 502, Bob Harris/Educational Testing Service; p. 507 (Fig. 13.1), from *Human biology: An introduction to human evolution, variation, and growth,* by G. A. Harrison, J. S. Weiner, J. M. Tanner, and N. A. Barnicott. Copyright 1977 by Oxford University Press; p. 510, Owen Franken/Stock, Boston; p. 511 (Fig. 13.3), from *l'année Psychologique,* Paris, 1905. The New York Public Library, Astor, Lenox, and Tilden Foundations; p. 512, The Bettman Archive; p. 521 (Fig. 13.5), from Genetics and intelligence: Recent data, by R. Plomin and J. C. DeFries. In *Intelligence,* Vol. 4. Copyright 1980 by Ablex Publishing, Norwood, N.J.; p. 523, Chuck Fishman/Woodfin Camp; p. 525, Ellis Herwig/Stock, Boston; p. 527, UPI/Bettman News Photos; p. 529 (Fig. 13.6), from W. Grant Dahlstrom et al., *An MMPI handbook,* Vol 1, revised edition, University of Minnesota Press, Minneapolis. Copyright © 1972 by The University of Minnesota; p. 531 (top), Courtesy of Henri F. Ellenberger, M.D.; (bottom), © Copyright of the Rorschach Ink Blots 1921 (renewed 1948) by Verlag Hans Huber, Bern, Switzerland.

Chapter 14 Page 541, Bob Daemmrich/Stock, Boston; p. 542, The Granger Collection, New York; p. 544, Steve Elmore/The Stock Market; p. 548, Courtesy Jane M. Murphy, Ph.D.; p. 549, *St. Catherine of Siena Exorcising a Possessed Woman,* Girolamo di Benvenuto. Denver Arts Museum, Denver, Colorado, Samuel H. Kress Foundation; p. 555, Bob Daemmrich/Stock, Boston; p. 560, John C. Chiasson/Gamma Liaison; p. 565, Photofest; p. 571, from *Abnormal psychology* (2nd ed.), by Ephraim Rosen et al. Copyright © 1972 by W. B. Saunders & Company. Reprinted by permission; p. 573 (top left), Victoria and Albert Museum, photograph Sally Chappell; (top center, bottom right), © Guttman Maclay Collection, Institute of Psychiatry, London; p. 574, E. S. Beckwith/Design Photographers International.

Chapter 15 Page 583, Stacy Pick/Stock, Boston; p. 584, National Mental Health Association; p. 586, BBC Hulton Picture Library; p. 587, The Bettman Archive; p. 591, © Edmund Engelman; p. 598, The Bettman Archive; p. 599, Jim Wilson/Woodfin Camp; p. 601, Stacy Pick/Stock, Boston; p. 607, Will McIntyre/Photo Researchers, Inc.; p. 611, Archive Pictures, Inc.; p. 613, Chie Nisho/Omni-Photo Communications.

Chapter 16 Page 619, Phoebe Dunn/DPI; p. 621, Charles Harbutt/Archive Pictures, Inc.; p. 623, Focus on Sports; p. 625, © Michael Cosson 1983; p. 628, Paramount Pictures Corp./Phototeque; p. 630, Charles Gupton/Stock, Boston; p. 633, American Cancer Society; p. 635, Will McIntyre/Photo Researchers; p. 637 (Fig. 16.1), adapted from Cognitive consequences of forced compliance, by L. Festinger and J. M. Carlsmith. In *Journal of Abnormal and Social Psychology,*

Vol. 58. Copyright 1959 by the American Psychological Association. Used by permission of the author; p. 640, © William Vandivert, published in *Scientific American,* November 1955; p. 641, Charles Gupton/The Stock Market; p. 643, Copyright 1965 by Stanley Milgram. From the film *Obedience,* distributed by the New York University Film Library; p. 647, Jerry Wachter/Photo Researchers; p. 647 (Fig. 16.4), reprinted from *Social pressures in informal groups* by Leon Festinger, Stanley Schachter, and Kurt Bach with the permission of the publishers, Stanford University Press. © 1950 by the Board of Trustees of the Leland Stanford Junior University; p. 649, Phoebe Dunn/DPI; p. 652 (Fig. 16.5), from Bystander intervention in emergencies: Diffusion of responsibilities, by J. Darley & B. Latane. In *Journal of Personality and Social Psychology,* Vol. 8. Copyright 1968 by the American Psychological Association; p. 654, John Lei/Omni-Photo Communications.

Chapter 17 Page 663, Charles Feil/Stock, Boston; p. 666, Michael L. Abramson/Woodfin Camp; p. 670, Donald Dietz/Stock, Boston; p. 672, John Feingersh/Click, Chicago; p. 676, Charles Feil/Stock, Boston; p. 679, John Keating/Photo Researchers; p. 681 (Fig. 17.1), adapted from Baum, A., & Valins, S. (1977). *Architecture and social behavior* (pp. 22, 82). Hillsdale, NJ: Lawrence Erlbaum Associates; p. 683, Charles Feil/Stock, Boston; p. 692, Ken Karp/Omni-Photo Communications; p. 694, M. Fennelli/Photo Researchers; p. 699, Frank Siteman/Stock, Boston.

AUTHOR INDEX

SUBJECT INDEX